Financial accounting

Reporting, analysis and decision making

SIXTH EDITION

Shirley Carlon

Rosina McAlpine

Chrisann Lee

Lorena Mitrione

Ngaire Kirk

Lily Wong

WILEY

Sixth edition published 2019 by
John Wiley & Sons Australia, Ltd
42 McDougall Street, Milton Qld 4064

Typeset in 10/12pt Times LT Std

Cover and internal design images: © HAKKI ARSLAN / Shutterstock.com

Typeset in India by Aptara

Printed in Singapore by
Markono Print Media Pte Ltd

10 9 8 7 6 5 4 3 2 1

BRIEF CONTENTS

Preface   xiv
About the authors   xvi
Key features   xviii

1. An introduction to accounting   1
2. The recording process   93
3. Accrual accounting concepts   159
4. Inventories   231
5. Reporting and analysing inventory   284
6. Accounting information systems   344
7. Reporting and analysing cash and receivables   426
8. Reporting and analysing non-current assets   500
9. Reporting and analysing liabilities   564
10. Reporting and analysing equity   620
11. Statement of cash flows   676
12. Financial statement analysis and decision making   756
13. Analysing and integrating GAAP   827
14. Technology concepts   897

Managerial accounting supplement   927

15. Introduction to management accounting   928
16. Cost accounting systems   976
17. Cost–volume–profit relationships   1047
18. Budgeting   1093

Appendix: Time value of money   1167
Index   1184

CONTENTS

Preface xiv
About the authors xvi
Key features xviii

CHAPTER 1

An introduction to accounting 1

Chapter preview 2
1.1 Introduction to accounting 2
 The business world 2
1.2 Accounting: the language of business 4
 The accounting process 4
 The diverse roles of accountants 5
1.3 Forms of business organisation 7
 Sole proprietorship 7
 Partnership 8
 Company 8
 Other forms of business organisation 9
 Not-for-profit organisations 10
1.4 Introduction to the *Conceptual Framework* 10
 The objective of general purpose financial
  reporting 11
 The reporting entity 11
1.5 Users and uses of financial information 13
 Internal users 14
 External users 14
 Financing activities 15
 Investing activities 15
 Operating activities 15
 Sustainability reporting 16
1.6 Financial statements 17
 Statement of profit or loss 19
 Statement of changes in equity 20
 Statement of financial position 21
 Statement of cash flows 22
 Interrelationships between the statements 23
1.7 The financial reporting environment 35
 Australian Securities and Investments
  Commission 35
 Financial Reporting Council 35
 Australian Accounting Standards Board 36
 Australian Securities Exchange 37
 Regulation in New Zealand 37
 Professional accounting bodies 38

1.8 Concepts, principles and qualitative
 characteristics 38
 Concepts and principles 39
 Qualitative characteristics 40
1.9 Analysing financial statements 43
 Analysis and decision making 44
 Profitability 45
 Liquidity 48
 Solvency 53
 Summary 60
 Decision-making toolkit — a summary 61
 Key terms 62
 Demonstration problem 66
 Self-study questions 68
 Questions 71
 Brief exercises 72
 Exercises 73
 Problem set A 78
 Problem set B 83
 Building business skills 88
 Acknowledgements 92

CHAPTER 2

The recording process 93

Chapter preview 94
2.1 Accounting transactions and events 94
 Analysing transactions 95
 Summary of accounting transactions 100
2.2 The account 101
2.3 Debits and credits 102
 Debit and credit procedures 103
 Equity relationships 105
 Expansion of the basic accounting equation 106
2.4 Steps in the recording process 107
2.5 The journal 109
 Chart of accounts 111
2.6 The general ledger 112
2.7 Posting 113
 The recording process illustrated 113
 Summary illustration of journalising and
  posting 124
2.8 The trial balance 127
 Limitations of a trial balance 128
 Summary 131

Decision-making toolkit — a summary   131
Key terms   132
Demonstration problem   132
Self-study questions   135
Questions   136
Brief exercises   137
Exercises   138
Problem set A   142
Problem set B   148
Building business skills   154
Acknowledgement   158

CHAPTER 3

Accrual accounting concepts   159

Chapter preview   160
3.1 Timing issues   160
Accrual versus cash basis of accounting   161
3.2 Revenue recognition criteria   163
New accounting standard for revenue
  recognition   164
Expense recognition criteria   165
3.3 The basics of adjusting entries   167
Types of adjusting entries   167
3.4 Adjusting entries for prepayments   168
Prepaid expenses   169
Revenues received in advance   173
Adjusting entries for accruals   175
Summary of basic relationships   181
3.5 The adjusted trial balance and financial
  statements   184
Preparing the adjusted trial balance   184
Preparing financial statements   185
3.6 Closing the books   186
Preparing closing entries   186
Preparing a post-closing trial balance   189
3.7 Summary of the accounting cycle   189
3.8 Adjusting entries — using a worksheet   190
Summary   194
Decision-making toolkit — a summary   195
Key terms   195
Demonstration problem 1   196
Demonstration problem 2   197
Self-study questions   199
Questions   201
Brief exercises   201
Exercises   203

Problem set A   209
Problem set B   218
Building business skills   226
Acknowledgements   230

CHAPTER 4

Inventories   231

Chapter preview   232
4.1 Merchandising operations   232
Operating cycles   232
Inventory systems   232
4.2 Recording purchases of inventories   235
Purchase returns and allowances   237
Freight costs   237
Purchase discounts   238
4.3 Recording sales of inventories   240
Sales returns and allowances   242
Sales discounts   243
4.4 Statement of profit or loss presentation   245
Sales revenue   245
Gross profit   245
Other revenue   246
Operating expenses   246
4.5 Evaluating profitability   247
Gross profit ratio   247
Operating expenses to sales ratio   249
4.6 The goods and services tax   250
Overview of the GST process   250
4.7 Accounting for GST   252
Purchasing inventory   253
Purchases returns   253
Selling inventory   253
Sales returns and allowances   254
Settlement discount   254
Remitting GST to the taxation authority   255
Summary   259
Decision-making toolkit — a summary   260
Key terms   260
Demonstration problem   261
Self-study questions   263
Questions   264
Brief exercises   265
Exercises   266
Problem set A   269
Problem set B   274
Building business skills   280
Acknowledgements   283

CHAPTER 5

Reporting and analysing inventory 284

Chapter preview 285
5.1 Classifying inventory 285
  Periodic inventory system 286
  Recording inventory transactions 286
  Recording purchases of inventory 286
  Recording sales of inventory 287
  Comparison of entries — perpetual vs. periodic 288
5.2 Cost of sales 289
  Determining cost of goods purchased 289
5.3 Determining inventory quantities 290
  Counting the physical inventory 290
  Determining ownership of goods 290
5.4 Statement of profit or loss presentation 292
5.5 Inventory cost flow methods — periodic system 293
  Specific identification 293
  Cost flow assumptions 294
5.6 Financial statement effects of cost flow methods 299
  Statement of profit or loss effects 299
  Statement of financial position effects 300
  Taxation effects 301
  Using inventory cost flow methods consistently 301
5.7 Valuing inventory at the lower of cost and net realisable value 301
5.8 Analysis of inventory 302
  Inventory turnover 303
5.9 Inventory cost flow methods — perpetual system 305
  First-in, first-out (FIFO) 305
  Last-in, first-out (LIFO) 306
  Average cost 306
  Demonstration problem for section 5.9 307
5.10 Inventory errors 309
  Effects on profit 309
  Effects on assets and equity 310
5.11 Closing entries for merchandising entities 311
  Perpetual inventory method 311
  Periodic inventory method 312
  Worksheet 313
  Summary 316
  Decision-making toolkit — a summary 317
  Key terms 317

Demonstration problem 318
Self-study questions 319
Questions 321
Brief exercises 322
Exercises 323
Problem set A 327
Problem set B 333
Building business skills 339
Acknowledgements 343

CHAPTER 6

Accounting information systems 344

Chapter preview 345
6.1 Basic concepts of accounting information systems 346
  Principles of accounting information systems 346
6.2 Developing an accounting system 347
6.3 Internal control systems 348
  Internal control 349
6.4 Management's responsibility for internal control 349
6.5 Principles of internal control 351
  Establishment of responsibility 351
  Segregation of duties 352
  Documentation procedures 352
  Physical, mechanical and electronic controls 353
  Independent internal verification 354
  Limitations of internal control 355
  Internal control and forensic accounting 356
6.6 Transformation of financial data 357
  Accounting processes underlying the generation of financial statements 357
6.7 Sales and receivables, and purchases and payments cycles illustrated 359
6.8 Internal control principles applied to the sales and receivables cycle and purchases and payments cycle 363
  Sales and receivables cycle 363
  Purchases and payments cycle 363
6.9 Control accounts, subsidiary ledgers and special journals 364
  Control accounts and subsidiary ledgers illustrated 365
  Advantages of subsidiary ledgers 367
6.10 Special journals 368
  Posting the special journals 369
  Advantages of special journals 370

6.11 Computerised accounting information
    systems   371
    Basic features of computerised systems   372
6.12 Advantages and disadvantages of
    computerised systems   373
    Advantages   373
    Disadvantages   373
6.13 Sales journal   374
    Journalising credit sales   374
    Posting the sales journal   375
    Checking the ledgers   377
    Advantages of the sales journal   377
6.14 Cash receipts journal   377
    Journalising cash receipts transactions   378
    Posting the cash receipts journal   380
    Purchases journal   381
    Cash payments journal   384
    Effects of special journals on general journal   386
    Summary   390
    Decision-making toolkit — a summary   391
    Key terms   392
    Demonstration problem   393
    Self-study questions   394
    Questions   396
    Brief exercises   396
    Exercises   398
    Problem set A   404
    Problem set B   412
    Comprehensive problem: chapters 3 to 6   421
    Building business skills   422
    Acknowledgements   425

CHAPTER 7

Reporting and analysing cash and receivables   426

Chapter preview   427
7.1 Cash and credit transactions   427
    Business transactions and cash   427
7.2 Credit and electronic banking   429
7.3 Safeguarding and managing cash   430
    Internal control over cash   430
7.4 Bank reconciliation   433
    Reconciling the bank account   434
7.5 Managing and monitoring cash   441
    Basic principles of cash management   442
    Cash budget   443
7.6 Assessing cash adequacy   447
    Ratio of cash to daily cash expenses   447

7.7 Recording and reporting receivables   449
    Accounting for receivables   450
7.8 Valuing accounts receivable   450
    Direct write-off method for uncollectable
      accounts   451
    Allowance method for uncollectable accounts   452
    GST and bad debt write-off   457
    Notes receivable   458
7.9 Financial statement presentation
    of receivables   461
7.10 Analysing and managing receivables   461
    Extending credit   461
    Establishing a payment period   462
    Monitoring collections   462
    Evaluating the receivables balance   464
    Accelerating cash receipts   465
7.11 Operation of the petty cash fund   468
    Establishing the fund   468
    Making payments from petty cash   469
    Replenishing the fund   469
    Summary   472
    Decision-making toolkit — a summary   473
    Key terms   474
    Demonstration problem 1   475
    Demonstration problem 2   476
    Self-study questions   477
    Questions   480
    Brief exercises   481
    Exercises   482
    Problem set A   486
    Problem set B   491
    Building business skills   496
    Acknowledgements   499

CHAPTER 8

Reporting and analysing non-current assets   500

Chapter preview   501
8.1 Business context and decision making:
    overview   501
8.2 Property, plant and equipment   502
    Determining the cost of property, plant and
      equipment   503
8.3 Depreciation   508
    Factors in calculating depreciation   509
8.4 Depreciation methods   510
    Straight-line depreciation   511
    Diminishing-balance depreciation   512

Units-of-production depreciation   514
Management's choice: comparison of methods   515
Depreciation disclosure in the notes   516
Revising periodic depreciation   516
8.5 Subsequent expenditure   517
8.6 Impairments   518
Accounting for impairments   518
Reversal of impairments   519
8.7 Revaluations   520
Revaluation journal entries   520
Reversals of increases and decreases   521
8.8 Disposals of PPE assets   522
Sale of PPE assets   522
Scrapping of PPE assets   524
8.9 Property, plant and equipment records   524
8.10 Intangible assets   525
Accounting for intangible assets   525
8.11 Types of intangible assets   528
Patents   528
Research and development costs   528
Copyright   528
Trademarks and brand names   528
Franchises and licences   529
Goodwill   530
8.12 Other non-current assets   530
Agricultural assets   530
8.13 Natural resources   532
Amortisation (depletion)   532
8.14 Reporting and analysing issues   533
Reporting non-current assets in the financial statements   533
Analysis and decision making   533
Summary   540
Decision-making toolkit — a summary   541
Key terms   542
Demonstration problem 1   543
Demonstration problem 2   544
Self-study questions   545
Questions   547
Brief exercises   547
Exercises   548
Problem set A   551
Problem set B   555
Building business skills   559
Acknowledgements   563

CHAPTER 9

Reporting and analysing liabilities   564

Chapter preview   565
9.1 Current liabilities   565
9.2 Notes payable   566
Payroll and payroll deductions payable   567
Revenues received in advance   569
9.3 Non-current liabilities   570
Why issue unsecured notes or debentures?   571
Determining the market value of unsecured notes and debentures   572
Accounting for issues of unsecured notes and debentures   573
Redeeming unsecured notes and debentures at maturity   574
Redeeming unsecured notes and debentures before maturity   574
9.4 Loans payable by instalment   575
Accounting for loans payable by instalment   575
Current and non-current components of long-term debt   579
9.5 Leasing   580
What is a lease?   581
9.6 Accounting for leases   582
Operating leases   582
Finance leases   582
Reporting leases   584
9.7 Provisions and contingent liabilities   585
9.8 Recording provisions for warranties   587
Reporting provisions for warranties   589
9.9 Financial statement analysis   589
Liquidity ratios   589
Solvency ratios   592
Summary   597
Decision-making toolkit — a summary   598
Key terms   599
Demonstration problem   600
Self-study questions   602
Questions   604
Brief exercises   605
Exercises   606
Problem set A   609
Problem set B   613
Building business skills   617
Acknowledgements   619

CHAPTER 10

Reporting and analysing equity   620

Chapter preview   621
10.1 Business context and decision making: overview   621
10.2 The corporate form of organisation   622
  Characteristics of a corporation   622
  Forming a company   625
  Shareholder rights   625
10.3 Share issues   626
  Issue of shares   626
  Accounting for the private issue of shares   627
  Accounting for the public issue of shares   627
10.4 Share splits   628
10.5 Dividends   629
  Cash dividends   630
  Share dividends   631
10.6 Earning power and irregular items   633
  Errors   634
  Changes in accounting estimates   636
  Changes in accounting policies   637
  Discontinuing operations   638
10.7 Reporting on equity   639
  Statement of profit or loss and other comprehensive income   640
  Statement of changes in equity   642
  Statement of financial position — equity section   642
10.8 Retained earnings   644
10.9 Financial statement analysis and decision making   646
  Dividend record   647
  Earnings performance   648
10.10 Debt versus equity financing decision making   648
  Summary   652
  Decision-making toolkit — a summary   653
  Key terms   654
  Demonstration problem 1   655
  Demonstration problem 2   656
  Self-study questions   657
  Questions   659
  Brief exercises   660
  Exercises   661
  Problem set A   664

Problem set B   668
Building business skills   672
Acknowledgements   675

CHAPTER 11

Statement of cash flows   676

Chapter preview   677
11.1 The statement of cash flows: purpose   677
  Purpose of the statement of cash flows   678
11.2 Classification of cash flows   678
  Significant non-cash activities   680
  Format of the statement of cash flows   680
  Usefulness of the statement of cash flows   682
11.3 Preparing the statement of cash flows   683
  Determining the net increase (decrease) in cash (step 1)   685
  Determining net cash provided (used) by operating activities (step 2)   686
  Determining net cash provided (used) by investing activities (step 3)   695
  Determining net cash provided (used) by financing activities (step 4)   696
  Completing the statement of cash flows   697
  Indirect method for determining cash flows from operating activities   697
  Summary of indirect method for determining cash flows from operating activities   702
11.4 Using cash flows to evaluate an entity   705
  The entity life cycle   705
11.5 Free cash flow   707
  Capital expenditure ratio   709
  Assessing liquidity, solvency and profitability using cash flows   710
  Summary   716
  Decision-making toolkit — a summary   716
  Key terms   717
  Demonstration problem 1   718
  Demonstration problem 2 — comprehensive   720
  Self-study questions   727
  Questions   729
  Brief exercises   730
  Exercises   731
  Problem set A   735
  Problem set B   743
  Building business skills   751
  Acknowledgements   755

CHAPTER 12

Financial statement analysis and decision making   756

Chapter preview   757
12.1 Comparative analysis   757
12.2 Horizontal analysis   758
12.3 Vertical analysis   762
12.4 Ratio analysis   766
   Liquidity ratios   767
   Solvency ratios   771
   Profitability ratios   773
12.5 Limitations of financial statement analysis   780
   Estimates   780
   Cost   780
   Alternative accounting methods   781
   Atypical data   781
   Diversification   781
   Summary   785
   Decision-making toolkit — a summary   785
   Key terms   786
   Demonstration problem   787
   Self-study questions   793
   Questions   795
   Brief exercises   796
   Exercises   797
   Problem set A   802
   Problem set B   810
   Building business skills   819
   Acknowledgements   826

CHAPTER 13

Analysing and integrating GAAP   827

Chapter preview   828
13.1 Concepts and principles underlying accounting   829
   Monetary principle   829
   Accounting entity concept   830
   Accounting period concept   830
   Going concern principle   831
   Cost principle   831
   Full disclosure principle   831
13.2 Conceptual frameworks   834
   Historical developments   835
   Future developments   837
   Overview of the Conceptual Framework   838

13.3 The objective of general purpose financial reporting   839
   Stewardship and accountability objectives   839
   Decision-usefulness objective   840
   The Conceptual Framework   840
13.4 Users and uses of financial reports   841
   The Conceptual Framework — primary users   841
   The Conceptual Framework — other users   842
13.5 The reporting entity   843
   The reporting entity — defined   843
   The reporting entity — indicators   844
   ED/2010/2 Conceptual Framework for Financial Reporting: The Reporting Entity   844
   Differential financial reporting   845
13.6 Qualitative characteristics and constraint on financial reporting   846
   Fundamental qualitative characteristics   847
   Enhancing qualitative characteristics   849
   Constraint on financial reporting   851
13.7 Definition, recognition and measurement of elements in financial reports   852
   Assets — definition and recognition criteria   852
   Liabilities — definition and recognition criteria   855
   Equity — definition   856
   Income — definition and recognition criteria   857
   Standards for revenue recognition   859
   Expenses — definition and recognition criteria   859
   Measurement of the elements of financial reports   862
13.8 Integrating principles, concepts, standards and the Conceptual Framework   863
   Summarising GAAP   864
   Integrating GAAP   865
13.9 Future developments in financial reporting   865
   Integrated reporting   865
   Summary   871
   Decision-making toolkit — a summary   873
   Key terms   874
   Demonstration problem   875
   Self-study questions   877
   Questions   880
   Brief exercises   881
   Exercises   884
   Problem set   889
   Building business skills   893
   Acknowledgements   896

CHAPTER 14

Technology concepts   897

Chapter preview   898

14.1 Computerised accounting information
systems   898
Xero accounting software   898

14.2 Enterprise resource planning (ERP)   902
Why an ERP system?   902

14.3 Business processes supported by ERP
systems   903

14.4 ERP systems — SAP modules   904

14.5 eXtensible Business Reporting Language
(XBRL)   905
XBRL and its role in reporting systems and
decision making   905

14.6 Different ways to apply XBRL tags   907
XBRL tags in the accounting system   907
Tagging accounts after reports have been
produced   907

14.7 Benefits of XBRL   907
Reduced data manipulation   908
Paperless reporting   908
Industry-accepted standards   909
Reduced accounting time   909
Recognition by major accounting software
vendors   909
Interchangeable data   909
Comparisons across companies   909
Improved audit quality   909
Stakeholder benefits   909

14.8 XBRL concepts   910

14.9 Cloud computing   911
Cloud Infrastructure as a Service (IaaS)   912
Cloud Platform as a Service (PaaS)   912
Software as a Service (SaaS)   912

14.10 New technologies   914
Big data   914
Artificial intelligence   915
Blockchain   916
Bitcoin   917
Other technologies   918
Summary   919
Key terms   921
Self-study questions   922
Questions   923
Exercises   923
Building business skills   925
Acknowledgements   926

Managerial accounting supplement   927

CHAPTER 15

Introduction to management accounting   928

Chapter preview   929

15.1 Management accounting basics   929
Comparing management accounting and financial
accounting   930
Ethical standards for management
accountants   930

15.2 Management functions   931
Management cost concepts   932

15.3 Manufacturing costs   932
Direct materials   932
Direct labour   933
Manufacturing overhead   933

15.4 Product vs. period costs   934

15.5 Manufacturing costs in financial
statements   935
Statement of profit or loss   935

15.6 Statement of financial position   936

15.7 Determining the cost of goods manufactured
and cost of sales   937
Cost concepts: a review   940

15.8 Evolution and improvements in management
accounting   941
Service industry needs   942
Globalisation   943
Effects of technological change on business
infrastructure   943
E-commerce   944
New management systems and concepts   945

15.9 Accounting cycle for a manufacturing
entity   947
Worksheet   947
Closing entries   948
Summary   952
Decision-making toolkit — a summary   953
Key terms   953
Demonstration problem   954
Self-study questions   956
Questions   957
Brief exercises   958
Exercises   959

Problem set A   964
Problem set B   968
Building business skills   972
Acknowledgements   975

CHAPTER 16

Cost accounting systems   976

Chapter preview   977
16.1 Cost accounting systems   977
   Non-manufacturing entities   978
   Overhead application   978
   Job order costing and process costing   978
16.2 Job order costing   980
   Job cost flows   980
16.3 Job cost sheet   982
   Determining overhead rates   983
   Accounting procedures   984
   Reporting job cost data   986
   Under- or overapplied manufacturing
      overhead   986
   Non-manufacturing entities   988
   Process costing   990
16.4 Process cost flow   990
16.5 Accounting procedures   991
   Assignment of manufacturing costs — journal
      entries   991
   Equivalent units   994
16.6 Production cost report   996
16.7 Activity-based costing (ABC)   999
   Traditional costing systems   999
   The need for a new costing system   1000
   Activities and cost drivers   1000
   Activity-based costing in manufacturing
      industries   1000
   Activity-based costing in service industries   1003
16.8 Benefits and limitations of activity-based
      costing   1006
   Benefits of ABC   1006
   Limitations of ABC   1006
   When to switch to ABC   1007
16.9 Value-added vs. non-value-added
      activities   1007
   Hierarchy of activity levels   1009
16.10 Just-in-time processing (JIT)   1010
   Objective of JIT processing   1011
   Elements of JIT processing   1012
   Benefits of JIT processing   1012
   Summary   1015

Decision-making toolkit — a summary   1016
Key terms   1017
Demonstration problem   1018
Self-study questions   1020
Questions   1022
Brief exercises   1022
Exercises   1024
Problem set A   1029
Problem set B   1036
Building business skills   1043
Acknowledgements   1046

CHAPTER 17

Cost–volume–profit relationships   1047

Chapter preview   1048
17.1 Cost behaviour analysis   1048
   Variable costs   1048
   Fixed costs   1049
   Mixed costs   1051
17.2 Absorption vs. variable costing   1054
   Comparison of statements of profit or loss   1055
   Rationale for variable costing   1056
17.3 Cost–volume–profit analysis   1057
   Basic assumptions   1057
17.4 Contribution margin   1057
   Break-even analysis   1059
   Margin of safety   1063
17.5 Target profit   1064
   Mathematical equation   1064
   Contribution margin technique   1065
   Graphic presentation   1065
   CVP for profit planning   1065
17.6 Using CVP analysis with multiple
      products   1067
   Break-even sales   1067
   Limited resources   1068
17.7 CVP statement of profit or loss   1069
   Summary   1073
   Decision-making toolkit — a summary   1073
   Key terms   1074
   Demonstration problem   1075
   Self-study questions   1076
   Questions   1077
   Brief exercises   1078
   Exercises   1079
   Problem set A   1082
   Problem set B   1086

Building business skills   1089
Acknowledgements   1092

CHAPTER 18

Budgeting   1093

Chapter preview   1094
18.1 Budgeting basics   1094
   Budgeting and accounting   1094
   The benefits of budgeting   1095
   Essentials of effective budgeting   1095
   Length of the budget period   1096
   The budgeting process   1096
   Budgeting vs. long-range planning   1096
18.2 The master budget   1097
   Preparing the operating budgets   1098
18.3 Cash budget   1102
18.4 Preparing the budgeted financial
   statements   1106
   Budgeted statement of profit or loss   1106
   Budgeted statement of financial position   1106
18.5 Budgeting in non-manufacturing entities   1108
   Merchandising entities   1108
   Service entities   1109
   Not-for-profit entities   1109
   Government entities   1109
18.6 Budgetary control   1110
   Static budget reports   1111
18.7 Flexible budgets   1112
   Developing the flexible budget   1114

Flexible budget — a case study   1116
Flexible budget reports   1118
Management by exception   1119
18.8 The concept of responsibility
   accounting   1120
   Controllable vs. non-controllable revenues
     and costs   1121
   Responsibility reporting system   1122
   Types of responsibility centres   1123
18.9 Responsibility accounting for cost
   centres   1125
   Responsibility accounting for profit centres   1126
   Responsibility accounting for investment
     centres   1129
   Principles of performance evaluation   1130
   Summary   1134
   Decision-making toolkit — a summary   1135
   Key terms   1135
   Demonstration problem   1137
   Self-study questions   1138
   Questions   1139
   Brief exercises   1139
   Exercises   1141
   Problem set A   1146
   Problem set B   1153
   Building business skills   1161
   Acknowledgements   1166

Appendix: Time value of money   1167
Index   1184

PREFACE

In recent years accounting education has seen numerous changes to the way financial accounting is taught. These changes reflect the demands of an ever-changing business world, opportunities created by new technology and instructional technologies, and an increased understanding of how you (students) learn. The foundation of this text is based on a number of unique principles and innovations in accounting education.

'Less is more.'

The objective of this text is to provide you with an understanding of those concepts that are fundamental to the preparation and use of accounting information. Most will forget procedural details within a short period of time. On the other hand, concepts, if well taught, should be remembered for a lifetime. Concepts are especially important in a world where the details are constantly changing.

'Don't just sit there — do something.'

You learn best when you are actively engaged. The overriding pedagogical objective of this text is to provide you with continual opportunities for active learning. One of the best tools for active learning is strategically placed questions. Our discussions are framed by questions, often beginning with rhetorical questions and ending with review questions, and our analytical devices, called 'Decision-making toolkits', use key questions to demonstrate the purpose of each.

'I'll believe it when I see it.'

You will be more willing to commit time and energy to a topic when you believe that it is relevant to your future career. There is no better way to demonstrate relevance than to ground discussion in the real-world. Consistent with this, we adopted a macro-approach — starting in chapter 1, you are shown how to use financial statements of companies, demonstrating the relevance of accounting. As you become acquainted with the financial successes and fluctuations of these companies, many will begin to follow business news more closely, making their learning a dynamic, ongoing process. We also discuss small to medium-sized companies to highlight the challenges they face as they try to grow.

'You'll need to make a decision.'

In a business environment there are many and varied decisions to be made. Illustrative examples of the types of decisions internal management and external financial statement users make are discussed throughout the text. Decision making involves identifying and sourcing the relevant information, analysing data and critically evaluating alternatives, and this takes practice.

In addition, to develop your analysis and decision-making skills we have integrated important analytical tools throughout the text. After each new decision-making tool is presented, we summarise the key features of that tool in a decision-making toolkit. At the end of each chapter, we provide a comprehensive demonstration of an analysis of a real or hypothetical company using the decision tools presented in the chapter. The presentation of these tools throughout the text is logically sequenced to take full advantage of the tools presented in earlier chapters.

'It's a small world.'

Business operates in a global environment. Rapid and ever-changing improvements in information technology, logistics and transport continue to strive toward a single global economy. The internet has made it possible for even small businesses to sell their products virtually anywhere in the world. Few business decisions can be made without consideration of international factors. To heighten your awareness of the issues that concern business most we have included a range of case studies that explore international, environmental, financial analysis and ethical issues in the 'Building business skills' section.

'Apply what you learn.'

In developing this text, we have been mindful of the Accounting Threshold Learning Outcomes and, accordingly, we have integrated case studies into the resources available for instructors. The case studies feature a series of capstone cases aligned to the first 12 chapters of the text, and have been designed to challenge you to apply analytical skills, exercise judgement and communicate a financial decision.

ABOUT THE AUTHORS

Shirley Carlon

Shirley Carlon MCom (Hons), CA, is a senior lecturer in the Business School at the University of New South Wales. Her teaching interests include financial and managerial accounting, auditing and tax. Shirley has considerable experience in the delivery of both external and internal programs, including web-based courses. Shirley has received a national teaching citation award for outstanding contributions to student learning for innovations in curriculum development and the creation of peer support mechanisms for off-campus students. She has taught extensively in China and has been a guest speaker on accounting issues at government functions. Shirley's research interests are in financial reporting where she has published several articles on peer mentoring, risk reporting, intangible assets, accounting policy choice and tax in Australian and international journals. She is a chartered accountant with experience in both large and medium-sized audit firms.

Rosina McAlpine

Rosina McAlpine BCom, MCom (Hons), MHEd, PhD, is a social entrepreneur and CEO of Win Win Parenting. Rosina is a former associate professor at the University of Sydney Business School and holds a Masters degree and a PhD in education. She is an internationally recognised, award-winning researcher and educator, having received 5 outstanding teaching awards at the faculty, university and national levels as well as 5 international best paper awards. Since becoming a parent, Rosina has been developing programs to help parents overcome the challenges of modern-day parenting using the latest research in child development. Rosina's research interests include navigating and negotiating work–life balance, gender equality and parenting education. Rosina's workplace education programs are delivered across a variety of corporations and government organisations to support working parents better manage the work–family interface. Rosina is the contributing editor of the book entitled *Inspired children: how the leading minds of today raise their children.*

Chrisann Lee

Chrisann Lee is a lecturer in accountancy at Queensland University of Technology. She is a CPA and has a PhD (QUT), a Master of Commerce (CSU) and a Graduate Diploma in Management (AGSM). She lectures in introductory accounting, management accounting, superannuation and personal financial planning. Prior to joining the tertiary sector in 2004, Chrisann worked as a management accountant for a manufacturing company in Hong Kong as well as in the financial services industry in Sydney. Chrisann is passionate about teaching and learning. She was awarded the QUT Vice-Chancellor's Performance Award 2009 and 2015 in teaching excellence. Her research interests are in the areas of accounting education, financial literacy and superannuation where she has published numerous articles in Australian and international journals and has received several grants and awards.

Lorena Mitrione

Lorena Mitrione BCom, MBus, PGrad DipEc&Comm, is a lecturer in accounting at the Monash Business School. Prior to joining Monash in 2009, Lorena worked at CPA Australia. From 2001 she was the CPA Program Manager responsible for the development and maintenance of CPA Program materials and examinations. In this role Lorena developed a sound sense of the requirements for accounting learning materials while maintaining an up-to-date knowledge of accounting standards, accounting research, technical accounting matters and business practices. She is currently enrolled in a PhD. Her thesis title is 'Motivation and self-regulated learning strategies applied by accounting students in a blended learning environment'.

Ngaire Kirk

Ngaire Kirk BBS, BBS (Honours), MBS, CA, has a background in sheep and cattle farming and in the public and private health sectors. Her recent teaching responsibilities at Massey included coordinating and teaching introductory and intermediate financial accounting papers and teaching advanced auditing. Her research interests focused mainly on financial accounting, financial reporting and accounting education, in particular the use of electronic and online resources to enhance both internal and distance learning. Ngaire retired from Massey University at the end of April 2017, but prior to her retirement, she was a member of two key Massey Business College committees whose role is to enhance assurance of learning, and teaching and learning development across the college. Despite retiring, Ngaire accepted a request from Victoria University of Wellington to coordinate their large first-year accounting class for nonaccountants (ACCY130) in trimester 2, 2017 and has continued as a teaching fellow, teaching ACCY130 and the second-year financial accounting paper in trimester 1, 2018.

Lily Wong

Lily Wong BBus, MBus, PhD, CPA is an honorary professor in the College of Business, Victoria University, Australia. Lily is a recipient of international best paper awards, as well as university and national teaching excellence awards for her contribution to student learning in accounting education. Lily's key research interests relate to improving the learning experience and academic outcomes for first-year accounting students. Current areas of interest include blended learning, development of online teaching resources and examining the impact of technology-enhanced teaching options on student learning outcomes.

KEY FEATURES

Print text

This text is designed for students studying accounting for the first time. Real and hypothetical company financial information to support your understanding of accounting as an information system is presented in a clear, easy-to-follow way.

- Financial data from various companies are used to highlight comparative financial results and measure financial performance.
- There is a clear, well-developed balance between the perspectives of the users and the preparers of financial statements.
- In several chapters, 'Review it' questions relate chapter topics to real-world scenarios.
- In the 'Building business skills' section at the end of each chapter, financial reporting problems use financial statements to align the chapter material to the real-world.
- Analysis and decision making incorporated throughout the chapters reinforce applications to decision making and use of accounting information by management.

Pedagogical framework

We have used many constructive pedagogical tools to help you learn accounting concepts and apply them to decision making in the business world.

Understanding the context

- **Learning objectives**, listed at the beginning of each chapter, form a framework throughout the text, with each objective repeated in the main body of the chapter and again in the **Summary**. Also, end-of-chapter assignment materials are linked to the learning objectives.
- A **chapter preview** provides an overview of the major topics of the chapter. First, an introductory paragraph explains how the story relates to the topics to be discussed, and then a graphic outline of the chapter provides a 'road map', useful for seeing the big picture as well as the connections between subtopics.

Learning the material

- This text emphasises the accounting experiences of real entities throughout, from chapter preview to the chapter's last item of homework material. Details on these many features follow. In addition, every financial accounting chapter uses **financial statements** from companies.
- **Illustrations** support and reinforce the concepts of the text. Infographics help you visualise and apply accounting concepts to the real-world. The infographics often portray important concepts in entertaining and memorable ways.
- **Learning reflection and consolidation** sections occur at the end of each key topic and consist of two parts. *Review it* serves as a learning check within the chapter by asking you to stop and answer knowledge and comprehension questions about the material just covered. These exercises help cement your understanding of how topics covered in the chapter are reported in financial statements. Answers to questions using financial statements appear at the end of the chapter. *Do it* is a brief demonstration problem that gives immediate practice using the material just covered. Solutions are provided in the text to help you understand the reasoning involved in reaching an answer.
- **Accounting equation analyses** are included in each chapter underneath key journal entries. This feature reinforces your understanding of the impact of an accounting transaction on the financial statements.
- **Helpful hints** in italicised text throughout the chapters expand on or help clarify concepts under discussion in the surrounding text. Sometimes the hints also provide alternative terminology — synonymous

terms that students may come across in subsequent accounting courses and in business — or international notes — exposing international issues in accounting, reporting and decision making.

- Each chapter presents decision tools that are useful for analysing the financial statement components discussed in that chapter. At the end of the text discussion relating to the decision tool, a **Decision-making toolkit** summarises the key features of that decision tool and reinforces its purpose. For example, chapter 7 presents the receivables turnover and average collection period as tools for use in analysing receivables. At the end of that discussion the toolkit shown below appears.

DECISION-MAKING TOOLKIT

Decision/issue	Info needed for analysis	Tool or technique to use for decision	How to evaluate results to make decision
Are collections being made in a timely fashion?	Net credit sales and average receivables balance	Receivables turnover $= \dfrac{\text{Net credit sales}}{\text{Average net receivables}}$ Average collection period $= \dfrac{365 \text{ days}}{\text{Receivables turnover}}$	Receivables turnover and average collection period should be consistent with the entity's credit policy. Any significant deviation which results in a slower receivables turnover or a longer collection period may suggest a decline in the financial integrity of credit customers.

- A **Using the decision-making toolkit** exercise, which follows the final **Learning reflection and consolidation** section in the chapter, asks you to use the decision tools presented in that chapter. You will need to evaluate the financial situation of a company, often using ratio analysis to do so.

Putting it together

- At the end of each chapter, between the body of the text and the homework materials, are several useful features for review and reference: the **Summary** lists the main points of the chapter under each learning objective; the **Decision-making toolkit — a summary** presents in one place the decision tools used throughout the chapter; and the **Key terms** section provides a concise list of all important terms in the text and gives their definitions.
- Next, a **Demonstration problem** gives you another opportunity to refer to a detailed solution to a representative problem before you do homework assignments. Problem-solving strategies help establish logic for approaching similar problems and assist you in understanding the solution.

Developing skills through practice

Throughout the homework material, certain questions, exercises and problems make use of the decision tools presented in the chapter.

- **Self-study questions** comprise a practice test to enable you to check your understanding of important concepts. These questions are keyed to the learning objectives, so you can go back and review sections of the chapter for which you find you need further work.
- **Questions** provide a full review of chapter content and help you prepare for class discussions and testing situations.
- **Brief exercises** build your confidence and test your basic skills. Each brief exercise focuses on one of the learning objectives.
- Each of the **Exercises** focuses on one or more of the learning objectives. These tend to take a little longer to complete, and they present more of a challenge than the brief exercises. The exercises help to make a manageable transition to more challenging problems.

- **Problem sets** stress the applications of the concepts presented in the chapter. Problems are keyed to the learning objectives. Certain problems help build business writing skills.
- Each brief exercise, exercise and problem has a description of the concept covered and is keyed to the learning objectives.

Building business skills

This is a unique section at the end of each chapter that offers a wealth of resources to help you pull together the learning for the chapter. This section offers problems and projects for those who want to broaden the learning experience by bringing in more real-world decision-making and critical-thinking activities.

- **Financial reporting and analysis** problems use financial statements of companies or other sources, such as journals, for further practice in understanding and interpreting financial reporting. A selection of some of the following types of problems is used in each chapter. A *Financial reporting problem* directs you to study various aspects of the financial statements. A *Comparative analysis problem* offers the opportunity to compare and contrast the financial reporting of two companies. Since the ability to read and understand business publications is an asset in one's career, *Research cases* direct you to articles published in popular business periodicals for further study and analysis of key topics. The *Interpreting financial statements* problems ask you to read parts of financial statements of actual companies and use the decision tools presented in the chapter to interpret this information. A *Global focus* or *Real-world* problem asks you to apply concepts presented in the chapter to specific situations faced by actual international companies. *Financial analysis on the web* exercises guide you to web sites from which you can obtain and analyse financial information related to the chapter topic.
- **Critical thinking** problems offer additional opportunities and activities. A selection of the following types of problems is used in each chapter. The *Group decision cases* help promote group collaboration and build decision-making skills by analysing accounting information in a less structured situation. These cases require teams of you to analyse a manager's decision or to make a decision from among alternative courses of action. They also give practice in building business communication skills. *Communication activities* provide practice in written communication — a skill much in demand among employers. *Ethics cases* describe typical ethical dilemmas and ask you to analyse the situation, identify the ethical issues involved, and decide on an appropriate course of action.

Interactive eBook

Students who purchase a new print copy of *Financial accounting: Reporting, analysis and decision making*, 6th edition will have access to the interactive eBook version (a code is provided on the inside of the front cover). The eBook integrates the following media and interactive elements into the narrative content of each chapter.

- **Practitioner videos** provide insights into the application of financial accounting concepts.
- **Animations of worked examples** talk you through the steps in solving financial accounting problems.
- **Interactive questions** provide you with the scaffolding to attempt and solve problems.

CHAPTER 1

An introduction to accounting

LEARNING OBJECTIVES

After studying this chapter, you should be able to:

1.1 explain the business context and the need for decision making

1.2 define accounting, describe the accounting process and define the diverse roles of accountants

1.3 explain the characteristics of the main forms of business organisation

1.4 understand the *Conceptual Framework* and the purpose of financial reporting

1.5 identify the users of financial reports and describe users' information needs

1.6 identify the elements of each of the four main financial statements

1.7 describe the financial reporting environment

1.8 explain the accounting concepts, principles, qualitative characteristics and constraints underlying financial statements

1.9 calculate and interpret ratios for analysing an entity's profitability, liquidity and solvency.

Chapter preview

Welcome to the accounting journey, it is not just about recording numbers. Throughout this text you will explore the concepts and regulations that underlie the preparation of the accounting reports and the various decisions that need to be made in preparing the financial information and reports. As well, we will examine the decisions made using the accounting information as inputs into the decision-making process, both inside and outside the business organisation. Accounting information can help you understand a business entity's past performance and its current financial position, and provide some insight into its future prospects.

It is an exciting ever-changing business environment which keeps pace with the changes in technology and knowledge management. For example, Domino's Pizza Enterprises Ltd commenced as a single franchise in Australia and now is the largest franchisor of the US's largest pizza chain, with operations in Europe, Japan, Australia and New Zealand. How did this occur? Why did it embrace technologies such as online ordering, including a mobile phone app and Facebook? Domino's effectively obtains information from customers using this technology, which feeds into the sale growth predictions and the strategic future directions of the business.

In this chapter we introduce the business environment, including the role of accounting, the forms of business organisation, the regulatory environment, the financial statements, and some tools that can help you analyse financial statements for decision making. The content and organisation of this chapter are as follows.

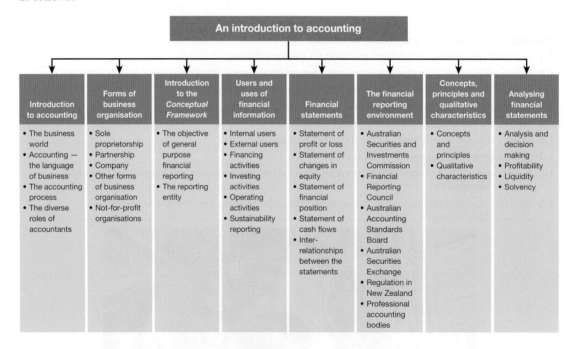

1.1 Introduction to accounting

LEARNING OBJECTIVE 1.1 Explain the business context and the need for decision making.

The business world

What's your favourite business? Apple, Google, Nike? Would you like to start your own business? How do you start a business? How do you make it grow and become widely recognised like Domino's? How do you determine whether your business is making or losing money? How do you manage your resources?

When you need to expand your operations, where do you get money to finance the expansion — should you borrow, should you issue shares, should you use your own funds? How do you convince lenders to lend you money or investors to buy your shares? Success in business requires countless decisions, and decisions require financial and other information. A **decision** is a choice among alternative courses of action.

Architects use technical and structural knowledge of the building codes together with their creative ability to design a model or plan of a building. Just like architects, in order to start and run a business you need not only your creative ideas and marketing plan, but also information on the business environment in order to understand the context of your business. Accounting provides an economic model of the business world. It plays a key role in the provision of financial information for decisions made by people inside and outside a business. The continued growth of Domino's in both the European and the Australian and New Zealand markets required a variety of information including the past and current performance of the Domino's operations. Projections on future store sales growth and potential market share growth from opening new stores was also required in order to plan ahead and to help towards the achievement of targets. The provision of accounting information within the business entity is referred to as **management accounting**. **Financial accounting** is the term used to describe the preparation and presentation of financial reports for external users. However, both financial accounting and management accounting draw on the same information system used to record and summarise the financial implications of transactions and events. Businesses also need to provide information on the environment and the community within which the business operates. The concept of sustainability is explained later in this chapter.

The business environment is ever changing. Driven by technology, life cycles of businesses are shortening. New technologies, new processes, new products, faster information flows are driving changes. How often do you update your mobile phone? Everyone in society is affected by technology change. Computers provide the technology to process the information so more time is devoted to the analysis of the information to make the best informed decisions. Accountants work in businesses as part of management teams who analyse the information gathered to make decisions. So how do we go about the decision making?

The first step in the process of decision making is to identify the issue or the decision to be made. The next step is to gather the relevant information required for the analysis. Once gathered, you identify the tool or technique that will assist analysis of the issue so a decision can be made. The final step is to evaluate the results of the analysis and make the decision. The decision-making toolkit summarises this process.

DECISION-MAKING TOOLKIT

Decision/issue	Info needed for analysis	Tool or technique to use for decision	How to evaluate results to make decision
Which film your friends wish to see	Cinema times and films showing Who are the lead actors Personal preferences	Eliminate unsuitable times and films Discuss which preferences are left and rank in popularity	Film most wish to see is the one chosen If none suitable, re-evaluate or select another social activity and start the decision process again.

Note: Each chapter presents useful information about how decision makers use financial statements. Decision-making toolkits summarise discussions of key decision-making contexts and techniques.

For example, if you were wanting to choose which film a group of friends wish to watch, you would need information concerning each of your preferences for the genre and how flexible you are in your preferences, maybe who is in the leading roles and the times the movie is being shown. The tool would be to rank the films in order of preference starting with what is showing at the times your group is available, then reducing the alternatives to which films are showing, and then eliminating any alternative which one of your group didn't want to see. You may end up with no suitable film or you may go back and change the parameters, which may include looking for another social activity. Even with this analysis your group may not enjoy the film as it was a dud, but that is the risk you take. Decisions are future oriented and you need to make informed judgements.

Similar to the social activity decision, in the business world, even with all the information available, the final outcome of the decision may not be what was expected. Next, we are going to consider what accounting is and how it is used in the decision-making process in the business environment.

1.2 Accounting: the language of business

LEARNING OBJECTIVE 1.2 Define accounting, describe the accounting process and define the diverse roles of accountants.

The primary function of accounting is to provide reliable and relevant financial information for decision making. Accounting has been around for centuries and has developed significantly since its humble beginnings in ancient times when scribes recorded simple agreements between parties and other information on clay tablets. Today, almost every person engages in business transactions in relation to the financial aspects of life such as purchasing products and paying bills. This means that accounting plays a significant role in society.

Accounting can be referred to as the 'language of business' as it is a means of common communication where information flows from one party to others. In order for information to be effective it must be understood. Accounting, like many other professions, has its own terminology or jargon that is unique to the profession and can have alternative meanings in different contexts. Accounting terms, concepts and symbols are used to provide financial information to a variety of users including managers, shareholders and employees. You will need to learn these specialised terms and symbols in order to be able to prepare and use accounting information effectively. The definitions of key terms listed at the end of each chapter will support your learning. Providing reliable and relevant accounting information is a complex process.

The accounting process

Accounting is the process of identifying, measuring, recording and communicating the economic transactions and events of a business operation. Table 1.1 summarises these main steps.

TABLE 1.1 The accounting process

Identifying	Measuring	Recording	Communicating
Taking into consideration all transactions which affect the business entity	Quantifying in monetary terms	Analysing, recording, classifying and summarising the transactions	Preparing the accounting reports; analysing and interpreting

Identifying involves determining which economic events represent transactions. **Transactions** are economic activities relevant to a particular business and include, for example, the sale of a good to a customer or the purchase of office stationery from a supplier. Transactions are the basic inputs into the accounting process. **Measurement** is the process of quantifying transactions in monetary terms and must be completed in order to record transactions. The recording process results in a systematic record of all of the transactions of an entity and provides a history of business activities. To enhance the usefulness of the recorded information, it must be classified and summarised.

Classification allows for the reduction of thousands of transactions into meaningful groups and categories. For example, all transactions involving the sales of goods can be grouped as one total sales figure and all cash transactions can be grouped to keep track of the amount of money remaining in the business's bank account. The process of summarisation allows the classified economic data to be presented in financial reports for decision making by a variety of users. These reports summarise business information for a specific period of time such as a year, 6 months, one quarter or even a month. Domino's provides 6-monthly reports that are available to the general public via the securities exchange web site.

Communicating is the final stage in the accounting cycle. Communicating involves preparing accounting reports for potential users of the information. There are many reasons for maintaining accurate financial accounting records, including legal and other reporting requirements. The Australian Taxation Office (ATO) and the New Zealand Inland Revenue (NZIR) require businesses to provide a variety of financial information to comply with legal requirements. Users of financial information, both internal and external to the entity, will require financial information to make decisions in relation to the business. Once the users have acquired the information, they can use a variety of techniques to analyse and interpret the data. In most of the chapters, there are sections which demonstrate a variety of techniques that are useful for analysing and interpreting financial statements. These sections are intended to support the development of your skills in analysis and interpretation of financial information, and to enhance your understanding of accounting.

To recap this section, accounting provides an economic model of the business world and plays a key role in the provision of financial information for decision making. Accounting is the process of identifying, measuring, recording and communicating the economic transactions and events of a business operation to users of financial information. The first three activities of identifying, measuring and recording the business information are commonly referred to as **bookkeeping**. Bookkeeping forms the foundation of the activities underlying accounting and these processes are explained in detail in the early chapters of this text, using a manual accounting system. In the early part of the twentieth century, the role of the accountant did not extend much beyond this bookkeeping function. Today, however, the roles and responsibilities extend far beyond preparing accounting records.

The diverse roles of accountants

Accountants practise accounting in four main areas: commercial accounting, public accounting, government accounting and not-for-profit accounting.

Commercial accounting

Commercial accountants work in industry and commerce. Companies like Domino's and Qantas employ a number of accountants in different roles, such as management accounting and financial accounting. The accounting information system provides these accountants with the information they need for planning, decision making, and compiling reports for a range of users. The **chief financial officer (CFO)** is a senior manager in an organisation and directs the accounting operations. Financial accountants oversee the recording of all of the transactions and prepare reports for users external to the business entity, such as shareholders and creditors. Management accountants focus on providing information for internal decision making as they prepare specifically tailored reports for use by management. Commercial accountants are employed within organisations, and their work is directed by their employers. Public accountants, on the other hand, run their own businesses and are therefore more autonomous.

Public accounting

Public accountants, as the name suggests, provide their professional services to the public. They can practise in business organisations that range from small single-person-run offices to very large organisations with branches all over the world and thousands of employees. Public accountants tend to specialise in one or more areas of accounting when providing services to the public. Auditing is one of the primary services provided by large public accounting firms such as Deloitte and KPMG. An **audit** is an independent examination of the accounting data presented by an entity in order to provide an opinion as to whether the financial statements fairly present the results of the operations and the entity's financial position. Public accounting firms also provide a wide range of taxation services including advice for minimising an entity's tax liability, of course within the law, and preparation of tax returns, among other things. In more recent years, management advisory services have been a growing area for public accountants. Services include provision of advice on improving their clients' business efficiency and effectiveness, design and installation of accounting information systems, and assistance with strategic planning. Public accounting firms may also provide advisory services to government organisations or be employed by the government.

Government accounting

Government accountants, employed within government entities, engage in a variety of roles and activities, such as financial accounting and auditing. Local councils, state governments and federal government receive and pay out large amounts of funds each year and these activities need to be accounted for. Nowadays, many of the issues and decisions faced by government entities are the same as those in the commercial sector. As a result, these entities often follow accounting policies and practices similar to those in the private sector. Although most government entities are not-for-profit, some government departments, such as the Brisbane City Council, run profit-making businesses.

Not-for-profit accounting

Not-for-profit accountants, working in the not-for-profit sector, engage in many activities including planning, decision making, and preparing financial and management reports for both internal and external users. Management processes, accounting systems and operational methods are often similar between profit-making and not-for-profit entities. However, there is one major difference and that is the *profit motive*.

A **not-for-profit entity** focuses on successfully fulfilling its mission and administrative goals, rather than focusing on making a profit. Not-for-profit entities include public hospitals, clubs, some schools and charities. For example, the World Vision charity works with poor, marginalised people and communities to improve their lives and help them take control of their futures. Not-for-profit entities are exempt from income taxes on activities related to their exempt purpose and have fiduciary responsibilities to members, contributors and other constituents, and their activities may require reporting to supervising government entities.

In summary, accountants have many diverse roles and can work in different forms of organisation from small one-person businesses to large corporations with a worldwide presence. Once trained as an accountant, you can also work in organisations in non-traditional accounting roles or be better equipped to run your own business.

Would you like to run your own business? How would you decide how to structure your business and what resources would be required? In the next section, we explore the different forms of business organisation in more depth.

LEARNING REFLECTION AND CONSOLIDATION

Review it
1. What information would you require to set up and run your own business?
2. What is the primary objective of accounting?
3. Accountants practise accounting in four main areas. Describe these areas, with examples.

Note: Review it questions at the end of major text sections prompt you to stop and review the key points you have just studied. Sometimes these questions stand alone; other times they are accompanied by practice exercises called *Do it*.

1.3 Forms of business organisation

LEARNING OBJECTIVE 1.3 Explain the characteristics of the main forms of business organisation.

Business organisations can be classified into profit-oriented businesses such as sole proprietorship, partnership or company, and not-for-profit entities such as charities and government departments. Throughout this text, we concentrate on preparing financial reports for the profit sector. However, many of the concepts and regulations apply equally to the not-for-profit sector.

Suppose you graduate with a marketing degree and open your own marketing agency. One of the first important business decisions you will need to make is the organisational structure under which the business will operate. You have three choices: sole proprietorship, partnership or company. Figure 1.1 outlines the three main forms of business organisation. In selecting a suitable business structure, some of the factors to consider are:

- establishment fees and maintenance costs
- asset protection (business and personal assets)
- the type of business and how it impacts on your record keeping
- legitimate tax minimisation.

FIGURE 1.1 Characteristics of the main forms of business organisation

Sole proprietorship

- Simple to establish
- Owner controlled

Partnership

- Simple to establish
- Shared control
- Broader skills and resources

Company

- Easier to transfer ownership
- Easier to raise funds
- Limited liability

Sole proprietorship

A **sole proprietorship** is a business owned by one person. It is the simplest form of business structure and has very few legal formalities. It is quick and inexpensive to establish and inexpensive to wind down. Under this structure, the owner of the business has *no separate legal existence* from the business. You might choose the sole proprietorship form if you have a marketing agency. You would be referred to as a *sole trader*. As a sole trader, the business is fully owned by you and you have total autonomy over the business's strategic direction and all business decisions. The assets and profits completely belong to you. The business's income is treated as the business owner's individual income (hence, no separate legal existence). Sole traders pay the same tax as individual taxpayers, according to the marginal tax rates. Depending on the level of profits from the business, this could be a disadvantage. In the 2017 year, at an income level of around $137 000, the effective average tax rate of an individual is equal to the 30% company tax rate, so for any profits above this level the sole trader is paying more income tax than if the business was organised as a company. Other disadvantages are that the business is limited by the owner's skills, the funds available to invest, and the time available for running the business, as well as bearing full personal liability for the business's debts. Small owner-operated businesses such as restaurants, dentists and panel beaters are often sole proprietorships, as are farms and small retail shops.

Partnership

Another possibility for your new marketing agency is for you to join forces with other individuals to form a partnership, in which all partners share control. A **partnership** is a relationship or association between two or more entities carrying on a business in common with a view to making a profit. Entities forming the partnership may be individuals or companies.

There is little formality involved in creating a partnership. Partnerships are often formed because one individual does not have enough economic resources to initiate or expand the business, or because partners bring unique skills or resources to the partnership. You and your partner(s) should formalise your duties and contributions in a written partnership agreement. All partnerships should be formed on the basis of an agreement (which may be made in writing, verbally or by implication). In Australia, partnerships are governed on a state-by-state basis by the Partnership Act in each Australian state. In New Zealand, the *Partnership Act 1908* is the national legislation. Partners must also decide how profit (or losses) should be allocated among the partners. Accounting information is often used to determine each partner's share, as specified in the partnership agreement.

Traditionally, partnerships have *not* been incorporated. This means that, like a sole proprietorship structure, the business structure has **unlimited liability**, so each partner is personally liable for all the debts of the partnership even if they are caused by decisions made by other partners. More recently, changes to state and territory legislation have allowed for limited liability partnerships (LLPs). Similarly, New Zealand introduced limited partnerships in 2008. These are an emerging trend and are often used for raising venture capital for new businesses, such as a new mining venture. However, because *limited partnerships* are taxed as companies and the general partner still bears unlimited liability, this form of business structure is not very popular. Another disadvantage of a partnership structure is that a partnership has a limited life. If a partner wishes to sell or leave the partnership, or a partner dies, a new partnership agreement must be formed. The partnership agreement often has conditions on who can be admitted as a new partner in the event of a partner wishing to sell their share of the business. Finally, if there are disputes between the partners, it can be costly and damaging to the business, as well as to friendships.

Partnerships are often used to organise retail and service-type businesses, including professional services such as accounting, medical and legal practices.

Company

As a third alternative, a marketing agency can be organised as a company. A **company** or corporation is a separate legal entity formed under the *Corporations Act 2001* (Cwlth) in Australia or the New Zealand *Companies Act 1993* (Public Act). The process of setting up a company is called *incorporation*. The owners of a company are called **shareholders** (or *stockholders* in the US) and their ownership interests are represented by the number of shares they own in the company.

Under a company structure, the company can sue and be sued and enter into contracts in its own name. As a result, the shareholders of most companies have *limited liability*. **Limited liability** means the shareholders are liable for the debts of the business only to the extent of amounts unpaid on their shares. If a company breaches an agreement, it is generally solely liable — unless there is some misconduct by the directors or officers, such as misrepresentation or misleading or deceptive conduct. If misconduct or misrepresentation is proven, it is possible for the company directors to be held personally liable for debts. Another advantage of the corporate form is that a company has an indefinite life. The owners can more easily transfer their ownership interest by selling their shares in the company to other investors.

Companies vary in size from small privately owned and often family-run companies (proprietary limited companies — Pty Ltd) to large public companies listed on a securities exchange (limited companies — Ltd) managed by directors, with thousands of shareholders. If you use a company structure, there are establishment costs and ongoing fees and regulations to comply with. These make it more expensive to run than unincorporated business structures. We will discuss these issues in more depth in chapter 10.

When considering the business structure of your marketing agency, you need to decide on two factors: the decision-making structure you want for your business (sole trader, partnership or company) and the financial and legal ramifications of the structure you choose. Will the business be an incorporated or unincorporated business? A sole trader, for example, has all the decision-making power but also has full responsibility (is liable) for the actions of the business. A company, on the other hand, has limited liability but, if there is more than one director, the decision making is usually a shared responsibility. Thus, the decision to incorporate or to remain unincorporated has distinct legal and financial ramifications. Many businesses start as sole proprietorships or partnerships and eventually incorporate. For example, R.M. Williams was established as a small proprietary family company, was subsequently floated as a public company and, more recently, the family members repurchased the shares and delisted the company — so now it operates once again as a family business.

Other forms of business organisation

Although the sole proprietorship, partnership and company are the most common forms of business structure, others such as trusts, cooperatives and not-for-profit forms are discussed below.

Trusts

A **trust** is a relationship or association between two or more parties, whereby one party holds property in trust for the other; i.e. they are vested with the property. A trust, in its simple form, has:

- a settlor (who sets up the trust)
- a trustee (who is the legal owner and manages the trust property — investments, assets etc. — and pays out any net income for the benefit of the beneficiaries); and
- beneficiaries (the person or people who are the equitable owners and for whom the investments or assets are held and to whom income is paid).

The trustee has full control over the assets held by the trust, so it is important that the trustee be entirely trustworthy and able to manage all aspects of trust administration. Trusts may be made expressly in writing or implied from the circumstances. Trusts can range from relatively simplified structures to more complex structures. It is possible, for example, for a family member to act as a trustee for a family trust. It is very common in family-owned small businesses for a Pty Ltd company to be the trustee and the family members the beneficiaries, which means the business has the protection of limited liability for asset protection but profits can be split effectively for taxation. It is also possible for a company to trade as the trustee of a trust. For example, DEXUS Property Group is a property trust listed on the Australian Securities Exchange, with total funds under management as at 30 June 2016 of approximately $22.2 billion. The listed property portfolio comprises almost $11 billion of direct property assets in Australia, New Zealand, the United States and Europe.

Cooperatives

A **cooperative** is a form of business organisation that is member-owned, controlled and used. It must consist of five or more people. Cooperatives are legislated at state level in Australia. They are distinctive for fostering a highly participative and democratic style of work, pooling resources to be more competitive and sharing skills. Cooperatives play an important role in the community. They supply goods and services to their members and to the general public in areas as diverse as retailing, recycling, manufacturing, labour hiring, printing and agriculture. Examples include Australian Forest Growers, South Gippsland Herd Improvement Association Inc., Ballina Fishermen's Co-operative Ltd and Bermagui Pre School Co-operative Society Limited.

Not-for-profit organisations

Not-for-profit is one of the more interesting forms of business organisation. This sector includes associations such as clubs, charities and the government sector.

Associations

Small non-profit, community-based groups often form **associations**. Associations can be, but are not always, incorporated. There are currently more than 142 000 incorporated associations on the public register. An incorporated association provides a relatively inexpensive and easier means of establishing a legal entity than forming a company. In other words, an association is an alternative to a company. An incorporated association has similar advantages to a company but is not as expensive to set up or maintain. An association can trade as a profit organisation, but this cannot be its main objective. Any profit from the trading must be put back into the association and not given to its members. Although associations tend to be small community groups, they can be specialist interest groups such as sports associations, industry associations, animal breeder associations and hobby associations. The Australian Medical Association and the Epilepsy Association of Australia are two examples of groups that are focused on a particular area.

Government

The government sector is also called the **public sector**. The distinguishing feature is that the organisations are owned by the government, whether it be federal, state or local. Within this sector there may be departments or segments which are operated as business enterprises and have a profit-making objective or aim to generate a return on the resources they control. Examples include public hospitals, public schools and the ATO.

Because the majority of business is transacted by companies, the emphasis in this text is on the corporate form of business structure. Generally, the techniques for recording transactions, the basic accounting equation, the principles underlying accounting and financial reporting, and the major financial statements are common to all business forms. Recall that the primary role of accounting is to provide financial information for decision making. How do accountants know what information to provide? The *Conceptual Framework* provides guidance to preparers of financial information by defining who is required to report and who the users are likely to be.

1.4 Introduction to the *Conceptual Framework*

LEARNING OBJECTIVE 1.4 Understand the *Conceptual Framework* and the purpose of financial reporting.

In this section we introduce the ***Conceptual Framework***. We will piece it together frame by frame throughout the chapter. A conceptual framework consists of a set of concepts to be followed by preparers of financial statements and standard setters. We will use the image of a window to present the *Conceptual Framework*, because a window is a lens through which we can view the world, in the same way as preparing external financial statements using a conceptual framework allows us to view the economic world in a particular way.

The historical development of the *Conceptual Framework* is outlined in chapter 13. It is important to note that, at the time of writing, the 2010 version of the *Conceptual Framework* is being updated, with the new version expected to be released mid-2018. Throughout this text, the *Conceptual Framework* content is based on the 2010 version. In 2015, the International Accounting Standards Board (IASB) issued the *Conceptual Framework*'s Exposure Draft (ED). A summary of this ED and its potential effects on the financial statements of reporting entities is explored in chapter 13.

The *Conceptual Framework* that has been developed to date consists of four sections. Section 1 is the objective of general purpose financial reporting, as represented in figure 1.2.

FIGURE 1.2 Building the *Conceptual Framework* — section 1

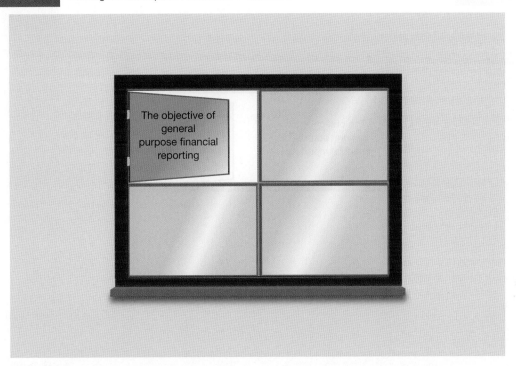

The objective of general purpose financial reporting

The objective of general purpose financial reporting forms the foundation of the *Conceptual Framework*. All the other elements flow from the objective. If we know why we need to report, then it follows we can determine who needs to report and what and how information is to be reported. The objective of general purpose financial reporting is to provide financial information about the reporting entity that is useful to existing and potential equity investors, lenders and other creditors in making their decisions about providing resources to the entity. This definition highlights the primary users of **general purpose financial reports** to be existing and potential shareholders, lenders and other creditors. It also acknowledges that other groups may also be interested in the financial information. The management of the reporting entity is one such group, but it was decided that management does not need to rely on general purpose financial reports because it can obtain the financial information it needs internally. Other parties such as regulators and members of the public may also find general purpose financial reports useful.

It is acknowledged that general purpose financial reports do not provide an evaluation of an entity but provide information that, together with other sources of information such as general economic conditions, political climate and industry conditions, allows primary users to estimate the value of the reporting entity.

Now that the objective of general purpose financial reporting has been discussed, the next step is to decide who needs to prepare general purpose financial reports.

The reporting entity

Another piece in the *Conceptual Framework* is represented in figure 1.3.

At the time of writing, the IASB's project to develop the new *Conceptual Framework* had not completed the section on the reporting entity and therefore Australian business entities and standard setters use that section from the previous Australian conceptual framework developed by the Australian Accounting Standards Board.

FIGURE 1.3 Building the *Conceptual Framework* — section 2

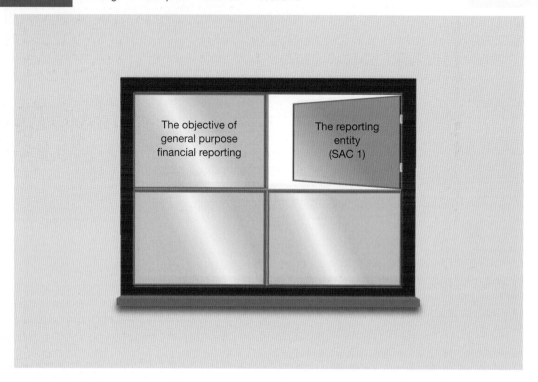

In the previous section, we described a number of different forms of business organisation. While each of these forms of business prepares some kind of information for a variety of users, not all businesses are classified as reporting entities. The Australian conceptual framework defines the **reporting entity** in Statement of Accounting Concept 1 (SAC 1) as an entity in which it is reasonable to expect the existence of users who depend on general purpose financial reports for information to enable them to make economic decisions.

Three main indicators determine which of the forms of business organisation discussed so far in this chapter fall into the category of a reporting entity. That is, an entity is more likely to be classified as a reporting entity if it is (1) managed by individuals who are not owners of the entity, (2) politically or economically important, and (3) sizable in any of the following ways — sales, assets, borrowings, customers or employees. It appears then, in applying the indicators, subjective judgements must be made. For example, what value of sales or how many employees are considered sizable enough for the business to be a reporting entity? In the main, reporting entities include public companies, some large private companies and government authorities.

It is important to determine whether an organisation is a reporting entity as reporting entities must prepare *external* general purpose financial reports that comply with accounting standards. All other entities will prepare information for internal use.

Reporting entities tend to be larger organisations and the financial information provided in external general purpose financial reports tends to be quite condensed. Both reporting and non-reporting entities also prepare internal reports that contain more detailed information. Examples of both internal and external reports are provided in the latter part of this chapter. Possible new developments and differential reporting are explored in chapter 13.

The information arising from businesses, regardless of their structure, is useful to a variety of users. In the next section, we explore the users of financial statements and users' information needs.

1.5 Users and uses of financial information

LEARNING OBJECTIVE 1.5 Identify the users of financial reports and describe users' information needs.

Now that we know which entities are required to prepare general purpose financial reports and the objective for financial reporting, let's take a closer look at the users of financial reports and their information needs. We begin with an exploration of the users and their information needs as outlined in the *Conceptual Framework* for financial reporting and then discuss other users of financial reporting.

Figure 1.4 sets out the primary users of the general purpose financial reports being those users who provide resources to the entity and therefore require information to make decisions concerning the provision of those resources.

FIGURE 1.4 Categories of primary users of general purpose financial reports

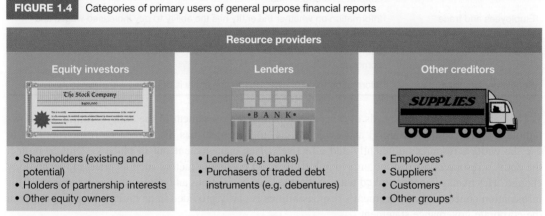

*Only in their capacity as resource providers, otherwise they are not considered primary users.

Equity investors contribute to the equity of an entity by investing resources (usually cash) for the purpose of receiving a return and include shareholders, holders of partnership interests and other equity owners. **Lenders** contribute to an entity by lending resources (usually cash) for the purpose of receiving a return in the form of interest. Some questions that may be asked by investors and creditors about a company include the following.
- Is the company earning satisfactory profit?
- How does the company compare in size and profitability with its competitors?
- Will the company be able to pay its debts as they fall due?
- Is the company paying regular dividends to its shareholders?

Other creditors may provide resources to an entity as a result of their relationship with the entity, even though they are not primarily resource providers. For example, suppliers extend credit to facilitate a sale, employees provide their services (human capital) in exchange for remuneration and customers may prepay for goods or services which are to be provided in the future. These parties are only considered resource providers to the extent that they provide the entity with resources in the form of credit, and they make decisions based on providing such resources. When they are not in this capacity they are referred to as other users.

Other users include government agencies, members of the public, suppliers, customers and employees (when not resource providers). While these other users have specialised information needs, they may find the financial information that meets the needs of resource providers useful. However, it is made clear that financial reporting is not primarily directed to other users but rather to resource providers. The information needs and questions of other external users vary considerably. For example, taxation authorities such as the ATO want to know whether the entity complies with the tax laws. Regulatory agencies such as the Australian Securities and Investments Commission (ASIC) or the Australian Competition and Consumer

Commission (ACCC) want to know whether the entity is operating within prescribed rules. Table 1.2 provides a list of external users and examples of their information needs.

TABLE 1.2 External users of accounting information and their information needs

Users	Information needs
Investors	Information to determine whether to invest based on future profitability, return or capital growth
Creditors	Information to determine whether to grant credit based on risks and ability of the entity to repay debts
Customers	Information on whether an entity will continue to honour product warranties and support its product lines
Employees and trade unions	Information on whether the entity has the ability to pay increased wages and benefits, and offer job security
Government authorities	Information to calculate the amount of tax owing and whether the entity complies with tax laws
Regulatory agencies	Information to determine whether the entity is operating within prescribed rules

The common information needs of other users include an assessment of the entity's future cash flows (amount, timing and uncertainty) and evidence that management has discharged its responsibilities to use the entity's resources efficiently and effectively. Has management put in place systems to protect the entity's resources against the unfavourable effects of economic factors such as price and technology change? Has management complied with applicable laws, regulations and contractual commitments? This information concerning management's responsibilities is partly provided in an entity's financial report in the corporate governance statement.

Internal users

Internal users of accounting information are managers who plan, organise and run a business. They do not need to rely on general purpose financial reports as they can obtain the financial information they need internally. Internal users include marketing managers, production supervisors, directors and other managers. In running a business, managers of large companies like Domino's must answer many important questions, including the following.

- Is there sufficient cash to pay debts?
- What is the cost of manufacturing each unit of product?
- Can we afford to give employees pay rises this year?
- How should we finance our expansion into Europe?

To answer these and other questions, users need detailed information on a timely basis. For internal users, accounting provides internal reports, such as financial comparisons of alternative plans, projections of revenue from new sales campaigns, and forecasts of cash needs for the next year. In addition, internal users rely on summarised financial information presented in the form of financial statements.

External users

Although the needs of the various users differ, there are some common information needs that are intended to be met by external general purpose financial reports, i.e. the published financial statements of an entity prepared in accordance with applicable accounting standards.

External users have an interest in financial information about the three main types of activities — financing, investing and operating. These activities are common to all businesses. The accounting information system keeps track of the results of each of these business activities. Let's look in more detail at each type of business activity.

Financing activities

It takes money to make money. The two main sources of outside funds for companies are borrowing money from lenders and selling shares to investors. For example, Domino's may borrow money in a variety of ways. It can take out a loan at a bank or borrow from many lenders by issuing debt securities. Two types of debt securities are unsecured notes and debentures. The main difference is that debentures are secured by a charge over the issuer's assets. This means that specified assets can be sold to pay the debenture holders if the issuer defaults.

A company may also obtain funds by selling shares to investors. When a business initially becomes a company, shares are often issued to a small group of individuals who have an interest in starting the company. However, as the business grows, it becomes necessary to sell shares more broadly to obtain additional financing. **Share capital** is the term used to describe the total amount paid in by shareholders for the shares. The shareholders are the owners of the company.

Helpful hint: Companies may issue several types of shares, but the shares that represent the main ownership interest are called **ordinary shares**.

The claims of creditors differ from those of shareholders. If you lend money to a company, you are one of its creditors. In lending money, you specify a payment schedule (for example, payment at the end of 3 months). As a creditor, you have a legal right to be paid at the agreed time. In the event of non-payment, you may legally force the company to take action, such as selling its property to pay its debts. The law requires that creditors' claims be paid before ownership claims, i.e. owners have no claim on corporate resources until the claims of creditors are satisfied. If you buy a company's shares instead of lending it money, you have no right to expect any payments until all of its creditors are paid. However, many companies make payments to shareholders on a regular basis as long as they are solvent — that is, after the dividend is paid there are sufficient resources to cover expected payments to creditors. These payments to shareholders are called **dividends**. Dividends are a distribution of profit; they are not repayment of capital.

Investing activities

Investing activities involve purchasing the resources an entity needs in order to operate. During the early stages of an entity's life it must acquire many assets. For example, computers, delivery trucks, furniture and buildings are assets obtained from investing activities. Different types of assets are given different names. Domino's plant and equipment are referred to as *property, plant and equipment*, but can also be known as *fixed assets* or *non-current assets*.

While many of the entity's assets are purchased through investing activities, others result from operating activities. For example, if Domino's sells goods to a customer and does not receive cash immediately, it has a right to expect payment from that customer in the future. This right to receive money in the future is an asset called **accounts receivable**.

Operating activities

Once a business has the assets it needs to get started, it can begin its operations. Domino's is in the business of selling fast food. We call the results from the sale of these products *revenues*. **Revenues** are sales and other increases in equity that arise from the ordinary activities of an entity. For example, Domino's records revenue when it sells a pizza.

Revenues arise from different sources and are identified by various names depending on the nature of the business. For instance, Domino's main source of revenue is the sale of goods. However, it also generates store asset rental revenue and revenue from royalties. Sources of revenue common to many businesses are sales revenue, service revenue and interest revenue.

Before the business can sell a single pizza, it must purchase the ingredients to make the product. It also incurs costs such as salaries, rent and electricity. All these costs are necessary to sell the product. In accounting language, **expenses** are the cost of assets consumed or services used in the process of generating revenues.

Expenses take many forms and are identified by various names depending on the type of asset consumed or service used. For example, the business keeps track of these types of expenses: cost of sales, selling expenses (such as the costs associated with delivering pizzas), marketing expenses (such as the cost of advertising), administrative expenses (such as the salaries of administrative staff, and telephone and heating costs incurred in the office), and interest expense (amount of interest paid on various debts).

Domino's compares the revenues of a period with the expenses of that period to determine whether it has earned a profit. When revenues exceed expenses, a **profit** results. When expenses exceed revenues, a **loss** results.

Accountants today not only need to record the transactions and events which are then recognised and reported in the financial statements, but also need to be aware of sustainability issues for business and how to report them.

Sustainability reporting

It's constantly in the news; there have been many documentaries about it, numerous television programs, scientific research. What is IT? The environment and humanity's impact on it. While each of us makes an imprint on our environment with daily use of electricity, driving of cars and adding huge amounts of household waste to public waste facilities, businesses have the capacity to have an even larger effect on the environment.

Mining, deforestation, toxic wastes in rivers and oceans, and natural resource consumption are only some of the negative impacts that businesses all around the world have on our natural environment. It is not sufficient just to talk about it; it is more important to look at what we are doing to try to reduce the effects? Have you ever thought about your impact on the environment? Are you doing anything to reduce your environmental footprint?

Sustainability is about making sure the social, economic and environmental needs of our community are met and kept healthy for future generations. Sustainable development must not be only about economic growth, but also environmental quality and social equity. Measuring environmental impact is a difficult task. Accounting has traditionally measured business activities in dollar terms. How can accountants measure the impact that businesses have on the environment? How do we measure the impact of an open-cut mine on the landscape? How do we measure the effects of an oil spill that kills marine life? With the use of eXtensible Business Reporting Language (XBRL) we are attempting to standardise our measurements of financial information. Is it possible to standardise our measurement of environmental impacts?

Many companies disclose information on the impact of their business on the environment. Mostly this has been on a voluntary basis. Just access some large company web sites and you will find information on how they are trying to reduce their impact on the environment. However, we need to do more.

Currently, social and environmental disclosures are voluntary. However, there are increasing pressures on companies from shareholders and other stakeholders to measure, report on and reduce their environmental impact. There are also increasing pressures on governments to take appropriate actions. In order to improve the situation, we need reliable measurement systems. Can accountants meet the challenge?

LEARNING REFLECTION AND CONSOLIDATION

Review it
1. What are the three main forms of business organisation and the advantages of each?
2. What is the purpose of the *Conceptual Framework*?
3. Distinguish between internal and external users of financial information? Give examples of each.
4. Identify three categories of users identified by the *Conceptual Framework*. Give examples of each.
5. What are the three types of business activity?
6. What is meant by sustainability?

Do it

Classify the following activities as financing, investing or operating: (1) issuing shares, (2) purchasing a building, (3) selling pizza, and (4) repaying a loan.

Solution

(1) financing, (2) investing, (3) operating, and (4) financing.

Note: *Do it* exercises, like the one here, ask you to put newly acquired knowledge to work. Sometimes, they outline the reasoning necessary to complete the exercise and show a solution.

1.6 Financial statements

LEARNING OBJECTIVE 1.6 Identify the elements of each of the four main financial statements.

Financial position, financial performance and cash flows are of interest to users of accounting information. How does an entity decide on the content of the financial statements? The definition of the elements of financial statements is another piece in the *Conceptual Framework* as represented in figure 1.5.

FIGURE 1.5 Building the *Conceptual Framework* — section 3

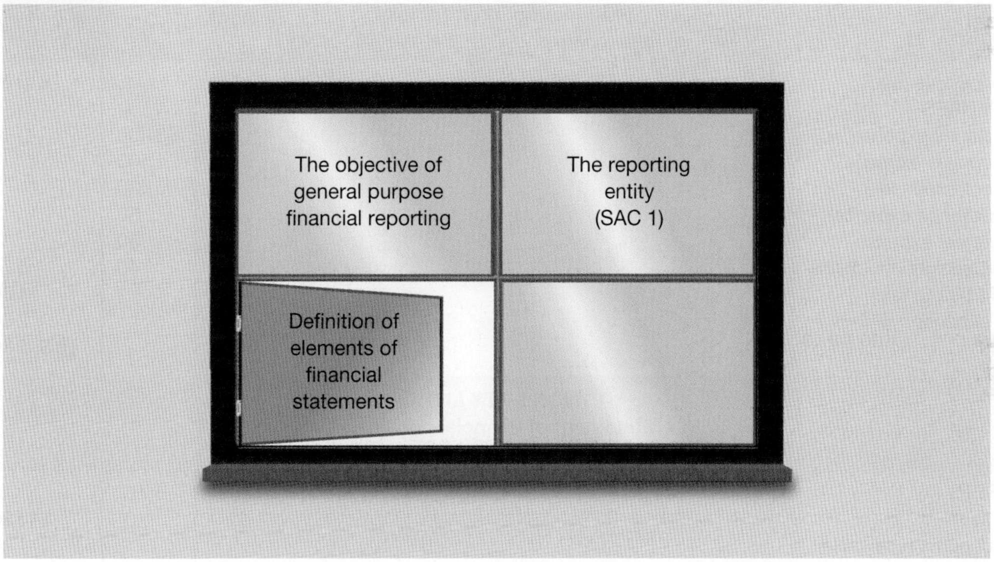

The *Conceptual Framework for Financial Reporting 2010* defines the elements of financial statements. In this section, we explore the **financial statements** that provide vital information to users when making a variety of decisions. This information is presented in four main financial statements that form the backbone of financial accounting.

To present a picture at a point in time of what your business controls (its assets), what it owes (its liabilities) and the owner's investment in the business (equity), you would prepare a **statement of financial position**. **Assets** are formally defined in the *Conceptual Framework* as a resource controlled by the entity as a result of past events from which future economic benefits are expected by the entity. **Liabilities** are formally defined in the *Conceptual Framework* as outflows of economic benefits that the entity is presently obliged to make as a result of past events. We will look at assets and liabilities in more detail in later chapters.

To show how successfully your business performed during a period of time, you would report its revenues and expenses in the *statement of profit or loss*. The **statement of changes in equity** explains all changes in equity during a period of time. Finally, of particular interest to bankers and other creditors is the **statement of cash flows**, which shows where the business obtained cash during a period of time and how that cash was used. The statement of cash flows is considered in more detail in chapter 11.

The next section of this chapter outlines and explains the regulation of external financial reporting in detail. To introduce you to the main financial statements, we have prepared the financial statements for a marketing agency, Wong Pty Ltd (figure 1.6). Take some time now to look at their general form and categories in preparation for the more detailed discussion that follows. Note that:

- a simplified statement of profit or loss is shown; a fully classified statement of profit or loss is provided in figure 4.6.
- a simplified statement of financial position is shown; a fully classified statement of financial position is provided in figure 1.15
- Wong's financial statements are internal reports generated for internal use. External financial statements are presented in a different format as illustrated in the Giorgina's Pizza Limited statements later in the chapter.

FIGURE 1.6	Wong Pty Ltd's financial statements

WONG PTY LTD Statement of profit or loss for the month ended 31 October 2019		
Service revenues		$10 600
EXPENSES		
Salaries expense	$3 200	
Supplies expense	1 500	
Rent expense	900	
Insurance expense	50	
Interest expense	50	
Depreciation expense	40	5 740
Profit before tax		4 860
Tax expense		2 000
Profit		❶ $ 2 860

WONG PTY LTD Statement of financial position as at 31 October 2019		
ASSETS		
Cash		$15 200
Accounts receivable		200
Advertising supplies		1 000
Prepaid insurance		550
Office equipment		4 960
Total assets		21 910
LIABILITIES		
Accounts payable	$2 500	
Interest payable	50	
Revenue received in advance	800	
Salaries payable	1 200	
Bank loan	5 000	
Total liabilities		9 550
Net assets		$12 360
EQUITY		
Share capital		$10 000
Retained earnings 31/10/19		**2 360**
Total equity		$12 360

WONG PTY LTD Calculation of retained earnings for the month ended 31 October 2019		
Retained earnings, 1/10/19	$	0
Profit		**2 860**
Less: Dividends		(500)
Retained earnings, 31/10/19	② $	**2 360**

WONG PTY LTD Statement of cash flows for the month ended 31 October 2019		
CASH FLOWS FROM OPERATING ACTIVITIES		
Cash receipts from operating activities	$11 200	
Cash payments for operating activities	(5 500)	
Net cash provided by operating activities		$ 5 700
CASH FLOWS FROM INVESTING ACTIVITIES		
Purchased office equipment	(5 000)	
Net cash used by investing activities		(5 000)
CASH FLOWS FROM FINANCING ACTIVITIES		
Issue of shares	10 000	
Proceeds from bank loan	5 000	
Payment of dividend	(500)	
Net cash provided by financing activities		14 500
Net increase in cash		15 200
Cash at beginning of period		–
Cash at end of period		**$15 200**

① Note that final sums in the statements are double-underlined. Also note the interrelationships of the four financial statements as illustrated by the amounts in bold.

② The calculation of retained earnings is part of the statement of changes in equity, but is usually shown as a note in the financial statements (see figure 1.14).

Statement of profit or loss

The purpose of the statement of profit or loss is to report the success or failure of the entity's operations for a period of time. To indicate that Wong's statement reports the results of operations for a period of time, the statement is dated 'for the month ended 31 October 2019'. The **statement of profit or loss** lists the entity's income (i.e. revenues and gains), followed by its expenses. Finally, the profit (or loss) is determined by deducting expenses from income. This result is the famed *bottom line* often referred to in business.

Why are financial statement users interested in the bottom line? We explain this using the 'decision-making toolkit' that follows. Resource providers (investors and lenders) use the statement of profit or loss to determine if the entity is profitable. If the revenues exceed the expenses, then a profit is reported; but if expenses exceed the revenues, then it is a loss. If investors believe that Wong Pty Ltd will be even more successful in the future, they may be willing to invest more funds. Investors are interested in an entity's past profit because it provides some information about future profit. Similarly, creditors also use the statement of profit or loss to predict future performance. When a bank lends money to an entity, it does so in the belief that it will be repaid in the future. If it didn't think it was going to be repaid, it wouldn't lend the money. Therefore, before making the loan, the bank loan officer will use the statement of profit or loss as a source of information to predict whether the entity will be profitable enough to repay its loan. Note also that managers allocate resources based on their beliefs about an entity's future performance.

The issue of shares and dividend distributions are not used in determining profit. For example, $10 000 of cash received from issuing new shares was not treated as revenue by Wong Pty Ltd, and dividends paid of $500 were not regarded as a business expense.

For external financial reports, the statement of profit or loss must also include all changes in equity other than owner/shareholder changes. This statement is called a 'statement of profit or loss and other comprehensive income'. The new standard permits an option of presenting one statement of profit or loss and other comprehensive income in two sections or two statements (a separate profit or loss section and a separate comprehensive income section). If a company does not have any additional items (such as asset revaluations), the statement of profit or loss and the statement of profit or loss and other comprehensive income are identical. The statement of profit or loss and other comprehensive income is illustrated in chapter 10.

Helpful hint: The heading of every statement of profit or loss includes the name of the entity, the name of the statement and the time period covered by the statement. Usually, another line is added to indicate the unit of measure; when it is used, this fourth line usually indicates that the data are presented 'in thousands' ($'000) or 'in millions'.

DECISION-MAKING TOOLKIT

Decision/issue	Info needed for analysis	Tool or technique to use for decision	How to evaluate results to make decision
Are the entity's operations profitable?	Statement of profit or loss	The statement of profit or loss reports on the success or failure of the entity's operations by reporting its revenues and expenses.	If the entity's revenues exceed its expenses, it will report a profit; if expenses exceed revenues, it will report a loss.

Statement of changes in equity

The *statement of changes in equity* reports the total comprehensive income for the period and other changes in equity, such as adjustments to retained earnings (accumulated prior-year profits) for changes in accounting standards, changes in accounting policies and corrections of errors. The statement of changes in equity must also report details of transactions with the owners of the company (share capital movements and dividend payments) and, finally, a reconciliation of the movement in each component of equity. However, for simplicity we will illustrate only that part of the statement that reports on retained earnings; a full statement of changes in equity is illustrated later in this chapter using Giorgina's Pizza Limited. **Retained earnings** refers to the accumulated profit that has not been distributed as dividends to owners. This is an important part of the statement of changes in equity because it reports on dividends and explains the link between the statement of profit or loss and the statement of financial position.

As shown in figure 1.6, the statement of changes in equity shows the profit for the current period, which is the same as the amount reported in the statement of profit or loss. In this simple example, there are no other income or expense items or adjustments to retained earnings. The current period profit is the only item increasing retained earnings during the reporting period. The amount of retained earnings at the start of the period, which is nil for Wong Pty Ltd as it only commenced business at the beginning of the month, is added to profit.

Dividends reduce equity because they are a distribution to owners. In the Wong Pty Ltd example, dividends of $500 are deducted to calculate the closing amount of retained earnings. Note that this is equal to the amount of retained earnings reported in the statement of financial position.

Shareholders can see how much profit has been distributed as dividends by reading the statement of changes in equity. An entity could pay all of its profits for a period as dividends to shareholders. But few entities choose to do this. Why? Because they want to retain part of the profits to allow for further expansion. High-growth entities often choose to pay low or no dividends.

Statement of financial position

The *statement of financial position* reports assets and claims to those assets at a specific point in time. Claims are subdivided into two categories: claims of creditors and claims of owners. Claims of creditors are called *liabilities*. Claims of owners are called **equity** (or *shareholders' equity*). This relationship is shown in equation form in figure 1.7. This equation is referred to as the **basic accounting equation**.

FIGURE 1.7   Basic accounting equation

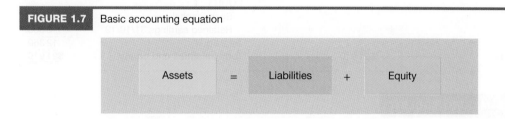

Assets = Liabilities + Equity

Assets must be in balance with the claims to the assets. As you can see from looking at Wong Pty Ltd's statement of financial position in figure 1.6, assets are listed first, followed by liabilities and equity. Equity comprises two parts: (1) share capital and (2) retained earnings and reserves. As noted earlier, share capital results when the entity issues shares. Wong Pty Ltd has share capital of $10 000. (Other names for share capital are *paid-up capital, issued capital* and *contributed equity*.)

Without any complex adjustments, which are considered in later chapters, the amount of retained earnings reported in the statement of financial position at the end of the period is the amount of retained earnings at the beginning of the period, plus profit after tax for the period, less any amount distributed as a dividend during the period.

Reserves also form part of equity. Some reserves are accumulated profit and result from transferring amounts from retained earnings to reserves. Other reserves result from the application of accounting standards involving, for example, asset revaluations.

Wong Pty Ltd has no reserves. The equity of Wong Pty Ltd is $12 360, consisting of share capital of $10 000 and retained earnings of $2360.

In figure 1.6 the statement of financial position is shown in a vertical format, which is the method used in the published financial statements of listed companies. An alternative format is the horizontal (or account) format shown in figure 1.8, where the layout of the statement of financial position is closely aligned to the basic accounting equation shown in figure 1.7.

Using the decision-making toolkit, creditors can use the statement of financial position as another source of information to determine the likelihood that they will be repaid. They carefully evaluate the nature of an entity's assets and liabilities. For example, does the entity have assets that could easily be sold to repay its debts? Managers use the statement of financial position with the statement of profit or loss to determine, for example, whether inventory is adequate to support future sales. The statement of financial position is also useful in assessing whether cash on hand is sufficient for immediate cash needs. The decision demonstrated in the toolkit looks at the relationship between debt (liabilities) and equity to determine whether the entity relies more on creditors or owners for its financing. Managers use this analysis to determine whether they have the best proportion of debt and equity financing.

Helpful hint: The heading of a statement of financial position includes the name of the entity, the name of the statement and the date.

FIGURE 1.8 Horizontal format of the statement of financial position

WONG PTY LTD
Statement of financial position
as at 31 October 2019

ASSETS		LIABILITIES	
Cash	$15 200	Accounts payable	$ 2 500
Accounts receivable	200	Interest payable	50
Advertising supplies	1 000	Revenue received in advance	800
Prepaid insurance	550	Salaries payable	1 200
Office equipment	4 960	Bank loan	5 000
		Total liabilities	9 550
		EQUITY	
		Share capital	10 000
		Retained earnings 31/10/19	2 360
		Total equity	12 360
Total assets	**$21 910**	**Total liabilities and equity**	**$21 910**

DECISION-MAKING TOOLKIT

Decision/issue	Info needed for analysis	Tool or technique to use for decision	How to evaluate results to make decision
Does the entity rely mainly on debt or equity to finance its assets?	Statement of financial position	The statement of financial position reports the entity's resources and claims to those resources. There are two types of claims: liabilities and equity.	Compare the amount of liabilities (debt) with the amount of equity to determine whether the entity relies more on creditors or owners for its financing.

Statement of cash flows

The main purpose of a *statement of cash flows* is to provide financial information about the cash receipts and cash payments of a business for a specific period of time. To help investors, creditors and others in their analysis of an entity's cash position, the statement of cash flows reports the cash effects of an entity's: (1) operating activities, (2) investing activities and (3) financing activities. In addition, the statement of cash flows shows the net increase or decrease in cash during the period, and the cash amount at the end of the period.

Users are interested in the statement of cash flows because they want to know what is happening to an entity's most important resource. The statement of cash flows provides answers to the following simple but important questions.

- Where did cash come from during the period?
- How was cash used during the period?
- What was the change in the cash balance during the period?

The statement of cash flows for Wong Pty Ltd in figure 1.6 shows that cash increased by $15 200 during the year. This resulted because operating activities (services to clients) increased cash by $5700; financing activities increased cash by $14 500; and investing activities used $5000 cash for the purchase of equipment. The decision demonstrated in the decision-making toolkit is to determine if the entity is generating enough cash from its operations to fund its investing activities. Comparing the cash provided from operating activities with the amount of cash used in investing activities provides the answer.

If there is any deficiency, i.e. cash used by investing activities is greater than that generated from operating, then the funds must be provided from financing activities.

Helpful hint: The heading of a statement of cash flows must identify the entity, the type of statement and the time period covered by the statement.

Interrelationships between the statements

Because the results on some statements are used as inputs to other statements, the statements are interrelated. These interrelationships are evident in Wong Pty Ltd's statements in figure 1.6.

1. The statement of financial position depends on the results of the statement of profit or loss and statement of changes in equity. Wong Pty Ltd reported profit of $2860 for the period. This amount is added to the beginning amount of retained earnings as part of the process of determining ending retained earnings.
2. The statement of cash flows and the statement of financial position are also interrelated. The statement of cash flows shows how the cash account changed during the period by showing the amount of cash at the beginning of the period, the sources and uses of cash during the period, and the $15 200 of cash at the end of the period. The ending amount of cash shown on the statement of cash flows is reflected in amounts reported on the statement of financial position.

Study these interrelationships carefully. To prepare financial statements you must understand the sequence in which these amounts are determined and how each statement affects the next.

The classified statement of financial position

As explained above, the statement of financial position shows a snapshot of an entity's financial position at a point in time. (Prior to periods commencing 1 January 2009, the statement of financial position was called a balance sheet.) To improve users' understanding of an entity's financial position, entities group similar assets and similar liabilities together. This is useful because it tells you that items within a group have similar economic characteristics. International accounting standard IAS 1/Australian accounting standard AASB 101 *Presentation of Financial Statements* prescribes minimum disclosures on the face of a classified statement of financial position. A **classified statement of financial position** is one in which assets and liabilities are classified as current and non-current (see figure 1.15). The most commonly reported items are listed in table 1.3.

TABLE 1.3   Minimum disclosures on the statement of financial position

Assets	Liabilities
Cash assets	Trade and other payables
Trade and other receivables	Financial liabilities
Other financial assets	Tax liabilities
Inventories	Provisions
Investment in property	**Equity**
Property, plant and equipment	Capital and reserves
Tax assets	Retained earnings or accumulated losses
Intangible assets	

Before we dive in, we need to explain three points.

1. To demonstrate a classified statement of financial position, we use a fictitious company, Giorgina's Pizza Limited.
2. Giorgina's Pizza Limited, like most entities, presents its financial statements for more than one year. This allows users to compare the business's financial position and performance for an accounting period with that of the previous period.
3. Note that numbers are reported in thousands on Giorgina's financial statements — i.e. numbers are rounded to the nearest thousand. Thus, the entity's total inventories for 2019 were $5 014 000 not $5014 (see figure 1.9).

IAS 1/AASB 101 also requires that the assets and liabilities be classified as current and non-current, unless categorisation by liquidity provides more relevant information. Almost all entities, other than financial institutions and insurance companies, choose the current/non-current categories for presentation of the statement of financial position. Although not as informative as liquidity categories, the current/non-current categories provide a crude measure of: (1) whether the entity has enough assets to pay its debts as they come due, and (2) the claims of short-term and long-term creditors on the entity's total assets. This is discussed in more detail in the section on analysing financial statements (section 1.9). Current and non-current categories are used extensively for internal and external reporting. These categories can be seen in the statement of financial position for our example company, Giorgina's Pizza Limited. Each of the categories is explained below.

Helpful hint: Liquidity — the sooner an asset converts to cash, the more liquid it is said to be.

Current assets

Current assets include assets that are cash, held for the purpose of being traded, or expected to be converted to cash or used in the business within 1 year or within the operating cycle, whichever is longer. The **operating cycle** is the average time taken to acquire goods and services and convert them to cash in producing revenues. Giorgina's reported current assets of $45 286 000 in 2019. For most businesses the cut-off for classification as current assets is 1 year from the end of the reporting period. For example, accounts receivable are included in current assets because they will be converted to cash through collection within 1 year. Inventories are current assets because we expect that they will be used in the business within 1 year (hopefully, the raw materials sooner!).

Common types of current assets are: (1) cash, (2) marketable securities, such as shares held as a short-term investment, (3) receivables (notes receivable, accounts receivable and interest receivable), (4) inventories, and (5) prepaid expenses (insurance and supplies). Figure 1.9 shows the current assets that are reported in Giorgina's 2019 consolidated financial statements.

An entity's current assets are important in assessing its short-term debt-paying ability, as explained later in the chapter.

FIGURE 1.9 Current assets section of Giorgina's statement of financial position

GIORGINA'S PIZZA LIMITED
Statement of financial position (partial)
as at 30 June 2019

	Note	2019 $'000	2018 $'000
CURRENT ASSETS			
Cash and cash equivalents	14	14 017	30 255
Trade and other receivables	15	19 809	15 764
Inventories	16	5 014	4 280
Current tax assets	17	143	0
Other current assets	22	5 701	4 673
		44 684	54 972
Assets held for sale	18	602	528
Total current assets		**45 286**	**55 500**

Non-current assets

Non-current assets are assets that are not expected to be consumed or sold within 1 year or the operating cycle. They encompass a diverse range of assets. The most common types of non-current assets include receivables that are due more than 1 year from the date of the statement of financial position; property, plant and equipment; and intangible assets. Figure 1.10 shows the non-current assets reported in Giorgina's 2019 financial statements.

FIGURE 1.10 Non-current assets section of Giorgina's statement of financial position

	Note	2019 $'000	2018 $'000
GIORGINA'S PIZZA LIMITED Statement of financial position (partial) as at 30 June 2019			
NON-CURRENT ASSETS			
Property, plant & equipment	19	37 270	26 273
Deferred tax assets	17	30	622
Goodwill	20	42 835	35 195
Other intangible assets	21	13 070	9 607
Other non-current assets	22	3 821	4 294
Total non-current assets		**97 026**	**75 991**

Property, plant and equipment

Property, plant and equipment (sometimes called *fixed assets*) are assets with relatively long useful lives that are used in operating the business. This category includes land, buildings, machinery and equipment, delivery vehicles, and furniture. Giorgina's reported property, plant and equipment of $37 270 000, as shown in its statement of financial position in figure 1.10.

Depreciation is the practice of allocating the cost of assets to a number of periods, rather than simply expensing the full purchase price of the asset in the year of purchase. Assets that the entity depreciates should be reported on the statement of financial position at cost less accumulated depreciation. For example, Giorgina's reported accumulated depreciation of $17 069 000 for property, plant and equipment will be reported in the notes to the financial statements. The accumulated depreciation is the total amount of depreciation to date over the *life of the asset*.

Intangible assets

Many entities have assets, other than financial assets, that have no physical substance yet often are very valuable. These assets are referred to as **intangible assets**. They include patents, copyrights and trademarks or trade names that give the entity exclusive right of use for a specified period of time. Goodwill is included in intangible assets. Giorgina's reported goodwill of $42 835 000, as shown in figure 1.10. Non-current assets will be discussed further in chapter 8.

Current liabilities

In the liabilities section of the statement of financial position, the first grouping is current liabilities. **Current liabilities** are obligations that are to be paid within the coming year or the entity's operating cycle. Common examples are accounts payable, wages payable, bank loans payable, interest payable, taxes payable, and current maturities of long-term obligations (payments to be made within the next year on long-term obligations).

Within the current liabilities section of the statement of financial position, payables are usually listed first, followed by short-term borrowings, tax liabilities and provisions. Figure 1.11 shows the current liabilities reported in Giorgina's 2019 consolidated financial statements.

Non-current liabilities

Obligations that are not classified as current liabilities must be classified as **non-current liabilities**. Liabilities in this category include debentures payable, mortgages payable, unsecured notes payable and lease liabilities. Many entities report long-term borrowings maturing after 1 year as a single amount in the statement of financial position and show the details of the debt in notes to the financial statements. Others list the various types of long-term liabilities. In its statement of financial position, Giorgina's reported non-current liabilities as shown in figure 1.12. Liabilities will be discussed further in chapter 9.

FIGURE 1.11 Current liabilities section of Giorgina's statement of financial position

GIORGINA'S PIZZA LIMITED Statement of financial position (partial) as at 30 June 2019			
	Note	2019 $'000	2018 $'000
CURRENT LIABILITIES			
Trade and other payables	23	28 541	25 629
Borrowings—short term	24	5 312	8 651
Current tax liabilities	25	1 913	2 658
Provisions—short term	26	2 332	1 770
Other current liabilities	27	381	0
Total current liabilities		**38 479**	**38 708**

FIGURE 1.12 Non-current liabilities section of Giorgina's statement of financial position

GIORGINA'S PIZZA LIMITED Statement of financial position (partial) as at 30 June 2019			
	Note	2019 $'000	2018 $'000
NON-CURRENT LIABILITIES			
Borrowings—long term	24	24 442	1 882
Provisions—long term	26	331	431
Deferred tax liabilities	25	1 796	2 324
Other non-current liabilities	27	330	365
Total non-current liabilities		**26 899**	**5 002**

LEARNING REFLECTION AND CONSOLIDATION

Review it

1. What are the major sections in a classified statement of financial position?
2. Explain the difference between current assets and non-current assets?
3. What was Giorgina's largest type of current asset at 30 June 2019? (The answer to this question is at the end of the chapter.)

Do it

The following information relates to Hoffman Ltd's statement of financial position at 30 June 2019. All receivables are due within 30 days.

Short-term investments	$ 2 300
Cash	800
Property, plant and equipment	10 700
Inventory	3 400
Accumulated depreciation	2 700
Accounts receivable	1 100

Prepare the assets section of a classified statement of financial position for Hoffman Ltd.

▶

Solution

HOFFMAN LTD
Statement of financial position (partial)
as at 30 June 2019

ASSETS		
Current assets		
Cash	$ 800	
Accounts receivable	1 100	
Inventory	3 400	
Short-term investments	2 300	
Total current assets		$ 7 600
Non-current assets		
Property, plant and equipment	10 700	
Less: Accumulated depreciation	2 700	
Total non-current assets		8 000
Total assets		**$15 600**

A quick look at Giorgina's financial reports

So far we have examined Giorgina's classified statement of financial position. Now let's put all the financial statements together. The same relationships that you observed among the internal financial statements of Wong Pty Ltd are evident in Giorgina's financial statements, which are presented in figures 1.13 to 1.18. We have simplified the financial statements to assist your learning — but they may look complicated anyway. Do not be alarmed by their apparent complexity. (If you could already read and understand them, there would be little reason to take this course!) By the end of this text, you'll have a great deal of experience in reading and understanding financial statements such as these.

Statement of profit or loss

Giorgina's statement of profit or loss is presented in figure 1.13. It reports total revenues and other gains in 2019 of $223 840 000 ($141 473 000 + $79 694 000 + $2 673 000). It then subtracts 11 types or categories of expenses to arrive at a profit of $21 400 000. This is a 5% decrease from the profit of $22 560 000 for the previous year.

Helpful hint: The percentage change in any amount from one year to the next is calculated as follows:

$$\frac{\text{Change during period}}{\text{Previous value}} \times \frac{100}{1}$$

Thus, the percentage change in profit is:

$$\frac{\text{Change in profit}}{\text{Previous year's profit}} \times \frac{100}{1}$$

Statement of changes in equity

To refresh your memory about this statement you might like to review the earlier 'Statement of changes in equity' section. Giorgina's presents information about its retained earnings in the notes to the financial statements in 2019 (figure 1.14). The amount of $47 784 000 reported as retained earnings at 30 June 2019 reflects the retained profits of $45 857 000 at the beginning of the reporting period, plus $21 400 000 profit for the year, less dividends of $19 473 000.

FIGURE 1.13 Giorgina's statement of profit or loss (partial)

GIORGINA'S PIZZA LIMITED
Statement of profit or loss (partial)
for the year ended 30 June 2019

	Note	2019 $'000	2018 $'000
Sales revenue	3	141 473	126 350
Other revenue	4	79 694	72 316
Other gains and losses	5	2 673	2 371
Food and packaging expenses	8	(63 863)	(59 009)
Employee benefits expense	9	(57 195)	(44 954)
PPE maintenance expenses		(6 998)	(6 441)
Depreciation and amortisation expense	10	(9 594)	(7 522)
Rent expense		(6 827)	(5 878)
Finance expenses		(304)	(338)
Marketing expenses		(8 573)	(8 608)
Restaurant expenses		(5 387)	(4 415)
Telephone expenses		(4 763)	(5 002)
Other expenses	11	(29 764)	(26 642)
Profit before tax		**30 572**	**32 228**
Income tax expense	12	(9 172)	(9 668)
Profit from continuing operations	**13**	**21 400**	**22 560**

Note: Prior to 1 July 2012, the statement of profit or loss and other comprehensive income was called the statement of comprehensive income, and if the separate statement of profit or loss was presented it was called an income statement. Some companies still use the old terminology when labelling their external reports. See chapter 10 for further discussion.

FIGURE 1.14 Note 30, Movement in retained earnings, from Giorgina's financial statements

GIORGINA'S PIZZA LIMITED
Notes to the financial statements
for the year ended 30 June 2019

	2019 $'000	2018 $'000
30. RETAINED EARNINGS		
Balance at beginning of year	45 857	36 013
Net profit	21 400	22 560
Payment of dividends (note 31)	(19 473)	(12 716)
Balance at end of year	**47 784**	**45 857**

Statement of financial position

Giorgina's statement of financial position is shown in figure 1.15. In the previous section, we examined the components of the statement of financial position separately. Now let's look at the full picture. The entity's total assets increased from $131 491 000 on 1 July 2018 to $142 312 000 on 30 June 2019. Its liabilities include trade and other payables as well as interest-bearing liabilities, such as borrowings.

You can see that Giorgina's has slightly more equity financing than debt — 54% of its assets are financed by equity. As you learn more about financial statements, we will discuss how to interpret the relationships and changes in financial statement items.

Helpful hint: A statement of financial position which reports current and non-current categories for assets and liabilities is known as a fully classified statement of financial position.

FIGURE 1.15 Giorgina's statement of financial position

GIORGINA'S PIZZA LIMITED
Statement of financial position
as at 30 June 2019

	Note	2019 $'000	2018 $'000
ASSETS			
Current assets			
Cash and cash equivalents	14	14017	30255
Trade and other receivables	15	19809	15764
Inventories	16	5014	4280
Current tax assets	17	143	0
Other current assets	22	5701	4673
Assets held for sale	18	602	528
Total current assets		45286	55500
Non-current assets			
Property, plant & equipment	19	37270	26273
Deferred tax assets	17	30	622
Goodwill	20	42835	35195
Intangible assets	21	13070	9607
Other non-current assets	22	3821	4294
Total non-current assets		97026	75991
Total assets		142312	131491
LIABILITIES			
Current liabilities			
Trade and other payables	23	28541	25629
Borrowing—short term	24	5312	8651
Current tax liabilities	25	1913	2658
Provisions—short term	26	2332	1770
Other current liabilities	27	381	0
Total current liabilities		38479	38708
Non-current liabilities			
Borrowing—long term	24	24442	1882
Provisions—long term	26	331	431
Deferred tax liabilities	25	1796	2324
Other non-current liabilities	27	330	365
Total non-current liabilities		26899	5002
Total liabilities		65378	43710
Net assets		**76934**	**87781**
EQUITY			
Capital and reserves			
Issued capital	28	30640	52404
Reserves	29	(1490)	(10480)
Retained earnings	30	47784	45857
Total equity		**76934**	**87781**

Statement of cash flows

Giorgina's statement of cash flows is shown in figure 1.16. We can see that Giorgina's cash decreased by $17 836 000 during the year ended 30 June 2019. The reasons for this can be determined by examining the statement of cash flows in figure 1.16. The company generated $24 885 000 from its operating activities during the year. Its investing activities included capital expenditures (purchases of property, plant and equipment) as well as proceeds from the sale of non-current assets. The net effect of its investing activities was a decrease of cash of $22 797 000. Its financing activities involved the payment of cash dividends, repayment of borrowings, the return of share capital and proceeds from borrowings and share issues using net cash of $19 924 000. In all, the net effect of the cash generated from its operating activities, less the cash used in its investing and financing, plus the translation gain from cash held in foreign currencies was a decrease in cash of $16 238 000.

FIGURE 1.16	Giorgina's statement of cash flows

GIORGINA'S PIZZA LIMITED
Statement of cash flows
for the year ended 30 June 2019

	Note	2019 $'000	2018 $'000
CASH FLOWS FROM OPERATING ACTIVITIES			
Receipts from customers		245 357	221 324
Payments to suppliers and employees		(212 148)	(188 094)
Interest received		827	1 339
Interest paid		(304)	(338)
Income taxes paid		(8 847)	(5 972)
Net cash generated by operating activities	35	24 885	28 259
CASH FLOWS FROM INVESTING ACTIVITIES			
Payment for investment and business operations		(14 308)	(8 907)
Loans repaid by third parties		1 887	1 580
Payments for property, plant & equipment		(18 778)	(13 244)
Proceeds from sale of non-current assets		15 802	17 193
Payments for intangible assets		(7 400)	(5 606)
Net cash used in investing activities	36	(22 797)	(8 984)
CASH FLOWS FROM FINANCING ACTIVITIES			
Proceeds from borrowings		32 791	0
Repayment of borrowings		(15 380)	(18)
Return of share capital		(22 532)	0
Dividends paid		(19 473)	(12 716)
Proceeds from issue of equity securities		4 670	4 012
Net cash used in financing activities	37	(19 924)	(8 722)
Net increase (decrease) in cash and cash equivalents		(17 836)	10 553
Cash and cash equivalents at the beginning of the year		30 255	21 064
Effects of changes in exchange rates on cash held in foreign currencies	38	1 598	(1 362)
Cash and cash equivalents at the end of the year	35	**14 017**	**30 255**

Note: The movement in cash is $17 836 000 less exchange rate differences of cash held in foreign currencies $1 598 000, a total net reduction of $16 238 000.

Other elements of an annual report

Companies that are publicly traded must provide their shareholders with an *annual report* each year. The **annual report** always includes the financial statements introduced in this chapter as well as other important sources of information such as notes to the financial statements, corporate governance statement the directors' report and an independent auditor's report. If the concise form of financial reporting is used to report to shareholders, a general discussion and analysis section must be included. This is instead of some of the notes to the financial statements, which are included in the full financial report. No analysis of an entity's financial situation and prospects is complete without a review of each of these items.

Notes to the financial statements

An entity's published financial statements are accompanied by explanatory notes and supporting schedules that form part of the statements. The **notes to the financial statements** clarify information presented in the financial statements, as well as expand on it where additional detail is needed. Information in the notes does not always have to be quantifiable (numeric). Examples of notes are descriptions of the accounting policies and methods used in preparing the statements, explanations of uncertainties and contingencies, and statistics and details too voluminous to be included in the statements. The notes are essential to understanding an entity's operating performance and financial position.

Figure 1.17 is an extract from the notes to Giorgina's financial statements for 2019. It describes the methods the company uses to account for revenues.

FIGURE 1.17 Extract from the notes to Giorgina's financial statements

GIORGINA'S PIZZA LIMITED
Notes to the financial statements (extract from Note 2.2)
for the year ended 30 June 2019

2.2 REVENUE RECOGNITION
Revenue is measured at the fair value of the consideration paid or to be received.

2.2.1 Sale of goods
Revenue from the sale of goods is recognised when the entity transfers to the purchaser the significant risks and rewards of ownership of the goods.

2.2.2 Other revenue
Dividend revenue from investments is recognised when it is established that the shareholders have the right to receive payment.

Interest revenue is accrued on a time basis, by reference to the principal outstanding and at the effective interest rate applicable.

Corporate governance statement

In 2002, the Australian Securities Exchange (ASX) established the ASX Corporate Governance Council, which produced a document entitled Principles of good corporate governance and best practice recommendations (released in March 2003). The guidelines were updated in 2007 (Corporate governance principles and recommendations, 2nd edition) and 2010 (Corporate governance principles and recommendations with 2010 amendments). In 2012, there was a comprehensive review and a third edition of the principles and recommendation was released. All Australian listed entities as part of the ASX listing requirements (LR4.10.3) are required to disclose the extent to which they have followed the ASX corporate governance recommendations, and, if they have not followed the recommendations, the reasons for adopting alternative governance practices. For some smaller listed entities, the **corporate governance statement** is part of the directors' report.

Directors' report

The **directors' report** section covers a number of issues which might affect users' interpretation of the financial statements. The contents of the report in Australia are governed by the Corporations Act, ss. 298–300. Information required to be disclosed in the report helps shareholders assess the performances of the entity and the directors. Among the things that must be included are a description of the business(es) undertaken by the entity; details of dividends; a description of anything important that has happened after the date of the financial statements (but before they were released); and various information about directors, including how many directors' meetings each one attended. In their report, directors will try to avoid disclosing things that might give competitors an advantage. Figure 1.18 presents a part of Giorgina's directors' report.

Auditor's report

Another important source of information is the auditor's report. An **auditor** is an accountant who conducts an independent examination of the accounting data presented by an entity. Only accountants who are registered auditors may perform audits. If the auditor is satisfied that the financial statements present fairly the financial position, results of operations and cash flows in accordance with generally accepted accounting principles, then an unqualified opinion is expressed. If the auditor expresses anything other than an unqualified opinion, the financial statements should be used only with caution. That is, without an unqualified opinion, we cannot have complete confidence that the financial statements give an accurate picture of the entity's financial health.

GIORGINA'S PIZZA LIMITED
Directors' report (extract)

PRINCIPAL ACTIVITIES
The entity's principal activities in the course of the financial year were the operation of retail food outlets. During the financial year there were no significant changes in the nature of those activities.

REVIEW OF OPERATIONS
The result for the financial year ended 30 June 2019 was as follows:

	2019 $'000	2018 $'000
Profit before income tax expense	30 572	32 228
Income tax expense	(9 172)	(9 668)
Profit after income tax expense	**21 400**	**22 560**

Changes in state of affairs
There were no significant changes in the state of affairs of the entity that occurred during the financial year.

Future developments
The focus is on the opening of two additional stores, building our online business, and putting additional resources into staff development to maximise our efficiencies.

Dividends
In respect of the financial year ended 30 June 2018, as detailed in the Directors' Report for the financial year, a final dividend of 31.8 cents per share was paid to the holders of fully paid ordinary shares on 12 August 2018.

In respect of the financial year ended 30 June 2019, an interim dividend of 12.1 cents per share was paid to the holders of fully paid ordinary shares on 18 February 2019.

In respect of the financial year ended 30 June 2019, the Company will be paying a final dividend of 14.5 cents per share to the holders of fully paid ordinary shares on 21 October 2019.

LEARNING REFLECTION AND CONSOLIDATION

Review it

1. What are the content and purpose of each statement: statement of profit or loss, statement of changes in equity, statement of financial position and statement of cash flows?
2. The accounting equation is: Assets = Liabilities + Equity. Replacing words in the equation with dollar amounts, what is Giorgina's accounting equation at 30 June 2019? (*Hint:* Use comparative 2019 data in figure 1.15.) (The answer to this question is at the end of the chapter.)
3. Why are notes to the financial statements necessary? What kinds of items are included in these notes?
4. What is the purpose of the directors' report in the annual report?
5. What is the purpose of the auditor's report?

Do it

Pink Music Store Pty Ltd began operations on 1 July 2019. The following information is available for Pink Music Store on 30 June 2020: service revenue $17 000; accounts receivable $4000; accounts payable $2000; building rental expense $9000; bank loan $5000; share capital $10 000; retained earnings; equipment $16 000; insurance expense $1000; supplies (asset) $1800; supplies expense $200; cash $1500; dividends $500.

▶

Prepare a statement of profit or loss, a statement of financial position and a calculation of retained earnings for Pink Music Store Pty Ltd using this information.

Reasoning

A statement of profit or loss reports the success or failure of an entity's operations for a period of time. A statement of financial position presents the assets, liabilities and equity of an entity at a specific point in time. The statement of changes in equity shows the items affecting each component of equity (in this case, retained earnings) during the period.

Solution

PINK MUSIC STORE PTY LTD Statement of profit or loss for the year ended 30 June 2020		
REVENUES		
Service revenue		$17 000
EXPENSES		
Rent expense	$9 000	
Insurance expense	1 000	
Supplies expense	200	
Total expenses		10 200
Profit		**$ 6 800**

PINK MUSIC STORE PTY LTD Statement of financial position as at 30 June 2020		
ASSETS		
Cash		$ 1 500
Accounts receivable		4 000
Supplies		1 800
Equipment		16 000
Total assets		23 300
LIABILITIES		
Accounts payable	$2 000	
Bank loan	5 000	
Total liabilities		7 000
Net assets		**$16 300**
EQUITY		
Share capital		$10 000
Retained earnings 30/6/20		6 300
Total equity		**$16 300**

PINK MUSIC STORE PTY LTD Calculation of retained earnings for the year ended 30 June 2020	
Retained earnings, 1 July 2019	$ 0
Profit	6 800
Less: Dividends	(500)
Retained earnings, 30 June 2020	**$6 300**

1.7 The financial reporting environment

LEARNING OBJECTIVE 1.7 Describe the financial reporting environment.

Accounting has developed over time and the accounting rules have been developed to suit the needs of the ever-changing business environment. For example, as a result of the failure of many joint venture entities in the eighteenth century and loss of investors' funds, there arose a need for regulation to protect the investors and to encourage economic development. In most cases, until the mid-nineteenth century, an Act of Parliament was required to permit the raising of funds. The early *Companies Act 1856* set out rules for company formation, the roles of the directors, and rules protecting the distribution of the capital invested, but the accounting rules were left to the accountants. These rules and accounting practices were known as *generally accepted accounting principles (GAAP)* and the authority was derived from use by the business community and the accounting profession. However, as the business environment became more complex and the capital markets were globalised, there emerged many deviations in practice and the accounting profession recognised the need for standardised guidelines for accounting practices and procedures. The current GAAP in Australia is a combination of statutory rules (accounting standards) and interpretations as well as the concepts and principles which have been developed over time.

Companies registered in Australia must comply with the Corporations Act. This Act prescribes the preparation of external general purpose financial reports by certain categories of companies and this preparation is subject to regulations from several sources. The various users of financial information were discussed earlier in this chapter, where it was established that the provision of information is essential for decision making. However, there is a need for regulations and monitoring to ensure that the information provided to such users is reliable and unbiased. Let's take a closer look at each of these key players in the financial reporting environment, as well as a few others with whom they interact.

Australian Securities and Investments Commission

The **Australian Securities and Investments Commission (ASIC)** administers the Corporations Act. The Act requires certain companies, such as listed public companies, to prepare financial statements in accordance with Australian accounting standards. Among other functions, ASIC monitors compliance with accounting standards and the Corporations Act. This involves investigating companies that are suspected of not complying with the Act or of publishing financial reports that do not comply with accounting standards. The surveillance program of ASIC is assisted by auditors who access the internal records of companies and report on compliance. More details about ASIC can be found on its web site, www.asic.gov.au.

The structure of accounting standard setting is illustrated in figure 1.19, which refers to the two key bodies: the Financial Reporting Council and the Australian Accounting Standards Board. The roles of these bodies in regulating financial reporting are discussed below.

Financial Reporting Council

The **Financial Reporting Council (FRC)** is responsible for the broad oversight of the accounting standard-setting process for the private and public sectors. It comprises key stakeholders from the business community, the professional accounting bodies, governments and regulatory agencies. Members of the FRC are appointed by the treasurer. The FRC oversees the **Australian Accounting Standards Board (AASB)**, which is the organisation with authority to issue accounting standards in Australia, and the **Auditing and Assurance Standards Board (AUASB)**, which is the organisation with authority to issue auditing and assurance standards for use by auditors and providers of other assurance services. It advises the Commonwealth Government on the accounting standard-setting and auditing standard-setting processes. The FRC also monitors developments in international accounting standards and determines the AASB's broad strategic direction. The FRC may give the AASB directions, advice and feedback on matters of general policy and is responsible for approving its priorities, business plan, budget and staffing arrangements. However, the FRC cannot influence the AASB's technical deliberations and, hence, the content of particular accounting standards. More information about the FRC can be found on its web site, www.frc.gov.au.

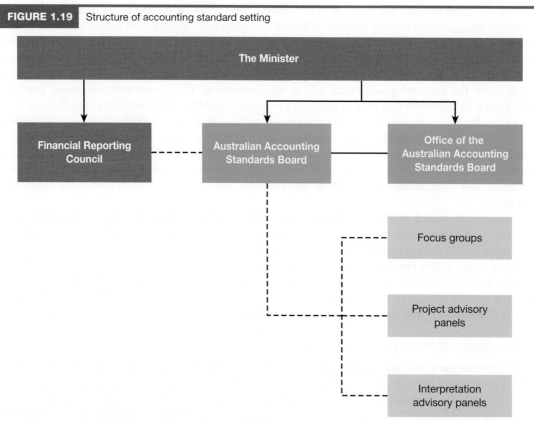

FIGURE 1.19 Structure of accounting standard setting

Source: Australian Accounting Standards Board web site, www.aasb.gov.au.

Australian Accounting Standards Board

The AASB issues accounting standards for all types of reporting entities, business, not-for-profit and government (public) sectors. The members of the AASB are appointed by the FRC. In 2002, the FRC exercised its authority in determining the AASB's direction by endorsing Australia's convergence with international accounting standards from 1 January 2005. The standards issued by the AASB are consistent and include all options that currently exist under those issued by the International Accounting Standards Board. The **International Accounting Standards Board (IASB)** is the organisation with the authority to issue international financial reporting standards, commonly referred to as IFRSs. The standards issued by the IASB are intended for the preparation of general purpose financial reports of profit-seeking entities, but in Australia and New Zealand (until recently) the same standards are applied to public sector entities and not-for-profit entities that prepare external general purpose financial reports. Where necessary, the AASB adds its own paragraphs to the international accounting standards only if they are considered particularly relevant in the Australian reporting environment, e.g. exclusions and alternatives to make the standards applicable to public sector entities. Not all entities need to comply with full accounting standards. AASB 1053 *Application of Tiers of Australian Accounting Standards* sets out the reduced disclosure requirements for some entities. More on this differential reporting regime will be covered in chapter 13.

Until 2004, in addition to setting standards, the AASB was developing a conceptual framework. The conceptual framework consisted of a set of concepts to be followed by preparers of financial statements and standard setters. It comprised statements of accounting concepts (SACs), which provided guidance but did not have mandatory status. The AASB had issued four statements of accounting concepts prior to the decision to converge with international accounting standards. The four statements addressed the scope and objective of general purpose financial reporting, qualitative characteristics, and the elements of financial statements. Some of the Australian conceptual framework differed from the IASB framework for presentation of financial statements. As part of the international convergence program, the AASB issued the *Framework*, which is equivalent to the *Conceptual Framework* issued by the IASB.

Since 2005 the conceptual framework that was developed in Australia has no longer been used in its entirety. The statements concerned with the objective (SAC 2) of general purpose financial reporting, qualitative characteristics (SAC 3) and the elements of financial statements (SAC 4) were encompassed in the framework. The statements that cover the scope (SAC 1) of general purpose financial reporting has been temporarily retained, but it is expected that the requirements of these statements will be incorporated into a later version of the *Framework*. At the time of writing, the conceptual framework is under review. The new developments are explored in chapter 13. More information about the AASB can be found on its web site, www.aasb.gov.au.

Australian Securities Exchange

Another source of regulation for listed public companies is the Australian Securities Exchange (ASX). Listed entities must comply with the listing rules of the exchange or exchanges on which they are listed. The listing rules relating to financial reporting typically focus on disclosure of information. The ASX, through its Corporate Governance Council, publishes corporate governance guidelines for Australian listed entities. They also include industry-specific disclosure requirements. For example, the ASX requires listed companies operating in the mining industry to disclose details of mineral reserves. Details about the ASX can be found on its web site, www.asx.com.au.

Regulation in New Zealand

Accounting and auditing standards in New Zealand are set by the External Reporting Board. The **External Reporting Board (XRB)** is an independent Crown Entity, established under section 22 of the Financial Reporting Act 1993, and subject to the Crown Entities Act 2004. For more information about the XRB, refer to its web site, www.xrb.govt.nz.

In 2011, the New Zealand government announced changes to the financial reporting requirements for New Zealand entities. These changes are enacted in the Financial Reporting Act 2013. The main change is that many small and medium sized New Zealand companies will no longer need to prepare accounting reports using New Zealand generally accepted accounting practice (GAAP). Complementary to this, the XRB announced that, for financial reporting, New Zealand would change from a single set of sector neutral accounting standards to a multi-sector and standards approach. The full effect of these changes took place in 2016. Prior to these changes the reporting requirements between Australia and New Zealand were similar, particularly having sector-neutral accounting standards. Now, New Zealand is similar to the international standards where the for-profit publicly accountable entities will use New Zealand equivalents to the International Financial Reporting Standards (NZ IFRS) and public benefit entities (not-for-profit and government sector) will report using PBE standards, which are based primarily on International Public Sector Accounting Standards (IPSAS), modified as necessary for the New Zealand environment by the XRB. Also within the two-sector reporting regime there are four tiers. Tier one in both sectors will use the full standards with fewer requirements as the tiers go down. More on this differential reporting regime will be covered in chapter 13.

Public companies listed on the New Zealand Stock Exchange (NZX) must also comply with NZX listing rules. The listing rules relating to financial reporting typically focus on disclosure of information. They also include industry-specific disclosure requirements. For example, the NZX requires listed companies operating in the mining industry to provide quarterly reports with full details of production, development and exploration activities. For more information about the NZX refer to its web site, www.nzx.com.

Professional accounting bodies

The three largest professional accounting bodies are CPA Australia, Chartered Accountants Australia and New Zealand, and the Institute of Public Accountants.

CPA Australia is the largest of the three professional bodies, with more than 150 000 members. The national office is in Melbourne with divisions throughout Australia and other countries, including Fiji, China (Hong Kong and Beijing), Indonesia, Malaysia, New Zealand, Papua New Guinea and Singapore. CPA Australia's web site, www.cpaaustralia.com.au, provides useful information for students of accounting. The web site provides information to its members and the public about accounting-related issues, such as financial planning including superannuation, financial reporting, changes in accounting standards, tax laws, auditing, finance and treasury, corporate governance, environmental and social reporting, business management and e-business. The web site also caters for students by providing information about study options in Australia and Asia, how to become a Certified Practising Accountant (CPA), business news and careers.

In 2013, the Australian and New Zealand chartered accounting associations voted to merge their associations. The new institute brand, Chartered Accountants Australia and New Zealand, was launched on 1 July 2014 and is expected to have more than 100 000 members in total with 17 000-plus candidates. The Australian national office is in Sydney. There are regional offices throughout Australia and New Zealand with overseas members' groups in Hong Kong, Malaysia, Singapore, Switzerland and the United Kingdom. Further information on the combined professional accounting body can be found at www.charteredaccountantsanz.com.

The new professional accounting body has common admission programs for membership. The most common way is for a person to complete academic study (an undergraduate business degree), have practical experience and complete the professional competence program for Chartered Accountants (CA program).

CPAs and CAs are employed at all levels of government and the private sector, including not-for-profit entities, commerce and industry, and in public practice. CPAs and CAs working in commerce and industry may be chief financial officers (CFOs), specialists in financial reporting or management accounting, or do other specialised work in areas such as information technology, corporate treasury and internal auditing. Accountants in public practice engage in a variety of work, including taxation, financial planning, financial reporting, management consulting, auditing and reviewing. In medium and large accounting firms, accountants usually specialise in one area.

The Institute of Public Accountants (IPA) caters for accounting practitioners who do not have a university degree in accounting. It also has a higher category of membership that requires completion of a degree as part of the professional qualification requirements. Like the two professional bodies discussed above, the IPA is a member of the International Federation of Accountants (IFAC). The IPA offers student membership and provides information about its membership categories and requirements, as well as developments in accounting, such as taxation and superannuation, on its web site, www.publicaccountants.org.au.

1.8 Concepts, principles and qualitative characteristics

LEARNING OBJECTIVE 1.8 Explain the accounting concepts, principles, qualitative characteristics and constraints underlying financial statements.

In the previous section the statutory regulation of accounting was outlined. Now let's examine the practices which underlie accounting.

Concepts and principles

Monetary principle

In looking at Giorgina's financial statements you will notice that everything is stated in terms of dollars. The **monetary principle** requires that only those things that can be expressed in money be included in the accounting records. This might seem so obvious that it doesn't bear mentioning, but in fact it has important implications for financial reporting. Because the exchange of money is fundamental to business transactions, it makes sense that we measure a business in terms of money. However, it also means that certain important information needed by investors, creditors and managers is not reported in the financial statements. For example, customer satisfaction is important to every business, but it is not easily quantified in dollar terms, thus it is not reported in the financial statements.

Accounting entity concept

The **accounting entity concept** states that every entity can be separately identified and accounted for. For example, suppose you are a shareholder in Giorgina's, the amount of cash you have in your personal bank account and the balance owed on your personal car loan are not reported in the company's financial statements. The reason is that, for accounting purposes, you and the company are separate accounting entities. In order to accurately assess Giorgina's performance and financial position, it is important that you not confuse it with your personal transactions, or the transactions of any other entity. This is particularly important for sole proprietorships and partnerships as they are not separate legal entities. In addition, the business owners are often the managers of the business enterprises so it is easier to confuse the business and private transactions.

The accounting period concept

If you look at Giorgina's 2019 financial statements you will notice that the company reports on cash flows and performance for periods of 1 year, and on the financial position at the end of each period. The **end of the reporting period** for many Australian entities is 30 June and for many New Zealand entities is 31 March (NZ financial year-end). The **accounting period concept** states that the life of a business can be divided into artificial periods and that useful reports covering those periods can be prepared for the business. All entities report at least annually. Listed companies report at least every 6 months to shareholders and many prepare monthly statements for internal purposes.

Going concern principle

The **going concern principle** states that the business will remain in operation for the foreseeable future. Of course, many businesses do fail but, in general, it is reasonable to assume that the business will continue operating. Management must make an assessment of the validity of the going concern principle when preparing financial statements in accordance with accounting standards. The going concern principle underlies much of what we do in accounting. To give you just one example, if going concern is not assumed, then plant and equipment should be stated at their liquidation value (selling price less cost of disposal), not at their cost. The going concern principle is inappropriate only when liquidation of the business appears likely.

Cost principle

The **cost principle** states that all assets are initially recorded in the accounts at their purchase price or cost. This is applied not only at the time the asset is purchased, but also over the time the asset is held. For example, if Giorgina's was to purchase land for $500 000, it would initially be recorded at $500 000. But what would the company do if, by the end of the next year, the land had increased in value to $600 000? The answer is that under the cost principle the land would continue to be reported at $500 000.

The use of cost for measurement of assets is often criticised as being irrelevant. Critics contend that market value would be more useful to financial decision makers. Proponents of cost measurement say that cost is the best measure because it can be verified easily from transactions between two parties, whereas market value is often subjective.

Helpful hint: Recently, some accounting rules have been changed, requiring that certain assets be measured at market value at the end of the reporting period.

Numerous departures from the cost principle are permitted by accounting standards. For example, asset revaluations are permitted for most tangible non-current assets. Asset revaluations are discussed in chapter 8.

Full disclosure principle

Some important financial information is not easily reported on the face of the statements. For example, an entity might be sued by one of its customers. Investors and creditors might not know about this lawsuit. The **full disclosure principle** requires that all circumstances and events that could make a difference to the decisions financial statement users might make be disclosed. If an important item cannot reasonably be reported directly in the financial statements, then it should be discussed in notes that accompany the statements.

The accounting concepts and principles are shown graphically in figure 1.20.

FIGURE 1.20 Accounting concepts and principles

Monetary principle

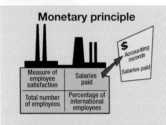

Only those things that can be expressed in terms of money should be included in the accounting records.

Accounting entity concept

Ford

Toyota

GMH

Every entity can be separately identified and accounted for.

Accounting period concept

The economic life of an entity can be divided into artificial time periods.

Going concern principle

Now   Future

The entity will continue to operate in the foreseeable future.

Cost principle

Assets should be recorded at cost.

Full disclosure principle

Circumstances and events that could make a difference to financial statement users' decisions should be disclosed.

Qualitative characteristics

Now let's turn our attention to the needs of external users of accounting information. The *Conceptual Framework* identifies the *objective of general purpose financial reporting* as the provision of information to a wide range of users for making and evaluating decisions about the allocation of scarce resources. But how is that objective best served? In what format should financial information be presented? These questions are addressed by another piece of the *Conceptual Framework*. The *Conceptual Framework* provides guidance on the qualitative characteristics that information contained in general purpose financial reports should have in order to achieve the objective of providing useful information for decision making. Figure 1.21 below represents the final piece of the *Conceptual Framework* we introduce in this chapter.

FIGURE 1.21   Building the *Conceptual Framework* — section 4

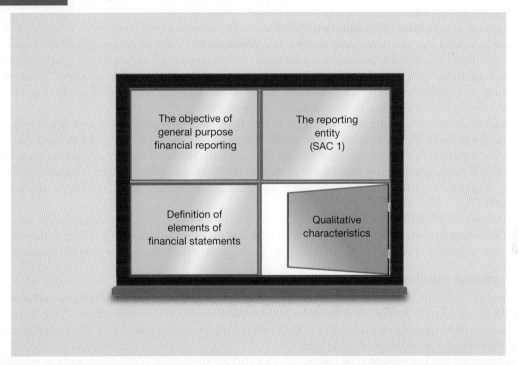

While the objective of general purpose financial reporting is to provide useful information for decision making, the qualitative characteristics outline what it is about the financial information contained in the financial statements that primary users will find most useful. That is, the qualitative characteristics are the attributes that make the information in financial statements useful.

According to the *Conceptual Framework*, the qualitative characteristics are classified as either fundamental or enhancing depending on how they affect the usefulness of financial information. Enhancing qualitative characteristics and fundamental qualitative characteristics are complementary.

Fundamental qualitative characteristics

For the information in general purpose financial reports to be useful, it must be relevant and provide a faithful representation of the economic phenomena it represents. Relevance and faithful representation are therefore classified as fundamental qualitative characteristics.

Relevance

Information is considered **relevant** if it is capable of making a difference in the decisions made by users. Information that has predictive value and/or confirmatory value is considered to be relevant. Information is considered to have predictive value if it can be used to develop expectations for the future. Information is considered to have confirmatory value if it confirms or corrects users' past or present expectations. Information can often be both predictive and confirmatory.

For example, when Giorgina's issues financial statements, the information in the statements is considered relevant because it provides a basis for forecasting future profits. Accounting information is also relevant to business decisions because it confirms or corrects previous expectations. Thus, Giorgina's financial statements help predict future events and provide feedback about previous expectations of the financial health of the company. The relevance of the information is affected by its **materiality**. Information is material if its omission or misstatement could affect users' decisions. Information that is immaterial need not be separately identified. For example, if Giorgina's purchased a stapler for $5 this would be considered immaterial; the purchase would be recorded in the accounting records as a business expense, although it would not be separately identified in the financial statements.

Faithful representation

Information is a **faithful representation** of the economic phenomena it purports to represent if it is complete, neutral and free from material error. It is important that the information depicts the economic substance of the transactions, events or circumstances. At times, economic substance may not be the same as the legal form. To be complete, all of the information needed to represent the economic phenomena faithfully is included and there is no omission which could make the information misleading. Hence, faithful representation is linked to the full disclosure principle.

Information that is considered to be neutral is free from bias. Information is biased if it is intended to attain or induce a particular behaviour or result. Some of the information in general purpose financial reports is measured using estimates in conditions of uncertainty. Hence, it is not reasonable to expect that reports will be completely error free. However, despite this limitation, faithful representation is achieved when the inputs used to make the judgements and estimates reflect the best available information at the time.

Relevance and faithful representation work together in enhancing the decision usefulness of information. Relevance is applied to determine which economic phenomena to represent and then faithful representation is applied to determine which depictions best represent the underlying economic phenomena.

Enhancing qualitative characteristics

Enhancing qualitative characteristics include **comparability**, **verifiability**, **timeliness** and **understandability** and are used to distinguish more useful information from less useful information. These characteristics are called enhancing characteristics as they enhance the decision usefulness of relevant information faithfully represented in financial statements.

Information that is comparable facilitates users identifying similarities and differences between different economic phenomena. Consistency refers to the use of the same accounting policies between entities, at the same point in time, or the same entity over time. Consistency supports the achievement of comparability.

Information is verifiable if it represents the economic phenomena without bias or material error and has been prepared with appropriate recognition and measurement methods.

Timeliness is measured by whether the information is available to users before it ceases to be relevant; that is, the information is received while it is still capable of influencing the decisions users make based on the information.

Understandability is the last of the enhancing qualitative characteristics and relates to the quality of information that assists users to understand the meaning of the information provided. It is important to recognise that understandability is highly dependent upon the capabilities of the users of the financial statements, and that users are assumed to have a reasonable knowledge of business activities and economic phenomena. However, classifying, characterising and presenting comparable information clearly and concisely will enhance understandability.

While enhancing qualitative characteristics improve the usefulness of financial information and should be maximised where possible, they cannot make information decision useful if the information is irrelevant or not faithfully represented.

Constraint on financial reporting

Cost constraints limit the information provided by financial reporting. Providing decision-useful information imposes costs, and the benefits of providing the information should outweigh the costs. Costs can include those associated with collecting, processing, verifying and disseminating information. Assessing whether benefits outweigh costs is usually more qualitative than quantitative and is often incomplete. In an attempt to ensure benefits outweigh costs, it is important to consider whether one or more enhancing qualitative characteristics may be sacrificed to reduce costs.

Table 1.4 summarises the fundamental and enhancing qualitative characteristics of financial information and the constraint of providing financial information in the *Conceptual Framework*.

TABLE 1.4	Fundamental and enhancing qualitative characteristics and constraint of financial information	
Fundamental qualitative characteristics	**Enhancing qualitative characteristics**	**Constraint of providing financial information**
Relevance	Comparability	Cost
Faithful representation*	Verifiability	
	Timeliness	
	Understandability	

*Complete, neutral, free from material error

The accounting concepts and principles and the qualitative characteristics, together with accounting standards, are collectively referred to as Australian **generally accepted accounting principles (GAAP)**. Australian GAAP is different from GAAP in other countries, such as the United States. The differences arise mainly in the detailed prescriptions of accounting standards. Any differences are specified in the statement of conformity. Australian GAAP is almost identical to New Zealand's generally accepted accounting practices (GAAP). They include financial reporting standards, statements of accounting practice, exposure drafts, IASB exposure drafts, technical practice aids and research bulletins. Both Australia and New Zealand have introduced reduced reporting requirements depending on the type and size of the organisation. There will be more discussion of differential reporting in chapter 13.

LEARNING REFLECTION AND CONSOLIDATION

Review it
1. What are generally accepted accounting principles (GAAP)?
2. Describe the concepts, principles and constraints underlying financial statements.
3. Explain the two main qualitative characteristics of information in general purpose financial reports.

1.9 Analysing financial statements

LEARNING OBJECTIVE 1.9 Calculate and interpret ratios for analysing an entity's profitability, liquidity and solvency.

So far, we have introduced the four main financial statements and discussed how these statements provide information about an entity's financial performance and position. As outlined in the *Conceptual Framework*, the objective of general purpose financial reporting is to provide financial information about the reporting entity that is useful to existing and potential equity investors, lenders and other creditors in making their decisions about providing resources to the entity. Now it is time to extend our discussion by showing you specific tools that can be used to analyse financial statements to make a more meaningful evaluation of an entity to assist investors and lenders' investment decisions. The analysis of financial statements is covered in more detail in chapter 12. For this section, we use the 2019 accounts of two furniture retailers: Original Furnishings Limited and Artistry Furniture Limited.

Analysis and decision making

Ratios are a valuable source of information when making resource allocation decisions. A **ratio** expresses the mathematical relationship between one quantity and another. **Ratio analysis** therefore expresses the relationship among selected items of financial statement data found in general purpose financial statements. The relationship between financial data points is expressed in terms of a percentage, a rate or a simple proportion. To illustrate, in 2019 Original Furnishings Limited had current assets of $187 470 000 and current liabilities of $123 975 000. The relationship between these accounts is determined by dividing current assets by current liabilities to get 1.51. The alternative means of expression are:

Percentage: Current assets are 151% of current liabilities.
Rate:　　　Current assets are 1.51 times as great as current liabilities.
Proportion: The relationship of current assets to current liabilities is 1.51:1.

For analysis of the main financial statements, ratios can be classified as shown in figure 1.22.

When making a decision to lend money or to invest in an entity, users of general purpose financial statements find it helpful to use ratios. Ratios can provide clues as to underlying conditions that may not be apparent from simply inspecting the individual components of a particular ratio as provided in the financial statements. The ratios can be classified into profitability ratios, liquidity ratios and solvency ratios, which we discuss in detail below with reference to furniture retailers Artistry Furniture Limited and Original Furnishings Limited. While ratios are useful inputs into resource allocation decisions, a single ratio by itself is not very meaningful. Accordingly, in this and the following chapters we will augment ratios with data and information from a wide variety of sources including:

1. *intracompany comparisons* covering two years for the same entity
2. *intercompany comparisons* based on comparisons with a competitor in the same industry
3. *other relevant information* such as general economic conditions, industry trends or averages, information from directors' reports and media releases.

FIGURE 1.22 Financial ratio classifications

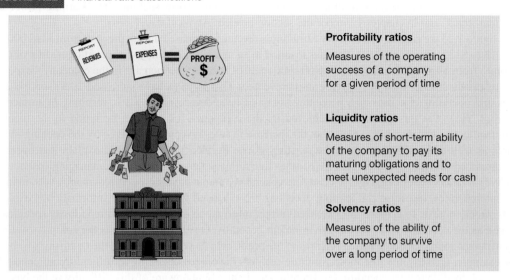

Profitability ratios

Measures of the operating
success of a company
for a given period of time

Liquidity ratios

Measures of short-term ability
of the company to pay its
maturing obligations and to
meet unexpected needs for cash

Solvency ratios

Measures of the ability of
the company to survive
over a long period of time

Profitability

Original Furnishings aims to generate a profit for its shareholders by manufacturing and selling furniture. Artistry Furniture aims to generate profits for its shareholders as a furniture retailer. The statement of profit or loss for Artistry Furniture reports how successful it is at generating a profit from its sales and other revenue. The statement reports the revenue for the period and the expenses incurred during the period. Figures relating to profitability are taken from Artistry Furniture's statement of profit or loss for the year ended 30 June 2019 and summarised in figure 1.23.

FIGURE 1.23 Extract from Artistry Furniture Limited's statement of profit or loss

ARTISTRY FURNITURE LIMITED Statement of profit or loss (extract) for the year ended 30 June 2019		
	2019 $'000	2018 $'000
Revenues	135 000	112 000
Expenses	(113 600)	(98 500)
Profit before income tax	**21 400**	**13 500**
Income tax expense	(4 800)	(4 050)
Profit	**16 600**	**9 450**

Before we begin the analysis, it is important to note that, when identifying the numbers to be used in ratio calculations, a close examination of the notes to the financial statements is required. For example, Artistry Furniture reports net profit after tax for the year ended 30 June 2019 as $21 900 000. However, this figure includes a one-off item in other income that needs to be excluded from the ratio calculations. Artistry Furniture received a one-off compensation benefit of $5 300 000 (net of tax) from the State Government. This income does not represent income generated by the day-to-day operations of the business and is unlikely to be received in the future, hence it should be excluded in calculating profitability for the company. Users of financial information make decisions about current and future profitability based on past data using trends over time. Removing items that distort trends and hinder users' assessments of the true earning capacity of the company assists in the analysis of the company and improves the decision-making process. This is discussed further in chapter 10 in section 10.6 'Earning power and irregular items' and in chapter 12 under the section headed 'Atypical data'.

In figure 1.23 we can see that Artistry Furniture's revenues increased during the year from $112 000 000 in 2018 to $135 000 000 in 2019. This has resulted in an increase in the adjusted profit figure (net of other income) from $9 450 000 in 2018 to $16 600 000 in 2019 because the increase in the company's expenses was relatively smaller than the increase in its revenues. That is, sales have increased 20.5% on the 2018 sales and operating expenses as a percentage of sales have decreased by 3.8%, resulting in an increase in profit. How was this great result achieved by the company? Insights can be found in the financial statement notes, which could explain that the increase in sales revenue was driven by the opening of new stores as well as growth in sales in the existing stores. Further, the notes could explain that operating expenses had decreased as a percentage of sales due to management's success in managing costs.

Given retailers are affected by the changing general economic conditions, employment levels, inflation and interest rates, investing and lending decisions are enhanced when company information is explored in its wider context. To achieve this, we need further information about the furniture industry specifically, as well as the economy and business environment generally. One helpful source is the company's annual report; other sources include media releases in the press, data on competitors and the company's web site. For example, let's assume that these furniture retailers have been operating in difficult retail conditions due to subdued consumer spending on discretionary items. Being aware of this difficulty in the business environment would prompt the decision makers to evaluate an increase in sales as even more impressive than first thought from the figures alone.

To evaluate the profitability of Artistry Furniture further, ratio analysis would be used. **Profitability ratios** measure the operating success of an entity for a given period of time. We will look at two examples of profitability ratios: return on assets and profit margin.

Return on assets

An overall measure of profitability is the **return on assets (ROA)**. This ratio is calculated by dividing profit by average assets. (Average assets are commonly calculated by adding the beginning and ending values of assets and dividing by 2.) Profit refers to profit after income tax unless stated otherwise. The return on assets indicates the amount of profit generated by each dollar invested in assets. Thus, the higher the return on assets, the more profitable the entity. Selected figures from the 2019 statement of profit or loss for Artistry Furniture are presented in figure 1.23. The 2019 and 2018 return on assets of Original Furnishings and Artistry Furniture Limited (entities operating in the same industry) are presented in figure 1.24.

FIGURE 1.24	Return on assets

	Return on assets $= \dfrac{\text{Profit}}{\text{Average total assets}}$	
($'000)	**2019**	**2018**
Original Furnishings	$\dfrac{\$35\,900}{(\$287\,370 + \$233\,280)/2} = 0.138{:}1 \text{ or } 13.8\%$	$\dfrac{\$38\,875}{(\$233\,280 + \$255\,050)/2} = 0.159{:}1 \text{ or } 15.9\%$
Artistry Furniture	$\dfrac{\$16\,600}{(\$65\,250 + \$51\,840)/2^{*}} = 0.284{:}1 \text{ or } 28.4\%$	$\dfrac{\$9\,450}{(\$51\,840 + \$41\,472)/2^{*}} = 0.203{:}1 \text{ or } 20.3\%$

*Amounts used to calculate average assets are taken from the statement of financial position (see figure 1.26). Total assets in 2017 were $41 472 000. Also note that amounts in the ratio calculations have been rounded to the nearest thousand.

We can evaluate Original Furnishings' 2019 and 2018 return on assets in a number of ways. First, we can compare the ratio across time. That is, did its performance improve? The decrease from 15.9% in 2018 to 13.8% in 2019 suggests a decline in profitability. The ratio tells us that in 2018 Original Furnishings generated 15.9 cents on every dollar invested in assets and in 2019 it generated 13.8 cents on every dollar invested in assets. Then we can compare the ratios with those of another operator in the industry, Artistry Furniture. In both 2018 and 2019, Original Furnishings' return on assets is below that of Artistry Furniture's. Thus, based on the return on assets, Original Furnishings' profitability appears weaker than Artistry Furniture's. In 2018, Artistry Furniture has a higher return on assets because it generated almost one-quarter of the amount of profits in dollar terms compared with Original Furnishings' profits, whilst using about one-fifth of the assets used by Original Furnishings. In 2019, Artistry Furniture has a larger return on assets because it generated around one-half of profits in dollar terms compared with Original Furnishings' profits, but Original Furnishings has around four and a half times the assets used by Artistry Furniture. In other words, put simply, Artistry Furniture was able to generate more profits using fewer assets.

Profit margin

The **profit margin** measures the percentage of each dollar of sales that results in profit. It is calculated by dividing profit by net sales (revenue) for the period. Businesses with high turnover, such as supermarkets and grocers (Coles or Woolworths) and discount stores (The Reject Shop or Crazy Prices) generally experience low profit margins. Low-turnover businesses, such as jewellery stores (Tiffany's) or shipbuilders (Australian Defence Industries), usually have high profit margins. Profit margins for Original Furnishings and Artistry Furniture are shown in figure 1.25. The figure for sales revenue used in calculating the profit margin is the same as total revenue reported in the statement of profit or loss. For simplicity it is assumed that all revenue is sales revenue.

| FIGURE 1.25 | Profit margin |

($'000)	Profit margin $= \dfrac{\text{Profit}}{\text{Net sales}}$	
	2019	**2018**
Original Furnishings	$\dfrac{\$35\,900}{\$562\,500} = 0.064$ or 6.4%	$\dfrac{\$38\,875}{\$510\,300} = 0.076$ or 7.6%
Artistry Furniture	$\dfrac{\$16\,600}{\$135\,000} = 0.123$ or 12.3%	$\dfrac{\$9\,450}{\$112\,000} = 0.084$ or 8.4%

Original Furnishing's profit margin decreased from 7.6% in 2018 to 6.4% in 2019. This means that in 2019 the company generated 6.4 cents on each dollar of sales and in 2018 it generated 7.6 cents on each dollar of sales. As we said earlier, single numbers have more meaning when they are combined with other data. Let's start by evaluating Original Furnishings' results by comparing them to those of its competitor, Artistry Furniture. Original Furnishings' profit margin was lower than Artistry Furniture's in both years. What could explain the difference in mark-up between businesses in the same industry? To answer this, we need to know a little more about the two companies. In 2019, Original Furnishings has 75 stores, with 55 of those being their Fun Furniture stores. A plausible explanation is that Original Furnishings has established itself in the marketplace as 'best value' and therefore sets a lower mark-up. Artistry Furniture, on the other hand, has 20 stores, with only 4 stores in the 'best value' market. Artistry Furniture branded stores may be perceived by the marketplace as 'better quality' and the company is therefore able to command a higher mark-up on its furniture sales.

In addition to the structure of the store holdings, further information provided in the financial statements and results presentations for each of these companies (available on the company web sites) sheds further light on the difference in mark-up. Artistry Furniture purchases its stock from overseas and was able to maintain its profit margin as supplier increases were offset by a stronger Australian dollar resulting in larger buying power. On the other hand, Original Furnishings explained that its profit margin was down due to its strategy of discounting its stock to clear excessive inventory. Furthermore, Artistry Furniture noted that it had decreased its expenses as a percentage of sales, illustrating management's focus on managing its operating costs. Original Furnishings reported quite a different story, claiming that its cost of business actually increased with higher property costs, higher employment costs and increased depreciation, as well as the development of an e-commerce platform.

As you can see, there is a lot of information users can draw upon to analyse, evaluate and make decisions about an entity. The decision-making and analysis processes are summarised in the decision-making toolkit below. In subsequent chapters you will learn more about evaluating an entity and the various forms of analysis for evaluating an entity's profitability, as introduced in this section.

Potential investors, shareholders, lenders and other users are interested in evaluating a company's profitability when making decisions about providing resources to a company. As you can imagine, potential investors and lenders feel more confident investing resources in a company that is profitable rather than one that is unprofitable. Calculating the return on assets ratio using profit and average total assets data from financial reports and then interpreting the results using multiple sources of information assists users in answering questions like: is the entity using its assets effectively? Recall that a higher value for the ratio indicates a better or more efficient use of assets, as was seen for Artistry Furniture when compared with Original Furnishings.

Another question decision makers might like to answer when making resource allocation decisions includes: is the entity maintaining an adequate margin between sales and expenses? By calculating the profit margin ratio using the profit and net sales figures from the statement of profit or loss, resource providers can evaluate whether the entity has a sufficient mark-up on its inventory and whether it is managing its operating costs effectively. All other things being equal, the higher the value of the ratio, the more favourable the return on each dollar of sales; thus the more attractive the company is to investors and the safer it is to lenders.

DECISION-MAKING TOOLKIT

Decision/issue	Info needed for analysis	Tool or technique to use for decision	How to evaluate results to make decision
Is the entity using its assets effectively?	Profit and average assets	$\text{Return on assets} = \dfrac{\text{Profit}}{\text{Average total assets}}$	Higher value suggests efficient use of assets.
Is the entity maintaining an adequate margin between sales and expenses?	Profit and net sales	$\text{Profit margin} = \dfrac{\text{Profit}}{\text{Net sales}}$	Higher value suggests favourable return on each dollar of sales.

LEARNING REFLECTION AND CONSOLIDATION

Review it

1. What are the three ways that ratios can be expressed?
2. What is the purpose of profitability ratios? Explain the return on assets and the profit margin ratios and how they inform the decisions that users make about resource allocations.

Liquidity

Profitability ratios are helpful in evaluating and making decisions about an entity. However, these ratios do not provide users of financial information with a complete picture of the entity to support their resource allocation decisions, so including liquidity and solvency ratios is helpful. **Liquidity ratios** measure the short-term ability of the entity to pay its maturing obligations and to meet unexpected needs for cash.

You can learn a lot about an entity's financial health by evaluating the relationship between its various assets and liabilities. However, any analysis of liquidity is incomplete without looking at cash flows. In this section, we will look at some ratios that use numbers from the statement of financial position of Artistry Furniture (figure 1.26). This will be followed by cash flow analysis.

FIGURE 1.26 Artistry Furniture statement of financial position

ARTISTRY FURNITURE LIMITED Statement of financial position (extract) as at 30 June 2019		
	2019 $'000	2018 $'000
ASSETS		
Current assets		
Cash	24 000	19 800
Trade and other receivables	4 420	2 700
Inventories	12 500	10 300
Other financial assets	520	100
Other assets	210	540
Total current assets	41 650	33 440
Non-current assets		
Deferred tax assets	2 100	2 400
Property, plant & equipment	19 500	14 000
Intangible assets	2 000	2 000
Total non-current assets	23 600	18 400
Total assets	65 250	51 840
LIABILITIES		
Current liabilities		
Trade and other payables	23 150	16 300
Current tax liabilities	4 800	4 050
Provisions	1 180	900
Total current liabilities	29 130	21 250
Non-current liabilities		
Deferred tax liabilities	270	20
Provisions	1 940	2 610
Borrowings	7 800	5 200
Total non-current liabilities	10 010	7 830
Total liabilities	39 140	29 080
Net assets	**26 110**	**22 760**
EQUITY		
Issued capital	2 000	2 000
Reserves	680	15
Retained earnings	23 430	20 745
Total equity	**26 110**	**22 760**

Suppose you are a banker considering lending money to Artistry Furniture, or you are a computer manufacturer interested in selling computers to the company. You would be concerned about Artistry Furniture's **liquidity** — its ability to pay obligations that are expected to become due within the next year or operating cycle. You would look closely at the relationship of its current assets to current liabilities before lending the entity money or supplying the entity with goods or services on credit.

Working capital

One measure of liquidity is **working capital**, which is the difference between the amounts of current assets and current liabilities:

$$\text{Working capital} = \text{Current assets} - \text{Current liabilities}$$

When working capital is positive, there is greater likelihood that the entity will be able to pay its liabilities. When working capital is negative, the entity will be unable to pay short-term creditors from existing current assets. Short-term creditors may not be paid unless the entity can draw on other sources of cash, and the entity may ultimately be forced into liquidation. Artistry Furniture had a positive working capital in 2019 of $12 520 000 ($41 650 000 − $29 130 000) and is therefore in a good position to pay its short-term debts as they fall due.

Current ratio

One liquidity ratio is the **current ratio**, which is calculated by dividing current assets by current liabilities.

The current ratio is a more dependable indicator of liquidity than working capital. Two entities with the same amount of working capital may have significantly different current ratios. The 2019 and 2018 current ratios for Original Furnishings and Artistry Furniture are shown in figure 1.27.

| **FIGURE 1.27** | Current ratios of Original Furnishings and Artistry Furniture |

	$\text{Current ratio} = \dfrac{\text{Current assets}}{\text{Current liabilities}}$	
($'000)	**2019**	**2018**
Original Furnishings	$\dfrac{\$187\,470}{\$123\,975} = 1.51{:}1 \text{ or } \$1.51$	$\dfrac{\$150\,480}{\$95\,625} = 1.57{:}1 \text{ or } \$1.57$
Artistry Furniture	$\dfrac{\$41\,650}{\$29\,130} = 1.43{:}1 \text{ or } \$1.43$	$\dfrac{\$33\,440}{\$21\,250} = 1.57{:}1 \text{ or } \$1.57$

Calculating the ratio is only the first step in the analysis process when making a decision. It is important to take the time to *interpret* the data. Decision makers need to answer the question 'what does this ratio actually mean?' Original Furnishings' 2019 current ratio of 1.51:1 means that, for every dollar of current liabilities, it has $1.51 of current assets. This indicates that the company will have funds available to pay debts as they fall due. Original Furnishings' current ratio decreased slightly from 1.57 in 2018 to 1.51 in 2019, decreasing its liquidity. However, compared with Artistry Furniture's 2019 current ratio of 1.43:1, Original Furnishings appears to have better liquidity.

What is considered to be an *acceptable* ratio varies from industry to industry. However, 1:1 is generally considered to be an acceptable current ratio for most industries. In this case both Original Furnishings' and Artistry Furniture's liquidity ratios are well above the *acceptable* ratio. These results would become *part* of the information resource providers use to make resource allocation decisions. For example, these ratios increase a lender's confidence that the companies will be able to repay any funds lent to them.

The current ratio is only one measure of liquidity. It does not take into account the *composition* of the current assets. For example, a satisfactory current ratio does not disclose whether a portion of the current assets is tied up in slow-moving inventory, i.e. inventory that is held in stock for a long period of time and is difficult to sell. The composition of the assets matters because a dollar of *cash* is more readily available to pay the bills than is a dollar of inventory. Inventory generally will be converted into cash in time, which will then be available to pay debts; however, only *after* the item is sold *and* the cash has been collected from the customer. This can take days, weeks, months or years depending on how quickly inventories sell.

Explaining why examining the composition of current assets is so important is best demonstrated using an example. Suppose an entity's cash balance declined while its inventory increased substantially. If inventory increased because the entity was having difficulty selling its products, then even though the current ratio might increase, the current ratio might not fully reflect the reduction in the entity's liquidity. In a later chapter you will learn about other measures of liquidity and how to analyse the liquidity of certain assets using turnover ratios.

Using the statement of cash flows

The statement of cash flows provides financial information about the sources and uses of an entity's cash. Investors, creditors and others want to know what is happening to an entity's most liquid resource — its cash. In fact, it is often said that 'cash is king' because if an entity can't generate cash, it won't survive, and for this reason cash is often referred to as the *life blood* of the business. To aid in the analysis of cash, the statement of cash flows reports the cash effects of: (1) an entity's *operating activities*, (2) its *investing activities* and (3) its *financing activities*.

The sources of cash matter. For example, you would feel much better about an entity's health if you knew that its cash was generated from the operations of the business rather than borrowed from the bank. The statement of cash flows for Artistry Furniture for the year ended 30 June 2019 is provided in figure 1.28.

FIGURE 1.28	Artistry Furniture Limited cash flows

ARTISTRY FURNITURE LIMITED Statement of cash flows for the year ended 30 June 2019	2019 $'000	2018 $'000
CASH FLOWS FROM OPERATING ACTIVITIES		
Receipts from customers	137 200	121 500
Payments to suppliers and employees	(115 300)	(106 400)
Interest received	950	900
Income taxes paid	(4 050)	(3 450)
Net cash flows from operating activities	18 800	12 550
CASH FLOWS FROM INVESTING ACTIVITIES		
Payments for property, plant & equipment	(9 000)	(2 000)
Net cash used in investing activities	(9 000)	(2 000)
CASH FLOWS FROM FINANCING ACTIVITIES		
Dividends paid	(8 200)	(7 200)
Proceeds from borrowings	3 400	0
Interest paid	(800)	(225)
Net cash used in financing activities	(5 600)	(7 425)
Net increase/(decrease) in cash held	4 200	3 125
Cash at the beginning of the year	19 800	16 675
Cash at the end of the year	**24 000**	**19 800**

In the long term, it is generally desirable that an entity be able to generate enough cash from its operating activities to pay dividends and finance its investing needs. This information is important when potential investors and creditors are deciding whether to provide resources to the entity. Cash flows from operations needs to be assessed over a number of years because the timing of major capital investment expenditures and, to a lesser extent, cash paid for operating activities can cause considerable variation in the relationship between operating and investing cash flows from year to year.

To illustrate, let's consider Artistry Furniture's operating cash flows. Cash generated by operating activities for 2019 was $18 800 000 compared with $12 550 000 for 2018. There was an increase in cash receipts, and payments to suppliers and employees increased at a lesser rate. This resulted in an increase in net cash from operations of $6 250 000. Net cash spent on investing activities, which consisted solely of purchases of property, plant and equipment in 2019, was $9 000 000 compared with $2 000 000 in 2018. The funds for investing activities were provided partly from operating activities and partly by the proceeds from borrowings; you can see this in the investing and financing sections of the statement of cash flows. The outflow of cash for property, plant and equipment was largely due to a $6 500 000 purchase of property. No additional funds were obtained from new share issues during 2018 or 2019. Dividends accounted for the main outflow of funds for 2019 and 2018 financing activities in the amounts of $8 200 000 and $7 200 000 respectively.

Earlier we introduced you to the current ratio. The statement of cash flows can also be used to calculate additional measures of liquidity. The **current cash debt coverage** is a measure of liquidity that is calculated as *net cash provided by operating activities* divided by *average current liabilities*. It indicates the entity's ability to generate sufficient cash to meet its short-term needs. Cash debt coverage is the best measure of liquidity given it shows whether the cash generated by operating activities is sufficient to cover the current liabilities as they fall due. Statement of financial position measures of liquidity, such as the current ratio, include items in the calculation that are not yet cash, such as receivables or inventories. Inventories and receivables cannot be used to pay liabilities until the cash is collected, which can take time. While the acceptable level for the current cash debt coverage will vary between industries, in general a value below 0.40 times is considered cause for additional investigation of an entity's liquidity. Figure 1.29 shows the current cash debt coverage for Original Furnishings and Artistry Furniture for 2019 and 2018.

FIGURE 1.29 Current cash debt coverage

$$\text{Current cash debt coverage} = \frac{\text{Net cash provided by operating activities}}{\text{Average current liabilities}}$$

($'000)	2019	2018
Original Furnishings	$\dfrac{\$79\,425}{(\$123\,975 + \$95\,625)/2} = 0.72{:}1 \text{ or } 0.72$	$\dfrac{\$56\,475}{(\$95\,625 + \$71\,720)/2} = 0.68{:}1 \text{ or } 0.68$
Artistry Furniture	$\dfrac{\$18\,800}{(\$29\,130 + \$21\,250)/2^*} = 0.75{:}1 \text{ or } 0.75$	$\dfrac{\$12\,550}{(\$21\,250 + \$17\,000)/2^*} = 0.66{:}1 \text{ or } 0.66$

*Amounts used to calculate average current liabilities are taken from the statement of financial position (figure 1.26). Current liabilities at year-end 2017 were $17 000. Also note that amounts in the ratio calculations have been rounded to the nearest thousand.

We can use these cash measures of liquidity to supplement the analysis of liquidity using the statement of financial position figures. Original Furnishings' current cash debt coverage of 0.72 in 2019 is higher than in 2018.

The recommended minimum level for current cash debt coverage is 0.40. This is a general guide that decision makers can use when making resource allocation decisions. A current debt coverage of greater than 0.40 gives potential investors and creditors more confidence in the company than a ratio below 0.40. 'Can the entity meet its short-term obligations?' is the primary question decision makers ask about liquidity, as outlined in the decision-making toolkit. By drawing on information from the statement of financial position (current assets and current liabilities) as well as information from the statement of cash flows (cash flows from operating activities) decision makers can calculate the current ratio and cash debt coverage ratio to assess liquidity. In both cases, a higher ratio indicates more favourable liquidity. Recall liquidity is the entity's ability to repay current obligations as they fall due. If the entity can't pay its obligations, then it could be forced into liquidation, which might result in the resource providers (e.g. lenders, suppliers or investors) losing money. Let's explore cash measures of liquidity using the data from Original Furnishings' and Artistry Furniture's financial statements.

As at June 2019, Artistry Furniture's current liabilities were covered 0.75 by cash flows from operations. This result is almost twice the general guide used to evaluate an entity's liquidity for the current cash debt coverage ratio, indicating more favourable liquidity for the company. Both companies' current cash debt coverage ratios are above 0.40, which indicates the companies have a favourable liquidity position and should be able to generate sufficient cash flows from operations to meet current liabilities as they fall due. The steps in the decision-making process are summarised in the decision-making toolkit next.

Decision/issue	Info needed for analysis	Tool or technique to use for decision	How to evaluate results to make decision
Can the entity meet its short-term obligations?	Current assets and current liabilities	$\text{Current ratio} = \dfrac{\text{Current assets}}{\text{Current liabilities}}$	Higher ratio indicates more favourable liquidity.
Can the entity meet its short-term obligations?	Current liabilities and cash provided by operating activities	$\text{Current cash debt coverage} = \dfrac{\text{Cash provided by operations}}{\text{Average current liabilities}}$	A higher value indicates more favourable liquidity.

Solvency

When deciding how to allocate resources, decision makers need to consider how the entity will fare in the short term as well as the long term. Now suppose that instead of being a short-term creditor, you are interested in either buying Artistry Furniture's shares or extending the company a long-term loan. Long-term creditors and shareholders are interested in an entity's long-term **solvency** — its ability to pay interest as it comes due and to repay the debt at maturity. **Solvency ratios** measure the ability of the business to survive over a long period of time. The debt to total assets ratio is one source of information about long-term debt-paying ability. Cash flow ratios, such as the cash debt coverage, are also useful tools of analysis. By looking at an entity's profitability, liquidity and solvency with other data like general economic and business information, decision makers can construct a more complete picture of the entity's performance and position when analysing and making decisions about lending or investing their funds.

Helpful hint: Some users evaluate solvency using a ratio of liabilities divided by equity. The higher this ratio, the lower an entity's solvency.

Debt to total assets ratio

Recall that Assets = Liabilities + Equity. This equation shows that the assets can either be funded through equity or debt. The **debt to total assets ratio** measures the *percentage* of assets financed by creditors rather than shareholders. Debt financing is more risky than equity financing because debt must be repaid at specific points in time, whether the entity is performing well or not. Thus, the higher the percentage of debt financing, the riskier the entity. What risk means in this instance is that, all other things being equal, the higher the debt is, the more interest that needs to be repaid each period and the greater the principal to be repaid at the end of the loan period. In practical terms, the company has to generate sufficient profits to repay the interest and debt, and if it cannot and the company goes into liquidation, existing resource providers (lenders or investors) may not be able to claim their investment or loan from the company if it has insufficient funds. Thus, the higher the debt is, the riskier it is for resource providers.

The debt to total assets ratio is calculated by dividing total debt (both current and non-current liabilities) by total assets. The information for this ratio is taken from the statement of financial position. Calculating this ratio is a tool that helps users of financial information assess whether the entity can meet its long-term obligations, as summarised in the decision-making toolkit above. The higher the percentage of total liabilities (debt) to total assets, the greater the risk that the entity may be unable to pay its debts as they become due. The ratios of debt to total assets for Original Furnishings and Artistry Furniture for 2019 and 2018 are presented in figure 1.30.

The 2019 ratio of 59% means that 59 cents of every dollar invested in assets by Original Furnishings has been provided by its creditors. The 2019 ratio of 60% means that 60 cents of every dollar invested in assets by Artistry Furniture has been provided by its creditors. The higher the ratio, the lower the equity 'buffer' available to creditors if the company becomes insolvent, i.e. the less chance the creditors might have their debts repaid out of shareholders' funds if the company goes into liquidation. Thus, from a lender's or creditor's point of view, a high ratio of debt to total assets is undesirable. Based on the 2019 data, Original Furnishings is slightly more solvent than Artistry Furniture. Examination of the statement of financial position indicates that Artistry Furniture has less long-term debt than Original Furnishings.

FIGURE 1.30	Debt to total assets ratio	
	$\text{Debt to total assets ratio} = \dfrac{\text{Total liabilities}}{\text{Total assets}}$	
($'000)	2019	2018
Original Furnishings	$\dfrac{\$170\,235}{\$287\,370} = 0.59{:}1 \text{ or } 0.59$	$\dfrac{\$130\,860}{\$233\,280} = 0.56{:}1 \text{ or } 0.56$
Artistry Furniture	$\dfrac{\$39\,140}{\$65\,250} = 0.60{:}1 \text{ or } 0.60$	$\dfrac{\$29\,080}{\$51\,840} = 0.56{:}1 \text{ or } 0.56$

Based on these ratios, Original Furnishings appears to be solvent in that its assets exceed its liabilities. Artistry Furniture, on the other hand, is only near solvent given its debt to total assets ratio of 0.60:1. However, the adequacy of this ratio is often judged in the light of the entity's profits, cash flows and ability to pay interest when it falls due. Generally, entities with relatively stable profit can support higher debt to total assets ratios than can cyclical entities with widely fluctuating profits, such as many high-tech companies. The profitability, liquidity and solvency ratios calculated thus far, as well as the other information on the company's management, suggest that Artistry Furniture is a safe investment for potential shareholders and lenders.

The **cash debt coverage** is another measure of solvency that is calculated as cash provided by operating activities divided by average total liabilities. It indicates the entity's ability to generate sufficient cash to meet its long-term needs. Figure 1.31 presents the cash debt coverage for Original Furnishings and Artistry Furniture for 2019 and 2018. Although what is considered an acceptable ratio varies between industries, a general rule of thumb is that a ratio below 0.20 is considered cause for additional investigation.

FIGURE 1.31	Cash debt coverage	
	$\text{Cash debt coverage} = \dfrac{\text{Net cash provided by operating activities}}{\text{Average total liabilities}}$	
($'000)	2019	2018
Original Furnishings	$\dfrac{\$79\,425}{(\$170\,235 + \$130\,860)/2} = 0.53{:}1 \text{ or } 0.53$	$\dfrac{\$56\,475}{(\$130\,860 + \$98\,147)/2} = 0.49{:}1 \text{ or } 0.49$
Artistry Furniture	$\dfrac{\$18\,800}{(\$39\,140 + \$29\,080)/2*} = 0.55{:}1 \text{ or } 0.55$	$\dfrac{\$12\,550}{(\$29\,080 + \$23\,264)/2*} = 0.48{:}1 \text{ or } 0.48$

*Amounts used to calculate average total liabilities are taken from Artistry Furniture's statement of financial position (figure 1.26). Total liabilities at year-end 2017 were $23 264 (in thousands). Also note that amounts in the ratio calculations have been rounded to the nearest thousand.

Original Furnishings' cash debt coverage of 0.53 in 2019 is well above the recommended minimum level of 0.20, suggesting it is solvent consistent with the results of the debt to total assets ratio. Note the differences between the current debt coverage and the cash debt coverage for both Original Furnishings and Artistry Furniture. This difference reflects the levels of non-current liabilities. Artistry Furniture experienced a substantial increase in cash debt coverage in 2019, whereas Original Furnishings experienced only a slight increase. However, while Artistry Furniture maintained higher cash debt coverage in

2019, both companies are above the minimum level of 0.20, indicating they are both solvent. We will investigate other measures of liquidity and solvency in later chapters.

The decision-making toolkit below summarises the decision-making processes for determining whether an entity can meet its long-term obligations. Calculating the cash debt coverage ratio is a useful tool for users of financial statements when making decisions about lending money to an entity or purchasing shares. A higher ratio indicates better solvency because the entity is generating cash to meet its long-term needs. The solvency ratios for both Original Furnishings and Artistry Furniture indicate that the entities are solvent and therefore low risk for investors and creditors.

In this section, we have explored some of the decision-making processes users of general purpose financial statements undertake when making choices about whether to lend money or to invest in an entity. We saw that ratios could provide clues as to underlying conditions that may not be apparent from simply inspecting the individual figures provided in financial statements. The ratios were classified into profitability ratios, liquidity ratios and solvency ratios, which were employed to conduct an in-depth analysis of two companies, Artistry Furniture Limited and Original Furnishings Limited. By now you can clearly see that, while ratios are useful inputs into resource allocation decisions, a single ratio by itself is not very meaningful. Augmenting ratios with data and information from a wide variety of sources makes the data more meaningful and gives the analysis some context. Recall that *intracompany comparisons* (covering two years for the same entity), *intercompany comparisons* (based on comparisons with a competitor in the same industry) and *other relevant information* such as general economic conditions, industry trends or averages, and information from directors' reports and media releases provided great insights for interpreting the data.

You may find it helpful to consolidate your knowledge by taking some time now to work through the decision-making toolkit activity. Then, review the steps in the decision-making toolkit summary to ensure you understand how to calculate and evaluate profitability, liquidity and solvency ratios.

DECISION-MAKING TOOLKIT

Decision/issue	Info needed for analysis	Tool or technique to use for decision	How to evaluate results to make decision
Can the entity meet its long-term obligations?	Total liabilities and total assets	Debt to total assets ratio $= \dfrac{\text{Total liabilities}}{\text{Total assets}}$	A higher ratio indicates solvency risk because the entity has fewer assets available for creditors.
Can the entity meet its long-term obligations?	Total liabilities and cash provided by operating activities	Cash debt coverage $= \dfrac{\text{Cash provided by operations}}{\text{Average total liabilities}}$	A higher ratio indicates better solvency as the entity is generating cash to meet its long-term needs.

LEARNING REFLECTION AND CONSOLIDATION

Review it

1. What is liquidity? How can it be measured using a classified statement of financial position?
2. What is solvency? How can it be measured using (a) a statement of financial position? (b) a statement of cash flows?
3. What information does the statement of cash flows provide that is not available in an income statement or statement of financial position?
4. What does the current cash debt coverage measure? What does the cash debt coverage measure?

▶

Do it

Selected financial data for Drummond Ltd at 30 June 2019 are as follows: cash $60 000; receivables (net) $80 000; inventory $70 000; total assets $540 000; current liabilities $140 000; and total liabilities $270 000. Calculate the current ratio and debt to total assets ratio.

Reasoning

The formula for the current ratio is: Current assets ÷ Current liabilities. The formula for the debt to total assets ratio is: Total liabilities ÷ Total assets.

Solution

The current ratio is 1.5:1 ($210 000 ÷ $140 000). The debt to total assets ratio is 0.5:1 ($270 000 ÷ $540 000).

USING THE DECISION-MAKING TOOLKIT

Roaming Limited operates in the travel and leisure industry. Assume that you are considering the purchase of shares in Roaming.

Required

Answer these questions related to your decision whether to invest.
(a) What financial statements should you be interested in?
(b) What should these financial statements tell you?
(c) Should you request audited financial statements? Explain.
(d) Will the financial statements show the market value of Roaming's assets? Explain.
(e) Compare Roaming's profit for 2019 with its profit for 2018. The statement of profit or loss with comparative 2018 figures is provided in figure 1.32.

FIGURE 1.32 Roaming's statement of profit or loss

ROAMING LIMITED
Statement of profit or loss (extract)
for the year ended 30 June 2019

	Consolidated	
	2019 $'000	2018 $'000
REVENUE FROM CONTINUING OPERATIONS		
Revenue from the sale of travel services	778 950	695 491
Other revenue from ordinary activities	20 000	15 200
Total for revenue from continuing operations	798 950	710 691
OTHER INCOME	3 230	1 470
EXPENSES		
Selling expenses	(611 670)	(554 240)
Administration/support expenses	(85 457)	(58 278)
Finance costs	(13 282)	(13 585)
Share of loss of joint venture accounted for using the equity method	(463)	(415)
Profit before income tax expense	**91 308**	**85 643**
Income tax expense	(27 392)	(25 693)
Profit attributable to members of Roaming Limited	**63 916**	**59 950**

(f) How much of Roaming's assets were financed by creditors at 30 June 2019? Roaming's statement of financial position is shown in figure 1.33.

FIGURE 1.33 Roaming's statement of financial position

ROAMING LIMITED
Statement of financial position (extract)
as at 30 June 2019

	Consolidated	
	2019 $'000	2018 $'000
ASSETS		
Current assets		
Cash and cash equivalents	261 843	240 357
Available for sale financial assets	204 831	—
Receivables	244 987	211 200
Other financial assets	—	192 738
Current tax receivables	5 596	—
Assets of disposal group classified as held for sale	12 179	—
Total current assets	729 436	644 295
Non-current assets		
Property, plant and equipment	78 486	91 239
Intangible assets	207 431	165 671
Deferred tax assets	13 206	15 998
Other financial assets	—	—
Investments accounted for using the equity method	2 248	2 750
Total non-current assets	301 371	275 658
Total assets	1 030 807	919 953
LIABILITIES		
Current liabilities		
Payables	465 000	424 942
Borrowings	43 662	37 793
Provisions	3 400	3 116
Current tax liabilities	2 533	3 144
Total current liabilities	514 595	468 995
Non-current liabilities		
Payables	34 682	17 844
Borrowings	27 000	15 000
Deferred tax liabilities	378	1 025
Provisions	8 442	8 729
Total non-current liabilities	70 502	42 598
Total liabilities	585 097	511 593
Net assets	**445 710**	**408 360**
EQUITY		
Share capital	260 000	260 000
Reserves	7 770	4 940
Retained earnings	177 940	143 420
Total equity	**445 710**	**408 360**

(g) Did Roaming generate sufficient cash flows from its operating activities to finance its investing activities in 2019? A simplified statement of cash flows is provided in figure 1.34.

FIGURE 1.34 Roaming's statement of cash flows

ROAMING LIMITED Statement of cash flows for the year ended 30 June 2019		
	2019 $'000	2018 $'000
Net cash inflow from operating activities	122 974	117 596
Net cash (outflow) from investing activities	(62 497)	(22 970)
Net cash (outflow) from financing activities	(38 991)	(97 433)
Net increase (decrease) in cash held	**21 486**	**(2 807)**

(h) Calculate Roaming's return on assets for 2019 and profit margin for 2019 and 2018. Has profitability improved in the 2-year period?
(i) Calculate Roaming's current ratio for 2019 and 2018 and the current cash debt coverage for 2019. Does Roaming have liquidity problems?
(j) Calculate Roaming's debt ratio for 2019 and 2018 and the cash debt coverage for 2019. Has solvency improved since 2018?
(k) What other information would be useful to review when looking at Roaming's operations?
(Using the decision-making toolkit exercises, which follow the final set of Review it questions in the chapter, ask you to use information from financial statements to make financial decisions. We encourage you to think through the questions related to the decision before you study the solution.)

Solution
(a) Before you invest, you should investigate the statement of profit or loss, statement of financial position and statement of cash flows.
(b) You would probably be most interested in the statement of profit or loss because it tells about past performance and thus gives an indication of future performance. The statement of cash flows reveals where the entity is getting and spending its cash. This is especially important for an entity that wants to grow. Finally, the statement of financial position reveals the types of assets and liabilities and the relationship between assets and liabilities.
(c) You would want audited financial statements — statements that an independent accountant has examined and expressed the opinion that the statements present fairly the entity's financial position and results of operations. Investors and creditors should not make decisions without studying audited financial statements of entities required to appoint auditors.
(d) The financial statements will not show the market value of all of the entity's assets. One important principle of accounting is the cost principle, which states that assets should be recorded at cost. Cost has an important advantage over other valuations: it is objective and reliable.
(e) Roaming's profit for 2019 is $63 916 000, an increase of $3 966 000 on the 2018 profit of $59 950 000. This is a 6.6% increase. Revenue from the sale of travel services increased 12%, but during the year there was an expansion in the corporate travel service network to internationalise the business and added costs came with this expansion. The future aims are to reduce global costs and improve the profit margin.
(f) Roaming's debt ratio at 30 June 2019 was 0.57:1 or 57%, indicating that 57 cents of every dollar of assets was financed by creditors. The debt ratio is calculated as total liabilities divided by total assets ($585 097 000/$1 030 807 000).
(g) Roaming generated net cash flows of $122 974 000 from its operations in 2019 and spent $62 497 000 (net) on investing activities that year, so there were sufficient cash flows from operations to finance the investing activities.

(h) The return on assets for 2019 is 0.066 or 6.6% [$63 916 000/($1 030 807 000 + $919 953 000)/2]. The profit margin for 2019 was 0.08 or 8% ($63 916 000/$798 950 000) and for 2018 it was 0.084 or 8.49% ($59 950 000/$710 691 000). Thus profitability decreased marginally in 2019.

(i) Roaming's current ratio was 1.42:1 ($729 436 000/$514 595 000) in 2019 and 1.37:1 ($644 295 000/$468 995 000) in 2018. The current cash debt coverage for 2019 was 0.25 or 25% [$122 974 000/($514 595 000 + $468 995 000)/2]. Roaming generated positive net cash flows from operating activities in 2019 and 2018. The current ratio improved only slightly during the year. The improvement was because of a growth in cash and trade receivables. However, the current cash coverage is only 0.25, which is below the general rule of thumb of 0.40, so the actual liquidity should be investigated.

(j) Roaming's debt ratio for 2019 was 57%, as calculated in part (f), and 0.556 or 55.6% for 2018 ($511 593 000/$919 953 000). This indicates that solvency hasn't changed from 2018 to 2019. The cash debt coverage for 2019 was 0.224 or 22.4% [$122 974 000/($585 097 000 + $511 593 000)/2]. A ratio of 0.20 times is the bare minimum, so the cash debt coverage indicates barely adequate solvency and should be monitored, as most of the liabilities are current (short term).

(k) Other useful information would be information from the company such as directors' reports and media releases; intercompany comparisons with a competitor in the same industry; information on general economic conditions; and industry trends or averages.

SUMMARY

1.1 Explain the business context and the need for decision making.

Accounting provides an economic model of the business world. It plays a key role in the provision of financial information for decisions made by people inside and outside the business. The process of decision making is first to identify the issue or the decision to be made. The next step is to gather the relevant information required for the analysis. Once gathered, you then identify the tool or technique that can provide the analysis of the issue so a decision may be made. The final step is to evaluate the results of the analysis and make the decision.

1.2 Define accounting, describe the accounting process and define the diverse roles of accountants.

Accounting is the process of identifying, measuring, recording and communicating the economic transactions and events of a business operation to provide reliable and relevant financial information for decision making. Accountants practise accounting in four main areas: commercial accounting, public accounting, government and not-for-profit accounting.

1.3 Explain the characteristics of the main forms of business organisation.

A sole proprietorship is a business owned by one person. A partnership is a business owned by two or more people. A company is a separate legal entity for which evidence of ownership is provided by shares. Other forms include trusts, cooperatives and not-for-profit forms. A trust is a relationship or association between two or more parties whereby one party holds property in trust for the other. A cooperative is a form of business organisation which is member-owned, controlled and used. It must consist of five or more people. The not-for-profit sector includes clubs, charities and the government sector.

1.4 Understand the *Conceptual Framework* and the purpose of financial reporting.

The *Conceptual Framework* consists of a set of concepts to be followed by preparers of financial statements and standard setters. A reporting entity is defined as an entity for which it is reasonable to expect the existence of users who depend on general purpose financial reports for information to enable them to make economic decisions. It is important to determine whether an organisation is a reporting entity as reporting entities must prepare external general purpose financial reports which comply with accounting standards. Reporting entities tend to be larger organisations and the financial information provided in external general purpose financial reports tends to be quite condensed. Both reporting and non-reporting entities also prepare internal reports which have more detailed information. The objective of general purpose financial reporting is to provide financial information about the reporting entity that is useful to existing and potential equity investors, lenders and other creditors in making their decisions about providing resources to the entity.

1.5 Identify the users of financial reports and describe users' information needs.

Internal users are managers who need accounting information for planning, controlling and evaluating business operations. The main external users are investors and creditors. Investors (shareholders) use accounting information to help them decide whether to buy, hold or sell shares. Creditors (suppliers and bankers) use accounting information to assess the risk of granting credit or lending money to a business. Other groups who have an indirect interest in a business are customers and regulatory agencies. Users of financial reports are interested in information about financing activities, which involve collecting the necessary funds to support the business; investing activities, which involve acquiring the resources necessary to run the business; and operating activities, which involve putting the resources of the business into action to generate a profit.

1.6 Identify the elements of each of the four main financial statements.

A statement of profit or loss presents the income (revenues and gains) and expenses of an entity for a specific period of time. A statement of changes in equity reports the amount of comprehensive income for the period and other changes in equity. A statement of financial position reports the assets, liabilities and equity of a business at a specific date. A statement of cash flows summarises information concerning the cash inflows (receipts) and outflows (payments) for a specific period of time.

1.7 Describe the financial reporting environment.

The Corporations Act regulates the activities of companies. ASIC administers the Corporations Act. The financial reporting regulations are contained in the Australian accounting standards. The FRC oversees the AASB and advises the Commonwealth Government on the standard-setting process and developments in international standard setting. The AASB issues accounting standards which certain entities, such as listed companies, must apply when preparing published financial statements. Listed companies must also comply with additional financial reporting requirements of the Australian Securities Exchange. Key professional bodies include CPA Australia, Chartered Accountants Australia and New Zealand and IPA. The accounting standards issued by both the Australian and New Zealand standard-setting bodies are consistent with those issued by IASB and are commonly referred to as IFRSs.

1.8 Explain the accounting concepts, principles, qualitative characteristics and constraints underlying financial statements.

The basic accounting concepts and principles are the monetary principle, the accounting entity concept, the accounting period concept, the going concern principle, the cost principle and the full disclosure principle. The *Conceptual Framework* states that for information included in general purpose financial reports to be useful it must be relevant and provide a faithful representation of the economic phenomena it represents. Relevance and faithful representation are therefore classified as fundamental qualitative characteristics. Enhancing qualitative characteristics include comparability, verifiability, timeliness and understandability and are used to distinguish more useful information from less useful information. Cost is the constraint that limits the information provided by financial reporting.

1.9 Calculate and interpret ratios for analysing an entity's profitability, liquidity and solvency.

Profitability ratios, such as profit margin and return on assets, measure different aspects of the operating success of an entity for a given period of time. Liquidity ratios, such as the current ratio, measure an entity's short-term ability to pay its maturing obligations and to meet unexpected needs for cash. The current cash debt coverage is another measure of an entity's liquidity. Solvency ratios, such as the debt to total assets ratio and the cash debt coverage, measure an entity's ability to survive in the long term.

DECISION-MAKING TOOLKIT — A SUMMARY

DECISION-MAKING TOOLKIT

Decision/issue	Info needed for analysis	Tool or technique to use for decision	How to evaluate results to make decision
Are the entity's operations profitable?	Statement of profit or loss	The statement of profit or loss reports on the success or failure of the entity's operations by reporting its revenues and expenses.	If the entity's revenues exceed its expenses, it will report profit; if expenses exceed revenues, it will report a loss.
Does the entity rely mainly on debt or equity to finance its assets?	Statement of financial position	The statement of financial position reports the entity's resources and claims to those resources. There are two types of claims: liabilities and equity.	Compare the amount of liabilities (debt) with the amount of equity to determine whether the entity relies more on creditors or owners for its financing.

Decision/issue	Info needed for analysis	Tool or technique to use for decision	How to evaluate results to make decision
Does the entity generate sufficient cash from operations to fund its investing activities?	Statement of cash flows	The statement of cash flows shows the amount of cash provided or used by operating activities, investing activities and financing activities.	Compare the amount of cash provided by operating activities with the amount of cash used by investing activities. Any deficiency in cash from operating and investing activities must be made up with cash from financing activities.
Is the entity using its assets effectively?	Profit and average assets	$\text{Return on assets} = \dfrac{\text{Profit}}{\text{Average total assets}}$	Higher value suggests efficient use of assets.
Is the entity maintaining an adequate margin between sales and expenses?	Profit and net sales	$\text{Profit margin} = \dfrac{\text{Profit}}{\text{Net sales}}$	Higher value suggests favourable return on each dollar of sales.
Can the entity meet its short-term obligations?	Current assets and current liabilities	$\text{Current ratio} = \dfrac{\text{Current assets}}{\text{Current liabilities}}$	Higher ratio indicates more favourable liquidity.
Can the entity meet its short-term obligations?	Current liabilities and cash provided by operating activities	$\text{Current cash debt coverage} = \dfrac{\text{Cash provided by operations}}{\text{Average current liabilities}}$	A higher value indicates more favourable liquidity.
Can the entity meet its long-term obligations?	Total liabilities and total assets	$\text{Debt to total assets ratio} = \dfrac{\text{Total liabilities}}{\text{Total assets}}$	A higher ratio indicates solvency risk because the entity has fewer assets available for creditors.
Can the entity meet its long-term obligations?	Total liabilities and cash provided by operating activities	$\text{Cash debt coverage} = \dfrac{\text{Cash provided by operations}}{\text{Average current liabilities}}$	A higher ratio indicates better solvency as the entity is generating cash to meet its long-term needs.

KEY TERMS

accounting The process of identifying, measuring, recording and communicating the economic transactions and events of a business operation.

accounting entity concept A concept that every entity can be separately identified and accounted for. Economic events can be identified with a particular unit of accountability, so that financial statements are prepared from the perspective of the entity, not its owners or other parties.

accounting period concept An accounting concept that the economic life of an entity can be divided into discrete periods of time and that useful reports covering those periods can be prepared by the entity.

accounts receivable Amounts due from customers for the sale of goods or services on credit. Also called debtors or trade debtors.

annual report A report prepared by corporate management that presents financial information including financial statements, notes and the directors' report.

assets Resources controlled by an entity as a result of past events and from which future economic benefits are expected to flow to the entity.

associations Small, non-profit, community-based groups. Associations can be, but are not always, incorporated as an alternative to a company. An incorporated association has similar advantages to a company but is not as expensive to set up or maintain. An association can trade as a profit organisation, but this cannot be its main objective.

audit An audit is an independent examination of the accounting data presented by an entity in order to provide an opinion as to whether the financial statements fairly present the results of the operation and the entity's financial position.

Auditing and Assurance Standards Board (AUASB) The organisation with authority to issue auditing and assurance standards for use by auditors and providers of other assurance services.

auditor An accountant who conducts an independent examination of the accounting data presented by the entity and expresses an opinion as to the fairness of the presentation of an entity's financial position and results of operations, and the entity's conformance with accounting standards.

Australian Accounting Standards Board (AASB) The organisation with authority to issue accounting standards in Australia.

Australian Securities and Investments Commission (ASIC) The body that administers the Corporations Act.

basic accounting equation Assets = Liabilities + Equity.

bookkeeping The activities of identifying, measuring and recording the business information are commonly referred to as bookkeeping. Bookkeeping forms the foundation of the activities underlying accounting.

cash debt coverage A cash-basis ratio used to evaluate solvency, calculated as net cash provided by operating activities divided by average total liabilities.

chief financial officer (CFO) A senior manager in an organisation who directs the accounting operations.

classified statement of financial position A statement of financial position in which assets and liabilities are classified as current and non-current.

commercial accountants Commercial accountants work in industry and commerce in different roles such as management accounting and financial accounting.

company A company or corporation is a separate legal entity formed under the Corporations Act. The process of setting up a company is called incorporation. The owners of a company are called shareholders.

comparability Ability to compare the accounting information of different entities or the same entity over time because the same accounting measurement and principles are used.

Conceptual Framework The conceptual framework consists of a set of concepts to be followed by the preparers of financial statements and standard setters.

cooperative A form of business organisation which is member-owned, controlled and used. It must consist of five or more people. Cooperatives are legislated at state level. They are distinctive for fostering a highly participative and democratic style of work, pooling resources to be more competitive and sharing skills.

corporate governance statement A separate section of a company's annual report containing disclosures relating to the extent to which the company has followed the ASX's corporate governance principles and recommendations.

cost constraints A constraint on the pursuit of qualitative characteristics of financial reporting so that the costs of preparing and reporting financial information does not exceed the benefits to users.

cost principle All assets are initially recorded in the accounts at their purchase price or cost.

current assets Cash and other assets that are reasonably expected to be converted to cash or used in the business within 1 year or the operating cycle, whichever is longer.

current cash debt coverage A cash-basis ratio used to evaluate liquidity, calculated as net cash provided by operating activities divided by average current liabilities.

current liabilities Obligations reasonably expected to be paid within the next year or operating cycle, whichever is longer, e.g. wages payable or loan payable.

current ratio A measure used to evaluate an entity's liquidity and short-term debt-paying ability, calculated as current assets divided by current liabilities.

debt to total assets ratio Measures the percentage of total financing provided by creditors; calculated as total liabilities divided by total assets.

decision A choice among alternative courses of action.

directors' report A section of the annual report that provides information about the directors and their views on the company's performance.

dividends A distribution of profits by a company to its shareholders in an amount proportional to each shareholder's percentage ownership. The most common form is a cash distribution.

end of the reporting period The last date of each reporting period.

equity The residual interest in the assets of the entity after deducting all its liabilities; also known as shareholders' or owners' equity.

equity investors People who make decisions to buy, hold or sell shares.

expenses Assets consumed or services used in the process of generating revenues, and losses incurred.

External Reporting Board (XRB) An independent New Zealand Crown Entity that sets accounting and auditing standards in New Zealand.

faithful representation Information is a faithful representation of the economic phenomena it purports to represent if it is complete, neutral and free from material error.

financial accounting The preparation and presentation of financial reports for external users.

Financial Reporting Council (FRC) Body that oversees the AASB.

financial statements Section in the annual report that contains the summarised financial information of an entity prepared in accordance with applicable accounting standards.

full disclosure principle Accounting principle dictating that circumstances and events that make a difference to financial statement users should be disclosed.

general purpose financial reports Financial reports intended to meet the information needs of users who are unable to command reports to suit their specific needs.

generally accepted accounting principles (GAAP) A set of rules and practices, having substantial authoritative support, that are recognised as a general guide for financial reporting purposes. In New Zealand GAAP stands for generally accepted accounting *practices*.

going concern principle States that the financial statements are prepared on a going concern basis unless management either intends to or must liquidate the business or cease trading.

government accountants Are employed within government enterprises and engage in a variety of roles and activities, such as financial accounting and auditing.

intangible assets Identifiable non-monetary assets that have no physical substance (e.g. patents and copyrights).

International Accounting Standards Board (IASB) The organisation with the authority to issue international financial reporting standards (IFRSs).

lenders Suppliers, bankers and others who grant credit or lend money.

liabilities The outflows of economic benefits that the entity is presently obliged to make as a result of past events.

limited liability The limit of liability of owners of a company to any unpaid amount of capital.

liquidity The ability of an entity to pay obligations that are expected to become due within the next year or operating cycle.

liquidity ratios Measures of the short-term ability of an entity to pay its maturing obligations and to meet unexpected needs for cash.

loss The amount by which expenses exceed revenues and gains.

management accounting A field of accounting that provides economic and financial information for managers and other internal users.

materiality The condition on reporting information if its omission or misstatement could influence the decisions of users of financial reports.

measurement The process of determining the monetary amounts at which the elements of the financial reports are to be recognised and carried in the statement of financial position and the statement of profit or loss.

monetary principle A principle stating that the items included in an entity's accounting records must be able to be expressed in monetary terms.

non-current assets Assets that are not expected to be consumed or sold within 1 year or the operating cycle and have not been purchased for trading purposes.

non-current liabilities Liabilities that are not expected to be paid within 1 year or the operating cycle, e.g. mortgage payable.

not-for-profit accountants Accountants working in the not-for-profit sector who engage in many activities including planning, decision making, and preparing financial and management reports for both internal and external users.

not-for-profit entity A not-for-profit entity focuses on successfully fulfilling its mission and administrative goals, rather than focusing on making a profit. Not-for-profit entities include public hospitals, clubs, some schools and charities.

notes to the financial statements Notes that clarify information presented in the financial statements, as well as expand on information where additional detail is needed.

operating cycle The length of time it takes for a business to acquire goods, sell them to customers and collect the cash from the sale.

ordinary shares Shares representing the residual ownership interests in a company.

partnership A business relationship or association between two or more people or entities carrying on a business in common with a view to making a profit.

profit The amount by which revenues and gains exceed expenses.

profit margin A measure of the profit generated by each dollar of sales, calculated as profit divided by net sales.

profitability ratios Measures of the profit or operating success of an entity for a given period of time.

property, plant and equipment Tangible assets that have physical substance, are used in the operations of the business for more than one period, and are not intended for sale to customers (e.g. land and buildings).

public accountants Accountants who provide their professional services to the public. They can practise in business organisations that range from small, single-person run offices to very large organisations, with branches all over the world and thousands of employees.

public sector The public sector is also called the government sector. The distinguishing feature is that the organisations are owned by the government, whether it be federal, state or local.

ratio An expression of the mathematical relationship between one quantity and another; may be expressed as a percentage, a rate or a proportion.

ratio analysis A technique for evaluating financial statements that expresses the relationship among selected financial statement data.

relevant Accounting information is considered to be relevant if the information makes a difference to a decision.

reporting entity An entity in which it is reasonable to expect the existence of users who depend on general purpose financial reports for information to enable them to make economic decisions.

retained earnings The accumulated profit from the current and previous accounting periods that has not been distributed to owners.

return on assets (ROA) An overall measure of profitability, calculated as profit divided by average total assets.

revenues Sales and other increases in equity that arise from the ordinary activities of an entity.

share capital The total amount paid in by shareholders for shares in the company. Alternative terminology includes: paid-up capital, issued capital and contributed equity.

shareholders The owners of a company are called shareholders and their ownership interests are represented by the number of shares they own in the company.

sole proprietorship A business owned by one person.

solvency An entity's ability to pay interest as it comes due and to repay the face value of debt at maturity.

solvency ratios Measures of the ability of the entity to survive over a long period of time.

statement of cash flows A basic financial statement that provides information about the cash receipts and cash payments of an entity during a period, classified as operating, investing and financing activities, in a format that reconciles the beginning and ending cash balances.

statement of changes in equity A statement that reports the amount of total comprehensive income for the period and all other changes in equity.

statement of financial position A statement that reports on the assets, liabilities and equity of an entity at a specific date.

statement of profit or loss A statement that reports revenues, gains and expenses, and the resulting profit or loss; previously known as the statement of financial performance or the profit and loss statement.

sustainability Making sure social, economic and environmental factors are considered and kept healthy for future generations.

timeliness Whether the communication of financial information is in the time frame within which decisions are made.

transactions Economic activities relevant to a particular business, such as the sale of a good to a customer or the purchase of office stationery from a supplier. Transactions are the basic inputs into the accounting process.

trust A relationship or association between two or more parties whereby one party holds property in trust for the other, i.e. they are vested with the property.

understandability The extent to which information can be understood by proficient users.

unlimited liability Like a sole proprietorship structure, a partnership has unlimited liability, so each partner is personally liable for all the debts of the partnership even if they are caused by decisions made by other partners.

verifiability The extent to which independent observers could reach a consensus that a particular depiction is a faithful representation of the economic phenomena it is meant to represent.

working capital The difference between the amounts of current assets and current liabilities.

DEMONSTRATION PROBLEM

Jeff Andringa, a former Aussie Rules player, quit his job and started Footy Camp, a football camp for children aged 8 to 17. Eventually he would like to open football camps nationwide. Jeff has asked you to help him prepare financial statements at the end of his first year of operations. He relates the following facts about his business activities.

In order to get the business off the ground, he decided to incorporate. He issued shares in Footy Camp Pty Ltd to a few close friends, as well as buying some of the shares himself. He initially raised $75 000 through the issue of these shares. In addition, the company took out a $100 000 loan at a local bank. A bus for transporting children was purchased for $40 000 cash. Balls and other miscellaneous equipment were purchased with $3000 cash. The company earned camp fees during the year of $200 000, but had collected only $140 000 of this amount. Thus, at the end of the year it was still owed $60 000. The company rents time at a local school oval for $150 per day. Total oval rental costs during the year were $8000, insurance was $20 000, salary expense was $45 000, and administrative expenses totalled $15 700, all of which were paid in cash. The company incurred $2000 in interest expense on the bank loan; the interest was still owed at the end of the year.

The company paid dividends during the year of $16 000 cash. The balance in the company's bank account at the end of the year, 30 June 2019, was $167 300.

Required

Using the format of Wong Pty Ltd's statements, prepare a statement of profit or loss, a statement of changes in equity (retained earnings section only), a statement of financial position and a statement of cash flows. (*Hint:* Prepare statements in this order to take advantage of the flow of information from one statement to the next — see figure 1.6.) Ignore depreciation and tax for this problem.

(*Demonstration problems* are a final review before you begin homework. Problem-solving strategies that appear before the solution give you tips about how to approach the problem and the solution provided illustrates both the form and content of complete answers.)

PROBLEM-SOLVING STRATEGIES

From the information given you need to identify which reports the items are entered in to.

1. The statement of profit or loss shows revenues and expenses for a period of time. Revenues are reported when billed or the invoice is prepared.
2. The statement of changes in equity reports the amount of profit for a period of time and other changes in equity. The calculation of the movement in retained earnings was required here and the ending balance is entered into the equity section of the statement of financial position together with the shares issued at the beginning of the period.
3. The statement of financial position reports assets, liabilities and equity at a specific date.
4. The statement of cash flows reports sources and uses of cash from operating, investing and financing activities for a period of time. This statement reports only the actual cash flows and the ending balance of the cash is also reported in the statement of financial position.

SOLUTION TO DEMONSTRATION PROBLEM

FOOTY CAMP PTY LTD Statement of profit or loss for the year ended 30 June 2019		
REVENUES		
Camp fees revenue		$200 000
EXPENSES		
Salaries expense	$45 000	
Insurance expense	20 000	
Administrative expenses	15 700	
Oval rental expense	8 000	
Interest expense	2 000	
Total expenses		90 700
Profit		**$109 300**

FOOTY CAMP PTY LTD Calculation of retained earnings for the year ended 30 June 2019	
Retained earnings, 1 July 2018	$ —
Profit	109 300
Less: Dividends	(16 000)
Retained earnings, 30 June 2019	**$ 93 300**

FOOTY CAMP PTY LTD		
Statement of financial position		
as at 30 June 2019		
ASSETS		
Cash		$167 300
Accounts receivable		60 000
Bus		40 000
Equipment		3 000
Total assets		270 300
LIABILITIES		
Bank loan payable	$100 000	
Interest payable	2 000	
Total liabilities		102 000
Net assets		**$168 300**
EQUITY		
Share capital		$ 75 000
Retained profits		93 300
Total equity		**$168 300**

FOOTY CAMP PTY LTD		
Statement of cash flows		
for the year ended 30 June 2019		
CASH FLOWS FROM OPERATING ACTIVITIES		
Cash receipts from operating activities	$140 000	
Cash payments for operating activities	(88 700)	
Net cash provided by operating activities		$ 51 300
CASH FLOWS FROM INVESTING ACTIVITIES		
Purchase of bus	(40 000)	
Purchase of equipment	(3 000)	
Net cash used by investing activities		(43 000)
CASH FLOWS FROM FINANCING ACTIVITIES		
Proceeds from bank loan	100 000	
Issue of shares	75 000	
Dividends paid	(16 000)	
Net cash provided by financing activities		159 000
Net increase in cash		167 300
Cash at beginning of period		—
Cash at end of period		**$167 300**

SELF-STUDY QUESTIONS

1.1 The steps, in order, in the decision-making process are: **LO1**

    (a) identify issue, analyse information, gather information, identify decision-making tool, evaluate results; make a decision.

    (b) gather information; identify decision-making tool; identify issue, evaluate results; analyse information; make a decision.

    (c) identify issue; gather information; identify decision-making tool; analyse information; evaluate results; make a decision.

    (d) gather information; identify issue; identify decision-making tool, evaluate results; analyse; make a decision.

1.2 Accounting is the process of: **LO2**
- (a) recognising, measuring, recording and communicating.
- (b) identifying, measuring, recording and communicating.
- (c) identifying, recording, classifying and communicating.
- (d) analysing, identifying, recording and interpreting.

1.3 Which of the following is not a typical accountant's role?   **LO2**
- (a) A financial controller.
- (b) A marketing manager.
- (c) An auditor.
- (d) All of the above are roles of an accountant.

1.4 Which is *not* one of the three main forms of business organisation?   **LO3**
- (a) Sole proprietorship.
- (b) Unincorporated trust.
- (c) Partnership.
- (d) Company.

1.5 Which is an advantage of companies relative to partnerships and sole proprietorships from the perspective of owners?   **LO3**
- (a) Separation of ownership and control.
- (b) Harder to transfer ownership.
- (c) Reduced legal liability.
- (d) Most common form of organisation.

1.6 Which is *not* an indicator that the entity is a reporting entity?   **LO4**
- (a) Separation of ownership from management.
- (b) It has substantial borrowings.
- (c) It trades overseas.
- (d) It is economically important.

1.7 Which of the following statements concerning general purpose financial reports is correct?   **LO5**
- (a) General purpose financial reports are more detailed than the internal reports.
- (b) General purpose financial reports are prepared in accordance with accounting standards.
- (c) General purpose financial reports are the only accounting reports entities prepare.
- (d) Government enterprises do not need to prepare general purpose financial reports.

1.8 Which is *not* one of the three main business activities?   **LO5**
- (a) Financing.
- (b) Operating.
- (c) Advertising.
- (d) Investing.

1.9 Which statement about users of accounting information is *incorrect*?   **LO6**
- (a) Management is considered an internal user.
- (b) Taxing authorities are considered external users.
- (c) Present creditors are considered external users.
- (d) Regulatory authorities are considered internal users.

1.10 Profit will result when: **LO6**
- (a) assets exceed liabilities.
- (b) assets exceed revenues.
- (c) expenses exceed revenues.
- (d) revenues exceed expenses.

1.11 What section of a statement of cash flows indicates the cash spent on new equipment during the past accounting period?   **LO6**
- (a) The investing section.
- (b) The operating section.

(c) The financing section.

(d) The statement of cash flows does not give this information.

1.12 Which financial statement reports assets, liabilities and equity? **LO6**

(a) Statement of changes in equity.

(b) Statement of profit or loss.

(c) Statement of financial position.

(d) Statement of cash flows.

1.13 The amount of retained earnings is not affected by: **LO6**

(a) profit.

(b) loss.

(c) the issue of shares.

(d) dividends.

1.14 In a classified statement of financial position, assets are usually classified as: **LO6**

(a) current assets and cash.

(b) current assets, non-current assets and equity.

(c) current assets and non-current assets.

(d) current assets and intangible assets.

1.15 As of 31 December 2018, Smithers Pty Ltd has assets of $7500 and equity of $3000. What are the liabilities for Smithers Pty Ltd as of 31 December 2018? **LO5**

(a) $10 500.

(b) $4500.

(c) $7500.

(d) $3000.

1.16 The AASB is overseen by: **LO7**

(a) ASIC.

(b) the IASB.

(c) the FRC.

(d) the ASX.

1.17 Generally accepted accounting principles are: **LO7**

(a) a set of standards and rules that are recognised as a general guide for financial reporting.

(b) usually established by the Australian Taxation Office.

(c) the guidelines used to resolve ethical dilemmas.

(d) fundamental truths that can be derived from the laws of nature.

1.18 What organisation issues Australian accounting standards? **LO7**

(a) Australian Accounting Standards Board.

(b) External Reporting Board.

(c) Australian Securities and Investments Commission.

(d) None of the above.

1.19 What organisation issues New Zealand accounting standards? **LO7**

(a) New Zealand Institute of Chartered Accountants.

(b) New Zealand Inland Revenue.

(c) External Reporting Board.

(d) None of the above.

1.20 Which of the following is a main qualitative characteristic of information reported in financial statements in accordance with the *Conceptual Framework*? **LO8**

(a) Comparability.

(b) Understandability.

(c) Relevance.

(d) Confidentiality.

1.21 Cost measurement means that: **LO8**
   (a) assets should be recorded at cost and adjusted when the market value changes.
   (b) activities of an entity should be kept separate and distinct from its owner.
   (c) assets should be recorded at their cost.
   (d) only transaction data capable of being expressed in terms of money should be included in the accounting records.

1.22 Valuing assets at their market value rather than at their cost is inconsistent with the: **LO8**
   (a) accounting period concept.
   (b) accounting entity concept.
   (c) cost principle.
   (d) All of the above.

1.23 Which is *not* an indicator of profitability? **LO9**
   (a) Current ratio.
   (b) Profit margin.
   (c) Profit.
   (d) Return on assets.

1.24 For 2019 Carman Ltd reported profit $48 000; net sales $400 000; and average assets $800 000. What was the 2019 profit margin? **LO9**
   (a) 6%.
   (b) 12%.
   (c) 40%.
   (d) 200%.

1.25 Which of these measures is an evaluation of an entity's ability to pay current liabilities? **LO9**
   (a) Profit margin.
   (b) Current ratio.
   (c) Both (a) and (b).
   (d) None of the above.

QUESTIONS

1.1 Describe the decision-making process.

1.2 What are some of the financial decisions owners need to make when running a new business?

1.3 What are the advantages to a business of being formed as a company? What are the disadvantages?

1.4 Who are the external users of accounting data? Give examples.

1.5 Listed here are some items found in the financial statements of Ruth Weber Ltd. Indicate in which financial statement(s) each item would appear.
   (a) Sales revenue.
   (b) Office equipment.
   (c) Accounts receivable.
   (d) Interest expense.
   (e) Share capital.
   (f) Loan payable.

1.6 What is a conceptual framework and what purpose does it serve?

1.7 Why is it important to determine if a business entity is a reporting entity? Outline the three main indicators that determine if an entity is a reporting entity.

1.8 What are the three main categories of the statement of cash flows? Why do you think these categories were chosen?

1.9 What is retained earnings? What items increase the balance in retained earnings? What items decrease the balance in retained earnings?

1.10 What purpose does the going concern principle serve?

1.11 Shirl Lee, the managing director of Whitegoods Pty Ltd, is pleased. Whitegoods substantially increased its profit in 2018 while keeping its unit inventory relatively the same. Rose Ena, chief accountant, cautions Shirl Lee, explaining that since Whitegoods changed its method of inventory valuation, there is a comparability problem and it is difficult to determine whether Whitegoods is better off. Is Rose correct? Why or why not?

1.12 What is meant by the term *operating cycle*?

1.13 (a) Tia Kim believes that the analysis of financial statements is directed at two characteristics of an entity: liquidity and profitability. Is Tia correct? Explain.

(b) Are short-term creditors, long-term creditors, and shareholders mainly interested in the same characteristics of an entity? Explain.

1.14 Holding all other factors constant, indicate whether each of the following signals generally good or bad news about an entity.

(a) Increase in the profit margin.

(b) Increase in the current ratio.

(c) Decrease in the debt to total assets ratio.

(d) Increase in the current cash debt coverage.

BRIEF EXERCISES

BE1.1 **Explain the characteristics of the main forms of business organisation.** **LO3**

Match each of the following forms of business organisation with a set of characteristics: sole proprietorship (SP), partnership (P), company (C).

(a) _____ Shared control, increased skills and resources.

(b) _____ Simple to set up and maintains control with founder.

(c) _____ Easier to transfer ownership and raise funds, no personal liability.

BE1.2 **Describe the financial reporting environment.** **LO7**

Indicate whether each statement is *true* or *false*.

(a) Accounting standards are set by the Financial Reporting Council.

(b) The ASX Listing Rules are only applicable to entities listed on the ASX.

(c) The Corporations Act is administered by the ATO.

BE1.3 **Identify users of accounting financial reports and describe their information needs.** **LO5**

Match each of the following types of evaluation with one of the listed users of accounting information.

1. Trying to determine whether the company complied with the Corporations Act.

2. Trying to determine whether the entity can pay its obligations.

3. Trying to determine whether a major investment proposal will be cost-effective.

4. Trying to determine whether the company's profit will result in a share price increase.

5. Trying to determine whether the entity should use debt or equity financing.

(a) _____ Executive directors.

(b) _____ Bank managers.

(c) _____ Shareholders.

(d) _____ Chief financial officer.

(e) _____ Australian Securities and Investments Commission.

BE1.4 Prepare a statement of financial position. **LO6**

In alphabetical order below are items for ABC Pty Ltd at 31 December 2018. Prepare a statement of financial position following the format of figure 1.6.

Accounts payable	$32 500
Accounts receivable	10 000
Cash	30 000
Inventory	7 500
Share capital	15 000

BE1.5 Determine the proper financial statement. **LO6**

Indicate which statement you would examine to find each of the following items: statement of financial position (SFP), statement of profit or loss (P/L) or statement of cash flows (SCF).
(a) Revenues during the period.
(b) Accounts receivable at the end of the year.
(c) Cash received from borrowing during the period.
(d) Cash payments for the purchase of property, plant and equipment.

BE1.6 Prepare the assets section of a classified statement of financial position. **LO6**

A list of financial statement items for Swift Ltd includes the following: accounts receivable $15 000; prepaid rent $1000; cash $4500; supplies $2000; short-term investments $12 000; property, plant and equipment $40 000. Prepare the asset section of the statement of financial position, showing appropriate classifications.

BE1.7 Calculate return on assets and profit margin. **LO9**

The following information is available for Ware Ltd for 2018: sales revenue $7 840 000; cost of sales $3 528 000; profit $1 176 000; total equity $2 233 300; average total assets $5 113 000. Calculate the return on assets and profit margin for Ware Ltd for 2018.

EXERCISES

E1.1 Match items with descriptions. **LO1, 3, 5, 6**

Here is a list of words or phrases discussed in this chapter:
1. Auditor's opinion
2. Accounts payable
3. Accounts receivable
4. Sole trader
5. Partnership
6. Decision
7. Company
8. Equity investors
9. Share capital

Required

Match each word or phrase with the best description of it.

_____ (a) An expression about whether financial statements are presented in a reasonable fashion.
_____ (b) Obligations to suppliers of goods.
_____ (c) The portion of equity that results from contributions from investors.
_____ (d) An entity that raises money by issuing shares.
_____ (e) Amounts due from customers.
_____ (f) People who make decisions to buy, hold, or sell shares.
_____ (g) A person operating and owning a business with no other owners.

_____ (h) A business that is owned jointly by two or more individuals but that does not issue shares.

_____ (i) A choice among alternative courses of action.

E1.2 Prepare a statement of profit or loss and a calculation of retained earnings.   **LO6**

This information relates to Rosie's Rentals Pty Ltd for the year 2018:

Retained earnings, 1 January 2018	$ 90 000
Advertising expense	3 000
Dividends paid during 2018	14 000
Rent expense	20 200
Hire revenue	140 000
Electricity expense	4 800
Wages expense	56 000
Share capital	40 000

Required

After analysing the data, prepare a statement of profit or loss and a calculation of retained earnings for the year ending 31 December 2018.

E1.3 Correct an incorrectly prepared statement of financial position.   **LO6**

Deanna Veale is the bookkeeper for Quality Products Ltd. Deanna has been trying to make the statement of financial position of Quality Products Ltd balance. It is finally balanced, but now she's not sure it is correct.

QUALITY PRODUCTS LTD Statement of financial position as at 30 June 2018			
ASSETS		**LIABILITIES AND EQUITY**	
Cash	$15 000	Accounts payable	$15 000
Supplies	5 600	Accounts receivable	(6 000)
Inventory	28 400	Share capital	25 000
Dividends	3 000	Retained earnings	18 000
Total assets	**$52 000**	**Total liabilities and equity**	**$52 000**

Required

Prepare a correct statement of financial position.

E1.4 Identify financial statement components and calculate profit.   **LO6**

The following items were taken from Black Ltd's financial statements for 2018. (All dollars are in thousands.)

_____	Retained earnings	$ 2 000	_____	Non-current borrowings	$22 000
_____	Cost of sales	24 600	_____	Inventories	4 500
_____	Wages expense	18 300	_____	Sales revenue	66 000
_____	Cash	11 200	_____	Accounts receivable	12 000
_____	Current payables	14 500	_____	Reserves	8 000
_____	Interest expense	6 200	_____	Income tax expense	4 200
_____	Other expense	1 100	_____	Contributed equity	30 000
_____	Depreciation	1 800	_____	Property and equipment	20 000

Required

Perform each of the following:

(a) In each case identify whether the item is an asset (A), liability (L), equity (Eq), revenue (R) or expense (Ex).

(b) Calculate profit for Black Ltd for the year ended 30 June 2018.

E1.5 **Calculate missing amounts.** LO6

Here are incomplete financial statements for Road Ltd:

ROAD LTD
Statement of financial position

ASSETS		LIABILITIES AND EQUITY	
Cash	$ 10 500	Liabilities	
Inventory	15 500	Accounts payable	$ 26 000
Property	80 000	Equity	
		Contributed equity	(a)
		Retained earnings	(b)
Total assets	**$106 000**	**Total liabilities and equity**	**$106 000**

Statement of profit or loss

Revenues	$200 000
Cost of sales	(c)
Administrative expenses, including tax	14 000
Profit	**$ (d)**

Statement of changes in equity

Beginning retained earnings	$12 000
Profit	(e)
Less: Dividends	(8 000)
Ending retained earnings	**$45 000**

Required

Calculate the missing amounts.

E1.6 **Identify the concept or principle that has been violated.** LO8

Cheong Pty Ltd had three major business transactions during 2018.

(a) Merchandise inventory with a cost of $68 000 is reported at its market value of $100 000.

(b) The owner of Cheong Pty Ltd, Cheong Kong, purchased a computer for personal use and charged it to his expense account.

(c) Cheong Pty Ltd wanted to make its 2018 profit look better, so it added in sales that occurred on the first two days of 2019.

Required

In each situation, identify the assumption or principle that has been violated, if any, and discuss what should have been done.

E1.7 **Classify items as current or non-current, and prepare assets section of statement of financial position.** LO6

The following items were taken from the 30 June 2019 consolidated statement of financial position of Maximum Energy Limited. (All dollars are in millions.)

Inventories—current	$ 199.5	Intangibles	$4 724.1
Receivables—due after 30/06/2020	70.9	Other current assets	586.6
Oil and gas assets (non-current)	742.6	Property, plant and equipment	7 997.4
Investments (long term)	49.6	Cash and cash equivalents	421.5
Other long-term financial assets	507.7	Current receivables	2 766.0
Other financial assets (short term)	280.3	Other non-current assets	41.1
		Exploration and evaluation assets	
Deferred tax assets (non-current)	1 093.8	(non-current)	523.5
		Inventories (non-current)	43.8

Required

Prepare the assets section of a classified statement of financial position.

E1.8 Classify items as current or non-current, and prepare the assets section of the statement of financial position. **LO6**

The following items were taken from the 30 June 2019 consolidated statement of financial position of Field Limited. (All dollars are in millions.)

Inventories	$ 138.9	Other current assets	$ 16.6
Trade and other receivables	182.9	Deferred tax assets (non-current)	57.1
Property, plant and equipment	521.5	Cash and cash equivalents	603.1
Other non-current assets	1.0	Current tax receivable	8.1
Intangible assets	1 410.5	Derivative financial instruments (current)	0.1
Investments in jointly controlled entities			
(non-current)	6.5	Receivable (non-current)	0.9
Assets held for sale (current)	1.9		

Required

Prepare the assets section of a classified statement of financial position.

E1.9 Prepare financial statements. **LO6**

These financial statement items are for Christchurch Flooring Pty Ltd at year-end, 31 July 2018:

Cost of sales	$30 000
Salaries expense	25 000
Other expenses	18 000
Building	70 000
Accounts payable	8 000
Sales revenue	62 000
Rent revenue	30 000
Rent revenue received in advance	2 000
Share capital	90 000
Cash	33 000
Bank loan	80 000
Accumulated depreciation	12 000
Land	80 000
Depreciation expense	4 000
Retained earnings (beginning of the year)	2 000
Inventory	26 000

Required

(a) Prepare a statement of profit or loss for the year.

(b) Prepare a classified statement of financial position at 31 July 2018.

E1.10 Prepare financial statements. **LO6**

These financial statement items are for Teddy Pty Ltd at year-end, 30 June 2020:

Cost of sales	$ 42 000
Salaries expense	27 000
Other expenses	26 600
Building	196 000
Accounts payable	39 400
Sales revenue	100 000
Rent revenue	36 000
Rent revenue received in advance	5 800
Share capital	221 000
Cash	42 500

Bank loan	208 000
Accumulated depreciation	19 600
Land	265 000
Depreciation expense	5 400
Retained earnings (beginning of the year)	10 900
Inventory	36 200

Required

(a) Prepare a statement of profit or loss for the year.

(b) Prepare a calculation of retained earnings for the year.

(c) Prepare a classified statement of financial position at 30 June 2020.

E1.11 Calculate liquidity ratios and compare results. **LO9**

Retail Ltd operates stores in numerous states. Selected financial statement data (in thousands of dollars) for the year ended 30 June 2019 are as follows:

	End of year	Beginning of year
Cash	$ 8 995	$ 17 807
Receivables (net)	10 711	15 992
Merchandise inventory	184 872	187 890
Other current assets	3 848	1 624
Total current assets	$208 426	$223 313
Total current liabilities	$129 941	$169 549

For the year, net sales revenue was $1 109 934 and cost of sales was $628 197 (in thousands).

Required

(a) Calculate the working capital and current ratio at the beginning of the year and at the end of the current year.

(b) Did Retail Ltd's liquidity improve or worsen during the year?

E1.12 Calculate and interpret solvency ratios. **LO9**

The following data were taken from the 2019 financial statements of Energy Limited. (All dollars in millions.)

	2019	2018
Current assets	$ 2 838.0	$ 4 231.9
Total assets	13 367.8	15 738.4
Current liabilities	2 291.8	7 609.8
Total liabilities	9 026.8	8 605.5
Total equity	8 339.0	8 132.9
Cash provided by operating activities	621.8	467.5
Cash generated by (used in) investing activities	(559.6)	(532.3)

Required

Perform each of the following:

(a) Calculate the debt to assets ratio for each year.

(b) Calculate the cash debt coverage for each year. (*Note:* Total liabilities at year-end 2017 were $7804 million.)

(c) Discuss Energy Limited's solvency in 2019 versus 2018.

(d) Discuss Energy Limited's ability to finance its investment activities with cash provided by operating activities, and how any deficiency would be met.

E1.13 Calculate and interpret solvency ratios.   **LO9**

The following data were taken from the 2019 financial statements of Oldfield Limited. (All dollars in millions.)

	2019	2018
Current assets	$ 726.4	$ 719.8
Total assets	2 756.8	2 694.8
Current liabilities	392.8	534.1
Total liabilities	1 324.5	1 328.7
Total equity	1 652.3	1 376.1
Cash provided by operating activities	188.7	130.0
Cash generated by (used in) investing activities	158.9	(85.6)

Required

Perform each of the following:

(a) Calculate the debt to assets ratio for each year.

(b) Calculate the cash debt coverage for each year. (*Note:* Total liabilities at year-end 2017 were $1405 million.)

(c) Discuss Oldfield Limited's solvency in 2019 versus 2018.

(d) Discuss Oldfield Limited's ability to finance its investment activities with cash provided by operating activities, and how any deficiency would be met.

PROBLEM SET A

PSA1.1 Determine forms of business organisation.   **LO3**

Presented below are five independent situations.

(a) Three information systems lecturers have formed a business to improve the speed of information transfer over the internet for securities exchange transactions. Each has contributed an equal amount of cash and knowledge to the venture. Although their approach looks promising, they are concerned about the legal liabilities that their business might confront.

(b) Sarah and Andrew wish to purchase a taxi licence. One has a suitable motor vehicle and the other has enough cash to buy the licence.

(c) Robert Steven and Tom Cheng each owned separate shoe manufacturing businesses. They have decided to combine their businesses. They expect that within the coming year they will need significant funds to expand their operations.

(d) Darcy Becker, Ellen Sweet and Meg Dwyer recently graduated with marketing degrees. They have been friends since childhood. They have decided to start a consulting business focused on marketing sporting goods over the internet.

(e) Anthony Troy wants to rent CD players and CDs in airports across the country. His idea is that customers will be able to rent equipment and CDs at one airport, listen to the CDs on their flights, and return the equipment and CDs at their destination airport. Of course, this will require a substantial investment in equipment and CDs, as well as employees and locations in each airport. Anthony has no savings or personal assets. He wants to maintain control over the business.

Required

In each case explain what form of organisation the business is likely to take — sole proprietorship, partnership or company. Give reasons for your choice.

PSA1.2 Identify users and uses of financial statements.   **LO5**

Financial decisions often place heavier emphasis on one type of financial statement over the others. Consider each of the following hypothetical situations independently.

(a) North Sales Ltd is considering extending credit to a new customer. The terms of the credit would require the customer to pay within 30 days of receipt of goods.

(b) An investor is considering purchasing shares in Giorgina's. The investor plans to hold the investment for at least 5 years.

(c) Otago Bank is considering extending a loan to a small company. The company would be required to make interest payments at the end of each year for 5 years, and to repay the loan at the end of the fifth year.

(d) The finance director of Pacific Pipes Ltd is trying to determine whether the company is generating enough cash to increase the amount of dividends paid to investors in this and future years, and still have enough cash to buy plant and machinery as needed.

Required

Although the decision makers should refer to all financial statements, for each situation, state whether the decision maker would be most likely to place the main emphasis on information provided by the statement of profit or loss, statement of financial position or statement of cash flows. In each case provide a brief justification for your choice. Choose only one financial statement in each case.

PSA1.3 Comment on proper accounting treatment and prepare a corrected statement of financial position.   **LO6, 8**

Smart Travel Goods Pty Ltd was formed on 1 July 2018. At 30 June 2019, Mark Austin, the managing director and major shareholder, decided to prepare a statement of financial position, which appeared as follows:

SMART TRAVEL GOODS PTY LTD			
Statement of financial position			
as at 30 June 2019			
ASSETS		LIABILITIES AND EQUITY	
Cash	$ 30 000	Accounts payable	$ 30 000
Accounts receivable	23 000	Notes payable	12 000
Inventory	40 000	Bank loan	350 000
Villa	450 000	Equity	151 000

Mark willingly admits that he is not an accountant by training. He is concerned that his statement of financial position might not be correct. He has provided you with the following additional information:

1. The villa is on the Sunshine Coast and actually belongs to Mark, not to Smart Travel Goods Pty Ltd. However, because he thinks he might allow executives to use it sometimes, he decided to list it as an asset of the company. To be consistent he also listed as a liability of the company his personal loan that he took out at the bank to buy the villa.

2. The inventory was originally purchased for $15 000, but due to a surge in demand Mark now thinks he could sell it for $40 000. He thought it would be best to record it at $40 000.

3. Included in the accounts payable balance is $6000 that Mark owes for his personal telephone account. Mark included this in the accounts payable of Smart Travel Goods Pty Ltd because he will probably use a company cheque to pay for it.

Required

(a) Comment on the proper accounting treatment of the three items above.

(b) Provide a corrected statement of financial position for Smart Travel Goods Pty Ltd. (*Hint:* To get the statement of financial position to balance, adjust equity.)

PSA1.4 Prepare financial statements.   **LO6**

PQR Pty Ltd was started on 1 October with an investment of $65 000 cash. Following are the assets and liabilities of the company on 31 October 2018, and the revenues and expenses for the month of October, its first month of operations.

Cash	$ 9 200	Bank loan	$40 000
Accounts receivable	28 500	Rent expense	4 000
Equipment	80 000	Repair expense	800
Service revenue	25 000	Fuel expense	8 700
Advertising expense	1 200	Insurance expense	1 000
Accounts payable	5 400		

No further shares were issued in October, but a dividend of $2000 in cash was paid.

Required

Prepare a statement of profit or loss and a calculation of retained earnings for the month of October, and prepare a statement of financial position as at 31 October 2018.

PSA1.5 Determine items included in a statement of cash flows and prepare the statement.   **LO6**

Presented below are selected financial statement items for Daisy Ltd for 31 December 2018:

Inventory	$ 32 000
Cash paid to suppliers	195 000
Building	400 000
Share capital	20 000
Share issued for cash this current year	10 000
Cash dividends paid	15 000
Cash paid to purchase equipment	35 000
Equipment	40 000
Revenues	300 000
Cash received from customers	264 000

Required

Determine which items should be included in a statement of cash flows, and then prepare the statement for Daisy Ltd.

PSA1.6 Prepare financial statements.   **LO6**

Ultra Pty Ltd was started on 1 May with an investment of $75 000 cash. Following are the assets and liabilities of the company on 31 May 2019, and the revenues and expenses for the month of May, its first month of operations.

Cash	$30 500	Bank loan	$40 000
Accounts receivable	25 400	Rent expense	12 500
Equipment	87 000	Repair expense	1 800
Service revenue	42 800	Fuel expense	3 600
Advertising expense	800	Insurance expense	2 600
Accounts payable	8 400		

No further shares were issued in May, but a dividend of $2000 in cash was paid.

Required

Prepare a statement of profit or loss and statement of changes in equity for the month of May, and prepare a statement of financial position as at 31 May 2019.

PSA1.7 Determine items included in a statement of cash flows and prepare the statement. **LO6**

Presented below are selected financial statement items for Liddy Ltd for 30 June 2019.

Inventory	$ 40 000
Cash	101 000
Cash paid to suppliers	85 000
Building	320 000
Share capital	25 000
Cash dividends paid	9 000
Cash paid to purchase equipment	25 000
Equipment	35 000
Revenues	160 000
Cash received from customers	148 000

Required

Determine which items should be included in a statement of cash flows, and then prepare the statement for Liddy Ltd.

PSA1.8 Prepare a classified statement of financial position. **LO6**

The following items are taken from the 30 June 2019 statement of financial position of Cement Ltd (in millions):

Cash on deposit (short term)	$ 80.6
Issued capital	2 533.8
Property, plant and equipment	3 367.1
Payables (short term)	761.1
Intangible assets	859.9
Non-controlling interests (part of equity)	99.3
Current tax liabilities	29.1
Other non-current assets	58.5
Other current assets	32.8
Investments accounted for using the equity method (non-current assets)	44.6
Deferred tax assets (non-current)	153.7
Other financial assets (current)	21.6
Other financial liabilities (non-current)	35.5
Other long-term financial assets	13.5
Receivables (short term)	877.8
Other financial liabilities (current)	66.1
Receivables due after 30 June 2020	26.8
Retained earnings	588.0
Cash and cash equivalents	249.9
Loans and borrowings	1 639.6
Provisions (short term)	242.1
Inventories (current)	620.0
Payables (long term)	8.4
Reserves	75.4
Loans and borrowings (due before June 2020)	136.9
Deferred tax liabilities (non-current)	58.6
Provisions (long term)	146.5
Inventories (non-current)	13.6

Required

Prepare a statement of financial position, appropriately classified, for Cement Ltd as at 30 June 2019.

PSA1.9 Calculate liquidity, solvency and profitability ratios.   **LO9**

Here are the comparative statements of City Sales Pty Ltd:

CITY SALES PTY LTD Statement of profit or loss for the year ended 30 June 2019		
	2019	2018
Net sales	$2 200 000	$2 000 000
Cost of sales	1 120 000	996 000
Selling and administrative expense	830 000	824 000
Interest expense	31 000	30 000
Income tax expense	104 000	50 000
Profit	**$ 115 000**	**$ 100 000**

CITY SALES PTY LTD Statement of financial position as at 30 June 2019		
	2019	2018
ASSETS		
Current assets		
Cash	$ 100 500	$ 60 000
Short-term investments	90 000	50 000
Accounts receivable (net)	139 000	125 000
Inventory	145 000	115 500
Total current assets	474 500	350 500
Property, plant and equipment (net)	540 300	440 300
Total assets	1 014 800	790 800
LIABILITIES		
Current liabilities		
Accounts payable	146 000	65 400
Income taxes payable	104 000	34 600
Total current liabilities	250 000	100 000
Debentures payable	210 000	200 000
Total liabilities	460 000	300 000
Net assets	**$ 554 800**	**$490 800**
EQUITY		
Contributed equity	$ 350 000	$300 000
Retained earnings	204 800	190 800
Total equity	**$ 554 800**	**$490 800**

The cash provided by operating activities for 2019 was $260 000.

Required

Calculate these values and ratios for 2019:

(a) Working capital.
(b) Current ratio.
(c) Current cash debt coverage.
(d) Debt to total assets ratio.
(e) Cash debt coverage.
(f) Profit margin.
(g) Return on assets.

PSA1.10 Calculate ratios and compare liquidity, solvency and profitability for two entities.　　　**LO9**

Selected financial data (in thousands) of two competitors, AKA Ltd and UFO Ltd, for 2018 are presented here:

	AKA Ltd	UFO Ltd
	Selected statement of profit or loss data for year	
Net sales	$120 000	$100 000
Cost of sales	65 000	51 000
Borrowing costs (interest expense)	10 500	30 000
Income tax expense	14 000	4 000
Profit	16 000	5 000
	Condensed statement of financial position (end of year)	
Current assets	$ 33 000	$ 20 000
Non-current assets	127 000	175 000
Total assets	**$160 000**	**$195 000**
Current liabilities	$ 15 000	$ 10 000
Non-current liabilities	70 000	160 000
Total equity	75 000	25 000
Total liabilities and equity	**$160 000**	**$195 000**
	Beginning-of-year balances	
Total assets	$140 000	$155 000

Required

For each entity, calculate these values and ratios:
(a) Working capital.
(b) Current ratio.
(c) Debt to total assets ratio.
(d) Return on assets.
(e) Profit margin.
(f) Compare the liquidity, solvency and profitability of the two entities.

PROBLEM SET B

PSB1.1 Determine forms of business organisation.　　　**LO3**

Presented below are five independent situations.
(a) Fiona has just graduated with a media and communications degree and wants to start an events management business. She has some savings and her family is willing to support her in her endeavours. Although she has had offers to work for several established businesses, Fiona wants to try it on her own and she wants to maintain control over the business.
(b) Mark has been operating as a sole trader for a number of years. Profits are slowly increasing and he expects his gross profit before income tax this year to be around $200 000. Mark also has an opportunity to expand operations and will need to borrow larger sums from a bank or similar financial institution.
(c) Maurice, Jacob and Emily have all just graduated with commerce degrees, one in accounting, another in IT and the third in marketing. They want to combine their skills and start a business selling goods over the internet.
(d) Amanda and Jessica have been friends since school and want to make a go of their hobby of jewellery making. They already have fashion stores interested in stocking their product, plus they have a web site and sell goods over the internet.

(e) Michael Murphy and Steve Elks each own separate printing businesses. They have decided to combine their businesses. They expect that within the coming year they will need significant funds to expand their operations.

Required

In each case explain what form of organisation the business is likely to take — sole proprietorship, partnership or company. Give reasons for your choice.

PSB1.2 Identify users and uses of financial statements. **LO5**

Financial decisions often place heavier emphasis on one type of financial statement over the others. Consider each of the following hypothetical situations independently.

(a) The finance director of Organic Products Ltd is trying to determine whether the company is generating enough cash to buy new equipment for the business without borrowing and still have enough left to pay dividends to investors.

(b) An investor is considering purchasing shares in Woolworths Limited. The investor plans to hold the investment for at least 4 years.

(c) Datt Ltd is considering extending credit to a new customer. The terms of the credit would require the customer to pay within 30 days of receipt of the goods.

(d) Intrigue Finance is considering extending a loan to a company. The company would be required to make interest payments at the end of each year for 8 years, and to repay the loan at the end of the eighth year.

Required

Although the decision makers should refer to all financial statements, for each situation, state whether the decision maker would be most likely to place the main emphasis on information provided by the statement of profit or loss, statement of financial position or statement of cash flows. In each case provide a brief justification for your choice. Choose only one financial statement in each case.

PSB1.3 Comment on proper accounting treatment and prepare a corrected statement of financial position. **LO6, 8**

Jupiter Pty Ltd was formed on 1 July 2018. At 30 June 2019, Mary Eagle, the managing director and major shareholder, decided to prepare a statement of financial position, which appeared as follows:

JUPITER PTY LTD Statement of financial position as at 30 June 2019			
ASSETS		LIABILITIES AND EQUITY	
Cash	$ 56 000	Accounts payable	$ 65 000
Accounts receivable	84 000	Notes payable	30 000
Inventory	75 000	Bank loan	320 000
Villa	500 000	Equity	72 000

Mary willingly admits that she is not an accountant by training. She is concerned that her statement of financial position might not be correct. She has provided you with the following additional information:

1. The villa is in Port Macquarie and actually belongs to Mary, not to Jupiter Pty Ltd. However, because she thinks she might allow executives to use it sometimes, she decided to list it as an asset of the company. To be consistent, she also listed, as a liability of the company, her personal loan that she took out at the bank to buy the villa.

2. The inventory was originally purchased for $25 000, but due to a surge in demand Mary now thinks she could sell it for $75 000. She thought it would be best to record it at $75 000.

3. Included in the accounts payable balance is $2000 that Mary owes for her personal electricity account. Mary included this in the accounts payable of Jupiter Pty Ltd because she will probably use a company cheque to pay for it.

Required

(a) Comment on the proper accounting treatment of the three items above.

(b) Provide a corrected statement of financial position for Jupiter Pty Ltd.

PSB1.4 Prepare financial statements. **LO6**

Evans Ltd was started on 1 July 2018 with an investment of $150 000 cash. Following are the assets and liabilities of the company on 30 June 2019, and the revenues and expenses for the year of operations.

Cash	$155 100	Bank loan	$90 000
Accounts receivable	43 000	Rent expense	37 500
Equipment (net)	120 000	Repair expense	700
Service revenue	250 000	Office expense	68 000
Advertising expense	16 500	Depreciation expense	30 000
Accounts payable	24 800	Insurance expense	24 000

No further shares were issued during the year, but a dividend of $20 000 in cash was paid.

Required

Prepare a statement of profit or loss, a calculation of retained earnings for the year, and a statement of financial position as at 30 June 2019.

PSB1.5 Determine items included in a statement of cash flows and prepare the statement. **LO6**

Presented below are selected financial statement items for Buzzy Bee Ltd for 31 December 2018:

Inventory	$ 80 000
Cash paid to suppliers	301 500
Building	1 800 000
Share capital	200 000
Cash received—issue of shares	50 000
Cash dividends paid	15 000
Cash paid to purchase equipment	210 000
Equipment	240 000
Revenues	560 000
Cash received from customers	509 200

Required

Determine which items should be included in a statement of cash flows, and then prepare the statement for Buzzy Bee Ltd.

PSB1.6 Prepare financial statements. **LO6**

Goodwin Ltd was started on 1 May 2019 with an investment of $60 000 cash. Following are the assets and liabilities of the company on 31 May 2019, and the revenues and expenses for the month of May, its first month of operation.

Cash	$38 350	Bank loan	$40 000
Accounts receivable	14 800	Rent expense	3 800
Equipment	63 000	Repair expense	600
Service revenue	30 000	Office expense	8 200
Advertising expense	2 000	Insurance expense	1 200
Accounts payable	2 700		

No further shares were issued in May, but a dividend of $750 in cash was paid.

Required

Prepare a statement of profit or loss and calculate retained earnings for the month of May and prepare a statement of financial position as at 31 May 2019.

PSB1.7 Determine items included in a statement of cash flows and prepare the statement.   **LO6**

Presented below are selected financial statement items for Spoon Ltd as at 30 June 2019.

Inventory	$ 65 000
Cash	270 000
Cash paid to suppliers	205 000
Building	640 000
Share capital	50 000
Cash dividends paid	77 000
Cash paid to purchase equipment	105 000
Equipment	140 000
Revenues	605 000
Cash received from customers	515 000

Required

Determine which items should be included in a statement of cash flows, and then prepare the statement for Spoon Ltd.

PSB1.8 Prepare financial statements.   **LO6**

An extract from the general ledger of Retail Limited for the year ended 30 June 2018 appears as follows:

Item	$	Item	$
Accounts payable	3 300	Inventory	21 500
Accounts receivable	8 320	Other expenses	6 250
Advertising expense	5 000	Rent expense	2 500
Bank loan	15 000	Repairs expense	15 000
Cash	24 250	Opening retained earnings	12 500
Cost of sales	82 000	Salaries expense	35 000
Equipment	83 000	Sales	167 420
Insurance expense	1 300	Share capital	100 000
Intangibles	6 300	Dividends paid	7 800

Additional information:
- Cash paid to suppliers $84 500
- All other expenses were paid in cash
- Cash received from customers $172 350
- Cash paid to purchase equipment $36 000
- The bank loan was taken out in the current year and is repayable in May 2020.

Required

(a) Prepare a statement of profit or loss for the year ended 30 June 2018.
(b) Prepare a calculation of retained earnings for the year ended 30 June 2018.
(c) Prepare a statement of financial position as at 30 June 2018.
(d) Prepare a statement of cash flows for the year ended 30 June 2018.
(e) Calculate the cash account balance at 1 July 2017 (i.e. the opening balance).

PSB1.9 Calculate liquidity, solvency and profitability ratios. **LO9**

Here are the comparative statements of Nixon Pty Ltd:

NIXON PTY LTD Statement of profit or loss for the year ended 30 June 2019		
	2019	2018
Net sales	$3 300 000	$3 000 000
Cost of sales	1 680 000	1 494 000
Selling and administrative expense	1 245 000	1 236 000
Interest expense	46 500	45 000
Income tax expense	156 000	75 000
Profit after tax	**$ 172 500**	**$ 150 000**

NIXON PTY LTD Statement of financial position as at 30 June 2019		
	2019	2018
ASSETS		
Current assets		
Cash	$ 150 750	$ 90 000
Short-term investments	135 000	75 000
Accounts receivable (net)	208 500	187 500
Inventory	217 500	173 250
Total current assets	711 750	525 750
Property, plant and equipment (net)	810 450	660 450
Total assets	1 522 200	1 186 200
LIABILITIES		
Current liabilities		
Accounts payable	219 000	98 100
Income taxes payable	156 000	51 900
Total current liabilities	375 000	150 000
Debentures payable	315 000	300 000
Total liabilities	690 000	450 000
Net assets	**$ 832 200**	**$ 736 200**
EQUITY		
Contributed equity	525 000	450 000
Retained earnings	307 200	286 200
Total equity	**$ 832 200**	**$ 736 200**

The cash provided by operating activities for 2019 was $375 000.

Required

Calculate these values and ratios for 2019:

(a) Working capital.
(b) Current ratio.
(c) Current cash debt coverage.
(d) Debt to total assets ratio.
(e) Cash debt coverage.
(f) Profit margin.
(g) Return on assets.

PSB1.10 Calculate ratios and compare liquidity, solvency and profitability for two entities.   **LO9**

Selected financial data (in thousands) of two competitors, NEW Ltd and OLD Ltd, for 2018 are presented here:

	NEW Ltd	OLD Ltd
	Selected statement of profit or loss data for year	
Net sales	$420 000	$350 000
Cost of sales	227 500	178 500
Borrowing costs (interest expense)	36 750	105 000
Income tax expense	49 000	14 000
Profit	56 000	17 500
	Condensed statement of financial position (end of year)	
Current assets	$115 500	$ 70 000
Non-current assets	444 500	612 500
Total assets	**$560 000**	**$682 500**
Current liabilities	$ 52 500	$ 35 000
Non-current liabilities	245 000	560 000
Total equity	262 500	87 500
Total liabilities and equity	**$560 000**	**$682 500**
	Beginning-of-year balances	
Total assets	$490 000	$542 500

Required

For each entity, calculate these values and ratios:

(a) Working capital.
(b) Current ratio.
(c) Debt to total assets ratio.
(d) Return on assets.
(e) Profit margin.
(f) Compare the liquidity, solvency and profitability of the two entities.

BUILDING BUSINESS SKILLS

FINANCIAL REPORTING AND ANALYSIS

Financial reporting problem: Giorgina's Pizza Limited

BBS1.1 Giorgina's 2019 financial statements were provided earlier in this chapter in figures 1.13, 1.15 and 1.16.

Required

Use Giorgina's financial data to answer these questions:

(a) What were Giorgina's total assets at 30 June 2019? 1 July 2018?
(b) How much inventory did Giorgina's have on 30 June 2019?
(c) What amount of accounts payable (payables) did Giorgina's report on 30 June 2019? on 1 July 2018?
(d) What were Giorgina's sales in 2019? in 2018?
(e) What is the amount of the change in profit before tax from 2018 to 2019?
(f) The accounting equation is: Assets = Liabilities + Equity. Replacing the words in that equation with dollar amounts, give Giorgina's accounting equation at 30 June 2019.
(g) What were the current liabilities on 1 July 2018?

Comparative analysis problem: Giorgina's Pizza Limited vs. Classic Food Ltd

BBS1.2 Extracts from the 2019 financial statements of Classic Food Ltd (a hypothetical company) are presented below, and Giorgina's 2019 financial statements are in figures 1.13, 1.15 and 1.16.

CLASSIC FOOD LTD Statement of profit or loss (extract) for the year ended 30 June 2019		
	2019 $'000	2018 $'000
Revenue	650 738	237 735
Borrowing costs expense	(4 463)	(574)
Profit from ordinary activities before income tax expense	37 265	19 330
Income tax expense	(13 713)	(7 078)
Profit from ordinary activities after income tax expense	23 552	12 252

CLASSIC FOOD LTD Statement of financial position as at 30 June 2019		
	2019 $'000	2018 $'000
Current assets		
Cash	25 000	5 220
Receivables	7 842	4 112
Inventories	139 412	70 055
Other	2 446	1 951
Total current assets	174 700	81 338
Non-current assets		
Property, plant and equipment	86 158	40 729
Deferred tax assets	6 900	3 205
Intangible assets	96 085	44 530
Other	384	494
Total non-current assets	189 527	88 958
Total assets	364 227	170 296
Current liabilities		
Payables	139 500	60 797
Interest-bearing liabilities	35 016	17 895
Current tax liabilities	6 743	5 623
Provisions	13 741	8 522
Total current liabilities	195 000	92 837
Non-current liabilities		
Interest-bearing liabilities	60 891	31 634
Deferred tax liabilities	1 712	1 421
Provisions	6 917	5 105
Total non-current liabilities	69 520	38 160
Total liabilities	264 520	130 997
Net assets	**99 707**	**39 299**
EQUITY		
Contributed equity	77 663	31 442
Retained earnings	22 044	7 857
Total equity	**99 707**	**39 299**

Required

(a) For each entity calculate the return on assets and profit margin.

(b) Which entity appears to have stronger profitability?

(c) For each entity calculate working capital and the current ratio.

(d) Which entity appears to have stronger liquidity?

(e) What additional information would you require to make a better decision about the future profitability and liquidity of the two companies?

Interpreting financial statements

BBS1.3 NuSmart Technology Ltd launched its latest wireless communications product in 2019. The company spent much of 2018 developing and testing software so that its equipment could operate seamlessly in the public switched telephone network. Information from the company's statement of cash flows for the year ended 31 December 2019 follows.

	2019	2018
Cash received from customers	–	–
Cash generated (used) by operating activities	$(8 700 703)	$(11 265 540)
Cash generated (used) by investing activities	183 160	(42 968)
Cash provided (used) by financing activities	8 489 104	11 226 587
Net change in cash	$ (28 439)	$ (81 921)

The most significant source of cash generation was borrowing in 2018 and share issues in 2019. Despite delays, management has expressed confidence that the company is now positioned with a considerable competitive advantage.

Required

Use the information provided to answer each of the following:

(a) If you were a creditor of NuSmart Technology, what reaction might you have to the 2018 and 2019 statements of cash flows?

(b) If you were a shareholder of NuSmart Technology, what reaction might you have to the cash flows in 2019?

(c) If you were evaluating the company as either a creditor or a shareholder, what other information would you be interested in reviewing?

Financial analysis on the web

BBS1.4 *Purpose:* This exercise is an introduction to some large accounting firms.

Addresses:	Deloitte	www2.deloitte.com/au *or* www2.deloitte.com/nz
	Ernst & Young	www.ey.com/au/en/home
	KPMG	www.kpmg.com.au
	PricewaterhouseCoopers	www.pwc.com.au *or* www.pwc.co.nz

Steps: Go to the homepage of a firm that is of interest to you.

Required

Answer the following questions:

(a) Name two services provided by the firm.

(b) What countries or regions does it operate in?

(c) Does it provide information for students? If so, briefly describe the type of information.

(d) Summarise one recent news item discussed on the firm's web site.

CRITICAL THINKING

Group decision case

BBS1.5 Permanent Press provides laundry services to hotels and hospitals. In a recent annual report, Permanent Press chronicled its contributions to community services over the past 10 years. The following excerpts illustrate the variety of services provided:

1. At a local festival, Permanent Press sponsored the event by providing T-shirts, stationery and office decorations featuring the company's name and logo.

2. In support of the 'Clean Up Australia' campaign in 2018, the company donated, and its employees planted, grevillea gardens in cities across Australia.

3. The company held a competition in which customers throughout Australia and New Zealand nominated their favourite children's charities. Winning charities in the draw received a monetary donation from Permanent Press in the name of the customer.

4. Permanent Press executives often volunteer their time and resources to serve as role models and mentors to young people in Auckland.

Required

With the class divided into groups, answer the following:

(a) The entity assumption requires that a company keep the personal expenses of its employees separate from business expenses. Which of the activities listed above were expenses of the business, and which were personal expenses of the employees? Be specific. If part of the donation is business and part is personal, note which part is each.

(b) For those items that were business expenses, state whether the expense was probably categorised as an advertising expense, employee wages expense, grounds maintenance expense, or charitable contribution expense. You may use any or all of the categories. Explain your answer.

Communication activity

BBS1.6 Amy Joan is the bookkeeper for J.B. Hamilton Ltd. Amy has finally got the company's statement of financial position to balance, but she still isn't sure that it is correct. Before sending the statement to the board of directors, she asks you to check it.

J.B. HAMILTON LTD Statement of financial position for the month ended 30 June 2019			
ASSETS		LIABILITIES AND EQUITY	
Equipment	$30 750	Contributed equity	$ 40 000
Cash	12 000	Accounts receivable	(25 000)
Supplies	1 400	Inventory	(6 000)
Dividends	3 500	Accounts payable	21 650
		Retained earnings	17 000
Total assets	**$47 650**	**Total liabilities and equity**	**$ 47 650**

Required

Explain to Amy in a memo (a) the purpose of a statement of financial position and (b) why this statement is incorrect and what she should do to correct it.

Sustainability

BBS1.7 The following is an extract from the AGL Energy Limited web site:

> At AGL, sustainability means thinking about responsibilities we have to all our stakeholders — our employees, our customers, our investors, the community and the environment. In addition to our economic performance, AGL recognises that our future success and reputational standing is also shaped and measured by the social and environmental consequences our decisions and actions have for all our stakeholders.
>
> AGL has implemented a sustainability strategy to identify, manage, monitor and report on the material risks that affect our ability to protect and enhance AGL's long-term value. AGL has established a framework for ongoing public reporting to provide an accurate, transparent, responsive and timely account of our performance and commitments in relation to sustainability risks and opportunities.
>
> *Source:* AGL Energy Limited, www.agl.com.au/about-agl/what-we-stand-for/sustainability.

Required

What is meant by the term sustainability?

Access AGL Energy Limited's latest sustainability responsibility report and:

1. outline the company's approach to sustainability

2. summarise AGL's achievements in health and safety and the environment for the current period. Include a discussion of how these achievements are measured.

Ethics case

BBS1.8 As the chief financial officer of Mobile Phones Pty Ltd, you discover a significant misstatement that overstated assets in this year's financial statements. The misleading financial statements are contained in the company's annual report, which is about to be issued to banks and other creditors. After much thought about the consequences of telling the managing director, Jack Frost, about this misstatement, you gather your courage to tell him. Jack says, 'What they don't know won't hurt them. But just so we set the record straight, we'll adjust next year's financial statements for this year's misstatement. We can fix it next year when we make more profit. Just don't make that kind of mistake again.'

Required

(a) Who are the stakeholders in this situation?

(b) What are the ethical issues?

(c) What would you do as the chief financial officer?

ANSWERS

Answers to self-study questions

1.1 (c) 1.2 (b) 1.3 (b) 1.4 (b) 1.5 (c) 1.6 (c) 1.7 (b) 1.8 (c) 1.9 (d) 1.10 (d) 1.11 (a) 1.12 (c) 1.13 (c) 1.14 (c) 1.15 (b) 1.16 (c) 1.17 (a) 1.18 (a) 1.19 (c) 1.20 (c) 1.21 (c) 1.22 (c) 1.23 (a) 1.24 (b) 1.25 (b)

Answer to review it questions

Question 3, section 1.6: Trade and other receivables (from figure 1.9)

Question 2, section 1.6: Assets $142 312 000 = Liabilities $65 378 000 + Equity $76 934 000

ACKNOWLEDGEMENTS

Photo: © Joshua Hodge Photography / Getty Images

Photo: © Luiz Rocha / Shutterstock.com

Photo: © TW van Urk / Shutterstock.com

Figure 1.19: © 2018 Australian Accounting Standards Board AASB. The text, graphics and layout of this publication are protected by Australian copyright law and the comparable law of other countries. No part of the publication may be reproduced, stored or transmitted in any form or by any means without the prior written permission of the AASB except as permitted by law. For reproduction or publication permission should be sought in writing from the Australian Accounting Standards Board. Requests in the first instance should be addressed to the National Director, Australian Accounting Standards Board, PO Box 204, Collins Street West, Melbourne, Victoria, 8007.

Text: © AGL

CHAPTER 2

The recording process

After studying this chapter, you should be able to:

2.1 analyse the effect of accounting transactions and events on the basic accounting equation
2.2 explain what an account is and how it helps in the recording process
2.3 define debits and credits and explain how they are used to record accounting transactions
2.4 identify the basic steps in the recording process
2.5 explain what a journal is and how it helps in the recording process
2.6 explain what a general ledger is and how it helps in the recording process
2.7 explain what posting is and how it helps in the recording process
2.8 explain the purposes of a trial balance.

Chapter preview

An effective accounting information system is a necessity for any entity. The purpose of this chapter is to explain and illustrate the features of a recording information system. The organisation and content of the chapter are as follows.

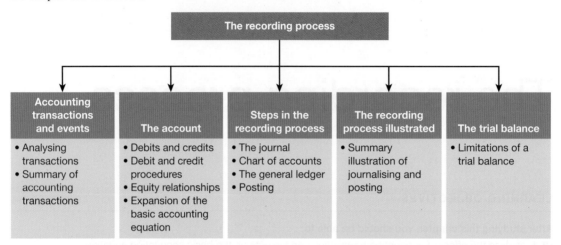

The system of collecting and processing transaction data and communicating financial information to interested parties is known as the **accounting information system**. Accounting information systems vary widely from one business to another. Factors that shape these systems include: the nature of the business, the types of transactions in which the business engages, the size of the business, the volume of data to be handled, and the information demands that management and others place on the system.

In reading this chapter, it is important to note that most businesses of any size today use computerised accounting systems. These systems handle all the steps involved in the recording process, from initial data entry to preparation of the financial statements. In order to remain competitive, companies like Domino's Pizza Enterprises Ltd, Freedom Foods Group Limited and Nike are continually updating and improving their accounting systems to provide accurate and timely data for decision making. Continual developments in technology allow for greater speed and efficiency in sharing information between groups of people. For example, the growth in the use of Bluetooth wireless technology means that people can work anywhere and everywhere. This technology has completely revolutionised our ability to be connected and share information. Bluetooth eliminates the need for cables and wires while providing connectivity on a level we've never experienced before. This low-cost solution links computers, mobile phones and any manner of other Bluetooth-enabled devices quickly and easily. We no longer need to be in our office to stay in touch.

In this chapter we focus on a manual accounting system because the accounting concepts and principles do not change whether a system is computerised or manual, and manual systems are easier to illustrate. Note, however, that many of the problems in this and subsequent chapters can also be completed using a computerised accounting package or even a simple spreadsheet program.

The transactions demonstrated in this chapter do not include the effects of the goods and services tax (GST). GST is first introduced in chapter 4, section 4.6.

2.1 Accounting transactions and events

LEARNING OBJECTIVE 2.1 Analyse the effect of accounting transactions and events on the basic accounting equation.

To use an accounting information system to develop financial statements, you need to know which economic transactions and events to record (recognise). Not all transactions and events are recorded and reported in the financial statements. A *transaction* is an external exchange of something of value between two or more entities. *Events* include price increases in business assets during an accounting period or the allocation of the cost of the long-lived assets of a business to different accounting periods. Events like these will be discussed in later chapters. For example, suppose Freedom Foods Group hired a new employee or purchased office equipment. Are these transactions and events entered in its accounting records? The hiring of a new employee (event) would not be recorded, but the purchase of office equipment (transaction) would. How to account for these and many other events and transactions is explained in detail in this chapter.

Helpful hint: Accountants often speak about 'recognising' the effects of transactions in the accounts. In this sense, to 'recognise' simply means to record the effects of transactions in the financial statements.

Accounting transactions and events are those occurrences which must be recorded because they have an effect on the assets, liabilities or equity items of a business. Recall from chapter 1 that the *Conceptual Framework* outlines the definition and recognition criteria for assets, liabilities and equity items. These help us to record transactions. The purchase of a computer, the payment of rent and the sale of advertising space are examples of transactions that change an entity's assets, liabilities or equity. In this chapter we will focus on transaction analysis and in later chapters we will explore in more depth the definition and recognition criteria for assets, liabilities and equity from the *Conceptual Framework*. Figure 2.1 summarises the decision process used to decide whether or not to record transactions and events.

| **FIGURE 2.1** | Accounting transaction and event identification process |

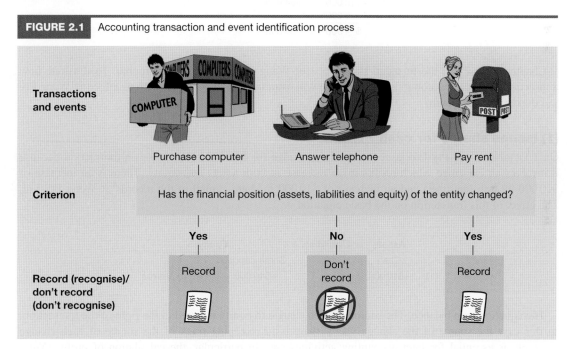

Analysing transactions

In chapter 1 you were introduced to the basic accounting equation:

In this chapter you will learn how to analyse transactions, in terms of their effect on assets, liabilities and equity, in order to decide whether or not to record the transactions. **Transaction analysis** is the process of identifying the specific effects of transactions and events on the accounting equation. In subsequent chapters we will look at different events. Meanwhile, the focus of this chapter is on recording accounting transactions.

The accounting equation must always balance. Therefore, each transaction has a dual (double-sided) effect on the equation. For example, if an individual asset is increased, there must be a corresponding:

- decrease in another asset, *or*
- increase in a specific liability, *or*
- increase in equity.

It is quite possible that two or more items could be affected when an asset is increased. For example, if an entity purchases office furniture for $10 000 by paying $6000 in cash and the remaining $4000 on credit, one asset (office furniture) increases $10 000, another asset (cash) decreases $6000, and a liability (accounts payable) increases $4000. The result is that the accounting equation remains in balance as assets increased by a net $4000 and liabilities increased by $4000, as shown below:

Assets	=	Liabilities	+	Equity
+$10 000		+$4 000		
−6 000				
$ 4 000		$4 000		

Chapter 1 presented the financial statements for Wong Pty Ltd for its first month. To illustrate how transactions affect the accounting equation, we will examine a variety of transactions affecting Wong Pty Ltd during its first month.

(1) Issues shares for cash

On 1 October Wong Pty Ltd issues shares in exchange for $10 000 cash. This is a transaction because it involves an exchange which results in an increase in both assets and equity. There is an increase of $10 000 in cash (an asset) and an increase of $10 000 in share capital in the records of Wong Pty Ltd. The effect of this transaction on the basic equation is:

	Assets	=	Liabilities	+	Equity	
	Cash	=			Share capital	
(1)	+$10 000	=			+$10 000	Issued shares

The equation is in balance. The source of each change to equity is noted to the right of the transaction. In this case the source of the change was a share issue. Keeping track of the source of each change in equity is essential for later accounting activities and, in particular, the calculation of profit. (*Note:* An alternative term for share capital is *contributed equity*. In the United States, share capital is called *stock.*)

(2) Borrows money from a bank

On 1 October Wong Pty Ltd borrows $5000 from the ANZ Bank. This transaction results in an equal increase in assets and liabilities: cash (an asset) increases $5000, and bank loan (a liability) increases $5000.

The specific effect of this transaction and the cumulative effect of the first two transactions are shown below.

		Assets	=	Liabilities	+	Equity
				Bank		Share
		Cash	=	loan	+	capital
	Old balance	$10 000				$10 000
(2)		+5 000		+$5 000		
	New balance	$15 000	=	$5 000	+	$10 000
					$15 000	

Note that total assets are now $15 000, and equity plus the new liability also total $15 000.

(3) Purchase of office equipment for cash

On 2 October Wong Pty Ltd acquires office equipment by paying $5000 cash to Superior Equipment Sales Ltd. This transaction results in an equal increase and decrease in Wong's assets. Office equipment (an asset) increases $5000, and cash (an asset) decreases $5000.

			Assets		=	Liabilities	+	Equity
				Office		Bank		Share
		Cash	+	equipment	=	loan	+	capital
	Old balance	$15 000				$5 000		$10 000
(3)		−5 000		+$5 000				
	New balance	$10 000	+	$5 000	=	$5 000	+	$10 000
			$15 000				$15 000	

The total assets are now $15 000, and equity plus the liability also total $15 000.

(4) Receipt of cash in advance from customer

On 2 October Wong Pty Ltd receives a $1200 cash advance from R. Knox, a client. In this transaction, cash (an asset) is received for advertising services that are expected to be completed by Wong Pty Ltd by 31 December. In the magazine and airline industries, customers are expected to prepay. These businesses have a liability to the customer until the magazines are delivered or the flight is provided. As soon as the product or service is provided, revenue can be recorded. Since Wong Pty Ltd received cash before performing the service, Wong Pty Ltd has a liability for the work due. Determining when to record revenue and when to record revenue received in advance (also called *unearned revenue*) is discussed further in chapter 3. In this example, cash increases by $1200, and a liability, service revenue received in advance (abbreviated as revenue received in advance), increases by an equal amount on 2 October:

			Assets		=		Liabilities		+	Equity
							Revenue			
				Office		Bank	received in			Share
		Cash	+	equipment	=	loan	+	advance	+	capital
	Old balance	$10 000		$5 000		$5 000				$10 000
(4)		+1 200						+$1 200		
	New balance	$11 200	+	$5 000	=	$5 000	+	$1 200	+	$10 000
			$16 200					$16 200		

(5) Renders services for cash

On 3 October Wong Pty Ltd receives $10 000 in cash from Copa & Co. for advertising services performed. In this transaction Wong Pty Ltd receives cash (an asset) in exchange for services. Advertising services is the principal revenue-producing activity of Wong Pty Ltd. *Revenue increases equity*. Both assets and equity are, then, increased by this transaction. Cash is increased by $10 000, and retained earnings is increased by $10 000. The new balances in the equation are:

		Assets		=	Liabilities	+		Equity		
			Office		Bank		Revenue received in	Share	Retained	
		Cash +	equipment	=	loan +		advance +	capital +	earnings	
	Old balance	$11 200	$5 000		$5 000		$1 200	$10 000		
(5)		+10 000								+$10 000 Service revenue
	New balance	$21 200 +	$5 000	=	$5 000 +		$1 200	+ $10 000 +	$10 000	
			$26 200				$26 200			

Helpful hint: Recall from chapter 1 that, although a capital contribution by owners increases equity, it is not revenue.

Often businesses sell goods or provide services 'on account' (this can also be known as buying and selling goods 'on credit'). That is, they provide services or goods for which they are paid at a later date. Instead of receiving cash, the business receives a different type of asset, an account receivable. **Accounts receivable** represent the right to receive payment at a later date. Suppose that Wong Pty Ltd had provided these services on account rather than for cash. This transaction would have been reported using the accounting equation as:

Assets	= Liabilities +	Equity	
Accounts		Retained	
receivable =		earnings	
+$10 000		+$10 000	Service revenue

Later, when the $10 000 is collected from the customer, accounts receivable would decrease by $10 000, and cash would increase by $10 000.

Assets		= Liabilities + Equity
	Accounts	
Cash	receivable	
+$10 000	−$10 000	

Note that in this case, equity is not affected by the collection of cash. Instead we record an exchange of one asset (accounts receivable) for a different asset (cash).

(6) Payment of rent in cash

On 3 October Wong Pty Ltd pays its office rent for the month of October in cash, $900. Rent is an expense incurred by Wong Pty Ltd in its effort to generate revenues. *Expenses decrease equity*. This transaction results in a decrease in cash and an increase in rent expense. It is recorded by decreasing cash and decreasing equity (specifically, retained earnings) to maintain the balance of the accounting equation. To record this transaction, cash is decreased by $900, and retained earnings is decreased by $900. The effect of the payment on the accounting equation is:

		Assets	=	Liabilities	+	Equity		
		Office		Bank	Revenue received in		Share	Retained
	Cash +	equipment =		loan +	advance +		capital +	earnings
Old balance	$21 200	$5 000		$5 000	$1 200		$10 000	$10 000
(6)	−900							−900 Rent expense
New balance	$20 300 +	$5 000	= $5 000 +		$1 200	+ $10 000 +		$ 9 100
		$25 300			$25 300			

(7) Payment of insurance in cash

On 4 October Wong Pty Ltd pays $600 for a 1-year insurance policy that will expire next year on 30 September. In this transaction one asset is exchanged for another. The asset cash is decreased by $600. The asset prepaid insurance is increased by $600. This is an asset because the insurance extends beyond the current month. Payments for benefits that continue for more than the current accounting period are identified as pre-paid expenses or prepayments. Note that the balance in total assets did not change; one asset account decreased by the same amount that another increased.

		Assets		=	Liabilities	+	Equity	
		Prepaid	Office	Bank	Revenue received in		Share	Retained
	Cash +	insurance +	equipment =	loan +	advance +		capital +	earnings
Old balance	$20 300		$5 000	$5 000	$1 200		$10 000	$9 100
(7)	−600	+$600						
New balance	$19 700 +	$600 +	$5 000	= $5 000 +	$1 200	+ $10 000 +		$9 100
		$25 300			$25 300			

(8) Purchase of supplies on credit

On 5 October Wong Pty Ltd purchases an estimated 3-month supply of advertising materials on account from Aero Supply for $2500. Assets are increased by this transaction because supplies represent a resource that will be used in the process of providing services to customers. Liabilities are increased by the amount owing to Aero Supply. The asset supplies is increased by $2500, and the liability accounts payable is increased by the same amount. **Accounts payable** represent amounts owing to suppliers for the purchase of goods or services on credit. The effect of the transaction on the accounting equation is:

			Assets			=		Liabilities		+	Equity	
				Prepaid	Office	Bank	Accounts	Revenue received in		Share	Retained
	Cash +	Supplies +	insurance +	equipment =		loan +	payable +	advance +		capital +	earnings
Old balance	$19 700		$600	$5 000		$5 000		$1 200		$10 000	$9 100
(8)		+$2 500					+$2 500				
New balance	$19 700 +	$2 500 +	$600 +	$5 000	= $5 000 +		$2 500 +	$1 200	+ $10 000 +		$9 100
			$27 800					$27 800			

Helpful hint: Recall that the term 'on account' means that the supplies will be provided now but the payment will be made at a later date.

(9) Hiring of new employees

On 9 October Wong Pty Ltd hires four new employees to begin work on 15 October. Each employee is to receive a weekly salary of $500 for a 5-day working week, payable every 2 weeks. Employees are to receive their first pay on 26 October. There is no effect on the accounting equation because the assets, liabilities and equity of Wong Pty Ltd have not changed. A transaction has not occurred. At this point there is only an agreement that the employees will begin work on 15 October. (See transaction (11) for the first payment.)

(10) Payment of dividend

On 20 October Wong Pty Ltd pays a $500 dividend. Dividends are a distribution of profit and not an expense. A dividend transaction affects assets and equity as cash and retained earnings are decreased by $500.

		Assets				=	**Liabilities**			+	**Equity**		
		Cash	+ Supplies	+ Prepaid insurance	+ Office equipment	=	Bank loan	+ Accounts payable	+ Revenue received in advance	+	Share capital	+ Retained earnings	
(10)	Old balance	$19 700	$2 500	$600	$5 000		$5 000	$2 500	$1 200		$10 000	$9 100	
		−500										−500	Dividends
	New balance	$19 200 +	$2 500 +	$600 +	$5 000	=	$5 000 +	$2 500 +	$1 200 +		$10 000 +	$8 600	
				$27 300					$27 300				

(11) Payment of cash for employee salaries

Employees have worked 2 weeks, earning $4000 in salaries, which are paid on 26 October. Like the costs that were incurred for rent, salaries are an expense. They are a cost of generating revenues, and decrease equity. Cash and retained earnings are each decreased by $4000.

		Assets				=	**Liabilities**			+	**Equity**		
		Cash	+ Supplies	+ Prepaid insurance	+ Office equipment	=	Bank loan	+ Accounts payable	+ Revenue received in advance	+	Share capital	+ Retained earnings	
(11)	Old balance	$19 200	$2 500	$600	$5 000		$5 000	$2 500	$1 200		$10 000	$8 600	
		−4 000										−4 000	Salaries expense
	New balance	$15 200 +	$2 500 +	$600 +	$5 000	=	$5 000 +	$2 500 +	$1 200 +		$10 000 +	$4 600	
				$23 300					$23 300				

Summary of accounting transactions

The transactions of Wong Pty Ltd, which you analysed to decide if they are to be recognised in the accounting records, are summarised in figure 2.2 to show their cumulative effect on the basic accounting equation. The transaction number, the specific effects of the transaction, and the balances after each transaction are indicated. Remember that (9) has no effect on the accounting equation, so no entry is included. The illustration demonstrates three significant facts:

1. Each transaction is analysed in terms of its effect on assets, liabilities and equity.
2. The two sides of the equation must always be equal (assets must equal liabilities plus equity).
3. The cause of each change in equity must be indicated.

FIGURE 2.2   Summary of transactions

	Cash	+ Supplies	+ Prepaid insurance	+ Office equipment	=	Bank loan	+ Accounts payable	+ Revenue received in advance	+ Share capital	+ Retained earnings	
(1)	+$10 000				=				+$10 000		Issued shares
(2)	+5 000					+$5 000					
	15 000				=	5 000			+ 10 000		
(3)	−5 000			+$5 000							
	10 000			+ 5 000	=	5 000			+ 10 000		
(4)	+1 200							+$1 200			
	11 200			+ 5 000	=	5 000		+ 1 200	+ 10 000		
(5)	+10 000									+$10 000	Service revenue
	21 200			+ 5 000	=	5 000		+ 1 200	+ 10 000	+ 10 000	
(6)	−900									−900	Rent expense
	20 300			+ 5 000	=	5 000		+ 1 200	+ 10 000	+ 9 100	
(7)	−600		+$600								
	19 700	+ 600		+ 5 000	=	5 000		+ 1 200	+ 10 000	+ 9 100	
(8)		+$2 500					+$2 500				
	19 700 +	2 500 +	600 +	5 000	=	5 000 +	2 500 +	1 200 +	10 000 +	9 100	
(10)	−500									−500	Dividends
	19 200 +	2 500 +	600 +	5 000	=	5 000 +	2 500 +	1 200 +	10 000 +	8 600	
(11)	−4 000									−4 000	Salaries expense
	$15 200 +	$2 500 +	$600 +	$5 000	=	$5 000 +	$2 500 +	$1 200 +	$10 000 +	$4 600	

$23 300 $23 300

DECISION-MAKING TOOLKIT

Decision/issue	Info needed for analysis	Tool or technique to use for decision	How to evaluate results to make decision
Has an accounting transaction occurred?	Details of the event	Accounting equation	Determine the effect, if any, on assets, liabilities and equity. A transaction has occurred if the accounting equation is affected.

2.2 The account

LEARNING OBJECTIVE 2.2 Explain what an account is and how it helps in the recording process.

Rather than using a tabular summary like the one in figure 2.2 for Wong Pty Ltd, an accounting information system uses accounts. An **account** is an individual accounting record of increases and decreases in a specific asset, liability or equity item. For example, Wong Pty Ltd has separate accounts for cash, accounts receivable, accounts payable, service revenue, salaries expense, and so on. (Note that whenever we are referring to a specific account, we use title case for the name.)

In its simplest form, an account consists of three parts: (1) the name of the account, (2) a left, or debit, side, and (3) a right, or credit, side. Because the alignment of these parts of an account resembles the letter T, it is referred to as a **T account**. The basic form of an account is shown in figure 2.3.

FIGURE 2.3 Basic or T form of account

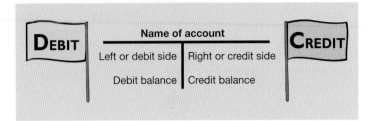

The T-account form is used often throughout this text to explain basic accounting relationships. However, another common form of account is the running balance account, illustrated in figure 2.4. The running balance form provides a balance for the account after each transaction.

FIGURE 2.4   Tabular summary and account forms for Wong Pty Ltd's cash account

Tabular summary		T-account form				Running balance account form			
Cash		**Cash**				**Cash**			
$10 000		(Debits)	10 000	(Credits)	5 000	**Debit**	**Credit**	**Balance**	
5 000			5 000		900	10 000		10 000	
−5 000			1 200		600	5 000		15 000	
1 200			10 000		500		5 000	10 000	
10 000					4 000	1 200		11 200	
−900						10 000		21 200	
−600							900	20 300	
−500		The balance of the T account is $15 200 Dr					600	19 700	
−4 000		as the debit side exceeds the credit side by					500	19 200	
$15 200		$15 200.					4 000	15 200 Dr	

2.3 Debits and credits

LEARNING OBJECTIVE 2.3 Define debits and credits and explain how they are used to record accounting transactions.

The term **debit** refers to the left side and the term **credit** refers to the right side when recording accounting transactions and events. They are commonly abbreviated as Dr for debit and Cr for credit. These terms are directional signals; they do *not* mean increase or decrease or good or bad as is commonly thought. The terms *debit* and *credit* are used repeatedly in the recording process to describe where entries are made in accounts. For example, the act of entering an amount on the left side of an account is called *debiting* the account. Making an entry on the right side is *crediting* the account. When the totals of the two sides of the T account are compared, an account will have a debit balance if the total of the debit amounts exceeds the total of the credits. Conversely, an account will have a credit balance if the total of the credit amounts exceeds the total of the debits. Note the position of the debit or credit balances in figure 2.3.

The procedure for recording debits and credits in an account is shown in figure 2.4 for the transactions affecting the cash account of Wong Pty Ltd. The data are taken from the cash column of the tabular summary in figure 2.2.

Every positive item in the tabular summary represents a receipt of cash; every negative amount represents a payment of cash. Note that in the account forms the increases in cash are recorded as debits and the decreases in cash are recorded as credits. In the T-account form, having increases on one side and decreases on the other side reduces recording errors and helps in determining the totals of each side of the account as well as the balance in the account. The account balance, a debit of $15 200, indicates that Wong Pty Ltd has $15 200 in its cash account. Since it started with a balance of zero, it has $15 200 more increases than decreases in cash.

Debit and credit procedures

Each transaction must affect two or more accounts to keep the basic accounting equation in balance. In other words, for each transaction, debits must equal credits. The equality of debits and credits provides the basis for the double-entry accounting system.

Under the universally used **double-entry system**, the dual (two-sided) effect of each transaction is recorded in appropriate accounts. This system provides a logical method for recording transactions. The double-entry system also offers a means of ensuring the accuracy of the recorded amounts. If every transaction is recorded with equal debits and credits, then the sum of all the debits to the accounts must equal the sum of all the credits. The double-entry system for determining the equality of the accounting equation is much more efficient than the plus/minus procedure used earlier. There, it was necessary after each transaction to compare total assets with total liabilities and equity to determine the equality of the two sides of the accounting equation.

Dr/Cr procedures for assets and liabilities

In figure 2.4 for Wong Pty Ltd, increases in cash (an asset) were entered on the left side of a T account, and decreases in cash were entered on the right side. We know that both sides of the basic equation (Assets = Liabilities + Equity) must be equal. Therefore, increases and decreases in liabilities will have to be recorded *opposite from* increases and decreases in assets. Thus, increases in liabilities must be entered on the right or credit side, and decreases in liabilities must be entered on the left or debit side. The effects that debits and credits have on assets and liabilities are summarised in figure 2.5.

FIGURE 2.5 Debit and credit effects — assets and liabilities

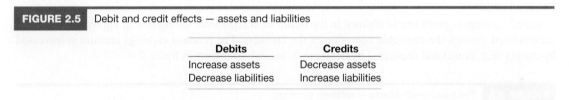

Debits	Credits
Increase assets	Decrease assets
Decrease liabilities	Increase liabilities

Asset accounts normally show debit balances. That is, debits to a specific asset account should exceed credits to that account. Likewise, liability accounts normally show credit balances. That is, credits to a liability account should exceed debits to that account. The normal balances are illustrated in figure 2.6.

FIGURE 2.6 Normal balances — assets and liabilities

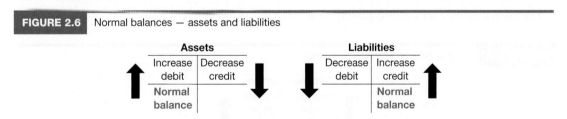

Knowing which is the normal balance in an account may help when you are trying to find errors. For example, a credit balance in an asset account such as land or a debit balance in a liability account such as wages payable usually indicates errors in recording. Occasionally, however, an abnormal balance may be correct. The cash account, for example, will have a credit balance when an entity has overdrawn its bank balance, i.e. when an entity has taken more money out of the bank account than it has put in. This is discussed further in later chapters.

Dr/Cr procedures for equity

Subdivisions of equity include share capital, retained earnings, dividends, revenues and expenses. In a double-entry system, accounts are kept for each of these subdivisions.

Share capital

Share capital is issued in exchange for the owners' investment. The share capital account is increased by credits and decreased by debits. For example, when cash is invested in the business, cash is debited and share capital is credited. The effects of debits and credits on the share capital account are shown in figure 2.7.

FIGURE 2.7 Debit and credit effects — share capital

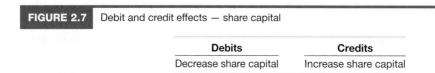

Debits	Credits
Decrease share capital	Increase share capital

The normal balance in the share capital account may be illustrated as in figure 2.8.

FIGURE 2.8 Normal balance — share capital

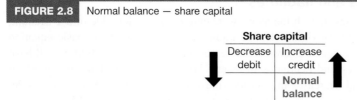

Share capital

Decrease debit	Increase credit
	Normal balance

Retained earnings

Retained earnings is profit that is retained in the business. It represents the portion of equity that has been accumulated through the profitable operation of the business. The retained earnings account is increased by credits (e.g. profit) and decreased by debits (e.g. losses), as shown in figure 2.9.

FIGURE 2.9 Debit and credit effects — retained earnings

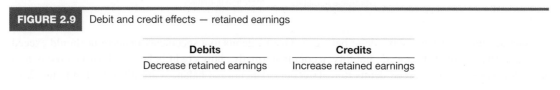

Debits	Credits
Decrease retained earnings	Increase retained earnings

The normal balance for retained earnings may be illustrated as in figure 2.10.

FIGURE 2.10 Normal balance — retained earnings

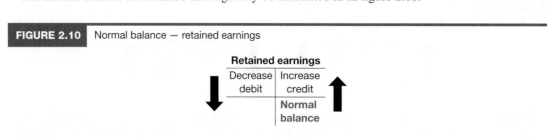

Retained earnings

Decrease debit	Increase credit
	Normal balance

Dividends

A **dividend** is a distribution by a company to its shareholders in an amount proportional to each investor's percentage ownership. The most common form of distribution is a cash dividend. Dividends result in a reduction of the shareholders' claims on retained earnings. Because dividends reduce equity, increases in the dividends account are recorded with debits. As shown in figure 2.11, the dividends account normally has a debit balance.

FIGURE 2.11   Normal balance — dividends

Dividends

Increase debit	Decrease credit
Normal balance	

Revenues and expenses

When revenues are recognised, equity is increased. Accordingly, the effect of debits and credits on revenue accounts is identical to their effect on equity. Revenue accounts are increased by credits and decreased by debits.

On the other hand, expenses decrease equity. As a result, expenses are recorded by debits. Since expenses are the negative factor in the calculation of profit and revenues are the positive factor, it is logical that the increase and decrease sides of expense accounts should be the reverse of revenue accounts. Thus, expense accounts are increased by debits and decreased by credits. The effects of debits and credits on revenues and expenses are shown in figure 2.12.

FIGURE 2.12   Debit and credit effects — revenues and expenses

Debits	**Credits**
Decrease revenues	Increase revenues
Increase expenses	Decrease expenses

Credits (increases) to revenue accounts normally exceed debits (decreases), and debits (increases) to expense accounts should exceed credits (decreases). Thus, revenue accounts normally show credit balances, and expense accounts normally show debit balances. The normal balances may be illustrated as in figure 2.13.

FIGURE 2.13   Normal balances — revenues and expenses

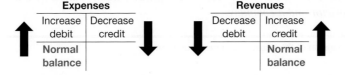

Equity relationships

As indicated in chapter 1, share capital, dividends and retained earnings for Wong Pty Ltd are reported in the equity section of the statement of financial position. Revenues and expenses are reported on the statement of profit or loss. Dividends, revenues and expenses are eventually transferred to retained earnings at the end of the period. The balance in the retained earnings account at the end of the period is calculated as follows: beginning balance in retained earnings plus profit (or minus loss) minus dividends. The relationships of the accounts affecting equity are shown in figure 2.14.

FIGURE 2.14 Equity relationships

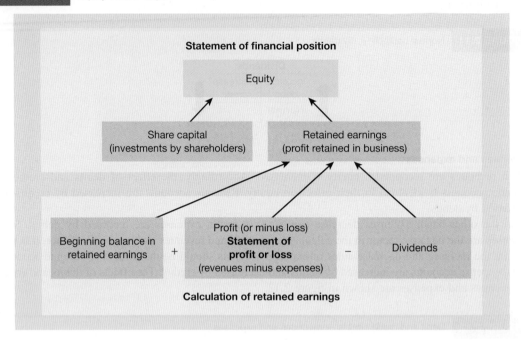

Helpful hint: The revenue and expenses are used to calculate profit in the period. The resulting profit is added to the retained earnings account. The retained earnings account is an equity account that is increased by profit and decreased by dividends — that is, when profit is distributed to shareholders. This will be expanded upon in chapter 10.

Expansion of the basic accounting equation

You have already learned the basic accounting equation. Figure 2.15 expands this equation to show the accounts that make up equity. In addition, the debit/credit rules and effects on each type of account are illustrated. Study this diagram carefully. It will help you understand the fundamentals of the double-entry system. Like the basic equation, the expanded basic equation must be in balance; total debits must equal total credits.

Helpful hint: The accounting equation Assets = Liabilities + Equity can be used to analyse transactions for both a sole proprietor and a company.

FIGURE 2.15 Expansion of the basic accounting equation

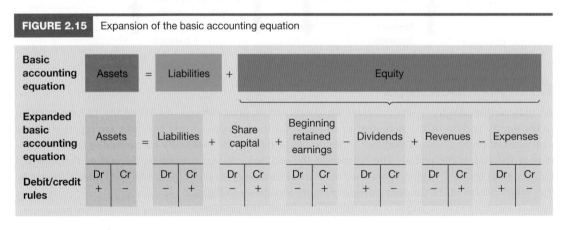

Review it

1. What do the terms *debit* and *credit* mean?
2. Explain the debit and credit effects on assets, liabilities and equity.
3. What are the debit and credit effects on revenues, expenses and dividends?
4. What are the *normal* balances for the following accounts of Giorgina's Pizza Limited: trade and other receivables, income tax expense, sales revenue, food and paper expenses? (The answer to this question is at the end of the chapter.)

Do it

Kate Brown, managing director of Hair Affair Pty Ltd, has just rented space in a Westfield shopping centre for the purpose of opening and operating a hairdressing salon. Long before opening day and before purchasing equipment, hiring assistants and renovating the space, Kate was strongly advised to set up a double-entry set of accounting records in which to record the business transactions.

Identify the accounts that Hair Affair Pty Ltd is likely to need to record the transactions necessary to establish and open for business. Also, indicate whether the normal balance of each account is a debit or a credit.

Reasoning

To start the business, Hair Affair Pty Ltd will need to have asset accounts for each different type of asset invested in the business. In addition, the company will need liability accounts for debts incurred by the business. Hair Affair Pty Ltd will need only one equity account for share capital when it begins the business. The other equity accounts will be needed only after business has commenced.

Solution

Hair Affair Pty Ltd is likely to need the following accounts in which to record the transactions necessary to establish and ready the salon for opening day: cash (debit balance); equipment (debit balance); supplies (debit balance); accounts payable (credit balance); bank loan (credit balance), if the business borrows money; and share capital (credit balance).

2.4 Steps in the recording process

LEARNING OBJECTIVE 2.4 Identify the basic steps in the recording process.

Although it is possible to enter transaction information directly into the accounts, few businesses do so. Practically every business uses these three basic steps in the recording process.

1. Analyse each transaction in terms of its effect on the accounts.
2. Enter the transaction information in a journal.
3. Transfer the journal information to the appropriate accounts in the ledger.

The actual sequence of events begins with the transaction. Evidence of the transaction comes in the form of a **source document**, such as a purchase order (evidence of goods ordered from a supplier), a purchase invoice (evidence from a supplier of a purchase of goods or services on credit), a cheque (evidence of a payment), cash register tape (evidence of cash sales made through a cash register) or a sales invoice (evidence of a credit sale). Figure 2.16 is an example of a sales invoice, which provides evidence that the business has made a credit sale to a customer. The original sales invoice is sent to the customer for the customer's records, and the copy provides the evidence of a credit sale in the business's records. (Sales invoices are called tax invoices when the goods and services tax (GST) is payable. The GST is first introduced in chapter 4, section 4.6.)

Each source document is analysed to determine the effect of the transaction on specific accounts. The transaction is then entered in the journal. Finally, the journal entry is transferred to the designated accounts in the ledger. The sequence of events in the recording process is shown in figure 2.17.

FIGURE 2.16   A sales invoice

TAX INVOICE

No. 204403

M.BROWN & ASSOCIATES (i.e. name of entity)

ABN 33 123 689 701

Charge to:

Smith & Retton
21 Edinburgh Street
BOOVAL QLD 4304

Send to:

Smith & Retton
21 Edinburgh Street
BOOVAL QLD 4304

Account No.	Terms	Customer Order Ref.
210337	Net 30 days	25/8/2016

Stock No.	Quantity	Description	Unit Price	TOTAL
63147	20	XC M-type gear boxes	$27.50	$550.00
21003	40	XC Gear box brackets	$ 1.10	$ 44.00
		Total amount payable		**$594.00**
		Total includes GST of		**$ 54.00**

FIGURE 2.17   The recording process

The recording process

Analyse each transaction

Enter transaction in a journal

Transfer journal information to ledger accounts

The basic steps in the recording process occur repeatedly in every business. The analysis of transactions has already been illustrated, and more examples of this step are given in this and later chapters. The other steps in the recording process are explained in the next sections.

2.5 The journal

LEARNING OBJECTIVE 2.5 Explain what a journal is and how it helps in the recording process.

Transactions are initially recorded in chronological order in a **journal** before they are transferred to the accounts. For each transaction the journal shows the debit and credit effects on specific accounts. Businesses may use various kinds of journals to record transactions; these are explored in detail in chapter 6. Every business has at least the most basic form of journal, a **general journal**. The general journal makes two significant contributions to the recording process.
1. It provides a chronological record of all transactions.
2. It discloses in one place the complete effect of a transaction. This helps to prevent or locate errors.

Entering transaction data in the journal is known as **journalising**. To illustrate the technique of journalising, let's look at the first three transactions of Wong Pty Ltd. These transactions were: 1 October, shares were issued in exchange for $10 000 cash; 1 October, $5000 was borrowed from a bank; 2 October, purchased office equipment costing $5000 for cash. In equation form, these transactions appeared in our earlier discussion as follows:

Assets	**= Liabilities +**		**Equity**	
			Share	
Cash	=		capital	
+$10 000			+$10 000	Issued shares

Assets	**= Liabilities +**	**Equity**
	Bank	
Cash =	loan	
+$5 000	+$5 000	

	Assets		**= Liabilities +**	**Equity**
	Office			
Cash	equipment			
−$5 000	+$5 000			

Separate journal entries are made for each transaction. A complete entry consists of: (1) the date of the transaction, (2) the accounts and amounts to be debited and credited, and (3) a brief explanation of the transaction, referred to as a **narration**. Wong Pty Ltd's first three transactions are journalised in figure 2.18.

Note the following features of the journal entries.
1. The date of the transaction is entered in the Date column.
2. The account to be debited is always entered first at the left. The account to be credited is then entered on the next line, indented under the line above. The indentation differentiates debits from credits and decreases the possibility of switching the debit and credit amounts.
3. The amounts for the debits are recorded in the debit (left) column, and the amounts for the credits are recorded in the credit (right) column.

4. A brief explanation of the transaction is given (narration). The narration is found directly below the transaction.
5. The posting reference column (abbreviated to Post ref.) contains the account number as it appears in the chart of accounts (discussed in the next section).

FIGURE 2.18 Recording transactions in journal form

	General journal			
Date	Account name (narration)	Post ref.	Debit	Credit
2019 Oct. 1	Cash	100	10 000	
	Share capital	300		10 000
	(Issued shares for cash)			
1	Cash	100	5 000	
	Bank loan	230		5 000
	(Borrowed money from a bank)			
2	Office equipment	130	5 000	
	Cash	100		5 000
	(Purchased office equipment for cash)			

It is important to use correct and specific account names and numbers in journal entries. Since all accounts are used in preparation of the financial statements, erroneous account names lead to incorrect financial statements. Some flexibility exists initially in selecting account names. For example, a business could use any of these account names for recording the cost of delivery trucks: delivery vehicles, delivery trucks or trucks. The main criterion is that each name must appropriately describe the type of asset, liability, revenue, expense or equity represented in the account. You would expect entities that have similar business transactions, like Domino's and Freedom Foods Group to have similar account names. Once the business chooses the specific account name, all subsequent transactions involving the account should be recorded under that account name. An entity's chart of accounts facilitates the consistent recording of transactions as it provides a list of all the account names used to record transactions for that business.

LEARNING REFLECTION AND CONSOLIDATION

Review it
1. What is the correct sequence of steps in the recording process?
2. What contribution does the journal make to the recording process?
3. What are the standard form and content of a journal entry made in the general journal?

Do it
The following events occurred during the first month of business of Hair Affair Pty Ltd, Kate Brown's hairdressing salon:
1. issued shares to shareholders in exchange for $20 000 cash
2. purchased $4800 of hair supplies inventory on account (to be paid in 30 days)
3. interviewed three people for the position of hairdresser.
   In what form (type of record) should the entity initially record these three activities? Prepare the entries to record the transactions.

Reasoning

Kate should record the transactions in a journal, which is a chronological record of the transactions. The record should be a complete and accurate representation of the transactions' effects on the assets, liabilities and equity of her business.

Solution

Each transaction that is recorded is entered in the general journal. The three activities are recorded as follows:

1.	Cash	20 000	
	Share capital		20 000
	(Issued shares for cash)		
2.	Inventory	4 800	
	Accounts payable		4 800
	(Purchased hair supplies inventory on account)		
3.	No entry because no transaction occurred.		

Helpful hint: If you are unsure of the solution to part 3 here, review transaction 9 in section 2.1 for Wong Pty Ltd.

Chart of accounts

All transactions for a business are recorded in accounts set up in the general ledger. The **chart of accounts** is a list of all these accounts. *Account numbers* as well as *account names* are often used for each account. One of the most important decisions when setting up the recording system is ensuring the information system is suitable to meet the needs of the users of the accounting information. In order to ensure the data is 'sorted and summarised' so the accounting reports provide the relevant information, you start with the required outputs and design the recording system to meet those needs. When you are designing the numbering system it should be flexible to allow for additional accounts to be added when required.

When establishing or modifying a chart of accounts, you should be careful to make sure that similar names are not used for different accounts. For example, the account name Motor Vehicle does not indicate whether a posting should be made to an asset account or an expense account, whereas including an account number and using names, such as motor vehicle asset account and motor vehicle expense account, leave no room for doubt. Using account numbers as well as account names is recommended, as it is easier to make sure the correct account is selected if similar names are used and you are unable to change them to make them more distinctive.

The number and type of accounts used differ for each business, depending on the size, complexity and type of business. For example, the number of accounts depends on the amount of detail desired by management. The management of one business may want one single account for all types of service expense. Another may keep separate expense accounts for each type of service expense, such as gas, electricity and water. Similarly, a small business like Wong Pty Ltd will not have many accounts compared with a large company like Domino's. Wong Pty Ltd may be able to manage and report its activities in 20 to 30 accounts, whereas companies such as Vodafone, Wesfarmers and Freedom Foods Group require thousands of accounts to keep track of their worldwide activities.

The chart of accounts for Wong Pty Ltd is shown in figure 2.19. Accounts shown in red are used in this chapter; accounts shown in black are explained in later chapters. New accounts may be created as needed during the life of the business.

FIGURE 2.19 Chart of accounts for Wong Pty Ltd

WONG PTY LTD — Chart of accounts

Assets		Liabilities		Equity		Revenues		Expenses	
No.	Account name	No.	Account name	No.	Account name	No.	Account name	No.	Account name
100	Cash	200	Accounts payable	300	Share capital	400	Service revenue	500	Salaries expense
104	Accounts receivable	210	Interest payable	310	Retained earnings	405	Commissions revenue	505	Supplies expense
105	Commissions receivable	213	Revenue received in advance	320	Dividends			510	Rent expense
110	Advertising supplies	215	Salaries payable	330	Profit or loss summary			515	Insurance expense
112	Prepaid insurance	230	Bank loan					518	Interest expense
130	Office equipment							520	Depreciation expense
131	Acc. depreciation— office equipment								

2.6 The general ledger

LEARNING OBJECTIVE 2.6 Explain what a general ledger is and how it helps in the recording process.

The general journal provides a chronological list of all of the transactions for a business. A chronological list on its own, however, is of limited use. Classifying and summarising data improves their usefulness for decision making. For example, a business's general journal could contain hundreds of purchases, cash receipts and cash payments transactions in any given month. If a sales manager wants to know the total sales revenue for any particular month, this information cannot be easily obtained from the general journal, but it can be obtained from the sales revenue account in the ledger. The ledger accumulates all the information about changes in specific account balances such as sales revenue, cash, and wages expense.

FIGURE 2.20 The general ledger

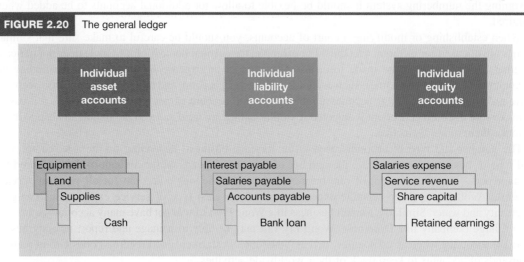

The entire group of accounts maintained by a business is referred to collectively as the general ledger. A **general ledger** contains all the assets, liabilities and equity accounts, as shown in figure 2.20. A business can use a loose-leaf binder or card file for the ledger, with each account kept on a separate sheet or card. Most businesses today, however, use a computerised accounting system. Computerised accounting systems are illustrated in chapter 6. Whenever the term *ledger* is used in this text without additional specification, it will mean the general ledger.

2.7 Posting

LEARNING OBJECTIVE 2.7 Explain what posting is and how it helps in the recording process.

The procedure of transferring journal entries to ledger accounts is called **posting**. This phase of the recording process accumulates the effects of journalised transactions in the individual asset, liability, equity, revenue and expense accounts. Posting involves the following steps.

1. Using the account number in the posting reference column, locate in the ledger the account to be debited and enter the date the transaction occurred.
2. To the right of the date, enter the name of the ledger account to which the credit entry will be posted. This is called the cross-reference.
3. Enter the amount to be debited to the debit side of the ledger account. (If a running balance ledger account is used, enter the amount in the debit column of the ledger account and calculate the new balance in the balance column.)
4. In the general journal, place a tick beside the account number in the posting reference column. This signifies that the entry has now been posted to the ledger.
5. Repeat steps 1–4 for the credit side of the entry.
   These steps are illustrated in figures 2.22 to 2.32 in the next section.

A cross-reference in a ledger account is very useful as it provides additional information on each amount recorded in an individual ledger account. For example, figure 2.4 illustrates the transactions affecting the cash account for Wong Pty Ltd for the month of October. In this very simple form of the cash ledger account, cross-references are not given and so no details are available on what the amounts represent. This simple cash ledger T account is reproduced in figure 2.21. Also in figure 2.21 is the same cash ledger account with cross-references included. *The cross-references serve two important purposes: (1) they indicate the corresponding ledger accounts to which the entries are posted, and (2) at a glance, they provide information on the nature of each transaction in the ledger account.* For example, in the cash ledger account in figure 2.21 the cross-reference indicates the nature of each cash outlay (credit entries) and the nature of the amount of incoming cash (debit entries). When you compare the cash ledger account which includes cross-references with the account that does not include cross-references, it is easy to see which is more useful and why cross-references are so important. In some chapters, where a very basic form of the ledger account is used due to space constraints, ledger cross-references may not always be shown. In practice, however, in businesses using computerised accounting packages, the cross-referencing is usually complete.

FIGURE 2.21 Wong Pty Ltd's cash account with and without dates and cross-references

No cross-references		Cross-references included				
Cash		**Cash**				
(Debits) 10 000	**(Credits)** 5 000	Oct. 1	Share capital	10 000	Oct. 2 Office equipment	5 000
5 000	900	1	Bank loan	5 000	3 Rent expense	900
1 200	600	2	Revenue received		4 Prepaid insurance	600
10 000	500		in advance	1 200	20 Dividends	500
	4 000	3	Service revenue	10 000	26 Salaries expense	4 000

The recording process illustrated

Figures 2.22 to 2.32 show the basic steps in the recording process using the October transactions of Wong Pty Ltd. Its accounting period is a month. A basic analysis and a debit–credit analysis precede the journalising and posting of each transaction. Study these transaction analyses carefully. The purpose of transaction analysis is first to identify the type of account involved and then to determine whether a debit or a credit to the account is required. You should always perform this type of analysis before preparing a journal entry. Doing so will help you understand the journal entries discussed in this chapter as well as more complex journal entries to be described in later chapters.

FIGURE 2.22   Shares issued for cash

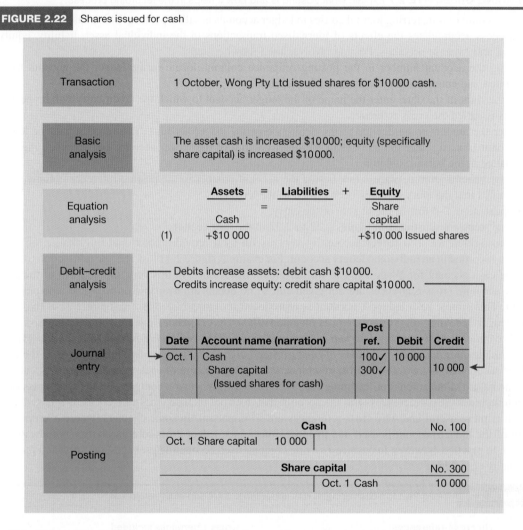

Helpful hint: Remember to place a ✓ beside the account number in the general journal once the entry has been posted to the ledger. Note that the cross-references indicate the ledger account to which the opposite side of the entry is posted.

FIGURE 2.23 Bank loan

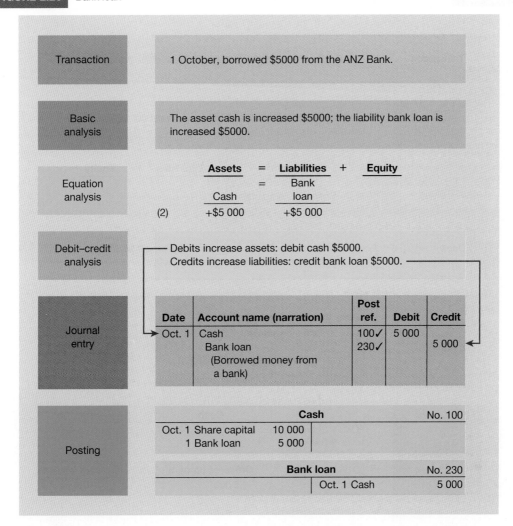

Transaction	1 October, borrowed $5000 from the ANZ Bank.	
Basic analysis	The asset cash is increased $5000; the liability bank loan is increased $5000.	

Equation analysis

	Assets	=	Liabilities	+	Equity
		=	Bank		
	Cash		loan		
(2)	+$5 000		+$5 000		

Debit–credit analysis

Debits increase assets: debit cash $5000.
Credits increase liabilities: credit bank loan $5000.

Journal entry

Date	Account name (narration)	Post ref.	Debit	Credit
Oct. 1	Cash	100✓	5 000	
	Bank loan	230✓		5 000
	(Borrowed money from a bank)			

Posting

Cash			**No. 100**
Oct. 1 Share capital	10 000		
1 Bank loan	5 000		

	Bank loan	**No. 230**
	Oct. 1 Cash	5 000

Helpful hint: In the cash ledger account, note that the cross-references indicate the nature of the cash received — $10 000 from a share issue and $5000 from a bank loan.

FIGURE 2.24 Purchase of office equipment for cash

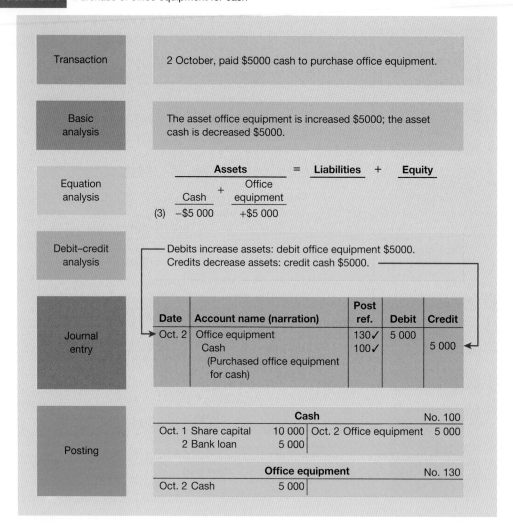

Transaction

2 October, paid $5000 cash to purchase office equipment.

Basic analysis

The asset office equipment is increased $5000; the asset cash is decreased $5000.

Equation analysis

	Assets		=	**Liabilities**	+	**Equity**
	Cash	+	Office equipment			
(3)	−$5 000		+$5 000			

Debit–credit analysis

Debits increase assets: debit office equipment $5000.
Credits decrease assets: credit cash $5000.

Journal entry

Date	Account name (narration)	Post ref.	Debit	Credit
Oct. 2	Office equipment	130✓	5 000	
	Cash	100✓		5 000
	(Purchased office equipment for cash)			

Posting

Cash			No. 100	
Oct. 1 Share capital	10 000	Oct. 2 Office equipment	5 000
2 Bank loan	5 000		

Office equipment		No. 130
Oct. 2 Cash	5 000	

FIGURE 2.25 Receipt of cash in advance from customer

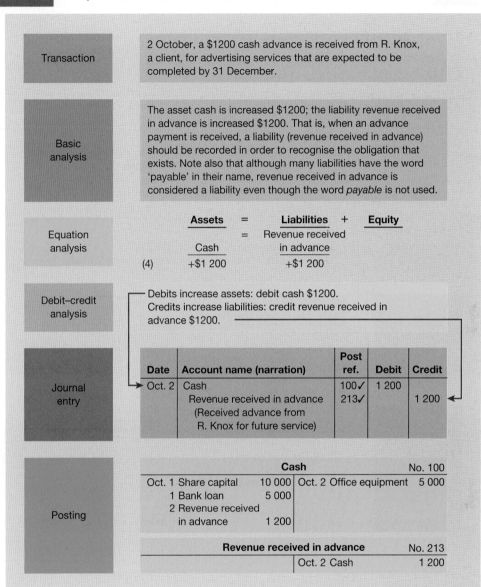

	Transaction	2 October, a $1200 cash advance is received from R. Knox, a client, for advertising services that are expected to be completed by 31 December.

Basic analysis — The asset cash is increased $1200; the liability revenue received in advance is increased $1200. That is, when an advance payment is received, a liability (revenue received in advance) should be recorded in order to recognise the obligation that exists. Note also that although many liabilities have the word 'payable' in their name, revenue received in advance is considered a liability even though the word *payable* is not used.

Equation analysis

	Assets	=	**Liabilities**	+	**Equity**
		=	Revenue received		
	Cash		in advance		
(4)	+$1 200		+$1 200		

Debit–credit analysis — Debits increase assets: debit cash $1200.
Credits increase liabilities: credit revenue received in advance $1200.

Journal entry

Date	Account name (narration)	Post ref.	Debit	Credit
Oct. 2	Cash	100✓	1 200	
	Revenue received in advance	213✓		1 200
	(Received advance from			
	R. Knox for future service)			

Posting

Cash   No. 100

Oct. 1	Share capital	10 000	Oct. 2	Office equipment	5 000
1	Bank loan	5 000			
2	Revenue received in advance	1 200			

Revenue received in advance   No. 213

		Oct. 2 Cash	1 200

Helpful hint: Use the chart of accounts to help you analyse each transaction before you record it in the general journal. The chart of accounts lists all the account names and numbers used in the business.

FIGURE 2.26 Services rendered for cash

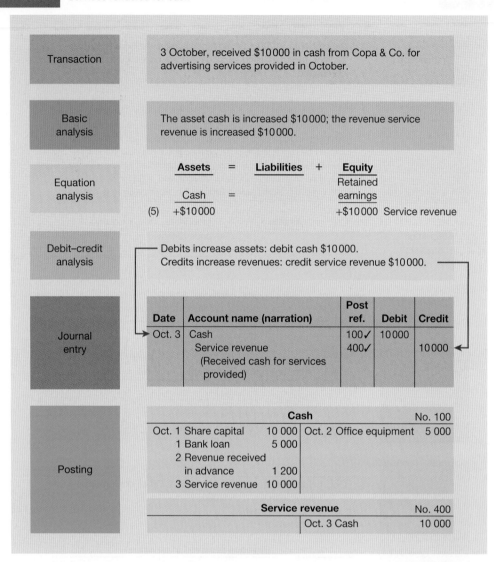

Transaction

3 October, received $10 000 in cash from Copa & Co. for advertising services provided in October.

Basic analysis

The asset cash is increased $10 000; the revenue service revenue is increased $10 000.

Equation analysis

Assets	=	Liabilities	+	Equity
				Retained
Cash	=			earnings
(5) +$10 000				+$10 000 Service revenue

Debit–credit analysis

Debits increase assets: debit cash $10 000.
Credits increase revenues: credit service revenue $10 000.

Journal entry

Date	Account name (narration)	Post ref.	Debit	Credit
Oct. 3	Cash	100✓	10 000	
	Service revenue	400✓		10 000
	(Received cash for services provided)			

Posting

Cash			No. 100
Oct. 1 Share capital	10 000	Oct. 2 Office equipment	5 000
1 Bank loan	5 000		
2 Revenue received in advance	1 200		
3 Service revenue	10 000		

Service revenue		No. 400
	Oct. 3 Cash	10 000

FIGURE 2.27 Payment of rent in cash

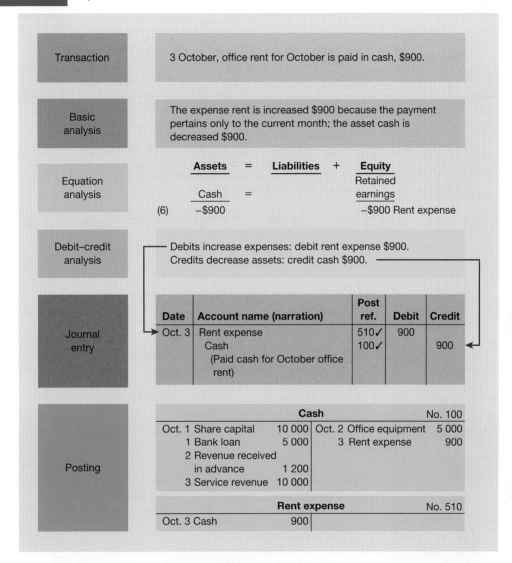

Transaction	3 October, office rent for October is paid in cash, $900.	
Basic analysis	The expense rent is increased $900 because the payment pertains only to the current month; the asset cash is decreased $900.	

Equation analysis

	Assets	=	**Liabilities**	+	**Equity**
					Retained
	Cash	=			earnings
(6)	−$900				−$900 Rent expense

Debit–credit analysis

Debits increase expenses: debit rent expense $900.
Credits decrease assets: credit cash $900.

Journal entry

Date	Account name (narration)	Post ref.	Debit	Credit
Oct. 3	Rent expense	510✓	900	
	Cash	100✓		900
	(Paid cash for October office rent)			

Posting

Cash			**No. 100**		
Oct. 1 Share capital	10 000	Oct. 2 Office equipment	5 000		
1 Bank loan	5 000	3 Rent expense	900		
2 Revenue received in advance	1 200				
3 Service revenue	10 000				

Rent expense		**No. 510**
Oct. 3 Cash	900	

Helpful hint: The narration provides additional information about the transaction. In this case, it indicates the period covered by the rent payment, i.e. the month of October.

FIGURE 2.28 Payment of insurance in cash

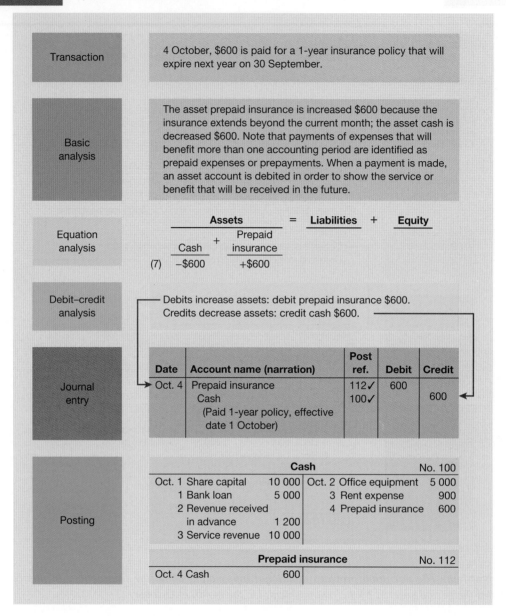

Transaction

4 October, $600 is paid for a 1-year insurance policy that will expire next year on 30 September.

Basic analysis

The asset prepaid insurance is increased $600 because the insurance extends beyond the current month; the asset cash is decreased $600. Note that payments of expenses that will benefit more than one accounting period are identified as prepaid expenses or prepayments. When a payment is made, an asset account is debited in order to show the service or benefit that will be received in the future.

Equation analysis

	Assets		= Liabilities + Equity
	Cash	+ Prepaid insurance	
(7)	−$600	+$600	

Debit–credit analysis

Debits increase assets: debit prepaid insurance $600.
Credits decrease assets: credit cash $600.

Journal entry

Date	Account name (narration)	Post ref.	Debit	Credit
Oct. 4	Prepaid insurance	112✓	600	
	Cash	100✓		600
	(Paid 1-year policy, effective date 1 October)			

Posting

Cash				No. 100
Oct. 1 Share capital	10 000	Oct. 2 Office equipment	5 000
1 Bank loan	5 000	3 Rent expense	900
2 Revenue received in advance	1 200	4 Prepaid insurance	600
3 Service revenue	10 000		

Prepaid insurance		No. 112
Oct. 4 Cash	600	

Helpful hint: Prepayments are discussed and illustrated in more detail in the next chapter.

FIGURE 2.29 Purchase of supplies on credit

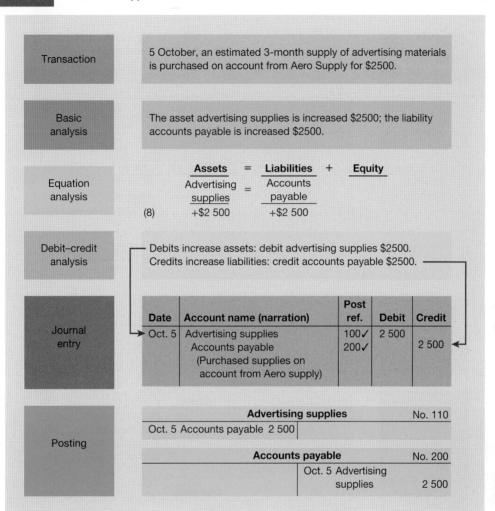

| Transaction | 5 October, an estimated 3-month supply of advertising materials is purchased on account from Aero Supply for $2500. |

| Basic analysis | The asset advertising supplies is increased $2500; the liability accounts payable is increased $2500. |

Equation analysis

	Assets	=	**Liabilities**	+	**Equity**
	Advertising supplies	=	Accounts payable		
(8)	+$2 500		+$2 500		

Debit–credit analysis

Debits increase assets: debit advertising supplies $2500.
Credits increase liabilities: credit accounts payable $2500.

Journal entry

Date	Account name (narration)	Post ref.	Debit	Credit
Oct. 5	Advertising supplies	100✓	2 500	
	Accounts payable	200✓		2 500
	(Purchased supplies on account from Aero supply)			

Posting

Advertising supplies		No. 110
Oct. 5 Accounts payable 2 500		

Accounts payable		No. 200
	Oct. 5 Advertising supplies	2 500

FIGURE 2.30 Hiring of new employees

| Transaction/ event | 9 October, hired four employees to begin work on 15 October. Each employee is to receive a weekly salary of $500 for a 5-day working week, payable every 2 weeks — first payment made on 26 October. |

| Basic analysis | An accounting transaction has not occurred. There is only an agreement that the employees will begin work on 15 October. Thus, a debit–credit analysis is not needed because there is no accounting entry. (See transaction of 26 October for first salaries entry.) |

FIGURE 2.31   Payment of dividend

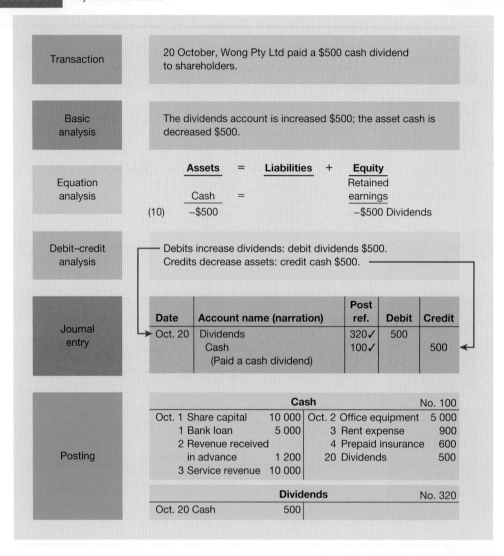

			Post ref.	Debit	Credit
Date	Account name (narration)				
Oct. 20	Dividends		320✓	500	
	Cash		100✓		500
	(Paid a cash dividend)				

Transaction

20 October, Wong Pty Ltd paid a $500 cash dividend to shareholders.

Basic analysis

The dividends account is increased $500; the asset cash is decreased $500.

Equation analysis

Assets	=	**Liabilities**	+	**Equity**
Cash	=			Retained earnings
(10) −$500				−$500 Dividends

Debit–credit analysis

Debits increase dividends: debit dividends $500.
Credits decrease assets: credit cash $500.

Posting

Cash   No. 100

Oct. 1 Share capital	10 000	Oct. 2 Office equipment	5 000
1 Bank loan	5 000	3 Rent expense	900
2 Revenue received		4 Prepaid insurance	600
in advance	1 200	20 Dividends	500
3 Service revenue	10 000		

Dividends   No. 320

Oct. 20 Cash	500	

FIGURE 2.32 Payment of cash for employee salaries

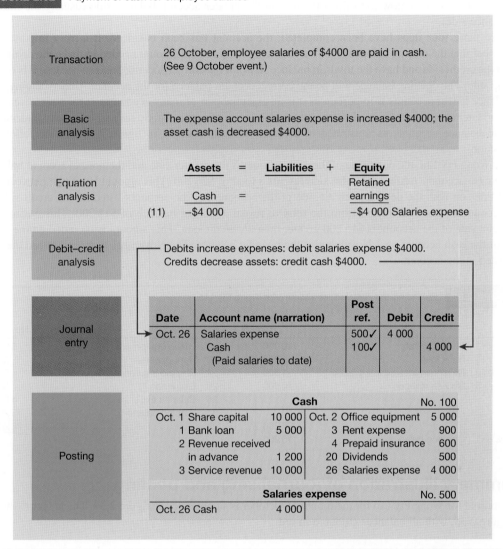

Transaction	26 October, employee salaries of $4000 are paid in cash. (See 9 October event.)

Basic analysis	The expense account salaries expense is increased $4000; the asset cash is decreased $4000.

Equation analysis

	Assets	=	Liabilities	+	Equity
					Retained
	Cash	=			earnings
(11)	−$4 000				−$4 000 Salaries expense

Debit–credit analysis

Debits increase expenses: debit salaries expense $4000.
Credits decrease assets: credit cash $4000.

Journal entry

Date	Account name (narration)	Post ref.	Debit	Credit
Oct. 26	Salaries expense	500✓	4 000	
	Cash	100✓		4 000
	(Paid salaries to date)			

Posting

Cash				**No. 100**
Oct. 1 Share capital	10 000	Oct. 2 Office equipment	5 000
1 Bank loan	5 000	3 Rent expense	900
2 Revenue received		4 Prepaid insurance	600
in advance	1 200	20 Dividends	500
3 Service revenue	10 000	26 Salaries expense	4 000

Salaries expense		**No. 500**
Oct. 26 Cash	4 000	

Figures 2.22 to 2.32 illustrate the basic steps in the recording process using the October transactions of Wong Pty Ltd. Once recording is complete, a trial balance is prepared. To facilitate this process, the balance of each account in the general ledger must be calculated. The process of balancing a T account is illustrated using the cash account from figure 2.32. Balancing involves the following main steps.

1. For each account, add each side. Generally, the normal account balance side will be the side with the greater amount. If you need to review the normal balances for each type of account, refer to figures 2.6, 2.8, 2.10, 2.11 and 2.13.
2. Leaving a blank line, rule lines as illustrated in figure 2.33 and write in the greater amount calculated in step 1 on both the debit and credit sides of the account (between the ruled lines).
3. The closing balance for the account can now be determined by subtracting the amounts listed on the lesser side from the total. The words 'closing balance' and the amount calculated in this step are recorded on the lesser side (generally the side opposite to the normal balance side).

4. The date (the first day of the next month), the words 'opening balance' and the balance calculated in step 3 are written below the ruled-off lines on the greater account balance side (usually the normal balance side).

Once these four steps have been completed, the account has been balanced. It is very important to remember that the closing balance is *only* a balancing item, i.e. the amount needed to make the debit side equal the credit side and have the totals in balance. It is *not* the correct account balance because it is on the wrong side. The opening balance will be the correct account balance for the account. Understanding how to balance ledger accounts is important as it is an essential part of many accounting processes covered in this and later chapters and is used in later years of an accounting course. So take some time to understand how to balance accounts as illustrated in the cash account example in figure 2.33 and the following discussion.

For Wong Pty Ltd, the debit side of the cash account is the greater side and the normal account balance of the cash account. Adding the debit side reveals a total of $26 200. This amount is written between the ruled lines on both the debit and credit side of the account. All the amounts listed on the credit side of the account are then subtracted from the total to reveal a closing balance of $15 200. This means that the debit side of the account is $15 200 greater than the credit side. This amount is recorded on the debit side of the cash account on 1 November as the opening balance. The November transactions can then be recorded in the account.

FIGURE 2.33 Balancing the cash ledger account for Wong Pty Ltd

			Cash					No. 100
Oct.	1	Share capital	10 000	Oct.	2	Office equipment		5 000
	1	Bank loan	5 000		3	Rent expense		900
	2	Revenue received in advance	1 200		4	Prepaid insurance		600
	3	Service revenue	10 000		20	Dividends		500
					26	Salaries expense		4 000
					31	Closing balance		15 200
			26 200					26 200
Nov.	1	Opening balance	15 200					

Summary illustration of journalising and posting

The journal for Wong Pty Ltd for the month of October is summarised in figure 2.34. The ledger is shown in figure 2.35, with all balances coloured in red.

FIGURE 2.34 General journal for Wong Pty Ltd

	General journal			
Date	Account name (narration)	Post ref.	Debit	Credit
2019				
Oct. 1	Cash	100	10 000	
	Share capital	300		10 000
	(Issued shares for cash)			
1	Cash	100	5 000	
	Bank loan	230		5 000
	(Borrowed money from a bank)			
2	Office equipment	130	5 000	
	Cash	100		5 000
	(Purchased office equipment for cash)			

Date	Account name (narration)	Post ref.	Debit	Credit
2019				
Oct. 2	Cash	100	1 200	
	Revenue received in advance	213		1 200
	(Received advance from R. Knox for future service)			
3	Cash	100	10 000	
	Service revenue	400		10 000
	(Received cash for services rendered)			
3	Rent expense	510	900	
	Cash	100		900
	(Paid cash for October office rent)			
4	Prepaid insurance	112	600	
	Cash	100		600
	(Paid 1-year policy; effective date 1 October)			
5	Advertising supplies	110	2 500	
	Accounts payable	200		2 500
	(Purchased supplies on account from Aero Supply)			
20	Dividends	320	500	
	Cash	100		500
	(Declared and paid a cash dividend)			
26	Salaries expense	500	4 000	
	Cash	100		4 000
	(Paid salaries to date)			

Helpful hint: Enter the account number in the posting reference column at the time you record the general journal entry. Put the ✓ in the posting reference column once the amount has been posted to the ledger.

FIGURE 2.35   General ledger for Wong Pty Ltd

General ledger

Cash   **No. 100**

Oct.	1	Share capital	10 000	Oct.	2	Office equipment	5 000
	1	Bank loan	5 000		3	Rent expense	900
	2	Revenue received in advance	1 200		4	Prepaid insurance	600
	3	Service revenue	10 000		20	Dividends	500
					26	Salaries expense	4 000
					31	Closing balance	15 200
			26 200				26 200
Nov.	1	Opening balance	15 200				

Advertising supplies   **No. 110**

Oct.	5	Accounts payable	2 500	Oct.	31	Closing balance	2 500
			2 500				2 500
Nov.	1	Opening balance	2 500				

Prepaid insurance   **No. 112**

Oct.	4	Cash	600	Oct.	31	Closing balance	600
			600				600
Nov.	1	Opening balance	600				

Office equipment   **No. 130**

Oct.	2	Cash	5 000	Oct.	31	Closing balance	5 000
			5 000				5 000
Nov.	1	Opening balance	5 000				

Accounts payable   No. 200

Oct.	31	Closing balance	2 500	Oct.	5	Advertising supplies	2 500
			2 500				2 500
				Nov.	1	Opening balance	2 500

Revenue received in advance   No. 213

Oct.	1	Closing balance	1 200	Oct.	2	Cash	1 200
			1 200				1 200
				Nov.	1	Opening balance	1 200

Bank loan   No. 230

Oct.	31	Closing balance	5 000	Oct.	1	Cash	5 000
			5 000				5 000
				Nov.	1	Opening balance	5 000

Share capital   No. 300

Oct.	31	Closing balance	10 000	Oct.	1	Cash	10 000
			10 000				10 000
				Nov.	1	Opening balance	10 000

Dividends   No. 320

Oct.	20	Cash	500	Oct.	31	Closing balance	500
			500				500
Nov.	1	Opening balance	500				

Service revenue   No. 400

Oct.	31	Closing balance	10 000	Oct.	3	Cash	10 000
			10 000				10 000
				Nov.	1	Opening balance	10 000

Salaries expense   No. 500

Oct.	26	Cash	4 000	Oct.	31	Closing balance	4 000
			4 000				4 000
Nov.	1	Opening balance	4 000				

Rent expense   No. 510

Oct.	3	Cash	900	Oct.	31	Closing balance	900
			900				900
Nov.	1	Opening balance	900				

Helpful hints:

1. *Due to space constraints the ledger cross-references to the source journals are not shown. The journal cross-references are demonstrated in chapters 3 and 6.*
2. *Post each of the entries from the general journal to the general ledger, then balance each of the accounts before preparing a trial balance.*
3. *In this example, only the cash account needed to be balanced as all the other accounts had only one transaction. However, all accounts were balanced to clearly demonstrate the procedure.*

LEARNING REFLECTION AND CONSOLIDATION

Review it

1. How does journalising differ from posting?
2. What is the purpose of (a) the ledger and (b) a chart of accounts?

Do it

On 5 January, the day of her successful grand opening of Hair Affair Pty Ltd, Kate Brown collected $2280 in cash for hair styling services, and paid $400 in wages and $92 for rent. Kate recorded these transactions in a general journal and posted the entries to the general ledger.

1. Explain the purpose and process of journalising and posting these transactions.
2. Journalise the three transactions (ignore post references).
3. Balance the cash account.

Cash				No. 100
Jan. 5 Service revenue	2 280	Jan. 5 Salaries expense		400
		5 Rent expense		92

Use the chart of accounts for Wong Pty Ltd (figure 2.19).

Reasoning

Every business must keep track of its financial activities (receipts, payments, receivables, payables, etc.); journalising does this. However, just recording every transaction in chronological order does not make the entries useful. To be useful, the entries need to be classified and summarised; posting the entries to specific ledger accounts does this.

Solution

1. The purpose of journalising is to record every transaction in chronological order. Journalising involves dating every transaction, measuring the dollar amount of each transaction, identifying or labelling each amount with account names, and recording in a standard format equal debits and credits. Posting involves transferring the journalised debits and credits to specific accounts in the ledger.

2.

Date	Account name (narration)	Post ref.	Debit	Credit
Jan. 5	Cash	100	2 280	
	Service revenue	400		2 280
	(Received cash for services provided)			
5	Salaries expense	500	400	
	Cash	100		400
	(Paid wages to date)			
5	Rent expense	510	92	
	Cash	100		92
	(Paid rent bill)			

3.

Cash				No. 100
Jan. 5 Service revenue	2 280	Jan. 5 Salaries expense		400
		5 Rent expense		92
		31 Closing balance		1 788
	2 280			2 280
Feb. 1 Opening balance	1 788			

2.8 The trial balance

LEARNING OBJECTIVE 2.8 Explain the purposes of a trial balance.

A **trial balance** is a list of accounts and their balances at a given time. Customarily, a trial balance is prepared at the end of an accounting period. The accounts are listed in the order in which they appear in the ledger. Debit balances are listed in the left column and credit balances in the right column. The totals of the two columns must be equal.

The main purpose of a trial balance is to prove the mathematical equality of debits and credits after posting. Under the double-entry system, this equality will occur when the sum of the debit account balances equals the sum of the credit account balances. A trial balance also uncovers some types of errors in journalising and posting, such as omitting one side of a journal entry and posting unequal amounts. The trial balance can facilitate the identification of a posting error that results in an account having a credit balance when it would normally have a debit balance, or a debit balance when it would normally have a credit balance. In addition, a trial balance is useful in the preparation of financial statements, as explained in the next chapter.

These are the procedures for preparing a trial balance.
1. List the account numbers, names and their balances.
2. Total the debit and credit columns.
3. Verify the equality of the two columns.

The trial balance prepared from the ledger of Wong Pty Ltd is presented in figure 2.36. Note that the total debits, $28 700, equal the total credits, $28 700.

FIGURE 2.36 Trial balance of Wong Pty Ltd

	WONG PTY LTD **Trial balance** as at 31 October 2019		
No.	Account name	Debit	Credit
100	Cash	$15 200	
110	Advertising supplies	2 500	
112	Prepaid insurance	600	
130	Office equipment	5 000	
200	Accounts payable		$ 2 500
213	Revenue received in advance		1 200
230	Bank loan		5 000
300	Share capital		10 000
320	Dividends	500	
400	Service revenue		10 000
500	Salaries expense	4 000	
510	Rent expense	900	
		$28 700	$28 700

Helpful hint: The trial balance for Wong Pty Ltd does not contain any end of period adjustments that may need to be made to ensure the accuracy of accounting information. It is an 'unadjusted' trial balance. Chapter 3 illustrates and explains end of period adjustments.

Limitations of a trial balance

A trial balance does not guarantee that all transactions have been recorded or that the ledger is correct. Numerous errors may exist even though the trial balance columns agree. For example, the trial balance may balance even when any of the following occurs: (1) a transaction is not journalised, (2) a correct journal entry is not posted, (3) a journal entry is posted twice, (4) incorrect accounts are used in journalising or posting, or (5) offsetting errors are made in recording the amount of a transaction. In other words, as long as equal debits and credits are posted, even to the wrong account or in the wrong amount, the total debits will equal the total credits. Nevertheless, despite its limitations, the trial balance is a useful screen for finding errors and is frequently used in practice.

Helpful hint: Extracting a trial balance is essential when a manual accounting system is used to ensure debits equal credits. Companies like Domino's employ sophisticated computerised accounting systems where transactions are only processed when debits equal credits. These companies are less likely to prepare a trial balance but instead prepare complex accounting reports.

Review it

1. What is a trial balance, and how is it prepared?
2. What is the main purpose of a trial balance?
3. What are the limitations of a trial balance?

DECISION-MAKING TOOLKIT

Decision/issue	Info needed for analysis	Tool or technique to use for decision	How to evaluate results to make decision
How do you determine that debits equal credits?	All account balances	Trial balance	List the account names and their balances; total the debit and credit columns; verify equality. If not equal, look for error.

USING THE DECISION-MAKING TOOLKIT

The Western Farmers' Cooperative Ltd was formed in the late 1990s. Its purpose is to use raw materials, mainly grain and meat products grown by its members, to process this material into consumer food products and to distribute the products nationally. Profits not needed for expansion or investment are returned to the members annually, on a pro rata basis, according to the market value of the grain and meat products received from each farmer.

Assume that the following information was prepared for the company's trial balance.

WESTERN FARMERS' COOPERATIVE LTD
Trial balance
as at 31 December 2019

Account name	Debit $'000	Credit $'000
Accounts receivable	712 000	
Accounts payable		37 000
Advertising and promotion payable		141 000
Buildings	365 000	
Cash	32 000	
Cost of sales	2 384 000	
Current portion of long-term debt		12 000
Freight expense	500 000	
Inventories	1 291 000	
Land	110 000	
Long-term debt		1 368 000
Machinery and equipment	63 000	
Retained earnings		822 000
Sales revenue		3 741 000
Salaries and wages payable		62 000
Selling and administrative expense	651 000	
	6 108 000	6 183 000

Helpful hint: The current portion of the long-term debt is the amount of the debt due to be paid within 12 months.

Because the trial balance is not in balance, you have checked with various people responsible for entering accounting data and have discovered the following.
1. The purchase of five new trucks, costing $7 million and paid for with cash, was not recorded.
2. A data entry clerk accidentally deleted the account name for an account with a credit balance of $472 million, so the amount was added to the long-term debt account in the trial balance.
3. December cash sales revenue of $75 million was credited to the sales revenue account, but the other half of the entry was not made.
4. $50 million of selling expenses were mistakenly charged to freight expense.

Required

Answer these questions:
(a) Which mistake or mistakes have caused the trial balance to be out of balance?
(b) Should all the items be corrected? Explain.
(c) What is the name of the account the data entry clerk deleted?
(d) Make the necessary corrections and balance the trial balance.
(e) On your trial balance, write SFP beside the accounts that should be shown on the statement of financial position and P/L beside those that should be shown on the statement of profit or loss.

Solution

(a) Only mistake 3 (sales revenue of $75 million not posted) has caused the trial balance to be out of balance.
(b) All the items should be corrected. The misclassification error (mistake 4) on the selling expense would not affect bottom line profit, but it does affect the amounts reported in the two expense accounts, and should, therefore, be corrected.
(c) There is no share capital account, so that must be the account that was deleted by the data entry clerk.
(d) and (e):

WESTERN FARMERS' COOPERATIVE LTD
Trial balance
as at 31 December 2019

Account name	Debit $'000	Credit $'000	
Accounts receivable	712 000		SFP
Accounts payable		37 000	SFP
Advertising and promotion payable		141 000	SFP
Buildings	365 000		SFP
Cash ($32 000 − $7000 + $75 000)	100 000		SFP
Cost of sales	2 384 000		P/L
Current portion of long-term debt		12 000	SFP
Freight expense ($500 000 − $50 000)	450 000		P/L
Inventories	1 291 000		SFP
Land	110 000		SFP
Long-term debt ($1 368 000 − $472 000)		896 000	SFP
Machinery and equipment ($63 000 + $7000)	70 000		SFP
Retained earnings		822 000	SFP
Sales revenue		3 741 000	P/L
Salaries and wages payable		62 000	SFP
Selling and administrative expense ($651 000 + $50 000)	701 000		P/L
Share capital		472 000	SFP
	6 183 000	6 183 000	

Helpful hint: The effects of the mistakes on the original unadjusted account balances are given in parentheses in the solution.

SUMMARY

2.1 Analyse the effect of accounting transactions and events on the basic accounting equation.
Each business transaction must have a dual effect on the accounting equation. For example, if an individual asset is increased, there must be a corresponding (a) decrease in another asset or (b) increase in liabilities or (c) increase in equity.

2.2 Explain what an account is and how it helps in the recording process.
An account is an individual accounting record of increases and decreases in specific asset, liability, revenue, expense and equity items.

2.3 Define debits and credits and explain how they are used to record accounting transactions.
The terms *debit* and *credit* refer to the *left* and *right* sides of accounts. Assets, dividends and expenses are increased by debits and decreased by credits. Liabilities, share capital, retained earnings and revenues are increased by credits and decreased by debits.

2.4 Identify the basic steps in the recording process.
The basic steps in the recording process are: (a) analyse each transaction in terms of its effect on the accounts, (b) enter the transaction information in a journal, and (c) transfer the journal information (post) to the appropriate accounts in the ledger.

2.5 Explain what a journal is and how it helps in the recording process.
The initial accounting record of a transaction is entered in a journal before the data are entered in the accounts. A journal provides a chronological record of all transactions. It records in one place the complete effect of a transaction, and this helps to prevent or locate errors.

2.6 Explain what a general ledger is and how it helps in the recording process.
The entire group of accounts maintained by an entity is referred to collectively as a general ledger. The ledger keeps in one place all the information about changes in specific account balances.

2.7 Explain what posting is and how it helps in the recording process.
Posting is the procedure of transferring journal entries to the ledger accounts. This phase of the recording process accumulates the effects of journalised transactions in the individual accounts.

2.8 Explain the purposes of a trial balance.
A trial balance is a list of accounts and their balances at a given time. The main purpose of the trial balance is to prove the mathematical equality of debits and credits after posting. A trial balance also uncovers some types of errors in journalising and posting and is useful in preparing financial statements.

DECISION-MAKING TOOLKIT — A SUMMARY

DECISION-MAKING TOOLKIT

Decision/issue	Info needed for analysis	Tool or technique to use for decision	How to evaluate results to make decision
Has an accounting transaction occurred?	Details of the event	Accounting equation	Determine the effect, if any, on assets, liabilities and equity. A transaction has occurred if the accounting equation is affected.
How do you determine that debits equal credits?	All account balances	Trial balance	List the account names and their balances; total the debit and credit columns; verify equality. If not equal look for error.

KEY TERMS

account An individual accounting record of increases and decreases in a specific asset, liability or equity item.

accounting information system The system of collecting and processing transaction data and communicating financial information to interested parties.

accounting transactions and events Occurrences which affect the assets, liabilities and equity items in a business and must be recognised (recorded). A transaction is an external exchange of something of value between two or more entities. The allocation of the cost of an entity's long-lived assets over different accounting periods is an example of an event.

accounts payable Amounts owed to suppliers for the purchase of goods or services on credit. Also called creditors or trade creditors.

accounts receivable Amounts due from customers for the sale of goods or services on credit. Also called debtors or trade debtors.

chart of accounts A list of all an entity's ledger account names and account numbers.

credit The right side of an account.

debit The left side of an account.

dividend A distribution of profits by a company to its shareholders in an amount proportional to each shareholder's percentage ownership. The most common form is a cash distribution.

double-entry system A system that records the dual effect of each transaction in appropriate accounts.

general journal The most basic form of journal where the transactions are initially recorded in chronological order.

general ledger A ledger that contains all asset, liability, and equity accounts maintained by each individual business.

journal An accounting record in which transactions are initially recorded in chronological order.

journalising The procedure of entering transaction data in the journal.

narration A brief explanation of each transaction recorded in the general journal. The narration is generally found directly below the transaction it relates to.

posting The procedure of transferring journal entries to the ledger accounts.

source document A form that provides written evidence that a transaction has occurred, e.g. sales invoice, purchase order, cash register tape.

T account The basic form of an account.

transaction analysis The process of identifying the specific effects of transactions and events on the accounting equation (Assets = Liabilities + Equity).

trial balance A list of accounts and their balances at a given time.

DEMONSTRATION PROBLEM

Nikola Subotic and his brothers opened Niky's Dry Cleaning Pty Ltd on 1 September 2019. During the first month of operations the following transactions occurred:

Sept.	1	The business issued shares and shareholders invested $20 000 cash in the business.
	2	Paid $1000 cash for shop rent for the month of September.
	3	Purchased industrial dry-cleaning equipment for $25 000, paying $10 000 in cash and $15 000 on credit.
	4	Paid $1200 for 1-year accident insurance policy.
	10	Received bill from the *Daily Telegraph* for advertising the opening of the cleaning service, $200.
	15	Performed services on account for $6200.
	20	Paid a $700 cash dividend to shareholders.
	30	Received $5000 from customers invoiced on 15 September.

The chart of accounts for the entity is the same as for Wong Pty Ltd except for the following: cleaning equipment (account number 132) and advertising expense (account number 512).

Required

(a) Journalise the September transactions.

(b) Open ledger accounts and post the September transactions.

(c) Prepare a trial balance at 30 September 2019.

PROBLEM-SOLVING STRATEGIES

1. Make separate journal entries for each transaction.
2. Note that all debits precede all credit entries.
3. In journalising, make sure debits equal credits.
4. Use specific account names and numbers taken from the chart of accounts.
5. Provide a narration explaining each entry.
6. Arrange ledger in statement order beginning with the statement of financial position.
7. Post in chronological order, place a ✓ in the post reference column and balance each account.
8. Prepare a trial balance, which lists accounts in the order in which they appear in the ledger.
9. List debit balances in the left column and credit balances in the right column.

SOLUTION TO DEMONSTRATION PROBLEM

(a)

General journal				
Date	Account name (narration)	Post ref.	Debit	Credit
2019 Sept. 1	Cash	100✓	20 000	
	Share capital	300✓		20 000
	(Issued shares)			
2	Rent expense	510✓	1 000	
	Cash	100✓		1 000
	(Paid September rent)			
3	Cleaning equipment	131✓	25 000	
	Cash	100✓		10 000
	Accounts payable	200✓		15 000
	(Purchased cleaning equipment part paid for in cash and part on account)			
4	Prepaid insurance	112✓	1 200	
	Cash	100✓		1 200
	(Paid 1-year insurance policy)			
10	Advertising expense	512✓	200	
	Accounts payable	200✓		200
	(Received invoice from *Daily Telegraph* for advertising)			
15	Accounts receivable	104✓	6 200	
	Service revenue	400✓		6 200
	(To record credit sale)			
20	Dividends	320✓	700	
	Cash	100✓		700
	(Paid a cash dividend)			
30	Cash	100✓	5 000	
	Accounts receivable	104✓		5 000
	(To record collection of accounts receivable)			

Helpful hint: Remember that a ✓ is placed in the post reference column after the journal entry has been posted to the general ledger. The ✓ indicates that the journal entry has been posted to the general ledger.

(b)

General ledger								

Cash — **No. 100**

Sept.	1	Share capital	20 000	Sept.	2	Rent expense	1 000
	30	Accounts receivable	5 000		3	Cleaning equipment	10 000
					4	Prepaid insurance	1 200
					20	Dividends	700
					30	Closing balance	12 100
			25 000				25 000
Oct.	1	Opening balance	12 100				

Accounts receivable — **No. 104**

Sept.	15	Service revenue	6 200	Sept.	30	Cash	5 000
					30	Closing balance	1 200
			6 200				6 200
Oct.	1	Opening balance	1 200				

Prepaid insurance* — **No. 112**

Sept.	4	Cash	1 200	Sept.	30	Closing balance	1 200
			1 200				1 200
Oct.	1	Opening balance	1 200				

Cleaning equipment* — **No. 131**

Sept.	3	Cash/accounts payable	25 000	Sept.	30	Closing balance	25 000
			25 000				25 000
Oct.	1	Opening balance	25 000				

Accounts payable — **No. 200**

				Sept.	3	Cleaning equipment	15 000
Sept.	30	Closing balance	15 200		10	Advertising expense	200
			15 200				15 200
				Oct.	1	Opening balance	15 200

Share capital* — **No. 300**

Sept.	30	Closing balance	20 000	Sept.	1	Cash	20 000
			20 000				20 000
				Oct.	1	Opening balance	20 000

Dividends* — **No. 320**

Sept.	20	Cash	700	Sept.	30	Closing balance	700
			700				700
Oct.	1	Opening balance	700				

Service revenue* — **No. 400**

Sept.	30	Closing balance	6 200	Sept.	15	Accounts receivable	6 200
			6 200				6 200
				Oct.	1	Opening balance	6 200

Rent expense* — **No. 510**

Sept.	2	Cash	1 000	Sept.	30	Closing balance	1 000
			1 000				1 000
Oct.	1	Opening balance	1 000				

Advertising expense* — **No. 512**

Sept.	10	Accounts payable	200	Sept.	30	Closing balance	200
			200				200
Oct.	1	Opening balance	200				

*These accounts did not need to be balanced as there was only one transaction. However, all accounts were balanced to show 1 Oct. balances more clearly.

(c)

	NIKY'S DRY CLEANING PTY LTD Trial balance as at 30 September 2019		
No.	Account name	Debit	Credit
100	Cash	$12 100	
104	Accounts receivable	1 200	
112	Prepaid insurance	1 200	
131	Cleaning equipment	25 000	
200	Accounts payable		$15 200
300	Share capital		20 000
320	Dividends	700	
400	Service revenue		6 200
510	Rent expense	1 000	
512	Advertising expense	200	
		$41 400	$41 400

SELF-STUDY QUESTIONS

2.1 The effects on the basic accounting equation of performing services for cash are to: **LO1**
  (a) increase assets and decrease equity.
  (b) increase assets and increase equity.
  (c) increase assets and increase liabilities.
  (d) increase liabilities and increase equity.

2.2 Which statement about an account is *true*? **LO2**
  (a) In its simplest form, an account consists of two parts.
  (b) An account is an individual accounting record of increases and decreases in specific asset, liability or equity items.
  (c) There are separate accounts for specific assets and liabilities but only one account for equity items.
  (d) The left side of an account is the credit or decrease side.

2.3 Debits: **LO3**
  (a) increase both assets and liabilities.
  (b) decrease both assets and liabilities.
  (c) increase assets and decrease liabilities.
  (d) decrease assets and increase liabilities.

2.4 A revenue account: **LO3**
  (a) has a normal balance of a debit.
  (b) is decreased by credits.
  (c) is increased by debits.
  (d) is increased by credits.

2.5 Which accounts normally have debit balances? **LO3**
  (a) Assets, expenses and revenues.
  (b) Assets, expenses and retained earnings.
  (c) Assets, liabilities and dividends.
  (d) Assets, dividends and expenses.

2.6 Which of these statements about a journal is *false*? **LO5**
  (a) It contains only revenue and expense accounts.
  (b) It provides a chronological record of transactions.
  (c) It helps to prevent or locate errors because both debit and credit amounts for each entry are in one place.
  (d) It records in one place the complete effect of a transaction.

2.7 A general ledger: LO6
  (a) contains only asset and liability accounts.
  (b) should show accounts in alphabetical order.
  (c) is a collection of the entire group of accounts maintained by an entity.
  (d) provides a chronological record of transactions.

2.8 Posting: LO7
  (a) normally occurs before journalising.
  (b) transfers ledger transaction data to the journal.
  (c) is an optional step in the recording process.
  (d) transfers journal entries to ledger accounts.

2.9 A trial balance: LO8
  (a) is a list of accounts with their balances at a given time.
  (b) proves the accuracy of all journalised transactions in the ledger.
  (c) will not balance if a correct journal entry is posted twice.
  (d) proves that all transactions have been recorded.

2.10 A trial balance will not balance if: LO8
  (a) a correct journal entry is posted twice.
  (b) the purchase of supplies on credit is debited to supplies and credited to cash.
  (c) a $200 cash dividend is debited to dividends for $2000 and credited to cash for $200.
  (d) a $450 payment on account is debited to accounts payable for $45 and credited to cash for $45.

QUESTIONS

2.1 Describe the accounting information system and the steps in the recording process.

2.2 Are the following events recorded in the accounting records? Explain your answer in each case.
  (a) A major shareholder of the company dies.
  (b) Supplies are purchased on account.
  (c) An employee is fired.
  (d) The company pays a cash dividend to its shareholders.

2.3 Indicate how each business transaction affects the basic accounting equation.
  (a) Paid cash for cleaning services.
  (b) Purchased equipment for cash.
  (c) Issued shares to investors in exchange for cash.
  (d) Paid an account payable in full.

2.4 Charles Nguyen, a fellow student, contends that the double-entry system means each transaction must be recorded twice. Is Charles correct? Explain.

2.5 Tanya Nikolic, an introductory accounting student, believes debit balances are favourable and credit balances are unfavourable. Is Tanya correct? Discuss.

2.6 State the rules of debit and credit as applied to (a) asset accounts, (b) liability accounts, (c) the share capital account, (d) revenue accounts, (e) expense accounts and (f) dividend account.

2.7 What is the normal balance for each of these accounts?
  (a) Equipment.
  (b) Cash.
  (c) Advertising expense.
  (d) Accounts payable.
  (e) Service revenue.
  (f) Accounts receivable.
  (g) Share capital.

2.8 (a) What is a ledger?

(b) Why is a chart of accounts important?

2.9 What is a trial balance and what are its purposes?

2.10 Two students are discussing the use of a trial balance. They wonder whether the following errors, each considered separately, would prevent the trial balance from balancing. If the trial balance did balance, does this mean the transactions were entered correctly? What would you tell them?

(a) The bookkeeper debited accounts receivable for $900 and credited cash for $900 for receipt of monies from sales made on account, previously recorded.

(b) Cash collected on account was debited to cash for $900, and service revenue was credited for $90.

BRIEF EXERCISES

BE2.1 Determine effect on basic accounting equation.   **LO1**

Presented here are three economic events. On a sheet of paper, list the letters (a), (b) and (c) with columns for assets, liabilities and equity. In each column, indicate whether the event increased (+), decreased (−) or had no effect (NE) on assets, liabilities and equity.

(a) Purchased equipment on account.

(b) Received cash for providing a service.

(c) Received cash from a customer who had purchased goods the previous week on account.

BE2.2 Indicate debit and credit effects.   **LO3**

For each of the following accounts indicate the effect of a debit or a credit on the account and the normal balance.

(a) Accounts payable.

(b) Advertising expense.

(c) Service revenue.

(d) Accounts receivable.

(e) Retained earnings.

(f) Dividends.

BE2.3 Indicate basic debit–credit analysis.   **LO4**

Dudley Advertising Ltd had the following transactions during August of the current year. Indicate (a) the basic analysis and (b) the debit–credit analysis.

Aug.	1	Issued shares to investors in exchange for $15 000 cash.
	4	Paid insurance in advance for 6 months, $1800.
	16	Received $9000 from clients for services rendered.
	27	Paid secretary $500 salary.

BE2.4 Journalise transactions.   **LO5**

Use the data in BE2.3 and journalise the transactions. (Include narrations.)

BE2.5 Post journal entries to T accounts.   **LO7**

Selected transactions for Gonzales Ltd are presented in journal form (without narrations). Post the transactions to T accounts.

Date	Account name	Debit	Credit
May 5	Accounts receivable	13 200	
	Service revenue		13 200
12	Cash	12 400	
	Accounts receivable		12 400
15	Cash	12 000	
	Service revenue		12 000

BE2.6 Prepare a trial balance. **LO8**

From the ledger balances below, prepare a trial balance for Evans Ltd at 30 June 2019. All account balances are normal.

Accounts payable	$ 8 650	Service revenue	$11 500
Cash	6 400	Accounts receivable	5 600
Share capital	30 000	Salaries expense	9 000
Dividends	2 200	Rent expense	3 950
Equipment	23 000		

BE2.7 Prepare a corrected trial balance. **LO8**

An inexperienced bookkeeper prepared the following trial balance that does not balance. Prepare a correct trial balance, assuming all account balances are normal.

TIMARU LTD **Trial balance** as at 31 December 2019	Debit	Credit
Cash	$32 100	
Prepaid insurance		$ 1 500
Accounts payable		8 700
Revenue received in advance	3 500	
Share capital		25 000
Retained earnings		9 000
Dividends		4 500
Service revenue		34 800
Insurance expense	8 700	
Salaries expense	18 900	
Rent expense		15 300
	$63 200	$98 800

EXERCISES

E2.1 Analyse the effect of transactions. **LO1**

Selected transactions for Speedy Lawn Care Pty Ltd are listed here:
1. Issued shares to investors in exchange for cash.
2. Paid monthly rent.
3. Received cash from customers when service was rendered.
4. Invoiced customers for services performed.
5. Paid dividend to shareholders.
6. Incurred advertising expense on account.
7. Received cash from customers invoiced in (4).
8. Purchased additional equipment for cash.
9. Purchased equipment on account.

Required

Describe the effect of each transaction on assets, liabilities and equity. For example, the first answer is: (1) Increase in assets and increase in equity.

E2.2 Analyse transactions and calculate profit. **LO1**

An analysis of transactions for Foxes Ltd in August 2019, its first month of operations, is shown as follows. Each change in equity is explained.

	Cash	+	Accounts receivable	+	Supplies	+	Office equipment	=	Accounts payable	+	Equity	
1.	+$34 000										+$34 000	Issued share capital
2.	−4 000						+$10 000		+$6 000			
3.	−1 100				+$1 100							
4.	+21 800		+$5 600								+27 400	Service revenue
5.	−3 000								−3 000			
6.	−1 000										−1 000	Dividends
7.	−2 750										−2 750	Rent expense
8.	+3 200		−3 200									
9.	−5 700										−5 700	Salaries expense
10.									+1 500		−1 500	Electricity expense

Required

(a) Describe each transaction.

(b) Determine how much equity increased for the month.

(c) Calculate the profit for the month.

(d) Explain the relationship between profit and equity which is shown in the statement of financial position.

E2.3 Prepare financial statements.   LO1

The analysis of transactions for Foxes Ltd is presented in E2.2.

Required

Prepare a statement of profit or loss for August, a statement of financial position as at 31 August 2019 and a calculation of retained earnings.

E2.4 Identify debits, credits and normal balances.   LO3

Selected transactions for Expensive Designs Pty Ltd, an interior decorator in its first month of business, are as follows:

1. Issued shares to investors for $10 000 in cash.

2. Purchased used car for $5000 cash for use in business.

3. Purchased supplies on account for $500.

4. Invoiced customers $1800 for services performed.

5. Paid $200 cash for advertising start of business.

6. Received $700 cash from customers invoiced in transaction (4).

7. Paid creditor $300 cash on account.

8. Paid dividends of $400 cash to shareholders.

Required

For each transaction, indicate (a) the basic type of account debited and credited (asset, liability, equity), (b) the specific account debited and credited (cash, rent expense, service revenue etc.), (c) whether the specific account is increased or decreased, and (d) the normal balance of the specific account. Use the following format, in which transaction 1 is given as an example:

	Account debited				Account credited			
Transaction	(a) Basic type	(b) Specific account	(c) Effect	(d) Normal balance	(a) Basic type	(b) Specific account	(c) Effect	(d) Normal balance
1	Asset	Cash	Increase	Debit	Equity	Share capital	Increase	Credit

E2.5 Journalise transactions.   LO5

Data for Expensive Designs Pty Ltd, interior decorator, are presented in E2.4.

Required

Journalise the transactions. Narrations are required.

E2.6 Identify debits, credits and normal balances.   **LO3**

Selected transactions for Bookit Pty Ltd, a bookkeeping service in its first month of business, are as follows:

1. Issued shares to investors for $10 000 in cash.
2. Purchased used photocopier for $3000 on account, for use in business.
3. Purchased supplies on account for $400.
4. Invoiced customers $1800 for services performed.
5. Paid $300 cash for advertising start of business.
6. Received $1500 cash from customers invoiced in transaction (4).
7. Paid creditor $3400 cash on account.
8. Paid rent for month, $600 cash.

Required

For each transaction, indicate (a) the basic type of account debited and credited (asset, liability, equity), (b) the specific account debited and credited (cash, rent expense, service revenue etc.), (c) whether the specific account is increased or decreased, and (d) the normal balance of the specific account. Use the following format, in which transaction (1) is given as an example:

	Account debited				Account credited			
Transaction	(a) Basic type	(b) Specific account	(c) Effect	(d) Normal balance	(a) Basic type	(b) Specific account	(c) Effect	(d) Normal balance
1	Asset	Cash	Increase	Debit	Equity	Share capital	Increase	Credit

E2.7 Journalise transactions.   **LO5**

Data for Bookit Pty Ltd, a bookkeeping service, are presented in E2.6.

Required

Journalise the transactions. Narrations are required.

E2.8 Post journal entries and prepare a trial balance.   **LO7, 8**

Selected transactions from the journal of Ink Pad Printers Ltd during its first month of operations are presented here:

Date	Account name	Debit	Credit
Aug. 1	Cash	17 000	
	Share capital		17 000
10	Cash	12 400	
	Service revenue		12 400
12	Office equipment	4 000	
	Cash		1 000
	Bank loan		3 000
25	Accounts receivable	1 500	
	Service revenue		1 500
31	Cash	600	
	Accounts receivable		600

Required

(a) Post the transactions to T accounts.
(b) Prepare a trial balance as at 31 August 2020.

E2.9 Journalise transactions from T accounts and prepare a trial balance. **LO5, 8**

These simple T accounts summarise the ledger of Zebra Tours Ltd at the end of the first month of operations:

	Cash					Revenue received in advance	
Apr. 1	10 000	Apr. 15	750			Apr. 30	700
12	1 900	25	3 500				
29	200						
30	700						

	Accounts receivable					Share capital	
Apr. 7	2 400	Apr. 29	200			Apr. 1	10 000

	Supplies				Service revenue	
Apr. 4	4 800				Apr. 7	2 400
					12	1 900

	Accounts payable					Salaries expense	
Apr. 25	3 500	Apr. 4	4 800	Apr. 15	750		

Required

(a) Prepare in the order they occurred in the journal entries (including narrations) that resulted in the amounts posted to the account.

(b) Prepare a trial balance as at 30 April 2019.

E2.10 Analyse transactions, prepare journal entries, and post transactions to T accounts. **LO1, 5, 7**

Selected transactions for Ranch Ltd during its first month in business are presented below:

Sept.	1	Issued shares in exchange for $45 000 cash received from investors.
	5	Purchased equipment for $25 000, paying $10 000 in cash and the balance on account.
	25	Paid $7500 cash on balance owed for equipment.
	30	Paid $1000 cash dividend.

Ranch Ltd's chart of accounts shows: Cash (no. 100), Equipment (no. 120), Accounts payable (no. 200), Share capital (no. 300), and Dividends (no. 320).

Required

(a) Prepare an analysis of the September transactions. The column headings should be: Cash + Equipment = Accounts payable + Equity. For transactions affecting equity, provide explanations at the side, as shown in figure 2.2.

(b) Journalise the transactions. Narrations are required.

(c) Post the transactions to T accounts.

E2.11 Analyse errors and their effects on trial balance. **LO8**

The bookkeeper for Equipment Repair Pty Ltd made these errors in journalising and posting:

1. A credit posting of $600 to accounts payable was omitted.

2. A debit posting of $750 for prepaid insurance was debited to insurance expense.

3. A collection on account of $100 was journalised and posted as a debit to cash $100 and a credit to service revenue $100.

4. A credit posting of $300 to rates and taxes payable was made twice.

5. A cash purchase of supplies for $250 was journalised and posted as a debit to supplies $25 and a credit to cash $25.

6. A debit of $465 to advertising expense was posted as $456.

Required

(a) For each error, indicate (a) whether the trial balance will balance; if the trial balance will not balance, indicate (b) the amount of the difference and (c) the trial balance column that will have the greater total. Consider each error separately. Use the following form, in which error 1 is given as an example:

	(a)	(b)	(c)
Error	In balance	Difference	Column with larger total
1	No	$600	Debit

(b) Describe the types of errors a trial balance will not detect.

E2.12 Prepare a trial balance.   **LO8**

The accounts in the ledger of Sushi To Go Ltd contain the following balances on 31 July 2019:

Accounts receivable	$ 27 184	Prepaid insurance	$ 3 836
Accounts payable	14 692	Repair expense	1 822
Cash	?	Service revenue	31 220
Delivery equipment	118 620	Dividends	1 300
Fuel expense	1 416	Share capital	79 900
Insurance expense	946	Salaries expense	8 756
Bank loan	56 800	Salaries payable	1 530
		Retained earnings	9 172

Required

Prepare a trial balance with the accounts arranged as illustrated in this chapter, and fill in the missing amount for cash.

E2.13 Prepare a trial balance.   **LO8**

The accounts in the ledger of Boxer Ltd contain the following balances on 31 March 2020:

Accounts receivable	$ 13 450	Prepaid insurance	$ 6 345
Accounts payable	23 774	Repair expense	3 421
Cash	76 526	Service revenue	67 589
Delivery equipment	165 000	Dividends	2 700
Fuel expense	7 890	Share capital	112 000
Insurance expense	4 568	Salaries expense	23 700
Bank loan	75 000	Salaries payable	3 460
		Retained earnings	?

Required

Prepare a trial balance with the accounts arranged as illustrated in the chapter, and fill in the missing amount for retained earnings.

PROBLEM SET A

PSA2.1 Analyse transactions and calculate profit.   **LO1**

On 1 April, Let's Go Travel Agency Ltd was established. These transactions were completed during the month:

1. Shareholders invested $40 000 cash in the company in exchange for shares.
2. Paid $800 cash for April office rent.
3. Purchased office equipment for $5000 cash.
4. Incurred $600 of advertising costs in *The Australian*, on account.
5. Paid $1200 for office supplies.
6. $18 000 of services was provided: cash of $2000 was received from customers, and the balance of $16 000 was invoiced to customers on account.

7. Paid $400 cash dividends.
8. Paid *The Australian* amount due in transaction (4).
9. Paid employees' salaries, $2400.
10. Received $16 000 in cash from customers who had previously been invoiced in transaction (6).

Required

(a) Prepare a transaction analysis using these column headings: Cash, Accounts receivable, Supplies, Office equipment, Accounts payable, Share capital, and Retained earnings. Include in the margin all explanations for any changes in retained earnings.

(b) From an analysis of the column Retained earnings, calculate profit or loss for April.

PSA2.2 Analyse transactions and prepare financial statements.   **LO1**

Aurora Goodwin started her own consulting firm, Best Consulting Pty Ltd, on 1 May 2019. The following transactions occurred during the month of May:

May	1	Shareholders invested $10 000 cash in the business.
	2	Paid $1050 for office rent for the month.
	3	Purchased $250 of supplies on account.
	5	Paid $75 to advertise in the *Auckland News*.
	9	Received $1250 cash for services provided.
	12	Paid $100 for telephone.
	15	Performed $3500 of services on account.
	17	Paid $2000 for employee salaries.
	20	Paid for the supplies purchased on account on 3 May.
	23	Received a cash payment of $2250 for services provided on account on 15 May.
	26	Borrowed $2500 from the bank.
	29	Purchased office equipment for $1200 on account.
	30	Paid $125 for electricity.

Required

(a) Show the effects of the previous transactions on the accounting equation using the following format:

			Assets					Liabilities			Equity	
Date	Cash	+	Accounts receivable	+	Supplies	+	Office equipment	=	Bank loan	+	Accounts payable	+	Share capital	+	Retained earnings

Include margin explanations for any changes in retained earnings.

(b) Prepare a statement of profit or loss for the month of May.

(c) Prepare a statement of financial position as at 31 May 2019.

PSA2.3 Analyse transactions and prepare financial statements.   **LO1**

Ivan Izo started a business providing legal services, Ivan Izo Pty Ltd, on 1 July 2019. On 31 July the statement of financial position showed: cash $4000; accounts receivable $1500; supplies $500; office equipment $5000; accounts payable $4200; share capital $6500; and retained earnings $300. During August the following transactions occurred:

1. Collected $1400 of amounts owing from accounts receivable.
2. Paid $2700 cash of the balance of accounts payable.
3. Recorded revenue of $6400, of which $3000 was collected in cash and the balance is due in September.
4. Purchased additional office equipment for $1000, paying $400 in cash and the balance on account.
5. Paid salaries $1500, rent for August $900, and advertising expenses $350.

6. Declared and paid a cash dividend of $550.

7. Borrowed $2000 from Kati Kati Bank.

8. Incurred electricity expense for the month of $250 on account.

Required

(a) Prepare a transaction analysis of the August transactions beginning with 31 July balances. The column headings should be: Cash + Accounts receivable + Supplies + Office equipment = Bank loan + Accounts payable + Share capital + Retained earnings. Include in the margin explanations for any changes in retained earnings.

(b) Prepare a statement of profit or loss for August, and a classified statement of financial position as at 31 August.

PSA2.4 **Journalise a series of transactions.** **LO3, 5**

Fantasy Miniature Golf and Driving Range Pty Ltd was opened on 1 March by Jim Zarle. These selected events and transactions occurred during March:

Mar.	1	Shareholders invested $60 000 cash in the business in exchange for shares in the company.
	3	Purchased Lee's Golf Land for $38 000 cash. The price consists of land $23 000, building $9000, and equipment $6000.
	5	Advertised the opening of the driving range and miniature golf course, paying advertising expenses of $1600 cash.
	6	Paid cash $1480 for a 1-year insurance policy.
	10	Purchased golf clubs and other equipment for $1600 from Golf Australia, payable in 30 days.
	18	Received golf fees of $800 in cash for games played in March.
	19	Sold 100 voucher books for $15.00 each in cash. Each book contains 10 vouchers that enable the holder to play one round of miniature golf or to hit one bucket of golf balls. (*Hint:* The revenue is recorded as revenue received in advance until the customers use the vouchers.)
	25	Paid a $500 cash dividend.
	30	Paid salaries of $600.
	30	Paid Golf Australia in full.
	31	Received $800 of fees in cash.

The company uses these accounts: Cash (no. 100), Prepaid insurance (no. 112), Land (no. 130), Buildings (no. 135), Equipment (no. 138), Accounts payable (no. 200), Golf revenue received in advance (no. 213), Share capital (no. 300), Retained earnings (no. 310), Dividends (no. 320), Golf revenue (no. 400), Advertising expense (no. 500) and Salaries expense (no. 510).

Required

Journalise the March transactions. Include narrations.

PSA2.5 **Journalise transactions, post, and prepare a trial balance.** **LO3, 5, 6, 7, 8**

Mahon Consultants Pty Ltd opened as licensed architects on 1 April 2019. During the first month of the operation of the business, these events and transactions occurred:

Apr.	1	Shareholders invested $76 500 cash in exchange for shares.
	1	Hired a personal assistant at a salary of $5850 per month, payable monthly.
	2	Paid office rent for the month, $2850.
	3	Purchased drawing supplies on account from Speedy Supplies Ltd, $7650.
	10	Completed a contract and invoiced client $4050 for services.
	11	Received $1650 cash advance from R. Welk for the design of an extension.
	20	Received $9450 cash for services completed for P. Donahue.
	30	Paid assistant for the month, $5850.
	30	Paid $3450 owed to Speedy Supplies Ltd.

Mahon Consultants Pty Ltd uses these accounts: Cash (no. 100), Accounts receivable (no. 110), Supplies (no. 115), Accounts payable (no. 200), Revenue received in advance (no. 209), Share capital (no. 300), Service revenue (no. 400), Salaries expense (no. 500), and Rent expense (no. 510).

Required

(a) Journalise the transactions. Include narrations.

(b) Post to the ledger T accounts.

(c) Prepare a trial balance on 30 April 2019.

PSA2.6 Journalise transactions, post and prepare a trial balance.   **LO3, 5, 6, 7, 8**

This is the trial balance of Lou Lou's Beauty Centre Pty Ltd on 30 September:

	LOU LOU'S BEAUTY CENTRE PTY LTD Trial balance as at 30 September 2019		
No.	Account name	Debit	Credit
100	Cash	$32 800	
115	Accounts receivable	7 600	
120	Supplies	5 600	
130	Equipment	30 800	
200	Accounts payable		$18 800
210	Revenue received in advance		1 600
300	Share capital		56 400
		$76 800	$76 800

The October transactions were as follows:

Oct.	5	Received $2400 cash from customers on account.
	10	Invoiced customers for services performed, $12 800.
	15	Paid employee salaries, $3600.
	17	Performed $1200 of services for customers who paid in advance in September for suntanning sessions to be used in October.
	20	Paid $5200 to creditors on account.
	29	Paid a $800 cash dividend.
	31	Paid electricity, $1600.

Required

(a) Prepare a general ledger using T accounts. Enter the opening balances in the ledger accounts as of 1 October. Provision should be made for these additional accounts: Dividends (no. 310), Service revenue (no. 400), Salaries expense (no. 500), and Electricity expense (no. 510).

(b) Journalise the transactions, including narrations.

(c) Post to the ledger accounts, which you prepared in part (a).

(d) Prepare a trial balance as at 31 October 2019.

PSA2.7 Journalise transactions, post, and prepare a trial balance.   **LO3, 5, 6, 7, 8**

This is the trial balance of Western Laundry Services Pty Ltd on 30 April:

	WESTERN LAUNDRY SERVICES PTY LTD Trial balance as at 30 April 2019		
No.	Account name	Debit	Credit
100	Cash	$ 4 250	
115	Accounts receivable	1 100	

No.	Account name	Debit	Credit
120	Supplies	850	
130	Equipment	4 000	
200	Accounts payable		$ 2 500
210	Revenue received in advance		350
300	Share capital		7 350
		$10 200	$10 200

The May transactions were as follows:

May	2	Received $450 cash from customers on account.
	8	Invoiced customers for services performed, $1750.
	12	Paid employee salaries, $600.
	15	Performed $300 of services for customers who paid in advance in April for services to be performed in May.
	18	Paid $800 to creditors on account.
	25	Paid a $250 cash dividend.
	31	Paid electricity, $350.

Required

(a) Prepare a general ledger using T accounts. Enter the opening balances in the ledger accounts as of 1 May. Provision should be made for these additional accounts: Dividends (no. 310), Service revenue (no. 400), Salaries expense (no. 500), and Electricity expense (no. 510).

(b) Journalise the transactions, including narrations.

(c) Post to the ledger accounts, which you prepared in part (a).

(d) Prepare a trial balance as at 31 May 2019.

PSA2.8 **Journalise transactions, post, and prepare a trial balance.** **LO3, 5, 6, 7, 8**

The Drive-in Movie Palace Ltd was recently formed. It began operations in March 2019. The Movie Palace is unique in that it is a drive-in theatre and will show only triple features of sequential theme movies. As of 28 February, the ledger of The Drive-in Movie Palace Ltd showed: (100) Cash $19 100; (110) Equipment $19 100; (120) Land $45 100; (130) Buildings $21 100; (200) Accounts payable $15 100; and (300) Share capital $89 300. During the month of March the following events and transactions occurred:

Mar.	2	Acquired the first three *Bourne* movies (*The Bourne Identity*, *The Bourne Supremacy* and *The Bourne Ultimatum*) to be shown for the first 3 weeks of March. The film rental was $15 100; $8000 was paid in cash and $7100 will be paid on 10 March.
	3	Ordered the *Iron Man* trilogy to be shown on the last 10 days of March. It will cost $500 per night.
	9	Received $11 600 cash from admissions.
	10	Paid balance due on the *Bourne* movies rental and $7100 on 28 February accounts payable.
	11	Hired B. Barista to operate a coffee cart. Barista agrees to pay The Drive-in Movie Palace Ltd 20% of gross receipts, payable monthly.
	12	Paid advertising expenses, $3900.
	20	Received $10 300 cash from admissions.
	20	Received the *Iron Man* movies and paid rental fee of $5000.
	31	Paid salaries of $6900.
	31	Received statement from B. Barista showing gross receipts from coffee cart sales of $11 100 and the balance due to The Drive-in Movie Palace Ltd of $2220 for March. B. Barista paid half the balance due and will remit the remainder on 5 April.
	31	Received $21 600 cash from admissions.

In addition to the accounts identified above, the chart of accounts includes: (105) Accounts receivable, (400) Admission revenue, (410) Coffee cart revenue, (500) Advertising expense, (510) Film rental expense, and (520) Salaries expense.

Required

(a) Using T accounts, enter the beginning balances in the ledger.

(b) Journalise the March transactions, including narrations.

(c) Post the March journal entries to the ledger accounts you prepared in part (a).

(d) Prepare a trial balance as at 31 March 2019.

PSA2.9 Prepare a correct trial balance. **LO8**

This trial balance of Queenstown Ltd does not balance.

QUEENSTOWN LTD Trial balance as at 30 June 2020		
Account name	Debit	Credit
Cash		$ 17 940
Accounts receivable	$21 093	
Supplies	5 700	
Equipment	18 900	
Accounts payable		16 896
Revenue received in advance	8 100	
Share capital		60 000
Dividends	5 700	
Service revenue		15 180
Salaries expense	21 300	
Office expense	6 360	
	$87 153	$110 016

Each of the listed accounts has a normal balance. An examination of the ledger and journal reveals the following errors:

1. Cash received from a customer on account was debited to cash for $3420, and accounts receivable was credited for the same amount. The actual collection was for $4320.

2. The purchase of a scientific calculator on account for $500 was recorded as a debit to supplies for $500 and a credit to accounts payable for $500.

3. Services were performed on account for a client for $6240. Accounts receivable was debited for $6240 and service revenue was credited for $624.

4. A debit posting to salaries expense of $4500 was omitted.

5. A payment on account for $2136 was credited to cash for $2136 and credited to accounts payable for $2163.

6. Payment of a $3300 cash dividend to Queenstown Ltd's shareholders was debited to salaries expense for $3300 and credited to cash for $3300.

Required

(a) Prepare the correct trial balance.

(b) Explain what adjustments were made and why they were necessary.

PSA2.10 Prepare a correct trial balance.

This trial balance of Helpful Services Ltd does not balance.

HELPFUL SERVICES LTD Trial balance as at 30 June 2019		
Account name	Debit	Credit
Cash		$ 5 680
Accounts receivable	$ 6 462	
Supplies	1 600	
Equipment	6 000	
Accounts payable		5 332
Revenue received in advance	2 400	
Share capital		18 000
Dividends	1 600	
Rental revenue		4 760
Salaries expense	6 800	
Office expense	1 820	
	$26 682	$33 772

Each of the listed accounts has a normal balance. An examination of the ledger and journal reveals the following errors:

1. Cash received from a customer on account was debited to cash for $1140, and accounts receivable was credited for the same amount. The actual collection was for $1500.
2. The purchase of a printer on account for $680 was recorded as a debit to supplies for $680 and a credit to accounts payable for $680.
3. Services were performed on account for a client for $1780. Accounts receivable was debited for $1780 and service revenue was credited for $178.
4. A debit posting to salaries expense of $1200 was omitted.
5. A payment on account for $412 was credited to cash for $412 and credited to accounts payable for $520.
6. Payment of an $800 cash dividend to shareholders was debited to salaries expense for $800 and credited to cash for $800.

Required

(a) Prepare the correct trial balance.
(b) Explain what adjustments were made and why they were necessary.

PROBLEM SET B

PSB2.1 Analyse transactions and calculate profit.

Crazy Bob's Repair Shop Ltd was started on 1 May. Here is a summary of the May transactions:

1. Shareholders invested $16 000 cash in the company in exchange for shares.
2. Purchased equipment for $5000 cash.
3. Paid $400 cash for May office rent.
4. Paid $500 cash for supplies.
5. Incurred $550 of advertising costs in the *North Shore Times* on account.
6. Received $4100 in cash from customers for repair service.
7. Declared and paid a $500 cash dividend.
8. Paid part-time employee salaries, $1200.
9. Paid electricity bill, $140.
10. Provided repair service on account to customers, $400.
11. Collected cash of $120 for services invoiced in transaction (10).

Required

(a) Prepare a transaction analysis using these column headings: Cash, Accounts receivable, Supplies, Equipment, Accounts payable, Share capital, and Retained earnings. Revenue is called service revenue. Include in the margin explanations for any changes in retained earnings.

(b) From an analysis of the column retained earnings, calculate the profit or loss for May.

PSB2.2 Analyse transactions and prepare financial statements. **LO1**

Alex Rogers started his own delivery service, Rogers Deliveries Ltd, on 1 June 2019. The following transactions occurred during the month of June:

June	1	Shareholders invested $30 000 cash in the business in exchange for shares.
	2	Purchased a used van for deliveries for $20 000. Rogers paid $4000 cash and the remaining balance was on account.
	3	Paid $1000 for office rent for the month.
	5	Performed $2000 of services on account.
	9	Paid $400 in cash dividends.
	12	Purchased supplies for $300 on account.
	15	Received a cash payment of $1500 for services provided on 5 June.
	17	Purchased petrol for $200 on account.
	20	Received a cash payment of $3000 for services provided.
	23	Made a cash payment of $1000 on the amount owing for the delivery van purchased on 2 June.
	26	Paid $500 for electricity.
	29	Paid for the petrol purchased on account on 17 June.
	30	Paid $1000 for employee salaries.

Required

(a) Show the effects of the previous transactions on the accounting equation using the following format:

		Assets					Liabilities		Equity		
Date	Cash	+	Accounts receivable	+	Supplies	+	Delivery van	=	Accounts payable	+	Share capital	+	Retained earnings

Include in the margin explanations for any changes in retained earnings.

(b) Prepare a statement of profit or loss for the month of June.

(c) Prepare a statement of financial position at 30 June 2019.

PSB2.3 Analyse transactions and prepare a statement of profit or loss and a statement of financial position. **LO1**

Donna Corso opened Healthy Paws Ltd, a veterinary business, on 1 August 2019. On 31 August the statement of financial position showed: Cash $9000; Accounts receivable $1700; Supplies $600; Office equipment $6000; Accounts payable $3600; Share capital $13 000; and Retained earnings $700. During September the following transactions occurred:

1. Paid $3100 cash on accounts payable.
2. Collected $1300 of accounts receivable.
3. Purchased additional office equipment for $4100, paying $800 in cash and the balance on account.
4. Earned a revenue of $8900, of which $2500 was paid in cash and the balance is due in October.
5. Declared and paid a $600 cash dividend.
6. Paid salaries $700, rent for September $900, and advertising expense $300.
7. Incurred electricity expense for month on account, $170.
8. Borrowed $7000 from Westpac Bank.

Required

(a) Prepare a transaction analysis of the September transactions beginning with 31 August balances. The column headings should be: Cash + Accounts receivable + Supplies + Office equipment = Bank loan + Accounts payable + Share capital + Retained earnings. Include in the margin explanations for any changes in retained earnings.

(b) Prepare a statement of profit or loss for September, a calculation of retained earnings for September, and a classified statement of financial position at 30 September 2019.

PSB2.4 Journalise a series of transactions. **LO3, 5**

Just for Fun Park was started on 1 April by Greg Winters. These selected events and transactions occurred during April:

Apr.	1	Shareholders invested $90 000 cash in the business in exchange for shares.
	4	Purchased land costing $45 000 for cash.
	8	Incurred advertising expense of $2700 on account.
	11	Paid salaries to employees, $2550.
	12	Hired park manager at a salary of $6000 per month, effective 1 May.
	13	Paid $4500 for a 1-year insurance policy.
	17	Paid $900 cash dividends.
	20	Received $8550 in cash for admission fees.
	25	Sold 150 voucher books for $25 each. Each book contains 10 vouchers that entitle the holder to one admission to the park. (*Hint:* The revenue is recorded as revenue received in advance until the vouchers are used.)
	30	Received $11 850 in cash admission fees.
	30	Paid $1050 on account for advertising incurred on 8 April.

Just for Fun Park uses the following accounts: Cash, Prepaid insurance, Land, Accounts payable, Revenue received in advance, Share capital, Dividends, Admission revenue, Advertising expense, and Salaries expense.

Required

Journalise the April transactions, including narrations.

PSB2.5 Journalise transactions, post, prepare a trial balance and financial statements.

LO3, 5, 6, 7, 8

Diane Smith incorporated Accurate Accountants, an accounting practice, on 1 May 2019. During the first month of operations of her business, these events and transactions occurred:

May	1	Shareholders invested $156 000 cash in exchange for shares in the company.
	2	Hired a receptionist at a salary of $3000 per month.
	3	Purchased $3600 of supplies on account from Read Supply Ltd.
	7	Paid office rent of $2700 for the month.
	11	Completed a tax return and invoiced the client $3300 for services provided.
	12	Received $13 500 advance on a management consulting engagement.
	17	Received cash of $3600 for services completed for H. Arnold Ltd.
	31	Paid receptionist $3000 salary for the month.
	31	Paid 40% of balance owing to Read Supply Ltd.

The following chart of accounts is used: (100) Cash, (110) Accounts receivable, (115) Supplies, (200) Accounts payable, (210) Revenue received in advance, (300) Share capital, (400) Service revenue, (500) Salaries expense, and (510) Rent expense.

Required

(a) Journalise the transactions, including narrations.

(b) Post to the ledger T accounts.

(c) Prepare a trial balance on 31 May 2019.

(d) Prepare a statement of profit or loss for the month of May and a classified statement of financial position as at 31 May 2019.

PSB2.6 Journalise transactions, post, prepare a trial balance and financial statements. LO3, 5, 6, 7, 8

The trial balance of Wellington Dry Cleaners on 30 June is given here:

No.	Account name	Debit	Credit
	WELLINGTON DRY CLEANERS **Trial balance** **as at 30 June 2019**		
100	Cash	$25 064	
110	Accounts receivable	21 072	
120	Supplies	9 688	
130	Equipment	51 900	
200	Accounts payable		$31 756
210	Revenue received in advance		3 460
300	Share capital		72 508
		$107 724	$107 724

The July transactions were as follows:

July	8	Collected $9872 in cash for previous month's credit sales.
	9	Paid employee salaries, $4200.
	11	Received $9850 in cash for services provided.
	14	Paid 30 June creditors $21 500 on account.
	17	Purchased supplies on account, $1108.
	22	Invoiced customers for services provided, $9400.
	30	Paid employee salaries $6228, electricity $3168, and repairs $984.
	31	Paid $1000 cash dividend.

Required

(a) Prepare a general ledger using T accounts. Enter the opening balances in the ledger accounts as of 1 July. Provision should be made for the following additional accounts: (310) Dividends, (400) Dry cleaning revenue, (500) Repair expense, (510) Salaries expense, and (520) Electricity expense.
(b) Journalise the transactions.
(c) Post to the ledger accounts, which you prepared in part (a).
(d) Prepare a trial balance on 31 July 2019.
(e) Prepare a statement of profit or loss for July and a classified statement of financial position as at 31 July 2019.

PSB2.7 Journalise transactions, post, prepare a trial balance and financial statements.

LO3, 5, 6, 7, 8

Maria George incorporated Busy Bookkeepers Pty Ltd, a bookkeeping practice, on 1 January 2019. During the first month of operations, these events and transactions occurred:

Jan.	2	Shareholders invested $88 000 cash in exchange for shares in the company.
	3	Hired a receptionist at a salary of $2000 per month.
	4	Purchased $1600 of supplies on account from Abbey Supply Ltd.
	7	Paid office rent of $2400 for the month.
	11	Invoiced clients $3800 for services provided.
	12	Received $3000 advance on a management consulting engagement.
	17	Received cash of $1600 for services completed for Pete's Plumbing. (These services were not included in the 11 January transaction.)
	31	Paid receptionist $2000 salary for the month.
	31	Paid 40% of balance owing to Abbey Supply Ltd.

The following chart of accounts is used: (100) Cash, (110) Accounts receivable, (115) Supplies, (200) Accounts payable, (210) Revenue received in advance, (300) Share capital, (400) Service revenue, (500) Salaries expense, and (510) Rent expense.

Required

(a) Journalise the transactions, including narrations.

(b) Post to the ledger T accounts.

(c) Prepare a trial balance as at 31 January 2019.

(d) Prepare a statement of profit or loss for the month of January and a classified statement of financial position as at 31 January 2019.

PSB2.8 Journalise transactions, post, prepare a trial balance and financial statements.

LO3, 5, 6, 7, 8

Lights Out Theatre Ltd was recently formed. All facilities were completed on 31 March 2019. On 1 April, the ledger showed: (100) Cash $6000; (120) Land $10 000; (130) Buildings $8000; (140) Equipment $6000; (200) Accounts payable $2000; (210) Mortgage payable $8000; and (300) Share capital $20 000. During April, the following events and transactions occurred:

Apr.	2	Paid film rental of $800 on first movie.
	3	Ordered two additional films at $700 each.
	9	Received $3800 cash from admissions.
	10	Made $2000 payment on mortgage and $1000 on accounts payable.
	11	Hired R. Thoms to operate a candy bar. Thoms agreed to pay Lights Out Theatre 17% of gross receipts, payable monthly.
	12	Paid advertising expenses, $300.
	20	Received one of the films ordered on 3 April and was invoiced $500. The film will be shown in April.
	25	Received $3200 cash from admissions.
	29	Paid salaries, $1600.
	30	Received statement from R. Thoms showing gross receipts of $1000 and the balance due to Lights Out Theatre of $170 for April. Thoms paid half of the balance due and will remit the remainder on 5 May.
	30	Prepaid $700 rental on special film to be run in May.

In addition to the accounts identified above, the chart of accounts shows: (105) Accounts receivable, (107) Prepaid rentals, (400) Admission revenue, (410) Candy bar revenue, (510) Advertising expense, (520) Film rental expense, (530) Salaries expense.

Required

(a) Enter the beginning balances in the ledger T accounts as of 1 April.

(b) Journalise the April transactions, including narrations.

(c) Post the April journal entries to the ledger T accounts prepared in part (a).

(d) Prepare a trial balance on 30 April 2019.

(e) Prepare a statement of profit or loss for April and a classified statement of financial position as at 30 April 2019.

PSB2.9 Prepare a correct trial balance.

LO8

This trial balance for Theatre Adelaide Ltd does not balance.

THEATRE ADELAIDE LTD Trial balance as at 31 May 2019		
Account name	Debit	Credit
Cash	$ 5 850	
Accounts receivable		$ 2 750
Prepaid insurance	700	
Equipment	8 000	

Account name	Debit	Credit
Accounts payable		4 500
Rates and taxes payable	560	
Share capital		5 700
Retained earnings		6 000
Service revenue	6 690	
Salaries expense	4 200	
Advertising expense		1 100
Rates and taxes expense	800	
	$26 800	$20 050

Your review of the ledger reveals that each account has a normal balance. You also discover the following errors:

1. The totals of the debit sides of prepaid insurance, accounts payable, and rates and taxes expense were each understated $100.
2. Transposition errors were made in accounts receivable and service revenue. Based on postings made, the correct balances were $2570 and $6960, respectively.
3. A debit posting to salaries expense of $200 was omitted.
4. A $700 cash dividend was debited to share capital for $700 and credited to cash for $700.
5. A $420 purchase of supplies on account was debited to equipment for $420 and credited to cash for $420.
6. A cash payment of $250 for advertising was debited to advertising expense for $25 and credited to cash for $25.
7. A collection from a customer for $210 was debited to cash for $210 and credited to accounts payable for $210.

Required

(a) Prepare the correct trial balance. (*Note:* The chart of accounts also includes the following: Dividends, Supplies, and Supplies expense.)
(b) Explain what adjustments were made and why they were necessary.

PSB2.10 **Prepare a correct trial balance.**   **LO8**
This trial balance for Glasgow Pty Ltd does not balance.

GLASGOW PTY LTD Trial balance as at 31 December 2019		
Account name	Debit	Credit
Cash		$ 7 804
Accounts receivable	$ 9 736	
Supplies	3 640	
Equipment	9 560	
Accounts payable		10 798
Revenue received in advance	3 200	
Share capital		18 000
Dividends	1 200	
Service revenue		19 808
Salaries expense	12 600	
Office expense	4 820	
	$44 756	$56 410

Each of the listed accounts has a normal balance. An examination of the ledger and journal reveals the following errors:

1. Cash received from a customer on account was debited to cash for $1680 and accounts receivable was credited for the same amount. The actual collection was for $960.
2. The purchase of a printer on account for $440 was recorded as a debit to supplies for $440 and a credit to accounts payable for $440.
3. Services were performed on account for a client for $1280. Accounts receivable was debited $1280 and service revenue was credited $128.
4. A debit posting to salaries expense of $1800 was omitted.
5. A payment made on account for $818 was credited to cash for $818 and credited to accounts payable for $980.
6. Payment of a $1200 cash dividend to shareholders was debited to salaries expense for $1200 and credited to cash for $1200.

Required

(a) Prepare the correct trial balance.
(b) Explain what adjustments were made and why they were necessary.

BUILDING BUSINESS SKILLS

FINANCIAL REPORTING AND ANALYSIS

Financial reporting problem: Giorgina's Pizza Limited

BBS2.1 The financial statements of Giorgina's (found in chapter 1, figures 1.13 and 1.15) contain the following selected accounts, all in thousands of dollars:

	2019 $'000
Issued capital	30 640
Trade and other payables (accounts payable)	28 541
Trade and other receivables (accounts receivable)	19 809
Marketing expenses	8 573
Inventories	5 014
Property, plant and equipment (net book value)	37 270
Sales revenue	141 473

Required

(a) What is the increase and decrease side for each account? What is the normal balance for each account?
(b) Identify the probable other account in the transaction and the effect on that account when:
1. Accounts receivable is decreased.
2. Accounts payable is decreased.
3. Prepaid expenses (prepayments) is increased.
(c) Identify the other account(s) that ordinarily would be involved when:
1. Marketing expense is increased.
2. Property, plant and equipment is increased.

Comparative analysis problem: Giorgina's Pizza Limited vs. Freedom Foods Group Limited

BBS2.2 Refer to the financial statements for Giorgina's Pizza Limited from chapter 1 and to the financial statements of Freedom Foods Group (www.freedomfoods.com.au).

Required

(a) Determine the normal balance for each of the accounts listed as follows for Giorgina's Pizza Limited and Freedom Foods Group Limited.

Giorgina's Pizza Limited	Freedom Foods Group Limited
1. Cash	1. Inventories
2. Goodwill	2. Current tax liabilities
3. Borrowings	3. Provisions
4. Retained earnings	4. Issued capital
5. Sales revenue	5. Administrative expenses

(b) Identify the other account ordinarily involved when:
1. Accounts receivable is decreased.
2. Bank loan is increased.
3. Equipment is increased.
4. Sales revenue is increased.

Interpreting financial statements

BBS2.3 Obtain the latest annual report of a public company.

Address: www.asx.com.au or www.nzx.com

Steps:
1. On the Australian Securities Exchange home page, you will notice a blue banner across the top of the page. Click on the **Prices and research** button and a drop down menu will appear. Click on **Company information** which will take you to a page where you can search for individual companies.

   There is also a heading for New Zealand-based companies dual listed in Australia and New Zealand.
2. You are now at the index for listed companies. Choose a letter and select a particular company (don't just choose the first company) by clicking on the ASX code.
3. From this page browse down to the internet address and click on the address which will take you to the company's web site.
4. From the web site, search around and find the latest annual report.

OR

For the New Zealand Stock Exchange:
1. Go to the home page and click on **MARKETS** on the top menu and select **NZX Main Board**.
2. This will take you to a side menu. Click on **All Securities**. You are now at the index for listed entities.
3. Scroll down the names and click on a company. This will take you to its page, click on the company name at the right and under Contact information you will see the company's web site address.

Required

Answer the following questions:
(a) What company did you select? Please also provide the web address and date you accessed the web site.
(b) Search the annual report you selected and provide the following information and reference in the annual report where you found the information; for example, trade and other receivables in the statement of financial position, page 31.
   1. Principal activities.
   2. The number of controlled entities/subsidiaries and the countries in which they operate.
   3. The percentage ownership in the company of the 20 largest shareholders.
   4. The number of directors.
   5. The accounting policy for depreciation.
   6. The amount of income tax expense and the profit for the year.
   7. Name of its auditors.
   8. List the business segments.

9. The amount of current assets.
10. The amount of net cash flows from operating activities.
11. The amount of dividends paid.
12. Describe any related party transactions.

CRITICAL THINKING
Group decision case
BBS2.4 Mark Dingo operates Supreme Riding School Pty Ltd. The riding school's main sources of revenue are riding fees and lesson fees, which are provided on a cash basis. Mark also boards horses for owners, who are invoiced monthly for boarding fees. In a few cases, boarders pay in advance of expected use. For its revenue transactions, the riding school maintains these accounts: Cash, Accounts receivable, Revenue received in advance, Riding revenue, Lesson revenue, and Boarding revenue.

The riding school owns 20 horses, a stable, a riding field, riding equipment and office equipment. These assets are accounted for in accounts: Horses, Building, Riding field, Riding equipment, and Office equipment.

The riding school employs stable helpers and an office worker, who receive weekly salaries. At the end of each month, the mail usually brings invoices for advertising, electricity and veterinary services. Other expenses include feed for the horses and insurance. The riding school also maintains the following accounts: Hay and feed supplies, Prepaid insurance, Accounts payable, Salaries payable, Salaries expense, Advertising expense, Electricity expense, Veterinary expense, Hay and feed expense, and Insurance expense.

Mark Dingo's sole source of personal income is dividends from the riding school. Thus, the business declares and pays periodic dividends. To record equity in the business and dividends, two accounts are maintained: Share capital and Dividends.

During the first month of operations an inexperienced bookkeeper was employed. Mark asks you to review the following nine general journal entries of the 50 entries made during the month. In each case, the explanation for the entry is correct.

May	1	Cash	200 000	
		Share capital		200 000
		(Issued shares in exchange for $200 000 cash)		
	2	Salaries expense	10 000	
		Salaries payable		10 000
		(Hired employees' services for the month)		
	5	Cash	5 000	
		Accounts receivable		5 000
		(Received $5000 cash for lesson fees)		
	7	Cash	5 000	
		Boarding revenue		5 000
		(Received $5000 for boarding of horses beginning 1 June)		
	9	Hay and feed expense	10 000	
		Cash		10 000
		(Purchased estimated 5 months' supply of feed and hay for $10 000 on account)		
	14	Riding equipment	2 500	
		Cash		2 500
		(Purchased desk and other office equipment for $2500 cash)		
	15	Salaries expense	6 000	
		Cash		6 000
		(Issued cheque to Mark Dingo for personal use)		

May	20	Cash	13 500	
		Riding revenue		13 500
		(Received $13 500 cash for riding fees)		
	31	Veterinary expense	6 750	
		Accounts receivable		6 750
		(Received invoice of $6750 from veterinarian for services provided)		

Required

With the class divided into groups, answer the following:

(a) State which journal entries are correct. For each journal entry that is incorrect, prepare the entry that should have been made by the bookkeeper.

(b) Which of the incorrect entries would prevent the trial balance from balancing?

(c) What was the correct profit for May, assuming the bookkeeper originally reported profit of $15 100 after posting all 50 entries? (*Hint:* Assume errors occurred only in the nine entries reported, i.e. the remaining 41 entries were recorded correctly.)

(d) What was the correct cash balance at 31 May, assuming the bookkeeper reported a balance of only $20 650 after posting all 50 entries?

Communication activity

BBS2.5 Fancy Flowers Ltd provides a flower delivery service. Two recurring transactions for the business are invoicing customers for services provided and paying employee salaries. For example, on 15 March invoices totalling $8500 were sent to customers, and $3200 was paid in salaries to employees.

Required

Write a memorandum to the new assistant accountant at Fancy Flowers that explains and illustrates the steps in the recording process for each of the 15 March transactions. Use the format demonstrated in this text under the heading 'The recording process illustrated' (in section 2.7).

BBS2.6 John Jones, a new university graduate, has just been appointed as an assistant accountant in the small business division of a public accounting practice. One of John's first tasks is to verify the balances in the ledger of a new client. A trial balance listing was completed but it did not balance.

Required

Write a memorandum to John Jones explaining the purpose of the trial balance, outlining the types of recording errors a trial balance will and will not detect.

Ethics case

BBS2.7 Answer the following questions on ethics by conducting research using the library and/or internet and reflecting on your knowledge of ethics, your life experiences and beliefs.

(a) What does the word 'ethics' mean and what is its origin (e.g. does the word come from a Latin or Greek word)?

(b) Now that you have a definition of ethics, explain in your own words what is considered 'ethical behaviour'.

(c) List five criteria you feel would indicate that an accountant was behaving ethically. Two examples of criteria are (i) the accountant has respect for the law and (ii) the accountant acts with discretion, i.e. not revealing private business affairs to outside parties.

(d) What are the 'costs', both personal and financial, of unethical behaviour?

(e) Provide an example from your own life experiences to illustrate how someone has behaved unethically in relation to you or with someone you know.

ANSWERS

Answers to self-study questions

2.1 (b) 2.2 (b) 2.3 (c) 2.4 (d) 2.5 (d) 2.6 (a) 2.7 (c) 2.8 (d) 2.9 (a) 2.10 (c)

Answer to review it questions

Question 4, section 2.3: Trade and other receivables debit; Income tax expense debit; Revenue credit; Food and paper expenses debit.

ACKNOWLEDGEMENT

Photo: © Andrey_Popov / Shutterstock.com

CHAPTER 3

Accrual accounting concepts

LEARNING OBJECTIVES

After studying this chapter, you should be able to:

3.1 differentiate between the cash basis and the accrual basis of accounting

3.2 explain criteria for revenue recognition and expense recognition

3.3 explain why adjusting entries are needed and identify the major types of adjusting entries

3.4 prepare adjusting entries for prepayments and accruals

3.5 describe the nature and purpose of the adjusted trial balance

3.6 explain the purpose of closing entries

3.7 describe the required steps in the accounting cycle

3.8 describe the purpose and the basic form of a worksheet.

Chapter preview

Recording transactions in the correct accounting period is important and necessary. To do otherwise leads to a misstatement of assets, liabilities, revenues, expenses and equity. In this chapter we introduce you to the accrual accounting concepts and decision making involved in adjusting entries that are an important part of accrual accounting.

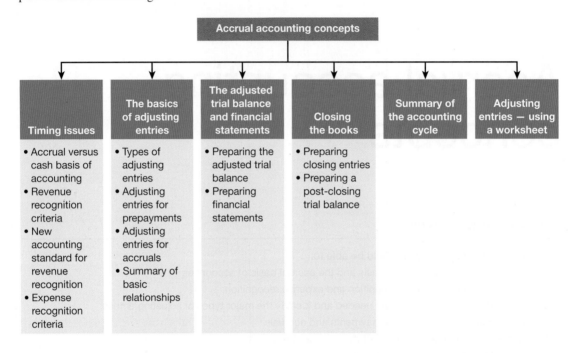

3.1 Timing issues

LEARNING OBJECTIVE 3.1 Differentiate between the cash basis and the accrual basis of accounting.

Consider this story:

> A fish and chip shop owner who had emigrated years ago from England kept his accounts payable in a shoe box, accounts receivable on a note pad, and cash in a cigar box. His daughter, having just completed the CPA program, chided her father: 'I don't understand how you can run your business this way. How do you know what your profits are?'
>
> 'Well,' her father replied, 'when I got off the boat 40 years ago, I had nothing but the pants I was wearing. Today your brother is a doctor, your sister is a university lecturer, and you are a CPA. Your mother and I have a nice car, a well-furnished house, and a holiday house. We have a good business and everything is paid for. So, you add all that together, subtract the pants, and there's your profit.'

Although the old fish and chip shop owner may be correct in his evaluation of how to calculate profit over his lifetime, most businesses need more immediate feedback about how well they are doing. For example, management usually needs monthly reports on financial results, most large entities are required to present 6-monthly and annual financial statements to shareholders, and taxation authorities require all businesses to lodge annual tax returns. Consequently, accounting divides the economic life of a business into artificial time periods. As indicated in chapter 1, this is the **accounting period concept**. Accounting periods are generally a month, a quarter, a half a year, or a year.

*Helpful hint: An accounting time period that is 1 year long is called a **financial year**.*

Many business transactions affect more than one of these arbitrary time periods. For example, a new building purchased by Domino's or a new machine purchased by Fisher & Paykel will be used for many years. It doesn't make good sense to expense the full amount of the building or the machine at the time it is purchased because each will be used for many subsequent periods. Therefore, it is necessary to determine the impact of each transaction on specific accounting periods.

Accrual versus cash basis of accounting

Revenues and expenses can be recorded or recognised on either a cash or an accrual basis. Under **cash-based accounting**, revenue is recorded only when the cash is received, and an expense is recorded only when cash is paid. When the majority of the transactions are carried out using cash (i.e. they have few receivables and payables), the cash basis will produce similar results to the accrual basis and is simpler to operate. However, it is not suitable where business organisations conduct a major part of their business on credit, because the statement of profit or loss produced under cash-based accounting would not represent the activities that relate to the current period.

Accrual-based accounting, on the other hand, records transactions and events in the accounting periods in which they occur rather than in the periods in which the entity receives or pays the related cash. Recall in chapter 1 we introduced the *Conceptual Framework*. One of the underlying assumptions described in the *Conceptual Framework* is that the statement of profit or loss and statement of financial position should be prepared on an accrual basis in order to best serve the function of providing relevant and reliable information for making decisions. For most merchandising businesses, using the accrual basis of accounting means recording revenues when goods are sold rather than when the cash is received. For entities that generate revenue by providing services, the accrual basis of accounting is typically applied by recording revenue when the service is performed rather than when the customer or client pays for the service. If services are part of a long-term contract, the revenue may need to be recognised progressively over several periods. The accounting reports prepared using the accrual-based system better reflect the true position and performance of the business for the period covered by the accounting period. Accountants are sometimes asked to convert cash-based records to the accrual basis. As you might expect, extensive adjustments to the accounting records are required for this task. (On an international note, although different accounting standards are often used by entities in other countries, the accrual basis of accounting is central to all of these standards.)

Figure 3.1 shows the relationship between accrual-based numbers and cash-based numbers, using a simple example. Suppose that the Blue Chip Painting Company paints a large building (Bob's Bait Barn) during year 1. In year 1 Blue Chip pays total expenses of $50 000, which include the cost of the paint and its employees' salaries. Now assume that Blue Chip billed Bob's Bait Barn $80 000 at the end of year 1 but was not paid until year 2. On an accrual basis, the revenue and expenses would be recognised in the same period (year 1) when the work was performed, and costs and revenue can be measured reliably. Thus, Blue Chip's profit for year 1 would be $30 000, and no revenue or expense from this project would be reported in year 2.

The $30 000 profit reported for year 1 provides a useful indication of the profitability of Blue Chip during that period. If, instead, a cash basis of accounting was adopted, Blue Chip would report expenses of $50 000 in year 1 and revenues of $80 000 in year 2. The results would be a loss of $50 000 for year 1 and a profit of $80 000 for year 2. The cash-based measures are not very informative about the results of Blue Chip's efforts during years 1 and 2, but they are useful if you wish to know about the entity's cash flows.

Table 3.1 summarises when transactions are recorded under accrual- versus cash-based accounting. Under the accrual basis, all cash transactions are still recorded, but the difference lies in the analysis of the effect on the accounting equation. What you need to determine is whether the transaction has been partly recorded already in the books. For example, using accrual accounting, you record the service when the service has been performed and invoiced. Hence, you recognise the increase in the asset accounts receivable and an increase in equity, service fees revenue. When payment is received from the customer, the analysis of the transaction is that you have an increase in an asset, cash and, because you have already recognised the revenue when you billed the customer, the other side of the transaction is a decrease in an asset, accounts receivable.

FIGURE 3.1 Accrual- versus cash-based accounting

	Year 1	Year 2
Activity	Purchased paint, painted building, paid employees	Received payment for work done in year 1
Accrual basis	Revenue $80 000 Expense 50 000 Profit $30 000	Revenue $ — Expense — Profit $ —
Cash basis	Revenue $ — Expense 50 000 Loss $(50 000)	Revenue $80 000 Expense — Profit $80 000

TABLE 3.1 Timing of recording transactions using cash- and accrual-based accounting

		Transactions recorded in books of the seller	
Transaction	**Timing**	**Cash basis**	**Accrual basis**
Customer order received	1 August	Nothing recorded	Nothing recorded
Sold goods on credit and invoiced customer	5 August	Nothing recorded	Increase accounts receivable Increase sales revenue
Customer paid account	6 September	Increase cash Increase sales revenue	Increase cash Decrease accounts receivable
Ordered inventory (goods) from supplier	2 August	Nothing recorded	Nothing recorded
Received inventory and invoice from supplier	3 August	Nothing recorded	Increase inventory Increase accounts payable
Paid amount owing to supplier	7 September	Increase inventory Decrease cash	Decrease accounts payable Decrease cash

Determining the amount of revenues and expenses to be reported in a given accounting period can be difficult. Proper reporting requires a thorough understanding of the nature of the entity's business. Accountants have developed criteria for the recognition of revenues and expenses to facilitate the recording process. These criteria form part of generally accepted accounting principles (GAAP).

3.2 Revenue recognition criteria

LEARNING OBJECTIVE 3.2 Explain criteria for revenue recognition and expense recognition.

In chapter 1 we introduced the *Conceptual Framework* which consists of four sections. One section outlines the definitions of the elements in the financial statements. Income is defined in the *Conceptual Framework* as encompassing both revenue and gains. The *Conceptual Framework* defines *revenue* as increases in economic benefits arising in the course of ordinary activities of an entity. It includes sales revenue, fees, interest, dividends, royalties and rent. *Gains* are other increases in economic benefits. They are no different in nature from revenue but are labelled as gains either because they do not arise in the ordinary course of business or because they are reported as a net amount, such as the gain on the sale of non-current assets.

A definition of revenue is helpful in determining *what* is to be recorded as revenue, but we also need guidelines on *when* to record or recognise revenues. For example, entities that sell goods (merchandising entities) need to first purchase goods, then sell them to customers and collect the cash. The **operating cycle** is the length of time it takes for a business to acquire goods, sell them to customers and collect the cash from the sales. The question that arises is: at which point in the operating cycle should revenue be recognised?

The recognition criteria for elements of financial statements are helpful in determining 'when' to record amounts. The *Conceptual Framework* provides **revenue recognition criteria**. Revenues should be recognised when and only when:

(a) it is probable that any future economic benefits associated with the revenue will flow to the entity, and

(b) the revenue can be measured with reliability.

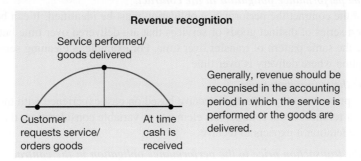

In the context of revenue recognition, the concept of probability refers to the degree of uncertainty that the future economic benefits will flow to the entity. The assessment of probability, or the degree of uncertainty, is made on the basis of evidence available when the financial statements are prepared. Ordinarily, this assessment is also made at the time that the transaction giving rise to the revenue occurs, thereby allowing the transaction to be recorded. However, when preparing the financial statements, the accountant must reconsider any information available at this time in order to assess whether the revenue should be reported as such in the financial statements.

The requirement that the revenue can be measured reliably does not mean that it must be measured with absolute certainty. In some routine transactions, such as cash sales, measurement may be certain. However, in many instances, revenue must be estimated.

In applying the recognition criteria, many businesses adopt procedures for recognising revenue when it is earned. For example, when a surgeon earns revenue by conducting surgery on a patient, a claim against the patient arises for the doctor's fee. At that time, the amount of the fee could be measured reliably because the doctor would know what has been performed, and the flow of benefits would be probable because the doctor would have a valid claim against the patient for the fee.

In a service entity, revenue is recognised at the time the service is performed. For example, assume a dry-cleaning business cleans clothing on 30 June, but customers do not pick up and pay for their clothes until the first week of July. Using the revenue recognition criteria, revenue is recorded in June when the service is performed, not in July when the cash is received. At 30 June, the tests for the recognition of revenue are met. The amount could be measured reliably because the entity would know how many items were cleaned. A claim to cash has been established by the provision of the agreed dry-cleaning service. This establishes probability. Before the service is performed, it is less probable that economic benefits will flow to the dry-cleaning business because the customer might cancel the dry-cleaning order. The stage of completion and costs incurred are known because the job is finished. The drycleaner would report a receivable on its statement of financial position and revenue in its statement of profit or loss for the service performed.

New accounting standard for revenue recognition

IFRS 15/AASB 15 *Revenue from Contracts with Customers* is mandatory for reporting periods commencing 1 January 2018 but may be adopted earlier. The new standard adopts a five-step model framework to identify when revenue should be recognised.

Step 1. Identify the contract(s) with a customer.
The contract must be approved by parties to the contract and each party's rights with regard to the goods or services to be transferred must be clearly identified as well as the terms for payment. The contract must have commercial substance, and it should be feasible that the consideration will be collected.

Helpful hint: A contract may be written or verbal.

Step 2. Identify the performance obligation in the contract.
At the inception of the contract the performance obligation must be identified. It can be either a distinct good or service or a series of distinct goods or services that are delivered over time but are substantially the same and have the same pattern of transfer over time. For example, a cleaning service provided or a magazine subscription where delivery is over time.

Step 3. Determine the transaction price.
This is the transfer price the entity expects to receive based on past experience with the customer, net of discounts, rebates or refunds. If the contract has elements of variable consideration, then it must estimate the amount of consideration it expects to receive.

Step 4. Allocate the transaction price to the performance obligation in the contract.

Step 5. Recognise revenue when (or as) the entity satisfies the performance obligation.

Essentially revenue is recognised when an entity satisfies a performance obligation. In order to recognise revenue from contracts with customers to supply goods or services, the following conditions must be met:
- the contract has been approved by parties to the contract
- each party's rights in relation to the goods to be transferred have been identified
- the payment terms have been identified
- the contract has commercial substance; and
- it is probable that the consideration to which the entity is entitled in exchange for the goods or services will be collected.

Decision/issue	Info needed for analysis	Tool or technique to use for decision	How to evaluate results to make decision
At what point should the entity recognise (record) revenue?	Need to understand the nature of the entity's business	Revenue is recognised when an entity satisfies a performance obligation in a contract. The following conditions must be met: the contract has been approved by parties to the contract; each party's rights in relation to the goods or services to be transferred have been identified; the payment terms have been identified; the contract has commercial substance; and it is probable that the consideration to which the entity is entitled to in exchange for the goods or services will be collected.	Recognising revenue too early overstates current period revenue; recognising it too late understates current period revenue.

Expense recognition criteria

There are many types of expenses, such as wages expense, rent expense, interest expense and electricity expense. The *Conceptual Framework* defines expenses as encompassing both losses and expenses. *Expenses* are decreases in economic benefits. They include expenses that arise in the ordinary activities of the entity, such as cost of sales, wages and payments for rent. The term *losses* refers to expenses that do not necessarily arise in the ordinary course of business, such as the loss from a fire or flood, as well as reductions in economic benefits that are reported on a net basis (i.e. net of any associated revenue), such as a loss on the sale of non-current assets.

Put simply, expenses are decreases in equity during an accounting period that are not due to distributions to the owner(s). Consumptions or losses of future economic benefits include reductions in assets such as cash, and increases in liabilities include payables such as salaries payable.

The consumption of economic benefits is easily determined for some transactions, such as using cash to pay rent for the current period. However, some economic benefits, such as buildings and equipment, last for numerous accounting periods. Measuring the amount of economic benefits consumed in each accounting period can be difficult. This makes it difficult to determine how much of the cost of assets such as buildings and equipment should be allocated to expenses in each accounting period. This is discussed further in the section 'Depreciation' (in section 3.4).

The definition of expenses is helpful in determining *what* is to be recorded as an expense but, as for revenues, we need guidelines on *when* to record or recognise expenses. The *Conceptual Framework* provides **expense recognition criteria**. Expenses should be recognised when and only when:

(a) the outflow of future economic benefits associated with the expense is probable, and

(b) the expense can be measured reliably.

Many expenses for merchandising and service entities involve little uncertainty as they result from the production or delivery of goods or services during an accounting period, such as the cost of employees' services (wages and salaries), supplies used (e.g. stationery) and electricity or gas used. It is important to note that an expense is recognised when the reduction in assets or the increase in liabilities is recognised, and that this may occur before, as or after cash is paid. Referring to the previous dry-cleaning business example, although wages may not be paid on 30 June for the hours worked by employees in providing dry-cleaning services, the expense is recognised as the increase in liabilities (wages payable) has occurred and the future outflow can be measured reliably.

Where the expenses result directly and jointly from the same transaction as the revenues, e.g. the cost of services provided or the cost of goods sold, expenses should be recognised on the basis of a direct association with revenues. This recognition technique is sometimes referred to as 'matching' of expenses with revenues — the simultaneous recognition of revenues and related expenses. The nature of and methods for recording cost of sales is further explored in chapters 4 and 5.

Determining the amount of revenues and expenses to be reported in each accounting period is facilitated by revenue and expense recognition criteria. Relationships between revenue recognition, expense recognition and the accounting period concept which form part of GAAP are depicted in figure 3.2.

FIGURE 3.2 Relationships between revenue recognition, expense recognition and the accounting period concept

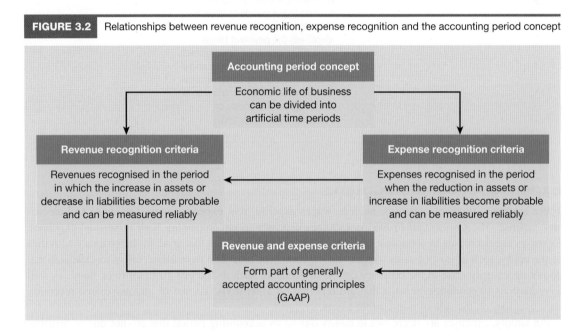

Although most entities use the accrual basis of accounting, some small businesses use the cash basis because they have few receivables and payables. For these businesses, the cash basis may approximate the accrual basis.

Note: The recognition criteria in figure 3.2 are the same as those in the *Conceptual Framework* which is currently under revision. The criteria in the decision-making toolkit are from the new accounting standard IFRS 15 *Revenue from Contracts with Customers*.

DECISION-MAKING TOOLKIT

Decision/issue	Info needed for analysis	Tool or technique to use for decision	How to evaluate results to make decision
At what point should the entity recognise (record) expenses?	Need to understand the nature of the entity's business	Expenses should be recognised when decreases in assets or increases in liabilities that result in a decrease in equity are probable and can be measured reliably.	Recognising expenses too early overstates current period expenses; recognising them too late understates current period expenses.

Review it

1. What are the differences between the cash and accrual bases of accounting?
2. Explain revenue recognition and expense recognition criteria.

Do it

During year 1, Services Ltd invoiced its customers $100 000 for services performed. It received $75 000 cash in year 1 and the balance in year 2. Expenses paid during year 1 amounted to $45 000 but another $13 000 of expenses were not paid until year 2. Calculate the profit for year 1 using (a) accrual-based accounting and (b) cash-based accounting.

Reasoning

Accrual-based accounting revenues and expenses are recognised in the period in which the revenues are earned and the expenses are incurred, whereas when cash-based accounting is used the receipt and payment of the cash triggers the recognition.

Solution

Accrual-based: Profit is the $100 000 (invoiced) less $45 000 (cash expenses paid) and $13 000 (incurred but still unpaid) = $100 000 − ($45 000 + $13 000) = $42 000. Cash-based: Profit is $75 000 (cash received) less $45 000 (cash expenses paid) = $30 000.

3.3 The basics of adjusting entries

LEARNING OBJECTIVE 3.3 Explain why adjusting entries are needed and identify the major types of adjusting entries.

In order for revenues and expenses to be recorded in the correct accounting period, adjusting entries are made to revenue and expense accounts at the end of the accounting period. In short, **adjusting entries** are needed to ensure that the recognition criteria are followed for assets, liabilities, revenues and expenses.

The use of adjusting entries makes it possible to produce accurate financial statements at the end of the accounting period. Thus, the statement of financial position reports appropriate assets, liabilities and equity at the end of the reporting period, and the statement of profit or loss shows the appropriate profit (or loss) for the period. Adjusting entries are necessary because the general ledger may not contain up-to-date and complete data, for the following reasons.

1. Some events are not journalised daily because it would not be useful or efficient to do so. Examples are the use of supplies and the earning of wages by employees.
2. Some costs are not journalised during the accounting period because the economic benefits expire with the passage of time rather than as a result of recurring daily transactions. Examples include building and equipment deterioration, rent and insurance.
3. Some items may be unrecorded. An example is an electricity or telephone bill that will not be received until the next accounting period.

Adjusting entries are required every time financial statements are prepared. An essential starting point is an analysis of each account in the trial balance to determine whether it is complete and up to date for financial statement purposes.

None of the transactions demonstrated in this chapter and the end-of-chapter activities include the effects of the goods and services tax (GST). Section 4.6 in chapter 4 introduces transactions with GST.

Types of adjusting entries

Adjusting entries can be classified as either prepayments or accruals. Each of these classes has two subcategories as shown in figure 3.3. (*Note:* Another term for prepayments is *deferrals*.)

FIGURE 3.3 Categories of adjusting entries

Prepayments

1. *Prepaid expenses:* Amounts paid in cash and recorded as assets until the economic benefits are used or consumed.
2. *Revenues received in advance:* Amounts received from customers and recorded as liabilities until the services are performed or the goods are provided and revenue is recognised.

Accruals

1. *Accrued revenues:* Amounts not yet received and not yet recorded for which the goods or services have been provided.
2. *Accrued expenses:* Amounts not yet paid and not yet recorded for which the consumption of economic benefits has occurred.

Alternatively, expenses when paid may be recorded as an expense, and the adjustment is to defer the expense to the next period and record it as an asset. Refer to table 3.2.

Specific examples and explanations of each type of adjustment are given in subsequent sections. Each example is based on the 31 October trial balance of Wong Pty Ltd, from chapter 2, reproduced in figure 3.4. Note that the retained earnings account has been added to this trial balance with a nil balance. We will explain its use later.

It will be assumed that Wong Pty Ltd uses an accounting period of 1 month for internal reporting. Thus, monthly adjusting entries will be made. The adjusting entries will be dated 31 October.

FIGURE 3.4 Trial balance of Wong Pty Ltd

No.	Account name	Debit	Credit
	WONG PTY LTD **Trial balance** as at 31 October 2019		
100	Cash	$15 200	
110	Advertising supplies	2 500	
112	Prepaid insurance	600	
130	Office equipment	5 000	
200	Accounts payable		$ 2 500
213	Service revenue received in advance		1 200
230	Bank loan		5 000
300	Share capital		10 000
310	Retained earnings		—
320	Dividends	500	
400	Service revenue		10 000
500	Salaries expense	4 000	
510	Rent expense	900	
		$28 700	$28 700

3.4 Adjusting entries for prepayments

LEARNING OBJECTIVE 3.4 Prepare adjusting entries for prepayments and accruals.

Prepayments are either prepaid expenses or revenues received in advance. Adjusting entries for prepayments are required at the end of the reporting period to record the portion of the prepayment that represents the expense or the revenue in the current accounting period. Adjusting entries for amounts recorded as prepayments are graphically depicted in figure 3.5.

FIGURE 3.5 Adjusting entries for prepayments

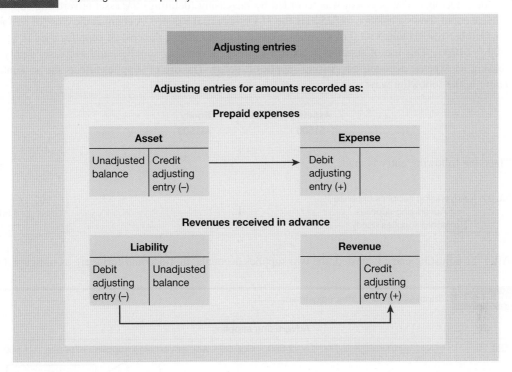

Prepaid expenses

Payments of amounts that will provide economic benefits for more than the current accounting period are called **prepaid expenses** or **prepayments**. When such a cost is incurred, an asset account is increased (debited) to show the service or benefit that will be received in the future. Examples of common prepayments are insurance, supplies, advertising and rent.

Prepaid expenses expire as the service is provided with the passage of time (e.g. rent and insurance) or through use (e.g. supplies). The expiration of these benefits does not require daily entries — that would be impractical and unnecessary. Accordingly, we postpone the recognition of the expiry of prepaid expenses until financial statements are prepared. At the end of each reporting period, adjusting entries are made to record the expenses applicable to the current accounting period and to show the remaining amounts in the asset accounts. Before adjustment, assets are overstated and expenses are understated. Therefore, an adjusting entry for prepaid expenses results in an increase (a debit) to an expense account and a decrease (a credit) to an asset account.

Alternatively, some entities may record the cost incurred immediately as an expense (debit) rather than as an asset. Therefore, the adjusting entry will be to increase (debit) the asset account for the future benefit which is unexpired and to decrease the expense (credit). Hence, the expense has been deferred.

Supplies

The purchase of supplies, such as paper and envelopes, results in an increase (a debit) to an asset account. During the accounting period, supplies are used or consumed. Rather than record supplies expense as the supplies are used, many entities recognise supplies expense at the *end* of the accounting period. At the end of the accounting period the entity must count the remaining supplies. The difference between the unadjusted balance in the supplies (asset) account and the actual cost of supplies on hand represents the supplies used (expense) for that period. That is, the cost of the supplies consumed during the period is an expense.

Recall from the facts presented in chapter 2 that Wong Pty Ltd purchased advertising supplies costing $2500 on 5 October. The payment was recorded by increasing (debiting) the asset advertising supplies, and this account shows a balance of $2500 in the 31 October trial balance. A count at the close of business on 31 October reveals that $1000 of supplies are still on hand. Thus, the cost of supplies used is $1500 ($2500 − $1000). This use of supplies decreases an asset, advertising supplies, and decreases equity by increasing an expense account, advertising supplies expense. The use of supplies affects the accounting equation in the following way:

Assets	=	Liabilities	+	Equity
−$1500				−$1500

Thus, the following entry is made:

Oct. 31	Advertising supplies expense	1 500	
	Advertising supplies		1 500
	(To record supplies used)		

After the adjusting entry is posted, the two supplies accounts, in T-account form, are as in figure 3.6.

FIGURE 3.6   Supplies accounts after adjustment

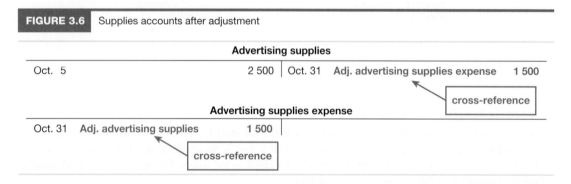

For simplicity, the posting references have not been included in the general journal entry shown above and in the illustrations that follow. A more comprehensive example utilising many general ledger accounts is provided in figure 3.16, where posting references are included to help you trace the entries to the ledger accounts illustrated in figure 3.17.

The asset account advertising supplies now shows a debit balance of $1000, which is equal to the cost of supplies on hand at the end of the reporting period. In addition, advertising supplies expense shows a debit balance of $1500, which equals the cost of supplies used in October. If the adjusting entry was not made, October expenses would be understated and profit overstated by $1500. Moreover, both assets and equity would be overstated by $1500 on the 31 October statement of financial position.

Recall from chapter 2 that the account names listed inside each general ledger account are called cross-references and indicate the other account affected. For the remainder of the examples, cross-references are not included due to limited space. However, cross-references are included in figure 3.23.

Insurance

Entities purchase insurance to protect themselves from losses due to fire, theft and other unforeseen events. Insurance must be paid in advance, usually for a period of 1 year. Insurance payments (premiums) made in advance are normally recorded in the asset account prepaid insurance. At the end of the reporting period it is necessary to increase (debit) insurance expense and decrease (credit) prepaid insurance for the cost of insurance that has expired during the period.

On 4 October Wong Pty Ltd paid $600 for a 1-year insurance policy. Coverage began on 1 October. The payment was recorded by increasing (debiting) prepaid insurance when it was paid. This account shows a balance of $600 in the 31 October trial balance. An analysis of the policy reveals that $50 ($600/12) of insurance expires each month. The expiration of prepaid insurance has the following effect on the accounting equation in October (and each of the next 11 months):

$$\underline{\textbf{Assets} = \textbf{Liabilities} + \textbf{Equity}}$$
$$-\$50 \qquad\qquad\qquad -\$50$$

Thus, the following adjusting entry is made:

Oct. 31	Insurance expense	50	
	Prepaid insurance		50
	(To record insurance expired)		

After the adjusting entry is posted, the accounts appear as in figure 3.7.

FIGURE 3.7   Insurance accounts after adjustment

Prepaid insurance				Insurance expense		
Oct. 4	600	Oct. 31 **Adj.**	50	Oct. 31 **Adj.**	50	

The asset prepaid insurance shows a debit balance of $550, which represents the costs allocated to the future economic benefits of the business for the remaining 11 months of coverage. At the same time, the balance in insurance expense is equal to the insurance benefit that was used in October. If this adjustment was not made, October expenses would be understated by $50 and profit overstated by $50. Moreover, as the accounting equation shows, both assets and equity would be overstated by $50 on the 31 October statement of financial position.

The examples shown illustrate the recording of prepayments — amounts paid which provide benefits for more than one period. The amounts paid were initially recorded as assets, for example, supplies and prepaid insurance. However, the recording of such payments as assets at the time of payment is only one way of recording these transactions. As discussed earlier, an alternative way is to record the amounts paid as expenses at the time of payment; for example, supplies expense and insurance expense.

At the time of payment, it does not matter whether the amount is recorded as an expense or an asset, as adjusting entries will be made at the end of the reporting period to record the expenses that relate to the current period and show the unexpired cost in the asset accounts. Demonstration problem 2 provides a comprehensive example illustrating the different ways in which these types of transactions can be recorded and the corresponding adjusting entries required at the end of the reporting period.

Depreciation

A business typically owns a variety of assets that have long lives, such as buildings, equipment and motor vehicles. These assets are called non-current assets as they provide future economic benefits to the business for more than one accounting period. The term **useful life** of the asset refers to the estimated total service potential or estimated period of time over which the future economic benefits are expected to be consumed by the entity. Because a building is expected to provide service for many years, it is recorded as an asset, rather than an expense, on the date it is acquired. As explained in chapter 1, such assets are recorded at cost, as required by the historical cost principle. According to expense recognition criteria, a portion of this cost should then be reported as an expense during each period of the asset's useful life. **Depreciation** is the process of allocating the cost of an asset to expense over its useful life.

Need for adjustment. From an accounting standpoint, the acquisition of long-lived assets is essentially a long-term prepayment for economic benefits. The need for making periodic adjusting entries for depreciation is therefore the same as described before for other prepaid expenses — that is, to recognise the cost of economic benefits that have been consumed during the period as expenses and to report the cost of economic benefits that remain at the end of the period as assets. One point is very important to understand: *depreciation is an allocation concept, not a valuation concept.* That is, we depreciate an asset to allocate its cost to the periods in which we use the asset. We are not attempting to reflect the actual change in the value of the asset.

For Wong Pty Ltd, assume that depreciation on the office equipment is estimated to be $480 a year, or $40 per month. This would have the following impact on the accounting equation:

Assets	=	Liabilities	+	Equity
−$40				−$40

Accordingly, depreciation for October is recognised by this adjusting entry:

Oct. 31	Depreciation expense	40	
	Accumulated depreciation—office equipment		40
	(To record monthly depreciation)		

After the adjusting entry is posted, the accounts appear as in figure 3.8.

FIGURE 3.8   Accounts after adjustment for depreciation

Office equipment

Oct. 2	5 000	

Accumulated depreciation—office equipment

	Oct. 31	Adj.	40

Depreciation expense

Oct. 31	Adj.	40	

The balance in the accumulated depreciation account will increase by $40 each month.

Statement presentation. Accumulated depreciation—office equipment is a **contra asset account**, which means that it is offset against office equipment on the statement of financial position, and its normal balance is a credit. This account is used instead of decreasing (crediting) office equipment in order to record *both* the original cost of the equipment and the total cost that has expired to date. In the statement of financial position, accumulated depreciation—office equipment is deducted from the related asset account as shown in figure 3.9.

Helpful hint: All contra accounts have increases, decreases, and normal balances opposite to the account to which they relate.

FIGURE 3.9   Statement of financial position presentation of accumulated depreciation

Office equipment	$5 000
Less: Accumulated depreciation—office equipment	40
	$4 960

The difference between the cost of any depreciable asset and its related accumulated depreciation is referred to as its **carrying amount** (also referred to as *book value*). In figure 3.9, the carrying amount of the equipment at the end of the reporting period is $4960. The carrying amount and the market value of the asset are generally two different values.

Note also that depreciation expense identifies the amount of an asset's cost that has expired in October. The accounting equation shows that, as in the case of other prepaid adjustments, the omission of this adjusting entry would cause total assets, total equity and profit to be overstated and depreciation expense to be understated.

As noted earlier, depreciation is a matter of cost allocation, not valuation. Property, plant and equipment, and intangible assets, such as a licence or franchise, are discussed at length in chapter 8.

Revenues received in advance

Cash received before the revenue recognition criteria have been met is recorded by increasing (crediting) a liability account called **revenues received in advance**. Items such as rent and customer deposits for future service result in revenues received in advance. Airlines such as Qantas and Virgin Australia treat receipts from the sale of tickets as revenue received in advance until the flight service is provided. Health clubs treat membership revenue as deferred income until the service has been provided in accordance with the membership contract. Revenues received in advance are the opposite of prepaid expenses. Indeed, revenue received in advance in the records of one entity is likely to be a prepayment in the records of the entity that has made the advance payment. For example, if identical accounting periods are assumed, a landlord will have rent revenue received in advance when a tenant has prepaid rent.

When payment is received for services to be provided in a future accounting period, a revenue received in advance (a liability) account should be credited to recognise the obligation that exists. Revenues received in advance are subsequently recognised as revenue when the service is provided to a customer. During the accounting period, it is not always practical to make daily entries to the revenue received in advance accounts as the services are provided. Instead, we delay recognition of revenue until the adjustment process. Then an adjusting entry is made to record the revenue during the period and to show the liability that remains at the end of the accounting period. Typically, before adjustment, liabilities are overstated and revenues are understated. Therefore, the adjusting entry for revenues received in advance results in a decrease (a debit) to a liability account and an increase (a credit) to a revenue account.

Wong Pty Ltd received $1200 on 2 October from R. Knox for advertising services expected to be completed by 31 December. The payment was credited to service revenue received in advance, and this liability account shows a balance of $1200 in the 31 October trial balance. An evaluation of the work performed by Wong for Knox indicated that services worth $400 were performed in October. This affects the accounting equation in the following way:

$$\underline{\textbf{Assets} = \textbf{Liabilities} + \textbf{Equity}}$$
$$-\$400 \qquad +\$400$$

The following adjusting entry is made:

Oct. 31	Service revenue received in advance	400	
	Service revenue		400
	(To record revenue)		

After the adjusting entry is posted, the accounts appear as in figure 3.10.

FIGURE 3.10 Service revenue accounts after adjustment

Service revenue received in advance			Service revenue		
Oct. 31 **Adj.**	400	Oct. 2 1 200		Oct. 3	10 000
				31 **Adj.**	400

The liability service revenue received in advance now shows a credit balance of $800, which represents the remaining advertising services expected to be performed in the future. At the same time, service revenue shows total revenue in October of $10 400. If this adjustment were not made, revenues and profit would be understated by $400 in the statement of profit or loss. Moreover, liabilities would be overstated and equity would be understated by $400 on the 31 October statement of financial position.

The example illustrates the initial recording of revenue received in advance as a liability. Alternatively, amounts received in advance of the provision of goods and services could be recorded initially as revenue. The adjusting entry at the end of the reporting period would then be to decrease revenue and recognise a liability for revenue received in advance.

LEARNING REFLECTION AND CONSOLIDATION

Review it

1. What are the four types of adjusting entries?
2. What is the effect on assets, equity, expenses and profit if a prepaid expense adjusting entry is not made when a portion of the economic benefits has expired?
3. What is the effect on liabilities, equity, revenues and profit if an adjusting entry for revenue received in advance is not made when services have been performed or goods have been delivered?

Do it

The ledger of Hammond Ltd on 31 March 2019 includes these selected accounts before adjusting entries are prepared:

	Debits	Credits
Prepaid insurance	$ 3 600	
Office supplies	2 800	
Office equipment	25 000	
Accumulated depreciation—office equipment		$5 000
Service revenue received in advance		9 200

An analysis of the accounts shows the following.
1. Insurance expires at the rate of $100 per month.
2. Supplies on hand total $800.
3. The office equipment depreciates by $200 each month.
4. In relation to the $9200 recorded as service revenue received in advance, $4000 of services were performed during March.
Prepare the adjusting entries for the month of March.

Reasoning

In order to record all revenues and all expenses in an accounting period, adjusting entries are made at the *end* of the accounting period. They record the portion of the prepayment that represents an expense or revenue for the current accounting period. The failure to adjust for the prepayment would lead to an overstatement of the asset or liability and a related understatement of the expense or revenue.

Solution

1. Insurance expense	100	
Prepaid insurance		100
(To record prepaid insurance expired)		
2. Office supplies expense	2 000	
Office supplies		2 000
(To record supplies used)		
3. Depreciation expense	200	
Accumulated depreciation—office equipment		200
(To record monthly depreciation)		
4. Service revenue received in advance	4 000	
Service revenue		4 000
(To record revenue)		

Adjusting entries for accruals

The second category of adjusting entries is *accruals*. Adjusting entries for accruals are required in order to record revenues and expenses in the current accounting period that have not been recognised through daily entries and thus are not yet reflected in the accounts. The revenue account (and the related asset account) or the expense account (and the related liability account) are understated if there are unrecorded revenues and expenses. Thus, the adjusting entry for accruals will increase the balances of accounts in both the statement of financial position and the statement of profit or loss. Adjusting entries for accruals are graphically depicted in figure 3.11.

Helpful hint: For accruals, there may have been no previous entry, and the accounts requiring adjustment may both have nil balances before adjustment.

FIGURE 3.11   Adjusting entries for accruals

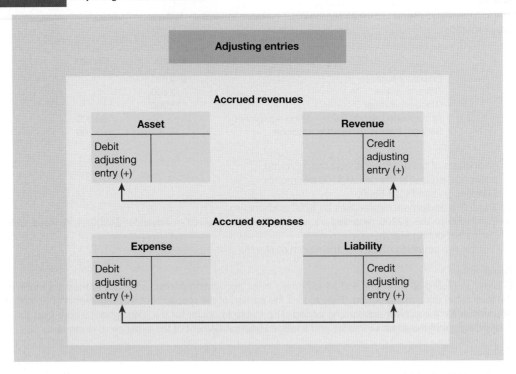

Accrued revenues

Accrued revenues are revenues that are recorded as adjusting entries because they have not been recorded in the daily recording of transactions. Accrued revenues may accumulate (accrue) over time, as in the case of rent revenue and interest revenue, or they may result from services that have been performed but neither invoiced nor collected, as in the case of commissions and fees. The former are unrecorded because the receipt of rent and interest revenues does not involve daily transactions. Fee revenue, or service revenue, may be unrecorded because only a portion of the total service has been provided and the clients won't be invoiced until the service has been completed. Alternatively, commissions revenue may be due but not received by the end of the reporting period.

An adjusting entry is required to show the receivable that exists at the end of the reporting period and to record the revenue for the period. Before adjustment, both assets and revenues are understated. Accordingly, an adjusting entry for accrued revenues results in an increase (a debit) to an asset account and an increase (a credit) to a revenue account.

Wong Pty Ltd earns commission of 1% of sales revenue from one of its advertising clients. Although the client has not yet paid, Wong has been advised that the amount for October is $200. As this revenue has not yet been recorded, revenue and assets are understated. The required adjusting entry affects the accounting equation as follows:

Assets	=	Liabilities	+	Equity
+$200				+$200

Thus, the following adjusting entry is made:

Oct. 31	Commissions receivable	200	
	Commissions revenue		200
	(To accrue commissions revenue not recorded or collected)		

After the adjusting entry is posted, the accounts appear as in figure 3.12.

Receivable and revenue accounts after accrual adjustments

Commissions receivable		Commissions revenue	
Oct. 31 Adj. 200			Oct. 31 Adj. 200

The commissions receivable asset shows that $200 is owed by a client at the end of the reporting period. The credit balance of $200 in commissions revenue represents the total commissions revenue for the month of October. If the adjusting entry were not made, assets and equity on the statement of financial position, and revenues and profit on the statement of profit or loss would be understated.

The client pays the commission of $200 on 10 November. This transaction should be recorded as an increase in cash and a decrease in commissions receivable. No revenue is recognised when the cash is received because the revenue belongs to, and was recognised in, the October accounting period. The accounting equation is affected as follows:

$$\text{Assets} = \text{Liabilities} + \text{Equity}$$
$$+\$200$$
$$-\$200$$

Thus, the following entry is made:

Nov. 10	Cash	200	
	Commissions receivable		200
	(To record receipt of commissions accrued in October)		

Accrued expenses

Expenses not yet paid or recorded at the end of the reporting period are called **accrued expenses**. Interest, rent, taxes and salaries are common examples of accrued expenses. Accrued expenses result from the same factors as accrued revenues. In fact, an accrued expense in the records of one business is likely to be an accrued revenue to another business. For example, the $200 accrual of service revenue by Wong Pty Ltd is an accrued expense to the client that received the service.

Adjustments for accrued expenses are necessary to record the obligations that exist at the end of the reporting period and to recognise the expenses that apply to the current accounting period. Before adjustment, both liabilities and expenses are understated. Therefore, an adjusting entry for accrued expenses results in an increase (a debit) to an expense account and an increase (a credit) to a liability account.

Accrued interest

On 1 October Wong Pty Ltd borrowed $5000 from a bank, with interest payments required quarterly. The bank charges Wong Pty Ltd interest at an annual rate of 12%. The amount of the interest accumulation is determined by three factors: (1) the principal borrowed, (2) the interest rate, which is always expressed as an annual rate, and (3) the length of time the loan is outstanding. In this instance, the interest for October has not been paid because interest is not due until 1 January, 3 months after the commencement of the loan. The formula for calculating interest and its application to Wong Pty Ltd for the month of October are shown in figure 3.13.

FIGURE 3.13 Formula for interest

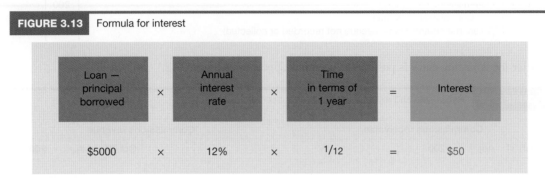

Note that the time period is expressed as a fraction of a year. The accrual of interest at 31 October would have the following impact on the accounting equation:

$$\underline{\textbf{Assets} = \textbf{Liabilities} + \textbf{Equity}}$$
$$+\$50 \qquad -\$50$$

This would be reflected in an accrued expense adjusting entry at 31 October as follows:

Oct. 31	Interest expense	50	
	Interest payable		50
	(To accrue interest on bank loan)		

After this adjusting entry is posted, the accounts appear as in figure 3.14.

FIGURE 3.14 Interest accounts after adjustment

Interest expense			Interest payable		
Oct. 31 Adj.	50			Oct. 31 Adj.	50

Interest expense shows the interest charges for the month of October. The amount of interest owed at the end of the reporting period is shown in interest payable. It will not be paid until the interest payment is due at the end of 3 months. The interest payable account is used, instead of crediting the bank loan account, to distinguish between the two different types of obligations — interest and principal — in the accounts and financial statements. If this adjusting entry were not made, liabilities and interest expense would be understated, and profit and equity would be overstated.

Accrued salaries

Some types of expenses, such as employee salaries and commissions, are paid for after the services have been performed. At Wong Pty Ltd, salaries were last paid on 26 October; the next payment of salaries will not occur until 9 November. As shown in the calendar, 3 working days remain in October (29–31 October). (Accrued salaries can also be termed *accrued wages*.)

Helpful hint: When you are preparing adjusting entries for accrued salaries you may find it helpful to draw a rough calendar and mark the dates for the start of the pay period, payday and the adjustment period as shown in this example.

At 31 October the salaries for 3 days represent an accrued expense and a related liability of Wong Pty Ltd. The employees receive total salaries of $2000 for a 5-day working week, or $400 per day. Thus, accrued salaries at 31 October are $1200 ($400 × 3). This accrual increases a liability, salaries payable, and an expense account, salaries expense, and has the following effect on the accounting equation:

Assets	=	Liabilities	+	Equity
		+$1200		−$1200

The adjusting entry is:

Oct. 31	Salaries expense	1 200	
	Salaries payable		1 200
	(To record accrued salaries)		

After this adjusting entry is posted, the accounts are as in figure 3.15.

FIGURE 3.15 Salary accounts after adjustment

Salaries expense			Salaries payable		
Oct. 26		4 000	Oct. 31	Adj.	1 200
31	Adj.	1 200			

After this adjustment, the balance in salaries expense of $5200 is the actual salary expense for October. The balance in salaries payable of $1200 is the amount of the liability for salaries owed as at 31 October. If the $1200 adjustment for salaries were not recorded, Wong Pty Ltd's expenses and liabilities would both be understated by $1200.

Wong Pty Ltd pays salaries every 2 weeks. Consequently, the next payday is 9 November, when total salaries of $4000 will again be paid. The payment consists of $1200 of salaries payable at 31 October plus $2800 of salaries expense for November (7 working days × $400). The following entry is made on 9 November:

Nov. 9	Salaries payable	1 200	
	Salaries expense	2 800	
	Cash		4 000
	(To record 9 November payroll)		

This entry eliminates the liability for salaries payable that was recorded by the 31 October adjusting entry and records the correct amount of salaries expense for the period between 1 November and 9 November.

An alternative entry to the 9 November entry can be done if reversing entries are entered. Some accountants prefer to reverse the accrual, adjusting entries at the beginning of a new accounting period. A **reversing entry** is made at the beginning of the next accounting period and is the exact opposite of the adjusting entry made in the previous period. The purpose of the reversing entry is to make the recording of the transaction in the new accounting period easier. That is, you do not have to keep track of which items were accrued. The following entries demonstrate this:

Nov. 1	Salaries payable	1 200	
	Salaries expense		1 200
	(To record reversing entry)		
Nov. 9	Salaries expense	4 000	
	Cash		4 000
	(To record 9 November payroll)		

After the payroll entry on 9 November, salaries payable has a nil balance and the salaries expense account has a $2800 debit balance.

Summary of basic relationships

Important data on each of the four basic types of adjusting entries are summarised in table 3.2. Take some time to study and analyse the adjusting entries. Note that each adjusting entry affects one revenue or expense account and one statement of financial position account.

TABLE 3.2   Summary of adjusting entries

Type of adjustment	Accounts before adjustment	Adjusting entry
Prepaid expenses		
If amount paid is initially recorded as an asset	Assets overstated Expenses understated	Dr Expenses Cr Assets
If amount paid is initially recorded as an expense	Expenses overstated Assets understated	Dr Assets Cr Expenses
Revenues received in advance		
If amount received is initially recorded as a liability	Liabilities overstated Revenues understated	Dr Liabilities Cr Revenues
If amount received is initially recorded as revenue	Revenues overstated Liabilities understated	Dr Revenues Cr Liabilities
Accrued revenues	Assets understated Revenues understated	Dr Assets Cr Revenues
Accrued expenses	Expenses understated Liabilities understated	Dr Expenses Cr Liabilities

The journalising and posting of adjusting entries for Wong Pty Ltd on 31 October are shown in figures 3.16 and 3.17. When reviewing the general ledger in figure 3.17, note that the adjustments are highlighted in colour and that the asset, liability and equity accounts have been balanced to facilitate the preparation of an adjusted trial balance.

FIGURE 3.16   General journal showing adjusting entries

General journal

Date	Account name (narration)	Post ref.	Debit	Credit
2019 Oct. 31	*Adjusting entries* Advertising supplies expense 　　　Advertising supplies 　　(To record supplies used)	505 110	1 500	1 500
31	Insurance expense 　　　Prepaid insurance 　　(To record insurance expired)	515 112	50	50
31	Depreciation expense 　　　Acc. depn—office equipment 　　(To record monthly depreciation)	520 131	40	40
31	Service revenue received in advance 　　　Service revenue 　　(To record revenue)	213 400	400	400
31	Commissions receivable 　　　Commissions revenue 　　(To accrue revenue not recorded or collected)	105 405	200	200

Date	Account name (narration)	Post ref.	Debit	Credit
Oct. 31	Interest expense	518	50	
	Interest payable	210		50
	(To accrue interest on bank loan)			
31	Salaries expense	500	1 200	
	Salaries payable	215		1 200
	(To record accrued salaries)			

FIGURE 3.17   General ledger after recording adjustments and balancing of share capital, asset and liability accounts

General ledger

Cash   **No. 100**

Oct. 1	Share capital	GJ	10 000	Oct. 2	Office equipment	GJ	5 000
1	Bank loan	GJ	5 000	3	Rent expense	GJ	900
2	Service rev. rec'd in advance	GJ	1 200	4	Prepaid insurance	GJ	600
3	Service revenue	GJ	10 000	20	Dividends	GJ	500
				26	Salaries expense	GJ	4 000
				31	Closing balance	GJ	15 200
			26 200				26 200
Nov. 1	Opening balance		15 200				

Commissions receivable*   **No. 105**

Oct. 31	Commissions revenue	GJ	200	Oct. 31	Closing balance		200
			200				200
Nov. 1	Opening balance		200				

Advertising supplies   **No. 110**

Oct. 5	Accounts payable	GJ	2 500	Oct. 31	Adv. supplies exp.	GJ	1 500
				31	Closing balance		1 000
			2 500				2 500
Nov. 1	Opening balance		1 000				

Prepaid insurance   **No. 112**

Oct. 4	Cash	GJ	600	Oct. 31	Insurance exp.	GJ	50
				31	Closing balance		550
			600				600
Nov. 1	Opening balance		550				

Office equipment*   **No. 130**

Oct. 2	Cash	GJ	5 000	Oct. 31	Closing balance		5 000
			5 000				5 000
Nov. 1	Opening balance		5 000				

Accumulated depreciation—office equipment*   **No. 131**

Oct. 31	Closing balance		40	Oct. 31	Depreciation exp.	GJ	40
			40				40
				Nov. 1	Opening balance		40

Accounts payable*   **No. 200**

Oct. 31	Closing balance		2 500	Oct. 5	Advertising supplies	GJ	2 500
			2 500				2 500
				Nov. 1	Opening balance		2 500

Interest payable*   **No. 210**

Oct. 31	Closing balance		50	Oct. 31	Interest expense	GJ	50
			50				50
				Nov. 1	Opening balance		50

Service revenue received in advance   No. 213

Oct. 31	Service revenue	GJ	400	Oct.	2	Cash	GJ	1 200
31	Closing balance		800					
			1 200					1 200
				Nov.	1	Opening balance		800

Salaries payable*   No. 215

Oct. 31	Closing balance		1 200	Oct. 31	Salaries expense	GJ	1 200
			1 200				1 200
				Nov. 1	Opening balance		1 200

Bank loan*   No. 230

Oct. 31	Closing balance		5 000	Oct. 1	Cash	GJ	5 000
			5 000				5 000
				Nov. 1	Opening balance		5 000

Share capital*   No. 300

Oct. 31	Closing balance		10 000	Oct. 1	Cash	GJ	10 000
			10 000				10 000
				Nov. 1	Opening balance		10 000

Retained earnings   No. 310

Oct. 1	Closing balance	—	

Dividends   No. 320

Oct. 20	Cash	GJ	500	

Service revenue   No. 400

Oct. 31	Closing balance		10 400	Oct.	3	Cash	GJ	10 000
					31	Service revenue received in advance	GJ	400
			10 400					10 400
				Oct.	31	Opening balance		10 400

Commissions revenue   No. 405

				Oct. 31	Commissions receivable	GJ	200

Salaries expense   No. 500

Oct. 31	Cash	GJ	4 000	Oct. 31	Closing balance		5 200
31	Salaries payable		1 200				
			5 200				5 200
Oct. 31	Opening balance		5 200				

Advertising supplies expense   No. 505

Oct. 31	Advertising supplies	GJ	1 500	

Rent expense   No. 510

Oct. 3	Cash	GJ	900	

Insurance expense   No. 515

Oct. 31	Prepaid insurance	GJ	50	

Interest expense   No. 518

Oct. 31	Interest payable	GJ	50	

Depreciation expense   No. 520

Oct. 31	Acc. depn—office equipment	GJ	40	

*If the balance in the general ledger is shown, there is no need to balance. The accounts are balanced here only to illustrate that the balances are the 1 November opening balances.

Helpful hint: Recall from chapter 2 that the amount shown as the closing balance is only a balancing item in the ledger account presentation and does not represent the correct account balance at the end of the period because it is shown on the opposite side of the ledger account. The account balance at the end of the period is equal to the opening balance for the new period. Adjusting entries are shown in red.

3.5 The adjusted trial balance and financial statements

LEARNING OBJECTIVE 3.5 Describe the nature and purpose of the adjusted trial balance.

Recall from chapter 2, figure 2.36, a trial balance was prepared. This was presented again in this chapter in figure 3.4. After all adjusting entries have been journalised and posted, another trial balance is prepared from the ledger accounts. This trial balance is called an **adjusted trial balance**. It shows the balances of all accounts, including those that have been adjusted, at the end of the accounting period. The purpose of an adjusted trial balance is to prove that the total debit balances equal the total credit balances in the ledger after all adjustments have been made. Because the accounts contain all the data that are needed for financial statements, the adjusted trial balance is the main basis for the preparation of financial statements.

Preparing the adjusted trial balance

The adjusted trial balance for Wong Pty Ltd presented in figure 3.18 has been prepared from the ledger accounts in figure 3.17. To facilitate the comparison of account balances, the trial balance data, labelled 'Before adjustment' (presented earlier in figure 3.4), are shown alongside the adjusted data, labelled 'After adjustment'. In addition, the amounts affected by the adjusting entries are highlighted in red in the 'After adjustment' columns. (The trial balance before adjustments can be called the *unadjusted trial balance*.)

FIGURE 3.18	Trial balance and adjusted trial balance compared

WONG PTY LTD
Trial balances
as at 31 October 2019

No.	Account name	Before adjustment Dr	Before adjustment Cr	After adjustment Dr	After adjustment Cr
100	Cash	$15 200		$15 200	
105	Commissions receivable			200	
110	Advertising supplies	2 500		1 000	
112	Prepaid insurance	600		550	
130	Office equipment	5 000		5 000	
131	Accumulated depreciation—office equipment				$ 40
200	Accounts payable		$ 2 500		2 500
210	Interest payable				50
213	Service revenue received in advance		1 200		800
215	Salaries payable				1 200
230	Bank loan		5 000		5 000
300	Share capital		10 000		10 000
310	Retained earnings		—		—
320	Dividends	500		500	
400	Service revenue		10 000		10 400
405	Commissions revenue		—		200
500	Salaries expense	4 000		5 200	
505	Advertising supplies expense			1 500	
510	Rent expense	900		900	
515	Insurance expense			50	
518	Interest expense			50	
520	Depreciation expense			40	
		$28 700	$28 700	$30 190	$30 190

Helpful hint: Use the opening *balances for November given in figure 3.17 to prepare the adjusted trial balance. Recall that the closing balances are only balancing items and are on the wrong side of the account.*

Preparing financial statements

Financial statements can be prepared directly from an adjusted trial balance. The interrelationships of data in the adjusted trial balance of Wong Pty Ltd are presented in figures 3.19 and 3.20. As figure 3.19 shows, the statement of profit or loss is prepared from the revenue and expense accounts. Similarly, the retained earnings calculation is derived from the retained earnings account, dividends account, and the profit (or loss) shown in the statement of profit or loss. As shown in figure 3.20, the statement of financial position is then prepared from the asset and liability accounts and the ending retained earnings, as shown in the calculation of retained earnings.

FIGURE 3.19 Preparation of the statement of profit or loss and calculation of retained earnings from the adjusted trial balance

WONG PTY LTD
Adjusted trial balance
as at 31 October 2019

Account name	Debit	Credit
Cash	$15 200	
Commissions receivable	200	
Advertising supplies	1 000	
Prepaid insurance	550	
Office equipment	5 000	
Accumulated depreciation— office equipment		$ 40
Accounts payable		2 500
Interest payable		50
Service revenue received in advance		800
Salaries payable		1 200
Bank loan		5 000
Share capital		10 000
Retained earnings		—
Dividends	500	
Service revenue		10 400
Commissions revenue		200
Salaries expense	5 200	
Advertising supplies expense	1 500	
Rent expense	900	
Insurance expense	50	
Interest expense	50	
Depreciation expense	40	
	$30 190	$30 190

WONG PTY LTD
Statement of profit or loss
for the month ended 31 October 2019

REVENUES		
Service revenue		$10 400
Commissions revenue		200
		10 600
EXPENSES		
Salaries expense	$5 200	
Advertising supplies expense	1 500	
Rent expense	900	
Insurance expense	50	
Interest expense	50	
Depreciation expense	40	
Total expenses		7 740
Profit		$ 2 860

WONG PTY LTD
Calculation of retained earnings
for the month ended 31 October 2019

Retained earnings, 1 October	$ —
Add: Profit	2 860
	2 860
Less: Dividends	500
Retained earnings, 31 October	$2 360

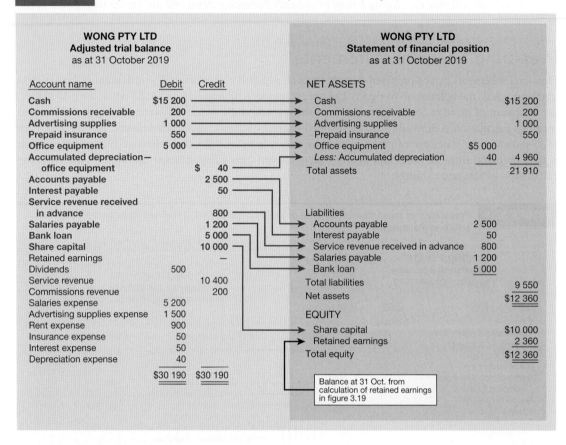

3.6 Closing the books

LEARNING OBJECTIVE 3.6 Explain the purpose of closing entries.

In previous chapters you learned that revenue and expense accounts and the dividends account are subdivisions of retained earnings, which is reported in the equity section of the statement of financial position. Because revenues, expenses and dividends relate to only a given accounting period, they are considered **temporary accounts** (sometimes called *nominal accounts*). In contrast, all statement of financial position accounts are considered **permanent accounts** because their balances are carried forward into future accounting periods. Figure 3.21 identifies the accounts in each category.

Preparing closing entries

At the end of the reporting period, the temporary account balances are transferred to the permanent equity account — retained earnings — through the preparation of closing entries. **Closing entries** formally recognise in the ledger the transfer of profit (or loss) and dividends to retained earnings, which will be shown in the retained earnings section of the statement of changes in equity. For example, notice that in figure 3.20 retained earnings has an adjusted balance of nil. This is because it was Wong Pty Ltd's first year of operations. Retained earnings started with a nil balance, and profit has not yet been calculated and closed to retained earnings. Therefore, the adjusted balance is still nil. Similarly, the nil balance does not reflect dividends declared during the period, since the dividends account has not yet been closed to retained earnings.

FIGURE 3.21 Temporary versus permanent accounts

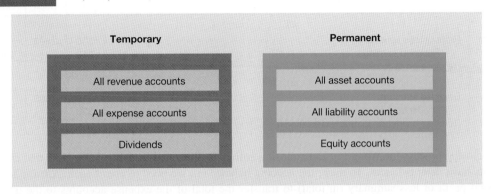

In addition to updating retained earnings to its correct ending balance, closing entries produce a _nil balance in each temporary account._ As a result, these accounts are ready to accumulate data about revenues, expenses and dividends in the next accounting period that is separate from the data in the previous periods. Permanent accounts are not closed. Closing entries are recorded in the general journal and then posted to the general ledger.

When closing entries are prepared, each statement of profit or loss account could be closed directly to retained earnings. However, to do so would result in excessive detail in the retained earnings account. Accordingly, the revenue and expense accounts are closed to another temporary account, **profit or loss summary**, and only the resulting profit or loss is transferred from this account to retained earnings. The closing entries for Wong Pty Ltd are shown in figure 3.22. For the purposes of this illustration, we have assumed that 31 October is the end of Wong Pty Ltd's reporting period.

Helpful hint: Total revenues are closed to profit or loss summary, total expenses are closed to profit or loss summary, and the balance in the profit or loss summary is a profit or loss.

FIGURE 3.22 Closing entries journalised

General journal				
Date	Account name (narration)	Post ref.	Debit	Credit
	Closing entries			
2019	_(1)_			
Oct. 31	Service revenue	400	10 400	
	Commissions revenue	405	200	
	Profit or loss summary	330		10 600
	(To close revenue accounts)			
	_(2)_			
31	Profit or loss summary	330	7 740	
	Salaries expense	500		5 200
	Advertising supplies expense	505		1 500
	Rent expense	510		900
	Insurance expense	515		50
	Interest expense	518		50
	Depreciation expense	520		40
	(To close expense accounts)			

Date	Account name (narration)	Post ref.	Debit	Credit
2019	*(3)*			
Oct. 31	Profit or loss summary	330	2 860	
	Retained earnings	310		2 860
	(To close profit to retained earnings)			
	(4)			
31	Retained earnings	310	500	
	Dividends	320		500
	(To close dividends to retained earnings)			

The closing process for Wong Pty Ltd's closing entries is illustrated in figure 3.23. Note that expense accounts have debit balances. To make the account balance nil, we need to credit each expense account and debit profit or loss summary (in total) to transfer the total of the expense accounts to the profit or loss summary account. As revenue accounts have credit balances, we need to debit revenue accounts to reduce them to a nil balance and transfer the revenue to the profit or loss summary account.

Helpful hint: Recall that the account names within each general ledger account are cross-references, e.g. 'Cash' in the salaries expense account. Cross-references indicate the ledger account to which the opposite side of the entry is posted. (See figure 2.21 and the associated text for more on cross-referencing.)

FIGURE 3.23   Posting of closing entries

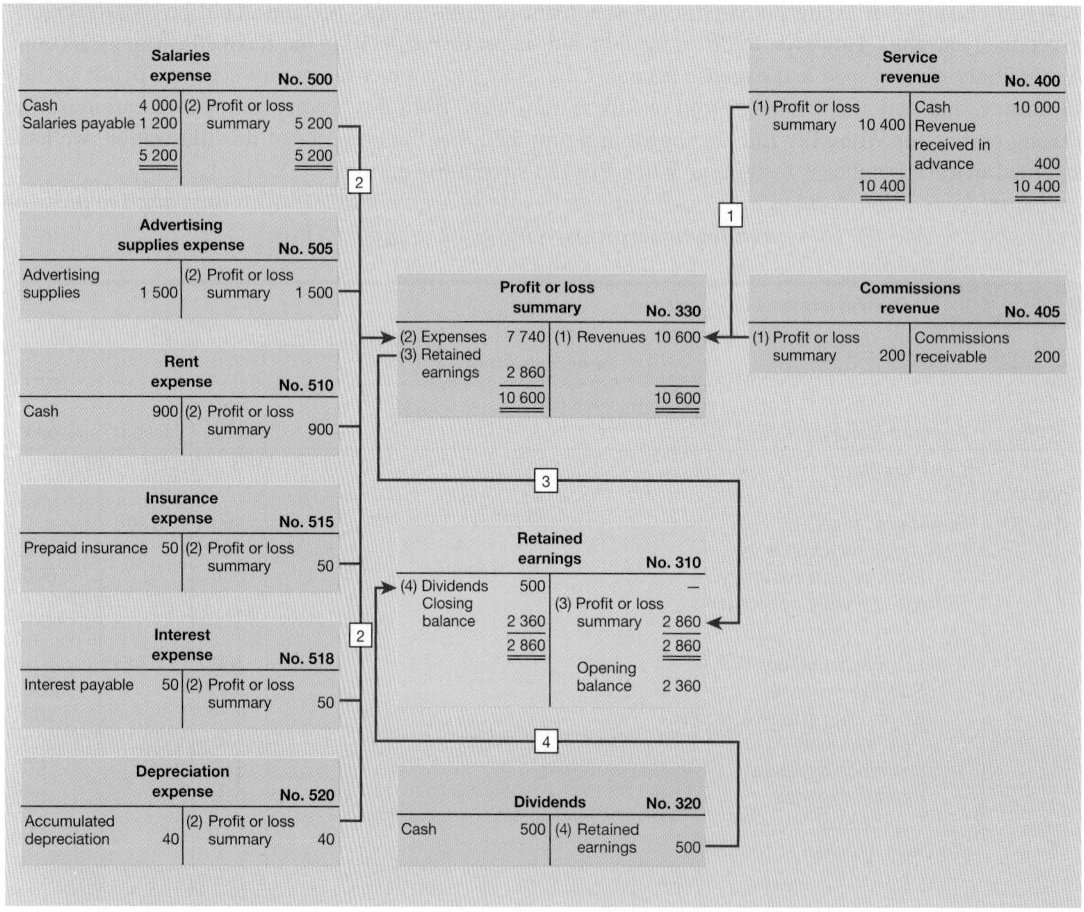

Preparing a post-closing trial balance

After all closing entries are journalised and posted, another trial balance, called a **post-closing trial balance**, is prepared from the ledger. A post-closing trial balance is a list of all permanent accounts and their balances after closing entries are journalised and posted. The purpose of this trial balance is to prove the sum of the debit balances equals the sum of the credit balances that are carried forward into the next accounting period. Since all temporary accounts will have nil balances, the post-closing trial balance will contain only permanent — statement of financial position — accounts.

3.7 Summary of the accounting cycle

LEARNING OBJECTIVE 3.7 Describe the required steps in the accounting cycle.

The required steps in the accounting cycle are shown graphically in figure 3.24. You can see that the cycle begins with the analysis of business transactions and ends with the preparation of a post-closing trial balance. The steps in the cycle are performed in sequence and are repeated in each accounting period.

FIGURE 3.24   Required steps in the accounting cycle

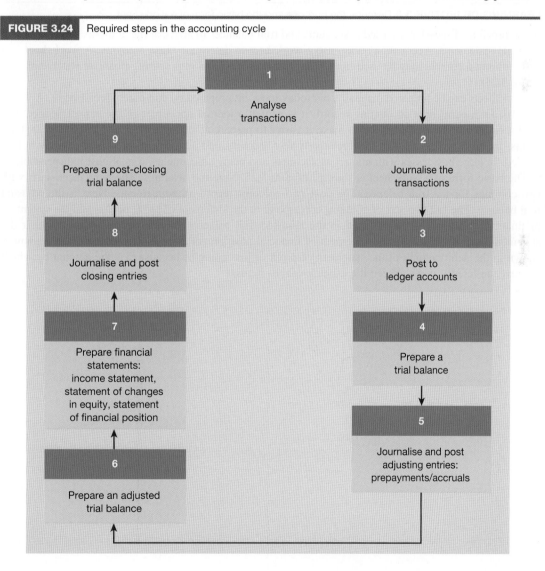

Steps 1–3 may occur daily during the accounting period, as explained in chapter 2. Steps 4–7 are performed on a periodic basis, such as monthly, 6-monthly or annually. Steps 8 and 9, closing entries and a post-closing trial balance, are usually prepared only at the end of a business's financial year.

3.8 Adjusting entries — using a worksheet

LEARNING OBJECTIVE 3.8 Describe the purpose and the basic form of a worksheet.

In the previous discussion we used T accounts and trial balances to arrive at the amounts used to prepare financial statements. Accountants often use a worksheet to determine these amounts. A **worksheet** is a multicolumn form that may be used in the adjustment process and in preparing financial statements (see figure 3.25).

Worksheets can be prepared manually, but today most are prepared on computer spreadsheets. A worksheet is not a permanent accounting record; it is neither a journal nor a part of the general ledger. The worksheet is merely a device used to make it easier to prepare adjusting entries and the financial statements. In small businesses that have relatively few accounts and adjustments, a worksheet may not be needed. In large businesses with numerous accounts and many adjustments, it is almost indispensable.

The basic form of a worksheet is shown in figure 3.25. Note the headings. The worksheet starts with two columns for the trial balance. The next two columns record all adjustments. Next is the adjusted trial balance. The last two sets of columns correspond to the statement of profit or loss and the statement of financial position. All items listed in the adjusted trial balance columns are recorded in either the statement of profit or loss or the statement of financial position columns. Note that the profit amount is shown in the debit column of the statement of profit or loss columns because it is the amount by which the revenue (credit) items exceed the expense (debit) items.

FIGURE 3.25 Form and procedure for a worksheet

WONG PTY LTD
Worksheet
for the month ended 31 October 2019

No.	Account names	Trial balance Dr	Trial balance Cr	Adjustments Dr	Adjustments Cr	Adjusted trial balance Dr	Adjusted trial balance Cr	Statement of profit or loss Dr	Statement of profit or loss Cr	Statement of financial position Dr	Statement of financial position Cr
100	Cash	15 200				15 200				15 200	
110	Advertising supplies	2 500			(a) 1 500	1 000				1 000	
112	Prepaid insurance	600			(b) 50	550				550	
130	Office equipment	5 000				5 000				5 000	
200	Accounts payable		2 500				2 500				2 500
230	Bank loan		5 000				5 000				5 000
213	Serv. rev. rec'd in advance		1 200	(d) 400			800				800
300	Share capital		10 000				10 000				10 000
310	Retained earnings		—				—				—
320	Dividends	500				500				500	
400	Service revenue		10 000		(d) 400		10 400		10 400		
405	Commissions revenue				(e) 200		200		200		
500	Salaries expense	4 000		(g) 1 200		5 200		5 200			
510	Rent expense	900				900		900			
	Totals	28 700	28 700								
505	Advertising supplies expense			(a) 1 500		1 500		1 500			
515	Insurance expense			(b) 50		50		50			
131	Accum. depn—off. equip.				(c) 40		40				40
520	Depreciation expense			(c) 40		40		40			
518	Interest expense			(f) 50		50		50			
105	Commissions receivable			(e) 200		200				200	
210	Interest payable				(f) 50		50				50
215	Salaries payable				(g) 1 200		1 200				1 200
	Totals			3 440	3 440	30 190	30 190	7 740	10 600	22 450	19 590
	Profit							2 860			2 860
	Totals							10 600	10 600	22 450	22 450

1. Prepare a trial balance on the worksheet

2. Enter adjustment data

3. Calculate adjusted balances

4. Extend adjusted balances to appropriate statement columns

5. Total the statement columns, calculate profit (or loss), and complete worksheet

People Care Ltd provides managed healthcare services to more than 12 000 people. With its head office in Auckland, it has over 160 employees throughout the North and South Islands. A simplified version of People Care's 31 December 2019 adjusted trial balance is shown below.

PEOPLE CARE LTD Adjusted trial balance as at 31 December 2019		
Account name	Dr $'000	Cr $'000
Cash	913	
Short-term investments	1 594	
Receivables	276	
Other current assets	336	
Property and equipment (net)	433	
Long-term investments	305	
Other non-current assets	1 639	
Medical costs payable		484
Trade creditors		1 865
Other current liabilities		294
Long-term borrowing		1 165
Share capital		935
Dividends	—	
Retained earnings		624
Revenues		9 781
Medical cost expense	8 041	
Selling and administrative expense	1 328	
Depreciation expense	128	
Other expenses	34	
Interest expense	47	
Income tax expense	74	
	15 148	15 148

Required

From the trial balance, prepare the following internal reports and calculations: a statement of profit or loss, a statement of changes in equity and a statement of financial position. Be sure to prepare them in that order, since the calculation of retained earnings depends on the profit that is determined in the statement of profit or loss, and the statement of financial position requires information generated by the calculation of retained earnings.

Solution

PEOPLE CARE LTD Statement of profit or loss for the year ended 31 December 2019		
	$'000	$'000
Revenues		9 781
EXPENSES		
Medical cost expense	8 041	
Selling and administrative expense	1 328	
Depreciation expense	128	
Interest expense	47	
Other expenses	34	
Income tax expense	74	9 652
Profit		**129**

PEOPLE CARE LTD Calculation of retained earnings for the year ended 31 December 2019	$'000
Beginning retained earnings	624
Profit	129
Less: Dividends	—
Ending retained earnings	753

PEOPLE CARE LTD
Statement of financial position
as at 31 December 2019

	$'000	$'000
ASSETS		
Current assets		
Cash	$ 913	
Short-term investments	1 594	
Receivables	276	
Other current assets	336	
Total current assets		$3 119
Non-current assets		
Long-term investments	305	
Property and equipment (net)	433	
Other non-current assets	1 639	
Total non-current assets		2 377
Total assets		5 496
LIABILITIES		
Current liabilities		
Medical costs payable	484	
Trade creditors	1 865	
Other current liabilities	294	
Total current liabilities		2 643
Non-current liabilities		
Long-term borrowing	1 165	
Total non-current liabilities		1 165
Total liabilities		3 808
Net assets		**$1 688**
EQUITY		
Share capital		935
Retained earnings		753
Total equity		**$1 688**

SUMMARY

3.1 Differentiate between the cash basis and the accrual basis of accounting.
Accrual-based accounting means that transactions and events are recognised in the periods in which they occur rather than when the associated cash flows occur. Under the cash basis, transactions and events are recognised only in the periods in which the business receives or pays the associated cash.

3.2 Explain criteria for revenue recognition and expense recognition.
Criteria for the recognition of revenues and expenses facilitate the recording of revenues and expenses in a given accounting period. Under the *Conceptual Framework*, revenues should be recognised when an inflow or saving in outflows of future economic benefits is probable and can be measured reliably. Generally, for a service business, revenue is recognised when the service is performed, and for a merchandising business, revenue is recognised when the goods are delivered. Expenses should be recognised when the decrease in assets or the increase in liabilities is probable and can be measured reliably.

The new accounting standard for recognising revenue, IFRS 15/AASB 15 *Revenue from Contracts with Customers*, became effective from 1 January 2018. Essentially, revenue is recognised when an entity satisfies a performance obligation in a contract. The following conditions must be met: the contract has been approved by parties to the contract; each party's rights in relation to the goods or services to be transferred have been identified; the payment terms have been identified; the contract has commercial substance; and it is probable that the consideration to which the entity is entitled in exchange for the goods or services will be collected.

3.3 Explain why adjusting entries are needed and identify the major types of adjusting entries.
Adjusting entries are made at the end of an accounting period. They ensure that all revenues and expenses are recorded in each accounting period. The major types of adjusting entries are prepaid expenses, revenues received in advance, accrued revenues and accrued expenses.

3.4 Prepare adjusting entries for prepayments and accruals.
Prepayments are either prepaid expenses or revenues received in advance. Adjusting entries for prepaid expenses and revenues that were originally recorded as assets and liabilities respectively are made by reducing the asset and increasing expenses and reducing the liability and increasing revenue. Accruals are either accrued revenues or accrued expenses. Adjusting entries for accruals record revenues and expenses and related assets and liabilities respectively in the current accounting period that have not been recognised through daily entries.

3.5 Describe the nature and purpose of the adjusted trial balance.
An adjusted trial balance is a trial balance that shows the balances of all accounts, including those that have been adjusted, at the end of an accounting period. The purpose of an adjusted trial balance is to show the effects of all financial events that have occurred during the accounting period, to check that debits equal credits, and to assist in preparing financial statements.

3.6 Explain the purpose of closing entries.
One purpose of closing entries is to transfer the results of operations for the reporting period to retained earnings. Additionally, it creates nil balances in all temporary accounts (revenue accounts, expense accounts and dividends), ready for the start of the next reporting period. To accomplish this, all temporary accounts are 'closed' at the end of the reporting period. Separate entries are made to close revenues and expenses to profit or loss summary, profit or loss summary to retained earnings, and dividends to retained earnings. Only temporary accounts are closed.

3.7 Describe the required steps in the accounting cycle.
The required steps in the accounting cycle are: (a) analyse business transactions, (b) journalise the transactions, (c) post to ledger accounts, (d) prepare a trial balance, (e) journalise and post adjusting entries, (f) prepare an adjusted trial balance, (g) prepare financial statements, (h) journalise and post closing entries, and (i) prepare a post-closing trial balance.

3.8 Describe the purpose and the basic form of a worksheet.

The worksheet is used to make it easier to prepare adjusting entries and the financial statements. It is often prepared on a computer spreadsheet. The sets of columns of the worksheet are, from left to right, the unadjusted trial balance, adjustments, adjusted trial balance, statement of profit or loss and statement of financial position.

DECISION-MAKING TOOLKIT — A SUMMARY

DECISION-MAKING TOOLKIT

Decision/issue	Info needed for analysis	Tool or technique to use for decision	How to evaluate results to make decision
At what point should the entity recognise (record) revenue?	Need to understand the nature of the entity's business	Revenue is recognised when an entity satisfies a performance obligation in a contract. The following conditions must be met: the contract has been approved by parties to the contract; each party's rights in relation to the goods or services to be transferred have been identified; the payment terms have been identified; the contract has commercial substance; and it is probable that the consideration to which the entity is entitled in exchange for the goods or services will be collected.	Recognising revenue too early overstates current period revenue; recognising it too late understates current period revenue.
At what point should the entity recognise (record) expenses?	Need to understand the nature of the entity's business	Expenses should be recognised when decreases in assets or increases in liabilities that result in a decrease in equity are probable and can be measured reliably.	Recognising expenses too early overstates current period expenses; recognising them too late understates current period expenses.

KEY TERMS

accounting period concept An accounting concept that the economic life of an entity can be divided into discrete periods of time and that useful reports covering those periods can be prepared by the entity.

accrual-based accounting The accounting basis in which transactions and events are recorded in the periods in which they meet the recognition criteria for assets, liabilities, revenues and expenses. Recognition can occur before, as or after cash is paid or received.

accrued expenses Amounts that are recorded as adjusting entries for expenses that are not yet paid and not yet recorded but for which the consumption of economic benefits has occurred.

accrued revenues Amounts recognised as adjusting entries for revenues that are not yet received and not yet recorded but for which the goods or services have been provided.

adjusted trial balance A list of accounts and their balances after all adjustments have been made.

adjusting entries Entries made at the end of an accounting period to ensure that recognition criteria are followed for assets, liabilities, revenues and expenses.

carrying amount The cost of an asset less accumulated depreciation. This is also referred to as book value.

cash-based accounting An accounting basis in which revenue is recorded only when cash is received, and an expense is recorded only when cash is paid.

closing entries Entries at the end of the reporting period to transfer the balances of temporary accounts to a permanent equity account, retained earnings.

contra asset account An account that is offset against another account on the statement of financial position.

depreciation The process of allocating to expense the cost of an asset over its useful life in a rational and systematic manner.

expense recognition criteria Expenses are recognised when the outflow of future economic benefits is probable and can be measured reliably.

financial year An accounting period that is 1 year in duration.

operating cycle The length of time it takes for a business to acquire goods, sell them to customers and collect the cash from the sale.

permanent accounts Statement of financial position accounts; accounts for which balances are carried forward to the next accounting period.

post-closing trial balance A list of permanent accounts and their balances after closing entries have been journalised and posted.

prepaid expenses (prepayments) Amounts paid in cash and recorded as assets until the economic benefits expire or are consumed.

profit or loss summary A temporary account used in closing revenue and expense accounts.

revenue recognition criteria Under the *Conceptual Framework*, revenues are recognised when an inflow of future economic benefits is probable and can be measured reliably. According to IFRS 15, revenue is recognised when an entity satisfies a performance obligation in a contract and it is probable that the consideration to which the entity is entitled in exchange for the goods or service will be collected.

revenues received in advance Amounts received from customers and recorded as liabilities until the services are performed or the goods are provided and the revenue is recognised.

reversing entry An entry made at the beginning of the next accounting period; the exact opposite of the adjusting entry made in the previous period.

temporary accounts Revenue, expense and dividend accounts; accounts for which balances are transferred to retained earnings at the end of a reporting period.

useful life The length of service of an asset to the entity.

worksheet A multicolumn spreadsheet, prepared either manually or electronically, that may be used in the adjustment process and in preparing financial statements.

DEMONSTRATION PROBLEM 1

Web Expert Consultants Pty Ltd began business on 1 April. At 30 April the trial balance shows the following balances for selected accounts:

110	Prepaid insurance	$ 7 200
120	Equipment	56 000
200	Bank loan	40 000
210	Service revenue received in advance	9 600
300	Service revenue	3 600
	Other accounts include:	
100	Accounts receivable	
121	Accumulated depreciation—equipment	
205	Interest payable	
400	Insurance expense	
405	Depreciation expense	
410	Interest expense	

Analysis reveals the following additional data pertaining to these accounts:
1. Prepaid insurance is the cost of a 2-year insurance policy, effective 1 April.
2. Depreciation on the equipment is $1000 per month.
3. Web Expert Consultants Pty Ltd took out the loan on 1 April for a period of 6 months at an annual interest rate of 6%.
4. Eight customers paid for Web Expert Consultants Pty Ltd's 6-month service package of $1200 beginning in April. These customers were serviced in April.
5. Services performed for other customers but not invoiced at 30 April totalled $3000.

Required

Prepare the adjusting entries for the month of April. Show calculations and provide post references and narrations.

PROBLEM-SOLVING STRATEGIES
1. Note that adjustments are being made for 1 month.
2. Make calculations carefully.
3. Select account names carefully.
4. Make sure debits are made first and credits are indented.
5. Check that debits equal credits for each entry.

SOLUTION TO DEMONSTRATION PROBLEM 1

	General journal			
Date	Account name (narration)	Post ref.	Debit	Credit
Apr. 30	Insurance expense	400	300	
	Prepaid insurance	110		300
	(To record insurance expired:			
	$7200 ÷ 24 = $300 per month)			
30	Depreciation expense	405	1 000	
	Accumulated depn—equipment	121		1 000
	(To record monthly depreciation)			
30	Interest expense	410	200	
	Interest payable	205		200
	(To accrue interest on loan:			
	$40 000 × 6% × 1/12 = $200)			
30	Service revenue received in advance	210	1 600	
	Service revenue	300		1 600
	(To record revenue: $1200 ÷ 6 = $200;			
	$200 per month × 8 = $1600 *or* $9600 ÷ 6)			
30	Accounts receivable	100	3 000	
	Service revenue	300		3 000
	(To accrue revenue not invoiced or collected)			

DEMONSTRATION PROBLEM 2

Rosy Narr is enrolled in an introductory accounting course at university. She is currently studying for a quiz on adjusting entries and has completed the following revision question from her textbook. She wasn't sure how to answer the question, so she answered it in three different ways. You are her tutor, and she has asked you to check and comment on her answers.

REVISION QUESTION

XYZ Ltd pays for a 1-year insurance policy commencing on 1 June 2019 in cash. The policy costs $12 000. This is the first time the entity has taken out an insurance policy. The end of the entity's reporting period is 30 June 2019.

Required

(a) Record the payment of insurance on 1 June 2019 in general journal format.

(b) Record the adjusting entry on 30 June 2019 in general journal format.

(c) Determine the balances in both the insurance expense and prepaid insurance general ledger accounts at 30 June 2019.

ROSY'S ANSWERS

Method 1

(a) 2019			
June 1	Dr Prepaid insurance	12 000	
	Cr Cash		12 000
(b) June 30	Dr Insurance expense	1 000	
	Cr Prepaid insurance		1 000

(c) Insurance expense $1000, prepaid insurance $11 000 (both are debit balances)

Method 2

(a) 2019			
June 1	Dr Insurance expense	12 000	
	Cr Cash		12 000
(b) June 30	Dr Prepaid insurance	11 000	
	Cr Insurance expense		11 000

(c) Insurance expense $1000, prepaid insurance $11 000 (both are debit balances)

Method 3

(a) 2019			
June 1	Dr Insurance expense	1 000	
	Dr Prepaid insurance	11 000	
	Cr Cash		12 000

(b) No adjusting entry required

(c) Insurance expense $1000, prepaid insurance $11 000 (both are debit balances)

TUTOR'S COMMENTS

All your answers are correct. Well done, Rosy! You have prepared a very comprehensive answer to the question and it shows that you have a very good understanding of recording adjusting entries for pre-payments. In method 1 you record the entire insurance payment as an asset; the adjusting entry then decreases the asset by the amount that has expired and increases the expense that relates to the reporting period. This leaves the correct balances of $1000 for the insurance expense for the period and $11 000 for prepaid insurance (asset).

In method 2 you record all the insurance payment as an expense; at the end of the reporting period, the adjusting entry reduces the expense and increases the asset account as you are deferring the amount that is still an asset. Once again, this results in the correct balance of $1000 for the insurance expense for the period and $11 000 for prepaid insurance (asset).

Method 3 is also correct as it has correctly allocated the amount paid between the expense for the period and the remaining asset. This method requires no adjusting entry as the initial entry results in a correct balance of $1000 for the insurance expense for the period and $11 000 in prepaid insurance that would be reported in the financial statements.

Well done, Rosy. Good luck in the quiz.

SELF-STUDY QUESTIONS

3.1 Under the cash basis of accounting: **LO1**

(a) cash must be received before income is recognised.

(b) profit is calculated by deducting liabilities from the assets.

(c) events that change a company's accounting reports are recognised in the period they occur rather than in the period in which cash is paid or received.

(d) the ledger accounts must be adjusted to reflect unrecorded transactions before the financial reports are prepared.

3.2 Using accrual-based accounting, expenses are recorded and reported only: **LO1**

(a) if they are paid before they are incurred.

(b) when they are incurred and paid at the same time.

(c) when they are incurred, whether or not cash is paid.

(d) if they are paid after they are incurred.

3.3 Betty's Bookkeeper Service uses cash-based accounting for the financial statements. Betty performs a bookkeeping service on 31 July. The client picks up their books and the financial reports on 1 August and mails the payment to Betty on 5 August. Betty receives the cheque in the mail on 6 August. When should Betty show that the income was earned? **LO1**

(a) 31 July.

(b) 1 August.

(c) 5 August.

(d) 6 August.

3.4 What is the accounting period concept? **LO2**

(a) A business will continue to operate for a long period of time.

(b) The economic life of a business can be divided into artificial time periods.

(c) The financial year should correspond with the calendar year.

(d) None of the above.

3.5 Adjusting entries are made to ensure that: **LO3**

(a) economic transactions and events affecting the business are recorded even if cash has not been received or paid.

(b) statement of profit or loss accounts have correct balances at the end of an accounting period.

(c) statement of financial position accounts have correct balances at the end of an accounting period.

(d) all of the above.

3.6 Each of the following is a major type (or category) of adjusting entry *except*: **LO3**

(a) prepaid expenses.

(b) accrued revenues.

(c) accrued expenses.

(d) earned expenses.

3.7 The trial balance shows Supplies $1350 and Supplies expense $0. If $600 of supplies are on hand at the end of the period, the adjusting entry is: **LO4**

(a) Supplies	600	
Supplies expense		600
(b) Supplies	750	
Supplies expense		750
(c) Supplies expense	750	
Supplies		750
(d) Supplies expense	600	
Supplies		600

3.8 Adjustments to decrease revenues received in advance: **LO4**
    (a) decrease liabilities and increase revenues.
    (b) increase liabilities and increase revenues.
    (c) increase assets and increase revenues.
    (d) decrease revenues and decrease assets.

3.9 Adjustments to accrue revenues: **LO4**
    (a) increase assets and increase liabilities.
    (b) increase assets and increase revenues.
    (c) decrease assets and decrease revenues.
    (d) decrease liabilities and increase revenues.

3.10 Kathy Kiska earned a salary of $1000 for the week ending Friday, 3 October. She will be paid on 2 October. The adjusting entry for Kathy's employer at 30 September is: **LO4**

| (a) | Salaries expense | 1 000 | |
| | Salaries payable | | 1 000 |

| (b) | Salaries expense | 600 | |
| | Salaries payable | | 600 |

| (c) | Salaries payable | 600 | |
| | Salaries expense | | 600 |

| (d) | Salaries expense | 400 | |
| | Salaries payable | | 400 |

3.11 Which statement is *incorrect* concerning the adjusted trial balance? **LO5**
    (a) An adjusted trial balance proves the equality of the total debit balances and the total credit balances in the ledger after all adjustments are made.
    (b) The adjusted trial balance provides the main basis for the preparation of financial statements.
    (c) The adjusted trial balance lists only permanent accounts.
    (d) The adjusted trial balance is prepared after the adjusting entries have been journalised and posted.

3.12 Which one of these statements about the accrual basis of accounting is *false*? **LO1**
    (a) Events that change an entity's financial statements are recorded in the periods in which the events occur.
    (b) For a service organisation, revenue is generally recognised in the period in which the service is performed.
    (c) This basis is in accord with generally accepted accounting principles.
    (d) Revenue is recorded only when cash is received, and expenses are recorded only when cash is paid.

3.13 The accounting cycle begins with the analysis of transactions and may end with the: **LO7**
    (a) preparation of financial statements.
    (b) posting of transactions to ledger accounts.
    (c) journalising of adjusting entries.
    (d) preparation of a post-closing trial balance.

3.14 Which account will have a nil balance after closing entries have been journalised and posted? **LO6**

    (a) Service revenue.
    (b) Advertising supplies.
    (c) Prepaid insurance.
    (d) Accumulated depreciation.

3.15 Which types of accounts will appear in the post-closing trial balance? **LO6, 7**
   (a) Permanent accounts.
   (b) Temporary accounts.
   (c) Accounts shown in the statement of profit or loss columns of a worksheet.
   (d) None of the above.

QUESTIONS

3.1 (a) How does the accounting period concept affect an accountant's analysis of accounting transactions?
   (b) Explain the term *financial year*.

3.2 Identify and state two generally accepted accounting principles that relate to adjusting the accounts.

3.3 Outline the revenue recognition criteria under IFRS 15/AASB 15 *Revenue from Contracts with Customers* and explain how they are applied to the sale of goods or performing a service.

3.4 Tony Gale, a solicitor, accepts a legal engagement in March, performs the work in April, and is paid in May. If Gale's law firm prepares monthly financial statements, when should it recognise revenue from this engagement? Why?

3.5 In completing the engagement in question 3.4, Gale incurs $2000 of expenses in March, $1000 in April and $600 in May. How much expense should be deducted from revenues in the month the revenue is recognised? Why?

3.6 Why might the financial information in a trial balance not be up to date and complete?

3.7 Distinguish between the two categories of adjusting entries, and identify the types of adjustments applicable to each category.

3.8 Explain the differences between depreciation expense and accumulated depreciation.

3.9 An entity has recognised revenue for which the services have not been performed but the cash has been received. Which of the following accounts are involved in the adjusting entry: (a) asset, (b) liability, (c) revenue or (d) expense? For the accounts selected, indicate whether they would be debited or credited in the entry.

3.10 An entity recognised some expenditure as an expense but the future benefits have not expired. Indicate which of the following accounts is debited and which is credited in the adjusting entry: (a) asset, (b) liability, (c) revenue or (d) expense.

3.11 For each of the following items before adjustment, indicate the type of adjusting entry — prepaid expense, revenue received in advance, accrued revenue, and accrued expense — that is needed to correct the misstatement. If the misstatement could result from more than one type of entry or unrecorded item, indicate each or all of the adjustments required.
   (a) Assets are understated.
   (b) Liabilities are overstated.
   (c) Liabilities are understated.
   (d) Expenses are understated.
   (e) Assets are overstated.
   (f) Revenue is understated.

3.12 What is the basic form and purpose of a worksheet?

BRIEF EXERCISES

BE3.1 Identify the impact of transactions on cash and retained earnings. **LO1**
   Transactions that affect profits do not necessarily affect cash.

Required

Identify the effect, if any, that each of the following transactions would have upon cash and retained earnings. The first transaction has been completed as an example.

	Cash	Retained earnings
(a) Purchased $120 supplies for cash.	$–120	$–
(b) Recorded an adjusting entry to record use of $60 of the above supplies.		
(c) Made sales of $1200, all on account.		
(d) Received $960 from customers in payment of their accounts.		
(e) Purchased a photocopier for cash, $3000.		
(f) Recorded depreciation of building for period used, $1200.		
(g) Purchased inventory, $2000 on account.		

BE3.2 Identify the major types of adjusting entries. **LO3**

Riko Ltd accumulates the following adjustment data at 31 March. Indicate (1) the type of adjustment (prepaid expense, accrued revenues, and so on) and (2) the status of the accounts before adjustment (overstated or understated).

(a) Supplies of $600 are on hand. Supplies account shows $1900 balance.

(b) Service provided to customers but not invoiced totals $900.

(c) Interest of $200 is due on a bank loan.

(d) The period for which rent had been collected in advance, totalling $800, has expired.

BE3.3 Prepare adjusting entry for depreciation. **LO4**

At the end of its first year, the trial balance of Shah Ltd shows equipment $25 000 and zero balances in accumulated depreciation—equipment and depreciation expense. Depreciation for the year is estimated to be $3000. Prepare the adjusting entry for depreciation at 30 June, post the adjustments to T accounts, and indicate the statement of financial position presentation of the equipment at 30 June.

BE3.4 Prepare adjusting entries for accruals. **LO4**

The bookkeeper for DeVoe Ltd asks you to prepare the following accrued adjusting entries at 30 June:

(a) Interest on loan of $200 is accrued.

(b) Services performed but not yet invoiced total $700.

(c) Salaries of $700 earned by employees have not been recorded.

Use these account names: Service revenue, Service revenue receivable, Interest expense, Interest payable, Salaries expense, and Salaries payable.

BE3.5 Analyse accounts in an adjusted trial balance. **LO5**

The trial balance of Hoi Ltd includes the following statement of financial position accounts. Identify the accounts that might require adjustment and for each indicate (1) the type of adjusting entry (prepaid expenses, revenue received in advance, accrued revenues, and accrued expenses) and (2) the related account in the adjusting entry.

(a) Accounts receivable.

(b) Prepaid insurance.

(c) Equipment.

(d) Accumulated depreciation—equipment.

(e) Bank loan.

(f) Interest payable.

(g) Service revenue received in advance.

(h) Interest receivable.

(i) Wages payable.

BE3.6 **Identify the financial statement for selected accounts; identify post-closing trial balance accounts.** **LO6, 7**

The following selected accounts appear in the adjusted trial balance for Khanna Ltd. Indicate the financial statement on which each balance would be reported, and identify the accounts that would be included in a post-closing trial balance.

(a) Accumulated depreciation.
(b) Depreciation expense.
(c) Retained earnings.
(d) Dividends.
(e) Service revenue.
(f) Supplies.
(g) Accounts payable.

BE3.7 **List the required steps in the accounting cycle sequence.** **LO7**

The required steps in the accounting cycle are listed in random order below. List the steps in proper sequence.

(a) Journalise the transactions.
(b) Post to ledger accounts.
(c) Prepare a post-closing trial balance.
(d) Prepare an adjusted trial balance.
(e) Analyse business transactions.
(f) Journalise and post closing entries.
(g) Journalise and post adjusting entries.
(h) Prepare financial statements.
(i) Prepare a trial balance.

EXERCISES

E3.1 **Determine cash-basis and accrual-basis revenue.** **LO1**

In its first year of operations, Tang Pty Ltd generated $78 000 for services provided, $12 000 of which was on account and still outstanding at year-end. The remaining $66 000 was received in cash from customers.

The company incurred operating expenses of $45 000. Of these expenses, $40 500 were paid in cash; $4500 was still on account at year-end. In addition, Tang Pty Ltd prepaid $6500 for insurance coverage that would not commence until the second year of operations.

Required

(a) Calculate the first year's profit under the cash basis of accounting, and calculate the first year's profit under the accrual basis of accounting.
(b) Which basis of accounting (cash or accrual) provides more useful information for decision makers?

E3.2 **Identify accounting concepts, principles, criteria and constraints.** **LO2**

These are the concepts, principles, criteria and constraints discussed in this and previous chapters:

1. Accounting entity concept.
2. Accounting period concept.
3. Cost principle.
4. Expense recognition criteria.
5. Full disclosure principle.
6. Going concern principle.
7. Materiality.
8. Monetary principle.
9. Revenue recognition criteria.

Required

Identify by number the accounting concept, principle or constraint that describes each situation below. Do not use a number more than once.

_____ (a) Is the rationale for why plant assets are not reported at liquidation value. (Do not use the cost principle.)

_____ (b) Indicates that personal and business record keeping should be separately maintained.

_____ (c) Ensures that all relevant financial information is reported.

_____ (d) Assumes that the dollar is the 'measuring stick' used to report on financial performance.

_____ (e) Requires that accounting standards be followed for items that are reasonably expected to affect decisions.

_____ (f) Separates financial information into time periods for reporting purposes.

_____ (g) Requires recognition of expenses when the flow of economic benefits from the entity is probable and able to be reliably measured.

_____ (h) Indicates that market value changes subsequent to purchase are not recorded in the accounts.

E3.3 Identify the violated concept, principle or criterion.   **LO2**

Here are some accounting reporting situations:

(a) Tercek Ltd recognises revenue at the end of the production cycle but before sale. The price of the product, as well as the amount that can be sold, is not certain.

(b) Bonilla Co. Ltd is in its fifth year of operation and has yet to issue financial statements. (Do not use the full disclosure principle.)

(c) Barton Ltd is carrying inventory at its current market value of $100 000. Inventory had an original cost of $110 000.

(d) Hospital Supply Co. Ltd reports only current assets and current liabilities on its statement of financial position. Property, plant and equipment and bills payable are reported as current assets and current liabilities, respectively. Property, plant and equipment is stated at the amount for which it could be sold at short notice. Liquidation of the entity is unlikely.

(e) Watts Ltd has inventory on hand that cost $400 000. Watts reports inventory on its statement of financial position at its current market value of $425 000.

(f) Steph Wolfson, manager of Classic Music Ltd, bought a computer for her personal use. She paid for the computer with company funds and debited the 'computers' account.

Required

For each situation, give the concept, principle, recognition criteria or constraint that has been violated, if any. Some of these concepts, principles and constraints were presented in the previous chapter. Give only one answer for each situation.

E3.4 Identify accounting concepts, principles and criteria.   **LO2**

Presented below are the concepts, principles and criteria used in this and previous chapters:

1. Accounting entity concept.
2. Going concern principle.
3. Monetary principle.
4. Accounting period concept.
5. Full disclosure principle.
6. Revenue recognition criteria.
7. Expense recognition criteria.
8. Cost principle.
9. Materiality test.

Required

Identify by number the accounting concept, principle or criteria that describes each of these situations. Do not use a number more than once.

_____ (a) Repair tools are expensed when purchased.

_____ (b) Recognises an expense for unpaid salaries.

_____ (c) Assumes that the dollar is the measuring unit used to report financial information.

_____ (d) Separates financial information into time periods for reporting purposes.

_____ (e) Market value changes subsequent to purchase are not recorded in the accounts. (Do not use the revenue recognition criteria.)

_____ (f) Indicates that personal and business record keeping should be separately maintained.

_____ (g) Ensures that all relevant financial information is reported.

_____ (h) Requires recognition of revenues when an entity has completed a performance obligation and it is probable that the consideration to which the entity is entitled in exchange for the goods will be collected.

E3.5 Identify types of adjustments and accounts before adjustment. **LO3, 4**

Zimbabwe Ltd accumulates the following adjustment data at 30 June:

(a) Services provided but not yet invoiced total $600.

(b) Store supplies of $300 are on hand. Supplies account shows $2300 balance.

(c) Electricity expenses of $225 are unpaid and unrecorded.

(d) Service for which payment of $260 was collected in advance has been performed.

(e) Salaries of $800 are unpaid and unrecorded.

(f) Benefits arising from prepaid insurance totalling $350 have expired.

Required

(a) For each item indicate (1) the type of adjustment (prepaid expense, revenue received in advance, accrued revenue or accrued expense) and (2) the accounts before adjustment (overstatement or understatement).

(b) Calculate the effect on profit if the adjustments were not recorded.

E3.6 Prepare adjusting entries from selected account data. **LO4**

The ledger of Uniform Ltd on 30 June of the current year includes these *selected* accounts and corresponding account numbers before adjusting entries have been prepared:

	Debits	Credits
100 Prepaid insurance	$14 040	
110 Supplies	8 400	
120 Equipment	97 500	
121 Accumulated depreciation — equipment		$ 31 800
200 Bank loan		78 000
210 Rent revenue received in advance		36 270
300 Rent revenue		234 000
400 Interest expense	—	
410 Wage expense	54 600	

An analysis of the accounts shows the following:

1. The equipment depreciates $1600 per month.

2. The rent revenue received in advance was for the 9 months commencing 1 April.

3. Interest of $975 is accrued on the bank loan.

4. Supplies on hand total $2800.

5. The benefits of prepaid insurance expire at the rate of $1170 per month.

Prepare the adjusting entries at 30 June, assuming that adjusting entries are made *quarterly*. Additional accounts and account numbers are: 420 Depreciation expense, 430 Insurance expense, 220 Interest payable, and 440 Supplies expense.

E3.7 Prepare adjusting entries. **LO4**

Con James commenced a dental practice on 1 January 2019. During the first month of operations the following transactions occurred:

(a) Performed services for patients and, at 31 January, $1500 was earned for these services but not yet billed to the patients.

(b) Electricity expense incurred and not paid or recorded prior to 31 January, $1040.

(c) Purchased dental equipment on 1 January 2019 for $160 000, paying $40 000 in cash and signing a $120 000 interest-bearing note payable. (Interest is payable on 31 December 2019.) The equipment depreciates at $1600 per month and interest on the note is $500 per month.

(d) Purchased a 1-year insurance policy on 1 January 2019 for $24 000.

(e) Purchased $3200 of dental supplies (recorded as an asset). On 31 January, $700 worth of supplies was still on hand.

Required

Prepare the adjusting entries on 31 January 2019. Use these account names: Accumulated depreciation—dental equipment, Depreciation expense, Service revenue, Accounts receivable, Interest expense, Insurance expense, Salaries expense, Interest payable, Prepaid insurance and Salaries payable.

E3.8 Prepare adjusting entries. **LO4**

The trial balance for Wong Pty Ltd is shown in figure 3.4. In lieu of the adjusting entries shown in the text at 31 October, assume the following adjustment data:

1. Advertising supplies on hand at 31 October total $1600.
2. Benefits of prepaid insurance of $100 have expired.
3. Depreciation for the month is $60.
4. Services performed in relation to cash received in advance total $300.
5. Services performed but not invoiced at 31 October total $700.
6. Interest accrued at 31 October is $80.
7. Accrued salaries at 31 October are $1300.

Required

Prepare the adjusting entries for these items. Use the account names and numbers from figure 2.19.

E3.9 Prepare a correct statement of profit or loss. **LO1, 3, 4, 5**

The statement of profit or loss of Wolfmother Ltd for the month of July 2020 shows a profit of $1400 based on service revenue $5500; wages expense $2300; supplies expense $1200; and electricity expense $600. In reviewing the statement, you discover:

1. the benefit consumed for prepaid insurance during July was not recorded — $300.
2. supplies expense includes $400 of supplies that are still on hand at 31 July.
3. depreciation on equipment of $150 was omitted.
4. accrued but unpaid wages at 31 July of $300 were not included.
5. services totalling $800 were performed but not invoiced.

Required

Prepare a correct statement of profit or loss for the month of July 2020.

E3.10 Analyse adjusted data.   LO3, 4, 5

This is a partial adjusted trial balance of Darcy Designs Pty Ltd.

	DARCY DESIGNS PTY LTD Adjusted trial balance (partial) as at 31 July 2019		
No.	Account name	Debit	Credit
110	Supplies	$1 500	
112	Prepaid insurance	2 400	
212	Salaries payable		$1 500
213	Service revenue received in advance		1 125
400	Service revenue		3 000
500	Salaries expense	7 300	
505	Supplies expense	1 220	
515	Insurance expense	800	

Required

Answer these questions, assuming the year begins on 1 July:

(a) If the amount in supplies expense is the 31 July adjusting entry, and $1320 of supplies was purchased in July, what was the balance in supplies on 1 July?

(b) If the amount in insurance expense is the July adjusting entry, and the original insurance premium was for 1 year, what was the total premium and when was the policy purchased?

(c) If $7500 of salaries was paid in July, what was the balance in salaries payable at 30 June 2019?

(d) There were no additional amounts of revenue received in advance during July. An amount of $2400 was received for services performed in July. What was the amount of service revenue received in advance at 1 July 2019/30 June 2019?

(*Hint:* Reconstruct the T accounts to help answer these questions.)

E3.11 Analyse adjusted data.   LO3, 4, 5

This is a partial adjusted trial balance of Martin Pty Ltd.

	MARTIN PTY LTD Adjusted trial balance as at 31 March 2020		
No.	Account name	Debit	Credit
110	Supplies	$ 700	
112	Prepaid insurance	2 400	
212	Salaries payable		$ 800
213	Service revenue received in advance		750
400	Service revenue		2 000
500	Salaries expense	1 800	
505	Supplies expense	950	
515	Insurance expense	400	

Required

Answer these questions, assuming the year begins on 1 March:

(a) If the amount in supplies expense is the 31 March adjusting entry, and $850 of supplies was purchased in March, what was the balance in supplies on 1 March?

(b) If the amount in insurance expense is the March adjusting entry, and the original insurance premium was for 1 year, what was the total premium and when was the policy purchased?

(c) If $2500 of salaries was paid in March, what was the balance in salaries payable at 1 March 2020?

(d) There were no additional amounts of revenue received in advance during March. An amount of $1600 was received in March for services performed in March. What was the amount of service revenue received in advance at 1 March 2020?

(*Hint:* Reconstruct the T accounts to help answer these questions.)

E3.12 **Journalise basic transactions and adjusting entries.** **LO4**

Selected accounts of Snowmass Ltd are shown here:

Supplies expense				Supplies			
July 31	500		July 1	Bal.	1 100	July 31	500
			10		200		

Salaries payable				Service revenue receivable			
		July 31	1 200	July 31	500		

Salaries expense				Service revenue received in advance			
July 15	1 200		July 31	900	July 1	Bal.	1 500
31	1 200				20		700

Service revenue		
	July 14	3 000
	31	900
	31	500

Required

After analysing the accounts, journalise (a) the July transactions and (b) the adjusting entries that were made on 31 July. (*Hint:* July transactions were for cash.)

E3.13 **Prepare adjusting entries.** **LO3, 4**

A review of the ledger of Monkey Ltd at 30 June 2019 produced the following data relating to the preparation of annual adjusting entries:

1. Prepaid insurance $37 260: the entity has separate insurance policies on its buildings and its motor vehicles. Policy B4564 on the building was purchased on 1 January 2018 for $33 300. The policy has a term of 3 years. Policy A2958 on the vehicles was purchased on 1 July 2018 for $9510. This policy has a term of 2 years.

2. Subscription revenue received in advance $135 200: the entity began selling magazine subscriptions on 1 April 2019 on an annual basis. The selling price of a subscription is $130. A review of subscription contracts reveals the following:

Subscription start date	Number of subscriptions
1 April	200
1 May	300
1 June	540
	1 040

The annual subscription is for 12 monthly issues. The June magazine for all of the subscriptions had been delivered to the subscribers at 30 June 2019.

3. Bank loan $100 000: the loan was taken out on 1 April at an annual interest rate of 6%.

4. Salaries payable: There are eight salaried employees. Salaries are paid every Friday for the current week. Four employees receive a salary of $1050 each per week, and three employees earn $1350 each per week. 30 June is a Tuesday. Employees do not work on weekends. All employees worked the last 2 days of June.

Required

(a) Prepare the adjusting journal entries at 30 June 2019.

(b) Explain why the business would not recognise the full subscription revenue when the customers sign up for the magazines and pay for the subscription.

PROBLEM SET A

PSA3.1 Prepare adjusting entries, post to ledger accounts, and prepare adjusted trial balance.

LO3, 4, 5

Ewok Ltd began operations on 1 May 2019. The trial balance at 30 June is as follows.

No.	Account name	Debit	Credit
	EWOK LTD **Trial balance** **as at 30 June 2019**		
100	Cash	$ 34 560	
104	Accounts receivable	26 040	
112	Prepaid insurance	9 600	
113	Supplies	13 600	
130	Office equipment	86 400	
200	Accounts payable		$ 19 800
213	Service revenue received in advance		4 800
300	Share capital		100 000
400	Service revenue		76 600
500	Salaries expense	23 800	
510	Rent expense	7 200	
		$201 200	$201 200

In addition to those accounts listed on the trial balance, the chart of accounts for Ewok Ltd also contains the following accounts: 131 Accumulated depreciation—office equipment, 218 Electricity payable, 215 Salaries payable, 520 Depreciation expense, 515 Insurance expense, 530 Electricity expense, and 505 Supplies expense.

Other data:
1. Supplies on hand at 30 June total $7200.
2. An electricity bill for $1200 has not been recorded and will not be paid until next month.
3. The insurance policy is for a year, commencing 1 May 2019.
4. Services were performed during the period in relation to $3000 of revenue received in advance.
5. Salaries of $6400 are owed at 30 June.
6. The office equipment has a 5-year life with no resale value and is being depreciated at $1440 per month for 60 months.
7. Invoices representing $8000 of services performed during the month have not been recorded as of 30 June.

Required
(a) Prepare the adjusting entries for the month of June.
(b) Using T accounts, enter the totals from the trial balance as beginning account balances and then post the adjusting entries to the ledger accounts.
(c) Prepare an adjusted trial balance as at 30 June 2019.
(d) Calculate the profit for the month.
(e) Discuss the impact on profit for the current period and year and future years if the equipment was depreciated over 2 years, not 5 years, and yet the business uses the equipment for the 5 years.

PSA3.2 **Prepare adjusting entries, post to ledger accounts, and prepare adjusted trial balance.**

LO3, 4, 5

The unadjusted trial balance at 30 June 2020 for Maxi Services Ltd is as follows.

No.	Account name	Debit	Credit
	MAXI SERVICES LTD **Trial balance** as at 30 June 2020		
100	Cash	$ 54 800	
104	Accounts receivable	15 000	
112	Prepaid insurance	3 200	
113	Supplies	1 500	
130	Office equipment	30 000	
131	Accumulated depreciation		$ 20 000
200	Accounts payable		7 400
213	Service revenue received in advance		4 000
300	Share capital		60 000
310	Retained earnings		7 500
400	Service revenue		46 800
500	Salaries expense	34 000	
510	Rent expense	2 000	
515	Insurance expense	1 200	
530	Electricity expense	4 000	
		$145 700	$145 700

The chart of accounts for Maxi Services Ltd contains the following accounts in addition to those listed on the trial balance: 218 Electricity payable, 215 Salaries payable, 520 Depreciation expense, and 505 Supplies expense.

Other data:
1. Supplies on hand at 30 June total $1000.
2. An electricity bill for $300 for June has not been recorded and will not be paid until next month.
3. The balance of the prepaid insurance account is the annual premium for insurance commencing 1 January 2020.
4. Services were performed during the current period in relation to $3000 of revenue received in advance.
5. Salaries of $4600 are owed at 30 June.
6. Depreciation expense for the year is $4000.
7. Invoices representing $4400 of services performed during the month have not been recorded as of 30 June 2020.

Required
(a) Prepare the adjusting entries from the information provided.
(b) Using T accounts, enter the totals from the trial balance as beginning account balances and then post the adjusting entries to the ledger accounts.
(c) Prepare an adjusted trial balance as at 30 June 2020.
(d) Calculate profit or loss for the year ended 30 June 2020.
(e) If the business wanted to report a higher profit, which of the adjusting entries above would be avoided? Which stakeholders would be affected by the misreported profit?

PSA3.3 Prepare adjusting entries and financial statements; identify accounts to be closed.

LO4, 5, 6, 7

Auckland Consulting Ltd began operations on 1 July 2019. Quarterly financial statements are prepared. The trial balance and adjusted trial balance on 30 September are shown below.

		Unadjusted		Adjusted	
	AUCKLAND CONSULTING LTD **Trial balances** **as at 30 September 2019**				
No.	Account name	Dr	Cr	Dr	Cr
100	Cash	$ 4 950		$ 4 950	
110	Accounts receivable	1 200		19 800	
120	Prepaid rent	4 500			
130	Supplies	1 350		900	
150	Equipment	45 000		45 000	
151	Accumulated depreciation—equipment				$ 2 250
200	Accounts payable		$ 4 530		4 530
210	Salaries payable				4 200
220	Interest payable				300
230	Rent revenue received in advance		4 200		1 800
250	Bank loan		15 000		15 000
300	Share capital		42 000		42 000
310	Retained earnings		—		—
311	Dividends	1 800		1 800	
400	Commission revenue		3 600		22 200
410	Rent revenue		30 000		32 400
500	Salaries expense	24 000		28 200	
510	Rent expense	15 000		19 500	
520	Depreciation expense			2 250	
530	Supplies expense			450	
540	Electricity expense	1 530		1 530	
550	Interest expense			300	
		$99 330	$99 330	$124 680	$124 680

Required

(a) Journalise the adjusting entries that were made.
(b) Prepare a statement of profit or loss and a calculation of retained earnings for the 3 months ending 30 September and prepare a statement of financial position as at 30 September.
(c) Identify which accounts should be closed on 30 September.
(d) If the interest rate on the loan is 12%, when did the entity take out the loan?

PSA3.4 Prepare adjusting entries from analysis of trial balances; prepare financial statements from adjusted trial balance.

LO4, 5, 6

The trial balances shown below are before and after adjustment for Frog Ltd at the end of its reporting period.

		Unadjusted		Adjusted	
	FROG LTD **Trial balances** **as at 30 June 2019**				
No.	Account name	Dr	Cr	Dr	Cr
100	Cash	$ 14 500		$ 14 500	
110	Accounts receivable	13 200		14 100	

		Unadjusted		Adjusted	
No.	Account name	Dr	Cr	Dr	Cr
120	Office supplies	3 450		1 050	
130	Prepaid insurance	6 000		3 750	
140	Office equipment	18 000		18 000	
141	Accumulated depreciation—office equipment		$ 3 600		$ 5 400
200	Accounts payable		8 700		8 700
210	Salaries payable		—		1 650
220	Rent revenue received in advance		2 250		1 050
300	Share capital		15 000		15 000
310	Retained earnings		5 600		5 600
400	Service revenue		51 000		51 900
410	Rent revenue		16 500		17 700
500	Salaries expense	25 500		27 150	
510	Office supplies expense	—		2 400	
520	Rent expense	22 000		22 000	
530	Insurance expense	—		2 250	
540	Depreciation expense	—		1 800	
		$ 102 650	$ 102 650	$ 107 000	$ 107 000

Required

(a) Prepare the adjusting journal entries that were made.

(b) Prepare the statement of profit or loss and the calculation of retained earnings for the year ended 30 June 2019 and prepare the statement of financial position as at 30 June 2019.

(c) Prepare the closing journal entries for the temporary accounts at 30 June.

PSA3.5 **Prepare adjusting entries and financial statements; identify accounts to be closed.**

LO4, 5, 6, 7

Nathan Ltd began operations on 1 July 2019. Quarterly financial statements are prepared. The trial balance and adjusted trial balance on 30 September are shown below.

		NATHAN LTD Trial balance as at 30 September 2019			
		Unadjusted		Adjusted	
No.	Account name	Dr	Cr	Dr	Cr
100	Cash	$ 114 450		$ 114 450	
110	Accounts receivable	5 400		12 900	
120	Prepaid rent	22 500		15 000	
130	Supplies	9 000		4 500	
150	Equipment	120 000		120 000	
151	Accumulated depreciation—equipment				$ 6 000
200	Accounts payable		$ 19 200		19 200
210	Salaries payable				10 800
220	Interest payable				900
230	Comm. rev. rec'd in advance		12 000		5 400
250	Bank loan		90 000		90 000
300	Share capital		105 000		105 000
310	Retained earnings				
311	Dividends	3 000		3 000	
400	Sales revenue		77 700		85 200
410	Commission revenue		45 000		51 600
500	Salaries expense	54 300		65 100	
510	Rent expense	15 000		22 500	

No.	Account name	Unadjusted Dr	Unadjusted Cr	Adjusted Dr	Adjusted Cr
520	Depreciation expense			6 000	
530	Supplies expense			4 500	
540	Electricity expense	5 250		5 250	
550	Interest expense			900	
		$348 900	$348 900	$374 100	$374 100

Required

(a) Journalise the adjusting entries that were made.

(b) Prepare a statement of profit or loss and a calculation of retained earnings for the 3 months ending 30 September and prepare a statement of financial position as at 30 September.

(c) Identify which accounts should be closed on 30 September.

(d) If the interest rate on the loan is 6%, when did the entity take out the loan?

(e) If the business uses straight-line depreciation and it was estimated the residual value of the equipment was zero, calculate the estimated useful life of the equipment.

PSA3.6 Prepare adjusting entries, and financial statements; identify accounts to be closed.

LO4, 5, 6, 7

Characters Ltd adjusted and unadjusted trial balances as of 30 June 2020 are as follows.

	CHARACTERS LTD Trial balances as at 30 June 2020				

No.	Account name	Unadjusted Dr	Unadjusted Cr	Adjusted Dr	Adjusted Cr
100	Cash	$ 24 520		$ 24 520	
110	Accounts receivable	22 400		24 080	
130	Supplies	9 400		5 600	
140	Prepaid insurance	3 750		2 800	
150	Printing equipment	67 200		67 200	
151	Accumulated depreciation		$ 31 360		$ 39 200
200	Accounts payable		5 600		5 600
220	Interest payable				120
230	Revenue received in advance		7 840		6 270
240	Salaries payable				1 400
250	Bank loan (long term)		18 000		18 000
300	Share capital		22 400		22 400
310	Retained earnings		6 160		6 160
311	Dividends	13 440		13 440	
400	Revenue		65 630		68 880
500	Salaries expense	11 200		12 600	
505	Insurance expense			950	
510	Interest expense	600		720	
520	Depreciation expense			7 840	
530	Supplies expense			3 800	
540	Rent expense	4 480		4 480	
		$156 990	$156 990	$168 030	$168 030

Required

(a) Journalise the annual adjusting entries that were made.

(b) Prepare a statement of profit or loss and a calculation of retained earnings for the year ended 30 June 2020 and prepare a statement of financial position as at 30 June 2020.

(c) Identify which accounts should be closed on 30 June.

(d) If the bank loan was taken out 6 months ago, what is the annual interest rate on the loan?

(e) If the entity paid $13 400 in salaries in 2020, what was the balance in Salaries Payable on 30 June 2019?

(f) What is the effect on profit as a result of these adjusting entries?

(g) The statement of profit or loss presents the performance of the business over the past year. What other information concerning the profitability of the business would be useful for the financial statement users?

PSA3.7 **Prepare adjusting entries, adjusted trial balance, and financial statements.**   **LO4, 5, 6**

Smart Rentals Ltd opened for business on 1 April 2020. Here is its trial balance before adjustment on 30 June 2020 presented on a worksheet.

SMART RENTALS LTD
Worksheet
as at 30 June 2020

No.	Account name	Trial balance Dr	Trial balance Cr	Adjustments Dr	Adjustments Cr	Adjusted trial balance Dr	Adjusted trial balance Cr	Statement of profit or loss Dr	Statement of profit or loss Cr	Statement of financial position Dr	Statement of financial position Cr
100	Cash	$ 15 000									
112	Prepaid insurance	10 800									
113	Supplies	11 400									
120	Land	90 000									
122	Building	420 000									
130	Furniture	100 800									
200	Accounts payable		$ 28 200								
212	Rent revenue received in advance		21 600								
220	Mortgage payable		210 000								
300	Share capital		360 000								
400	Rent revenue		55 200								
505	Advertising expense	3 000									
510	Electricity expense	6 000									
525	Salaries expense	18 000									
	Totals	**$675 000**	**$675 000**								

In addition to those accounts listed on the trial balance, the chart of accounts for Showroom Rentals Ltd also contains the following accounts: 123 Accumulated depreciation—building, 131 Accumulated depreciation—furniture, 506 Depreciation expense, 512 Insurance expense, 515 Interest expense, and 530 Supplies expense.

Other data:

1. Insurance expires at the rate of $900 per month and is an annual premium commencing 1 April 2020.

2. An inventory of supplies shows $7200 of unused supplies on 30 June.

3. Depreciation is $5400 on the building and $4500 on furniture (depreciation to 30 June 2020).

4. The mortgage interest rate is 6%. (The mortgage was taken out on 1 April.)

5. $9000 of the rent revenue received in advance pertains to June. The remainder pertains to July.

6. Salaries of $1800 are unpaid at 30 June.

Required

(a) Using the information provided complete the above worksheet.

(b) Journalise the adjusting entries on 30 June.

(c) Prepare a ledger using T accounts. Enter the trial balance amounts as opening balances and post the adjusting entries.

(d) Prepare an adjusted trial balance on 30 June.

(e) Prepare the statement of profit or loss and a calculation of retained earnings for the quarter ended 30 June 2020, and prepare the statement of financial position as at 30 June 2020.

(f) Identify which accounts should be closed on 30 June.

PSA3.8 Complete all steps in accounting cycle. **LO4, 5, 6, 7**

Central Cleaning Ltd began operations on 1 July 2019. During July the following transactions were completed:

July	1	Issued 60 000 shares at $1 each.
	1	Purchased used truck for $48 000, paying $15 000 cash and the balance on account.
	3	Purchased cleaning supplies for $3600 on account.
	5	Paid $14 400 cash on 1-year insurance policy effective 1 July.
	12	Invoiced customers $15 720 for cleaning services.
	18	Paid $9000 cash of amount owed on truck and $2400 of amount owed on cleaning supplies.
	20	Paid $9600 cash for employee salaries.
	21	Collected $12 000 cash from customers invoiced on 12 July.
	25	Invoiced customers $10 800 for cleaning services.
	31	Paid petrol and oil for month on truck $1200.
	31	Paid $2250 cash dividend.

The chart of accounts for Central Cleaning Ltd contains the following accounts and account numbers: 100 Cash, 110 Accounts receivable, 120 Cleaning supplies, 130 Prepaid insurance, 170 Truck, 171 Accumulated depreciation—truck, 200 Accounts payable, 210 Salaries payable, 300 Share capital, 310 Retained earnings, 315 Dividends, 320 Profit or loss summary, 400 Service revenue, 500 Petrol and oil expense, 510 Cleaning supplies expense, 520 Depreciation expense, 530 Insurance expense, and 540 Salaries expense.

Required

(a) Journalise the July transactions.

(b) Post to the ledger accounts (use T accounts).

(c) Prepare a trial balance as at 31 July.

(d) Journalise the following adjustments.
   1. Services provided but not invoiced and uncollected at 31 July were $6000.
   2. Depreciation on truck for the month was $750.
   3. One-twelfth of the insurance expired.
   4. An inventory count shows $1200 of cleaning supplies on hand at 31 July.
   5. Unpaid employee salaries were $900.

(e) Post adjusting entries to the T accounts prepared in part (b).

(f) Prepare an adjusted trial balance.

(g) Prepare the statement of profit or loss and a calculation of retained earnings for July, and prepare a classified statement of financial position as at 31 July.

(h) Journalise and post closing entries and complete the closing process as if it were the end of the financial year.

(i) Prepare a post-closing trial balance at 31 July.

(j) The business purchases cleaning supplies which are 'environmentally friendly' but cost twice the price of an alternative brand. Joe, a potential investor, doesn't understand why a business would not just try to reduce costs. Prepare a short response to Joe explaining why a business would choose to operate this way.

PSA3.9 Journalise transactions and follow through accounting cycle to preparation of financial statements. LO4, 5, 6, 7, 8

On 1 July 2019, the following were the account balances of Bulwara Ltd:

	Debits
Cash	$ 5 000
Accounts receivable	5 600
Supplies	2 000
Store equipment	20 000
	$32 600
	Credits
Accumulated depreciation	$ 1 000
Accounts payable	4 200
Service revenue received in advance	800
Salaries payable	1 000
Share capital	20 000
Retained earnings	5 600
	$32 600

During July the following summary transactions were completed:

July	8	Paid $3000 for salaries due to employees, of which $2000 is for July and $1000 is for June.
	10	Received $2000 cash from customers in payment of their accounts.
	12	Received $800 cash for services performed in July 2019.
	15	Purchased store equipment on account $8000.
	17	Purchased supplies on account $3400.
	24	Paid accounts payable $2000.
	24	Paid July/August rent $800.
	25	Paid salaries $3000.
	27	Performed services on account and invoiced customers for services provided $2300.
	27	Received $1300 from customers for future service.

Other data:
1. Supplies on hand are valued at $3200.
2. Accrued salaries payable are $1000.
3. Depreciation for the month is $240.
4. Services have been performed in relation to $600 recorded in service revenue received in advance.

Required
(a) Prepare a chart of accounts. (*Hint:* Refer to Wong Pty Ltd in chapter 2 of this text.)
(b) Enter the 1 July balances in the ledger accounts (use T accounts).
(c) Journalise the July transactions.
(d) Post to the ledger accounts you prepared for part (c) above. Use service revenue, depreciation expense, supplies expense, salaries expense and rent expense.
(e) Prepare a trial balance at 31 July before adjusting entries.
(f) Journalise and post adjusting entries.

(g) Prepare an adjusted trial balance.

(h) Prepare a statement of profit or loss and a calculation of retained earnings for July and prepare a statement of financial position as at 31 July 2019.

(i) *Optional:* Using the information in this problem starting at part (e), prepare a worksheet using the format in figure 3.25.

PSA3.10 Complete all steps in accounting cycle. **LO3, 4, 5, 6, 7, 8**

Willard Cleaning Ltd began operations on 1 April 2020. During April the following transactions were completed:

April	1	Issued $37 500 shares for cash.
	1	Purchased used truck for $22 500, paying $12 500 cash and the balance on account.
	5	Purchased cleaning supplies for $4875 on account.
	7	Paid $5820 cash on 1-year insurance policy effective 1 April.
	14	Invoiced customers $6850 for cleaning services.
	21	Paid $10 000 cash of amount owed on truck and $2125 of amount owed on cleaning supplies.
	21	Paid $3400 cash for employee salaries.
	23	Collected $3250 cash from customers invoiced on 14 April.
	25	Invoiced customers $5975 for cleaning services.
	30	Paid petrol and oil for month on truck $432.
	30	Paid $600 cash dividend.

The chart of accounts for Cortex Cleaning Ltd contains the following accounts and account numbers: 100 Cash, 110 Accounts receivable, 120 Cleaning supplies, 130 Prepaid insurance, 171 Motor vehicles, 172 Accumulated depreciation—motor vehicles, 200 Accounts payable, 210 Salaries payable, 300 Share capital, 310 Retained earnings, 315 Dividends, 320 Profit or loss summary, 400 Service revenue, 500 Petrol and oil expense, 510 Cleaning supplies expense, 520 Depreciation expense, 530 Insurance expense, and 540 Salaries expense.

Required

(a) Journalise the April transactions.

(b) Post to the ledger accounts (use T accounts).

(c) Prepare a trial balance as at 30 April.

(d) Journalise the following adjustments.

1. Services provided but not invoiced and uncollected at 30 April were $1150.
2. Depreciation on the truck for the month was $375.
3. One-twelfth of the insurance expired.
4. An inventory count shows $750 of cleaning supplies on hand at 30 April.
5. Unpaid employee salaries were $1200.

(e) Post adjusting entries to the T accounts prepared in part (b).

(f) Prepare an adjusted trial balance.

(g) Prepare the statement of profit or loss and a calculation of retained earnings for April, and prepare a classified statement of financial position as at 30 April.

(h) Journalise and post closing entries and complete the closing process, as if it were the end of the financial year.

(i) Prepare a post-closing trial balance at 30 April.

(j) *Optional:* Using the information in this problem starting at part (e), prepare a worksheet using the format in figure 3.25.

PROBLEM SET B

PSB3.1 **Prepare adjusting entries, post to ledger accounts, and prepare adjusted trial balance.**

Solo Ltd began operations on 1 June 2019. The trial balance at 30 June is as follows.

	SOLO LTD Trial balance as at 30 June 2019		
No.	Account name	Debit	Credit
100	Cash	$ 7 750	
104	Accounts receivable	6 000	
112	Prepaid insurance	2 400	
113	Supplies	2 000	
130	Office equipment	15 000	
200	Accounts payable		$ 4 500
213	Service revenue received in advance		4 000
300	Share capital		21 750
400	Service revenue		7 900
500	Salaries expense	4 000	
510	Rent expense	1 000	
		$38 150	$38 150

In addition to those accounts listed on the trial balance, the chart of accounts for Solo Ltd also contains the following accounts: 131 Accumulated depreciation—office equipment, 218 Electricity payable, 215 Salaries payable, 520 Depreciation expense, 515 Insurance expense, 530 Electricity expense, and 505 Supplies expense.

Other data:
1. Supplies on hand at 30 June total $1300.
2. An electricity bill for $150 has not been recorded and will not be paid until next month.
3. The insurance policy is for a year.
4. Services were performed during the period in relation to $2500 of revenue received in advance.
5. Salaries of $1500 are owed at 30 June.
6. The office equipment has a 5-year life with no resale value and is being depreciated at $250 per month for 60 months.
7. Invoices representing $3000 of services performed during the month have not been recorded as of 30 June.

Required
(a) Prepare the adjusting entries for the month of June.
(b) Using T accounts, enter the totals from the trial balance as beginning account balances and then post the adjusting entries to the ledger accounts.
(c) Prepare an adjusted trial balance as at 30 June 2019.
(d) Calculate the profit for the month
(e) Discuss the impact on profit for the current period and year and future years if the equipment was depreciated over 2 years instead of 5 years and yet the business used the equipment for 5 years.

PSB3.2 Prepare adjusting entries, post to ledger accounts, and prepare adjusted trial balance.

LO3, 4, 5

Brothers Ltd began operations on 1 February 2019. The trial balance at 30 June is as follows.

	BROTHERS LTD Trial balance as at 30 June 2019		
No.	Account name	Debit	Credit
100	Cash	$ 9 480	
104	Accounts receivable	3 150	
112	Prepaid insurance	2 520	
113	Supplies	2 350	
130	Office equipment	22 500	
200	Accounts payable		$ 1 550
213	Service revenue received in advance		1 500
300	Share capital		20 000
400	Service revenue		25 495
500	Salaries expense	3 295	
510	Rent expense	5 250	
		$48 545	$48 545

In addition to those accounts listed on the trial balance, the chart of accounts for Brothers Ltd also contains the following accounts: 131 Accumulated depreciation—office equipment, 218 Electricity payable, 215 Salaries payable, 520 Depreciation expense, 515 Insurance expense, 530 Electricity expense, and 505 Supplies expense.

Other data:

1. Supplies on hand at 30 June total $490.
2. An electricity bill for $110 has not been recorded and will not be paid until next month.
3. The insurance policy is for a year, commencing 1 February 2019.
4. Services were performed during the period in relation to $800 of revenue received in advance.
5. Salaries of $770 are owed at 30 June.
6. The office equipment has a 5-year life with no resale value and is being depreciated at $375 per month for 60 months.
7. Invoices representing $1500 of services performed during the month have not been recorded as of 30 June.

Required

(a) Prepare the adjusting entries for the month of June.
(b) Using T accounts, enter the totals from the trial balance as beginning account balances and then post the adjusting entries to the ledger accounts.
(c) Prepare an adjusted trial balance as at 30 June 2019.
(d) If the business wanted to report a higher profit, which of the adjusting entries would be avoided? Which stakeholders would be affected by the misreported profit?

PSB3.3 **Prepare adjusting entries, and financial statements; identify accounts to be closed.**

LO4, 5, 6, 7

Matrix Ltd began operations on 1 July 2019. Quarterly financial statements are prepared. The trial balance and adjusted trial balance on 30 September are shown below.

			MATRIX LTD			
			Trial balances			
			as at 30 September 2019			
		Unadjusted		**Adjusted**	
No.	Account name	Dr	Cr	Dr	Cr
100	Cash	$ 8 710		$ 8 710	
110	Commissions receivable	520		1 300	
120	Prepaid rent	1 950		1 170	
130	Supplies	1 560		1 300	
150	Equipment	19 500		19 500	
151	Accumulated depreciation—equipment				$ 455
200	Accounts payable		$ 1 963		1 963
210	Salaries payable				520
220	Interest payable				65
230	Rent revenue received in advance		1 170		780
250	Bank loan		6 500		6 500
300	Share capital		18 200		18 200
310	Retained earnings		—		—
311	Dividends	780		780	
400	Commission revenue		18 200		18 980
410	Rent revenue		520		910
500	Salaries expense	11 700		12 220	
510	Rent expense	1 170		1 950	
520	Depreciation expense			455	
530	Supplies expense			260	
540	Electricity expense	663		663	
550	Interest expense			65	
		$46 553	$46 553	$48 373	$48 373

Required

(a) Journalise the adjusting entries that were made.
(b) Prepare a statement of profit or loss and a calculation of retained earnings for the 3 months ending 30 September, and prepare a statement of financial position as at 30 September.
(c) Identify which accounts should be closed on 30 September.
(d) If the interest rate on the loan is 12%, when did Matrix Ltd take out the loan?

PSB3.4 **Prepare adjusting entries from analysis of trial balances; prepare financial statements from adjusted trial balance.**

LO4, 5, 6

The trial balances shown below are before and after adjustment for Aurora Pty Ltd at the end of its reporting period.

			AURORA PTY LTD			
			Trial balances			
			as at 30 June 2020			
		Unadjusted		**Adjusted**	
No.	Account name	Dr	Cr	Dr	Cr
100	Cash	$ 5 200		$ 5 200	
110	Accounts receivable	4 400		4 700	
120	Office supplies	1 150		350	

No.	Account name	Unadjusted Dr	Unadjusted Cr	Adjusted Dr	Adjusted Cr
130	Prepaid insurance	2 000		1 250	
140	Office equipment	7 000		7 000	
141	Acc. depn—office equipment		$ 1 800		$ 2 400
200	Accounts payable		2 900		2 900
210	Salaries payable		—		550
220	Rent rev. rec'd in advance		750		350
300	Share capital		5 000		5 000
310	Retained earnings		2 800		2 800
400	Service revenue		17 000		17 300
410	Rent revenue		5 500		5 900
500	Salaries expense	8 500		9 050	
510	Office supplies expense	—		800	
520	Rent expense	7 500		7 500	
530	Insurance expense	—		750	
540	Depreciation expense	—		600	
		$35 750	$35 750	$37 200	$37 200

Required

(a) Prepare the adjusting entries that were made.

(b) Prepare the statement of profit or loss and the calculation of retained earnings for the year ended 30 June 2020 and prepare the statement of financial position as at 30 June 2020.

(c) Prepare the closing entries for the temporary accounts at 30 June.

PSB3.5 **Prepare adjusting entries and financial statements; identify accounts to be closed.**

LO4, 5, 6, 7

McPherson Ltd began operations on 1 January 2019. Quarterly financial statements are prepared. The trial balance and adjusted trial balance on 31 March are shown below.

McPHERSON LTD
Trial balances
as at 31 March 2019

No.	Account name	Unadjusted Dr	Unadjusted Cr	Adjusted Dr	Adjusted Cr
100	Cash	$15 750		$15 750	
110	Accounts receivable	1 300		6 800	
120	Prepaid rent	2 000		—	
130	Supplies	1 500		600	
150	Equipment	32 000		32 000	
151	Accumulated depreciation—equipment				$ 1 750
200	Accounts payable		$ 1 840		1 840
210	Salaries payable				1 800
220	Interest payable				250
230	Rent revenue received in advance		1 000		500
250	Bank loan		15 000		15 000
300	Share capital		25 000		25 000
310	Retained earnings				
311	Dividends	600		600	
400	Sales revenue		13 100		18 600
410	Rent revenue		11 500		12 000
500	Salaries expense	9 540		11 340	
510	Rent expense	4 000		6 000	

		Unadjusted		Adjusted	
No.	Account name	Dr	Cr	Dr	Cr
520	Depreciation expense			1 750	
530	Supplies expense			900	
540	Electricity expense	750		750	
550	Interest expense			250	
		$67 440	$67 440	$76 740	$76 740

Required

(a) Journalise the adjusting entries that were made.

(b) Prepare a statement of profit or loss and a calculation of retained earnings for the 3 months ending 31 March, and prepare a statement of financial position as at 31 March.

(c) Identify which accounts should be closed on 31 March.

(d) If the interest rate on the loan is 10%, when did the entity take out the loan?

PSB3.6 **Prepare adjusting entries and financial statements; identify accounts to be closed.**

LO4, 5, 6, 7

Lou's Advertising Agency Pty Ltd was founded by Louise Lou in 2011. Presented here are both the adjusted and unadjusted trial balances as of 31 December 2020.

	LOU'S ADVERTISING AGENCY PTY LTD **Trial balances** as at 31 December 2020				
		Unadjusted		Adjusted	
No.	Account name	Dr	Cr	Dr	Cr
100	Cash	$ 30 800		$ 30 800	
110	Accounts receivable	56 000		60 200	
130	Art supplies	23 520		14 000	
140	Prepaid insurance	9 380		7 000	
150	Printing equipment	168 000		168 000	
151	Accumulated depreciation		$ 78 400		$ 98 000
200	Accounts payable		14 000		14 000
220	Interest payable				420
230	Advertising revenue received in advance		19 600		15 680
240	Salaries payable				3 640
250	Bank loan (long term)		14 000		14 000
300	Share capital		56 000		56 000
310	Retained earnings		15 400		15 400
311	Dividends	33 600		33 600	
400	Advertising revenue		164 080		172 200
500	Salaries expense	28 000		31 640	
505	Insurance expense			2 380	
510	Interest expense	980		1 400	
520	Depreciation expense			19 600	
530	Art supplies expense			9 520	
540	Rent expense	11 200		11 200	
		$361 480	$361 480	$389 340	$389 340

Required

(a) Journalise the annual adjusting entries that were made.

(b) Prepare a statement of profit or loss and a calculation of retained earnings for the year ended 31 December 2020, and prepare a statement of financial position as at 31 December 2020.

(c) Identify which accounts should be closed on 31 December.

(d) If the bank loan was taken out 10 months ago, what is the annual interest rate on the loan?

(e) If the entity paid $31 200 in salaries in 2020, what was the balance in salaries payable on 31 December 2019?

(f) What is the effect on profit as a result of these adjusting entries?

PSB3.7 **Prepare worksheet, adjusting entries, adjusted trial balance, and financial statements.**

LO3, 4, 5, 6, 8

The Palpatine Hotel Ltd opened for business on 1 May 2019. A worksheet as at 31 May 2019 for Palpatine Hotel has been started as follows.

PALPATINE HOTEL LTD
Worksheet
as at 31 May 2019

No.	Account name	Trial balance Dr	Trial balance Cr	Adjustments Dr	Adjustments Cr	Adjusted trial balance Dr	Adjusted trial balance Cr	Statement of profit or loss Dr	Statement of profit or loss Cr	Statement of financial position Dr	Statement of financial position Cr
100	Cash	$ 4 500									
112	Prepaid insurance	2 520									
113	Supplies	2 660									
120	Land	21 000									
122	Building	98 000									
130	Furniture	23 520									
200	Accounts payable		$ 6 580								
212	Rent rev. rec'd in advance		5 040								
220	Mortgage payable		50 000								
300	Share capital		84 000								
400	Rent revenue		12 880								
505	Advertising expense	700									
510	Electricity expense	1 400									
525	Salaries expense	4 200									
	Totals	$158 500	$158 500								

In addition to those accounts listed on the trial balance, the chart of accounts for Palpatine Hotel also contains the following accounts: 123 Accumulated depreciation—building, 131 Accumulated depreciation—furniture, 506 Depreciation expense, 512 Insurance expense, 515 Interest expense, and 530 Supplies expense.

Other data:

1. Insurance expires at the rate of $210 per month.
2. An inventory of supplies shows $1680 of unused supplies on 31 May.
3. Annual depreciation is $5040 on the building and $4200 on furniture.
4. The mortgage interest rate is 12%. (The mortgage was taken out on 1 May.)
5. $2100 of the rent revenue received in advance relates to May and is now earned.
6. Salaries of $420 are unpaid at 31 May.

Required

(a) Using information provided complete the above worksheet.

(b) Journalise the adjusting entries on 31 May.

(c) Prepare the general ledger using T accounts. Enter the trial balance amounts and post the adjusting entries.

(d) Prepare an adjusted trial balance on 31 May.

(e) Prepare the statement of profit or loss and a calculation of retained earnings for the month of May and prepare the statement of financial position as at 31 May 2019.

(f) Identify which accounts should be closed on 31 May.

PSB3.8 Complete all steps in accounting cycle.   **LO3, 4, 5, 6, 7**

Contract Cleaners Pty Ltd began operations on 1 July 2019. During July the following transactions were completed:

July	1	Issued $27 000 shares for cash.
	1	Purchased used truck for $18 000, paying $9000 cash and the balance on account.
	3	Purchased cleaning supplies for $2700 on account.
	5	Paid $3600 cash on 1-year insurance policy effective 1 July.
	12	Invoiced customers $7500 for cleaning services.
	18	Paid $3000 cash of amount owed on truck and $1500 of amount owed on cleaning supplies.
	20	Paid $3600 cash for employee salaries.
	21	Collected $4200 cash from customers invoiced on 12 July.
	25	Invoiced customers $6000 for cleaning services.
	31	Paid petrol and oil for month on truck $600.
	31	Paid $1800 cash dividend.

The chart of accounts for Contract Cleaners Pty Ltd contains the following accounts and account numbers: 100 Cash, 110 Accounts receivable, 120 Cleaning supplies, 130 Prepaid insurance, 171 Motor vehicles, 172 Accumulated depreciation—motor vehicles, 200 Accounts payable, 210 Salaries payable, 300 Share capital, 310 Retained earnings, 315 Dividends, 320 Profit or loss summary, 400 Service revenue, 500 Petrol and oil expense, 510 Cleaning supplies expense, 520 Depreciation expense, 530 Insurance expense, and 540 Salaries expense.

Required

(a) Journalise the July transactions.
(b) Post to the ledger accounts (use T accounts).
(c) Prepare a trial balance as at 31 July.
(d) Journalise the following adjustments.
    1. Services provided but not invoiced and uncollected at 31 July were $3300.
    2. Depreciation on the truck for the month was $600.
    3. One-twelfth of the insurance expired.
    4. An inventory count shows $1800 of cleaning supplies on hand at 31 July.
    5. Unpaid employee salaries were $1200.
(e) Post adjusting entries to the T accounts you prepared in part (b).
(f) Prepare an adjusted trial balance.
(g) Prepare the statement of profit or loss and a calculation of retained earnings for July, and prepare a classified statement of financial position as at 31 July.
(h) Journalise and post closing entries and complete the closing process, as if it were the end of the financial year.
(i) Prepare a post-closing trial balance at 31 July.
(j) What is the change in reported profit as a result of the adjusting entries?

PSB3.9 Journalise transactions and follow through accounting cycle to preparation of financial statements and a worksheet.   **LO3, 4, 5, 6, 7, 8**

On 1 November 2019, the following were the account balances of Naboo Equipment Ltd.

	Debits
Cash	$ 3 348
Accounts receivable	3 012
Supplies	1 200
Store equipment	12 000
	$19 560

	Credits
Accumulated depreciation	$ 600
Accounts payable	2 520
Service revenue received in advance	480
Salaries payable	600
Share capital	12 000
Retained earnings	3 360
	$ 19 560

During November the following summary transactions were completed:

Nov.	8	Paid $1320 for salaries due to employees, of which $720 was for November and $600 was for October.
	10	Received $1440 cash from customers on account.
	12	Received $1680 cash for services performed in November.
	15	Purchased store equipment on account $3600.
	17	Purchased supplies on account $1800.
	20	Paid creditors on account $3000.
	22	Paid November rent $360.
	25	Paid salaries $1200.
	27	Performed services on account and invoiced customers for services provided $1080.
	29	Received $660 from customers for future service.

Other data:
1. Supplies on hand are valued at $1920.
2. Accrued salaries payable are $600.
3. Depreciation for the month is $144.
4. Services have been performed in relation to $360 recorded in service revenue received in advance.

Required
(a) Prepare a chart of accounts. (*Hint:* Refer to Wong Pty Ltd in chapter 2 of this text.)
(b) Enter the 1 July balances in the ledger accounts (use T accounts).
(c) Journalise the November transactions.
(d) Post to the ledger accounts you prepared for part (c) above. Use service revenue, depreciation expense, supplies expense, salaries expense, and rent expense.
(e) Prepare a trial balance at 30 November before adjusting entries.
(f) Journalise and post adjusting entries.
(g) Prepare an adjusted trial balance.
(h) Prepare a statement of profit or loss and a calculation of retained earnings for November, and prepare a statement of financial position as at 30 November 2019.
(i) *Optional:* Using the information in this problem starting at part (e), prepare a worksheet using the format in figure 3.25.

PSB3.10 Complete all steps in accounting cycle. LO3, 4, 5, 6, 7, 8

On Call Services Ltd began operations on 1 September 2018. During September the following transactions were completed:

September	1	Issued $150 000 shares for cash.
	1	Purchased used truck for $90 000, paying $45 000 cash and the balance on account.
	5	Purchased cleaning supplies for $18 600 on account.
	7	Paid $27 000 cash on 1-year insurance policy effective 1 September.
		Invoiced customers $26 700 for cleaning services.

▶

September	14	Paid $45 000 cash of amount owed on truck and $10 500 of amount owed on cleaning supplies.
	21	Paid $15 300 cash for employee salaries.
	23	Collected $18 000 cash from customers invoiced on 14 September.
	25	Invoiced customers $28 500 for cleaning services.
	30	Paid petrol and oil for month on truck $1980.
	30	Paid $900 cash dividend.

The chart of accounts for On Call Services Ltd contains the following accounts and account numbers: 100 Cash, 110 Accounts receivable, 120 Cleaning supplies, 130 Prepaid insurance, 171 Motor vehicles, 172 Accumulated depreciation—motor vehicles, 200 Accounts payable, 210 Salaries payable, 300 Share capital, 310 Retained earnings, 315 Dividends, 320 Profit or loss summary, 400 Service revenue, 500 Petrol and oil expense, 510 Cleaning supplies expense, 520 Depreciation expense, 530 Insurance expense, and 540 Salaries expense.

Required

(a) Journalise the September transactions.

(b) Post to the ledger accounts (use T accounts).

(c) Prepare a trial balance as at 30 September.

(d) Journalise the following adjustments.

1. Services provided but not invoiced and uncollected at 30 September were $5400.
2. Depreciation on the truck for the month was $1500.
3. One-twelfth of the insurance expired.
4. An inventory count shows $3600 of cleaning supplies on hand at 30 September.
5. Unpaid employee salaries were $5400.

(e) Post adjusting entries to the T accounts prepared in part (b).

(f) Prepare an adjusted trial balance.

(g) Prepare the statement of profit or loss and a calculation of retained earnings for September, and prepare a classified statement of financial position as at 30 September.

(h) Journalise and post closing entries and complete the closing process, as if it were the end of the financial year.

(i) Prepare a post-closing trial balance at 30 September.

(j) *Optional:* Using the information in this problem starting at part (e), prepare a worksheet using the format in figure 3.25.

BUILDING BUSINESS SKILLS

FINANCIAL REPORTING AND ANALYSIS

Financial reporting problem: Giorgina's Pizza Limited

BBS3.1 Refer to the financial statements of Giorgina's Pizza Limited in chapter 1 — figures 1.13, 1.15 and 1.16.

Required

(a) Using the statement of profit or loss and the statement of financial position, identify any two items that may result in adjusting entries for accruals. (*Hint:* Review the adjusting entries for accruals explained in the chapter.)

(b) What was the total amount of the provision (a liability) at the end of the 2019 reporting period? How much was current and how much was non-current?

(c) What was the cash paid for income taxes during 2019? Where was this reported? What was the income tax expense for 2019? Where was this reported?

Financial reporting problem: MYOB Group Limited

BBS3.2 Go to the ASX website (www.asx.com.au) and search for the latest annual report for a company in the Software and Services industry group. Select **Prices and research**, then **Company information**, then select **View all companies** under the Company directory. Search for the latest annual report for MYOB Group Limited.

Required

(a) Review the Notes to the Financial Statements sections, specifically 'Note 4 Revenue'. Explain the different forms of revenue recorded by MYOB and the different ways the company recognises each type of revenue.

(b) Are MYOB's methods of revenue recognition consistent with the revenue recognition criteria discussed in the chapter?

(c) What are the sources and amounts of revenues in the latest annual report? Explain the distinction between revenue and other income as disclosed in the financial statements.

Interpreting financial statements

BBS3.3 Micro Ltd, based in Perth, manufactures computers. Micro Ltd's products are distributed through both independent and company-owned distribution entities, which are located throughout Australasia. Micro Ltd's partial statement of profit or loss for 2019 is shown below.

MICRO LTD **Statement of profit or loss (partial)** for the year ended 30 June 2019		
	$'000	$'000
REVENUES		
Net sales	8 607	
Interest revenue and other income	418	
		9 025
COST AND EXPENSES		
Cost of sales	7 050	
Selling, general and administrative	1 121	
Research and development	336	
Interest expense	360	
		8 867
Profit before income tax		**158**

Assume that this partial statement of profit or loss was prepared before all adjusting entries had been made, and that the internal audit staff identified the following items that require adjustments:

1. Depreciation on the administrative offices of $50 million needs to be recorded.
2. A physical inventory determined that $2 million in office supplies had been used in 2019.
3. $30 million in salaries have been incurred but not recorded. Half of this amount is for the salaries of R&D staff; the other half is for the administrative staff.
4. $4.5 million in insurance premiums was prepaid on 1 May 2018. The premiums were for one year and insurance has not been renewed.
5. $12 million in prepaid rent is no longer prepaid at year-end.
6. Interest of $20 million has been incurred but not paid at year-end.

Required

(a) Make the adjusting entries required. Use standard account names.

(b) For each of the accounts in these adjusting entries that will be posted to the general ledger, show which item on the statement of profit or loss will be increased or decreased.

(c) Prepare a new partial statement of profit or loss based on the adjusting entries prepared.

(d) What information concerning the revenues and expenses would be useful to disclosure for the users of the financial statements?

Financial analysis on the web

BBS3.4 **Purpose:** This exercise explores information contained in notes to financial statements.

Address: www.fairfaxmedia.com.au

Steps:

1. *Choose* **Investors**.
2. Then select **Annual reports**.
3. Choose the most recent annual report.

Required

(a) In the annual report, find 'Note 1 Summary of significant accounting policies', and read the sections on revenue recognition. Explain Fairfax Media's policy for recognising revenue.

(b) Which items referred to in the revenue recognition policy require accrual adjustments and which items require adjustments for prepaid revenue?

(c) Is the way Fairfax Media recognises revenue consistent with the revenue recognition criteria discussed in the chapter?

CRITICAL THINKING

Group decision case

BBS3.5 Holiday Travel Australasia commenced business on 1 April 2019. Alice Adare is a good manager but a poor accountant. From the trial balance prepared by a part-time bookkeeper, Alice prepared the following statement of profit or loss for the year ended 31 March 2020. Alice knew something was wrong with the statement because profit up to February had not exceeded $40 000. Knowing that you are an experienced accountant, she asks you to review the statement of profit or loss and other data.

You first look at the trial balance. In addition to the account balances reported in the statement of profit or loss, the general ledger contains these selected balances at 31 March 2020.

Advertising supplies on hand	$15 000
Prepaid insurance	21 000
Bank loan	20 000

HOLIDAY TRAVEL AUSTRALASIA
Statement of profit or loss
for the year ended 31 March 2020

REVENUES		
Service revenue		$150 000
OPERATING EXPENSES		
Advertising	$ 8 700	
Wages	56 400	
Electricity	4 600	
Depreciation	1 200	
Repairs	4 000	
Total operating expenses		74 900
Profit		**$ 75 100**

You then make enquiries and discover the following:

1. Service revenues include advanced money for holidays after March, $16 000.
2. There was only $5200 of advertising supplies on hand at 31 March.
3. Prepaid insurance resulted from the payment of a 1-year policy on 1 July 2019.
4. The following invoices had not been paid or recorded: advertising for week of 24 March, $3200; repairs made 10 March, $2000; and electricity expense, $320.
5. At 31 March, 2 days' wages had not been paid or recorded, amounting to $300.
6. The business took out the loan on 1 January 2020 at an annual interest rate of 10%.

Required

With the class divided into groups, answer the following:

(a) Prepare a correct statement of profit or loss for the year ended 31 March 2020.

(b) Explain to Alice the generally accepted accounting principles that she did not follow in preparing her statement of profit or loss and their effect on her results.

Communication activity

BBS3.6 For the past 7 years, Sam Portafello has been running a small business and has been using the cash basis of accounting to record transactions. He is thinking about inviting family members to invest in the business as he feels the business has potential to expand if there were more funds. His daughter, Maria, who has just completed a commerce degree at the University of Sydney, urges him to adopt the accrual basis of accounting so he can better understand the profitability of his business and increase his chances of raising the funds required.

Being a stubborn man, he refuses to listen to his daughter and claims that cash is what is important. Maria decides to seek help from a third party to convince her father of the merits of accrual accounting, so she consults an accountant. You are that accountant and Maria asks you to write a report to explain the benefits of accrual accounting to her father.

Required

Prepare a report on the benefits of accrual accounting. In your report, cover the following issues:

(a) Explain the difference between accrual and cash accounting.

(b) List the items that are not recorded under cash accounting which are recorded under accrual accounting.

(c) Sam's plans to expand the business require the purchase of more equipment. He will be able to pay for some of it in cash but will need to apply for credit. Explain the implications of the purchase on the accounting reports under the accrual basis and cash basis of accounting.

(d) Conclude the report by summarising the advantages and disadvantages of accrual accounting and cash accounting, and give your recommendation on whether Sam Portafello should use accrual or cash accounting in his business.

Ethics case

BBS3.7 Wellcovered Insurance Ltd sells general insurance policies. At the end of the reporting period, the business information system manager, Mark Duncan, found that the company's accounting system had been infected by a computer virus and any general ledger account balances could not be relied upon. Mark advised the chief financial officer, Ben Nguyen, and the chief executive officer, Sarah Chan, that the profit reports would be delayed extensively while the software was disinfected.

Sarah said that she needed to issue a press release for the profit figures and didn't want this to be delayed because stakeholders would think something was wrong with the company. She explained to Ben that it was not in the shareholders' best interests to delay profit figures and asked him to estimate them so that the press release would not be late. Ben argued that he did not have documentation or other sources of information on which to base the estimates because they depended on the computer to determine how many insurance contracts had been sold. Sarah countered that this should not be a problem because accounting uses a lot of estimates and judgements. She added that this was what was meant by *timeliness*, which Sarah recalled was mentioned in an accounting textbook she had read a long time ago.

Required

(a) Who are the stakeholders in this situation?

(b) Is Sarah correct about the estimation of revenue, expenses and profit for the period being consistent with the timeliness constraint?

(c) Would the actions requested by Sarah be consistent with accounting principles?

(d) Would reporting the estimated figures be ethical?

(e) What do you think would be the consequences of a significant error in the estimation that overestimated profit?

Communication activity

BBS3.8 Woolworths Group published a sustainability strategy report, *Corporate Responsibility Strategy 2020*, which can be found on Woolworths' web site, www.woolworthsgroup.com.au.

This document outlines the company's approach and major commitments and targets.

Required

Access the sustainability strategy report and the priority of the environmental sustainability issues. Then access Woolworths' latest corporate responsibility report and summarise Woolworths' achievements in the areas of contribution to the community and environmental stewardship.

ANSWERS

Answers to self-study questions

3.1 (a) 3.2 (c) 3.3 (d) 3.4 (b) 3.5 (d) 3.6 (d) 3.7 (c) 3.8 (a) 3.9 (b) 3.10 (d) 3.11 (c) 3.12 (d) 3.13 (d) 3.14 (a) 3.15 (a)

ACKNOWLEDGEMENTS

Photo: © Slawomir Fajer / iStockphoto
Photo: © Uber Images / Shutterstock.com

CHAPTER 4

Inventories

LEARNING OBJECTIVES

After studying this chapter, you should be able to:

4.1 identify the differences between a service business and a merchandising business

4.2 explain the recording of purchases under a perpetual inventory system

4.3 explain the recording of sales revenues under a perpetual inventory system

4.4 prepare a fully classified statement of profit or loss

4.5 use ratios to analyse profitability

4.6 understand the basic process and main features of the goods and services tax (GST)

4.7 complete journal entries to record GST.

Chapter preview

JB Hi-Fi, Harvey Norman and Woolworths are called merchandising businesses because they buy and sell merchandise (known as **inventory**) rather than perform services as their main source of revenue. Inventories or stocks are goods acquired for the purpose of resale in the ordinary course of business activities. Businesses that sell inventories directly to consumers are called *retailers*. Businesses that sell inventories to retailers are known as *wholesalers*.

Retail businesses make up a significant proportion of Australian businesses. Understanding the financial statements of these businesses is important. The content and organisation of the chapter are as follows.

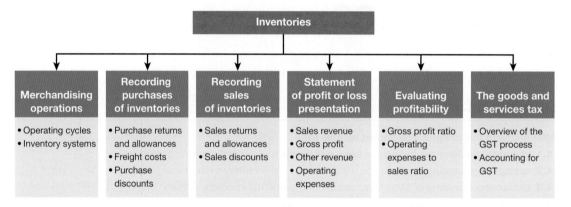

4.1 Merchandising operations

LEARNING OBJECTIVE 4.1 Identify the differences between a service business and a merchandising business.

The main source of revenues for merchandising businesses is the sale of inventory, often referred to simply as **sales revenue** or sales. Expenses for a merchandising business are divided into two categories: the cost of sales and operating expenses.

The **cost of sales (COS)** (which can also be called *cost of goods sold (COGS)*) is the total cost of inventory sold during the period. This expense is directly related to the revenue recognised from the sale of goods. The profit measurement process for a merchandising business is shown in figure 4.1. Determination of profit is one of the major objectives of accounting for inventories. The items in the two blue boxes in figure 4.1 are unique to a merchandising business; they are not used by a service business.

Operating cycles

The operating cycle of a merchandising business ordinarily is longer than that of a service business. The purchase of inventory and its eventual sale lengthen the cycle. The operating cycles of service and merchandising businesses are contrasted in figure 4.2. Note that the added asset account for a merchandising business is the Inventory account.

Inventory systems

A merchandising business keeps track of its inventory to determine what is available for sale and what has been sold. One of two systems is used to account for inventory: a perpetual inventory system or a periodic inventory system.

FIGURE 4.1   Profit measurement process for a merchandising business

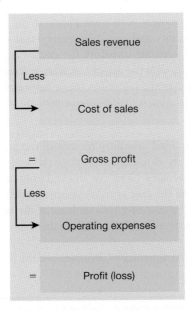

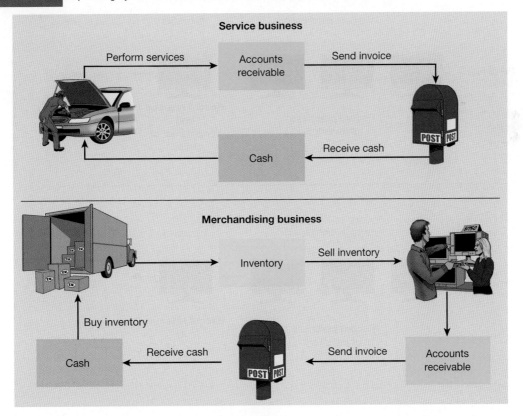

Perpetual system

In a **perpetual inventory system**, detailed records of the cost of each inventory purchase and sale are maintained. The perpetual inventory system is so named because the accounting records continuously — that is, perpetually — show the quantity and cost of inventory that should be on hand at any time. For example, a Mercedes dealership has separate inventory records for each car, truck and van in its car yard and on the showroom floor. Similarly, with the use of barcodes and optical scanners, JB Hi-Fi can keep a daily running record of every computer and television that it buys and sells. Under a perpetual inventory system, the cost of sales is *determined each time a sale occurs.*

Periodic system

In a **periodic inventory system**, detailed inventory records of the goods on hand are not kept throughout the period. The cost of sales is *determined only at the end of the accounting period* — i.e. periodically — when a physical inventory count (or stocktake) is taken to determine the quantity and cost of goods on hand. To determine the cost of sales under a periodic inventory system, the following steps are necessary: (1) determine the cost of goods on hand at the beginning of the accounting period; (2) add to it the cost of goods purchased; and (3) subtract the cost of goods on hand at the end of the accounting period.

Figure 4.3 graphically compares the sequence of activities and the timing of the cost of sales calculation under the two inventory systems.

FIGURE 4.3   Cost of sales — comparing periodic and perpetual inventory systems

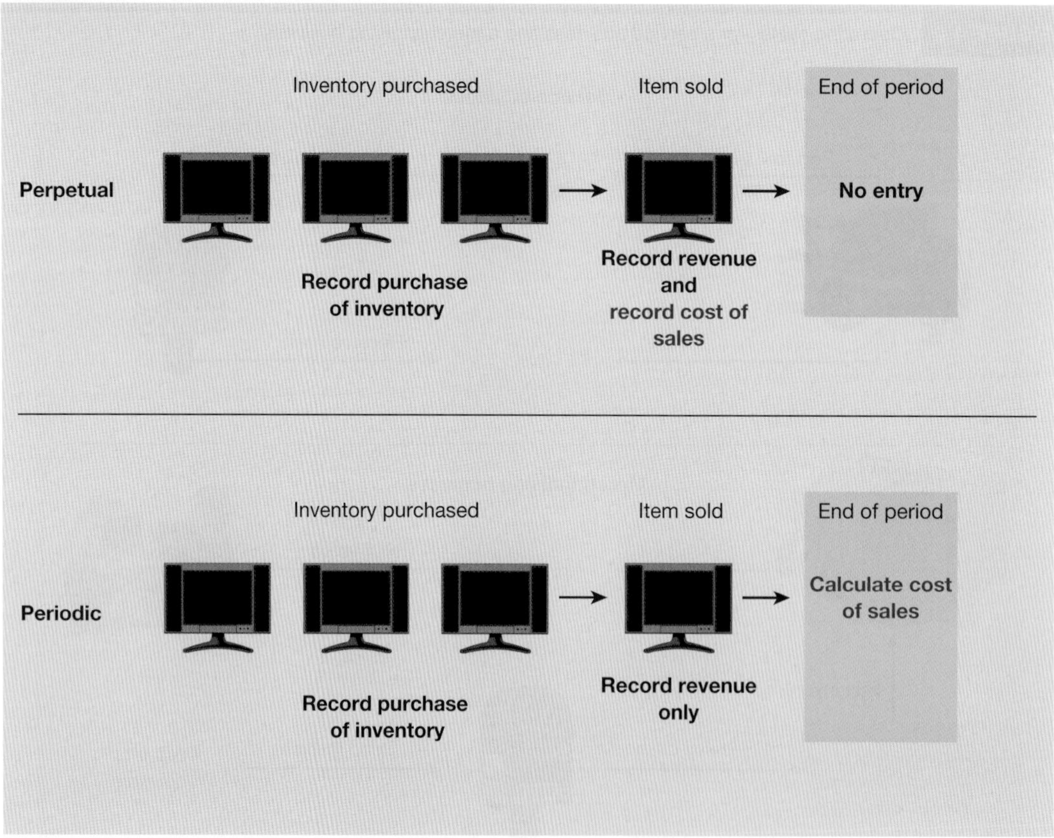

Computerised inventory systems

An increasing number of businesses are adopting computerised inventory systems to take advantage of technology improvements in recent years. An integrated inventory system is linked with accounts payable and purchases and with accounts receivable and sales to record the number of units purchased, number of units sold and quantities of goods on hand. For example, the cash register or the self-checkout counter at a JB Hi-Fi store or a Woolworths supermarket is a computer terminal that records a sale and updates inventory records instantly. Commonly, barcodes, which represent the inventory and cost data of each stock item, are scanned by a laser as part of the computerised inventory system. As the computerised inventory system keeps up-to-the-minute records, managers can access the most current inventory information at any time. Having the most current inventory information available at any time also assists managers in making decisions about when to replenish and reorder inventory to ensure that enough is available to meet customer sales.

Additional considerations

A perpetual inventory system provides better control over inventories than a periodic system. Since the inventory records show the quantities that should be on hand, the goods can be counted at any time to see whether the amount of goods on hand agrees with the inventory records. Any shortages uncovered can be investigated immediately. Although a perpetual inventory system requires additional clerical work and additional cost to maintain the records, a computerised system can minimise this cost.

Helpful hint: For control purposes a physical inventory count is taken under the perpetual system, even though it is not needed to determine cost of sales.

Some businesses find it either unnecessary or uneconomical to invest in a computerised perpetual inventory system. Many small retail businesses, in particular, find that a perpetual inventory system costs more than it is worth. Managers of small businesses, such as greengrocers, cafés, restaurants and convenience stores, can control their inventories and manage day-to-day operations without detailed inventory records by simply looking at their shelves.

The perpetual inventory system, which is growing in popularity and use, is illustrated in this chapter. The periodic system, still widely used among small businesses, is described in the next chapter.

4.2 Recording purchases of inventories

LEARNING OBJECTIVE 4.2 Explain the recording of purchases under a perpetual inventory system.

Merchandising businesses purchase inventories for resale. For example, JB Hi-Fi purchases inventories from suppliers (also called *sellers* or *vendors*), such as Apple and LG, to sell to customers. Purchases of inventories may be made for cash or on credit (on account). Purchases made for cash are those that are paid for when the goods are delivered. Payments at the time of delivery may be made by cash, by cheque, by credit card or by electronic funds transfer. They are referred to as cash purchases because the payment is made at the time of delivery.

Credit purchases are those that are paid for after delivery of the goods, i.e. the purchase is on credit terms. Common credit terms are 30 days and 7 days. If purchases are on 7-day terms, the supplier allows the purchaser up to 7 days to pay for the goods. Similarly, if purchases are on terms of 30 days, the purchaser has up to 30 days from the date of the invoice (which is usually on or close to the delivery date) to pay for the goods.

Purchases are normally recorded when the goods are received from the seller. Every purchase should be supported by source documents that provide written evidence of the transaction. Each cash purchase should be supported by a cheque payment, a cash receipt and/or a supplier's invoice indicating the items purchased and amounts paid. Cash purchases are recorded by an increase in inventory and a decrease in cash.

Each credit purchase should be supported by a supplier's invoice. The **supplier's invoice** is a document evidencing the supplier's claim against the purchaser. It states the quantity and cost of each item supplied, the total purchase price and the terms of payment.

In this chapter, to illustrate inventory recording processes, we will follow a series of transactions between PW Audio Supply Ltd and Sauk Stereo. PW Audio Supply Ltd sells inventories to Sauk Stereo. We begin with Sauk Stereo's purchase of inventory. Figure 4.4 shows the sales invoice prepared by PW Audio Supply Ltd (the seller) which is sent to Sauk Stereo (the buyer). Sauk Stereo uses the invoice to record the purchase.

Helpful hint: As we are ignoring the effects of GST in this section of the chapter, GST is not included on this invoice. GST is discussed in sections 4.6 and 4.7.

FIGURE 4.4 Sales invoice from PW Audio Supply Ltd

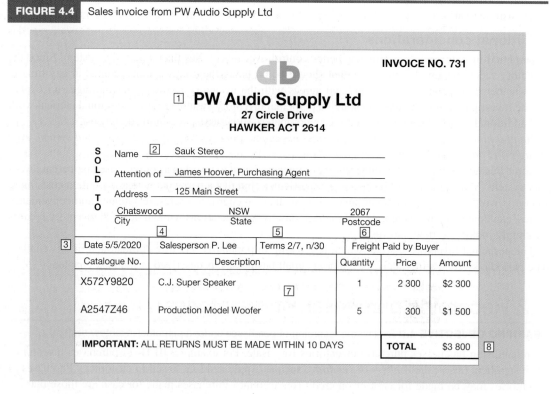

The important elements of this invoice are numbered in figure 4.4 and explained as follows.
1. The seller (supplier) is PW Audio Supply Ltd.
2. The purchaser is Sauk Stereo.
3. The invoice date is 5 May 2020 and is needed for determining whether the purchaser receives a discount for prompt payment (see point 5).
4. The salesperson is P. Lee and is important for calculation of sales commission, if any.
5. The credit terms of the transaction are 2/7, n/30; that is, if Sauk Stereo pays within 7 days of the invoice date, it may deduct a 2% discount. Otherwise, the full invoice amount is due in 30 days. (The discussion of discounts appears later in this section.)
6. The freight terms are that Sauk Stereo is responsible for the transportation costs. (Freight costs are discussed in a section next.)
7. The details of the goods sold are one unit of item C.J. Super Speaker and five units of the item Production Model Woofer.
8. The total invoice amount is $3800.

The associated entry for Sauk Stereo for the invoice from PW Audio Supply Ltd is:

May 5	Inventory	3 800	
	Accounts payable		3 800
	(To record goods purchased on account from PW Audio Supply Ltd)		

A	=	L	+	E
+3800		+3800		

Helpful hint: After key journal entries are equation analyses *that summarise the effects of the transaction on the three elements of the accounting equation.*

Under the perpetual inventory system, purchases of goods for resale are recorded in the Inventory account. Thus, JB Hi-Fi, for example, would increase (debit) inventory for televisions, computers and anything else purchased for resale to customers. Not all purchases are debited to inventory. Purchases of assets acquired for use by JB Hi-Fi, such as stationery, equipment and similar items, are recorded as increases to specific asset accounts rather than to inventory. For example, JB Hi-Fi would increase supplies to record the purchase of materials used to make shelf signs or for cash register receipt paper.

Purchase returns and allowances

A purchaser may be dissatisfied with the inventory received because the goods are damaged or defective, of inferior quality, or do not meet the purchaser's specifications. In such cases, the purchaser may return the goods to the seller for credit if the sale was made on credit, or for a cash refund if the purchase was for cash. This transaction is known as a *purchase return*. Alternatively, the purchaser may choose to keep the inventory if the seller is willing to grant an allowance (deduction) from the purchase price. This transaction is known as a *purchase allowance*.

Assume that Sauk Stereo returned goods costing $300 to PW Audio Supply Ltd on 8 May. The entry by Sauk Stereo for the returned merchandise is:

May 8	Accounts payable	300	
	Inventory		300
	(To record return of goods received from PW Audio Supply Ltd)		

A	=	L	+	E
−300		−300		

Because Sauk Stereo increased inventory when the goods were received, inventory is decreased when Sauk returns the goods.

Freight costs

The sales invoice indicates whether the seller or the buyer pays the cost of transporting the goods to the buyer's place of business. When the buyer pays the transport costs, these costs are considered part of the cost of purchasing inventory and are called **freight-in**. Conceptually, the cost of inventory includes the invoice price plus freight charges. However, in practice, freight costs are often recorded in a freight-in account because of the difficulty of allocating freight costs to individual inventory items when several different items are delivered at the same time. As a result, the freight-in account is increased. Although freight-in costs are not directly debited to inventory, they are included in the cost of inventory. How this is achieved is illustrated in chapter 5.

In this example, on delivery of the goods on 6 May, Sauk Stereo pays We Deliver Freight Co. $150 for freight charges, and the entry in Sauk Stereo's records is:

May 6	Freight-in	150	
	Cash		150
	(To record payment of freight on goods purchased)		

$$A = L + E$$
$$-150 \qquad -150$$

In contrast, freight costs incurred by the seller on outgoing inventory are called **freight-out** and are an operating expense to the seller. These costs increase an expense account entitled freight-out or delivery expense. For example, if the freight terms on the invoice in figure 4.4 had required that PW Audio Supply Ltd pay the $150 freight charges, the entry by PW Audio Supply Ltd would be:

May 5	Freight-out	150	
	Cash		150
	(To record payment of freight on goods sold)		

$$A = L + E$$
$$-150 \qquad -150$$

When the freight charges are paid by the seller, the seller may establish a higher invoice price for the goods to cover the delivery expense.

Purchase discounts

Many businesses offer discounts to their customers. Discounts fall into two categories: settlement discounts (can also be called *cash discounts*) and trade discounts.

Settlement discounts

The credit terms of a purchase on account may permit the buyer to claim a discount for prompt payment. The buyer calls this settlement discount **discount received**. This incentive offers advantages to both parties — the purchaser saves money, and the seller is able to shorten the operating cycle by converting the accounts receivable into cash earlier.

The credit terms specify the amount of the cash discount and time period during which it is offered. They also indicate the time within which the purchaser is expected to pay the full invoice price. In the sales invoice in figure 4.4, credit terms are 2/7, n/30, which is read as 'two-seven, net thirty'. This means that a 2% cash discount may be taken on the invoice price, less ('net of') any returns or allowances, if payment is made within 7 days of the invoice date (the *discount period*); otherwise, the invoice price, less any returns or allowances, is due 30 days from the invoice date.

Helpful hint: The term net *in 'net 30' means the remaining amount due after subtracting any returns or allowances and partial payments.*

When the seller elects not to offer a settlement discount for prompt payment, credit terms will specify only the maximum time period for paying the balance due. For example, the time period may be stated as n/30, meaning that the net amount must be paid in 30 days from the invoice date.

When an invoice is paid within the discount period, the amount of the discount is credited to discount received. Discounts are recorded by the buyer as revenue, as a discount represents a saving in outflows and a consequential reduction in liabilities and an increase in equity. To illustrate, assume Sauk Stereo pays the balance due of $3500 (gross invoice price of $3800 less purchase returns and allowances of $300) on 12 May, the last day of the discount period. The settlement discount is $70 ($3500 × 2%), and the amount of cash paid by Sauk Stereo is $3430 ($3500 − $70). The entry to record the 12 May payment by Sauk Stereo is shown next.

May 12	Accounts payable				3 500	
	Cash					3 430
	Discount received					70
	(To record payment within discount period)					

A	=	L	+	E
−3430		−3500		+70

If Sauk Stereo failed to take the discount and instead made full payment on 3 June, Sauk's entry is:

June 3	Accounts payable				3 500	
	Cash					3 500
	(To record payment with no discount taken)					

A	=	L	+	E
−3500		−3500		

In Australia and in New Zealand the treatment of settlement discounts can be interpreted and recorded in a number of ways, which is in accordance with IAS 2/AASB 102 *Inventories*. One way is to record the purchase discount as a credit to discount received, as demonstrated in the 12 May journal entry above. Under this method, the discount is considered to be related to the management of accounts receivable and therefore is treated as revenue. Another way is to credit inventory by the amount of the discount when an invoice is paid within the discount period. Entities justify this approach by arguing that inventory is recorded at cost and, by paying within the discount period, the buyer has reduced its cost.

The recording of a settlement discount as a credit to inventory is illustrated below, using the same information as given for the 12 May payment where Sauk Stereo pays the balance due of \$3500 (gross invoice price of \$3800 less purchase returns and allowances of \$300) and the settlement discount is \$70 (3500 × 2%). The entry to record the payment is:

May 12	Accounts payable				3 500	
	Cash					3 430
	Inventory					70
	(To record payment within discount period)					

A	=	L	+	E
−3430		−3500		
−70				

Companies such as Woolworths Limited and Harvey Norman Holdings Limited treat settlement discounts as a credit to inventory. Given that both approaches are acceptable, which approach do you prefer — the credit to discount received or the credit to inventory? Why?

Note: When completing the exercises and problems at the end of the chapters, use only the first method illustrated. That is, record all purchase discounts as a credit to discount received unless the question explicitly requires you to record the purchase discount as a credit to inventory.

Businesses can save money by taking advantage of settlement discounts, provided that they are not paying more in interest than they are saving with the discount. For example, Sauk Stereo could pay \$3430 on 12 May (taking the discount) or pay \$3500 on 4 June, 23 days later.

Helpful hint: So as not to miss settlement discounts, unpaid invoices should be filed by due dates. This procedure helps the purchaser remember the discount date, prevents early payment of bills, and maximises the time that cash can be used for other purposes. With computerised accounting systems, payments can be automated to ensure they are made by due dates.

Another way of looking at the discount is to say that it would cost Sauk Stereo an additional \$70 to have the use of the money (\$3430) for another 23 days. How does \$70 (or 2%) interest for 23 days compare with the interest that Sauk Stereo would pay for money it borrows from the bank? We can convert the 2% for 23 days to an annual interest rate as follows:

$$\frac{365}{23} \times 2\% = 31.7\% \text{ p.a.}$$

Thus, unless Sauk Stereo pays more than 31.7% interest p.a. for the money that it uses (such as a bank overdraft), it will save money by taking advantage of the discount. Obviously, it would be better for Sauk Stereo to borrow money at the prevailing bank interest rates of 6% to 10% than to lose the discount.

Trade discounts

Trade discounts, unlike settlement discounts, do not depend on early payment of the amount due and are not recorded in the records of either the buyer or the seller. Trade discounts are disclosed on the sales invoice as a percentage reduction in the list price of the inventories sold. For example, assume that a seller quotes a list price of $500 per item and allows a trade discount of 10% for buyers who purchase in large quantities (in this example, assume that 8 items or more are considered a large purchase). If the buyer purchases 10 items of inventory on 19 May, taking a trade discount of 10%, the invoice price would be $4500 (10 × $500 × 90%). The purchase would be recorded in the buyer's records as:

May 19	Inventory	4 500	
	Accounts payable		4 500
	(To record purchase of inventory on account with a trade discount of $500)		

A	=	L	+	E
+4500		+4500		

Helpful hint: In the records of the seller, the sale of inventory would be recorded in the amount of $4500. Hence, the $500 trade discount is not recorded in the records of either the buyer or the seller.

LEARNING REFLECTION AND CONSOLIDATION

Review it

1. How does the measurement of profit in a merchandising business differ from that in a service business?
2. In what ways is a perpetual inventory system different from a periodic system?
3. Under the perpetual inventory system, what entries are made to record purchases, purchase returns and allowances, discounts received, and freight costs?

4.3 Recording sales of inventories

LEARNING OBJECTIVE 4.3 Explain the recording of sales revenues under a perpetual inventory system.

Sales revenues, like service revenues, are recognised (recorded) when the inflow of economic benefits is probable and can be measured reliably. There are set criteria for the recognition of revenue for the sale of goods under IFRS 15/AASB 15 *Revenue from Contracts with Customers*. Please refer to section 3.2 to review these criteria. Typically, revenue recognition occurs when the goods are transferred from the seller to the buyer. At this point the sales transaction is completed, a claim arises against the buyer, and the sales price has been established.

Sales may be made on credit or for cash. Every sales transaction should be supported by a source document that provides written evidence of the sale. Cash register tapes or cash receipts provide evidence of cash sales. A **sales invoice**, like the one that was shown in figure 4.4, provides support for a credit sale. The original copy of the invoice goes to the customer, and a copy is kept by the seller for use in

---

recording the sale. The invoice shows the date of sale, customer name, total sales price and other relevant information.

Under a perpetual inventory system, two entries are made for each sale. The first entry records the sale: assuming a cash sale, cash is increased by a debit, and sales is increased by a credit at the selling (invoice) price of the goods. The second entry records the cost of the inventory sold: cost of sales is increased by a debit, and inventory is decreased by a credit for the cost of those goods. For example, assume that on 5 May PW Audio Supply Ltd made cash sales of $2200, and that the goods sold cost $1400. The entries to record the day's cash sales are as follows:

May 5	Cash	2 200	
	Sales		2 200
	(To record daily cash sales)		
5	Cost of sales	1 400	
	Inventory		1 400
	(To record cost of inventories sold for cash)		

$$A = L + E$$
$$+2200 \qquad\qquad +2200$$

$$A = L + E$$
$$-1400 \qquad\qquad -1400$$

For credit sales (1) accounts receivable is increased and sales is increased, and (2) cost of sales is increased and inventory is decreased. As a result, the inventory account will show at all times the amount of inventory that should be on hand. To illustrate a credit sales transaction, PW Audio Supply Ltd's sale of $3800 on 5 May to Sauk Stereo (see figure 4.4) is recorded as follows (assume the goods sold cost PW Audio Supply Ltd $2400):

May 5	Accounts receivable	3 800	
	Sales		3 800
	(To record credit sale to Sauk Stereo per invoice no. 731)		
5	Cost of sales	2 400	
	Inventory		2 400
	(To record cost of inventories sold on invoice no. 731 to Sauk Stereo)		

A	=	L	+	E
+3800				+3800

A	=	L	+	E
−2400				−2400

For internal decision-making purposes, businesses may use more than one sales account. For example, JB Hi-Fi keeps separate sales accounts for its various computers and home theatre products, and PW Audio Supply Ltd may decide to keep separate sales accounts for its sales of TV sets and DVD players. By using separate sales accounts for major product lines, rather than a single combined sales account, management can monitor sales trends more closely and respond in a more appropriate strategic manner to changes in sales patterns. For example, if TV sales are increasing while DVD player sales are decreasing, the business should re-evaluate both its advertising and pricing policies on each of these items to ensure they are the best possible. However, on its statement of profit or loss, presented to outside investors, a retail entity would normally report only total sales revenue as part of an aggregate revenue figure.

Helpful hint: The sales account is credited only for sales of goods held for resale. Sales of assets not held for resale, such as equipment or land, are accounted for separately.

Sales returns and allowances

We now look at purchase returns and allowances from the supplier's perspective. When a customer returns goods, the seller may give a cash refund or a credit note. A credit note reduces the amount owed by the customer. Cash refunds and credit notes are recorded as **sales returns and allowances** in the records of the seller. PW Audio Supply Ltd's entries to record a credit for returned goods from sales to Sauk Stereo that are not faulty or damaged involve (1) an increase in sales returns and allowances and a decrease in accounts receivable at the $300 selling price, and (2) an increase in inventory (assume a $140 cost) and a decrease in cost of sales as follows:

May 8	Sales returns and allowances	300	
	Accounts receivable		300
	(To record credit granted to Sauk Stereo for returned goods)		
8	Inventory	140	
	Cost of sales		140
	(To record cost of goods returned)		

A	=	L	+	E
−300				−300

A	=	L	+	E
+140				+140

Helpful hint: Returned goods are debited to Inventory only if they are not damaged or faulty.

If PW Audio Supply Ltd gave Sauk Stereo a cash refund, the cash account would be credited for $300 instead of accounts receivable. All other entries would be the same. The effect on the accounting equation would be the same because both cash and accounts receivable are asset accounts.

Let's assume that the goods returned were, in fact, faulty. Faulty and damaged goods cannot be returned to inventory for resale. PW Audio Supply Ltd's entries to record a credit for faulty goods returned would involve (1) an increase in sales returns and allowances and a decrease in accounts receivable (or cash if a refund is given) at the $300 selling price, and (2) an increase in an expense account called **inventory write-down** and a decrease in cost of sales ($140 cost) as follows:

May 8	Sales returns and allowances	300	
	Accounts receivable		300
	(To record credit granted to Sauk Stereo for returned goods)		
8	Inventory write-down	140	
	Cost of sales		140
	(To record cost of faulty goods returned)		

$$A = L + E$$
$$-300 \qquad\qquad -300$$

$$A = L + E$$
$$\qquad\qquad -140$$
$$\qquad\qquad +140$$

The inventory write-down account can also be used to record inventory shrinkage (e.g. evaporation of inventories such as ink or fuel), inventory waste (e.g. offcuts of fabric or building materials), inventory obsolescence or inventory that has been lost or stolen. (*Note:* Inventory write-down expense can also be referred to as inventory write-off expense, damaged inventory expense or obsolete inventory expense.)

Sales returns and allowances is a **contra revenue account** to sales. The normal balance of sales returns and allowances is a debit. A contra account is used, instead of debiting sales, to separately identify in the accounts and in the statement of profit or loss the amount of sales returns and allowances. This information is important to management as it may impact on decisions made with regards to inventory. For example, if excessive returns are due to inferior inventory, then management may decide to source their products or raw materials for making those products from different suppliers. Excessive returns and allowances may not be indicative only of inferior inventories, but could be due also to inefficiencies in filling orders, errors in invoicing customers, or mistakes in delivery and shipment of goods. Moreover, a decrease (debit) recorded directly to sales would obscure the relative importance of sales returns and allowances as a percentage of sales. It also could distort comparisons between total sales in different accounting periods.

Helpful hint: Remember that the increases, decreases and normal balances of contra accounts are the opposite of the accounts to which they correspond.

Sales discounts

As mentioned in our discussion of purchase transactions, the seller may offer the customer a settlement discount for the prompt payment of the balance due. Like a purchase discount, a sales discount is based on the invoice price less returns and allowances, if any. Businesses decide on the percentage of discount to be offered to customers based on many factors, including rewarding valuable customers and encouraging speedy payment. Businesses decide on the amount of discount to offer based on how much cash they are willing to forgo while ensuring that the discount provides enough incentive for the customer to pay within the discount period. The discount allowed account is increased (debited) for discounts that are taken by customers. The entry by PW Audio Supply Ltd to record the cash receipt on 12 May from Sauk Stereo within the discount period is shown next.

May 12	Cash	3 430	
	Discount allowed	70	
	Accounts receivable		3 500
	(To record collection within 2/7, n/30 discount period from Sauk Stereo)		

$$A = L + E$$
$$+3430$$
$$-3500 \qquad\qquad -70$$

If Sauk Stereo pays the amount owing outside the discount period, PW Audio Supply Ltd increases cash for $3500 and decreases accounts receivable for the same amount on the day payment is received.

Discount allowed is reported as an expense in the statement of profit or loss and provides information to management on the amount of discount taken by customers. Sellers offer customers settlement discounts to encourage early payment of the account and have the cash available for use by the business before the end of the credit period.

Helpful hint: A sales discount, recorded as discount allowed in the seller's accounts, is a mirror reflection of the settlement discount, recorded as discount received in the buyer's accounts.

LEARNING REFLECTION AND CONSOLIDATION

Review it

1. Under a perpetual inventory system, what are the two entries that must be recorded at the time of each sale?
2. Why is it important to use the sales returns and allowances account, rather than simply reducing the sales account, when goods are returned?

Do it

On 5 September, De La Hoya Ltd buys inventories on account from Junot Ltd. The selling price of the goods is $1500, and the cost to Junot Ltd was $800. Due to an error in filling the order, incorrect goods with a selling price of $200 and a cost of $80 are returned on 8 September. Prepare journal entries to record these transactions for each entity.

Reasoning

Under a perpetual inventory system the purchaser will record goods at cost. The seller will record both the sale and the cost of goods sold at the time of the sale. When goods are returned, the purchaser will directly reduce inventory, but the seller will record the return in a contra account, sales returns and allowances.

Solution

DE LA HOYA LTD (THE PURCHASER)			
Sept. 5	Inventory	1 500	
	Accounts payable		1 500
	(To record goods purchased on account)		
Sept. 8	Accounts payable	200	
	Inventory		200
	(To record return of incorrect goods)		

JUNOT LTD (THE SELLER)			
Sept. 5	Accounts receivable	1 500	
	Sales		1 500
	(To record credit sale)		
5	Cost of sales	800	
	Inventory		800
	(To record cost of goods sold on account)		

Sept. 8	Sales returns and allowances	200	
	Accounts receivable		200
	(To record credit granted for receipt of returned goods)		
8	Inventory	80	
	Cost of sales		80
	(To record cost of goods returned)		

Helpful hint: The goods returned in the example are incorrect, not faulty or damaged, so they are returned into inventory by debiting the Inventory account. Recall that damaged goods are not returned to inventory but debited to the inventory write-down expense account.

4.4 Statement of profit or loss presentation

LEARNING OBJECTIVE 4.4 Prepare a fully classified statement of profit or loss.

A fully classified statement of profit or loss generated for internal use contains a number of main components including sales revenue, gross profit, operating expenses and profit. Note that income tax expense is reported in a separate section of the statement and is deducted from profit before tax to determine profit after tax. The following discussion provides additional information about some of the main components of a fully classified statement of profit or loss as shown in figure 4.6.

Sales revenue

The statement of profit or loss for a merchandising business typically presents gross sales revenue for the period and provides details about deductions from that total amount. Sales returns and allowances, a contra revenue account, is deducted from sales in the statement of profit or loss to arrive at **net sales**. The sales revenue section of the statement for PW Audio Supply Ltd is shown in figure 4.5.

FIGURE 4.5   Statement of profit or loss presentation of sales revenue section

PW AUDIO SUPPLY LTD Statement of profit or loss (extract)	
SALES REVENUE	
Sales	$480 000
Less: Sales returns and allowances	(20 000)
Net sales	$460 000

Gross profit

Cost of sales is deducted from sales revenue to determine **gross profit** (sometimes referred to as gross margin).

On the basis of the sales data presented in figure 4.5 (net sales of $460 000) and the cost of sales (assume a balance of $316 000), the gross profit for PW Audio Supply Ltd is $144 000, calculated as follows:

Net sales	$ 460 000
Less: Cost of sales	(316 000)
Gross profit	$ 144 000

It is important to understand what gross profit is — and what it is not. Gross profit is the surplus of sales revenue over the cost of sales. It is *not* a measure of the overall profit of a business because operating expenses have not been deducted. Nevertheless, the amount and trend of gross profit are closely watched by management and other interested parties. Comparisons of current gross profit with gross profit in previous periods and with gross profit of other businesses in the industry indicate the effectiveness of a business's purchasing and pricing policies.

Other revenue

Revenue items other than sales revenue are included *after* gross profit. **Other revenue** includes items such as rent revenue and discount received. The other revenue for PW Audio Supply Ltd (see figure 4.6) consists of:

Rent revenue	$12 000
Interest revenue	9 000
Discount received	3 000

Operating expenses

Operating expenses are the next component in measuring profit for a merchandising business. These expenses are similar in merchandising and service businesses. At PW Audio Supply Ltd, operating expenses were $125 000.

Subgrouping of operating expenses

In a fully classified statement of profit or loss, operating expenses are subdivided into selling, administrative and financial expenses (as shown in the statement in figure 4.6). *Selling expenses* are those associated with making sales. They include advertising expenses and storage costs as well as expenses of completing the sale, such as delivery and shipping expenses. *Administrative expenses* relate to the operating activities of the general, accounting and personnel offices, and are sometimes called *general expenses*. They include office salaries expense and rent expense. *Financial expenses* are those associated with the financing of the firm's operations and debt collection. They include interest expense and discount allowed.

In figure 4.6 we have provided a fully classified statement of profit or loss of PW Audio Supply Ltd.

Note: For homework problems, the fully classified form of the statement of profit or loss should be used unless the requirements state otherwise.

FIGURE 4.6 | Fully classified statement of profit or loss

PW AUDIO SUPPLY LTD Statement of profit or loss for the year ended 30 June 2020			
OPERATING REVENUE			
Sales revenue			
Gross sales revenue			$ 480 000
Less: Sales returns and allowances			(20 000)
Net sales revenue			460 000
Less: Cost of sales			(316 000)
Gross profit			144 000
OTHER OPERATING REVENUE			
Rent revenue		$12 000	
Interest revenue		9 000	
Discount received		3 000	24 000
			168 000

OPERATING EXPENSES			
Selling expenses			
Sales salaries and commission expense	$45 000		
Advertising expense	16 000		
Freight-out	8 000		
Rent expense—store space	7 000		
Depn expense—store equipment	5 000	81 000	
Administrative expenses			
Office salaries expense	19 000		
Electricity expense	4 000		
Rent expense—office space	10 000		
Depn expense—office equipment	3 000		
Insurance expense	2 000	38 000	
Financial expenses			
Interest expense	2 000		
Discount allowed	4 000	6 000	
			(125 000)
Profit before income tax			**43 000**
Less: Income tax expense			(12 900)
Profit after tax			$ 30 100

Helpful hint: This is an internal report. External reports differ in their presentation style to internal reports, as illustrated in chapter 1.

  What is and is not reported?

1. *Did the entity sell on credit? Yes, it had discount allowed.*
2. *Did the entity take all available purchase discounts? Don't know; discounts not taken are not reported.*

LEARNING REFLECTION AND CONSOLIDATION

Review it

1. Under the perpetual inventory system, what entries are made to record sales, sales returns and allowances, and discount allowed?
2. How are sales and contra revenue accounts reported in the statement of profit or loss?
3. What is the significance of gross profit?

4.5 Evaluating profitability

LEARNING OBJECTIVE 4.5 Use ratios to analyse profitability.

Gross profit ratio

An entity's gross profit may be expressed as a percentage by dividing the amount of gross profit by net sales; this is referred to as the **gross profit ratio**. For PW Audio Supply Ltd the gross profit ratio is 31.3% (Gross profit $144 000 ÷ Net sales $460 000). The gross profit *ratio* is generally considered to be more informative than the gross profit *amount* because it expresses a more meaningful relationship between gross profit and net sales. For example, a gross profit amount of $1 000 000 may sound impressive. But if it was the result of sales of $100 000 000, the business's gross profit ratio was only 1%. Such a low gross profit ratio is acceptable in only a few industries.

A decline in a business's gross profit ratio might have several causes. The business may have begun to sell products with a lower 'mark-up' — for example, budget blue jeans versus designer blue jeans. Increased competition may have resulted in a lower selling price. Or the business may be forced to pay higher prices to its suppliers without being able to pass these costs on to its customers.

In chapter 1 we introduced ratio analysis using 2019 data from Artistry Furniture Limited and Original Furnishings Limited to illustrate how to calculate and interpret profitability, liquidity and solvency ratios. In order to continue our analysis and understanding of these companies, the gross profit ratios are presented in figure 4.7.

FIGURE 4.7 Gross profit ratio

$$\text{Gross profit ratio} = \frac{\text{Gross profit}}{\text{Net sales}}$$

($'000)	2019	2018
Original Furnishings	$\frac{\$212\,500}{\$562\,500} = 0.38$ or 38%	$\frac{\$200\,300}{\$510\,300} = 0.39$ or 39%
Artistry Furniture	$\frac{\$55\,000}{\$135\,000} = 0.41$ or 41%	$\frac{\$46\,000}{\$112\,000} = 0.41$ or 41%

Original Furnishings reported a 10% increase in net sales from $510 300 000 in 2018 to $562 500 000 in 2019 and a 6% increase in gross profit from $200 300 000 in 2018 to $212 500 000 in 2019. This resulted in a small decrease of 1% in the gross profit ratio over the 2 years. The company attributed this drop in sales and profit to a challenging year in difficult retail trading conditions. Due to fixed and rising costs, the reduction in expected sales had a larger than normal impact on profit. In contrast, Artistry Furniture reported a substantial (20.5%) increase in net sales from $112 000 000 in 2018 to $135 000 000 in 2019 and almost the same level of increase (19.6%) in gross profit from $46 000 000 in 2018 to $55 000 000 in 2019. As a consequence, the gross profit ratio remained constant at 41% over the 2 years. Artistry Furniture attributed this relatively high profit margin to record sales revenue from newly opened stores, an increase in marketing activity, and careful selection of the product range and pricing for its furniture items.

Despite a challenging and competitive retail environment, Artistry Furniture achieved a gross profit ratio of 41% in 2019, which is higher than Original Furnishings (38%). This comparison reveals that Artistry Furniture can command a larger mark-up on its furniture items than Original Furnishings. The difference may be explained by the fact that Original Furnishings prides itself as being the 'best value' company in the furniture market segment. Artistry Furniture, on the other hand, may be perceived by the marketplace as 'better quality' and is therefore able to command a higher mark-up on its furniture sales.

Potential investors, shareholders, lenders and other users are interested in evaluating a company's profitability when making decisions about providing resources to a company. For example, potential investors and lenders would have greater confidence in investing resources in a profitable company. One of the key measures of profitability is the gross profit. As shown in the decision-making toolkit, calculating the gross profit ratio using the gross profit and net sales data from financial statements assists users in determining whether the entity is maintaining an adequate margin between the selling price and the cost of inventory. A higher gross profit ratio suggests that the average margin between selling price and inventory cost is increasing. Management should take caution in determining an appropriate mark-up on inventory as too high a margin may result in lower sales.

Decision/issue	Info needed for analysis	Tool or technique to use for decision	How to evaluate results to make decision
Is management maintaining an adequate margin between the selling price and the cost of inventory?	Gross profit and net sales	Gross profit ratio $=\dfrac{\text{Gross profit}}{\text{Net sales}}$	Higher ratio suggests the average margin between selling price and inventory cost is increasing. Too high a margin may result in lower sales.

Operating expenses to sales ratio

A useful measure of operating expenses is the **operating expenses to sales ratio**. Over the last decade many entities have improved the efficiency of their operations, thus reducing the ratio of operating expenses to sales. As a consequence, they have increased their profitability. The record profits of many entities in the 1990s were achieved as much by reducing costs as by increasing revenues. The use of computers and changes in organisational structure have brought added efficiency. For example, one study of a thousand businesses that successfully re-engineered their warehouse operations by using new technologies found savings on labour costs averaging 25%. Epson, a company which sells printers, scanners and other computer accessories, reported space savings of 50%, labour savings of 43%, and operating cost savings of 25% on their warehouses. Operating costs have been reduced to such low levels for so many entities that many investors believe further improvements in profits from cost reductions will be difficult to accomplish.

The ratios of operating expenses to sales for Original Furnishings and Artistry Furniture are presented in figure 4.8.

FIGURE 4.8 Operating expenses to sales ratio

	Operating expenses to sales ratio $=\dfrac{\text{Operating expenses}}{\text{Net sales}}$	
($'000)	2019	2018
Original Furnishings	$\dfrac{\$155\,000}{\$562\,500}=0.28$ or 28%	$\dfrac{\$143\,200}{\$510\,300}=0.28$ or 28%
Artistry Furniture	$\dfrac{\$33\,600}{\$135\,000}=0.25$ or 25%	$\dfrac{\$32\,500}{\$112\,000}=0.29$ or 29%

As shown in figure 4.7, the gross profit margins for both companies remained much the same for 2018 and 2019. In figure 4.8 we can see that, for both 2019 and 2018, Original Furnishings incurred 28 cents of operating costs for every dollar of sales. In contrast, Artistry Furniture incurred 29 cents of operating costs for every dollar of sales for 2018, but for 2019, incurred only 25 cents of operating costs for every dollar of sales. These figures suggest that Artistry Furniture was better at controlling its operating costs during 2019 when compared with Original Furnishings. Artistry Furniture's increase in operating costs from 2018 to 2019 was 3% compared to an increase in operating costs for Original Furnishings of 8%. This information is helpful for management as it provides some insight into how future profits can be improved. One option for Original Furnishings could be to review its operating costs and take measures to reduce them where possible.

We will introduce other measures of operational efficiency, in terms of inventory management, in chapter 5.

Review it

1. How is the gross profit ratio calculated? What might cause it to decline?
2. What effect does improved efficiency of operations have on the operating expenses to sales ratio?

Another important measure of profitability is the operating expenses to sales ratio. By comparing the entity's operating expenses to net sales data from financial statements, users can determine whether management is effective in controlling operating costs. A higher operating expenses to sales ratio should be investigated to determine whether greater control of expenses is required by management.

DECISION-MAKING TOOLKIT

Decision/issue	Info needed for analysis	Tool or technique to use for decision	How to evaluate results to make decision
Is management effective in controlling operating costs?	Net sales and operating expenses	Operating expenses to sales ratio $= \dfrac{\text{Operating expenses}}{\text{Net sales}}$	Higher ratio should be investigated to determine whether greater control of expenses is required.

4.6 The goods and services tax

LEARNING OBJECTIVE 4.6 Understand the basic process and main features of the goods and services tax (GST).

Generally, businesses have to deal with a variety of taxes, both direct and indirect. In previous chapters, we have introduced company income tax, which is a direct tax on income. The focus of this section is the **goods and services tax (GST)** which is an indirect tax, i.e. a tax on some other measure of activity rather than directly on income. In Australia, the government introduced the GST, as part of its tax reform package, which took effect on 1 July 2000. The GST is a value-added tax, as explained below. Value-added taxes are also levied in other countries, e.g. in New Zealand and Canada where it is also called the GST, and in the United Kingdom where it is called the VAT (value-added tax).

Overview of the GST process

The GST is a **value-added tax** which means that the tax is levied on the *value added* by a business at each stage in the production and distribution chain, i.e. at each stage from the initial purchase of supplies for production to the final stage where goods and services are provided to consumers. For example, the price paid by a furniture manufacturer for timber purchased includes GST, the price paid by a furniture retailer to the furniture manufacturer includes GST and the price paid by a consumer for goods purchased from the furniture retailer also includes GST.

A business is defined broadly in the legislation to include any profession, trade, religious institution and charitable organisation. This makes the GST a broad-based tax, i.e. the GST is included in the selling price of most goods and services at each stage in the production and distribution chain. Goods and services which attract a GST are referred to as **taxable supplies**. In Australia, the rate levied on taxable supplies is 10% and in New Zealand it is 15%.

There are two exceptions where the consumer does not pay GST — **GST-free supplies (zero rated supplies in New Zealand)** and **input taxed supplies (exempt supplies in New Zealand)**. GST-free supplies include basic food, education, health services and exported goods, which are non-taxable under GST legislation. Input taxed supplies include financial services and residential rents. The difference between GST-free supplies and input taxed supplies is that the supplier can obtain an input tax credit from the taxation authority for GST-free supplies but cannot obtain a credit for input taxed supplies.

It is important to note that, even though GST may be paid on taxable supplies at each stage in the commercial chain, in most cases it is the final consumer who bears the cost. That is, if the supplier (seller) includes GST in the final selling price, the GST is imposed on the final private consumption of goods and services, so the supplier does not bear the cost of the GST but effectively acts as a collector of GST for the **taxation authority**. The Australian Taxation Office (ATO) and the New Zealand Inland Revenue (IR) are the appropriate authorities in Australia and New Zealand. In relation to taxable supplies, registered suppliers receive a credit (called an **input tax credit**) for all the GST paid on goods or services purchased in the commercial chain. At regular intervals (monthly, quarterly or yearly) businesses must report the amount of GST paid and collected during a period and discharge any GST liability owing to the taxation authority. The information is provided by filling in a report called a **business activity statement (BAS) (GST return in New Zealand)**. Thus, the accounting system of the business must provide all the information necessary to complete this return.

Helpful hint: The GST a business pays is received back from the ATO, thus GST paid is an asset (GST receivable). On the other hand, the GST a business collects is a liability (GST payable) because the GST is collected on behalf of the ATO.

In summary, GST is generally collected by a business from its customers and clients when goods or services are supplied (taxable supplies). The business also pays GST on goods and services it purchases (creditable acquisitions) from its suppliers for which it may claim a tax credit. The difference between the total amount of GST the business collects on sales and the total it pays on purchases is remitted to the taxation authority at regular intervals along with the BAS. If the GST paid is greater than the GST collected, the taxation authority refunds the amount to the business.

Review it

1. At which stage(s) of the production and distribution chain is GST paid and who ultimately bears the cost of the GST?
2. What type of tax is the GST?

Each of the various stages in the process is explained in the following text in this section.

A simple case

A timber merchant sells timber to a furniture manufacturer for $220 (this amount includes 10% GST). The furniture manufacturer then makes a table and sells it to Fabulous Furniture Ltd, a furniture retailer, for $440 (including GST). The retailer sells the table to a consumer for $550 (including GST). How is the GST remitted to the taxation authority when it has been collected at various stages in the supply and distribution chain? Let's look at the effects of GST in this case.

The total amount of GST that needs to be paid to the taxation authority is $50, i.e. the amount of GST levied on the final consumer. The final sale is to the consumer who buys the table for $550 (including GST). To calculate the amount of GST levied, we divide the selling price of $550 by 11. The answer is $50, which represents the 10% GST included in the price. This is the total amount owing to the taxation authority. The $50 is collected by the taxation authority as described below.

The timber merchant

The timber merchant sells timber to the furniture manufacturer for $220 (including $20 GST), so the timber merchant collects $20 of GST from the manufacturer on behalf of the taxation authority. As no GST has been *paid* by the merchant, the whole amount is remitted to the taxation authority. The taxation authority now has $20.

The manufacturer

The manufacturer sells $440 worth of goods to the retailer (including $40 GST) and so the manufacturer collects $40 of GST from the retailer on behalf of the taxation authority. As the manufacturer has already paid $20 GST to the timber merchant, the manufacturer remits only the difference between the amount collected and the amount paid to the taxation authority — $20 — thus the taxation authority now has $40 ($20 from the timber merchant and $20 from the manufacturer).

The retailer

The retailer sells $550 worth of goods to a customer (including $50 GST) and so the retailer collects $50 GST from the consumer on behalf of the taxation authority. The retailer has already paid $40 GST to the manufacturer. Thus, the retailer need remit only $10 to the taxation authority. Once this is remitted, the taxation authority has the final $10 of the $50 GST.

4.7 Accounting for GST

LEARNING OBJECTIVE 4.7 Complete journal entries to record GST.

The basic journal entries used by businesses to record GST transactions are demonstrated in this section. For the purposes of demonstrating the recording it will be assumed that the accrual (non-cash) basis is used for accounting and GST purposes. The transactions will be demonstrated using general journals.

To record the GST two separate accounts will be used, one for GST collected and one for GST paid. However, some businesses prefer to use one GST clearing account rather than two separate accounts. The debits to the GST clearing account represent the GST paid and the credit to the GST clearing account represents the GST collected. The GST clearing account could be an asset or a liability, depending on whether its balance represents an amount owing to or owing from the taxation authority.

Purchasing inventory

Roger Retailer (who uses a perpetual inventory system) purchases 10 tables on credit from the manufacturer for $440 each (including $40 GST per item).

Inventory (10 × $400)	4 000	
GST paid (an asset account)	400	
Accounts payable		4 400
(To record purchase of furniture from the manufacturer)		

A	=	L	+	E
+4000	=	+4400		
+400				

Helpful hint: In a periodic system, the debit is to purchases not to inventory.

Note that the $400 debit to the GST paid account represents an asset, a future economic benefit for the firm, as this amount can be offset against any future GST liability owing to the taxation authority. The inventory is recorded net of GST, as the $400 is not part of the cost of acquiring inventory. The full amount is payable to the manufacturer, including the GST, as the manufacturer acts as a collecting agent for the taxation authority.

Purchases returns

Roger Retailer ordered the incorrect quantity and returned 3 of the tables to the manufacturer and received an adjustment credit note from the manufacturer. The tables originally cost $440 each (including $40 GST per item).

Accounts payable	1 320	
Inventory (3 × $400)		1 200
GST paid (an asset account)		120
(To record return of furniture to the manufacturer)		

A	=	L	+	E
−1200	=	−1320		
−120				

Note that the effect of the purchase return is the reverse of the purchase. Inventory and the GST paid accounts are reduced and the amount owing to the supplier is now only $3080 ($4400 − $1320). The balance of the GST paid account is now $280 debit. The inventory balance is $2800 (7 tables × $400).

Selling inventory

Roger Retailer sells 5 tables on credit to a customer, who was buying the goods for family members, for $550 including $50 GST. Credit terms of 2% cash discount apply if the account is settled within 10 days from date of invoice, and the amount is due by 30 days.

Accounts receivable	2 750	
GST collected (a liability account)		250
Sales (5 × $500)		2 500
(To record sale of furniture to a customer)		

A	=	L	+	E
+2750	=	+250	+	+2500

Cost of sales	2 000	
Inventory (5 × $400)		2 000
(To record the cost of inventories sold)		

A	=	L	+	E
−2000				−2000

The $250 GST collected represents an amount owing to the taxation authority based on GST collected. The sales account is credited only for $2500 net of the GST; the $250 GST is not sales revenue but was collected on behalf of the taxation authority. A debit of $2750 (5 × $550) is made to accounts receivable to recognise amount due from the customer. When the goods are sold an entry is made to record the cost of sales. This does not involve GST as the inventory is recorded net of any GST.

Sales returns and allowances

The next day the customer returned one of the tables as they realised they needed only 4 of the tables purchased the day before. Roger Retailer issued an adjustment note and credited their account.

Sales returns and allowances	500	
GST collected (a liability account)	50	
Accounts receivable		550
(To record sales return of furniture from a customer)		

A	=	L	+	E
−550		−50		−500

Inventory	400	
Cost of sales		400
(To record the cost of goods returned)		

A	=	L	+	E
+400				+400

The $50 GST collected represents an amount which is no longer owed to the taxation authority. The sales account is debited only for $500 as the original sales transaction was net of GST. A credit of $550 is made to accounts receivable to recognise the amount no longer due from the customer. As the goods were returned into inventory, inventory is increased and cost of sales decreased, again net of any GST as the asset inventory is recorded net of the GST paid.

Settlement discount

A week later Roger Retailer's customer wishes to settle their account. The amount owing from the original sale of 5 tables less the 1 table returned is $2200. The terms of the sale were a settlement discount of 2%, granted if the customer paid within 10 days. So the amount the customer will pay is $2156 (the $2200 less 2% ($44)). The original supply due of $2200 includes $200 for the GST collected from the customer to be remitted by Roger Retailer to the taxation authority. As a settlement discount was offered and taken by the customer, the GST collected (liability) will need to be adjusted. Roger Retailer will not be required to issue an adjustment as the original tax invoice is sufficient evidence. Therefore, the discount given of $44 is split $4 against the GST collected account ($200 × 2%) and the $40 is the discount allowed expense.

Cash ($2200 × 98%)	2 156	
Discount allowed ($2000 × 2%)	40	
GST collected ($200 × 2%)	4	
Accounts receivable		2 200
(To record payment of the account by the customer within the discount period)		

A	=	L	+	E
−2200		−4		−40
+2156				

Review it

In recording GST transactions, a business can use the following accounts: GST clearing, GST paid and GST collected. Explain the nature of each account and how it is used to record collections and payments of GST.

Do it

The preceding illustration demonstrated the purchase and sale transactions for Roger Retailer. Assume Roger Retailer paid to the manufacturer the balance owing and was entitled to claim a 5% settlement discount. Record the journal entry to pay the amount owing to the manufacturer (supplier).

Reasoning

Using the same logic as illustrated for discount allowed, the discount received by Roger Retailer will need to be adjusted for the input tax credits not available as Roger Retailer paid to their supplier the amount per the invoice less the discount amount. The amount owing to the supplier is the original purchase of 10 tables ($4400) less the purchase return of 3 tables ($1320). The amount owing is $3080. This amount is subject to a 5% discount, so $2926 is payable. The amount of GST paid in the balance owing is $280 (7 tables × $40) or $3080 ÷ 11 = $280. So, the increasing adjustment is $280 × 5% = $14. The discount revenue is $140 ($3080 × 5% × 10 ÷ 11).

Solution

Accounts payable	3 080	
Discount received*		140
GST paid		14
Cash		2 926
(To record payment of the account by Roger Retail within the discount period)		

A	=	L	+	E
−2926		−3080		+140
−14				

*Discount revenue is often credited to inventory to reduce the cost of inventory purchased.

Remitting GST to the taxation authority

At the end of each taxation reporting period, the business is required to report to the taxation authority and pay the GST liability. Assume the GST collected is $4000 and the GST paid is $3000. This will leave a net balance owing to the tax authority of $1000, which is remitted. If the amount of GST paid is greater than the amount of GST collected, a refund will be paid to the business.

Continuing the example above for Roger Retailer, as an illustration, requires a debit to GST Collected for the total amount of GST collected during the period (this sets the liability account to nil); a credit to the GST paid account for the total GST paid for the reporting period; and a debit to cash, which is the refund due from the taxation authority. The GST paid balance is $266 ($400 − $120 − $14) and the GST collected is $196 ($250 − $50 − $4).

GST collected (a liability account)	196	
Cash	70	
GST paid (an asset account)		266
(To record refund of GST owing from the taxation authority)		

$$A \quad = \quad L \quad + \quad E$$
$$-266 \qquad -196$$
$$+70$$

If the amount collected exceeds the paid amount collected during a period, then a different entry would be recorded. For example, let's assume that during the reporting period a service firm collected $200 GST from customers and paid $160 GST to suppliers — the amount paid to the taxation authority would be $40. This would be recorded as follows:

GST collected (a liability account)	200	
GST paid (an asset account)		160
Cash		40
(To record payment of GST paid to taxation authority)		

$$A \quad = \quad L \quad + \quad E$$
$$-160 \qquad -200$$
$$-40$$

The accumulated amounts of GST collected and GST paid in each taxation reporting period are cleared by the payment of the GST to the taxation authority. In the next period, the GST collected and GST paid accounts accumulate amounts for that taxation reporting period.

Helpful hint: The business could initially record a receivable for the amount owing from the taxation authority. Then, once the refund is actually received, the business would debit cash and credit the receivable.

Some businesses prefer to use one GST clearing account rather than two separate accounts — one for GST collected and one for GST paid. The GST clearing account could be an asset or a liability, depending on whether its balance represents an amount owing to or owing from the taxation authority. Typically, the GST clearing account is a liability account because most businesses collect more GST from customers than they pay to suppliers.

LEARNING REFLECTION AND CONSOLIDATION

Review it

In recording GST transactions, a business can use the following accounts — GST clearing, GST paid, GST collected. Explain the nature of each account and how it is used to record collections and payments of GST.

Do it

Games Mania made sales of $11 000 (including GST) and purchases of $7700 (including GST) in the quarter ending December 2020. All transactions were on credit and all purchases and sales were subject to GST. Record the relevant transactions to record the collection of GST, payment of GST and the discharge of the liability to the taxation authority.

Solution

Inventory	7 000	
GST paid (an asset account)	700	
Accounts payable		7 700
(To record purchase of games discs)		
Accounts receivable	11 000	
GST collected (a liability account)		1 000
Sales		10 000
(To record sales of games discs to customers)		
GST collected (a liability account)	1 000	
GST paid (an asset account)		700
Cash		300
(To record payment of GST owing to taxation authority)		

A	=	L	+	E
+7000		+7700		
+700				

A	=	L	+	E
+11 000		+1000		+10 000

A	=	L	+	E
−700		−1000		
−300				

USING THE DECISION-MAKING TOOLKIT

Sophie Limited is a retail company with 40 department stores, three warehouse outlets and Sophie Online. The following financial data are for the 2018 and 2019 reporting periods. Follow the instructions below and comment on profitability over the 2-year period.

	2019 $'000	2018 $'000
Profit after income tax	101 500	100 600
Ending total assets	1 330 000	1 340 000
Beginning total assets	1 340 000	1 318 000
Sales	1 900 000	1 920 000
Cost of sales	1 440 000	1 450 000
Operating expenses	620 000	600 000

Required
(a) Using the details from the table, calculate the following components of Sophie's profitability for the years 2019 and 2018:
   i. Return on assets ratio
   ii. Profit margin ratio
   iii. Gross profit ratio
   iv. Operating expenses to sales ratio.
(b) Compare Sophie's gross profit ratio and operating expenses to sales ratio with the results for Original Furnishings and Artistry Furniture.

▶

Solution

(a)

Sophie Limited	2019 ('000)	2018 ('000)
Return on assets ratio		
Profit after income tax	$101 500	$100 600
Average total assets[(i)]	$1 335 000	$1 329 000
	7.6%	7.6%
Profit margin ratio		
Profit after income tax	$101 500	$100 600
Sales	$1 900 000	$1 920 000
	5.3%	5.2%
Gross profit ratio		
Gross profit[(ii)]	$460 000	$470 000
Sales	$1 900 000	$1 920 000
	24.2%	24.5%
Operating expenses to sales ratio		
Operating expenses	$620 000	$600 000
Sales	$1 900 000	$1 920 000
	32.6%	31.3%

[(i)]Average total assets = (Beginning total assets + Ending total assets)/2
[(ii)]Gross profit = Sales − Cost of sales

The return on assets ratio for Sophie Limited remained constant at 7.6% from 2018 to 2019. This was due to a marginal increase (0.1%) in profit after income tax from $100 600 000 to $101 500 000 with the same increase (0.1%) in average total assets between 2018 and 2019. The profit margin ratio increased slightly from 5.2% to 5.3% despite a drop in sales, which were down 1% on the prior year reflecting a challenging trading environment in 2019. The gross profit ratio decreased slightly from 24.5% to 24.2% in 2019 despite a $20 000 000 decline in sales. The gross profit of $460 000 000 was impacted by an $8 500 000 charge related to the write down of inventory associated with the Sophie Limited brand. The operating expenses to sales ratio showed an increase from 31.3% to 32.6% over the 2-year period. This increase relates to higher employee costs, higher lease and occupancy costs and higher depreciation charges. The increase in lease and occupancy costs reflects the opening of a new store and higher occupancy costs. The higher depreciation charge reflects the company's significant investment in technology in 2018 and 2019.

(b)

2019	Sophie Limited	Original Furnishings	Artistry Furniture
Gross profit ratio	24.2%	38%	41%
Operating expenses to sales ratio	32.6%	28%	25%

Sophie Limited's gross profit ratio of 24.2% in 2019 is significantly lower than Original Furnishings (38%) and Artistry Furniture (41%), suggesting that, on average across all of its inventory items, it applies a lower mark-up on its goods across a more diverse range of products. Sophie Limited's operating expenses to sales ratio of 32.6% suggests that it has less control over its costs in comparison to Original Furnishings (28%) and Artistry Furniture (25%).

SUMMARY

4.1 Identify the differences between a service business and a merchandising business.
Because of the presence of inventory, a retail business has sales revenue, cost of sales and gross profit. To account for inventory, a retail business must choose between a perpetual inventory system and a periodic inventory system.

4.2 Explain the recording of purchases under a perpetual inventory system.
The inventory account is debited for all purchases of inventories, and it is credited for purchase returns and allowances.

4.3 Explain the recording of sales revenues under a perpetual inventory system.
When inventory is sold, accounts receivable (or cash) is debited and sales is credited for the selling price of the inventories. At the same time, cost of sales is debited and inventory is credited for the cost of inventory items sold.

4.4 Prepare a fully classified statement of profit or loss.
A fully classified statement of profit or loss is an internal report which shows numerous steps in determining profit including the calculation of gross profit, other revenue, expenses classified by function into three categories — selling, administrative and financial expenses — and profit before and after income tax expense.

4.5 Use ratios to analyse profitability.
Profitability is affected by gross profit, as measured by the gross profit ratio, and by management's ability to control costs, as measured by the ratio of operating expenses to sales.

4.6 Understand the basic process and main features of the goods and services tax (GST).
The GST is essentially a 10% (15% in New Zealand) value-added tax imposed on most goods and services. The tax is paid at each stage in the production and supply chain, but it is the final consumer who bears the cost. Businesses that supply goods and services are generally eligible for a credit from the taxation authority on the tax paid. Suppliers essentially act as tax collectors for the taxation authority. The difference between how much GST a business has collected and paid determines whether the business will have a GST liability to pay to the taxation office or will receive a refund from the taxation authority.

4.7 Complete journal entries to record GST.
GST included in amounts paid to suppliers is debited to a GST paid account (an asset account). GST collected from customers is credited to a GST collected account (a liability account). At the end of the reporting period, if the amount of GST collected exceeds the amount paid, the business pays the net amount to the taxation authority. The payment is recorded as a debit to GST collected, a credit to GST paid and a credit to cash to discharge the GST liability with the taxation authority. If the amount of GST paid exceeds GST collected, the business will receive a refund from the taxation authority. This is recorded as a debit to cash, a debit to GST collected and a credit to GST paid.

DECISION-MAKING TOOLKIT — A SUMMARY

Decision/issue	Info needed for analysis	Tool or technique to use for decision	How to evaluate results to make decision
Is management maintaining an adequate margin between the selling price and the cost of inventory?	Gross profit and net sales	Gross profit ratio $= \dfrac{\text{Gross profit}}{\text{Net sales}}$	Higher ratio suggests the average margin between selling price and inventory cost is increasing. Too high a margin may result in lower sales.
Is management effective in controlling operating costs?	Net sales and operating expenses	Operating expenses to sales ratio $= \dfrac{\text{Operation expenses}}{\text{Net sales}}$	Higher ratio should be investigated to determine whether greater control of expenses is required.

KEY TERMS

business activity statement (BAS) (GST return in New Zealand) A report filed at regular intervals (monthly, quarterly or yearly) by a business with the taxation authority. It details the amount of GST collected by a business on taxable supplies, the amount of GST paid on purchases, and the amount owing to or the refund due from the taxation authority.

contra revenue account An account that is offset against a revenue account on the statement of profit or loss, e.g. sales returns and allowances.

cost of sales (COS) The total cost of inventories sold during the period.

discount allowed A settlement discount given by a seller for prompt payment of a balance due.

discount received A settlement discount claimed by a buyer for prompt payment of a balance due.

freight-in An expense incurred by the buyer of inventory which is considered part of the cost of inventory.

freight-out An expense incurred by the seller of inventory which is classified as a selling expense.

goods and services tax (GST) A broad-based indirect tax levied on most supplies of goods and services. In Australia the rate applied is 10% and in New Zealand it is 15%.

gross profit The excess of net sales revenue over the cost of sales.

gross profit ratio Gross profit expressed as a percentage by dividing the amount of gross profit by net sales.

GST-free supplies (zero rated supplies in New Zealand) Goods and services that do not attract GST under GST legislation, such as basic food, education, health services and exported goods.

input tax credit The credit received by registered suppliers from the taxation authority for the amount of GST paid on all goods and services purchased in the supply chain.

input taxed supplies (exempt supplies in New Zealand) Goods and services that do not attract GST under GST legislation such as residential rents and financial supplies.

inventory Goods acquired by a retail business for the purposes of resale in the ordinary course of business activities.

inventory write-down An expense account used to record damaged, stolen, obsolete or lost inventory as well as inventory shrinkage or waste that occurs.

net sales Sales less sales returns and allowances.

operating expenses to sales ratio A measure of the costs incurred to support each dollar of sales, calculated as operating expenses divided by net sales.

other revenue Revenue items other than sales revenue, such as interest revenue and rent revenue.

periodic inventory system An inventory system in which detailed records are not maintained and the cost of sales and inventory on hand is determined only at the end of an accounting period.

perpetual inventory system A detailed inventory system in which the cost of each inventory item is maintained and the records continuously show the cost of sales and inventory that should be on hand.

sales invoice A document prepared by the seller evidencing a claim for payment for goods or services provided to a customer.

sales returns and allowances Cash refunds or credit notes recorded in the books of the seller for merchandise returned or discounted if faulty or incorrect.

sales revenue Revenue generated from the sale of inventory.

supplier's invoice A document prepared by the supplier, evidencing a claim for payment for goods and services provided.

taxable supply Goods and services that have GST included in the selling price.

taxation authority The body that administers tax legislation. In Australia, this is the Australian Taxation Office (ATO). In New Zealand it is the Inland Revenue department.

trade discount A reduction in the list price granted to certain customers. The discount is shown as a reduction from the list price on the invoice but is not recorded in the accounts of either the buyer or the seller.

value-added tax An indirect tax levied on the value added by a business at each stage of the production and distribution chain, i.e. from the purchase of raw materials to the sale of the finished product or supply of the service to the final consumer. GST is a value-added tax.

DEMONSTRATION PROBLEM

The adjusted trial balance as at 30 June 2020 for Zhang Ltd is shown below.

ZHANG LTD Adjusted trial balance as at 30 June 2020		
	Dr	Cr
Cash	$ 15 950	
Accounts receivable	12 210	
Inventory	31 900	
Prepaid insurance	2 750	
Store equipment	94 600	
Accumulated depreciation		$ 19 800
Accounts payable		11 660
Bank loan		27 500
Share capital		77 000
Retained earnings		12 100
Dividends	13 200	
Sales		590 480
Sales returns and allowances	7 370	
Discount allowed	5 500	
Cost of sales	399 740	
Freight-out	8 360	
Advertising expense	13 200	
Salaries expense		
—Store	39 600	
—Office	22 000	

	Dr	Cr
Electricity expense	19 800	
Rent expense		
—Store	13 200	
—Office	13 200	
Depreciation expense		
—Store	3 300	
—Office	6 600	
Income tax expense	9 900	
Insurance expense	4 950	
Interest expense	3 960	
Interest revenue		2 200
Discount received		550
	$ 741 290	$ 741 290

Required

Prepare a fully classified statement of profit or loss for Zhang Ltd.

PROBLEM-SOLVING STRATEGIES

1. In preparing the statement of profit or loss, remember that the key components are net sales, cost of sales, gross profit, total operating expenses, and profit (loss). These components are reported in the right-hand column of the statement.
2. Operating expenses are classified into three subgroups: selling expenses, administrative expenses and financial expenses.

SOLUTION TO DEMONSTRATION PROBLEM

ZHANG LTD
Statement of profit or loss
for the year ended 30 June 2020

OPERATING REVENUE			
Sales revenue			
Gross sales revenue			$ 590 480
Less: Sales returns and allowances			(7 370)
Net sales revenue			583 110
Less: Cost of sales			(399 740)
Gross profit			183 370
OTHER OPERATING REVENUE			
Interest revenue		$ 2 200	
Discount received		550	2 750
			186 120
OPERATING EXPENSES			
Selling expenses			
Store salaries expense	$39 600		
Advertising expense	13 200		
Rent expense—store space	13 200		
Freight-out	8 360		
Depn expense—store equipment	3 300	77 660	
Administrative expenses			
Office salaries expense	22 000		
Electricity expense	19 800		
Rent expense—office space	13 200		
Depn expense—office equipment	6 600		
Insurance expense	4 950	66 550	

Financial expenses			
Discount allowed		5 500	
Interest expense		3 960	9 460
			(153 670)
Profit before income tax			**32 450**
Less: Income tax expense			(9 900)
Profit after income tax			$ __22 550__

SELF-STUDY QUESTIONS

4.1 Which of the following statements about a periodic inventory system is true? **LO2**
    (a) Cost of sales is determined only at the end of the accounting period.
    (b) Detailed records of the cost of each inventory purchase and sale are maintained continuously.
    (c) The periodic system provides better control over inventories than a perpetual system.
    (d) The increased use of computerised systems has increased the use of the periodic system.

4.2 Which of the following statements is true for the perpetual inventory system? **LO2**
    (a) The increased use of computerised systems has increased the use of the perpetual system.
    (b) Cost of sales is determined only at the end of the accounting period.
    (c) The periodic inventory system provides better control over inventories than the perpetual system does.
    (d) The Purchases account is updated after each purchase of inventory.

4.3 Which of the following items does *not* result in an adjustment in the Inventory account under a perpetual system? **LO2**
    (a) A purchase of inventory.
    (b) A return of inventory to the supplier.
    (c) Payment of freight costs for goods shipped to a customer.
    (d) A return from a customer of inventory that is not faulty.

4.4 Which of the following accounts normally has a credit balance? **LO3**
    (a) Discount received.
    (b) Purchase returns and allowances.
    (c) Both (a) and (b).
    (d) Neither (a) nor (b).

4.5 A credit sale of $750 is made on 13 June, terms 2/7, n/30, on which a return of $50 is granted on 16 June. The customer paid the amount owing on 17 June. What amount did the customer pay? **LO3**
    (a) $700.
    (b) $686.
    (c) $685.
    (d) $650.

4.6 Gross profit will result if: **LO4**
    (a) operating expenses are less than profit.
    (b) sales revenue is greater than operating expenses.
    (c) sales revenue is greater than cost of sales.
    (d) operating expenses are greater than cost of sales.

4.7 If net sales revenue is $420 000, cost of sales is $320 000, and operating expenses are $60 000, what is the gross profit? **LO4**
    (a) $340 000.
    (b) $100 000.
    (c) $40 000.
    (d) $420 000.

4.8 Which of the following are reported on the statement of profit or loss of a merchandising business? **LO4**
  (a) Gross profit.
  (b) Cost of sales.
  (c) A sales revenue section.
  (d) All of the above.

4.9 Which of the following would affect the gross profit ratio? **LO5**
  (a) An increase in sales returns.
  (b) An increase in the depreciation expense.
  (c) A decrease in the electricity expense.
  (d) An increase in interest revenue.

4.10 Which of the following would *not* affect the operating expenses to sales ratio? (Assume sales remains constant.) **LO5**
  (a) An increase in advertising expense.
  (b) A decrease in depreciation expense.
  (c) An increase in cost of sales.
  (d) A decrease in insurance expense.

4.11 The gross profit ratio is equal to: **LO5**
  (a) profit divided by net sales.
  (b) cost of sales divided by net sales.
  (c) net sales minus cost of sales, divided by net sales.
  (d) net sales minus cost of sales, divided by cost of sales.

4.12 Which factor would *not* affect the gross profit ratio? **LO5**
  (a) An increase in sales staff salaries.
  (b) An increase in the sales price of luxury items.
  (c) An increase in the use of 'discount pricing' to sell inventories.
  (d) An increase in the cost of inventory items.

4.13 When a business pays GST to suppliers it records: **LO6, 7**
  (a) an asset.
  (b) a liability.
  (c) an expense.
  (d) a revenue.

4.14 If a business uses a GST clearing account to record GST transactions, then GST paid would: **LO7**
  (a) be recorded as a credit to the GST clearing account.
  (b) be recorded as a debit to the GST clearing account.
  (c) not be recorded in the GST clearing account.
  (d) be recorded as both a debit and a credit to the GST clearing account.

QUESTIONS

4.1 (a) 'The steps in the accounting cycle for a merchandising business are different from the steps in the accounting cycle for a service business.' Do you agree or disagree?
  (b) Is the measurement of profit in a merchandising business conceptually the same as in a service business? Explain.

4.2 (a) Explain the profit measurement process in a merchandising business.
  (b) How does profit measurement differ between a merchandising business and a service business?

4.3 Frasier Ltd has net sales revenue of $220 000, cost of sales of $154 000, and operating expenses of $44 000. What is its gross profit?

4.4 Peter Freeman believes revenues from credit sales may be recognised before they are collected in cash. Do you agree? Explain.

4.5 (a) What is a primary source document for recording (1) cash sales and (2) credit sales?

(b) Using XXs for amounts, give the journal entry for each of the transactions in part (a).

4.6 Goods costing $2240 are purchased on account on 18 July with credit terms of 2/7, n/30. On 20 July a $140 credit note is received from the supplier for damaged goods. Give the journal entry on 24 July to record payment of the balance due within the discount period.

4.7 MBA Ltd reports net sales of $480 000, gross profit of $348 000, and profit before tax of $180 000. What are its operating expenses?

4.8 What types of businesses are most likely to use:

(a) a perpetual inventory system?

(b) a periodic system?

4.9 What factors affect a business's gross profit ratio, i.e. what can cause the gross profit ratio to increase and what can cause it to decrease?

4.10 Which of the following statements relating to GST is true? Give reasons for your answers.

(a) The first purchaser bears the cost of the GST.

(b) GST is not a tax on business income.

BRIEF EXERCISES

BE4.1 Calculate missing amounts in determining profit. **LO4**

Presented here are the components in Felix Ltd's statement of profit or loss. Determine the missing amounts.

Sales	Cost of sales	Gross profit	Operating expenses	Profit
$195 000	(b)	$113 100	(d)	$28 080
$280 800	$169 000	(c)	(e)	$76 700
(a)	$186 940	$284 960	$102 700	(f)

BE4.2 Journalise perpetual inventory entries. **LO2, 3**

Neo Ltd buys inventory on account from Gruff Ltd. The selling price of the goods is $1800 and the cost of goods to Mayo Ltd is $1200. Both entities use perpetual inventory systems. Journalise the transactions in the records of both entities.

BE4.3 Journalise sales transactions. **LO3**

Prepare the journal entries to record the following transactions in Simon Ltd's records using a perpetual inventory system.

(a) On 2 March Simon Ltd sold $450 000 of inventory to Finkle Ltd, terms 2/7, n/30. The cost of the inventory sold was $300 000.

(b) On 6 March Finkle Ltd returned $65 000 of the inventory purchased on 2 March because it was incorrect. The cost of the inventory returned was $40 000.

(c) On 8 March Simon Ltd received the balance due from Finkle Ltd.

BE4.4 Prepare sales revenue section of the statement of profit or loss. **LO4**

Aditya Ltd provides this information for the month ended 31 October 2018: sales on credit $363 000; cash sales $121 000; discount allowed $6050; and sales returns and allowances $24 200. Prepare the sales revenue section of the statement of profit or loss based on this information.

BE4.5 Identify placement of items on a fully classified statement of profit or loss. **LO4**

Explain where each of these items would appear on a fully classified statement of profit or loss: interest revenue, cost of sales, depreciation expense, sales returns and allowances, purchase returns and allowances, discount received, and discount allowed.

BE4.6 Calculate profitability ratios. **LO5**

Long Pty Ltd reported net sales of $275 000, cost of sales of $110 000, operating expenses of $55 000, profit after tax of $88 000, beginning total assets of $550 000, and ending total assets of $660 000. Calculate each of these values:

(a) Return on assets ratio.

(b) Profit margin ratio.

(c) Gross profit ratio.

(d) Operating expenses to sales ratio.

BE4.7 Calculate GST and revenue earned. **LO7**

Maori Jewellery is a respected jeweller in Christchurch. For the month of June, Maori Jewellery sold NZ$25 000 (excluding GST) worth of merchandise to customers for cash. The GST was 15%. How much cash did Maori Jewellery receive? How much sales revenue did Maori Jewellery earn?

BE4.8 Understanding GST journal entries. **LO7**

The following journal entry was recorded in the books of Sellers Limited.

Dr		GST collected	100
	Cr	GST paid	90
	Cr	Cash	10

Explain the nature of this journal entry.

EXERCISES

E4.1 Journalise sales transactions. **LO3**

The following transactions are for Unique Artworks Ltd.

1. On 7 December Unique Artworks Ltd sold $792 000 of inventory to Cambridge Collectables Ltd, terms 2/7, n/30. The cost of the inventory sold was $528 000.
2. On 8 December Cambridge Collectables Ltd was granted an allowance of $33 000 for inventory purchased on 7 December.
3. On 13 December Unique Artworks Ltd received the balance due from Cambridge Collectables Ltd.

Required

(a) Prepare the journal entries to record these transactions in the records of Unique Artworks Ltd.

(b) Assume that Unique Artworks Ltd received the balance due from Cambridge Collectables Ltd on 2 January of the following year instead of 13 December. Prepare the journal entry to record the receipt of payment on 2 January.

(c) What are the advantages and disadvantages associated with granting a discount for early payment?

E4.2 Journalise perpetual inventory transactions. **LO2, 3**

On 1 July Queenscliff Pty Ltd sold inventory to Stokers Pty Ltd for $20 000. The credit terms were 3/10, n/30. Stokers Pty Ltd paid the account promptly on 10 July and uses the perpetual inventory system to record transactions.

Required

(a) Record the purchase and payment of inventory in the accounts of Stokers Pty Ltd.

(b) Assume Stokers Pty Ltd decided to record the discount as a credit to inventory. Record the journal entry.

(c) What is the difference between the effect on (i) profit and (ii) assets between the treatment of the discount in parts (a) and (b)?

E4.3 Journalise sales transactions.   **LO3**

Use the information provided in E4.2 to complete the following activities.

Required

(a) Record the sales of inventory in the accounts of Queenscliff Pty Ltd. The cost of the inventory sold was $12 000.

(b) What are the journal entries on 10 July when Queenscliff Pty Ltd received the amount from Stokers Pty Ltd?

E4.4 Journalise perpetual inventory entries.   **LO2, 3**

On 1 September Cambell's Office Supplies had an inventory of 30 deluxe pocket calculators at a cost of $22 each. The business uses a perpetual inventory system. During September these transactions occurred:

Sept.	6	Purchased 80 calculators at $22 each from Digital Ltd for cash.
	9	Paid freight of $88 to We Deliver on calculators purchased from Digital Ltd.
	10	Returned two calculators to Digital Ltd for $44 credit because they did not meet specifications.
	12	Sold 26 calculators costing $22 for $33 each to Techno Store, terms n/30.
	14	Granted credit of $33 to Techno Store for the return of one calculator that was not ordered.
	20	Sold 30 calculators costing $22 for $33 each to Uni Card Shop, terms n/30.

Required

Journalise the September transactions.

E4.5 Journalise purchase transactions.   **LO2**

The following information relates to Hampton Pty Ltd.

1. On 5 April purchased inventory from R. Ward & Co. for $9000, terms 2/7, n/30.
2. On 6 April paid freight costs to Freight Masters of $450 on inventories purchased from R. Ward & Co.
3. On 7 April purchased equipment on account for $52 000.
4. On 8 April returned incorrect inventories to R. Ward & Co. and was granted a $1500 allowance.
5. On 11 April paid the amount due to R. Ward & Co.

Required

(a) Prepare the journal entries to record the transactions listed in the records of Hampton Pty Ltd.

(b) Assume that Hampton Pty Ltd paid the balance due to R. Ward & Co. on 4 May instead of 11 April. Prepare the journal entry to record this payment.

E4.6 Journalise purchase transactions.   **LO2**

On 10 June Grand Accessories Ltd purchased $5400 of inventories from Highend Distributors Ltd, terms 2/7, n/30. Grand Accessories Ltd pays the freight costs of $270 to Freight Masters on 11 June. Goods totalling $270 are returned to Highend Distributors Ltd for credit on 12 June. On 17 June Grand Accessories Ltd pays Highend Distributors Ltd the amount owing. Both entities use a perpetual inventory system.

Required

(a) Prepare separate entries for each transaction in the records of Grand Accessories Ltd.

(b) Prepare separate entries for each transaction for Highend Distributors Ltd. The inventory purchased by Grand Accessories on 10 June cost Highend Distributors $2700, and the goods returned cost Highend Distributors $135.

(c) Explain the difference between freight-in and freight-out. How are they classified in the statement of profit or loss?

E4.7 **Prepare a statement of profit or loss and calculate profitability ratios.** **LO4, 5**

Presented is information related to Dawson Ltd for the month of January 2018:

Cost of sales	$416 000	Discount allowed	$ 16 000
Freight-out	14 000	Sales returns and allowances	26 000
Insurance expense	12 000	Sales	700 000
Salary expense—office	61 000	Bank charges	100
Discount received	14 000	Income tax expense	45 270
Rent expense—store space	20 000	Rent revenue	2 000

Required

(a) Prepare a fully classified statement of profit or loss using the format presented in figure 4.6. Operating expenses should be segregated into selling, administrative and financial expenses.

(b) Calculate the following: profit margin ratio, gross profit ratio, and the operating expenses to sales ratio.

(c) Why is it useful to calculate ratios? Provide examples to support your answer.

E4.8 **Calculate missing amounts and calculate profitability ratios.** **LO4, 5**

Financial information is presented here for two entities:

	Bright Ltd	Dull Ltd
Sales	$180 000	?
Sales returns	?	$ 10 000
Net sales	162 000	190 000
Cost of sales	112 000	?
Gross profit	?	76 000
Operating expenses	30 000	?
Profit	?	30 000

Required

(a) Fill in the missing amounts. Show all calculations.

(b) Calculate the profit margin ratio, gross profit ratio, and operating expenses to sales ratio for each entity.

E4.9 **Prepare a fully classified statement of profit or loss and calculate profitability ratios.** **LO4, 5**

In its statement of profit or loss for the year ended 30 June 2019, Lulu Ltd reported the following condensed data:

Administrative expenses	$261 000	Income tax expense	$ 37 980
Cost of sales	593 400	Selling expenses	414 000
Financial expenses	42 000	Net sales	1 410 000
Other operating revenue	27 000		

Required

(a) Prepare a fully classified statement of profit or loss.

(b) Calculate the profit margin ratio, gross profit ratio, and operating expenses to sales ratio.

E4.10 **Prepare sales revenue section of a statement of profit or loss.** **LO4**

The adjusted trial balance of Snuffy Pty Ltd shows these data pertaining to sales at the end of its financial year, 30 June 2018: sales $585 000; freight-out $7800; sales returns and allowances $9100; and discount allowed $7800.

Required

Prepare the sales revenue section of the statement of profit or loss.

E4.11 **Prepare journal entries for GST.** **LO7**

Ezios Earthenware Ltd lodges quarterly business activity statements with the taxation authority.

Required

(a) Record the journal entries during the March 2019 quarter for sales $6600 (including GST) and purchases $1210 (including GST).

(b) What is the journal entry to discharge the GST liability?

E4.12 Prepare journal entries for GST.   **LO7**

Phams Pottery Ltd reported the following transactions for May:

May	3	Purchased inventory for $440 (including $40 GST).
	10	Sold inventory for $550 (including $50 GST).

Required

Record the journal entries for May and the journal entry to discharge the GST liability.

E4.13 Prepare journal entries for GST.   **LO7**

Use the data provided in E4.11 to answer the following questions.

Required

(a) Record the journal entries for the March quarter assuming the company uses a GST clearing account.

(b) Record the journal entry to discharge the GST liability assuming the company uses a GST clearing account.

PROBLEM SET A

PSA4.1 Journalise, post, prepare partial statement of profit or loss and calculate ratios.   LO2, 3, 4, 5

Papermark Ltd completed the following inventory transactions in the month of May. At the beginning of May, Papermark Ltd's ledger showed Cash $3500 and Share Capital $3500.

May	2	Sold inventory on account for $3150, terms 2/7, n/30. The cost of the inventory sold was $2100.
	3	Purchased inventory on account from Pen & Paper Wholesale Supply for $4200, terms 2/7, n/30.
	5	Returned inventory and received credit from Pen & Paper Wholesale Supply for $140.
	9	Received amounts owing from customers invoiced for sales of $3150 on 2 May.
	10	Paid Pen & Paper Wholesale Supply the amount owing.
	11	Purchased supplies for cash $630.
	12	Purchased inventory for cash $1680.
	15	Returned goods and received a refund for poor-quality inventory from supplier on cash purchase $161.
	20	Purchased inventory from Harlow Distributors for $1330, terms 2/7, n/30.
	21	Paid freight to DHL on 20 May purchase $175.
	24	Sold inventory for cash $4340. The cost of the inventory sold was $3038.
	25	Purchased inventory from Art World Ltd for $700, terms 2/7, n/30.
	27	Paid Harlow Distributors the amount outstanding.
	29	Made refunds to cash customers for inventory sold for $70. The returned inventory had cost $49. The inventory returned was not faulty.
	31	Sold inventory on account for $1120, terms n/30. The cost of the inventory sold was $784.

Papermark Ltd's chart of accounts includes 100 Cash, 110 Accounts receivable, 120 Inventory, 130 Supplies, 200 Accounts payable, 300 Share capital, 400 Sales, 405 Sales returns and allowances, 410 Discount received, 500 Discount allowed, 505 Cost of sales, and 510 Freight inwards.

Required

(a) Journalise the transactions using a perpetual inventory system.

(b) Post the transactions to T accounts. Be sure to enter the beginning cash and share capital balances.

(c) Prepare a statement of profit or loss up to gross profit for the month of May 2018.

(d) Calculate the profit margin ratio and the gross profit ratio. (Assume operating expenses were $980 and the income tax expense was $133.)

PSA4.2 **Journalise purchase and sale transactions under a perpetual inventory system.**   **LO2, 3**

The Novelty Bookstore distributes hardback books to retail stores and extends credit terms of 2/7, n/30 to all of its customers. During the month of June the following inventory transactions occurred.

June	2	Purchased 130 books on account for $6 each from Reader's World Publishers, terms 1/7, n/30. Also made a cash payment to Classic Couriers of $60 for the freight on this date.
	3	Sold 140 books on account to the Book Nook for $12 each.
	6	10 books returned to Reader's World Publishers. Received $60 credit.
	9	Paid Reader's World Publishers the amount owing.
	15	Received payment from the Book Nook.
	17	Sold 120 books on account to Read-A-Lot Bookstore for $12 each.
	20	Purchased 120 books on account for $6 each from Read More Publishers, terms 2/7, n/30.
	24	Received payment of account from Read-A-Lot Bookstore.
	26	Paid Read More Publishers the amount owing.
	28	Sold 110 books on account to Readers Bookstore for $12 each.
	30	Granted Readers Bookstore $180 credit for 15 books returned costing $90. The books were returned into inventory.

Required

(a) Journalise the transactions for the month of June for The Novelty Bookstore, using a perpetual inventory system. Assume the cost of each book sold was $6.

(b) What are the advantages and disadvantages for The Novelty Bookstore of using a perpetual inventory system as opposed to a periodic system?

PSA4.3 **Prepare financial statements and calculate profitability ratios.**   **LO4, 5**

Harrots Department Store Pty Ltd is located in the city centre. During the past several years, profit has been declining because suburban shopping centres have been attracting business away from city areas. At the end of the company's financial year on 30 June 2018, the accounts shown below appeared in its adjusted trial balance:

Accounts payable	$ 39 053
Accounts receivable	16 830
Accumulated depreciation—office equipment	28 142
Accumulated depreciation—store equipment	59 774
Bank loan	65 780
Cash	11 440
Cost of sales	905 505
Depreciation expense—office equipment	5 720
Depreciation expense—store equipment	13 585
Discount received	1 430
Dividends	17 160
Electricity expense	15 158
Freight-out	11 726
Income tax expense	28 314
Income tax payable	28 314
Insurance expense	12 870
Interest expense	11 440

Interest revenue	5 720
Inventory	51 766
Office equipment	81 510
Prepaid insurance	6 435
Rates and taxes expense	5 005
Rates and taxes payable	5 005
Rent expense	
—Store	12 870
—Office	28 600
Retained earnings	20 306
Salaries expense	
—Sales	100 100
—Office	57 200
Sales	1 301 300
Sales commissions expense	20 020
Sales commissions payable	8 580
Sales returns and allowances	14 300
Share capital	42 900
Store equipment	178 750

Required

(a) Prepare a fully classified statement of profit or loss, a calculation of retained earnings (refer to figure 1.6) and a classified statement of financial position.

(b) Calculate the return on assets ratio, profit margin ratio, gross profit ratio, and operating expenses to sales ratio. Assume that total assets at the beginning of the year were $228 800.

(c) Why is it helpful to fully classify items in the statement of profit or loss?

PSA4.4 Journalise, post, and prepare trial balance and partial statement of profit or loss.　　**LO2, 3, 4**

On 1 April the ledger of Alexander's Tennis Pro Shop Pty Ltd showed cash $4500, inventory $6300, and share capital $10 800. The following transactions occurred during April 2019:

Apr.	7	Purchased racquets and balls on account from Tennis Australia Ltd $3060, terms 2/7, n/60.
	8	Paid freight on Tennis Australia Ltd purchase $144.
	9	Returned inventory and received credit from Tennis Australia Ltd for $360.
	10	Sold inventory on account $1620, terms n/30. The inventory sold had a cost of $1134.
	14	Purchased tennis shoes, T-shirts and other accessories on account from Sharp Sporting Goods $1188, terms 1/7, n/30.
	14	Paid Tennis Australia Ltd the amount due.
	17	Returned inventory and received credit from Sharp Sporting Goods for $108.
	20	Made sales on account to customers $1260, terms n/30. The cost of the inventory sold was $882.
	21	Paid Sharp Sporting Goods the amount owing.
	27	Granted an allowance to customers for clothing that did not fit properly $108.
	30	Received payments on account, $1980.

The chart of accounts for the shop includes 100 Cash, 105 Accounts receivable, 115 Inventory, 200 Accounts payable, 300 Share capital, 400 Sales, 405 Sales returns and allowances, 410 Discount received, 500 Cost of sales, and 505 Freight inwards.

Required

(a) Journalise the April transactions using a perpetual inventory system.

(b) Using T accounts, enter the beginning balances in the ledger accounts and post the April transactions.

(c) Prepare a trial balance as at 30 April 2019.

(d) Prepare a statement of profit or loss to gross profit.

PSA4.5 **Prepare a fully classified statement of profit or loss.** **LO4**

An inexperienced accountant prepared this statement of profit or loss for Peninsula Pty Ltd, a merchandising firm that has been in business for a number of years.

PENINSULA PTY LTD Statement of profit or loss for the year ended 30 June 2018		
REVENUES		
Net sales		$ 462 000
Other revenues		13 200
		475 200
Less: Cost of sales		(305 250)
Gross profit		169 950
OPERATING EXPENSES		
Selling expenses	$57 200	
Administrative expenses	44 000	
Financial expenses	4 950	
		(106 150)
Profit before tax		$ **63 800**

As an experienced, knowledgeable accountant, you review the statement and determine the following facts:

1. Net sales consist of sales $495 000, less delivery expense on inventory sold $16 500, and sales returns and allowances $16 500.
2. Other revenues consist of discount received $8800 and rent revenue $4400.
3. Selling expenses consist of salespersons' salaries $44 000; depreciation on office equipment $4400; advertising $5500; and sales commissions $3300. The commissions represent commissions paid. At 30 June, $2200 of commissions have been earned by salespersons but have not been paid.
4. Administrative expenses consist of office salaries $20 350; dividends $2750; electricity $6600; interest expense $1100; and rent expense $13 200, which includes prepayments totalling $3300 for rent for the first quarter of 2019.
5. Financial expenses consist of bank charges $550, and discount allowed $4400.
6. The company tax rate is 30%.

Required

Prepare a fully classified statement of profit or loss.

PSA4.6 **Journalise, post and prepare adjusted trial balance and financial statements.** **LO4**

The trial balance of Rankins Ltd contained the accounts shown at 30 June, the end of the company's reporting period:

RANKINS LTD Trial balance as at 30 June 2019	Debit	Credit
Cash	$ 50 100	
Accounts receivable	56 400	
Inventory	165 000	
Land	138 000	
Buildings	295 500	
Accumulated depreciation—buildings		$ 85 500
Store equipment	125 250	
Accumulated depreciation—store equipment		63 600

	Debit	Credit
Accounts payable		56 250
Bank loan		75 000
Share capital		300 000
Retained profits		101 700
Dividends	15 000	
Interest revenue		1 500
Sales		1 381 650
Sales returns and allowances	1 500	
Discount allowed	5 400	
Cost of sales	1 064 850	
Salaries expense		
—Office	82 500	
—Sales	22 200	
Electricity expense	14 100	
Repair expense (computers)	13 350	
Petrol and oil expense	10 800	
Insurance expense	5 250	
	$2 065 200	$2 065 200

Adjustment data:

1. Depreciation is $15 000 on buildings and $13 500 on store equipment.
2. Interest of $10 500 is due and unpaid on bank loan at 30 June.

Other data: $22 500 of the bank loan is payable next year. The income tax rate is 30%.

Required

(a) Journalise the adjusting entries.
(b) Create T accounts for all accounts used in part (a). Enter the trial balance amounts into the T accounts and post the adjusting entries.
(c) Prepare an adjusted trial balance.
(d) Prepare a fully classified statement of profit or loss, a calculation of retained earnings (refer to figure 1.6) and a classified statement of financial position as at 30 June 2019.
(e) Explain why the statement of profit or loss is prepared for a period of time while the statement of financial position is prepared as at a particular date.

PSA4.7 Journalise, post, prepare partial statement of profit or loss, and calculate ratios. LO2, 3, 4, 5
Belle Boutique Fashion Pty Ltd completed these inventory transactions in the month of April 2018. At the beginning of April, the ledger of Belle Boutique Fashion showed cash of $4950 and share capital of $4950.

Apr.		
	4	Purchased inventory on account from Upmarket Supply Ltd $3245, terms 2/7, n/30.
	6	Sold inventory on account $2750, terms 2/7, n/30. The cost of the inventory sold was $2200.
	6	Received credit from Upmarket Supply Ltd for inventory returned $165.
	7	Paid $110 freight to We Deliver on 6 April sale.
	11	Paid Upmarket Supply Ltd the amount outstanding.
	13	Received payments from customers invoiced on 6 April.
	14	Purchased inventory for cash $2420.
	16	Received refund from supplier on cash purchase of 14 April, $275.
	21	Purchased inventory from French Fashion Ltd $3150, terms 2/7, n/30.
	22	Paid freight $55 to Fast Delivery Ltd for the 21 April purchase.
	23	Sold inventory for cash $4070. The cost of the inventory sold was $3366.
	26	Purchased inventory for cash $1265.
	27	Paid French Fashion Ltd the amount owing.
	29	Made refunds to cash customers for inventory sold for $50. The returned inventory had a cost of $38.
	30	Sold inventory on account $2035, terms n/30. The cost of the inventory sold was $1650.

Belle Boutique Fashion Pty Ltd's chart of accounts includes Cash, Accounts receivable, Inventory, Accounts payable, Share capital, Sales, Sales returns and allowances, Discount received, Discount allowed, Cost of sales, Freight-out, and Freight-in.

Required

(a) Journalise the transactions using the perpetual inventory system.

(b) Post the transactions to T accounts. Be sure to enter the beginning cash and share capital balances.

(c) Prepare the statement of profit or loss up to gross profit for the month of April.

(d) Calculate the profit margin ratio and the gross profit ratio. (Assume operating expenses were $495 and ignore the effects of income tax for this question.)

PSA4.8 Journalise GST transactions. LO7

Kids + Kites Ltd sells all kinds of children's toys. The entity's accountant, Fred Heights, was preparing the information needed to account for the GST and report to the taxation authority for the quarter ending 31 March 2019, when he came down with a nasty flu and had to stay at home. You have been hired to take over Fred's role until he recovers. Before Fred fell ill, he prepared the following information for the quarter:

Total sales (including GST)	$70 700
Total sales returns (including GST)	1 400
Total purchases (including GST)	28 560
Purchase returns (including GST)	3 360

Required

(a) Journalise the sales and purchases transactions, as well as payment of GST to the taxation authority, using the GST paid and GST collected accounts.

(b) Journalise the sales and purchases transactions, as well as payment of GST to the taxation authority, using the GST clearing account.

(c) Assuming the total net sales for the quarter were $28 560 (including GST) and the total net purchases were $70 700 (including GST), journalise the sales and purchases transactions, as well as the refund from the taxation authority, using the GST paid and GST collected accounts.

(d) Using the same information as in part (c), journalise the sales and purchases transactions, as well as the refund from the taxation authority, using the GST clearing account.

PROBLEM SET B

PSB4.1 Journalise, post, prepare partial statement of profit or loss, and calculate ratios. LO2, 3, 4, 5

Clucker Poultry Distributing Company completed these inventory transactions in the month of April. At the beginning of April, the ledger of Clucker Poultry showed cash of $4500 and share capital of $4500.

Apr.	4	Purchased inventory on account from Leghorn Supply Ltd $2950, terms 2/7, n/30.
	6	Sold inventory on account $2500, terms 2/7, n/30. The cost of the inventory sold was $2000.
	7	Paid $100 freight on 6 April sale.
	8	Received credit from Leghorn Supply Ltd for inventory returned $150.
	11	Paid Leghorn Supply Ltd in full, less discount.
	13	Received collections in full, less discounts, from customers billed on 6 April.
	14	Purchased inventory for cash $2200.
	16	Received refund from supplier on cash purchase of 14 April, $250.
	21	Purchased inventory from Pigeon Distributors $2100, terms 2/7, n/30.

Apr. 22	Paid freight on 21 April purchase $50.
23	Sold inventory for cash $3700. The cost of the inventory sold was $3060.
26	Purchased inventory for cash $1150.
27	Paid Pigeon Distributors in full, less discount.
29	Made refunds to cash customers for inventory sold for $45. The returned inventory had a cost of $35.
30	Sold inventory on account $1850, terms n/30. The cost of the inventory sold was $1500.

Clucker Poultry Distributing Company's chart of accounts includes Cash, Accounts receivable, Inventory, Accounts payable, Share capital, Sales, Sales returns and allowances, Discount allowed, Cost of sales, Freight-in, and Freight-out.

Required

(a) Journalise the transactions.

(b) Post the transactions to T accounts. Be sure to enter the beginning cash and share capital balances.

(c) Prepare the statement of profit or loss up to gross profit for the month of April 2019.

(d) Calculate the profit margin ratio and the gross profit ratio. (Assume operating expenses were $450 and ignore the effects of income tax for this question.)

PSB4.2 Journalise purchase and sale transactions under a perpetual inventory system. **LO2, 3**

Wen Goh Warehouse distributes miniature paintings to retail stores and extends credit terms of 1/7, n/30 to all of its customers. During the month of January, the following inventory transactions occurred:

July 1	Purchased 50 paintings on account for $15 each from Reproductions R Us, terms 1/7, n/30.
3	Sold 40 paintings on account to Mini Paintings Ltd for $25 each.
6	Paid Reproductions R Us in full.
9	Received payment in full from Mini Paintings Ltd.
17	Sold 30 paintings on account to Little Painters for $25 each.
18	Purchased 60 paintings on account for $15 each from Small Artistry, terms 2/7, n/30. Also made a cash payment of $100 for freight on this date.
20	Received $150 credit for 10 paintings returned to Small Artistry.
21	Received payment in full from Little Painters.
22	Sold 40 paintings on account to The Paint Box for $25 each.
30	Paid Small Artistry in full.
31	Granted The Paint Box $125 credit for 5 paintings returned costing $75.

Required

(a) Journalise the transactions for the month of January for Wen Goh Warehouse, using a perpetual inventory system. Assume the cost of each painting sold was $15.

(b) What are the advantages and disadvantages for Wen Goh Warehouse of using a perpetual inventory system as opposed to a periodic system?

PSB4.3 Prepare financial statements and calculate profitability ratios. **LO4, 5**

Enoteca Department Store is located near the Village Shopping Mall. At the end of Enoteca's financial year on 30 June 2018, the following accounts appeared in its adjusted trial balance.

Accounts payable	$ 87 230
Accounts receivable	55 330
Accumulated depreciation—building	57 750
Accumulated depreciation—equipment	47 190
Building	209 000
Cash	36 300
Cost of sales	453 970
Depreciation expense—building	11 440

▶

Depreciation expense—equipment	14 630
Dividends	30 800
Electricity expense	12 100
Equipment	110 000
Insurance expense	7 920
Interest expense	12 100
Interest payable	8 800
Interest revenue	4 400
Inventory	82 500
Mortgage payable	88 000
Office salaries expense	35 200
Prepaid insurance	2 640
Rates and taxes payable	5 280
Rates and taxes expense	5 280
Retained earnings	29 260
Sales salaries expense	83 600
Sales	690 800
Sales commissions expense	15 950
Sales commissions payable	3 850
Sales returns and allowances	8 800
Share capital	165 000

Additional data: $22 000 of the mortgage payable is due for payment next year.

Required

(a) Prepare a fully classified statement of profit or loss, a calculation of retained earnings (refer figure 1.6), and a classified statement of financial position. (Ignore income tax expense.)

(b) Calculate the return on assets ratio, profit margin ratio, gross profit ratio, and operating expenses to sales ratio. Assume total assets at the beginning of the year were $352 000.

(c) Why is it helpful to fully classify items in the statement of profit or loss?

PSB4.4 **Journalise, post, and prepare trial balance and partial statement of profit or loss.** **LO2, 3, 4**

At the beginning of April 2019, the ledger of Racquets 'R' Us Tennis Shop showed Cash $3750; Inventory $2550; and Share Capital $6300. The following transactions were completed during April.

Apr.	6	Purchased racquets and balls from Robert Ltd $1260, terms 3/7, n/30.
	7	Paid freight on Robert Ltd purchase $60.
	8	Sold inventory to members $1350, terms n/30. The inventory sold cost $900.
	10	Received credit of $60 from Robert Ltd for a racquet that was returned.
	11	Purchased tennis shoes from Niki Sports for cash $450.
	13	Paid Robert Ltd in full.
	14	Purchased tennis shirts and shorts from Martina's Sportswear $750, terms 2/7, n/60.
	15	Received cash refund of $75 from Niki Sports for damaged inventory that was returned.
	17	Paid freight on Martina's Sportswear purchase $45.
	18	Sold inventory to members $1350, terms n/30. The cost of the inventory sold was $795.
	20	Received $750 in cash from members in settlement of their accounts.
	21	Paid Martina's Sportswear in full.
	27	Granted an allowance of $45 to members for tennis clothing that did not fit properly.
	30	Received cash payments on account from members $750.

The chart of accounts for the tennis shop includes Cash, Accounts receivable, Inventory, Accounts payable, Share capital, Sales, Sales returns and allowances, Cost of sales and Freight inwards.

Required

(a) Journalise the April transactions.

(b) Using T accounts, enter the beginning balances in the ledger accounts and post the April transactions.

(c) Prepare a trial balance on 30 April 2019.

(d) Prepare a statement of profit or loss up to gross profit.

(e) What is the purpose of the chart of accounts? Why is it helpful in recording transactions?

PSB4.5 **Prepare a correct statement of profit or loss.**   **LO4**

A part-time bookkeeper prepared the statement of profit or loss for Sirimon Ltd for the year ending 30 June 2019. As an experienced, knowledgeable accountant, you review the statement and determine the following facts.

1. Sales include $15 000 of deposits from customers for future sales orders.
2. Other revenues contain one item: interest revenue $7950.
3. Selling expenses consist of sales salaries $114 000; advertising $15 000; depreciation on store equipment $11 250; and sales commissions expense $9750.
4. Administrative expenses consist of office salaries $28 500; electricity expense $12 000; rent expense $24 000; and insurance expense $10 500. Insurance expense includes $1800 of prepaid insurance. Financial expenses consist of bank charges $1500 and interest expense $6000.

SIRIMON LTD Statement of profit or loss for the year ended 30 June 2019		
REVENUES		
Sales		$ 1 053 000
Freight-out	$ 15 000	
Discount allowed	16 950	(31 950)
Net sales		1 021 050
Other revenues (net)		1 950
Total revenues		1 023 000
EXPENSES		
Cost of sales	705 000	
Selling expenses	150 000	
Administrative expenses	73 500	
Financial expenses	1 500	
Dividends	18 000	
Total expenses		948 000
Profit		$ 75 000

Required

Prepare a corrected fully classified statement of profit or loss.

PSB4.6 **Journalise, post, and prepare adjusted trial balance and financial statements.**   **LO4**

The unadjusted trial balance of Daniela's Fashion House contained the following accounts at 30 June, the end of the company's financial year:

DANIELA'S FASHION HOUSE Trial balance as at 30 June 2020		
	Debit	Credit
Cash	$ 18 350	
Accounts receivable	16 850	
Inventory	22 500	

	Debit	Credit
Store supplies	2 750	
Store equipment	42 500	
Accumulated depreciation—store equipment		$ 19 000
Office equipment	19 000	
Accumulated depreciation—office equipment		3 000
Notes payable		20 500
Accounts payable		24 250
Share capital		40 000
Retained earnings		15 000
Dividends	6 000	
Sales		373 600
Sales returns and allowances	2 100	
Cost of sales	253 700	
Salaries expense		
—Administrative staff	50 000	
—Sales staff	15 000	
Advertising expense	13 200	
Electricity expense	7 000	
Repair expense	6 050	
Freight-out	8 350	
Rent (office space)	12 000	
	$ 495 350	$ 495 350

Adjustment data:
1. Store supplies on hand total $1750.
2. Depreciation is $4500 on the store equipment and $3500 on the office equipment.
3. Interest of $5500 is accrued on notes payable at 30 June.

Other data: $15 000 of notes payable are due for payment next year. (Ignore income tax for this question.)

Required

(a) Journalise the adjusting entries.
(b) Prepare T accounts for all accounts used in part (a). Enter the trial balance into the T accounts and post the adjusting entries.
(c) Prepare an adjusted trial balance.
(d) Prepare a fully classified statement of profit or loss and a calculation of retained earnings (refer to figure 1.6), and a classified statement of financial position at 30 June 2020.
(e) Explain why the statement of profit or loss is prepared for a period of time while the statement of financial position is prepared as at a particular date.

PSB4.7 Journalise, post, prepare fully classified statement of profit or loss, and calculate ratios.

LO3, 4, 5

Fixit Hardware Pty Ltd completed the following inventory transactions in the month of May. At the beginning of May, Fixit Hardware Pty Ltd's ledger showed cash $2500 and share capital $2500.

May	2	Sold inventory on account for $2250, terms 2/7, n/30. The cost of the inventory sold was $1500.
	3	Purchased inventory on account from Depot Wholesale Supply for $3000, terms 2/7, n/30.
	5	Returned inventory and received credit from Depot Wholesale Supply for $100.
	9	Received amounts owing from customers invoiced on sales of $2250 on 2 May.
	10	Paid Depot Wholesale Supply the amount owing.
	11	Purchased supplies for cash $450.
	12	Purchased inventory for cash $1200.

May 15	Returned goods and received a refund for poor-quality inventory from supplier on cash purchase $115.
20	Purchased inventory from Harlow Distributors for $950, terms 2/7, n/30.
21	Paid freight to We Deliver on 20 May purchase $125.
24	Sold inventory for cash $3100. The cost of the inventory sold was $2170.
25	Purchased inventory from Horicon Ltd for $500, terms 2/7, n/30.
27	Paid Harlow Distributors the amount outstanding.
29	Made refunds to cash customers for inventory sold for $50. The returned inventory had cost $35. The inventory returned was not faulty.
31	Sold inventory on account for $800, terms n/30. The cost of the inventory sold was $560.

Fixit Hardware Pty Ltd's chart of accounts includes 100 Cash, 110 Accounts receivable, 120 Inventory, 130 Supplies, 200 Accounts payable, 300 Share capital, 400 Sales, 405 Sales returns and allowances, 410 Discount received, 500 Discount allowed, 505 Cost of sales, and 510 Freight inwards.

Required

(a) Journalise the transactions using a perpetual inventory system.
(b) Post the transactions to T accounts. Be sure to enter the beginning cash and share capital balances.
(c) Prepare a statement of profit or loss up to gross profit for the month of May.
(d) Calculate the profit margin and the gross profit ratio. (Assume operating expenses were $700 and ignore the effects of income tax for this question.)

PSB4.8 Journalise GST transactions.   **LO7**

Nguyen Electronics is a wholesaler of electrical products. Jinli Nguyen supplies many retailers but Bing Lee and Retravision are his two largest clients. Jinli has completed an introductory accounting course and has prepared the following information required for the GST calculations and the report to the taxation authority for the quarter ending 30 June 2018.

Total sales (including GST)	$50 500
Total sales returns (including GST)	1 000
Total purchases (including GST)	20 400
Total purchase returns (including GST)	2 400

Jinli is unable to prepare the journal entries for GST transactions and has turned to you, as a public accountant, to assist him.

Required

(a) Journalise the sales and purchases transactions, as well as the payment of GST to the taxation authority, using the GST paid and GST collected accounts.
(b) Journalise the sales and purchases transactions, as well as the payment of GST to the taxation authority, using the GST clearing account.
(c) Assuming total net sales for the quarter were $20 400 (including GST) and the total net purchases were $50 500 (including GST), journalise the sales and purchases transactions, as well as the payment of GST to the taxation authority, using the GST paid and GST collected accounts.
(d) Using the same information as in (c), journalise the sales and purchases transactions, as well as the payment of GST to the taxation authority, using the GST clearing account.

BUILDING BUSINESS SKILLS

FINANCIAL REPORTING AND ANALYSIS

Financial reporting problem

BBS4.1 Go to the ASX website (www.asx.com.au) and search for the latest annual report for a company in the Software and Services industry group. Select **Prices and research**, then **Company information**, then select **View all companies** under the Company directory. You may select the same company you chose from one of the learning reflection and consolidation boxes in chapter 3.

Required

Answer these questions using your chosen company's consolidated statement of profit or loss.

(a) What was the percentage change in revenue from sale of goods and in profit after tax from the previous year to the current year?

(b) What was the operating expenses to sales ratio for each year? Comment on any trend in this percentage.

Comparative analysis problem: Nike vs. Adidas Group

BBS4.2 Refer to the latest financial statements of Nike (http://investors.nike.com/investors/news-events-and-reports/). Select **Annual Reports**. Also refer to the latest financial statements for adidas Group (www.adidas-group.com). Select **Investors**, then **Download Center**, then select the year which has the completed FY results (e.g. 2017). (Ignore the different currencies, € vs. US$ when calculating ratios.)

Required

(a) Based on the information contained in these financial statements, determine the following values for each entity:

1. Profit margin ratio for year.
2. Gross profit for year.
3. Gross profit ratio for year.
4. Operating profit after tax for year.
5. Percentage change in operating profit after tax from the previous year to the current year.
6. Operating expenses to sales ratio for year.

(b) What conclusions concerning the relative profitability of the two entities can be drawn from these data?

Community and social perspective

BBS4.3 As the corporate community is increasingly aware of the impact of business activities on society and the environment, many entities are adopting strategies to counter such impact and contribute to the wider community. One such strategy is concerned with inventory management, whereby companies donate excess, overstocked, obsolete or outdated inventories to charitable organisations, which pass on the donated inventory to those in need.

NAEIR (National Association for the Exchange of Industrial Resources) is a US not-for-profit organisation that facilitates donated inventory to schools and not-for-profits. Schools and not-for-profits have access to thousands of brand new, high-quality products such as office supplies, clothes, toys, toiletries, electronics and books absolutely free. Another overseas organisation, Operation Give, is a charity that organises donated inventory for individuals in developing countries. Visit their web sites at www.naeir.org and www.operationgive.org.

Required

(a) Identify the benefits to businesses that make donations of excess inventory.

(b) Outline the procedures for making donations of excess inventory.

A global focus

BBS4.4 In this chapter we have calculated and compared a number of profitability ratios for two fictional retailers — Artistry Furniture and Original Furnishings. This exercise involves comparing retailers from different countries. Empire Limited is a large clothing retailer with stores all over America and Jacaranda Limited is a large clothing retailer in Australia.

Below are basic financial data for Jacaranda (in Australian dollars) and Empire (in US dollars). Even though their results are presented in different currencies, by using ratios we can make some basic comparisons.

	Jacaranda A$ (in millions)	Empire US$ (in millions)
Sales	58 000	470 000
Gross profit	15 000	115 000
Operating expenses	12 000	93 000
Profit (after tax)	2 100	15 400
Total assets	22 000	204 000
Average total assets	21 000	202 000
Current assets	6 000	61 000
Current liabilities	7 500	69 000
Total liabilities	13 000	123 000

Required

Compare the two entities by answering the following:

(a) Calculate the gross profit ratio and operating expense to sales ratio for each of the entities, and discuss their relative abilities to control cost of sales and operating expenses.

(b) Calculate the return on assets ratio and profit margin ratio, and discuss their relative profitability.

(c) Calculate the current ratio and debt to total assets ratio for the two entities, and discuss their relative liquidity and solvency.

(d) What concerns might you have in relying on this comparison?

Financial analysis on the web

BBS4.5 Purpose: No financial decision maker should ever rely solely on the financial information reported in the annual report to make decisions. It is important to keep abreast of financial news. This activity demonstrates how to search for financial news on the Web.

Address: www.news.com.au/finance

Steps:

1. In the search box, type in Harvey Norman, Woolworths or Coles.
2. Select an article that sounds interesting to you and that would be relevant to an investor in these companies.

You could also try: www.smh.com.au/business or https://finance.nine.com.au/. Company web sites often have press releases or Australian Securities Exchange information as well.

Required

(a) What was the source of the article (e.g. Reuters, nine Finance, *Sydney Morning Herald*)?

(b) Pretend that you are a personal financial planner and that one of your clients owns shares in the company. Write a brief memo to your client summarising the article and explaining the implications of the article for your client's investment.

CRITICAL THINKING

Group decision case

BBS4.6 Three years ago Fiona Jones and her brother-in-law, Frank Woolley, opened Grosby Music Store which sells musical instruments and sheet music. For the first 2 years, business was good, but the following summarised statement of profit or loss results for 2019 were disappointing:

GROSBY MUSIC STORE Statement of profit or loss for the year ended 30 June 2019		
Net sales		$ 700 000
Cost of sales		(546 000)
Gross profit		154 000
OPERATING EXPENSES		
Selling expenses	$ 100 000	
Administrative expenses	20 000	
Financial expenses	5 000	
Total expenses		(125 000)
Profit		**$ 29 000**

Fiona believes the problem lies in the relatively low gross profit ratio (gross profit divided by net sales) of 22%. Frank believes the problem is that operating expenses are too high. Fiona thinks the gross profit rate can be improved by making two changes: (1) increase average selling prices by 17% — this increase is expected to lower sales volume so that total sales will increase only 6%; (2) buy inventory in larger quantities to take advantage of all trade discounts — these changes are expected to increase the gross profit ratio by 3%. Fiona does not anticipate that these changes will have any effect on operating expenses.

Frank thinks expenses can be cut by making these two changes: (1) cut 2020 sales salaries of $60 000 in half and give sales personnel a commission of 2% of net sales; (2) reduce store deliveries to one day per week rather than twice a week — this change would reduce 2020 delivery expenses of $30 000 by 40%. Frank feels that these changes would not have any effect on net sales.

Fiona and Frank come to you for help in deciding the best way to improve profit.

Required

With the class divided into groups, answer the following:

(a) Prepare a summarised statement of profit or loss for 2020 assuming (1) Fiona's changes are implemented and (2) Frank's ideas are adopted.

(b) What is your recommendation to Fiona and Frank?

(c) Prepare a summarised statement of profit or loss for 2020 assuming both sets of proposed changes are made.

(d) Discuss the impact that other factors might have. For example, would increasing the quantity of inventory increase costs? Would a salary cut affect employee morale? Would decreased morale affect sales? Would decreased store deliveries decrease customer satisfaction? What other suggestions might be considered?

Ethics case

BBS4.7 Sonya Packovski was hired as the assistant accountant of Delicacy Foods, a gourmet food business that has nine retail stores concentrated in one city. Her main responsibility is to maintain the business's high credit rating by paying all bills when due and to take advantage of all settlement discounts. Among other things, the payment of all invoices is centralised in one of the departments Sonya manages.

Adam Fox, the former assistant accountant, who has been promoted to accountant, is training Sonya in her new duties. He instructs Sonya that she is to continue the practice of preparing all cheques 'net of discount' and dating the cheques the last day of the discount period. 'But,' Adam continues, 'we always hold the cheques at least 4 days beyond the discount period before mailing them. That way we get another 4 days of interest on our money. Most of our suppliers need our business and don't complain. And, if they scream about our missing the discount period, we blame it on the mail room or the post office. We only lose one discount out of every hundred we take that way. I think everybody does it.'

Required

(a) What are the ethical considerations in this case?

(b) What stakeholders are harmed or benefited?

(c) Should Sonya continue the practice started by Adam? Does she have any choice?

ANSWERS

Answers to self-study questions

4.1 (a) 4.2 (a) 4.3 (c) 4.4 (c) 4.5 (b) 4.6 (c) 4.7 (b) 4.8 (d) 4.9 (a) 4.10 (c) 4.11 (c) 4.12 (a)
4.13 (a) 4.14 (b)

ACKNOWLEDGEMENTS

Photo: © Hero Images / Getty Images
Photo: © gpointstudio / Shutterstock.com
Photo: © Diego Cervo / Shutterstock.com

CHAPTER 5

Reporting and analysing inventory

LEARNING OBJECTIVES

After studying this chapter, you should be able to:

5.1 record purchases and sales of inventory under a periodic inventory system

5.2 determine cost of sales under a periodic inventory system

5.3 describe the steps in determining inventory quantities

5.4 identify the unique features of the statement of profit or loss for a merchandising business under a periodic inventory system

5.5 explain the basis of accounting for inventories and apply the inventory cost flow methods under a periodic inventory system

5.6 explain the financial statement effects of each of the inventory cost flow methods

5.7 explain the lower of cost and net realisable value basis of accounting for inventories

5.8 calculate and interpret inventory turnover

5.9 apply the inventory cost flow methods to perpetual inventory records

5.10 indicate the effects of inventory errors on the financial statements

5.11 record the closing entries for merchandising entities.

Chapter preview

In the previous chapter, we discussed accounting for inventory using a perpetual inventory system. In this chapter, we explain the periodic inventory system and methods used to calculate the cost of inventory on hand at the end of the reporting period. We conclude by illustrating methods for analysing inventory.

The content and organisation of this chapter are as follows.

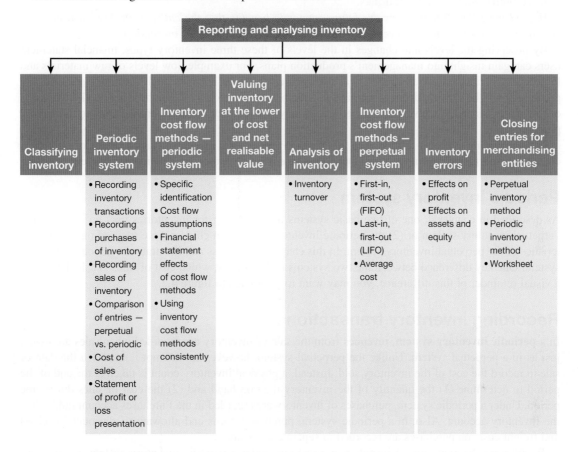

5.1 Classifying inventory

LEARNING OBJECTIVE 5.1 Record purchases and sales of inventory under a periodic inventory system.

How a business classifies its inventory depends on whether the entity is a merchandiser like JB Hi-Fi or a manufacturer like Coca-Cola Amatil. In merchandising businesses, such as those described in chapter 4, inventory consists of many different items. For example, in a supermarket, canned goods, dairy products, meats and produce are just a few of the inventory items on hand. These items have two common characteristics: (1) they are owned by the entity, and (2) they are in a form ready for sale to customers in the ordinary course of business. Thus, only one inventory classification, *inventory*, is needed to describe the many different items that make up the total inventory.

In a manufacturing business, some inventory may not yet be ready for sale. As a result, inventory is usually classified into three categories: finished goods, work in process and raw materials. Regardless of the classification, most inventories are reported under current assets on the statement of financial position. **Finished goods inventory** comprises manufactured items that are completed and ready for sale. **Work in process** is that portion of manufactured inventory that has been placed into the production process but is not yet complete (work in process can also be called *work in progress*). **Raw materials** are the basic materials that will be used in manufacturing but have not yet been placed into the production process. For example, Coca-Cola Amatil classifies beverages, food and equipment ready for sale as finished goods. Work in progress, spare parts (manufacturing and cold drink equipment) and fountain stock (post-mix products) are classified as other inventories. Raw materials include items such as the various syrups used to make bottled and canned soft drinks.

Helpful hint: Recall that assets are future economic benefits that the entity controls as a result of a past transaction or event. For inventory, control is usually established by ownership.

By observing the levels and changes in the levels of these three inventory types, financial statement users can gain insight into management's production plans. For example, low levels of raw materials and high levels of finished goods suggest that management believes it has enough inventory on hand and production will be slowing down — perhaps in anticipation of a recession. On the other hand, high levels of raw materials and low levels of finished goods may indicate that management is planning to increase production.

The accounting concepts discussed in this chapter apply to the inventory classifications of both merchandising and manufacturing entities. Our focus here is on inventory for a merchandising entity.

Periodic inventory system

As described in chapter 4, one of two basic systems of accounting for inventories may be used: (1) the perpetual inventory system or (2) the periodic inventory system. In chapter 4 we focused on the characteristics of the perpetual inventory system. In this chapter we discuss and illustrate the periodic inventory system. One key difference between the two systems is the point at which cost of sales is calculated. For a visual reminder of this difference, you may want to refer back to figure 4.3.

Recording inventory transactions

In a **periodic inventory system**, revenues from the sale of inventory are recorded when sales are made, just as in a perpetual system. Unlike the perpetual system, however, no attempt is made on the date of sale to record the cost of the inventory sold. Instead, a physical inventory count is taken at the end of the period to determine (1) the quantity of the inventory then on hand and (2) the cost of sales during the period. Under a periodic system, purchases of inventory are recorded in the Purchases account rather than the Inventory account. Also, in a periodic system, purchase returns and allowances, discounts received and freight costs on purchases are recorded in separate accounts.

To illustrate the recording of inventory transactions under a periodic inventory system, we will use purchase/sale transactions between PW Audio Supply Ltd and Sauk Stereo, as illustrated for the perpetual inventory system in chapter 4.

Recording purchases of inventory

On the basis of the sales invoice (figure 4.4) and receipt of the inventory ordered from PW Audio Supply Ltd, Sauk Stereo records the $3800 purchase as follows:

May 5	Purchases				3 800	
	Accounts payable					3 800
	(To record goods purchased on account, terms 2/7, n/30)					
	A	=	L	+	E	
			+3800		−3800	

Purchases is a temporary account whose normal balance is a debit. The **purchases account** is used to accumulate the cost of all inventory purchased for resale during the period.

Purchase returns and allowances

Because $300 of inventory received from PW Audio Supply Ltd is incorrect, Sauk Stereo returns the goods and prepares the entry below to recognise the return.

May 8	Accounts payable	300	
	Purchase returns and allowances		300
	(To record return of incorrect goods purchased from PW Audio Supply Ltd)		

$$A \quad = \quad L \quad + \quad E$$
$$-300 \qquad +300$$

Purchase returns and allowances is a contra purchases account whose normal balance is a credit. The **purchase returns and allowances account** is credited to record all returns and allowances rather than directly crediting the purchases account. This provides management with information on the magnitude of returns and allowances in one account. It is also important for management to keep track of goods being returned as it may require management to source goods from different suppliers if the return of goods is due to inferior quality.

Freight costs

When the purchaser directly incurs the freight costs, the account freight-in (or transportation-in) is debited. For example, if upon delivery of the goods on 6 May, Sauk pays We Deliver Freight Co. $150 for freight charges on its purchase from PW Audio Supply Ltd, the entry in Sauk's records is:

May 6	Freight-in	150	
	Cash		150
	(To record payment of freight on goods purchased)		

$$A \quad = \quad L \quad + \quad E$$
$$-150 \qquad -150$$

Like purchases, Freight-in is a temporary account whose normal balance is a debit. Freight-in is part of cost of goods purchased. The reason is that cost of goods purchased should include any freight charges necessary to bring the goods to the purchaser. Freight costs are not subject to a purchase discount. Purchase discounts apply on the invoice cost of the inventory.

Purchase discounts

On 12 May Sauk Stereo pays the balance due on account to PW Audio Supply Ltd, taking the 2% cash discount allowed by PW Audio Supply Ltd for payment within 7 days. The payment and discount are recorded by Sauk Stereo as follows:

May 12	Accounts payable ($3800 – $300)	3 500	
	Cash		3 430
	Discount received ($3500 × $0.02)		70
	(To record payment to PW Audio Supply Ltd within the discount period)		

$$A \quad = \quad L \quad + \quad E$$
$$-3430 \qquad -3500 \qquad +70$$

Discount received is a revenue account whose normal balance is a credit.

Recording sales of inventory

The sale of $3800 of merchandise to Sauk Stereo on 5 May (sales invoice no. 731, figure 4.4) is recorded by the seller, PW Audio Supply Ltd, as follows:

May 5	Accounts receivable	3 800	
	Sales		3 800
	(To record credit sales per invoice no. 731 to Sauk Stereo)		

A = L + E
+3800   +3800

Sales returns and allowances

To record the returned goods received from Sauk Stereo on 8 May, PW Audio Supply Ltd records the $300 sales return as follows:

May 8	Sales returns and allowances	300	
	Accounts receivable		300
	(To record return of goods from Sauk Stereo)		

A = L + E
−300   −300

Sales discounts

On 12 May, PW Audio Supply Ltd receives payment of $3430 on account from Sauk Stereo. PW Audio Supply Ltd honours the 2% cash discount and records the payment of Sauk's account receivable in full as follows:

May 12	Cash	3 430	
	Discount allowed ($3500 × 0.02)	70	
	Accounts receivable ($3800 − $300)		3 500
	(To record collection from Sauk Stereo within 2/7, n/30 discount period)		

A = L + E
+3430   −70
−3500

Comparison of entries — perpetual vs. periodic

The periodic inventory system entries above are shown in figure 5.1 next to those that were illustrated in chapter 4 (sections 4.2 and 4.3) under the perpetual inventory system for both Sauk Stereo and PW Audio Supply Ltd.

FIGURE 5.1   Comparison of journal entries under perpetual and periodic inventory systems

ENTRIES IN SAUK STEREO'S RECORDS (PURCHASER)

Transaction		Perpetual inventory system			Periodic inventory system		
May 5	Purchase of inventory on credit.	Inventory	3 800		Purchases	3 800	
		Accounts payable		3 800	Accounts payable		3 800
May 6	Freight costs on purchases.	Freight-in/Inventory	150		Freight-in	150	
		Cash		150	Cash		150
May 8	Purchases returns and allowances.	Accounts payable	300		Accounts payable	300	
		Inventory		300	Purchase returns and allowances		300
May 12	Payment on account with a discount.	Accounts payable	3 500		Accounts payable	3 500	
		Cash		3 430	Cash		3 430
		Discount received		70	Discount received		70

ENTRIES IN PW AUDIO SUPPLY LTD'S RECORDS (SELLER)					
Transaction	**Perpetual inventory system**			**Periodic inventory system**	
May 5 Sale of inventory on credit.	Accounts receivable Sales	3 800	3 800	Accounts receivable Sales	3 800 3 800
	Cost of sales Inventory	2 400	2 400	No entry for cost of sales	
May 8 Return of inventory sold.	Sales returns and allowances Accounts receivable	300	300	Sales returns and allowances Accounts receivable	300 300
	Inventory Cost of sales	140	140	No entry for cost of sales	
May 12 Cash received on account with a discount.	Cash Discount allowed Accounts receivable	3 430 70	3 500	Cash Discount allowed Accounts receivable	3 430 70 3 500

5.2 Cost of sales

LEARNING OBJECTIVE 5.2 Determine cost of sales under a periodic inventory system.

Under a periodic inventory system, a running account of the changes in inventory is not recorded when either purchases or sales transactions occur. Neither the daily amount of inventory on hand nor the cost of sales is known. To determine the **cost of sales (COS)** under a periodic inventory system, it is necessary to (1) record purchases of inventory, (2) determine the cost of goods purchased, and (3) determine the cost of goods on hand at the beginning and end of the accounting period. The cost of goods on hand must be determined by (1) a physical inventory count and (2) an application of costs to the items counted in the inventory.

Determining cost of goods purchased

Under a periodic inventory system, various accounts, such as purchases, freight-in, and purchase returns and allowances, are used to record the cost of goods purchased. (A perpetual system usually uses only one account, inventory, although in practice a freight-in account may be used.) These accounts, with their impact on cost of goods purchased, are listed in table 5.1.

TABLE 5.1   Accounts used to record purchases of inventory

Item	Periodic account title	Debit or credit entry	Effect on cost of goods purchased
Invoice price	Purchases	Debit	Increase
Freight charges paid by purchaser	Freight-in	Debit	Increase
Purchase returns and allowances granted by seller	Purchase returns and allowances	Credit	Decrease

To determine cost of goods purchased we begin with gross purchases. This amount is then adjusted for any returns of unwanted goods. The result is **net purchases**. Because freight charges are a necessary cost incurred to acquire inventory, freight-in is added to net purchases to arrive at **cost of goods purchased**. To summarise:

1. Purchase returns and allowances is subtracted from purchases to get *net purchases*.
2. Freight-in is added to net purchases to arrive at *cost of goods purchased*.

To illustrate, assume that PW Audio Supply Ltd shows these balances for the accounts above: purchases $325 000; purchase returns and allowances $17 200; and freight-in $12 200. Net purchases and cost of goods purchased are $307 800 and $320 000, as calculated in figure 5.2.

FIGURE 5.2 Calculation of net purchases and cost of goods purchased

	Purchases	$325 000
(1)	*Less:* Purchase returns and allowances	(17 200)
	Net purchases	**307 800**
(2)	*Add:* Freight-in	12 200
	Cost of goods purchased	**$320 000**

All three of the accounts (purchases, purchase returns and allowances, and cost of sales) used in the periodic system are temporary accounts. They are used to determine cost of sales. Therefore, the balances in these accounts are reduced to nil at the end of each accounting period (i.e. annually). Cost of sales must be provided in the annual report. For example, Artistry Furniture Limited reported cost of sales of $80 million for 2019.

5.3 Determining inventory quantities

LEARNING OBJECTIVE 5.3 Describe the steps in determining inventory quantities.

Businesses that use a periodic inventory system do a physical inventory count to determine the inventory on hand at the end of the reporting period and to calculate cost of sales. Even businesses that use a perpetual inventory system do this. They do so to check the accuracy of the accounting records and to determine the amount of inventory shortage or shrinkage due to wasted raw materials, shoplifting or employee theft.

Determining inventory quantities involves two steps: (1) counting the physical inventory of goods on hand (stocktake) and (2) determining the ownership of goods.

Counting the physical inventory

Counting the physical inventory involves actually counting, weighing or measuring each type of inventory on hand. In many businesses, counting inventory is a formidable task. Companies such as Coca-Cola Amatil, Woolworths Ltd and Mitre 10 have thousands of different inventory items. An inventory count is generally more accurate when goods are not being sold or received during the counting. Consequently, merchandisers often perform the stocktake when the business is closed or when business is slow. Under a periodic inventory system, the stocktake is done at the end of the accounting period.

The quantity of each type of inventory is listed on inventory summary sheets. To ensure the accuracy of the summary sheets, the listing should be verified by a second employee or supervisor. Subsequently, unit costs will be applied to the quantities to determine a total cost of the inventory (which is the topic of later sections). An accurate inventory count is important to help companies provide accurate inventory and profit figures in the financial statements.

Determining ownership of goods

To determine ownership of goods, two questions must be answered: Do all of the goods included in the count belong to the entity? Does the entity own any goods that were not included in the count?

Goods in transit

A complication in determining ownership is **goods in transit** (on board a truck, train, ship or plane) at the end of the period. A business may have purchased goods that have not yet been received, or it may have sold goods that have not yet been delivered. To arrive at an accurate count, ownership of these goods must be determined.

Goods in transit should be included in the inventory of the business that has legal title to the goods. Legal title is determined by the terms of the sale, as shown in figure 5.3 and described in the text that follows.

Terms of sale

1. When the terms are **FOB (free on board) shipping point**, ownership of the goods passes to the buyer when the delivery entity accepts the goods from the seller.
2. When the terms are **FOB destination**, ownership of the goods remains with the seller until the goods reach the buyer.

Consigned goods

In some lines of business, it is customary to hold the goods of other parties and try to sell the goods for them for a fee, but without taking ownership of the goods. These are called **consigned goods** (other terms for consigned goods are *consignment stock* and *goods on consignment*). For example, you might have a used car that you would like to sell. If you take the car to a dealer, the dealer might be willing to put the car in its car sales yard and charge you a commission if it is sold. But under this agreement the dealer would not take ownership of the car, which would still belong to you. Therefore, if an inventory count were taken, the car would not be included in the dealer's inventory. Many car, boat and antique dealers sell goods on consignment to keep their inventory costs down and to avoid the risk of purchasing an item that they won't be able to sell.

Calculating cost of sales

We have now reached the point where we can calculate cost of sales. Doing so involves two steps.
1. Add the cost of goods purchased to the cost of goods on hand at the beginning of the period (beginning inventory; also known as *opening inventory*) to obtain the **cost of goods available for sale**.
2. Subtract the cost of goods on hand at the end of the period (ending inventory) from the cost of goods available for sale to arrive at the *cost of sales*.

For example, assume PW Audio Supply Ltd has beginning inventory of $36 000 and ending inventory of $40 000, and that the cost of goods purchased during the period is $320 000. The cost of goods available for sale and cost of sales can be calculated as shown in figure 5.4.

FIGURE 5.4 Calculation of cost of goods available for sale and cost of sales

	Beginning inventory	$ 36 000
(1)	*Add:* Cost of goods purchased	320 000
	Cost of goods available for sale	356 000
(2)	*Less:* Ending inventory	(40 000)
	Cost of sales	$316 000

5.4 Statement of profit or loss presentation

LEARNING OBJECTIVE 5.4 Identify the unique features of the statement of profit or loss for a merchandising business under a periodic inventory system.

The statement of profit or loss for a merchandising business is the same whether a periodic or perpetual inventory system is used, except for the cost of sales section. Under a periodic inventory system, the cost of sales section generally contains more detail. A statement of profit or loss for PW Audio Supply Ltd, using a periodic inventory system, is shown in figure 5.5.

FIGURE 5.5 Statement of profit or loss for a merchandising business using a periodic inventory

PW AUDIO SUPPLY LTD Statement of profit or loss for the year ended 30 June 2020			
SALES REVENUE			
Gross sales revenue			$ 480 000
Less: Sales returns and allowances			(20 000)
Net sales			460 000
COST OF SALES			
Inventory, 1 July 2019		$ 36 000	
Purchases	$325 000		
Less: **Purchase returns and allowances**	(17 200)		
Net purchases	307 800		
Add: **Freight-in**	12 200		
Cost of goods purchased		320 000	
Cost of goods available for sale		356 000	
Inventory, 30 June 2020		(40 000)	
Cost of sales			(316 000)
Gross profit			144 000
Other operating revenue			24 000
			168 000
Operating expenses			(125 000)
Profit before income tax			43 000
Less: Income tax expense			(12 900)
Profit after income tax			$ 30 100

Helpful hint: The far-right column identifies the major subdivisions of the statement of profit or loss. The middle column identifies the main items that make up cost of sales of $316 000. The first column explains cost of goods purchased of $320 000.

The use of the periodic inventory system does not affect the content of the statement of financial position. Inventory is reported at the same amount in the current assets section under both the perpetual and periodic inventory systems.

In the remainder of this chapter we discuss additional issues related to inventory costing. To simplify our presentation, we assume a periodic inventory accounting system.

LEARNING REFLECTION AND CONSOLIDATION

Review it
1. Discuss the three steps in determining cost of sales in a periodic inventory system.
2. What accounts are used in determining the cost of goods purchased?
3. In what ways is a perpetual inventory system different from a periodic inventory system?

Do it

Aussie Mac's accounting records show the following at year-end: freight-in $6100; sales $240 000; purchases $162 500; beginning inventory $18 000; ending inventory $20 000; sales returns and allowances $10 000; purchase returns $8600; and operating expenses $57 000. Calculate these amounts for Aussie Mac:

(a) Net sales.
(b) Cost of goods purchased.
(c) Cost of sales.
(d) Gross profit.
(e) Profit before tax.

Reasoning

To calculate the required amounts, it is important to know the relationships in measuring profit for a merchandising business. For example, it is necessary to know the difference between sales and net sales, goods available for sale and cost of sales, and gross profit and profit.

Solution

(a) Net sales: Sales – Sales returns and allowances
$240 000 – $10 000 = $230 000
(b) Cost of goods purchased:
Purchases – Purchase returns + Freight-in
$162 500 – $8600 + $6100 = $160 000
(c) Cost of sales:
Beginning inventory + Cost of goods purchased – Ending inventory
$18 000 + $160 000 – $20 000 = $158 000
(d) Gross profit: Net sales – Cost of sales
$230 000 –$158 000 = $72 000
(e) Profit before income tax: Gross profit – Operating expenses
$72 000 – $57 000 = $15 000

5.5 Inventory cost flow methods — periodic system

LEARNING OBJECTIVE 5.5 Explain the basis of accounting for inventories and apply the inventory cost flow methods under a periodic inventory system.

Purchases, purchase returns and allowances, and freight-in are all costs included in the cost of goods available for sale. Cost of goods available for sale must be allocated between cost of sales and ending inventory at the end of the accounting period. First, the costs assignable to the ending inventory are determined. Second, the cost of the ending inventory is subtracted from the cost of goods available for sale to determine the cost of sales. (Refer to figure 5.4 to see this calculation.)

Determining ending inventory can be complicated if the units on hand for a specific item of inventory have been purchased at different times. This is particularly so in periods of changing price levels. In the following sections we explore the effect of purchasing inventory at different prices. To illustrate, assume that Crivitz TV purchases three televisions at costs of $700, $750 and $800 and, during the year, two sets are sold at $1200 each. Ending inventory might be $700, $750 or $800, and corresponding cost of sales might be $1550 ($750 + $800), $1500 ($700 + $800), or $1450 ($700 + $750), depending on how Crivitz measures the cost flows of the inventory purchased and sold. In this section we discuss alternative inventory costing methods. To simplify our presentation, we assume a periodic inventory system. Inventory costing methods are applied to the perpetual inventory system in section 5.9.

Specific identification

If we determine that the television in Crivitz's inventory is the one originally purchased for $750, then the ending inventory is $750 and cost of sales is $1500 ($700 + $800). If Crivitz can positively identify which particular units were sold and which are still in ending inventory, it can use the **specific identification method** of inventory costing (see figure 5.6). In this case ending inventory and cost of sales are easily and accurately determined.

Specific identification is possible when a business sells a limited variety of high-unit-cost items that can be identified clearly from the time of purchase to the time of sale. Examples of such businesses are motor vehicle dealerships (cars, trucks and vans), jewellery stores (diamond rings and gold necklaces), and antique shops (tables and cabinets).

| **FIGURE 5.6** | Specific identification method |

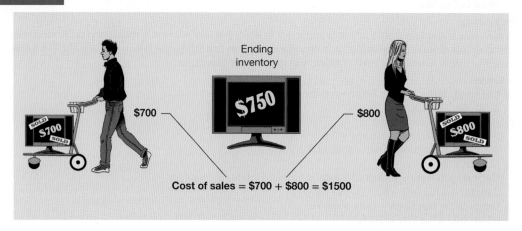

Helpful hint: A major disadvantage of the specific identification method is that management may be able to manipulate profit by choosing to supply a good with a low or high unit cost, once the sale is made to a customer.

But what if we cannot specifically identify particular inventory units? For example, supermarkets, newsagents and hardware stores sell thousands of relatively low-unit-cost items of inventory. These items are often indistinguishable from one another, making it impossible or impractical to track each item's cost. In that case, we must make assumptions, called *cost flow assumptions*, about which units were sold.

Cost flow assumptions

Because specific identification is often impractical, other cost flow methods are used. These differ from specific identification in that they *assume* flows of costs that may be unrelated to the physical flow of goods. There are three assumed cost flow methods:
1. first-in, first-out (FIFO)
2. last-in, first-out (LIFO)
3. average cost.

There is no accounting requirement that the cost flow assumption be consistent with the physical movement of the goods. The selection of the appropriate cost flow method is made by management and depends on many factors including the type of inventory, the effect that each method has on the financial statements, accounting standards, income tax laws, cost, and the information needs of management and financial statement users. Under the international accounting standard IAS 2/AASB 102 *Inventories*, some costing methods are acceptable and others are not. This standard applies in Australia and New Zealand as these countries, along with many other countries, have adopted international accounting standards. Specific identification, FIFO and average cost methods are acceptable, but the standards exclude the use of the LIFO method. The standards require organisations to use the same costing method for all inventories of a similar nature but permit different costing methods for inventories that have a different nature or use. For example, Coca-Cola Amatil uses the FIFO method and average cost method for its inventories — whichever is the most appropriate in each case.

While use of the LIFO method is not permitted under Australian and New Zealand standards, it is permitted in the United States, as shown in an extract from the Financial Accounting Standards Board (FASB) General Standards:

> Cost for inventory purposes shall be determined under any one of several assumptions as to the flow of cost factors (such as first-in, first-out; average; and last-in, first-out); the major objective in selecting a method shall be to choose the one that most clearly reflects periodic income. (FASB Inventory — Section I78, paragraph 107.)

Given that we operate in a global economy, it is possible that you could work for a company with an Australian subsidiary, whose head office is in the United Sates and uses the LIFO inventory method. In this case, it would be helpful for you to understand the LIFO inventory method. You may also be interested in examining and/or comparing financial statements of international companies for investment purposes. Understanding how inventory figures can be affected by different inventory cost flows will assist your decision-making processes.

The FIFO, LIFO and average cost flow methods are illustrated using Dubbo Electronics which uses a periodic inventory system and has the information shown in figure 5.7 for its Astro condenser.

FIGURE 5.7	Cost of goods available for sale

DUBBO ELECTRONICS Astro condensers				
Date	Explanation	Units	Unit cost	Total cost
Jan. 1	Beginning inventory	100	$10	$ 1 000
Apr. 15	Purchase	200	11	2 200
Aug. 24	Purchase	300	12	3 600
Nov. 27	Purchase	400	13	5 200
	Total	1 000		$12 000

The business had a total of 1000 units available that it could have sold during the period. The total cost of these units was $12 000. A physical inventory at the end of the year determined that during the year 550 units were sold and 450 units were in inventory at 31 December. The question, then, is how to determine what costs should be allocated to the goods sold and to the ending inventory. The sum of the cost allocated to the units sold plus the cost of the units in inventory must add up to $12 000, the total cost of all goods available for sale.

First-in, first-out (FIFO)

The **FIFO method** assumes that the first goods purchased are the first to be sold. FIFO often parallels the actual physical flow of merchandise because it generally is good business practice to sell the oldest units first, especially with perishable goods. Under the FIFO method, therefore, the costs of the earliest goods purchased are the first to be recognised as cost of sales. (Note that this does not necessarily mean that the oldest units *are* sold first, but that the costs of the oldest units are recognised first. In a bin of picture hangers at the hardware store, for example, no one really knows, nor would it matter, which hangers are sold first.) The allocation of the cost of goods available for sale at Dubbo Electronics under FIFO is shown in figure 5.8.

Note that under FIFO, since it is assumed that the first goods purchased were the first goods sold, ending inventory is based on the costs of the most recent units purchased. That is, under FIFO, the cost of the ending inventory is obtained by taking the unit cost of the most recent purchase and working backwards until all units of inventory have been costed. In this example, the 450 units of ending inventory must be costed using the most recent costs. The last purchase was 400 units at $13 on 27 November. The remaining 50 units are allocated the cost of the second most recent purchase, $12, on 24 August. Next, cost of sales is calculated by subtracting the cost of the units not sold (ending inventory) from the cost of all goods available for sale.

FIGURE 5.8	Allocation of costs — FIFO method

Cost of goods available for sale

Date	Explanation	Units	Unit cost	Total cost
Jan. 1	Beginning inventory	100	$10	$ 1 000
Apr. 15	Purchase	200	11	2 200
Aug. 24	Purchase	300	12	3 600
Nov. 27	Purchase	400	13	5 200
	Total	1 000		$12 000

Step 1: Ending inventory

Date	Units	Unit cost	Total cost
Nov. 27	400	$13	$5 200
Aug. 24	50	12	600
Total	450		$5 800

Step 2: Cost of sales

Cost of goods available for sale	$12 000
Less: Ending inventory	5 800
Cost of sales	$ 6 200

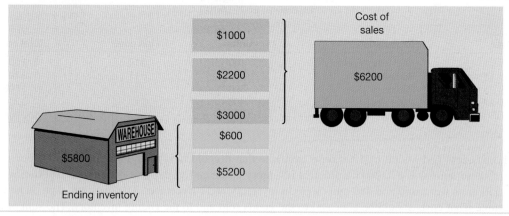

Helpful hint: Note the sequencing of the allocation in the above figure — (1) calculate ending inventory and (2) determine cost of sales.

Figure 5.9 demonstrates that cost of sales can also be calculated by accounting for the 550 units sold using the costs of the first 550 units acquired. Note that of the 300 units purchased on 24 August, only 250 units are assumed sold. This agrees with our calculation of the cost of ending inventory, where 50 of these units were assumed unsold and thus included in ending inventory.

FIGURE 5.9	Proof of cost of sales

Date	Units	Unit cost	Total cost
Jan. 1	100	$10	$1 000
Apr. 15	200	11	2 200
Aug. 24	250	12	3 000
Total	550		$6 200

Last-in, first-out (LIFO)

The **LIFO method** assumes that the last goods purchased are the first to be sold. LIFO seldom coincides with the actual physical flow of inventory. (Exceptions include goods stored in piles, such as coal or hay, where goods are removed from the top of the pile as sold.) Under the LIFO method, the costs of the last goods purchased are the first to be recognised as cost of sales. The allocation of the cost of goods available for sale at Dubbo Electronics under LIFO is shown in figure 5.10.

FIGURE 5.10	Allocation of costs — LIFO method

Cost of goods available for sale				
Date	Explanation	Units	Unit cost	Total cost
Jan. 1	Beginning inventory	100	$10	$ 1 000
Apr. 15	Purchase	200	11	2 200
Aug. 24	Purchase	300	12	3 600
Nov. 27	Purchase	400	13	5 200
	Total	1 000		$12 000

Step 1: Ending inventory				Step 2: Cost of sales	
Date	Units	Unit cost	Total cost		
Jan. 1	100	$10	$1 000	Cost of goods available for sale	$12 000
Apr. 15	200	11	2 200	*Less:* Ending inventory	5 000
Aug. 24	150	12	1 800		
Total	450		$5 000	Cost of sales	$ 7 000

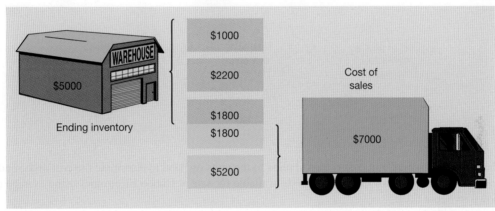

Under LIFO, since it is assumed that the first goods sold were those that were most recently purchased, ending inventory is based on the costs of the oldest units purchased. That is, under LIFO, the cost of the ending inventory is obtained by taking the unit cost of the earliest goods available for sale and working forward until all units of inventory have been costed. In this example, the costs of the earliest purchases are allocated to the 450 units of ending inventory. The first purchase was 100 units at $10 in the 1 January beginning inventory. Then 200 units were purchased at $11. The remaining 150 units needed cost $12 per unit (24 August purchase). Next, cost of sales is calculated by subtracting the cost of the unsold units (ending inventory) from the cost of all goods available for sale.

Helpful hint: In some cases, the 'unit' might be a litre of petrol or a kilogram of sand rather than a single item of inventory such as a car tyre or a fridge.

Figure 5.11 demonstrates that cost of sales can also be calculated by allocating the cost of the most recent purchases to the 550 units sold. Note that of the 300 units purchased on 24 August, only 150 units are assumed sold. This agrees with our calculation of the cost of ending inventory, where 150 of these units were assumed unsold and thus included in ending inventory.

FIGURE 5.11 Proof of cost of sales

Date	Units	Unit cost	Total cost
Nov. 27	400	$13	$5 200
Aug. 24	150	12	1 800
Total	550		$7 000

Under a periodic inventory system, which we are using here, all goods purchased during the period are assumed to be available for the first sale, regardless of the date of purchase. No attempt is made to compare the dates of sales with purchase dates, as is done when using the perpetual system. Hence, it is possible to allocate the cost of an item that has not yet been purchased at the time of the sale.

Average cost

The **average cost method** allocates the cost of goods available for sale on the basis of the **weighted average unit cost** incurred. The average cost method assumes that goods are similar in nature. The formula and a sample calculation of the weighted average unit cost are given in figure 5.12.

FIGURE 5.12 Formula for weighted average unit cost

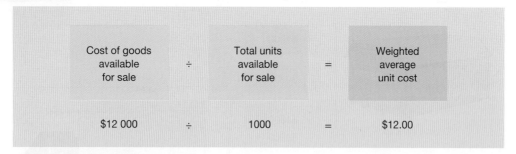

The weighted average unit cost is then applied to the units on hand to determine the cost of the ending inventory. The allocation of the cost of goods available for sale at Dubbo Electronics using average cost is shown in figure 5.13.

We can verify the cost of sales under this method by multiplying the units sold by the weighted average unit cost ($550 \times \$12 = \$6600$). Note that this method does not use the simple average of the unit costs. That average is $11.50 ($10 + $11 + $12 + $13 = $46; $46 ÷ 4). The average cost method instead uses the average *weighted* by the quantities purchased at each unit cost.

FIGURE 5.13 Allocation of costs — average cost method

	Cost of goods available for sale			
Date	Explanation	Units	Unit cost	Total cost
Jan. 1	Beginning inventory	100	$10	$ 1 000
Apr. 15	Purchase	200	11	2 200
Aug. 24	Purchase	300	12	3 600
Nov. 27	Purchase	400	13	5 200
	Total	1 000		$12 000

Step 1: Ending inventory				Step 2: Cost of sales	
$12 000	÷ 1000 =	$12.00		Cost of goods available for sale	$12 000
Units	**Unit cost**	**Total cost**		*Less:* Ending inventory	5 400
450	$12.00	$5 400		Cost of sales	$ 6 600

Ending inventory

Cost of sales

5.6 Financial statement effects of cost flow methods

LEARNING OBJECTIVE 5.6 Explain the financial statement effects of each of the inventory cost flow methods.

Only two of the three assumed cost flow methods are acceptable in Australia and New Zealand. Domino's Pizza Enterprises Ltd, for example, uses the FIFO method of inventory costing. Kathmandu and Woolworths use the average cost method for all or part of their inventory. Indeed, a business may use more than one cost flow method at the same time. For example, Coca-Cola Amatil value their inventory by applying either FIFO or average cost to each particular class of inventory. As the use of inventory cost flow methods varies among businesses, it is important to note that the use of each of these methods has varying effects on:

1. the statement of profit or loss
2. the statement of financial position
3. taxation.

Statement of profit or loss effects

To understand why businesses might choose a particular cost flow method, let's examine the effects of the different cost flow assumptions on the financial statements of Dubbo Electronics. The statements of profit or loss in figure 5.14 assume that Dubbo Electronics sold its 550 units for $11 500, had operating expenses of $2000, and is subject to an income tax rate of 30%.

Although the cost of goods available for sale ($12 000) is the same under each of the three inventory cost flow methods, both the ending inventories and costs of sales are different. This difference is due to the unit costs that are allocated to cost of sales and to ending inventory. Each dollar of difference in ending inventory results in a corresponding dollar difference in profit before income tax. For Dubbo, an $800 difference exists between FIFO and LIFO cost of sales.

In periods of changing prices, the cost flow assumption can have a significant impact on profit and on evaluations based on profit. In most instances, prices are rising (inflation). In a period of inflation, FIFO produces a higher profit because the lower unit costs of the first units purchased are matched against revenues. In a period of rising prices (as is the case here for Dubbo), FIFO reports the highest profit ($2310) and LIFO the lowest ($1750); average cost falls in the middle ($2030). If prices are falling, the results from the use of FIFO and LIFO are reversed where FIFO will report the lowest profit and LIFO the highest. To management, higher profit is an advantage as it causes external users to view the business more favourably. In addition, if management bonuses are based on profit, FIFO will provide the basis for higher bonuses.

FIGURE 5.14 Comparative effects of cost flow methods

DUBBO ELECTRONICS Statements of profit or loss			
	FIFO	LIFO	Average cost
Sales	$11 500	$11 500	$11 500
Beginning inventory	1 000	1 000	1 000
Purchases	11 000	11 000	11 000
Cost of goods available for sale	12 000	12 000	12 000
Less: Ending inventory	(5 800)	(5 000)	(5 400)
Cost of sales	6 200	7 000	6 600
Gross profit	5 300	4 500	4 900
Less: Operating expenses	(2 000)	(2 000)	(2 000)
Profit before income tax	**3 300**	**2 500**	**2 900**
Less: Income tax expense (30%)	(990)	(750)	(870)
Profit after income tax	**$ 2310**	**$ 1750**	**$ 2030**

Some argue that the use of LIFO in a period of inflation enables an entity to avoid reporting paper profit or phantom profit. To illustrate, assume that Kralik Ltd buys 200 units of a product at $20 per unit on 10 January and 200 more on 31 December at $24 each. During the year, 200 units are sold at $30 each. The results under FIFO and LIFO are shown in figure 5.15.

Helpful hint: Managers of different businesses in the same industry may reach different conclusions as to the most appropriate inventory method.

FIGURE 5.15 Statement of profit or loss effects compared

	FIFO	LIFO
Sales (200 × $30)	$6 000	$6 000
Cost of sales	4 000 (200 × $20)	4 800 (200 × $24)
Gross profit	$2 000	$1 200

Under LIFO, Kralik Ltd has recovered the current replacement cost ($4800) of the units sold. Thus, the gross profit in economic terms is real. However, under FIFO, the entity has recovered only the 10 January cost ($4000). To replace the units sold, it must reinvest $800 (200 × $4) of the gross profit. Thus, $800 of the gross profit is said to be phantom or illusory. As a result, reported profit is also overstated in real terms.

Statement of financial position effects

A major advantage of the FIFO method is that, in a period of inflation, the costs allocated to ending inventory will approximate their current cost. For example, for Dubbo Electronics, 400 of the 450 units in the ending inventory are costed under FIFO at the higher 27 November unit cost of $13.

Conversely, a major shortcoming of the LIFO method is that, in a period of inflation, the costs allocated to ending inventory may be significantly understated in terms of current cost. This is true for Dubbo

Electronics, where the cost of the ending inventory includes the $10 unit cost of the beginning inventory. The understatement becomes greater over prolonged periods of inflation if the inventory includes goods purchased several years earlier.

Note: In the United States, a tax rule, often referred to as the LIFO conformity rule, requires that if LIFO is used for tax purposes it must also be used for financial reporting purposes. This means that if a company chooses the LIFO method to reduce its tax expense it will also have to report lower profit in its financial statements.

Taxation effects

We have seen that both inventory on the statement of financial position and profit on the statement of profit or loss are higher when FIFO is used in a period of inflation. In the United States, many companies have switched to LIFO. The reason is that LIFO results in the lowest income taxes (because of lower profit) during times of rising prices. For example, at Dubbo Electronics, income tax would be $750 under LIFO, compared with $990 under FIFO. The tax saving of $240 makes more cash available for use in the business. Recall, however, that LIFO is not allowed in Australia or New Zealand.

Using inventory cost flow methods consistently

Whatever cost flow method a business chooses, it should be used consistently from one accounting period to another. Consistent application enhances the comparability of financial statements over successive periods. In contrast, using the FIFO method one year and the average cost method the next year makes it difficult to compare the profits of the two years.

Helpful hint: As you learned in chapter 1, comparability is an important characteristic of accounting information.

Although consistent application is preferred, it does not mean that a business may *never* change its method of inventory costing. When a business adopts a different method, the change and its effects on profit should be disclosed in the financial statements.

For retail businesses, determining the cost of inventory can be difficult where the inventory comprises a large number of items with high turnover and the cost of individual items is not readily available. In these circumstances IAS 2/AASB 102 permits the use of the **retail inventory method**. This method uses the current selling prices of inventory and *reduces* selling prices to cost by subtracting average mark-up ratios.

5.7 Valuing inventory at the lower of cost and net realisable value

LEARNING OBJECTIVE 5.7 Explain the lower of cost and net realisable value basis of accounting for inventories.

Cost is the main basis for recording and reporting most assets, including inventory. When the cost of inventory fluctuates, inventory costing methods can be used to determine inventory cost. However, when there has been a decrease in the selling price of inventory, in certain circumstances it is necessary to report inventory at an amount below its original cost. The decline in selling price may be due to a decrease in demand, increase in competition, or to obsolescence or damage.

The value of the inventory of businesses selling high-technology or fashion goods can drop very quickly due to changes in technology or changes in fashions. For example, suppose you are the owner of a retail store that sells computers. Imagine that during the last 12 months the selling price of the computers has dropped $500 per unit and the selling price is now below the original cost. At the end of your financial year, you have some of these computers in inventory. Do you think your inventory should be stated at cost, in accordance with historical cost measurement, or at its lower selling value?

As you probably reasoned, this situation requires a departure from the cost basis of accounting. When the selling value of inventory is lower than its cost, the inventory is written down to its net realisable value. This is done by debiting inventory write-down expense, crediting inventory, and reporting inventory at the **lower of cost and net realisable value (LCNRV)** in the period in which the decline in net realisable value occurs.

LCNRV is applied to the items in inventory after one of the cost flow methods (specific identification, FIFO, LIFO or average cost) has been used to determine cost. Under the LCNRV rule, net realisable value is not just the selling price. IAS 2/AASB 102 defines **net realisable value (NRV)** as the estimated selling price in the ordinary course of business *less*, where applicable, estimated further costs to be incurred in completing, marketing, selling and distributing to customers.

LEARNING REFLECTION AND CONSOLIDATION

Review it

1. What factors should be considered by management in selecting an inventory cost flow method?
2. What inventory cost flow method does Domino's Pizza Enterprises Ltd use for its inventories? (*Hint:* You will need to access the latest annual report for Domino's and review the notes to the financial statements.)
3. Which inventory cost flow method produces the highest profit in a period of rising prices?
4. When should inventory be reported at a value other than cost?

Do it

The accounting records of U-Beaut Compute show the following data.

Beginning inventory	4000 units at $3
Purchases	6000 units at $4
Sales	5000 units at $12

Determine the cost of sales during the period under a periodic inventory system using (a) the FIFO method, (b) the LIFO method and (c) the average cost method.

Reasoning

Because the units of inventory on hand and available for sale may have been purchased at different prices, a systematic method must be adopted to allocate the costs between the goods sold and the goods on hand (ending inventory).

Solution

(a) FIFO: (4000 @ $3) + (1000 @ $4) = $12 000 + $4000 = $16 000
(b) LIFO: 5000 @ $4 = $20 000
(c) Average cost: [(4000 @ $3) + (6000 @ $4)] ÷ 10 000
     = ($12 000 + $24 000) ÷ 10 000
     = $3.60 per unit; 5000 @ $3.60 = $18 000

5.8 Analysis of inventory

LEARNING OBJECTIVE 5.8 Calculate and interpret inventory turnover.

For businesses that sell goods, managing inventory levels can be one of the most critical tasks. Having too much inventory on hand costs the business money in storage costs, interest cost (on funds tied up in inventory), and costs associated with the obsolescence of technical goods (e.g. computer chips) or shifts in fashion for products like clothes. So, for example, most retailers tend to hold higher inventory levels during November and December to provide better service to customers over the Christmas period. In this section we discuss some issues related to evaluating inventory levels.

Inventory turnover

Inventory turnover is calculated as the cost of sales divided by average inventory. The cost of sales is used rather than sales, as the cost of sales and inventory are stated at cost. **Days in inventory** indicates the average number of days inventory is held by the entity. It is calculated as 365 days divided by inventory turnover. Both measures indicate how quickly an entity sells its goods, i.e. how many times the inventory 'turns over' (is sold) during the year. High inventory turnover or low days in inventory indicates the entity is tying up little of its funds in inventory as it has a minimal amount of inventory on hand at any one time. Although minimising the funds tied up in inventory is efficient, too high an inventory turnover may indicate that the entity is losing sales opportunities due to inventory shortages. Management should therefore monitor inventory turnover closely to achieve the optimal balance between too much and too little inventory held.

In chapter 1 we introduced ratio analysis using 2019 data from Artistry Furniture and Original Furnishings to illustrate how to calculate and interpret profitability, liquidity and solvency ratios. To continue our analysis and our understanding of these companies, figure 5.16 presents inventory turnover and days in inventory for those two entities, using data from their financial statements for 2019 and 2018.

Amounts used to calculate average inventory are taken from the respective columns in the 2019 statement of financial position. Inventory at year-end for 2017 for Original Furnishings and Artistry Furniture respectively was $44 980 and $8240 (in thousands). The amounts in the ratio calculations have been rounded to the nearest thousand.

The calculations in figure 5.16 show that Original Furnishings' inventory turnover improved slightly from 6.79 times in 2018 to 6.82 times in 2019. However, even though there was a slight improvement in the inventory turnover, it wasn't enough to improve the average time an item of furniture spent on an Original Furnishings showroom floor or in the warehouse. For both 2018 and 2019 the days in inventory remained at 54 days.

FIGURE 5.16   Inventory turnover and days in inventory

$$\text{Inventory turnover} = \frac{\text{Cost of sales}}{\text{Average inventory}}$$

$$\text{Days in inventory} = \frac{365}{\text{Inventory turnover}}$$

		2019 ('000)	2018 ('000)
Original Furnishings	Inventory turnover	$\dfrac{\$350\,000}{(\$56\,250 + \$46\,350)/2} = 6.82$ times	$\dfrac{\$310\,000}{(\$46\,350 + \$44\,980)/2} = 6.79$ times
	Days in inventory	$\dfrac{365 \text{ days}}{6.82} = 54$ days	$\dfrac{365 \text{ days}}{6.79} = 54$ days
Artistry Furniture	Inventory turnover	$\dfrac{\$80\,000}{(\$12\,500 + \$10\,300)/2} = 7.02$ times	$\dfrac{\$66\,000}{(\$10\,300 + \$8\,240)/2} = 7.12$ times
	Days in inventory	$\dfrac{365 \text{ days}}{7.02} = 52$ days	$\dfrac{365 \text{ days}}{7.12} = 51$ days

In contrast, Artistry Furniture held higher levels of inventory in proportion to cost of sales. Artistry Furniture's inventory turnover ratio decreased from 7.12 times in 2018 to 7.02 times in 2019, thereby increasing days in inventory from 51 days to 52 days.

LEARNING REFLECTION AND CONSOLIDATION

Review it

What is the purpose of calculating inventory turnover? What is the relationship between inventory turnover and average days in inventory?

Using the decision-making toolkit below, managers and external users can evaluate the entity's ability to sell its inventory. The decision focuses on the length of time that inventory is held before it is sold. Using the cost of sales and inventory figures, two measures can be calculated. The inventory turnover measures the number of times per annum an entity sells its inventory. The days in inventory ratio converts the inventory turnover into days. A high inventory turnover or a low number of days inventory held both indicate that the entity is efficient in selling its inventory quickly. Slow moving inventory may be of concern to managers and potential investors as any increase in the costs associated with wastage and obsolescence may have an adverse effect on profitability.

DECISION-MAKING TOOLKIT

Decision/issue	Info needed for analysis	Tool or technique to use for decision	How to evaluate results to make decision
How long is an item held in inventory?	Cost of sales; beginning and ending inventory	$\text{Inventory turnover} = \dfrac{\text{Cost of sales}}{\text{Average inventory}}$ $\text{Days in inventory} = \dfrac{365 \text{ days}}{\text{Inventory turnover}}$	A higher inventory turnover ratio or lower average days in inventory suggests that the entity is efficient in managing and selling its inventory.

5.9 Inventory cost flow methods — perpetual system

LEARNING OBJECTIVE 5.9 Apply the inventory cost flow methods to perpetual inventory records.

Each of the inventory cost flow methods described in the chapter for a periodic inventory system may be used in a perpetual inventory system. To illustrate the application of the three assumed cost flow methods (FIFO, LIFO and average cost), we will use the data shown below in figure 5.17 and in this chapter for Dubbo Electronics' Astro Condensers.

FIGURE 5.17 Inventories — units and costs

	DUBBO ELECTRONICS Astro condensers				
Date	Explanation	Units	Unit cost	Total cost	Balance in units
Jan. 1	Beginning inventory	100	$10	$ 1 000	100
Apr. 15	Purchases	200	11	2 200	300
Aug. 24	Purchases	300	12	3 600	600
Sept. 10	Sale	550			50
Nov. 27	Purchases	400	13	5 200	450
				$12 000	

First-in, first-out (FIFO)

Under FIFO, the cost of the earliest purchases of goods *on hand before* each sale is charged to cost of sales. Therefore, the cost of sales on 10 September consists of the units in beginning inventory on 1 January and the units purchased on 15 April and 24 August. The inventory in a FIFO method perpetual system is shown in figure 5.18.

FIGURE 5.18 Perpetual system — FIFO

Date	Purchases	Sales	Balance
Jan. 1			(100 @ $10) $1 000
Apr. 15	(200 @ $11) $2 200		(100 @ $10) ⎫ $3 200 (200 @ $11) ⎭
Aug. 24	(300 @ $12) $3 600		(100 @ $10) ⎫ (200 @ $11) ⎬ $6 800 (300 @ $12) ⎭
Sept. 10		(100 @ $10) ⎫ (200 @ $11) ⎬ $6 200 (250 @ $12) ⎭	(50 @ $12) $ 600
Nov. 27	(400 @ $13) $5 200		(50 @ $12) ⎫ $5 800 (400 @ $13) ⎭

The ending inventory in this situation is $5800, and the cost of sales is $6200 [(100 @ $10) + (200 @ $11) + (250 @ $12)].

Regardless of the system (periodic or perpetual), the first costs in are the costs assigned to cost of sales. Recall that, under a perpetual system, stock losses and shortages can be separately identified and recorded, whereas under a periodic system, stock losses are included as part of cost of sales.

The results under FIFO in a perpetual system are the same as in a periodic system if there are no stock shortages/losses (see figure 5.8 where, similarly, the ending inventory is $5800 and cost of sales is $6200).

Last-in, first-out (LIFO)

Under the LIFO method using a perpetual system, the costs of the most recent purchases before each sale are allocated to the units sold. Therefore, the cost of sales on 10 September consists of all the units from the 24 August and 15 April purchases and 50 of the units in beginning inventory. The ending inventory on a LIFO method is calculated in figure 5.19.

FIGURE 5.19 Perpetual system — LIFO

Date	Purchases	Sales	Balance
Jan. 1			(100 @ $10) $1 000
Apr. 15	(200 @ $11) $2 200		(100 @ $10) ⎫ $3 200 (200 @ $11) ⎭
Aug. 24	(300 @ $12) $3 600		(100 @ $10) ⎫ (200 @ $11) ⎬ $6 800 (300 @ $12) ⎭
Sept. 10		(300 @ $12) ⎫ (200 @ $11) ⎬ $6 300 (50 @ $10) ⎭	(50 @ $10)
Nov. 27	(400 @ $13) $5 200		(50 @ $10) ⎫ (50 @ $10) ⎬ $5 700 (400 @ $13) ⎭

The use of LIFO in a perpetual system will usually produce cost allocations that differ from using LIFO in a periodic system. In a perpetual system, the latest units purchased *before each sale* are allocated to cost of sales. In contrast, in a periodic system, the latest units purchased *during the period* are allocated to cost of sales. Costs are allocated to goods sold, commencing with the most *recent* purchases and working backwards to the earlier purchases, irrespective of whether individual purchase transactions predate individual sales transactions. Thus, when a purchase is made after the last sale, the LIFO periodic system will apply costs from this purchase to the previous sale. See figure 5.11 where the proof shows the cost of the 400 units at $13 purchased on 27 November applied to the sale of 550 units on 10 September.

As shown above under the LIFO perpetual system, the costs of the 400 units at $13 purchased on 27 November are all applied to the ending inventory.

The ending inventory in this LIFO perpetual example is $5700 and cost of sales is $6300, as compared with the LIFO periodic example where the ending inventory is $5000 and cost of sales is $7000.

Average cost

The average cost method in a perpetual inventory system is called the **moving weighted average method**. Under this method a new weighted average unit cost is calculated after each purchase. The average cost is calculated by dividing the cost of goods available for sale by the units on hand. The average cost is then applied to (1) the units sold, to determine the cost of sales, and (2) the remaining units on hand, to determine the ending inventory amount. The application of the average cost method by Dubbo Electronics is shown in figure 5.20.

FIGURE 5.20 Perpetual system — average cost method

Date	Purchases	Sales	Balance
Jan. 1			(100 @ $10) $1 000
Apr. 15	(200 @ $11) $2 200		(300 @ $10.67) $3 200
Aug. 24	(300 @ $12) $3 600		(600 @ $11.33) $6 800
Sept. 10		(550 @ $11.33) $6 233	(50 @ $11.33) $ 567
Nov. 27	(400 @ $13) $5 200		(450 @ $12.82) $5 767

As indicated previously, a new average is calculated each time a purchase is made. On 15 April, after 200 units are purchased for $2200, a total of 300 units costing $3200 ($1000 + $2200) are on hand. The average unit cost is $10.67 ($3200 ÷ 300). On 24 August, after 300 units are purchased for $3600, a total of 600 units costing $6800 ($1000 + $2200 + $3600) are on hand at an average cost per unit of $11.33 ($6800 ÷ 600). This unit cost of $11.33 is used in costing sales until another purchase is made, when a new unit cost is calculated. Accordingly, the unit cost of the 550 units sold on 10 September is $11.33, and the total cost of sales is $6233. On 27 November, following the purchase of 400 units for $5200, there are 450 units on hand costing $5767 ($567 + $5200) with a new average cost of $12.82 ($5767 ÷ 450).

This moving average cost under the perpetual inventory system should be compared with figure 5.13 showing the weighted average method under a periodic inventory system.

Demonstration problem for section 5.9

The demonstration problem revolves around the New Zealand Souvenir Shop Pty Ltd which uses a perpetual inventory system. The New Zealand Souvenir Shop Pty Ltd has the following inventory, purchases and sales data for the month of March. Later in the chapter (in the end-of-chapter section) this problem will then show cost of sales calculations for the New Zealand Souvenir Shop assuming it uses the periodic system. (*Note:* It will have the same inventory, purchases and sales data for the month of March as shown here.)

Inventory, March 1	200 units @ $4.00	$ 800
Purchases		
March 10	500 units @ $4.50	2 250
March 20	400 units @ $4.75	1 900
March 30	300 units @ $5.00	1 500
Sales		
March 15	500 units	
March 25	400 units	

The physical inventory count on 31 March shows 500 units on hand.

Required

Under a *perpetual inventory system*, determine the cost of inventory on hand at 31 March and the cost of sales for March under the (a) first-in, first-out (FIFO) method, (b) last-in, first-out (LIFO) method, and (c) average cost method.

PROBLEM-SOLVING STRATEGIES

1. For FIFO, the first costs are allocated to cost of sales.
2. For LIFO, the most recent costs are allocated to cost of sales.
3. For average costs, use a weighted average for periodic and a moving weighted average for perpetual.
4. Remember, the costs allocated to ending inventory can be proved.
5. Total purchases are the same under all three cost flow methods.

SOLUTION TO DEMONSTRATION PROBLEM

The cost of goods available for sale is $6450:

Inventory	200 units @ $4.00	$ 800
Purchases		
March 10	500 units @ $4.50	2 250
March 20	400 units @ $4.75	1 900
March 30	300 units @ $5.00	1 500
Total cost of goods available for sale	1 400 units	$6 450

Under a *perpetual inventory system*, the cost of sales under each cost flow method is as follows:

FIFO method

Date	Purchases	Sales	Balance
March 1			(200 @ $4.00) $ 800
March 10	(500 @ $4.50) $2 250		(200 @ $4.00) ⎱ $3 050 (500 @ $4.50) ⎰
March 15		(200 @ $4.00) ⎱ $2 150 (300 @ $4.50) ⎰	(200 @ $4.50) $ 900
March 20	(400 @ $4.75) $1 900		(200 @ $4.50) ⎱ $2 800 (400 @ $4.75) ⎰
March 25		(200 @ $4.50) ⎱ $1 850 (200 @ $4.75) ⎰	(200 @ $4.75) $ 950
March 30	(300 @ $5.00) $1 500		(200 @ $4.75) ⎱ $2 450 (300 @ $5.00) ⎰

Ending inventory $2 450. Cost of sales: $6 450 − $2 450 = $4 000
         500 units   900 units

Helpful hint: The physical number of units remains the same whichever inventory cost flow method is used. It is the inventory cost ($) that is different.

LIFO method

Date	Purchases	Sales	Balance
March 1			(200 @ $4.00) $ 800
March 10	(500 @ $4.50) $2 250		(200 @ $4.00) ⎱ $3 050 (500 @ $4.50) ⎰
March 15		(500 @ $4.50) $2 250	(200 @ $4.00) $ 800
March 20	(400 @ $4.75) $1 900		(200 @ $4.00) ⎱ $2 700 (400 @ $4.75) ⎰
March 25		(400 @ $4.75) $1 900	(200 @ $4.00) $ 800
March 30	(300 @ $5.00) $1 500		(200 @ $4.00) ⎱ $2 300 (300 @ $5.00) ⎰

Ending inventory $2 300. Cost of sales: $6 450 − $2 300 = $4 150
         500 units   900 units

Moving average cost method

Date	Purchases	Sales	Balance
March 1			(200 @ $4.00) $ 800
March 10	(500 @ $4.50) $2 250		(700 @ $4.357) $3 050
March 15		(500 @ $4.357) $2 179	(200 @ $4.357) $ 871
March 20	(400 @ $4.75) $1 900		(600 @ $4.618) $2 771
March 25		(400 @ $4.618) $1 847	(200 @ $4.618) $ 924
March 30	(300 @ $5.00) $1 500		(500 @ $4.848) $2 424

Ending inventory $2 424. Cost of sales: $6 450 − $2 424 = $4 026
         500 units   900 units

5.10 Inventory errors

LEARNING OBJECTIVE 5.10 Indicate the effects of inventory errors on the financial statements.

Unfortunately, errors occasionally occur in accounting for inventory. In some cases, errors are caused by failure to count or price the inventory correctly. In other cases, errors occur because proper recognition is not given to the transfer of legal title to goods that are in transit. When errors occur, they affect both the statement of profit or loss and statement of financial position.

Effects on profit

As you know, both the beginning and ending inventories appear in the statement of profit or loss. The ending inventory of one period automatically becomes the beginning inventory of the next period. Inventory errors affect the determination of cost of sales and profit in two periods.

The effects on cost of sales can be determined by entering incorrect data in the formula in figure 5.21 and then substituting the correct data.

| **FIGURE 5.21** | Formula for cost of sales |

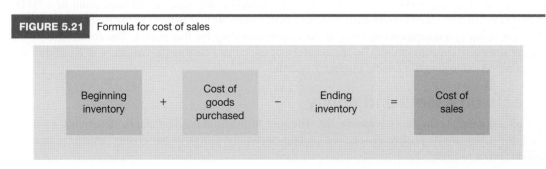

If beginning inventory is understated, cost of sales will be understated. On the other hand, understating ending inventory will overstate cost of sales. The effects of inventory errors on the current year's statement of profit or loss are shown in table 5.2.

TABLE 5.2   **Effects of inventory errors on current year's statement of profit or loss**

Inventory error	Cost of sales	Profit
Understate beginning inventory	Understated	Overstated
Overstate beginning inventory	Overstated	Understated
Understate ending inventory	Overstated	Understated
Overstate ending inventory	Understated	Overstated

An error in the ending inventory of the current period will have a reverse effect on profit of the next accounting period. This is shown in figure 5.22. Note that the understatement of ending inventory in 2018 results in an understatement of beginning inventory in 2019 and an overstatement of profit in 2019.

FIGURE 5.22   Effects of inventory errors on two years' statements of profit or loss

SAMPLE COMPANY
Statement of profit or loss (condensed)

	2018			2019		
	Incorrect	Correct		Incorrect	Correct	
Sales		$80 000	$80 000		$90 000	$90 000
Beginning inventory	$20 000	$20 000		$12 000	$15 000	
Cost of goods purchased	40 000	40 000		68 000	68 000	
Cost of goods available for sale	60 000	60 000		80 000	83 000	
Ending inventory	12 000	15 000		23 000	23 000	
Cost of sales		48 000	45 000		57 000	60 000
Gross profit		32 000	35 000		33 000	30 000
Operating expenses		10 000	10 000		20 000	20 000
Profit		$22 000	$25 000		$13 000	$10 000

$(3 000)
Profit
understated

$3 000
Profit
overstated

The errors cancel. Thus the combined total profit for the
2-year period is correct, but profit in each period is incorrect.

Over the two years, total profit is correct because the errors offset each other. Notice that total profit using incorrect data is $35 000 ($22 000 + $13 000), which is the same as the total profit of $35 000 ($25 000 + $10 000) using correct data. Also note in this example that an error in the beginning inventory does not result in a corresponding error in the ending inventory for that period. The correctness of the ending inventory depends entirely on the accuracy of taking and costing the inventory at the end of the reporting period under the periodic inventory system.

Effects on assets and equity

The effect of ending inventory errors on the statement of financial position can be determined by using the basic accounting equation: Assets = Liabilities + Equity. Errors in the ending inventory have the effects shown in table 5.3.

TABLE 5.3	Effects of ending inventory errors on the statement of financial position			
Ending inventory error	Assets	Liabilities	Equity	
Overstated	Overstated	No effect	Overstated	
Understated	Understated	No effect	Understated	

The effect of an error in ending inventory on the subsequent period was shown in figure 5.22. Recall that if the error is not discovered and corrected, the combined total profit for the two periods is correct. Thus, total equity (shareholders' equity) reported on the statement of financial position at the end of 2019 will also be correct.

5.11 Closing entries for merchandising entities

LEARNING OBJECTIVE 5.11 Record the closing entries for merchandising entities.

In chapter 3 we demonstrated the closing entries for a service entity. In this section we briefly explain the closing entries for merchandising entities by illustrating the journal entries for both the perpetual and periodic inventory methods.

Perpetual inventory method

You might recall that all temporary accounts (revenue, expense and drawings/dividends accounts) are closed to the profit or loss summary at the end of the period. If you cannot recall this process clearly, please review the text in section 3.6 before reading further. While some of the closing entries are the same for both types of entity, merchandising entities have extra accounts such as sales returns and allowances and cost of sales that need to be closed at the end of the period. Further, merchandising entities employing the perpetual method for recording inventory transactions have different accounts to entities employing the periodic method. The difference between the two methods is evident in the statements of profit or loss and closing entries shown in figure 5.23.

FIGURE 5.23	Perpetual inventory method

Statement of profit or loss (extract) Perpetual inventory method	
Sales revenue	$85 000
Less: Sales returns and allowances	5 000
Net sales revenue	80 000
Less: Cost of sales	57 600
Gross profit	**$22 400**

Under the perpetual inventory method, the various temporary credit and debit accounts are closed at the end of the period as illustrated below.

Dr Sales revenue	85 000	
Cr Profit or loss summary		85 000
(To close various credit accounts — sales revenue — to the profit or loss summary account)		

$$A \quad = \quad L \quad + \quad E$$
$$-85\,000$$
$$+85\,000$$

Dr Profit or loss summary		62 600	
Cr Cost of sales			57 600
Cr Sales returns and allowances			5 000
(To close various debit accounts — cost of sales and sales returns & allowances — to the profit or loss summary)			

A	=	L	+	E
				−62 600
				+57 600
				+5 000

Profit or loss summary

		Closing entry (various credit accounts)	85 000
Closing entry (various debit accounts)	62 600		

Balance = 22 400 (Gross profit)

Periodic inventory method

The closing process using the periodic method is not as simple as for the perpetual method, as there is no one cost of sales account that can be closed off to the profit or loss summary account. As shown in figure 5.24, cost of sales is calculated using a number of different accounts including: beginning inventory *plus* purchases *plus* freight-in *minus* ending inventory *minus* purchase returns *equals* cost of sales.

FIGURE 5.24	Periodic inventory method

Statement of profit or loss (extract) Periodic inventory method			
Sales revenue			$85 000
Less: Sales returns and allowances			5 000
Net sales revenue			80 000
COST OF SALES			
Cost of beginning inventory		$14 000	
Add: Cost of purchases	$60 000		
Freight-in	600		
	60 600		
Less: Purchases returns and allowances	1 000		
Cost of net purchases		59 600	
Cost of goods available for sale		73 600	
Less: Cost of ending inventory		16 000	
Cost of sales			57 600
Gross profit			**$22 400**

So, in *essence*, the following accounts are closed off to the profit or loss summary.

Profit or loss summary

		Sales	85 000
Sales returns	5 000		
Beginning inventory	14 000		
Purchases	60 000	Purchase returns	1 000
Freight-in	600	Ending inventory	16 000

Balance = 22 400 (Gross profit)

However, the amounts are *not* entered individually in the profit or loss summary, but in total as shown in the closing general journal entries below.

Dr Profit or loss summary	79 600	
Cr Beginning inventory		14 000
Cr Sales returns and allowances		5 000
Cr Purchases		60 000
Cr Freight-in		600
(To close various debit accounts to the profit or loss summary)		

$$
\begin{array}{ccccc}
A & = & L & + & E \\
-14\,000 & & & & -79\,600 \\
& & & & +5\,000 \\
& & & & +60\,000 \\
& & & & +600
\end{array}
$$

Dr Ending inventory	16 000	
Dr Sales	85 000	
Dr Purchase returns and allowances	1 000	
Cr Profit or loss summary		102 000
(To close various credit accounts to the profit or loss summary)		

$$
\begin{array}{ccccc}
A & = & L & + & E \\
+16\,000 & & & & -85\,000 \\
& & & & -1\,000 \\
& & & & +102\,000
\end{array}
$$

Profit or loss summary

Closing entry		Closing entry	
(various debit accounts)	79 600	(various credit accounts)	102 000

Balance = 22 400 (Gross profit)

After closing entries have been posted to the general ledger, balances in the various debit and credit accounts are zero and the balance in the profit or loss summary account represents the gross profit (i.e. the net effect of transferring all of the balances of these accounts to the profit or loss summary). The remaining temporary accounts such as interest income or rent expense must also be closed, as illustrated in chapter 3.

Worksheet

You may recall that we introduced the worksheet in section 3.8. Please refer to this section if you need to refresh your memory. Entering the closing entries on a worksheet before preparing journal entries can be helpful. To illustrate, we have entered the closing entries journalised above onto the worksheet (extract) in figure 5.25.

FIGURE 5.25 Worksheet (extract) closing entries for merchandising organisations

Perpetual account	Adjusted trial balance Dr	Adjusted trial balance Cr	Closing entries Dr	Closing entries Cr	Post-closing trial balance Dr	Post-closing trial balance Cr
Sales revenue		85 000	85 000			—
Cost of sales	57 600			57 600	—	
Sales returns and allowances	5 000			5 000	—	
Sales revenue		85 000	85 000			—

	Adjusted trial balance		Closing entries		Post-closing trial balance	
Periodic account	Dr	Cr	Dr	Cr	Dr	Cr
Sales returns and allowances	5 000			5 000	—	
Inventory	14 000		16 000	14 000	16 000	
Purchases	60 000			60 000	—	
Freight-in	600			600	—	
Purchase returns and allowances		1 000	1 000			—

It is important to observe that under the periodic system the inventory account is both credited and debited. The opening balance of Inventory is credited to clear this old balance and the closing balance is debited to ensure the correct closing inventory is recorded in the inventory general ledger account and then subsequently transferred to the financial statements.

USING THE DECISION-MAKING TOOLKIT

Conway Ltd is a leading manufacturing company and supplier of building products. Figures for inventory from the 2019 annual report for Conway Ltd are shown below.

CONWAY LTD
Notes to the financial statements

NOTE 10. INVENTORIES
The components of inventories are summarised at 30 June as follows (in millions):

	2019	2018
Current		
Raw and process materials and stores	$ 41.1	$ 41.4
Work in progress	6.5	6.3
Finished goods	87.8	88.4
Land held for sale	26.5	20.5
Total current inventories	$161.9	$156.6

In the note on the significant accounting policies of the 2019 annual report for Conway Ltd, the section on inventories specifies that the inventories are valued at the lower of cost and net realisable value and that the most appropriate valuation method is used for each class of inventory. The majority of Conway Ltd's inventory has been valued using either the first-in-first-out basis or the average cost basis.
Some additional facts are ($ millions):

	2019	2018
Current liabilities	$212.6	$204.5
Current assets	318.1	319.5
Cost of sales	618.1	619.8
Sales revenue	873.3	841.2

Required
Answer the following questions:
(a) Why does Conway Ltd report its inventory in four components?
(b) Why might Conway Ltd use more than one method to account for its inventory?
(c) Calculate each of the following ratios and analyse the changes from 2019 to 2018.
　　1. Inventory turnover and average days in inventory. (*Hint:* When calculating average inventory, use *only* the finished goods component of inventory. The finished goods inventory for 2017 was $92.3 million.)
　　2. Current ratio.
　　3. Gross profit ratio.

Solution

(a) Conway Ltd is a manufacturer, so it purchases and produces raw materials and makes them into finished products. At the end of each period, it has some goods that have been started but are not yet complete, referred to as work in process. By reporting components of inventory, Conway reveals important information about its inventory position. For example, if amounts of raw materials have increased significantly compared with the previous year, we might assume the entity is planning to step up production. On the other hand, if levels of finished goods have increased relative to last year and raw materials have declined, we might conclude that sales are slowing down — that the entity has too much inventory on hand and is cutting back production.

(b) Entities are free to choose different cost flow assumptions for different types of inventory. An entity might choose to use FIFO for a class of inventory (e.g. perishable item like sugar) and average cost for another (e.g. roof tiles) due to the different nature of the inventory.

(c)

Ratio	2019	2018
1. Inventory turnover $= \dfrac{\text{Cost of sales}}{\text{Average inventory}}$	$\dfrac{\$618.1}{(\$87.8 + \$88.4)/2}$ $= 7.02$ times	$\dfrac{\$619.8}{(\$88.4 + \$92.3)/2}$ $= 6.86$ times
Days in inventory $= \dfrac{\text{365 days}}{\text{Inventory turnover}}$	$\dfrac{365 \text{ days}}{7.02} = 52$ days	$\dfrac{365 \text{ days}}{6.86} = 53$ days

Conway Ltd's inventory turnover improved from 6.86 times in 2018 to 7.02 times in 2019. Consequently, the average time inventory was held by Conway decreased from 53 days in 2018 to 52 days in 2019. This was due to an increase in sales and lower levels of inventory held in 2019.

	2019	2018
2. Current ratio $= \dfrac{\text{Current assets}}{\text{Current liabilities}}$	$\dfrac{\$318.1}{\$212.6} = 1.5$	$\dfrac{\$319.5}{\$204.5} = 1.56$

Conway Ltd's current ratio of 1.56 in 2018 indicates it had $1.56 in current assets to cover each dollar of current liabilities. The decrease in the current ratio to 1.5 in 2019 was attributed to a decrease in current assets and an increase in current liabilities. The overall liquidity of Conway has weakened slightly; however, these results are still within the acceptable range of 1:1 for most industries.

	2019	2018
3. Gross profit ratio $= \dfrac{\text{Sales} - \text{Cost of sales}}{\text{Sales}}$	$\dfrac{\$873.3 - \$618.1}{\$873.3} = 29\%$	$\dfrac{\$841.2 - \$619.8}{\$841.2} = 26\%$

Conway's gross profit margin showed an increase from 26% in 2018 to 29% in 2019. This improvement was due to a 4% increase in sales revenue with only a marginal increase in the cost of sales. More efficient management of inventory resulted in lower levels of inventory held.

SUMMARY

5.1 Record purchases and sales of inventory under a periodic inventory system.
In the records of the purchaser, entries are required for (a) cash and credit purchases, (b) purchase returns and allowances, (c) purchase discounts and (d) freight costs. In the records of the seller, entries are required for (a) cash and credit sales, (b) sales returns and allowances and (c) sales discounts.

5.2 Determine cost of sales under a periodic inventory system.
The steps in determining cost of sales are (a) recording the purchase of inventory, (b) determining the cost of goods purchased and (c) determining the cost of goods on hand at the beginning and end of the accounting period.

5.3 Describe the steps in determining inventory quantities.
The steps are (1) counting the physical inventory of goods on hand and (2) determining the status and quantity of goods in transit or on consignment.

5.4 Identify the unique features of the statement of profit or loss for a merchandising business under a periodic inventory system.
The statement of profit or loss for a merchandising business contains three features not found in a service business's statement of profit or loss: sales revenue, cost of sales, and a gross profit line. The cost of sales section generally shows more detail under a periodic than a perpetual inventory system by reporting beginning and ending inventories, net purchases and total goods available for sale.

5.5 Explain the basis of accounting for inventories and apply the inventory cost flow methods under a periodic inventory system.
The main basis of accounting for inventories is cost. Cost includes all expenditures necessary to acquire goods and place them in condition ready for sale. Cost of goods available for sale includes (a) cost of beginning inventory and (b) cost of goods purchased. The inventory cost flow methods are: specific identification and three assumed cost flow methods — FIFO, LIFO and average cost.

5.6 Explain the financial statement effects of each of the inventory cost flow methods.
The cost of goods available for sale may be allocated to cost of sales and ending inventory by specific identification or by a method based on an assumed cost flow. When prices are rising, the first-in, first-out (FIFO) method results in lower cost of sales and higher profit than the average cost and the last-in, first-out (LIFO) methods. The reverse is true when prices are falling. In the statement of financial position, FIFO results in an ending inventory that is closest to current purchase cost, whereas the inventory under LIFO is the furthest from current purchase cost.

5.7 Explain the lower of cost and net realisable value basis of accounting for inventories.
The lower of cost and net realisable value (LCNRV) basis means that when the net realisable value of inventory is less than cost, the inventory should be reported at net realisable value. Under LCNRV, the loss is recognised in the period in which the decline in realisable value occurs.

5.8 Calculate and interpret inventory turnover.
Inventory turnover is calculated as cost of sales divided by average inventory. It can be converted to average days in inventory by dividing 365 days by the inventory turnover. A higher turnover or lower average days in inventory suggests that management is efficient in managing and selling its inventory.

5.9 Apply the inventory cost flow methods to perpetual inventory records.
Under FIFO, the cost of the earliest goods on hand before each sale is charged to cost of sales. Under LIFO, the cost of the most recent purchases before sale is charged to cost of sales. Under the average cost method, a new average cost is calculated after each purchase.

5.10 Indicate the effects of inventory errors on the financial statements.
In the statement of profit or loss of the current year: (a) an error in beginning inventory will have the opposite effect on profit (overstatement of inventory results in understatement of profit and vice versa) and

(b) an error in ending inventory will have a similar effect on profit (e.g. overstatement of inventory results in overstatement of profit). If ending inventory errors are not detected and corrected in the following period, their effect on profit for that period is reversed, and total profit for the two years will be correct. In the statement of financial position, ending inventory errors will have the same effect on total assets and total equity (shareholders' equity) and no effect on liabilities.

5.11 Record the closing entries for merchandising entities.

One purpose of closing entries is to transfer the results of the operations for the year to retained earnings and render all temporary account balances zero. The closing entries for merchandising entities are similar to those for service entities; however, merchandising entities have extra accounts related to the sale of inventory, such as sales returns and allowances and cost of sales, that need to be closed at the end of the period.

DECISION-MAKING TOOLKIT — A SUMMARY

DECISION-MAKING TOOLKIT

Decision/issue	Info needed for analysis	Tool or technique to use for decision	How to evaluate results to make decision
How long is an item held in inventory?	Cost of sales; beginning and ending inventory	$\text{Inventory turnover} = \dfrac{\text{Cost of sales}}{\text{Average inventory}}$ $\text{Days in inventory} = \dfrac{365 \text{ days}}{\text{Inventory turnover}}$	A higher inventory turnover or lower average days in inventory suggests that the entity is efficient in managing and selling its inventory.

KEY TERMS

average cost method An inventory costing method that uses the weighted average unit cost to allocate the cost of goods available for sale to ending inventory and cost of sales.

consigned goods Goods held for sale by one party (the consignee) although ownership of the goods is retained by another party (the consignor).

cost of goods available for sale The sum of the beginning inventory and the cost of goods purchased.

cost of goods purchased The sum of net purchases and freight-in.

cost of sales (COS) The total cost of inventories sold during the period.

days in inventory Measure of the average number of days inventory is held; calculated as 365 divided by the inventory turnover.

finished goods inventory Manufactured items that are completed and ready for sale.

first-in, first-out (FIFO) method An inventory costing method which assumes that the costs of the earliest goods purchased are the first to be recognised as cost of sales.

FOB destination Freight terms indicating that the goods are placed free on board the carrier by the seller, but the seller pays the freight cost; goods belong to the seller while in transit.

FOB shipping point Freight terms indicating that the goods are placed free on board the carrier by the seller, but the buyer pays the freight cost; goods belong to the buyer while in transit.

goods in transit Goods moving between the buyer and the seller on board a truck, train, ship or plane.

inventory turnover A measure of the liquidity of inventory, calculated as cost of sales divided by average inventory.

last-in, first-out (LIFO) method An inventory costing method that assumes that the costs of the latest units purchased are the first to be allocated to cost of sales.

lower of cost and net realisable value (LCNRV) basis A basis whereby inventory is stated at the lower of cost and net realisable value.

moving weighted average method An inventory costing method used in a perpetual inventory system, where a moving weighted average unit cost is used to allocate the cost of goods available for sale to ending inventory and cost of sales.

net purchases Purchases less purchase returns and allowances.

net realisable value (NRV) IAS 2/AASB 102 defines net realisable value as the estimated selling price in the ordinary course of business less the estimated costs of completion and the estimated costs necessary to make the sale.

periodic inventory system An inventory system in which detailed records are not maintained and the cost of sales and inventory on hand is determined only at the end of an accounting period.

purchase returns and allowances account Account used to accumulate the cost of all inventory returned to suppliers.

purchases account Account used to accumulate the cost of all inventory purchased for resale during the period.

raw materials Materials that will be used in production but have not yet been placed in production.

retail inventory method A method used to estimate the ending inventory value based on the relationship of cost to retail prices.

specific identification method An inventory costing method that uses actual physical flow of inventory to determine cost of sales; items still in inventory are specifically costed to arrive at the total cost of the ending inventory.

weighted average unit cost Average cost that is weighted by the number of units purchased at each unit cost.

work in process That portion of manufactured inventory that has begun the production process but is not yet complete.

DEMONSTRATION PROBLEM

The New Zealand Souvenir Shop Pty Ltd has the following inventory, purchases and sales data for the month of March:

Inventory, March 1	200 units @ $4.00	$ 800
Purchases		
March 10	500 units @ $4.50	2 250
March 20	400 units @ $4.75	1 900
March 30	300 units @ $5.00	1 500
Sales		
March 15	500 units	
March 25	400 units	

The physical inventory count on 31 March shows 500 units on hand.

Required

Under a *periodic inventory system*, determine the cost of inventory on hand at 31 March and the cost of sales for March under (a) the first-in, first-out (FIFO) method, (b) the last-in, first-out (LIFO) method, and (c) the average cost method.

PROBLEM-SOLVING STRATEGIES

1. For FIFO, the latest costs are allocated to inventory.
2. For LIFO, the earliest costs are allocated to inventory.
3. For average costs, use a weighted average.
4. Remember, the costs allocated to cost of sales can be proved.
5. Total purchases are the same under all three cost flow methods.

SOLUTION TO DEMONSTRATION PROBLEM

The cost of goods available for sale is $6450:

Inventory	200 units @ $4.00	$ 800
Purchases		
March 10	500 units @ $4.50	2 250
March 20	400 units @ $4.75	1 900
March 30	300 units @ $5.00	1 500
Total cost of goods available for sale	1 400 units	$6 450

Helpful hint: The physical number of units remains the same whichever inventory cost flow method is used. It is the inventory cost ($) that is different.

(a)

FIFO method

Ending inventory:

Date	Units	Unit cost	Total cost
Mar. 30	300	$5.00	$1 500
Mar. 20	200	4.75	950
	500		2 450

Cost of sales: $6 450 − $2 450 = $4 000
900 units

(b)

LIFO method

Ending inventory:

Date	Units	Unit cost	Total cost
Mar. 1	200	$4.00	$ 800
Mar. 10	300	4.50	1 350
	500		2 150

Cost of sales: $6 450 − $2 150 = $4 300
900 units

(c)

Average cost method

Weighted average unit cost: $6 450 ÷ 1 400 = $4.607
Ending inventory: 500 × $4.607 = $2 303.50
Cost of sales: $6 450 − $2 303.50 = $4 146.50
900 units

SELF-STUDY QUESTIONS

5.1 When goods are purchased for resale by a business using a periodic inventory system: **LO1**
    (a) purchases on account are debited to inventory.
    (b) purchases on account are debited to purchases.
    (c) purchase returns are debited to purchase returns and allowances.
    (d) freight costs are debited to purchases.

5.2 In determining cost of sales: **LO2**
   (a) purchase discounts are deducted from net purchases.
   (b) freight-out is added to net purchases.
   (c) purchase returns and allowances are deducted from net purchases.
   (d) freight-in is added to net purchases.

5.3 If beginning inventory is $60 000, cost of goods purchased is $380 000, and ending inventory is $50 000, what is cost of sales?   **LO2**
   (a) $390 000.
   (b) $370 000.
   (c) $330 000.
   (d) $420 000.

5.4 Which of the following should not be included in the physical inventory of an entity?   **LO3**
   (a) Goods held on consignment from another entity.
   (b) Goods shipped on consignment to another entity.
   (c) Goods in transit from another entity shipped FOB shipping point.
   (d) All of the above should be included.

5.5 Lim Ltd has the following units and costs: **LO5**

	Units	Unit cost
Inventory, 1 Jan.	8 000	$11
Purchase, 19 June	13 000	12
Purchase, 8 Nov.	5 000	13

If 9000 units are on hand at 31 December, what is the cost of the ending inventory under FIFO?
   (a) $99 000.
   (b) $108 000.
   (c) $113 000.
   (d) $117 000.

5.6 From the data in question 5.5, what is the cost of the ending inventory under LIFO?   **LO5**
   (a) $113 000.
   (b) $108 000.
   (c) $99 000.
   (d) $100 000.

5.7 In periods of rising prices, LIFO will produce: **LO6**
   (a) higher profit than FIFO.
   (b) the same profit as FIFO.
   (c) lower profit than FIFO.
   (d) higher profit than average costing.

5.8 Considerations that affect the selection of an inventory costing method include: **LO6**
   (a) nature of the inventory (e.g. perishable or non-perishable).
   (b) statement of financial position effects.
   (c) statement of profit or loss effects.
   (d) all of the above.

5.9 Which of the following events could result in the cost of an item of inventory being higher than its net realisable value?   **LO7**
   (a) Inventory obsolescence.
   (b) A fall in the demand for inventory.
   (c) Water or fire damage to inventory.
   (d) All of the above.

5.10 Which of these would cause inventory turnover to increase the most?　　　　**LO8**

(a) Increasing the amount of inventory on hand.

(b) Keeping the amount of inventory on hand constant but increasing sales.

(c) Keeping the amount of inventory on hand constant but decreasing sales.

(d) Decreasing the amount of inventory on hand and increasing sales.

5.11 In a perpetual inventory system:　　　　**LO9**

(a) LIFO cost of sales will be the same as in a periodic inventory system.

(b) average costs are based entirely on unit-cost simple averages.

(c) a new average is calculated under the average cost method after each sale.

(d) FIFO cost of sales will be the same as in a periodic inventory system.

5.12 Neville Pty Ltd's ending inventory is understated by $4000. The effects of this error on the current year's cost of sales and profit, respectively, are:　　　　**LO10**

(a) understated and overstated.

(b) overstated and understated.

(c) overstated and overstated.

(d) understated and understated.

5.13 Firth Pty Ltd's ending inventory is overstated by $10 000. The effect on the current year's assets, liabilities and equity respectively, are:　　　　**LO10**

(a) overstated, no effect and overstated.

(b) understated, no effect and overstated.

(c) overstated, no effect and understated.

(d) overstated, overstated and overstated.

5.14 Which of the following statements is true?　　　　**LO11**

(a) Using a periodic method, the cost of sales account is closed to the profit or loss summary at the end of the accounting period with a credit to the cost of sales account.

(b) Using a perpetual method, the cost of sales account is closed to the profit or loss summary at the end of the accounting period with a credit to the cost of sales account.

(c) Using a periodic method, the cost of sales account is closed to the profit or loss summary at the end of the accounting period with a debit to the cost of sales account.

(d) Using a perpetual method, the cost of sales account is closed to the profit or loss summary at the end of the accounting period with a debit to the cost of sales account.

5.15 Using a periodic inventory system, Cost of Sales is calculated as follows:　　　　**LO11**

(a) Beginning inventory + purchases + freight-in + purchase returns and allowances − ending inventory.

(b) Beginning inventory + purchases − freight-in − purchase returns and allowances − ending inventory.

(c) Beginning inventory − purchases + freight-in − purchase returns and allowances − ending inventory.

(d) Beginning inventory + purchases + freight-in − purchase returns and allowances − ending inventory.

QUESTIONS

5.1 Goods costing $1600 are purchased on account on 18 July with credit terms of 2/7, n/30. On 19 July a $100 credit memo is received from the supplier for damaged goods. Give the journal entry on 24 July to record payment of the balance due within the discount period assuming a periodic inventory system.

5.2 Assuming a periodic inventory system, identify the item designated by the letter X in the following:

   (a) Purchases − X = Net purchases.

   (b) Beginning inventory + X = Cost of goods available for sale.

   (c) Cost of goods available for sale − Cost of sales = X.

5.3 (a) Shields Ltd ships inventory to Francine Ltd on 30 June. The inventory reaches the buyer on 5 July. Indicate the terms of sale that will result in the goods being included in (1) Shields Ltd's 30 June inventory and (2) Francine Ltd's 30 June inventory.

   (b) Under what circumstances should Shields Ltd include consigned goods in its inventory?

5.4 What is the main basis of accounting for inventories? What is the major objective in accounting for inventories?

5.5 'The selection of an inventory cost flow method is a decision made by accountants.' Do you agree? Explain. Once a method has been selected, what accounting requirement applies?

5.6 Which assumed inventory cost flow method:

   (a) usually parallels the actual physical flow of inventory?

   (b) assumes that goods available for sale during an accounting period are similar in nature?

   (c) assumes that the latest units purchased are the first to be sold?

5.7 In a period of decreasing prices, the inventory reported in Lee Ltd's statement of financial position is close to the current cost of the inventory, whereas Lam Ltd's inventory is considerably above its current cost. Identify the inventory cost flow method used by each entity.

5.8 Nancy Drews is studying for the next accounting examination. What should Nancy know about (a) departing from the cost basis of accounting for inventories and (b) the meaning of net realisable value in relation to accounting for inventories?

5.9 'When perpetual inventory records are kept, the results under the FIFO and LIFO methods are the same as they would be in a periodic inventory system.' Do you agree? Explain.

5.10 Peta Ltd discovers in 2020 that its ending inventory at 30 June 2019 was $5000 understated. What effect will this error have on (a) 2019 profit, (b) 2020 profit, and (c) the combined profit for the 2 years?

BRIEF EXERCISES

BE5.1 **Identify inventory systems and inventory cost flow methods.**   **LO1, 5**

Suggest the most appropriate inventory system and inventory cost flow method for each of the following businesses and products:

   (a) Textbook sales in the co-op bookshop.

   (b) Petrol sales in the local petrol station.

   (c) Antique mirror sales in an antique furniture shop.

   (d) Bottled juice in a fruit bar.

   (e) Necklace sales in a jewellery shop.

BE5.2 **Calculate cost of sales and gross profit.**   **LO2**

Assume that Jess Ltd uses a periodic inventory system and has the following account balances: Beginning inventory $45 000, Ending inventory $67 500, Sales $472 500, Purchases $300 000, Purchase returns $14 250, and Freight-in $12 000. Determine the amounts to be reported for cost of net purchases, cost of sales and gross profit.

BE5.3 **Calculate ending inventory using FIFO and LIFO.**   **LO5**

In its first month of operations, Cushion Ltd made three purchases of inventory in the following sequence: (1) 300 units at $12, (2) 400 units at $14, and (3) 500 units at $18. Assuming there are 400 units on hand, calculate the cost of the ending inventory under (a) the FIFO method and (b) the LIFO method. Cushion Ltd uses a periodic inventory system.

BE5.4 **Determine the lower of cost and net realisable value basis of accounting for inventories.** **LO7**

Olynda Garden Centre accumulates the following data at 30 June:

Inventory categories	Cost data	Net realisable value
Native trees	$16 800	$14 280
Potting mix	12 600	13 300
Garden statues	19 600	17 920

Calculate the lower of cost and net realisable value for Olynda's total inventory.

BE5.5 **Calculate inventory turnover and days in inventory.** **LO8**

At 30 June, the following information (in thousands) was available for sunglasses manufacturer, Che Eyewear Ltd: Ending inventory $53 322; Beginning inventory $39 300; Cost of sales $129 201; Sales revenue $347 901. Calculate inventory turnover and days in inventory for Che Eyewear Ltd.

BE5.6 **Apply cost flow methods to perpetual records.** **LO9**

Harrots Department Store uses a perpetual inventory system. Data for product E2–D2 include the following purchases:

Date	Number of units	Unit price
May 7	50	$12
July 28	30	18

On 1 June Harrots sold 30 units, and on 27 August, 33 more units. Calculate the cost of sales using (1) FIFO, (2) LIFO and (3) average cost.

BE5.7 **Determine correct financial statement amount.** **LO10**

Williams Ltd reports profit of $180 000 in 2018. However, ending inventory was understated by $14 000. What is the correct profit for 2018? What effect, if any, will this error have on total assets as reported in the statement of financial position at 30 June 2018?

EXERCISES

E5.1 **Journalise purchase transactions.** **LO1**

This information relates to Peters Ltd.

1. On 5 April purchased inventory from D. Nicks Ltd for $9000, terms 2/7, n/30, FOB shipping point.
2. On 6 April paid freight costs of $450 on inventory purchased from D. Nicks Ltd.
3. On 7 April purchased equipment on account for $13 000.
4. On 8 April returned damaged inventory to D. Nicks Ltd and was granted a $1500 allowance.
5. On 9 April paid the amount due to D. Nicks Ltd in full.

Required

(a) Prepare the journal entries to record these transactions on the books of Peters Ltd using a periodic inventory system.
(b) Assume that Peters Ltd paid the balance due to D. Nicks Ltd on 4 May instead of 9 April. Prepare the journal entry to record this payment.

E5.2 **Prepare cost of sales section.** **LO2**

The trial balance of Francine Pty Ltd at the end of its financial year, 30 June 2019, includes these accounts: Beginning inventory $56 760; Purchases $469 920; Sales $627 000; Sales returns and allowances $9900; Freight-out $3300; Purchase returns and allowances $6600. The ending inventory is $85 800.

Required

Prepare the cost of sales section of the statement of profit or loss for the year ending 30 June 2019.

E5.3 Prepare cost of sales section. **LO2**

Below is a series of cost of sales sections for companies X, F, L and S.

	X	F	L	S
Beginning inventory	250	120	1 000	(j)
Purchases	1 500	1 080	(g)	43 590
Purchase returns and allowances	40	(d)	290	(k)
Net purchases	(a)	1 030	7 210	42 090
Freight-in	110	(e)	(h)	2 240
Cost of goods purchased	(b)	1 230	7 940	(l)
Cost of goods available for sale	1 820	1 350	(i)	49 530
Ending inventory	310	(f)	1 450	6 230
Cost of sales	(c)	1 230	7 490	43 300

Required

(a) Fill in the lettered blanks to complete the cost of sales sections.

(b) Explain the purpose of this exercise. (*Hint:* What is the main skill you have been developing?)

E5.4 Determine the correct inventory amount. **LO3**

Bank of Epping is considering giving Hooton Ltd a loan. Before doing so, the bank decides that further discussions with Hooton's accountant may be desirable. One area of particular concern is the inventory account, which has a year-end balance of $147 500. Discussions with the accountant reveal the following:

1. Hooton Ltd sold goods costing $17 500 to Moghul Ltd FOB shipping point on 28 June. The goods are not expected to arrive in India until 12 July. The goods were not included in the physical inventory because they were not in the warehouse.
2. The physical count of the inventory did not include goods costing $47 500 that were shipped to Hooton Ltd FOB destination on 27 June and were still in transit at year-end.
3. Hooton received goods costing $12 500 on 2 July. The goods were shipped FOB shipping point on 26 June by Cellar Ltd. The goods were not included in the physical count.
4. Hooton sold goods costing $20 000 to Sterling of Canada FOB destination on 30 June. The goods were received in Canada on 8 July. They were not included in Hooton's physical inventory.
5. Hooton received goods costing $22 000 on 2 July that were shipped FOB destination on 29 June. The shipment was a rush order that was supposed to arrive on 30 June. This purchase was included in the ending inventory of $147 500.
6. Goods costing $25 000 have been in inventory for more than 12 months and are unlikely to be sold.

Required

(a) Determine the correct inventory amount on 30 June.

(b) Why is it important for the Bank of Epping to determine the correct amount for inventory before granting a loan to Hooton Ltd?

E5.5 Prepare a statement of profit or loss. **LO4**

Presented here is information related to Djuric Ltd for the month of January 2019.

Freight-in	$ 14 300
Rent expense	
—store space	14 300
—office space	14 300
Freight-out	10 010

Salary expense	
—sales	30 030
—office	57 200
Insurance expense	17 160
Discount allowed	11 440
Purchases	286 000
Sales returns and allowances	18 590
Sales	446 160
Purchase returns and allowances	12 870

Beginning inventory was $60 060, and ending inventory was $90 090.

Required

Prepare a fully classified statement of profit or loss for Djuric Ltd.

E5.6 **Calculate inventory and cost of sales using FIFO and LIFO.** **LO5**

SurfsUp Ltd sells a snowboard, Xpert, that is popular with snowboard enthusiasts. Below is information relating to SurfsUp's purchases of Xpert snowboards during May. During the same month, 124 Xpert snowboards were sold. SurfsUp uses a periodic inventory system.

Date	Explanation	Units	Unit cost	Total cost
May 1	Inventory	26	$ 97	$ 2 522
12	Purchases	45	102	4 590
19	Purchases	28	104	2 912
26	Purchases	40	105	4 200
	Totals	139		$14 224

Required

(a) Calculate the ending inventory at 31 May using the FIFO and LIFO methods. Prove the amount allocated to cost of sales under each method.

(b) For both FIFO and LIFO, calculate the sum of ending inventory and cost of sales. What do you notice about the answers you found for each method?

E5.7 **Calculate inventory and cost of sales using FIFO, LIFO and average cost.** **LO5**

Fenning Pty Ltd reports the following for the month of June:

Date	Explanation	Units	Unit cost	Total cost
June 1	Inventory	200	$10	$2 000
12	Purchases	300	12	3 600
23	Purchases	500	14	7 000
30	Inventory	180		

Required

(a) Calculate cost of the ending inventory and the cost of sales under (1) FIFO, (2) LIFO and (3) average cost.

(b) Which costing method gives the highest ending inventory and the highest cost of sales? Why?

(c) How do the average cost values for ending inventory and cost of sales compare with ending inventory and cost of sales for FIFO and LIFO?

(d) Explain why the average cost is not $12.

E5.8 **Calculate and explain the lower of cost and net realisable value basis of accounting for inventories.** **LO7**

The following data are available for Fashionista Hair Accessories Pty Ltd at 31 December:

	Cost	Net realisable value
Silk ribbons	$25 200	$21 420
Gold-plated hair clips	18 900	19 950
Crystal hair jewels	29 400	26 880

Required

(a) Calculate the lower of cost and net realisable value for Fashionista Hair Accessories total inventory.

(b) Why is it important to account for inventory using the lower of cost and net realisable value basis?

E5.9 Calculate inventory turnover, days in inventory and gross profit rate.   **LO8**

The following information is available for BJ Electronics Ltd for 2018, 2019 and 2020.

(in millions)	2018	2019	2020
Beginning inventory	$ 1051	$ 853	$ 732
Ending inventory	853	732	1016
Cost of sales	8452	8525	9330
Sales	20337	20917	22348

Required

(a) Calculate the inventory turnover ratio, days in inventory, and gross profit ratio (from chapter 4) for BJ Electronics Ltd for 2018, 2019 and 2020.

(b) Comment on any trends.

E5.10 Apply cost flow methods to perpetual records.   **LO9**

Information about SurfsUp Ltd is presented in E5.6. Additional data regarding SurfsUp's sales of Xpert snowboards are provided below. Assume that SurfsUp uses a perpetual inventory system.

Date	Explanation	Units	Unit price	Total cost
May 5	Sale	12	$199	$ 2388
16	Sale	50	199	9950
29	Sale	62	209	12958
	Totals	124		$25296

Required

(a) Calculate ending inventory at 31 May using FIFO, LIFO and average cost.

(b) Compare ending inventory using a perpetual inventory system with ending inventory using a periodic inventory system (from E5.6).

(c) Which inventory cost flow method (FIFO, LIFO) gives the same ending inventory value under both periodic and perpetual? Which method gives different ending inventory values?

E5.11 Prepare correct statements of profit or loss.   **LO10**

Goddard Pty Ltd reported the following statement of profit or loss data for a 2-year period.

	2018	2019
Sales	$420000	$500000
Beginning inventory	64000	80000
Cost of goods purchased	346000	404000
Cost of goods available for sale	410000	484000
Ending inventory	80000	104000
Cost of sales	330000	380000
Gross profit	$ 90000	$120000

Goddard Pty Ltd uses a periodic inventory system. The inventories at 1 July 2018 and 30 June 2019 are correct. However, the ending inventory at 30 June 2018 is overstated by $12000.

Required

(a) Prepare correct statements of profit or loss data for the 2 years.

(b) What is the cumulative effect of the inventory error on total gross profit for the 2 years?

(c) Explain in a letter to the financial controller of Goddard Pty Ltd what has happened, i.e. the nature of the error and its effect on the financial statements.

E5.12 Journalise closing entries. **LO11**

Statement of profit or loss data for Goddard Pty Ltd were provided for 2018 and 2019 in E5.11.

Required

Using the 2019 data, prepare closing entries up to gross profit.

E5.13 Prepare closing entries on a worksheet. **LO11**

Statement of profit or loss data for Goddard Pty Ltd were provided for 2018 and 2019 in E5.11.

Required

Using the 2018 data, enter the closing entries up to gross profit on a worksheet. (*Hint:* See figure 5.25 for an example.)

PROBLEM SET A

PSA5.1 Journalise, post and prepare trial balance and partial statement of profit or loss. **LO1, 2, 4**

At the beginning of the current season on 1 October, the ledger of Eagle Ridge Golf Pty Ltd showed cash $5250; inventory $7350; and share capital $12 600. The following transactions occurred during October 2018.

Oct.	5	Purchased golf bags, clubs and balls on account from Balata Ltd $5460, FOB shipping point, terms 2/7, n/60.
	7	Paid freight on Balata Ltd purchases $168.
	9	Received credit from Balata Ltd for inventory returned $210.
	10	Sold inventory on account $2520, terms n/30.
	12	Purchased golf shoes, sweaters and other accessories on account from Arrow Sportswear $1386, terms 1/7, n/30.
	12	Paid Balata Ltd the amount owed.
	17	Received credit from Arrow Sportswear for inventory returned $126.
	18	Paid Arrow Sportswear in full.
	20	Made sales on account $1890, terms n/30.
	27	Granted credit to customers for clothing that did not fit $63.
	30	Made cash sales $1260.
	30	Received payments on account from customers $2310.

The chart of accounts for Eagle Ridge Golf includes Cash, Accounts receivable, Inventory, Accounts payable, Share capital, Sales, Sales returns and allowances, Purchases, Purchase returns and allowances, Discount received, and Freight-in.

Required

(a) Journalise the October transactions using a periodic inventory system.

(b) Using T accounts, enter the beginning balances in the ledger accounts and post the October transactions.

(c) Prepare a trial balance as at 31 October 2018.

(d) Prepare closing entries, assuming inventory on hand at 31 October is $8820.

(e) Prepare a statement of profit or loss up to gross profit.

PSA5.2 Prepare a fully classified statement of profit or loss. **LO2, 4**

Pumpkin Patchwork Ltd is located in New Zealand. At the end of the entity's financial year on 30 November 2019, the following accounts appeared in its adjusted trial balance.

Accounts payable	$ 38 841
Accounts receivable	15 147
Accumulated depreciation—office equipment	21 648
Accumulated depreciation—store equipment	45 980
Bank charges	1 100
Cash	8 800
Depreciation expense—office equipment	4 400
Depreciation expense—store equipment	10 450
Freight-in	5 566
Freight-out	9 020
Share capital	77 000
Retained earnings	18 920
Dividends	13 200
Insurance expense	9 900
Inventory	37 796
Loan payable	50 600
Office equipment	62 700
Prepaid insurance	4 950
Purchases	693 000
Discount received	7 700
Purchase returns and allowances	3 300
Rates and taxes expense	3 850
Rates and taxes payable	3 850
Rent expense—office space	20 900
Salaries expense—office	154 000
Sales	1 056 000
Sales commissions expense	13 200
Sales commissions payable	8 800
Sales returns and allowances	11 000
Store equipment	137 500
Electricity expense	22 660

Additional facts:

1. Inventory at 30 November 2018 is $39 820.
2. Note that Pumpkin Patchwork Ltd uses a periodic inventory system.
3. Income tax rate is 28%.

Required

Prepare a fully classified statement of profit or loss for the year ended 30 November 2019.

PSA5.3 **Determine cost of sales and ending inventory using FIFO, LIFO, and average cost.**   **LO5, 6**

Modelmania Ltd sells model cars. At the beginning of March, Modelmania Ltd had in beginning inventory 90 model cars with a unit cost of $35. During March Modelmania Ltd made the following purchases of model cars.

March 5	210 @ $40	March 21	240 @ $50
March 13	330 @ $45	March 26	90 @ $55

During March, 810 units were sold. Modelmania Ltd uses a periodic inventory system.

Required

(a) Determine the cost of goods available for sale.
(b) Determine (1) the ending inventory and (2) the cost of sales under each of the assumed cost flow methods (FIFO, LIFO and average cost). Prove the accuracy of the cost of sales under the FIFO and LIFO methods.
(c) Which cost flow method results in (1) the highest inventory amount for the statement of financial position and (2) the highest cost of sales for the statement of profit or loss?

PSA5.4 Calculate ending inventory, prepare statements of profit or loss, and analyse effects of accounting policy choices. **LO5, 6**

The management of Canterbury Ltd, a US-based company, is reassessing the appropriateness
of its present inventory costing method, which is average cost. Management asks your help in
determining the results of operations for 2019 if either the FIFO or the LIFO method had been
used. For 2019 the accounting records show the following data.

Inventories		Purchases and sales	
Beginning (10 000 units)	$52 500	Total net sales (95 000 units)	$997 500
		Total cost of goods purchased	
Ending (? units)		(120 000 units)	$753 000

Purchases were made quarterly as follows.

Quarter	Units	Unit cost	Total cost
1	40 000	$6.00	$240 000
2	60 000	6.30	378 000
3	20 000	6.75	135 000
4	0		0
	120 000		$753 000

Operating expenses were $180 000, and the company's income tax rate is 30%.

Required

(a) Prepare comparative condensed statements of profit or loss for 2019 under FIFO and LIFO.
(Show calculations of ending inventory.)
(b) Answer the following questions for management:
1. Which inventory cost flow method produces the most meaningful inventory amount for
the statement of financial position? Why?
2. Which inventory cost flow method produces the most meaningful profit? Why? (*Hint:*
How much of the gross profit under FIFO is illusory in comparison with the gross profit
under LIFO?)
3. Which inventory cost flow method is most likely to approximate the actual physical flow
of the goods? Why?
4. How much more cash will be available for management under LIFO than under FIFO?
Why?
5. Will gross profit under the average cost method be higher or lower than FIFO? Than
LIFO? (*Note:* It is not necessary to quantify your answer.)

PSA5.5 Calculate inventory turnover, days in inventory, and current ratio based on FIFO. **LO8**

This information is available for the European Division of World Building Products Ltd for
2018. World Building Products uses the FIFO inventory method.

(in millions)	2018
Beginning inventory	$ 31 465.20
Ending inventory	31 738.20
Current assets	115 343.80
Current liabilities	124 295.60
Cost of sales	306 729.80
Sales	365 125.80

Required

(a) Calculate inventory turnover, days in inventory, and current ratio for World Building
Products for 2018.
(b) What do inventory turnover and days in inventory indicate?

(c) If an organisation has high inventory turnover or low days in inventory, is it considered a good or a bad sign? Explain your answer.

PSA5.6 Determine ending inventory under a perpetual inventory system.   **LO9**

Fontana Ltd began operations on 1 July. It uses a perpetual inventory system. During July the business had the following purchases and sales.

Date	Purchases Units	Purchases Unit cost	Sales units
July 1	5	$ 95	
6			3
11	4	106	
14			3
21	3	112	
27			4

Required

(a) Determine the ending inventory under a perpetual inventory system using (1) FIFO, (2) average cost and (3) LIFO.

(b) Which costing method produces the highest cost allocation to ending inventory?

PSA5.7 Journalise, post and prepare trial balance and partial statement of profit or loss.   **LO1, 2, 4**

At the beginning of the current season, the ledger of Kids Sportstore Ltd showed Cash $5250; Inventory $3570; and Share Capital $8820. The following transactions were completed during October 2019.

Oct.	4	Purchased bats and balls from Robert & Co. $1974, FOB shipping point, terms 3/7, n/30.
	6	Paid freight on Robert & Co. purchase $84.
	8	Sold inventory to customers $1890, terms n/30.
	10	Received credit of $84 from Robert & Co. for a damaged bat that was returned.
	11	Purchased cricket shoes from Niki Sports for cash $1260.
	11	Paid Robert & Co. amount due.
	14	Purchased shirts and shorts from Cash's Sportswear $1050, FOB shipping point, terms 2/7, n/60.
	15	Received cash refund of $105 from Niki Sports for damaged inventory that was returned.
	17	Paid freight on Cash's Sportswear purchase $63.
	18	Sold inventory $1680, terms n/30.
	20	Received $1050 in cash from customers in settlement of their accounts.
	20	Paid Cash's Sportswear amount due.
	27	Granted credit of $63 for clothing that did not fit.
	30	Sold inventory to customers $1890, terms n/30.
	30	Customers paid amounts owing on accounts, $1050.

The chart of accounts for Kids Sportstore Ltd includes Cash, Accounts receivable, Inventory, Accounts payable, Share capital, Sales, Sales returns and allowances, Purchases, Purchase returns and allowances, Discount received, and Freight-in.

Required

(a) Journalise the October transactions using a periodic inventory system.

(b) Using T accounts, enter the beginning balances in the ledger accounts and post the October transactions.

(c) Prepare a trial balance as at 31 October 2019.

(d) Journalise the closing entries.

(e) Prepare a statement of profit or loss up to gross profit, assuming inventory on hand at 31 October is $3780.

PSA5.8 **Prepare a fully classified statement of profit or loss.** **LO2, 4**

Fashionista Ltd is located near the Southworld Shopping Centre. At the end of the entity's financial year on 30 June 2020, the following accounts appeared in its adjusted trial balance.

Accounts payable	$ 139 308
Accounts receivable	78 468
Accumulated depreciation—building	81 900
Accumulated depreciation—equipment	66 924
Building	296 400
Cash	35 880
Depreciation expense—building	16 224
Depreciation expense—equipment	20 748
Equipment	171 600
Freight-in	8 736
Insurance expense	11 232
Inventory	63 180
Mortgage payable	124 800
Office salaries expense	49 920
Prepaid insurance	3 744
Rates and taxes payable	7 488
Purchases	689 520
Discount received	18 720
Purchase returns and allowances	9 984
Sales salaries expense	118 560
Sales	1 120 080
Sales commissions expense	22 620
Sales commissions payable	5 460
Sales returns and allowances	12 480
Share capital	234 000
Retained earnings	42 960
Dividends	43 680
Rates and taxes expense	10 608
Electricity expense	17 160
Interest expense	3 120

Additional facts:

1. Inventory on 30 June 2019 is $117 000.
2. Note that Fashionista Ltd uses a periodic system.
3. The income tax rate is 30%.

Required

(a) Prepare a fully classified statement of profit or loss for the year ended 30 June 2020.
(b) If you are not told that a particular company employs the periodic or the perpetual inventory method to account for its inventories, what accounts in the trial balance indicate which system is in use? Use the trial balance provided in this question as a starting point, and provide examples to support your discussion.

PSA5.9 **Determine cost of sales and ending inventory using FIFO, LIFO and average cost with analysis.** **LO5, 6**

Movieworld Ltd sells old movies on DVD. At the beginning of October, Movieworld had in beginning inventory 1100 DVDs with a unit cost of $10. During October, Movieworld made the following purchases of DVDs:

Oct. 3	3850 @ $12	Oct. 19	3300 @ $16
Oct. 9	4400 @ $14	Oct. 25	2200 @ $18

During October 12 100 units were sold. Movieworld uses a periodic inventory system.

Required

(a) Determine the cost of goods available for sale.

(b) Determine (1) the ending inventory and (2) the cost of sales under each of the assumed cost flow methods (FIFO, LIFO and average cost). Prove the accuracy of the cost of sales under the FIFO and LIFO methods.

(c) Which cost flow method results in (1) the highest inventory amount for the statement of financial position and (2) the highest cost of sales for the statement of profit or loss?

PSA5.10 Calculate inventory turnover, days in inventory, and current ratio based on LIFO.   **LO8**

Sweet Cookies Ltd in Thailand manufactures and sells a full line of equipment for baking cookies. Many of these systems are computer-controlled. This information is available for Sweet Cookies for 2018. Sweet Cookies uses the LIFO inventory cost flow method.

(in thousands)	2018
Beginning inventory (finished goods)	$139 851.60
Ending inventory (finished goods)	142 257.40
Current assets	187 663.00
Current liabilities	81 019.40
Cost of sales	328 942.60
Sales	450 970.80

Required

(a) Calculate inventory turnover, days in inventory and current ratio for Sweet Cookies Ltd.

(b) Choco Chip is an Australian-based manufacturer of equipment for baking cookies. Choco Chip has an inventory turnover of 5.4 times, days in inventory of 67.6 and a current ratio of 0.75:1. You are an investment adviser providing advice to a client interested in investing in these companies. Write a short report to highlight the differences between the companies in light of the information available in part (a) and (b) of this question.

PSA5.11 Record closing entries for the periodic and perpetual inventory methods.   **LO11**

The following statement of profit or loss extracts are from entities employing different inventory recording methods.

MICHAEL LTD Statement of profit or loss (extract) Perpetual inventory method	
Sales revenue	$154 275
Less: Sales returns and allowances	9 075
Net sales revenue	145 200
Less: Cost of sales	104 544
Gross profit	**$ 40 656**

SONYA LTD Statement of profit or loss (extract) Periodic inventory method			
Sales revenue			$154 275
Less: Sales returns and allowances			9 075
Net sales revenue			145 200
COST OF SALES			
Cost of beginning inventory		25 410	
Add: Cost of purchases	108 900		
Freight inwards	1 089		
	109 989		
Less: Purchases returns and allowances	1 815		

Cost of net purchases	108 174	
Cost of goods available for sale	133 584	
Less: Cost of ending inventory	29 040	
Cost of sales		104 544
Gross profit		$ **40 656**

Required

(a) Using the information above, prepare closing general journal entries for both the periodic and perpetual inventory systems.

(b) Post these entries to the appropriate general ledger accounts.

PSA5.12 **Journalise inventory entries under a perpetual inventory system with GST.**　　　　　**LO9**

On 1 September, Better Office Supplies had an inventory of 30 deluxe pocket calculators at a cost of $20 each. The business uses a perpetual inventory system and FIFO inventory cost flow method. During September, the following transactions occurred:

Sept.	6	Purchased 80 calculators at $22 each from Digital Ltd for cash.
	9	Paid freight of $88 to We Deliver on calculators purchased from Digital Ltd.
	10	Returned two calculators to Digital Ltd for $44 credit because they did not meet specifications.
	12	Sold 26 calculators for $33 each to Reader Book Store, terms n/30.
	14	Granted credit of $33 to Reader Book Store for the return of one calculator that was not ordered.
	20	Sold 30 calculators for $33 each to Mega Ltd, terms n/30.

Required

Journalise the September transactions, assuming all businesses were registered for GST and the GST rate was 10%.

PROBLEM SET B

PSB5.1 **Journalise, post and prepare trial balance and partial statement of profit or loss.**　　**LO1, 2, 4**

At the beginning of the current season on 1 October, the ledger of Hancock's Pro Shop Pty Ltd showed Cash $5000; Inventory $7000; and Share capital $12 000. The following transactions occurred during October 2018.

Oct.	5	Purchased golf bags, clubs and balls on account from Balata Ltd $5200, FOB shipping point, terms 2/7, n/60.
	7	Paid freight on Balata Ltd purchases $160.
	9	Received credit from Balata Ltd for inventory returned $200.
	10	Sold inventory on account $2400, terms n/30.
	12	Purchased golf shoes, sweaters and other accessories on account from Arrow Sportswear $1320, terms 1/7, n/30.
	12	Paid Balata Ltd the amount owed.
	17	Received credit from Arrow Sportswear for inventory returned $120.
	18	Paid Arrow Sportswear in full.
	20	Made sales on account $1800, terms n/30.
	27	Granted credit to customers for clothing that did not fit $60.
	30	Made cash sales $1200.
	30	Received payments on account from customers $2200.

The chart of accounts for the pro shop includes Cash, Accounts receivable, Inventory, Accounts payable, Share capital, Sales, Sales returns and allowances, Purchases, Purchase returns and allowances, Discount received, and Freight-in.

Required

(a) Journalise the October transactions using a periodic inventory system.

(b) Using T accounts, enter the beginning balances in the ledger accounts and post the October transactions.

(c) Prepare a trial balance as at 31 October 2018.

(d) Prepare a statement of profit or loss up to gross profit, assuming inventory on hand at 31 October is $8400.

PSB5.2 Prepare a fully classified statement of profit or loss.   **LO2, 4**

Bargains Department Store is located in Sydney. At the end of the entity's financial year on 30 November 2019, the following accounts appeared in its trial balance:

Accounts payable	$ 52 965
Accounts receivable	20 655
Accumulated depreciation — office equipment	29 520
Accumulated depreciation — store equipment	62 700
Bank charges	1 500
Cash	12 000
Depreciation expense — office equipment	6 000
Depreciation expense — store equipment	14 250
Freight-in	7 590
Freight-out	12 300
Share capital	105 000
Retained profits	25 800
Dividends	18 000
Insurance expense	13 500
Inventory	51 540
Loan payable	69 000
Office equipment	85 500
Prepaid insurance	6 750
Purchases	945 000
Discount received	10 500
Purchase returns and allowances	4 500
Rates and taxes expense	5 250
Rates and taxes payable	5 250
Rent expense — office space	28 500
Salaries expense — office	210 000
Sales	1 440 000
Sales commissions expense	18 000
Sales commissions payable	12 000
Sales returns and allowances	15 000
Store equipment	187 500
Electricity expense	30 900

Additional facts:

1. Inventory at 30 November 2018 is $54 300.

2. Note that Bargains Department Store uses a periodic inventory system.

3. Income tax rate is 30%.

Required

Prepare a fully classified statement of profit or loss for the year ended 30 November 2019.

PSB5.3 Determine cost of sales and ending inventory using FIFO, LIFO, and average cost.   LO5, 6

Rye Sails sells model boats. At the beginning of March, Rye Sails had in beginning inventory 150 model boats with a unit cost of $35. During March Rye Sails made the following purchases of model boats.

| March 5 | 350 @ $40 | March 21 | 400 @ $50 |
| March 13 | 550 @ $45 | March 26 | 150 @ $55 |

During March, 1350 units were sold. Rye Sails uses a periodic inventory system.

Required

(a) Determine the cost of goods available for sale.

(b) Determine (1) the ending inventory and (2) the cost of sales under each of the assumed cost flow methods (FIFO, LIFO and average cost). Prove the accuracy of the cost of sales under the FIFO and LIFO methods.

(c) Explain which cost flow method results in (1) the highest inventory amount for the statement of financial position and (2) the highest cost of sales for the statement of profit or loss.

PSB5.4 **Calculate ending inventory, prepare statements of profit or loss and answer questions using FIFO and LIFO.** **LO5, 6**

The management of Peoria Ltd, a US-based company, is reassessing the appropriateness of using its present inventory cost flow method, which is average cost. Management requests your help in determining the results of operations for 2019 if either the FIFO or the LIFO method had been used. For 2019 the accounting records show these data:

Inventories		Purchases and sales	
Beginning (15 000 units)	$34 000	Total net sales (225 000 units)	$865 000
		Total cost of goods purchased	
Ending (? units)		(230 000 units)	$578 500

Purchases were made quarterly as follows:

Quarter	Units	Unit cost	Total cost
1	60 000	$2.30	$138 000
2	50 000	2.50	125 000
3	50 000	2.60	130 000
4	70 000	2.65	185 500
	230 000		$578 500

Operating expenses were $147 000, and the company's income tax rate is 32%.

Required

(a) Prepare comparative condensed statements of profit or loss for 2019 under FIFO and LIFO. (Show calculations of ending inventory.)

(b) Answer the following questions for management in business-letter form:

1. Which cost flow method (FIFO or LIFO) produces the more meaningful inventory amount for the statement of financial position? Why?

2. Which cost flow method (FIFO or LIFO) produces the more meaningful profit? Why?

3. Which cost flow method (FIFO or LIFO) is more likely to approximate the actual physical flow of goods? Why?

4. How much more cash will be available for management under LIFO than under FIFO? Why?

5. Will gross profit under the average cost method be higher or lower than FIFO? Than LIFO? (*Note:* It is not necessary to quantify your answer.)

PSB5.5 **Calculate inventory turnover, days in inventory, and current ratio based on FIFO.** **LO8**

This information is available for the Automotive and Electronics Divisions of Prestige Motors Ltd for 2018. Prestige Motors uses the FIFO inventory method.

(in millions)	2018
Beginning inventory	$ 36 306
Ending inventory	36 621
Current assets	133 089
Current liabilities	143 418
Cost of sales	353 919
Sales	421 299

Required

(a) Calculate inventory turnover, days in inventory, and current ratio for Prestige Motors Ltd for 2018.

(b) If a company has a low inventory turnover or high days in inventory, is it considered to be a good or bad sign for the entity's shareholders? Explain your answer.

PSB5.6 **Determine ending inventory under a perpetual inventory system.** **LO9**

Watson Pty Ltd began operations on 1 July. It uses a perpetual inventory system. During July the business had the following purchases and sales:

	Purchases		
Date	Units	Unit cost	Sales units
July 1	5	$ 90	
6			3
11	4	99	
14			3
21	3	106	
27			4

Required

(a) Determine the ending inventory under a perpetual inventory system using (1) FIFO, (2) average cost and (3) LIFO.

(b) Which costing method produces the highest cost allocation to ending inventory?

PSB5.7 **Journalise, post and prepare trial balance and partial statement of profit or loss.** **LO1, 2, 4**

At the beginning of the current season, the ledger of Mill Park Tennis Shop Pty Ltd showed Cash $5000; Inventory $3400; and Share capital $8400. The following transactions were completed during October 2019.

Oct.	4	Purchased racquets and balls from Robert & Co. $1880, FOB shipping point, terms 3/7, n/30.
	6	Paid freight on Robert & Co. purchase $80.
	8	Sold inventory to members $1800, terms n/30.
	10	Received credit of $80 from Robert & Co. for a damaged racquet that was returned.
	11	Purchased tennis shoes from Niki Sports for cash $1200.
	11	Paid Robert & Co. amount due.
	14	Purchased tennis shirts and shorts from Cash's Sportswear $1000, FOB shipping point, terms 2/7, n/60.
	15	Received cash refund of $100 from Niki Sports for damaged inventory that was returned.
	17	Paid freight on Cash's Sportswear purchase $60.
	18	Sold inventory $1600, terms n/30.
	20	Received $1000 in cash from customers in settlement of their accounts.
	20	Paid Cash's Sportswear amount due.
	27	Granted credit of $60 for tennis clothing that did not fit.
	30	Sold inventory to customers $1800, terms n/30.
	30	Customers paid amounts owing on accounts, $1000.

The chart of accounts for the tennis shop includes Cash, Accounts receivable, Inventory, Accounts payable, Share capital, Sales, Sales returns and allowances, Purchases, Purchase returns and allowances, Discount received, and Freight-in.

Required

(a) Journalise the October transactions using a periodic inventory system.

(b) Using T accounts, enter the beginning balances in the ledger accounts and post the October transactions.

(c) Prepare a trial balance as at 31 October 2019.

(d) Journalise the closing entries.

(e) Prepare a statement of profit or loss up to gross profit, assuming inventory on hand at 31 October is $3600.

PSB5.8 **Prepare a fully classified statement of profit or loss.**   **LO2, 4**

Westfields Ltd is located near the St Ives Village Shopping Centre. At the end of Westfields Ltd's financial year on 30 June 2020, the following accounts appeared in its adjusted trial balance.

Accounts payable	$ 98 230
Accounts receivable	55 330
Accumulated depreciation—building	57 750
Accumulated depreciation—equipment	47 190
Building	209 000
Cash	25 300
Depreciation expense—building	11 440
Depreciation expense—equipment	14 630
Equipment	121 000
Freight-in	6 160
Insurance expense	7 920
Inventory	82 500
Mortgage payable	88 000
Office salaries expense	35 200
Prepaid insurance	2 640
Rates and taxes payable	5 280
Purchases	486 200
Discount received	13 200
Purchase returns and allowances	7 040
Sales salaries expense	83 600
Sales	789 800
Sales commissions expense	15 950
Sales commissions payable	3 850
Sales returns and allowances	8 800
Share capital	165 000
Retained profits	30 360
Dividends	30 800
Rates and taxes expense	7 480
Electricity expense	12 100
Interest expense	2 200

Additional facts:

1. Inventory on 30 June 2019 is $44 550.

2. Note that Westfields Ltd uses a periodic system.

3. The income tax rate is 30%.

Required

Prepare a fully classified statement of profit or loss for the year ended 30 June 2020.

PSB5.9 Determine cost of sales and ending inventory using FIFO, LIFO and average cost with analysis.
LO5, 6

Movies Abound Pty Ltd sells DVDs of the performing artist Edwin Drood. At the beginning of October, Movies Abound had in beginning inventory 1000 Drood DVDs with a unit cost of $10. During October, Movies Abound made the following purchases of Drood DVDs.

Oct. 3	3500 @ $12	Oct. 19	3000 @ $16
Oct. 9	4000 @ $14	Oct. 25	2000 @ $18

During October 11 000 units were sold. Movies Abound uses a periodic inventory system.

Required

(a) Determine the cost of goods available for sale.
(b) Determine (1) the ending inventory and (2) the cost of sales under each of the assumed cost flow methods (FIFO, LIFO and average cost). Prove the accuracy of the cost of sales under the FIFO and LIFO methods.
(c) Which cost flow method results in (1) the highest inventory amount for the statement of financial position and (2) the highest cost of sales for the statement of profit or loss?

PSB5.10 Calculate inventory turnover, days in inventory, and current ratio based on LIFO.   **LO8**

Plant Food Ltd in Auckland manufactures and sells a full line of equipment that is used to apply fertiliser. Many of these systems are computer-controlled. This information is available for Make-it-Grow for 2018. Plant Food uses the LIFO inventory cost flow method.

('000)	2018
Beginning inventory (finished goods)	$ 99 894
Ending inventory (finished goods)	101 751
Current assets	134 045
Current liabilities	57 871
Cost of sales	234 959
Sales	322 122

Required

(a) Calculate inventory turnover, days in inventory and current ratio for Plant Food Ltd.
(b) Green Thumb Ltd is an Australian-based manufacturer of equipment that is used to apply fertiliser. Green Thumb has an inventory turnover of 8.5 times, days in inventory of 42.9 and a current ratio of 0.8:1. You are an investment adviser providing advice to a client interested in investing in these companies. Write a short report to highlight the differences between the companies in light of the information available in parts (a) and (b) of this question.

PSB5.11 Record closing entries for the periodic and perpetual inventory methods.   **LO11**

The following statement of profit or loss extracts are from entities employing different inventory recording methods.

MASTRILLI LTD Statement of profit or loss (extract) Perpetual inventory method	
Sales revenue	$46 750
Less: Sales returns and allowances	2 750
Net sales revenue	44 000
Less: Cost of sales	31 680
Gross profit	**$12 320**

ERRICA LTD			
Statement of profit or loss (extract)			
Periodic inventory method			
Sales revenue			$46 750
Less: Sales returns and allowances			2 750
Net sales revenue			44 000
COST OF SALES			
Cost of beginning inventory		7 700	
Add: Cost of purchases	33 000		
Freight inwards	330		
	33 330		
Less: Purchases returns and allowances	550		
Cost of net purchases		32 780	
Cost of goods available for sale		40 480	
Less: Cost of ending inventory		8 800	
Cost of sales			31 680
Gross profit			**$12 320**

Required

(a) Using the information provided, prepare closing general journal entries for both the periodic and perpetual inventory systems.

(b) Post these entries to the appropriate general ledger accounts.

PSB5.12 **Journalise inventory entries under a perpetual inventory system with GST.** **LO9**

On 1 September Petrocelli Office Supplies had an inventory of 45 USBs at a cost of $30 each. The business uses a perpetual inventory system and FIFO inventory cost flow method. During September, the following transactions occurred.

Sept. 6	Purchased 120 USBs at $32 each from Storetek Ltd for cash.
9	Paid freight of $132 to Speedy Delivery Ltd on USBs purchased from Storetek Ltd.
10	Returned two USBs to Storetek Ltd for $64 credit because they did not meet specifications.
12	Sold 39 USBs for $43 each to Sunny Store, terms n/30.
14	Granted credit of $43 to Sunny Store for the return of one USB that was not ordered.
20	Sold 45 calculators for $43 each to Martins Ltd, terms n/30.

Required

Journalise the September transactions, assuming all businesses were registered for GST and the GST rate was 10%.

BUILDING BUSINESS SKILLS

FINANCIAL REPORTING AND ANALYSIS

Financial reporting problem: Domino's Pizza Enterprises Ltd

BBS5.1 The notes that accompany an entity's financial statements provide informative details that would clutter the amounts and descriptions presented in the statements. Look up the latest annual report for Domino's. Go to www.dominos.com.au, scroll down to the bottom right of the home page and select **Domino's Corporate Site**, then select **Investors** and click on **click here** where the annual report and presentations are discussed.

Required

Answer the following questions. (Give the amounts in thousands of dollars, as shown in the consolidated figures in the financial statements in the annual report.)

(a) What did Domino's report for the amount of inventories in its consolidated statement of financial position as at the beginning of the current period?

(b) Calculate the dollar amount of change and the percentage change in inventories between the current period and the previous period. Calculate inventory as a percentage of current assets for the current period.

Comparative analysis problem: Soft Drink Co. vs. Soda Pop Inc.

BBS5.2 The following data are from recent financial statements of Soft Drink Co. and Soda Pop Inc.

	Soft Drink Co. (A$ in millions)	Soda Pop Inc. (US$ in millions)
Cost of sales	$1 422	$16 750
Finished goods inventory, start of the year	172	755
Finished goods inventory, end of the year	178	751

Required

(a) Based on the information in the financial statements, calculate these values for each entity:
   1. Inventory turnover.
   2. Days in inventory.
(b) What conclusions concerning the management of the inventory can be drawn from these data?

A global focus and interpreting financial statements

BBS5.3 Cross Trainers Group and Fitness Shoes Limited compete toe-to-toe in the sport shoe and sport apparel business. For both companies, inventory is a significant portion of total assets. The following information was taken from each entity's financial statements and notes to those financial statements for the year ended 31 December 2019.

CROSS TRAINERS GROUP
Notes to the financial statements

Inventory valuation (extract). Inventories are stated at lower of cost or net realisable value and valued on a first-in, first-out (FIFO) or average cost basis. Inventory costs include the product cost from suppliers, insurance, import duties, taxes, freight, and other handling fees.
Inventory summary for Cross Trainers Group (in US$ millions):

	31 December	
	2019	2018
Inventory	1 717	1 611
Cost of sales	7 140	6 592

FITNESS SHOES LIMITED
Notes to the financial statements

Inventory valuation (extract). Our merchandise and finished goods are valued at the lower of cost or net realisable value. Costs are determined using the average cost method. Finished goods costs include raw materials, direct labour and direct manufacturing overheads.

Inventory	2019 (AUD in millions)	2018 (AUD in millions)
Finished goods and merchandise on hand	902	818
Goods in transit	400	408
Raw materials	15	13
Work in progress	2	3
Total	1 319	1 242

Inventory summary for Fitness Shoes Limited (AUD in millions):

	31 December	
	2019	**2018**
Inventory	1 319	1 242
Cost of sales	3 676	3 890

Required

Answer each of these questions on how these two entities manage inventory:

(a) What challenges of inventory management might Cross Trainers and Fitness Shoes face in the international sport apparel industry?

(b) What inventory cost flow assumptions does each entity use?

(c) Fitness Shoes provides more detail regarding the nature of its inventory (e.g. raw materials, work in progress and finished goods) than does Cross Trainers. How might this additional information be useful in evaluating Fitness Shoes?

(d) Calculate and interpret inventory turnover and days in inventory for each company for the latest year using the figures for total inventory.

Financial analysis on the web

BBS5.4 Purpose: Use an entity's annual report to identify the inventory method used and analyse the effects on the statement of profit or loss and statement of financial position.

Address: www.jbhifi.com.au

Steps:

1. Scroll down to the bottom of JB Hi-Fi's home page, in the bottom right-hand corner of the page, choose **Investors**.

2. Choose **Financial and Annual Reports**.

3. Use the latest annual report (financial statements and notes to the financial statements) to answer the questions below.

Required

Answer the following questions:

(a) At JB Hi-Fi's year-end, what was the inventory on the statement of financial position? What was the cost of sales for the year?

(b) Refer to note 1. How is inventory valued?

(c) What proportion of total assets was made up of inventory?

(d) Calculate inventory turnover and days in inventory for the latest year. How does this compare with Original Furnishings and Artistry Furniture in figure 5.16?

CRITICAL THINKING

Group decision case

BBS5.5 Chem Products International Ltd manufactures specialty chemicals and vehicle airbags. Recently, its specialty chemicals business was reorganised, and two manufacturing plants were closed. Profits were generally high, however, mostly because of an improved product mix. The vehicle airbag business did very well, with sales more than 30% higher than the previous year. However, towards the end of the year, questions were being raised about the safety of airbags, and this put the future of this business in some jeopardy.

The current assets portion of Chem Products International's statement of financial position for the year ended 30 June 2019 is shown next.

CHEM PRODUCTS INTERNATIONAL LTD		
Statement of financial position (partial)		
as at 30 June 2019		
(in millions)		
CURRENT ASSETS		
Cash and cash equivalents		$ 138.0
Accounts receivable	$479.2	
Less: Allowance for doubtful debts	10.6	468.6
Inventories		381.0
Other current assets		125.4
Total current assets		**$1 113.0**

Assume that the following transactions occurred during June and July 2019.

1. Office supplies were shipped to Chem Products by Office Max, FOB destination. The goods were shipped on 29 June and received on 30 June.
2. Chem Products purchased specialty plastic from Uniroyal Technology for use in airbag manufacture. The goods were shipped FOB shipping point on 1 July, and were received by Chem Products on 4 July.
3. Johnson Motor Company purchased 10 000 airbags to be used in the manufacture of new cars. These were shipped FOB shipping point on 30 June, and were received by Johnson on 2 July.
4. Bassett Furniture shipped office furniture to Chem Products, FOB destination, on 29 June. The goods were received on 3 July.
5. Inland Specialty Chemicals shipped chemicals that Chem Products uses in the manufacture of airbags and other items. The goods were sent FOB shipping point on 29 June, and were received on 1 July.
6. Chem Products purchased new cars for its executives from MAC. The cars were shipped FOB destination on 19 June, and were received on 2 July.
7. Chem Products shipped specialty chemicals to A1Chemicals, FOB destination. The shipment arrived at A1Chemicals on 2 July.
8. Chem Products purchased steel to be used in expanding its manufacturing plant. The steel arrived on 6 July, shipped FOB shipping point.

Required

With the class divided into groups, answer the following:

(a) Which items would be owned by Chem Products International Ltd as of 30 June 2019?
(b) Identify which transactions involve Chem Products's inventory account as of 30 June 2019 and which affect it after 30 June 2019.

Communication activity (J, CT)

BBS5.6 You are the accountant of City Jeans Ltd. Su Lee, the managing director, recently mentioned to you that she had found an error in the 2018 financial statements which she believed had corrected itself. She was convinced, in discussions with the purchasing department, that the 2018 ending inventory was overstated by $1 million. Su says, however, that the 2019 ending inventory is correct, and she assumes that the 2019 profit is correct. Su says to you, 'What happened has happened — there's no point in worrying about it anymore.'

Required

You conclude that Su is incorrect. Write a brief, tactful memo, clarifying the situation.

ANSWERS

Answers to self-study questions

5.1 (b) 5.2 (d) 5.3 (a) 5.4 (a) 5.5 (c) 5.6 (d) 5.7 (c) 5.8 (d) 5.9 (d) 5.10 (d) 5.11 (d) 5.12 (b)
5.13 (a) 5.14 (b) 5.15 (d)

ACKNOWLEDGEMENTS

Photo: © Monkey Business Images / Shutterstock.com
Photo: © Pressmaster / Shutterstock.com
Photo: © Alistair Berg / Getty Images

CHAPTER 6

Accounting information systems

LEARNING OBJECTIVES

After studying this chapter, you should be able to:

6.1 identify the basic principles of accounting information systems

6.2 explain the major phases in the development of an accounting system

6.3 define internal control

6.4 appreciate management's responsibility in relation to internal control

6.5 identify the principles and limitations of internal control

6.6 understand the accounting processes underlying the generation of financial statements

6.7 describe the sales and receivables cycle and the purchases and payments cycle

6.8 apply internal control principles to the sales and receivables cycle and purchases and payments cycle for transforming data

6.9 describe the nature and purpose of control accounts and subsidiary ledgers

6.10 explain how special journals are used in recording transactions

6.11 understand the basic features of computerised accounting systems and appreciate the role and use of non-integrated systems

6.12 identify the advantages and disadvantages of computerised accounting systems

6.13 record transactions for sales, purchases, cash receipts and cash payments in special journals

6.14 understand how multi-column special journals are posted.

Chapter preview

A reliable accounting information system is a necessity for any business. Whether a manual or computerised system is used in maintaining accounting records, certain principles and procedures apply. In order to introduce basic accounting procedures, the exercises and illustrations given in previous chapters have been limited to manually operated accounting systems. However, large entities like McDonald's and even smaller businesses require more sophisticated accounting systems. The purpose of this chapter is to explain and illustrate accounting information systems used to enable efficient and dependable processing of numerous transactions into useful information for decision making. The chapter begins by explaining some basic concepts of accounting information systems and the importance of having good internal controls within such a system. It is important to have good internal controls so that the accounting information derived from the accounting system is reliable. We will explain how transactions are transformed into financial data as well as some refinements to manual accounting systems. In the latter part of the chapter we take a look at the impact of computers on accounting information systems. Chapter 14 provides additional in-depth information on Xero, an accounting software system.

The content and organisation of this chapter are as follows.

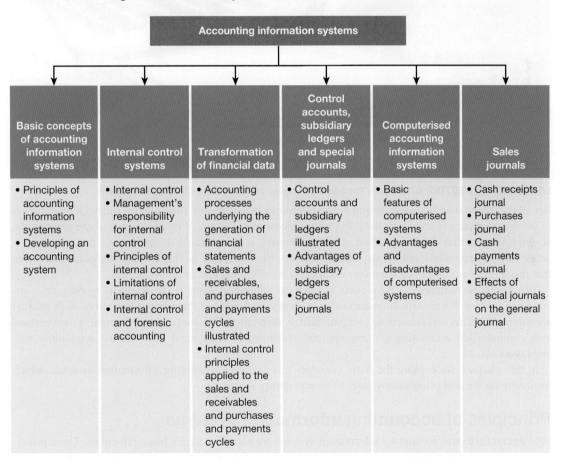

Accounting information systems					
Basic concepts of accounting information systems	**Internal control systems**	**Transformation of financial data**	**Control accounts, subsidiary ledgers and special journals**	**Computerised accounting information systems**	**Sales journals**
• Principles of accounting information systems • Developing an accounting system	• Internal control • Management's responsibility for internal control • Principles of internal control • Limitations of internal control • Internal control and forensic accounting	• Accounting processes underlying the generation of financial statements • Sales and receivables, and purchases and payments cycles illustrated • Internal control principles applied to the sales and receivables and purchases and payments cycles	• Control accounts and subsidiary ledgers illustrated • Advantages of subsidiary ledgers • Special journals	• Basic features of computerised systems • Advantages and disadvantages of computerised systems	• Cash receipts journal • Purchases journal • Cash payments journal • Effects of special journals on the general journal

6.1 Basic concepts of accounting information systems

LEARNING OBJECTIVE 6.1 Identify the basic principles of accounting information systems.

Recall that the system that collects and processes transaction data and disseminates financial information to interested parties is known as the accounting information system. It includes each of the steps in the accounting cycle that you have studied in earlier chapters. It also includes the documents that provide evidence of the transactions and events, and the records, trial balances, worksheets and financial statements that result. An accounting information system may be either manual or computerised.

You might be wondering, 'Why cover manual accounting systems if the business world uses computerised systems?' First, small businesses still abound and most of them begin operations with manual accounting systems and convert to computerised systems as the business grows. Second, to understand how computerised accounting systems operate, you need to understand how manual accounting systems work.

In this chapter, we explore the basic concepts that underlie accounting information systems, which from here on we will often simply refer to as accounting systems.

Principles of accounting information systems

Efficient and effective accounting information systems are based on certain basic principles. These principles are: (1) cost effectiveness (2) usefulness and (3) flexibility, as described in figure 6.1. If the accounting system is cost effective, provides useful output and has the flexibility to meet future needs, it can contribute to both individual and organisational goals.

Cost effectiveness
The accounting system must be cost effective. Benefits of information must outweigh the costs of providing it.

Useful output
To be useful, information must be relevant, faithfully representative, comparable, verifiable, timely and understandable, and satisfy the test of materiality. Designers of accounting systems must consider the needs and knowledge of various users.

Flexibility
The accounting system should accommodate a variety of users and changing information needs. The system should be sufficiently flexible to meet the resulting changes in the demands made upon it.

6.2 Developing an accounting system

LEARNING OBJECTIVE 6.2 Explain the major phases in the development of an accounting system.

Accounting systems, which are used by many Australian businesses, do not just happen. Good accounting systems are carefully planned, designed, installed, managed and refined. Within all businesses, senior executives such as the finance director will continually review and modify the accounting system in use to improve its usability and to streamline business processes as the business environment changes. Generally, an accounting system is developed in the following four phases.

1. *Analysis.* The starting point is to determine the information needs of internal and external users. The system analyst then identifies the sources of the needed information and the records and procedures for collecting and reporting the data. If an existing system is being analysed, its strengths and weaknesses must be identified.
2. *Design.* A new system must be built from the ground up — forms and documents designed, methods and procedures selected, job descriptions prepared, controls integrated, reports formatted, and equipment selected. Redesigning an existing system may involve only minor changes or a complete overhaul.
3. *Implementation.* Implementation of new or revised systems requires that documents, procedures and processing equipment be installed and made operational. Also, personnel must be trained and closely supervised throughout a start-up period.
4. *Follow-up.* After the system is up and running, it must be monitored for weaknesses or breakdowns. Also, its effectiveness must be compared with design and organisational objectives. Changes in design or implementation may be necessary.

Figure 6.2 highlights the relationship of these four phases in the life cycle of the accounting system. These phases represent the life cycle of an accounting system. They suggest that few systems remain the same forever. As experience and knowledge are obtained, and as technological and organisational changes occur, the accounting system may also have to grow and change.

FIGURE 6.2 Phases in the development of an accounting system

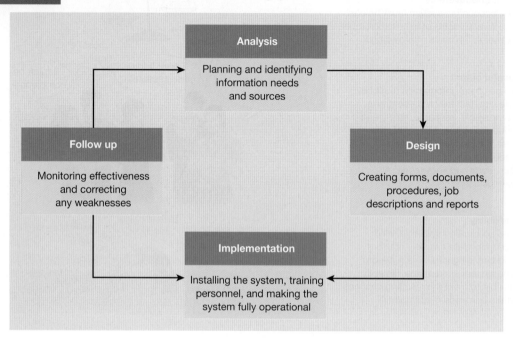

An accounting system must have adequate controls built into it, including mechanisms which will protect and safeguard the assets of the business and ensure that the information provided by the system is faithfully represented, relevant and timely so that it meets the decision-making needs of both management and external users. This is what is referred to as a system of internal control and is discussed in the next section.

6.3 Internal control systems

LEARNING OBJECTIVE 6.3 Define internal control.

One of the primary functions of those who are managing and running the business is to ensure that the assets of the business are used as efficiently as possible and that they are always protected. Assets include, for example, inventory and equipment, which are physical assets, and data and information, which are collected in and disseminated from the accounting information system. In a sole trader business, the owner will often be involved in running the business and therefore will have adequate controls in place. However, as the business becomes larger, the owner may have to rely on others to help manage and control the operations of the business, which will mean putting in place systems to assist in ensuring assets are used efficiently and that they are protected. This means that management will need to implement a risk management system. Risk management involves identifying and putting in place processes that will lessen the risks faced by the business. Internal control is an essential part of risk management, i.e. the policies adopted to reduce the likelihood or severity of potential losses. Failure to maintain an adequate system of internal control can be considered as negligence on the part of management.

Internal control

Internal control consists of all the processes used by management and staff to provide effective and efficient operations, and compliance with laws, regulations and internal policies. It incorporates policies adopted by a business to:

- safeguard its assets from employee theft, robbery and unauthorised use
- enhance the completeness, accuracy and reliability of its accounting records by reducing the risk of errors (unintentional mistakes) and irregularities (intentional mistakes and misrepresentations) in the accounting process, and permit the timely preparation of financial information.

There are two aspects of internal control: (1) administrative controls and (2) accounting controls. Administrative controls are those which provide operational efficiency and adherence to policies and procedures which have been prepared by the management of the business. For example, documents that identify purchasing and sales procedures, or policies that are required to be followed when hiring employees.

Accounting controls are the methods and procedures used to protect assets and to ensure that the accounting records are reliable, such as procedures for ensuring transactions are recorded as necessary and ensuring that the record keeping for assets is kept separate from those who have physical custody of the assets.

Before we consider the principles of internal control systems that are required to protect assets and enhance the reliability of accounting records, let us briefly consider management's responsibility in relation to internal control.

6.4 Management's responsibility for internal control

LEARNING OBJECTIVE 6.4 Appreciate management's responsibility in relation to internal control.

Large businesses, such as companies, are managed and run by senior employees, such as the Chief Executive Officer, Chief Financial Officer and other senior managers. These senior employees, known collectively as management, act on behalf of the owners of the business. Companies also have a board of directors that is made up of elected members who jointly oversee the activities of the company. One of the key roles of the board of directors is to establish objectives for the organisation. Management is then responsible for developing policies and practices that align with the organisation's objectives which are then ratified by the board of directors. These broad policies and practices form part of the environment that companies operate in, and they should reflect the overall attitude of the senior executives, directors and owners of the company. The board of directors is independent of management, with the members of the board delegating responsibility to management and charged with the responsibility of regularly assessing how management adheres to these objectives.

The framework of rules, relationships, systems and processes within and by which authority is exercised and controlled within corporations is known as **corporate governance**. Corporate governance, therefore, is the system by which entities are directed or controlled, managed and administered. It includes every aspect of management from action plans and internal controls to performance measurement and corporate disclosure. It influences how the objectives of the company are set and achieved, how risk is monitored and assessed, and how performance of the company is optimised. Governance is largely about the decision-making process of the entity, ensuring that the goals and hence the decisions made by management are aligned with those of the shareholders. The board of directors plays a key role in effective corporate governance as the board is ultimately responsible for making sure that management carries out the policies and procedures as previously set. Better quality accounting information can be provided to shareholders if entities adopt good corporate governance principles.

In recent years, corporate governance practices have increasingly focused on identifying and managing business risk, and internal control is considered an important element of a good corporate governance structure. In response to corporate failures, such as HIH and One.Tel, the Australian Securities Exchange (ASX) Corporate Governance Council issued guidelines in 2003 called *Principles of Good Corporate Governance and Best Practice Recommendations*. The second edition of the guidelines, *Corporate Governance Principles and Recommendations 2nd Edition*, was released in August 2007, and amendments to this edition were released in June 2010. The third edition of the guidelines, *Corporate Governance Principles and Recommendations (Third Edition)* was released in March 2014. The guidelines contain eight principles of good corporate governance. Among these principles is 'Principle 7: Recognise and manage risk'. Recognising and managing risk is a crucial part of the role of the board of directors and management of the company.* To enable the board and management to put in place good risk management practices, the company must have an appropriate risk management framework and needs to manage that risk on an ongoing basis through periodic reviews.

As previously noted, the board delegates the running of the business to management, including responsibility for internal control, but the board needs to regularly monitor what management is doing. To assist the board in its monitoring and oversight, the board creates a number of committees, namely an audit committee and a risk committee. The audit committee is responsible for the oversight of financial reporting and disclosure and also assesses management processes that support the preparation of the external reports. Further, the audit committee assesses the performance and independence of the external auditors and is responsible for maintaining communication with both the external and internal auditors. **Internal auditors** are employees of the business who evaluate on a continuous basis the effectiveness of the system of internal control. They periodically review the activities of departments and individuals to determine whether prescribed internal controls are being followed.

Creation of a risk committee is one of the recommendations in Principle 7 of the *Corporate Governance Principles and Recommendations (Third Edition)*, and it is the committee created to oversee and manage the risks that organisations face.

The ASX believes that good corporate governance promotes investor confidence, so complying with these principles is good for investors.

---

* ASX Corporate Governance Council 2014, *Corporate Governance Principles and Recommendations (Third Edition)*, www.asx.com.au.

6.5 Principles of internal control

LEARNING OBJECTIVE 6.5 Identify the principles and limitations of internal control.

To safeguard assets and enhance the accuracy and reliability of its accounting records, a business follows internal control principles. The specific control measures used vary with the size and nature of the business and with management's control philosophy. However, the five principles in figure 6.3 apply to most businesses. Each principle is explained in the following sections.

FIGURE 6.3	Principles of internal control

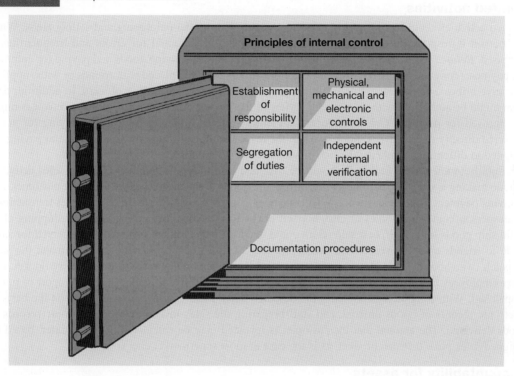

Establishment of responsibility

Two essential characteristics of internal control are the assignment of responsibility to specific individuals and the appointment of supervisors to monitor compliance with procedures. Control is most effective when only one person is responsible for a given task. If two or more individuals share the same responsibility and something goes wrong, it will be very difficult to determine who is at fault and therefore difficult to take corrective action to ensure that the problem does not occur again.

When assigning responsibility to individuals, management should ensure that employees are appropriately qualified or trained. Some responsibilities require licences, for example truck drivers must hold the class of licence for the truck they are to drive. Some companies invest a lot of money training staff. For example, Domino's Pizza Enterprises Ltd has developed a Safe Delivery Program as well as initiating a self-paced online staff training program called Domino's Team Member and Management Training (Pizza College). Establishing responsibility includes the authorisation and approval of transactions. For example, establishing an account for a new customer ordinarily requires a creditworthiness check and approval from the credit department.

Segregation of duties

Segregation of duties is indispensable in a system of internal control. There are two common applications of this principle:

- The responsibility for related activities should be assigned to different individuals.
- The responsibility for keeping the records for an asset should be separate from the physical custody of that asset. This is an example of an accounting control.

The rationale for segregation of duties is that the work of one employee should, without a duplication of effort, provide a reliable basis for checking the work of another employee.

Related activities

Related activities should be assigned to different people in both the purchasing and selling areas. When one person is responsible for all of the related activities, the potential for errors and irregularities is increased. *Related purchasing activities* include ordering goods, receiving goods and paying (or authorising payment) for goods. In purchasing, for example, orders could be placed with friends or with suppliers who give bribes, such as cash, gifts or other personal benefits to purchasing officers. In addition, payment might be authorised without a careful review of the invoice or, even worse, fictitious invoices might be approved for payment. One large Australian entity suffered losses because it was paying for goods delivered directly to employees' homes. When the responsibilities for ordering, receiving and paying are assigned to different individuals, the risk of such abuses is minimised.

Similarly, *related sales activities* should be assigned to different individuals. Related sales activities include making a sale, despatching (or delivering) the goods to the customer, invoicing the customer, and receiving payment from the customer. When one person is responsible for these related sales transactions, a salesperson could make sales at unauthorised prices to increase sales commissions, a shipping clerk could ship goods to himself, or a sales clerk could understate the amount invoiced and received for sales made to friends and relatives. These abuses are less likely to occur when salespeople make the sale, despatch (warehousing) department employees send the goods on the basis of the delivery docket, and other employees prepare the sales invoice after comparing the delivery docket with the report of goods despatched. With computerised systems, the despatch department employees send goods on the basis of electronic records of goods ordered, and staff preparing the sales invoice rely on electronic records of goods delivered. The amount that the customer is invoiced may be calculated by a computer, based on assigned sales price for each product, as is the case at most supermarket checkouts.

Accountability for assets

If accounting is to provide a valid basis of accountability for an asset, the accountant (as record keeper) should have neither physical custody of the asset nor access to it. Moreover, the custodian of the asset should not maintain or have access to the accounting records. An asset is not likely to be converted to personal use if one employee maintains the record of the asset that should be on hand and a different employee has physical custody of the asset. The separation of accounting responsibility from the custody of assets is especially important for cash and inventories because these assets are very vulnerable to unauthorised use or misappropriation.

Documentation procedures

Documents provide evidence that transactions and events have occurred. For example, the delivery document (also referred to as a picking slip) indicates that the goods have been shipped, and the sales invoice indicates that the customer has been invoiced for the goods. By adding signatures (or initials) to the documents, the people responsible for the transaction or event can be identified.

Procedures should be established for documents. First, whenever possible, documents should be prenumbered (e.g. cheques, sales invoices and cash receipts) and all documents should be accounted for. Prenumbering helps to prevent a transaction from being recorded more than once or, conversely, to prevent the transactions from not being recorded. It facilitates an audit trail, i.e. evidence of transactions and how they are recorded. Second, documents that are source documents for accounting entries should be promptly forwarded to the accounting department to help ensure timely recording of the transaction and event. Computers can produce prenumbered documents, record them and create an audit trail. For example, an audit trail may indicate that a customer's order has been received, which goods have been sent, and how much the customer has been invoiced, because related transactions can easily be identified by the use of prenumbered documents. A computer report can also identify unprocessed documents. This control measure contributes directly to the accuracy, reliability and timeliness of the accounting records.

In some computerised systems, multiple copies of documents are not used. Instead, an order or job is created and employees responsible for each function enter information on completion of each task. For example, a warehouse employee may enter data to confirm despatch of goods. Control is maintained by electronically limiting access with passwords.

Physical, mechanical and electronic controls

Use of physical, mechanical and electronic controls is essential. Physical controls such as safes and locked cabinets relate mainly to the safeguarding of assets. Mechanical and electronic controls safeguard assets and enhance the accuracy and reliability of the accounting records. Examples of these controls are shown in figure 6.4.

| **FIGURE 6.4** | Physical, mechanical and electronic controls |

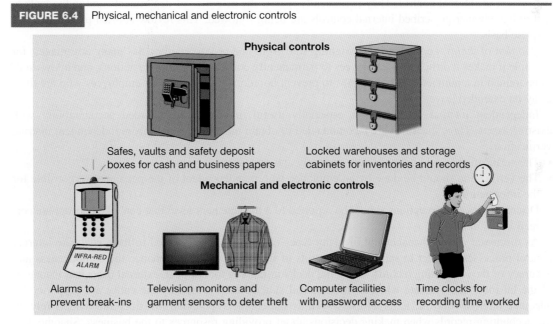

Physical controls

Safes, vaults and safety deposit boxes for cash and business papers

Locked warehouses and storage cabinets for inventories and records

Mechanical and electronic controls

Alarms to prevent break-ins

Television monitors and garment sensors to deter theft

Computer facilities with password access

Time clocks for recording time worked

A crucial consideration in programming computerised systems is building in controls that limit unauthorised or unintentional tampering. Several books and films have been produced with computer system tampering as a major theme. Most programmers would agree that tamper-proofing and debugging programs are the most difficult and time-consuming phases of their jobs. Program controls built into the computer prevent intentional or unintentional errors or unauthorised access. To prevent unauthorised access, the computer system may require that passwords be entered and that passwords be changed regularly. Once access has been allowed, other program controls identify data having a value higher or lower than a predetermined amount (limit checks), validate calculations (maths checks), and detect improper processing order (sequence checks). For example, the MYOB accounting package does not allow a journal entry to be posted unless debits equal credits. Another example is the Xero accounting package where the total of a supplier's invoice must be entered when entering a new bill. The system will not allow the bill to be approved unless the total of the individual line items (including any GST) equals this invoice total.

Independent internal verification

Most systems of internal control provide for independent internal verification. This principle involves the review, comparison and reconciliation of data prepared by employees. There are four common forms of internal verification:

- checking procedures facilitated by segregation of duties, such as the employee who receives inventory into the warehousing (receiving) department ensures that the amount of inventory actually received is the same amount as recorded by another employee on the purchase order
- monitoring by the employee's supervisor, such as a shop manager observing that the shop assistants do not remove inventory for their own personal use
- verification by an internal auditor
- rotation of duties.

Larger businesses would normally use all four forms of internal verification.

In large businesses, independent internal verification is assigned to internal auditors. Recall that internal auditors are employees of the business who evaluate on a continuous basis the effectiveness of the system of internal control. They periodically review the activities of departments and individuals to determine whether prescribed internal controls are being followed. This review is often performed on a surprise basis.

Rotation of duties, i.e. regularly reassigning staff from one task to another, has many advantages, for example it makes it difficult for employees to permanently conceal any improper actions, and allows staff to be trained in a number of different jobs to prevent boredom and to cover for employees who are ill or away on extended leave.

Independent internal verification is especially useful in comparing recorded accountability with existing assets. Three measures are recommended to obtain maximum benefit from independent internal verification.

- The verification should be made both routinely and on a surprise basis.
- The verification should be done by an employee who is independent of the personnel responsible for the information.
- Discrepancies and exceptions should be reported to a management level that can take appropriate corrective action.

As discussed above, management of many types of business entities need to have adequate internal control processes in order to safeguard the assets of the business and to enhance the completeness and accuracy of the accounting records. Using the decision-making toolkit next, external users and managers of the business can evaluate whether the financial statements prepared by the entity are supported by adequate internal controls. External users such as shareholders, potential investors and lenders rely on the accounting records when making decisions about providing resources to the business. Shareholders and potential investors need reliable information when making decisions about whether to continue to invest in the business. External users can place greater reliance on the financial statements if the auditor states in the auditor's report that the financial statements are a true and fair representation of the entity's operations. Reviewing the auditor's report, therefore, is an important step in the decision-making process for shareholders. Shareholders and potential investors also scan the financial press regularly for any articles that suggest there has been a misappropriation of assets through theft or irregularities as this may indicate that the internal control processes within the business entity are lacking. Internal reports from the internal auditors are an important source of information for senior management of the business as they may highlight the need for improvement in all or one of the internal control measures. If the auditor's report indicates that internal control processes are found wanting or reports in the financial papers regarding misappropriation of assets are a common occurrence, then external users need to review the financial statements with caution when using the financial statements to make resource allocation decisions.

The application of internal control to cash, an asset which is the most susceptible to misappropriation, is discussed in chapter 7.

DECISION-MAKING TOOLKIT

Decision/issue	Info needed for analysis	Tool or technique to use for decision	How to evaluate results to make decision
Are the business's financial statements supported by adequate internal controls?	Auditor's report, articles in financial press (external parties); reports on asset losses from theft, errors, customer complaints (internal parties)	The required measures of internal control are to (1) establish responsibility, (2) segregate duties, (3) document procedures, (4) use physical or automated controls, and (5) use independent internal verification.	If any indication is given that these or other controls are lacking, the financial statements should be used with caution.

Limitations of internal control

A system of internal control is generally designed to provide reasonable assurance that assets are properly safeguarded and that the accounting records are reliable. The concept of reasonable assurance rests on the premise that the costs of establishing control procedures should not exceed their expected benefit. To illustrate, consider shoplifting losses in retail stores. Such losses could be completely eliminated by having a security guard assigned to each customer entering the store. Store managers have concluded, however, that the negative effects of this procedure cannot be justified. Instead, stores have attempted to 'control' shoplifting losses by less costly procedures such as (1) posting signs saying, 'We reserve the right to inspect all bags' and 'Shoplifters will be prosecuted', (2) using hidden TV cameras and store detectives to monitor customer activity, and (3) using sensor equipment at exits, such as tags, to detect goods not paid for.

The human element is an important factor in every system of internal control. A good system can become ineffective as a result of employee fatigue, carelessness or indifference. For example, a receiving clerk in the warehousing department may not bother to count goods received from a supplier or may just 'fudge' the counts. Occasionally, two or more individuals may work together to get around prescribed controls. Such collusion can significantly impair the effectiveness of a system because it eliminates the protection anticipated from segregation of duties. If a supervisor and a receiving clerk collaborate to understate receipt of inventory, the system of internal control may be subverted (at least in the short run). No system of internal control is perfect.

The size of the business may impose limitations on internal control. In a small business, for example, it may be difficult to apply the principles of segregation of duties and some forms of independent internal verification because of the small number of employees. Small businesses rely more on supervision of employees.

It has been suggested that the most important and inexpensive measure any business can take to reduce employee theft and fraud is to conduct thorough background checks before employing people. Here are two tips: (1) check to see whether job applicants actually hold the qualifications they list; and (2) never use the telephone numbers for previous employers given on the reference sheet; always look them up yourself as you could be speaking to a relative or friend rather than a previous employer.

Internal control and forensic accounting

Internal control is an integral part of risk management and, as the previous section demonstrates, weaknesses in internal controls can have adverse consequence for business in terms of damage to profitability and reputation. Business is increasingly faced with challenges posed by fraudsters both within and external to organisations. Corporate fraud varies in shape and size, ranging from small-scale stealing to computer fraud committed by organised crime syndicates. A specialised strand of accounting service, called forensic accounting, has developed over the past decade in response to the growing complexity of the business environment and the increasing number of business-related investigations.

Forensic accounting is about the application of accounting knowledge and skills to issues arising in the context of civil and criminal litigations and investigation. More specifically, forensic accounting integrates accounting, auditing and investigative skills to provide accounting analysis in litigation support, dispute analysis, litigation services and expert witness services.

So what does a forensic accountant do, you may ask? Some of the common forensic investigation areas include:
- transaction reconstruction and measurement
- asset identification and valuation
- falsifications and manipulations of accounts
- bankruptcy and insolvency
- divorce and family law
- recovering proceeds of crime.

In addition to forensic investigation, forensic accounting is also concerned with more proactive risk reduction roles such as fraud prevention and management. This may include fraud awareness training for employees, managers and directors. Forensic accountants often perform fraud risk assessment and assist business in developing fraud control strategies. Further, forensic accountants are often advisers to audit committees, risk committees and governance committees for larger organisations.**

LEARNING REFLECTION AND CONSOLIDATION

Review it
1. What basic principles are followed in designing and developing an effective accounting information system?
2. What are the major phases in the development of an accounting information system?
3. Define internal control. What are the two main objectives of internal control?
4. Identify and describe the principles of internal control.
5. What are the limitations of internal control?
6. What are some of the tasks of forensic accountants?

Do it
Li Song owns a small retail store. Li wants to establish good internal control procedures but is confused about the difference between segregation of duties and independent internal verification. Explain the differences to Li.

Reasoning
In order to help Li, you need to thoroughly understand each principle. From this knowledge, you should be able to explain the differences between the two principles.

** D. Larry Crumbley 2008, *Journal of Forensic Accounting: Auditing, Fraud, and Risk*, vol. IX, www.rtedwards.com/journals/JP.

> **Solution**
> Segregation of duties pertains to the assignment of responsibility so that (1) related activities are assigned to different people, thus enabling the work of one employee to serve to confirm the accuracy of the work of another employee and (2) the custody of assets is separated from the records that keep track of the assets. Segregation of duties occurs daily in using assets and in executing and recording transactions. In contrast, independent internal verification involves reviewing, comparing and reconciling data prepared by one or several employees. Independent internal verification occurs after the fact, as in a supervisor ensuring inventory is counted regularly to ensure that the amount of inventory on hand matches the data held in the accounting records.

6.6 Transformation of financial data

LEARNING OBJECTIVE 6.6 Understand the accounting processes underlying the generation of financial statements.

This chapter has emphasised the importance of reliable accounting records and how good internal controls help to achieve reliability. We will now consider how data from transactions is transformed into financial data through the use of an accounting system. As part of this discussion we will also consider two major cycles, i.e. the sales and receivables, and purchases and payments cycles. We will then apply the principles of internal control to these cycles.

Accounting processes underlying the generation of financial statements

Recall that the system that collects and processes transaction data and disseminates financial information to interested parties is known as the accounting information system. An accounting information system has three phases: input, processing and output. The input refers to source documents such as sales invoices, purchase invoices, cheque butts and bank deposit slips. The source documents are used to record transactions as they occur into the journals. The journal serves as the chronological record of the transactions because transactions are entered into the journal in date order. In previous chapters we discussed the general journal as the journal where transactions are recorded. However, we need to recognise that most businesses will have several types of repetitive transactions, such as sales, purchases, receipts, and payments of cash. The journal entries for these similar transactions will be essentially the same. The accounting system can therefore be enhanced to be more streamlined and efficient through the reduction of the amount of duplication when recording in the general journal with the introduction and use of special journals, which are discussed later in the chapter. These journals are then posted to the general ledger periodically, which is the processing phase. Recall that the general ledger is made up of assets, liabilities, equity, income and expense accounts. The output of the system is the generation of the financial statements, which are prepared from the data in the general ledger. As discussed in chapter 1, the four financial statements that are prepared from the accounting data include:

1. The *statement of profit or loss*, which presents the income and expenses and resulting profit or loss for a specified period of time.
2. The *statement of changes in equity*, which summarises the changes in equity for a specific period of time.
3. The *statement of financial position*, which reports the assets, liabilities and equity at a specific date.
4. The *statement of cash flows*, which summarises information about the cash inflows (receipts) and outflows (payments) for a specific period of time.

Accompanying the financial statements are explanatory notes and supporting schedules. The financial statements and the notes are provided to external users such as shareholders, creditors and customers for decision-making purposes.

In the conversion of input to output, data are transformed into information that is useful to an external user. For example, each time a sale is made an invoice is generated and is then used as the source document for entry into the accounting system, and then summarised and totalled to be reported as sales information in the form of revenue in the statement of profit or loss. The transformation of data into useful information in an accounting system occurs as we move through the accounting cycle, as shown in figure 6.5.

| **FIGURE 6.5** | The transformation of accounting data to accounting information |

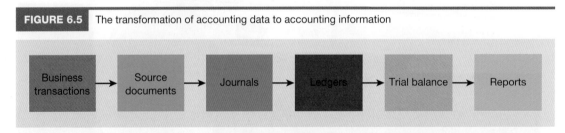

The number of transactions for small businesses would be low so a manual accounting system would be used to record the transactions and then generate the financial statements. As the number of transactions increases, owners of the business would need to decide whether to continue with a manual accounting system or move to a computerised accounting system. Owners of the business would decide to use a computerised accounting system instead of a manual system if the number of transactions had increased substantially. In these situations, the decision to move to a computerised system would be more efficient and more cost effective. It would be more cost effective as it would reduce the time taken to record transactions and possibly lead to a reduction of errors. This would therefore give the owners more confidence in the final reports prepared. It is important to realise that the design, structure and operation of both manual and computerised accounting systems are essentially the same. So an understanding of the manual accounting system is necessary in order to operate a computerised accounting system effectively. Computerised accounting systems are discussed later in this chapter and in greater detail in chapter 14.

6.7 Sales and receivables, and purchases and payments cycles illustrated

LEARNING OBJECTIVE 6.7 Describe the sales and receivables cycle and the purchases and payments cycle.

The sales and receivables cycle, also known as the revenue cycle, provides a flow of how sales are made and recorded within an organisation. As we know, a sales transaction can be a cash sale or a credit sale. A cash sale creates a sales invoice that initiates the recording of the sale transaction through the journal, which is then posted to the general ledger with a debit to the bank account and a corresponding credit to the sales account. Many goods have a barcode on their packaging. When this barcode is scanned for a sale transaction, the scanning process will automatically reduce the respective amount of inventory on hand so that the system keeps a running record of the quantities of the item of inventory on hand. As we know, many sales transactions are sales on credit. And often, for example, the sale may be made online. Figure 6.6 is a simplified diagram of the sales and receivables cycle. (Remember that inventory is also known as *stock*.)

A sales order from the customer initiates the cycle. A sales order can be received electronically, i.e. either online or via email. Alternatively, a sales order can be phoned through to the business by the customer. The sales department prepares an internal sales order which lists the inventory that has been ordered by the customer. The internal sales order is the internal record that initiates the process. The internal sales order is also known as the picking slip. The picking slip is then sent to the warehousing department. The warehousing department is the section of the business that controls the inventory held by the organisation. The warehousing department checks that inventory is available to meet the customer demand, and then personnel within this department fill the order by preparing a delivery docket and packing the inventory for delivery to the customer as per the picking slip. For example, assume a customer has ordered five heart rate monitors. This would be listed on the picking slip. The warehousing department would fill this order by packing five heart rate monitors, which would then be delivered to the customer. Once the inventory was despatched, the inventory records would be updated to reflect the removal of inventory from the warehouse. A copy of the delivery docket would be sent to the accounting department who would then generate a sales invoice, which would be sent to the customer. The generation of the sales invoice results in the recording of the sale in the accounting system of a debit to the accounts receivable account and a credit to the sales account.

The preceding paragraph has explained the process as though it were a manual process. However, many large organisations have fully integrated systems, i.e. every step in the process is automatic and computer generated. In an integrated system the sales order would be received online, which would initiate the process in the computerised system. Once initiated, a picking slip would be automatically generated and the computerised system would automatically determine if the order could be filled, i.e. that the inventory ordered is available to be despatched. A delivery docket would be automatically generated once the inventory had been picked and electronic sign-off would occur, which would then generate the sales invoice.

Depending on the geographical location of the customer and the delivery schedule, the goods could be received on the same day as despatched, or if the customer were located a long distance away from the business, the goods would be received some time later. When the customer receives the goods, the customer checks that what they have received matches what they have ordered and that the goods are in good condition. The customer will then sign the delivery docket as proof of delivery. On receipt of the signed delivery docket the warehouse will file it away for completeness.

Payment for the goods will be sent by the customer, according to the credit terms that were arranged previously between the business and the customer. The setting of credit terms is discussed in more detail in chapter 7. However, at this point, you should note that there would be a time lag between the sales order, delivery of the goods and the receipt of cash from the customer. This time lag is due to the credit terms.

Briefly, before a sales order is filled it is common practice for the accounting department to carry out a credit check on new customers to ensure that the risk of non-payment for goods is minimised. Existing customers who have already had their credit checks will usually have their orders filled automatically. The responsibility for credit checks rests with the accounting department, which will review each customer separately taking into account their past history in terms of sales and receipts of cash. Once the cash is received from the customer, the transaction will be entered into the journal and posted to the general ledger, resulting in a reduction in accounts receivable through a credit to this account and a corresponding debit to the cash account.

FIGURE 6.6 Sales and receivables cycle

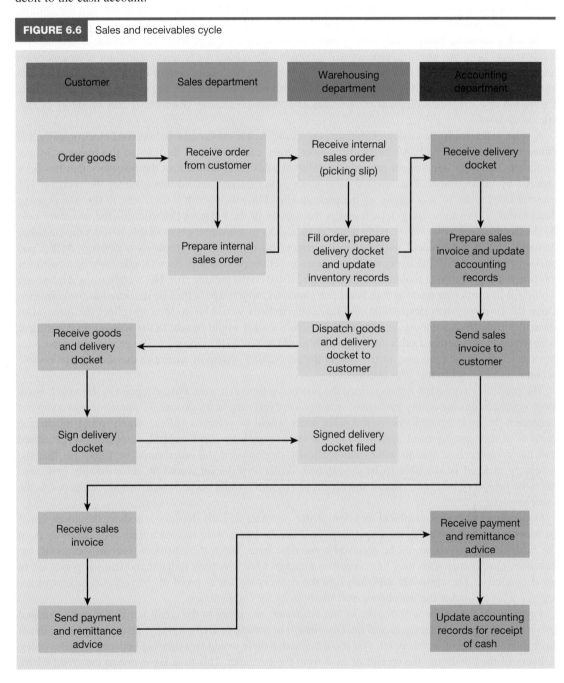

Figure 6.7 outlines the purchases and payments cycle, showing the flow of purchases of inventory and payments for inventory within organisations.

The warehousing department within an organisation is responsible for ensuring that there is enough inventory on hand to meet sales demands. This department will have a number of measures in place to assist them in determining when items of inventory need to be replenished or added to. A computerised system will advise when the item of inventory has reached a point where it needs to be reordered — this is known as the reorder point. The reorder point is determined and set by the business through a review of prior sales for each item of inventory. Once it has been identified that inventory levels for a particular item of inventory are low, the warehouse clerk in the warehousing department will complete a purchase requisition to order the replacement or additional inventory needed. The purchase requisition will list the quantity and the item of inventory that is being reordered and therefore repurchased. This requisition will be signed off by a supervisor before the order is forwarded on to the purchasing department. The purchasing department will ensure that all details are complete with regard to the inventory being ordered and will prepare a purchase order. This purchase order will then be sent to the supplier. There will usually be additional copies of the purchase order — one for each of the following departments: the accounting department and the warehousing department. Once the purchase order has been sent to the supplier, a copy of this is sent to the accounting department so that it can be used to check against the goods received note (discussed below) and the supplier invoice when received.

Once the supplier receives the purchase order, the supplier will fill the purchase order and despatch the goods ordered to the business. A delivery docket will be attached to the boxed goods. The supplier will also send an invoice to the business so that payment can be made by the business once the goods are received and checked.

The warehousing department will receive the goods accompanied by the delivery docket. The warehouse clerk will ensure that the goods received match both the delivery docket and the purchase order exactly. The clerk will also check that the goods received are in good condition. Once the clerk confirms that the goods match the purchase order, the clerk will complete a goods received note, which will be forwarded to the accounting department. The delivery docket will also be signed to reflect the goods have been received and this signed copy will be forwarded to the supplier. Also at this point, the inventory will be added to the shelves in the warehouse and the inventory levels will be updated.

On receipt of the supplier's invoice, the accounting department will check that the details on the purchase order, the goods received note and the supplier's invoice are all the same. As the goods and the supplier's invoice have been received by the business, the accounting system will be updated, which will result in a debit to the inventory account and a credit to the accounts payable account.

Prior to making payment to the supplier, the accounting department will check the payment terms that were arranged previously between the two businesses and will authorise payment. Once the payment is made to the supplier, the accounts payable account will be debited and the bank account will be credited. There will be a time lag between the time the goods are ordered, received and paid for. This time lag is due to the credit terms that the business has arranged with the supplier of the goods.

The preceding paragraphs in relation to the purchases and payments cycle have explained the purchasing process as though it were a manual process. Many large organisations have fully integrated inventory systems where many of the steps are automatically generated. For example, in an integrated system, when the inventory has reached its minimum level it would automatically set in train the process of ordering the goods for replenishment. In fact, advancements in information technology in recent years have enabled businesses to integrate inventory ordering systems with sophisticated supply chain management systems. In some inventory systems regular suppliers of specific items would have access to the purchasing entity's inventory database via the internet so that the supplier can monitor and replenish their customers' inventory levels automatically.

Now that we have reviewed the respective cycles for purchases of inventory and sales of inventory, let us consider some internal control principles that business may apply with regard to these respective cycles.

FIGURE 6.7 Purchases and payments cycle

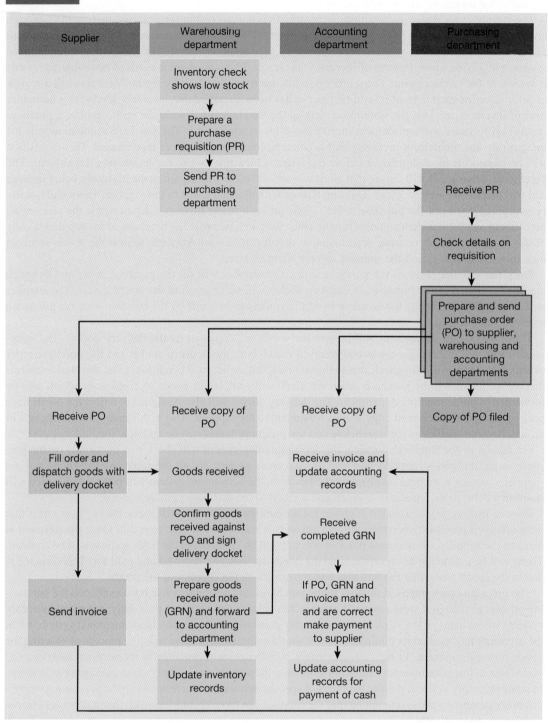

6.8 Internal control principles applied to the sales and receivables cycle and purchases and payments cycle

LEARNING OBJECTIVE 6.8 Apply internal control principles to the sales and receivables cycle and purchases and payments cycle for transforming data.

Recall that the principles of internal control include establishment of responsibility for staff; segregation of duties; documentation procedures; physical, mechanical and internal controls; and independent internal verification. Let us now apply these principles firstly to the sales and receivables cycle and then to the purchases and payments cycle.

Sales and receivables cycle

It is important to note that each person involved in the cycle within each of the respective departments needs to be authorised to carry out their task and is appropriately qualified to do so. For example, the warehouse clerk needs to have the authority to fill the customer order and update the inventory records.

Similarly, in executing a sales transaction, the entity needs to assign responsibility for the sale to various personnel within the different departments, as shown in figure 6.6. Recall that this is known as segregation of duties. Remember, the sale is made by a salesperson, while filling and despatching the sales order is carried out by a warehouse clerk, while other staff within the accounting department will send the invoice to the customer. Within the accounting department it will also be necessary to ensure that the same staff member does not process the cash received and also update the customer record. Having various personnel involved with the sales transaction ensures that there is independent verification at each step of the transaction. The segregation of duties will ensure that fictitious sales are not created or that the salesperson does not make a sale at unauthorised prices, and that a warehouse clerk in the warehousing department does not send the goods to himself or herself. Also, segregation of duties within the accounting department will ensure that cash is not misappropriated.

Also note in figure 6.6, when the warehouse clerk fills the sales order he or she will sign the picking slip to confirm that the amount of goods despatched matches the goods on the sales order — this is an example of a documentation procedure. This will ensure that the person responsible for the shipment of goods can be identified.

A business will ensure that its inventory records can only be accessed by authorised personnel with password access. Often businesses will also have alarm systems in place to safeguard their inventory.

Let us now turn to the purchases and payments cycle.

Purchases and payments cycle

Recall that the establishment of responsibility is an important internal control principle. This is also true for the purchases and payments cycle. The warehouse clerk needs to have the required skills and experience to initiate the purchases cycle, while this staff member needs to have an appreciation of when the inventory levels are low and require replenishment. In a computerised system the warehouse clerk would need to be experienced in checking that the system is reordering inventory when inventory levels are low. The warehouse clerk also needs to have the authority to check the goods received against the purchase order, complete a goods received note and ensure inventory levels are updated on receipt of the goods.

Also in the purchases and payments cycle, related activities need to be assigned to different personnel. When one person is responsible for all the related activities, the potential for errors or irregularities increases. Related purchasing activities include ordering goods, receiving of goods and paying for goods. Referring to figure 6.7, goods are ordered by a purchasing clerk within the purchasing department, and the warehouse clerk within the warehousing department is then responsible for receiving the goods and ensuring that the received goods match the order placed against the delivery docket (an example of independent verification). An accounting staff member is then responsible for paying the supplier for the goods. Note that the accounting department does not have physical custody of the goods nor access to the goods. Goods are kept in the warehousing department and the accounting records are in the accounting department. This is an important internal control to safeguard the inventory. Note that within this cycle there is also a requirement for the warehouse clerk to complete and sign the goods received note, before it is sent to the accounting department, to confirm the receipt of goods, an example of a documented procedure.

LEARNING REFLECTION AND CONSOLIDATION

Review it
1. Explain how financial data is transformed into financial statements.
2. Describe the sales and receivables cycle.
3. Describe the purchases and payments cycle.

In earlier chapters, we illustrated basic accounting procedures by recording each transaction with one entry in the general journal and later posting the debit and credit from the general journal to the appropriate general ledger accounts. While this accounting system, as illustrated in the first five chapters, is satisfactory in a business where the volume of transactions is extremely low, as noted earlier most businesses will have several types of repetitive transactions, such as sales, purchases, receipts and payments of cash. The journal entries for these similar transactions will be essentially the same, such that the accounting system will be enhanced with the introduction of special journals. The accounting system will also find it necessary to add additional ledgers and journals to the accounting system to record transaction data efficiently.

6.9 Control accounts, subsidiary ledgers and special journals

LEARNING OBJECTIVE 6.9 Describe the nature and purpose of control accounts and subsidiary ledgers.

The discussion in previous chapters was limited to only one ledger, the general ledger. A more efficient and effective way for businesses to process a large number of transactions is to use control accounts and subsidiary ledgers. For example, Flashback Entertainment is a wholesaler in Kirawee, a suburb of Sydney, that sells CDs and DVDs on credit to many stores (including JB Hi-Fi Ltd, Crazy Clark's, Big W and IGA) in New South Wales. It has a customer base of around 100 stores. If the entity recorded all its credit sales and cash receipts in one accounts receivable general ledger account, it would be very difficult to determine how much inventory each customer had purchased, which customers had paid their accounts and which customers had unpaid balances at any point in time. The one general ledger account would not provide sufficient detail to easily answer these questions. One solution to this problem is to have individual general ledger accounts for each customer. However, this too would be inappropriate as large entities like Coca-Cola Amatil may have thousands of customers and the general ledger and trial balance would become huge and unmanageable. It might also be useful to know the aggregate amount of all accounts receivable. This situation is further compounded by the fact that other accounts such as accounts payable, plant and equipment, and inventory also comprise many items on which separate information may be required.

Instead of using a single general ledger account, most businesses use subsidiary ledgers to keep track of individual balances. A **subsidiary ledger** is a group of accounts with a common characteristic (e.g. all accounts receivable). The subsidiary ledger frees the general ledger from the details of individual balances.

Two common subsidiary ledgers are:

1. the **accounts receivable** (or **customers'**) **subsidiary ledger**, which collects transaction data of individual customers
2. the **accounts payable** (or **suppliers'**) **subsidiary ledger**, which collects transaction data of individual creditors.

In each of these subsidiary ledgers, individual accounts are usually arranged in alphabetical order or by customer or creditor account number. (*Note:* The accounts receivable subsidiary ledger can also be called the *debtors' subsidiary ledger*. The accounts payable subsidiary ledger can also be called the *creditors' subsidiary ledger*.)

The detailed data from a subsidiary ledger are summarised in a general ledger account. For example, the detailed data from the accounts receivable subsidiary ledger are summarised in accounts receivable in the general ledger. The general ledger account that summarises subsidiary ledger data is called a **control account**. An overview of the relationship of subsidiary ledgers to the general ledger is shown in figure 6.8. The general ledger control accounts and subsidiary ledger accounts are shown in green. Note that cash and share capital in this illustration are not control accounts because there are no subsidiary ledger accounts related to these accounts.

FIGURE 6.8 Relationship of general ledger and subsidiary ledgers

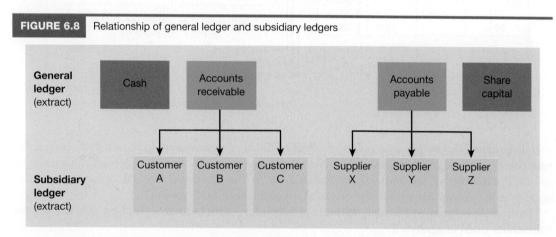

It is important to understand that the subsidiary ledger is *outside* the general ledger and is not used in extracting the trial balance. If the trial balance included *both* the summarised balances from a general ledger control account and the detailed balances from the corresponding subsidiary ledger, it would be double counting (note that the control account provides the same information as the subsidiary ledger, but in summary).

Each general ledger control account balance must equal the composite balance of the individual accounts in the related subsidiary ledger at the end of an accounting period. This provides an element of control within the system and facilitates accuracy in account balances. For example, the balance in the accounts payable general ledger in figure 6.8 must equal the total of the subsidiary balances of suppliers X + Y + Z.

Control accounts and subsidiary ledgers illustrated

An example of a control account and subsidiary ledger for Larson Ltd is provided in figure 6.9. (The explanation column in these accounts is not shown in this and subsequent illustrations due to space considerations.)

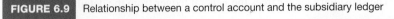

FIGURE 6.9 Relationship between a control account and the subsidiary ledger

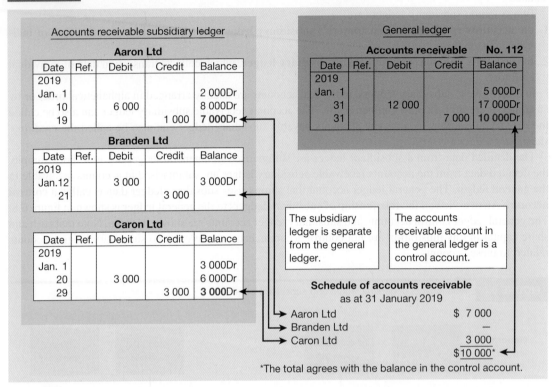

Helpful hint: The schedule of accounts receivable is a list of all balances in the subsidiary ledger. The total can be compared with the total in the control account. Also, the 'Posting reference' column can be abbreviated as 'Post ref.', as illustrated in chapter 2, or 'Ref.' as illustrated here. The accounts receivable account in the general ledger can also be called 'Accounts receivable control'.

The example is based on 1 January balances of $2000 for Aaron Ltd and $3000 for Caron Ltd and the transactions listed in figure 6.10.

FIGURE 6.10 Sales and collection transactions

Credit sales			Collections on account		
Jan. 10	Aaron Ltd	$ 6 000	Jan. 19	Aaron Ltd	$1 000
12	Branden Ltd	3 000	21	Branden Ltd	3 000
20	Caron Ltd	3 000	29	Caron Ltd	3 000
		$12 000			$7 000

The opening balance of $5000 on 1 January in the accounts receivable control account is the total of the opening balances in the accounts receivable subsidiary ledger ($2000 Aaron Ltd and $3000 Caron Ltd).

The total debits ($12 000) and credits ($7000) in the accounts receivable control account in the general ledger are reconcilable to the detailed debits and credits in the subsidiary accounts. Also, the 31 January balance of $10 000 in the control account agrees with the total of the balances in the individual accounts (Aaron Ltd $7000 + Branden Ltd $0 + Caron Ltd $3000) in the subsidiary ledger and the schedule of accounts receivable. A **schedule of accounts receivable** is a list of all accounts and their balances in the subsidiary ledger for accounts receivable at a particular date (see figure 6.9). Similarly, a **schedule of accounts payable** is a list of all accounts and their balances in the subsidiary ledger for accounts payable at a particular date.

As shown, postings are made monthly to the control accounts in the general ledger. This practice allows monthly financial statements to be prepared. Postings to the individual accounts in the subsidiary ledger are made daily. Daily posting ensures that account information is current. This enables the business to monitor credit limits, invoice customers, and answer enquiries from customers about their account balances. Using the decision-making toolkit below, managers can evaluate whether the recording of transactions for customers and suppliers has resulted in accurate balances in the respective ledger accounts. Managers within the business will check at the end of every month that the balances in the general ledger control accounts equals the total of the individual balances in the subsidiary ledgers for both accounts receivable and accounts payable. This function is carried out by management in order to ensure that entries have been entered correctly in both ledgers. This provides an element of control to the process of entering transactions. It also provides verification that the balances of the control accounts that are carried through to the trial balance are correct. If the balance in the general ledger control account and the corresponding subsidiary ledger schedule are not the same, then it indicates that an error in recording has occurred. If this is the case, then the error must be identified and a correcting entry actioned.

DECISION-MAKING TOOLKIT

Decision/issue	Info needed for analysis	Tool or technique to use for decision	How to evaluate results to make decision
Does the balance in the general ledger control account equal the total of the individual balances in the subsidiary ledger?	General ledger control account (e.g. accounts receivable) and corresponding subsidiary ledger (e.g. subsidiary ledger for accounts receivable)	Balance in the general ledger control account (e.g. accounts receivable) and a schedule of the corresponding subsidiary ledger (e.g. schedule of accounts receivable)	Compare the balance in the general ledger control account with the total of the corresponding subsidiary ledger schedule. A discrepancy indicates an error in the accounting records. The error must be identified and corrected.

Advantages of subsidiary ledgers

Subsidiary ledgers have several advantages.
1. They show transactions affecting one customer or one creditor in a single account, thus providing up-to-date information on specific account balances.
2. They free the general ledger of excessive details. As a result, a trial balance of the general ledger does not contain vast numbers of individual account balances.
3. They provide effective control through periodic comparison of the total of the schedule of the subsidiary ledger with the balance in the corresponding control account.
4. They make possible a segregation of duties in posting. One employee can post to the general ledger while someone else posts to the subsidiary ledgers.

An efficient and effective accounting information system is a critical part of a business. Early detection of overdue customer accounts prompting action to collect outstanding debts can be achieved with a well-functioning accounts receivable subsystem. The timely collection of accounts receivable is a significant factor for entity success. A variety of reports can be generated to enable management to monitor whether customer accounts are being paid on time and, if not, to take prompt action to collect outstanding amounts. Monitoring cash flows is vital in any business. Ensuring outstanding accounts are paid on time is a critical part of maintaining adequate cash inflows and enables a business to have sufficient cash to meet payments as they fall due and to continue to grow a successful business.

Review it

1. What is a subsidiary ledger, and what purpose does it serve?
2. Explain the relationship between a control account in the general ledger and its corresponding subsidiary ledger.

Do it

Presented below is information related to Sims Ltd for its first month of operations. Determine the balances that appear in the accounts payable subsidiary ledger. What accounts payable control balance appears in the general ledger at the end of January?

Credit purchases			Cash paid		
Jan. 5	Devon Ltd	$11 000	Jan. 9	Devon Ltd	$7 000
11	Shelby Pty Ltd	7 000	14	Shelby Pty Ltd	2 000
22	Taylor Ltd	15 000	27	Taylor Ltd	9 000

Problem-solving strategies

• To determine the balances that appear in the accounts payable subsidiary ledger, subtract cash paid from credit purchases. (Note that there are no opening balances as it is the first month of operations for Sims Ltd.)
• To determine the accounts payable control balance in the general ledger, sum the individual balances.

Solution

Subsidiary ledger balances: Devon Ltd $4000 ($11 000 − $7000); Shelby Pty Ltd $5000 ($7000 − $2000); Taylor Ltd $6000 ($15 000 − $9000). General ledger accounts payable balance: $15 000 ($33 000 credit purchases less $18 000 cash paid).

6.10 Special journals

LEARNING OBJECTIVE 6.10 Explain how special journals are used in recording transactions.

So far you have learned to journalise transactions in a two-column general journal and post each entry to the general ledger. This procedure is satisfactory in only the very smallest businesses and is inappropriate for entities such as JB Hi-Fi Ltd and Harvey Norman which process thousands of transactions each month. To expedite journalising and posting, most businesses use special journals in addition to the general journal.

A **special journal** is used to record similar types of transactions. Examples would be all sales of inventory on account, or all cash receipts. What special journals a business uses depends largely on the types of transactions that occur frequently. Most merchandising businesses use the journals shown in figure 6.11 to record transactions daily.

The sales journal is used to record sales of inventory on account, i.e. on credit. All receipts of cash are recorded in the cash receipts journal, including cash sales and collections of accounts receivable. All purchases of inventory on account, i.e. on credit, are recorded in the purchases journal. All payments of cash are entered in the cash payments journal. Further discussion on each of the special journals is provided in sections 6.13 and 6.14. A general journal is used to record transactions that cannot be entered in one of the special journals.

FIGURE 6.11 Use of special journals and the general journal

Sales journal	Cash receipts journal	Purchases journal	Cash payments journal	General journal
Used for: All sales of inventory on account	*Used for:* All cash received (including cash sales)	*Used for:* All purchases of inventory on account	*Used for:* All cash paid (including cash purchases)	*Used for:* Transactions that cannot be entered in a special journal, including correcting, adjusting and closing entries

You might like to familiarise yourself with the form of each of these special journals by taking a quick look at sections 6.13 and 6.14. You will notice that each special journal will have a number of columns such as a column to record the date of the transaction, a posting reference column (which is used when posting to the ledger) and an account credited column which is the column where you record information about the transaction, for example the customer name if the transaction is a sales transaction or the receipt of money from the customer. Within each special journal you will have separate columns to record amounts for similar transactions. For example, in the sales journal in section 6.13 you will have a column to record the sales amount to the customer at its selling price (accounts receivable/sales) and a column to record the cost price of the sale to cost of sales/inventory accounts as Karns Wholesale Supply uses the perpetual inventory system.

Each daily transaction is recorded in the respective journal as a one-line entry. For example, if the transaction is the receipt of cash from a customer, then this entry would be journalised in the cash receipts journal in one entry, with the amount of cash received in the cash column and in the accounts receivable column. It is important to realise that the general debit and credit rules used to record transactions, as discussed in previous chapters, still applies. Every journal entry must have at least one debit and one credit entry, so the need for equality of debits and credits remains. As noted, examples of each special journal and illustrations of journalising for each special journal are provided and further explained in sections 6.13 and 6.14.

If a transaction cannot be recorded in a special journal, it is recorded in the general journal. For example, if you had special journals for only the four types of transactions shown in figure 6.11, purchase returns and allowances would be recorded in the general journal as would sales returns and allowances. A further example of a transaction entered in the general journal is for the purchase of a fixed asset such as equipment on credit. Similarly, correcting, adjusting and closing entries are recorded in the general journal. Other types of special journals may be used in some situations. For example, when sales returns and allowances are frequent, special journals may be used to record these transactions.

We will now summarise the posting process for special journals. A detailed discussion of the posting process for each of the special journals as identified in figure 6.11 can be found in sections 6.13 and 6.14.

Posting the special journals

When posting from the special journals, column totals are posted at the end of each month to the corresponding general ledger account as noted in the column heading. Account numbers are entered below the column totals to show that they have been posted to the general ledger. This holds true for all columns except for the other accounts column which is found in the cash receipts and cash payments journals. The other accounts column is used for transactions that do not fit into other specified columns within the respective journal. Therefore, the other accounts column will include entries for different types of transactions, for example in the cash receipts journal columns will usually exist for credit entries to accounts receivable, sales, and other accounts. If, for example, the transaction being entered into this journal is for the contribution of capital, then the amount will be credited in the other accounts column. The individual amounts comprising the other accounts total are posted separately to the general ledger accounts specified in the account credited column. The symbol (✗) is inserted below the total of the other accounts column to indicate that the total amount has not been posted.

Sales transactions from the sales journal are posted daily to the individual accounts receivable account in the subsidiary ledger. The column total of this journal is posted to the general ledger, accounts receivable control account, at the end of each month, and when posted the account numbers are entered below the column totals to show that they have been posted.

Receipts of cash from customers will be recorded in the cash receipts journal and this column will be posted in total at the end of the month to the accounts receivable control account in the general ledger; the individual amounts are posted daily to the subsidiary ledger accounts.

Purchase transactions from the purchases journal and corresponding payments of cash to suppliers in the cash payments journal are posted daily to the individual accounts payable account in the subsidiary ledger, and as a total amount to the control account in the general ledger at the end of each month.

A tick (✓) (or the appropriate subsidiary ledger account number for the customer or the supplier) is inserted in the posting reference (Ref.) column to indicate that the daily posting to the customer's (or supplier's) account has been made.

In both the subsidiary ledger and the general ledger accounts, a reference to the journal and the corresponding page number is written in the reference column of the ledger, for example, CR1 indicates that the posting came from page 1 of the cash receipts journal.

You might like to refer to sections 6.13 and 6.14 for a detailed illustration of posting from each of the respective special journals.

Advantages of special journals

Special journals permit greater segregation of duties because several people can record entries in different journals at the same time. For example, one employee may journalise all cash receipts, and another may journalise all credit sales. Also, the use of special journals reduces the time needed to complete the posting process as totals for each column in the special journals are posted to the general ledger at the end of each month. Each transaction is recorded on a single line and narrations are not required as transactions within the journals (e.g. the sales journal and the purchases journal) are of the same type (i.e. sales and purchases respectively).

LEARNING REFLECTION AND CONSOLIDATION

Review it

1. What types of special journals are used to record transactions? Why are special journals used?
2. Explain how special journals are posted.
3. The use of special journals has several advantages. Discuss this statement.

Do it

Chiara Accessories Ltd uses special journals and a general journal. Identify the journal in which each of the following transactions is recorded.
(a) Purchased equipment on account.
(b) Purchased inventory on account.
(c) Paid utility expense in cash.
(d) Sold inventory on account.
(e) Received cash from a customer.
(f) Closing rent expense to the profit or loss summary account.

6.11 Computerised accounting information systems

LEARNING OBJECTIVE 6.11 Understand the basic features of computerised accounting systems and appreciate the role and use of non-integrated systems.

A manual accounting system is sufficient for a small business with a limited number of transactions, although most businesses are at least partially computerised due to the popularity of computers and their affordability. Businesses may choose to employ 'off-the-shelf' accounting packages like Xero and MYOB or develop their own customised information subsystems that can require ongoing refinements and upgrades to improve usability and streamline business processes.

Companies such as Domino's Pizza Enterprises Ltd and JB Hi-Fi Ltd have large volumes of transactions to process and need computers to increase the accuracy and speed of data processing. In addition to the huge volumes of sales and purchases recorded, these companies are required to make various payments to and on behalf of their employees for salaries, personal income tax and superannuation. To be able to account for all of these different transactions, large companies employ highly sophisticated computerised accounting information systems and subsystems. For example, transactions for employee salaries can be made using a specialised payroll subsystem. Other small businesses which have fewer transactions and fewer employees can use accounting software like MYOB or Xero to process their transactions. Supermarkets such as Coles and Woolworths sell thousands of items each day and the use of computer technology and product code scanners allows these entities to update inventories and sales efficiently. Different businesses employ a variety of computerised accounting systems to satisfy their information recording and reporting needs. While these systems can vary in terms of cost and their level of sophistication, the basic features of computerised systems are outlined below, with more detailed information provided in chapter 14.

Basic features of computerised systems

The model underlying all computer accounting packages is based on the underlying framework of a manual double-entry accounting system. In a **manual accounting system**, each of the steps in the accounting cycle is performed by hand. For example, each accounting transaction is entered manually in the journal; each is posted manually to the ledger. Other manual calculations must be made to obtain ledger account balances and to prepare a trial balance and financial statements.

In a computerised accounting system, there are programs for performing the steps in the accounting cycle, such as journalising, posting, and preparing a trial balance and accounting reports.

The system of special journals, control accounts and subsidiary ledgers used in a manual accounting system is also evident in computerised accounting systems. Most computerised systems today are **integrated accounting systems**. Integrated systems are made up of subsystems commonly referred to as *modules*, examples of which include general ledger, inventory, non-current assets, accounts receivable and payable, and payroll modules. In a fully integrated accounting system, when data are entered into one module the computer automatically updates the information in other relevant modules. For example, when a purchase is made, the computer automatically updates the accounts payable and inventory accounts in the general ledger module. Accounting reports such as the statement of financial position and the statement of profit or loss are also automatically updated.

There are many computerised accounting systems available on the market. Examples of the best known packages include Sage, ACCPAC, Attaché, MYOB, QuickBooks, Xero and Sybiz. These accounting systems offer computer packages with various subsystems covering all the accounting functions. Most accounting software providers also sell a range of subpackages consisting of various modules that can be purchased separately to suit the needs of the particular business. For example, a business providing only services would not require an inventory subsystem, whereas a business selling goods would find an inventory module useful in recording and managing inventories. Thus, integrated accounting packages and various modules can be purchased based on the nature of the business (service, manufacturing or merchandising), its size (small, medium or large) and the number of employees.

Some computerised accounting systems are cloud-based systems which can be accessed anywhere, anytime, on a PC, Mac, tablet or phone. An example of this is the Xero accounting package and MYOB AccountRight Live. Where packages can be run on a desktop or as a cloud-based system, management needs to decide which access they wish to have and would base their decision on considerations such as accessibility (anywhere, anytime would be available if it was a cloud-based solution) and risk.

As we know, an accounting information system is concerned with financial data and accounting transactions. For example, a sale will be captured by the accounting system through the accounting software package, resulting in a debit to accounts receivable and a credit to sales. However, other potentially useful non-financial information about the sale, for example the time of day the sale was made, may also be important. Such information can be gathered in an enterprise resource planning (ERP) system. An ERP system integrates all aspects of a company's operations with the accounting information system.

It collects, processes and stores data in a centralised database and shares up-to-date information across business processes so that business activities can be coordinated. It is an effective means of capturing data and providing information to managers so that they can assess the company. SAP is an example of an ERP system, and is a leading provider of enterprise business applications which allow businesses to manage operations and customer relations. SAP products are available for small and large businesses.

Recall that not all businesses run fully integrated accounting systems. This means that data from reports produced in one subsystem need to be entered into other subsystems either manually or via data export/import processes. In addition to computerised accounting packages like Xero and MYOB, companies will also use other subsystems such as Excel spreadsheets. Electronic spreadsheets, such as an Excel spreadsheet, can be an important part of the accounting function in some businesses. For example, spreadsheets can be used to develop business budgets, monitor inventory movements and calculate depreciation on fixed assets. A spreadsheet is a powerful tool, as rows and columns of data can be added, deleted or changed. The use of spreadsheets for budgets allows the accountant to experiment with the budget by applying and testing 'what if?' questions by changing one number of one formula in the spreadsheet. This saves hours of manual calculations.

6.12 Advantages and disadvantages of computerised systems

LEARNING OBJECTIVE 6.12 Identify the advantages and disadvantages of computerised accounting systems.

Computerised accounting systems offer many advantages, but it is important to recognise that there are also problems associated with their use.

Advantages

The main advantages of computerised accounting systems are the ability to process numerous transactions quickly, the built-in automatic posting of transactions, error reduction, a fast response time, and flexible and fast report production. Fast processing speed allows thousands of transactions to be processed quickly. Posting is performed automatically and so it is virtually error-free. This means that up-to-date information is available to answer day-to-day queries such as customer account balances and inventory levels. However, adequate procedures should be in place to ensure that input errors do not occur or, if they do, that they can be detected. Manual systems are much more susceptible to human error than are computerised systems.

Computerised accounting systems can be programmed to produce automatically various accounting documents such as invoices, and a wide range of specialised reports in addition to the statement of profit or loss and statement of financial position. Computerised reports are much more sophisticated and flexible than reports produced in a manual system. For example, computerised systems can produce reports of sales by geographical region, expenses by department or purchases from major suppliers for a certain period. The wide variety of reports provides owners and managers with the information needed to make decisions. In the past, high cost and sophistication of computerised accounting systems put them out of reach of small business owners. However, the cost of hardware and software has fallen considerably, and the availability of user-friendly accounting packages like Xero, MYOB and QuickBooks has resulted in increased use of computerised accounting systems by all businesses.

Disadvantages

As we have seen from the discussion above, computerised accounting systems have many advantages over manual accounting systems. However, some of the advantages outlined may not be achieved if the hardware and software are inappropriate, incompatible or faulty. Furthermore, employees need to be able to operate the system, and people lacking the skills could cause problems in the system or not make full use of the system's capabilities.

All computerised systems need good back-up mechanisms to ensure that important data are not lost during power failures or system crashes. Computer viruses and computer hackers can also have devastating effects on data, and highly skilled computer programmers can manipulate computerised accounting systems to commit fraud or embezzlement. Even though computerised accounting systems have many advantages and benefits, it is important to be aware of the potential problems associated with their use.

Using the decision-making toolkit for Aussie Roo Ltd at the end of the chapter, managers can compare the balance of the accounts receivable and the accounts payable control accounts with the respective subsidiary ledger schedules as at 30 June 2020. This comparison will highlight if there are discrepancies between both control accounts and subsidiary ledger schedules and identify where the errors have occurred. This will then allow for errors to be corrected, which will result in new balances.

6.13 Sales journal

LEARNING OBJECTIVE 6.13 Record transactions for sales, purchases, cash receipts and cash payments in special journals.

The general journal described in earlier chapters can be used to record all types of transactions — sales, sales returns, purchases, purchase returns, cash receipts and cash payments. However, recording these transactions in the general journal requires that each debit and credit recorded must be posted to the ledger accounts individually, which will require a large amount of posting time and may increase the risk of errors being recorded. Each transaction will also need its own narration, adding more time to the recording of the transaction. It also means you cannot have segregation of duties as only one person at a time can record the effects of transactions and post debits and credits to the ledger. To avoid these limitations, similar transactions are recorded in special journals. The common special journals used by a retail business, i.e. the sales journal, purchases journal, cash receipts journal and cash payments journal, are now illustrated in more detail.

The **sales journal** is used to record sales of inventory on account. Cash sales of inventory are entered in the cash receipts journal. Credit sales of assets other than inventory are entered in the general journal. Although most products and services attract GST, the effects of GST are not illustrated in this chapter. GST was covered in chapter 4 (sections 4.6 and 4.7).

Helpful hint: Postings are also made daily to individual ledger accounts in the inventory subsidiary ledger to maintain a perpetual inventory system.

Journalising credit sales

Karns Wholesale Supply uses a perpetual inventory system. Under this system, each entry in the sales journal results in one entry at selling price and another entry at cost. The entry *at selling price* is a debit to accounts receivable (a control account) and a credit of equal amount to Sales. The entry *at cost* is a debit to cost of sales and a credit of equal amount to inventory (a control account). A sales journal with two amount columns can show on only one line a sales transaction at both selling price and cost. The two-column sales journal of Karns Wholesale Supply is shown in figure 6.12, using assumed credit sales transactions (for sales invoice nos. 101–107).

It is important to understand that, even though the number of journals used to record business transactions has changed (from one general journal to many special journals), the general debit and credit rules used to record transactions in previous chapters still apply. Every journal entry must have at least one debit and one credit entry, so the need for the equality of debits and credits remains.

FIGURE 6.12 Journalising the sales journal — perpetual inventory system

	KARNS WHOLESALE SUPPLY Sales journal					S1
Date	Account debited	Invoice no.	Ref.	Accounts receivable Dr Sales Cr	Cost of sales Dr Inventory Cr	
2019						
May 3	Abbot Sisters Ltd	101		10 600	6 360	
7	Babson Ltd	102		11 350	7 370	
14	Carson Ltd	103		7 800	5 070	
19	Deli Ltd	104		9 300	6 510	
21	Abbot Sisters Ltd	105		15 400	10 780	
24	Deli Ltd	106		21 210	15 900	
27	Babson Ltd	107		14 570	10 200	
				90 230	62 190	

Let's illustrate this point by using the 3 May transaction in figure 6.12. If we were to record the general journal entry for a credit sale to Abbot Sisters Ltd for $10 600 with a cost of sales of $6360, it would look like this:

May 3	Dr Accounts receivable				10 600	
	Cr Sales					10 600
	Dr Cost of sales				6 360	
	Cr Inventory					6 360

	A	=	L	+	E	
	+10 600				+10 600	

	A	=	L	+	E	
	−6360				−6360	

As the amount to be debited and credited is the *same* for the first two lines of the journal entry and the amount to be debited and credited is the *same* for the last two lines of the journal entry, we can use two columns to record the whole journal entry and still have the same effect. This is illustrated in figure 6.12, where the second last column is used to record the first two lines of the journal entry (Dr accounts receivable and Cr sales) and the last column is used to record the last two lines of the journal entry (Dr cost of sales and Cr inventory).

The posting reference (Ref.) column is not used in journalising. It is used in posting the sales journal, as explained in the next section. Also, note that, unlike the general journal, an explanation is not required for each entry in a special journal as the title of the special journal explains the transaction. Finally, note that each invoice is prenumbered to ensure that all invoices are journalised.

Helpful hint: When recording sales in the journal, check that you have entered all sales invoice numbers in consecutive order to ensure that all transactions have been entered.

Posting the sales journal

Postings from the sales journal are made daily to the individual accounts receivable in the subsidiary ledger. Posting to the general ledger is made monthly. Figure 6.13 shows both the daily and monthly postings.

FIGURE 6.13 Posting the sales journal

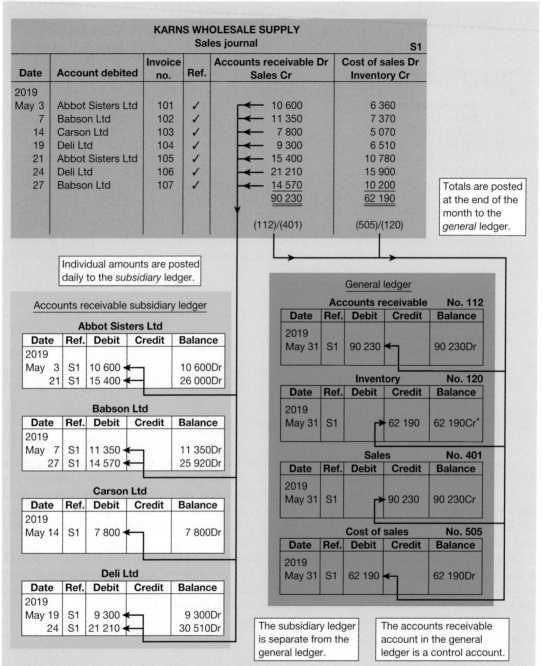

*The normal balance for inventory is a debit. But, because of the sequence in which we have posted the special journals, with the sales journals first, the credits to inventory are posted before the debits. This posting sequence explains the credit balance in inventory which exists only until the other journals are posted.

A tick (✓) is inserted in the posting reference (Ref.) column to indicate that the daily posting to the customer's account has been made. A tick (✓) is used in this illustration because the subsidiary ledger accounts are not numbered. When subsidiary ledger accounts are numbered, the account number can be recorded in the posting reference column to indicate that the amount has been posted and to which subsidiary ledger account it has been posted. At the end of the month, the column totals of the sales journal are posted to the general ledger. Here, the column totals are a debit of $90 230 to accounts receivable (account no. 112), a credit of $90 230 to sales (account no. 401), a debit of $62 190 to cost of sales (account no. 505), and a credit of $62 190 to inventory (account no. 120). Recording the account numbers below the column total indicates that the postings have been made and provides a reference for easy identification of the account. In both the general ledger and subsidiary ledger accounts, the reference (Ref.) **S1** indicates that the posting came from page 1 of the sales journal.

Checking the ledgers

The next step is to check the ledgers. To do so, we must determine two things: (1) the total of the general ledger debit balances must equal the total of the general ledger credit balances; (2) the sum of the subsidiary ledger balances must equal the balance in the control account in the general ledger. The check of the postings from the sales journal to the general and subsidiary ledger is shown in figure 6.14.

FIGURE 6.14 Checking the equality of the postings from the sales journal

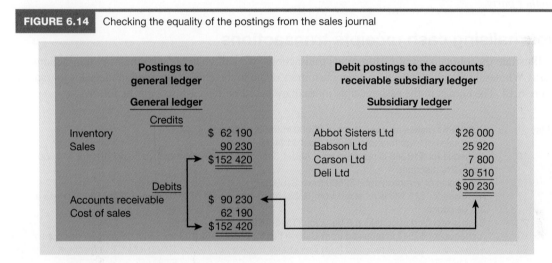

Advantages of the sales journal

The use of a special journal to record sales on account has a number of advantages. First, the one-line entry for each sales transaction saves time. In the sales journal, it is not necessary to write out the four account names for each transaction. Second, only totals, rather than individual entries, are posted to the general ledger. This saves posting time and reduces the possibilities of errors in posting. Finally, a segregation of duties can be achieved, because one person can take responsibility for the sales journal, while someone else takes responsibility for the general journal or any of the other special journals (purchases, cash receipts or cash payments).

6.14 Cash receipts journal

LEARNING OBJECTIVE 6.14 Understand how multi-column special journals are posted.

All receipts of cash are recorded in the **cash receipts journal**. The most common types of cash receipts are cash sales of inventory and collections of accounts receivable. Many other possibilities exist, such as receipt of money from bank loans, rent revenue, interest revenue, dividend revenue and cash proceeds from disposal of equipment. A one- or two-column cash receipts journal would not have space enough for all possible cash receipt transactions. Therefore, a multiple-column cash receipts journal is used.

Generally, a cash receipts journal includes the following columns: debit columns for cash and discount allowed; and credit columns for accounts receivable, sales, and other accounts. The other accounts category is used when the cash receipt does not involve a cash sale or a collection of accounts receivable. Under a perpetual inventory system, each sales entry is accompanied by another entry that debits cost of sales and credits inventory for the cost of the inventory sold. This entry may be recorded separately. A six-column cash receipts journal is shown in figure 6.15.

Additional credit columns may be used if they significantly reduce postings to a specific account. To illustrate, assume that two entities, Company A and Company B, sublet part of their office space. This means that they rent part of their office space to other businesses. Company A sublets office space to a number of different businesses, and Company B rents a part of its office space to only one business. If Company A used a manual accounting system, a significant saving in posting would result from using a separate credit column for rent revenue rather than using the other accounts credit column. In contrast, if Company B used a manual system, with only one rent collection a month, a separate column for rent revenue would not be as useful.

Helpful hint: Subletting is when one party, who is a lessee, rents out the leased premises to another party.

Journalising cash receipts transactions

To illustrate the journalising of cash receipts transactions, we will continue with the May transactions of Karns Wholesale Supply. Collections from customers relate to the entries recorded in the sales journal in figure 6.12. The entries in the cash receipts journal are based on the cash receipts as follows.

May 1	D.A. Karns makes an investment of $5000 in the business.
7	Cash sales of inventory total $1900 (cost $1240).
10	A cheque for $10 388 is received from Abbot Sisters Ltd in payment of invoice no. 101 for $10 600 less a 2% discount.
12	Cash sales of inventory total $2600 (cost $1690).
17	A cheque for $11 123 is received from Babson Ltd in payment of invoice no. 102 for $11 350 less a 2% discount.
22	Cash is received upon taking a bank loan for $6000.
23	A cheque for $7644 is received from Carson Ltd for invoice no. 103 for $7800 less a 2% discount.
28	A cheque for $9114 is received from Deli Ltd for invoice no. 104 for $9300 less a 2% discount.

Further information about the columns in the cash receipts journal (see figure 6.15) is given below.

Helpful hint: When is an account name entered in the 'Account credited' column of the cash receipts journal?

Answer: A subsidiary ledger name is entered there whenever the entry involves a collection of accounts receivable. A general ledger account name is entered there whenever the entry involves an account that is not the subject of a special column (and an amount must be entered in the other accounts column). No account name is entered there if neither applies.

Debit columns

1. *Cash.* The amount of cash actually received in each transaction is entered in this column. The column total indicates the total cash receipts for the month.
2. *Discount allowed.* Karns includes a discount allowed column in its cash receipts journal. By doing so, it is not necessary to enter sales discount items in the general journal. As a result, the collection of an account receivable within the discount period is expressed on one line in the appropriate columns of the cash receipts journal.

FIGURE 6.15   Journalising and posting the cash receipts journal

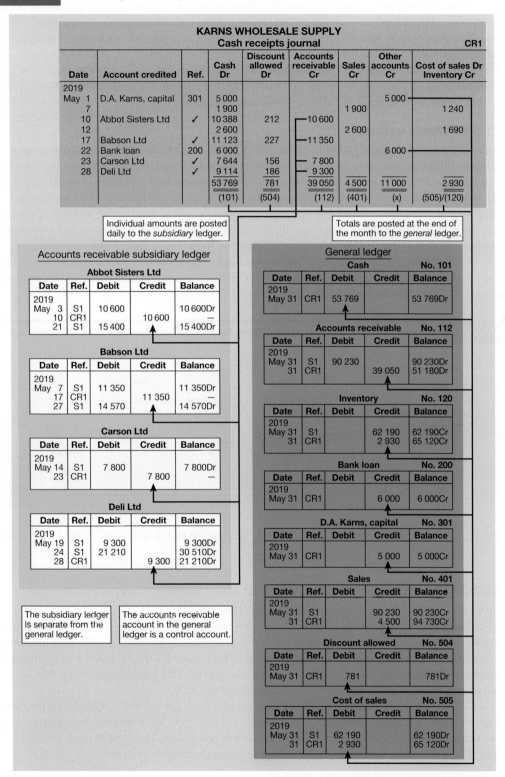

Credit columns

3. *Accounts receivable.* The accounts receivable column is used to record cash collections on account. The amount entered here is the amount to be credited to the individual customer's account.
4. *Sales.* The sales column records all cash sales of inventory. Cash sales of other assets (equipment, for example) are not reported in this column.
5. *Other accounts.* The other accounts column is used whenever the credit is other than to accounts receivable or sales. For example, in the first entry, $5000 is entered as a credit to D.A. Karns, Capital. This column is often referred to as the *sundry accounts column.*

Debit and credit column

6. *Cost of sales and inventory.* This column records debits to cost of sales and credits to inventory.

In a multicolumn journal, generally only one line is needed for each entry. Debit and credit amounts for each line must be equal. For example, when the collection from Abbot Sisters Ltd on 10 May is journalised, the two debit entries to discount allowed and cash equal the credit entry to accounts receivable. Note also that the 'Account credited' column is used to identify both general ledger and subsidiary ledger account names. General ledger accounts are illustrated in the 1 May and 22 May entries. A subsidiary account is illustrated in the 10 May entry for the collection from Abbot Sisters Ltd.

When the journalising of a multicolumn journal has been completed, the amount columns are totalled, and the totals are compared to check the equality of debits and credits. The check of the equality of Karns's cash receipts journal is shown in figure 6.16.

FIGURE 6.16 | Checking the equality of the debit and credit totals in the cash receipts journal (cross-footing)

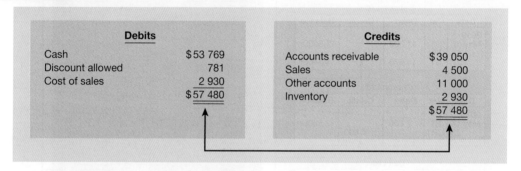

Debits		Credits	
Cash	$53 769	Accounts receivable	$39 050
Discount allowed	781	Sales	4 500
Cost of sales	2 930	Other accounts	11 000
	$57 480	Inventory	2 930
			$57 480

Totalling the columns of a journal and checking the equality of the debit and credit totals is called *cross-footing* a journal.

Posting the cash receipts journal

Posting a multicolumn journal involves the following steps.

1. All column *totals* except for the other accounts total are posted once at the end of the month to the account(s) specified in the column heading (such as cash or accounts receivable). Account numbers are entered below the column totals to show that they have been posted. Cash is posted to account no. 101, accounts receivable to account no. 112, inventory to account no. 120, sales to account no. 401, discount allowed to account no. 504, and cost of sales to account no. 505.
2. The individual amounts comprising the other accounts total are posted separately to the general ledger accounts specified in the 'Account credited' column. See, for example, the credit posting to D.A. Karns, Capital. The total amount of this column is not posted. The symbol (x) is inserted below the total of this column to indicate that the *total amount* has not been posted.

3. The individual amounts in a column, posted in total to a control account (accounts receivable, in this case), are posted daily to the subsidiary ledger account specified in the 'Account credited' column. See, for example, the credit posting of $10 600 to Abbot Sisters Ltd.

In both the subsidiary ledger and the general ledger accounts, the reference **CR1** indicates that the posting came from page 1 of the cash receipts journal.

Checking the ledgers

After the posting of the cash receipts journal is completed, it is necessary to check the ledgers. As shown in figure 6.17, the general ledger totals are in agreement. Also, the sum of the subsidiary ledger balances equals the control account balance.

FIGURE 6.17 Checking the ledgers after posting the sales and the cash receipts journals

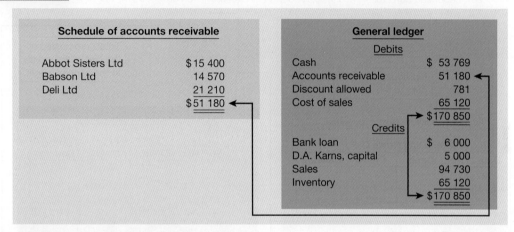

Purchases journal

All purchases of inventory on account are recorded in the **purchases journal**. Each entry in this journal results in a debit to inventory or purchases (depending on whether a perpetual or periodic inventory system is used) and a credit to accounts payable. When a single-column purchases journal is used (as in figure 6.18), other types of purchases on account and cash purchases cannot be journalised in it. For example, credit purchases of equipment or supplies must be recorded in the general journal. Likewise, all cash purchases are entered in the cash payments journal. As illustrated later, where credit purchases for items other than inventory are numerous, the purchases journal is often expanded to a multicolumn format. The purchases journal for Karns Wholesale Supply is shown in figure 6.18.

Helpful hint: Recall that if a business uses the perpetual inventory system, inventory is debited for purchases of inventory. If a business uses a periodic system, purchases is debited for purchases of inventory.

Helpful hint: A single-column purchases journal is not added to check the equality of debits and credits as the total will be posted once as a debit and then as a credit in the general ledger. However, it is a good idea to add the total twice before posting to ensure the total posted is, in fact, correct. Also, the accounts payable account in the general ledger can also be called the Accounts payable control *account.*

Journalising credit purchases of inventory

Entries in the purchases journal are made from suppliers' invoices. The journalising procedure is similar to that used for the sales journal. In contrast to the sales journal, the purchases journal may not have an invoice number column because invoices received from different suppliers will not be in numerical sequence. To ensure that all purchase invoices are recorded, some entities consecutively number each invoice upon receipt and then use an internal document number column in the purchases journal.

FIGURE 6.18 Journalising and posting the purchases journal

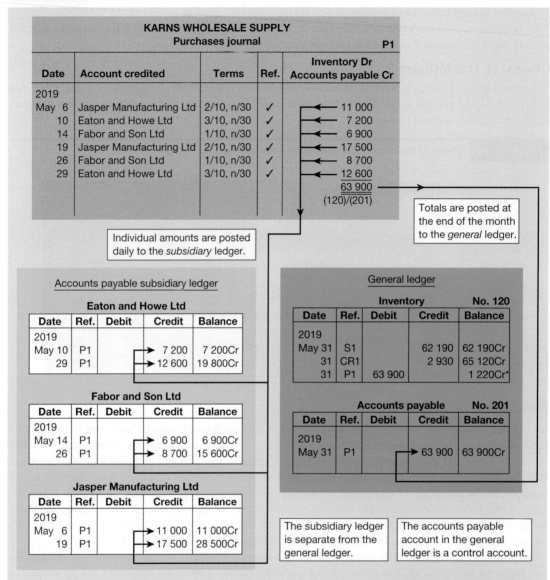

*The normal balance for inventory is a debit. But, because of the sequence in which we have posted the special journals, with the sales and cash receipts journals first, the credits to Inventory are posted before the debits. Once the purchases and cash payments journals are posted, the balance in the Inventory account will be a debit.

The entries for Karns Wholesale Supply are based on the assumed credit purchases shown in figure 6.19.

Posting the purchases journal

The procedures for posting the purchases journal are similar to those for the sales journal. In this case, postings are made daily to the accounts payable subsidiary ledger and monthly to inventory and accounts payable in the general ledger. In both the subsidiary and general ledgers, **P1** is used in the reference column to show that the postings are from page 1 of the purchases journal.

Helpful hint: Postings to subsidiary ledger accounts are done daily because it is often necessary to know a current balance for the subsidiary accounts.

FIGURE 6.19 Credit purchases transactions

Date	Supplier	Amount
May 6	Jasper Manufacturing Ltd	$11 000
10	Eaton and Howe Ltd	7 200
14	Fabor and Son Ltd	6 900
19	Jasper Manufacturing Ltd	17 500
26	Fabor and Son Ltd	8 700
29	Eaton and Howe Ltd	12 600

The check on the equality of the postings from the purchases journal to both ledgers is shown in figure 6.20.

FIGURE 6.20 Checking the equality of the purchases journal

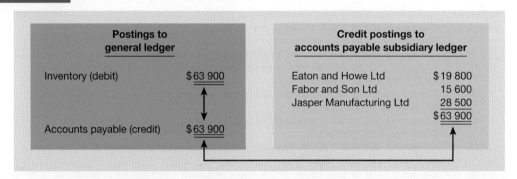

Postings to general ledger		Credit postings to accounts payable subsidiary ledger	
Inventory (debit)	$63 900	Eaton and Howe Ltd	$19 800
		Fabor and Son Ltd	15 600
		Jasper Manufacturing Ltd	28 500
			$63 900
Accounts payable (credit)	$63 900		

Expanding the purchases journal

Some businesses expand the purchases journal to include all types of purchases on account. Instead of one column for inventory and accounts payable, they use a multicolumn format. The multicolumn format usually includes a credit column for accounts payable and debit columns for purchases of inventory, office supplies and store supplies, and for other accounts. Figure 6.21 is an example of a multicolumn purchases journal for Hangover Ltd. The posting procedures are similar to those illustrated earlier for posting the cash receipts journal.

FIGURE 6.21 Multicolumn purchases journal

							Other accounts Dr		
Date	Account credited	Ref.	Accounts payable Cr	Inventory Dr	Office supplies Dr	Store supplies Dr	Account	Ref.	Amount
2019									
June 1	Signe Audio	✓	2 000		2 000				
3	Wright Ltd	✓	1 500	1 500					
5	Orange Tree Ltd	✓	2 600				Equipment	157	2 600
30	Sue's Business Forms	✓	800						
			56 600	43 000	7 500	1 200			4 900

HANGOVER LTD
Purchases journal

Helpful hint: A multicolumn purchases journal must be added and cross-footed to check the equality of debits and credits.

Cash payments journal

All payments are entered in a **cash payments journal** (sometimes called the *cash disbursements journal*). Businesses make most of their payments by cheque. Payments made in currency (notes and coins) are usually small in amount. The recording of small currency payments, called petty cash payments, is discussed in chapter 7 (section 7.11). Entries are made from prenumbered cheques. Because cash payments are made for various purposes, the cash payments journal has multiple columns. A four-column journal is shown in figure 6.22.

Journalising cash payments transactions

The procedures for journalising transactions in this journal are similar to those described earlier for the cash receipts journal. Each transaction is entered on one line, and for each line there must be equal debit and credit amounts. The entries in the cash payments journal in figure 6.22 are based on the following transactions for Karns Wholesale Supply.

May	1	Cheque no. 101 for $1200 issued for the annual premium on a fire insurance policy.
	3	Cheque no. 102 for $100 issued in payment of freight when terms were FOB shipping point.
	8	Cheque no. 103 for $4400 issued for the purchase of inventory.
	10	Cheque no. 104 for $10 780 sent to Jasper Manufacturing Ltd in payment of 6 May invoice for $11 000 less a 2% discount.
	19	Cheque no. 105 for $6984 mailed to Eaton and Howe Ltd in payment of 10 May invoice for $7200 less a 3% discount.
	23	Cheque no. 106 for $6831 sent to Fabor and Son Ltd in payment of 14 May invoice for $6900 less a 1% discount.
	28	Cheque no. 107 for $17 150 sent to Jasper Manufacturing Ltd in payment of 19 May invoice for $17 500 less a 2% discount.
	30	Cheque no. 108 for $500 issued to D.A. Karns as a cash withdrawal for personal use.

Note that whenever an amount is entered in the other accounts column, a specific general ledger account must be identified in the 'Account debited' column. The entries for cheque numbers 101, 102 and 103 illustrate this situation. Similarly, a subsidiary account must be identified in the 'Account debited' column whenever an amount is entered in the accounts payable column. See, for example, the entry for cheque no. 104.

After the cash payments have been entered in the journal, the columns are totalled. The totals are then balanced to check the equality of debits and credits.

Posting the cash payments journal

The procedures for posting the cash payments journal are similar to those for the cash receipts journal. The amounts recorded in the accounts payable column are posted individually on a daily basis to the subsidiary ledger and in total at the end of the month to the control account. Inventory and cash are posted only in total at the end of the month. Transactions in the other accounts column are posted individually to the appropriate general ledger account(s) at the end of the month. No totals are posted for this column.

The posting of the cash payments journal is shown in figure 6.22. Note that the symbol **CP1** is used as the posting reference to show that the postings are from page 1 of the cash payments journal. After postings are completed, the equality of the debit and credit balances in the general ledger should be determined. In addition, the control account balances should agree with the subsidiary ledger total balance. The agreement of these balances is shown in figure 6.23.

FIGURE 6.22 Journalising and posting the cash payments journal

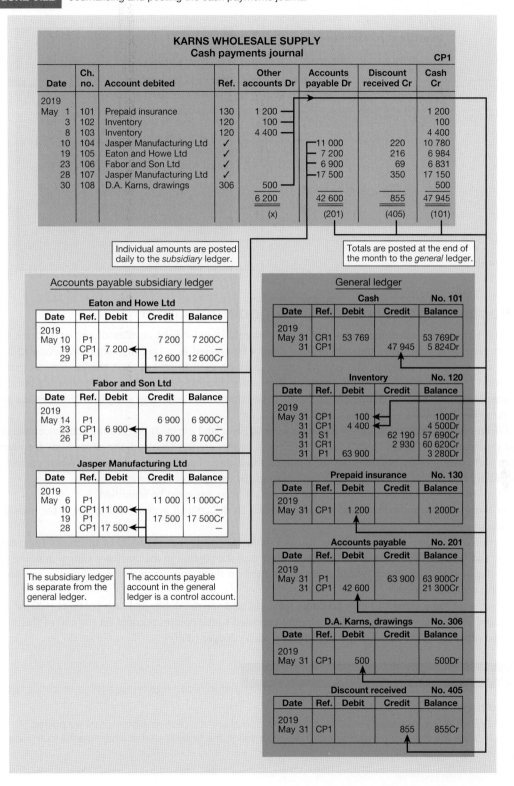

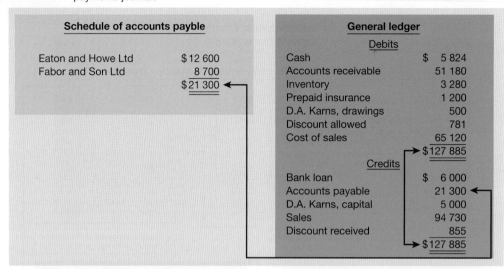

Effects of special journals on general journal

Special journals for sales, purchases and cash substantially reduce the number of entries that are made in the general journal. Only transactions that cannot be entered in a special journal are recorded in the general journal. For example, the general journal may be used to record such transactions as granting of credit to a customer for a sales return or allowance, obtaining credit from a supplier for purchases returned, and purchase of equipment on credit. Also, correcting, adjusting and closing entries are made in the general journal.

The general journal has columns for date, account name and explanation, posting reference, and debit and credit amounts. When control and subsidiary accounts are not involved, the procedures for journalising and posting of transactions are the same as those described in earlier chapters. When control and subsidiary accounts are involved, two changes from the earlier procedures are required.

1. In *journalising*, both the control and the subsidiary accounts must be identified.
2. In *posting*, there must be a dual posting — once to the control account and once to the subsidiary account.

To illustrate, assume that on 31 May Karns Wholesale Supply returns $500 of inventory for credit to Fabor and Son Ltd. The entry in the general journal and the posting of the entry are shown in figure 6.24. Note that if cash is received instead of credit granted on this return, then the transaction is recorded in the cash receipts journal.

Observe in the journal that two accounts are indicated for the debit, and two postings ('201/✓') are indicated in the reference column. One amount is posted to the control account (at the end of the month) and the other to the creditor's account in the subsidiary ledger (daily).

LEARNING REFLECTION AND CONSOLIDATION

Review it

1. Explain how transactions recorded in the sales journal and the cash receipts journal are posted.
2. Indicate the types of transactions that are recorded in the general journal when special journals are used.

FIGURE 6.24 Journalising and posting the general journal

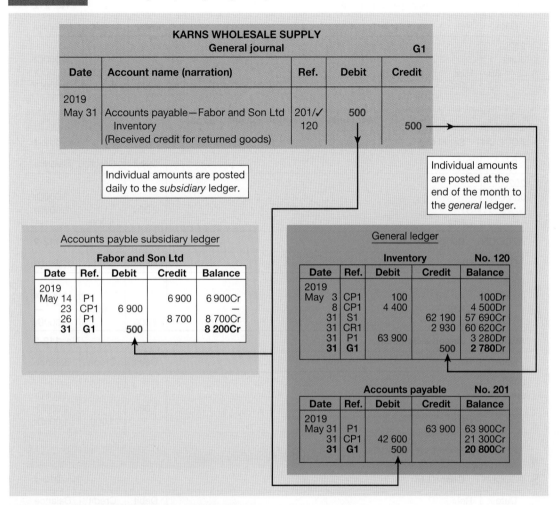

USING THE DECISION-MAKING TOOLKIT

The accounts receivable control and accounts payable control accounts and subsidiary ledgers for Aussie Roo Ltd are given below.

General ledger					
ACCOUNT **Accounts receivable control**					No. **112**
Date	Ref.		Debit	Credit	Balance
2020					
June 1					5 000Dr
30	S1		6 000		11 000Dr
30	CR12			7 000	4 000Dr

ACCOUNT   **Accounts payable control**   No. **212**

Date	Ref.	Debit	Credit	Balance
2020				
June 1				6 000Cr
30	P12		8 000	14 000Cr
30	CP12	5 000		9 000Cr

Accounts receivable subsidiary ledger

ACCOUNT   **Segal Ltd**   No. **112-1**

Date	Ref.	Debit	Credit	Balance
2020				
June 1				3 000Dr
5	S1	2 000		5 000Dr
	CR12		5 000	—

ACCOUNT   **Bongo Pty Ltd**   No. **112-2**

Date	Ref.	Debit	Credit	Balance
2020				
June 1				1 000Dr
15	CR12		1 000	—
23	S1	2 000		2 000Dr

ACCOUNT   **Jetson & Sons Ltd**   No. **112-3**

Date	Ref.	Debit	Credit	Balance
2020				
June 1				1 000Dr
5	S1	1 000		2 000Dr
	CR12		1 000	1 000Dr

Accounts payable subsidiary ledger

ACCOUNT   **Crisco Ltd**   No. **212-1**

Date	Ref.	Debit	Credit	Balance
2020				
June 1				3 000Cr
10	P12		5 000	8 000Cr
23	CP12	3 000		5 000Cr

ACCOUNT   **Petre Pty Ltd**   No. **212-2**

Date	Ref.	Debit	Credit	Balance
2020				
June 1				2 000Cr
9	CP12	2 000		—
30	P12		2 000	2 000Cr

ACCOUNT   **Cooloo Ltd**   No. **212-3**

Date	Ref.	Debit	Credit	Balance
2020				
June 1				1 000Cr
3	P12		2 000	3 000Cr

There are two errors in the ledgers, one in the accounts receivable subsidiary ledger and the other in the accounts payable control account.

Required

(a) Prepare a schedule of accounts receivable and a schedule of accounts payable as at 30 June 2020. Compare the total of each schedule with the balance in the corresponding control account.

(b) Explain how each error may have occurred.

Solution

(a)

Schedule of accounts receivable as at 30 June 2020		
112-1	Segal Ltd	$ —
112-2	Bongo Pty Ltd	2 000
112-3	Jetson & Sons Ltd	1 000
	Total	$ 3 000

The balance of $3000 in the subsidiary ledger does not agree with the $4000 total in the accounts receivable control account.

Schedule of accounts payable as at 30 June 2020		
212-1	Crisco Ltd	$ 5 000
212-2	Petre Pty Ltd	2 000
212-3	Cooloo Ltd	3 000
	Total	$10 000

The balance of $10 000 in the subsidiary ledger does not agree with the $9000 total in the accounts payable control account.

(b) The discrepancy between the accounts receivable control account and the subsidiary ledger appears to be due to a credit sale *not* posted to the subsidiary ledger. Credit sales totalling $6000 were debited to the accounts receivable control account but only $5000 was debited to the accounts receivable subsidiary ledger. The sales journal should be reviewed to determine which customer's account should be debited. Alternatively, the error may be in the addition of the sales journal. If the sales journal total should have been $5000 instead of $6000, the accounts receivable control account and the sales account would be overstated by $1000 as a result of the addition error. We can tell that the error is not in the posting of cash receipts because the amount credited to accounts receivable control is equal to the sum of the amounts credited to the accounts receivable subsidiary ledgers.

The discrepancy between the accounts payable control account and subsidiary ledger appears to be due to an error in totalling the purchases journal or an error in posting to the accounts payable control account. Credit purchases totalling $9000 were credited to the accounts payable subsidiary ledger but only $8000 was credited to the control account. To correct this error, the total of the purchases journal should be checked and the correct total posted to the general ledger. Alternatively, the error may have been caused by incorrect posting to the subsidiary ledger. If the subsidiary ledger is incorrect, it should be corrected and a new balance calculated.

SUMMARY

6.1 Identify the basic principles of accounting information systems.

The basic principles in developing an accounting information system are cost effectiveness, useful output and flexibility.

6.2 Explain the major phases in the development of an accounting system.

The major phases in the development of an accounting system are analysis, design, implementation and follow-up.

6.3 Define internal control.

The plan of organisation and all the related methods and measures adopted within a business to safeguard its assets and enhance the accuracy and reliability of its accounting records.

6.4 Appreciate management's responsibility in relation to internal control.

Senior management of companies, on behalf of shareholders, are responsible for developing policies and practices which align with the company's overall objectives. Good risk management practices, including a system of internal control, are one of the responsibilities of management in order to ensure that the business is being run as efficiently and effectively as possible.

6.5 Identify the principles and limitations of internal control.

The principles of internal control are the establishment of responsibility; segregation of duties; documentation procedures; physical, mechanical and electronic controls; and independent internal verification, including rotation of duties. The limitations of internal control are the costs of measures required by the entity to safeguard its assets and ensure accounting records are reliable; impact of human fatigue, carelessness or indifference; possibility of collusion amongst two or more members of staff; and the size of the business, i.e. if a business is too small it may not be able to implement the measures required.

6.6 Understand the accounting processes underlying the generation of financial statements.

An accounting information system has three phases: input, processing and output. These phases transform data into information that is useful for decision making by external users. Source documents are the input to the accounting system which allows for the transactions to be recorded in the journals. Posting from the journals to the general ledger and the subsidiary ledgers is the processing phase. The output of the accounting system is the financial statements.

6.7 Describe the sales and receivables cycle and the purchases and payments cycle.

The sales and receivables cycle provides a flow of how sales are made and recorded, and the purchases and payments cycle provides a flow of how purchases and payments of inventory are made within an organisation.

6.8 Apply internal control principles to the sales and receivables cycle and purchases and payments cycle for transforming data.

Establishment of responsibility; segregation of duties; documentation procedures; physical, mechanical and electronic controls; and independent internal verification are important principles of internal control in relation to the sales and receivables cycle and the purchases and payments cycle.

6.9 Describe the nature and purpose of control accounts and subsidiary ledgers.

A subsidiary ledger is a group of accounts with a common characteristic. It facilitates the recording process by freeing the general ledger control account from details of individual balances.

6.10 Explain how special journals are used in recording transactions.

A special journal is used to group similar types of transactions. In a special journal, generally only one line is used to record a complete transaction.

6.11 Understand the basic features of computerised accounting systems and appreciate the role and use of non-integrated systems.

Manual and computerised accounting systems are essentially the same in terms of design, structure and operation — they are both based on double-entry accounting. Most computerised systems are integrated accounting systems with subsystems or modules, so that when data is entered into one of the modules it automatically updates the information in other relevant modules and the accounting reports. Computerised systems allow for efficient and dependable processing of numerous transactions and provide instant and flexible reports.

Not all businesses run fully integrated accounting systems. For example, Excel spreadsheets may be used by businesses for budgeting purposes. A non-integrated system means that data from reports produced in one subsystem needs to be entered either manually or as an import/export process to other subsystems.

6.12 Identify the advantages and disadvantages of computerised accounting systems.

Advantages include the ability to process numerous transactions quickly, automatic posting of transactions, error reduction, fast response time, and flexible and fast report production. Disadvantages include software and hardware incompatibilities, higher staff training costs as employees need to be trained to use computerised systems, effects of power failures and viruses on accounting data, and the increasing incidence of hacking, computer fraud and computer viruses.

6.13 Record transactions for sales, purchases, cash receipts and cash payments in special journals.

Similar repetitive transactions such as sales, purchases, receipts and payments of cash are recorded in the respective special journals.

6.14 Understand how multi-column special journals are posted.

In posting a multicolumn journal:
(a) All column totals except for the other accounts column are posted once at the end of the month to the account name specified in the column heading.
(b) The total of the other accounts column is not posted. Instead, the individual amounts comprising the total are posted separately to the general ledger accounts specified in the account credited column.
(c) The individual amounts in a column posted in total to a control account are posted daily to the subsidiary ledger accounts specified in the account credited column.

DECISION-MAKING TOOLKIT — A SUMMARY

DECISION-MAKING TOOLKIT

Decision/issue	Info needed for analysis	Tool or technique to use for decision	How to evaluate results to make decision
Are the business's financial statements supported by adequate internal controls?	Auditor's report, articles in financial press (external parties); reports on asset losses from theft, errors, customer complaints (internal parties)	The required measures of internal control are to (1) establish responsibility, (2) segregate duties, (3) document procedures, (4) use physical or automated controls, and (5) use independent internal verification.	If any indication is given that these or other controls are lacking, the financial statements should be used with caution.

Decision/issue	Info needed for analysis	Tool or technique to use for decision	How to evaluate results to make decision
Does the balance in the general ledger control account equal the total of the individual balances in the subsidiary ledger?	General ledger control account (e.g. accounts receivable) and corresponding subsidiary ledger (e.g. subsidiary ledger for accounts receivable)	Balance in the general ledger control account (e.g. accounts receivable) and a schedule of the corresponding subsidiary ledger (e.g. schedule of accounts receivable)	Compare the balance in the general ledger control account with the total of the corresponding subsidiary ledger schedule. A discrepancy indicates an error in the accounting records. The error must be identified and corrected.

KEY TERMS

accounts payable (suppliers') subsidiary ledger A subsidiary ledger that contains accounts of individual creditors.

accounts receivable (customers') subsidiary ledger A subsidiary ledger that contains individual customer accounts.

cash payments journal A special journal used to record all cash payments.

cash receipts journal A special journal used to record all cash received.

control account An account in the general ledger that is supported by the detail of a subsidiary ledger.

corporate governance The system in which entities are directed or controlled, managed and administered.

forensic accounting The application of accounting knowledge and skills to issues arising in the context of civil and criminal litigations and investigation.

integrated accounting system A computerised accounting package consisting of several modules which perform different accounting functions (e.g. payroll). Once an entry is made in one module, all other relevant modules are updated.

internal auditors Employees of the business who evaluate on a continuous basis the effectiveness of the business's system of internal control.

internal control The plan of organisation and all the related methods and measures adopted within a business to safeguard its assets and enhance the accuracy and reliability of its accounting records.

manual accounting system A system in which each of the steps in the accounting cycle is performed by hand.

purchases journal A special journal used to record all purchases of inventory on account.

sales journal A special journal used to record all sales of inventory on account.

schedule of accounts payable A list of all accounts and their balances in the accounts payable subsidiary ledger at a particular date.

schedule of accounts receivable A list of all accounts and their balances in the accounts receivable subsidiary ledger at a particular date.

special journal A journal that is used to record similar types of transactions, such as all credit sales.

subsidiary ledger A group of accounts with a common characteristic, the total of which should equal the balance in the related general ledger control account.

DEMONSTRATION PROBLEM

Dion Designs uses a six-column cash receipts journal with the following columns: cash (Dr), discount allowed (Dr), accounts receivable (Cr), sales (Cr), other accounts (Cr), cost of sales (Dr) and inventory (Cr). Cash receipts transactions for the month of July 2021 are as follows.

July	3	Cash sales total $5800 (cost $3480).
	4	A cheque for $6370 is received from Arena Ltd in payment of an invoice dated 29 June for $6500, terms 2/7, n/30.
	9	An additional investment of $5000 in cash is made in the business by Debbie Dion, the owner.
	10	Cash sales total $12 519 (cost $7511).
	12	A cheque for $7275 is received from Eliot Ltd in payment of a $7500 invoice dated 10 July, terms 3/7, n/30.
	15	A customer paid a deposit of $700 cash for goods to be delivered in August.
	20	Cash sales total $15 472 (cost $9283).
	22	A cheque for $5880 is received from Beck Pty Ltd in payment of $6000 invoice dated 13 July, terms 2/10, n/30.
	29	Cash sales total $17 660 (cost $10 596).
	31	Cash of $200 is received for interest earned for July.

Required

(a) Journalise the transactions in the cash receipts journal.

(b) Contrast the posting of the accounts receivable and other accounts columns.

SOLUTION TO DEMONSTRATION PROBLEM

(a)

DION DESIGNS
Cash receipts journal   CR12

Date	Account credited	Post ref.	Cash Dr	Discount allowed Dr	Accounts receivable Cr	Sales Cr	Other accounts Cr	Cost of sales Dr Inventory Cr
2021								
July 3			5 800			5 800		3 480
4	Arena Ltd		6 370	130	6 500			
9	Dion, capital		5 000				5 000	
10			12 519			12 519		7 511
12	Eliot Ltd		7 275	225	7 500			
15	Revenue rec'd in adv.		700				700	
20			15 472			15 472		9 283
22	Beck Pty Ltd		5 880	120	6 000			
29			17 660			17 660		10 596
31	Interest revenue		200				200	
			76 876	475	20 000	51 451	5 900	30 870

(b) The total of the accounts receivable column is posted as a credit to the accounts receivable account in the general ledger. The individual amounts are credited to the accounts receivable subsidiary ledger accounts identified in the 'Account credited' column.

The amounts in the other accounts column are only posted individually. They are credited to the account names identified in the 'Account credited' column.

SELF-STUDY QUESTIONS

6.1 The basic principles of an accounting information system include all of the following *except:*
LO1
(a) cost-effectiveness.
(b) flexibility.
(c) useful output.
(d) periodicity.

6.2 To be useful, accounting information must be:
LO1
(a) understandable.
(b) relevant.
(c) timely.
(d) all of the above.

6.3 Which of the following is *not* a major phase in the development of an accounting information system?
LO2
(a) Design.
(b) Responsiveness.
(c) Implementation.
(d) Follow-up.

6.4 In developing an accounting information system, which of the following could be considered to be part of the implementation phase?
LO2
(a) Determine the information needs of the external and internal users.
(b) Design forms and documents.
(c) Install equipment and make it operational.
(d) Monitor for weaknesses and breakdowns.

6.5 Internal control is used in a business to enhance the accuracy and reliability of its accounting records and to:
LO3
(a) safeguard its assets.
(b) prevent mistakes.
(c) produce correct financial statements.
(d) ensure the business never makes a loss.

6.6 The principles of internal control do *not* include:
LO5
(a) establishment of responsibility.
(b) documentation procedures.
(c) external auditors.
(d) independent internal verification.

6.7 Which of the following is the correct sequence in transforming transactions into financial statements?
LO6
(a) Ledgers, journals, trial balance, financial statements.
(b) Journals, ledgers, trial balance, financial statements.
(c) Journals, trial balance, ledgers, financial statements.
(d) Ledgers, trial balance, journals, financial statements.

6.8 Which of the following is *incorrect* concerning subsidiary ledgers?
LO9
(a) The purchases ledger is a common subsidiary ledger for creditor accounts.
(b) The accounts receivable subsidiary ledger is a subsidiary ledger for customer accounts.
(c) A subsidiary ledger is a group of accounts with a common characteristic.
(d) An advantage of the subsidiary ledger is that it permits a division of labour in posting.

6.9 Which of the following is *not* an advantage of subsidiary ledgers?
LO9
(a) They allow a segregation of duties in posting.
(b) They result in too much detail in the general ledger.

(c) They can provide all details relating to one customer in one account.

(d) None of the above.

6.10 When special journals are used: **LO10**

(a) all purchase transactions are recorded in the purchases journal.

(b) all cash received, except from cash sales, is recorded in the cash receipts journal.

(c) all payments are recorded in the cash payments journal.

(d) a general journal is not necessary.

6.11 Postings from the purchases journal to the subsidiary ledger are generally made: **LO10**

(a) yearly.

(b) monthly.

(c) weekly.

(d) daily.

6.12 Which of the following is *correct* in relation to computerised accounting systems?   **LO11**

(a) They are based on the framework of a manual accounting system.

(b) Accounting transactions are entered automatically but posted manually.

(c) There is no need for control accounts and subsidiary ledgers.

(d) Manual calculations must be made to generate account balances.

6.13 Which of the following are advantages of computerised accounting systems?   **LO12**

(a) Ability to process numerous transactions quickly.

(b) Built-in automatic posting of transactions.

(c) Error reduction.

(d) All of the above.

6.14 Which of the following are *not* disadvantages of computerised accounting systems?   **LO12**

(a) Incompatible hardware and software.

(b) Computer viruses and hackers.

(c) Error reduction.

(d) Loss of data due to power failure.

6.15 A cash receipts journal is used for: **LO13**

	Credit sales	Cash sales	Discount allowed
(a)	no	yes	yes
(b)	yes	no	yes
(c)	yes	no	no
(d)	yes	yes	no

6.16 Which statement is *incorrect* regarding the general journal?   **LO13**

(a) Only transactions that cannot be entered in a special journal are recorded in the general journal.

(b) Transactions are initially posted in the general journal.

(c) The general journal may be used to record closing entries.

(d) Correcting and adjusting entries are made in the general journal.

6.17 Which of the following statements is correct?   **LO13**

(a) The 'Discount allowed' column is included in the cash receipts journal.

(b) The purchases journal records all purchases of inventory whether for cash or on account.

(c) The cash receipts journal records credit sales.

(d) Inventory returned by the buyer is recorded by the seller in the purchases journal.

6.18 Which of the following is *incorrect* concerning the posting of the cash receipts journal?   **LO14**

(a) The total of the 'Other accounts' column is not posted.

(b) All column totals except the total for the 'Other accounts' column are posted once at the end of the month to the account name(s) specified in the column heading.

(c) The totals of all columns are posted daily to the accounts specified in the column heading.

(d) The individual amounts in a column posted in total to a control account are posted daily to the subsidiary ledger account specified in the 'Account credited' column.

QUESTIONS

6.1 (a) What is an accounting information system?

(b) 'An accounting information system applies only to a manual system.' Do you agree? Explain.

6.2 Generally, an accounting system is developed in phases. Identify and explain each of the phases.

6.3 What is meant by corporate governance?

6.4 'Corporate governance does not apply to small business.' Do you agree? Explain.

6.5 Explain the role of an internal auditor.

6.6 Internal control is concerned only with enhancing the accuracy of the accounting records. Do you agree? Explain.

6.7 Identify the process of how accounting data is transformed into financial statements.

6.8 Describe the internal control principles applicable to the sales and receivables cycle and the purchases and payments cycle.

6.9 What are the advantages of using subsidiary ledgers?

6.10 (a) When are postings normally made to (1) the subsidiary ledgers and (2) the general ledger control accounts?

(b) Describe the relationship between a control account and a subsidiary ledger.

6.11 A $500 purchase of merchandise on account from Julia Ltd was properly recorded in the purchases journal. When posted, however, the amount recorded in the subsidiary ledger was $50. How might this error be discovered?

6.12 Give some examples of appropriate general journal transactions for an organisation using special journals.

6.13 Identify and explain the four specific journals discussed in sections 6.13 and 6.14. List an advantage of using each of these journals rather than using only a general journal.

6.14 The 'Cash' and the 'Accounts receivable' columns in the cash receipts journal were incorrectly added by $4000 at the end of the month.

(a) Will the customers' ledger agree with the accounts receivable control account?

(b) Assuming no other errors, will the trial balance totals be equal?

6.15 In what journal would the following transactions be recorded? (Assume that a two-column sales journal and a single-column purchases journal are used.)

(a) Recording of depreciation expense for the year.

(b) Credit given to a customer for inventory purchased on credit and returned.

(c) Sales of inventory for cash.

(d) Sales of inventory on account.

(e) Collection of cash on account from a customer.

(f) Purchase of office supplies on account.

6.16 Give an example of a transaction in the general journal that causes an entry to be posted twice (i.e. to two accounts), one in the general ledger, the other in the subsidiary ledger. Does this affect the debit/credit equality of the general ledger?

BRIEF EXERCISES

BE6.1 Identify basic principles of accounting information system development. **LO1**

Indicate whether each of the following statements is true or false.

(a) When designing an accounting system, we need to think about the needs and knowledge of both the top management and various other users.

(b) When the environment changes as a result of technological advances, increased competition or government regulation, an accounting system does not have to be sufficiently flexible to meet the changes in order to save money.

(c) In developing an accounting system, cost is relevant. The system must be cost effective. That is, the benefits obtained from the information disseminated must outweigh the cost of providing it.

BE6.2 Identify major phases in accounting system development.   **LO2**

The development of an accounting system involves four phases: analysis, design, implementation and follow-up. Identify the statement that best describes each of these four phases.

(a) Determining internal and external information needs, identifying information sources and the need for controls, and studying alternatives.

(b) Evaluation and monitoring of effectiveness and efficiency, correction of weaknesses, implementation and design.

(c) Creation of forms and documents, selection of procedures, and preparation of job descriptions.

(d) Implementing new or revised documents, procedures, reports and processing equipment; hiring and training personnel through a start-up or transition period.

BE6.3 Identify the principles and limitations of internal control.   **LO5, 8**

Several of the internal control procedures of Cumin Ltd are listed below. Identify the principles of internal control that are being followed in each case.

(a) Employees who have physical control of assets do not have access to the accounting records.

(b) Each month the assets on hand are compared with the accounting records by an internal auditor.

(c) A prenumbered delivery docket is prepared for each shipment of goods to customers.

BE6.4 Identify subsidiary ledger accounts.   **LO9**

Identify in which ledger (general or subsidiary) each of the following accounts is shown.

(a) Rent expense.

(b) Accounts receivable — Melbourne Pty Ltd.

(c) Bank loan.

(d) Accounts payable — Sydney Pty Ltd.

BE6.5 Identify special journals.   **LO10, 13**

Identify the journal in which each of the following transactions is recorded.

(a) Cash sales.

(b) Owner withdrawal of cash.

(c) Cash purchase of land.

(d) Credit sales.

(e) Purchase of inventory on account.

(f) Receipt of cash for services performed.

BE6.6 Identify entries to cash receipts journal.   **LO13**

Indicate whether each of the following debits and credits is included in the cash receipts journal. (Use 'Yes' or 'No' to answer this question.)

(a) Debit to sales.

(b) Credit to inventory.

(c) Credit to accounts receivable.

(d) Debit to accounts payable.

BE6.7 Indicate postings to cash receipts journal.   **LO10, 14**

Computer Components Ltd uses a multicolumn cash receipts journal. Indicate which column(s) is/are posted only in total, only daily, or both in total and daily.

(a) Accounts receivable.

(b) Discount allowed.

(c) Cash.

(d) Other accounts.

BE6.8 Identify transactions for special journals. **LO10, 13**

Identify the special journal(s) in which the following column headings appear.

(a) Discount allowed Dr.

(b) Accounts receivable Cr.

(c) Cash Dr.

(d) Sales Cr.

(e) Inventory Dr.

EXERCISES

E6.1 Identify the principles and limitations of internal control. **LO5, 8**

Rotundo's Pizza operates strictly on a takeaway basis. Customers pick up their orders at a counter where a clerk exchanges the pizza for cash. At the counter, the customer can see other employees making the pizzas and the large ovens in which the pizzas are baked.

Required

Identify the five principles of internal control and give an example of each principle that you might observe when picking up your pizza. (*Note:* It may not be possible to observe all the principles.)

E6.2 Identify the principles and limitations of internal control. **LO5, 8**

Caterpilla Tractors buys wheels from Wheels R Us in order to complete the manufacture of its tractors. The Mina brothers work for Caterpilla Tractors. Sam works in the purchasing department while Peter works in the accounting department. The business is starting out and has a system in place such that the purchasing department also receives the wheels when they are delivered to the business. Sam orders the wheels from his best friend's business, Wheels R Us. The order for the parts is processed through the accounting system by Sam, and Peter pays Wheels R Us once notified by Sam that the wheels have been received.

Required

Identify which of the five principles of internal control you feel is lacking in the aforementioned scenario. (*Note:* It may not be possible to observe all the principles.)

E6.3 Determine control account balances, and explain posting of special journals. **LO9, 10, 14**

Tessa Ltd uses both special journals and a general journal as described in this chapter. On 30 June, after all monthly postings had been completed, the accounts receivable control account in the general ledger had a debit balance of $200 000; the accounts payable control account had a credit balance of $45 000.

The July transactions recorded in the special journals are summarised below. No entries affecting accounts receivable and accounts payable were recorded in the general journal for July.

Sales journal	Total sales	$125 150
Purchases journal	Total purchases	$ 27 180
Cash receipts journal	Accounts receivable column total	$ 63 500
Cash payments journal	Accounts payable column total	$ 23 750

Required

(a) What is the balance of the accounts receivable control account after the monthly postings on 31 July?

(b) What is the balance of the accounts payable control account after the monthly postings on 31 July?

(c) To what account(s) is the column total of $125 150 in the sales journal posted?

(d) To what account(s) is the accounts receivable column total of $63 500 in the cash receipts journal posted?

E6.4 Post various journals to control and subsidiary accounts.   **LO9, 10, 14**

On 1 September the balance of the accounts receivable control account in the general ledger of Teone Ltd was $5980. The customers' subsidiary ledger contained account balances as follows: Edmonds $1220, Lee $1320, Roemer $1030, Schulz $2410, Henry $0. At the end of September the various journals contained the following information.

- *Sales journal:* Sales to Schulz $400; to Edmonds $675; to Henry $515; to Roemer $550.
- *Cash receipts journal:* Cash received from Roemer $655; from Schulz $1150; from Henry $205; from Lee $900; from Edmonds $620.
- *General journal:* An allowance is granted to Schulz $110.

Required

(a) Set up control and subsidiary ledger accounts and enter the beginning balances. Do not construct the journals.

(b) Post the various journals. Post the items as individual items or as totals, whichever would be the appropriate procedure. (No discount was given for early payment.)

(c) Prepare a list of customers and check that the control account balance agrees with a schedule of accounts in the subsidiary ledger at 30 September 2019.

(d) Why is it important to ensure that the balance in the control account agrees with the schedule of accounts receivable?

E6.5 Record transactions in sales and purchases journal.   **LO9, 10, 13**

Duckstein Ltd uses special journals and a general journal. The following transactions occurred during September 2020.

Sept. 2	Sold inventory on account to R. Crow, invoice no. 101 for $960, terms n/30. The cost of the inventory sold was $600.
10	Purchased inventory on credit from L. Dayne $1200, terms 2/7, n/30.
12	Purchased office equipment on account from B. Piazza $13 000.
21	Sold inventory on account to Buffy Ltd, invoice no. 102 for $1600, terms 2/14, n/30. The cost of the inventory sold was $960.
25	Purchased inventory on account from F. Sage $1800, terms n/30.
27	Sold inventory to Harold Ltd for $1400 cash. The cost of the inventory sold was $840.

Required

(a) Draw up a sales journal (see figure 6.13) and a single-column purchases journal (see figure 6.18). (Use page 1 for each journal.)

(b) Record the transaction(s) for September that should be journalised in the sales journal and the purchases journal.

(c) What is the advantage of having a multicolumn purchases journal as opposed to a single-column purchases journal?

E6.6 Record transactions in cash receipts and cash payments journal.   **LO9, 10, 13**

Vanessa Bosnat uses special journals and a general journal. The following transactions occurred during May 2019.

May 1	V. Bosnat invested $30 000 cash in the business.
2	Sold inventory to J. Simon for $12 000 cash. The cost of the inventory sold was $8400.
3	Purchased inventory for $18 000 from L.M. Farr using cheque no. 101.
14	Paid salary to S. Little $1400 by issuing cheque no. 102.
16	Sold inventory on account to B. Jones for $1800, terms n/30. The cost of the inventory sold was $1260.
22	A cheque for $18 000 is received from R. Dusto in full for invoice 101; no discount given.

Required

(a) Draw up a multicolumn cash receipts journal (see figure 6.15) and a multicolumn cash payments journal (see figure 6.22). (Use page 1 for each journal.)

(b) Record the transaction(s) for May that should be journalised in the cash receipts journal and cash payments journal.

E6.7 Explain journalising in cash journals.   **LO10, 13**

Jamie's Hardware uses the columnar cash journals illustrated in the text. In April, the following selected cash transactions occurred.

1. Gave a refund to a customer for the return of damaged goods.
2. Received payment from a customer. The payment was received within the discount period and the customer received a 3% discount.
3. Purchased inventory for cash.
4. Paid a creditor within the discount period and received 3% discount.
5. Received collection from customer after the discount period had expired.
6. Paid freight on inventory purchased.
7. Paid cash for office equipment.
8. Received cash refund from supplier for inventory returned.
9. Withdrew cash for personal use of owner.
10. Made cash sales.

Required

Indicate (a) the journal and (b) the columns in the journal that should be used in recording each transaction.

E6.8 Journalise transactions in general journal and post.   **LO10, 13, 14**

Opera House Ltd has the following selected transactions during March.

Mar. 2	Purchased equipment costing $6000 from Harbour Ltd on account.
5	Received credit note for $300 from Boat & Co. for inventory damaged in shipment to Opera House Ltd.
7	Issued a credit note for $400 to Luna Ltd for inventory the customer returned. The returned inventory had a cost of $260.

Opera House Ltd uses a single-column purchases journal, a sales journal, the multicolumn cash journals used in this text, and a general journal.

Required

(a) Journalise the transactions in the general journal.
(b) As the accountant, prepare a brief memo to the managing director of Opera House Ltd, Mr Peterson, to explain all postings to the control and subsidiary accounts.

E6.9 Indicate journalising in special journals.   **LO10**

Below are some typical transactions incurred by Rotunda Printworks.

1. Payment of creditors on account.
2. Return of inventory sold for credit.
3. Collection from customers for amounts owing on account.
4. Sale of land for cash.
5. Sale of inventory on credit.
6. Sale of inventory for cash.
7. Received credit for inventory originally purchased on credit.
8. Discount allowed for early payment by customer.
9. Payment of employee wages.
10. Profit or loss summary closed to capital account.
11. Depreciation on building.
12. Purchase of office supplies for cash.
13. Purchase of inventory on account.

Required

For each transaction, indicate whether it would normally be recorded in a cash receipts journal, cash payments journal, sales journal, single-column purchases journal, or a general journal.

E6.10 Explain posting to control account and subsidiary ledger.   **LO9**

The general ledger of Frenchy Ltd contained the following accounts payable control account (in T-account form). Also shown is the related subsidiary ledger.

General ledger						
Accounts payable control						
Feb. 15	General journal	1 400	Feb. 1	Balance		26 025
28	?	?	5	General journal		265
			11	General journal		550
28	Ending balance	9 840	28	Purchases		13 900
		40 740				40 740
			Mar. 1	Balance		9 840

Accounts payable subsidiary ledger					
Sealy			**Wang**		
	Mar. 1 Bal.	4 600		Mar. 1 Bal.	?
Gates					
	Mar. 1 Bal.	2 000			

Required

(a) Indicate the missing posting reference and amount in the control account, and the missing ending balance in the subsidiary ledger.

(b) Indicate the amounts in the control account that were also posted to the subsidiary accounts.

E6.11 Prepare purchases and general journals.   **LO10, 13**

Selected accounts from the ledgers of Peterson Ltd at 31 July showed the following.

General ledger					
ACCOUNT	**Store equipment**				**No. 153**
Date	Explanation	Ref.	Debit	Credit	Balance
July 1		G11	1 800		1 800

ACCOUNT	**Accounts payable**				**No. 201**
Date	Explanation	Ref.	Debit	Credit	Balance
July 1		G11		1 800	1 800
15		G11		200	2 000
18		G11	50		1 950
25		G11	100		1 850
31		P10		4 200	6 050

ACCOUNT	**Inventory**				**No. 120**
Date	Explanation	Ref.	Debit	Credit	Balance
July 15		G11	200		200
18		G11		50	150
25		G11		100	50
31		P10	4 200		4 250

ACCOUNT **Alou Equipment Ltd**

Date	Explanation	Ref.	Debit	Credit	Balance
July 1		G11		1 800	1 800

ACCOUNT **Benton Ltd**

Date	Explanation	Ref.	Debit	Credit	Balance
July 3		P10		1 000	1 000
20		P10		350	1 350

ACCOUNT **Comerica Materials**

Date	Explanation	Ref.	Debit	Credit	Balance
July 17		P10		700	700
18		G11	50		650
29		P10		1 050	1 700

ACCOUNT **Dunlap Pty Ltd**

Date	Explanation	Ref.	Debit	Credit	Balance
July 14		P10		550	550
25		G11	100		450

ACCOUNT **Emerick Ltd**

Date	Explanation	Ref.	Debit	Credit	Balance
July 12		P10		250	250
21		P10		300	550

ACCOUNT **Galant Transit**

Date	Explanation	Ref.	Debit	Credit	Balance
July 15		G11		200	200

Required

(a) From the data prepare the single-column purchases journal for July.

(b) From the data prepare the general journal entries for July.

(c) What are the advantages of using specialised journals? Are there any circumstances where it would be better not to use specialised journals?

E6.12 Determine correct posting amount to control account. **LO9, 14**

Musac Hi Fi Ltd uses both special journals and a general journal as described in this chapter. Musac Hi Fi Ltd also posts customers' accounts in the accounts receivable subsidiary ledger. The postings for the most recent month are included in the subsidiary T accounts below.

	Viola Ltd				**Cellos Pty Ltd**	
Bal.	204	150		Bal.	90	90
	120				174	

	Harps Ltd				**Pianos & Co.**	
Bal.	0	87		Bal.	72	72
	87				141	
					102	

Required

Determine the correct amount of the end-of-month posting from the sales journal to the accounts receivable control account.

E6.13 Determine control account balances, and explain posting of special journals.   **LO9, 10, 14**

Ruby Ltd uses both special journals and a general journal as described in this chapter. On 30 June, after all monthly postings had been completed, the accounts receivable control account in the general ledger had a debit balance of $300 000; the accounts payable control account had a credit balance of $67 500. The December transactions recorded in the special journals are summarised below. No entries affecting accounts receivable and accounts payable were recorded in the general journal for December.

Sales journal	Total sales	$187 725
Purchases journal	Total purchases	$ 40 770
Cash receipts journal	Accounts receivable column total	$ 95 250
Cash payments journal	Accounts payable column total	$ 35 625

Required

(a) What is the balance of the accounts receivable control account after the monthly postings on 31 December?
(b) What is the balance of the accounts payable control account after the monthly postings on 31 December?
(c) To what account(s) is the column total of $187 725 in the sales journal posted?
(d) To what account(s) is the accounts receivable column total of $95 250 in the cash receipts journal posted?
(e) What is the purpose of preparing a schedule of accounts receivable?

E6.14 Explain posting to control account and subsidiary ledger.   **LO9, 10, 14**

The general ledger of Bing Ltd contained the following accounts receivable control account (in T-account form). Also shown is the related subsidiary ledger.

General ledger					
Accounts receivable control					
Feb. 1	Balance	28 628	Feb. 15	Cash	15 000
18	Sales	15 290	21	General journal	896
28	?	?	28	Ending balance	33 022
		48 918			48 918
Mar. 1	Balance	33 022			

Accounts receivable subsidiary ledger			
Ding		**Ring**	
Mar. 1 Bal. 15 060		Mar. 1 Bal. ?	
King			
Mar. 1 Bal. 12 200			

Required

(a) Indicate the missing cross-reference and the amount in the control account, and the missing opening balance in the subsidiary ledger.
(b) Indicate the amounts in the control account that were also posted to the subsidiary accounts during February.

E6.15 Determine correct posting amount to control account. **LO9, 10, 14**

Building Blocks Pty Ltd uses both special journals and a general journal to record transactions. Building Blocks also posts creditors' accounts in the accounts payable subsidiary ledger. The postings for the most recent month are included in the subsidiary T accounts below.

Cement for U Ltd		
300	Bal.	408
		240

Brick-a-Brack Pty Ltd		
180	Bal.	180
		348

Building Materials Ltd		
174	Bal.	0
		174

Ladders Pty Ltd		
144	Bal.	144
		228
		204

Required

(a) Determine the correct amount of the end-of-month posting from the purchases journal to the accounts payable control account.

(b) Assume that Building Blocks has one creditor only and does not expect there to be any other creditors in the future. Would there be any advantage to Building Blocks setting up an accounts payable subsidiary ledger?

PROBLEM SET A

PSA6.1 Journalise transactions in cash receipts journal; post to control account and subsidiary ledger.
LO9, 10, 13, 14

Computer Supplies Ltd chart of accounts includes the following selected accounts.

101	Cash		401	Sales
112	Accounts receivable		414	Discount allowed
120	Inventory		505	Cost of sales
301	Selma Wiggle, capital			

On 1 April the accounts receivable ledger of Computer Supplies Ltd showed the following balances: East PC Ltd $4650, Office Supplies Ltd $3600, PC West Ltd $8700, and Computers for U Ltd $5100. The April transactions involving the receipt of cash were as follows.

Apr. 1	The owner, Selma Wiggle, invested additional cash in the business $18 000.
4	Received cheque for payment of account from Computers for U Ltd less 2% cash discount.
5	Received cheque for $1860 in payment of invoice no. 307 from PC West Ltd.
8	Made cash sales of inventory totalling $21 736. The cost of the inventory sold was $13 040.
10	Received cheque for $2400 in payment of invoice no. 309 from East PC Ltd.
11	Received cash refund from a supplier for damaged inventory returned $1650.
23	Received cheque for $4500 in payment of invoice no. 310 from PC West Ltd.
29	Received cheque for payment of account from Office Supplies Ltd.

Required

(a) Journalise the transactions above in a six-column cash receipts journal with columns for Cash Dr, Discount allowed Dr, Accounts receivable Cr, Sales Cr, Other accounts Cr, and Cost of sales Dr/Inventory Cr. Total and cross-foot the journal.

(b) Enter the beginning balances in the accounts receivable control and subsidiary accounts, and post the April transactions to these accounts.

(c) Check that the control account and subsidiary account balances agree.

PSA6.2 Journalise transactions in cash payments journal; post to control account and subsidiary ledgers.
LO9, 10, 13, 14

Antique Jewels Pty Ltd's chart of accounts includes the following selected accounts.

101	Cash	201	Accounts payable
120	Inventory	306	Amy Amethyst, drawings
130	Prepaid insurance	405	Discount received
157	Equipment	505	Cost of sales

On 1 October the accounts payable ledger of Antique Jewels Pty Ltd showed the following balances: Diamond Factory Ltd $3740, Precious Stones Ltd $5500, Rubys R Us Ltd $3080, and Angus and Bandicoot $11 100. The October transactions involving the payment of cash were as follows.

Oct.	1	Purchased inventory, cheque no. 63, $1540.
	3	Purchased equipment, cheque no. 64, $1760.
	5	Paid Diamond Factory Ltd balance due of $3740, less 2% discount, cheque no. 65, $3665.
	10	Purchased inventory, cheque no. 66, $4950.
	15	Paid Rubys R Us Ltd balance due of $3080, cheque no. 67.
	16	Amy Amethyst, the owner, pays her personal insurance premium of $880, cheque no. 68.
	19	Paid Precious Stones Ltd for invoice no. 610, $3080 less 2% cash discount, cheque no. 69, $3018.
	29	Paid Angus and Bandicoot in full for invoice no. 264, $5720, cheque no. 70.

Required

(a) Journalise the transactions above in a five-column cash payments journal with columns for Other accounts Dr, Accounts payable Dr, Inventory Cr, Discount received Cr, and Cash Cr. Total and cross-foot the journal.

(b) Insert the beginning balances in the accounts payable control and subsidiary accounts, and post the October transactions to these accounts.

(c) Check that the control account and the subsidiary account balances agree.

(d) Amy Liu, the managing director of Antique Jewels Pty Ltd, recently found out that its major supplier, Angus and Bandicoot, supplied them with stolen diamonds. The information is not public knowledge and Valentine's Day, when a large amount of stock is sold, is approaching. Discuss what actions Amy could take and the social and financial implications of her actions for the company.

PSA6.3 Journalise transactions in multicolumn purchases journal; post to the general and subsidiary ledgers.
LO9, 10, 13, 14

The chart of accounts of Raquets 'R' Us Ltd includes the following selected accounts.

112	Accounts receivable	401	Sales
120	Inventory	412	Sales returns and allowances
126	Supplies	505	Cost of sales
157	Equipment	610	Advertising expense
201	Accounts payable		

In July the following selected transactions were completed. All purchases and sales were on account. The cost of all inventory sold was 70% of the sales price.

July	1	Purchased inventory from Tennis Australia Ltd $8800.
	2	Received invoice for freight inwards from Johnson Shipping on Tennis Australia purchase $550.
	3	Made sales to Squash Club Ltd $1980, and to Teeny Tennis Ltd $2200.

▶

July	5	Purchased inventory from Grant and Sons $5500.
	8	Received credit on inventory returned to Grant and Sons $550.
	13	Purchased store supplies from Raquet Supplies $990.
	15	Purchased inventory from Tennis Australia Ltd $3960 and from Lepa Ltd $3190.
	16	Made sales to Martin Ltd $3795 and to Teeny Tennis Ltd $1507.
	18	Received invoice for advertising from Dennisen Advertisements $594.
	21	Sales were made to Squash Club Ltd $341 and to Randee Ltd $3080.
	22	Granted allowance to Squash Club Ltd for inventory damaged in shipment $55.
	24	Purchased inventory from Grant and Sons $3960.
	26	Purchased equipment from Raquet Supplies $330.
	28	Received an invoice for freight from Johnson Shipping on Grant purchase of 24 July, $462.
	30	Sales were made to Martin Ltd $4290.

Required

(a) Journalise the transactions above in a purchases journal, a sales journal and a general journal. The purchases journal should have the following column headings: Date, Account credited (debited), Post ref., Other accounts Dr, and Inventory Dr/Accounts payable Cr.

(b) Post to both the general and subsidiary ledger accounts. (Assume that all accounts have nil opening balances.)

(c) Check that the control and subsidiary account balances agree.

PSA6.4 Journalise transactions in special journals.   **LO9, 10, 13, 14**

Selected accounts from the chart of accounts of Bouncing Balls Ltd are shown below.

101	Cash		401	Sales
112	Accounts receivable		412	Sales returns and allowances
120	Inventory		416	Discount received
126	Supplies		505	Cost of sales
157	Equipment		716	Discount allowed
201	Accounts payable		726	Salaries expense
202	Sundry accounts payable			

The cost of all inventory sold was 60% of the sales price. During January, Bouncing Balls Ltd completed the following transactions.

Jan.	3	Purchased inventory on account from Ball Supplies Ltd $15 000.
	4	Purchased supplies for cash $120.
	4	Sold inventory on account to Toys 4 U $10 875, invoice no. 371, terms 1/7, n/30.
	5	Returned $450 worth of damaged goods to Ball Supplies Ltd.
	6	Made cash sales for the week totalling $4725.
	8	Purchased inventory on account from Balls Ltd $6750.
	9	Sold inventory on account to Mays Ltd $8700, invoice no. 372, terms 1/7, n/30.
	11	Purchased inventory on account from Hoble $5550.
	13	Paid Ball Supplies Ltd on account less a 2% discount.
	13	Made cash sales for the week totalling $8010.
	14	Received payment from Mays Ltd for invoice no. 372.
	15	Paid fortnightly salaries of $21 450 to employees.
	17	Received payment from Toys 4 U for invoice no. 371.
	17	Sold inventory on account to Kids Time Ltd $1800, invoice no. 373, terms 1/10, n/30.
	19	Purchased equipment on account from Johnson Ltd $8250.
	20	Cash sales for the week totalled $4800.
	20	Paid in full Balls Ltd on account less a 2% discount.
	23	Purchased inventory on account from Ball Supplies Ltd $11 700.
	24	Purchased inventory on account from Levine $7035.
	27	Made cash sales for the week totalling $5595.
	30	Received payment from Kids Time Ltd for invoice no. 373.
	31	Paid fortnightly salaries of $19 800 to employees.
	31	Sold inventory on account to Toys 4 U $13 995, invoice no. 374, terms 1/7, n/30.

Bouncing Balls Ltd uses the following journals.
1. Sales journal.
2. Single-column purchases journal.
3. Cash receipts journal with columns for Cash Dr, Discount allowed Dr, Accounts receivable Cr, Sales Cr, Other accounts Cr, and Cost of sales Dr/Inventory Cr.
4. Cash payments journal with columns for Other accounts Dr, Accounts payable Dr, Inventory Cr, Discount received Cr and Cash Cr.
5. General journal.

Required

Using the selected accounts provided:
(a) Record the January transactions in the appropriate journal noted.
(b) Total and cross-foot all special journals.
(c) Show how postings would be made by placing ledger account numbers and ticks (✓) as needed in the journals. (Actual posting to ledger accounts is not required.)
(d) Explain the purpose of cross-footing special journals.

PSA6.5 **Journalise in sales and cash receipts journals; post; prepare a trial balance; check control with subsidiary; prepare adjusting entries; prepare an adjusted trial balance.** **LO9, 10, 13, 14**
Presented below are the purchases and cash payments journals for Mill Park Heights Bikes for its first month of operations.

Purchases journal				P14
Date	Account credited		Post ref.	Inventory Dr Accounts payable Cr
July 4	Dixon's Bikes			4 080
5	Bike Supplies Ltd			4 500
11	R. Gamble			2 352
13	M. Hill			9 180
20	D. Jacob			5 280
				25 392

Cash payments journal						CP16
Date	Account debited	Post ref.	Other accounts Dr	Accounts payable Dr	Discount received Cr	Cash Cr
July 4	Store supplies		360			360
10	Bike Supplies Ltd			4 500	45	4 455
11	Prepaid rent		3 600			3 600
15	Dixon's Bikes			4 080		4 080
19	R. Williams, drawings		1 500			1 500
21	M. Hill			9 180	92	9 088
			5 460	17 760	137	23 083

In addition, the following transactions have not been journalised for July. The cost of all inventory sold was 65% of the sales price.

July	1	The owner, R. Williams, invests $48 000 in cash.
	6	Sell inventory on account to Toy World Ltd $3240 terms 1/7, n/30.
	7	Make cash sales totalling $2400.
	8	Sell inventory on account to Biker Ltd $2160, terms 1/7, n/30.
	10	Sell inventory on account to L. Lemansky $2940, terms 1/14, n/30.
	13	Receive payment from Biker Ltd.
	16	Receive payment from L. Lemansky.

July 20	Receive payment from Toy World Ltd.	
21	Sell inventory on account to S. Kane $2400, terms 1/7, n/30.	
29	Returned damaged goods to Dixon's Bikes and received cash refund of $270.	

Required

(a) Open the following accounts in the general ledger.

101	Cash	306	R. Williams, drawings
112	Accounts receivable	401	Sales
120	Inventory	405	Discount received
127	Store supplies	505	Cost of sales
131	Prepaid rent	614	Discount allowed
201	Accounts payable	631	Supplies expense
301	R. Williams, capital	729	Rent expense

(b) Journalise the transactions that have not been journalised in the sales journal (S15), the cash receipts journal (CR16) (see figure 6.15), and the general journal (G5). (*Note:* Round all figures to nearest whole dollar.)

(c) Post to the accounts receivable and accounts payable subsidiary ledgers. Follow the sequence of transactions as shown in the problem.

(d) Post the individual entries and totals to the general ledger.

(e) Prepare an unadjusted trial balance as at 31 July 2020.

(f) Determine whether the subsidiary ledgers agree with the control accounts in the general ledger.

(g) The following adjustments at the end of July are necessary:
  1. A count of supplies indicates that $84 is still on hand.
  2. Recognise rent expense for July, $300.
     Prepare the necessary entries in the general journal. Post the entries to the general ledger.

(h) Prepare an adjusted trial balance as at 31 July 2020.

(i) Assume your trial balance does not balance. List some of the steps you could take to discover the error(s).

PSA6.6 **Journalise in special journals; post; prepare a trial balance.** **LO9, 10, 13, 14**

The post-closing trial balance for Party Shop Ltd is as follows.

PARTY SHOP LTD Post-closing trial balance as at 31 December 2019		
	Debit	Credit
Cash	$21 500	
Accounts receivable	8 250	
Commissions receivable	23 250	
Inventory	12 250	
Equipment	3 975	
Accumulated depreciation—equipment		$ 2 250
Accounts payable		22 250
B. Beatle, capital		44 725
	$69 225	$69 225

The subsidiary ledgers contain the following information: (1) Accounts receivable—Party Time Ltd $1500, Celebrations Pty Ltd $4000, S. Devine $2750; (2) Accounts payable—Toys 4 U $5250, R. Grilson $9250, D. Harms $7750. The cost of all inventory sold was 65% of the sales price.

The transactions for January 2020 are as follows.

Jan.	5	Sell inventory to W. Wong $2750, terms 2/7, n/30.
	5	Purchase inventory from S. Warren $1500, terms 2/7, n/30.
	7	Receive a cheque from S. Devine $1750.
	11	Pay freight inwards on inventory purchased $250.
	12	Pay rent of $1000 for January.
	12	Receive payment from W. Wong for amount due.
	14	Issue a credit note to acknowledge receipt of damaged inventory of $350 returned by Party Time Ltd.
	15	Send D. Harms a cheque for $7500 in payment of account, discount $250.
	17	Purchase inventory from D. Lapeska $750, terms 2/7, n/30.
	18	Pay sales salaries of $1250 and office salaries $500.
	20	Send R. Grilson a cheque for $9250 in payment of account payable.
	23	Total cash sales amount to $5000.
	24	Sell inventory on account to Celebrations Pty Ltd $3850, terms 1/7, n/30.
	27	Send S. Warren a cheque for $475.
	29	Receive $23 250 of the commissions revenue receivable at 31 December 2019.
	30	Return inventory of $250 to D. Lapeska for credit.

Required

(a) Open general and subsidiary ledger accounts for the following:

101	Cash	412	Sales returns and allowances
112	Accounts receivable	415	Discount received
115	Commissions receivable	505	Cost of sales
120	Inventory	506	Freight inwards
157	Equipment	714	Discount allowed
158	Accumulated depreciation—equipment	726	Sales salaries expense
201	Accounts payable	727	Office salaries expense
301	B. Beatle, capital	729	Rent expense
401	Sales	750	Inventory write-down expense
405	Commissions revenue		

(b) Record the January transactions in a sales journal, a single-column purchases journal, a cash receipts journal (see figure 6.15), a cash payments journal (see figure 6.22) and a general journal.

(c) Post the appropriate amounts to the general ledger.

(d) Prepare a trial balance as at 31 January 2020.

(e) Determine whether the subsidiary ledgers agree with the corresponding control accounts in the general ledger.

PSA6.7 **Journalise transactions in cash receipts journal; post to control account and subsidiary ledger.**

LO9, 10, 13, 14

Wyatt Sports' chart of accounts includes the following selected accounts.

101	Cash	401	Sales
112	Accounts receivable	505	Cost of sales
120	Inventory	614	Discount allowed
301	J. Wyatt, capital		

On 1 June the accounts receivable ledger of Wyatt Sports showed the following balances: Block & Son $1750, Field Ltd $950, Green Bros. $800, and Mastin Pty Ltd $500. The June transactions involving the receipt of cash were as follows.

June	1	The owner, J. Wyatt, invested additional cash in the business $5000.
	3	Received cheque from Mastin Pty Ltd less 2% cash discount.
	6	Received cheque from Field Ltd less 2% cash discount.
	7	Made cash sales of inventory totalling $3068. The cost of the inventory sold was $2045.
	9	Received cheque from Block & Son less 2% cash discount.
	11	Received cash refund from a supplier for damaged inventory $100.
	15	Made cash sales of inventory totalling $2625. The cost of the inventory sold was $1750.
	20	Received cheque in full from Green Bros. $800.

Required

(a) Journalise the transactions above in a six-column cash receipts journal with columns for Cash Dr, Discount allowed Dr, Accounts receivable Cr, Sales Cr, Other accounts Cr, and Cost of sales Dr/Inventory Cr. Total and cross-foot the journal.

(b) Insert the opening balances in the accounts receivable control and subsidiary accounts, and post the June transactions to these accounts.

(c) Determine whether the control account and subsidiary account balances agree.

PSA6.8 **Journalise in special journals; post; prepare a trial balance; check control with subsidiary; prepare adjusting entries; prepare an adjusted trial balance.**   **LO9, 10, 13, 14**

Presented below are the sales and cash receipts journals for Clover Hill for its first month of operations.

Sales journal				S1
Date	Account debited	Post ref.	Accounts receivable Dr Sales Cr	Cost of sales Dr Inventory Cr
Feb. 3	D. Adams		8 250	5 445
9	P. Babcock		9 750	6 435
12	D. Chambers		12 000	7 920
26	K. Dawson		9 000	5 940
			39 000	25 740

Cash receipts journal								CR1
Date	Account credited	Post ref.	Cash Dr	Discount allowed Dr	Accounts receivable Cr	Sales Cr	Other accounts Cr	Cost of sales Dr Inventory Cr
Feb. 1	J. Hill, capital		45 000				45 000	
2			9 750			9 750		6 435
13	D. Adams		8 167	83	8 250			
18	Inventory		225				225	
26	P. Babcock		9 750		9 750			
			72 892	83	18 000	9 750	45 225	6 435

In addition, the following transactions have not been journalised for February 2019.

Feb.	6	Purchased inventory on account from S. Healy for $6000, terms 1/7, n/30.
	9	Purchased inventory on account from L. Held for $45 000, terms 1/10, n/30.
	9	Paid cash of $1500 for purchase of supplies.
	12	Paid $5940 to S. Healy in payment of $6000 invoice, less 1% discount.
	15	Purchased equipment for $12 000 cash.
	16	Purchased inventory on account from R. Landly $3600, terms 2/7, n/30.
	17	Paid $44 550 to L. Held in payment of $45 000 invoice, less 1% discount.
	20	Withdrew cash of $1650 from business for personal use.
	21	Purchased inventory on account from J. Able for $9750, terms 1/7, n/30.
	28	Paid $3600 to R. Landly in payment of $3600 invoice.

Required

(a) Open the following accounts in the general ledger.

101	Cash	306	J. Hill, drawings
112	Accounts receivable	401	Sales
120	Inventory	405	Discount received
126	Supplies	505	Cost of sales
157	Equipment	614	Discount allowed
158	Accumulated depreciation—equipment	631	Supplies expense
201	Accounts payable	711	Depreciation expense
301	J. Hill, capital		

(b) Journalise the transactions that have not been journalised in a one-column purchases journal and the cash payments journal (see figure 6.22).

(c) Post to the accounts receivable and accounts payable subsidiary ledgers. Follow the sequence of transactions as shown in the problem.

(d) Post the individual entries and totals to the general ledger.

(e) Prepare a trial balance as at 28 February 2019.

(f) Determine that the subsidiary ledgers agree with the control accounts in the general ledger.

(g) The following adjustments at the end of February are necessary:

    1. A count of supplies indicates that $450 is still on hand.

    2. Depreciation on equipment for February is $300.

       Prepare the adjusting entries and then post the adjusting entries to the general ledger.

(h) Prepare an adjusted trial balance as at 28 February 2019.

PSA6.9 Journalise transactions in cash receipts journal; post to control account and subsidiary ledger.

LO9, 10, 13, 14

Lacquer Nail Supplies chart of accounts includes the following selected accounts.

101	Cash	201	Accounts payable
120	Inventory	306	P. Pinky, drawings
130	Prepaid insurance	405	Discount received
157	Equipment		

On 1 November the accounts payable ledger of Lacquer Nail Supplies showed the following balances: Cotton Balls Ltd $4500, Nail Polish Professionals $2350, Plastic Nails Pty Ltd $1000, and Creams and Oils R Us $1900. The November transactions involving the payment of cash were as follows.

Nov. 1	Purchased inventory, cheque no. 11, $900.
3	Purchased store equipment, cheque no. 12, $1700.
5	Paid Creams and Oils R Us balance due of $1900, less 1%, cheque no. 13, $1881.
11	Purchased inventory, cheque no. 14, $2000.
15	Paid Plastic Nails Pty Ltd balance due of $1000, less 3% discount, cheque no. 15, $970.
16	V. Pinky, the owner, withdrew $500 cash for own use, cheque no. 16.
19	Paid Nail Polish Professionals in full for invoice no. 1245, $1300 less 2% discount, cheque no. 17, $1274.
25	Paid premium due on one-year insurance policy, cheque no. 18, $3000.
30	Paid Cotton Balls Ltd in full for invoice no. 832, $2500, cheque no. 19.

Required

(a) Journalise the transactions above in a five-column cash payments journal with columns for Date, Cheque number, Amount debited (credited), Post reference, Other accounts Dr, Accounts payable Dr, Inventory Cr, Discount received Cr and Cash Cr. Total and cross-foot the journal.

(b) Enter the beginning balances in the accounts payable control and subsidiary accounts, and post the November transactions to these accounts.

(c) Agree the control account and the subsidiary account balances.

PSA6.10 **Journalise transactions in multicolumn purchases journal; post to the general and subsidiary ledgers.** **LO9, 10, 13, 14**

The chart of accounts of Fancy Footware Ltd includes the following selected accounts.

112	Accounts receivable		401	Sales
120	Inventory		412	Sales returns and allowances
126	Supplies		505	Cost of sales
157	Equipment		506	Freight inwards
201	Accounts payable		610	Advertising expense

In July the following selected transactions were completed. All purchases and sales were on account. The cost of all inventory sold was 70% of the sales price.

July	1	Purchased inventory from Little Feet Ltd $9600.
	2	Received invoice for freight inwards from Quick Shipping on Little Feet purchase $600.
	3	Made sales to Pete's Shoes Ltd, $2160, and to Teeny Feet Ltd $2400.
	5	Purchased inventory from Grant and Sons $6000.
	8	Received credit on inventory returned to Grant and Sons $600.
	13	Purchased store supplies from Shoe Supplies $1080.
	15	Purchased inventory from Little Feet Ltd $4320 and from Lepa Ltd $3480.
	16	Made sales to Martin's Spartans Ltd $4140 and to Teeny Feet Ltd $648.
	18	Received invoice for advertising from Shoe Advertisements Pty Ltd $372.
	21	Sales were made to Pete's Shoes Ltd $310 and to Sandles Ltd $3360.
	22	Granted allowance to Pete's Shoes Ltd for inventory damaged in shipment $60.
	24	Purchased inventory from Grant and Sons $4320.
	26	Purchased equipment from Shoe Supplies $360.
	28	Received an invoice for freight from Quick Shipping on Grant purchase of 24 July, $504.
	30	Sales were made to Martin's Spartans Ltd $4680.

Required

(a) Journalise these transactions in a purchases journal, a sales journal and a general journal. The purchases journal should have the following column headings: Date, Account credited (debited), Post ref., Other accounts Dr, and Inventory Dr/Accounts payable Cr.

(b) Post to both the general and subsidiary ledger accounts. (Assume that all accounts have nil opening balances.)

(c) Check that the control and subsidiary accounts balances agree.

(d) Explain the advantages and disadvantages of computerised accounting systems or manual accounting systems.

PROBLEM SET B

PSB6.1 **Journalise transactions in cash payments journal; post to the general and subsidiary ledgers.** **LO9, 10, 13, 14**

South Morange Hardware's chart of accounts includes the following selected accounts:

101	Cash		201	Accounts payable
120	Inventory		306	V. Morange, drawings
130	Prepaid insurance		405	Discount received
157	Equipment			

On 1 November the accounts payable ledger of South Morange's Hardware showed the following balances: R. Huff $2250, G. Paul $1175, R. Snyder $500, and Wald Bros $950. The November transactions involving the payment of cash were as follows.

Nov. 1	Purchased inventory, cheque no. 11, $450.	
3	Purchased store equipment, cheque no. 12, $850.	
5	Paid Wald Bros balance due of $950, less 1%, cheque no. 13, $941.	
11	Purchased inventory, cheque no. 14, $1000.	
15	Paid R. Snyder balance due of $500, less 3% discount, cheque no. 15, $485.	
16	V. Morange, the owner, withdrew $250 cash for own use, cheque no. 16.	
19	Paid G. Paul in full for invoice no. 1245, $650 less 2% discount, cheque no. 17, $637.	
25	Paid premium due on one-year insurance policy, cheque no. 18, $1500.	
30	Paid R. Huff in full for invoice no. 832, $1250, cheque no. 19.	

Required

(a) Journalise the transactions above in a five-column cash payments journal with columns for Date, Cheque number, Amount debited (credited), Post reference, Other accounts Dr, Accounts payable Dr, Inventory Cr, Discount received Cr and Cash Cr. Total and cross-foot the journal.

(b) Enter the beginning balances in the accounts payable control and subsidiary accounts, and post the November transactions to these accounts.

(c) Agree the control account and the subsidiary account balances.

(d) R. Snyder, a good friend of Mr Dodgy, the purchasing officer for South Morange's Hardware, has offered Mr Dodgy a fully paid overseas holiday if South Morange's Hardware increase their purchases from R. Snyder by 100% in the next financial year. How would you advise Mr Dodgy?

PSB6.2 Journalise transactions in multicolumn purchases journal; post to the general and subsidiary ledgers.
                                                                                     LO9, 10, 13, 14

The chart of accounts of Victoria Ltd includes the following selected accounts.

112	Accounts receivable		401	Sales
120	Inventory		412	Sales returns and allowances
126	Supplies		505	Cost of sales
157	Equipment		510	Freight inwards
201	Accounts payable		610	Advertising expense

In May the following selected transactions were completed. All purchases and sales were on account except as indicated. The cost of all inventory sold was 70% of the sales price.

May 2	Purchased inventory from Vons Ltd $10 450.
3	Received invoice for freight from The Freight People on Vons purchase $440.
5	Sales were made to Penner Ltd $1925, Hend Ltd $2970, and Nelles Ltd $1650.
8	Purchased inventory from Golden Ltd $8800 and Dorn Ltd $9570.
10	Received credit on inventory returned to Dorn Ltd $550.
15	Purchased supplies from Engle Supply $990.
16	Purchased inventory from Vons Ltd $4950, and Golden Ltd $6600.
17	Returned supplies to Engle Supply, receiving credit note for $110. (*Hint*: Credit supplies.)
18	Received invoice for freight on 16 May purchases from The Freight People $550.
20	Returned inventory to Vons Ltd receiving credit note for $330.
23	Made sales to Hend Ltd $2640 and to Nelles Ltd $2420.
25	Received invoice for advertising from Ball Advertising $990.
26	Granted allowance to Nelles Ltd for inventory damaged in shipment $220.
28	Purchased equipment from Engle Supply $275.

Required

(a) Journalise the transactions above in a purchases journal, a sales journal, and a general journal. The purchases journal should have the following column headings: Date, Accounts credited (debited), Post ref., Other accounts Dr, and Inventory Dr/Accounts payable Cr.

(b) Post to both the general and subsidiary ledger accounts. (Assume that all accounts have nil beginning balances.)

(c) Agree the control account and subsidiary ledger balances.

PSB6.3 **Journalise transactions in special journals.** **LO9, 10, 13, 14**

Selected accounts from the chart of accounts of Allegra Pty Ltd are shown below.

101	Cash		201	Accounts payable
112	Accounts receivable		401	Sales
120	Inventory		405	Discount received
126	Supplies		505	Cost of sales
140	Land		610	Advertising expense
145	Buildings		614	Discount allowed

The cost of all inventory sold was 60% of the sales price. During October, Allegra Pty Ltd completed the following transactions.

Oct.	2	Purchased inventory on account from Mason Ltd $9250.
	4	Sold inventory on account to Parker Ltd $4500. Invoice no. 204, terms 2/7, n/30.
	5	Purchased supplies for cash $40.
	7	Made cash sales for the week totalling $4580.
	9	Paid in full the amount owed to Mason Ltd less a 2% discount.
	10	Purchased inventory on account from Quinn Ltd $2100.
	10	Received payment from Parker Ltd for invoice no. 204.
	13	Returned $125 worth of damaged goods to Quinn Ltd.
	14	Made cash sales for the week totalling $4090.
	16	Sold a parcel of land for $54 000 cash, the land's book value.
	17	Sold inventory on account to L. Boyton Ltd $2675, invoice no. 205, terms 2/7, n/30.
	18	Purchased inventory for cash $1065.
	21	Made cash sales for the week totalling $4235.
	23	Paid in full the amount owed Quinn Ltd for the goods kept (no discount).
	25	Purchased supplies on account from Frey Ltd $130.
	25	Sold inventory on account to Green Ltd $2610, invoice no. 206, terms 2/7, n/30.
	25	Received payment from L. Boyton Ltd for invoice no. 205.
	26	Purchased for cash a small parcel of land and a building on the land to use as a storage facility. The total cost of $70 000 was allocated $42 000 to the land and $28 000 to the building.
	27	Purchased inventory on account from Schmid Ltd $4250.
	28	Made cash sales for the week totalling $4270.
	30	Purchased inventory on account from Mason Ltd $7000.
	30	Paid advertising for the month from the *Herald* $200.
	30	Sold inventory on account to L. Boyton Ltd $2300, invoice no. 207, terms 2/7, n/30.

Allegra Pty Ltd uses the following journals:

1. Sales journal.
2. Single-column purchases journal.
3. Cash receipts journal with columns for Cash Dr, Discount allowed Dr, Accounts receivable Cr, Sales Cr, Other accounts Cr, and Cost of Sales Dr/Inventory Cr.
4. Cash payments journal with columns for Other accounts Dr, Accounts payable Dr, Inventory Cr, Discount received Cr and Cash Cr.
5. General journal.

Required

Using the selected accounts provided:

(a) Record the October transaction in the appropriate journals.

(b) Total and cross-foot all special journals.

(c) Show how postings would be made by placing ledger account numbers and ticks (✓) as needed in the journals. (Actual posting to ledger accounts is not required.)

(d) Explain why it is helpful to place ledger account numbers and ticks (✓) in the journals.

PSB6.4 Journalise transactions in cash receipts journal; post to control account and subsidiary ledger.

LO9, 10, 13, 14

Illuminate Lighting's chart of accounts includes the following selected accounts:

101	Cash		401	Sales
112	Accounts receivable		414	Discount allowed
120	Inventory		505	Cost of sales
301	F. Francis, capital			

On 1 April the accounts receivable ledger of Illuminate Lighting showed the following balances: Horn $3100, Harris $2400, North Ltd $5800, and Smith $3400. The April transactions involving the receipt of cash were as follows.

Apr.	1	The owner, F. Francis, invested additional cash in the business $12 000.
	4	Received cheque for payment of account from Smith less 2% cash discount.
	5	Received cheque for $1240 in payment of invoice no. 307 from North Ltd.
	8	Made cash sales of inventory totalling $14 490. The cost of the inventory sold was $8694.
	10	Received cheque for $1600 in payment of invoice no. 309 from Horn.
	11	Received cash refund from a supplier for damaged inventory $1100.
	23	Received cheque for $3000 in payment of invoice no. 310 from North Ltd.
	29	Received cheque for payment of account from Harris.

Required

(a) Journalise the transactions provided in a six-column cash receipts journal with columns for Cash Dr, Discount allowed Dr, Accounts receivable Cr, Sales Cr, Other accounts Cr, and Cost of sales Dr/Inventory Cr. Total and cross-foot the journal.

(b) Enter the beginning balances in the accounts receivable control and subsidiary accounts, and post the April transactions to these accounts.

(c) Check that the control account and subsidiary account balances agree.

(d) What are the advantages and disadvantages of settlement discounts?

PSB6.5 Journalise transactions in cash payments journal; post to control account and subsidiary ledgers.

LO9, 10, 13, 14

Findon Pty Ltd's chart of accounts includes the following selected accounts:

101	Cash		201	Accounts payable
120	Inventory		306	L. Findon, drawings
130	Prepaid insurance		405	Discount received
157	Equipment		505	Cost of sales

On 1 October the accounts payable ledger of Findon Pty Ltd showed the following balances: Hester Ltd $6800, Milos Ltd $10 000, Tario Ltd $5600, and Pagan and Sons $14 800. The October transactions involving the payment of cash were as follows:

Oct.	1	Purchased inventory, cheque no. 63, $2800.
	3	Purchased equipment, cheque no. 64, $3200.
	5	Paid Hester Ltd balance due of $6800, less 2% discount, cheque no. 65, $6664.

▶

Oct. 10	Purchased inventory, cheque no. 66, $9000.
15	Paid Tario Ltd balance due of $5600, cheque no. 67.
16	L. Findon, the owner, pays her personal insurance premium of $1600, cheque no. 68.
19	Paid Milos Ltd for invoice no. 610, $5600 less 2% cash discount, cheque no. 69, $5488.
29	Paid Pagan and Sons in full for invoice no. 264, $10 400, cheque no. 70.

Required

(a) Journalise the transactions above in a five-column cash payments journal with columns for Other accounts Dr, Accounts payable Dr, Inventory Cr, Discount received Cr, and Cash Cr. Total and cross-foot the journal.

(b) Insert the beginning balances in the accounts payable control and subsidiary accounts, and post the October transactions to these accounts.

(c) Check that the control account and the subsidiary account balances agree.

PSB6.6 Journalise transactions in special journals.   **LO9, 10, 13, 14**

Selected accounts from the chart of accounts of Ruby Ltd are shown below.

101	Cash	401	Sales
112	Accounts receivable	412	Sales returns and allowances
120	Inventory	416	Discount received
126	Supplies	505	Cost of sales
157	Equipment	716	Discount allowed
201	Accounts payable	726	Salaries expense

The cost of all inventory sold was 60% of the sales price. During January, Ruby Ltd completed the following transactions.

Jan. 3	Purchased inventory on account from Bell Bros. $11 000.
4	Purchased supplies for cash $88.
4	Sold inventory on account to Gilbert $7975, invoice no. 371, terms 1/7, n/30.
5	Returned $330 worth of damaged goods to Bell Bros.
6	Made cash sales for the week totalling $3465.
8	Purchased inventory on account from Law Ltd $4950.
9	Sold inventory on account to Mays Ltd $6380, invoice no. 372, terms 1/7, n/30.
11	Purchased inventory on account from Hoble $4070.
13	Paid Bell Bros on account less a 2% discount.
13	Made cash sales for the week totalling $5874.
14	Received payment from Mays Ltd for invoice no. 372.
15	Paid fortnightly salaries of $15 730 to employees.
17	Received payment from Gilbert for invoice no. 371.
17	Sold inventory on account to Amber Ltd $1320, invoice no. 373, terms 1/7, n/30.
19	Purchased equipment on account from Johnson Ltd $6050.
20	Cash sales for the week totalled $3520.
20	Paid in full Law Ltd on account less a 2% discount.
23	Purchased inventory on account from Bell Bros $8580.
24	Purchased inventory on account from Levine $5160.
27	Made cash sales for the week totalling $4103.
30	Received payment from Amber Ltd for invoice no. 373.
31	Paid fortnightly salaries of $14 520 to employees.
31	Sold inventory on account to Gilbert $10 265, invoice no. 374, terms 1/7, n/30.

Ruby Ltd uses the following journals:

1. Sales journal.
2. Single-column purchases journal.
3. Cash receipts journal with columns for Cash Dr, Discount allowed Dr, Accounts receivable Cr, Sales Cr, Other accounts Cr, and Cost of sales Dr/Inventory Cr.

4. Cash payments journal with columns for Other accounts Dr, Accounts payable Dr, Inventory Cr, Discount received Cr, and Cash Cr.

5. General journal.

Required

Using the selected accounts provided:

(a) Record the January transactions in the appropriate journal.

(b) Total and cross-foot all special journals.

(c) Show how postings would be made by placing ledger account numbers and ticks (✓) as needed in the journals. (Actual posting to ledger accounts is not required.)

PSB6.7 Journalise in special journals; post; prepare a trial balance. LO9, 10, 13, 14

The post-closing trial balance for Camperdown Carpets is as follows.

CAMPERDOWN CARPETS Post-closing trial balance as at 31 December 2019		
	Debit	Credit
Cash	$ 41 500	
Accounts receivable	15 000	
Commissions receivable	45 000	
Inventory	23 000	
Equipment	6 450	
Accumulated depreciation—equipment		$ 1 500
Accounts payable		43 000
S. Alomar, capital		86 450
	$130 950	$130 950

The subsidiary ledgers contain the following information: (1) Accounts receivable—R. Barton $2500, B. Cole $7500, S. Devine $5000; (2) Accounts payable—S. Field $10 000, R. Grilson $18 000, D. Harms $15 000. The cost of all inventory sold was 65% of the sales price.

The transactions for January 2020 are as follows.

Jan. 5	Sell inventory to B. Senton $4000, terms 2/7, n/30.
5	Purchase inventory from S. Warren $2500, terms 2/7, n/30.
7	Receive a cheque from S. Devine $3500.
11	Pay freight on inventory purchased $300.
12	Pay rent of $1000 for January.
12	Receive payment from B. Senton for amount due.
14	Issue a credit note to acknowledge receipt of damaged inventory of $700 returned by R. Barton.
15	Send D. Harms a cheque for $14 850 in payment of account, discount $150.
17	Purchase inventory from D. Lapeska $1600, terms 2/7, n/30.
18	Pay sales salaries of $2800 and office salaries $1500.
20	Send R. Grilson a cheque for $18 000 in payment of account payable.
23	Total cash sales amount to $8600.
24	Sell inventory on account to B. Cole $7700, terms 1/7, n/30.
27	Send S. Warren a cheque for $950.
29	Receive $40 000 of the commissions revenue receivable at 31 December 2019.
30	Return inventory of $500 to D. Lapeska for credit.

Required

(a) Open general and subsidiary ledger accounts for the following:

101	Cash	412	Sales returns and allowances
112	Accounts receivable	415	Discount received
115	Commissions receivable	505	Cost of sales
120	Inventory	506	Freight inwards
157	Equipment	714	Discount allowed
158	Accumulated depreciation—equipment	726	Sales salaries expense
201	Accounts payable	727	Office salaries expense
301	S. Alomar, capital	729	Rent expense
401	Sales	750	Inventory write-down expense
405	Commissions revenue		

(b) Record the January transactions in a sales journal, a single-column purchases journal, a cash receipts journal (see figure 6.15), a cash payments journal (see figure 6.22) and a general journal.

(c) Post the appropriate amounts to the general ledger.

(d) Prepare a trial balance as at 31 January 2020.

(e) Determine whether the subsidiary ledgers agree with the corresponding control accounts in the general ledger.

PSB6.8 **Journalise in sales and cash receipts journals; post; prepare a trial balance; check control with subsidiary; prepare adjusting entries; prepare an adjusted trial balance.**   **LO9, 10, 13, 14**

Presented below are the purchases and cash payments journals for Collins Bikes for its first month of operations.

Purchases journal				P14
Date	Account credited	Post ref.		Inventory Dr Accounts payable Cr
July 4	J. Dixon			6 800
5	W. Engel			7 500
11	R. Gamble			3 920
13	M. Hill			15 300
20	D. Jacob			8 800
				42 320

Cash payments journal						CP16
Date	Account debited	Post ref.	Other accounts Dr	Accounts payable Dr	Discount received Cr	Cash Cr
July 4	Store supplies		600			600
10	W. Engel			7 500	75	7 425
11	Prepaid rent		6 000			6 000
15	J. Dixon			6 800		6 800
19	Collins, drawings		2 500			2 500
21	M. Hill			15 300	153	15 147
			9 100	29 600	228	38 472

In addition, the following transactions have not been journalised for July. The cost of all inventory sold was 65% of the sales price.

July	1	The owner, R. Collins, invests $80 000 in cash.
	6	Sell inventory on account to Hardy Ltd $5400 terms 1/7, n/30.
	7	Make cash sales totalling $4000.
	8	Sell inventory on account to D. Wasburn $3600, terms 1/7, n/30.
	10	Sell inventory on account to L. Lemansky $4900, terms 1/14, n/30.
	13	Receive payment from D. Wasburn.
	16	Receive payment from L. Lemansky.
	20	Receive payment from Hardy Ltd.
	21	Sell inventory on account to S. Kane $4000, terms 1/7, n/30.
	29	Returned damaged goods to J. Dixon and received cash refund of $450.

Required

(a) Open the following accounts in the general ledger:

101	Cash	306	Collins, drawings
112	Accounts receivable	401	Sales
120	Inventory	405	Discount received
127	Store supplies	505	Cost of sales
131	Prepaid rent	614	Discount allowed
201	Accounts payable	631	Supplies expense
301	Collins, capital	729	Rent expense

(b) Journalise the transactions that have not been journalised in the sales journal, the cash receipts journal (see figure 6.15) and the general journal.

(c) Post to the accounts receivable and accounts payable subsidiary ledgers. Follow the sequence of transactions as shown in the problem.

(d) Post the individual entries and totals to the general ledger.

(e) Prepare a trial balance as at 31 July 2019.

(f) Determine whether the subsidiary ledgers agree with the control accounts in the general ledger.

(g) The following adjustments at the end of July are necessary:

1. A count of supplies indicates that $140 is still on hand.
2. Recognise rent expense for July, $500. Prepare the necessary entries in the general journal. Post the entries to the general ledger.

(h) Prepare an adjusted trial balance as at 31 July 2019.

(i) Part (g) required the journal entries for two adjustments. What is the purpose of adjusting entries? What are the implications of not completing adjusting entries?

PSB6.9 **Journalise transactions in cash receipts journal; post to control account and subsidiary ledger.**

LO9, 10, 13, 14

Beachcombers Supplies Pty Ltd chart of accounts includes the following selected accounts.

101	Cash	401	Sales
112	Accounts receivable	414	Discount allowed
120	Inventory	505	Cost of sales
301	Beach Boy, capital		

On 1 April the accounts receivable ledger of Beachcombers' Supplies showed the following balances: Board Barn Ltd $2325, I'm Board Ltd $1800, Sand Wedge Ltd $4350 and Wet Suits Gallore Pty Ltd $2550. The April transactions involving the receipt of cash were as follows.

Apr.	1	The owner, Beach Boy, invested additional cash in the business $9000.
	4	Received cheque for payment of account from Wet Suits Gallore Pty Ltd less 2% cash discount.
	5	Received cheque for $930 in payment of invoice no. 307 from Sand Wedge Ltd.
	8	Made cash sales of inventory totalling $10 868. The cost of the inventory sold was $6520.
	10	Received cheque for $1200 in payment of invoice no. 309 from Board Barn Ltd.
	11	Received cash refund from a supplier for damaged inventory returned $825.
	23	Received cheque for $2250 in payment of invoice no. 310 from Sand Wedge Ltd.
	29	Received cheque for payment of account from I'm Board Ltd.

Required

(a) Journalise the transactions above in a six-column cash receipts journal with columns for Cash Dr, Discount allowed Dr, Accounts receivable Cr, Sales Cr, Other accounts Cr, and Cost of sales Dr/Inventory Cr. Total and cross-foot the journal.

(b) Enter the beginning balances in the accounts receivable control and subsidiary accounts, and post the April transactions to these accounts.

(c) Check that the control account and subsidiary account balances agree.

PSB6.10 Journalise transactions in multicolumn purchases journal; post to the general and subsidiary ledgers. **LO9, 10, 13, 14**

The chart of accounts of Richards Ltd includes the following selected accounts.

112	Accounts receivable	401	Sales
120	Inventory	412	Sales returns and allowances
126	Supplies	505	Cost of sales
157	Equipment	510	Freight inwards
201	Accounts payable	610	Advertising expense

In December the following selected transactions were completed. All purchases and sales were on account except as indicated. The cost of all inventory sold was 70% of the sales price.

Dec.	2	Purchased inventory from Celtic Ltd $14 250.
	3	Received invoice for freight from Fast Delivery on Celtic purchase $600.
	5	Sales were made to Wang Ltd $2625, Singh Ltd $4050, and Smith Ltd $2250.
	8	Purchased inventory from Ripping Ltd $12 000 and Lamb Ltd $13 050.
	10	Received credit on inventory returned to Lamb Ltd $750.
	15	Purchased supplies from Office Supply $1350.
	16	Purchased inventory from Celtic Ltd $6750, and Ripping Ltd $9000.
	17	Returned supplies to Office Supply, receiving credit note for $150.
	18	Received invoice for freight on 16 December for purchases from Celtic Ltd, $600.
	20	Returned inventory to Celtic Ltd, receiving credit note for $450.
	23	Made sales to Singh Ltd $1200, and to Smith Ltd $3300.
	25	Received invoice for advertising from Striking Advertising $1350.
	26	Granted allowance to Smith Ltd for inventory damaged in shipment $300.
	28	Purchased equipment from Office Supply $375.

Required

(a) Journalise the transactions above in a purchases journal, a sales journal and a general journal. The purchases journal should have the following column headings: Date, Accounts credited (debited), Post ref., Other accounts Dr, and Inventory Dr/Accounts payable Cr.

(b) Post to both the general and subsidiary ledger accounts. (Assume that all accounts have nil beginning balances.)

(c) Agree the control account and subsidiary ledger balances.

(d) Explain the advantages and disadvantages of computerised accounting systems over manual accounting systems.

COMPREHENSIVE PROBLEM: CHAPTERS 3 TO 6

Greta's Furniture Pty Ltd has the following opening account balances in its general and subsidiary ledgers on 1 January. All accounts have normal debit and credit balances.

No.	Account name	1 January opening balance
	General ledger	
101	Cash	$ 64 350
112	Accounts receivable	23 400
115	Commissions receivable	70 200
120	Inventory	32 400
125	Office supplies	1 800
130	Prepaid insurance	3 600
157	Equipment	11 610
158	Accumulated depreciation	2 700
201	Accounts payable	63 000
301	P. Greta, capital	141 660

Customer	1 January opening balance
	Accounts receivable subsidiary ledger
Couch City	$ 2 700
Table Tops Ltd	13 500
Lowell Chairs	7 200

Creditor	1 January opening balance
	Accounts payable subsidiary ledger
Lee Importers	$16 200
Ikeah	27 000
Nordin Office Furniture	19 800

Jan.	3	Sell inventory on credit to The Furniture Warehouse $5580, invoice no. 510, and Beautiful Homes Ltd $3240, invoice no. 511.
	5	Purchase inventory from Walden & Co. $5400 and D. Landell $3960.
	7	Receive cheques for $7200 from Lowell Chairs and $3600 from Table Tops Ltd. Discount allowed $72 and $36, respectively.
	8	Pay freight on inventory purchased $324.
	9	Send cheques to Lee Importers for $16 200 and Nordin Office Furniture for $19 800. Discount received $162 and $297 respectively.
	9	Issue credit note for $540 to Beautiful Homes Ltd for inventory returned (goods were not damaged and were returned to inventory).
	10	Summary cash sales total $27 900.
	11	Sell inventory on credit to Couch City for $2340, invoice no. 512, and to Lowell Chairs $1620, invoice no. 513.
	12	Pay rent of $1800 for January.
	13	Receive payment in full from The Furniture Warehouse and Beautiful Homes Ltd.
	15	Withdraw $1440 cash by P. Greta for personal use.
	16	Purchase inventory from Nordin Office Furniture for $27 000, from Lee Importers for $25 560, and from Walden & Co. for $2700.
	17	Pay $720 cash for office supplies.
	18	Return $360 of inventory to Lee Importers and receive credit.
	20	Summary cash sales total $31 500.

▶

Jan.	21	Send cheque to Ikeah in payment of balance due.
	21	Receive payment in full from Lowell Chairs, discount allowed $162.
	22	Sell inventory on credit to The Furniture Warehouse for $3060, invoice no. 514, and to Couch City for $1440, invoice no. 515.
	23	Send cheques to Nordin Office Furniture and Lee Importers in full payment.
	25	Sell inventory on credit to Table Tops Ltd for $6300, invoice no. 516, and to Beautiful Homes Ltd for $10 980, invoice no. 517.
	27	Purchase inventory from Nordin Office Furniture for $26 100, from D. Landell for $2160, and from Walden & Co. for $5040.
	28	Pay $360 cash for office supplies.
	31	Summary cash sales total $38 340.
	31	Pay sales salaries of $7740 and office salaries of $4680.
	31	Received $70 200 commission revenue owing at the end of December 2020.

The chart of accounts includes the following accounts: 306 P. Greta, drawings, 350 Profit or loss summary, 401 Sales, 412 Sales returns and allowances, 415 Discount received, 417 Commissions revenue, 510 Purchases, 512 Purchases returns and allowances, 516 Freight inwards, 627 Sales salaries expense, 711 Depreciation expense, 722 Insurance expense, 725 Discount allowed, 727 Office salaries expense, 728 Office supplies expense and 729 Rent expense.

Required

(a) Record the January transactions in the appropriate journal: sales, purchases, cash receipts, cash payments and general.

(b) Post the journals to the general and subsidiary ledgers. New accounts should be added and numbered in an orderly fashion as needed.

(c) Prepare a trial balance as at 31 January 2021 using a worksheet. Complete the worksheet using the following additional information.

1. Office supplies at 31 January total $900.
2. Insurance cover expires on 31 October 2021.
3. Annual depreciation on the equipment is $2700.
4. Commissions revenue of $39 600 has accrued during January.
5. Inventory at 31 January is $28 800.

(d) Prepare a fully classified statement of profit or loss for January and a classified statement of financial position at the end of January.

(e) Prepare and post the adjusting and closing entries.

(f) Prepare a post-closing trial balance, and determine whether the subsidiary ledgers agree with the control accounts in the general ledger.

BUILDING BUSINESS SKILLS

FINANCIAL REPORTING AND ANALYSIS

Financial reporting problem: Sky Network Television Limited

BBS6.1 Information about which control accounts, subsidiary ledgers and special journals an entity uses is not disclosed in the financial statements. However, by looking at the nature of the entity's activities and the types of accounts used, you can infer which subsystems it might use. Go to www.asx.com.au/asx/share-price-research/company/SKT to access the latest annual report of Sky Network Television Limited.

Required

(a) Look at the annual report and, from the information disclosed, list the control accounts, subsidiary ledgers and special journals that you think Sky Network might use. Explain why you believe they might use each of these.

(b) List the advantages and disadvantages for Sky Network in using control accounts, subsidiary ledgers and special journals.

(c) Review the Corporate Governance section of the annual report. Using the ASX *Corporate Governance Principles and Recommendations (Third Edition)*, discuss whether Sky Network's corporate governance statement meets the ASX guidelines.

CRITICAL THINKING

Group decision case

BBS6.2 Ling & Jessop is a retail outlet for antique books that provides a book repair service and also sells rare music manuscripts. Ling & Jessop is operated by Cam Ling and Tim Jessop. Mildred Mildew is a repair specialist who works for Ling & Jessop on a fixed salary. Revenues are generated through the sale of antique books (approximately 75% of total revenues), rare manuscripts (10%) and the repair of old books brought to the store (15%). Book sales are made on both a credit and a cash basis. Customers receive prenumbered sales invoices. Credit terms are always net/30 days. All manuscript sales and repair work are cash only.

Inventory is purchased on account from various antique book and manuscript dealers. Virtually all suppliers offer cash discounts for prompt payment, and it is company policy to take all discounts. Most cash payments are made by cheque. Cheques are most frequently issued to suppliers, to transport companies for freight on inventory purchases, and to newspapers, radio and TV stations for advertising. All invoices for advertising are paid as received. Cam and Tim each make a monthly drawing in cash for personal living expenses. The salaried repair woman is paid fortnightly.

Ling & Jessop currently has a manual accounting system. Cam Ling is concerned about the inefficiencies in journalising and posting transactions with the manual system. Two additional bookkeepers were employed a month ago, but the inefficiencies have continued at an even higher rate. However, Tim is old-fashioned and refuses to install an electronic accounting system.

Required

With the class divided into groups, answer the following.

(a) Identify the special journals that Ling & Jessop should have in its manual system. List the column headings appropriate for each of the special journals.

(b) What control and subsidiary accounts should be included in Ling & Jessop's manual system? Why?

(c) Explain why the additional personnel did not help.

(d) What changes should be made to improve the efficiency of the accounting system?

Communication activity

BBS6.3 CRM stands for customer relationship management. As customers are at the centre of business success, it is essential for companies to understand and satisfy customer needs.

Your friend, Marlene Jones, is going to start a computer dating business and wants you to prepare a report on CRM using the Web as a research tool. You will be paid $5000 and your friend would like you to include answers to the following questions in your report.

(a) What is CRM?

(b) What technologies can be used in CRM?

(c) What are the goals of CRM?

(d) What are the benefits of CRM?

Ethics case

BBS6.4 Tyler Products Ltd operates three divisions, each with its own manufacturing factories and marketing/sales force. The corporate headquarters and central accounting office are in Sydney, and the factories are in Moorebank, Smithfield and Tempe, all within 50 kilometres of Sydney. Corporate management treats each division as an independent profit centre and encourages competition among them. They each have similar but different product lines. As a competitive incentive, bonuses are awarded each year to the employees of the fastest growing and most profitable division.

Don Henke is the manager of Tyler's centralised computer accounting operation that records the sales transactions and maintains the accounts receivable for all three divisions. Don came up in the accounting ranks from the Tempe division where his wife, several relatives and many friends still work.

As sales documents are entered into the computer, the originating division is identified by code. Most sales documents (95%) are coded, but some (5%) are not coded or are coded incorrectly. As the manager, Don has instructed the data entry staff to assign the Tempe code to all uncoded and incorrectly coded sales documents. This is done, he says, 'in order to expedite processing and to keep the computer files current since they are updated daily'. All receivables and cash collections for all three divisions are handled by Tyler as one subsidiary accounts receivable ledger.

Required

(a) Who are the stakeholders in this situation?

(b) What are the ethical issues in this case?

(c) How might the system be improved to prevent this situation?

Research case

BBS6.5 In the 2016 annual report for Domino's Pizza Enterprises Ltd, Chairman Jack Cowin, together with Don Meij, Managing Director / Group Chief Executive Officer of Domino's, stated in the Directors' Report:

> **Future Developments**
>
> In ANZ [Australia and New Zealand], we will be unveiling our biggest menu launch since 2008 and driving product innovation through the introduction of new food categories and delivering a menu, free of preservatives and artificial colouring. Further development of DRU (Domino's automated robotic unit) and the launch of "Zero Click" ordering will continue to drive our digital innovation allowing for continued focus on maximising online sales and sustained increase in our network of stores.
>
> We have upgraded our future store network guidance in ANZ to 1,200 stores by 2025, up from 900, on the basis of continued demand.
>
> In Europe, we will continue to focus on delivering a number of new initiatives that have been put in place to optimise logistics and drive operational efficiencies. The logistics optimization will include the opening of the new Paris (France) commissary and is expected to be the most automated Domino's commissary in the world, yielding substantial cost savings through production benefits. Operational efficiencies include the continuing rollout of the global point of sale ("POS") and "One Digital" online ordering systems in France. The GPS Driver Tracker will be fully rolled out in the Netherlands and we are expecting record organic new store growth in the FY17 year...
>
> In Japan, the key areas of focus in FY17 will be the continuation of new store rollouts. Stores will also be relocated to pick up friendly locations and the new Point of sale (POS) system will be rolled out. "One Digital" online ordering system will be rolled out within FY17 and we will continue to seek further expansion opportunities into new regional markets in FY17.

Required

Using the internet as a research tool, access multiple types of information available that indicate whether or not Jack Cowin and Don Meij have been successful in achieving the goals listed in the 2016 annual report. As a start, you can search the company's web site at www.dominos.com.au, then select **Domino's Corporate Site** and/or **Investors** and/or **Domino's annual report** where you will find company reports and presentations that will assist

you in answering these questions. Please reference your information sources appropriately by including:
- document name
- web address
- date accessed.

You might also like to keep a hard or soft copy of the data you access, as information that is currently available may not be available at a later date when the site is updated.

Sustainability

BBS6.6 Jewels, Jewels and More Jewels Ltd is one of the largest sellers of diamonds in Australia. It has more than 50 stores nationwide and sells on the internet as well. This morning, Jane Peterson, one of the senior managers of Jewels, Jewels and More Jewels Ltd, read an article in the press accusing Big Diamond Factory, one of its major suppliers, of having acquired 'blood diamonds'. Blood diamonds are also called conflict diamonds because they are mined in war-torn African countries by the rebels to fund their efforts. The rebels are known to abuse human rights by murdering and enslaving the local populations to mine the diamonds. Jane can't believe it and calls you into her office to prepare a report for all senior staff.

Required

(a) Explain the concept Corporate Social Responsibility (CSR).
(b) Discuss in detail, the impact this information could have on Jewels, Jewels and More Jewels Ltd.
(c) What could the management of Jewels, Jewels and More Jewels Ltd do to avoid negative consequences?

ANSWERS

Answers to self-study questions

6.1 (d) 6.2 (d) 6.3 (b) 6.4 (c) 6.5 (a) 6.6 (c) 6.7 (b) 6.8 (a) 6.9 (b) 6.10 (c) 6.11 (d) 6.12 (a) 6.13 (d) 6.14 (c) 6.15 (a) 6.16 (b) 6.17 (a) 6.18 (c)

ACKNOWLEDGEMENTS

Photo: © mrmohock / Shutterstock.com
Photo: © Robert Daly / Getty Images
Photo: © Blend Images / Getty Images
Photo: © Pressmaster / Shutterstock.com
Text: © Domino's Pizza Enterprises Limited

CHAPTER 7

Reporting and analysing cash and receivables

LEARNING OBJECTIVES

After studying this chapter, you should be able to:

7.1 identify the effect of business transactions on cash

7.2 describe electronic banking processes

7.3 explain the application of internal control principles for handling cash

7.4 prepare a bank reconciliation

7.5 discuss the basic principles of cash management

7.6 assess the adequacy of cash

7.7 identify the different types of receivables

7.8 describe how to value receivables

7.9 describe how receivables are reported in financial statements

7.10 analyse and manage receivables

7.11 explain the operation of a petty cash fund.

Chapter preview

Cash is the lifeblood of any business. It is typically the most common asset with which all entities begin and is the basis for measuring and accounting for all business transactions. As cash is the most liquid asset and can be easily transferred from one person to another, large and small businesses alike must therefore guard it carefully. Managers must know both how to use cash efficiently and how to protect it.

Another current asset closely associated with cash is accounts receivable. Increasingly, many business transactions are conducted on a credit basis. Manufacturers, wholesalers, retailers and service organisations regularly extend credit to buyers of their goods and services as a means of increasing sales. A common feature of all receivables is that they are generally regarded as highly liquid assets that are expected to be collected and converted into cash in the short term. There are possibilities that some debtors may not make payment on time and some may not pay at all due to insolvency or bankruptcy. As such, it is important that business owners and managers have the tools to analyse and manage credit risk.

In this chapter you will learn ways to reduce the risk of theft of cash, how to report cash and receivables in the financial statements, and how to manage these assets through the course of the entity's operating cycle. The content and organisation of the chapter are as follows.

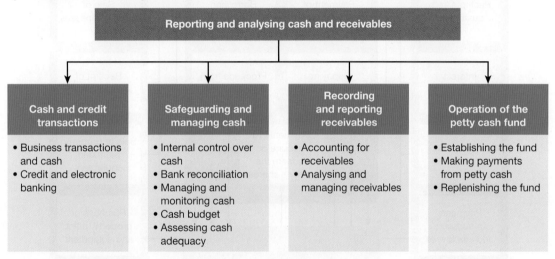

7.1 Cash and credit transactions

LEARNING OBJECTIVE 7.1 Identify the effect of business transactions on cash.

Cash is an essential part of a business's assets. Broadly, for accounting purposes, **cash** includes cash on hand (i.e. coin and paper money held), cash at bank (i.e. a cheque account) and cash equivalents, which are highly liquid investments (i.e. quickly converted to cash), such as bank overdrafts, deposits on the money market and 90-day bank acceptance bills. Credit card and electronic banking has become increasingly important for settling transactions in the past decade. As such, cash also consists of duplicates of credit card and electronic funds transfer at point of sale (EFTPOS) sales that a bank or financial institution will normally accept as a deposit to an account.

Business transactions and cash

Many transactions have implications on an entity's cash flows in that almost every business transaction eventually results in an inflow or outflow of cash. Let's analyse the cash effect through a business cycle. Consider, for example, you are planning to start a mobile coffee kiosk business while you are studying at university. You will need to carefully consider the cash flow requirements in your business plan; for instance, how much cash you need to inject into the business (cash inflow) to invest in buying assets such as the coffee machine and the van (cash outflow). If you have limited cash available to contribute to the business, you may need to borrow funds from your parents or friends or even from a bank (cash inflow). During the normal course of operation, the business needs to purchase supplies such as coffee beans and cups either by cash purchase or purchase on account (cash outflow). Of course, every cup of coffee it sells brings in cash to the business (cash inflow). In a few years' time when you complete your degree, you may decide to sell the business as you want to travel the world. At that stage of the business lifecycle, there is cash inflow from selling the business assets. As you wind up the business, returning the capital to you or repaying the loan to the lenders represents the final cash outflow.

| **FIGURE 7.1** | Effect of major accounting transactions on cash |

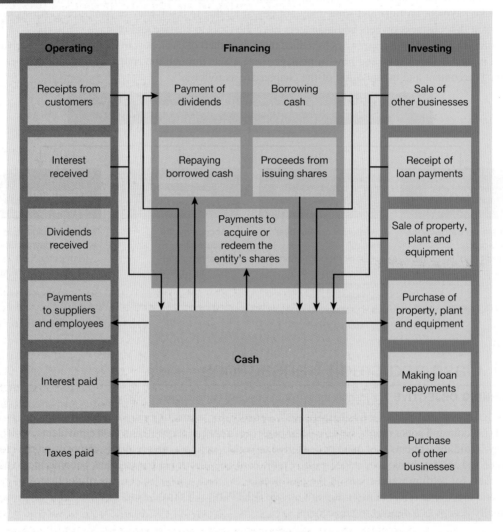

Cash is at the heart of the business as it impacts on a number of profit or loss and statement of financial position accounts. For example, cash sales increase both cash (asset) and revenue (profit or loss), while cash payment for purchases of inventory decreases cash but increases inventory (asset). Figure 7.1 depicts the effects of major accounting transactions on cash. Essentially, all these transactions will be reported in the operating, investing or financing activities in the statement of cash flows, which you will learn about in chapter 11. In summary, examples of transactions with inflows of cash include:

- revenue from cash sales of goods and services
- collection of cash from credit sales
- cash proceeds from divestment of assets
- cash received from business owners through issuance of shares
- cash received from borrowings.

 Examples of transactions that cause outflows of cash include:
- cash payment for purchases of inventory
- cash payment for investment in assets such as property, plant and equipment
- cash payment for business expenses such as payroll and rent
- payment to business owners in the form of dividend or return of capital
- interest and loan payments to financial institution.

7.2 Credit and electronic banking

LEARNING OBJECTIVE 7.2 Describe electronic banking processes.

Increasingly, business transactions nowadays are settled electronically thanks to the convenience brought about by 'plastic money'. Having access to credit cards and bank cards means that customers can shop without physically carrying cash. What's more, in the last couple of years, advances in mobile phone technology have made it possible for people to move from credit card to mobile phone for payments. Perhaps you have a smartphone and have downloaded apps to allow you to conduct transactions whenever and wherever you like with a touch of the screen on your phone.

The convenience of easy access to credit cards has also brought about ballooning credit card debts in the last decade. Because of the high interest rate charged on credit cards, it is very important for us to be 'money smart'. Here are some smart ways to use credit cards: (1) shop around to get a card with the lowest annual fee (some banks may offer no fees cards); (2) negotiate to get as long an interest-free period as possible; (3) use a credit card, rather than EFTPOS from your savings account, to pay for everyday expenses; (4) once you receive the credit card statements, make sure that you pay the outstanding balance in full by the due date. In this way, you can essentially use the credit card for free while you can keep earning interest on your savings account. Better still, some credit cards also come with reward programs so that you can accumulate reward points to redeem gift cards or products of your choosing. But the catch is that you should always pay the outstanding balance in full and, importantly, by the due date. Failing to do that will result in not only a late fee being charged, but also it means that you will be incurring interest on any new purchases made on your card until the full balance is paid in full.

For business owners, although a merchant or bank fee is involved in using electronic funds transfer at point of sale (EFTPOS), accepting payments electronically can bring in several benefits, the most obvious being a possible saving in staffing cost as there is less handling of cash required. For internal control purposes, cash presents a high risk of being misappropriated. Linking the business's accounting system to its electronic banking provider(s) enables the business to establish a clearer paper trail and thus reduces the possibility of mishandling cash. We will discuss credit card sales in more detail later in the chapter. For the moment, let's take a closer look at how electronic banking works.

Electronic banking is an electronic payment system that enables customers of a financial institution to conduct financial transactions on a web site operated by the institution, such as a bank, credit union or building society. (It is also referred to as *internet banking*, *e-banking*, *virtual banking* and *online banking*.) To access a financial institution's online banking facility, a customer with internet access would need to register with the institution for the service and set up a password for customer verification. Once registered, a bank customer can transact banking tasks through online banking, including transferring funds between the customer's linked accounts and paying third parties, including bill payments through BPAY. A bank customer can also perform non-transactional tasks through online banking, including viewing account balances, viewing recent transactions, downloading bank statements, ordering cheque books and so on.

In the last decade, **electronic funds transfer (EFT)** has gained widespread acceptance as the cost of processing cheques through the banking system is high. Considerable delays of up to 5 working days exist in the clearing process for cheques. With EFT, money is transferred almost instantaneously from one location to another via the internet. Electronic banking not only speeds up the transfer of money, but also helps to reduce the transactional cost as there is less documentation of writing cheques and deposit slips, and less labour required.

7.3 Safeguarding and managing cash

LEARNING OBJECTIVE 7.3 Explain the application of internal control principles for handling cash.

Cash is the one asset that is readily convertible into any other type of asset; it is easily concealed and transported; and it is highly desired. Moreover, because of the large volume of cash transactions, numerous errors may occur in executing and recording cash transactions. Therefore, having an effective mechanism in place to safeguard cash assets is essential. An internal control procedure such as performing a bank reconciliation regularly is one such measure to safeguard cash. Further, monitoring cash in terms of striking a balance between keeping too much cash on hand and running a low cash balance, and managing cash through careful cash budgeting are also important tools for keeping businesses afloat. We will also look at ways to analyse the adequacy of cash to aid making informed business decisions.

Internal control over cash

Because cash is the asset most susceptible to misappropriation, i.e. improper use and theft, it is important to set up a strong internal control system for handling and recording cash transactions. Such a system must contain procedures for protecting cash on hand as well as for handling both cash receipts and cash payments.

Internal control over cash receipts

Cash receipts result from a variety of sources such as cash sales, cash in the form of cheques received from customers through the mail, the receipt of other income including interest, rents and dividends, cash from owners' capital contributions, bank loans, and proceeds from the sale of non-current assets.

Procedures for the control of cash receipts from cash sales are based heavily on the principle of segregation of duties for record keeping and custodianship (discussed in chapter 6). Briefly, cash received from cash sales, on EFTPOS or on credit cards should be rung up on a cash register located in a position that permits the customer to see the amount recorded. The register prints a receipt that is given to the customer. Registers are usually linked directly to computers used by the accounting department or have a locked-in tape on which each cash sale is recorded. The cash in the register plus EFTPOS and credit card slips are counted and recorded on a preprinted form that is sent to the accounting department. The cash and slips are then forwarded to the cashier for deposit, and the tape is sent to the accounting department for preparing accounting entries.

Similarly, procedures for the control of cash received in the mail are based heavily on separation of record keeping and custodianship. The employee who opens the mail should prepare a list of the amounts received. One copy of the list is sent to the cashier along with the cash amounts. These amounts are combined with those from the cash registers in preparing the daily bank deposit. Another copy of the list is forwarded to the accounting department for preparing entries in the cash receipts journal and in customers' accounts.

With both cash sales and cash received in the mail, it should be emphasised that neither the mail clerk nor the cashier should have access to the accounting records. Likewise, the accounting staff should not have access to cash. If properly carried out, these internal control procedures should minimise fraud unless there is collusion by two or more employees. The internal control principles applicable to cash receipts transactions are shown in figure 7.2. As might be expected, businesses vary considerably in how they apply these principles.

FIGURE 7.2 Application of internal control principles for cash receipts

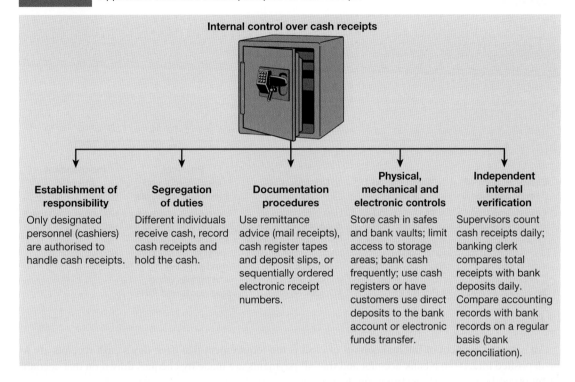

Internal control over cash receipts

Establishment of responsibility	Segregation of duties	Documentation procedures	Physical, mechanical and electronic controls	Independent internal verification
Only designated personnel (cashiers) are authorised to handle cash receipts.	Different individuals receive cash, record cash receipts and hold the cash.	Use remittance advice (mail receipts), cash register tapes and deposit slips, or sequentially ordered electronic receipt numbers.	Store cash in safes and bank vaults; limit access to storage areas; bank cash frequently; use cash registers or have customers use direct deposits to the bank account or electronic funds transfer.	Supervisors count cash receipts daily; banking clerk compares total receipts with bank deposits daily. Compare accounting records with bank records on a regular basis (bank reconciliation).

Internal control over cash payments

Cash is disbursed (paid out) for a variety of reasons, such as to pay for cash purchases, to pay suppliers for goods and services bought on credit, to pay for expenses and liabilities or to purchase assets. Determining appropriate procedures for authorisation of electronic payments and the issue of cheques is key to effective control over cash payments. Similar to control over cash receipts, the establishment of responsibility and segregation of duties are important principles for internal control over cash payments.

Generally, internal control over cash payments is more effective when payments are made by *using a bank account* rather than cash on hand, except for incidental amounts that are paid out of petty cash (discussed in section 7.11). Whether payment is through petty cash, by cheque or by using some form of EFT, it is generally made only after specified control procedures have been followed. For example, consider the payment of invoices received from suppliers for purchases made. Staff designated to approve invoices for payments should have no responsibility for preparing cheques or other payment instruments. They should verify that the goods or services represented by the invoice were properly ordered and actually received before authorising payment. On the other hand, employees responsible for signing cheques or approving electronic fund transfers should have no invoice approval or accounting responsibilities. Cheques should be signed only on receipt of a properly approved invoice. For payments exceeding a certain larger amount, some businesses require two signatories to approve these payments as an extra security check. Another control procedure is to cancel supporting documents after payment so that they are not used to support another payment.

Approved invoices, copies of the cheques and approved electronic transfers are then sent to the accounting department for preparing the appropriate entries to record the payments. If properly carried out, these internal control procedures would make it difficult for a fraudulent payment to be made without collusion by two or more employees. The principles of internal control apply to cash payments as shown in figure 7.3.

FIGURE 7.3 Application of internal control principles to cash payments

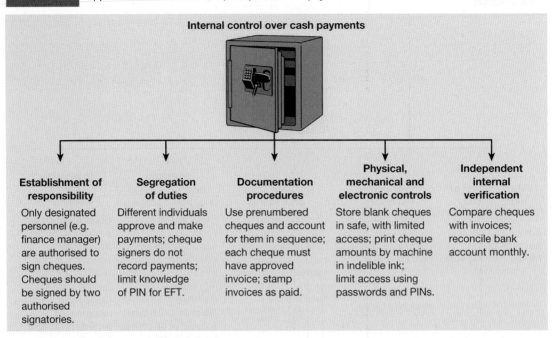

Internal control over cash payments

Establishment of responsibility	Segregation of duties	Documentation procedures	Physical, mechanical and electronic controls	Independent internal verification
Only designated personnel (e.g. finance manager) are authorised to sign cheques. Cheques should be signed by two authorised signatories.	Different individuals approve and make payments; cheque signers do not record payments; limit knowledge of PIN for EFT.	Use prenumbered cheques and account for them in sequence; each cheque must have approved invoice; stamp invoices as paid.	Store blank cheques in safe, with limited access; print cheque amounts by machine in indelible ink; limit access using passwords and PINs.	Compare cheques with invoices; reconcile bank account monthly.

An essential element of internal control of cash is the requirement that each day's cash receipts are to be deposited intact into a bank account and that all payments are made by cheques drawn on that account or by properly authorised electronic funds transfer.

Petty cash fund

Better internal control over cash disbursements is possible when payments are made by cheque or electronic funds transfer. However, using cheques to pay such small amounts as those for postage, employees' working lunches and taxi fares is both impractical and a nuisance. A common way of handling such payments while maintaining satisfactory control is to use a petty cash fund. A **petty cash fund** is a cash fund used to pay relatively small amounts. Information regarding the operation of a petty cash fund is provided in section 7.11.

LEARNING REFLECTION AND CONSOLIDATION

Review it
1. How do the principles of internal control apply to cash receipts?
2. How do the principles of internal control apply to cash disbursements?
3. What is the purpose of a petty cash fund?

Do it
Liam Jeffery is concerned about control over cash receipts in his fast-food restaurant, Healthy Snap. The restaurant has two cash registers. At no time do more than two employees take customer orders and ring up sales. Work shifts for employees range from 4 to 8 hours. Liam asks for your help in installing a good system of internal control over cash receipts.

Reasoning
Liam needs to understand the principles of internal control, especially establishing responsibility, the use of electronic controls, and independent internal verification. With this knowledge, an effective system of control over cash receipts can be designed and implemented.

7.4 Bank reconciliation

LEARNING OBJECTIVE 7.4 Prepare a bank reconciliation.

The use of a bank contributes significantly to good internal control over cash. The business deposits money with the bank to open a bank account. The business can add to its bank account by making deposits, thus increasing its asset, cash at bank. From the bank's point of view, its customer's deposit is a liability because it is money that the bank is obliged to return to its customer.

A business can use the money in its bank account to pay other parties, such as suppliers, by writing a cheque or by EFT. In the case of a cheque, the business is the payer, and the supplier who is to receive the cheque is the payee. The cheque is drawn on the business's bank. This means that the bank is obligated to pay the amount shown on the cheque to the payee. When the bank pays the amount of the cheque, this is known as honouring the cheque (some banks refer to this as *clearing cheques*). When a bank honours a customer's cheque, it deducts the money from the customer's bank account.

The asset account cash at bank, maintained by the business, is the reciprocal of the bank's liability account for that business. Conversely, if the business has overdrawn its bank account, the cash at bank account is a liability from the point of view of the business and a receivable, i.e. an asset, from the point of view of the bank. It should be possible to reconcile these accounts — make them agree — at any time.

Many businesses have more than one bank account. For efficiency of operations and better control, some businesses may have state or regional bank accounts. In addition, a business may maintain accounts with several different banks in order to have more than one source for obtaining short-term loans when needed.

Each month, the business receives from the bank a **bank statement** showing its bank transactions and balances. A list of bank transactions can also be downloaded from the bank's web site directly into accounting systems such as QuickBooks, MYOB and SAP. The statement for Justco Pty Ltd in figure 7.4 shows (1) cheques that have been presented and paid, electronic payments (e.g. Autopay, BPay) made during the month, and other debits that reduce the balance in Justco's account; (2) deposits (card entry), direct-deposit electronic transfers, other third-party deposits paid directly to the bank, and other credits that increase the balance in Justco's account; and (3) the account balance after each day's transactions.

Helpful hint: Essentially, the bank statement is a copy of the bank's records sent to the customer for periodic review.

Remember that bank statements are prepared from the *bank's* perspective. Therefore, every deposit received from Justco Pty Ltd by the Regional Bank of Australia is *credited* by the bank to Justco Pty Ltd. The reverse occurs when the bank honours, i.e. pays, a cheque issued by Justco Pty Ltd. Payments reduce the bank's liability and are therefore *debited* to Justco's account with the bank. This is the opposite of the entity's records, where payments reduce the entity's assets and are therefore credited to the cash at bank account.

All honoured cheques are listed on the bank statement in the order in which they are paid by the bank, along with the amount. The date refers to when the cheque is honoured by the bank. In addition, the bank statement explains other debits and credits made by the bank to its customer's account.

When a previously deposited customer's cheque 'bounces', it is called a **dishonoured cheque**. This means that the customer's bank has not honoured the cheque. This may occur if the customer does not have sufficient funds. In such a case, the cheque is returned to the depositor's bank. The bank then debits (decreases) the depositor's account, as shown in figure 7.4 (RET of $25 on 26 August). The bank typically charges the account holder a fee for having deposited a cheque that was subsequently dishonoured. The dishonoured cheque and the dishonoured cheque fee reduce the amount of cash in the bank account.

Helpful hint: Bank fees are financial supplies and no GST is charged.

Reconciling the bank account

A bank reconciliation involves a comparison between the bank's records and the business's cash receipts journal, cash payments journal and cash at bank ledger account. Because the bank and the business maintain independent records of the business's bank account, you might assume that the respective balances will always agree. In fact, the two balances are seldom the same at any given time. Therefore, it is necessary to make the balance in the business's records agree with the balance as per the bank — a process called reconciling the bank account. The lack of agreement between the balances has two causes:

* *timing differences*, when one of the parties records the transaction in a different period from the period used by the other party
* *errors* by either party in recording transactions.

Helpful hint: All cheques drawn by the entity, even unpresented cheques, are recorded in the cash payments journal. This is because an unpresented cheque is one that has been drawn by the business as payment for an amount owing, but the party receiving the cheque did not present the cheque to the bank for payment before the bank statement was printed.

Timing differences occur frequently. For example, several days may elapse between the time a business pays by cheque and the date the cheque is honoured by the bank. A cheque that has been drawn by the payer but not yet paid by the bank is called an **unpresented cheque** (also called an *outstanding cheque*). Similarly, when a business uses the bank's night safe to make its deposits, there will be a difference of one day between the time the receipts are recorded by the business and the time they are recorded by the bank. Business deposits that do not yet appear in the bank records are called **outstanding deposits** (sometimes referred to as a *deposit in transit*). A time lag also occurs whenever the bank makes a direct entry, such as bank charges, to the business's bank account.

The incidence of errors depends on the effectiveness of the internal controls maintained by the business and the bank. Bank errors are infrequent. However, either party could inadvertently record a $450 cheque as $45 or $540. In addition, the bank might mistakenly deposit money to the wrong account.

Reconciliation procedure

To obtain maximum benefit from a bank reconciliation, the reconciliation should be prepared by an employee who has no other responsibilities pertaining to the bank account. When the internal control principle of independent internal verification is not followed in preparing the reconciliation, cash embezzlements may escape unnoticed.

Most businesses prepare a bank reconciliation at least monthly. Bank reconciliations are ongoing. The following steps should reveal all the reconciling items that cause the difference between the bank statement balance and the cash records of the business.

Helpful hint: Outstanding deposits and unpresented cheques are reconciling items that result from timing differences.

Step 1

Compare the amounts listed on the bank statement (bank records) to the *previous* month's bank reconciliation statement and to the *current* month's cash receipts and cash payments journals (business records).

First, review the previous month's bank reconciliation statement and place a tick beside any amounts appearing on the current month's bank statement that were recorded as outstanding on the bank reconciliation statement from last month (i.e. unpresented cheques and/or outstanding deposits). Place a tick beside the figures on *both* the bank statement and the previous bank reconciliation statement. After this process is complete, any amounts that remain outstanding (e.g. unpresented cheques) must be carried forward, i.e. entered on the *current* bank reconciliation statement. These should then be investigated to determine the reason they remain outstanding.

Second, match the individual deposits recorded on the bank statement with the deposits recorded in the cash receipts journal and place a tick near each of the items appearing in both places. Match the individual presented cheques recorded on the bank statement with the cheques issued by the business and recorded in the cash payments journal. Place a tick near each of the items appearing in both places, and check that *both* the cheque numbers and the cheque amounts correspond exactly. Similarly, match the individual electronic fund transfer items (e.g. Autopay, BPay) recorded on the bank statement and recorded in the cash payments journal.

As the first and second parts of this step are completed, discrepancies may be uncovered. Such discrepancies may be due to errors made in the recording of cheques or deposits either by the business or by the bank. For example, if a presented cheque correctly written by the entity for $195 is mistakenly recorded in the cash payments journal as $159 (transposition error), the resulting error of $36 should be corrected. Errors made by the business should be corrected in the cash journals. In the example above, the understated cheque should be corrected in the cash payments journal by recording an adjustment entry to increase cash payments by $36. Errors made by the bank are reconciling items. The business should inform the bank of the error so that it can be corrected by the bank, and the error should be listed in the business's current bank reconciliation statement.

Step 2

Identify items on the bank statement that remain unticked. These are items initiated by the bank and include dishonoured cheques and cash transactions made directly through the bank but not yet recorded in the business's records. These should be entered in the appropriate cash journals and ticked in these records and on the bank statement.

The remaining unticked items in the cash receipts journal are outstanding deposits. The remaining items in the cash payments journal are unpresented cheques. Both are reconciling items. Any unticked outstanding deposits or unpresented cheques from the previous bank reconciliation are carried forward as reconciling items.

Step 3

The cash journals should then be totalled and posted to the cash at bank ledger account. The balance of the account should then be determined.

Step 4

The balance as per cash at bank (as determined in step 3) is often different from the bank statement balance. The bank reconciliation statement accounts for the differences. The bank reconciliation statement can be completed, starting with the balance as per bank statement. Reconciliation items that increase the bank account, such as outstanding deposits, should be added to the balance as per bank statement. Reconciliation items that decrease the bank account, such as unpresented cheques drawn by the business, should be subtracted from the balance as per bank statement. If the balance as per bank statement is in debit, i.e. an overdraft, subtract the outstanding deposits and add unpresented cheques. The balance as per bank statement, adjusted for reconciliation items, should then equal the balance as per the cash at bank ledger account.

Bank reconciliation illustrated

The bank statement for Justco Pty Ltd is illustrated in figure 7.4. The bank statement shows a balance of $399.10 at 31 August 2019. Note that it is a credit balance from the perspective of the bank because the bank has a liability to Justco Pty Ltd. The previous month's bank reconciliation is illustrated in figure 7.5. Extracts from the cash receipts journal and cash payments journal for Justco Pty Ltd are illustrated in figures 7.6 and 7.7, respectively.

The first step in the bank reconciliation includes comparing the deposits on the bank statement with those shown as outstanding in the previous bank reconciliation and those subsequently listed in the entity's cash receipts journal. For example, the outstanding deposit of $119.50 shown on the July bank reconciliation (figure 7.5) corresponds to the deposit shown on the bank statement on 2 August. Both can now be ticked or otherwise marked. Note that cash receipts for the same day are entered separately in the cash receipts journal but have been combined to form one deposit as shown in the amount banked column. For example, cash receipts on 2 August of $110.60 and $195.18 are combined in the card entry deposit of 2 August of $305.78 shown on the bank statement. After completing the process of matching bank deposits with the entity's records of cash receipts, an outstanding deposit of $219.40 is identified. This was entered in the cash receipts journal on 31 August, but will not be recorded in the bank's records or appear on the bank statement until September. This outstanding deposit, marked o/s, will need to be added to the bank statement balance in the bank reconciliation statement (figure 7.9).

The first step also involves comparing presented cheques appearing on the bank statement with the cash payments journal and the unpresented cheques appearing on the previous bank reconciliation. The unpresented cheque from the July bank reconciliation (figure 7.5) was presented on 2 August and it can now be ticked on both the bank statement and the previous bank reconciliation. This process reveals timing differences — four cheques remain unpresented at the end of August. The four cheques, numbered 1922, 1923, 1924 and 1925, are marked o/s and therefore will be included in the bank reconciliation statement. Note also that cheque number 1916 was recorded in the cash payments journal as a payment of $31.80 but an amount of $32.80 was recorded on the bank statement. Assume for the purpose of this illustration that examination of the invoice reveals that the bank statement is correct and that the error was in the way that the cheque was recorded in the cash payments journal. In other words, this error originated from the company's record and therefore an adjusting entry must be made in the cash payments journal to increase cash payments by $1.00 for cheque 1916 dated 31 August, as shown in figure 7.7.

FIGURE 7.4   Bank statement

STATEMENT OF ACCOUNT WITH

Regional Bank of Australia
Melbourne, Vic.

NAME OF ACCOUNT	ACCOUNT NO.
Justco PTY LTD	801055
	PAGE
	30

DATE	PARTICULARS	DEBIT	CREDIT	BALANCE
2019				
August 1	Balance			312.40 Cr
2	1910	5.15 ✓		307.25 Cr
	Card entry St Kilda branch		119.50 ✓	426.75 Cr
	1899	56.00 ✓		370.75 Cr
	Card entry St Kilda branch		305.78 ✓	676.53 Cr
4	1911	298.30 ✓		378.23 Cr
5	1912	25.50 ✓		352.73 Cr
	Standing Order Autopay	275.00 ✓		77.73 Cr
	1914	25.00 ✓		52.73 Cr
	Direct transfer Hayden Ltd		60.00 ✓	112.73 Cr
8	1913	49.18 ✓		63.55 Cr
	Direct transfer F. Perry & Son		310.50 ✓	374.05 Cr
12	1915	112.15 ✓		261.90 Cr
	Standing Order Autopay	275.00 ✓		13.10 Dr
	Card entry Camberwell branch		391.95 ✓	378.85 Cr
14	1917	15.00 ✓		363.85 Cr
	1918	30.75 ✓		333.10 Cr
15	Direct entry D. Logovic		111.15 ✓	444.25 Cr
16	1916	32.80 ✓		411.45 Cr
19	1919	94.10 ✓		317.35 Cr
	Standing Order Autopay	275.00 ✓		42.35 Cr
	Card entry Camberwell branch		305.00 ✓	347.35 Cr
25	Card entry Camberwell branch		265.68 ✓	613.03 Cr
26	Standing Order Autopay	275.00		338.03 Cr
	1920	16.90 ✓		321.13 Cr
	Ret	25.00 ✓		296.13 Cr
29	1921	38.32 ✓		257.81 Cr
	Account fees	11.00 ✓		246.81 Cr
	External BPay-ATO	42.60 ✓		204.21 Cr
	Card entry St Kilda branch		204.39 ✓	408.60 Cr
	Transaction fees	9.50 ✓		399.10 Cr

DATE OF ISSUE	TOTAL DEBITS	TOTAL CREDITS	BALANCE
31 August 2019	1987.25	2073.95	399.10 Cr

(*Note:* Ticks have been added as part of the reconciliation procedure in the illustrative example next in this section.)

A number of abbreviations have been used. Some of the typical ones which may be used are set out below:

BC	Proceeds bill for collection	INT	Interest on account
Cr	Account in credit	MSC	Miscellaneous charge
CBK	Cheque book	PA	Payment under authority
CHQ	Deposit inc. cheque(s)	PCR	Periodic credit received
COM	Commission	PN	Promissory note
CSH	Cash deposit	REP	Unpaid cheque represented
CTI	Interest on Commonwealth Bonds	RET	Cheque returned unpaid debited
DEP	Deposit		to account (dishonoured cheque)
DIV	Dividend	REV	Reversal of entry
Dr	Account in debit	TRA	Transactions fee
FEE	Charge for keeping account	TFR	Transfer from other bank/branch

Note: A modern trend is the use of full descriptions of entries in the statement rather than abbreviations. These details differ from one financial institution to another.

FIGURE 7.5 Bank reconciliation for previous month

JUSTCO PTY LTD
Bank reconciliation
as at 31 July 2019 (previous month)

Balance as per bank statement	Cr	$312.40
Add: Outstanding deposit		119.50 ✓
		431.90
Less: Unpresented cheque no. 1899		56.00 ✓
Balance as per cash at bank account	**Dr**	**$375.90**

Note: Ticks are added as part of the reconciliation process.

The second step involves identifying items on the bank statement that have been initiated by the bank and entering them in the cash journals. This process reveals three items initiated by the bank: dishonoured cheque (RET) and account fees and transaction fees that have been charged by the bank. The treatment of these items is explained below.

The dishonoured cheque (RET) related to a cheque of $25 received from R. Richards (a customer on account) which was deposited in Justco's bank account on 19 August (as part of the card entry deposit of $305). This original transaction was recorded in the company's cash receipts journal as a debit to cash at bank and a credit to accounts receivable. When this cheque subsequently bounced, the company needed to 'reverse' the original transaction by reducing the cash at bank column by $25 (a negative cash receipt) and increasing the accounts receivable column by $25. This entry is shown on 27 August in figure 7.6.

FIGURE 7.6 Extract from cash receipts journal of Justco Pty Ltd

Cash receipts journal

Date	Account	Post ref.	Discount allowed Dr	Cash at bank Dr	Accounts receivable Cr	Sales Cr	Other accounts Cr	Amount banked
2019								
Aug. 2	M. Mason	✓		✓ $ 110.60	$ 110.60			
	Sales	✓		✓ 195.18		$195.18		$305.78
5	Hayden Ltd	✓		✓ 60.00	60.00			60.00
8	F. Perry & Son	✓		✓ 310.50	310.50			310.50
12	Sales			✓ 136.20		136.20		
	H. Lawson	✓		✓ 85.00	85.00			
	W. Wentworth	✓		✓ 170.75	170.75			391.95
15	Sales			✓ 111.15		111.15		111.15
19	R. Richards	✓		✓ 25.00	25.00			
	Morley Co-op	✓		✓ 280.00	280.00			305.00
25	Sales			✓ 77.18		77.18		
	M. Mason	✓		✓ 140.00	140.00			
	Hayden Ltd	✓		✓ 48.50	48.50			265.68
27	R. Richards							
	(dish. ch.)	✓		✓ (25.00)	(25.00)			
29	Sales			✓ 204.39		204.39		204.39
31	Sales			o/s 219.40		219.40		219.40
				$2 148.85	$1 205.35	$943.50		
				(100)	(110)	(400)		

Note: Ticks and o/s (for outstanding deposit) in the cash at bank column are added as part of the reconciliation process.

The two bank charges were deducted from the bank statement balance. However, the company's book balance has not recorded these deductions. Therefore, these two items should be entered in the cash payments journal. The entries are illustrated in figure 7.7.

FIGURE 7.7 Extract from cash payments journal of Justco Pty Ltd

Cash payments journal

Date	Chq. no.	Account debited	Post ref.	Accounts payable Dr	Other accounts Dr	Cash at bank Cr	
2019							
Aug. 1	1910	Office supplies	116		5.15	✓	5.15
	1911	Wm. Prince & Co. Ltd	✓	298.30		✓	298.30
4	1912	Advertising expense	560		25.50	✓	25.50
5	1913	R. Bill & Co.	✓	49.18		✓	49.18
		Standing order autopay—wages & salaries	550		275.00	✓	275.00
	1914	Petty cash	105		25.00	✓	25.00
8	1915	L. Edwards & Son	✓	112.15		✓	112.15
12	1916	Truck maintenance	545		31.80		31.80
		Standing order autopay—wages & salaries	550		275.00	✓	275.00
14	1917	Travel expenses	532		15.00	✓	15.00
16	1918	Commission expense	520		30.75	✓	30.75
18	1919	Wm. Prince & Co. Ltd	✓	94.10		✓	94.10
19		Standing order autopay—wages & salaries	550		275.00		275.00
24	1920	Light & power	540		16.90	✓	16.90
26		Standing order autopay—wages & salaries	550		275.00	✓	275.00
27	1921	J. Norton	✓	38.32		✓	38.32
		External BPay—ATO	570		42.60	✓	42.60
29	1922	Donation—Red Shield	575		10.00	o/s	10.00
	1923	L. Edwards & Son	✓	77.40		o/s	77.40
31	1924	Freight inwards	510			o/s	22.05
	1925	P. Perkins	✓	82.56	22.05	o/s	82.56
				752.01	1 324.75		2 076.76
	B/S	Account fees	569		11.00	✓	11.00
	B/S	Transaction fees	569		9.50	✓	9.50
	B/S	Truck maintenance (error adjustment cheque no. 1916)	545		1.00		1.00
				$752.01	$1 346.25	✓	$2 098.26
				(210)	(X)		(100)

The third step is to total the cash payments journal and the cash receipts journal and post the entries to the ledger accounts. This enables the cash at bank account to be balanced. After all entries have been posted, the balance of Justco Pty Ltd's cash at bank account shows a debit balance of $426.49, as shown in figure 7.8.

FIGURE 7.8 Cash account

Cash

2019				2019			
Aug. 1		Opening balance	375.90	Aug. 31		Cash payments	2 098.26
31		Cash receipts	2 148.85	31		Closing balance	426.49
			2 524.75				2 524.75
Sept. 1		Opening balance	426.49				

The last step is to prepare the bank reconciliation statement. This is illustrated in figure 7.9.

FIGURE 7.9	Bank reconciliation statement

JUSTCO PTY LTD
Bank reconciliation statement
as at 31 August 2019

Balance as per bank statement		$399.10 Cr
Add: Outstanding deposit		219.40
		618.50
Less: Unpresented cheques:		
1922	$10.00	
1923	77.40	
1924	22.05	
1925	82.56	192.01
Balance as per cash at bank account		**$426.49 Dr**

Note that the bank statement was the source of evidence for recording, in the cash payments journal, various bank charges, $20.50, and the error in cheque no. 1916, $1.00.

Helpful hint: Why is an outstanding deposit added to the bank statement balance in the bank reconciliation statement?

Answer: The deposit was first recorded in the cash at bank ledger account when the business placed the deposit with the bank. The bank has not yet added this deposit onto the statement because of timing differences but it will eventually. Therefore, the outstanding deposit needs to be added to the bank statement balance.

The reconciling items are the outstanding deposit and unpresented cheques, both caused by timing differences. Other potential reconciling items not illustrated in this example are bank errors.

What entries does the bank make? If any bank errors are discovered in preparing the reconciliation, the bank should be notified so it can make the necessary corrections on its records. The bank does not make any entries for outstanding deposits or unpresented cheques. Only when these items reach the bank will the bank record them.

LEARNING REFLECTION AND CONSOLIDATION

Review it

1. Why is it necessary to reconcile a bank account?
2. What steps are involved in the reconciliation procedure?
3. What information is included in a bank reconciliation statement?

Do it

Kirsty Harris owns Harris Linen Hire. Kirsty asks you to explain how the following differences between the bank statement and the cash at bank ledger account should be treated: (1) an entry on the bank statement for a dishonoured cheque, (2) unpresented cheques, and (3) an outstanding deposit.

Reasoning

Kirsty needs to understand that one cause of reconciling items is timing differences. The first item generates a difference between the bank records and the ledger because Harris Linen Hire has not yet recorded the dishonoured cheque. Items (2) and (3) are reconciling items because the bank has not recorded the transactions.

7.5 Managing and monitoring cash

LEARNING OBJECTIVE 7.5 Discuss the basic principles of cash management.

Many businesses struggle, not because they can't generate sales, but because they can't manage their cash. For example, Doris Tam starts up her own clothing manufacturing business. Soon she has more orders from large stores than she can fill. Yet she finds herself on the brink of financial disaster, having mortgaged her house and owing a lot of money to the taxation authority. Her business can generate sales, but it isn't collecting cash fast enough to support its operations. The bottom line is that a business must have cash.

To understand cash management, consider the operating cycle of Doris's clothing manufacturing business. To begin with, it must purchase cloth. Let's assume that it purchases the cloth on credit provided by the supplier, so the business owes its supplier money. Next, employees convert the cloth to clothing. Now the business also owes its employees money. Next, it sells the clothing to retailers on credit. Doris's business has no money to pay suppliers or employees until its customers pay it. In a manufacturing operation there may be a significant lag between the original purchase of raw materials and the ultimate receipt of cash from customers. Managing the often precarious balance created by the ebb and flow of cash during the operating cycle is one of an entity's greatest challenges. The objective is to ensure that a business has sufficient cash to meet payments as they come due, yet minimise the amount of surplus cash on hand because the money could be invested more profitably in operations.

A merchandising entity's operating cycle is generally shorter than that of a manufacturing entity's, depending on how long the inventory is held for sale. The cash to cash operating cycle of a retail operation is shown graphically in figure 7.10.

FIGURE 7.10 Operating cycle of a retail business

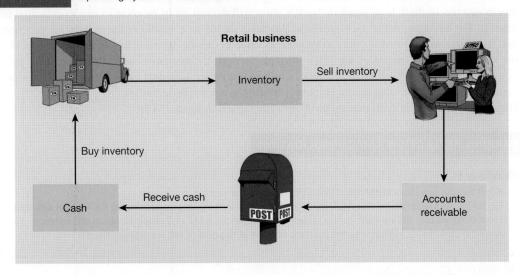

Basic principles of cash management

Management of cash is typically the responsibility of an entity's finance director or finance manager. A business can improve its chances of having adequate cash by following five basic principles of cash management.

1. *Increase the speed of collection of receivables.* Money owed to Doris by her customers is money she can't use. The sooner customers pay her, the sooner she can use those funds. Thus, rather than have an average collection period of 60 days, she may want an average collection period of 40 days. However, any attempt to force her customers to pay earlier must be carefully weighed against the possibility that she may anger or alienate customers. Perhaps her competitors are willing to provide a 30-day grace period. As noted in chapter 4, one way to encourage customers to pay more quickly is to offer cash discounts for early payment under such terms as 2/7, n/30.

2. *Keep inventory levels low.* Maintaining a large inventory of cloth and finished clothing is costly. It requires that large amounts of cash be tied up, as well as warehouse space. Increasingly, businesses are using techniques to reduce inventory on hand, thus conserving their cash. Of course, if Doris has inadequate inventory, she will lose sales. The proper level of inventory is an important decision.

3. *Don't pay earlier than necessary.* By keeping track of when her payments are due, Doris can avoid paying accounts too early. Let's say her supplier allows 30 days for payment. If she pays in 10 days, she has lost the use of cash for 20 days. Therefore, she should use the full payment period but should not 'stretch' payment past the point that could damage her credit rating (and future borrowing ability). Doris should conserve cash by taking cash discounts offered by suppliers, when the benefit of the discount exceeds the cost of not having the use of the cash (such as additional interest paid on an overdraft).

4. *Plan the timing of major expenditures.* To maintain operations or to grow, all business entities must make major expenditures, which normally require some form of outside financing. In order to increase the likelihood of obtaining outside financing, the timing of major expenditures should be carefully considered in light of the entity's operating cycle and cash flows. Expenditure that is made at a time when the entity normally has excess cash places less stress on the entity's cash resources.

5. *Invest idle cash.* Cash on hand earns little, if anything at all. An important part of the finance manager's job is to ensure that any excess cash is invested, even if it is only overnight. Many businesses, such as Doris's clothing business, are seasonal. When she has excess cash, she should invest it. To avoid a cash crisis, it is very important that these investments be highly liquid and risk-free. A *liquid investment* is one with a market in which someone is always willing to buy or sell the investment. A *risk-free investment* means there is no concern that the party will default on its promise to pay its principal and interest. For example, using excess cash to purchase shares in a small company because you heard that the shares were probably going to increase in value in the short term is totally inappropriate. First, the shares of small companies are often illiquid. Second, if the shares suddenly decrease in value, you might be forced to sell them at a loss in order to pay your accounts as they come due. The most common form of liquid investment is interest-bearing government securities.

These five principles of cash management are summarised in figure 7.11.

LEARNING REFLECTION AND CONSOLIDATION

Review it

1. What are the five main elements of sound cash management?
2. Go to the ASX website (www.asx.com.au) and search for the latest annual report for **Webjet Limited**. How does Webjet define cash in the statement of financial position? (*Hint:* Refer to the notes to the financial statements.) What was the balance of cash at the end of the reporting period?

FIGURE 7.11 Five principles of sound cash management

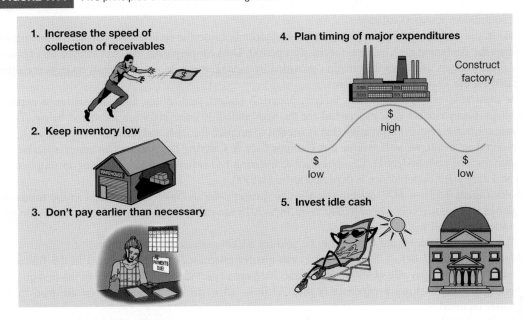

Cash budget

Cash is at the heart of a business, which needs to ensure that it has adequate cash to pay its suppliers, employees and creditors on time to ensure the business can operate efficiently. But how does it decide how much cash is needed and when payments are required? Planning the entity's cash needs is important to enable possible cash shortfalls to be covered and to make use of idle funds. Let's see how a small café business uses cash budgets to help it plan cash flow activities.

A cash budget shows anticipated cash receipts and payments. The cash budget generally contains three sections (cash receipts, cash payments, and financing), and the beginning and ending cash balances, as shown in figure 7.12.

FIGURE 7.12	Basic form of a cash budget

ANY ENTITY Cash budget	
Beginning cash balance	$XXX
Add: Cash receipts (itemised)	XXX
Total available cash	XXX
Less: Cash payments (itemised)	XXX
Excess (deficiency) of available cash over cash payments	XXX
Financing	XXX
Ending cash balance	**$XXX**

The *cash receipts section* includes expected receipts from the entity's main source(s) of revenue such as cash sales and collections from customers on credit sales. This section also shows anticipated receipts of interest and dividends, and proceeds from planned sales of investments, plant and equipment, and the issue of shares.

The *cash payments section* shows expected payments for materials and selling and administrative expenses. This section also includes projected payments for income tax, dividends, investments, and plant and equipment.

The *financing section* shows expected borrowings and the repayment of the borrowed funds plus interest. This section is needed when there is a cash deficiency or when the cash balance is below management's minimum required balance.

Data in the cash budget must be prepared in sequence because the ending cash balance of one period becomes the beginning cash balance for the next period. Data for preparing the cash budget are obtained from other budgets and from information provided by management. In practice, cash budgets are often prepared for the year on a monthly basis.

For illustrative purposes, the sales budget, materials budget, and selling and administrative expense budget for Campus Café & Catering Ltd for the year ended 30 June 2019 are presented below. These budgets contain essential information that is needed to prepare the cash budget.

To minimise detail, we will assume that Campus Café & Catering Ltd prepares an annual cash budget by quarters. The cash budget for Campus Café & Catering Ltd is based on the following assumptions.
1. The 1 July 2018 cash balance is expected to be $10 000.
2. Sales (figure 7.13) — 60% are collected in the quarter sold and 40% are collected in the following quarter. Accounts receivable of $7000 at 30 June 2018 are expected to be collected in full in the first quarter of 2018–19.
3. Marketable investments are expected to be sold for $2000 cash in the first quarter.
4. Materials (figure 7.14) — 50% is paid in the quarter purchased and 50% is paid in the following quarter. Accounts payable of $5000 at 30 June 2018 are expected to be paid in full in the first quarter.
5. Selling and administrative expenses (figure 7.15) — all items except depreciation are paid in the quarter incurred.
6. Management plans to purchase a new coffee machine in the first quarter for $8000 cash.
7. Management plans to purchase a dishwasher in the third quarter for $15 000 cash.
8. Loans are repaid in the first subsequent quarter in which there is sufficient cash; interest of $100 is payable with repayments.
9. It is Campus Café & Catering Ltd's policy to maintain a minimum cash level of $10 000.

FIGURE 7.13 Sales budget

CAMPUS CAFÉ & CATERING LTD
Sales budget
for the year ended 30 June 2019

	Quarter				
	1	2	3	4	Year
Expected unit sales	6 000	6 500	7 000	7 500	27 000
Unit selling price ($)	5	5	5	5	5
Total sales ($)	30 000	32 500	35 000	37 500	135 000

FIGURE 7.14 Materials budget

Materials budget
for the year ended 30 June 2019

	Quarter				
	1	2	3	4	Year
Units to be sold (figure 7.13)	6 000	6 500	7 000	7 500	
Materials (kg) per unit	0.1	0.1	0.1	0.1	
Total materials (kg) required	600	650	700	750	
Cost per kilogram ($)	20	20	20	20	
Total cost of materials purchases ($)	12 000	13 000	14 000	15 000	54 000

FIGURE 7.15 Selling and administrative expense budget

CAMPUS CAFÉ & CATERING LTD
Selling and administrative expense budget
for the year ended 30 June 2019

	Quarter ($)				($)
	1	2	3	4	Year
Advertising	1 000	1 000	1 000	1 000	4 000
Salaries	7 500	7 500	7 500	7 500	30 000
Depreciation	500	500	500	500	2 000
Rent	3 000	3 000	3 000	3 000	12 000
Total selling and administrative expenses	12 000	12 000	12 000	12 000	48 000

Schedules for collections from customers (assumption no. 2 given previously) and cash payments for materials (assumption no. 4 given previously) are useful in preparing the cash budget. The schedules are shown in figures 7.16 and 7.17.

FIGURE 7.16 Collection from customers

Schedule of expected collections from customers

	Quarter ($)			
	1	2	3	4
Accounts receivable, 30/6/18	7 000			
Sales, first quarter ($30 000)*	18 000*	12 000**		
Sales, second quarter ($32 500)		19 500*	13 000**	
Sales, third quarter ($35 000)			21 000*	14 000**
Sales, fourth quarter ($37 500)				22 500*
Total collections	25 000	31 500	34 000	36 000

*See assumption 2 above, $30 000 × 60% = $18 000 or 60% of current quarter's sales
**40% of previous quarter's sales

FIGURE 7.17 Payments for materials

Schedule of expected payments for materials

	Quarter ($)			
	1	2	3	4
Accounts payable, 30/6/18	5 000			
Purchases, first quarter ($12 000)	6 000*	6 000		
Purchases, second quarter ($13 000)		6 500	6 500	
Purchases, third quarter ($14 000)			7 000	7 000
Purchases, fourth quarter ($15 000)				7 500
Total payments	11 000	12 500	13 500	14 500

*See assumption 4 above, $12 000 ↔ 50% = $6000

The cash budget for Campus Café & Catering Ltd is shown in figure 7.18. The budget indicates that $3500 and $2100 of financing will be needed in the first and the third quarter to maintain a minimum cash balance of $10 000. Since there is an excess of available cash over payments of $17 500 and $20 500 at the end of the second and fourth quarters, the borrowings are repaid in these quarters plus $100 interest.

FIGURE 7.18 Cash budget

CAMPUS CAFÉ & CATERING LTD
Cash budget
for the year ended 30 June 2019

| | Assumption | Quarter ($) | | | |
		1	2	3	4
Beginning cash balance	1	10 000	10 000	13 900	10 000
Add: Receipts					
Collections from customers	2	25 000	31 500	34 000	36 500
Sale of investments	3	2 000	–	–	–
Total receipts		27 000	31 500	34 000	36 500
Total available cash		37 000	41 500	47 900	46 500
Less: Payments					
Materials	4	11 000	12 500	13 500	14 500
Selling and administrative expenses	5	11 500*	11 500	11 500	11 500
Purchase of coffee machine	6	8 000	–	–	–
Purchase of dishwasher	7	–	–	15 000	–
Total payments		30 500	24 000	40 000	26 000
Excess (deficiency) of available cash over payments		6 500	17 500	7 900	20 500
Financing					
Borrowings		3 500	–	2 100	–
Repayments — plus $100 interest	8	–	3 600	–	2 200
Ending cash balance		**10 000**	**13 900**	**10 000**	**18 300**

*$12 000 – $500 depreciation

A cash budget contributes to more effective cash management. For example, it can show when additional financing will be necessary well before the actual need arises, and arrangements can be made with the bank ahead of time or you may be able to delay the payment of your suppliers in the short term. Conversely, it can indicate when excess cash will be available for investments or other purposes.

DECISION-MAKING TOOLKIT

Decision/issue	Info needed for analysis	Tool or technique to use for decision	How to evaluate results to make decision
Will the entity need to borrow funds in the coming quarter?	Beginning cash balance, cash receipts, cash payments, and desired cash balance	Cash budget	The entity will need to borrow money if the cash budget indicates a projected cash deficiency of available cash over cash payments for the quarter.

We have used a small café business to illustrate how cash budgets are prepared. Obviously, for retail and service businesses, the process is less taxing. Nonetheless, it is important for these businesses to prepare a cash budget as it assists decision making by:
* detailing the timing of all estimated cash inflows and outflows
* identifying periods of expected cash shortfalls so corrective actions, such as borrowing, can be arranged
* identifying periods of expected cash surpluses so short-term investments, such as term deposits, can be considered.

7.6 Assessing cash adequacy

LEARNING OBJECTIVE 7.6 Assess the adequacy of cash.

In evaluating an entity's cash management practices we are interested in whether the amount of cash it has on hand is adequate. This can be evaluated using the ratio of cash to daily cash expenses.

Ratio of cash to daily cash expenses

Company managers, as well as outside investors, closely monitor a company's cash position. Announcement of a projected cash shortfall can send shock waves through the sharemarket. For example, in early December 2013, Qantas flagged deteriorating trading conditions and a potential A$300 million half-year loss in a media release that sent its share price tumbling on the Australian sharemarket. To improve its financial performance, Qantas flagged further cost-cutting plans including 1000 job cuts over the next 12 months, a review of capital expenditure, and a pay cut for the board and CEO in a bid to save $2 billion over three years. Qantas announced that it no longer expected to generate a positive net free cash flow in that financial year.

One measure of the adequacy of cash is the **ratio of cash to daily cash expenses**. In this ratio, 'cash' includes cash plus cash equivalents. It calculates the number of days of cash expenses the cash on hand can cover. Dividing the balance in cash by average daily cash expenses, as shown in figure 7.19, gives the number of days the entity can operate without an additional injection of cash. Average daily cash expenses can be calculated by dividing cash payments for the provision of services, interest and taxes by 365 days.

FIGURE 7.19 | Ratio of cash to daily cash expenses

$$\text{Cash to daily cash expenses ratio} = \frac{\text{Cash}}{\text{Average daily cash expense}}$$

Helpful hint: Cash equivalents are highly liquid investments that can be quickly converted to cash.

Users of external financial reports can obtain the data needed to calculate this ratio from the statement of cash flows (chapter 11 discusses the preparation and analysis of the statement of cash flows). The cash balance is also reported in the statement of financial position. (*Note:* The statement of financial position may also be called the *balance sheet* and the statement of cash flows may also be called the *cash flow statement.*)

Note that the ratio of cash to daily cash expenses is a short-term measure of the adequacy of cash because it ignores other cash outgoings, such as loan repayments, the timing of cash flows and access to financing facilities, such as an overdraft facility or borrowings. Longer term measures such as liquidity and solvency ratios are discussed in chapter 12.

The cash to daily expenses ratio provides management and external users such as shareholders some insight into the entity's ability to cover its daily expenditure. By comparing the cash on hand with the average daily expenses, users can determine whether the entity's cash level is adequate by the number of days covered. If the ratio indicates a low level of coverage this may need further investigation to avert potential liquidity issues. In contrast, a very high level of coverage may indicate excessive cash held. In this case, management can consider alternative investment opportunities to maximise the returns on any cash in surplus of its daily needs. The relevance of this information in assisting management to determine the appropriate level of cash to be held is summarised in the decision-making toolkit next.

Decision/issue	Info needed for analysis	Tool or technique to use for decision	How to evaluate results to make decision
Does the business have adequate cash to meet its daily needs?	Cash, average daily expenses	Cash to daily cash expenses ratio $= \dfrac{\text{Cash}}{\text{Average daily cash expenses}}$	A low level of cash coverage should be investigated. If this measure is very low, it may be necessary to source additional financing.

Referring back to our sample company in chapter 1, Artistry Furniture Limited, the ratio of cash to daily cash expenses for Artistry Furniture is shown in figure 7.20.

FIGURE 7.20 Cash to daily cash expenses ratio for Artistry Furniture

	2019 $'000	2018 $'000
Cash to daily cash expenses ratio	$\dfrac{\$24\,000}{\$327} = 73$ days	$\dfrac{\$19\,800}{\$301} = 66$ days
Average daily cash expenses (Payments to suppliers and employees + Income taxes paid)	$\dfrac{\$119\,350}{365} = \$327$	$\dfrac{\$109\,850}{365} = \$301$

The cash adequacy of Artistry Furniture in 2019 improved from 2018 due to an increase in cash on hand even though there was a slight increase in the daily cash expenses. The ratio of cash to daily cash expenses indicates that at the end of the 2019 reporting period its cash was sufficient to meet the needs of 73 days of normal operating activity, an improvement on 2018 when its cash balance would cover 66 days of operating activity without further cash injection.

LEARNING REFLECTION AND CONSOLIDATION

Review it

What is the formula for the cash to daily cash expenses ratio? What does it tell management about the entity's cash position?

USING THE DECISION-MAKING TOOLKIT

Presented below are financial data for the year ended 31 July 2019 for two companies that operate in New Zealand: Timaru Limited and Orbost Group.

Name of entity	Timaru Ltd $'000	Orbost Group $'000
Cash ($NZ)	1 172	165 000
Cash expenses for the year ($NZ)	169 445	268 000

Required
(a) Use the selected data to calculate the ratio of cash to daily cash expenses for each entity.
(b) Rank the entities in terms of their ability to meet cash expenses from cash available.
(c) Comment on why it is not enough to just look at the cash balance to analyse the adequacy of cash reserves.

Solution
(a)

($NZ)	Timaru $'000	Orbost $'000
Cash to daily cash expenses ratio	$\dfrac{\$1\,172}{\$464} = 3$ days	$\dfrac{\$165\,000}{\$734} = 225$ days
Average daily cash expenses	$\dfrac{\$169\,445}{365} = \$464$	$\dfrac{\$268\,000}{365} = \$734$

(b) Orbost's cash to daily cash expenses ratio shows an extremely high level of coverage with sufficient cash to cover 225 days of normal operating activity. In contrast, Timaru manages its business with a very low coverage with sufficient cash to cover only 3 days of normal operating activity.
(c) It is not enough to look at the cash balance in isolation to determine the adequacy of cash reserves; the average daily cash expenses need to also be considered. Although the cash to daily cash expenses ratio considers cash needs, it does not take into account the timing of cash flows and therefore should be used with other cash flow ratios to give a more comprehensive overview of the entities' cash position.

7.7 Recording and reporting receivables

LEARNING OBJECTIVE 7.7 Identify the different types of receivables.

The term **receivables** refers to amounts due from individuals and businesses. Receivables are claims that are expected to be collected in cash. Management of receivables is a very important activity for any entity that sells goods on credit. Receivables are important because they represent one of an entity's most liquid assets. For many businesses, receivables are also one of the largest assets. Figure 7.21 lists receivables as a percentage of total assets for three entities in 2019.

FIGURE 7.21	Receivables as a percentage of assets

Company	Receivables as a percentage of total assets
Giorgina's Pizza Limited	14%
Artistry Furniture Limited	7%
Original Furnishings Limited	7%

The relative significance of an entity's receivables as a percentage of its assets differs depending on its industry, the time of year, whether it extends long-term financing, and its credit policies. For external financial reporting, receivables are classified as current or non-current assets on the statement of financial position. Details of receivables and their maturity are disclosed in the notes to the financial statements.

Accounts receivable are amounts owed by customers on account. More specifically, accounts receivable refer to those accounts that arise from the sale of goods and services on credit in the course of business. Credit is often extended to business customers and these receivables generally are expected to be collected within 30 to 60 days. They are usually the most significant type of claim held by a business. (*Note:* Accounts receivable from customers are also referred to as *trade debtors*.)

Notes receivable represent claims for which formal instruments of credit are issued as evidence of the debt. Notes receivable are an asset of a company, bank or other organisation that holds a written promissory note from another party. For example, if a company lends a supplier $10 000 and the supplier signs a written promise to repay the amount, the company will enter the amount in its asset account notes receivable. The credit instrument normally requires the debtor to pay interest and extends for time periods of 60–90 days or longer. The supplier will also enter the amount in its current liability account notes payable.

Other receivables include non-trade receivables such as interest receivable, loans to officers, advances to employees, and GST receivable.

Accounting for receivables

Accounts receivable are classified as a current asset because they represent resources controlled by the entity from which future economic benefits are expected to flow to the entity within a normal operating cycle. Accounts receivable arise from the sale of goods or services on account. The future economic benefits result from the right of the entity to collect cash from customers who have been extended credit. Even though many business owners may prefer to receive cash at the time of sale, due to competitive market conditions they may have no choice but to extend credit to customers. Two issues associated with accounting for accounts receivable are:
- recognising accounts receivable
- valuing accounts receivable.

Helpful hint: Another way to describe the buying and selling of goods 'on account' is buying and selling goods 'on credit'.

A third issue, accelerating cash receipts from receivables, is discussed later in the chapter.

Initial recognition of accounts receivable is relatively straightforward. For a service entity, a receivable is recorded when service is provided on account. For a merchandiser, accounts receivable are recorded at the point of sale of goods on account. When a merchandiser sells goods on credit, both accounts receivable and sales are increased by debiting accounts receivable and crediting Sales.

Receivables also are reduced as a result of sales discounts and sales returns. The seller may offer terms that encourage early payment by providing a discount. For example, terms of 2/7, n/30 provide the buyer with a 2% discount if paid within 7 days. If the buyer chooses to pay within the discount period, the seller's accounts receivable is reduced. Also, the buyer might find some of the goods unacceptable and choose to return the unwanted goods. For example, if goods with a selling price of $100 are returned, the seller reduces accounts receivable by $100 upon receipt of the returned goods.

7.8 Valuing accounts receivable

LEARNING OBJECTIVE 7.8 Describe how to value receivables.

Accounts receivable are reported on the statement of financial position as an asset. At what amount? The amount owing by the customer? Not always. Let's see why not.

Although each customer must satisfy the credit requirements of the seller before the credit sale is approved, inevitably some accounts receivable become uncollectable, i.e. the customer defaults and never pays the account. For example, one of your customers may not be able to pay because it experienced a decline in sales due to a downturn in the economy. Similarly, individuals may be laid off from their jobs or be faced with unexpected hospital bills. Unrecoverable receivables are written off by debiting **bad debts expense** (also referred to as *bad and doubtful debts expense*). Such losses are considered a normal and necessary risk of doing business on a credit basis.

Two methods are used in accounting for uncollectable accounts: (1) the direct write-off method and (2) the allowance method.

Direct write-off method for uncollectable accounts

Under the **direct write-off method**, when a particular account is determined to be uncollectable, the loss is charged to bad debts expense. Assume, for example, that Warden Pty Ltd writes off M.E. Doran's $200 balance as uncollectable on 12 December. The entry is:

Dec. 12	Bad debts expense	200	
	Accounts receivable—M.E. Doran		200
	(To record write-off of M.E. Doran account)		

A	=	L	+	E
−200				−200

When this method is used, bad debts expense will be recognised when the uncollectable account is specifically identified and written off. Accounts receivable will be reported at its gross amount. Note that the credit to accounts receivable must be recorded in both the general ledger and the subsidiary ledger (refer to chapter 6).

Use of the direct write-off method can reduce the usefulness of both the statement of profit or loss and statement of financial position if bad debts are material. Consider the following example. In 2018, Quick Buck Computers Ltd decided it could increase its revenues by offering computers to university students without requiring any deposit, and with no credit-approval process. It distributed 10 000 computers with a selling price of $800 each. This increased Quick Buck's revenues and receivables by $8 million. The promotion was a huge success! The 2018 statement of financial position and statement of profit or loss looked wonderful. Unfortunately, during 2019, nearly 40% of the student customers defaulted on their loans. This made the 2019 statement of financial position and statement of profit or loss look terrible. Figure 7.22 shows the effect of these events on the financial statements when the direct write-off method is used.

FIGURE 7.22   Effects of direct write-off method

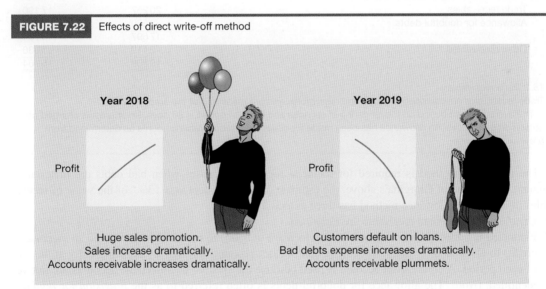

Year 2018

Profit

Huge sales promotion.
Sales increase dramatically.
Accounts receivable increases dramatically.

Year 2019

Profit

Customers default on loans.
Bad debts expense increases dramatically.
Accounts receivable plummets.

Under the direct write-off method, bad debts expense is often recorded in the period following that in which the revenue was recorded. It is not until the account receivable has been outstanding for a while that it becomes apparent that it is uncollectable. The direct write-off method makes no attempt to show accounts receivable in the statement of financial position at the amount actually expected to be received. Consequently, unless bad debts losses are insignificant, the direct write-off method is not acceptable for financial reporting purposes.

Allowance method for uncollectable accounts

The **allowance method** of accounting for bad debts is used in order to give financial statement users a more accurate picture as to the amount of accounts receivable expected to be collectable at the end of the reporting period. At the end of the accounting period, before the accounting records are closed and the financial reports prepared, managers need to estimate the amount of receivables expected to be uncollectable, i.e. doubtful debts. An adjusting entry is prepared with a debit to the bad debts expense account and a credit to an account called allowance for doubtful debts. (For external reporting purposes, this allowance is sometimes called an 'allowance for impairment of receivables'.) IAS 37/ AASB 137 *Provisions, Contingent Liabilities and Contingent Assets* requires that the 'provision' or 'allowance' be reviewed at the end of each reporting period and adjusted to reflect the current best estimate. An entity is required to assess at the end of each reporting period whether there is any evidence of impairment to (or deterioration in) the value of the accounts receivable on its statement of financial position.

To illustrate these concepts, let's see how Giorgina's reported accounts receivable in its 2019 financial statements. An extract from the notes to the financial statements is shown in figure 7.23, which indicates that at the end of the reporting period on 30 June 2019, the management of Giorgina's estimated an impairment of $2 560 000 to its trade receivables of $20 257 000.

FIGURE 7.23 Note on accounts receivable from the notes to the financial statements of Giorgina's for 2019

GIORGINA'S PIZZA LTD
Notes to the financial statements (extract)

	2019 $'000	2018 $'000
15. TRADE AND OTHER RECEIVABLES		
Trade receivables	20 257	17 190
Allowance for doubtful debts	(2 560)	(2 456)
	17 697	14 734
Other receivables	2 112	1 030
	19 809	15 764

15.1 Trade receivables
Trade receivables are classified as loans and receivables and are measured at the amortised cost.
   The average credit period on the rendering of services and sales of goods is 30 days. No interest is charged on outstanding balances. An allowance has been made for estimated irrecoverable amounts as determined from previous experience.

The allowance method is required for financial reporting purposes when bad debts are material in amount. In the case of Giorgina's above, the estimate of doubtful debt was 13%* of the value of receivables in 2019. The allowance method has three essential features.
1. Uncollectable accounts receivable are *estimated*.
2. Estimated uncollectables are recorded as an increase (a debit) to bad debts expense and an increase (a credit) to allowance for doubtful debts (a contra asset account) through an adjusting entry at the end of each period. A contra asset account is used because the specific uncollectable accounts are not yet identified. (*Note:* The allowance for doubtful debts is often referred to as the *provision for doubtful debts.*)
3. Actual uncollectables are debited to allowance for doubtful debts and credited to accounts receivable at the time the specific account is written off as uncollectable.

---

*Giorgina's policy of allowance for doubtful debts is based on trade receivables 60 days and over. In 2019, the amount written off as uncollectable was $318 000, representing 1.6% of the value of trade receivables.

Recording estimated uncollectables

To illustrate the allowance method, assume that Hampson Furniture Ltd has credit sales of $1 200 000 in 2019, of which $200 000 remains uncollected at 31 December. The credit manager estimates that $12 000 of these sales will prove uncollectable. The adjusting entry to record the estimated uncollectables is:

Dec. 31	Bad debts expense	12 000	
	Allowance for doubtful debts		12 000
	(To record estimate of uncollectable accounts)		

A	=	L	+	E
−12 000				−12 000

Bad debts expense is reported in the statement of profit or loss as an operating expense (usually as a finance expense). Thus, the estimated reduction in the recoverable amount of accounts receivable is recognised as an expense when it can be reliably measured.

The allowance for doubtful debts shows the estimated amount of claims on customers that are expected to become uncollectable in the future. A contra account is used instead of a direct credit to accounts receivable because we do not know which customers will not pay. The credit balance in the allowance account will absorb the specific write-offs when they occur. It is deducted from accounts receivable in the current asset section of the statement of financial position as shown in figure 7.24.

FIGURE 7.24 Presentation of allowance for doubtful debts

HAMPSON FURNITURE LTD
Statement of financial position (partial)

CURRENT ASSETS		
Cash		$ 14 800
Accounts receivable	$200 000	
Less: Allowance for doubtful debts	(12 000)	188 000
Inventory		310 000
Prepaid expense		25 000
Total current assets		**$537 800**

The amount of $188 000 in figure 7.24 represents the expected recoverable amount of the accounts receivable at the statement date. Allowance for doubtful debts is not closed at the end of the financial year, because it is a permanent account. This contra account records the extent to which the gross amount of accounts receivable has been written down. Bad debts expense is closed to profit or loss summary at the end of the financial year.

Recording the write-off of an uncollectable account

Entities use various methods of collecting past-due accounts, such as letters, calls and legal action. When all means of collecting a past-due account have been exhausted and collection appears impossible, the account should be written off. To prevent premature or unauthorised write-offs, each write-off should be formally approved in writing by authorised management personnel. To maintain good internal control, authorisation to write off accounts should not be given to someone who also has daily responsibilities related to cash or receivables because that person might keep the money paid by the customer and write off the account receivable.

To illustrate a receivables write-off, assume that the credit manager of Hampson Furniture Ltd authorises a write-off of the $500 balance owed by R.A. Ware on 1 March 2020. The entry to record the write-off is as follows.

Mar. 1	Allowance for doubtful debts	500	
	Accounts receivable—R.A. Ware		500
	(Write-off of R.A. Ware account)		

A = L + E
+500
−500

Bad debts expense is not increased when the write-off occurs. Under the allowance method, every bad debt write-off is debited to the allowance account and not to bad debts expense. A debit to bad debts expense would be incorrect because the expense was already recognised when the adjusting entry was made for estimated bad debts. Instead, the entry to record the write-off of an uncollectable account reduces both accounts receivable and the allowance for doubtful debts. After posting, the general ledger accounts will appear as in figure 7.25.

Helpful hint: The credit to accounts receivable must be posted to both the general ledger account and the subsidiary ledger account.

FIGURE 7.25 General ledger balances after write-off

Accounts receivable						Allowance for doubtful debts					
2020			2020			2020			2020		
Jan. 1	Bal.	200 000	Mar. 1		500	Mar. 1		500	Jan. 1	Bal.	12 000
					199 500			11 500			
		200 000			200 000			12 000			12 000
Mar. 1	Bal.	199 500							Mar. 1	Bal.	11 500

A write-off affects only statement of financial position accounts. The net receivable amount in the statement of financial position, therefore, remains the same, as shown in figure 7.26.

FIGURE 7.26 Recoverable amount comparison

	Before write-off	After write-off
Accounts receivable	$200 000	$199 500
Allowance for doubtful debts	12 000	11 500
Net receivable amount	$188 000	$188 000

Recovery of an uncollectable account

Occasionally, a business collects from a customer after the account has been written off as uncollectable. Two entries are required to record the recovery of a bad debt: (1) the entry made in writing off the account is reversed to reinstate the customer's account; (2) the collection is journalised in the usual manner. To illustrate, assume that on 1 July 2020 R.A. Ware pays the $500 amount that had been written off on 1 March 2020. These are the entries:

(1)

July 1	Accounts receivable—R.A. Ware	500	
	Allowance for doubtful debts		500
	(To reverse write-off of R.A. Ware account)		

A = L + E
+500
−500

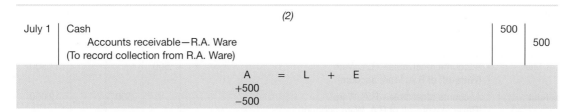

		(2)		
July 1	Cash		500	
	Accounts receivable—R.A. Ware			500
	(To record collection from R.A. Ware)			

A   =   L   +   E
+500
−500

The second journal entry will be recorded in the cash receipts journal if specialised journals are used.

Note that the recovery of a bad debt, like the write-off of a bad debt, affects only statement of financial position accounts. The net effect of the two entries above is an increase in cash and an increase in allowance for doubtful debts of $500. Accounts receivable and the allowance for doubtful debts both increase in entry (1) for two reasons: the entity made an error in judgement when it wrote off the account receivable; R.A. Ware did pay and therefore the accounts receivable account should show this collection for possible future credit purposes.

Estimating the allowance

For Hampson Furniture Ltd in figure 7.25, the amount of the expected uncollectables was given. However, in 'real life', businesses must estimate that amount if they use the allowance method. Two methods are used: (1) the percentage of net sales and (2) ageing the accounts receivable.

Under the percentage of net sales method, the increment to the allowance for doubtful debts for each period is determined as a percentage of sales. This method is used by some entities for monthly internal reporting. However, at year-end and for external reporting purposes, the allowance for doubtful debts should be estimated by **ageing the accounts receivable**. This involves preparing a schedule in which customer balances are classified by the length of time they have been unpaid.

After the accounts are arranged by age, the expected bad debt losses are determined by applying percentages based on past experience to the totals of each category. The longer a receivable is past due, the less likely it is to be collected. As a result, the estimated percentage of uncollectable debts increases as the number of days past due increases. An ageing schedule for Hampson Furniture Ltd as at 31 December 2019 is shown in figure 7.27. Note the increasing uncollectable percentages from 2% to 40%.

FIGURE 7.27 Accounts receivable ageing schedule as at 31 December 2019

			Number of days past due			
Customer	Total	Not yet due	1–30	31–60	61–90	Over 90
T.E. Adert	$ 60 000		$30 000	$24 000		$ 6 000
R.C. Bortz	20 000	$20 000				
B.A. Carl	45 000		22 500	22 500		
O.L. Diker	55 000				$33 000	22 000
T.O. Ebbet	43 000	43 000				
R.A. Ware	12 000	6 000	6 000			
	$235 000	$69 000	$58 500	$46 500	$33 000	$28 000
Estimated percentage uncollectable		2%	4%	10%	20%	40%
Total estimated bad debts	$ 26 170	$ 1 380	$ 2 340	$ 4 650	$ 6 600	$11 200

Total estimated bad debts for Hampson Furniture Ltd ($26 170) represent the existing customer claims expected to become uncollectable in the future. Thus, this amount represents the *required balance* in allowance for doubtful debts at year-end. Accordingly, the amount of the bad debts adjusting entry is the difference between the required balance and the existing balance in the allowance account. So, what is the existing balance in the allowance account? The allowance account is presented in a running-balance format next.

Allowance for doubtful debts				Balance	
Date	Particular	Dr	Cr	Dr	Cr
1 Jan. 2020	Opening balance				12 000
1 Mar.	Accounts receivable—R.A. Ware	500			11 500
	(Write-off of R.A. Ware account)				
1 Jul.	Accounts receivable—R.A. Ware		500		12 000
	(Reverse write-off of R.A. Ware account)				

The existing balance of the allowance account was $12 000 in credit. In order to bring the account to a credit balance of $26 170 to match the estimated bad debt from the ageing schedule, a credit of $14 170 is required, as shown in the following adjusting entry:

Dec. 31	Bad debts expense	14 170	
	Allowance for doubtful debts		14 170
	(To adjust allowance account to total estimated uncollectables)		

$$A \quad = \quad L \quad + \quad E$$
$$-14\,170 \qquad\qquad -14\,170$$

After the adjusting entry is posted, the accounts of Hampson Furniture Ltd will appear as in figure 7.28, in running-balance format.

Bad debts expense				Balance	
Date	Particular	Dr	Cr	Dr	Cr
31 Dec. 2020	Allowance for doubtful debts	14 170		14 170	
	(Adjusting entry)				

FIGURE 7.28   Bad debts accounts after posting

Allowance for doubtful debts				Balance	
Date	Particular	Dr	Cr	Dr	Cr
1 Jan. 2020	Opening balance				12 000
1 Mar.	Write-off of R.A. Ware account	500			11 500
1 Jul.	Reverse write-off of R.A. Ware account		500		12 000
31 Dec.	Bad debts expense		14 170		26 170

The review at year-end should also consider specific debtors. Accounts that are unlikely to be recovered should be written off.

An important aspect of accounts receivable management is simply maintaining a close watch on the accounts. Studies have shown that accounts more than 60 days past due lose approximately 50% of their value if no payment activity occurs within the next 30 days. For each additional 30 days that pass, the collectable value halves once again because the probability of collection is lower.

Occasionally, the allowance account will have a debit balance before adjustment because write-offs during the year have exceeded the previous allowance for bad debts. In such a case, the debit balance is added to the required balance when the adjusting entry is made. Thus, if there was a $12 000 debit balance in the account before adjustment, the adjusting entry would be for $38 170 ($26 170 + $12 000) to arrive at a credit balance of $26 170. In other words, a bigger amount of bad debts expense needs to be recognised because of larger write-offs during the year.

The percentage of receivables basis provides an estimate of the *recoverable amount* of the receivables. It also provides for the recognition of an expense in the period that the expected future cash flows from accounts receivable decline.

GST and bad debt write-off

The basic recording for the GST was demonstrated in sections 4.6 and 4.7 in chapter 4. The sale and subsequent payment from the customer was illustrated, and you will recall that the accounts receivable account included the GST charged. Just as settlement discount alters the amount of GST liability, similarly when the GST is recognised on the non-cash basis a bad debt write-off also affects the amount of the GST liability. Assume Jones Enterprises Pty Ltd uses the provisioning method to account for impairment of receivables. For the year ended 30 June 2019, it was estimated that the allowance for doubtful debts was $4000. This entry is illustrated below.

June 30	Bad debts expense	4 000	
	Allowance for doubtful debts		4 000
	(To record the year-end allowance to write down accounts		
	receivable to net realisable value)		

$$A = L + E$$
$$-4\,000 \qquad\qquad -4\,000$$

This entry would be reported as an expense in the 2019 statement of profit or loss. The allowance account does not recognise any adjustment to the GST at this stage. On 2 February 2020, after efforts to collect a debt from G. Antoniou for $2200, the manager decided to write the debt off as bad.

Feb. 2	Allowance for doubtful debts	2 000	
	GST collected	200	
	Accounts receivable (subsidiary ledger also credited)		2 200
	(To record the debt being written off in accordance with the manager's decision)		

$$A = L + E$$
$$+2\,000 \qquad -200$$
$$-2\,200$$

The debit to the GST collected account is a decreasing adjustment. When the amount owing was originally invoiced, the GST liability was recorded in the ledger as if it had been collected. As the customer G. Antoniou did not settle the account, the GST collected is also reduced as well as reducing the accounts receivable. The second demonstration problem at the end of this chapter will further illustrate the GST.

DECISION-MAKING TOOLKIT

Decision/issue	Info needed for analysis	Tool or technique to use for decision	How to evaluate results to make decision
Is the amount of past due accounts increasing? Which accounts require management's attention?	List of outstanding receivables and their due dates	Prepare an ageing schedule showing the receivables in various stages: outstanding 1–30 days, 31–60 days, 61–90 days, and over 90 days.	Accounts in the older categories require follow-up: letters, phone calls and possible renegotiation of terms.

LEARNING REFLECTION AND CONSOLIDATION

Review it

1. To maintain adequate internal controls over receivables, who should authorise receivables write-offs?
2. What are the essential features of the allowance method?

▶

3. What is the main criticism of the direct write-off method?
4. What is the effect on the GST liability for a bad debt write-off?

Do it

Jet Ltd has been in business for 5 years. The ledger at the end of the current year shows: accounts receivable $30 000, sales $180 000, and allowance for doubtful debts with a debit balance of $2000. After ageing the accounts receivable, bad debts are estimated to be 10% of accounts receivable. Prepare the entry necessary to adjust the allowance for doubtful debts.

Helpful hint: The debit of $5000 to bad debts expense is calculated as follows:

Allowance for doubtful debts			
Op. bal.	2 000	Adj.	5 000
Cl. bal.	3 000		
	5 000		5 000
		Op. bal.	3 000

Reasoning

Receivables are to be reported net of allowance for doubtful debts. The allowance reflects the current best estimate of any amount the entity does not expect it will collect. The estimated uncollectable amount should be recorded in an allowance account.

Solution

The following entry should be made to bring the balance in the allowance for doubtful debts up to a balance of $3000 (10% × $30 000):

Bad debts expense		5 000	
Allowance for doubtful debts			5 000
(To record estimate of uncollectable accounts)			

Notes receivable

Notes receivable captures receivables that differ from trade debtors in that they involve a formal credit instrument and do not always arise from transactions with customers. In this section we will use promissory notes to illustrate accounting procedures for short-term notes receivable.

Credit may also be granted in exchange for a formal credit instrument known as a promissory note. A **promissory note** is a written promise to pay a specified amount of money at a definite time. Promissory notes may be used (1) when individuals and businesses lend or borrow money, (2) when the amount of the transaction and the credit period exceed normal limits, and (3) in settlement of accounts receivable.

In a promissory note, the party making the promise to pay is called the issuer; the party to whom payment is to be made is called the payee. The payee may be specifically identified by name or may be designated simply as the bearer of the note.

In the promissory note shown in figure 7.29, Brent Ltd is the issuer and Wilma Ltd is the payee. To Wilma Ltd, the promissory note is a note receivable; to Brent Ltd, it is a note payable.

Notes receivable give the holder a more expedient legal claim to assets than accounts receivable. Notes receivable can be readily sold to another party. Promissory notes are negotiable instruments (as are cheques), which means that, when sold, they can be transferred to another party by endorsement.

Helpful hint: Who are the two key parties to a note, and what entry does each party make when the note is issued?

Answer: 1) The issuer, Brent Ltd, credits notes payable; and 2) the payee, Wilma Ltd, debits notes receivable.

FIGURE 7.29 Promissory note

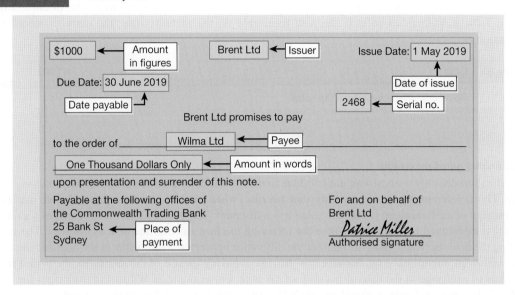

Notes receivable may be accepted from customers who need to extend the payment of an outstanding account receivable, and are often required from high-risk customers. The majority of notes, however, originate from lending transactions.

Recognising notes receivable

To illustrate the basic entry for notes receivable, we will use Brent Ltd's $1000, 2-month promissory note dated 1 May. Assuming that the note was written to settle an outstanding debtor's account, we record this entry for the receipt of the note by Wilma Ltd:

Mar. 1	Notes receivable	1 000	
	Accounts receivable—Brent Ltd		1 000
	(To record acceptance of Brent Ltd note)		

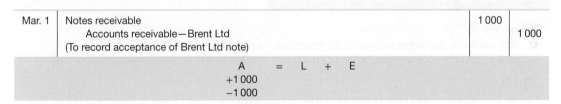

The note receivable is recorded at its *face value*, i.e. the value shown on the face of the note.

Valuing notes receivable

Like accounts receivable, short-term notes receivable are reported at their recoverable amount. The notes receivable allowance account is allowance for doubtful debts. Valuing short-term notes receivable is the same as valuing accounts receivable. The calculations and estimations involved in determining the recoverable amount and in recording the proper amount of bad debts expense and related allowance are similar. However, given the formality of the legal claim, bad debts on notes receivable are less common.

Disposing of notes receivable

Notes may be held to their maturity date, at which time the face value is collected. In some situations, the maker of the note defaults and appropriate adjustment must be made. In other situations, the holder of the note speeds up the conversion to cash by exchanging the note. The entries for honouring and exchanging notes are illustrated next.

Honouring notes receivable

A note is *honoured* when it is paid in full at its maturity date. To illustrate, using the example from figure 7.29, if Wilma Ltd collects the note receivable on the maturity date, the entry to record the collection is:

June 30	Cash	1 000	
	Notes receivable		1 000
	(To record collection of Brent Ltd note)		

$$A \quad = \quad L \quad + \quad E$$
$$+1\,000$$
$$-1\,000$$

Exchanging notes receivable

If Wilma Ltd does not wish to wait until 30 June to receive the face value of the note, it may exchange the note. This is referred to as discounting the note because, when a holder exchanges a note before maturity, the amount of cash received is the face value less a discount. The purchaser of the note makes a gain by paying a discounted amount for the note but receiving the face value of the note at maturity. The party selling the note receivable must account for the difference between the face value of the note and the cash received as an interest expense, because it is the cost of having the use of the money for the period from the date of exchange to the date of maturity of the note. For example, if Wilma Ltd exchanges the note at a 1% discount on 1 June it would receive $990. The entry to record this exchange would be:

June 1	Cash	990	
	Interest expense	10	
	Notes receivable		1 000
	(To record discounting the note from Brent at 1%)		

$$A \quad = \quad L \quad + \quad E$$
$$-1\,000 \qquad\qquad\qquad -10$$
$$+990$$

LEARNING REFLECTION AND CONSOLIDATION

Review it

1. Why are notes receivable accounted for separately from accounts receivable?
2. Explain the difference between holding a promissory note to maturity and exchanging it before maturity.

Do it

Taylor Stores Ltd accepts from Leonard Ltd a $3400, 90-day note dated 10 May in settlement of Leonard Ltd's overdue account. What is the maturity date of the note? What entry is made by Taylor Stores Ltd at the maturity date, assuming Leonard Ltd pays the note in full at that time?

Reasoning

When the due date is stated in terms of days, it is necessary to count the exact number of days to determine the maturity date. The date the note is issued is omitted from the count, but the due date is included. The entry to record interest at maturity in this solution assumes that no interest has previously accrued on this note.

Solution

The maturity date is 8 August, calculated as follows:

Term of note		90 days
May (31 − 10)	21	
June	30	
July	31	82
Maturity date, August		8

This entry is recorded by Taylor Stores Ltd at the maturity date:

Aug. 8	Cash	3 400	
	Notes receivable		3 400
	(To record collection of Leonard Ltd note)		

7.9 Financial statement presentation of receivables

LEARNING OBJECTIVE 7.9 Describe how receivables are reported in financial statements.

Each of the major types of receivables should be identified in the notes to the financial statements. Receivables that mature within 12 months or within the entity's operating cycle (whichever is the longer) are reported in the current assets section of the statement of financial position. Receivables not classified as current assets are classified as non-current. Both the gross amount of receivables and the allowance for doubtful debts should be reported in the notes to the financial statements. Figure 7.30 shows an extract from the 2019 financial report of Giorgina's.

FIGURE 7.30	Presentation of receivables in the notes to the financial statements of Giorgina's for 2019

GIORGINA'S PIZZA ENTERPRISES LTD
Notes to the financial statements (extract)

15.1 TRADE RECEIVABLES (CONTINUED)
The directors believe there is no further allowance required in addition to the allowance for doubtful debts.

If an entity has significant risk of uncollectable accounts or other problems with its receivables, it is required to discuss this possibility in the notes to the financial statements.

LEARNING REFLECTION AND CONSOLIDATION

Review it
Distinguish between current and non-current receivables.

7.10 Analysing and managing receivables

LEARNING OBJECTIVE 7.10 Analyse and manage receivables.

Managing accounts receivable involves five steps.
1. Determine to whom to extend credit.
2. Establish a payment period.
3. Monitor collections.
4. Evaluate the receivables balance.
5. Accelerate cash receipts from receivables when necessary.

Extending credit

A critical part of managing receivables is determining who should be extended credit and who should not. Many businesses increase sales by being generous with their credit policy, but they may end up extending credit to risky customers who do not pay. If the credit policy is too tight, they will lose sales; if it is too loose, they may sell to customers who will pay either very late or not at all.

Certain steps can be taken to help minimise losses as credit standards are relaxed. Risky customers may be required to provide letters of credit or bank guarantees. Then if the customer does not pay, the bank that provided the guarantee will. Particularly risky customers may be required to pay cash on delivery. In addition, potential customers may be asked for references from banks and suppliers to determine their payment history. It is important to check the references of potential customers as well as periodically checking the financial health of continuing customers. Many resources are available for investigating customers. For example, *The Dun & Bradstreet Reference Book* lists millions of companies and provides credit ratings for many of them.

Establishing a payment period

Businesses that extend credit should determine a required payment period and communicate that policy to their customers. It is important to make sure that the payment period is consistent with that of competitors. For example, if you decide to require payment within 15 days, but your competitors require payment within 45 days, you may lose sales to your competitors. However, as noted in chapter 4, you might allow up to 45 days to pay but offer a settlement discount of 2% for people paying within 15 days to match competitors' terms and encourage prompt payment of accounts; in this case, the payment term would be 2/15, n/45.

Monitoring collections

Credit risk is the threat of non-payment of receivables that could adversely affect an entity's financial position. One initial step that can be taken to monitor receivables is to calculate an entity's **credit risk ratio**, which is found by dividing the allowance for doubtful debts by accounts receivable, as shown in figure 7.31.

FIGURE 7.31	Credit risk ratio

$$\text{Credit risk ratio} = \frac{\text{Allowance for doubtful debts}}{\text{Accounts receivable}}$$

Changes in this ratio over time may suggest that the overall credit risk is increasing or decreasing, and differences across entities may suggest differences in each entity's overall credit risk. A high credit risk ratio may indicate that a business is extending credit to questionable customers.

To illustrate the use of the credit risk ratio, we will evaluate the receivables of Giorgina's, reported in figure 7.23. The credit risk ratio for Giorgina's is shown in figure 7.32.

FIGURE 7.32	Credit risk ratio for Giorgina's

	2019 $'000	2018 $'000
$\text{Credit risk ratio} = \dfrac{\text{Allowance for doubtful debts}}{\text{Accounts receivable}}$	$\dfrac{\$2\,560}{\$20\,257} = 12.6\%$	$\dfrac{\$2\,456}{\$17\,190} = 14.3\%$

Giorgina's credit risk ratio improved slightly, with the level of risk decreasing from 14.3% in 2018 to 12.6% in 2019.

Preparation of the accounts receivable ageing schedule was discussed in the text before and after figure 7.27. In addition to estimating the allowance for bad debts, the ageing schedule has other uses for management. It aids estimation of the timing of future cash inflows, which is very important to the finance manager's efforts to prepare a cash budget. It provides information about the overall collection experience of the business and identifies problem accounts. Problem accounts need to be pursued through phone calls, letters and occasionally legal action. Sometimes special arrangements must be made with problem accounts, such as discontinuing credit. This means that all further sales are on a cash on delivery (COD) basis until the outstanding account is paid.

As credit sales represent a significant proportion of total sales for many business entities, it is important for management to monitor receivables to minimise credit risk and to strengthen its overall cash position. One measure of assessing the integrity of the receivables is to evaluate the entity's credit risk ratio, by comparing the allowance for doubtful debts to accounts receivable. Management and potential investors would be concerned if the entity were exposed to a high level of credit risk ratio as this may indicate that credit has been extended to customers who are not creditworthy. Lower amounts of cash collected would have an adverse impact on the entity's liquidity and the increased likelihood of bad debts would have a similar impact on profitability. The relevance of the credit risk ratio is summarised in the decision-making toolkit below.

DECISION-MAKING TOOLKIT

Decision/issue	Info needed for analysis	Tool or technique to use for decision	How to evaluate results to make decision
Is the entity's credit risk increasing?	Allowance for doubtful debts and accounts receivable	$$\text{Credit risk ratio} = \frac{\text{Allowance for doubtful debts}}{\text{Accounts receivable}}$$	Increase in ratio may suggest increased credit risk, requiring evaluation of credit policies.

Companies must report on credit risk in their published financial statements. The amount and likelihood of significant credit risks should be considered. An excerpt from the credit risk note from the 2019 annual report of Giorgina's is shown in figure 7.33.

FIGURE 7.33 Note on credit risk in the notes to the financial statements of Giorgina's for 2019

GIORGINA'S PIZZA LIMITED
Notes to the financial statements (extract)

40.5 CREDIT RISK MANAGEMENT
Credit risk refers to the risk that a supplier will default on its contractual obligations, resulting in financial loss to the entity. The entity has a policy of only dealing with creditworthy suppliers and obtaining sufficient financial security as is appropriate to minimise the risk of financial loss from defaults. Credit controls are continually reviewed to limit the exposure to risk.

This note to Giorgina's financial statements suggests that, although the entity extends significant amounts of credit, its exposure to any individual customer or group of customers is limited.

DECISION-MAKING TOOLKIT

Decision/issue	Info needed for analysis	Tool or technique to use for decision	How to evaluate results to make decision
Does the business have significant concentrations of credit risk?	Notes to the financial statements on credit risk	The potential impact of the credit risk should be evaluated in terms of amount and likelihood.	If a material loss appears likely, the potential negative impact of that loss should be carefully evaluated, along with the adequacy of the allowance for doubtful debts.

Evaluating the receivables balance

Investors and managers keep a watchful eye on the relationship among sales, accounts receivable and cash collections. If sales increase, then accounts receivable are also expected to increase. But a disproportionate increase in accounts receivable might signal trouble. Perhaps the business increased its sales by loosening its credit policy, and these receivables may be difficult or impossible to collect. Such receivables are considered less liquid. Recall that liquidity is measured by how quickly certain assets can be converted to cash. The ratio used to assess the liquidity of the receivables is the **receivables turnover**. This ratio measures the number of times, on average, receivables are collected during the period. The receivables turnover is usually calculated by dividing net credit sales (net sales less cash sales) by the average net receivables during the year. Unless seasonal factors are significant, *average* receivables outstanding can be calculated from the beginning and ending balances of the net receivables.**

Helpful hint: An alternative method of calculating the receivables turnover is to use average gross receivables in the denominator.

A popular variant of the receivables turnover is to convert it into an **average collection period** in terms of days. This is done by dividing the receivables turnover into 365 days. The average collection period is often used to assess the effectiveness of credit and collection policies. The general rule is that the collection period should not greatly exceed the credit term period (i.e. the time allowed for payment). The following data (in millions) are available for Soft Drink Co.

	For the year ended 30 June		
	2019 ($ millions)	2018 ($ millions)	2017 ($ millions)
Sales	2 518.2	2 548.7	2 400.6
Accounts receivable	444.9	443.6	388.0

The receivables turnover and average collection period for Soft Drink Co. are shown in figure 7.34.

FIGURE 7.34 Receivables turnover and average collection period

$$\text{Receivables turnover} = \frac{\text{Net credit sales}}{\text{Average net receivables}}$$

$$\text{Average collection period} = \frac{365}{\text{Receivables turnover}}$$

		2019 $'000	2018 $'000
Soft Drink Co.	Receivables turnover	$\dfrac{\$2\,518.2}{(\$444.9 + \$443.6)/2} = 5.67$ times	$\dfrac{\$2\,548.7}{(\$443.6 + \$388.0)/2} = 6.13$ times
	Average collection period	$\dfrac{365}{5.67} = 64$ days	$\dfrac{365}{6.13} = 60$ days

These calculations assume that all sales were credit sales.

The receivables turnover for Soft Drink Co. was 6.13 times in 2018 with a corresponding average collection period of 60 days. In 2019, the receivables turnover had slowed down to 5.67 times per annum which lengthened the collection period to 64 days. These results indicate a 7% increase in the collection time, while the dollar value of credit sales decreased by 1%. Soft Drink Co. was not able to improve its

---

** If seasonal factors are significant, the average receivables balance might be determined by using monthly amounts. However, this would be useful only for users of internal information, as disclosures in published financial statements do not include monthly debtors' balances.

---

receivables turnover by increasing credit sales revenue and decreasing the average time taken to collect cash during this period.

One of the practical strategies for better debt collection is to monitor the efficiency of the cash collection process and have procedures in place to follow up on slow-paying accounts. One measure used to assess whether the cash is collected within a reasonable timeframe is the receivables turnover. The receivables turnover ratio compares the net credit sales to the average net receivable. This ratio determines the number of times that cash is collected from credit customers during the year: the higher the receivables turnover ratio, the faster the cash collection. This ratio can also be expressed in days as the average collection period by calculating the number of days in the year divided into the receivables turnover: the lower the number of days, the quicker the cash collection. The decision-making and analysis process in determining the efficiency in managing accounts receivable and cash collection is summarised in the decision-making toolkit below.

DECISION-MAKING TOOLKIT

Decision/issue	Info needed for analysis	Tool or technique to use for decision	How to evaluate results to make decision
Are collections being made in a timely fashion?	Net credit sales and average receivables balance	$$\text{Receivables turnover} = \frac{\text{Net credit sales}}{\text{Average net receivables}}$$ $$\text{Average collection period} = \frac{365 \text{ days}}{\text{Receivables turnover}}$$	Receivables turnover and average collection period should be consistent with the entity's credit policy. Any significant deviation which results in a slower receivables turnover or a longer collection period may suggest a decline in the financial integrity of credit customers.

Accelerating cash receipts

In the normal course of events, accounts receivable are collected in cash. However, as credit sales and receivables have grown in size and significance, the 'normal course of events' has changed. Two common expressions apply to the collection of receivables: (1) time is money — i.e. waiting for the normal collection process costs money; (2) a bird in the hand is worth two in the bush — i.e. getting the cash now is better than getting it later or not at all. Therefore, in order to accelerate the receipt of cash from receivables, businesses often sell their receivables to another business for cash, thereby shortening the cash-to-cash operating cycle.

There are three reasons for the sale of receivables. The first is their size. In recent years, for competitive reasons, sellers (retailers, wholesalers and manufacturers) often have provided financing to purchasers of their goods. For example, many major businesses in the vehicles, industrial and farm equipment, computer, and appliance industries offer finance to their customers. However, the entities involved do not necessarily want to hold large amounts of receivables.

Second, receivables may be sold because they may be the only reasonable source of cash. When money is tight, businesses may not be able to borrow money in the usual credit markets. If money is available, the cost of borrowing may be prohibitive.

A final reason for selling receivables is that invoicing and collection are often time-consuming and costly. As a result, it is often easier for businesses to sell the receivables to another party that has expertise in invoicing and collection matters.

Sale of receivables to a factor

A common way to accelerate receivables collection is by a sale to a factor. A **factor** is a financial institution or bank that buys receivables from businesses for a fee and then collects the payments directly from the customers. Factoring was traditionally associated with the textiles, apparel, footwear, furniture and home furnishing industries.

Credit card sales

Three parties are involved when credit cards are used in making retail sales: (1) the credit card issuer, who is independent of the retailer, (2) the retailer, and (3) the customer. A retailer's acceptance of a credit card is another form of selling — factoring — the receivable by the retailer.

The use of credit cards translates to more sales without bad debts for the retailer. Both are powerful reasons for a retailer to accept such cards. The major advantages of credit cards to the retailer are shown in figure 7.35. In exchange for these advantages, the retailer pays the credit card issuer a fee of 2% to 6% of the invoice price for its services.

FIGURE 7.35	Advantages of credit cards to the retailer

Sales resulting from the use of VISA, Bankcard and MasterCard are considered cash sales by the retailer. These cards are issued by banks. Upon receipt of credit card sales slips from a retailer, the bank immediately adds the amount to the seller's bank balance. These credit card sales slips are therefore recorded in the same manner as cheques deposited from a cash sale.

The basic principles of managing accounts receivable are summarised in figure 7.36.

FIGURE 7.36 Managing receivables

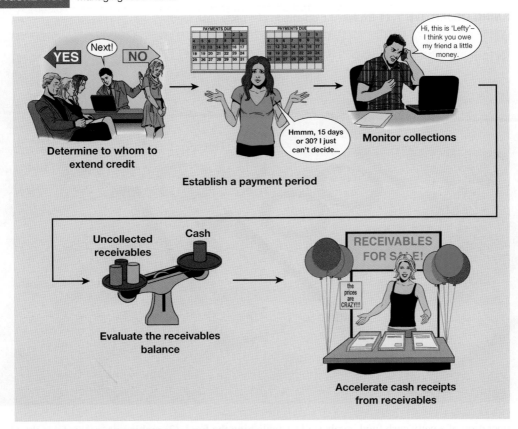

LEARNING REFLECTION AND CONSOLIDATION

Review it

1. What is the interpretation of the receivables turnover and the average collection period?
2. Why do some businesses sell their receivables?
3. For whom is the service charge on a credit card sale an expense?

Do it

Grayson Ltd has been expanding faster than it can raise capital. According to its local banker, the entity has reached its debt ceiling. Grayson customers are slow in paying (60–90 days), but its suppliers (creditors) are demanding 30-day payment. Grayson has a cash flow problem.

Grayson needs to raise $120 000 in cash to safely cover next Friday's employee payroll. Grayson's present balance of outstanding receivables totals $750 000. What might Grayson do to alleviate this cash crisis?

Reasoning

Grayson has an urgent need for cash to pay the payroll.

Solution

One source of immediate cash at a competitive cost is the sale of receivables to a factor. Rather than waiting until it can collect receivables, Grayson may raise immediate cash by selling its receivables. The last thing Grayson (or any employer) wants to do is miss a payroll.

7.11 Operation of the petty cash fund

LEARNING OBJECTIVE 7.11 Explain the operation of a petty cash fund.

The operation of a petty cash fund involves (1) establishing the fund, (2) making payments from the fund, and (3) replenishing the fund.

Establishing the fund

Two essential steps in establishing a petty cash fund are appointing a petty cash custodian who will be responsible for the fund and determining the size of the fund. Ordinarily, the amount is expected to cover anticipated disbursements for a short period ranging from one day to several months, depending on the size of the entity. The fund is established by withdrawing cash from the bank account. Larger entities usually do this by cashing a cheque. If Justco Pty Ltd decides to establish a $100 fund on 1 March, the entry in general journal form is:

Mar. 1	Petty cash	100	
	Cash at bank		100
	(To establish a petty cash fund)		

		A	=	L	+	E
		+100				
		−100				

However, this entry would usually be made in the cash payments journal.

The cheque is then cashed and the proceeds are placed in a locked petty cash box or drawer. Most petty cash funds are established on a fixed amount basis. Moreover, no additional entries will be made to the petty cash account unless the stipulated amount of the fund is changed. For example, if Justco Pty

Ltd decides on 1 July to increase the size of the fund to $250, it would debit petty cash $150 and credit cash $150.

Making payments from petty cash

The cashier, who is the custodian of the petty cash fund, makes payments from the fund that conform to prescribed management policies. Usually management limits the size of expenditures that may be reimbursed through petty cash. Each petty cash claim must be documented on a petty cash voucher, usually supported by evidence of the claimant's expenditure. For example, if an employee claimed reimbursement for the purchase of petrol while driving the employer's motor vehicle, the receipt from the petrol station should be attached to the petty cash voucher. The petty cash voucher should be signed by the manager who authorises the expenditure. The petty cash voucher satisfies two principles of internal control: (1) establishing responsibility through authorisation, and (2) documentation procedures.

The receipts are kept in the petty cash box until the fund is replenished. As a result, the sum of the petty cash receipts and money in the fund should equal the established total at all times. This means that surprise counts can be made at any time by an independent person, such as an internal auditor, to determine whether the fund is being maintained intact.

No accounting entry is made to record a payment at the time it is taken from petty cash. It is considered both time consuming and unnecessary to do so. Instead, the accounting effects of each payment are recognised when the fund is replenished. The fund is replenished at the end of each reporting period to ensure that all expenses are recognised.

Replenishing the fund

When the money in the petty cash fund reaches a minimum level and at the end of each accounting period, the fund is replenished. The request for reimbursement is initiated by the cashier. This person prepares a schedule (or summary) of the payments that have been made and sends the schedule, supported by petty cash receipts and other documentation, to the financial accountant or other designated authority. The receipts and supporting documents are examined to verify that they were proper payments from the fund. The replenishment of the petty cash fund is then approved and a cheque is prepared. At the same time, all supporting documentation is stamped 'paid' so that it cannot be submitted again for payment.

To illustrate, assume that on 15 March the cashier requests a cheque for $87. The fund contains $13 cash and petty cash receipts for postage $44, supplies $38 and miscellaneous expenses $5. The entry, in general journal form, to record the cheque is:

Mar. 15	Postage expense	44	
	Supplies	38	
	Miscellaneous expense	5	
	Cash at bank		87
	(To replenish petty cash fund)		

A	=	L	+	E
+38				−44
−87				−5

This entry would usually be recorded in a cash payments journal.

Note that the petty cash account is not affected by the reimbursement entry. Replenishment changes the composition of the fund by replacing the petty cash receipts with cash, but it does not change the balance of the fund.

Occasionally, in replenishing a petty cash fund it may be necessary to recognise a cash shortage or surplus. To illustrate, assume in the preceding example that the custodian had only $12 in cash in the fund plus the receipts as listed. The request for reimbursement would therefore be for $88, and the following entry would be made:

Mar. 15	Postage expense	44	
	Supplies	38	
	Miscellaneous expense	5	
	Cash over and short	1	
	Cash at bank		88
	(To replenish petty cash fund)		

$$
\begin{array}{ccccc}
A & = & L & + & E \\
+38 & & & & -44 \\
-88 & & & & -5 \\
& & & & -1
\end{array}
$$

Conversely, if the custodian had $14 in cash, the reimbursement request would be for $86, and **cash over and short** would be credited for $1. A debit balance in cash over and short is reported in the statement of profit or loss as an expense; a credit balance is reported as revenue. Cash over and short is closed to the profit or loss summary at the end of the year.

Replenishing petty cash involves three internal control procedures: segregation of duties, documentation procedures and independent internal verification. Internal control over a petty cash fund is strengthened by (1) having a supervisor make surprise counts of the fund to ascertain whether the petty cash vouchers and fund cash equal the designated amount, and (2) cancelling the paid vouchers so they cannot be resubmitted for reimbursement.

USING THE DECISION-MAKING TOOLKIT

The following information was taken from the 2019 financial statements of Bradman Ltd, a manufacturer and distributor of high-quality cricket bats.

BRADMAN LTD
Selected financial information

		2019 $'000		2018 $'000
Sales		1 300		1 200
CURRENT ASSETS				
Cash and cash equivalents		200		200
Accounts receivable	600		550	
Allowance for doubtful debts	(80)		(50)	
Net accounts receivable		520		500
Inventories		300		280
Other current assets		80		20
Total current assets		**1 100**		**1 000**

All sales are on credit. The industry average credit ratio is 10% and the industry average collection period is 70 days. The industry averages have been constant during 2019 and 2018.

Required

Comment on Bradman Ltd's accounts receivable management relative to that of the industry, with consideration given to (a) the credit risk ratio and (b) the receivables turnover and average collection period.

Solution

(a) Here are the credit risk ratios of Bradman Ltd:

2019	2018
$\dfrac{\$80}{\$600} = 13\%$	$\dfrac{\$50}{\$550} = 9\%$

Bradman Ltd's increase in sales has come at the expense of credit risk. The ratio has increased from 9%, which was below the industry average, to 13% in 2019, which was well above the industry average.

(b) The receivables turnover ratio and average collection period for Bradman Ltd for 2019 are:

$$\text{Receivables turnover ratio} = \frac{\$1\,300}{(\$520 + \$500)/2} = 2.5 \text{ times}$$

$$\text{Average collection period} = \frac{365}{2.5} = 146 \text{ days}$$

Bradman Ltd's receivables turnover of 2.5 is much lower than the industry average. Its average collection days of 146 days compared to the industry average of 70 days suggests that Bradman Ltd's credit customers take longer to pay.

SUMMARY

7.1 Identify the effect of business transactions on cash.

Many transactions have implications for an entity's cash flows in that almost every business transaction eventually results in an inflow or outflow of cash. It is therefore important to carefully consider the cash flow requirements in any business plan and operation.

7.2 Describe electronic banking processes.

Electronic banking is an electronic payment system that enables customers of a financial institution to conduct financial transactions on a web site operated by the financial institution. To access a financial institution's online banking facility, a customer with internet access would need to register with the institution for the service, and set up a password for customer verification. Once registered, a bank customer can transact banking tasks through online banking, including transferring funds between the customer's linked accounts and paying third parties, including bill payments through BPAY.

7.3 Explain the application of internal control principles for handling cash.

Internal controls over cash include: (a) designating only personnel such as cashiers to handle cheques and cash; (b) assigning the duties of receiving and disbursing cash, recording cash, and having custody of cash to different people; (c) obtaining remittance advice for mail receipts, cash register tapes, sequential electronic receipt numbers and deposit slips for bank deposits, and prenumbered cheques; (d) using safes and bank vaults to store cash with access limited to authorised personnel, direct deposits, and cash registers when dealing with over-the-counter receipts; (e) making independent daily counts of register receipts, daily comparisons of total receipts with total deposits, and adhering to cheque-signing procedures; (f) requiring personnel who handle cash to take annual leave, and to stamp invoices 'paid'.

7.4 Prepare a bank reconciliation.

The steps in determining the reconciling items are to ascertain outstanding deposits, unpresented cheques and errors by the depositor or the bank, updating and, if necessary, correcting cash records, and preparing a bank reconciliation statement.

7.5 Discuss the basic principles of cash management.

The basic principles of cash management include: (a) increase collection of receivables, (b) keep inventory levels low, (c) don't pay earlier than necessary, (d) plan timing of major expenditures, and (e) invest idle cash. The cash to daily expense ratio indicates how many days of expenses the current cash resources will cover.

7.6 Assess the adequacy of cash.

In evaluating an entity's cash management practices, one of the key considerations is whether the amount of cash held is adequate to cover its daily operational needs. One measure of the adequacy of cash is the ratio of cash to daily cash expenses. This ratio provides management and external decision makers with some insight into the entity's ability to cover its daily expenditure. A low level of coverage may require further investigation to avert potential liquidity issues. In contrast, a very high level of coverage may indicate excessive cash held. In this case, management may consider alternative investment opportunities to maximise the returns on any cash in surplus of its daily needs.

7.7 Identify the different types of receivables.

Receivables are frequently classified as accounts, notes and other. Accounts receivable are amounts owed by customers on account. Notes receivable represent claims that are evidenced by formal instruments of credit. Other receivables include non-trade receivables such as interest receivable, loans to officers, advances to employees, and goods and services tax refundable.

7.8 Describe how to value receivables.

Accounts receivable are recorded at the invoice price and reduced by sales returns and allowances. The two methods of accounting for uncollectable accounts are the direct write-off method and the allowance method, which emphasises the net amount of accounts receivable estimated to be received. The percentage of sales revenue basis can be used to estimate uncollectable accounts in the allowance method for monthly internal reports. The ageing of the accounts receivable method must be used at the end of the year. A decreasing adjustment must be made to the GST liability account when a bad debt is written off if GST was charged to the customer. Notes receivable can be held to maturity, at which time the face value of the note is received. Collecting a note receivable is accounted for by debiting cash and crediting notes receivable. Alternatively, the note receivable may be discounted earlier. The discount is allocated to interest expense.

7.9 Describe how receivables are reported in financial statements.

Each major type of receivable should be identified in the notes to the financial statements. Receivables maturing within 1 year or the operating cycle are considered current assets. The gross amount of receivables and allowance for doubtful debts should be reported in the notes to the financial statements.

7.10 Analyse and manage receivables.

To properly manage receivables, management must (a) determine to whom to extend credit, (b) determine a payment period, (c) monitor collections, (d) evaluate the receivables balance, and (e) accelerate cash receipts from receivables when necessary. The receivables turnover and the average collection period are useful in analysing management's effectiveness in managing receivables. The accounts receivable ageing schedule also provides useful information. If the business needs additional cash, management can accelerate the collection of cash from receivables by selling (factoring) its receivables or by allowing customers to pay with credit cards.

7.11 Explain the operation of a petty cash fund.

In operating a petty cash fund, an entity establishes the fund by appointing a custodian and determining the size of the fund. Payments from the fund are made for documented expenditures, and the fund is replenished as needed and at the end of each accounting period. Accounting entries to record payments are made at that time.

DECISION-MAKING TOOLKIT — A SUMMARY

DECISION-MAKING TOOLKIT

Decision/issue	Info needed for analysis	Tool or technique to use for decision	How to evaluate results to make decision
Will the entity need to borrow funds in the coming quarter?	Beginning cash balance, cash receipts, cash payments, and desired cash balance	Cash budget	The entity will need to borrow money if the cash budget indicates a projected cash deficiency of available cash over cash payments for the quarter.
Does the business have adequate cash to meet its daily needs?	Cash, average daily expenses	$\text{Cash to daily cash expenses ratio} = \dfrac{\text{Cash}}{\text{Average daily cash expenses}}$	A low level of cash coverage should be investigated. If this measure is very low, it may be necessary to source additional financing.
Is the amount of past due accounts increasing? Which accounts require management's attention?	List of outstanding receivables and their due dates	Prepare an ageing schedule showing the receivables in various stages: outstanding 1–30 days, 31–60 days, 61–90 days, and over 90 days.	Accounts in the older categories require follow-up: letters, phone calls and possible renegotiation of terms.

Decision/issue	Info needed for analysis	Tool or technique to use for decision	How to evaluate results to make decision
Is the entity's credit risk increasing?	Allowance for doubtful debts and accounts receivable	$$\text{Credit risk ratio} = \frac{\text{Allowance for doubtful debts}}{\text{Accounts receivable}}$$	Increase in ratio may suggest increased credit risk, requiring evaluation of credit policies.
Does the business have significant concentrations of credit risk?	Notes to the financial statements on credit risk	The potential impact of the credit risk should be evaluated in terms of amount and likelihood.	If a material loss appears likely, the potential negative impact of that loss should be carefully evaluated, along with the adequacy of the allowance for doubtful debts.
Are collections being made in a timely fashion?	Net credit sales and average receivables balance	$$\text{Receivables turnover} = \frac{\text{Net credit sales}}{\text{Average net receivables}}$$ $$\text{Average collection period} = \frac{365 \text{ days}}{\text{Receivables turnover}}$$	Receivables turnover and average collection period should be consistent with the entity's credit policy. Any significant deviation which results in a slower receivables turnover or a longer collection period may suggest a decline in the financial integrity of credit customers.

KEY TERMS

accounts receivable Amounts due from customers for the sale of goods or services on credit. Also called debtors or trade debtors.

ageing the accounts receivable A method of determining the allowance for doubtful debts by analysing customer balances by the length of time they have been unpaid.

allowance method A method of accounting for bad debts that involves estimating uncollectable accounts at the end of each period and recognising an allowance account as a contra accounts receivable account.

average collection period The average number of days that receivables are outstanding, calculated as receivables turnover divided into 365 days.

bad debts expense An expense account to record uncollectable receivables.

bank statement A statement received from the bank that shows the depositor's bank transactions and balances for a period.

cash Resources that consist of cash on hand, cash at bank, cheque account, and highly liquid investments such as deposits on the money market and 90-day bank acceptance bills.

cash over and short A general ledger account for recording surplus or deficit of petty cash.

credit risk The threat of non-payment of receivables that could adversely affect the financial health of a business.

credit risk ratio A measure of the risk that a business's customers may not pay their accounts, calculated as the allowance for doubtful debts divided by accounts receivable.

direct write-off method A method of accounting for bad debts that involves expensing accounts receivable at the time they are determined to be uncollectable.

dishonoured cheque A cheque that is not paid by the bank because of insufficient funds in the payer's bank account or because it has been cancelled by the payer.

electronic funds transfer (EFT) A cash transfer system that uses telephone, telegraph or computer to transfer cash from one location to another.

factor A financial institution that buys receivables from businesses for a fee and then collects the payments directly from the customers.

notes receivable Claims for which formal instruments of credit are issued as evidence of the debt.

outstanding deposits Deposits that have been made but do not yet appear on the bank statement because of timing differences.

petty cash fund A cash fund used to pay relatively small amounts.

promissory note A written promise to pay a specified amount of money on a defined date.

ratio of cash to daily cash expenses A measure that indicates the number of days of expenses that available cash can cover. Calculated as cash divided by average daily expenses.

receivables Amounts due from individuals and businesses that are expected to be collected in cash.

receivables turnover A measure of the liquidity of receivables, calculated as net credit sales divided by average net trade receivables.

unpresented cheque A cheque that has been issued by the payer but not yet paid by the bank.

DEMONSTRATION PROBLEM 1

Presented here are selected transactions related to Dylan Ltd.

Mar.	1	Sold $20 000 of merchandise to Potter Pty Ltd, terms 2/7, n/30.
	8	Received payment in full from Potter Pty Ltd for balance due.
	12	Accepted Juno Pty Ltd's $20 000, 6-month note for balance due.
	13	Made credit sales to Grainger Ltd for $13 200.
	15	Made Visa credit sales totalling $6700. A 5% service fee is deducted from the bank deposit by Visa.
Apr.	11	Sold accounts receivable of $8000 to Harcot Factor. Harcot Factor assesses a service charge of 2% of the amount of receivables sold.
	13	Received collections of $8200 from Grainger Ltd.
May	10	Wrote off as uncollectable $16 000 account receivable from Wesley Ltd. Dylan Ltd uses the allowance method to account for bad debts.
June	30	The balance in accounts receivable at the end of the first 6 months is $200 000 and the bad debt percentage is 10%, determined by ageing the accounts receivable. At 30 June the credit balance in the allowance account before adjustment is $3500.
July	16	The account receivable written off in May pays part of the amount due, $4000. No further payment is expected.

Required

Prepare the entries for the transactions in general journal format. Discuss what information is required for a business to evaluate the quality of its accounts receivable asset.

PROBLEM-SOLVING STRATEGIES

1. Accounts receivable are generally recorded at invoice price.
2. Sales returns and allowances and cash discounts reduce the amount received on accounts receivable.
3. When accounts receivable are sold, a service charge expense is incurred by the seller.
4. Under the allowance method, bad debts expense is recognised when the allowance for doubtful debts is increased.
5. The ageing accounts receivable method of estimating the allowance considers any existing balance in the allowance account.
6. Write-offs of accounts receivable affect only statement of financial position accounts.

Mar. 1	Accounts receivable—Potter Pty Ltd	20 000	
	Sales		20 000
	(To record sales on account)		
8	Cash	19 600	
	Discount allowed (2% × $20 000)	400	
	Accounts receivable—Potter Pty Ltd		20 000
	(To record collection of accounts receivable)		
12	Notes receivable	20 000	
	Accounts receivable—Juno Pty Ltd		20 000
	(To record acceptance of Juno Pty Ltd note)		
13	Accounts receivable	13 200	
	Sales		13 200
	(To record credit sales)		
15	Cash	6 365	
	Service charge expense (5% × $6700)	335	
	Sales		6 700
	(To record credit card sales)		
Apr. 11	Cash	7 840	
	Service charge expense (2% × $8000)	160	
	Accounts receivable		8 000
	(To record sale of accounts receivable to Harcot Factor)		
13	Cash	8 200	
	Accounts receivable—Grainger Ltd		8 200
	(To record collection of accounts receivable)		
May 10	Allowance for doubtful debts	16 000	
	Accounts receivable—Grainger Ltd		16 000
	(To record write-off of accounts receivable)		
June 30	Bad debts expense	16 500	
	Allowance for doubtful debts		16 500
	[($200 000 × 10%) − $3500]		
	(To record estimate of uncollectable accounts)		
July 16	Accounts receivable—Wesley Ltd	4 000	
	Allowance for doubtful debts		4 000
	(To reverse write-off of accounts receivable)		
	Cash	4 000	
	Accounts receivable—Wesley Ltd		4 000
	(To record collection of accounts receivable)		

A number of factors would influence the quality of the accounts receivable asset of an entity. Most importantly, how likely the receivables are to be collected in cash is affected by how long the accounts have been unpaid, in other words, the ageing of the account; the credit worthiness of the customers who were given credit; the relationship with the customers; and the effort by the relevant sales staff to follow up with the customers to 'chase up' their accounts, and so on.

DEMONSTRATION PROBLEM 2

Walker Pty Ltd is a consultant and is registered for GST in New Zealand. Assume a GST rate of 15%. The terms of business are that a 2% settlement discount is offered if the customer pays their account within 30 days.
- Total fees for September were $460 000 (including GST).
- Walker Pty Ltd received payment for half of the fees within the discount period.

- One customer, Fred Beard, went into liquidation owing $28 750 and there was no chance of recovery, so Walker Pty Ltd wrote the debt off in December.
- The balance of the monies owing of $201 250 were paid in December.

Required

Prepare the general journal format for the entries to record the above information, including narrations.

PROBLEM-SOLVING STRATEGIES

1. Accounts receivable are generally recorded at invoice price.
2. The fees revenue is net of the GST included in the invoice price.
3. Cash settlement discounts reduce the amount received on accounts receivable and also the GST liability.
4. Write-offs of accounts receivable affect only statement of financial position accounts which includes the GST liability account.

SOLUTION TO DEMONSTRATION PROBLEM

Reasoning and workings

1. The GST included in the invoices to customers is at 15% fee revenue, i.e. $460 000 ÷ 1.15 = $400 000.
2. Settlement discount is at 2%. This is applied to half of the accounts receivable balance of $460 000 × 50% = $230 000. This means that 2% of the accounts receivable will not be collected so the GST collected liability account needs to be reduced also by 2%.
3. The bad debt to be written off also represents GST charged which will not be collected. Therefore, the GST liability needs a decreasing adjustment represented by the GST charged on the invoice.
4. The total collections for the September billings were $225 400 + $201 250 = $426 650. Therefore, the net GST collected will be $426 650 × (115 − 100)/115 = $55 650; or $60 000 − $600 − $3750 = $55 650.

Solution

1.	During Sept.	Account receivable	460 000	
		Fees revenue		400 000
		GST collected		60 000
		(To record fees for the period, GST charged at 15%)		
2.	Sept.	Cash ($230 000 × 98%)	225 400	
		Discount allowed ($200 000 × 2%)	4 000	
		GST collected ($30 000 × 2%)	600	
		Accounts receivable ($460 000 × 50%)		230 000
		(To record payment of account by customers within the discount period)		
3.	Dec.	Allowance for doubtful debts ($28 750/1.15)	25 000	
		GST collected ($28 750 − $25 000)	3 750	
		Accounts receivable		28 750
		(To record write-off of bad debt)		
4.	Dec.	Cash	201 250	
		Accounts receivable		201 250
		(To record balance of monies due from customers)		

SELF-STUDY QUESTIONS

7.1 Which of the following business transactions do not involve cash?   **LO1**

    (a) Collecting accounts receivable.

    (b) Buying office supplies.

    (c) Paying wages to workers.

    (d) Accruing depreciation expense.

7.2 Permitting only designated personnel such as cashiers to handle cash receipts is an application of the principle of: **LO3**
    (a) segregation of duties.
    (b) establishment of responsibility.
    (c) independent internal verification.
    (d) rotation of duties.

7.3 The use of prenumbered cheques in disbursing cash is an application of the principle of: **LO3**
    (a) establishment of responsibility.
    (b) segregation of duties.
    (c) physical, mechanical and electronic controls.
    (d) documentation procedures.

7.4 In a bank reconciliation, when the bank statement shows a credit balance, outstanding deposits are:
    (a) deducted from the business records balance. **LO4**
    (b) added to the business records balance.
    (c) added to the balance as per bank statement.
    (d) deducted from the balance as per bank statement.

7.5 Which of the following is not an effective way to manage cash? **LO5**
    (a) Invest idle cash.
    (b) Hold excessive inventory.
    (c) Speed up collection of accounts receivable.
    (d) Stretch payment for accounts payable.

7.6 Which of the following ratios is an indication of the effectiveness of cash management? **LO6**
    (a) Inventory turnover ratio.
    (b) Gross margin ratio.
    (c) Cash to daily cash expenses ratio.
    (d) Return on assets.

7.7 A cheque is written to replenish a $100 petty cash fund when the fund contains receipts of $94 and $3 in cash. In recording the cheque: **LO11**
    (a) Cash over and short should be debited for $3.
    (b) Petty cash should be debited for $94.
    (c) Cash should be credited for $94.
    (d) Petty cash should be credited for $3.

7.8 Jones Pty Ltd on 15 June sells inventory on account to Bullock Ltd for $1000, terms 2/7, n/30. On 20 June Bullock Ltd returns inventory worth $300 to Jones Pty Ltd. On 21 June payment is received from Bullock Ltd for the balance due. What is the amount of cash received? **LO8**
    (a) $700.
    (b) $680.
    (c) $686.
    (d) None of the above.

7.9 Net credit sales for the month are $800 000. The accounts receivable balance is $160 000. The allowance is calculated as 7.5% of the receivables balance using the ageing of receivables method. If the allowance for doubtful debts has a credit balance of $5000 before adjustment, what is the balance after adjustment? **LO8**
    (a) $12 000.
    (b) $7000.
    (c) $17 000.
    (d) $31 000.

7.10 In 2020 Norman Pty Ltd had net credit sales of $75 000. On 1 July 2019, the allowance for doubtful debts had a credit balance of $1800. During 2020, $3000 of uncollectable accounts receivable were written off. Ageing of accounts receivable revealed that the allowance should be 8% of the balance in receivables. If the accounts receivable balance at 30 June 2020 was $20 000, what is the required adjustment to the allowance for doubtful debts at 30 June 2020? **LO8**

(a) $1600.
(b) $7500.
(c) $2800.
(d) $3000.

7.11 An analysis and ageing of the accounts receivable of Machiavelli Ltd at 31 December reveal these data: **LO9**

Accounts receivable	$800 000
Allowance for doubtful debts per business	
records before adjustment (credit)	50 000
Amounts expected to become uncollectable	65 000

What is the recoverable amount of the accounts receivable at 31 December after adjustment?

(a) $685 000.
(b) $750 000.
(c) $800 000.
(d) $735 000.

7.12 Which of these statements about promissory notes is *incorrect*? **LO7**

(a) The party making the promise to pay is called the issuer.
(b) The party to whom payment is to be made is called the payee.
(c) A promissory note is not a negotiable instrument.
(d) A promissory note is more liquid than an account receivable.

7.13 Tyres R Us Ltd accepts a $1400, 3-month promissory note in settlement of an account with Parton Ltd. The entry to record this transaction is: **LO8**

(a) Accounts receivable | 1 400 |
    Notes receivable | | 1 400

(b) Notes receivable | 1 400 |
    Accounts receivable | | 1 400

(c) Notes receivable | 1 400 |
    Sales | | 1 400

(d) Bank | 1 400 |
    Notes receivable | | 1 400

7.14 Schlicht Ltd holds Osgrove Ltd's $10 000, 120-day note. The entry made by Schlicht Ltd when the note is collected at maturity is: **LO8**

(a) Cash | 10 000 |
    Notes receivable | | 10 000

(b) Cash | 10 000 |
    Accounts receivable | | 10 000

(c) Accounts receivable | 10 000 |
    Notes receivable | | 10 000

(d) Notes receivable | 10 000 |
    Accounts receivable | | 10 000

7.15 Moore Ltd had net credit sales during the year of $800 000 and cost of sales of $500 000. The balance in receivables at the beginning of the year was $100 000 and at the end of the year was $150 000. What was the receivables turnover? **LO10**

(a) 6.4
(b) 8.0
(c) 5.3
(d) 4.0

7.16 Hoffman Pty Ltd sells its goods on terms of 2/7, n/30. It has a receivables turnover of 7. What is its average collection period (days)? **LO10**

(a) 2555

(b) 30

(c) 52

(d) 210

7.17 Morgan Retailers accepted $50 000 of Citibank Visa credit card charges for inventory sold. Citibank deducts charges of 4% for its credit card use. The entry to record this transaction by Morgan Retailers will include a credit to Sales of $50 000 and a debit(s) to: **LO10**

(a) Cash $48 000 and Service charge expense $2000.

(b) Accounts receivable $48 000 and Service charge expense $2000.

(c) Cash $50 000.

(d) Accounts receivable $50 000.

QUESTIONS

7.1 Edward Lee is about to start a business selling smartphone accessories on campus. Explain the impact of business transactions on cash by giving examples of the transactions that involve cash at the start-up phase of the business.

7.2 Continue with question 7.1 above. Describe the electronic banking processes to Edward as he is setting up his business on campus.

7.3 'Internal control for handling cash is concerned only with enhancing the accuracy of the accounting records.' Do you agree? Explain.

7.4 Highland Ltd owns these assets at year-end:

Cash at bank—savings account	$15 000
Cash on hand	1 850
GST refund due	4 000
Cheque account balance	22 000

What amount should be reported as Cash in the statement of financial position?

7.5 Dent Department Stores has just installed new electronic cash registers in its stores. How do cash registers improve internal control over cash receipts?

7.6 Describe the basic principles of cash management.

7.7 Johnny Harris asks your help concerning a dishonoured cheque. Explain to Johnny (a) what a dishonoured cheque is, (b) how it is treated in a bank reconciliation and (c) whether it will require an adjusting entry in the business's records.

7.8 (a) Identify the three activities that pertain to a petty cash fund, and indicate an internal control principle that is applicable to each activity.

(b) When are journal entries required in the operation of a petty cash fund?

7.9 What is the difference between an account receivable and a note receivable?

7.10 Soo Eng cannot understand why the net amount of accounts receivable does not decrease when an uncollectable account is written off under the allowance method. Clarify this point for Soo Eng.

7.11 Simona Ltd's operating cycle is 1 year. How would the following receivables be classified on the statement of financial position?

(a) Trade debtor account of $500 000, of which 70% is due within 1 month with the balance due in 18 months.

(b) A 90-day promissory note.

7.12 Jayne's Gourmet Delivery is in its second year of operation. All sales are on credit and the business has a credit term of 30 days. You have just worked out that the receivables turnover is 8 times this year. Comment on the effectiveness of the collection policy.

BRIEF EXERCISES

BE7.1 Distinguish cash flows from assets. **LO1**

Identify which of the following items are (a) cash flows, (b) assets and (c) liabilities accounts.
- Inventory.
- Bank loan.
- Monthly loan payment.
- GST receivable.
- Motor vehicle.
- Car loan.
- Car loan payment.

BE7.2 Identify costs and benefits of electronic banking. **LO2**

Harry Ford is starting a fruit juice bar on campus. He is wondering whether he should accept EFTPOS payments at his juice bar. Identify some of the costs and benefits of using electronic banking for this business.

BE7.3 Apply internal control principles to handling cash. **LO3**

Aaron Tso is the merchandising manager for Franklin Office Supplies Ltd. During the month of April when the Franklin's accounts payable manager was on holiday, Aaron was responsible for receiving the goods that he ordered as well as approving payments for the purchases. Evaluate the internal controls in this situation.

BE7.4 Prepare partial bank reconciliation. **LO3**

At 31 July Ridley Pty Ltd has this bank information: cash balance as per bank $8420; unpresented cheques $862; outstanding deposits $2700; and a bank service charge $20. Determine the balance of the cash at bank account after any required adjustments.

BE7.5 Prepare entry to replenish a petty cash fund. **LO11**

On 20 March Sazin's petty cash fund of $200 is replenished when the fund contains $120 in cash and receipts for postage $32, supplies $26, and travel expense $22. Prepare the journal entry in general journal form to record the replenishment of the petty cash fund.

BE7.6 Identify different types of receivables. **LO7**

Presented below are three receivables transactions. Indicate whether these receivables are reported as accounts receivable, notes receivable, or other receivables on a statement of financial position.
(a) Advanced $10 000 to an employee.
(b) Received a promissory note of $57 000 for services performed.
(c) Sold inventory on account for $60 000 to a customer.

BE7.7 Prepare entry using allowance method. **LO8**

Massey Ltd uses the allowance method to record bad debts expense and concludes, using the ageing of accounts receivable method, that 1% of accounts receivable will become uncollectable. Accounts receivable are $500 000 at the end of the year, and the allowance for doubtful debts has a credit balance of $3000.
(a) Prepare the adjusting journal entry to record bad debts expense for the year.
(b) If the allowance for doubtful debts had a debit balance of $800 instead of a credit balance of $3000, determine the amount to be reported for bad debts expense.

BE7.8 Prepare entry for estimated uncollectables and classifications, and calculate ratios. LO8, 9, 10

During its first year of operations, Wendy Ltd had credit sales of $3 million, of which $600 000 remained uncollected at year-end. The credit manager estimates that $40 000 of these receivables will become uncollectable.
(a) Prepare the journal entry to record the estimated uncollectables. (Assume the allowance account has an unadjusted balance of nil.)

(b) Prepare the current assets section of the statement of financial position for Wendy Ltd, assuming that in addition to the receivables it has cash of $90 000, inventory of $130 000, and prepaid expenses of $13 000.

(c) Calculate the credit risk ratio, receivables turnover, and average collection period. Assume that average net receivables were $530 000.

BE7.9 Prepare entries for credit card sale and sale of accounts receivable. **LO2, 10**

Consider these transactions:

(a) Bella Restaurant accepted MasterCard for payment of a $200 dinner. The bank charges a 4% fee. What entry should Bella Restaurant make?

(b) Frantella Ltd sold its accounts receivable of $50 000. What journal entry should Frantella make, given a service charge of 4% on the amount of receivables sold?

EXERCISES

E7.1 Distinguish cash flows from assets. **LO1**

As a recent graduate of a fashion design and business degree, Edith Leung is planning to buy a fashion boutique from Keitha Jones, a family friend. Following are selected items from the financial records of the fashion boutique:

Credit card sales	$56 000	GST receivable	$ 3 800
Inventory	28 000	Cash at bank	8 760
Outstanding bank loan	12 000	Accounts payable	8 400
Loan payment	5 800	Cash sales	18 500
Rent payable	2 400	Accounts receivable	6 800
Operating expenses paid	24 000	Payment to suppliers	16 000

Required

(a) Calculate (i) cash inflows, (ii) cash outflows, (iii) assets and (iv) liabilities for Keitha Jones's fashion boutique.

(b) Based on requirement (a), what can Edith infer in relation to purchasing the fashion boutique?

E7.2 Identify the principles of internal control for handling cash. **LO3**

Gerry's Pizza operates strictly on a takeaway basis. Customers pick up their orders at a counter where a clerk exchanges the pizza for cash. At the counter, the customer can see other employees making the pizzas and the large ovens in which the pizzas are baked.

Required

Identify the five principles of internal control for handling cash and give an example of each principle that you might observe when picking up your pizza. (*Note:* It may not be possible to observe all the principles.)

E7.3 List internal control weaknesses over cash receipts and suggest improvements. **LO3**

The following control procedures are used for over-the-counter cash receipts:

1. All over-the-counter receipts are registered by three clerks who share a cash register with a single cash drawer.
2. To minimise the risk of robbery, cash in excess of $100 is stored in an unlocked attaché case in the stockroom until it is deposited in the bank.
3. At the end of each day the total receipts are counted by the cashier on duty and reconciled to the cash register tape total.
4. The accountant deposits the cash received in the bank and then records the day's receipts.

Required

(a) For each procedure, explain the weakness in internal control and identify the control principle that is violated.

(b) For each weakness, suggest a change in procedure that will result in good internal control.

E7.4 Prepare bank reconciliation statement and adjusting entries. **LO4**

Shoe City Pty Ltd's bank reconciliation clerk is unable to reconcile the bank balance at 31 January. The balance of the cash at bank account, before any entries for transactions initiated by the bank, was $4770.20 in the company records. The clerk's attempt at the bank reconciliation statement is as follows:

Cash balance as per bank statement	$4 392.20 Cr
Add: Dishonoured cheque	516.00
Less: Bank charges	30.00
Less: Outstanding deposits	708.00
Add: Unpresented cheques	876.00
Cash balance as per company records	**$5 046.20**

Required

(a) Prepare a correct bank reconciliation.

(b) Journalise the entries required by the reconciliation.

E7.5 Calculate and comment on the cash to daily cash expenses ratio. **LO6**

Green Dot Furniture reported the following financial data in its latest annual report:

	$'000
Cash and cash equivalents	17 312
Total cash expenses	92 728
Net cash provided by operating activities	15 520

Required

Calculate and comment on the cash to daily cash expenses ratio.

E7.6 Prepare journal entries for a petty cash fund. **LO11**

During October, Hair Styles Pty Ltd experiences the following transactions in establishing a petty cash fund.

Oct.	1	A petty cash fund is established with a cheque for $130 issued to the petty cash custodian.	
	31	A count of the petty cash fund disclosed the following items:	
	31	Currency (notes)	$ 7.80
		Coins	0.50
		Expenditure receipts (vouchers):	
		Office supplies	36.50
		Telephone and internet	21.30
		Postage	53.70
		Freight-out	8.80
		A cheque was written to reimburse the fund and increase the fund to $260.	

Required

Journalise the entries in October that pertain to the petty cash fund.

E7.7 Determine bad debts expense, and prepare the adjusting entry. **LO8**

Marc Pty Ltd has accounts receivable of $92 500 at 31 March 2019. An analysis of the accounts shows these amounts:

	Balance, 31 March	
Month of sale	**2019**	**2018**
March	$65 000	$75 000
February	12 600	8 000
December and January	8 500	2 400
November and October	6 400	1 100
	$92 500	$86 500

Credit terms are 2/7, n/30. At 31 March 2019 there is a $1600 credit balance in allowance for doubtful debts before adjustment. The entity uses the ageing of accounts receivable basis for estimating uncollectable accounts. Marc Pty Ltd's estimates of bad debts are as follows:

Age of accounts	Estimated percentage uncollectable
Current	2.0%
1–30 days past due	5.0
31–90 days past due	30.0
Over 90 days	50.0

Required

(a) Determine the total estimated uncollectables.

(b) Prepare the adjusting entry at 31 March 2019 to record bad debts expense.

(c) Discuss the implications of the changes in the ageing schedule from 2018 to 2019.

E7.8 Prepare journal entries for GST for bad debts expense.   **LO8**

Brian Bazaar had sold goods on credit in September 2019 for $5500 (including 10% GST). In November 2019 he became aware that the debtor M. Waters was bankrupt and the creditors were unlikely to receive any amounts due. On 28 November, the accountant for Brian Bazaar wrote the debt off against the allowance for bad debts account. Brian Bazaar uses the non-cash (accruals) basis for reporting and remitting the GST obligations.

Required

(a) Prepare the journal entry to record the bad debt write-off.

(b) Prepare a brief memo to the general manager explaining the effect of the bad debt write-off on the GST liabilities and the difference between reporting the GST on the cash and non-cash (accruals) basis in regard to bad debts.

E7.9 Report on receivables in financial statements.   **LO9**

Spring & Co Ltd had the following balances in receivable accounts at 30 June 2018 (in millions): Allowance for doubtful debts $11; Accounts receivable $290; Other receivables $22; Notes receivable $95.

Required

Prepare the presentation of Spring & Co Ltd's receivables in the notes to the financial statements.

E7.10 Calculate ratios to evaluate an entity's receivables balance.   **LO10**

The following information was taken from the 2020 financial statements of Honey Factory Ltd:

(in millions)	2020	2019	2018
Accounts receivable	$ 146.6	$ 104.3	$ 126.0
Allowance for doubtful debts	6.3	5.7	8.2
Sales	1 113.0	899.3	756.9
Total current assets	367.2	285.8	258.7

Required

Answer each of the following questions.

(a) Calculate the receivables turnover and average collection period for 2020 and 2019 for the entity, assuming all sales are on credit.

(b) Calculate the credit risk ratio for the entity for 2020 and 2019.

(c) Comment on the entity's credit and collection policies.

E7.11 Prepare entry for sale of accounts receivable. **LO9**

On 3 March Virtual Appliances sells $900 000 of its receivables to Fundamental Factors Ltd. Fundamental Factors Ltd assesses a finance charge of 4% of the amount of receivables sold.

Required

Prepare the entry in Virtual Appliances' records for the sale of the receivables.

E7.12 Prepare entry for credit card sale. **LO2**

On 10 May New Mark Ltd sold inventory for $2400 and accepted the customer's Business Bank MasterCard. At the end of the day, the Business Bank MasterCard receipts were deposited in New Mark Ltd's bank account. Business Bank charges a 1.5% service charge for credit card sales.

Required

Prepare the entry in New Mark Ltd's records for the sale of goods.

E7.13 Determine cash adequacy. **LO6**

You are considering investing in the bed and breakfast (B&B) industry. Two B&Bs, Burleigh Heaven and Miami Paradise, have been shortlisted for your consideration. Both companies are about the same size, with similar assets and sales. The following is extracted from their statements of cash flows for the year ended 31 December 2019:

	Burleigh Heaven	Miami Paradise
Receipts from customers	$ 91 380	$ 63 288
Cash payment to suppliers and employees	(63 905)	(55 802)
Interest received	489	288
Interest and other costs of finance paid	(6 780)	(16 383)
Income tax paid	(17 672)	(12 239)

The statements of financial position as at 31 December 2019 show the following balance for cash and cash equivalent for the two companies:

	Burleigh Heaven	Miami Paradise
Cash and cash equivalent	7 110	4 289

Required

(a) Calculate the cash to daily expenses ratio for both companies.
(b) If the adequacy of cash is the only factor in your investment decision, which company would you invest in?

E7.14 Calculate ratios to evaluate two divisions' credit risk and receivable balances. **LO10**

Advanced Lifestyle Ltd has stores in Auckland and Queenstown. The following information was taken from the 2019 financial statements, showing the results of its two divisions:

(in NZ$ millions)	Auckland	Queenstown
Total sales	1 653	1 596
Credit sales	1 498	1 388
Gross profit	215	174
Allowance for doubtful debts (2018)	7.2	6.2
Allowance for doubtful debts (2019)	10	5.2
Accounts receivable (2018)	152	128
Accounts receivable (2019)	197	120
Total current assets	322	285

Required

(a) Calculate for each division:
 1. receivables turnover for 2019
 2. average collection period for 2019
 3. credit risk ratio for 2019 and 2018.

(b) As the Managing Director of Advanced Lifestyle Ltd, what conclusion can you make about the performance of the two divisions' management in terms of their collection policy and credit risk?

PROBLEM SET A

PSA7.1 Calculate ratios to make business decisions.   **LO1**

As a recent graduate of a cooking course, James Brady is considering investing in a café that his best friend, Toby Dwyer, owns. Following are selected items from financial records of the café.

Credit card sales	$56 000	Operating expenses paid	$18 000
Accounts payable	12 400	GST receivable	4 900
Food supplies	29 500	Cash at bank	13 200
Outstanding bank loan	22 000	Loan payment	12 000
Rent payable	14 800	Cash sales	28 500
Accounts receivable	7 200	Payment to suppliers	21 000

Required

(a) Calculate (i) cash inflows, (ii) cash outflows, (iii) assets and (iv) liabilities for Toby's cafe business.

(b) Based on requirement (a), what can James infer in relation to investing in Toby's cafe?

(c) What other business information should James seek to make the decision of whether to invest in Toby's business?

PSA7.2 Identify internal control weaknesses over cash receipts.   **LO3**

Burlington Theatre is in the Burlington Mall. A cashier's booth is located near the entrance to the theatre. Two cashiers are employed. One works from 1 to 5 p.m., the other from 5 to 9 p.m. The cashiers receive cash from customers and operate a machine that ejects serially numbered tickets. The rolls of tickets are inserted and locked into the machine by the theatre manager at the beginning of each cashier's shift.

After purchasing a ticket, the customer takes the ticket to a doorperson stationed at the entrance of the theatre lobby some 18 metres from the cashier's booth. The doorperson tears the ticket in half, admits the customer, and returns the ticket stub to the customer. The other half of the ticket is dropped into a locked box by the doorperson.

At the end of each cashier's shift, the theatre manager removes the ticket rolls from the machine and makes a cash count. The cash count sheet is initialled by the cashier. At the end of the day, the manager deposits the receipts in total in a bank night deposit vault located in the mall. In addition, the manager sends copies of the deposit slip and the initialled cash count sheets to the theatre accountant for verification and to the accounting department. Receipts from the first shift are stored in a safe located in the manager's office.

Required

(a) Identify the internal control principles and their application to the cash receipts transactions of Burlington Theatre.

(b) If the doorperson and cashier decided to collaborate to misappropriate cash, what actions might they take?

PSA7.3 Prepare bank reconciliation and adjusting entries from detailed data. **LO4**

The bank reconciliation statement for Jona Ltd at 30 November 2019 is shown below.

JONA LTD Bank reconciliation statement as at 30 November 2019			
Cash balance per bank statement			$14 367.90
Add: Outstanding deposits			2 530.20
			16 898.10
Less: Unpresented cheques			
	Cheque number	Cheque amount	
	3451	$2 260.40	
	3470	720.10	
	3471	844.50	
	3472	1 426.80	
	3474	1 050.00	6 301.80
Cash balance as per ledger			**$10 596.30**

The December bank statement showed the following cheques and deposits:

Information from bank statement					
Cheques				Deposits	
Date	Number	Amount	Date		Amount
1/12	3451	$ 2 260.40	1/12		$ 2 530.20
2/12	3471	844.50	4/12		1 211.60
7/12	3472	1 426.80	8/12		2 365.10
4/12	3475	1 640.70	16/12		2 672.70
8/12	3476	1 300.00	21/12		2 945.00
10/12	3477	2 130.00	26/12		2 567.30
15/12	3479	3 080.00	29/12		2 836.00
27/12	3480	600.00	30/12		1 025.00
30/12	3482	475.50			
29/12	3483	1 140.00			
31/12	3485	540.80			
		Total $15 438.70			**Total $18 152.90**

Jona Ltd's cash records for December showed the following:

Cash payments journal (extract)							Cash receipts journal (extract)	
Date	Cheque number	Amount	Date	Cheque number	Amount		Date	Amount banked
1/12	3475	$1 640.70	20/12	3482	$ 475.50		3/12	$ 1 211.60
2/12	3476	1 300.00	22/12	3483	1 140.00		7/12	2 365.10
2/12	3477	2 130.00	23/12	3484	832.00		15/12	2 672.70
4/12	3478	538.20	24/12	3485	450.80		20/12	2 954.00
8/12	3479	3 080.00	30/12	3486	1 389.50		25/12	2 567.30
10/12	3480	600.00					28/12	2 836.00
17/12	3481	807.40					30/12	1 025.00
							31/12	1 190.40
				Total	$14 384.10		Total	$16 822.10

The bank statement contained two items:

1. A credit of $3145 for the collection of a $3000 note for Jona Ltd; interest of $160; a collection fee of $15.00. Jona Ltd has not accrued any interest on the note.
2. A debit of $647.10 for a dishonoured cheque written by A. Jordan, a customer. At 31 December the cheque had not been redeposited in the bank.

Helpful hint: NSF stands for not sufficient funds, that is, a dishonoured cheque.

At 31 December the cash balance per Jona Ltd's records was $13 034.30, and the cash balance per bank statement was $19 580.00. The bank did not make any errors, but two errors were made by Jona Ltd.

Required

(a) Using the procedure described under the heading 'Reconciliation procedure' (in section 7.4), prepare a bank reconciliation at 31 December.
(b) Prepare the adjusting entries based on the reconciliation. (*Note:* The correction of any errors pertaining to recording cheques should be made to accounts payable. The correction of any errors relating to recording cash receipts should be made to accounts receivable.)

PSA7.4 Prepare comprehensive bank reconciliation statement with internal control deficiencies.

LO3, 4

Delicious Pies Pty Ltd is a very profitable small business. It has not, however, given much consideration to internal control. For example, in an attempt to keep clerical and office expenses to a minimum, the jobs of cashier and bookkeeper have been combined. As a result, Rob Rowe handles all cash receipts, keeps the accounting records, and prepares the monthly bank reconciliations.

The balance as per the bank statement on 31 October 2020 was $25 732. Unpresented cheques were: no. 62 for $177.45, no. 183 for $210, no. 284 for $354.55, no. 862 for $266.99, no. 863 for $317.52, and no. 864 for $231.39. Included on the bank statement was a credit entry of $280 indicating the collection of a note receivable for Delicious Pies Pty Ltd by the bank on 25 October. This entry had not been recorded by Delicious Pies Pty Ltd.

The entity's ledger showed one cash account with a balance of $30 369.81. The balance included undeposited cash on hand. Because of the lack of internal controls, Rowe took for personal use all of the undeposited receipts in excess of $5313.71. He then prepared the following bank reconciliation statement in an effort to conceal his theft of cash:

Cash balance as per company records, 31 October		$30 369.81
Add: Unpresented cheques		
No. 862	$266.99	
No. 863	317.52	
No. 864	231.39	675.90
		31 045.71
Less: Undeposited receipts		5 313.71
Cash balance as per bank statement, 31 October		**$25 732.00**

Required

(a) Prepare a correct bank reconciliation statement. (*Hint:* Deduct the amount of the theft from the balance as per company records.)
(b) Indicate the three ways that Rowe attempted to conceal the theft and the dollar amount involved in each method.
(c) What principles of internal control were violated in this case?

PSA7.5 Prepare bank reconciliation statement and adjusting entries.   **LO4**

On 31 May 2018 Computec Ltd had a cash balance as per company records of $5681.50 debit. The bank statement from Community Bank on that date showed a credit balance of $7784.60. A comparison of the statement with the cash account revealed the following facts.

1. The statement included a debit entry of $60 for the printing of additional company cheques.
2. Cash sales of $836.15 on 12 May were deposited in the bank. The cash receipts journal entry and the deposit slip were incorrectly made for $846.15. The bank credited Computec Ltd for the correct amount.
3. Unpresented cheques at 31 May totalled $1276.25, and outstanding deposits were $836.15.
4. On 18 May Computec Ltd issued cheque no. 1181 for $685 to M. Helms on account. The cheque, which cleared the bank in May, was incorrectly journalised and posted by Computec Ltd for $658.
5. A $3000 note receivable was collected by the bank for Computec Ltd on 31 May plus $80 interest. The bank charged a collection fee of $20. No interest has been accrued on the note.
6. Included with the cheques paid was a cheque issued by Teller Pty Ltd to P. Jonet for $600 that was incorrectly charged to Computec Ltd by the bank.
7. On 31 May the bank statement showed a dishonoured cheque of $700 that had been issued by W. Hoad, a customer, to Computec Ltd.

Required
(a) Prepare the bank reconciliation as at 31 May 2018.
(b) Prepare the necessary adjusting entries as at 31 May 2018.

PSA7.6 Journalise transactions related to bad debts.   **LO8**

The following is an accounts receivable ageing schedule for Chin Ltd.

| Customer | Total | Not yet due | Number of days past due | | | |
			1–30	31–60	61–90	Over 90
Lee	$ 22 000		$10 000	$12 000		
Lu	40 000	$ 40 000				
Sing	57 000	16 000	6 000		$35 000	
Wong	34 000					$34 000
Others	126 000	96 000	16 000	14 000		
	279 000	152 000	32 000	26 000	35 000	34 000
Estimated percentage uncollectable		4%	7%	13%	25%	50%
Total estimated bad debts	$ 37 450	$ 6 080	$ 2 240	$ 3 380	$ 8 750	$17 000

At 31 December 2019 the unadjusted balance in Allowance for Doubtful Debts is a credit of $12 000.

Required
(a) Journalise and post the adjusting entry for bad debts at 31 December 2019.
(b) Journalise and post to the allowance account these 2020 events and transactions. (Use running-balance format.)
   1. 31 March, a $500 customer balance originating in 2020 is determined to be uncollectable.
   2. 31 May, a cheque for $500 is received from the customer whose account was written off as uncollectable on 31 March.
(c) Journalise the adjusting entry for bad debts at 31 December 2020, assuming that the unadjusted balance in allowance for doubtful debts is a debit of $800 and the ageing schedule indicates that total estimated bad debts will be $30 300.

PSA7.7 **Calculate bad debt amounts using different methods.** **LO8**

The following information relates to Eason Ltd for 2019:

Total credit sales	$200 000
Accounts receivable at 31 December 2019	46 000
Bad debts written off	2 900

Required

(a) What amount of bad debts expense will Eason Ltd report if it uses the direct write-off method of accounting for bad debts?

(b) Assume that Eason Ltd decides to estimate its bad debts expense based on 5% of accounts receivable. What amount of bad debts expense will the business record if it has an allowance for doubtful debts credit balance of $1600 at 31 December 2018?

(c) Assume the same facts as in part (b), except that there is a debit balance of $1150 in allowance for doubtful debts. What amount of bad debts expense will Eason Ltd record?

(d) What is the weakness of the direct write-off method of reporting bad debts expense?

PSA7.8 **Journalise entries to record transactions related to bad debts.** **LO8**

At 31 December 2019, the trial balance of Lexington Pty Ltd contained the following amounts before adjustment:

	Debits	**Credits**
Accounts receivable	$400 000	
Allowance for doubtful debts		$ 1 000
Sales		950 000

Required

(a) Based on the information given, which method of accounting for bad debts is Lexington Pty Ltd using — the direct write-off method or the allowance method? How can you tell?

(b) Prepare the adjusting entry at 31 December 2019, for bad debts expense assuming that the ageing schedule indicates that $11 750 of accounts receivable will be uncollectable.

(c) Repeat part (b) assuming that instead of a credit balance there is a $1000 debit balance in the allowance for doubtful debts.

(d) During the next month, January 2020, a $5000 account receivable is written off as uncollectable. Prepare the journal entry to record the write-off.

(e) Repeat part (d) assuming that Lexington uses the direct write-off method instead of the allowance method in accounting for uncollectable accounts receivable.

(f) What type of account is the allowance for doubtful debts? How does it affect how accounts receivable is reported on the statement of financial position at the end of the accounting period?

PSA7.9 **Journalise various receivables transactions.** **LO8, 9**

On 1 January 2020, Diego Ltd had accounts receivable $146 000, notes receivable $15 000 and allowance for doubtful debts $13 200. The note receivable is from Annabelle Ltd. It is a 4-month, 12% note dated 31 December 2019. Diego Ltd prepares financial statements annually. During the year the following selected transactions occurred.

Jan.	5	Sold $16 000 of merchandise to George Pty Ltd, terms n/15.
	20	Accepted George Pty Ltd's $16 000, 3-month, 9% note for balance due.
Feb.	18	Sold $8000 of merchandise to Swaim Ltd and accepted Swaim's $8000, 6-month, 10% note for the amount due.
Apr.	20	Collected George Pty Ltd note in full.
	30	Received payment in full from Annabelle Ltd on the amount due.

May	25	Accepted Avery Ltd $6000, 3-month, 8% note in settlement of a past-due balance on account.
Aug.	18	Received payment in full from Swaim Ltd on note due.
	25	The Avery Ltd note was dishonoured. Avery Ltd is not bankrupt and future payment is anticipated.
Sept.	1	Sold $10 000 of merchandise to Young Pty Ltd and accepted a $10 000, 6-month, 10% note for the amount due.

Required

Journalise the transactions.

PSA7.10 Calculate and interpret various ratios. **LO10**

Presented below is basic financial information from recent annual reports of Jumbo Airlines and Comfort Air:

	Jumbo Airlines (A$ million)	Comfort Air (NZ$ million)
Sales (assume all sales were credit sales)	$13 772	$4 046
Allowance for doubtful debts, start of year	27	2
Allowance for doubtful debts, end of year	6	3
Accounts receivable balance (gross), start of year	1 054	274
Accounts receivable balance (gross), end of year	1 088	322

Required

(a) Calculate the receivables turnover and average collection period for both entities. Comment on the difference in their collection experiences.

(b) Calculate the ratio of allowance for doubtful debts to gross accounts receivable (credit risk ratio) for each entity for the start of the year and at the end of the year. Comment on any apparent differences in their credit-granting practices.

PROBLEM SET B

PSB7.1 Calculate ratios to make business decisions. **LO1**

Samantha Perry is considering investing in a bakery that her friend, Caylie Lewis, owns. Following are selected items from financial records of the bakery.

Credit card sales	$46 000	Operating expenses paid	$22 000
Accounts payable	14 400	GST receivable	2 900
Food supplies	18 500	Cash at bank	9 200
Outstanding bank loan	15 000	Loan payment	4 000
Rent payable	4 800	Cash sales	22 500
Accounts receivable	7 200	Payment to suppliers	18 000

Required

(a) Calculate (i) cash inflows, (ii) cash outflows, (iii) assets and (iv) liabilities for Caylie's bakery business.

(b) Based on requirement (a), what can Samantha infer in relation to investing in Caylie's bakery?

(c) What other business information should Samantha seek to make the decision of whether to invest in Caylie's business?

PSB7.2 Identify internal control principles over cash disbursements. **LO3**

Rabbit Ears Pet Food Ltd recently changed its system of internal control over cash disbursements. The system includes the following features.

Instead of being unnumbered and manually prepared, all cheques must now be prenumbered. Before a cheque can be issued, each invoice must have the approval of Cindy Morris, the purchasing manager, and Ray Mills, the receiving department supervisor. Cheques must be signed by either Frank Malone, the accountant, or Mary Arno, the assistant accountant. Before signing a cheque, the signer is expected to compare the amounts of the cheque with the amounts on the invoice.

After signing a cheque, the signer stamps the invoice 'paid' and inserts within the stamp, the date, cheque number and amount of the cheque. The 'paid' invoice is then sent to the accounting department for recording.

Blank cheques are stored in a safe in the accountant's office. The combination to the safe is known by only the accountant and assistant accountant. Each month the bank statement is reconciled with the bank balance per books by the assistant managing director.

Required

Identify the internal control principles and their application to cash disbursements of Rabbit Ears Pet Food Ltd.

PSB7.3 **Prepare bank reconciliation statement and adjusting entries from detailed data.** **LO4**

The bank reconciliation statement for Watson Pty Ltd at 31 October 2018 is shown here:

WATSON PTY LTD Bank reconciliation statement as at 31 October 2018			
Cash balance as per bank statement			$12 367.90 Cr
Add: Outstanding deposits			1 530.20
			13 898.10
Less: Unpresented cheques			
	Cheque number	Cheque amount	
	2451	$1 260.40	
	2470	720.10	
	2471	844.50	
	2472	426.80	
	2474	1 050.00	4 301.80
Cash balance as per ledger			**$ 9 596.30 Dr**

The November bank statement showed the following cheques and deposits:

Information from bank statement					
Cheques				Deposits	
Date	Number	Amount	Date		Amount
1/11	2470	$ 720.10	1/11		$ 1 530.20
4/11	2471	844.50	4/11		1 211.60
4/11	2474	1 050.00	8/11		990.10
5/11	2475	1 640.70	13/11		2 575.00
8/11	2476	2 830.00	18/11		1 472.70
8/11	2477	600.00	21/11		2 945.00
15/11	2479	1 750.00	25/11		2 567.30
18/11	2480	1 330.00	28/11		1 650.00
27/11	2481	695.40	29/11		1 186.00
28/11	2483	575.50			
29/11	2486	900.00			
		$12 936.20			$16 127.90

The company's cash records for November showed the following:

Cash payments journal (extract)						Cash receipts journal (extract)	
Date	Cheque number	Amount	Date	Cheque number	Amount	Date	Amount banked
1/11	2475	$1 640.70	20/11	2483	$ 575.50	3/11	$ 1 211.60
2/11	2476	2 830.00	22/11	2484	829.50	7/11	990.10
2/11	2477	600.00	23/11	2485	974.80	12/11	2 575.00
4/11	2478	538.20	24/11	2486	900.00	17/11	1 472.70
8/11	2479	1 570.00	29/11	2487	398.00	20/11	2 954.00
10/11	2480	1 330.00	30/11	2488	800.00	24/11	2 567.30
15/11	2481	695.40				27/11	1 650.00
18/11	2482	612.00				29/11	1 186.00
						30/11	1 225.00
				Total	$14 294.10	Total	$15 831.70

The bank statement contained the following two items:
1. A credit of $1905 for the collection of an $1800 note for Watson Pty Ltd; interest of $120; a collection fee of $15. Watson Pty Ltd has not accrued any interest.
2. A debit for the printing of additional company cheques, $70.

At 30 November the cash balance as per company records was $11 133.90 and the cash balance as per bank statement was $17 394.60. The bank did not make any errors, but two errors were made by Watson Pty Ltd.

Required

(a) Using the procedure described under the heading 'Reconciliation procedure' (in section 7.4), prepare a bank reconciliation as at 30 November.

(b) Prepare the adjusting entries based on the reconciliation. (*Note:* The correction of any errors pertaining to recording cheques should be made to accounts payable. The correction of any errors relating to recording cash receipts should be made to accounts receivable.)

PSB7.4 **Prepare comprehensive bank reconciliation statement with internal control deficiencies.**

LO3, 4

Wizards and Dragons Pty Ltd is a very profitable small business. It has not, however, given much consideration to internal control. For example, in an attempt to keep clerical and office expenses to a minimum, the jobs of cashier and bookkeeper have been combined. As a result, Rob Rowe handles all cash receipts, keeps the accounting records, and prepares the monthly bank reconciliations.

The balance as per the bank statement on 31 October 2019 was $18 380. Unpresented cheques were: no. 62 for $126.75, no. 183 for $150, no. 284 for $253.25, no. 862 for $190.71, no. 863 for $226.80, and no. 864 for $165.28. Included on the bank statement was a credit entry of $200 indicating the collection of a note receivable for Wizards and Dragons Pty Ltd by the bank on 25 October. This entry had not been recorded by Wizards and Dragons Pty Ltd.

The entity's ledger showed one cash account with a balance of $21 892.72. The balance included undeposited cash on hand. Because of the lack of internal controls, Rowe took for personal use all of the undeposited receipts in excess of $3795.51. He then prepared the following bank reconciliation statement in an effort to conceal his theft of cash.

Cash balance as per company records, 31 October		$21 692.72
Add: Unpresented cheques		
No. 862	$190.71	
No. 863	226.80	
No. 864	165.28	482.79
		22 175.51
Less: Undeposited receipts		3 795.51
Cash balance as per bank statement, 31 October		**$18 380.00**

Required

(a) Prepare a correct bank reconciliation statement. (*Hint:* Deduct the amount of the theft from the balance as per company records.)

(b) Indicate the three ways that Rowe attempted to conceal the theft and the dollar amount involved in each method.

(c) What principles of internal control were violated in this case?

PSB7.5 Prepare bank reconciliation statement and adjusting entries. **LO4**

On 31 May 2019 Interactive Ltd had a cash balance as per company records of $10 949 debit. The bank statement from Community Bank on that date showed a credit balance of $15 569.20. A comparison of the statement with the cash account revealed the following facts:

1. The statement included a debit entry of $120 for the printing of additional company cheques.

2. Cash sales of $1672.30 on 12 May were deposited in the bank. The cash receipts journal entry and the deposit slip were incorrectly made for $1692.30. The bank credited Interactive Ltd for the correct amount.

3. Unpresented cheques at 31 May totalled $2552.50, and outstanding deposits were $1672.30.

4. On 18 May Interactive Ltd issued cheque no. 1181 for $1370 to M. Helms on account. The cheque, which cleared the bank in May, was incorrectly journalised and posted by Interactive Ltd for $1730.

5. A $6000 note receivable was collected by the bank for Interactive Ltd on 31 May plus $160 interest. The bank charged a collection fee of $40. No interest has been accrued on the note.

6. Included with the cheques paid was a cheque issued by Teller Pty Ltd to P. Jonet for $1200 that was incorrectly charged to Interactive Ltd by the bank.

7. On 31 May the bank statement showed a dishonoured cheque of $1400 that had been issued by W. Hoad, a customer, to Interactive Ltd.

Required

(a) Prepare the bank reconciliation as at 31 May 2019.

(b) Prepare the necessary adjusting entries as at 31 May 2019.

PSB7.6 Journalise transactions related to bad debts. **LO8**

The following is an accounts receivable ageing schedule for Cain Ltd.

Customer	Total	Not yet due	Number of days past due			
			1–30	31–60	61–90	Over 90
Aber	$ 20 000		$ 9 000	$11 000		
Bohr	30 000	$ 30 000				
Case	50 000	15 000	5 000		$30 000	
Datz	38 000					$38 000
Major Ltd	120 000	92 000	15 000	13 000		
	258 000	137 000	29 000	24 000	30 000	38 000
Estimated percentage uncollectable		3%	6%	12%	24%	50%
Total estimated bad debts	$ 34 930	$ 4 110	$ 1 740	$ 2 880	$ 7 200	$19 000

At 31 December 2019 the unadjusted balance in allowance for doubtful debts is a credit of $10 000.

Required

(a) Journalise and post the adjusting entry for bad debts at 31 December 2019.

(b) Journalise and post to the allowance account these 2020 events and transactions. (Use running-balance format.)

    1. 1 March, a $600 customer balance originating in 2020 is judged uncollectable.

    2. 1 May, a cheque for $600 is received from the customer whose account was written off as uncollectable on 1 March.

(c) Journalise the adjusting entry for bad debts at 31 December 2020, assuming that the unadjusted balance in allowance for doubtful debts is a debit of $1100 and the ageing schedule of accounts receivable indicates that total estimated bad debts will be $29 100.

PSB7.7 **Calculate bad debt amounts using different methods.**   **LO8**

The following information relates to Benson Ltd for 2019.

Total credit sales	$250 000
Accounts receivable at 31 December 2019	57 500
Bad debts written off	3 625

Required

(a) What amount of bad debts expense will Benson Ltd report if it uses the direct write-off method of accounting for bad debts?

(b) Assume that Benson Ltd decides to estimate its bad debts expense based on 5% of accounts receivable. What amount of bad debts expense will the business record if it has an allowance for doubtful debts credit balance of $2000 at 31 December 2018?

(c) Assume the same facts as in part (b), except that there is a debit balance of $1438 in allowance for doubtful debts. What amount of bad debts expense will Benson Ltd record?

(d) What is the weakness of the direct write-off method of reporting bad debts expense?

PSB7.8 **Journalise entries to record transactions related to bad debts.**   **LO8, 9**

At 30 June 2019, the trial balance of Shine Ltd contained the following amounts before adjustment.

	Debits	Credits
Accounts receivable	$350 000	
Allowance for doubtful debts		$ 1 500
Sales		875 000

Required

(a) Based on the information given which method of accounting for bad debts is Shine Ltd using — the direct write-off method or the allowance method? How can you tell?

(b) Prepare the adjusting entry at 30 June 2019 to record bad debts expense assuming that the ageing schedule indicates that $16 750 of accounts receivable will be uncollectable.

(c) Repeat part (a) assuming that instead of a credit balance there is a $1500 debit balance in the allowance for doubtful debts.

(d) During the next month, July 2019, a $4500 account receivable is written off as uncollectable. Prepare the journal entry to record the write-off.

(e) Repeat part (c) assuming that Shine Ltd uses the direct write-off method instead of the allowance method in accounting for uncollectable accounts receivable.

(f) What type of account is the allowance for doubtful debts? How does it affect how accounts receivable is reported on the statement of financial position at the end of the reporting period?

PSB7.9 **Journalise various receivables transactions.** **LO8, 9**

On 1 January 2020, Elam Ltd had accounts receivable $54 200 and allowance for doubtful debts $4700. During the year the selected transactions shown below occurred.

Jan.	5	Sold $6000 of inventory to Brooks Pty Ltd, terms n/30.
Feb.	2	Accepted a $6000, 4-month promissory note from Brooks Pty Ltd for balance due.
	12	Sold $7800 of inventory to Gage Pty Ltd and accepted Gage's $7800, 2-month note for the balance due.
	26	Sold $4000 of inventory to Mathias Ltd, terms n/10.
Apr.	12	Collected Gage Pty Ltd note in full.
June	2	Collected Brooks Pty Ltd note in full.
July	15	Sold $3000 of merchandise to Tritt Pty Ltd and accepted Tritt's $3000, 3-month note for the amount due.
Aug.	15	Tritt Pty Ltd's note was discounted for $2940.

Required

Journalise the transactions.

PSB7.10 **Calculate and interpret various ratios.** **LO10**

Presented below is basic financial information from recent annual reports of Sugar Mills Ltd and Tropico Ltd:

	Sugar Mills Ltd ($ million)	Tropico Ltd ($ million)
Sales (assume all sales were credit sales)	$3 754.9	$4 546.8
Allowance for doubtful debts, start of year	9.0	7.8
Allowance for doubtful debts, end of year	7.5	9.0
Accounts receivable balance (gross), start of year	562.1	671.0
Accounts receivable balance (gross), end of year	491.9	777.6

Required

(a) Calculate the receivables turnover and average collection period for both entities. Comment on the difference in their collection experiences.
(b) Calculate the ratio of allowance for doubtful debts to gross accounts receivable (credit risk ratio) for each entity for the start of the year and at the end of the year. Comment on any apparent differences in their credit-granting practices.

BUILDING BUSINESS SKILLS

FINANCIAL REPORTING AND ANALYSIS

Financial reporting problem: Health Care Equipment and Services Industry

BBS7.1 Go to the ASX website (www.asx.com.au) and search for the latest annual report for a company in the Health Care Equipment & Services industry group. Select **Prices and research**, then **Company information**, then select **View all companies** under the Company directory.

Required

Using the financial statements and reports, answer these questions about your chosen entity's internal controls and cash:

(a) What is the balance of cash shown in the statement of financial position at the beginning of the current period?
(b) How is cash defined in the notes to the financial statements?
(c) How much cash was provided by operating activities during the current period?
(d) Calculate the ratio of cash to daily cash expenses for the current period using the amount of cash reported in the statement of financial position.

Comparative analysis problem: Giorgina's Pizza Ltd

BBS7.2 The 2019 financial statements of Giorgina's Pizza are presented in chapter 1. The cash flow statement for Giorgina's for 2019 is reproduced below.

Required

(a) Calculate the ratio of cash to daily cash expenses for each year using the closing consolidated cash balance reported in the cash flow statement.

(b) Which year has the stronger cash position based on the ratios calculated?

	Note	2019 $'000	2018 $'000
GIORGINA'S PIZZA LIMITED Statement of cash flows for the year ended 30 June 2019			
CASH FLOWS FROM OPERATING ACTIVITIES			
Receipts from customers		245 357	221 324
Payments to suppliers and employees		(212 148)	(188 094)
Interest received		827	1 339
Interest paid		(304)	(338)
Income taxes paid		(8 847)	(5 972)
Net cash generated by operating activities	35	24 885	28 259
CASH FLOWS FROM INVESTING ACTIVITIES			
Payment for investment and business operations		(14 308)	(8 907)
Loans repaid by third parties		1 887	1 580
Payments for property, plant & equipment		(18 778)	(13 244)
Proceeds from sale of non-current assets		15 802	17 193
Payments for intangible assets		(7 400)	(5 606)
Net cash used in investing activities	36	(22 797)	(8 984)
CASH FLOWS FROM FINANCING ACTIVITIES			
Proceeds from borrowings		32 791	0
Repayment of borrowings		(15 380)	(18)
Return of share capital		(22 532)	0
Dividends paid		(15 572)	(12 716)
Proceeds from issue of equity securities		769	4 012
Net cash used in financing activities	37	(19 924)	(8 722)
Net increase (decrease) in cash and cash equivalents		(17 836)	10 553
Cash and cash equivalents at the beginning of the year		30 255	21 064
Effects of changes in exchange rates on cash held in foreign currencies	38	1 598	(1 362)
Cash and cash equivalents at the end of the year	35	**14 017**	**30 255**

CRITICAL THINKING

Group decision case

BBS7.3 Johanna and Jake Berkvom own Campus Fashions. From its inception Campus Fashions has sold goods on either a cash or credit basis, but no credit cards have been accepted. During the past several months, the Berkvoms have begun to question their credit sales policies. First, they have lost some sales because of their refusal to accept credit cards. Second, representatives of two banks have convinced them to accept their credit cards. One bank, City Bank, has stated that (1) its credit card fee is 4% and (2) it pays the retailer 96 cents on each $1 of sales within 3 days of receiving the credit card billings.

The Berkvoms decide that they should determine the cost of carrying their own credit sales. From the accounting records of the past 3 years they accumulate the following data.

	2020	2019	2018
Net credit sales	$600 000	$720 000	$480 000
Collection agency fees for slow-paying customers	2 940	3 000	1 920
Wages of part-time accounts receivable clerk	4 560	4 560	4 560

Credit and collection expenses as a percentage of net credit sales are as follows: uncollectable accounts 1.6%, invoicing and mailing costs 0.5%, and credit investigation fee on new customers 0.15%.

Johanna and Jake also determine that the average accounts receivable balance outstanding during the year is 5% of net credit sales. The Berkvoms estimate that they could earn an average of 10% annually on cash invested in other business opportunities.

Required

With the class divided into groups, answer the following:

(a) Present calculations for each year showing total credit and collection expenses in dollars and as a percentage of net credit sales.

(b) Determine the net credit and collection expenses in dollars and as a percentage of sales after considering the revenue not earned from other investment opportunities. (*Note:* The interest revenue lost on the cash held by the bank for 3 days is considered to be immaterial.)

(c) Discuss both the financial and non-financial factors that are relevant to the decision.

Ethics case

BBS7.4 The chief accountant of Shirts Galore Ltd believes that the entity's yearly allowance for doubtful debts should be 2% of net credit sales. The managing director of Shirts Galore Ltd, nervous that the shareholders might expect the entity to sustain its 10% growth rate, suggests that the chief accountant increase the allowance for doubtful debts to 4%. The managing director thinks that the lower profit, which reflects a 6% growth rate, will be a more sustainable rate for Shirts Galore Ltd.

Required

(a) Who are the stakeholders in this case?

(b) Does the managing director's request pose an ethical dilemma for the chief accountant?

(c) Should the chief accountant be concerned with Shirts Galore Ltd's growth rate in estimating the allowance? Explain your answer.

Communication activity

BBS7.5 As a new auditor for Farmers Chartered Accountants, you have been assigned to review the internal controls over cash receipts of Aardvark Pty Ltd. Your review reveals that cheques are promptly endorsed 'For account of Aardvark Pty Ltd only' so that they can be deposited only to Aardvark's bank account, but no list of the cheques is prepared by the person opening the mail. The mail is opened either by the cashier or by the employee who maintains the accounts receivable records. Mail receipts are deposited in the bank each week by the cashier.

Required

Write a letter to Izzy Rich, manager of Aardvark Pty Ltd, explaining the weaknesses in internal control and your recommendations for improving the system.

Communication activity

BBS7.6 With the growing sophistication of computers and technology, businesses are facing increasing risks from cyber attacks. Small to medium enterprises (SMEs) are particularly at risk of their financial data being compromised, and accountants can play an important role in implementing measures to help these businesses manage cyber security risks. An article published in INTHEBLACK, 'The accountant's role in combatting cyber crooks' by Jill Stewart (2016), discusses this very topic. Visit CPA Australia's INTHEBLACK website (www.intheblack.com/articles/2016/05/01/accountants-role-in-combatting-cyber-crooks) to view the article.

Required

Read the article and discuss the following questions in a group.

(a) Why are small to medium enterprises (SMEs) easy targets for hackers?

(b) What are some of the common forms of cybercrime?

(c) The article outlines some of the risk management strategies for deterring cybercrime. Briefly describe some of these detection and security solutions.

(d) Consider the various fields of accountancy such as management accounting, auditing and tax. In light of the growing demand for accountants who have data and IT expertise, would you consider taking on this specialty strand of accounting work?

ANSWERS

Answers to self-study questions

7.1 (d) 7.2 (b) 7.3 (d) 7.4 (c) 7.5 (b) 7.6 (c) 7.7 (a) 7.8 (c) 7.9 (a) 7.10 (c) 7.11 (d) 7.12 (c) 7.13 (c) 7.14 (a) 7.15 (a) 7.16 (c) 7.17 (a)

ACKNOWLEDGEMENTS

Photo: © michaeljung / Shutterstock.com
Photo: © TK Kurikawa / Shutterstock.com
Photo: © Jamie Farrantes / Shutterstock.com

Reporting and analysing non-current assets

After studying this chapter, you should be able to:

8.1 explain the business context of non-current assets and the need for decision making for these assets

8.2 describe how the cost principle applies to property, plant and equipment assets

8.3 explain the concept of depreciation

8.4 calculate depreciation using various methods and contrast the expense patterns of the methods

8.5 account for subsequent expenditures

8.6 account for asset impairments

8.7 account for the revaluation of property, plant and equipment assets

8.8 account for the disposal of property, plant and equipment assets

8.9 describe the use of an asset register

8.10 identify the basic issues related to reporting intangible assets

8.11 describe the common types of intangible assets

8.12 explain the nature and measurement of agricultural assets

8.13 account for the acquisition and depletion of natural resources

8.14 indicate how non-current assets are reported in the statement of financial position, and explain the methods of evaluating the use of non-current assets.

Chapter preview

For many business entities, making the right decision regarding non-current assets is critical because these assets represent huge capital investments. In this chapter we discuss this and other issues surrounding non-current assets. Our discussion is presented in three parts: property, plant and equipment; intangible assets; and other non-current assets. Property, plant and equipment (physical assets) are what commonly come to mind when we think of a business. However, business entities may also have important intangible assets. These assets, such as patents and brand names, lack physical substance but in some types of entities they are extremely valuable and are vital to the success of the business. Other non-current assets include natural resources such as minerals, oil and gas; and agricultural assets such as livestock, timber forests and vineyards.

The content and organisation of this chapter are as follows.

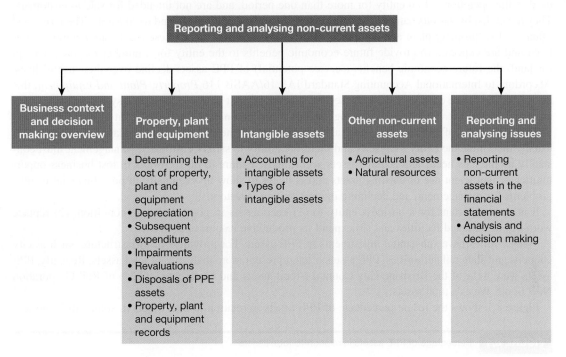

8.1 Business context and decision making: overview

LEARNING OBJECTIVE 8.1 Explain the business context of non-current assets and the need for decision making for these assets.

As chapter 1 explained, non-current assets are assets that are not expected to be consumed or sold within 1 year or the operating cycle. Thus, one simple way to define non-current assets is in the context of current assets, i.e. any asset that is not current. The proportion of current assets to non-current assets is highly dependent on the nature of a business and the way it structures its operations. Entities such as LG, Qantas and Air New Zealand have high proportions of their capital tied up in non-current assets and their choices can make a very big difference to their long-term sustainability.

Decision making is crucial for non-current assets. Throughout this chapter we discuss some of the key non-current asset issues requiring the decision-making skills first introduced in chapter 1. These decisions relate to both the internal and external context of the business. Examples relating to non-current assets include, 'What non-current assets does the business need to sustain and/or expand its future operations and profitability? How much of the businesses resources should be tied up in non-current assets?

Should the business buy or lease?' Such decisions can make the difference between success and failure. Other decisions pertain to the determination of the cost of non-current assets, estimates for depreciation, amortisation and impairment, accounting policies such as cost or revaluation models, depreciation methods, and primarily external decision-making tools such as analysis and interpretation based on financial statements.

You will find answers to some of these questions in this chapter.

8.2 Property, plant and equipment

LEARNING OBJECTIVE 8.2 Describe how the cost principle applies to property, plant and equipment assets.

Property, plant and equipment are assets that have physical substance (a definite size and shape), are used in the operations of an entity for more than one period, and are not intended for sale to customers. They are called by various names — tangible assets, plant and equipment, and fixed assets. The term most often used is 'property plant and equipment (PPE)'. By whatever name, these assets are generally long-lived and are expected to provide future economic benefits to the entity for a number of years. Except for land, the future economic benefits (service potential) of PPE assets decline over their useful lives. According to International Accounting Standard IAS 16/AASB 116 *Property, Plant and Equipment*, this decline in the future economic benefits (service potential) must be recognised on a systematic basis over an asset's useful life. This decline is recognised as depreciation expense in the profit or loss statement.

The acquisition of PPE assets is critical to the success of nearly all entities because these resources usually determine the entity's capacity and therefore ability to satisfy customers. Management must constantly monitor its needs and acquire assets accordingly. Failure to do so results in lost business opportunities or inefficient use of existing assets and is likely to show up eventually in poor financial results, problems for management, and declining interest among investors.

It is also important for a business entity to (1) keep assets in good operating condition, (2) replace worn-out or outdated facilities and (3) expand its productive resources as needed.

Many entities have substantial investments in PPE assets. For providers of infrastructure, such as city councils and state rail authorities, PPE assets often represent more than 75% of total assets. Recently, PPE assets were 81% of the Brisbane City Council's total assets and represented 97.3% of Rail Corporation New South Wales's total assets.

Figure 8.1 shows the recent percentage of PPE assets in relation to total assets in some other entities.

FIGURE 8.1 Percentage of PPE assets in relation to total assets

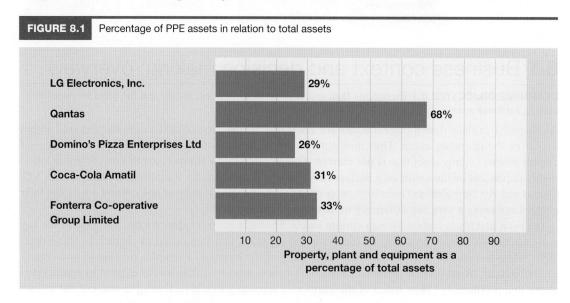

LG Electronics, Inc. — 29%
Qantas — 68%
Domino's Pizza Enterprises Ltd — 26%
Coca-Cola Amatil — 31%
Fonterra Co-operative Group Limited — 33%

Property, plant and equipment as a percentage of total assets

PPE assets are often subdivided into two classes:

- *property*, including land (such as a building site, and land improvements such as driveways and fences) and buildings (such as stores, offices, factories and warehouses)
- *plant and equipment*, such as cash registers, computers, office furniture, factory machinery and motor vehicles.

Note that land held for resale or other assets held for resale are excluded from the PPE category, and are classified as inventory.

Determining the cost of property, plant and equipment

PPE assets are initially recorded at cost in accordance with the cost principle of accounting. According to IAS 16/AASB 116, para. 6, '*Cost* is the amount of cash or cash equivalents paid or the fair value of the other consideration given to acquire an asset'. For assets that are constructed or built, costs (including interest on borrowed funds) are accumulated until the asset is ready for its intended use. IFRS 13, para. 9 defines **fair value** as 'the price that would be received to sell an asset or paid to transfer a liability in an orderly transaction between market participants at the measurement date'.

Cost consists of the fair value of all expenditures necessary to acquire the asset and make it ready for its intended use. For example, the purchase price, freight costs paid by the purchaser, and installation costs are all considered part of the cost of factory machinery. When an entity buys a non-current asset, it must decide whether to debit an asset account or an expense account. Examples of such spending range from LG's extension of its existing manufacturing plant to you replacing the flat tyre of your car.

Expenditures that increase an asset's capacity or efficiency or extend its useful life are called **capital expenditure**. So in the above example, the cost of LG's extension of its existing manufacturing plant should be classified as a capital expenditure as it enhances the capacity of the plant (an asset). The cost of a major overhaul that extends an asset's useful life is also classified as capital expenditure. These types of expenditures are capitalised and are debited to an asset account.

On the other hand, expenditures that do not extend an asset's capacity but merely maintain the asset in its working order are classified as **revenue expenditure**. These costs are expenses and are immediately matched against revenue. So, the costs of replacing the flat tyre of your car is considered a revenue expenditure as it does not extend the useful life of your car but merely maintains it in working order. These types of costs are said to be expensed and are debited to an expense account.

Determining which costs to include in the asset account and which costs not to include is very important. If a cost is not included in an asset account, then it must be expensed immediately. This distinction is important because it has immediate, and often material, implications for the profit or loss statement. In order to boost current profit, some entities have been known to capitalise expenditures that should have been expensed. For example, suppose that $10 000 of maintenance costs incurred at the end of the year are improperly capitalised to the equipment account (i.e. they are included in the asset account delivery truck rather than being expensed immediately in the maintenance expense account). If the cost of the truck is being allocated as an expense (depreciated) over a 5-year life, then the maintenance cost of $10 000 will be incorrectly spread across 5 years instead of being expensed in the current year. Current-year expenses will be understated by $10 000, and current-year profit will be overstated by $10 000. Figure 8.2 illustrates the distinction between capital expenditures and expenses for several delivery truck expenditures and their effects on the statement of profit or loss and the asset.

After the initial recognition of an asset at cost, an entity may choose to revalue its non-current assets to fair value. Accounting for the revaluation of non-current assets is explained later in this chapter.

The application of the cost principle to each of the major items consisting of PPE assets is explained in the following section.

Property

The cost of land includes (1) the cash purchase price, (2) settlement costs such as solicitor's fees, (3) stamp duty, and (4) accrued property taxes on the land assumed by the purchaser. For example, if the cash price is $50 000 and the purchaser agrees to pay accrued rates and land taxes of $5000, the cost of the land is $55 000.

FIGURE 8.2	Effects of capitalising versus expensing

	Debit	Credit	Type of repair	Effect on statement of profit or loss	Effect on asset
Capital expenditure	Delivery truck account (Asset)	Cash/Accounts payable	Overhauling the engine Extending storage capacity	Expenditures spread across many periods via depreciation expense, therefore higher profit in the current period	Higher asset — delivery truck account
Expense	Repair and maintenance expense	Cash/Accounts payable	Replacing tyres or windscreen Changing oil filter or lubrication	Amounts fully expensed in the current period, therefore lower profit in the current period	No effect on delivery truck account

All necessary costs incurred in making land ready for its intended use are recorded as an increase (debit) in the land account. When vacant land is acquired, its cost includes expenditures for clearing, draining, filling and grading. If the land has a building on it that must be removed to make the site suitable for construction of a new building, all demolition and removal costs, less any proceeds (amounts received) from salvaged materials, are included in the cost of the land and charged to the Land account.

To illustrate, assume that Hayes Manufacturing Ltd acquires real estate at a cash cost of $100 000. The property contains an old warehouse that is demolished at a net cost of $6000 ($7500 in costs less $1500 proceeds from salvaged materials). Additional expenditures are for the solicitor's fee $1000 and the stamp duty $2000. The cost of the land is $109 000, calculated as shown in figure 8.3.

When the acquisition is recorded, land is debited for $109 000 and cash is credited for $109 000.

Sometimes expenditures are made for landscaping, driveways, parking lots and fences. These are usually charged to the land improvements account, and depreciated over their useful lives.

All necessary expenditures relating to the purchase or construction of a building are charged to the buildings account. When a building is purchased, such costs include the purchase price, solicitor's fees and stamp duty. Costs to make the building ready for its intended use consist of expenditures for remodelling rooms and offices and replacing or repairing the roof, floors, electrical wiring and plumbing.

Helpful hint: Capitalising interest means including interest in the carrying amount of an asset instead of recognising it as an expense in the period in which it occurs.

FIGURE 8.3 Calculation of cost of land

Land	
Cash price of property	$100 000
Net removal cost of warehouse	6 000
Solicitor's fee	1 000
Stamp duty	2 000
Cost of land	**$109 000**

When a new building is constructed, its cost consists of the contract price plus payments made by the owner for architects' fees, building permits, and excavation costs. In addition, borrowing costs (interest) incurred to finance the project are included in the cost of the asset when a significant period of time is required to get the asset ready for use. In these circumstances, interest costs are considered as necessary as materials and labour. However, the inclusion of interest costs in the cost of a constructed building is limited to the construction period. When construction has been completed, subsequent interest payments on funds borrowed to finance the construction are recorded as increases (debits) to interest expense. IAS 23/AASB 123 *Borrowing Costs* sets out detailed rules for capitalising the interest, but generally the amount capitalised is the interest during the construction period.

Plant and equipment

The cost of equipment included in the accounts consists of the purchase price, freight charges and insurance during transit paid by the purchaser. It also includes expenditures required in assembling, installing and testing the unit. However, motor vehicle registration and accident insurance on an entity's trucks and cars are treated as expenses as they are incurred because they represent annual recurring expenditures and do not benefit future periods. Two points to consider in determining the cost of equipment are (1) the frequency of the cost — one time or recurring, and (2) the benefit period — the life of the asset or 1 year.

To illustrate, assume that Lenard Ltd purchases a delivery truck at a purchase price of $22 000. Related expenditures are for air conditioning $1320, painting and lettering $500, motor vehicle registration $350, and a 3-year accident insurance policy $1600. The cost of the delivery truck is $23 820, calculated as shown in figure 8.4.

FIGURE 8.4 Calculation of cost of delivery truck

Delivery truck	
Purchase price	$22 000
Air conditioning	1 320
Painting and lettering	500
Cost of delivery truck	**$23 820**

The cost of a motor vehicle registration is treated as an expense, and the cost of an insurance policy is considered a prepaid asset until the future benefits are consumed. These benefits are consumed over time as the policy expires. Thus, the entry to record the purchase of the truck and related expenditures is as follows:

Delivery truck	23 820	
Motor vehicle registration expense	350	
Prepaid insurance	1 600	
Cash		25 770
(To record purchase of delivery truck and related expenditures)		

A	=	L	+	E
+23 820				−350
+1 600				
−25 770				

Impact of goods and services tax (GST) on non-current assets

Although GST is included on goods and services, for the purpose of this chapter, you can ignore the impact of GST unless it is specifically stated that the figures include GST. As with all other assets in the accounts, with the exception of accounts receivable and accounts payable, the cost of non-current assets excludes GST. The only time GST impacts on journal entries is when the assets are purchased or sold. However, the following example is included to illustrate the impact of GST on the purchase of assets.

Assume Merten Ltd purchases factory machinery on account at a purchase price of $55 000. Related expenditures are for insurance during shipping $550, and installation and testing $1100. All figures include GST of 10%. The cost of the factory machinery is $51 500, calculated as in figure 8.5.

FIGURE 8.5   Calculation of cost of factory machinery

Factory machinery

Machinery price	$55 000
Insurance during shipping	550
Installation and testing	1 100
Purchase price factory machinery (GST inclusive)	56 650
Less: GST	5 150
Cost of machinery	**$51 500**

Thus, the entry to record the purchase and related expenditures is as follows:

Factory machinery	51 500	
GST paid	5 150	
Sundry accounts payable		56 650
(To record purchase of factory machinery and related expenditures)		

A	=	L	+	E
+56 650		+56 650		

Helpful hint: The above example has used the current Australian GST rate of 10%. However, the same principle applies regardless of the rate as that can change. New Zealand's current rate is 15%.

To buy or lease?

In this chapter we focus on assets that are purchased, but we want to discuss briefly an alternative to purchasing — leasing. In a lease, a party that owns an asset (the **lessor**) agrees to allow another party (the **lessee**) to use the asset for an agreed period of time at an agreed price. Some advantages of leasing an asset versus purchasing it are as follows.

1. *Reduced risk of obsolescence.* Frequently, lease terms allow the party using the asset (the lessee) to exchange the asset for a more modern one if it becomes outdated. This is much easier than trying to sell an obsolete asset.

2. *Little or no deposit.* Assets cost money. Although most entities can borrow money to buy assets, they still need to pay a deposit, usually of at least 20%. Leasing an asset requires little or no deposit.

3. *Shared tax advantages.* New entities typically do not make much money in their early years, and so they have little need for the tax deductions available from owning an asset. In a lease, the lessor gets the tax advantage because it owns the asset. The lessor often will pass these tax savings on to the lessee in the form of lower lease payments.

The main accounting issue is whether or not the lease arrangement should appear in the statement of financial position. IFRS 16/AASB 16 *Leases* defines a lease as a contract that allows an entity to use an asset (referred to as an underlying asset) for a period of time in exchange for consideration. There are two parties to a lease contract. The lessor is the owner of the underlying asset and provides another entity, the lessee, with a right to use that asset.

The accounting treatment required by the standard differs between lessees and lessors. The lessee is required to recognise both a right-of-use asset and a lease liability provided the lease is more than a year and is not immaterial. The cost of the right-of-use asset is equal to the present value of the future lease payments, plus any initial payments paid at the commencement of the lease term, less any lease incentives received. The lessee amortises the underlying asset over the term of the lease. The lease liability is equal to the present value of the future lease payments and is treated similarly to a bank loan. Each lease payment is split between a reduction in the lease liability and an interest expense component.

However, a lessor will recognise the lease payments depending on whether the lease is classified as a finance lease or an operating lease. A **finance lease** is where the lessor transfers to the lessee substantially all the risks and rewards incidental to ownership of the underlying asset. Some of the situations that can lead to a lease contract being classified as a finance lease include:

• ownership is transferred to the lessee before the end of the lease term
• the lessee has the option to purchase the underlying asset at a price that is sufficiently lower than its fair value at the date of the option
• the lease term is for the majority of the economic life of the underlying asset
• the present value of the lease payments amounts to almost all of the fair value of the underlying asset.

At the commencement of the lease term the lessor will recognise a lease receivable. Each payment received will be credited to this receivable account, with the interest components of the lease payments being recognised as interest revenue.

An **operating lease** is where the lessor *does not* transfer substantially all the risks and rewards incidental to ownership of a leased asset. If the asset is an *operating* lease, then the lease payments received are recognised by the lessor as rental or lease income in the statement of profit or loss and the cash at bank is debited.

LEARNING REFLECTION AND CONSOLIDATION

Review it

1. What are property, plant and equipment (PPE) assets? What are the major classes of PPE assets? At what value should PPE assets be recorded?
2. What are capital expenditures?
3. What are the two main types of leases?
4. What are the main advantages of leasing?

Do it

Assume that a delivery truck is purchased for $15 000 cash plus delivery costs to the dealer of $500. The buyer also pays $200 for painting and lettering, $600 for an annual insurance policy, and $400 for truck registration. Explain how each of these costs is accounted for.

▶

Reasoning

The cost principle applies to all expenditures made in order to prepare the delivery equipment ready for its intended use. It does not apply to operating costs incurred during the useful life of the equipment, such as petrol and oil, motor repairs and maintenance, registration and insurance.

Solution

The first three payments ($15 000, $500 and $200) are considered to be expenditures necessary to make the truck ready for its intended use. Thus, the cost of the truck is $15 700. The payments for insurance and the registration are considered to be operating expenses incurred during the useful life of the asset.

8.3 Depreciation

LEARNING OBJECTIVE 8.3 Explain the concept of depreciation.

As introduced in chapter 3, **depreciation** is the process of allocating to expense the cost of a PPE asset over its useful (service) life in a rational and systematic manner. Such cost allocation is designed to properly recognise expenses in accordance with the period concept (see figure 8.6).

FIGURE 8.6	Depreciation as a cost allocation concept

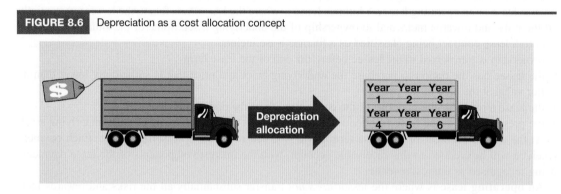

The journal entry to record depreciation for the period is to debit the depreciation expense account and credit *not* the asset account where the cost was recorded but a separate account entitled accumulated depreciation. Recognising depreciation for an asset does not result in the accumulation of cash for the asset's replacement. The balance in the **accumulated depreciation** account represents the total amount of the asset's cost that has been charged to depreciation expense since the asset was acquired; *it is not a cash fund.* The accumulated depreciation account is called a *contra account.* A **contra account** is reported as an offset to or reduction from a related account, being the PPE asset account where the cost was recorded. In the statement of financial position the **carrying amount** — cost less accumulated depreciation — is reported and in the notes to the accounts the original cost of the PPE asset and the accumulated depreciation are given to provide useful information concerning the age of the assets to the statement users. Carrying amount is also referred to as *book value.* It is important to understand that depreciation is a process of cost allocation, *not* a process of asset valuation. The carrying value of a PPE asset may differ significantly from its market value. In the final section of this chapter the reporting and analysing issues are shown in more detail.

Depreciation applies to land improvements, buildings, and plant and equipment. Each of these is considered to be a depreciable asset because its usefulness to the entity and its revenue-generating ability decline over the asset's useful life. Depreciation does not apply to land because its usefulness and revenue-generating ability generally remain intact as long as the land is owned. In fact, in many cases, the usefulness of land increases over time because of the scarcity of good sites. Thus, land is not a depreciable asset.

Helpful hint: Land does not depreciate because it does not wear out. However, its value may be impaired. This is discussed later in the chapter.

IAS 16/AASB 116 *Property, Plant and Equipment* outlines four factors that contribute to the decline in the future economic benefits of a depreciable asset.

1. *Usage of the asset.* The usage is determined by the expected capacity or physical output of the asset. A delivery truck's expected useful life, for example, would be the number of kilometres driven; for a photocopier it would be the number of copies made.
2. *Wear and tear through physical use of the asset.* A delivery truck that has been driven 100 000 kilometres will be less useful to an entity than one driven only 800 kilometres. Similarly, trucks and cars exposed to salt air and rain deteriorate faster than equipment not exposed to the elements. The maintenance program, and the type of care received by the asset when it is idle, will also affect an asset's capacity.
3. *Technical and commercial obsolescence.* Technical obsolescence is the process by which an asset becomes out of date before it physically wears out. Technological advances mean that new assets can produce the same goods or services more efficiently, giving a competitive advantage to entities having such assets. Many entities replace their computers long before originally planned because improvements in new computer technology make the old computers obsolete. Advances in robotic factory machinery make much of the older factory machinery and equipment obsolete. Today, many factories have fully automated production lines, with less human labour involved in the production process. Commercial obsolescence is where the revenue-producing ability of the asset declines because there is a fall in the market demand for the good or service produced by the PPE asset.
4. *Legal life or similar limits on the use of the asset.* If a lease on equipment expires and the equipment is returned to the lessor, then the period of the lease determines the maximum period that the economic benefits are obtained from the relevant asset.

Determining the useful life of the asset therefore requires judgement and reassessment each reporting period.

Factors in calculating depreciation

Three factors affect the calculation of depreciation, as shown in figure 8.7.

1. *Cost.* Considerations that affect the cost of a depreciable asset have been explained earlier in this chapter.
2. *Useful life.* **Useful life** is an estimate of the expected productive life (also called service life) of the asset to the entity. Useful life may be expressed in terms of time, units of activity (such as machine hours), or units of output. Useful life is an estimate. In making the estimate, management considers such factors as the intended use of the asset, repair and maintenance policies, vulnerability of the asset to obsolescence, and the legal life of the asset. The entity's past experience with similar assets is often helpful in deciding on expected useful life.
3. *Residual value.* **Residual value** is an estimate of the asset's value at the end of its useful life (and is also called *salvage value* or *trade-in value*). The value may be based on the asset's worth as scrap or salvage or on its expected trade-in value. Like useful life, residual value is an estimate. In making the estimate, management considers how it plans to dispose of the asset and its experience with similar assets.

FIGURE 8.7 Three factors in calculating depreciation

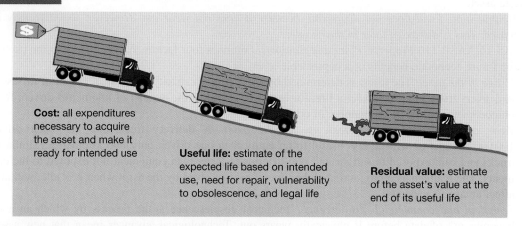

Cost: all expenditures necessary to acquire the asset and make it ready for intended use

Useful life: estimate of the expected life based on intended use, need for repair, vulnerability to obsolescence, and legal life

Residual value: estimate of the asset's value at the end of its useful life

---

LEARNING REFLECTION AND CONSOLIDATION

Review it

1. What is the relationship, if any, of depreciation to (a) cost allocation, (b) asset valuation, and (c) cash accumulation?
2. Explain the factors that contribute to the decline in the future economic benefits of a depreciated asset.

8.4 Depreciation methods

LEARNING OBJECTIVE 8.4 Calculate depreciation using various methods and contrast the expense patterns of the methods.

Depreciation is generally calculated using one of three methods:

- straight-line
- diminishing-balance
- units-of-production.

Like the alternative inventory methods discussed in chapter 5, each of these depreciation methods is acceptable under generally accepted accounting principles. Management selects the method it believes best measures an asset's decline in future benefits over its useful life. Once a method is chosen, it should be applied consistently over the useful life of the asset. Consistency enhances the comparability of financial statements between reporting periods. However, the depreciation method applied should be reviewed at the end of the reporting period and, if there is a significant change in the consumption of the future benefits, the depreciation method should be changed.

Depreciation affects the statement of financial position through accumulated depreciation, which is reported as a deduction from PPE assets. It affects the statement of profit or loss through depreciation expense.

Our illustration of the different depreciation methods is based on the following data relating to a small delivery truck purchased by Bill's Pizzas on 1 January 2018:

Cost	$ 13 000
Expected residual value	$ 1 000
Estimated useful life (in years)	5
Estimated useful life (in kilometres)	100 000

Straight-line depreciation

Under the **straight-line method**, depreciation is the same for each year of the asset's useful life because the future benefits are consumed at the same rate each year. To calculate the annual depreciation expense, we need to determine depreciable cost, which represents the total amount subject to depreciation. **Depreciable amount** is calculated as the cost of the asset or other amount substituted as cost, less its residual value. Depreciable amount is then divided by the asset's useful life to determine depreciation expense. Management must choose the useful life of an asset based on its own expectations and experience. The calculation of depreciation expense in the first year for Bill's Pizzas' delivery trucks is shown in figure 8.8.

FIGURE 8.8	Formula for straight-line method

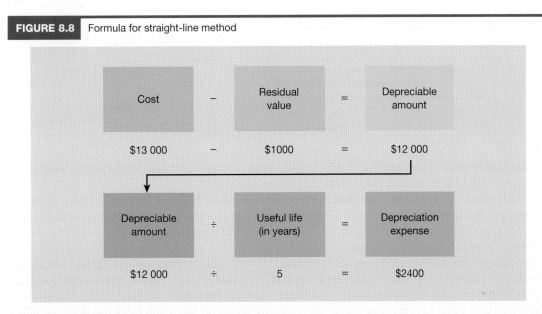

Alternatively, we can calculate an annual *rate* at which the delivery truck is being depreciated. In this case, the rate is 20% (100% ÷ 5 years). When an annual rate is used under the straight-line method, the percentage rate is applied to the *depreciable amount* (cost minus residual value) of the asset, as shown in the depreciation schedule in figure 8.9.

FIGURE 8.9	Straight-line depreciation schedule

BILL'S PIZZAS					
Calculation				**End of year**	
Year	Depreciable amount	× Depreciation rate	= Annual depreciation expense	Accumulated depreciation	Carrying amount
2018	$12 000	20%	$ 2 400	$ 2 400	$10 600*
2019	12 000	20	2 400	4 800	8 200
2020	12 000	20	2 400	7 200	5 800
2021	12 000	20	2 400	9 600	3 400
2022	12 000	20	2 400	12 000	1 000
			Total $12 000		

*Cost $13 000 – Year 1 depreciation $2400 = Carrying amount $10 600

The journal entry to record depreciation expense is:

Dec. 30	Depreciation expense—delivery truck	2 400	
	Accumulated depreciation—delivery truck		2 400
	(To record depreciation expense for the year)		

A	=	L	+	E
−2400				−2400

Note that the depreciation expense of $2400 is the same each year, and that the carrying amount at the end of the useful life is equal to the estimated $1000 residual value.

What happens when an asset is purchased *during* the year, rather than on 1 January, as in our example? In that case, the amount of depreciation for the first year is a proportion of the annual amount. If Bill's Pizzas had purchased the delivery truck on 1 April 2018, the depreciation for 2018 would have been $1800 ($12 000 × 20% × 9/12 of a year).

The straight-line method predominates in practice. For example, entities such as Qantas, Coca-Cola Amatil and Domino's use the straight-line method. It is simple to apply, and it writes down the asset appropriately when the use of the asset is reasonably uniform throughout the service life. The types of assets that give equal benefits over useful life generally are those for which daily use does not affect productivity. Examples are office furniture and fixtures, buildings, warehouses and garages for motor vehicles.

Diminishing-balance depreciation

The **diminishing-balance method** is called an 'accelerated method' because it results in more depreciation in the early years of an asset's life than does the straight-line approach. However, because the total amount of depreciation (the depreciable amount) taken over an asset's life is the same no matter which approach is used, the diminishing-balance method produces a decreasing annual depreciation expense over the useful life of the asset. That is, in early years, diminishing-balance depreciation expense will exceed straight-line, but in later years it will be less than straight-line. Managers might choose an accelerated approach if they think that an asset's usefulness will decline very quickly.

The depreciation rate remains constant from year to year, but the carrying amount to which the rate applies declines each year. The formula for calculating the annual depreciation rate is as follows:

$$\text{Depreciation rate} = 1 - \sqrt[n]{\frac{r}{c}}$$

where n = estimated useful life (in years)
      r = estimated residual value (in dollars)
      c = original cost of the asset (in dollars).

In relation to Bill's Pizzas:

$$\text{Depreciation rate} = 1 - \sqrt[5]{\frac{\$1000}{\$13\,000}}$$
$$= 1 - 0.5987$$
$$= 40\% \text{ (approximately)}.$$

Irrespective of which calculation is used to calculate the diminishing-balance depreciation rate, the accelerated method is justified when the future economic benefits are obtained in the earlier years rather than in the later years of an asset's useful life.

Using the rate of 40%, figure 8.10 presents the formula and the calculation for the first year of the delivery truck.

FIGURE 8.10 Formula for diminishing-balance method, after rate is determined

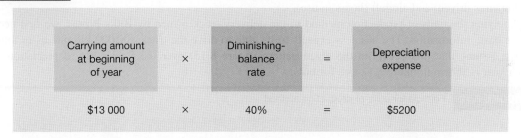

The depreciation schedule under this method is given in figure 8.11.

FIGURE 8.11 Diminishing-balance depreciation schedule

		BILL'S PIZZAS			
	Calculation			**End of year**	
Year	**Carrying amount beginning of year** ×	**Depreciation rate** =	**Annual depreciation expense**	**Accumulated depreciation**	**Carrying amount**
2018	$13 000	40%	$ 5 200	$ 5 200	$7 800*
2019	7 800	40	3 120	8 320	4 680
2020	4 680	40	1 872	10 192	2 808
2021	2 808	40	1 123	11 315	1 685
2022	1 685	40	685**	12 000	1 000
			Total $12 000		

*$13 000 − $5200
**Calculation of $674 ($1685 × 40%) is adjusted to $685 in order for carrying amount to equal residual value. This is because the rate was rounded to 40%, rather than 40.13% using the formula.

Another accelerated depreciation method is the sum-of-the-years-digits (SOYD). The depreciation charges are greater in the earlier years of an asset's life and become smaller as time goes on. Under the SOYD method, the depreciation rate changes each year. For example, if the useful life is 4 years, the sum of the years is calculated as $1 + 2 + 3 + 4 = 10$. The rate applied each year is a fraction of the remaining useful life at the beginning of the period — thus year 1 = 4/10 (40%), year 2 = 3/10 (30%), year 3 = 2/10 (20%), and year 4 = 1/10 (10%). Over the 4 years the depreciation equals 100% of the depreciable amount. This method is not used very often in practice, but it is another method which can be applied to vary the pattern of depreciation charges between the reporting periods.

Units-of-production depreciation

Under the **units-of-production method**, useful life is expressed in terms of the total units of production or the use expected from the asset. The units-of-production method is ideally suited to factory machinery — production can be measured in terms of units of output or in terms of machine hours used in operating the machinery. It is also possible to use the method for such items as delivery equipment (kilometres driven) and aircraft (hours in use).

Applying the units-of-production method to the delivery truck owned by Bill's Pizzas, we first need some basic information. The business expects to be able to drive the truck 100 000 kilometres in total. If we assume that this occurs in the given pattern (figure 8.13) over the 5-year life, depreciation in each year is shown in figure 8.12 as a formula.

FIGURE 8.12 Formula for units-of-production method

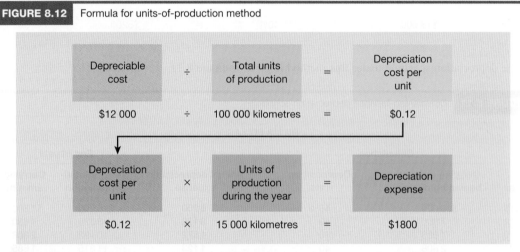

The depreciation schedule, using assumed kilometres data, is shown in figure 8.13.

FIGURE 8.13 Units-of-production depreciation schedule

		BILL'S PIZZAS			
	Calculation			End of year	
Year	Units of production (km) ×	Depreciation cost unit =	Annual depreciation expense	Accumulated depreciation	Carrying amount
2018	15 000	$0.12	$ 1 800	$ 1 800	$11 200*
2019	30 000	0.12	3 600	5 400	7 600
2020	20 000	0.12	2 400	7 800	5 200
2021	25 000	0.12	3 000	10 800	2 200
2022	10 000	0.12	1 200	12 000	1 000
	Total 100 000		$12 000		

*$13 000 − $1800

As the name implies, under units-of-production depreciation, the amount of depreciation is proportional to the production/activity that took place during that period. For example, the delivery truck was driven twice as many kilometres in 2019 as in 2018, and depreciation was exactly twice as much in 2019 as it was in 2018.

Management's choice: comparison of methods

Figure 8.14 presents a comparison of annual and total depreciation expense for Bill's Pizzas under the three methods.

	FIGURE 8.14	Comparison of depreciation methods	

Year	Straight-line	Diminishing-balance	Units-of-production
2018	$ 2 400	$ 5 200	$ 1 800
2019	2 400	3 120	3 600
2020	2 400	1 872	2 400
2021	2 400	1 123	3 000
2022	2 400	685	1 200
	$12 000	$12 000	$12 000

Periodic depreciation varies considerably among the methods, but total depreciation is the same for the 5-year period. Each method is acceptable in accounting because each recognises the decline in service potential of the asset in a rational and systematic manner. The depreciation expense pattern under each method is presented graphically in figure 8.15.

FIGURE 8.15 Patterns of depreciation

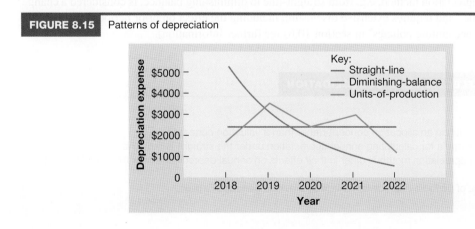

Depreciation disclosure in the notes

The choice of depreciation method must be disclosed in the notes to the financial statements. Figure 8.16 shows the depreciation and amortisation note from the 2019 financial statements of Giorgina's Pizza Limited.

FIGURE 8.16 Disclosure of depreciation policies

GIORGINA'S PIZZA LIMITED
Notes to the financial statements
for the year ended 30 June 2019

2.15 PROPERTY, PLANT AND EQUIPMENT
Plant and equipment are stated at cost less accumulated depreciation and impairment.
 Depreciation is calculated on a straight-line basis and is provided on property, plant and equipment. Land is not subject to depreciation.
 The gain or loss arising on disposal of any property, plant and equipment is determined as the difference between the sales proceeds and the carrying amount of the asset and is recognised in profit or loss.

The notes to the financial statements also disclose for each *class of non-current assets* the total amount of depreciation for the reporting period, the gross amount of depreciable assets and the related accumulated depreciation.

Revising periodic depreciation

Annual depreciation expense should be reviewed at least annually by an entity. If wear and tear or obsolescence indicates that annual depreciation is either inadequate or excessive, the depreciation expense amount should be changed.

When a change in an estimate is required, the change is made in current and future years but not to previous periods. Thus, when a change is made, (1) there is no correction of previously recorded depreciation expense, and (2) depreciation expense for current and future years is revised. The reason for this treatment is that continual restatement of previous periods would adversely affect users' confidence in financial statements.

Significant changes in estimates must be disclosed in the financial statements. Although an entity may have a legitimate reason for changing an estimated life, financial statement users should be aware that some entities might change an estimate simply to achieve financial statement goals. For example, extending an asset's estimated life reduces depreciation expense and increases current period profit.

A change in depreciation method, e.g. from straight-line to diminishing balance, is considered a change in accounting policy and requires extensive disclosure, including the effect on prior periods if practicable (see 'Changes in accounting policies' in section 10.6) for further information).

LEARNING REFLECTION AND CONSOLIDATION

Review it

1. Why is depreciation an allocation concept rather than a valuation concept?
2. What is the formula for calculating annual depreciation under the straight-line method?
3. How do the depreciation methods differ in their effects on annual depreciation over the useful life of an asset?
4. Are revisions of periodic depreciation made to previous periods? Explain.

Do it

On 1 July 2019, Snowy Ski Ltd purchased a new snow-making machine for $50 000. The machine is estimated to have a 10-year life with a $2000 residual value. What journal entry would Snowy Ski Ltd make at 30 June 2020 if it uses the straight-line method of depreciation?

Reasoning

Depreciation is an allocation concept. Under straight-line depreciation an equal amount of the depreciable cost is allocated to each period.

Solution

$$\text{Depreciation expense} = \frac{\text{Cost} - \text{Residual value}}{\text{Useful life}} = \frac{\$50\,000 - \$2000}{10} = \$4800$$

The entry to record the first year's depreciation would be:

June 30	Depreciation expense	4 800	
	Accumulated depreciation		4 800
	(To record annual depreciation on snow-making machine)		

8.5 Subsequent expenditure

LEARNING OBJECTIVE 8.5 Account for subsequent expenditures.

During the useful life of an asset, an entity may incur costs for ordinary repairs, additions and improvements. **Ordinary repairs** are expenditures to maintain the operating efficiency and expected productive life of the asset. They are usually fairly small amounts that occur frequently throughout the service life. Replacing parts on aircraft, painting buildings, and replacing worn-out gears on factory machinery are examples. They are debited to repair and maintenance expense as incurred, and are an expense in the statement of profit or loss. However, when businesses possess large values of plant assets, the repairs and maintenance costs can be material amounts.

Additions and improvements are costs incurred to increase the operating efficiency, productive capacity or expected useful life of the PPE asset. These expenditures are usually material in amount and occur infrequently during the period of ownership.

Helpful hint: These expenditures occur after all costs have been incurred to make the asset ready for its intended use when it was acquired.

When additional expenditure is incurred in relation to a non-current asset already in use, if the expenditure is material in amount and enhances the future economic benefits, such expenditure should be capitalised and depreciated over the remaining useful life of that asset.

8.6 Impairments

LEARNING OBJECTIVE 8.6 Account for asset impairments.

An additional measurement consideration in reporting the value of non-current assets is a test to ensure that the value reported in the statement of financial position is not above the present value of expected future cash flows the business will generate from the use of the assets. All items of PPE must be tested for impairment, in accordance with the requirements of IAS 36/AASB 136 *Impairment of Assets*. An **impairment loss** is the amount by which the carrying amount of an asset or a cash-generating unit exceeds its *recoverable amount*. The **recoverable amount** of an asset or a cash-generating unit is the higher of its fair value less costs of disposal and its value in use. **Value in use** is the present value of the future cash flows expected to be derived from an asset or cash-generating unit. When applying the impairment test it is recognised that at times the cash flows relating to individual assets are hard to identify, so the impairment test is applied to the *cash-generating unit*. A **cash-generating unit** is the smallest identifiable group of assets that generates cash inflows which are largely independent of the cash inflows from other assets or groups of assets.

Applying the impairment test to PPE assets is a two-step process. First, an entity must assess if there is any indication that an asset may be impaired, i.e. are there factors during the reporting period which would change the expected future cash flows that were originally estimated would flow to the business? Indicators include external factors such as a decline in the market value of the asset, changes in the technological, market, economic or legal environment, or an increase in the market interest rates; and internal factors such as physical damage, evidence of obsolescence, an adverse change or intended change in the intended use of the asset, or evidence from the internal reporting system indicating that the performance of the asset is worse than expected. The second step occurs if any of these indicators exist, and means that the *recoverable amount* must be estimated. This is described below.

Accounting for impairments

Applying the impairment test, you first need to calculate the fair value less costs of disposal and the value in use. It is the higher of these two values which must be compared to the carrying amount. It is only when the recoverable amount is lower that an impairment loss must be recognised. If the carrying value is below the recoverable amount, no entry is necessary, i.e. you do not write the asset up to the recoverable amount.

Helpful hint: If the fair value is easily determined and it is higher than the carrying value, then the value in use does not need to be calculated.

To illustrate how an impairment loss is accounted for, assume that on 30 June 2018 Microcloud has equipment with an original cost of $60 000 and accumulated depreciation of $35 000. Therefore the carrying amount is $25 000. The annual depreciation expense is $5000 per year, with 5 years of useful life remaining. The value in use (i.e. net present value from using the equipment) is $16 500 and the net selling price is $18 000 ($20 000 selling price less cost to sell of $2000). This is shown in figure 8.17.

FIGURE 8.17	Microcloud's original estimation for $60 000 asset, together with fair value and value in use information for 2018 and 2019

Year	Current depreciation	Accumulated depreciation	Carrying value	Fair value	Value in use
2018	$5 000	$35 000	$25 000	$18 000	$16 500
2019	5 000	40 000	20 000	18 000	21 500
2020	5 000	45 000	15 000		
2021	5 000	50 000	10 000		
2022	5 000	55 000	5 000		
2023	5 000	60 000	nil		

The recoverable amount is the *higher* of the net selling price ($18 000) and the value in use ($16 500), i.e. $18 000. This amount is then compared to the carrying value of the asset. Because the carrying value exceeds the recoverable amount, an impairment write-down of $7000 ($25 000 – $18 000) is required. The journal entry to record the impairment is:

June 30	Impairment loss	7 000	
	Accumulated impairment loss—computers		7 000
	(To record the impairment write-down on equipment)		

A	=	L	+	E
–7000				–7000

From 2019, the depreciation charge (after the impairment write-down) will be only $3600 ($18 000 ÷ 5) per year.

When the PPE asset is measured using the revaluation basis, any impairment loss is treated as a revaluation decrease. Revaluations are explained below.

Reversal of impairments

Reversal of impairment losses for PPE assets are permitted so long as the new carrying value is no greater than it would have been had no impairment loss been recognised in previous years.

To illustrate, consider the Microcloud example from earlier and refer to figure 8.17. The revised depreciation charge on equipment for 2019 is $3600. Accumulated depreciation is therefore $38 600 ($35 000 + $3600). The carrying value of the equipment at 30 June 2019 is:

Cost	$ 60 000
Less: Accumulated depreciation	(38 600)
Less: Accumulated impairment	(7 000)
Carrying value	$ 14 400

Assume that at 30 June 2019 the factors that caused the impairment write-down are no longer present, the net selling price is still $18 000 and the value in use is estimated to be $21 500. The recoverable amount is $21 500 (the higher of the net selling price and value in use). Can the impairment write-down be reversed? Yes, but only to what the equipment's carrying value would be if no impairment had taken place. Figure 8.17 shows that, had no impairment occurred, the carrying value on 30 June 2019 would have been $20 000 and this value is the maximum reversal permitted to a carrying value of $20 000. The adjustment is $5600 ($20 000 – $14 400). The journal entry necessary is:

July 1	Accumulated impairment loss—equipment	5 600	
	Income—impairment loss reversal		5 600
	(To record reversal of the impairment write-down on equipment)		

A	=	L	+	E
+5600				+5600

8.7 Revaluations

LEARNING OBJECTIVE 8.7 Account for the revaluation of property, plant and equipment assets.

A **revaluation** is a reassessment of the fair value of a non-current asset at a particular date. After initial recognition of a PPE asset at cost, IAS 16/AASB 116 requires each *class* of property, plant and equipment to be measured on either the cost basis or the revalued basis. A **class of non-current assets** is a category of non-current assets having a similar nature or function in the operations of the entity, and is shown without further dissection as a single line item in the notes to the statement of financial position. The cost model is the initial cost less accumulated depreciation and any impairment losses. The revaluation model permits the PPE asset — whose fair value can be measured reliably — to be carried at a revalued amount. This is the fair value at the date of the revaluation less any subsequent accumulated depreciation and impairments. If an entity chooses to measure its assets at fair value, then the revaluations must be kept up to date so that the carrying amount does not materially differ from fair value at the end of each reporting period. It is expected that revaluations be carried out every 3 to 5 years. This is sometimes described as a revaluation treadmill.

Revaluations may be either upwards or downwards. Any revaluation to a value above the up-to-date carrying amount is referred to as a revaluation increase, and any revaluation to a value below the up-to-date carrying amount is referred to as a revaluation decrease. If the asset is depreciable, then the carrying amount is the value net of the accumulated depreciation. Offsetting increases and decreases within the class of PPE assets is not permitted.

Revaluation increases must be credited directly to equity to an account called revaluation surplus rather than being treated as revenue in the profit or loss statement. Instead it forms part of comprehensive income. A revaluation decrease is treated as an expense in the statement of profit or loss.

Revaluation journal entries

The recording procedures for a revaluation are as follows:
1. Record depreciation to date of the asset revaluation.
2. Transfer the balance of the contra account, accumulated depreciation, to the asset account to give the asset's carrying amount.
3. Record the revaluation.

To illustrate, assume that the statement of financial position of Morris Decorators Ltd shows two classes of non-current assets on 31 December 2018, namely:

Land (Land A $150 000, Land B $150 000)		$300 000
Equipment	$75 000	
Accumulated depreciation	25 000	50 000

A decision is made on 1 January 2019 to revalue both assets: the land to a fair value of $290 000 (Land A $200 000 and Land B $90 000), and the equipment to a fair value of $45 000. The journal entries necessary for each asset are as follows.

Jan. 1	Land	50 000	
	Revaluation surplus		50 000
	(To record revaluation increase on Land A)		
1	Revaluation expense	60 000	
	Land		60 000
	(To record revaluation decrease on Land B)		
1	Accumulated depreciation—equipment	25 000	
	Revaluation expense	5 000	
	Equipment		30 000
	(To record revaluation decrease on equipment)		

A	=	L	+	E
+50 000				+50 000

A	=	L	+	E
−60 000				−60 000

A	=	L	+	E
+25 000				−5000
−30 000				

After the revaluation, the asset accounts would have the following balances:

Land	$290 000
Equipment	45 000

Helpful hint: To calculate the carrying amount of a depreciable asset, deduct accumulated depreciation from the asset cost account.

The equipment had a carrying amount of $50 000 ($75 000 − $25 000) before revaluation. The equipment had to be written down to the fair value of $45 000. Alternatively, the revaluation of the equipment can be split into two entries to make the journal entry a little clearer:

Jan. 1	Accumulated depreciation—equipment	25 000	
	Equipment		25 000
	(To close off accumulated depreciation against the asset)		
1	Revaluation expense	5 000	
	Equipment		5 000
	(To record revaluation decrease on equipment)		

A	=	L	+	E
+25 000				
−25 000				

A	=	L	+	E
−5000				−5000

Reversals of increases and decreases

If in a subsequent period the initial revaluations reverse, the revaluation increase (decrease) for an asset should be offset against the previous revaluation decrease (increase) to the extent of the amount of the previous revaluation. For reversals against the revaluation surplus, there must be balances relating to that asset available in the surplus. Using the previous example, assume that the piece of Land A owned by Morris Decorators is worth only $120 000 due to unforeseen contamination, and a decision is made to write down the land at 30 September 2021. The balance of the revaluation surplus is $50 000 credit arising from the previous revaluation of the land. The journal entry is as follows:

Sept. 30	Revaluation surplus	50 000	
	Revaluation expense	30 000	
	Land		80 000
	(To record the reversal of revaluation increase of Land A by writing down the revaluation surplus by $50 000 and recognising an expense of $30 000)		

A	=	L	+	E
−80 000				−50 000
				−30 000

In this example, Land A had an original cost of $150 000 and now has a carrying amount of $120 000. When the land is revalued downwards, the revaluation decrease of $80 000 reverses the previous increase ($50 000) recognised on 1 January 2019.

Impairment testing applies to assets held on the revalued basis. However, if the impairment is indicated, then the whole class of assets does not need to be adjusted. The asset which is impaired is written down and it is treated as a revaluation decrease.

The more complex issues relating to revaluations are covered in more advanced accounting courses.

8.8 Disposals of PPE assets

LEARNING OBJECTIVE 8.8 Account for the disposal of property, plant and equipment assets.

Entities dispose of PPE assets that are no longer useful to them. Figure 8.18 shows the three ways in which asset disposals are made: sale, scrapping, or exchange. (The accounting for exchanges is discussed in more advanced courses.)

FIGURE 8.18 Methods of PPE asset disposal

Sale
Equipment is sold to another party.

Scrapping
Equipment is scrapped or discarded.

Exchange
Existing equipment is traded for new equipment.

Whatever the disposal method, the entity must determine the carrying amount of the PPE asset at the time of disposal. Recall that the carrying amount is the difference between the cost of the PPE asset and the accumulated depreciation to date. If the disposal occurs at any time during the year, depreciation for the portion of the year to the date of disposal must be recorded. The carrying amount is then eliminated by reducing (debiting) accumulated depreciation for the total depreciation associated with that asset to the date of disposal and reducing (crediting) the asset account for the cost of the asset.

Sale of PPE assets

In a disposal by sale, the carrying amount of the asset is compared with the proceeds received from the sale. If the proceeds from the sale exceed the carrying amount of the asset, a gain on disposal occurs. If the proceeds from the sale are less than the carrying amount of the asset sold, a loss on disposal occurs.

Only by coincidence will the carrying amount and the proceeds from sale of the asset be the same. Gains and losses on sales of PPE assets are therefore quite common.

Gain on sale

To demonstrate a gain on sale of PPE assets, assume that on 1 July 2018 Wright Ltd sells office furniture for $16 000 cash. The office furniture originally cost $60 000 and as of 1 January 2018 had accumulated depreciation of $41 000. Depreciation for the first 6 months of 2018 is $8000. The entry to record depreciation expense and update accumulated depreciation to 1 July is as follows:

July 1	Depreciation expense	8 000	
	Accumulated depreciation—office furniture		8 000
	(To record depreciation expense for the first 6 months of 2018)		

A	=	L	+	E
−8000				−8000

After the accumulated depreciation balance is updated, a gain on disposal of $5000 is calculated as shown in figure 8.19.

FIGURE 8.19   Calculation of gain on disposal

Cost of office furniture	$60 000
Less: Accumulated depreciation ($41 000 + $8 000)	49 000
Carrying amount at date of disposal	11 000
Proceeds from sale	16 000
Gain on disposal of asset	**$ 5 000**

The entry to record the sale and the gain on sale of the PPE asset is as follows:

July 1	Cash	16 000	
	Accumulated depreciation—office furniture	49 000	
	Office furniture		60 000
	Gain on disposal		5 000
	(To record sale of office furniture at a gain)		

A	=	L	+	E
+16 000				+5000
+49 000				
−60 000				

Gains on disposal of PPE are classified as other income in the statement of profit or loss.

Loss on sale

Assume that instead of selling the office furniture for $16 000, Wright sells it for $9000. In this case, a loss of $2000 is calculated as in figure 8.20.

FIGURE 8.20   Calculation of loss on disposal

Cost of office furniture	$ 60 000
Less: Accumulated depreciation	49 000
Carrying amount at date of disposal	11 000
Proceeds from sale	9 000
Loss on disposal of asset	**$ (2 000)**

The entry to record the sale and the loss on sale of the asset is as follows:

July	1	Cash		9 000	
		Accumulated depreciation—office furniture		49 000	
		Loss on disposal		2 000	
		Office furniture			60 000
		(To record sale of office furniture at a loss)			

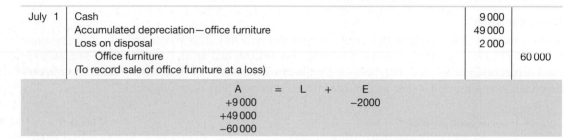

A = L + E
+9 000   −2000
+49 000
−60 000

Scrapping of PPE assets

Some assets are simply scrapped by the entity at the end of their useful life rather than sold. For example, some productive assets that are used in manufacturing may have very specific uses and consequently have no ready market when the entity no longer needs them. In this case the asset is simply scrapped.

Scrapping of an asset is recorded as a special case of a sale where no cash is received. Accumulated depreciation is decreased (debited) for the full amount of depreciation taken over the life of the asset. The asset account is reduced (credited) for the original cost of the asset. The loss on scrapping (a gain is not possible) is equal to the asset's carrying amount on the date of scrapping.

8.9 Property, plant and equipment records

LEARNING OBJECTIVE 8.9 Describe the use of an asset register.

Just as subsidiary ledgers are maintained for receivables, payables and inventory, as outlined in chapter 6, similarly a detailed asset register is maintained as an internal control procedure to protect and efficiently manage the property, plant and equipment (PPE).

The PPE assets in the general ledger are separated into functional asset groups, which means that there would normally be separate general ledger accounts for land, buildings, land improvements, motor vehicles, office equipment, office furniture, storage equipment and so on. Separate accounts may also be kept for different geographical locations, e.g. Christchurch and Perth. However, these general ledger accounts are summarised accounts and may contain many hundreds of individual items. Subsidiary ledgers are maintained to keep the details of the individual assets. The layout and content of a subsidiary ledger varies between entities, but at a minimum it would record the cost of the item, the depreciation rate and accumulated depreciation to date. For example, if the asset were a motor vehicle, the asset register information may include an asset identifying number (for stocktake and keeping track of its location), the date of purchase, the supplier, details of registration, insurance and maintenance information, depreciation method and rate, as well as depreciation each period. The master schedule from the asset register forms the source document for the journal entry to record depreciation for the period. Many entities use computerised asset registers which makes the detailed calculation of depreciation relatively easy.

4. How are the sales and scrapping of PPE assets accounted for?
5. What is the purpose of an asset register?

Do it

Overland Transport Ltd has an old truck that cost $30 000 and has accumulated depreciation of $16 000. Assume two different situations: (1) the entity sells the old truck for $17 000 cash; (2) the truck is worthless, so the entity simply scraps it. What entry should Overland use to record each scenario?

Reasoning
Gains and losses on the sale of PPE assets are determined by the difference between the carrying amount and the sale proceeds of the entity's asset. The expense on scrapping a PPE asset is the carrying amount at the time the asset is scrapped.

Solution
1. Sale of truck for cash:

Cash	17 000	
Accumulated depreciation—truck	16 000	
Truck		30 000
Gain on disposal [$17 000 – ($30 000 – $16 000)]		3 000
(To record sale of truck at a gain)		

Here the entity made a gain (profit) on sale of $3000, i.e. the proceeds of $17 000 less the carrying amount of $14 000.

2. Scrapping of truck:

Accumulated depreciation—truck	16 000	
Loss on disposal	14 000	
Truck		30 000
(To record scrapping of truck at a loss)		

8.10 Intangible assets

LEARNING OBJECTIVE 8.10 Identify the basic issues related to reporting intangible assets.

Intangible assets are defined in IAS 38/AASB 138 *Intangible Assets* as identifiable non-monetary assets that have no physical substance. Many valuable assets are intangible. Some widely known intangibles are the patents of the Apple iPod, the franchises of Domino's and the trademark 'swoosh' of Nike.

Financial statements do not report many intangibles. It is not uncommon for an entity's reported carrying amounts to differ from its market value because the financial statements are prepared using the cost principle. Although intangible assets account for most of the value of high-tech or so-called intellectual property entities, they are often not reported on the statement of financial position. Why not? Many intangibles are not recognised as assets because there is no external transaction

Accounting for intangible assets

Accounting standard IAS 38/AASB 138 *Intangibles* outlines the accounting rules for intangible assets.

Intangible assets can be separated into identifiable and unidentifiable. *Unidentifiable* intangible assets cannot be separated from the entity itself and are collectively referred to as goodwill. Goodwill can be recognised only if purchased in an external transaction. If an entity chooses not to separately identify an intangible asset, then the asset will be reflected in goodwill. The accounting treatment for goodwill is determined by IFRS 3 *Business Combinations*, which requires that goodwill be classified separately from other intangibles in the statement of financial position.

For an item to meet the criterion of an *identifiable* intangible, it must be capable of being separated or divided from an entity (whether sold, licensed, rented or exchanged), or it must arise from contractual or other legal rights. If an item does not meet the definition of an identifiable intangible then, unless it is part of a business combination, expenditure to acquire it or generate it internally must be recognised as an expense when incurred. Identifiable intangible assets include patents, development costs, copyrights, trademarks, brand names, franchises and licences.

Intangibles must be recognised at cost, the same as PPE assets. However, unlike PPE assets, intangibles cannot be subsequently measured at fair value or revalued unless there is an active market. An **active market** is one where the items traded in the market are homogeneous; willing buyers and sellers can normally be found at any time; and the prices are available to the public. By their nature, most intangibles would not have an active market and therefore would not be permitted to be revalued.

There is great variation in the recognition, valuation and reporting of intangibles. If the asset is generated from internal expenditure on research and development, the asset will not be recognised. However, when purchased in an external transaction it will be recognised.

Amortisation

The accounting treatment for intangibles is based on their useful life. If the intangible asset has a finite useful life then, as occurs with PPE assets, its cost will be systematically written down. The term used to describe the allocation of the cost of an intangible asset to expense is **amortisation** rather than depreciation. To record amortisation expense, the same accounting treatment applies as is used for depreciation. Intangible assets that are amortised are typically done so on the straight-line basis. For example, the legal life of a patent is 20 years. The cost of the patent should be amortised over its 20-year legal life or its useful life, whichever is shorter. To illustrate the calculation of patent amortisation, assume that National Labs Ltd purchases a patent at a cost of $60 000. If the useful life of the patent is estimated to be 8 years, the annual amortisation expense is $7500 ($60 000 ÷ 8). The following entry records the annual amortisation:

Dec. 31	Amortisation expense	7 500	
	Accumulated amortisation—patents		7 500
	(To record patent amortisation)		

A	=	L	+	E
−7500				−7500

When analysing an entity that has significant intangibles, the reasonableness of the estimated useful life should be evaluated. In determining useful life, the entity should consider obsolescence, inadequacy and other factors. These may cause a patent or other intangible asset to become economically ineffective before the end of its legal life. For example, suppose a computer hardware manufacturer obtained a patent on a new computer chip it had developed. The legal life of the patent is 20 years. From experience, however, we know that the useful life of a computer chip patent is rarely more than 5 years, because new superior chips are developed so rapidly, and existing chips become obsolete. Consequently, we would question the amortisation expense of an entity if it amortised its patent on a computer chip for longer than a 5-year period. Amortising an intangible over a period that is too long will understate amortisation expense, overstate the entity's profit, and overstate its assets.

Intangibles with indefinite useful lives are not amortised. This is discussed below.

Figure 8.21 contains an extract from the summary of significant accounting policies for a fictional company as an example of disclosure of accounting for different types of intangible assets.

FIGURE 8.21 Accounting policy note in financial statements

COMPANY X
Notes to the financial accounts
for the year ended 30 June 2019

INTANGIBLE ASSETS
The cost of acquiring an intangible asset with a finite life is amortised from the date the underlying asset is held ready for use on a straight-line basis over its estimated useful life, which is as follows:

Software	2–5 years
Other intangibles	4–20 years

   Amortisation is accelerated where the estimated useful life is deemed to have diminished due to technological change or market conditions.

IMPAIRMENT OF ASSETS
Goodwill
Goodwill is not subject to amortisation but is tested for impairment annually or whenever there is an indication that the asset may be impaired. For the purpose of impairment testing, assets are grouped into cash-generating units. If the recoverable amount of the cash-generating unit is less than the carrying amount of the unit, the impairment loss is firstly allocated to the carrying amount of any goodwill allocated to the unit. Impairment losses recognised for goodwill are not reversed in a subsequent period. The recoverable amount is the higher of fair value less costs to sell and value in use.

Subsequent expenditure

Any subsequent expenditure on intangible assets is rarely capitalised due to the nature of such assets, i.e. it is unlikely that you could replace part of an intangible asset. Therefore, most subsequent expenditures are likely to maintain the expected future economic benefits embodied in an existing intangible asset rather than meet the definition of an intangible asset, and hence the costs are expensed and not capitalised. IAS 38/AASB 138 requires any subsequent expenditure on brand names, mastheads, publishing titles, customer lists and items similar in substance (whether externally purchased or internally generated) to be recognised in profit or loss as incurred, thereby avoiding the recognition of internally generated goodwill.

Impairment

Intangibles with finite useful lives are subject to asset impairment write-downs using the same methodology described for PPE assets earlier in this chapter. Intangibles (including goodwill) with indefinite useful lives are *not amortised* but are subject to an *annual impairment test*, irrespective of whether any indicators of impairment exist. That is, the recoverable amount of intangibles with indefinite useful lives must be calculated annually. Reversal of impairment write-downs are permitted for identifiable intangibles but not for goodwill.

   Amortisation and impairment choices require a high degree of judgement. The following decision-making toolkit outlines an example of the decisions that need to be made when examining entities with high proportions of intangibles and the tools you can use to evaluate, compare and make decisions on such aspects as investing, extending credit or job security.

DECISION-MAKING TOOLKIT

Decision/issue	Info needed for analysis	Tool or technique to use for decision	How to evaluate results to make decision
Is the entity's amortisation of intangibles reasonable?	Estimated useful life of intangibles from notes to financial statements of this entity and its competitors	If the entity's estimated useful life significantly exceeds that of competitors or does not seem reasonable in light of the circumstances, the reason for the difference should be investigated.	Too high an estimated useful life will result in understating amortisation expense and overstating profit.

8.11 Types of intangible assets

LEARNING OBJECTIVE 8.11 Describe the common types of intangible assets.

Patents

A **patent** is an exclusive right granted by IP Australia, a federal government agency that enables the recipient to manufacture, sell or otherwise control an invention for a period of 20 years from the date of the grant. The New Zealand equivalent is IPONZ, a NZ government agency. The initial cost of a patent is the cash or cash equivalent price paid to acquire the patent.

The saying 'A patent is only as good as the money you're prepared to spend defending it' is very true. Many patents are subject to some type of litigation by competitors. If the owner incurs legal costs in successfully defending the patent in an infringement suit, such costs are considered necessary to establish the validity of the patent. Thus, they are added to the Patent account and amortised over the remaining useful life of the patent.

Research and development costs

Research and development costs are expenditures that may lead to patents, copyrights, new processes and new products. Many entities spend considerable sums of money on research and development in an ongoing effort to develop new products or processes. For example, LG spent 2.4 billion on research and development in 2016. There are uncertainties in identifying the extent and timing of the future benefits of these expenditures. As a result, research and development costs are usually recorded as an expense when incurred, whether the research and development is successful or not.

Research costs must be expensed when incurred. Development costs are permitted to be capitalised if certain criteria are met which demonstrate that the costs will be recovered in the future by the entity selling or using the intangible asset.

Assume that Laser Scanner Ltd spent $3 million on research and development that resulted in two highly successful patents. Only the development costs may be included in the cost of the patents. However, due to the uncertainty at the time they were incurred, the costs are recorded as an expense.

Many disagree with this accounting approach. They argue that to expense these costs leads to understated assets and understated profit. Others, however, argue that capitalising these costs would lead to highly speculative assets on the statement of financial position.

Copyright

Copyright gives the owner the exclusive right to reproduce and sell an artistic or published work. In Australia, copyright extends, in most cases, for the life of the creator plus 70 years. The cost of the copyright consists of the cost of acquiring and defending it. The useful life of a copyright generally is significantly shorter than its legal life. Therefore, it should be amortised over its useful life. However, in Australia it is often held at cost and not amortised.

Trademarks and brand names

A **trademark** or **brand name** is a word, phrase, jingle or symbol that distinguishes or identifies a particular business or product. Brand names like Domino's, LG, IKEA, Kleenex, Coca-Cola, Big Mac and iPod create immediate product identification and generally enhance the sale of the product. The creator or original user may obtain the exclusive legal right to the trademark or brand name by registering it with IP Australia. Such registration may be renewed indefinitely as long as the trademark or brand name is in use.

If the trademark or brand name is purchased, the cost is the purchase price. If it is developed by the entity itself, the cost must be expensed as these items cannot be distinguished from the expenditures incurred in developing the business as a whole.

Trademarks and brand names have indefinite useful lives and are not amortised but must be impairment-tested annually.

Franchises and licences

When you drive down the street in your RAV4 purchased from a Toyota dealer, fill up your petrol tank at the corner Mobil service station, eat lunch at Gloria Jean's, pick up a pizza from Domino's or make plans to holiday at a Club Med resort, you are dealing with franchises. A **franchise** is a contractual arrangement under which the franchisor grants the franchisee the right to sell certain products, to render specific services, or to use certain trademarks or brand names, usually within a designated geographic area.

Another type of franchise, granted by a government body, permits the entity to use public property in performing its services. Examples are the use of city streets for a bus service or taxi service; the use of public land for telephone, electric and cable television lines; and the use of airwaves for radio or TV broadcasting. Such operating rights are referred to as **licences**.

Franchises and licences may be granted for a definite period of time, an indefinite period, or perpetually. When costs can be identified with the acquisition of the franchise or licence, an intangible asset should be recognised. Annual payments made under a franchise agreement should be recorded as operating expenses in the period in which they are incurred. Where franchises and licences are for a limited period of time, the cost of a franchise (or licence) should be amortised as operating expense over the useful life.

Goodwill

Goodwill represents the value of all favourable attributes that relate to an entity and is defined as the future benefits from unidentifiable assets. These include exceptional management, desirable location, good customer relations, skilled employees, high-quality products, fair pricing policies, and harmonious relations with employees. Goodwill is associated with the entity *as a whole* — unlike other assets such as investments, PPE assets and even other intangibles which can be sold *individually* in the marketplace.

If goodwill can be associated only with the entity as a whole, how can it be determined? Certainly, many entities have many of the factors cited above (exceptional management, desirable location, and so on). However, to determine the amount of goodwill in these situations would be difficult and very subjective. In other words, to recognise goodwill without an exchange transaction that puts a value on the goodwill would lead to subjective valuations that do not contribute to the reliability of financial statements. Therefore, goodwill is recorded only when there is an exchange transaction that involves the purchase of an entire business entity. When an entire entity is purchased, goodwill is the excess of the cost of acquisition over the fair value of the identifiable net assets (assets less liabilities) acquired.

In recording the purchase of an entity, the net assets are shown at their fair values, cash is credited for the purchase price, and the difference is recorded as the cost of goodwill. Goodwill is not amortised but is subject to an annual impairment test.

LEARNING REFLECTION AND CONSOLIDATION

Review it

1. Identify the major types of identifiable intangible assets and the accounting treatment for them.
2. Explain the accounting for research and development costs.
3. What is goodwill? Explain the accounting treatment of goodwill.

8.12 Other non-current assets

LEARNING OBJECTIVE 8.12 Explain the nature and measurement of agricultural assets.

In this and the following section of the chapter we examine two types of assets related to specific industries: agricultural assets and natural resources.

Agricultural assets

An important issue for Australia and New Zealand is the accounting treatment of agricultural assets. IAS 41/AASB 141 *Agriculture* prescribes the accounting treatment and disclosures relating to agricultural activity. An **agricultural activity** is the management by an entity of the biological transformation of biological assets for sale, into agricultural produce, or into additional biological assets. A **biological asset** is a living animal or plant. Table 8.1 provides examples of biological assets, agricultural produce, and products that are the result of processing after harvest.

IAS 41/AASB 141 requires *biological assets* to be recognised when the assets can be reliably measured, it is probable that the future economic benefits will eventuate, and the fair value or cost of the asset can be reliably measured. The standard requires biological assets to be measured on initial recognition and at the end of each reporting period at fair value less estimated point-of-sale costs. Point-of-sale costs include commissions to brokers and dealers, charges by commodity exchanges, transfer taxes and duties. However, transport or other costs incurred to get the produce to market are not point-of-sale costs. Any changes in the measurement of biological assets at the end of each reporting period are included in the profit or loss in the period the change arises. Where no active market exists, then one or more of the following, when available, may be used as the best indicator of the fair value: the most recent market transaction price, provided there has been no significant change in economic circumstances between the date of that transaction and the end of the reporting period; market prices for similar assets with adjustment to reflect differences; and/or sector benchmarks such as the value of an orchard expressed per export tray, bushel or hectare, or the value of cattle expressed per kilogram of meat. The change in the value of the asset is reflected in the profit for the period. The journal entry to record the change in value debits (credits) the biological asset account to reflect the increase (decrease) in the value for the period, and credits (debits) a revenue (expense) account.

TABLE 8.1 Examples of agricultural produce

Biological assets	Agricultural produce	Products that are the result of processing after harvest
Sheep	Wool	Yarn, carpet
Trees in a timber plantation	Felled trees	Logs, lumber
Dairy cattle	Milk	Cheese
Pigs	Carcass	Sausages, cured hams
Cotton plants	Harvested cotton	Thread, clothing
Sugarcane	Harvested cane	Sugar
Tobacco plants	Picked leaves	Cured tobacco
Tea bushes	Picked leaves	Tea
Grape vines	Picked grapes	Wine
Fruit trees	Picked fruit	Processed fruit
Oil palms	Picked fruit	Palm oil
Rubber trees	Harve latex	Rubber products

Source: IAS 41/AASB 141 *Agriculture*, para. 4.

When harvested, biological assets become **agricultural produce** and are treated as inventory. The deemed cost when applying IAS 2/AASB 102 *Inventories* is the fair value less estimated point-of-sale costs at the point of harvest.

In the 2019 financial statements, Fresh Harvest Group disclosed biological assets (almond trees) of $46.1 million. The accounting policy and details of the biological assets are shown in figure 8.22.

FIGURE 8.22 Extract from accounting policy note in financial statements

FRESH HARVEST GROUP
Annual report 2019

(F) BIOLOGICAL ASSETS (extract only)
Almond trees
Almond trees are classified as a biological asset and valued in accordance with AASB 141 *Agriculture*.
   The fair value of almond trees is reviewed at the end of each period to ensure compliance with AASB 141. The fair value is measured using a discounted cash flow methodology of 12%.
   The discounted cash flow methodology incorporates the following factors.
- An estimated 25-year economic life for almond trees.
- Selling prices based on long-term averages of $5 per kg.
- Growing, processing and selling costs are based on long-term averages.
- Nursery trees are grown by the company for sale to external almond orchard owners and for use in almond orchards owned by the company. Nursery trees are carried at fair value.

8.13 Natural resources

LEARNING OBJECTIVE 8.13 Account for the acquisition and depletion of natural resources.

Natural resources or wasting assets are another special type of asset. Unlike agricultural assets, they are not regenerating. Entities in the extractive industries are involved in the search and extraction from the ground of natural substances of commercial value, such as minerals, oil and natural gas. These industries involve large investments and risk, as a viable deposit may not be found, and it can be many years (reporting periods) before the deposits are converted into inventory ready for sale. IFRS 6 *Exploration for and Evaluation of Mineral Resources* prescribes the accounting treatment for costs associated with extraction of natural resources. These include costs such as topographical and geophysical surveys, test drilling and evaluation of the quality of the resource found.

The standard does not prescribe valuation and recognition criteria for the mineral or oil deposits discovered. Although the statement of financial position does not reflect the value of the resources, extensive disclosures are made in annual reports concerning activities of these entities. The requirements of the accounting standard are complex and are covered in more advanced accounting courses. In general, however, the standard does permit, in certain cases, the capitalisation of the pre-production costs, until the resource is extracted. Then these capitalised costs are assigned (apportioned) as part of the inventory cost.

In the 2019 financial statements of Nature's Minerals Limited, $2153 million of exploration and evaluation assets were carried forward on the statement of financial position. This represents 8.5% of total assets.

Amortisation (depletion)

Once production has begun, the pre-production costs need to be charged to inventory by an appropriate amortisation. **Depletion** or amortisation is the periodic allocation of the cost of natural resources to reflect the units removed. The depletion rate is calculated in the same way as the units-of-production method for depreciation. The following example demonstrates this.

On 1 July 2018, Wallace Tin Mine had capitalised pre-production costs to the value of $150 million with a residual value of $10 million expected at the end of the mine lease. The mine is estimated to contain 7 million tonnes of ore. During the year the mine produced 2 million tonnes and direct production costs were $120 million. The depletable amount is $140 million ($150 million – $10 million). The depletion rate is calculated by dividing the depletable costs by the total estimated production. This rate is then applied to this year's production. Figure 8.23 presents the formula and calculation of depletion for 2019.

FIGURE 8.23   Formula for calculating depletion

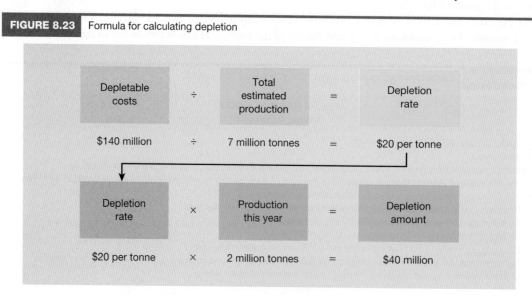

The journal entry to record the depletion is:

June 30	Inventory of ore	40 000 000	
	Accumulated depletion—tin mine		40 000 000
	(To record the depletion for the year)		

A	=	L	+	E
+40 m				
−40 m				

The pre-production costs are eventually expensed as part of cost of sales when the ore is sold. At the end of 2019, Wallace Tin Mine would show an asset of $110 million ($150 million − $40 million depletion).

8.14 Reporting and analysing issues

LEARNING OBJECTIVE 8.14 Indicate how non-current assets are reported in the statement of financial position, and explain the methods of evaluating the use of non-current assets.

Reporting non-current assets in the financial statements

IAS 1/AASB 101 *Presentation of Financial Statements* determines the minimum classification of assets that must be shown in the statement of financial position. Under the 'non-current assets' heading, property, plant and equipment, intangibles and land agricultural assets/biological assets are listed as separate categories. For an entity in the extractive industry, there would also be a separate line item for the oil and gas assets. There are requirements for extensive note disclosures of accounting policies and the break-up of the summarised accounts into separate categories.

If an entity has an asset/group of non-current assets, and it is highly probable that the future benefits will be derived from sale rather than from continued use, then depreciation ceases on this asset/group of assets. The asset/group of assets is measured at the lower of its/their carrying amount and fair value less costs of disposal.

Analysis and decision making

Decision makers can use information about PPE assets to analyse the entity's use of those assets. We will use three measures to analyse PPE assets: average useful life, average age of PPE assets, and asset turnover.

Average useful life

By selecting a longer estimated useful life, an entity spreads the cost of its PPE assets over a longer period of time. As a result, the amount of depreciation expense reported in each period is lower and profit is higher. A more conservative entity will choose a shorter estimated useful life and will have a lower reported profit.

Many entities do not provide precise disclosures about the estimated useful life of specific assets in the notes to financial statements. For example, a common disclosure might read: 'Plant and equipment assets are depreciated using the straight-line method over estimated useful lives ranging from 5 to 40 years.' This statement makes it difficult to determine whether an entity is using a conservative approach for depreciation. It is unclear, for example, how many assets are being depreciated using short lives and how many using long lives. To overcome this problem, we can estimate the **average useful life** of assets for an entity and compare it to that of its competitors. Again, we will use the two companies introduced in chapter 1, Original Furnishings Limited and Artistry Furniture Limited. The average useful life is estimated by dividing the average cost of property, plant and equipment by the depreciation expense. The following data are for Original Furnishings.

	Original Furnishings Limited ('000)
Total cost of plant, equipment and fixtures and fittings and leasehold improvements assets (2019)	$120 260
Total cost of plant, equipment and fixtures and fittings and leasehold improvements assets (2018)	126 750
Depreciation expense (2019)	13 400

Figure 8.24 presents a calculation of the average useful life of the entity's PPE assets.

FIGURE 8.24	Average useful life of PPE assets

$$\text{Average useful life of PPE assets} = \frac{\text{Average cost of PPE assets}}{\text{Depreciation expense}}$$

Original Furnishings Limited ('000)

$$\frac{\text{Average cost of PPE assets}}{\text{Depreciation expense}} = \frac{(\$120\,260 + \$126\,750)/2}{\$13\,400} = 9.2 \text{ years}$$

During the year there was a $6 490 000 reduction in Original Furnishing's PPE assets — a decrease of 5.1%. From this data, we can estimate an average useful life of the entity's PPE assets of 9.2 years. This estimate is consistent with the information published in its notes accompanying the financial statements, as 9.2 years indicates a rate of depreciation of around 11%. The estimated useful lives stated in its 2019 annual report indicate the following: buildings 40 years, plant and equipment 3–12 years, fixtures and fittings 5–12 years and leasehold improvements 10 years. Based on these details, the rates of depreciation for Original Furnishings' PPE assets range between 2.5% and 33%. The rough calculation indicates that most of the assets are depreciated around 5–10%. We recommend that, when analysing an entity, you use the estimate of the average useful life only as a check on the entity's published depreciable lives. It is a rough approximation at best, but it can be useful when an entity does not provide detailed disclosures for specific assets. Comparison can also be made with competitors in the same industry.

Using the decision-making toolkit next, management, along with other users such as potential investors, shareholders and lenders, can use this information to determine whether the estimated useful life for calculating depreciation is reasonable, as this will have an impact on the entity's reported profit. From the cost of PPE assets and their estimated useful life, users can evaluate if the estimated life or depreciation rate is within the range stated for the entity and its competitors. Too high an estimated useful life will result in understating depreciation expense and overstating profit.

Average age of PPE assets

Consider the importance of new equipment to a hospital or new planes to an airline. Not only are newer planes more fuel efficient, but they also require less maintenance and they are safer — key features for an airline, and one of the strengths of Air New Zealand and Qantas. Comparing the average age of PPE assets gives an indication of the potential effectiveness of an entity's PPE assets relative to others in the industry. Most entities do not report the age of their assets. But because most entities use straight-line depreciation in their financial reporting, the **average age of PPE assets** can be approximated by dividing accumulated depreciation by depreciation expense. For example, if XYZ Ltd has accumulated depreciation of $30 000 and depreciation expense of $10 000, the average age of PPE assets is 3 years ($30 000 ÷ $10 000). The following data are for Original Furnishings and Artistry Furniture for 2019:

	Original Furnishings Limited ($'000)	Artistry Furniture Limited ($'000)
Accumulated depreciation	39 260	14 625
Depreciation expense	13 400	3 035

The average age of PPE assets for these two companies is estimated in figure 8.25.

FIGURE 8.25 Average age of PPE assets

$$\text{Average age of PPE assets} = \frac{\text{Accumulated depreciation}}{\text{Depreciation expense}}$$

Original Furnishings Limited ('000)

$$\frac{\$39\,260}{\$13\,400} = 2.9 \text{ years}$$

Artistry Furniture Limited ('000)

$$\frac{\$14\,625}{\$3\,035} = 4.8 \text{ years}$$

Original Furnishings average age of PPE assets is 2.9 years and Artistry Furniture is 4.8 years. The comparison indicates that Original Furnishings PPE assets are newer. Care must be taken when interpreting this ratio because ratios can be informative but also misleading when the PPE assets have different estimated useful lives.

The relevance of the average age of PPE assets to users is shown in the decision-making toolkit next. This information provides an indication of the status of an entity's PPE assets; that is, are they relatively new or are they in need of replacement in the near future? These are potential investment decisions that impact on future cash flows and profitability. By comparing the accumulated depreciation to the depreciation expense, users are able to determine the average age of PPE assets. A high average age relative to competitors may be of concern as it may suggest that the entity's PPE assets are not as efficient, require higher maintenance costs, or are in need of updating or replacement.

DECISION-MAKING TOOLKIT

Decision/issue	Info needed for analysis	Tool or technique to use for decision	How to evaluate results to make decision
Are the entity's PPE assets outdated or in need of replacement?	Depreciation expense and accumulated depreciation	Average age of PPE assets $= \dfrac{\text{Accumulated depreciation}}{\text{Depreciation expense}}$	A high average age relative to competitors might suggest that the entity's assets are not as efficient, or that they may be in need of replacement.

Asset turnover

The **asset turnover** indicates how efficiently an entity uses its assets to generate sales. It is calculated by dividing net sales by average total assets. When we compare two entities in the same industry, the one with the higher asset turnover is operating more efficiently as it is generating more sales per dollar invested in assets. The following data are for Original Furnishings and Artistry Furniture:

	Original Furnishings Limited ($'000)	Artistry Furniture Limited ($'000)
Total assets (2019)	287 370	65 250
Total assets (2018)	233 280	51 840
Net sales (2019)	562 500	135 000

The asset turnovers for Original Furnishings and Artistry Furniture for 2019 are calculated in figure 8.26.

FIGURE 8.26 Asset turnover

$$\text{Asset turnover} = \frac{\text{Net sales}}{\text{Average total assets}}$$

Original Furnishings Limited ('000)

$$\frac{\$562\,500}{(\$287\,370 + \$233\,280)/2} = 2.16 \text{ times}$$

Artistry Furniture Limited ('000)

$$\frac{\$135\,000}{(\$65\,250 + \$51\,840)/2} = 2.31 \text{ times}$$

The asset turnovers tell us that, for each dollar invested in assets, Original Furnishings generates sales of $2.16 and Artistry Furniture $2.31. Artistry Furniture is more efficient in generating sales per dollar invested in assets. For a more comprehensive analysis, you could look at each entity's profit margin and the composition of its assets.

As shown in chapter 1, a review of the profit margins for each entity indicates that in 2019 Artistry Furniture's profit margin of 12.3% is significantly higher than Original Furnishings' profit margin of 6.4%. Closer examination of the composition of assets reveals that intangibles represent 3.1% of total assets for both Artistry Furniture and Original Furnishings. Original Furnishings turns its inventory over slightly slower at 6.82 times in comparison to Artistry Furniture at 7.02 times per annum, as shown in chapter 5. In summary, Artistry Furniture is slightly more efficient than Original Furnishings in using its assets to generate sales, its profit margin is significantly higher and its inventory turnover is marginally quicker than Original Furnishings. Asset turnovers vary considerably across industries. The asset turnover is comparable only within industries.

Asset turnovers provide users some insight into the productivity of an entity's assets. By calculating the asset turnover using the net sales figures and average total assets, users can determine the entity's level of efficiency in generating sales from its asset base. Due to the substantial investment required in assets, a high level of efficiency is desirable. The relevance of this information is summarised in the decision-making toolkit below.

DECISION-MAKING TOOLKIT

Decision/issue	Info needed for analysis	Tool or technique to use for decision	How to evaluate results to make decision
How efficient is the entity in generating sales from its assets?	Net sales and average total assets	$\text{Asset turnover} = \dfrac{\text{Net sales}}{\text{Average total assets}}$	A high value suggests the entity is effective in using its assets to generate sales. The asset turnover indicates the sales dollars generated per dollar of assets.

LEARNING REFLECTION AND CONSOLIDATION

Review it

1. What is the purpose of knowing the average age of PPE assets? How is this figure calculated?
2. What is the purpose of the asset turnover calculation? How is it calculated?

USING THE DECISION-MAKING TOOLKIT

Bruce Pharmaceuticals Ltd is a rapidly growing entity that acquires, develops and markets pharmaceuticals. In 2019 it reported a substantial increase in profit, after reporting a loss in 2017 and a small profit in 2018. The entity has acquired, rather than developed internally, a number of existing products from other entities. It reports significant intangible assets related to these acquisitions. You have noticed the improvement in Bruce's operating results and are considering investing in the company.

Required
Review the excerpts shown below and consider the entity's sensitivity to the amortisation of its intangibles and how that might affect your decision on whether to invest. Then answer these questions:
(a) What percentage of total assets are intangibles as at 30 June 2019?
(b) What method does the entity use to amortise intangibles, and over what period are they amortised?
(c) Calculate the average useful life that the entity is using to amortise its intangible assets.
(d) Comment on whether, in your opinion, the entity's intangibles amortisation policy is reasonable.
(e) What would 2019 profit have been if the entity had used a 15-year useful life for amortisation?
    (*Hint:* Base your calculation on the *average* intangible assets in 2019.)

▶

BRUCE PHARMACEUTICALS LTD
Statement of financial position (assets only)
for the years ended 30 June

Assets	2019 ('000)	2018 ('000)
Total current assets	$157 234	$137 987
PPE assets and other non-current assets	53 137	39 144
Intangible assets	315 865	194 317
Total assets	**$526 236**	**$371 448**

BRUCE PHARMACEUTICALS LTD
Profit or loss statement
for the years ended 30 June

	2019 ('000)	2018 ('000)
Total sales and revenue	$175 445	$122 508
Total operating costs and expenses	148 067	123 270
Operating profit (loss)	27 378	(762)
Other revenues, (expenses), gains and (losses)	(10 591)	3 279
Profit (loss)	**$ 16 787**	**$ 2 517**

BRUCE PHARMACEUTICALS LTD
Selected notes to the financial statements

SUMMARY OF SIGNIFICANT ACCOUNTING POLICIES
Intangible assets
Intangible assets are stated at cost less accumulated amortisation. Amortisation is determined using the straight-line method over the estimated useful lives of the related assets which are estimated to range from 5 to 40 years. It is the company's policy to review periodically and evaluate whether there has been an impairment in the value of intangibles. In the fourth quarter of 2019, the company recorded a charge against profits for an impairment of intangible assets and to expense purchased development products totalling $25.4 million.

Intangible assets consist of (in thousands):

	30 June	
	2019	2018
Product rights acquired	$349 282	$217 919
Less: Accumulated amortisation	33 417	23 602
	$315 865	$194 317

Notes
Amortisation expense for the years ended 30 June 2017, 2018 and 2019 was $6692, $6159 and $9815, respectively.

Solution
(a) As a percentage of the entity's total assets, intangibles represented 60% in 2019 ($315 865 000 ÷ $526 236 000).
(b) The entity uses the straight-line method to amortise intangibles. The notes state that they are amortised over a 5–40-year period.
(c) The average useful life being used to amortise intangible assets can be estimated by dividing the average cost of the intangible assets by the amortisation expense.

$$\frac{(\$349\,282\,000 + \$217\,919\,000) \div 2}{\$9\,815\,000} = 28.9 \text{ years}$$

(d) This is a matter of opinion. However, one factor to consider is that Bruce is purchasing the rights to existing products, so part of their useful life may already be gone. Additionally, because of rapidly changing technology, new drugs appear to be developed at a relatively rapid rate; thus, it seems unlikely that, on average, drugs would have a useful life of 40 years. Also, the notes state that the entity took a $25.4 million write-down in 2019 due to the impairment of its intangibles. This suggests its intangibles were not being amortised fast enough. A 15-year life would seem more appropriate.

(e) In order to estimate amortisation expense using a 15-year life, we would first need to calculate average intangibles for the year to approximate the amortisation:

$$\text{Average intangibles} = \frac{\$349\,282\,000 + \$217\,919\,000}{2} = \$283\,600\,500$$

Amortisation over a 15-year period would be:

$$\frac{\$283\,600\,500}{15} = \$18\,906\,700$$

The reduction in profit from the increased amortisation (revised amortisation minus actual amortisation) would be:

$$\$18\,906\,700 - \$9\,815\,000 = \$9\,091\,700$$

Therefore, with amortisation over a 15-year period, the resulting profit (reported profit minus increase in amortisation) for the year would be:

$$\$16\,787\,000 - \$9\,091\,700 = \$7\,695\,300$$

Conclusion: These calculations make it clear the entity's profit is very sensitive to the assumed useful life. Therefore, before investing, you would want to investigate further the reasonableness of the 5–40-year assumption currently being used.

SUMMARY

8.1 Explain the business context of non-current assets and the need for decision making for these assets.

The business context for non-current assets is very dependent on both internal and external factors in the business environment. The need for, focus and type of decisions are described throughout this chapter.

8.2 Describe how the cost principle applies to property, plant and equipment assets.

The cost of PPE assets includes all expenditures necessary to acquire the asset and make it ready for its intended use. Cost is measured by fair value of the consideration at the time of the acquisition.

8.3 Explain the concept of depreciation.

Depreciation is the process of allocating to expense the cost of a PPE asset over its useful (service) life in a rational and systematic manner. Depreciation is not a process of valuation, and it is not a process that results in an accumulation of cash. Depreciation is caused by wear and tear, technical and commercial obsolescence, and legal limit.

8.4 Calculate depreciation using various methods and contrast the expense patterns of the methods.

The expense patterns of the three main depreciation methods are as follows:

Method	Annual depreciation pattern
Straight-line	Constant amount
Diminishing-balance	Decreasing amount
Units-of-production	Varying amount

8.5 Account for subsequent expenditures.

Ordinary repairs are expenditures that maintain the efficiency and expected productive life of the asset. Additional improvements that increase the operating efficiency or useful life of the asset, if material, are capitalised.

8.6 Account for asset impairments.

When the asset's carrying amount is greater than the recoverable amount, the asset is said to be impaired and must be written down. Reversals of impairments of PPE assets and certain intangible assets are permitted but only to the extent the asset's carrying value would have been had the asset not been impaired.

8.7 Account for the revaluation of property, plant and equipment assets.

After initial recognition, property, plant and equipment assets may be measured at cost less accumulated depreciation or fair value. If fair value is chosen, then the valuation must be kept up to date.

8.8 Account for the disposal of property, plant and equipment assets.

The procedure for accounting for the disposal of an asset through sale or scrapping is: (a) eliminate the carrying amount of the asset at the date of disposal, (b) record cash proceeds, if any, and (c) account for the difference between the carrying amount and the cash proceeds as a gain or a loss on disposal.

8.9 Describe the use of an asset register.

An asset register is a subsidiary ledger in which individual asset details and depreciation are recorded.

8.10 Identify the basic issues related to reporting intangible assets.

Identifiable intangible assets are recognised at cost. After initial recognition, intangibles with finite useful lives are amortised. Intangibles with indefinite useful life and goodwill are tested for impairment annually. Intangibles cannot be revalued unless there is an active market.

8.11 Describe the common types of intangible assets.

Identifiable intangible assets include patents, development costs, copyrights, trademarks and brand names, franchises and licences. Goodwill is an unidentifiable intangible.

8.12 Explain the nature and measurement of agricultural assets.

Agricultural assets are living animals and plants that are a result of agricultural activity. While they are not in a state ready for sale, they are measured at fair value less estimated point-of-sale costs. Changes in value are reported directly to the statement of profit or loss as either revenue or expense. Once harvested or ready for sale, agricultural assets are classified as agricultural produce and form part of the inventory of an entity.

8.13 Account for the acquisition and depletion of natural resources.

Pre-production costs for the extractive industries are capitalised and depleted against future production.

8.14 Indicate how non-current assets are reported in the statement of financial position, and explain the methods of evaluating the use of non-current assets.

PPE assets are usually shown under property, plant and equipment; intangibles are shown under intangible assets. The balances of the major classes of assets, such as land, buildings and equipment, and accumulated depreciation by major classes or in total are disclosed in the notes to the financial statements. The depreciation and amortisation methods used should be described, and the amount of depreciation and amortisation expense for the period should be disclosed. PPE assets may be analysed using average useful life, average age and asset turnover ratios.

DECISION-MAKING TOOLKIT — A SUMMARY

DECISION-MAKING TOOLKIT

Decision/issue	Info needed for analysis	Tool or technique to use for decision	How to evaluate results to make decision
Is the entity's amortisation of intangibles reasonable?	Estimated useful life of intangibles from notes to financial statements of the entity and its competitors	If the entity's estimated useful life significantly exceeds that of competitors or does not seem reasonable in light of the circumstances, the reason for the difference should be investigated.	Too high an estimated useful life will result in understating amortisation expense and overstating profit.
Is the entity's estimated useful life for depreciation reasonable?	Estimated useful life of assets from notes to financial statements of the entity and its competitors; or cost of PPE assets and depreciation expense	If not provided in notes, average useful life can be estimated as: $$\text{Average useful life} = \frac{\text{Average cost of PPE assets}}{\text{Depreciation expense}}$$	Too high an estimated useful life will result in understating depreciation expense and overstating profit.
Are the entity's PPE assets outdated or in need of replacement?	Depreciation expense and accumulated depreciation	$$\text{Average age of PPE assets} = \frac{\text{Accumulated depreciation}}{\text{Depreciation expense}}$$	A high average age relative to that of competitors might suggest that the entity's assets are not as efficient, or that they may be in need of replacement.
How efficient is the entity in generating sales from its assets?	Net sales and average total assets	$$\text{Asset turnover} = \frac{\text{Net sales}}{\text{Average total assets}}$$	A high value suggests the entity is effective in using its assets to generate sales. The asset turnover indicates the sales dollars generated per dollar of assets.

KEY TERMS

accumulated depreciation The amount of depreciation that has been recorded as depreciation expense since the asset was acquired. It is not a cash fund.

active market A market where the items traded in it are homogeneous; willing buyers, and sellers, can normally be found at any time; and the prices are available to the public.

additions and improvements Costs incurred to increase the operating efficiency, productive capacity or expected useful life of a PPE asset.

agricultural activity The management by an entity of the biological transformation of biological assets for sale into agricultural produce, or into additional biological assets.

agricultural produce The harvested product of the entity's biological assets is agricultural produce, which is then classified as inventory.

amortisation The allocation of the cost of an intangible asset to expense.

asset turnover Measure of efficient use of assets, calculated as net sales divided by average total assets.

average age of PPE assets Measure of the age of an entity's PPE assets, calculated as accumulated depreciation divided by depreciation expense.

average useful life A comparative measure of PPE assets, calculated as the average cost of the assets divided by depreciation expense.

biological asset A living animal or plant.

capital expenditure Expenditure that increases the entity's investment in productive facilities.

carrying amount The cost of an asset less accumulated depreciation. This is also referred to as book value.

cash-generating unit The smallest identifiable group of assets that generate cash inflows which are largely independent of the cash inflows from other assets or groups of assets.

class of non-current assets Category of assets having similar nature or function in the operations of the entity. Shown as a single line item in the notes to the statement of financial position without further dissection.

contra account An account which is reported as an offset to or reduction from a related account.

copyright An exclusive right allowing the owner to reproduce and sell an artistic or published work.

cost Consists of the fair value of all expenditures necessary to acquire the asset and make it ready for its intended use.

depletion (amortisation) The periodic allocation of the cost of natural resources to reflect the units removed.

depreciable amount The cost of a PPE asset or other amount substituted at cost less its residual value.

depreciation The process of allocating to expense the cost of an asset over its useful life in a rational and systematic manner.

diminishing-balance method A depreciation method that results in a decreasing charge over the asset's useful life by applying a predetermined rate to the carrying amount of the asset. This is also referred to as accelerated depreciation.

fair value The price that would be received to sell an asset or paid to transfer a liability in an orderly transaction between market participants at the measurement date.

finance lease A long-term agreement where the lessor effectively transfers to the lessee substantially all the risks and rewards incidental to ownership of the leased asset. The arrangement is accounted for like a purchase.

franchise A contractual arrangement under which the franchisor grants the franchisee the right to sell certain products, to render specific services or to use certain trademarks or brand names, usually within a designated geographic area.

goodwill The future benefits from unidentifiable assets.

impairment loss The amount by which the carrying amount of an asset or a cash-generating unit exceeds its recoverable amount.

intangible assets Identifiable non-monetary assets that have no physical substance (e.g. patents and copyrights).

lessee A party that has made contractual arrangements to use another party's asset without purchasing it.

lessor A party that has agreed contractually to let another party use its asset.

licences Operating rights to use public property, granted by a government agency to a business.

operating lease An arrangement whereby the lessor effectively retains substantially all the risks and rewards incidental to ownership of a leased asset. The arrangement is accounted for as a rental.

ordinary repairs Expenditures to maintain the operating efficiency and expected productive life of the asset.

patent An exclusive right that enables the recipient to manufacture, sell or otherwise control an invention for a number of years from the date of the grant.

property, plant and equipment Tangible assets that have physical substance, are used in the operations of the business for more than one period, and are not intended for sale to customers (e.g. land and buildings).

recoverable amount The higher of an asset or a cash-generating unit's fair value less costs of disposal and its value in use.

research and development costs Expenditures that may lead to patents, copyrights, new processes and new products.

residual value An estimate of the asset's value at the end of its useful life. This is also called salvage value or trade-in value.

revaluation A reassessment of the fair value of a non-current asset at a particular date.

revenue expenditure Expenditures that do not extend an asset's capacity but merely maintain the asset in its working order.

straight-line method A method in which periodic depreciation is the same for each year of the asset's useful life.

trademark (brand name) A word, phrase, jingle or symbol that distinguishes or identifies a particular enterprise or product.

units-of-production method A depreciation method in which useful life is expressed in terms of the total units of production or use expected from the asset.

useful life An estimate of the expected productive life (also called service life) of the asset to the entity.

value in use The present value of net cash flows expected to be derived from using the asset.

DEMONSTRATION PROBLEM 1

DuPage Ltd purchased a factory machine at a cost of $18 000 on 1 January 2018. The machine was expected to have a residual value of $2000 at the end of its 4-year useful life. The entity's reporting period ends on 31 December. For the purposes of this question exclude GST.

Required
Prepare a depreciation schedule using the straight-line method.

PROBLEM-SOLVING STRATEGY
Under the straight-line method, the depreciation rate is applied to the depreciable amount.

SOLUTION TO DEMONSTRATION PROBLEM 1

		DUPAGE LTD				
		Depreciation schedule — straight-line method				
	Calculation				**End of year**	
Year	Depreciable amount	×	Depreciation rate	= Annual depreciation expense	Accumulated depreciation	Carrying amount
2018	$16 000		25%	$4 000	$ 4 000	$14 000*
2019	16 000		25	4 000	8 000	10 000
2020	16 000		25	4 000	12 000	6 000
2021	16 000		25	4 000	16 000	2 000

*Cost $18 000 − Year 1 depreciation $4000

DEMONSTRATION PROBLEM 2

(Including GST of 10%)

On 1 January 2018, Skyline Limousine Ltd purchased a vehicle at an acquisition cost of $30 800 (10% GST inclusive). The vehicle has been depreciated by the straight-line method using a 4-year service life and a $4000 residual value. The entity's reporting period ends on 31 December.

Required

1. Prepare the journal entry to record the purchase of the vehicle on 1 January 2018.
2. Prepare the journal entry or entries to record the disposal of the limousine assuming that it was:
   (a) scrapped with no residual value on 1 January 2022.
   (b) sold for $5500 cash on 1 July 2021.

PROBLEM-SOLVING STRATEGY

Accumulated depreciation is equal to depreciation expense per year times the number of years of use when the straight-line method is used.

SOLUTION TO DEMONSTRATION PROBLEM 2

1	Jan. 1 2018	Vehicle		28 000	
		GST paid		2 800	
		Accounts payable			30 800
		(To record purchase of vehicle)			
2 (a)	Jan. 1 2022	Accumulated depreciation—vehicle		24 000	
		Loss on disposal		4 000	
		Vehicle			28 000
		(To record scrapping of vehicle)			
(b)	July 1 2021	Depreciation expense		3 000	
		Accumulated depreciation—vehicle			3 000
		(To record depreciation to date of disposal—$24 000 × 25% × 6 months)			
		Cash		5 500*	
		Accumulated depreciation—vehicle		21 000	
		Loss on disposal		2 000	
		GST collected			500
		Vehicle			28 000
		(To record sale of vehicle)			

*6000 × 3.5 years = $21 000

SELF-STUDY QUESTIONS

8.1 Corrieten Ltd purchased equipment and these costs were incurred: **LO2**

Cash price	$18 000
Delivery costs	1 200
Insurance during transit	300
Installation and testing	500
Total costs	$20 000

What amount should be recorded as the cost of the equipment?
(a) $18 000.
(b) $19 500.
(c) $19 200.
(d) $20 000.

8.2 Harrington Ltd recently leased a number of trucks from Andre Ltd. In inspecting the books of Harrington Ltd, you notice that the trucks have not been recorded as assets on its statement of financial position. From this you can conclude that Harrington Ltd is accounting for this transaction as:
(a) an operating lease. **LO2**
(b) a finance lease.
(c) a purchase.
(d) none of the above.

8.3 Depreciation is a process of: **LO3**
(a) valuation.
(b) cost allocation.
(c) cash accumulation.
(d) appraisal.

8.4 Cuso Ltd purchased equipment on 1 January 2018 at a total invoice cost of $440 000 (including GST of 10%). The equipment has an estimated residual value of $20 000 and an estimated useful life of 5 years. What is the amount of accumulated depreciation at 31 December 2020 if the straight-line method of depreciation is used? **LO4**
(a) $160 000.
(b) $152 000.
(c) $228 000.
(d) $240 000.

8.5 An entity would minimise its depreciation expense in the first year of owning an asset if it used: **LO4**

(a) a high estimated life, a high residual value, and diminishing-balance depreciation.
(b) a low estimated life, a high residual value, and straight-line depreciation.
(c) a high estimated life, a high residual value, and straight-line depreciation.
(d) a low estimated life, a low residual value, and diminishing-balance depreciation.

8.6 When there is a change in estimated depreciation: **LO4**
(a) previous depreciation should be corrected.
(b) current and future years' depreciation should be revised.
(c) only future years' depreciation should be revised.
(d) none of the above.

8.7 Additions to PPE assets: **LO5**
(a) are expenses.
(b) increase a Repair expense account.
(c) increase a Purchases account.
(d) are capital expenditures.

8.8 Which of the following measures provides an indication of how efficient an entity is in using its assets? **LO14**

(a) Current ratio.

(b) Average useful life.

(c) Average age of PPE assets.

(d) Asset turnover.

8.9 Pierce Ltd incurred $150 000 of research and development costs in its laboratory to develop a new product. It spent $20 000 in legal fees for a patent granted on 2 January 2019. On 31 July 2022, Pierce paid $15 000 for legal fees in a successful defence of the patent. What is the total amount that should be debited to Patents up to 31 July 2022? Assume the figures are GST exclusive. **LO10**

(a) $150 000.

(b) $35 000.

(c) $185 000.

(d) Some other amount.

8.10 Indicate which one of these statements is *true*. **LO10**

(a) Since intangible assets lack physical substance, they need to be disclosed only in the notes to the financial statements.

(b) Goodwill should be reported as a contra account in the equity section.

(c) Totals of major classes of assets can be shown in the statement of financial position, with asset details disclosed in the notes to the financial statements.

(d) Intangible assets are typically combined with PPE assets and natural resources and then shown in the property, plant and equipment section.

8.11 If an entity reports goodwill as an intangible asset on its books, what is the one thing you know with certainty? **LO10**

(a) The entity is a valuable company worth investing in.

(b) The entity has a well-established brand name.

(c) The entity purchased another business.

(d) The goodwill will generate a lot of positive business for the entity for many years to come.

8.12 Kant Ltd purchased a truck for $11 000 on 1 January 2018. The truck will have an estimated residual value of $1000 at the end of 5 years. If you use the units-of-production method, the balance in accumulated depreciation at 31 December 2019 can be calculated by the following formula: **LO4**

(a) ($11 000 ÷ Total estimated production) × Units of production for 2019.

(b) ($10 000 ÷ Total estimated production) × Units of production for 2019.

(c) ($11 000 ÷ Total estimated production) × Units of production for 2018 and 2019.

(d) ($10 000 ÷ Total estimated production) × Units of production for 2018 and 2019.

8.13 In relation to agricultural assets, indicate which of the following statements is *true*. **LO12**

(a) The assets include only items purchased in an external transaction.

(b) The assets remain as agricultural assets until sold.

(c) The assets at the end of the reporting period are measured at fair value less estimated point-of-sale costs.

(d) The assets at the end of the reporting period are measured at fair value.

8.14 In relation to natural resources, indicate which of the following statements is *true*. **LO13**

(a) The value of the mineral or oil deposit is reflected on the statement of financial position.

(b) Similar to agricultural assets, the assets are regenerative.

(c) Preproduction costs must be expensed as incurred.

(d) Preproduction costs can be capitalised and depleted to inventory as the mineral or oil is extracted.

8.15 In relation to evaluating non-current assets indicate which of the following statements is *true*. **LO14**

(a) The older the assets are, the better the company is performing.

(b) Too high a depreciation rate will result in increased reported profits for the period.

(c) The higher the asset turnover, the more effective a company is in using its resources to generate sales.

(d) All non-current assets must be depreciated.

QUESTIONS

8.1 Identify three key decisions involving non-current assets.

8.2 James Knight is uncertain about how the cost principle applies to PPE assets. Explain this to James.

8.3 What impact does GST have on accounting for non-current assets?

8.4 What are the main advantages of leasing?

8.5 Contrast the effects of the three depreciation methods explained in this chapter on annual depreciation expense.

8.6 Distinguish between expenses and capital expenditures during an asset's useful life.

8.7 How is a gain or a loss on the sale of a PPE asset calculated?

8.8 What are the similarities and differences between depreciation, amortisation and depletion?

8.9 Goodwill could be described as the value of all favourable attributes that relate to a business as a whole. What types of attributes could result in goodwill?

8.10 Explain the accounting treatment for revaluation of assets.

8.11 What are agricultural assets?

8.12 You are comparing two entities in the same industry. You have determined that Amber Ltd depreciates its PPE assets over a 30-year life, whereas Jonty Ltd depreciates its PPE assets over a 40-year life. Discuss the implications this has for comparing the results of the two entities.

BRIEF EXERCISES

BE8.1 Determine the cost of land. **LO2**

These expenditures were incurred by Knight Ltd in purchasing land: cash price $180 000; rates $10 000; solicitor's fees $9500; real estate agent's commission $8100; clearing and grading $7000; and fencing $5000. What is the cost of the land, assuming all figures:

(a) are GST exclusive

(b) include GST at a rate of 10%

(c) include GST at a rate of 15%?

BE8.2 Calculate straight-line depreciation. **LO4**

Brianna Ltd acquires a delivery truck at a cost of $96 600 (GST exclusive) on 1 January 2019, the beginning of the company's financial year. The truck is expected to have a residual value of $4000 at the end of its 5-year useful life. Calculate annual depreciation for the first and second years using the straight-line method.

BE8.3 Calculate diminishing-balance depreciation. **LO4**

Depreciation information for Brianna Ltd is given in BE8.2. Assuming the diminishing-balance depreciation rate is one-and-a-half times the straight-line rate, calculate annual depreciation for the first and second years under the diminishing-balance method.

BE8.4 Journalise entries for disposal of PPE assets. **LO8**

Prepare journal entries to record the following:

(a) James Ltd scraps its delivery equipment, which cost $59 000. Accumulated depreciation is also $59 000 on this delivery equipment. No residual value was expected or taken into account when calculating depreciation for the delivery equipment.

(b) Assume the same information as in part (a), except that accumulated depreciation for James Ltd at the date of disposal is $56 000 instead of $59 000.

BE8.5 Account for intangibles — patents. LO10

Elliot Ltd purchases a patent for $220 000 on 1 July 2018. Its estimated useful life is 10 years. Assume Elliot Ltd's financial year ends on 30 June. Complete requirements (a) and (b) under two scenarios:

(i) assuming no GST

(ii) assuming GST at a rate of 10%.

(a) Prepare journal entries related to the patent for the year ending 30 June 2019.

(b) Show how this patent is reported on the statement of financial position as at 30 June 2019.

BE8.6 Calculate average life, average age of non-current assets, and asset turnover. LO1, 14

In its 2019 annual report, Fish Ltd reports beginning total assets of $37.42 billion; ending total assets of $35.58 billion; beginning property, plant and equipment (at cost) of $40.8 billion; ending property, plant and equipment (at cost) $39.2 billion; ending accumulated depreciation of $9.6 billion; depreciation expense of $1600 million; and net sales of $21.17 billion.

(a) Calculate the average useful life of Fish's property, plant and equipment.

(b) Calculate the average age of Fish's property, plant and equipment.

(c) Calculate Fish's asset turnover.

BE8.7 Prepare a partial statement of financial position. LO14

Irish Ltd reported the following property, plant and equipment and intangibles for the year ended 31 March 2020 (in thousands): land and buildings $782.4; plant and equipment $3294.6; goodwill $520.4; other intangibles $145.9; accumulated depreciation $2160.1; impairment of goodwill $321.5; accumulated amortisation $86.5. Prepare a partial statement of financial position for Irish Ltd for these items.

EXERCISES

E8.1 Determine cost of PPE acquisitions. LO2

The following expenditures relating to PPE assets were made by Sunny Ltd during the first 2 months of 2020.

1. Paid $6000 of accrued land taxes at time factory site was acquired.
2. Paid $750 air conditioning on new delivery truck.
3. Paid $18 000 for parking lots and driveways on new factory site.
4. Paid $900 for a 1-year accident insurance policy on new delivery truck.
5. Paid $350 to have company name and advertising slogan painted on new delivery truck.
6. Paid $7600 for installation of new factory machinery.
7. Paid $750 motor vehicle registration fee on new truck.
8. Paid $250 insurance to cover possible accident loss on new factory machinery while the machinery was in transit.

Required

(a) Explain the application of the cost principle in determining the acquisition cost of PPE assets.

(b) List the numbers of the foregoing transactions, and opposite each indicate the account name to which each expenditure should be debited.

E8.2 Calculate straight-line, diminishing-balance and units-of-production depreciation. LO4

Tops Ltd purchased a new machine on 1 October 2018 at a cost of $228 000. The entity estimated that the machine has a residual value of $28 000. The machine is expected to be used for 40 000 working hours during its 10-year life. Assume a 31 December year-end.

Required

Calculate the depreciation expense using the following methods in the year indicated:

(a) the straight-line method for 2018 and 2019.

(b) the diminishing-balance method using double the straight-line rate for 2018 and 2019.

(c) the units-of-production method for 2018, assuming the machine usage was 1800 hours.

E8.3 Calculate depreciation under units-of-production method.   **LO4**

AJ Bus Ltd uses the units-of-production method in depreciating its buses. One bus was purchased on 1 January 2018 at a cost of $268 000. Over its 5-year useful life, the bus is expected to be driven 120 000 kilometres. Residual value is expected to be $10 000.

Required

(a) Calculate the depreciation cost per unit.

(b) Prepare a depreciation schedule assuming actual distance travelled was: 2018, 29 000 km; 2019, 28 000 km; 2020, 30 000 km; 2021, 20 000 km; and 2022, 13 000 km.

E8.4 Account for subsequent expenditure and revised depreciation.   **LO4, 5**

Lion Ltd purchased equipment on 1 January 2019 at a cost of $180 000. It had an estimated useful life of 8 years and an estimated residual value of $20 000. Each year $1000 is spent on the maintenance of the equipment. On 1 July 2021, Lion paid $8800 cash for a major overhaul of the equipment, after which it had an expected useful life of 5 more years and nil residual value. The entity's reporting period ends on 30 June and it uses straight-line depreciation.

Required

(a) Calculate the depreciation expense for 2019 and 2020.

(b) Prepare the journal entry for the $8800 paid for the overhaul of the equipment, assuming:

　　(i) no GST

　　(ii) GST of 10%.

(c) Calculate the depreciation expense for 2022 based on assumption (i) in (b) above.

E8.5 Journalise entries for asset impairment.   **LO6**

Able Ltd purchased machinery on 1 November 2019 for $160 000. The estimated useful life of the machinery is 8 years, with an estimated residual of $10 000. The entity's reporting period ends on 30 June, and it uses the straight-line method of depreciation. On 1 July 2020, the value in use was estimated to be $90 000 and the net selling price was $98 750.

Required

Prepare the journal entries in relation to the equipment from the date of acquisition.

E8.6 Revaluation and disposal of non-current assets.   **LO7, 8**

On 1 January 2018, Wall Ltd purchased equipment for a total cost of $55 000. The estimated useful life of the equipment was 8 years, with an estimated residual value of $5000. The entity's reporting period ends on 30 June, and it uses straight-line depreciation. On 1 July 2020, Wall Ltd revalued the equipment upwards to reflect the fair value of $70 000. The revised useful life was 7 years and residual value was estimated at $nil. On 1 January 2022, Wall Ltd sold the equipment for $56 500.

Required

(a) Prepare the journal entries in relation to the equipment from the date of acquisition to the date of disposal assuming no GST.

(b) Prepare the journal entries in relation to the equipment from the date of acquisition to the date of disposal assuming GST at a rate of 10%.

E8.7 Revaluation, depreciation and reversal of PPE asset.   **LO4, 7**

On 1 July 2017, Capers Ltd purchased equipment for a total cost of $220 000 including 10% GST. The estimated useful life of the equipment was 10 years, with an estimated residual value of $15 000. The entity's reporting period ends on 30 June, and it uses straight-line depreciation. On 1 July 2019, the entity revalued the equipment upwards by $17 000 to reflect the fair value. The revised useful life was 8 years and residual value was estimated at $10 000. On 1 January 2021, Capers Ltd revalued the equipment downwards by $20 000 to reflect the fair value.

Required

(a) Prepare the journal entries in relation to the equipment from the date of acquisition.

(b) Calculate the new carrying value of the equipment immediately after the revaluation downwards.

E8.8 Journalise entries for disposal of PPE assets. **LO8**

Presented here are selected transactions for Zhou Ltd for the year ended 31 December 2019:

Jan.	1	Scrapped a piece of machinery that was purchased on 1 January 2009 at a cash price of $66 000. The machinery had a useful life of 10 years with no residual value.
June	30	Sold a computer that was purchased on 1 January 2016 for $33 000 cash. It had a useful life of 6 years with no residual value. The computer was sold for $13 200 cash.
Dec.	31	Discarded a delivery truck that was purchased on 1 January 2015 for $22 000 cash and was depreciated based on a 6-year useful life with a $2000 residual value.

Required

Journalise all entries required on the listed dates, including entries to update depreciation, where applicable, on assets disposed of. Zhou Ltd uses straight-line depreciation. (Assume depreciation is up to date as of 31 December 2018 and the GST rate is 10%.)

E8.9 Prepare entries to set up appropriate accounts for different intangibles; calculate amortisation. **LO10**

Wilkins Ltd, incorporated in 2018, has these transactions related to intangible assets in that year:

Jan.	1	Purchased patent (10-year life), $440 000.
July	1	Acquired an existing 10-year franchise; expiration date 1 July 2024, $330 000.
Sept.	1	Research and development costs, $155 000.

Required

Prepare the necessary entries to record these transactions. All costs incurred were for cash and included GST of 10%. Make the entries for 31 December 2018, the end of Wilkins Ltd's financial year, recording any necessary amortisation and indicating what the balances should be on 31 December 2018. Include any assumptions you made concerning the above expenditures.

E8.10 Answer questions on depreciation and intangibles. **LO4, 10, 11, 14**

The questions listed below are independent of one another.

Required

Provide a brief answer to each question.

(a) Why should an entity depreciate its buildings?

(b) How can an entity have a building that has a reported carrying amount of nil but a substantial market value?

(c) What are some examples of intangibles that you might find on the statement of financial position of your university?

(d) Give some examples of company or product trademarks or brand names. Are brand names and trademarks reported on an entity's statement of financial position?

E8.11 Discuss implications of amortisation period. **LO10**

MouseTrap Ltd in Canada noted in its 2019 annual report that, beginning that year, it changed the estimated life of its computer software for amortisation purposes from a 3-year life to a 12-year life.

Required

Write a short memo explaining the implications this has for the analysis of MouseTrap Ltd's results. Also, discuss whether this estimated life seems reasonable.

E8.12 Calculate average useful life, average age of property, plant and equipment, and asset turnover ratio. **LO14**

For the year ended 31 January 2018, Beta Ltd reported the following information (in thousands): net sales $1 663 970, profit $21 935, depreciation expense $6399. The statement of financial position showed total assets of $609 041 at the beginning of the year, and $515 357 at the end of the year; property, plant and equipment of $105 282 (cost) at the beginning of the year and $90 861 (cost) at the end of the year; and accumulated depreciation at year-end of $38 797.

Required

Calculate the following:

(a) average useful life of PPE assets.

(b) average age of PPE assets.

(c) asset turnover ratio.

Comment on how to interpret these ratios.

PROBLEM SET A

PSA8.1 Determine acquisition costs of land and building. **LO2**

Cameron Ltd commenced business on 1 April. During the first year of operations, the following property, plant and equipment asset expenditures and receipts were recorded in random order:

Debits	
1. Cost of real estate purchased as a factory site (land $180 000 and building $70 000)	$ 250 000
2. Installation of fences around property	4 900
3. Cost of demolishing building to make land suitable for construction of new building	27 000
4. Cost of filling and grading the land	7 270
5. Excavation costs for new building	21 900
6. Architects' fees on building plans	51 000
7. Full payment to building contractor	629 500
8. Cost of parking lots and driveways	31 800
9. Land taxes paid for the current year on land	5 320
	$1 028 690
Credits	
10. Proceeds from residual of demolished building	$ 12 700

Required

Analyse the transactions using the table column headings provided here.

Item	Land	Building	Other accounts

Enter the number of each transaction in the Item column, and enter the amounts in the appropriate columns. For amounts in the Other accounts column, also indicate the account name.

PSA8.2 Journalise equipment transactions related to purchase, sale, scrapping and depreciation.

LO2, 4, 8, 14

At 30 June 2018, Porter Ltd reported the following PPE assets.

Land		$ 4 000 000
Buildings	$28 500 000	
Less: Accumulated depreciation—buildings	12 100 000	16 400 000
Equipment	48 000 000	
Less: Accumulated depreciation—equipment	5 000 000	43 000 000
Total PPE assets		**$63 400 000**

During the financial year ending 30 June 2019, the following selected cash transactions occurred:

Aug.	1	Purchased land for $2 630 000.
Oct.	1	Sold equipment that cost $675 000 cash when purchased on 1 January 2012. The equipment was sold for $350 000 cash.
Dec.	1	Sold land purchased on 1 June 2004 for $1 800 000. The land cost cash $300 000.
Jan.	1	Purchased equipment for $1 000 000.
June	30	Scrapped equipment that cost $470 000 (GST exclusive) when purchased on 31 December 2007. No residual value was received.

Required

(a) For the transactions complete the following.
  1. Journalise the transactions. (*Hint:* You may wish to set up T accounts, post beginning balances, and then post 2018–19 transactions.) Porter uses straight-line depreciation for buildings and equipment. The buildings are estimated to have a 40-year useful life and no residual value; the equipment is estimated to have a 10-year useful life and no residual value. Update depreciation on assets disposed of at the time of sale or retirement.
  2. Record adjusting entries for depreciation for 2018–19.
  3. Prepare the PPE assets section of Porter Ltd's statement of financial position at 30 June 2019.
(b) Repeat requirement (a) assuming GST of 10% applied to all relevant transactions. (You should not need to repeat the T accounts, but could do so, adding GST accounts.)

PSA8.3 Journalise entries for disposals of PPE assets.

LO8

Presented here are selected transactions for CupCake Ltd for 2018.

Jan.	1	Scrapped a piece of machinery that was purchased on 1 January 2008. The machine cost $52 000 and had a useful life of 10 years with no residual value.
June	30	Sold a computer that was purchased on 1 January 2015. The computer cost $49 000 and had a useful life of 7 years with no residual value. The computer was sold for $31 000.
Dec.	31	Discarded a delivery truck that was purchased on 1 January 2014. The truck cost $27 000 and was depreciated based on an 8-year useful life with a $3000 residual value.

Required

Ignore GST. Journalise all entries required on the above dates, including entries to update depreciation on assets disposed of, where applicable. CupCake Ltd uses straight-line depreciation. The reporting period ends on 31 December.

PSA8.4 Prepare the entries to record revaluation, depreciation and disposal.

LO4, 7, 8

On 1 July 2018, Jupiter Ltd purchased land for $400 000 and buildings for $250 000. The estimated useful life of the buildings was 20 years, with a residual value of nil. On 1 October 2018, machinery was purchased at a total cost of $120 000. The estimated useful life of the machinery was 4 years with an estimated residual value of $9000. Jupiter Ltd uses straight-line depreciation for buildings and the diminishing-balance method for machinery. The entity's reporting period ends 30 June.

Required

(a) Prepare journal entries to record the purchase of the land, buildings and machinery during the year.

(b) Prepare journal entries to record the depreciation expense for the year ended 30 June 2019.

(c) Assume that on 1 July 2019 the entity revalued the land upwards by $80 000 and the buildings downwards by $50 000. Prepare the journal entries for the revaluations.

(d) On 31 December 2019, owing to a change in product mix, the machinery was sold for $50 000. Prepare journal entry(ies) to dispose of the machinery.

PSA8.5 Prepare journal entries for asset impairments and reversals.   **LO6**

On 1 July 2018, Shark Ltd purchased three machines, each used in a different production process in the factory. On 30 June 2019, there was an indication that the machines could be impaired due to a new competitor entering the market, so Shark Ltd calculated the recoverable amounts of the machines. Twelve months later this threat no longer existed and the recoverable amount was reassessed. Information concerning the machines is summarised in the following table. Shark Ltd uses straight-line depreciation over a 5-year period for all machinery. Assume that all three machines had nil residual values at the end of their useful lives.

Machine	Cost 1/7/18	Value in use 30/6/19	Net selling price 30/6/19	Value in use 30/6/20	Net selling price 30/6/20
1	$10 000	$ 7 500	$ 9 000	$ 6 000	$ 6 500
2	25 000	13 000	12 000	16 000	17 000
3	15 000	13 000	11 000	9 500	9 200
	50 000				

Required

(a) Prepare the journal entry to record depreciation for the year ended 30 June 2019.

(b) Prepare the journal entry to record any asset impairment at 30 June 2019.

(c) Prepare the journal entry to record depreciation for the year ended 30 June 2020.

(d) Prepare the journal entry to record any asset impairment or reversal at 30 June 2020.

PSA8.6 Prepare journal entries for asset revaluation and depreciation over periods increases and decreases.   **LO4, 7**

Toy Ltd has the following land and buildings in its accounts as at 30 June 2018:

	$'000
Land in Wellington, at cost	100
Land in Auckland, at valuation 2015	2 000
Buildings on land in Auckland, at valuation 2015	1 000
Accumulated depreciation	(150)

At 30 June 2018, the balance of the Revaluation Surplus is $800 000, of which $700 000 relates to the land in Auckland and $50 000 relates to the buildings (the balance relates to other PPE assets). An independent valuation carried out on this day determined the following fair values: land in Wellington $1 500 000, land in Auckland $2 400 000, buildings $750 000. The estimated remaining useful life of the buildings is 15 years with nil residual.

Required

(a) Record all entries relating to the revaluation of the assets on 30 June 2018.

(b) Record the depreciation for the year ended 30 June 2019.

PSA8.7 Calculate depreciation under different methods. **LO4**

In recent years Button Ltd has purchased three machines. Because of frequent employee turnover in the accounting department, a different accountant was in charge of selecting the depreciation method for each machine, and various methods have been used. Information concerning the machines is summarised in the table below.

Machine	Acquired	Cost	Residual value	Useful life (in years)	Depreciation method
1	1 Jan. 2015	$54 000	$10 500	10	Straight-line
2	1 Jan. 2016	38 400	9 000	8	Diminishing-balance*
3	1 Jan. 2016	26 000	6 000	5	Units-of-production

*Using $1\frac{1}{2}$ times the straight-line rate

For the units-of-production method, total machine hours are expected to be 10 000. Actual hours of use in the first 3 years were: 2016, 1000; 2017, 3000; and 2018, 4000.

Required

(a) Calculate the amount of accumulated depreciation on each machine at 31 December 2018.

(b) For Machine 3 in 2018, which depreciation method is the preferred method for tax purposes? Explain why.

(c) If you are the manager of Button Ltd and your bonus is linked to profit of the company, which depreciation method do you prefer for Machine 3 in 2018? Explain why in point form.

PSA8.8 Calculate depreciation under different methods. **LO4**

Carpet Ltd purchased machinery on 1 January 2018, at a cost of $400 000. The estimated useful life of the machinery is 4 years, with an estimated residual value at the end of that period of $40 000. The entity is considering different depreciation methods that could be used for financial reporting purposes for the year ended 31 December 2018.

Required

(a) Prepare separate depreciation schedules for the machinery using the straight-line method, and the diminishing-balance method. Round to the nearest dollar.

(b) Which method would result in the higher reported profit in 2018? In the higher total reported profit over the 4-year period?

PSA8.9 Prepare entries to record transactions related to acquisition and amortisation of intangibles; prepare the financial statement disclosures. **LO10**

The intangible assets information of Wang Ltd as at 30 June 2018 is presented here:

Patent ($80 000 cost less $10 000 amortisation)	$70 000
Copyright ($36 000 cost less $14 400 amortisation)	21 600
Total	**$91 600**

The patent was acquired in July 2017 and has a useful life of 8 years. The copyright was acquired in July 2014 and has a useful life of 10 years. The following cash transactions may have affected intangible assets during the year ending 30 June 2019:

Jul.	1	Paid $25 000 legal costs to successfully defend the patent against infringement by another entity.
Jul.–Dec.		Developed a new product, incurring $100 000 in development costs. A patent was granted for the product on 1 January 2019, and it is estimated that its useful life is equal to its legal life of 10 years.
Apr.	1	Incurred $30 000 to develop a brand for the new product.
May	1	Acquired a copyright for $250 000. The copyright has a useful life of 50 years.

Required

(a) Prepare journal entries to record the transactions for the year ending 30 June 2019.

(b) Prepare journal entries to record the 2019 amortisation expense for intangible assets.

(c) Calculate the carrying amount of the intangible assets reported in the statement of financial position at 30 June 2019.

(d) Prepare the note to the financial statements on Wang Ltd's intangible assets as of 30 June 2019.

PSA8.10 **Calculate and comment on average age, average useful life of PPE assets, and asset turnover.**
LO14

Ross Ltd and Yang Ltd, two entities of roughly the same size, are both involved in the manufacture of dancing shoes. Each entity depreciates its PPE assets using the straight-line approach. An investigation of their financial statements reveals this information:

	Ross Ltd	Yang Ltd
Profit	$ 560 000	$ 900 000
Sales	10 300 000	12 600 000
Total assets (average)	4 480 000	3 750 000
PPE assets (average)	3 360 000	2 000 000
Accumulated depreciation	1 420 000	937 500
Depreciation expense	420 000	130 000
Intangible assets (goodwill)	300 000	—
Amortisation expense	60 000	—

Required

(a) For each entity, calculate these values:
1. average age of PPE assets.
2. average useful life.
3. asset turnover.

(b) Based on your calculations in part (a), comment on the relative effectiveness of the two entities in using their assets to generate sales. What factors complicate your ability to compare the two entities?

PROBLEM SET B

PSB8.1 **Determine acquisition costs of land and building.**
LO2

Box Ltd was incorporated on 1 January. During the first year of operations, the following PPE asset expenditures and receipts were recorded in random order:

Debits	
1. Cost of real estate purchased as a factory site (land $235 000 and building $25 000)	$260 000
2. Installation cost of fences around property	6 750
3. Cost of demolishing building to make land suitable for construction of new building	19 000
4. Excavation costs for new building	23 000
5. Accrued land taxes paid at time of purchase of real estate	2 179
6. Cost of parking lots and driveways	29 000
7. Architects' fees on building plans	40 000
8. Land taxes paid for the current year on land	6 500
9. Full payment to building contractor	600 000
	$986 429
Credits	
10. Proceeds from residual of demolished building	$ 5 000

Required

Analyse the foregoing transactions using the following table column headings:

Item	Land	Building	Other accounts

Enter the number of each transaction in the Item column, and enter the amounts in the appropriate columns. For amounts in the Other accounts column, also indicate the account name.

PSB8.2 **Journalise equipment transactions related to purchase, sale, scrapping and depreciation.**

LO2, 4, 8

At 31 December 2018, King Ltd reported these PPE assets:

Land		$ 3 600 000
Buildings	$31 800 000	
Less: Accumulated depreciation—buildings	14 520 000	17 280 000
Equipment	48 000 000	
Less: Accumulated depreciation—equipment	6 000 000	42 000 000
Total PPE assets		**$62 880 000**

During 2019, the following selected cash transactions occurred:

Apr.	1	Purchased land for $2 400 000.
May	1	Sold equipment that cost $720 000 when purchased on 1 January 2015. The equipment was sold for $420 000.
June	1	Sold land for $1 800 000. The land cost $500 000.
July	1	Purchased equipment for $2 000 000.
Dec.	31	Scrapped equipment that cost $500 000 when purchased on 31 December 2009. No residual value was received.

Required

(a) For the transactions complete the following.
1. Journalise the transactions. (*Hint:* You may wish to set up T accounts, post beginning balances, and then post 2019 transactions.) King Ltd uses straight-line depreciation for buildings and equipment. The buildings are estimated to have a 40-year useful life and no residual value; the equipment is estimated to have a 10-year useful life and no residual value. Update depreciation on assets disposed of at the time of sale or scrapping.
2. Record adjusting entries for depreciation for 2019.
3. Prepare the PPE assets section of King Ltd's statement of financial position as at 31 December 2019.

(b) Repeat requirement (a) above assuming GST of 10% applies to all relevant transactions.

PSB8.3 **Journalise entries for disposals of PPE assets.** **LO8**

Presented here are selected transactions for Cox Ltd for 2019.

Jan.	1	Scrapped a piece of machinery that was purchased on 1 January 2009. The machine cost $78 000 and had a useful life of 10 years with no residual value.
Jun.	30	Sold office equipment that was purchased on 1 January 2016. The equipment cost $73 500 and had a useful life of 5 years with no residual value. The office equipment was sold for $30 000.
Dec.	31	Discarded a delivery truck that was purchased on 1 January 2015. The truck cost $40 500 and was depreciated based on an 8-year useful life with a $4500 residual value.

Required

Journalise all entries required on the above dates, including entries to update depreciation on assets disposed of, where applicable. Cox Ltd uses straight-line depreciation. The financial year-end is 31 December.

PSB8.4 **Prepare the entries to record revaluation, depreciation and disposal.** **LO4, 7, 8**

On 1 July 2018, Mars Ltd purchased land $1 200 000 and buildings $500 000. The estimated useful life of the buildings was 40 years, with a residual value of nil. On 1 October 2018, machinery was purchased at a total cost of $120 000. The estimated useful life of the machinery was 4 years with an estimated residual value of $9000. Mars Ltd uses straight-line depreciation for buildings and the diminishing-balance method for machinery at a rate of 48%. The entity's reporting period ends on 30 June.

Required

(a) Prepare journal entries to record the purchase of the land, buildings and machinery during the year.

(b) Prepare journal entries to record the depreciation expense for the year ended 30 June 2019.

(c) Assume that on 1 July 2019 the entity revalued the land upwards by $200 000 and the buildings downwards by $25 000. Prepare the journal entries for the revaluations.

(d) On 31 December 2019, owing to a change in product mix, the machinery was sold for $50 000. Prepare the journal entry(ies) to dispose of the machinery.

PSB8.5 **Prepare journal entries for asset impairments and reversals.** **LO6**

On 1 July 2018, Fox Ltd purchased equipment for $85 000 to manufacture a new product for sale overseas. The estimated useful life was 8 years, with a residual value of $5000. Fox Ltd uses straight-line depreciation. On 30 June 2019 there was an indication that the machine could be impaired due to fluctuations in the exchange rate, and Fox Ltd calculated the recoverable amount of the machine. The net selling price was $61 000 and the value in use was estimated to be $45 000. Twelve months later this threat no longer existed and the recoverable amount was reassessed. The net selling price was $70 000 and the value in use was estimated to be $65 000. Assume that the estimated residual value was $5000 throughout.

Required

(a) Prepare the journal entry to record the purchase of the machine and the depreciation for the year ended 30 June 2019.

(b) Prepare the journal entry to record any asset impairment at 30 June 2019.

(c) Prepare the journal entry to record depreciation for the year ended 30 June 2020.

(d) Prepare the journal entry to record any asset impairment or reversal at 30 June 2020.

PSB8.6 **Prepare journal entries for asset revaluation increases and decreases and depreciation over periods.** **LO4, 7**

Red Ltd has the following land and buildings in its accounts as at 30 June 2019:

	$'000
Land in Darwin, at valuation 2016	400
Land in Perth, at valuation 2016	1 200
Buildings in Perth, at valuation 2016	800
Accumulated depreciation	(150)

An independent valuation carried out on 30 June 2019 determined the following fair values: land in Darwin $600 000, land in Perth $1 000 000, buildings $500 000. At 30 June 2019, prior to the independent valuation, the balance of the revaluation surplus account was $400 000, of which $300 000 related to the land in Perth and $100 000 related to the buildings. Assume depreciation has been recorded for the year ending 30 June 2019.

Required

Record all entries relating to the revaluation of the assets on 30 June 2019.

PSB8.7 Calculate depreciation under different methods.   **LO4**

In recent years Winter Ltd has purchased three machines. Because of frequent employee turnover in the accounting department, a different accountant was in charge of selecting the depreciation method for each machine, and various methods have been used. Information concerning the machines is summarised in the table below.

Machine	Acquired	Cost	Residual value	Useful life (in years)	Depreciation method
1	1 Jan. 2015	$135 000	$26 250	10	Straight-line
2	1 Jan. 2016	96 000	22 500	8	Diminishing-balance*
3	1 Jan. 2016	65 000	15 000	5	Units-of-production

*Using $1\frac{1}{2}$ times the straight-line rate

For the units-of-production method, total machine hours are expected to be 10 000. Actual hours of use in the first 3 years were: 2016, 1000; 2017, 3000; and 2018, 4000.

Required

(a) Calculate the amount of accumulated depreciation on each machine at 31 December 2018.
(b) For Machine 3 in 2018, which depreciation method is the preferred method for tax purposes? Explain why.
(c) If you are the manager of Winter Ltd and your bonus is linked to profit of the company, which depreciation method do you prefer for Machine 3 in 2018? Explain why in point form.

PSB8.8 Calculate depreciation under different methods.   **LO4**

Buttercup Ltd purchased machinery on 1 January 2018, at a cost of $310 000. The estimated useful life of the machinery is 5 years, with an estimated residual value at the end of that period of $40 000. The entity is considering different depreciation methods that could be used for financial reporting purposes.

Required

(a) Prepare separate depreciation schedules for the machinery using the straight-line method, and the diminishing-balance method. Round to the nearest dollar.
(b) Which method would result in the higher reported profit in 2018? In the higher total reported profit over the 5-year period?

PSB8.9 Prepare entries to record transactions related to acquisition and amortisation of intangibles; prepare the financial statement disclosures.   **LO10**

The intangible assets information of Future Ltd as at 31 December 2019 is presented here:

Patent ($80 000 cost less $8000 amortisation)	$ 72 000
Copyright ($64 000 cost less $25 600 amortisation)	38 400
Total	**$110 400**

The patent was acquired in January 2019 and has a useful life of 10 years. The copyright was acquired in January 2013 and also has a useful life of 10 years. The following cash transactions may have affected intangible assets during 2020:

Jan.	1	Paid $13 500 legal costs to successfully defend the patent against infringement by another company.
Jan.–June		Developed a new product, incurring $180 000 in development costs.
July	1	A patent was granted for the new product. The patent's useful life is equal to its legal life of 20 years.
Sept.	1	Paid $45 000 to a rugby player to appear in commercials advertising the entity's products. The commercials will air in September and October.
Oct.	1	Acquired a copyright for $200 000. The copyright has a useful life of 50 years.

Required

(a) Prepare journal entries to record the transactions.

(b) Prepare journal entries to record the 2020 amortisation expense for intangible assets.

(c) Calculate the carrying amount of the intangible assets reported in the statement of financial position at 31 December 2020.

(d) Prepare the note to the financial statements on Future Ltd's intangible assets as of 31 December 2020.

PSB8.10 **Calculate and comment on average age, average useful life of PPE assets, and asset turnover.**

LO14

Zhou Ltd and Wang Ltd, two entities of roughly the same size, are both involved in the manufacture of canoes and kayaks. Each entity depreciates its PPE assets using the straight-line approach. An investigation of their financial statements reveals the following information.

	Zhou Ltd	Wang Ltd
Profit	$ 480 000	$ 720 000
Sales	3 680 000	3 440 000
Total assets (average)	2 840 000	2 000 000
PPE assets (average)	1 410 000	1 160 000
Accumulated depreciation	360 000	750 000
Depreciation expense	160 000	124 000
Intangible assets (goodwill)	360 000	—
Amortisation expense	72 000	—

Required

(a) For each entity, calculate these values:
   1. average age of PPE assets.
   2. average useful life.
   3. asset turnover.

(b) Based on your calculations in part (a), comment on the relative effectiveness of the two entities in using their assets to generate sales. What factors complicate your ability to compare the two entities?

BUILDING BUSINESS SKILLS

FINANCIAL REPORTING AND ANALYSIS

Financial reporting problem: Domino's Pizza Enterprises Ltd

BBS8.1 Look up the latest annual report for Domino's Pizza Enterprises Ltd at www.dominos.com.au, scroll down to bottom right of the home page and select **Domino's Corporate Site**, then select **Investors, Reports & Presentations**. Refer to the financial statements and the notes to the financial statements in the latest annual report.

Required

Answer the following questions:

(a) What were the total cost and book value of property, plant and equipment at the beginning of the current reporting period?

(b) What methods of depreciation are used by Domino's for financial reporting purposes?

(c) What were the amounts of depreciation and amortisation expense for the current reporting period and the comparative (previous) reporting period?

(d) What were the amounts of additions (if any) to plant and equipment, goodwill and other intangible assets in both reporting periods?

(e) Read the notes on leases. Does the entity engage mainly in finance or operating leases? What are the implications for analysis of its financial statements?

Comparative analysis problems

BBS8.2 Below are data from the 2019 annual reports of Sugar Mills Ltd and Bamboo Ltd.

($ in millions)	Sugar Mills Ltd	Bamboo Ltd
Total cost of plant and equipment, beginning of year	$2 105.1	$6 911.8
Total cost of plant and equipment, end of year	1 922.5	6 892.0
Depreciation expense	128.5	395.2
Accumulated depreciation	1 053.0	3 941.4
Total assets, end of year	3 049.0	9 474.6
Total assets, beginning of year	3 368.2	9 748.5
Net sales	2 523.6	7 814.1

Required

(a) Based on the above information, calculate:
   1. average useful life of the PPE assets.
   2. average age of the PPE assets.
   3. asset turnover ratio.

(b) What conclusions concerning the management of PPE assets can be drawn from these data?

BBS8.3 Meds4U Ltd and Hope Ltd are two leading producers of pharmaceutical drugs. Each has considerable assets and expends considerable funds each year in developing new products. The development of a new pharmaceutical drug is often very expensive and risky. New products must often undergo considerable testing before they are approved for distribution to the public. For example, it took Hope Ltd 5 years and $800 million to develop a new blood pressure drug.

Here are some basic data compiled from the 2019 financial statements of these entities:

($ in millions)	Meds4U Ltd	Hope Ltd
Total assets	$54 422	$63 706
Total revenue	47 314	53 796
Profit	6 118	10 496
Research and development expense	4 866	3 642
Intangible assets	14 418	16 574

Required

(a) What kinds of intangible assets might a pharmaceutical company have? Does the composition of these intangible assets matter to investors? That is, would Hope Ltd be perceived differently if all of its intangibles were goodwill instead of patents?

(b) Using the asset turnover, determine which entity is using its assets more effectively. (*Note:* In 2018 total assets were $51 472 million for Hope Ltd and $42 906 million for Meds4U Ltd.)

(c) Suppose that, by eliminating research and development expenditures, Hope Ltd could have reported $3.6 billion more in profit in 2019. Much of the research never results in a product or the products take years to develop, but shareholders are eager for higher returns. Therefore, the entity is considering eliminating research and development expenditures for at least a couple of years. What would you advise?

(d) The notes to Hope Ltd's financial statements indicate that Hope Ltd has goodwill of $8.6 billion. Where does recorded goodwill come from? Is it necessarily a good thing to have a lot of goodwill in the financial statements?

Financial analysis on the web

BBS8.4 **Purpose:** Use an annual report and identify a company's non-current assets and the depreciation and amortisation methods used.

Address: www.asx.com.au

Steps:

1. On the Australian Securities Exchange (ASX) home page, you will notice a menu on the left-hand side. Click on **Prices and Research** and then on **Company information** from the drop-down menu.

2. You will now see the listed Company directory. Click on a letter of the alphabet and select a particular company by clicking on the ASX code (don't just choose the first company).

3. On the page that appears, scroll down to the internet address and click on the address, which will take you to the company's web site.

4. On that web site, search around and find the latest annual report.

OR

Address: https://m.nzx.com/#

Steps:

1. Click on **Markets** on the top bar.

2. Then click on **NZX Main Board** from the drop-down menu.

3. You will now see the listed company directory. Select a particular company by clicking on the NZX code (don't just choose the first company).

4. Click on the name of the entity (usually towards the top right-hand corner of the page).

5. That should take you to a second page with their web site under contact information.

6. Click on the web site and search around and find the latest annual report.

Required

Answer the following questions:

(a) What is the company's name?

(b) What is the internet address of the annual report?

(c) From the statement of financial position, what is the net amount of property, plant and equipment?

(d) Does the company have any intangibles? List the intangibles by name.

(e) What is the accumulated depreciation, depreciation expense and amortisation expense?

(f) Does the company have any agricultural assets or natural resources?

(g) Outline the method of accounting for the various categories of non-current assets, including a description of the depreciation and amortisation methods.

CRITICAL THINKING

Communication activity

BBS8.5 This chapter has presented the current rule relating to the reporting of intangible assets. This rule prohibits internally generated brands, mastheads, publishing titles, customer lists and items similar in substance from being recognised as intangible assets, yet these are valuable assets that can be separately identified and sold. Applying this rule results in inconsistent treatment when two entities operate in the same industry with similar intangibles, but have statements of financial position that are not comparable because the intangible assets recognised depend on whether they were 'purchased' or 'internally generated'.

Required

Assume you are either (a) the CEO of an entity that has a large proportion of intangible assets and you find the current accounting rules not logically sound, or (b) an International Standard Setting Board member defending the current status of regulation regarding intangibles. Write a short report to the Standard Setting Board, putting forward an argument in favour of your views. (You may wish to include a discussion of goodwill.)

Ethics case

BBS8.6 Glass Ltd is suffering declining sales of its principal product, biodegradable recycled cardboard cartons. The managing director, Angela Smith, instructs the accountant, Jonty Upright, to lengthen asset lives to reduce depreciation expense. A processing line of automated cardboard pulping equipment, purchased for $7 million in January 2018, was originally estimated to have a useful life of 8 years and a residual value of $600 000. Depreciation has been recorded for 2 years on that basis. Angela wants the estimated life changed to 14 years total and the straight-line method continued. Jonty is hesitant to make the change, believing it is unethical to increase profit in this manner. Angela says, 'The life is only an estimate, and I've heard that our competition uses a 14-year life on their production equipment.'

Required

(a) Who are the stakeholders in this situation?

(b) Is the proposed change in asset life unethical, or is it simply a good business practice by an astute managing director?

(c) What is the effect of Angela Smith's proposed change on profit in the year of change?

Group decision case

BBS8.7 Auckland Ltd and Wellington Ltd are two entities that are similar in many respects except that Auckland Ltd uses the straight-line method and Wellington Ltd uses the diminishing-balance method at double the straight-line rate. On 2 January 2018, both entities acquired identical depreciable assets listed in the table below.

Asset	Cost	Residual	Useful life
Building	$460 000	$60 000	50 years
Equipment	200 000	15 000	8 years

Including the appropriate depreciation charges, annual profit for the entities in the years 2018, 2019 and 2020 was as follows:

	2018	2019	2020	Total
Auckland Ltd	$126 000	$123 800	$117 500	$367 300
Wellington Ltd	102 000	114 000	127 500	343 500

At 31 December 2020, the statements of financial position of the two entities are similar except that Wellington Ltd has more cash than Auckland Ltd.

Brianna James is interested in investing in one of the entities, and she comes to you for advice.

Required

With the class divided into groups, answer the following:

(a) Determine the annual and total depreciation recorded by both companies during the 3 years.

(b) Assuming that Wellington Ltd also uses the straight-line method of depreciation instead of the diminishing-balance method (i.e. Wellington's depreciation expense would equal Auckland's), prepare comparative profit data for the 3 years.

(c) Which entity should Brianna James invest in? Why?

Sustainability

BBS8.8 Many businesses are starting to focus on sustainability and are producing sustainability reports either as part of their annual report or as a separate stand-alone report. Often businesses now use the Global Reporting Institute's (GRI) guidelines as a benchmark to measure their progress towards sustainability

The following is an extract from Air New Zealand's website (2018): https://www.air newzealand.co.nz/sustainability.

> For more than 75 years, we've been part of the fabric of our society. To ensure we're a strong, vibrant business for at least another 75 years it's critical we commit to a purpose that's bigger than ourselves — that is to supercharge New Zealand's success socially, environmentally and economically.

Required

(a) What is meant by the term sustainability?

(b) Access Air New Zealand's latest sustainability report at www.airnewzealand.co .nz/sustainability. Scroll down to download the report, or go directly to https://p-airnz .com/cms/assets/PDFs/sustainability-report-2017-v2.pdf and complete the following requirements.

    1. Outline Air New Zealand's approach to sustainability and why it is important for the business.

    2. What are the main areas that its report focuses on?

    3. Scroll through the report to explore how Air New Zealand benchmarks its progress towards sustainability.

    4. Why do you think a company would choose to benchmark its progress against the GRI?

(c) How could climate change impact on the traditional financial reporting of non-current assets?

ANSWERS

Answers to self-study questions

8.1 (d) 8.2 (a) 8.3 (b) 8.4 (c) 8.5 (c) 8.6 (b) 8.7 (d) 8.8 (d) 8.9 (b) 8.10 (c) 8.11 (c) 8.12 (d) 8.13 (c) 8.14 (d) 8.15 (c)

ACKNOWLEDGEMENTS

Photo: © Hero Images / Getty Images
Photo: © Edi_Eco / Getty Images
Photo: © tiverylucky / Shutterstock.com

CHAPTER 9

Reporting and analysing liabilities

LEARNING OBJECTIVES

After studying this chapter, you should be able to:

9.1 explain the differences between current and non-current liabilities

9.2 identify common types of current liabilities and explain how to account for them

9.3 identify common types of non-current liabilities, such as debentures and unsecured notes, and explain how to account for them

9.4 prepare journal entries for loans payable by instalment and distinguish between current and non-current components of long-term debt

9.5 identify the advantages of leasing and explain the difference between an operating lease and a finance lease

9.6 complete basic journal entries for accounting for leases and explain how to report leases

9.7 explain the differences between provisions, contingencies and other types of liabilities and explain how to report contingent liabilities

9.8 prepare entries to record provisions for warranties

9.9 evaluate an entity's liquidity and solvency.

Chapter preview

Large entities like Domino's Pizza, Telstra and Telecom New Zealand, and even many small entities, do not rely solely on shareholders to finance their operations and investments. They also rely on debt to finance some of their operations. In this chapter we will look at different types of liabilities, how to account for liabilities, and the implications of alternative methods of finance for liquidity and solvency.

The content and organisation of this chapter are as follows.

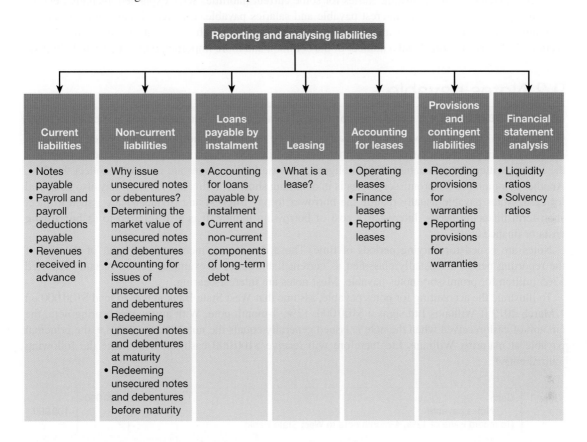

9.1 Current liabilities

LEARNING OBJECTIVE 9.1 Explain the differences between current and non-current liabilities.

As explained in chapter 1, liabilities are defined in the *Conceptual Framework* as outflows of economic benefits that the entity is presently obliged to make as a result of past events. The same definition is provided in IAS 37/AASB 137 *Provisions, Contingent Liabilities and Contingent Assets*. These obligations must be settled or paid at some time in the future by the transfer of assets or services. The future date on which they are due or payable (the maturity date) is a significant feature of liabilities.

A **current liability** is an obligation that can reasonably be expected to be paid within 1 year or within the operating cycle, whichever is the longer. Liabilities that do not meet this criterion are classified as non-current.

Financial statement users want to know whether an entity's obligations are current or non-current. An entity, for example, that has more current liabilities than current assets often lacks liquidity, or short-term debt-paying ability. In addition, users want to know the types of liabilities an entity has. If an entity becomes insolvent, i.e. unable to pay its debts as and when they fall due, then a specific, predetermined order of payment to creditors will have to be served. Thus, the amount and type of liabilities are of critical importance.

The different types of current liabilities include notes payable, accounts payable, revenue received in advance and accrued liabilities such as taxes, salaries and wages, provisions and interest. Many of these terms are already familiar to you. You may recall that in chapter 2 we introduced how to record the journal entries for borrowing money from the bank, for purchasing supplies on credit and for revenues received in advance. In chapter 3, the adjusting entries for some current liabilities were explained, including entries to record accrued expenses for interest payable and salaries payable. Chapters 4 and 5 focused on the accounting entries for recording trade accounts payable for the purchase inventories on credit. In this section we discuss in more detail a number of the common and more important types of current liabilities.

9.2 Notes payable

LEARNING OBJECTIVE 9.2 Identify common types of current liabilities and explain how to account for them.

Obligations in the form of written promissory notes are recorded as **notes payable**. When purchasing inventory on credit, notes payable are sometimes used instead of accounts payable because they give the lender written documentation of the obligation in case legal avenues are needed to collect the debt. Another common use for promissory notes is in obtaining short-term finance, i.e. they may also be issued for cash. Notes payable usually require the borrower to pay **interest** and frequently are issued to meet short-term financing needs. Interest is a cost of borrowing money. It is also referred to as **borrowing costs** or finance costs.

Notes are issued for varying periods of time. Those due for payment within 1 year of the end of the reporting period are usually classified as current liabilities. For example, Telstra recently reported $365 million for promissory notes payable. Most notes are interest-bearing.

To illustrate the accounting for notes payable, assume that West State Bank agrees to lend $100 000 on 1 March 2019 if Williams Ltd signs a $100 000, 12%, 4-month note. With an interest-bearing note, the amount of cash received when the note is issued generally equals the note's **face value**, i.e. the principal payable at maturity. Williams Ltd therefore will receive $100 000 cash and will make the following journal entry:

Mar. 1	Cash	100 000	
	Notes payable		100 000
	(To record issue of 12%, 4-month note to West State Bank)		

| | A | = | L | + | E |
| | +100 000 | | +100 000 | | |

Interest accrues over the life of the note and must be recorded periodically. If Williams Ltd's year-end is 30 June, an adjusting entry is required to recognise interest expense and interest payable of $4000 ($100 000 × 12% × 4/12) at 30 June. The adjusting entry is:

June 30	Interest expense	4 000	
	Interest payable		4 000
	(To accrue interest for 4 months on West State Bank note)		

| | A | = | L | + | E |
| | | | +4000 | | −4000 |

In the 30 June financial statements, the current liabilities section of the statement of financial position will include notes payable $100 000 and interest payable $4000. In addition, interest expense of $4000 will be reported in the statement of profit or loss.

At maturity, that is, when the principal payment is due (1 July), Williams Ltd must pay the face value of the note ($100 000) plus $4000 interest ($100 000 × 12% × 4/12). The entry to record payment of the note and accrued interest is:

July 1	Notes payable	100 000	
	Interest payable	4 000	
	Cash		104 000
	(To record payment of West State Bank interest-bearing note and accrued interest at maturity)		

A	=	L	+	E
−104 000		−100 000		
		−4 000		

Payroll and payroll deductions payable

Telstra, like every employer, incurs liabilities relating to employees' salaries and wages. The employer deducts amounts from employees' wages if they are required to be paid to other parties. For example, the employer is required by law to deduct tax from employees' gross pay and remit it to the taxation authority. Other payroll deductions include amounts paid to medical funds for health insurance and trade unions on behalf of employees. Until these payroll deductions, such as pay-as-you-go (PAYG) withheld tax, are remitted to the appropriate parties, they are recorded as increases (credited) to appropriate liability accounts. For example, accrual and payment of a $100 000 payroll on which an entity withholds tax from its employees' wages and salaries would be recorded as follows:

Mar. 7	Salaries and wages expense	100 000	
	Pay-as-you-go withheld tax payable		32 036
	Salaries and wages payable		67 964
	(To record payroll and withheld taxes for the week ending 7 March)		
	Salaries and wages payable	67 964	
	Cash		67 964
	(To record payment of the 7 March payroll)		

A	=	L	+	E
		+32 036		−100 000
		+67 964		

A	=	L	+	E
−67 964		−67 964		

When the payments are subsequently made, the payroll deduction liability accounts should be debited as follows:

Apr. 6	Pay-as-you-go withheld tax payable	32 036	
	Cash		32 036
	(To record payment of withheld taxes for March)		

A	=	L	+	E
−32 036		−32 036		

Taxation authorities impose substantial fines and penalties on employers if the taxes are not calculated correctly and paid on time.

Helpful hint: In Australia the taxation authority is the Australian Taxation Office (ATO), and in New Zealand it's the NZ Inland Revenue (IR).

In addition to PAYG withheld tax payable, a number of common payroll deductions may occur. These are illustrated in figure 9.1. Employers may deduct amounts from employees' wages for private health insurance to be paid to medical funds on behalf of their employees. For example, you may have heard of the medical funds such as Bupa and Medibank. Superannuation contributions are payments made to a superannuation fund. Superannuation contributions are required by law. The aim is to provide employees with a lump sum and/or regular payments on retirement. Other deductions may include payment of union fees if the employee is a member of a union, or donations to charitable and other organisations such as the Heart Foundation, Australian Cancer Research Foundation, Guide Dogs Australia and the Salvation Army.

FIGURE 9.1 Examples of payroll deductions that may occur

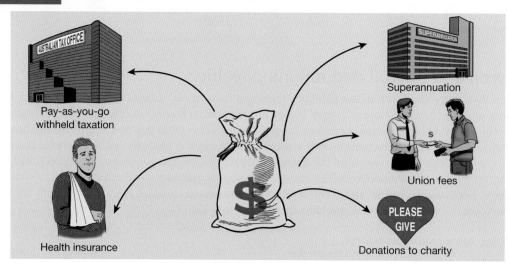

The payroll liability accounts are classified as current liabilities because they must be paid to employees or remitted to taxation authorities and other parties in the short term.

Recording the accrual and payment of the payroll deduction liabilities is illustrated using a simple example below. The general journal entry to record the various liabilities is:

Mar. 7	Salaries and wages expense	37 000	
	Pay-as-you-go withheld tax payable		32 000
	Superannuation payable		4 000
	Union fees payable		1 000
	(To record withheld taxes and deductions for the week ending 7 March)		

$$A \quad = \quad L \quad + \quad E$$
$$+32\,000 \qquad -37\,000$$
$$+4\,000$$
$$+1\,000$$

The entry in the cash payments journal to record the payment of the accrued liabilities is:

Cash payments journal					
Date	Description	Chq no.	Post ref.	Other accounts	Cash
Mar. 31	Pay-as-you-go withheld tax payable—Australian Taxation Office	101		32 000	32 000
	Superannuation payable—AMP	102		4 000	4 000
	Union fees payable—NTEU	103		1 000	1 000

Finally, employers may also incur other costs in relation to their employees such as annual leave, workers compensation, parental leave, sick leave and long service leave. Some of these costs are mandatory as required by legislation or specified in salary and wage awards and contracts. Employees are generally entitled to a number of paid weeks annual leave and a number of days of sick leave. As employees only become entitled to these benefits on a pro-rata basis as they work throughout the year, the employer generally accrues the liability at regular intervals. Workers compensation, on the other hand, is usually paid as a yearly premium as it is an insurance scheme to compensate employees for injuries or death at work. Long service leave is another substantial expense for an employer. It is generally granted after 10 years of service but is accrued only after the employees have completed a number of years of service. Long service leave may have a component that is classified as a current liability (i.e. for the portion to be paid within less than one year) and a non-current component (i.e. the amount to be paid after one year).

Helpful hint: Long service leave is discussed further in the section on provisions and contingent liabilities.

Revenues received in advance

A magazine publisher such as *Business Review Weekly* may receive a customer's payment when a customer subscribes for a period, such as a year. Qantas often receives cash when it sells tickets for future flights. How do these entities account for revenues that are received before goods are delivered or services are rendered?

1. When the advance is received, cash is increased (debited) and a current liability account identifying the source of the revenue received in advance is also increased (credited). The revenue received in advance account is a liability.
2. When the service is performed or the goods are delivered, the revenue received in advance account is decreased (debited) and a revenue account is increased (credited).

Helpful hint: Revenues received in advance is also referred to as unearned revenue.

To illustrate, assume that Suncorp Stadium Ltd sells 10 000 season football tickets at $50 each for its five-game home schedule. The entry for the sales of season tickets and receipt of cash on 6 August is:

Aug. 6	Cash	500 000	
	Ticket revenue received in advance		500 000
	(To record sale of 10 000 season tickets)		

$$A \qquad = \qquad L \qquad + \qquad E$$
$$+500\,000 \qquad +500\,000$$

As each game is completed, this entry is made:

Sept. 5	Ticket revenue received in advance	100 000	
	Football ticket revenue		100 000
	(To record football ticket revenues)		

$$A \qquad = \qquad L \qquad + \qquad E$$
$$-100\,000 \qquad +100\,000$$

The account ticket revenue received in advance represents revenue that belongs to a future period and is reported as a current liability in the statement of financial position. The cash received is accounted for as a liability because the entity has an obligation to provide the services paid for by the ticket holders. However, when the services have been performed, and subject to the criteria explained in chapter 3, the revenue is recognised and a transfer from revenue received in advance to revenue account occurs. Revenue received in advance is substantial for some entities.

Table 9.1 shows specific revenue received in advance and revenue accounts used in selected types of businesses.

TABLE 9.1 Revenue received in advance and revenue accounts

Type of business	Account name	
	Revenue received in advance	Revenue
Airline	Air fares received in advance	Air fare revenue
Magazine publisher	Subscriptions received in advance	Subscription revenue
Hotel	Rent received in advance	Rent revenue

Large entities as well as smaller businesses need to account for transactions involving both current and non-current liabilities. In the previous section we explored the nature of and the recording of common current liabilities. In this section we explore non-current liabilities or, as they are sometimes called, long-term liabilities.

9.3 Non-current liabilities

LEARNING OBJECTIVE 9.3 Identify common types of non-current liabilities, such as debentures and unsecured notes, and explain how to account for them.

Non-current liabilities are obligations that are expected to be paid after 1 year or outside the normal operating cycle. The normal operating cycle for payables is the time it takes from the purchase of inventory on credit to the payment of the liability. In this section we explain the accounting for the main types of obligations reported in the non-current section of the statement of financial position. These obligations are often in the form of bank loans or long-term notes.

Public companies may raise debt finance from the public. This can take the form of notes issued in small denominations (usually $1000 or multiples of $1000). Notes that are not subject to a security over assets of the issuing company are referred to as **unsecured notes**. Notes that are subject to a secured charge over some of the issuer's assets are called **debentures**. A security over assets is a right to have the assets liquidated to recover unpaid amounts of a debt if the debtor defaults on payment. The distinction between unsecured notes and debentures is illustrated in figure 9.2. Convertible notes are able to be converted into shares instead of being repaid at maturity.

| **FIGURE 9.2** | Distinction between secured and unsecured notes |

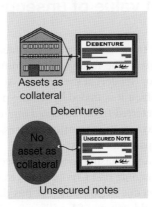

Why issue unsecured notes or debentures?

A company may use long-term financing, such as bank loans and leasing, other than unsecured notes (also known as *bonds*) or debentures. Both public and private companies may borrow money in this way. However, these other forms of financing involve an agreement between the company and an individual, creditor company, or financial institution.

From the standpoint of the company seeking long-term financing, notes offer advantages over shares as shown in figure 9.3.

| **FIGURE 9.3** | Advantages of debt financing over issuing ordinary shares |

Debt financing	Advantages
BALLOT BOX	**1. Shareholder control is not affected.** Noteholders do not have voting rights, so current owners (shareholders) retain full control of the company.
TAX BILL	**2. Tax savings result.** Interest is deductible for tax purposes; dividends on shares are not.
$ / 100 SHARES 100	**3. Earnings per share may be higher.** Although interest expense reduces profit, earnings per share is often higher under debt financing because no additional shares are issued.

The major disadvantage resulting from the use of unsecured notes or debentures is that the company locks in fixed payments that must be made in good times and bad. Interest must be paid on a periodic basis and the principal (face value) of the notes must be paid at maturity. A company with fluctuating earnings and a relatively weak cash position may experience great difficulty in meeting interest requirements in periods of low earnings. In the extreme, this can result in insolvency. With equity financing, on the other hand, the company can decide to pay low (or no) dividends if earnings are low.

Comparative analysis of debt and equity as alternative sources of finance will be considered in chapter 10 when you are more familiar with accounting for transactions with shareholders.

Determining the market value of unsecured notes and debentures

The market value of a note may differ from its face value. The face value of a note is the amount due at maturity, also referred to as the *principal*. The face value may differ from the **issue price**, which is the amount paid for the note by the investor (lender) at the time of issue. Throughout the term of the note its **market value**, which is the price at which it is traded by willing parties, may vary.

The **contract interest rate** (often referred to as the *stated interest rate*) is the rate used to determine the amount of interest the borrower pays and the investor receives. Usually the contract rate is stated as an annual rate, and interest is usually paid half-yearly.

If you were an investor interested in purchasing a note, how would the amount you pay for the note be determined? To be more specific, assume that Coronet Ltd issues a zero-interest debenture (pays no interest) with a face value of $1 million due in 20 years. For this debenture, the only cash you receive is $1 million at the end of 20 years. Would you pay $1 million for this debenture? We hope not, because $1 million received 20 years from now is not the same as $1 million received today. The reason you should not pay $1 million relates to what is called the *time value of money*. If you had $1 million today, you could invest it and earn interest such that at the end of 20 years your investment would be worth much more than $1 million. Thus, if someone will pay you $1 million 20 years from now, you would want to find its equivalent today, or its **present value**. In other words, you would want to determine how much must be invested today at current interest rates to have $1 million in 20 years.

The current market value (present value) of a debenture is therefore a function of three factors: (1) the dollar amounts to be received, (2) the length of time until the amounts are received, and (3) the market rate of interest. The **market interest rate** is the rate investors demand for lending funds to the entity. This, in turn, will depend on the risk-free interest rate (the rate that could be earned by investing in government bonds) and the risk of investing in the specific corporate bond or debenture. The process of finding the present value is referred to as **discounting** the future amounts.

To illustrate, assume that on 1 January 2019 Coronet Ltd issues $100 000 of 9% unsecured notes, due in 5 years, with interest payable annually at year-end. The purchaser of the notes would receive the following cash payments: (1) *principal* of $100 000 to be paid at maturity, and (2) five $9000 *interest payments* ($100 000 × 9%) over the term of the notes. A time diagram depicting both cash flows is shown in figure 9.4.

FIGURE 9.4   Time diagram depicting cash flows

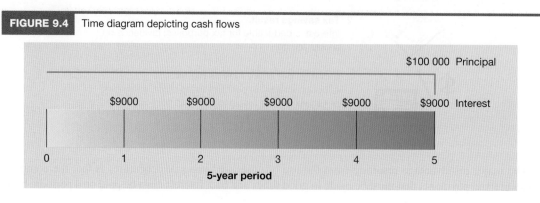

The current market value of an unsecured note or debenture is equal to the present value of all the future cash payments promised by the note. We will assume that the market interest rate for the notes is 9%. The present values of these amounts are listed in figure 9.5.

FIGURE 9.5	Calculation of present value of future payments

Present value of $100 000 received in 5 years	$ 64 993
Present value of $9000 received annually for 5 years	35 007
Market price of notes	**$100 000**

The contract interest rate on an issue of notes is not always the same as their market interest rate. For example, if the notes had zero interest and the market rate of interest were 9%, investors would have been prepared to pay only $64 993 for the right to receive $100 000 in 5 years. Tables are available to provide the present value factors to be used, or these values can be determined mathematically.*

LEARNING REFLECTION AND CONSOLIDATION

Review it
1. What are the advantages of unsecured notes and debentures versus equity financing?
2. Explain the terms *face value*, *contractual interest rate* and *market interest rate*.
3. Explain why you would prefer to receive $1 million today rather than 5 years from now.

Accounting for issues of unsecured notes and debentures

When a company receives payment for its unsecured notes and debentures, it makes journal entries to record their issue. If a note holder sells a note to another investor, the issuing company receives no further money on the transaction, nor is the transaction journalised by the issuing company.

The issue of debentures and unsecured notes at an amount different from their face value is quite common. By the time a company prints the certificates for the notes and markets them, it will be a coincidence if the market rate and the contractual rate are the same. Thus, the issue of notes at a discount (below face value) does not mean that the financial position of the issuer has declined. Likewise, the issue of notes at a premium (above face value) does not indicate that the financial strength of the issuer is exceptional. Prices for both new issues and existing issues are quoted as a percentage of the face value of the note, which is usually $1000. Thus, a $1000 unsecured note with a quoted price of 97 means that the selling price of the note is 97% of face value, or $970 in this case.

In this text we will consider only the issue of notes at face value. Accounting for issues at a premium or discount requires an understanding of present value calculations.

To illustrate the accounting for debentures issued at face value, assume that Devor Ltd issues 1000, 10-year, 10%, $1000 debentures on 30 June 2019 at 100 (100% of face value). The entry to record the $1 000 000 ($1000 × 1000) issue is:

June 30	Cash		1 000 000	
	Debentures payable			1 000 000
	(To record issue of debentures at face value)			

A	=	L	+	E
+1 000 000		+1 000 000		

---

*For those knowledgeable in the use of present value tables, the calculations in this example are: $100 000 × 0.64993 = $64 993 and $9000 × 3.88965 = $35 007 (rounded).

Debentures payable are usually reported in the non-current liabilities section of the statement of financial position because the maturity date is more than one year away. They are reclassified as current liabilities when maturity is within one year.

Over the term (life) of the debentures, entries are required for interest. Interest payable on debentures is calculated by multiplying the face value of the debenture by the interest rate stated in the contract. If it is assumed that interest is payable half-yearly on 31 December and 30 June on the debentures described above, interest of $50 000 ($1 000 000 × 10% × 6/12) must be paid on 31 December 2019. The entry for the payment, assuming no previous accrual of interest, is as shown below:

Dec. 31	Interest expense (borrowing costs)	50 000	
	Cash		50 000
	(To record payment of debenture interest)		

A	=	L	+	E
−50 000				−50 000

If interest payments do not coincide with the end of the reporting period, an end-of-period adjustment must be made to accrue unpaid interest. For instance, if the above interest payment were scheduled for 1 January, interest of $50 000 should be accrued by crediting interest payable instead of cash.

Interest payable is classified as a current liability because it is scheduled for payment within the next year.

Redeeming unsecured notes and debentures at maturity

Notes are redeemed when they are purchased (repaid) by the issuing company. Regardless of the issue price of notes, the carrying amount of the notes at maturity will equal their face value. Assuming that the interest for the last interest period is paid and recorded separately, the entry to record the redemption of debentures payable of $1 000 000 on 30 June 2029 is:

2029 June 30	Debentures payable	1 000 000	
	Cash		1 000 000
	(To record redemption of debentures at maturity)		

A	=	L	+	E
−1 000 000		−1 000 000		

Redeeming unsecured notes and debentures before maturity

Notes may be redeemed before maturity. A company may decide to redeem notes before maturity to reduce interest cost and remove debt from its statement of financial position. A company should redeem debt early only if it has sufficient cash resources. When notes are redeemed before maturity, it is necessary to: (1) eliminate the carrying amount of the notes at the redemption date, (2) record the cash paid, and (3) recognise the gain or loss on redemption. To illustrate, assume that Alpha Ltd issued debentures with a face value of $1 000 000 maturing on 30 June 2021. After paying interest for the year, Alpha Ltd redeems its debentures at 103 on 30 June 2018. The carrying amount of the debentures at the redemption date is $1 000 000. The amount that Alpha must pay is $1 030 000, being 103% of the face value. To record the redemption of the debentures on 30 June 2018, the entry is:

2018 June 30	Debentures payable	1 000 000	
	Loss on redemption of debentures	30 000	
	Cash		1 030 000
	(To record redemption of debentures at 103)		

A	=	L	+	E
−1 030 000		−1 000 000		−30 000

Note that the loss of $30 000 is the difference between the cash paid of $1 030 000 and the carrying amount of the debentures of $1 000 000.

Helpful hint: If a debenture is redeemed before its maturity date and its carrying amount exceeds its redemption price, will the redemption result in a gain or a loss?

Answer: Gain.

LEARNING REFLECTION AND CONSOLIDATION

Review it

1. What entry is made to record the issue of unsecured notes payable of $1 million at 100?
2. Why are notes issued at a discount? at a premium? at face value?
3. Explain the accounting for redemption of unsecured notes at maturity and before maturity by payment in cash.

Do it

Beta Ltd issued 500 $1000 unsecured notes at face value, maturing on 30 June 2018. On 30 June 2018, after payment of interest, the unsecured notes were redeemed at 96. Prepare the journal entry to record the redemption of the unsecured notes on 30 June 2018.

Reasoning

The journal entry should eliminate the carrying amount of the notes, record the payment of cash and recognise the resulting gain. Cash paid is 96% of face value.

Solution

2018			
June 30	Debentures payable	500 000	
	Gain on redemption of debentures		20 000
	Cash		480 000
	(To record redemption of notes at 96)		

9.4 Loans payable by instalment

LEARNING OBJECTIVE 9.4 Prepare journal entries for loans payable by instalment and distinguish between current and non-current components of long-term debt.

In addition to, or instead of, raising money by issuing debentures and unsecured notes to a large number of note holders, entities may borrow money from a single borrower in the form of a loan. It is common for loans, such as mortgages, to be repayable by instalment. A **mortgage** is a loan secured by a charge over property. If the borrower (mortgagor) is unable to repay the loan, the lender (mortgagee), may sell the property and use the proceeds to repay the loan. While the conditions of the loan may vary, mortgages usually require regular repayments of the principal (amount borrowed) and interest over the term of the loan.

When all the mortgage payments are added together over the term of the loan, the amount repaid exceeds the amount originally borrowed. The excess of payments over the original amount borrowed is interest. That is, not all of the money repaid is a reduction of the loan; a portion of the payments is interest expense. Interest expense is often referred to as 'borrowing costs' or 'finance costs' in published financial statements.

Accounting for loans payable by instalment

Each time the borrower makes a mortgage payment, it must be allocated between interest expense and a reduction of the loan liability. The reduction of the mortgage liability is also referred to as the reduction of the principal of the loan, or just the reduction of the principal. The effect of a mortgage payment on the accounting equation is as follows:

A	=	I	+		E
Cash ↓		Loan ↓			E ↓ (interest expense)

This would be recorded by debiting the loan payable account and interest expense account and crediting the cash at bank account.

Consider the effect on the accounting equation of a loan payment of $10 000:

A	=	L	+	E
−$10 000		−$?		−$?

How much of the payment should be allocated to interest expense and how much to the reduction of the principal of the loan?

Interest is the cost of borrowing money: the more that is borrowed, the greater the amount of interest expense. Interest expense is greater at the beginning of the loan than towards the end of the loan. This is because the amount of the loan outstanding is greater at the commencement of the loan. As more repayments are made, the loan principal is reduced and so is the interest. Thus the carrying amount of the liability is reduced progressively throughout the period of the loan. Measuring liabilities this way is known as the *amortised cost method using the effective interest rate*.

The interest expense for each period is determined by multiplying the balance of the loan at the beginning of the period by the interest rate for the period. The product is the amount of interest expense for the period. When recording the mortgage payment for the period, a debit entry is made to interest expense as calculated, and the balance of the payment is debited to the loan payable account.

For example, assume that CAS Ltd has a mortgage on which interest is payable at 12% per annum, with monthly payments of $10 000. At the beginning of March 2019, the balance of the loan payable account was $100 000. To record the payment of $10 000 in March, the accountant must determine how much should be interest expense and how much should be a reduction of the principal of the loan. This is calculated as follows:

$$\text{Interest expense} = \text{Balance at the beginning of the period} \times \text{interest rate}$$

The interest rate for one month is equal to the annual interest rate divided by 12. In this example, $12\% \div 12 = 1\%$ for the month. Thus the interest expense for March 2019 can be calculated as:

$$\text{Interest expense} = \$100\,000 \times 1\% = \mathbf{\$1000}$$

The payment of $10 000 in March should be accounted for as an interest expense of $1000 and a $9000 reduction in the principal of the loan. The payment would be recorded as follows:

March 31	Interest expense	1 000	
	Loan payable	9 000	
	Cash at bank		10 000
	(To record the loan payment for March)		

A	=	L	+	E
−10 000		−9000		−1000

This entry would usually be made in the cash payments journal if specialised journals are used. For simplification, the general journal form is used in the illustrations presented here.

Instead of performing this calculation every time a repayment is made, it is helpful to prepare a mortgage schedule. A mortgage schedule shows how much of each payment should be accounted for as an interest expense, and how much should be accounted for as a reduction in the principal of the loan.

The mortgage schedule in figure 9.6 is for a $106 220 loan obtained to purchase property that has been offered as security for the loan. Repayments of $5000 are made at the end of each month for two years. The interest rate is 12% per annum.

FIGURE 9.6 Mortgage schedule

Month ending	Beginning balance $	Payment $	Interest $	Reduction of principal $	Closing balance $
31.01.19	106 220	5 000	1 062	3 938	102 282
28.02.19	102 282	5 000	1 023	3 977	98 305
31.03.19	98 305	5 000	983	4 017	94 288
30.04.19	94 288	5 000	943	4 057	90 231
31.05.19	90 231	5 000	902	4 098	86 133
30.06.19	86 133	5 000	861	4 139	81 994
31.07.19	81 994	5 000	820	4 180	77 814
31.08.19	77 814	5 000	778	4 222	73 592
30.09.19	73 592	5 000	736	4 264	69 328
31.10.19	69 328	5 000	693	4 307	65 021
30.11.19	65 021	5 000	650	4 350	60 671
31.12.19	60 671	5 000	607	4 393	56 278
31.01.20	56 278	5 000	563	4 437	51 841
28.02.20	51 841	5 000	518	4 482	47 359
31.03.20	47 359	5 000	474	4 526	42 833
30.04.20	42 833	5 000	428	4 572	38 261
31.05.20	38 261	5 000	383	4 617	33 644
30.06.20	33 644	5 000	336	4 664	28 980
31.07.20	28 980	5 000	290	4 710	24 270
31.08.20	24 270	5 000	243	4 757	19 513
30.09.20	19 513	5 000	195	4 805	14 708
31.10.20	14 708	5 000	147	4 853	9 855
30.11.20	9 855	5 000	99	4 901	4 954
31.12.20	4 954	5 000	46	4 954	0

The first column lists the date of each payment. The second column lists the balance of the mortgage liability at the beginning of the period. The length of each period is determined by the frequency of the mortgage payments; payments are made at the end of each month in figure 9.6. Thus, at the beginning of the period, the balance of the mortgage in the second column is the balance of the loan at the beginning of each month. The third column lists the amount of each payment. The fourth column shows the amount of interest expense for each period. This is the amount of interest expense for each month because payments are made monthly. The interest is calculated by multiplying the mortgage's beginning-of-period balance (in the second column) by the interest rate for the period (i.e. the annual interest rate divided by the number of periods in the year). The fifth column lists the amount of each payment allocated to reducing the principal of the loan. It is the portion of the payment that is not interest. The amount in this column is determined by subtracting the interest expense (in the fourth column) from the mortgage payment in the third column. The last column lists the balance of the loan liability after each payment. The amount in this column is derived by subtracting the reduction of principal (in the fifth column) from the beginning-of-period balance in the second column. The closing balance of one month becomes the beginning balance of the next month. You should work through enough rows in figure 9.6 to ensure that you understand the calculations.

The mortgage schedule can be prepared quickly in an electronic spreadsheet. For example, we could view figure 9.6 as an Excel spreadsheet, as illustrated in figure 9.7. The column of dates in the figure would become column A in the spreadsheet, and the first row of numbers in the figure would become row 3 in the spreadsheet, with the headings in row 1 and the dollar signs in row 2. The formula for the interest column would take the form '=+B3*.01'. The formula for the reduction of principal in the fifth column would take the form '=+C3−D3', and the formula for the ending balance would be '=+B3−E3'.

FIGURE 9.7	Mortgage schedule as an electronic spreadsheet

	A	B	C	D	E	F
1	Month ending	Beginning balance	Payment	Interest	Reduction of principal	Closing balance
2		$	$	$	$	$
3	31.1.19	106 220	5 000	1 062	3 938	102 282
4	28.2.19	102 282	5 000	1 023	3 977	98 305
5	31.3.19	98 305	5 000	983	4 017	94 288
6	30.4.19	94 288	5 000	943	4 057	90 231
7	31.5.19	90 231	5 000	902	4 098	86 133
8	30.6.19	86 133	5 000	861	4 139	81 994
9	31.7.19	81 994	5 000	820	4 180	77 814
10	31.8.19	77 814	5 000	778	4 222	73 592

Figure 9.6 adopts a comprehensive form of the mortgage schedule for illustrative purposes. Simpler forms of the mortgage schedule can be used. Some of the columns do not need to be displayed. For example, the closing balance column could be omitted because it is reproduced as the opening balance for the next period.

The mortgage schedule forms the workings for the journal entry to record each mortgage payment. The first row in figure 9.6 provides the details needed to record the first mortgage payment on 31 January 2019. Of the first $5000 payment, $1062 should be recorded as interest expense and $3938 as a reduction in the mortgage liability. The journal entry to record the payment is:

2019 Jan. 31	Interest expense		1 062	
	Loan payable		3 938	
	Cash at bank			5 000
	(To record the loan payment for January)			

A	=	L	+	E
−5000		−3938		−1062

The journal entry to record the payment for February is:

2019 Feb. 28	Interest expense		1 023	
	Loan payable		3 977	
	Cash at bank			5 000
	(To record the loan payment for February)			

A	=	L	+	E
−5000		−3977		−1023

Rounding errors at the end of the mortgage schedule are very common. Rounding errors should be adjusted against the interest expense in the final period, rather than leaving a small debit or credit balance in the loan account. In figure 9.6 a rounding error of $4 has been adjusted against interest in the allocation of the last payment. The calculated interest expense is $50 (1% × $4954), with a reduction of principal, ($4950). This would leave a balance of $4 in the mortgage liability after all repayments have been made. This rounding error has been corrected by increasing the allocation to reduction of principal to $4954 and reducing the allocation to interest to $46.

Review it

1. What is the difference between the amount borrowed on a mortgage and the amount repaid?
2. How is the interest expense calculated on a mortgage for each period?

Do it

Using the mortgage schedule in figure 9.6, prepare the journal entry to record the mortgage payment on 31 March 2019.

Reasoning

The difference between the amount borrowed and the amount repaid is interest. The interest component of each repayment is calculated by multiplying the opening balance by the interest rate for the period. The interest should be recorded as an expense. The remainder of the payment should be recorded as a reduction in the principal of the mortgage.

Solution

2019 Mar. 31	Interest expense	983	
	Loan payable	4 017	
	Cash at bank		5 000
	(To record the loan payment for March)		

Current and non-current components of long-term debt

Liabilities are classified as current if they are due within one year or within the period of the entity's normal operating cycle. Entities often have a portion of long-term debt that falls due within the coming year (or operating cycle). For liabilities such as loans payable by instalment, a portion is usually due within one year of the financial statements in which they are reported. In the case of liabilities not paid by instalment, such as debentures and unsecured notes, the entire principal may be due within one year as the debt approaches maturity.

To the extent that long-term debt is payable within the same period as current liabilities, it should be classified as a current liability. For example, assume that during 2019 Charlie's Constructions Ltd entered into several long-term loans, two of which mature at the end of 2021, with the remainder maturing in later periods. In the statement of financial position as at 31 December 2019, all of the long-term loans would be classified as non-current. However, when the statement of financial position is prepared for 31 December 2020, the two loans that are due to be paid at the end of 2021 must be classified as current liabilities.

The calculation of the current portion of a liability payable by instalment is more complicated. Consider the example of a mortgage. The portion of the mortgage that falls due within one year (or operating cycle) of the end of the reporting period should be classified as a current liability in the statement of financial position. For example, assume that the entity with the mortgage schedule in figure 9.6 has a year-end of 31 March. The mortgage liability (see closing balance column) is $94 288 as at 31 March 2019. How much should be classified as current and how much as non-current at this date? The total liability of $94 288 represents the remaining amount of the principal borrowed that has not been repaid at that date. The amount to be reported as a current liability is the reduction in principal that occurs up to and including 31 March 2020. The reduction in principal after 31 March 2020 is the non-current portion of the mortgage liability.

Applying this technique to the mortgage liability in figure 9.6 as at 31 March 2019, the classification of the mortgage liability is calculated in figure 9.8.

Rather than adding long columns of figures, we can calculate the current portion of the mortgage liability as the reduction in the principal that occurs within the remaining year. In this example it is the difference between the amount of the liability at 31 March 2019 and 31 March 2020 ($94 288 − $42 833 = $51 455). Note that at 31 March 2019, the non-current portion of the mortgage liability is the sum of reductions in principal after 31 March 2020. This is equal to the closing amount of the liability at 31 March 2020, which is shown in figure 9.6 as $42 833.

FIGURE 9.8	Calculation of current and non-current portions of mortgage liability

Current portion of mortgage liability as at 31 March 2019	Non-current portion of mortgage liability as at 31 March 2019
$ 4 057	$ 4 572
4 098	4 617
4 139	4 664
4 180	4 710
4 222	4 757
4 264	4 805
4 307	4 853
4 350	4 901
4 393	4 954
4 437	
4 482	
4 526	
Current liability $51 455	Non-current liability $42 833

It is not necessary to prepare an adjusting entry to recognise the current maturity of the mortgage liability. The proper classification of each account is recognised when the statement of financial position is prepared for external financial reporting.

9.5 Leasing

LEARNING OBJECTIVE 9.5 Identify the advantages of leasing and explain the difference between an operating lease and a finance lease.

Mortgages are not the only liabilities payable by instalment. Leases are also liabilities payable by instalment. You may recall that we already introduced leases in chapter 8 when we discussed non-current assets. Leases are explored further in the following sections.

What is a lease?

Leasing is a popular way to acquire property, plant and equipment. Many assets including motor vehicles, aircraft, land, buildings and machinery can be leased. A **lease**, according to IFRS 16/AASB 16 *Leases*, is a contract that allows an entity to use an asset (referred to as an underlying asset) for a period of time in exchange for consideration. The **lessee** is the entity that has the right to use the underlying asset and the **lessor** is the entity that owns the underlying asset and provides it to the lessee. Both the lessor and the lessee must account for transactions involving assets leased between the entities.

Advantages of leasing

Leasing has become a common way of acquiring many non-current assets. The reason for its growth in popularity is that it offers numerous advantages to the lessee. For example, leasing provides the lessee with access to a wide variety of non-current assets and lease payments are a deductible expense for taxation purposes. Further, the risk of obsolescence of the non-current asset remains with the lessor, as some lease agreements allow the lessee to return old leased equipment in exchange for new equipment by cancelling the old lease and signing a new one. Another advantage is that lease contracts may be structured in a way so that they are less restrictive than many debt agreements for the lessee and, finally, operating leases are not required to be reported on the statement of financial position. This is advantageous for companies that do not want the liability to affect their financial ratios and borrowing capacity.

A central issue surrounding accounting for leases is whether the assets and the liabilities associated with leasing assets should be reported on the lessee's statement of financial position. This is where understanding the distinction between a finance lease and an operating lease is important.

Helpful hint: When leases are not reported on the statement of financial position of the lessee, this can be referred to as off-balance-sheet financing.

Finance and operating leases

During the term of the lease agreement the lessee acquires and uses the asset. However, the legal title to the asset remains with the lessor. The question is, should the lack of transfer of legal title or ownership preclude the lessee reporting the leased assets and the related liabilities on the statement of financial position when the lessee actually acquires and uses the asset for the term of the lease agreement?

IFRS 16/AASB 16 *Leases* requires the lessee to recognise both a right-of-use asset and a lease liability on their statement of financial position as they would have if the entity had borrowed funds to finance the purchase of the underlying asset. The cost of the right-of-use asset is recognised at the present value of the lease liability, plus any payments made at the commencement of the lease term, less any lease incentives received. The lessor, however, is required to classify their leases into one of two categories. A **finance lease** is where the *lessor* transfers substantially all the *risks and rewards of ownership* of the underlying asset to the lessee even though the *ownership remains with* the lessor. Some of the circumstances in which a lease contract would be classified as a finance lease were discussed in chapter 8. Under a finance lease, the lessor will recognise a lease receivable at the commencement of the lease term. Upon receipt of each payment from the lessee, the lessor will credit the lease receivable account with the principal amount and the interest component of the lease payment will be recognised as interest revenue. An **operating lease**, on the other hand, is where the *lessor* effectively retains the risks and rewards of owning the underlying asset and recognises the underlying asset in their statement of financial position. The lease payments received from the lessee will be recognised as either rental or lease income in their statement of profit or loss.

It is important to note that leasing is a complex and challenging area of accounting and is generally dealt with in some detail in later year accounting studies. This section is intended to provide an introduction to the topic area as opposed to an in-depth exploration. Simple examples illustrating how to account for leases are provided next.

9.6 Accounting for leases

LEARNING OBJECTIVE 9.6 Complete basic journal entries for accounting for leases and explain how to report leases.

Operating leases

A lessee will record the same transactions for both operating and finance leases. The journal entries recorded by the lessee are shown below in the example for financing leases. The transactions recorded by the lessor will differ based on the lease classification. Assets that are acquired under operating lease agreements are recorded by the lessor when the lease payment is due to be paid or is paid by the lessee. To illustrate, on 1 June Dome Pty Ltd (lessee) signed an 18-month lease agreement with U Bute Cars Ltd (lessor) to lease a car for $2000 per month. Payments are due every 3 months on the last day of the month. Both parties have a 30 June year-end. The first two journal entries, i.e. the lease accrual and the first lease payment, would be recorded as follows in the books of the lessor.

Lessor (U Bute Cars Ltd)

June 30	Car lease receivable—Dome Pty Ltd	2 000	
	Car lease revenue		2 000
	(To accrue the car lease revenue earned but not yet received and lease payment receivable as at 30 June)		
Aug. 31	Cash	6 000	
	Car lease receivable—Dome Pty Ltd		2 000
	Car lease revenue		4 000
	(Receipt of lease revenue for the amount accrued at 30 June and the current period car lease revenue)		

$$A = L + E$$
$$+2000 \qquad\qquad +2000$$

$$A = L + E$$
$$+6000 \qquad\qquad +4000$$
$$-2000$$

Finance leases

The accounting for finance leases is more complex than for operating leases. For example, the lessee is required at the beginning of the lease to recognise both the right-of-use asset and the lease liability. The amount recognised for the right-of-use asset is equal to the present value of the lease liability plus any payments made, less incentives received, at the commencement of the lease. Where possible, the implicit interest rate in the lease is used to calculate the present value of the lease liability. When the implicit interest rate cannot be determined, the lessee's incremental borrowing rate should be used. The **implicit interest rate** is the discount rate that results in the aggregate present value of the leased asset being equal to the fair value of the leased asset of the lessor at the inception of the lease. The **incremental borrowing rate** on the other hand is the rate of interest the lessee would have to pay to lease a similar asset or the interest rate that would be incurred by the lessee to borrow funds and purchase the asset outright.

These definitions may appear complex; however, to explain in simpler terms, a lessor purchases an asset and subsequently leases it to the lessee in order to make a profit. Therefore, in an uncomplicated finance lease, the lease payments are structured to include both the repayment of the cost price of the asset plus interest to provide the lessor with a rate of return. Otherwise there is no benefit to the lessor to be a part of the arrangement. As this chapter aims to present accounting for leases at the introductory level, the present value of all lease payments will be equal to the fair value of the underlying asset and this will be provided in all illustrations and questions. These calculations are generally explored in detail in intermediate accounting units.

An asset was leased on 1 July 2019 at a fair value of $50 000. In this example, we ignore GST implications and the direct lease costs and assume the lease is non-cancellable. The initial journal entry to record the lease in the books of both parties is as follows.

Lessee

July 1	Right-of-use asset	50 000	
	Lease liability		50 000
	(To record the asset and the liability related to the leased asset at the beginning of the lease)		

| A | = | L | + | E |
| +50 000 | | +50 000 | | |

Lessor

July 1	Lease receivable	50 000	
	Leased asset		50 000
	(To remove the leased asset and record the receivable related to the leased asset at the beginning of the lease)		

A	=	L	+	E
+50 000				
−50 000				

Assume that the lessor requires a rate of return of 10% on the leased asset over 4 years. Once each lease payment is made, the lessee records the lease expense and the lessor recognises the lease revenue. Lease payments consist of both interest and principal so the entries are similar to those illustrated in this chapter for mortgage payments and notes payable.

To illustrate, figure 9.9 presents the lease repayment schedule where each lease payment includes a repayment of principal and interest.

FIGURE 9.9 Lease repayment schedule

Date	Lease payment ($)	Interest 10% ($)	Principal reduction ($)	Balance lease obligation ($)
01.07.19				50 000.00
30.06.20	15 773.50	5 000.00	10 773.50	39 226.50
30.06.21	15 773.50	3 922.65	11 850.85	27 375.65
30.06.22	15 773.50	2 737.57	13 035.93	14 339.72
30.06.23	15 773.50	1 433.78	14 339.72	0.00
Total over 4 years	63 094.00	13 094.00	50 000.00	

Helpful hint: The interest calculation is the balance of the lease obligation multiplied by the interest rate. The principal reduction is the lease payment less the interest for the period.

The lease payments in the books of both the lessee and lessor are provided below.

Lessee

June 30	Lease liability	10 773.50	
	Interest expense	5 000.00	
	Cash		15 773.50
	(To record a lease payment)		

| A | = | L | + | E |
| −15 773.50 | | −10 773.50 | | −5000 |

Lessor

July 1	Cash		15 773.50	
	Lease receivable			10 773.50
	Interest revenue			5 000.00
	(To record the receipt of a lease payment)			

$$
\begin{array}{ccccc}
A & = & L & + & E \\
+15\,773.50 & & & & +5000 \\
-10\,773.50 & & & &
\end{array}
$$

Further, at the end of the year (30 June), in the books of the lessee only, the leased asset is amortised in the same way we depreciate other property, plant and equipment (PPE) assets, as illustrated in chapter 8. The leased asset is amortised over the economic life of the asset or over the period of the lease. Assume straight-line amortisation with no residual value. Hence the annual expense will be $12 500 (50 000 ÷ 4).

Lessee

June 30	Depreciation expense		12 500	
	Accumulated depreciation			12 500
	(To record the lease depreciation expense at the end of the period)			

$$
\begin{array}{ccccc}
A & = & L & + & E \\
-12\,500 & & & & -12\,500
\end{array}
$$

Over the lease period there will be four such payments as given above. The total interest paid and received will be $13 094 (the return to the lessor) and the total amortisation will be $50 000.

Reporting leases

In the statement of financial position the lessee is required to report the net amount of leased assets as well as both current and non-current portions of the lease liability (rounded figures) as illustrated in figure 9.10. The balance of the current and non-current portions of the lease are obtained from figure 9.9.

FIGURE 9.10   Statement of financial position — selected figures in relation to leases

Statement of financial position (selected figures) as at 30 June 2020	
NON-CURRENT ASSETS	
Leased asset	50 000
Less: Accumulated amortisation	(12 500)
	37 500
CURRENT LIABILITIES	
Lease liability	11 851
NON-CURRENT LIABILITIES	
Lease liability	27 375

IFRS 16/AASB 16 *Leases* also requires numerous note disclosures to be made by the lessee. These are not discussed in this text. However, if you continue your accounting studies, in later years you will study accounting for leasing in more depth and learn about how to account for the complexity of finance leases.

Review it

1. What is a lease?
2. List the advantages of leasing.
3. Explain the difference between an operating lease and a finance lease.

9.7 Provisions and contingent liabilities

LEARNING OBJECTIVE 9.7 Explain the differences between provisions, contingencies and other types of liabilities and explain how to report contingent liabilities.

You may recall that liabilities are defined as outflows of economic benefits that the entity is presently obliged to make as a result of past events. **Provisions** are defined as liabilities for which the amount of the outflows of economic benefits is uncertain. That is, whether a liability is a provision or some other type of liability (e.g. borrowings, trade creditors, accruals) depends upon the extent of uncertainty associated with the amount of the future outflows of economic benefits. For borrowings such as debentures, leases, unsecured notes and mortgages, the amount of the future outflows of economic benefits (i.e. the repayment) can be predicted with a high level of certainty. Similarly, the amount of the future outflows of economic benefits for trade creditors can be measured with a high level of certainty because it is quantified on the supplier's invoice. The uncertainty associated with the amounts of future outflows of economic benefits varies along a continuum ranging from very low uncertainty to very high uncertainty as indicated in figure 9.11.

FIGURE 9.11	Classification of liabilities based on uncertainty

UNCERTAINTY

Very low			Very high
Borrowings	Accruals	Provisions	Contingent liabilities
Accounts payable			

Accruals are liabilities to pay for goods or services that have been provided but for which a supplier's invoice has not yet been recorded as an account payable. Accruals often involve estimation, such as the amount of the next electricity bill or telephone account. Although higher than borrowings and trade creditors, the level of uncertainty of accruals is typically low because they are often for recurring services such as telephone connections, electricity usage and interest.

Helpful hint: To revise the accrual of expenses, refer back to chapter 3.

Provisions are liabilities for which there is significant uncertainty about the amount of the future outflows of economic benefits but which are considered able to be measured reliably by estimation. Examples include provisions for warranties, and provisions for employee entitlements such as long service leave. A **warranty** is an obligation of the supplier of goods or services to the purchaser that the product will be functional or that the work performed will remain satisfactory for a stated period after the sale of goods or the provision of services. There is significant uncertainty in the measurement of the future outflows of economic benefits that will be needed to satisfy existing warranties. This is due to two reasons:

1. The future outflows of economic benefits is conditional upon the customer making a claim.
2. The costs of satisfying claims vary with the nature of the fault. Some warranty claims may require the replacement of a small part, while other warranty claims may require replacement of the goods sold to the customer.

There is significant uncertainty about the future outflows of economic benefits required for employee entitlements, such as long service leave, because the amount payable is affected by the following:

- whether employees stay with the employer long enough to become entitled to long service leave
- when employees take long service leave
- the extent to which the employee is promoted before taking long service leave
- increases in general salaries between the time the liability is recorded and when it is paid.

The *Framework* not only defines liabilities but also sets out recognition criteria. For a liability to be reported in the statement of financial position, the future outflows or sacrifice of economic benefits must be *probable* and must be able to be *reliably* measured.

Helpful hint: Recognition in accounting means recording the transaction in the accounts. Hence, the amount of the liability is reported in the statement of financial position.

Liabilities for which the amount of the future sacrifices is so uncertain that it cannot be measured reliably are classified as **contingent liabilities**. Liabilities are also classified as contingent if they do not satisfy the probability criterion, or if they are dependent upon the occurrence of an uncertain future event outside the control of the entity. Examples include an unresolved lawsuit brought against the entity and the potential liability resulting from a tax audit in progress. Contingent liabilities are not recognised because they are not probable or are unable to be measured reliably, or both, i.e. they do not satisfy the probability criterion and the measurement criterion for the recognition of liabilities. However, information about contingent liabilities must be disclosed in the notes to the financial statements. The required disclosures include a description of their nature, an indication of the uncertainties associated with the amount or timing of any future sacrifice, the estimated financial effect (if practical) and the existence of any possible recovery of the future sacrifice.

LEARNING REFLECTION AND CONSOLIDATION

Review it
1. How is a provision different from other liabilities, such as accounts payable?
2. Why are contingent liabilities not recognised?

Do it
Match each item with a type of liability.

Liability	Type of liability
1. Debentures payable	A. Accounts payable and accruals
2. Legal proceedings against the entity for injuries from the use of its product	B. Interest-bearing liabilities (borrowings)
3. Trade creditors	C. Contingent liabilities
4. Warranties (unclaimed)	D. Provisions

Reasoning
Liabilities are classified as provisions if there is significant uncertainty about the amount of the future outflows of economic benefits. Liabilities are classified as contingent if they are conditional upon an uncertain future event outside the control of the entity or if they do not satisfy either or both of the recognition criteria for liabilities.

Solution
1B, 2C, 3A, 4D.

9.8 Recording provisions for warranties

LEARNING OBJECTIVE 9.8 Prepare entries to record provisions for warranties.

Manufacturers of certain types of goods provide a warranty with their sale to a consumer. Recall that a warranty is a promise in a contract that the goods will function properly for a stated period of time. For example, if you buy a new television, it will probably come with a one-year or two-year warranty from the manufacturer. Warranties may also be offered for the provision of services. For example, it is not uncommon for a tradesperson to provide a 3-month warranty for work performed.

From the manufacturer's point of view, providing a warranty creates an obligation to repair or replace the goods (free of charge) if certain faults arise within the warranty period. Unexpired warranties at the end of the reporting period are a liability from the manufacturer's point of view because they are a present obligation to make a future sacrifice (the repair or replacement of faulty goods) resulting from a past transaction (the sale of goods). Similarly, a service provider, such as a mechanic, may have a liability for unexpired warranty contracts because there is an obligation for future sacrifice (to repair work found to be faulty) resulting from a past transaction (the original provision of services).

Warranty liabilities are provisions because the amount of the future sacrifice is uncertain. It will vary with the amount of claims made and the cost of servicing warranty claims. Reporting entities that provide warranties estimate the cost of servicing unexpired warranty contracts at the end of the reporting period and record the amount in the warranty provisions account. Some entities use a heuristic (or rule-of-thumb) approach to estimating the warranty liabilities, such as a percentage of the current year's sales.

To illustrate, Electrobuz Ltd sells electronic equipment with a 12-month warranty. Its year-end is 30 June. At 30 June 2019, warranty contracts for sales made during the year have not expired. Electrobuz estimates from past experience that the cost of servicing outstanding warranties will be $200 000.

This reflects the percentage of sales resulting in warranty claims and the average cost of servicing warranty claims in the past. To record the liability for outstanding warranties, Electrobuz would make the following entry:

June 30	Warranty expense	200 000	
	Warranty provision		200 000
	(To record the liability for warranty contracts outstanding at year-end)		

| | A | = | L | + | E | |
| | | | +200 000 | | −200 000 | |

In the following year, the costs of servicing warranty claims are charged against the warranty provision account, e.g. on 12 July 2019, Electrobuz replaced goods under warranty at a cost of $1000 using goods from its own inventory. To record this transaction, the following entry is made:

July 12	Warranty provision	1 000	
	Inventory		1 000
	(To record replacement of goods under warranty)		

| | A | = | L | + | E | |
| | −1000 | | −1000 | | | |

The preceding example was simplified by assuming that Electrobuz Ltd did not already have a provision for warranty contracts when the liability was first recognised on 30 June 2019. Now let us assume that at 30 June 2020, after warranty claims have been made during the year, Electrobuz Ltd's warranty provision account has a credit balance of $5000. Electrobuz estimates that the cost of servicing unexpired warranty contracts will be $210 000. The warranty provision should be $210 000. To increase the credit balance in the account from $5000 to $210 000, Electrobuz needs to make the following entry:

June 30	Warranty expense	205 000	
	Warranty provision		205 000
	(To adjust the liability for warranty provision account to total estimated liability for contracts outstanding at year-end)		

| | A | = | L | + | E | |
| | | | +205 000 | | −205 000 | |

LEARNING REFLECTION AND CONSOLIDATION

Review it

What does the balance of the warranty provision account represent?

Do it

Wentworth Watches Ltd manufactures and sells watches with a 2-year warranty. The warranty provision account had a debit of $2000 before adjusting entries on 31 December 2018, which is Wentworth Watches' year-end. The estimated cost of servicing outstanding warranties is $25 000 at 31 December 2018. Prepare the adjusting journal entry to record the warranty provision as at 31 December 2018.

Reasoning

A provision of $25 000 is needed. A credit entry of $27 000 is needed to increase the warranty provision account from $2000 debit to $25 000 credit.

Reporting provisions for warranties

The warranty provision is reported in the liabilities section of the statement of financial position. Provisions are classified as current or non-current, depending on the expected timing of the future sacrifice. Electrobuz Ltd reports its warranty provision as current because the warranty contracts expire within one year. Entities that offer longer warranty contracts need to distinguish between current and non-current components of the warranty provision. Most entities classify liabilities as current if they are likely to be paid within one year of the end of the reporting period. In this case, an entity offering warranty periods longer than one year must estimate the amount of the warranty claims that are likely to occur within one year of the end of the reporting period and the amount expected to occur later than one year from the end of the reporting period.

LEARNING REFLECTION AND CONSOLIDATION

Review it

Refer back to chapter 1, figure 1.15, to the statement of financial position of Giorgina's Pizza Limited to answer the following questions.
1. What amount is reported for current provisions for 2019?
2. What amount is reported for non-current provisions for 2019?

9.9 Financial statement analysis

LEARNING OBJECTIVE 9.9 Evaluate an entity's liquidity and solvency.

In this chapter, liquidity and solvency evaluation will focus on items reported in the statement of financial position.

Liquidity ratios

Liquidity ratios measure the short-term ability of an entity to pay its maturing obligations and to meet unexpected needs for cash. Two measures of liquidity were examined in chapter 1 — working capital (Current assets − Current liabilities) and the current ratio (Current assets ÷ Current liabilities). In this section we add a third useful measure of liquidity, the quick ratio. In chapter 11 we will use cash flow measures to evaluate liquidity.

The current ratio is a frequently used ratio, but it can be misleading. Consider the current ratio's numerator, which can include some items in current assets that are not very liquid. For example, when an entity is having a difficult time selling its goods, its inventory increases. This will cause its current ratio to increase, even though the entity's liquidity has actually declined. Similarly, prepaid expenses are considered current assets, but generally cannot be sold and therefore do not contribute to liquidity. Consequently, the current ratio is often supplemented with the quick ratio.

The **quick ratio** (often referred to as the *acid test*) is a measure of an entity's immediate short-term liquidity. It is calculated by dividing the sum of cash, marketable securities such as shares in listed companies, and net receivables by current liabilities. Marketable securities, also called short-term investments, are investments that have a ready market and are intended to be sold within the next year. Cash, marketable securities and net receivables are usually highly liquid compared with inventory and prepaid expenses. Thus, because it measures *immediate* liquidity, the quick ratio should be calculated along with the current ratio. The 2019 statement of financial position for All Communications Group, a fictitious company, is shown in figure 9.12. Using this data from All Communications, working capital, current ratios and quick ratios have been calculated and are provided in figure 9.13.

FIGURE 9.12 Statement of financial position for All Communications Group

ALL COMMUNICATIONS GROUP
Statement of financial position
as at 30 June 2019

	Note	2019 $m	2018 $m
ASSETS			
Current assets			
Cash and cash equivalents	20	4958	7890
Trade and other receivables	10	9114	8692
Inventories	11	948	584
Current tax receivables		158	726
Prepayments		628	500
Assets classified as held for sale	12	0	1508
Total current assets		15806	19900
Non-current assets			
Trade and other receivables	10	1886	1702
Inventories	11	90	72
Investments	12	76	38
Property, plant and equipment	13	40652	41008
Intangible assets	14	18534	16318
Deferred tax assets	9	10	12
Total non-current assets		61248	59150
Total assets		77054	79050
LIABILITIES			
Current liabilities			
Trade and other payables	15	8482	8262
Provisions	16	1836	1884
Borrowings	17(a)	1590	7210
Current tax payables		888	1462
Revenue received in advance		2248	2550
Total current liabilities		15044	21368
Non-current liabilities			
Other payables	15	326	348
Provisions	16	552	528
Borrowings	17(a)	31876	28614
Deferred tax liabilities	9	2660	2214
Revenue received in advance	25	846	2600
Total non-current liabilities		36260	34304
Total liabilities		51304	55672
Net assets		**25750**	**23378**
EQUITY			
Share capital	19	11422	11270
Reserves		(1238)	(1734)
Retained profits		15038	13424
Equity available to shareholders		25222	22960
Non-controlling interests		528	418
Total equity		**25750**	**23378**

FIGURE 9.13 Liquidity measures

Ratio	Formula	All Communications Group	
($ in millions)		**2019**	**2018**
Working capital	Current assets − Current liabilities	$15 806 − $15 044 = $762	$19 900 − $21 368 = ($1468)
Current ratio	$\dfrac{\text{Current assets}}{\text{Current liabilities}}$	$\dfrac{\$15\,806}{\$15\,044} = 1.05{:}1$	$\dfrac{\$19\,900}{\$21\,368} = 0.93{:}1$
Quick ratio	$\dfrac{\text{Cash + Marketable securities +}}{\text{Net receivables}}$ _____ Current liabilities	$\dfrac{(\$4\,958 + \$9\,114)}{\$15\,044} = 0.94{:}1$	$\dfrac{(\$7\,890 + \$8\,692)}{\$21\,368} = 0.78{:}1$

According to our calculations in figure 9.13, All Communications' working capital was positive in 2019 as its current assets exceeded its current liabilities by $762 million. This is a significant improvement from the negative working capital of $1468 million in 2018. These results are reflected in All Communications' current ratio for these respective periods. The positive working capital of $762 million in 2019 can be expressed as a current ratio of 1.05:1, which indicates that All Communications had $1.05 in current assets to cover each $1 in current liabilities. In contrast, the negative working capital of $1468 million in 2018 can be expressed as a current ratio of 0.93:1, which indicates that All Communications had only $0.93 in current assets to cover each $1 in current liabilities. All Communications' quick ratio increased substantially from 0.78:1 in 2018 to 0.94:1 in 2019. Note that only cash and cash equivalents and accounts receivable (net receivables) are included in the numerator as All Communications did not have any short-term investments in marketable securities during this period.

Both the current ratio and quick ratio suggest that All Communications' liquidity improved in 2019. It is important to note that an analysis of liquidity is incomplete without consideration of cash flows. All Communications is able to operate with low or negative working capital because it has a healthy cash flow, aided by its ability to collect accounts receivable promptly.

Further insights about a company's ability to repay debt can also be found in its annual report. For example, All Communications' statement of cash flows, under cash flows from operating activities, shows that the receipts from customers increased by $794 million to $57 170 million in 2019.

Recall from chapter 1 that Artistry Furniture and Original Furnishings had much higher ratios compared to those of All Communications. In 2019, Original Furnishings' current ratio of 1.51:1 indicates that it had $1.51 of current assets for each $1 in current liabilities and had the capacity to pay debts as they fell due. Compared with Artistry Furniture's 2019 current ratio of 1.43:1 and All Communications' 2019 ratio of 1.05:1, Original Furnishings appears to have the highest level of liquidity. What is considered to be an *acceptable* ratio varies from industry to industry, so it would be helpful to compare All Communications' ratios to those of other similar companies in the telecommunications industry, as illustrated in the 'Using the decision-making toolkit' section of this chapter. However, a current ratio of 1:1 is generally considered an acceptable benchmark for most industries.

Using the decision-making toolkit next, management along with other users such as potential investors, shareholders and creditors can use this information to determine an entity's ability to pay its short-term obligations. One measure of liquidity is working capital, which represents the difference between an entity's current assets and current liabilities. A positive working capital is preferable as this means that the current assets are greater than the current liabilities. An alternative measure is the current ratio, which divides current assets by current liabilities. A current ratio above 1:1 means current assets exceed liabilities — a higher current ratio indicates a higher level of liquidity. The most rigorous measure of liquidity ratio is the quick ratio which focuses on those assets that are most quickly converted into cash: cash, marketable securities, and receivables. These quick assets are compared to current liabilities. Inventory is not included as it is generally more difficult to convert into cash on a shorter term basis. A higher quick ratio indicates a higher level of short-term liquidity.

Decision/issue	Info needed for analysis	Tool or technique to use for decision	How to evaluate results to make decision
Can the entity meet its current obligations?	Cash, accounts receivable, marketable securities, other current assets, current liabilities	$\text{Working capital} = \text{Current assets} - \text{Current liabilities}$	A positive working capital indicates that current assets are available to meet current liabilities.
		$\text{Current ratio} = \dfrac{\text{Current assets}}{\text{Current liabilities}}$	A current ratio above 1:1 means current assets exceed liabilities — a higher current ratio indicates a higher level of liquidity. Ratio should be compared with others in the same industry.
		$\text{Quick ratio} = \dfrac{\text{Cash} + \text{Marketable securities} + \text{Net receivable}}{\text{Current liabilities}}$	The quick ratio focuses on assets that are quickly converted into cash. A higher quick ratio indicates a higher level of short-term liquidity. The ratio should be compared with the others in the same industry.

Solvency ratios

Solvency ratios measure the ability of an entity to survive over a long period of time.

In chapter 1 you learned that one measure of an entity's solvency is the debt to total assets ratio. This ratio indicates the extent to which an entity's debt can be repaid by liquidating its assets. Other measures can also be useful. One such measure is **times interest earned** (also known as *interest coverage*), which provides an indication of an entity's ability to meet interest payments as they become due. It is calculated by dividing earnings before interest and tax (commonly abbreviated to EBIT) by interest expense (finance costs). This ratio uses EBIT as this represents the amount available to cover interest. Some companies report the EBIT figure as a line item in the statement of profit or loss. If this figure is not provided, it can be calculated using the profit before income tax and adding back interest expense to approximate EBIT. Note that, although there are some variations to this calculation, most companies generally use either interest expense or net finance costs as the denominator.

It is not uncommon for banks and other financial institutions to include terms in the loan agreement that restrict the amount of liabilities. Borrowing restrictions are often expressed in terms of the ratio of debt to total assets. For instance, an entity might be subject to a maximum debt to total assets ratio of 65%. So, if an entity had already borrowed to the maximum, any further expansion would need to be financed by additional equity.

We can use the information in figure 9.12 and the additional information below to calculate solvency ratios for All Communications Group.

($ in millions)	2019	2018
Profit before income tax	10 964	9 868
Interest expense (finance costs)	2 256	2 044

The debt to total assets ratios and times interest earned for All Communications Group are shown in figure 9.14.

FIGURE 9.14 Solvency measures

Ratio	Formula	All Communications Group	
($'000)		2019	2018
Debt to total assets ratio	Total liabilities / Total assets	$\dfrac{\$51\,304}{\$77\,054} = 0.67{:}1$	$\dfrac{\$55\,672}{\$79\,050} = 0.70{:}1$
Times interest earned	Profit before income tax + Interest expense / Interest expense	$\dfrac{(\$10\,964 + \$2\,256)}{\$2\,256} = 5.86$ times	$\dfrac{(\$9\,868 + \$2\,044)}{\$2\,044} = 5.83$ times

The debt to total assets ratio decreased slightly from 0.70:1 to 0.67:1 in 2019. The 2019 ratio of 0.67:1 indicates that 67 cents of each $1 invested in assets by All Communications was provided by its creditors. The higher the ratio, the lower the equity 'buffer' available to creditors if the company becomes insolvent, i.e. the less chance the creditors might have their debts repaid out of shareholders' funds if the company goes into liquidation. Therefore, from the creditors' point of view, a high ratio of debt to total assets is undesirable. If we compare All Communications' debt to total assets ratio of 0.67:1 to that of Original Furnishings' ratio of 0.59:1 and Artistry Furniture's ratio of 0.60:1 in 2019 as calculated in chapter 1, we can see that All Communications' reliance on debt finance appears to be significantly higher than that of these companies and higher than that of many other Australian companies. However, the adequacy of this ratio is often judged in light of the entity's profits and cash flows. Generally, entities with relatively stable profit can support higher debt to total assets ratios than can cyclical entities with widely fluctuating profits, such as many high-tech companies. All Communications' times interest earned increased slightly from 5.83 to 5.86 times in 2019. Creditors generally prefer the times interest earned to exceed 3.0 times and All Communications' interest coverage is well above this benchmark.

Once again, it is important to note that what is considered to be *acceptable* solvency ratios varies from industry to industry, so it would be helpful to compare All Communications' ratios with those of other similar companies. This is illustrated in the 'Using the decision-making toolkit' section of this chapter.

Using the decision-making toolkit below, management, along with other users such as potential investors, shareholders and creditors can use this information to determine an entity's ability to pay back debt. One measure of solvency is the debt to total assets ratio, which measures total liabilities as a percentage of total assets. A lower debt ratio is preferable as it implies a more stable business as less debt finance is used. Each industry has its own benchmarks for debt; however, a debt to total assets ratio of 50% is considered reasonable. Another indicator of solvency is the times interest earned ratio, which indicates how many times an entity can pay its interest expense with its profit before tax. It is preferable that this ratio should exceed 3 times as a higher interest coverage indicates that the entity has a greater capacity to pay its interest expense as it falls due.

DECISION-MAKING TOOLKIT

Decision/issue	Info needed for analysis	Tool or technique to use for decision		How to evaluate results to make decision
Can the entity meet its obligations in the long term?	Total liabilities, total assets	Debt to total assets ratio $=$	Total liabilities / Total assets	This ratio indicates the extent to which the entity's assets are financed by creditors. A low debt to total assets ratio is preferable.
	Interest expense, profit before income tax	Times interest earned $=$	Profit before income tax + Interest expense / Interest expense	This ratio should exceed 3 times — a higher interest coverage implies a greater capacity to meet interest payments.

Review it

1. What does the quick ratio measure, and how is it calculated?
2. What is meant by solvency?
3. What information does the times interest earned ratio provide and how is it calculated?

USING THE DECISION-MAKING TOOLKIT

Data Corporation of New Zealand Ltd operates in the telecommunications industry and has similar operations to All Communications Group. Data Corporation of New Zealand had profit before income tax of $682 million for 2019 and $846 million for 2018. Interest expense was $148 million in 2019 and $212 million in 2018. Data Corporation of New Zealand's statement of financial position as at 30 June 2019 with comparative figures for 2018 is provided below. Additional disclosures in the notes indicate the net short-term receivables were $738 million in 2019 and $844 million in 2018.

Required

(a) Evaluate Data Corporation New Zealand's liquidity using appropriate measures and compare it with that of All Communications Group reported in figure 9.13.

(b) Evaluate Data Corporation New Zealand's solvency using appropriate ratios and compare it with that of All Communications Group reported in figure 9.14.

DATA CORPORATION NEW ZEALAND Statement of financial position as at 30 June 2019			
	Notes	2019 NZ$m	2018 NZ$m
ASSETS			
Current assets			
Cash		246	372
Receivables	13	1 316	1 368
Taxation recoverable		8	106
Inventories	14	106	98
Total current assets		1 676	1 944
Non-current assets			
Long-term investments	15	154	114
Long-term receivables and prepayments	13	320	446
Intangible assets	16	2 142	1 800
Property, plant and equipment	17	2 694	3 030
Total non-current assets		5 310	5 390
Total assets		**6 986**	**7 334**
LIABILITIES AND EQUITY			
Current liabilities			
Accounts payable and accruals	18	1 638	1 550
Taxation payable		14	18
Short-term provisions	19	70	26
Debt due within one year	20	450	814
Total current liabilities		2 172	2 408
Non-current liabilities			
Deferred tax liabilities	21	336	364
Long-term payables and accruals	18	60	60
Long-term provisions	19	90	40
Long-term debt	22	1 502	1 210
Total non-current liabilities		1 988	1 674
Total liabilities		4 160	4 082

	Notes	2019 NZ$m	2018 NZ$m
Equity			
Share capital	23	1 798	1 980
Reserves	23	(1 008)	(990)
Retained earnings		2 024	2 252
Total equity attributable to equity holders of the company		2 814	3 242
Non-controlling interests		12	10
Total equity		2 826	3 252
Total liabilities and equity		**6 986**	**7 334**

Solution

(a) Data Corporation New Zealand's liquidity can be measured using the working capital, current ratio and quick ratio.

Ratio	Formula	Data Corporation New Zealand		All Communications Group
($ in NZ millions)		**2019**	**2018**	**2019**
Working capital	Current assets − Current liabilities	$1 676 − $2 172 = ($496)	$1 944 − $2 408 = ($464)	$15 806 − $15 044 = $762
Current ratio	$\dfrac{\text{Current assets}}{\text{Current liabilities}}$	$\dfrac{\$1\,676}{\$2\,172} = 0.77{:}1$	$\dfrac{\$1\,944}{\$2\,408} = 0.81{:}1$	$\dfrac{\$15\,806}{\$15\,044} = 1.05{:}1$
Quick ratio	$\dfrac{\text{Cash + Marketable securities + Net receivables}}{\text{Current liabilities}}$	$\dfrac{(\$246 + \$738^*)}{\$2\,172}$ $= 0.45{:}1$	$\dfrac{(\$372 + \$844^*)}{\$2\,408}$ $= 0.50{:}1$	$\dfrac{(\$4\,958 + \$9\,114)}{\$15\,044}$ $= 0.94{:}1$

*Given in the additional disclosure in the notes

Data Corporation New Zealand's working capital was negative in both years and by 2019 this amount had decreased a further $32 million. In contrast, All Communications recorded a positive working capital of $762 million for 2019 and a negative $1468 million in 2018. Data Corporation New Zealand's current ratio, which was less than 1:1 over the same period, indicates that its current liabilities are greater than its current assets. In 2019, it had 77 cents of current assets to cover each $1 of current liabilities, which is slightly lower than the 81 cents in 2018. Both figures are substantially lower than All Communications' current ratio of $1.05 in 2019. A similar trend can be seen in the quick ratio. In 2019, Data Corporation New Zealand's quick ratio declined from 45 cents of quick assets to cover each $1 of current liabilities, which is slightly lower than the 50 cents in 2018. Both figures are substantially lower than All Communications' quick ratio of 94 cents in 2019. A comparison of each entity's working capital, current ratio and quick ratio indicates that All Communications' liquidity is considerably better than that of Data Corporation New Zealand's across each of these measures. The decline in Data Corporation New Zealand's liquidity is due to the decrease in current and quick assets, which is proportionately larger than the decrease in current liabilities.

(b) Data Corporation New Zealand's solvency can be measured with the debt to total assets ratio and times interest earned.

Ratio	Formula	Data Corporation New Zealand		All Communications Group
($ in NZ millions)		2019	2018	2019
Debt to total assets ratio	$\dfrac{\text{Total liabilities}}{\text{Total assets}}$	$\dfrac{\$4\,160}{\$6\,986} = 0.60{:}1$	$\dfrac{\$4\,082}{\$7\,334} = 0.56{:}1$	$\dfrac{\$51\,304}{\$77\,054} = 0.67{:}1$
Times interest earned	$\dfrac{\text{Profit before income tax} + \text{Interest expense}}{\text{Interest expense}}$	$\dfrac{(\$682 + \$148)}{\$148}$ $= 5.61 \text{ times}$	$\dfrac{(\$846 + \$212)}{\$212}$ $= 4.99 \text{ times}$	$\dfrac{(\$10\,964 + \$2\,256)}{\$2\,256}$ $= 5.86 \text{ times}$

Data Corporation New Zealand's reliance on debt increased slightly over the 2-year period. In 2019, the debt to total assets ratio shows that it used 60 cents of debt finance for each $1 invested in assets, which is higher than the 56 cents in 2018. All Communications' debt to total assets ratio of 67 cents in 2019 suggests that it relies slightly more heavily on debt financing than Data Corporation New Zealand. The higher the ratio, the lower the equity 'buffer' available to creditors if the company becomes insolvent. Despite the slightly higher reliance on debt finance, Data Corporation New Zealand's times interest earned improved considerably from 4.99 times in 2018 to 5.61 times in 2019, which is similar to All Communications' coverage of 5.86 times. This was mainly attributed to the substantial decrease in interest expense which offset the decrease in profit before tax. Creditors prefer times interest earned exceeding 3.0 times — both Data Corporation New Zealand and All Communications are well above this benchmark.

SUMMARY

9.1 Explain the differences between current and non-current liabilities.

A current liability is an obligation that can reasonably be expected to be paid within 1 year or the normal operating cycle, whichever is the longer. A non-current liability is an obligation that is expected to be paid after 1 year or outside the normal operating cycle.

9.2 Identify common types of current liabilities and explain how to account for them.

The common types of current liabilities include notes payable, accounts payable, payroll and payroll deductions payable, and revenue received in advance. When a note is interest-bearing, the amount of cash received upon the issue of the note is generally equal to the face value of the note, and interest expense is accrued over the life of the note. At maturity, the amount paid is equal to the face value of the note plus accrued interest. Employee PAYG withheld tax and other payroll deductions are credited to appropriate liability accounts when recording the payroll. Revenues received in advance are initially recorded in a liability account. They are transferred from the liability account to revenue when the recognition criteria for revenue are satisfied.

9.3 Identify common types of non-current liabilities, such as debentures and unsecured notes, and explain how to account for them.

When unsecured notes and debentures are issued at face value, cash is debited and unsecured notes or debentures payable is credited for the face value of the issue. Interest payments are recognised as an expense. Interest is accrued if payment does not coincide with the end of the reporting period. When unsecured notes or debentures are redeemed at maturity, cash is credited and unsecured notes or debentures payable is debited for the face value of the issue. When unsecured notes or debentures are redeemed before maturity, it is necessary to (a) eliminate the carrying amount of the liability at the redemption date, (b) record the cash paid, and (c) recognise the gain or loss on redemption for the difference between the carrying amount of the unsecured notes or debentures and the amount paid to redeem them.

9.4 Prepare journal entries for loans payable by instalment and distinguish between current and non-current components of long-term debt.

When accounting for loans payable by instalment, each payment must be allocated between interest expense and the reduction in the liability (i.e. in the principal of the loan). A mortgage schedule may be prepared to facilitate calculation of the interest and principal component of each payment. The current component of the liability can be identified from the schedule as the sum of amounts allocated to the reduction of the principal during the first year (or operating cycle) after the end of the reporting period.

9.5 Identify the advantages of leasing and explain the difference between an operating lease and a finance lease.

A lease is an agreement where the lessor conveys to the lessee the right to use an asset for an agreed period of time in return for a payment or a series of payments. The advantages of leasing for the lessee include access to a wide variety of non-current assets, tax deductibility of lease payments, the risk of obsolescence of the non-current asset remains with the lessor, lease contracts may be less restrictive than many debt agreements, and some lease liabilities are not required to be reported on the statement of financial position. An operating lease is where the *lessor* effectively retains the risks and rewards of owning an asset and, consequently, the leased asset is reported in the statement of financial position of the lessor. A finance lease is where the substantial *risks and rewards of ownership* of the asset are effectively transferred to the lessee even though the *ownership remains with* the lessor. Consequently, the leased asset is reported in the statement of financial position of the lessee.

9.6 Complete basic journal entries for accounting for leases and explain how to report leases.

Assets that are acquired under operating lease agreements are recorded in the accounts of both the lessee and the lessor when the lease payment is due to be paid or is paid to the lessor by the lessee. The lessee records the lease expense and cash payment (or liability) and the lessor records the cash received (or receivable) and the lease revenue. Accounting for finance leases is more complex than operating leases and is covered in more depth in the later years of accounting studies. Simply put, at the beginning of the lease, the lessee is required to recognise both the asset and the liability for the leased assets at amounts equal to their fair value or, if lower, the present value of the minimum lease payments. Further, the lessee is required to record amortisation on the leased asset as well as the lease payments. The lessor records the lease receivable and the receipt of payments from the lessee.

9.7 Explain the differences between provisions, contingencies and other types of liabilities and explain how to report contingent liabilities.

Provisions are liabilities for which the amount of the future sacrifice is uncertain. Whether a liability is a provision or some other type of liability (e.g. borrowings, trade creditors, accruals) depends upon the extent of uncertainty associated with the amount of the future sacrifice. Liabilities are classified as contingent if they are conditional upon an uncertain future event outside the control of the entity, or if they do not satisfy either or both of the recognition criteria for liabilities.

Contingent liabilities are not recognised because they are not probable or are unable to be measured reliably, or both. Information about contingent liabilities must be disclosed in the notes to the financial statements. The required disclosures include a description of their nature, an indication of the uncertainties associated with the amount or timing of any future sacrifice, the estimated financial effect (if practical) and the existence of any possible recovery of the future sacrifice.

9.8 Prepare entries to record provisions for warranties.

Unexpired warranties at the end of the reporting period are a liability. The estimated cost of servicing unexpired warranty contracts at the end of the reporting period is reported as a warranty provision. Any existing balance in the warranty provision account is increased (or decreased) so that the amount of the provision equals the estimated cost of servicing warranties that have not expired at the end of reporting period. To increase the warranty provision account, warranty expense is debited and warranty provision is credited. Subsequent expenditure in servicing warranty claims is debited to the warranty provision account.

9.9 Evaluate an entity's liquidity and solvency.

The liquidity of an entity can be analysed using working capital, the current ratio and the quick ratio. The long-term solvency of an entity may be analysed by calculating the debt to total assets ratio and times interest earned. The relevance of these liquidity and solvency ratios in the decision-making process is summarised in the decision-making toolkit below.

DECISION-MAKING TOOLKIT — A SUMMARY

DECISION-MAKING TOOLKIT

Decision/issue	Info needed for analysis	Tool or technique to use for decision	How to evaluate results to make decision
Can the entity meet its current obligations?	Cash, accounts receivable, marketable securities, other current assets, current liabilities	$\text{Working capital} = \text{Current assets} - \text{Current liabilities}$	A positive working capital indicates that current assets are available to meet current liabilities.

Decision/issue	Info needed for analysis	Tool or technique to use for decision	How to evaluate results to make decision
		Current ratio $=\dfrac{\text{Current assets}}{\text{Current liabilities}}$	A current ratio above 1:1 means current assets exceed liabilities — a higher current ratio indicates a higher level of liquidity. Ratio should be compared with others in the same industry.
		Quick ratio $=\dfrac{\text{Cash + Marketable securities + Net receivables}}{\text{Current liabilities}}$	The quick ratio focuses on assets that are quickly converted into cash. A higher quick ratio indicates a higher level of short-term liquidity. The ratio should be compared with others in the same industry.
Can the entity meet its obligations in the long term?	Total liabilities, total assets	Debt to total assets ratio $=\dfrac{\text{Total liabilities}}{\text{Total assets}}$	This ratio indicates the extent to which the entity's assets are financed by creditors. A low debt to total assets ratio is preferable.
	Interest expense, profit before income tax	Times interest earned $=\dfrac{\text{Profit before income tax + Interest expense}}{\text{Interest expense}}$	This ratio should exceed 3 times — a higher interest coverage implies a greater capacity to meet interest payments.

KEY TERMS

borrowing costs Costs of borrowing money.

contingent liabilities Liabilities for which the amount of the future sacrifices (obligations) are dependent upon a future event (such as a law suit) or are so uncertain that their amount cannot be reliably measured.

contract interest rate Rate used to determine the amount of interest the borrower pays and the investor receives.

current liability An obligation that can reasonably be expected to be paid within 1 year or the operating cycle.

debentures Notes issued with security over some assets of the issuer.

discounting A reduction in value of a future amount to its present value reflecting the time value of money.

face value Amount of principal due at the maturity date of the note.

finance lease A long-term agreement where the lessor effectively transfers to the lessee substantially all the risks and rewards incidental to ownership of the leased asset. The arrangement is accounted for like a purchase.

implicit interest rate The discount rate that results in the aggregate present value of the leased asset being equal to the fair value of the leased asset of the lessor at the inception of the lease.

incremental borrowing rate The rate of interest the lessee would have to pay to lease a similar asset or the interest rate that would be incurred by the lessee to borrow funds and purchase the asset outright.

interest Cost of borrowing money.

issue price Amount paid by the investor on issue of a debenture or unsecured note.

lease An agreement where the lessor conveys to the lessee the right to use an asset for an agreed period of time in return for a payment or a series of payments.

lessee A party that has made contractual arrangements to use another party's asset without purchasing it.

lessor A party that has agreed contractually to let another party use its asset.

market interest rate The rate investors demand for lending funds to the entity.

market value The amount obtainable from the sale, or payable on the acquisition, of a financial instrument in an active market.

mortgage A loan secured by a charge over property.

non-current liability An obligation that is not classified as a current liability, i.e. an obligation expected to be paid after 1 year or outside the normal operating cycle.

notes payable A liability evidenced by notes.

operating lease An arrangement whereby the lessor effectively retains substantially all the risks and rewards incidental to ownership of a leased asset. The arrangement is accounted for as a rental.

present value The value today of an amount to be paid or received at some date in the future after taking into account current interest rates.

provision A liability for which the amount is uncertain but able to be measured reliably by estimation.

quick ratio A measure of an entity's immediate short-term liquidity, calculated by dividing the sum of cash, marketable securities and net receivables by current liabilities; also called the acid test.

times interest earned A measure of an entity's ability to meet interest payments as they come due, calculated as profit before income tax plus interest expense divided by interest expense.

unsecured notes Notes issued against the general credit of the issuer, i.e. not subject to any secured charge over assets.

warranty An obligation of the supplier of goods and services to the purchaser that the product will be functional or that work performed will remain satisfactory for a stated period after the sale of goods or the provision of services.

DEMONSTRATION PROBLEM

On 1 July 2018, Birds-Aflight Pet Store Ltd entered into a mortgage loan. The amount borrowed was $449 550, with $10 000 repayable at the end of each month over a 5-year period. The interest rate was 12% per annum.

Required

(a) Prepare a mortgage schedule for the loan.

(b) Use the information in the schedule to prepare journal entries to record mortgage payments on 31 July 2018 and 31 August 2018.

(c) Assuming Birds-Aflight Pet Store has a year-end of 30 June, calculate the amount of the liability as at 30 June 2019 that should be reported as current, and the amount that should be reported as non-current.

SOLUTION TO DEMONSTRATION PROBLEM

(a) Mortgage schedule

Month ending	Beginning balance	Payment	Interest	Reduction of principal	Closing balance
31.07.18	$449 550	$10 000	$4 496	$5 504	$444 046
31.08.18	444 046	10 000	4 440	5 560	438 486
30.09.18	438 486	10 000	4 385	5 615	432 871

Month ending	Beginning balance	Payment	Interest	Reduction of principal	Closing balance
31.10.18	432 871	10 000	4 329	5 671	427 200
30.11.18	427 200	10 000	4 272	5 728	421 472
31.12.18	421 472	10 000	4 215	5 785	415 687
31.01.19	415 687	10 000	4 157	5 843	409 844
28.02.19	409 844	10 000	4 098	5 902	403 942
31.03.19	403 942	10 000	4 039	5 961	397 981
30.04.19	397 981	10 000	3 980	6 020	391 961
31.05.19	391 961	10 000	3 919	6 081	385 880
30.06.19	385 880	10 000	3 859	6 141	379 739
31.07.19	379 739	10 000	3 797	6 203	373 536
31.08.19	373 536	10 000	3 735	6 265	367 271
30.09.19	367 271	10 000	3 673	6 327	360 944
31.10.19	360 944	10 000	3 609	6 391	354 553
30.11.19	354 553	10 000	3 546	6 454	348 099
31.12.19	348 099	10 000	3 481	6 519	341 580
31.01.20	341 580	10 000	3 416	6 584	334 996
28.02.20	334 996	10 000	3 350	6 650	328 346
31.03.20	328 346	10 000	3 284	6 716	321 630
30.04.20	321 630	10 000	3 216	6 784	314 846
31.05.20	314 846	10 000	3 148	6 852	307 994
30.06.20	307 994	10 000	3 080	6 920	301 074
31.07.20	301 074	10 000	3 011	6 989	294 085
31.08.20	294 085	10 000	2 941	7 059	287 026
30.09.20	287 026	10 000	2 870	7 130	279 896
31.10.20	279 896	10 000	2 799	7 201	272 695
30.11.20	272 695	10 000	2 727	7 273	265 422
31.12.20	265 422	10 000	2 654	7 346	258 076
31.01.21	258 076	10 000	2 581	7 419	250 657
29.02.21	250 657	10 000	2 507	7 493	243 164
31.03.21	243 164	10 000	2 432	7 568	235 596
30.04.21	235 596	10 000	2 356	7 644	227 952
31.05.21	227 952	10 000	2 280	7 720	220 232
30.06.21	220 232	10 000	2 202	7 798	212 434
31.07.21	212 434	10 000	2 124	7 876	204 558
31.08.21	204 558	10 000	2 046	7 954	196 604
30.09.21	196 604	10 000	1 966	8 034	188 570
31.10.21	188 570	10 000	1 886	8 114	180 456
30.11.21	180 456	10 000	1 804	8 196	172 260
31.12.21	172 260	10 000	1 723	8 277	163 983
31.01.22	163 983	10 000	1 640	8 360	155 623
28.02.22	155 623	10 000	1 556	8 444	147 179
31.03.22	147 179	10 000	1 472	8 528	138 651
30.04.22	138 651	10 000	1 386	8 614	130 037
31.05.22	130 037	10 000	1 300	8 700	121 337
30.06.22	121 337	10 000	1 213	8 787	112 550
31.07.22	112 550	10 000	1 125	8 875	103 675
31.08.22	103 675	10 000	1 037	8 963	94 712
30.09.22	94 712	10 000	947	9 053	85 659
31.10.22	85 659	10 000	857	9 143	76 516
30.11.22	76 516	10 000	765	9 235	67 281
31.12.22	67 281	10 000	673	9 327	57 954
31.01.23	57 954	10 000	580	9 420	48 534
28.02.23	48 534	10 000	485	9 515	39 019
31.03.23	39 019	10 000	390	9 610	29 409
30.04.23	29 409	10 000	294	9 706	19 703
31.05.23	19 703	10 000	197	9 803	9 900
30.06.23	9 900	10 000	100	9 900	0

(b) Journal entries

2018				
July 31	Interest expense	4 496		
	Loan payable	5 504		
	Cash at bank		10 000	
	(To record the loan payment for July)			
2018				
Aug. 31	Interest expense	4 440		
	Loan payable	5 560		
	Cash at bank		10 000	
	(To record the loan payment for August)			

(c) Current and non-current portions of mortgage liability at 30.06.19:

	$ 6 203
	6 265
	6 327
	6 391
	6 454
	6 519
	6 584
	6 650
	6 716
	6 784
	6 852
	6 920
Current portion of mortgage liability at 30.06.19	**$ 78 665**
Total mortgage liability at 30.06.19	$379 739
Less: Current portion of mortgage loan	78 665
Non-current portion of mortgage liability at 30.06.19	**$301 074**

SELF-STUDY QUESTIONS

9.1 To be classified as a current liability, a debt must be expected to be paid: **LO1**
(a) within 1 year.
(b) within the operating cycle.
(c) within 2 years.
(d) either (a) or (b).

9.2 Which of the following is *not* a current liability?   **LO1**
(a) Allowance for doubtful debts.
(b) Revenue received in advance.
(c) Current portion of long-term debt.
(d) Payroll deduction not yet remitted.

9.3 Which of the following would *not* be included in the numerator of the quick ratio?   **LO9**
(a) Inventory.
(b) Cash.
(c) Short-term investments.
(d) Accounts receivable.

9.4 Amounts deducted from employees' wages but not yet paid to a third party are recognised as:
(a) an asset.   **LO2**
(b) an expense.
(c) a liability.
(d) none of the above; they are not recognised.

9.5 An obligation for long service leave payable 6 years from now is recognised as: **LO3**
   (a) a contingent liability.
   (b) a non-current provision.
   (c) a current provision.
   (d) none of the above; it is not recognised.

9.6 Which of the following is *not* a measure of liquidity?   **LO9**
   (a) Debt to total assets ratio.
   (b) Working capital.
   (c) Current ratio.
   (d) Quick ratio.

9.7 Karson Ltd issues 10-year unsecured notes with a maturity value of $200 000. If the notes are issued at a premium, this indicates that: **LO3**
   (a) the face value exceeds the amount received.
   (b) the issue price exceeds the face value.
   (c) the contractual interest rate and the market interest rate are the same.
   (d) no relationship exists between the contractual and market interest rates.

9.8 Gester Ltd redeems its $100 000 face value debentures at 105 on 31 January, following the payment of half-yearly interest. The carrying amount of the debentures at the redemption date is $100 000. The entry to record the redemption will include a: **LO3**
   (a) credit of $5000 to gain on redemption of debentures.
   (b) debit of $5000 to loss on redemption of debentures.
   (c) credit of $100 000 to cash.
   (d) debit of $105 000 to debentures payable.

9.9 In a recent year Kennedy Ltd had profit after tax of $150 000, interest expense of $30 000, and tax expense of $20 000. What was Kennedy Ltd's times interest earned for the year?   **LO9**
   (a) 5.00.
   (b) 4.00.
   (c) 6.67.
   (d) 7.50.

9.10 Adelaide Boats Ltd had current liabilities of $5 million, non-current liabilities of $10 million and total assets of $20 million. What is Adelaide Boats Ltd's debt to total assets ratio?   **LO9**
   (a) 1.3:1.
   (b) 0.5:1.
   (c) 0.75:1.
   (d) 0.25:1.

9.11 Which of the following is *true* with regard to contingent liabilities?   **LO7**
   (a) Can be measured reliably.
   (b) Are recognised in the statement of financial position.
   (c) Are disclosed in the notes to the financial statements.
   (d) Are based on a past transaction or event.

9.12 Which of the following are considered to be advantages of operating leases for the lessee?   **LO5**
   (a) Access to a wide variety of non-current assets.
   (b) Tax deductibility of lease payments.
   (c) The risk of obsolescence of the non-current asset remains with the lessor.
   (d) All of the above.

9.13 Which of the following is *not* true in relation to leases?   **LO5**
   (a) An operating lease is where the *lessee* effectively retains the risks and rewards of owning an asset.
   (b) An operating lease is where the *lessor* effectively retains the risks and rewards of owning an asset.

(c) A finance lease is where the substantial risks and rewards of ownership of the asset are *not* transferred to the lessee.

(d) A finance lease is where the ownership is transferred to the *lessee*.

On 1 December, Braco Bros Pty Ltd (lessee) signed an 18-month operating lease agreement with U Bute Boats Ltd (lessor) to lease a boat for $100 per month. Payments are due every 3 months on the last day of the month. Both parties have a December year-end. Using this information, answer questions 9.14 and 9.15.

9.14 The entry to account for the lease payment accrual at the end of the period in the records of the lessee would be: **LO6**

(a) No accrual required, the transaction would be recorded on the date the lease payment was made.

(b)

June 30	Lease expense	100	
	Lease payable		100

(c)

Dec. 31	Lease expense	100	
	Lease payable		100

(d)

Dec. 31	Lease expense	100	
	Cash		100

9.15 Assuming the required lease accrual was made at 31 December, the payment of the first lease payment would be recorded as follows in the books of the lessee: **LO6**

(a)

Feb. 28	Lease payable	100	
	Lease expense	200	
	Cash		300

(b)

Feb. 28	Lease payable	200	
	Lease expense	100	
	Cash		300

(c)

Feb. 28	Lease expense	200	
	Cash		200

(d)

Feb. 28	Lease expense	300	
	Lease payable		300

QUESTIONS

9.1 Simon Harris believes a current liability is a debt that can be expected to be paid in 1 year. Is Simon correct? Explain.

9.2 Wellington University sold 5000 season football tickets at $50 each for its 5-game home schedule. What entries should be made (a) when the tickets are sold and (b) after each game?

9.3 Sandra Leung and Nikki Young are discussing how the market price of an unsecured note is determined. Nikki believes that the market price of a note is solely a function of the amount of the principal payment at the end of the term of a note. Is she right? Discuss.

9.4 Northumbria Ltd issued a $50 000, 8%, 3-month note on 1 October. Interest is payable on 1 January. How much interest should be accrued as at 31 December in relation to the note?

9.5 Explain the difference between a provision and other types of liabilities recognised on the statement of financial position.

9.6 Explain the difference between a provision and a contingent liability.

9.7 Ms Dwyer, the manager of Dwyer's Dryers, thinks that warranty liabilities should be recognised only when the customer makes a warranty claim. Is this consistent with generally accepted accounting principles?

9.8 What are the main features of a mortgage loan? How should a mortgage liability be reported on the statement of financial position?

9.9 Gotham Ltd has a current ratio of 1.25:1. Bruce Wayne has always been told that an entity's current ratio should exceed 2:0. Gotham Ltd argues that its ratio is low because it has a minimal amount of inventory on hand so as to reduce operating costs. What other measures might Bruce check to evaluate liquidity?

9.10 Explain the difference between a finance lease and an operating lease.

BRIEF EXERCISES

BE9.1 Identify whether obligations are current liabilities.   **LO1, 4**

Alvin Ltd has these obligations at 31 December: (a) a note payable for $50 000 due in 2 years, (b) a 10-year mortgage payable of $100 000 payable in ten $10 000 annual payments, (c) interest payable of $5000 on the mortgage, and (d) accounts payable of $60 000. For each obligation, indicate whether it should be wholly or partly classified as a current liability, or wholly classified as a non-current liability. Alvin Ltd has a 1-year operating cycle.

BE9.2 Prepare entries for an interest-bearing note payable.   **LO2**

Admiralty Pty Ltd borrows $160 000 on 1 July from the bank by signing a $160 000, 10%, 1-year note payable. Prepare the journal entries to record (a) the proceeds of the note and (b) accrued interest at 31 December, assuming adjusting entries are made only at the end of the year (31 December).

BE9.3 Prepare journal entries for loans payable by instalment.   **LO4**

Using the mortgage schedule in figure 9.6, prepare the journal entry to record the mortgage payment on 31 May 2019.

BE9.4 Prepare journal entries for loans payable by instalment.   **LO4**

Using the mortgage schedule in figure 9.6, prepare the journal entry to record the mortgage payment on 30 September 2019.

BE9.5 Prepare entries to record provisions for warranties.   **LO8**

Trish's Toasters Pty Ltd sells toasters with a 1-year warranty. At 30 June, it is estimated that the liability for unexpired warranties is $35 000. The warranty provision account has a debit balance of $1000. Prepare the adjusting entry to record the warranty provision at 30 June.

BE9.6 Prepare entries to record provisions for warranties.   **LO8**

Mac's Auto Repairs Pty Ltd provides a 3-month warranty for repairs. Mac's Auto Repairs estimates its warranty liabilities as 4% of the service revenue for the preceding quarter. For the 3 months from April to June, Mac's Auto Repairs' service revenue was $250 000. The warranty provision account has a credit balance of $700. Prepare the adjusting entry to record the warranty provision at 30 June.

BE9.7 Prepare journal entries for debentures issued at face value.   **LO3**

Eccencia Ltd issued 2000 8%, 5-year, $1000 debentures dated 1 January 2020 at 100.

(a) Prepare the journal entry to record the issue of these debentures on 1 January 2020.

(b) Prepare the journal entry to record the first interest payment on 1 July 2020 (interest payable half-yearly), assuming no previous accrual of interest.

(c) Prepare the adjusting journal entry on 31 December 2020, to record interest expense.

BE9.8 Analyse liquidity and solvency.   **LO9**

Johnson Ltd's 2019 financial statements contain the following selected data (in $'000).

Current assets	$ 294 705
Total assets	1 237 785
Current liabilities	301 830
Total liabilities	436 689
Cash	13 877
Short-term financial assets	941
Accounts receivable	19 092

Required

Calculate these values for Johnson Ltd:

(a) Working capital.

(b) Current ratio.

(c) Quick ratio.

(d) Debt to total assets ratio.

BE9.9 Prepare journal entries for leases.   **LO9**

On 1 June, Fresh Flowers Ltd (lessee) signed a 2-year operating lease agreement with Trucks R Us Pty Ltd (lessor) to lease a delivery truck for $100 per month. Payments are due every 3 months on the last day of the month. Trucks R Us Pty Ltd has a June year-end. In the books of Trucks R Us Pty Ltd, prepare the journal entries to record the accrued lease revenue at year-end and the receipt of the first lease payment.

EXERCISES

E9.1 Prepare entries for interest-bearing notes.   **LO2**

Ellie and Brad Nowland borrowed $12 000 on an 8-month, 10% note from a financial institution to open their business, EB's Café. The money was borrowed on 1 May 2019.

Required

(a) Prepare the entry to record the receipt of the funds from the loan.

(b) Prepare the entry to accrue the interest on 31 May.

(c) Assuming adjusting entries are made at the end of each month, what is the balance in the interest payable account at 31 December 2019?

(d) Prepare the entry required on 1 January 2020 when the loan is paid back.

E9.2 Journalise payroll entries.   **LO2**

During the month of June, Transfield Pty Ltd's employees earned wages of $105 000. Payroll deductions related to these wages were $6750 for General Health Fund, $11 250 for PAYG withheld tax, $9450 for superannuation, and $2000 for union fees.

Required

Prepare the necessary 30 June journal entry to record payroll. Assume that wages earned during June will be paid during July.

E9.3 Prepare journal entries for issue of notes and payment and accrual of interest.   **LO3**

On 1 January Fairy Wren Ltd issued $100 000, 10%, 10-year unsecured notes at face value. Interest is payable half-yearly on 1 July and 1 January. Interest is not accrued on 30 June. Fairy Wren Ltd's year-end is 31 December.

Required

Prepare journal entries to record these events:

(a) the issue of the unsecured notes.

(b) the payment of interest on 1 July.

(c) the accrual of interest on 31 December.

E9.4 Prepare journal entries for redemption of debentures. **LO3**

The situations presented below are independent.

Required

For each situation prepare the appropriate journal entry for the redemption of the debentures.

(a) Whitewater Rafting Ltd redeemed $130 000 face value, 12% debentures on 30 June 2019 at 102. The carrying amount of the debentures at the redemption date was $130 000. The debentures pay half-yearly interest, and the interest payment due on 30 June 2019 has been made and recorded.

(b) Coopers Ltd redeemed $180 000 face value, 12.5% debentures on 30 June 2020 at 98. The carrying amount of the debentures at the redemption date was $180 000. The debentures pay half-yearly interest, and the interest payment due on 30 June 2020 has been made and recorded.

E9.5 Record payment and identify components of a loan payable by instalment. **LO4**

Use the information in figure 9.6 to complete this exercise.

Required

Prepare a journal entry to record the mortgage payment on 30 June 2019.

(a) What is the carrying amount of the mortgage liability at that date, after the payment?

(b) What portion of the mortgage liability should be classified as a current liability?

(c) What portion of the mortgage liability should be classified as a non-current liability?

(d) Why is it important to classify liabilities as current and non-current? Explain how this is helpful for decision making. Provide examples.

E9.6 Record payment and identify components of a loan payable by instalment. **LO4**

Use the mortgage schedule in the 'Demonstration problem' section of this chapter to complete this exercise.

Required

(a) Prepare a journal entry to record the mortgage payment on 30 June 2019.

(b) What is the carrying amount of the mortgage liability at that date, after the payment?

(c) How much of the mortgage liability should be classified as a current liability?

(d) How much of the mortgage liability should be classified as a non-current liability?

E9.7 Categorise liabilities as provisions, contingent liabilities or other. **LO7**

Liabilities can be provisions, contingent liabilities or other liabilities.

Required

Categorise each of the following liabilities as (1) provisions, (2) contingent liabilities, or (3) other liabilities.

(a) An unquantifiable liability for restoring a polluted river

(b) Accounts payable

(c) Wages payable

(d) Obligation for unexpired warranty costs

(e) Trade creditors

(f) Obligations for employees' long service leave

(g) Accrued interest liability

(h) Mortgage loan

(i) Guarantee for another's loan, which will be payable if the other party defaults

E9.8 Prepare entries to record provisions for warranties. **LO7**

Olden Motor Vehicles Ltd offers a 12-month warranty for the sale of used motor vehicles. On 1 July 2018, there was a credit balance of $70 000 in its warranty provision account. During the year ended 30 June 2019, Olden Motor Vehicles incurred $65 000 in warranty costs, of which $30 000 was in the form of inventory and $35 000 was for labour costs. At 30 June 2019, Olden Motor Vehicles estimated its liability for unexpired warranty contracts as $75 000.

Required

(a) Prepare journal entries to record warranty claims during the period and end-of-period adjustments to the warranty provision account. (*Hint:* Credit wages payable for the labour costs.)

(b) Why do entities offer a warranty?

E9.9 Prepare entries to record provisions for warranties.   **LO7**

Benson Builder Pty Ltd provides a 12-month warranty on building work performed by the entity. On 1 January 2019, there was a credit balance of $80 000 in its warranty provision account. During the year ended 31 December 2019, Benson Builder Pty Ltd incurred $85 000 servicing warranty claims. All of the warranty costs were in the form of labour costs. During the year ended 31 December 2019, Benson Builder Pty Ltd's revenue from building contracts was $7 million. Warranty liabilities are estimated as 1% of building revenue for the previous 12 months.

Required

Prepare journal entries to record warranty claims during the period and end-of-period adjustments to the warranty provision account. (*Hint:* Credit wages payable for the labour costs.)

E9.10 Calculate liquidity and solvency ratios.   **LO7**

Investment Ltd's annual report 2019 contained the following selected data (in $'000).

Current assets	$ 422 275	Accounts receivable	$ 6 858
Total assets	1 562 014	Short-term investments	—
Current liabilities	89 588	Interest expense	6 988
Total liabilities	261 648	Profit before tax	245 956
Cash	313 157		

Required

(a) Calculate these values and provide an overview of Investment Ltd's liquidity and solvency.

1. Working capital.
2. Current ratio.
3. Quick ratio.
4. Debt to total assets ratio.
5. Times interest earned.

(b) Explain why it is helpful to compare ratios for individual entities to competitors' ratios or industry averages.

E9.11 Explain journal entries for leases.   **LO6**

The following entries were recorded in the accounts of Speedy Delivery Ltd.

June 30	Truck lease expense	200	
	Truck lease payable—Fast Trucks Ltd		200
Aug. 31	Truck lease payable—Fast Trucks Ltd	200	
	Truck lease expense	400	
	Cash		600

The following entries were recorded in the accounts of Fast Trucks Ltd.

June 30	Truck lease receivable—Speedy Delivery Ltd	200	
	Truck lease revenue		200
Aug. 31	Cash	600	
	Truck lease receivable—Speedy Delivery Ltd		200
	Truck lease revenue		400

Required

For the four journal entries recorded above, explain clearly the nature of each entry.

E9.12 Prepare journal entries for leases.   **LO6**

On 1 June, Sunny Nursery Ltd (lessee) signed a 2-year operating lease agreement with Bunning's Rentals Ltd (lessor) to lease gardening tools for $400 per month. Payments are due every 2 months on the last day of the month. Both the lessee and the lessor have a 30 June year-end.

Required

Record the first lease payment in the books of both the lessee and the lessor.

E9.13 Prepare journal entries for leases.   **LO6**

On 30 May, Grand Design Ltd (lessee) signed a 3-year operating lease agreement with Doby Ltd (lessor) to lease office space for $500 per month. Payments are due every 3 months on the last day of the month. Both the lessee and the lessor have a 30 June year-end.

Required

Record the first three journal entries, i.e. the lease accrual and the first two lease payments in the books of both the lessee and the lessor.

PROBLEM SET A

PSA9.1 Journalise and post note transactions; show statement of financial position presentation. LO2

Cling-on Ltd sells rock-climbing products and also operates an indoor climbing facility for climbing enthusiasts. During the last part of 2019, Cling-on Ltd had the following transactions related to notes payable.

Sept.	1	Issued a $16 000 note to Black Diamond to purchase inventory. The note payable bears interest of 9% and is due in 3 months.
	30	Recorded accrued interest for the Black Diamond note.
Oct.	1	Issued a $10 000, 12%, 3-month note to Montpelier Bank to finance the building of a new climbing area for advanced climbers.
	31	Recorded accrued interest for the Black Diamond note and the Montpelier Bank note.
Nov.	1	Issued an $18 000 note and paid $8000 cash to purchase a vehicle costing $26 000 to transport clients to nearby climbing sites as part of a new series of climbing classes. This note bears interest of 14% and matures in 12 months.
	30	Recorded accrued interest for the Black Diamond note, the Montpelier Bank note, and the vehicle note.
Dec.	1	Paid principal and interest on the Black Diamond note.
	31	Recorded accrued interest for the Montpelier Bank note and the vehicle note.

Required

(a) Prepare journal entries for the listed transactions.
(b) Post the entries to the notes payable, interest payable and interest expense accounts (use T accounts).
(c) Show the statement of financial position presentation of notes payable and interest payable at 31 December.
(d) How much interest expense relating to notes payable did Cling-on Ltd incur during the year? There were no other transactions relating to notes payable in 2019.
(e) Discuss the advantages and disadvantages of purchasing inventory by means of a note payable rather than accounts payable.

PSA9.2 Prepare current liability entries, adjusting entries, and current liability section.   **LO2**

On 1 July 2018, the ledger of Annie Clothing Ltd contained the following liability accounts.

Accounts payable	$78 000
PAYG withheld tax payable	1 750
Revenue received in advance	21 000

During July the following selected transactions occurred.

July 14	Provided services for customers who had made advance payments of $7500 (credit service revenue).
20	Paid taxation department $1750 for PAYG withheld tax deducted from wages in June 2018.
24	Borrowed $27 000 from South Coast Bank on a 6-month, 12%, $27 000 note.

During July the entity's employees earned wages of $20 000. Payroll deductions related to these wages were $1400 for a health fund, $1900 for PAYG withheld tax, and $1800 for super-annuation. Assume that wages earned during July will be paid during August.

Required

(a) Journalise the July transactions.

(b) Journalise the adjusting entries at 31 July for the note payable and for wages expense.

(c) Prepare the current liability section of the statement of financial position at 31 July 2018. Assume no change in accounts payable.

(d) Discuss some of the other costs employers may incur in relation to their employees.

PSA9.3 Prepare journal entries to record interest payments, and redemption of unsecured notes. LO3

The following section is taken from D100 Ltd's statement of financial position at 31 December 2019.

Current liabilities	
Interest payable on unsecured notes (for 6 months from 1 July to 31 December)	$ 240 000
Non-current liabilities	
Unsecured notes payable, 12% due 1 January 2023	4 000 000

Interest is payable half-yearly on 1 January and 1 July. Assume no interest is accrued on 30 June.

Required

(Round all calculations to the nearest dollar.)

(a) Journalise the payment of interest on 1 January 2020.

(b) Prepare the entry to pay the interest due on 1 July 2020.

(c) Assume on 1 July 2021, after paying interest, that D100 Ltd redeems half of the unsecured notes at 103. Record the redemption of the notes.

(d) Explain the advantages of debt financing over issuing shares.

PSA9.4 Prepare journal entries to record issue of debentures, and record redemption. LO3

Cameron Ltd issued $1 000 000 of 10%, 10-year debentures on 1 January 2018. The debentures were dated 1 January and pay interest on 1 July and 1 January. The debentures were issued at face value. Assume no interest is accrued on 30 June, and Cameron Ltd's year-end is 31 December.

Required

(a) Prepare the journal entry to record the issue of the debentures on 1 January 2018.

(b) Prepare journal entries to record the payment of interest on 1 July 2018 and the accrual of interest on 31 December 2018.

(c) At 31 December 2019, the entity redeemed the debentures at 104. Record the redemption of the debentures assuming that interest for the year had already been paid.

PSA9.5 Prepare a mortgage schedule and journal entries for loans payable by instalment. LO4

On 1 April 2018, Southbank Mechanic Ltd borrowed $112 550 from the bank at 12% per annum interest and offered its workshop premises in Southbank as security for the loan. The loan was for 1 year, repayable in amounts of $10 000 at the end of each month.

Required

(a) Prepare a journal entry to record the initial mortgage.

(b) Use an Excel spreadsheet to prepare a mortgage schedule.

(c) Use the schedule in part (b) to prepare the journal entries for loan repayments for April and May 2018.

PSA9.6 Prepare a mortgage schedule and journal entries for loans payable by instalment.   **LO4**

At the beginning of the month, Cherry Ltd had the following three loans outstanding:

Mortgagee	Balance owing at beginning of month	Annual interest rate	Monthly repayment
Eastpac Bank	$400 000	18%	$10 000
State Bank	$250 000	12%	$12 000
NZA Bank	$600 000	15%	$40 000

Required

(a) Prepare journal entries to record the interest payments on each loan for the month.

(b) What was Cherry Ltd's interest expense for mortgages for the current month?

(c) Assuming no new loans, will the interest expense for the next month be greater than, less than or the same as the current month's interest expense? Explain.

PSA9.7 Prepare journal entries to record provisions for warranties and discuss appropriateness of the provision.   **LO8**

Botch's Watches Ltd offers a 12-month guarantee with the watches that it sells. On 1 July 2019, the balance of the warranty provision account was $1200. During the year ended 30 June, warranty claims cost $1500, of which $500 was for parts and $1 000 was for labour. During the same year, revenue from the sale of watches was $14 000, an increase of more than 10% on the previous year. Management estimated that the liability for unexpired warranty contracts at 30 June was $1200. There have been no changes in suppliers, product quality or prices.

Required

(a) Prepare a journal entry to record the warranty claims during the year ended 30 June 2020. (*Hint:* Credit wages payable for the labour costs.)

(b) Prepare a journal entry to record the end-of-period adjustment to the warranty provision account.

(c) Comment on the appropriateness of the warranty provision at 30 June 2020. Do you think that the provision is adequate? Give reasons for your answer.

PSA9.8 Prepare journal entries to record provisions for warranties and reconstruct the provision for warranty account.   **LO8**

At the beginning of 2019, Lennox Plumbing Services Pty Ltd had a credit balance of $100 000 in its warranty provision account. The warranty expense for the year was $140 000 and the balance of the warranty provision account at the end of the year after adjusting entries was $130 000.

Required

(a) Calculate the cost of warranty claims during the period. It may be helpful to reconstruct the warranty provision account.

(b) Prepare journal entries to record the warranty claims during the period and end-of-period adjustments to the warranty provision account. Assume that all warranty costs were for the replacement of parts from spare parts inventory.

PSA9.9 **Evaluate liquidity and solvency.** LO9

Selected data from the June 2019 financial statements of Digital Ltd is presented below ($ in millions).

Cash	$ 5 530	Current liabilities	$ 8 680
Receivables	4 170	Total liabilities	25 400
Inventory	362	Total assets	39 360
Marketable securities	23	Profit before income tax	6 230
Current assets	10 085	Interest expense	1 115

Required

(a) Calculate the current ratio, quick ratio, debt to total assets ratio and times interest earned for Digital Ltd.
(b) Refer to the solution in the 'Using the decision-making toolkit' section of this chapter. Using the calculations and discussions prepared for Data Corporation New Zealand, compare and contrast the liquidity and solvency of Digital Ltd and Data Corporation New Zealand.

PSA9.10 **Evaluate liquidity and solvency.** LO9

The financial statements of Bayside Ltd revealed the following information.

Total current assets	$ 29 600
Total assets	357 875
Total current liabilities	15 390
Total liabilities	125 295
Cash	6 207
Marketable securities	3 400
Accounts receivable	10 840
Profit before income tax	246 950
Interest expense	11 440

Required

(a) Calculate each of the following:
  1. Working capital.
  2. Current ratio.
  3. Quick ratio.
  4. Debt to total assets ratio.
  5. Times interest earned.
(b) Discuss each of the ratios calculated in part (a).

PSA9.11 **Prepare journal entries to record payments for a long-term loan.** LO4

Steven Fu has just approached a venture capitalist for financing for his new business venture, the development of a wireless golf buggy. On 1 July 2017, Steven borrowed $200 000 at an annual interest rate of 12%. The loan is repayable over 5 years in annual instalments of $55 480, principal and interest, due on 30 June each year. The first payment is due on 30 June 2018. Steven uses the effective-interest method for amortising debt. His wireless golf buggy entity's year-end will be 30 June.

Required

(a) Prepare a mortgage schedule for the 5 years, 2017–2022. Round all calculations to the nearest dollar.
(b) Prepare all journal entries for Steven Fu for the first 2 fiscal years ended 30 June 2018 and 30 June 2019. Round all calculations to the nearest dollar.
(c) Show the statement of financial position presentation of the loan payable as of 30 June 2019. (*Hint:* Be sure to distinguish between the current and long-term portions of the loan.)

PSA9.12 Complete basic journal entries for accounting for leases. **LO6**

On 1 July 2018, Duncan Ltd entered a 3-year non-cancellable lease agreement with a finance company for equipment. The annual lease payments are $38 803 commencing on 30 June 2019. The fair value of the equipment was $100 000 and the rate implicit in the lease was 8%. Assume the lease was a finance lease. Duncan uses straight-line depreciation for similar equipment.

Required

(a) Prepare the lease repayment schedule. (*Hint:* See figure 9.9.)

(b) Prepare the journal entries in the books of Duncan Ltd for the year ending 30 June 2019.

(c) Prepare an extract from the statement of financial position as at 30 June 2019 providing the figures for the leased asset. (*Hint:* Ensure you identify the current and non-current portions of the loan.)

PROBLEM SET B

PSB9.1 Journalise and post note transactions; show statement of financial position presentation. **LO2**

Mountain Bikes Pty Ltd markets mountain-bike tours to clients vacationing in various locations in the Blue Mountains. In preparation for the upcoming winter biking season, the entity entered into the following transactions related to notes payable.

Mar.	1	Purchased Mongoose bikes for use as rentals by issuing an $8000, 9% note payable, which is due in 3 months.
	31	Recorded accrued interest for the Mongoose note.
Apr.	1	Issued a $20 000 note to Highland Property for the purchase of mountain property on which to build bike trails. The note bears 12% interest and is due in 9 months.
	30	Recorded accrued interest for the Mongoose note and the Highland Property note.
May	1	Issued a note to Telluride National Bank for $15 000 at 6%. The funds will be used for working capital for the beginning of the season; the note is due in 4 months.
	31	Recorded accrued interest for all three notes.
June	1	Paid principal and interest on the Mongoose note.
	30	Recorded accrued interest for the Highland Property note and the Telluride Bank note.

Required

(a) Prepare journal entries for the transactions.

(b) Post the entries to the notes payable, interest payable, and interest expense accounts. (Use T accounts.)

(c) Assuming that Mountain Bikes' year-end is 30 June, show the statement of financial position presentation of notes payable and interest payable at that date.

(d) How much interest expense relating to notes payable did Mountain Bikes incur during the year?

(e) Discuss the advantage and disadvantage of purchasing inventory by means of a note payable rather than accounts payable.

PSB9.2 Prepare current liability entries, adjusting entries, and current liability section. **LO2**

On 1 January 2019, the ledger of Jasmine Ltd contained the following liability accounts.

Accounts payable	$8 500
PAYG withheld tax payable	1 320
Service revenue received in advance	3 800

During January the following selected transactions occurred.

Jan.	1	Borrowed $30 000 in cash from East Coast Bank on a 6-month, 10% note.
	16	Provided services for customers who had made advance payments of $2000 (credit the service revenue account).
	22	Paid the tax office $1320 for PAYG tax withheld in December 2018.

During January the entity's employees earned wages of $16 000. Withholdings related to these wages were $2000 for a health fund, $1450 for PAYG tax withheld and $1440 for superannuation. Assume that wages earned during January will be paid during February. No entry has been recorded for wages or payroll tax expense as of 31 January.

Required

(a) Journalise the January transactions.

(b) Journalise the adjusting entries at 31 January for the outstanding note payable and for wages expense.

(c) Prepare the current liability section of the statement of financial position at 31 January 2019. Assume no change in Accounts Payable.

(d) Discuss some of the other costs employers may incur in relation to their employees.

PSB9.3 Prepare journal entries to record interest payments, and redemption of unsecured notes. LO3
The following extract is taken from Spring Hill Ltd's statement of financial position at 31 December 2018.

Current liabilities	
Interest payable on unsecured notes (for 6 months from 1 July to 31 December)	$ 360 000
Non-current liabilities	
Unsecured notes payable, 12% due 1 January 2022	6 000 000

Interest is payable half-yearly on 1 January and 1 July. Assume no interest is accrued on 30 June.

Required

(Round all calculations to the nearest dollar.)

(a) Journalise the payment of interest on 1 January 2019.

(b) Prepare the entry to pay the interest due on 1 July 2019.

(c) Assume on 1 July 2020, after paying interest, that Spring Hill Ltd redeems half of the unsecured notes at 103. Record the redemption of the notes.

(d) Explain the advantage of debt financing over issuing shares.

PSB9.4 Prepare journal entries to record issue of debentures and redemption of debentures.   LO3
Thompson Ltd issued $4 000 000, 9%, 20-year debentures at par (face) value on 1 July 2018. The debentures were dated 1 July 2018, and pay interest on 30 June and 31 December. Thompson's year-end is 30 June.

Required

(a) Prepare the journal entry to record the issue of the debentures on 1 July 2018.

(b) Prepare entries for the interest payments on 31 December 2018 and 30 June 2019.

(c) At 30 June 2020, Thompson Ltd redeemed the debentures at 102. Record the redemption of the debentures.

PSB9.5 Prepare a mortgage schedule and journal entries for loans payable by instalment.   LO4
On 1 April 2018, Sunflower Ltd borrowed $56 870 from the bank at 10% per annum interest and offered its florist studio as security for the loan. The loan was for 1 year, repayable in amounts of $5000 at the end of each month.

Required

(a) Prepare a journal entry to record the initial mortgage.
(b) Use an Excel spreadsheet to prepare a mortgage schedule.
(c) Use the schedule in part (b) to prepare the journal entries for loan repayments for April and May 2018.

PSB9.6 Prepare a mortgage schedule and journal entries for loans payable by instalment. LO4

Book City Ltd had the following three loans outstanding at the beginning of the month.

Mortgagee	Balance owing at beginning of month	Annual interest rate	Monthly repayment
Aussie Bank	$200 000	9%	$ 5 000
Kiwi Bank	$225 000	6%	$ 6 000
Bank Outback	$300 000	7%	$20 000

Required

(a) Prepare journal entries to record the interest payments on each loan for the month.
(b) What was Book City Ltd's interest expense for mortgages for the current month?
(c) Assuming no new loans, will the interest expense for the next month be greater than, less than or the same as the current month's interest expense? Explain.

PSB9.7 Prepare journal entries to record provisions for warranties and discuss appropriateness of the provision. LO8

Quinton Mechanics Ltd offers a 12-month guarantee with all car repairs and service. On 1 July 2018, the balance of the warranty provision account was $2400. During the year ended 30 June, warranty claims cost $3000, of which $1000 was for parts and $2000 was for labour. During the same year, revenue from car repairs was $280 000, an increase of more than 20% on the previous year. Management estimated that the liability for unexpired warranty contracts at 30 June was $2400. There have been no changes in suppliers, product quality or prices.

Required

(a) Prepare a journal entry to record the warranty claims during the year ended 30 June 2019. (*Hint:* Credit wages payable for the labour costs.)
(b) Prepare a journal entry to record the end-of-period adjustment to the warranty provision account.
(c) Comment on the appropriateness of the warranty provision at 30 June 2019. Do you think that the provision is adequate? Give reasons for your answer.

PSB9.8 Prepare journal entries to record provisions for warranties and reconstruct the provision for warranty account. LO8

At the beginning of 2019, Davis Builders Pty Ltd had a credit balance of $130 000 in its warranty provision account. The warranty expense for the year was $42 000 and the balance of the warranty provision account at the end of the year after adjusting entries was $39 000.

Required

(a) Calculate the cost of warranty claims during the period. (It may be helpful to reconstruct the warranty provision account.)
(b) Prepare journal entries to record the warranty claims during the period and end-of-period adjustments to the warranty provision account. Assume that all warranty costs were for the replacement of parts from spare parts inventory.

PSB9.9 **Evaluate liquidity and solvency.** **LO9**

Information from the June 2019 financial statements of Omni Co Ltd is presented below.

OMNI CO LTD ($ in millions)			
Cash	$ 61 086	Current liabilities	$175 896
Receivables	175 272	Total liabilities	392 638
Inventory	153 539	Total assets	982 180
Marketable securities	10 241	Profit before tax	165 877
Other	9 274	Interest expense	15 700
Current assets	501 581		

Required

(a) Calculate the current ratio, quick ratio, debt to total assets ratio and times interest earned for Omni Co Ltd for 2019.

(b) Refer to the solution in the 'Using the decision-making toolkit' section of this chapter. Using the calculations and discussions prepared for Data Corporation New Zealand, compare and contrast the liquidity and solvency of Omni Co Ltd and Data Corporation New Zealand.

PSB9.10 **Evaluate liquidity and solvency.** **LO9**

You have been presented with the following selected information taken from the financial statements of Matrix Ltd.

MATRIX LTD Statement of financial position (selected figures) (in millions)	2019	2018
Current assets	$ 5 450	$ 4 650
Non-current assets	27 250	25 100
Total assets	**$32 700**	**$29 750**
Current liabilities	$ 7 120	$ 5 760
Non-current liabilities	18 500	16 200
Total liabilities	25 620	21 960
Equity	7 080	7 790
Total liabilities and equity	**$32 700**	**$29 750**

Other information	2019	2018
Profit before interest and tax	$ 2 710	$ 2 670
Interest expense	450	390
Cash, marketable securities and receivables	2 860	3 145

Required

(a) Calculate each of the following for 2019 and 2018.
   1. Working capital.
   2. Current ratio.
   3. Quick ratio.
   4. Debt to total assets ratio.
   5. Times interest earned.

(b) Comment on the trend in each of the ratios.

PSB9.11 **Prepare journal entries to record payments for long-term loan.** **LO4**

Francis Lennon has just approached a venture capitalist for financing for her new business venture, the development of a waterslide. On 1 July 2018, Francis borrowed $100 000 at an annual interest rate of 10%. The loan is repayable over 5 years in annual instalments of $26 380, principal and interest, due on each 30 June. The first payment is due on 30 June 2019. Francis uses the effective-interest method for amortising debt. Her waterslide entity's year-end will be 30 June.

Required

(a) Prepare a mortgage schedule for the 5 years, 2018–2023. Round all calculations to the nearest dollar.

(b) Prepare all journal entries for Francis Lennon for the first 2 fiscal years ended 30 June 2019, and 30 June 2020. Round all calculations to the nearest dollar.

(c) Show the statement of financial position presentation of the loan payable as of 30 June 2020. (*Hint:* Be sure to distinguish between the current and long-term portions of the loan.)

PSB9.12 Complete basic journal entries for accounting for leases. **LO6**

On 1 July 2019, Cooper Ltd entered a 5-year non-cancellable lease agreement with a finance company for equipment. The annual lease payments are $20 805 commencing on 30 June 2020. The fair value of the equipment was $75 000 and the rate implicit in the lease was 12%. Assume the lease was a finance lease. Cooper uses straight-line depreciation for similar equipment.

Required

(a) Prepare the lease repayment schedule. (*Hint:* See figure 9.9.)

(b) Prepare the journal entries in the books of Cooper Ltd for the year ending 30 June 2020.

(c) Prepare the journal entries in the books of Cooper Ltd for the year ending 30 June 2021.

(d) Prepare an extract from the statement of financial position as at 30 June 2021 providing the figures for the leased asset. (*Hint:* Ensure you identify the current and non-current portions of the loan.)

BUILDING BUSINESS SKILLS

FINANCIAL REPORTING AND ANALYSIS

Financial reporting problem: Giorgina's Pizza Limited

BBS9.1 The financial statements of Giorgina's Pizza Limited are shown in figures 1.13, 1.15 and 1.16 in chapter 1. You will need to refer to these financial statements to find the data relevant to this problem.

Required

Answer the following questions.

(a) What is the amount of current liabilities at 30 June 2019?

(b) What is the amount of current provisions at 30 June 2019?

(c) What was the change in the value of total liabilities from 2018 to 2019?

(d) Calculate the working capital, current ratio, quick ratio, debt to total assets ratio and times interest earned for 2019.

Comparative analysis problem: Original Furnishings Limited and Artistry Furniture Limited

BBS9.2 Selected information from the 2019 financial statements of Original Furnishings and Artistry Furniture are presented below.

Original Furnishings Limited ($'000)			
Cash	108 000	Total current liabilities	123 975
Receivables	20 250	Total liabilities	170 235
Inventory	56 250	Total assets	287 370
Marketable securities	0	Profit before income tax	57 500
Total current assets	187 470	Interest expense	4 896

Artistry Furniture Limited ($'000)			
Cash	24 000	Total current liabilities	29 130
Receivables	4 420	Total liabilities	39 140
Inventory	12 500	Total assets	65 250
Marketable securities	724	Profit before income tax	21 400
Total current assets	41 650	Interest expense	214

Required

(a) Calculate the working capital, current ratio, quick ratio, debt to total assets ratio and times interest earned for each entity for 2019.

(b) What do the ratios indicate about the liquidity and solvency of the two entities?

A global focus

BBS9.3 Visit the Telstra web site and access the most recent annual report.

Address: http://telstra.com.au (Select **About Us** and then select **Investors**.)

Required

Refer to Telstra's latest annual report and the notes to the financial statements to identify the different countries and currencies in which Telstra has borrowings. Why might Australian entities borrow overseas or in other currencies? What risks are involved? (*Hint:* Refer to notes such as borrowings, interest-bearing liabilities and financial instrument disclosures.)

Financial analysis on the web

BBS9.4 Debentures or debt securities pay a stated rate of interest. This rate of interest depends on the risk associated with the investment. Moody's Investment Service provides ratings for companies that issue debt securities.

Address: www.moodys.com

Required

Answer the following questions:

(a) Select **About Moody's** at the top of the home page. Describe two types of services offered by Moody's.

(b) Copy the following address into your web browser: https://www.moodys.com/ratings-process/In-a-World-of-Short-Term-Outlooks-Long-Term-Opinions-are-Vital/002004003 to access Moody's statement about understanding risk titled 'In a world of short-term outlooks, long-term opinions are vital'. Why does Moody's take a long-term view and how is this achieved?

CRITICAL THINKING

Group decision case

BBS9.5 On 1 January 2019, Mall Ltd issued $1 200 000 of 5-year, 10% debentures at 93; the debentures pay interest half-yearly on 1 July and 1 January. By 1 January 2021, the market rate of interest for debentures of risk similar to those of Mall Ltd had risen. As a result, the market value of these debentures was $1 000 000 on 1 January 2021 — below their carrying amount of $1 144 000.

Jenny Payne, managing director of the Mall Ltd, suggests repurchasing all of these debentures in the open market at the $1 000 000 price. But to do so Mall Ltd will have to issue $1 000 000 (face value) of new 5-year, 17.36% debentures at face value. The managing director asks you as chief accountant: 'What is the feasibility of my proposed repurchase plan?'

Required

With the class divided into groups, answer the following:

(a) Prepare the journal entry to redeem the 5-year debentures on 1 January 2021. Prepare the journal entry to issue the new 10-year debentures.

(b) Prepare a short memo to the managing director in response to her request for advice. List the economic factors that you believe should be considered for the repurchase proposal.

Communication activity

BBS9.6 On 15 June 2018, Dundee Pty Ltd signed a contract to provide market research services to a client for $1 million. The research would be undertaken during the years ended 30 June 2019 and 30 June 2020. Half of the research would be performed in the year ended 30 June 2019 and an amount of $600 000 would be received that year. The remaining half of the research would be performed in the year ended 30 June 2020 and $300 000 would be received. The remaining $100 000 would be received in August 2020.

The managing director believes that the $1 million should be recognised as revenue in June 2018 because the contract has been signed. The finance director argues that no amount should be recognised in 2018; that $600 000 should be recognised as revenue in the year ending 30 June 2019 and $300 000 in the year ended 30 June 2020; and that the remaining $100 000 should be recognised in August 2020.

Required

Prepare a report to the board of directors outlining the appropriate treatment for the revenue arising from the research contract.

Ethics case

BBS9.7 Candy Bars Ltd produces several varieties of candy and chocolate bars. An action has been brought against the entity by a customer who broke a tooth while eating one of the entity's chewy chocolate bars. The managing director of Candy Bars Ltd has suggested that this should not be reported as a contingent liability because the entity might win the case, and any mention of this in the financial statements could encourage more law suits and increase the entity's liability.

Required

(a) Who are the stakeholders in this situation?
(b) Who would be potentially harmed or disadvantaged by non-disclosure of the contingent liability?
(c) Are the managing director's actions ethical?

ANSWERS

Answers to self-study questions

9.1 (d) 9.2 (a) 9.3 (a) 9.4 (c) 9.5 (b) 9.6 (a) 9.7 (b) 9.8 (b) 9.9 (c) 9.10 (c) 9.11 (c) 9.12 (d) 9.13 (a) 9.14 (c) 9.15 (a)

Answers to review it questions

Question 1, section 9.8: $2 332 000
Question 2, section 9.8: $331 000

ACKNOWLEDGEMENTS

Photo: © Blend Images / Getty Images
Photo: © Antonio Guillem / Shutterstock.com
Photo: © Hero Images / Getty Images

CHAPTER 10

Reporting and analysing equity

LEARNING OBJECTIVES

After studying this chapter, you should be able to:

10.1 explain the business context and the importance of decision making relating to equity

10.2 identify and discuss the main characteristics of a corporation (company)

10.3 record the issue of ordinary shares

10.4 describe the effects of share splits

10.5 prepare the entries for cash dividends and share dividends and describe the impact on equity and assets

10.6 understand the concept of earning power and indicate how irregular items are presented

10.7 identify components of comprehensive income and changes in equity

10.8 identify the items that affect retained earnings

10.9 evaluate a company's dividend and earnings performance from a shareholder's perspective

10.10 evaluate debt and equity as alternative sources of finance.

Chapter preview

Companies like Michael Hill International Limited, Fonterra Co-operative Group Limited, LG Electronics and Domino's Pizza Enterprises Ltd have substantial resources at their disposal. In fact, the corporation (company) is the dominant form of business organisation in Australia and New Zealand in terms of sales, profits and the number of employees. In this chapter we look at key decision making relating to the equity of corporations and the essential features of a corporation, and explain how to account for a corporation's capital transactions. When companies distribute profit to shareholders, that profit is referred to as a dividend. To the shareholders, the dividend is a return on their investment in the company. We will look at company dividend policies and how to account for different types of dividend payments.

In this chapter we will also revisit the statement of profit or loss and other comprehensive income and examine how to account for irregular items and other changes in equity. Lastly, in this chapter we will examine decision-making tools used by investors to evaluate earnings performance and learn how to compare debt and equity methods of finance for liquidity and solvency. The content and organisation of this chapter are as follows.

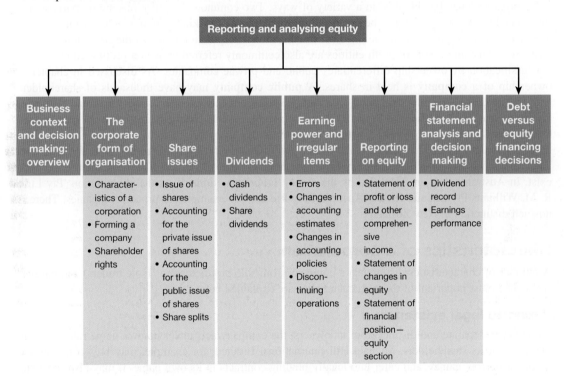

10.1 Business context and decision making: overview

LEARNING OBJECTIVE 10.1 Explain the business context and the importance of decision making relating to equity.

The business context for equity is very dependent on the nature of the entity, how it is funded, its ownership structure and its accountability beyond its direct owners. The objective of general purpose financial statements is to provide information that is useful particularly to existing and potential shareholders, the providers of equity, and other parties. However, equity investors are not the only group who use equity information in their decision marking. Ratios such as debt to equity are key metrics for lenders and form the basis of debt covenants. Directors and management have to make decisions such as whether to use debt or equity funding, how much to pay out to shareholders in dividends, or retain for future expansion, and when to raise more capital or return capital to investors. Shareholders will also base their decision making on metrics including return on equity (ROE) and dividend payout ratios when deciding to purchase, retain or sell shares. Throughout this chapter there is a strong focus on tools for decision making relating to equity.

10.2 The corporate form of organisation

LEARNING OBJECTIVE 10.2 Identify and discuss the main characteristics of a corporation (company).

A corporation is created by law. Companies are the most common type of corporation. Another type of corporation is a body corporate formed by the owners of strata-titled home units in a block. As a legal entity, a **corporation** has most of the rights and privileges of a person. The major exceptions relate to privileges that can be exercised only by a living person, such as the right to vote or to hold public office. Similarly, a corporation is subject to the same duties and responsibilities as a person; for example, it must abide by the laws and it must pay taxes.

Corporations may be classified in a variety of ways. Two common classifications are by purpose and by ownership. A corporation may be organised for the purpose of making a profit (such as Domino's), or it may be a not-for-profit charitable, medical or educational corporation (such as the Salvation Army or Red Cross Australia). Not-for-profit entities are also commonly referred to as non-profit entities.

Classification by ownership differentiates public and private companies. As discussed in chapter 1, ownership of a **company** is held in shares. A **public company** may have thousands of shareholders and, if listed, its shares may be traded on a national securities market such as the Australian Securities Exchange and the New Zealand Stock Exchange. Examples are Michael Hill International Limited and Qantas Airways Ltd. In contrast, a **proprietary company**, also referred to as a private company, has up to 50 non-employee shareholders, and it does not offer its shares for sale to the general public. Private companies are generally much smaller than public companies, although some notable exceptions exist. In Australia, they are identified by the words 'proprietary limited', or the abbreviation 'Pty Ltd'. R. M. Williams Pty Ltd and Rivers (Australia) Pty Ltd are two examples of private companies. There is no such distinction in New Zealand.

Characteristics of a corporation

A number of characteristics distinguish a company from sole proprietorships (sole traders) and partnerships. The most important of these characteristics are explained below.

Separate legal existence

As an entity separate and distinct from its owners, the company acts under its own name rather than in the name of its shareholders. Michael Hill International Limited, for example, may buy, own and sell property, borrow money, and enter into legally binding contracts in its own name. It may also sue or be sued, and it pays its own taxes.

In contrast to a partnership, in which the acts of the owners (partners) bind the partnership, the acts of the owners (shareholders) do not bind the company unless such owners are agents of the company. For example, if you owned Michael Hill shares, you would not have the right to purchase inventory for the company unless you were designated as an agent of the company, such as Michael Hill's purchasing officer.

Limited liability of shareholders

Since a company is a separate legal entity, creditors ordinarily have recourse only to company assets to satisfy their claims. Shareholders normally enjoy **limited liability**. This means that the liability of shareholders is normally limited to any unpaid capital, and creditors have no legal claim on the personal assets of the shareholders. Thus, even in the event of insolvency of the company, shareholders' losses are generally limited to the amount of capital they have invested in the company. Shareholders' privately owned assets, such as their cars, houses and bank accounts, are not required to be used to pay the company's debts.

Transferable ownership rights

Ownership of a company is shown in shares, which are transferable units. Shareholders may dispose of part or all of their interest in a company simply by selling their shares. In contrast to the transfer of an ownership interest in a partnership, which requires the consent of each partner, the transfer of shares is entirely at the discretion of the shareholder. It does not require the approval of either the company or other shareholders, unless specified in the company's own rules.

The transfer of ownership rights among shareholders normally has no effect on the operating activities of the company or on a company's assets, liabilities and total equity. That is, the company does not participate in the transfer of these ownership rights after the original sale of the shares. The company must maintain a register of shareholders and record any changes in share ownership in the register.

Continuous life

Since a company is a separate legal entity, the life of a company as a going concern is separate from its owners; it is not affected by the withdrawal, death or incapacity of a shareholder, employee or officer. As a result, a successful company can have a continuous and perpetual life.

Similarly, companies can restructure and change their direction without changing the owners of a business.

Ability to acquire capital

In general, it is relatively easy for a company to obtain capital through the issue of shares. Buying shares in a company is often more attractive to an investor than investing in a partnership because a shareholder has limited liability and shares are readily transferable. Moreover, individuals can become shareholders by investing small amounts of money. Successful companies find it very easy to obtain capital.

Listing publicly is a method to expand and obtain the requisite capital. During 2016, 129 new entities were listed on the ASX. At the end of December 2016, there were over 2100 entities listed on the ASX and the total capital raised for the calendar year ending December 2016 was $54 billion.

Company management

Although shareholders legally own the company, they manage it indirectly through a board of directors which they elect. The board of directors is headed by a chairperson. The board, in turn, formulates the operating policies for the company and selects officers, such as a managing director or chief executive officer and one or more division managers, to execute policy and to perform daily management functions.

A typical organisation chart showing the delegation of responsibility is shown in figure 10.1.

The managing director is the **chief executive officer (CEO)** with direct responsibility for managing the business. Although the CEO is usually a director, it is considered good corporate governance to ensure that the CEO is not also the chairperson of the board of directors. As the organisation chart in figure 10.1 shows, the managing director delegates responsibility to other officers, such as the finance manager/chief financial officer. The chief accounting officer is the **financial controller**. The financial controller's responsibilities include maintaining the accounting records and an adequate system of internal control, and preparing financial statements, tax returns and internal reports. The **treasurer** has custody of the company's funds and is responsible for maintaining the company's cash position. In smaller companies, the treasury function is the responsibility of the chief accountant. (Note that the titles given to people in the roles of chief executive officer, chief accounting officer and treasurer vary between organisations.)

The organisational structure enables a company to hire professional managers to run the business. The separation of ownership and management in large companies prevents owners from having an active role in managing the company, which some owners like to have. On the other hand, some view this separation as a weakness.

FIGURE 10.1   Company organisation chart

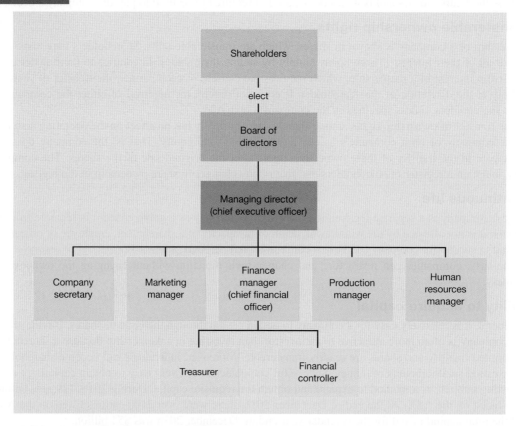

Government and other regulations

A company is subject to the Corporations Act and other government regulations in Australia and the equivalent Acts in New Zealand. Regulations do differ between the two countries but generally they serve a similar purpose and have similar provisions. For example, the (Australian) Corporations Act prescribes the requirements for public share issues, the distributions of profit permitted to shareholders, and buying back shares. A share buyback is when a company pays its shareholders an agreed sum in return for the cancellation of their shares. Also, public companies are required to make extensive disclosure of their financial affairs to the Australian Securities and Investments Commission (ASIC). For example, they are required to lodge financial statements. In addition, when a company is listed on a securities exchange, it must comply with the reporting requirements of the exchange.

The advantages and disadvantages of a company compared with a sole proprietorship and partnership are shown in table 10.1.

TABLE 10.1   **Advantages and disadvantages of a company**

Advantages	Disadvantages
• Separate legal existence • Limited liability of shareholders • Transferable ownership rights • Ability to acquire capital • Continuous life • Company management — professional managers	• Company management — separation of ownership and management • Government and other regulations

Decision/issue	Info needed for analysis	Tool or technique to use for decision	How to evaluate results to make decision
Should the business incorporate?	Capital needs, growth expectations, type of business	Companies have limited liability, easier capital-raising ability, continuous life and professional managers; but they suffer from government and other regulations, and separation of ownership from management.	Must carefully weigh the costs and benefits in light of the particular circumstances.

Forming a company

A company is formed by registration and is bound by the *Corporations Act 2001* (Cwlth). It is allocated an Australian business number (ABN) and an Australian company number (ACN). The ABN was introduced when Australia adopted the goods and services tax (GST). The ABN may now be used on company documentation in place of the ACN. The company may adopt a constitution, which is a set of rules governing the internal management of the company. It determines matters such as the authority to approve dividends and rules for shareholders' meetings. If a constitution is not adopted, the replaceable rules of the Corporations Act automatically apply as default rules for internal management. Similar provisions apply in New Zealand, with New Zealand companies bound by the Companies Act and allocated an IRD number that doubles as a GST number.

Shareholder rights

When registered, the company may begin issuing ownership rights in the form of shares. Different classes of shares carry different rights. The ownership rights of a share are stated in the company's constitution or the replaceable rules. The three major ownership rights are: the right to vote, the right to share in the company's profit, and the right to a residual claim in the event of the company being liquidated. At the company's annual general meeting, each shareholder has one vote by a show of hands. In the case of a poll, every fully paid share held by each shareholder entitles that shareholder to one vote. When a company has only one class of shares, these shares are referred to as **ordinary shares**. Each ordinary share gives the shareholder the ownership rights pictured in figure 10.2. Ordinary shares represent the residual ownership interest in a company.

Preference shares are a class of shares that have priority over ordinary shares with respect to dividends and/or repayment of capital in the event of the company being wound up, i.e. liquidated and ceasing to exist. Preference shares often do not have voting rights. In some cases, preference shares are disclosed as debt, but that is covered in more advanced accounting texts.

Review it

1. What are the advantages and disadvantages of a company compared with a sole proprietorship and a partnership?
2. Identify the principal steps in forming a company.
3. What rights are inherent in owning ordinary shares in a company?

FIGURE 10.2 | Ownership rights of shareholders

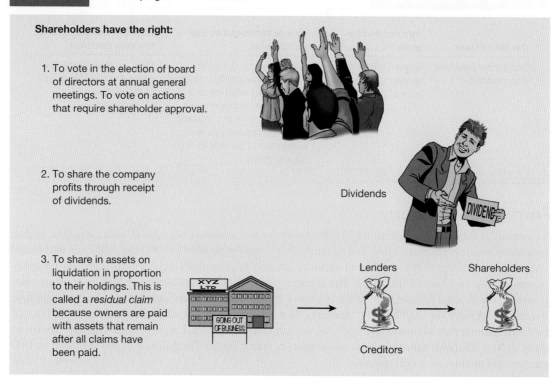

Shareholders have the right:

1. To vote in the election of board of directors at annual general meetings. To vote on actions that require shareholder approval.

2. To share the company profits through receipt of dividends.

3. To share in assets on liquidation in proportion to their holdings. This is called a *residual claim* because owners are paid with assets that remain after all claims have been paid.

10.3 Share issues

LEARNING OBJECTIVE 10.3 Record the issue of ordinary shares.

Michael Hill International Limited became a public company and listed on the New Zealand Stock Exchange in 1987. At that time, management evidently decided that the company would benefit from the injection of cash that a public issue of its shares would bring. When a company decides to issue shares, it must resolve a number of basic questions. How many shares should it issue? How should the shares be issued? At what price should the shares be issued? These questions are answered in the following sections.

Issue of shares

A company may issue shares by **private placement**, in which the invitation is made privately to certain potential investors. This may be arranged through a merchant bank that specialises in bringing securities to the attention of prospective investors. Public companies may also issue shares publicly. This requires a **prospectus**, which is a document reporting on the company's financial position, performance and plans. It contains reports from independent parties, such as independent accountants and other experts.

Helpful hint: While less common, shares may also be issued in return for services provided by professionals, such as lawyers and consultants.

How does a company set the **issue price** for a new issue of shares? Among the factors to be considered are (1) the company's anticipated future profits, (2) its expected dividend rate per share, (3) its current financial position, (4) the current state of the economy, and (5) the current state of the securities market. The calculation can be complex and is properly the subject of finance studies.

Accounting for the private issue of shares

When a company issues shares it normally receives some assets, typically cash, in return. The effect on the accounting equation is to increase assets and increase equity. The entire proceeds from the issue of shares are considered to be capital of the company. Throughout this chapter we use the share capital account to record the proceeds from the issue of shares, although this could also be referred to as **contributed equity** or **paid-up capital**.

When shares are issued by private placement, the proceeds are immediately available to the company. To illustrate, assume that Hydro-Slide Ltd issues 1000 shares for $1 each, payable in cash. The entry to record this transaction is:

Cash	1 000	
Share capital		1 000
(To record issue of 1000 shares at $1 each)		

A	=	L	+	E
+1000				+1000

If Hydro-Slide Ltd issues an additional 1000 shares for cash at $5 per share, the entry is:

Cash	5 000	
Share capital		5 000
(To record issue of 1000 shares at $5 each)		

A	=	L	+	E
+5000				+5000

The total share capital from these two transactions is $6000.

Accounting for the public issue of shares

When a company invites the public to subscribe to an issue of shares, it provides a prospectus, which includes an application form for prospective shareholders. The prospectus prescribes the number of shares that can be issued and the share price. When prospective investors apply to become shareholders, they send in an application form with the **application** money for the number of shares they are applying for. The administration of the share issue, including the receipt of application monies, may be handled by a third party. The entries illustrated below assume that the company is administering the public issue of its own shares.

When prospective investors apply to become shareholders, the application money is normally held in trust until the **allotment** (i.e. issue) of shares to the applicants (using a trust account is no longer legally required in New Zealand, but is good accounting practice and will be used in this text). At that time, the application money is transferred from a trust account into the company's own bank account and recorded as an increase in the share capital of the company.

Sometimes companies require only a partial payment of the share issue price on application, with the remainder due on allotment or subsequent calls on capital. A **call on capital** is when a company asks shareholders to pay some or all of the unpaid capital on issued shares. For example, a company may invite the public to subscribe for shares at $3.00 each with $1.00 payable on application, a further payment of $1.00 due on allotment, and the remainder on call. The company then has the right to call up part or all of the remaining $1.00 at any time in the future.

To illustrate, assume that Hydro-Slide Ltd invited the public to subscribe for 10 000 ordinary shares at $1.00 per share. The terms of the share issue are:
- $0.50 per share is payable on application by 30 September 2019
- $0.20 per share is payable on allotment by 31 October 2019.

Applications are received for 10 000 shares. The directors allot 10 000 shares on 1 October 2019 and all money due on allotment is received. The journal entries to record Hydro-Slide Ltd's share issue are:

2019			
Sept. 30	Cash trust	5 000	
	Application		5 000
	(To record the receipt of application money for 10 000 shares at $0.50 per share)		
Oct. 1	Application	5 000	
	Share capital		5 000
	(To record the application money as share capital on allotment of the shares to applicants)		
	Cash at bank	5 000	
	Cash trust		5 000
	(To record the transfer of the application money to the company's own bank account on allotment of the shares)		
	Allotment	2 000	
	Share capital		2 000
	(To record amounts owing on allotment of shares)		
Oct. 31	Cash at bank	2 000	
	Allotment		2 000
	(To record the receipt of monies due on allotment)		

$$A = L + E$$
$$+5000 \qquad\qquad +5000$$

$$A = L + E$$
$$\qquad\qquad +2000$$
$$\qquad\qquad -2000$$

$$A = L + E$$
$$+2000 \qquad\qquad +2000$$

Note that the effect of the call of $0.20 per share on allotment is shown as both increasing and decreasing equity. Although the call on allotment is accounted for by crediting capital, the amount of capital contributed by shareholders by 1 October 2019 was $5000. If a statement of financial position were prepared at 1 October 2019, the balance of the allotment account, a $2000 debit, would be shown as a reduction in contributed equity. The allotment account and any call accounts are *contra* equity accounts.

Share transactions, both the issue of shares and the payment of dividends, do not attract GST. However, if shares are exchanged for non-cash assets in New Zealand, GST registered entities can claim imputed GST for the fair value of the non-cash asset.

10.4 Share splits

LEARNING OBJECTIVE 10.4 Describe the effects of share splits.

A **share split** involves the issue of additional shares to shareholders according to their percentage ownership, and results in a reduction in the stated value per share. In a share split, the number of shares is increased in the reciprocal proportion as the stated value per share (the initial issue price) is decreased. For example, in a 2-for-1 split, one share with a stated value of $10 is exchanged for two shares which each have a stated value of $5. A share split does not affect the total share capital or equity of the company. Thus a company with share capital of $1000 comprising 1000 $1 shares may choose to do a 2-for-1 share split and divide its capital into 2000 $0.50 shares. After the share split, the share capital would still be $1000. There is no journal entry required to record a share split because it does not affect the amount of share capital or any other equity account. It affects only the number of shares and the stated value of each share. However, companies must keep some memorandum record of the share split because they will need to make disclosures in the annual financial reports in the form of a note about the composition of share capital. Michael Hill International Limited performed a 10 for 1 share split on 19 November 2007, increasing share numbers from 38 276 070 to 382 468 900 (excluding treasury shares).

The purpose of a share split is to increase the marketability of the shares by lowering the market value per share. This makes it easier for the corporation to issue additional shares. The effect of a share split on the market value of shares is generally inversely proportional to the size of the share split. For example, after Michael Hill International Limited performed the 10 for 1 share split, the market value of the shares fell from $10.50 to $1.10 overnight.

The trading of shares on securities exchanges involves the transfer of previously issued shares from an existing shareholder to another investor. Consequently, these transactions have no impact on a company's equity.

LEARNING REFLECTION AND CONSOLIDATION

Review it

1. What approaches may a company use to issue new shares to investors?
2. Distinguish between issue price and market value.
3. Explain the effect on the accounting equation of ordinary shares issued for cash.

Do it

Downunder Opals Ltd begins operations on 1 March by issuing 100 000 shares by private placement at $12 per share. Journalise the issue of the shares.

Reasoning

Upon issuing shares at $12, share capital is credited for $12 per share.

Solution

Mar. 1	Cash	1 200 000	
	Share capital		1 200 000
	(To record issue of 100 000 shares at $12 per share)		

10.5 Dividends

LEARNING OBJECTIVE 10.5 Prepare the entries for cash dividends and share dividends and describe the impact on equity and assets.

A **dividend** is a distribution of profit by a company to its shareholders on a pro rata basis. *Pro rata* means 'on a proportionate basis'. If you own, say, 10% of the ordinary shares, you will receive 10% of the dividend. Dividends can take three forms: cash, property or shares. Cash dividends, which predominate in practice, and share dividends, which are declared with some frequency, are the focus of our discussion. Many public companies pay dividends twice a year — a final dividend determined at the end of the company's financial year, and an interim dividend paid during the year.

Investors are very interested in a company's dividend practices. In the financial press, dividends are generally reported as a dollar amount per share. For example, Michael Hill International Limited's interim dividend for 2016 was 2.5 cents and its final dividend for that year was 2.5 cents per share. Dividends can also be expressed as a percentage of capital paid on the shares.

Cash dividends

A **cash dividend** is a pro rata distribution of profit paid in cash to shareholders. In Australia and New Zealand, companies can only pay a dividend if:
- the assets exceed liabilities by more than the amount of dividend proposed
- it is fair and reasonable to shareholders as a whole
- it does not materially prejudice the company's ability to pay its creditors.

A dividend subject to shareholder approval can now be paid from share capital. If a company is not required to prepare an annual financial report, eligibility to pay a dividend by being solvent can be determined from the accounting records.

The board of directors has full authority to determine the amount to be distributed in the form of dividends. However, a company may impose additional requirements, such as approval by shareholders at the annual general meeting for payment of a final dividend. Any such requirements would be specified in the company's constitution. Unlike interest, dividends on ordinary shares do not accrue or accumulate. They are not a legal liability until the date for payment arises.

The amount and the timing of a dividend are important issues for management to consider. The payment of a large cash dividend could lead to liquidity problems for the company. Conversely, a small dividend or a missed dividend may cause discontent among shareholders who expect to receive a reasonable cash payment from the company on a periodic basis. Many companies declare and pay cash dividends every 6 months. On the other hand, a number of high-growth companies pay no dividends, preferring to retain profits and use them to finance capital expenditures.

In order to remain in business, companies must honour their interest payments to suppliers, bankers and other creditors. But the payment of dividends to shareholders is another matter. Many companies can survive, and even thrive, without such payouts. Investors must keep an eye on the company's dividend policy and understand what it may mean. For most companies, for example, regular dividends in the face of irregular earnings can be a warning signal. Companies with high dividends and rising debt may be borrowing money to pay shareholders. On the other hand, low dividends may not be a negative sign because they may mean that profit is being retained for investment that will increase future profits.

Some companies pay regular dividends whereas other companies reinvest all profits. Presumably, investors for whom regular dividends are important tend to buy shares in companies that pay periodic dividends, and those for whom growth in the share price (capital gains) is more important tend to buy shares in companies that retain profits.

Entries for cash dividends

There are two important dates for the recording of dividends: (1) the declaration date and (2) the payment date.

On the **declaration date**, the board of directors formally declares (authorises) the cash dividend and announces it to shareholders. Although the declaration of a cash dividend does not commit the company to a binding legal obligation, Australian accounting standards require companies to recognise the decrease in retained earnings and the increase in the liability dividends payable if the dividend is proposed or declared before the end of the reporting period. This accounting treatment reflects a moral or equitable obligation and the high probability that the dividend will be paid. To illustrate, assume that on 1 December 2019, the directors of Media General Ltd declare a $0.50 per share cash dividend on 100 000 shares. The dividend is $50 000 (100 000 × $0.50), and the entry to record the declaration is:

	Declaration date		
Dec. 1	Retained earnings (or cash dividends declared)	50 000	
	Dividends payable		50 000
	(To record declaration of cash dividend)		

A	=	L	+	E
		+50 000		−50 000

Dividends payable is a current liability because it will normally be paid within the next 12 months. You may recall that, in chapter 2, instead of decreasing retained earnings, the dividends account was used. (The dividends account is also called *Cash dividend declared* or *Interim/final cash dividend declared*.) This account provides additional information in the ledger. For example, a company may have separate dividend accounts for each class of shares or each type of dividend. When a separate dividend account is used, its balance is transferred to retained earnings at the end of the year by a closing entry. Consequently, the effect of the declaration is the same — retained earnings is decreased and a current liability is increased. To avoid additional detail, we have chosen to use the retained earnings account.

On the **payment date**, dividend cheques are mailed to the shareholders or by EFT direct deposit and the payment of the dividend is recorded. If 20 January is the payment date for Media General Ltd, the entry on that date is:

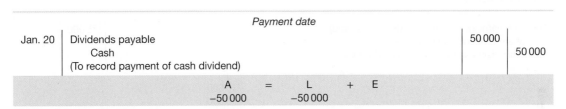

Note that payment of the dividend reduces both current assets and current liabilities but has no effect on equity. The cumulative effect of the declaration and payment of a cash dividend on a company's financial statements is to decrease both equity and total assets.

Share dividends

A **share dividend** (also be referred to as a *bonus share issue*) is a pro rata distribution of the company's own shares to shareholders. Whereas a cash dividend is paid in cash, a share dividend is paid in shares. A share dividend results in a decrease in retained earnings and an increase in share capital. Unlike a cash dividend, a share dividend does not decrease total equity or total assets.

Because a share dividend does not result in a distribution of assets, many view it as nothing more than a publicity gesture. Share dividends are often issued by companies that do not have adequate cash to issue a cash dividend. These companies may not want to announce that they will not issue a dividend at their normal time to do so. By issuing a share dividend they 'save face' by giving the appearance of distributing a dividend. Note that since a share dividend neither increases nor decreases the assets in the company, investors are not receiving anything they didn't already own.

To illustrate a share dividend, assume that you have a 2% ownership interest in Wing Ltd by virtue of owning 20 of its 1000 shares. In a 10% share dividend, 100 shares (1000 × 10%) would be issued. You would receive two shares (2% × 100), but your ownership interest would remain at 2% (22 ÷ 1100). You now own more shares, but your ownership interest has not changed. Moreover, no cash is paid out, and no liabilities have been assumed by the company.

What, then, are the purposes and benefits of a share dividend? Companies generally issue share dividends for one of the following reasons:
1. to satisfy shareholders' dividend expectations without spending cash
2. to emphasise that a portion of equity has been permanently reinvested in the business and therefore is unavailable for cash dividends.

However, in the long term, shareholders may benefit from the share dividend. If the company has a policy of maintaining constant dividends in terms of the amount per share, shareholders can look forward to more cash dividends in the future. For example, assume Bob holds 1000 shares in a company that has a policy of paying an annual cash dividend of 10 cents per share. Bob would usually receive a cash dividend of $100 (1000 × 10 cents). If the company issued a 10% share dividend, Bob would hold

1100 shares. In subsequent cash dividend payments of 10 cents per share by the company, Bob would receive $110 (1100 × 10 cents).

The size of the share dividend and the value to be assigned to each dividend share are determined by the board of directors when the dividend is declared.

Entries for share dividends (bonus shares)

To illustrate the accounting for share dividends, assume that Hawke's Bay Ltd has a balance of $300 000 in retained earnings and declares a 10% share dividend on its 50 000 shares. The current market price of Hawke's Bay shares is $15 per share and the directors have decided that this should be the value assigned to the bonus shares. The number of shares to be issued is 5000 (10% × 50 000), and the total amount to be debited to retained earnings is $75 000 (5000 × $15). The entry to record this transaction at the declaration date is:

Retained earnings (*or* share dividends declared)	75 000	
Share dividends payable		75 000
(To record declaration of 10% share dividend)		

$$A \quad = \quad L \quad + \quad E$$
$$-75\,000$$
$$+75\,000$$

Note that, at the declaration date, retained earnings is decreased (debited) for the assigned value of the shares issued and share dividends payable is increased (credited) for the same amount. Share dividends payable is an equity account. When the share dividend is paid, the share dividends payable account is decreased and the share capital account is increased as follows:

Share dividends payable	75 000	
Share capital		75 000
(To record the issue of 5000 shares as a share dividend)		

$$A \quad = \quad L \quad + \quad E$$
$$-75\,000$$
$$+75\,000$$

Effects of share dividends

How do share dividends affect equity? They change the composition of equity because a portion of retained earnings is transferred to share capital. The total equity remains the same but the number of issued shares increases. These effects are shown in figure 10.3.

FIGURE 10.3	Share dividend effects

		Before dividend	After dividend
	EQUITY		
	Contributed equity		
50 000	Ordinary shares	$500 000	$500 000
5 000	Ordinary shares	—	75 000
55 000	Total share capital	500 000	575 000
	Retained earnings	300 000	225 000
	Total equity	$800 000	$800 000
	Issued shares	$ 50 000	$ 55 000

In this example, total share capital is increased by $75 000 and retained earnings is decreased by the same amount. Note also that total equity remains unchanged at $800 000.

Review it

1. What factors affect the size of a company's cash dividend?
2. Why do companies issue share dividends?
3. How might a share dividend affect future cash dividends?

Do it

Linda CD Ltd issued 500 000 shares for $4 each. After 5 years of record profits, the company had a cash balance of $1 000 000, retained earnings of $2 500 000 and share capital of $2 000 000. The chief executive officer, Mandy Kang, is considering either a 10% cash dividend or a 10% share dividend with an assigned value of $4. She asks you for the 'before' and 'after' effects of each option on cash, retained earnings and equity.

Reasoning

Both a cash dividend and a share dividend would reduce retained earnings. The cash dividend would reduce cash and equity. The share dividend would not reduce equity because it would increase share capital instead of reducing cash.

Solution

The dividend amount is $200 000 (10% × $2 000 000). The balance of retained earnings after the payment of the dividend would be $2 300 000 ($2 500 000 − $200 000). If the dividend were paid in cash, Linda CD Ltd's cash balance would decrease to $800 000 ($1 000 000 − $200 000). Equity, which comprises share capital and retained earnings, would decrease from $4 500 000 ($2 000 000 + $2 500 000) to $4 300 000 ($2 000 000 + $2 300 000). If Mandy Kang chooses to pay a share dividend, there would be no reduction in equity because the reduction in retained earnings would be offset by an increase in share capital. The financial effects of the two dividend alternatives are summarised as follows:

	Original balances	After cash dividend	After share dividend
Share capital	$2 000 000	$2 000 000	$2 200 000
Retained earnings	2 500 000	2 300 000	2 300 000
Total equity	$4 500 000	$4 300 000	$4 500 000
Cash	$1 000 000	$ 800 000	$1 000 000

Before we examine how the equity section of the statement of financial position is presented we will further explore how irregular items that affect retained earnings are treated.

10.6 Earning power and irregular items

LEARNING OBJECTIVE 10.6 Understand the concept of earning power and indicate how irregular items are presented.

Ultimately, the value of an entity is a function of its future cash flows. When analysts use this year's profit to estimate future cash flows, they must be aware of any irregular revenues or expenses included in this year's profit. Profit adjusted for irregular items is referred to as **earning power**. Earning power is the most likely level of profit to be obtained in the future — that is, to the extent this year's profit is a good predictor of future years' profit. Earning power differs from actual profit by the amount of irregular revenues and expenses included in this year's profit.

Users are interested in earning power because it helps them derive an estimate of future earnings without the 'noise' of irregular items. For example, suppose Aust Ltd reports that this year's profit is $500 000 but included in that amount is a once-in-a-lifetime revenue of $400 000. In estimating next year's profit for Aust Ltd, we would be likely to ignore this $400 000 revenue and estimate that next year's profit will be in the neighbourhood of $100 000. That is, based on this year's results, the entity's earning power is roughly $100 000. Therefore, identifying irregular items has important implications for using reported profits as an input in estimating an entity's value.

Accounting standard IAS 1/AASB 101 *Presentation of Financial Statements* prescribes requirements for the presentation of the statement of profit or loss. IAS 8/AASB 108 *Accounting Policies, Changes in Accounting Estimates, and Errors* requires disclosures that aid the determination of earning power (or sustainable profit). This is achieved by requiring the identification of certain irregular items on the face of the statement of profit or loss or in the notes to the financial statements. In addition, disclosures about discontinued operations are required by IFRS 5/AASB 5 *Non-current Assets Held for Sale and Discontinued Operations*. Four types of irregular items are reported:

1. errors
2. changes in accounting estimates
3. changes in accounting policies
4. discontinuing operations.

These four categories are discussed in the following section. In addition, entities must also disclose revenues and expenses from ordinary activities that, because of their size, nature or incidence, are relevant to understanding financial performance. Examples include major inventory write-downs and the cost of settling a legal dispute.

Errors

Prior period errors are errors made in a previous period that have resulted in the presentation of incorrect information in financial statements. For example, it may be discovered in the current period that legal costs that should have been expensed were included in the carrying amount of an asset in the previous period. Such errors must be corrected retrospectively. This means that, when an error involves an income or expense item, the correction of the error is not recognised in the profit or loss of the period in which it is discovered. Instead, any effect on the profit of a prior period is recognised as an adjustment against opening retained earnings (which can also be called *retained profits*) in the statement of changes in equity, and comparative figures and any disclosed historical summaries are adjusted to include the correction.

In the period when the prior period error is corrected, the entity must disclose the nature of the error, the amount of the correction for each financial statement line item that is affected, and the amount of the correction at the beginning of the earliest prior period presented. Any information presented about prior periods, including any historical summaries of financial information, must be restated as far back as is practicable. If the entity reports earnings per share, this figure must be recalculated to reflect the effect of the error correction on profit. If it is impracticable to restate prior period figures, the entity must disclose the circumstances and a description of how the error has been corrected.

To illustrate, assume that during 2019 Aust Ltd paid legal fees of $200 000 associated with court proceedings, and that the fees were included in the cost of a parcel of land instead of being recognised as an expense. For simplicity, assume that the accounting treatment of the legal fees has not affected the income tax expense. Extracts from Aust Ltd's 2019 financial statements are illustrated in figures 10.4 to 10.6.

FIGURE 10.4 Extract from Aust Ltd's statement of profit or loss

AUST LTD Statement of profit or loss (extract) for the year ended 30 June 2019	
	$'000
Revenue	2 500
Expenses excluding finance costs	(1 200)
Finance costs	(100)
Profit before income tax expense	**1 200**
Income tax expense	(360)
Profit for the period	**840**

FIGURE 10.5 Extract from Aust Ltd's notes to the financial statements

AUST LTD
Notes to the financial statements (extract)
for the year ended 30 June 2019

	$'000
MOVEMENT IN RETAINED EARNINGS	
Balance at start of the period	1 600
Profit for the period	840
Total for the period	2 440
Dividends	(300)
Balance at end of period	**2 140**

FIGURE 10.6 Extract from Aust Ltd's statement of financial position

AUST LTD
Statement of financial position (extract)
as at 30 June 2019

	$'000
Land	4 700
Buildings, plant and equipment	8 000

The effect of the error is to understate expenses and to overstate profit and the carrying amount of the land in 2019. On discovery of the error in 2020, Aust Ltd would make the following journal entry to correct it:

2020	Retained earnings	200 000	
	Land		200 000
	(To correct a prior period error)		

A	=	L	+	E
−200 000				−200 000

The comparative financial statement information must also be corrected, as shown in figures 10.7 to 10.9. Note that the expenses reported as 2019 comparative figures in figure 10.7 differ from the expenses reported in the statement of profit or loss in the previous year shown in figure 10.4. Note also the carried down effect on profit for 2019.

FIGURE 10.7 Extract from Aust Ltd's statement of profit or loss

AUST LTD
Statement of profit or loss (extract)
for the year ended 30 June 2020

	2020 $'000	2019 $'000
Revenue	2 700	2 500
Expenses excluding finance costs	(1 300)	(1 400)
Finance costs	(300)	(100)
Profit before income tax expense	**1 100**	**1 000**
Income tax expense	(400)	(360)
Profit for the period	**700**	**640**

Compare the changes in retained earnings reported in figure 10.5 with the 2019 comparative data in figure 10.8. Both the profit for 2019 and the closing retained earnings are affected by the correction of the error. Note that this also changes the balance of retained earnings at the start of 2020.

FIGURE 10.8	Extract from Aust Ltd's notes to the financial statements

AUST LTD
Notes to the financial statements (extract)
for the year ended 30 June 2020

	2020 $'000	2019 $'000
MOVEMENT IN RETAINED EARNINGS		
Balance at start of the period	2 140	1 600
Correction of error	(200)	—
Restated balance	1 940	1 600
Profit for the period	700	640
Total for the period	2 640	2 240
Dividends	(300)	(300)
Balance at end of period	**2 340**	**1 940**

Helpful hint: In published external financial reports the movement in retained earnings is part of the statement of changes in equity.

Compare the carrying amount of the land reported in the 2019 statement of financial position in figure 10.6 with the 2019 comparative figures for land reported in the subsequent year shown in figure 10.9. The carrying amount of the land reported in the comparative 2019 column is $200 000 less than the amount reported in the statement of financial position in the previous year. It has been reduced by the correction of the error that had originally caused the land to be overstated.

FIGURE 10.9	Extract from Aust Ltd's statement of financial position, after correction of prior period error

AUST LTD
Statement of financial position (extract)
as at 30 June 2020

	2020 $'000	2019 $'000
Land	4 500	4 500
Buildings, plant and equipment	7 200	8 000

When comparing financial statements over several reporting periods, prior and current period profit should be adjusted for the effect of prior period errors. If we were to correct the error as an adjustment to current period profit (which is not permitted by IFRS 8/AASB 108), both years' reported profits would be incorrect. In the Aust Ltd example, profit would be overstated in 2019 and then understated in 2020 when the error was discovered and corrected. The retrospective adjustment required by the standard avoids this problem.

Changes in accounting estimates

A **change in accounting estimates** is a revision of estimates used in the preparation of previous-period financial statements. For example, the economic life of a depreciable asset may have been estimated as 10 years in the period of acquisition. A year later, this estimate of economic life may be revised to 5 years. The effect of the change must be included in the determination of profit in the period of the change. A revision of an estimate used in a previous year is not a correction of an error.

The effect of changes in accounting estimates on the current year's profit and, if practicable, future years' profit, must be disclosed if *material*. Information is considered material if its omission or misstatement has the potential to adversely affect decisions made by users of financial statements. Disclosure would typically be made in the notes to the financial statements rather than on the face of the statement of profit or loss. Information about changes in accounting estimates is useful when analysing trends in profit. The effect of the change — both on previous years' profit and the current year's profit — should be considered when analysing an entity's performance. This is because previous years' profit has been based on a different estimate to current year's profit, thus distorting the comparison. An apparent improvement in profitability may simply be the result of a change of accounting estimate.

DECISION-MAKING TOOLKIT

Decision/issue	Info needed for analysis	Tool or technique to use for decision	How to evaluate results to make decision
Have there been any changes to accounting estimates used in previous-period financial statements?	Effect of a change in accounting estimates in the notes to the financial statements	Items reported in this section indicate that the current profit is affected by a revision to an accounting estimate used in preparing previous-period financial statements.	Consistent accounting estimates should be applied when predicting future profits.

Changes in accounting policies

For ease of comparison, financial statements are expected to be prepared on a basis consistent with that used for the preceding period. That is, where a choice of accounting policies is available, the policy initially chosen should be applied consistently from period to period. A **change in accounting policy** occurs when the policy used in the current year is different from the one used in the preceding year. An example of a change in accounting policy is a change in inventory costing methods, such as from FIFO to average cost.

There are two types of changes in accounting policies: changes in accounting standards and voluntary changes. When an entity changes its accounting policies to comply with a new or revised accounting standard, it must follow any transitional provisions in the standard for the treatment of the effect of the change in accounting policy. For example, on initial application of IAS 38/AASB 138 *Intangible Assets*, a transitional provision permitted entities to charge against retained earnings the carrying amounts of any intangible assets that no longer qualified for recognition under the new standard. The following information, where applicable, must be disclosed in the notes to the financial statements for changes in accounting policies resulting from a change in accounting standards:
- the title of the standard
- confirmation that the change in accounting policy is made in accordance with its transitional provisions
- the nature of the change in accounting policy
- a description of the transition provisions
- any transitional provisions that might affect future periods
- the amount of the adjustment to each financial statement line item and, if reported, the effect on earnings per share
- the amount of the adjustment that relates to prior periods
- how the accounting policy change has been applied if any retrospective application required by the transitional provision was impracticable.

For voluntary changes in accounting policy, accounting standard IAS 8/AASB 108 requires the following disclosures in the notes to the financial statements:
- the nature of the change
- the reason(s) for the change
- the effect of the change on the current year's profit
- the effect of the change on each prior year's profit presented
- the effect of the change on all previous years that are not presented, to the extent practicable
- how the change has been applied if retrospective application is not practicable.

Comparative information, if practicable, must be restated for voluntary changes in accounting policies.

DECISION-MAKING TOOLKIT

Decision/issue	Info needed for analysis	Tool or technique to use for decision	How to evaluate results to make decision
Has the entity changed any of its accounting policies?	Prior period effect of change in accounting policy in the notes to the financial statements	Items reported in this section indicate that the entity has changed an accounting policy during the current year.	Consistent accounting policies should be applied when estimating future profits.

Discontinuing operations

A **discontinued operation** is a component of an entity that is being disposed of or is classified as held for sale. A component of an entity refers to operations and cash flows that can be clearly distinguished from the rest of the entity. For example, Coles can clearly identify its food and liquor operations and cash flows from other areas of its business, such as general merchandise and fuel. A discontinued operation will have been a cash-generating unit or group of cash-generating units while it was held for use.

Information about discontinuing operations is useful when estimating future profits. When certain steps have been taken towards discontinuing operations, such as entering into a binding agreement for the sale of part of the business, details about the discontinuing operations must be disclosed. When operations are classified as discontinuing, the carrying amounts of assets are measured at fair value less costs of disposal. IFRS 5/AASB 5 requires the sum of the after-tax profit or loss from discontinued operations and the after-tax gain or loss arising from the restatement of the assets of discontinued operations to be reported as a single line item on the face of the statement of profit or loss. When an operation is classified as a discontinued operation, the comparative statement of profit or loss is restated as if the operation had been discontinued from the start of the comparative period. This is useful information to users because it quantifies an amount of profit or loss included in the current profit that is not expected in future years because the source of that profit or loss has been discontinued.

The following disclosures must be made, either on the face of the statement of profit or loss or in the notes to the financial statements:
• revenue, expense and pre-tax profit or loss from discontinuing operations
• the gain or loss on measuring assets of discontinued operations at fair value and the associated tax effect
• net cash flows from the operating, investing and financing activities of the discontinuing operations.

Other information pertaining to discontinued operations that must be disclosed in the notes to the financial statements includes:
• identification of the discontinuing operations
• the business or geographic segment that had included the discontinuing operations
• a description of the facts and circumstances of the sale, or the facts and circumstances leading to the expected disposal
• when discontinuance is expected to be completed.

DECISION-MAKING TOOLKIT

Decision/issue	Info needed for analysis	Tool or technique to use for decision	How to evaluate results to make decision
Has the entity disposed of any major part of the business?	Statement of profit and loss and notes to the financial statements	Disclosures about discontinuing operations indicate that the source of some of the entity's profit is not continuing.	This source of profit should be ignored in estimating future profits.

LEARNING REFLECTION AND CONSOLIDATION

Review it
1. What is earning power?
2. What are irregular items and what effect might they have on the estimation of future profits and future cash flows?

10.7 Reporting on equity

LEARNING OBJECTIVE 10.7 Identify components of comprehensive income and changes in equity.

In chapter 1 we introduced you to the financial statements and illustrated a simple set of accounts for Wong Pty Ltd (see figure 1.6). In this example, the interrelationship between the statement of profit or loss, statement of changes in equity and statement of financial position was straightforward — the statement of changes in equity showed the movement in retained earnings accounting for profit and dividends. In this section of the chapter we will examine how movements in equity are presented in external general purpose financial statements.

The content and presentation of external general purpose financial statements is prescribed by IAS 1/ AASB 101 *Presentation of Financial Statements*.

A complete set of financial statements consists of a statement of profit or loss and other comprehensive income for the period, a statement of changes in equity for the period, a statement of cash flows for the period (see chapter 11), a statement of financial position as at the end of the period, and notes comprising a summary of significant accounting policies and other explanatory information. If an entity makes a retrospective change as a result of a change in an accounting policy or the correction of an error, or reclassifies items in its financial statements, a statement of financial position as at the beginning of the earliest comparative period must also be prepared. In other words, three statements of financial position and the related notes need to be prepared in the year these changes are made (i.e. as at the end of the current period, the end of the previous period and the beginning of the earliest comparative period). The names of the financial statements are not mandatory for the published financial statements. Therefore, in practice, there continues to be a variety of names used.

Statement of profit or loss and other comprehensive income

One of the main objectives in revising IAS 1/AASB 101 was to provide better information to users by aggregating information of items with common characteristics. Based on the concept of **total comprehensive income** as the change in equity during a period resulting from transactions and other events, other than those changes resulting from transactions with owners in their capacity as owners, IAS 1/AASB 101, paragraph 10(c) introduced the **statement of profit or loss and other comprehensive income**, which reports total comprehensive income for the period. This distinguishes changes in equity arising from transactions with owners/shareholders in their capacity as owners from all the other changes in equity from total comprehensive income representing changes in equity as a result of non-owner transactions.

Helpful hint: Prior to 1 July 2012, the statement of profit or loss and other comprehensive income was called the statement of comprehensive income.

So how does the statement of profit or loss relate to the statement of profit or loss and other comprehensive income? Consider figure 10.10.

The statement of profit or loss forms part of the statement of profit or loss and other comprehensive income. IAS 1/AASB 101 permits preparers to choose between presenting all items of profit or loss and other comprehensive income in a single statement divided into two sections, or presenting two separate statements, the first a statement of profit or loss and the second a statement of comprehensive income beginning with profit for the period and then adding other comprehensive income. The statement of profit or loss shows the income and expenses for the period resulting in the profit or loss, which is then transferred to retained earnings. Due to the rules set out in the accounting standards, some items of income and expenses are often not recognised in the statement of profit or loss. For example, you may recall from chapter 8 that when the revaluation basis is adopted for a class of non-current assets the upward revaluation increase is credited to the revaluation surplus and not to the statement of profit or loss. You will study other items of comprehensive income in later years of your accounting studies. IAS 1/AASB 101 paragraph 10 permits alternative names for the single statement and for the two separate statements. The alternative presentation of the statement of profit or loss and other comprehensive income is shown in figure 10.10. For ease of presentation, 2018 comparative figures are not shown.

Johanna's International Jewellery Limited's statement of comprehensive income is shown in figure 10.11. Note Johanna uses the single statement method. The profit for the year is obtained from the first part of the statement.

FIGURE 10.10 Alternative presentation of income

TWO STATEMENT PRESENTATION

ILLUSTRATIVE LTD
Statement of profit or loss
for the year ended 30 June 2019

CONTINUING OPERATIONS	
Revenue	$ 5 600
Cost of sales	(2 760)
Gross profit	2 840
Administrative expenses	(780)
Other expenses	(240)
Finance costs	(300)
Profit before income tax	**1 520**
Income tax expense	(450)
Profit for the period	**$ 1 070**

ILLUSTRATIVE LTD
Statement of comprehensive income
for the year ended 30 June 2019

Profit for the period	$ 1 070
Other comprehensive income	
Revaluation surplus	100
Income tax on other comprehensive income	30
Other comprehensive income for the period net of income tax	**70**
Total comprehensive income for the period	**$ 1 140**

ONE STATEMENT PRESENTATION

ILLUSTRATIVE LTD
Statement of profit or loss and other comprehensive income
for the year ended 30 June 2019

CONTINUING OPERATIONS	
Revenue	$ 5 600
Cost of sales	(2 760)
Gross profit	2 840
Administrative expenses	(780)
Other expenses	(240)
Finance costs	(300)
Profit before income tax	**1 520**
Income tax expense	(450)
Profit for the period	**1 070**
OTHER COMPREHENSIVE INCOME	
Revaluation surplus	100
Income tax on other comprehensive income	30
Other comprehensive income for the period net of income tax	**70**
Total comprehensive income for the period	**$ 1 140**

FIGURE 10.11 Johanna's International Jewellery Limited's 2019 statement of comprehensive income

JOHANNA'S INTERNATIONAL JEWELLERY LIMITED
Statement of comprehensive income
for the year ended 30 June 2019

	Notes	2019 $'000	2018 $'000
Revenue from continuing operations		274 762	255 749
Other income	1	206	747
Cost of sales	2	(99 676)	(97 287)
Employee benefits expenses		(70 353)	(62 197)
Occupancy costs		(26 042)	(23 766)
Selling expenses	3	(15 464)	(15 036)
Marketing expenses		(15 183)	(14 875)
Depreciation and amortisation expense	3	(6 516)	(6 119)
Loss on disposal of property, plant and equipment		(62)	(229)
Other expenses		(16 534)	(13 896)
Finance costs		(1 618)	(2 072)
Profit before income tax		**23 520**	**21 019**
Income tax (expense)/benefit	4	(3 504)	(2 764)
Profit for the year		**20 016**	**18 255**
OTHER COMPREHENSIVE INCOME			
Items that may be reclassified subsequently to profit or loss			
Currency translation differences arising during the year		(2 390)	(922)
Total comprehensive income for the year		**17 626**	**17 333**
Total comprehensive income for the year attributable to:			
Owners of Johanna's International Jewellery Limited		17 626	17 333

Statement of changes in equity

As the name suggests, the statement of changes in equity reflects the net changes in the equity accounts for the period. It shows the total comprehensive income for the period; the effects of any retrospective adjustments for accounting errors, changes in accounting policies and reclassification of amounts, as outlined in the previous section in this chapter; and the results of transactions with owners/shareholders in their capacity as owners, that is, contributions and distributions. The details of dividends or other distributions to owners can still be shown in a note to the financial statements. Lastly, the statement of changes in equity must show, for each equity account, a reconciliation between the opening and closing balances, separately disclosing each change. An extract of Johanna's International Jewellery Limited's statement of changes in equity as at 30 June 2019 is illustrated in figure 10.12. For ease of presentation, the non-controlling interests and the 2018 comparative figures are not shown.

FIGURE 10.12 Extract of Johanna's International Jewellery Limited's 2019 statement of changes in equity

JOHANNA'S INTERNATIONAL JEWELLERY LIMITED
Statement of changes in equity (extract)
for the year ended 30 June 2019

	Notes	Contributed equity $'000	Reserves $'000	Retained earnings $'000	Total $'000
Balance at 30 June 2018		2 042	896	94 242	97 180
Total comprehensive income		0	(2 390)	20 016	17 626
		2 042	(1 494)	114 258	114 806
Transactions with owners in their capacity as owners					
Dividends paid	17	0	0	(11 484)	(11 484)
Employee shares issued	21(b)	40	0	0	40
Option expense through share-based payment reserve	21(c)	0	70	0	70
		40	70	(11 484)	(11 374)
Balance at 30 June 2019		**2 082**	**(1 424)**	**102 774**	**103 432**

Now let's review how equity is reported in the statement of financial position.

Statement of financial position — equity section

The equity section of the statement of financial position of a corporation includes:
- share capital (often called *contributed equity* in external financial statements)
- retained earnings
- reserves.

Helpful hint: For reporting periods from 1 January 2009, the balance sheet is called the statement of financial position, but some companies continue to use the old title in their published financial statements.

The distinction between capital and retained earnings is important from both legal and economic perspectives. Share capital is the amount that has been paid into the company by shareholders in exchange for shares of ownership. **Retained earnings** represent a part of equity resulting from profit that has not been distributed as a dividend. Most reserves, such as the general reserve and the revaluation surplus, represent changes in equity that do not result from transactions with owners. The general reserve is an accumulation of profit, similar to retained earnings. The revaluation surplus was discussed in chapter 8, and is a component of other comprehensive income.

An extract from the equity section of Johanna's International Jewellery Limited's statement of financial position as at 30 June 2019 is illustrated in figure 10.13.

FIGURE 10.13 Equity section of Johanna's International Jewellery Limited's 2019 statement of financial position

JOHANNA'S INTERNATIONAL JEWELLERY LIMITED
Statement of financial position (extract)
as at 30 June 2019

	2019 $'000	2018 $'000
EQUITY		
Contributed equity	2 082	2 042
Reserves	(1 424)	896
Retained profits	102 774	94 242
Total equity	**103 432**	**97 180**

Share capital

The company must report the amount of share capital, often labelled contributed equity, on the face of the statement of financial position. Other information about share capital is also reported but is typically located in the notes to the financial statements.

Share capital may comprise several classes of shares. For each class of shares, the company reports the number of shares that are fully paid, the number of shares that are partly paid, and an explanation of any changes in the number of shares during the period.

Figure 10.14 shows extracts from the note disclosures of share capital in the 2019 annual report of AccountSoft Limited, a company funded entirely by equity. As can be seen from figure 10.14, AccountSoft Limited had 58 609 000 fully paid shares at the end of its 2019 financial year and the dollar amount of contributed equity, or paid-up capital, was $77 776 000. During 2019, the 5 218 000 increase in share capital came from three separate issues. The first was an issue of 5 million shares to Mater Capital and Valor Group, the second 45 000 to purchase Litehouse Limited, and the remaining 173 000 under employee long-term incentive plans.

FIGURE 10.14 Extract from the contributed equity note disclosure in the 2019 annual report of AccountSoft Limited

ACCOUNTSOFT LIMITED
Notes to the financial statements
for the year ended 30 June 2019

1. SUMMARY OF SIGNIFICANT ACCOUNTING POLICIES

(m) Share capital
Ordinary shares are classified as equity. Incremental costs directly attributable to the issue of new shares are deducted from equity, net of tax.

NOTE 10. SHARE CAPITAL (extract)

Movement in ordinary shares on issue

	Notes	Group 2019 shares $'000	Group 2018 shares $'000
Balance at 1 July		53 391	45 506
Issue of ordinary shares to Mater Capital and Valor Group		5 000	6 676
Issue of ordinary shares—purchase of PayCo assets	11	—	303
Issue of ordinary shares—purchase of Gem Solutions Limited		—	631
Issue of ordinary shares—purchase of Litehouse Limited		45	—
Issue of ordinary shares under employee long-term incentive plans		173	275
Ordinary shares on issue at 30 June		58 609	53 391
Treasury stock		(920)	(1 342)
Ordinary shares on issue at 30 June		**57 689**	**52 049**

All shares have been issued and fully paid.

In December 2018, the Company issued 5 million shares to Mater Capital and Valor Group. These shares were issued at $6.00. Transaction costs of $59 000 were incurred in this transaction.

For the current year, 173 719 shares were issued by the Company under the employee long-term incentive scheme, at an average price of $5.30.

For the current year, 196 195 options were granted to selected employees with exercise prices of $3.50 to $7.20 per share. The options are exercisable in equal amounts over two years from the grant date. No options can be exercised later than six months from the final vesting date. Any unvested and unexercised options will be cancelled should an employee cease to be employed.

Treasury stock includes shares issued in relation to the purchase of PayCo assets.

AccountSoft Limited's statement of changes in equity for the year ended 30 June 2019 showed total share capital of $77 776 000, an increase of $31 150 000 during the year. Of this, $30 000 000 related to the issue of shares on 12 December, $300 000 to the equity component of the purchase of Litehouse Limited, and $920 710 700 for the employee restricted share plan. In contrast, Johanna's International Jewellery Limited's share capital increase was limited to the $40 000 employee share scheme.

Reserves

Reserves are a component of equity. Most reserves of Australian and New Zealand companies are classified as **revenue reserves**, which mean they can be distributed as dividends. Management may choose to transfer retained earnings to a reserve account to signal that they have no intention of distributing it in the near future. This does not prevent the company from later distributing it as a dividend. Accounting standards require companies to disclose the nature and purpose of reserves, and to provide a reconciliation that explains the movement in each reserve during the reporting period. The aggregate amount of reserves at the end of the reporting period is shown on the face of the statement of financial position. See figure 10.15 for an example of the disclosure for reserves reported in the notes to the financial statements.

10.8 Retained earnings

LEARNING OBJECTIVE 10.8 Identify the items that affect retained earnings.

Retained earnings represent accumulated profits that have not been distributed to shareholders. The retained earnings account is increased by profits and decreased by losses and dividends. Amounts can also be transferred to reserve accounts from retained earnings; similarly, amounts can be transferred from reserve accounts to retained earnings.

Accounting standards require companies to report the opening amount of retained earnings and changes to retained earnings during the period. The amount of retained earnings at the end of the reporting period is also shown in the statement of financial position. To illustrate: Retainer Ltd had a credit balance of $120 000 in the retained earnings account at the beginning of the year. Retainer Ltd's profit for the year was $50 000. Dividends of $5000 were declared during the year and $20 000 was transferred to the general reserve. The movement in the retained earnings account and its closing balance can be determined as shown below.

Balance of retained earnings at the beginning of the period		$120 000
Add: Profit		50 000
		170 000
Less: Dividends declared	$ 5 000	
Transfer to general reserve	20 000	25 000
Balance of retained earnings at the end of the period		**$145 000**

Figure 10.15 illustrates an example of the disclosure for reserves and retained earnings reported in the notes to the financial statements.

GIORGINA's PIZZA LIMITED
Notes to the financial statements
for the year ended 30 June 2019

	2019 $'000	2018 $'000
29. RESERVES		
Foreign currency translation	(5 139)	(13 626)
Equity-settled share-based benefits	1 900	1 424
Hedging	1 749	1 722
	(1 490)	(10 480)
29.1 FOREIGN CURRENCY TRANSLATION RESERVE		
Balance at beginning of financial year	(13 626)	(10 792)
Translation of foreign operations	8 487	(2 834)
Balance at end of financial year	(5 139)	(13 626)

The foreign currency translation reserve represents the accumulation of exchange differences relating to the translation of the consolidated entity's foreign operations from functional currency to presentation currency (i.e. Australian dollars).

	2019 $'000	2018 $'000
29.2 EQUITY-SETTLED SHARE-BASED BENEFITS RESERVE		
Balance at beginning of financial year	1 424	1 264
Share-based payment	476	160
Balance at end of financial year	1 900	1 424

The equity settled share-based benefits reserve arises from the grant of share options to executives under the Executive Share Scheme ('ESS').

	2019 $'000	2018 $'000
29.3 HEDGING RESERVE		
Balance at beginning of financial year	1 722	1 533
Gain recognised:		
Net investment hedge	27	117
Interest rate swap	0	72
Balance at end of financial year	1 749	1 722

The hedging reserve represents gains and losses recognised on the net investment hedges of the Company.

	2019 $'000	2018 $'000
30. RETAINED EARNINGS		
Balance at beginning of financial year	45 857	36 013
Net profit attributable to members of the Company	21 400	22 560
Payment of dividends	(19 473)	(12 716)
Balance at end of financial year	47 784	45 857

LEARNING REFLECTION AND CONSOLIDATION

Review it

1. What are the differences between the statement of profit or loss, statement of profit or loss and other comprehensive income, and statement of changes in equity?
2. Identify the three components of equity.
3. Identify three items that decrease retained earnings.

Do it

Polar Equip Ltd operates a ski hire business. The company reported retained earnings of $80 000 and a general reserve of $250 000 in its statement of financial position at 30 June 2018. During the year ended 30 June 2019, Polar Equip Ltd generated profit of $30 000. It paid an interim dividend of $20 000 in January and declared a final dividend of $40 000 on 30 June 2019. The directors decided to transfer $50 000 from the general reserve account to the retained earnings account on 30 June 2019.

Calculate the closing balance of retained earnings and the general reserve at 30 June 2019 and prepare reconciliation statements showing the movement in each of these accounts.

Reasoning

The general reserve account is reduced by the transfer from the general reserve to retained earnings. The retained earnings account is increased by profit and the transfer from the general reserve dividends.

Solution

General reserve	
Balance 1 July 2018	$250 000
Transfer to retained earnings	(50 000)
Balance 30 June 2019	**$200 000**
Retained earnings	
Balance 1 July 2018	$ 80 000
Profit	30 000
Transfer from general reserve	50 000
Interim dividend	(20 000)
Final dividend	(40 000)
Balance 30 June 2019	**$100 000**

10.9 Financial statement analysis and decision making

LEARNING OBJECTIVE 10.9 Evaluate a company's dividend and earnings performance from a shareholder's perspective.

Investors are interested in both a company's dividend record and its earnings performance. Although they are often parallel, that is not always the case. Thus, each should be investigated separately.

Dividend record

One way that companies reward investors for their investment is to pay them dividends. The **dividend payout** measures the percentage of profit distributed in the form of cash dividends to ordinary shareholders. It is calculated by *dividing total cash dividends declared to ordinary shareholders by profit*. From the information shown below, the payout for Johanna's International Jewellery Limited in 2019 and 2018 is calculated in figure 10.16.

Helpful hint: Profit refers to profit after tax. Profit = revenue − expenses. Expenses include tax expense. For comparative purposes it excludes discontinuing items. Dividends paid include interim cash dividends plus any final cash dividends relating to the financial year even if declared after the end of the reporting period.

($ in millions)	2019	2018
Dividends	11 484	9 547
Profit	20 016	18 255

FIGURE 10.16   Johanna's International Jewellery Limited's dividend payout

	Cash dividends declared on ordinary shares	
Dividend payout =	Profit	
($ in millions)	2019	2018
Payout	$\dfrac{\$11\,484}{\$20\,016} = 57.4\%$	$\dfrac{\$9\,547}{\$18\,255} = 52.3\%$

Johanna's dividend payout increased by 5.1% from 2018 to 2019, indicating the company increased its payout less than the 9.6% increase in profits in 2019. This suggests that the company may be retaining some of its profit for investment in future growth.

Companies that have high growth rates are often characterised by low dividend payouts because they reinvest most of their profit in the business. Thus, a low payout rate is not necessarily bad news. Companies that believe they have many good opportunities for growth pay lower dividends and retain funds for investments. However, low dividend payments, or a cut in dividend payments, might signal that a company has liquidity or solvency problems and is trying to free up cash by not paying dividends. Thus, the reason for low dividend payments should be investigated. However, Johanna's does not appear to be in that situation. In deciding whether to invest in a company, potential investors and existing shareholders would be interested in the amount of dividends distributed to shareholders. The dividend payout ratio provides an indication of the proportion of profit that is distributed in dividends. It compares the cash dividends declared on ordinary shares to the profit available to ordinary shareholders. If investors are dividend focused, they may prefer a company with a high dividend payout. For those investors that are focused on capital gains, a low dividend payout may be preferable if the company is planning for future growth, which may lead to an increase in profit and share price in the future. The relevance of the dividend payout in the investment decision is summarised in the decision-making toolkit next.

Decision/issue	Info needed for analysis	Tool or technique to use for decision	How to evaluate results to make decision
What portion of its profit does the company pay out in dividends?	Profit and total cash dividends declared on ordinary shares	$$\text{Dividend payout} = \frac{\text{Cash dividend declared on ordinary shares}}{\text{Profit}}$$	A low rate suggests that the company is retaining its profit for investment in future growth or experiencing liquidity problems.

Earnings performance

Another way to measure corporate performance is through profitability. A widely used ratio that measures profitability from the shareholders' perspective is **return on ordinary shareholders' equity (ROE)**. This ratio shows how many dollars of profit were earned for each dollar invested by ordinary shareholders. It is calculated by dividing profit available to shareholders (Profit − Preference dividends) by average ordinary shareholders' equity. From the additional information presented below, Johanna's International Jewellery Limited's return on ordinary shareholders' equity is calculated for 2019 and 2018 in figure 10.17.

($ in millions)	2019	2018	2017
Profit	20 016	18 255	
Preference dividends	—	—	
Ordinary shareholders' equity	103 432	97 180	89 188

FIGURE 10.17 Johanna's International Jewellery Limited's return on ordinary shareholders' equity

$$\text{Return on ordinary shareholders' equity} = \frac{\text{Profit} - \text{Preference dividends}}{\text{Ordinary shareholders' average equity}}$$

($ in millions)	2019	2018
Return on ordinary shareholders' equity	$\dfrac{\$20\,016 - 0}{(\$103\,432 + \$97\,180)/2} = 20.0\%$	$\dfrac{\$18\,255 - 0}{(\$97\,180 + \$89\,188)/2} = 19.6\%$

From 2018 to 2019 Johanna's return on ordinary shareholders' equity increased slightly, as the increase in profit was 2% higher than the increase in average equity.

10.10 Debt versus equity financing decision making

LEARNING OBJECTIVE 10.10 Evaluate debt and equity as alternative sources of finance.

When undertaking major projects (e.g. purchasing a new vineyard), acquiring manufacturing facilities or expanding operations into international markets, management must consider how the investment will be financed. For small business, this usually involves a visit to the bank. For public companies, the decision is more complex because they have more alternatives — public companies can raise money from the public in the form of debt or equity.

The advantages of debt financing relative to issuing more shares are depicted in figure 10.18.

FIGURE 10.18 | Advantages of debt financing over issuing ordinary shares

Debt financing	Advantages
	**1. Shareholder control is not affected.** Noteholders do not have voting rights, so current owners (shareholders) retain full control of the company.
	**2. Tax savings result.** Interest is deductible for tax purposes; dividends on shares are not.
	**3. Return on ordinary shareholders' equity may be higher.** Although interest expense reduces profit, return on ordinary shareholders' equity is often higher under debt financing because equity is not increased by the issue of shares.

We will now focus on how the return on ordinary shareholders' equity can be increased by the effective use of debt. To illustrate the potential effect of debt on the return on ordinary shareholders' equity, assume that Magpie Ltd is considering two plans for financing the construction of a new $5 million factory. Plan A involves issuing 200 000 shares at the current market price of $25 per share. Plan B involves issuing $5 million, 12% unsecured notes. Assume that profit before interest and tax on the new factory will be $1.5 million; income tax is expected to be 30%. Magpie Ltd currently has equity of $2.5 million. The alternative effects on return on ordinary shareholders' equity are shown in figure 10.19.

FIGURE 10.19 | Effects on return on ordinary shareholders' equity — shares vs. notes payable

	Plan A: issue shares	Plan B: issue unsecured notes
Profit before interest and tax	$1 500 000	$1 500 000
Interest (12% × $5 000 000)	—	600 000
Profit before income tax	1 500 000	900 000
Income tax expense (30%)	450 000	270 000
Profit	$1 050 000	$ 630 000
Equity	$7 500 000	$2 500 000
Return on ordinary shareholders' equity	14%	25.2%

In calculating the estimated return on ordinary shareholders' equity for Plan A, the issue of shares, we include the increase in capital in equity. We do not include the change in retained earnings as this would involve numerous assumptions about dividend policy. We have no reason to expect that dividend policy will vary between financing alternatives. Implicitly, this approach assumes a dividend payout of 100% for both plans.

Note that with long-term debt financing (notes), profit is $420 000 less than with equity financing ($1 050 000 − $630 000). However, return on ordinary shareholders' equity is higher because equity is lower.

The major disadvantage resulting from the use of unsecured notes or debentures is that the company locks in fixed payments that must be made in good times and bad. Interest must be paid on a periodic basis, and the principal (face value) of the notes must be paid at maturity. A company with fluctuating earnings and a relatively weak cash position may experience great difficulty in meeting interest requirements in periods of low earnings. In the extreme, this can result in insolvency. With equity financing, on the other hand, the company can decide to pay low (or no) dividends if earnings are low. A potential disadvantage of equity finance is that issuing new shares may affect the control of existing shareholders.

In deciding whether to invest in a company, potential investors and existing shareholders would have a specific interest in the entity's ability to generate a satisfactory return from the funds invested by its owners. One key ratio that measures profitability from the shareholders' perspective is the return on ordinary shareholders' equity. It compares the profit available to ordinary shareholders to the amount of ordinary shareholders' equity. A company which generates a high rate of return would be a more attractive investment option as it provides investors greater confidence in the entity's ability to generate a high level of profit. The relevance of this information in the investment decision is summarised in the decision-making toolkit below.

DECISION-MAKING TOOLKIT

Decision/issue	Info needed for analysis	Tool or technique to use for decision	How to evaluate results to make decision
What is the company's return on ordinary shareholders' investment?	Profit available to ordinary shareholders and average ordinary shareholders' equity	Return on ordinary shareholders' equity $= \dfrac{\text{Profit} - \text{Preference dividends}}{\text{Average ordinary shareholders' equity}}$	A high measure suggests strong earnings performance from shareholders' perspective.

LEARNING REFLECTION AND CONSOLIDATION

Review it

1. What measure can be used to evaluate a company's dividend record, and how is it calculated?
2. What factors affect the return on ordinary shareholders' equity?
3. What are the advantages and disadvantages of debt and equity financing?

USING THE DECISION-MAKING TOOLKIT

The following facts are available for Prime Investments Limited. Using this information, evaluate its (1) dividend record and (2) earnings performance, and contrast them with those for Johanna's International Jewellery Limited 2019 and 2018 — calculated in section 10.9.

(rounded to $ millions except per share data)	2019	2018	2017
Dividends declared	30	28	
Profit	87	34	
Ordinary shareholders' equity	650	625	597

Solution

1. *Dividend record:* The payout ratio is a measure to evaluate a company's dividend record. For Prime, this measure was calculated for 2019 and 2018 as shown below.

	2019	2018
Dividend payout	$\dfrac{\$30}{\$87} = 34\%$	$\dfrac{\$28}{\$34} = 82\%$

Prime Investments' profit of $87 million in 2019 is substantially higher than the profit of $34 million reported in 2018. This 155% increase in profit was attributed to a reclassification adjustment of $52 million associated with a change in accounting for the entity's investment in Baker Group Limited. Excluding this adjustment, the entity's profit for 2019 was $35 million, which reflects a 3% increase compared to 2018. The dividend payout for 2019 using the unadjusted profit figure of $87 million was 34%, which appears significantly lower than the 82% payout for 2018. However, if the adjustment of $52 million is excluded from the profit, the dividend payout rates for 2019 and 2018 were around 86% and 82% respectively. These rates are much higher than Johanna's International Jewellery Limited's dividend payout rates for 2019 and 2018 of 57% and 52% respectively, as shown in figure 10.16.

2. *Earnings performance:* The return on ordinary shareholders' equity is one measure of earnings performance. The return on ordinary shareholders' equity for Prime Investments is calculated as shown below.

	2019	2018
Return on ordinary shareholders' equity	$\dfrac{\$87}{(\$650 + \$625)/2} = 13.6\%$	$\dfrac{\$34}{(\$625 + \$597)/2} = 5.6\%$

Prime Investments' return on ordinary shareholders' equity increased significantly from 5.6% in 2018 to 13.6% in 2019. This was mainly due to the 155% increase in profit associated with the reclassification adjustment of $52 million referred to previously. However, a strong performance from the entity's core brands as well as growth in the entity's online sales also contributed to this substantial improvement in 2019.

SUMMARY

10.1 Explain the business context and the importance of decision making relating to equity.

The business context for equity is very dependent on the nature of the entity and ownership structure. Decision making relating to equity is important for many stakeholders apart from owners, and relates to such issues as share issues, share splits, dividend policies, earning power, and so on.

10.2 Identify and discuss the main characteristics of a corporation (company).

The main characteristics of a corporation are separate legal existence, limited liability of shareholders, transferable ownership rights, ability to acquire capital, continuous life, company management, and the application of government and other regulations.

10.3 Record the issue of ordinary shares.

For a private placement, the proceeds of a share issue are directly credited to share capital. When the public is invited to subscribe to a share issue, application money is credited to the application account and the proceeds are held in a trust account until shares are allotted. At that time the proceeds become legal capital and are credited to the share capital account. The money received into the trust account is then transferred to the company's bank account.

10.4 Describe the effects of share splits.

Share splits increase the number of shares owned by each shareholder and decrease the assigned value of each share. Share splits do not affect the total amount of share capital.

10.5 Prepare the entries for cash dividends and share dividends and describe the impact on equity and assets.

Entries for both cash and share dividends are required at the declaration date and the payment date. At the declaration date, the entries are as follows — for a *cash dividend*, debit retained earnings and credit dividends payable; for a *share dividend*, debit retained earnings and credit share dividends payable. At the payment date, the entries for cash and share dividends are debit dividends payable and credit cash, and debit share dividends payable and credit share capital respectively. Cash dividends reduce reserves and thus total equity and assets, while share dividends make no difference to total equity or assets, but increase share capital while reducing reserves.

10.6 Understand the concept of earning power and indicate how irregular items are presented.

Earning power refers to an entity's ability to sustain its profits from operations. The effects of irregular items should be considered when evaluating earning power. Profit or loss from discontinued operations is reported in the statement of profit or loss, while effects of changes in accounting policies and accounting estimates used, if material, are disclosed in the notes to the financial statements.

10.7 Identify components of comprehensive income and changes in equity.

The statement of changes in equity provides a reconciliation of all changes in equity and shows details of movements in equity from transactions with owners/shareholders in their capacity as owners. The statement of profit or loss and other comprehensive income shows all changes in equity for a period other than those arising from transactions with owners/shareholders in their capacity as owners.

10.8 Identify the items that affect retained earnings.

Retained earnings are increased by profit and transfers from reserves, and decreased by losses, dividends and transfers to reserves.

10.9 Evaluate a company's dividend and earnings performance from a shareholder's perspective.

The dividend payout can be used to measure the portion of a company's profit distributed to shareholders as a dividend. A low dividend payout may indicate that the company is growing and that management has chosen to retain shareholders' funds for further investment. On the other hand, a low dividend payout could reflect liquidity problems. There are many measures of earnings performance, including the return on ordinary shareholders' equity.

10.10 Evaluate debt and equity as alternative sources of finance.

The return on ordinary shareholders' equity can be used to determine whether debt finance or the issue of more shares to finance an investment project would result in a better return to shareholders. However, other factors such as the fixed interest stream and shareholder control should also be considered.

DECISION-MAKING TOOLKIT — A SUMMARY

DECISION-MAKING TOOLKIT

Decision/issue	Info needed for analysis	Tool or technique to use for decision	How to evaluate results to make decision
Should the business incorporate?	Capital needs, growth expectations, type of business	Companies have limited liability, easier capital-raising ability, continuous life and professional managers; but they suffer from government and other regulations, and separation of ownership from management.	Must carefully weigh the costs and benefits in light of the particular circumstances.
Have there been any changes to accounting estimates used in previous-period financial statements?	Effect of a change in accounting estimates in the notes to the financial statements	Items reported in this section indicate that the current profit is affected by a revision to an accounting estimate used in preparing previous-period financial statements.	Consistent accounting estimates should be applied when predicting future profits.
Has the entity changed any of its accounting policies?	Prior period effect of change in accounting policy in the notes to the financial statements	Items reported in this section indicate that the entity has changed an accounting policy during the current year.	Consistent accounting policies should be applied when estimating future profits.
Has the entity disposed of any major part of the business?	Statement of profit or loss and notes to the financial statements	Disclosures about discontinuing operations indicate that the source of some of the entity's profit is not continuing.	This source of profit should be ignored in estimating future profits.
What portion of its profit does the company pay out in dividends?	Profit and total cash dividends declared on ordinary shares	$$\text{Dividend payout} = \frac{\text{Cash dividends declared on ordinary shares}}{\text{Profit}}$$	A low rate suggests that the company is retaining its profit for investment in future growth or experiencing liquidity problems.
What is the company's return on shareholders' investment?	Profit available to ordinary shareholders and average ordinary shareholders' equity	$$\text{Return on ordinary shareholders' equity} = \frac{\text{Profit} - \text{Preference dividends}}{\text{Average ordinary shareholders' equity}}$$	A high measure suggests strong earnings performance from shareholders' perspective.

KEY TERMS

allotment The issue of shares.

application The act of subscribing to a public issue of shares or other securities, such as debentures.

call on capital A claim for unpaid capital made by a company.

cash dividend A pro rata distribution of profit paid in cash to shareholders.

change in accounting estimates A revision of estimates used in the preparation of previous-period financial statements.

change in accounting policy Use of an accounting policy in the current year different from the one used in the preceding year.

chief executive officer (CEO) Mostly senior manager with direct responsibility for managing the business.

company A company or corporation is a separate legal entity formed under the Corporations Act. The process of setting up a company is called incorporation. The owners of a company are called shareholders.

contributed equity Another name for share capital.

corporation A separate legal entity, with most of the rights and privileges of a person.

declaration date The date the board of directors formally declares the dividend and announces it to shareholders.

discontinued operation A component of an entity that is being disposed of or classified as held for sale.

dividend A distribution of profits by a company to its shareholders in an amount proportional to each shareholder's percentage ownership. The most common form is a cash distribution.

dividend payout Total cash dividends declared to ordinary shareholders divided by profit.

earning power Profit adjusted for irregular items.

financial controller The chief accounting officer in a business.

issue price Amount paid by the investor on issue of a debenture or unsecured note.

limited liability The limit of liability of owners of a company to any unpaid amount of capital.

ordinary shares Shares representing the residual ownership interest in a company.

paid-up capital An alternative name for share capital.

payment date The date dividends are paid to shareholders.

prior period errors IAS 8 para. 5 defines prior period errors as 'omissions from, and misstatements in, the entity's financial statements for one or more prior periods arising from a failure to use, or misuse of, reliable information that: (a) was available when financial statements for those periods were authorised for issue; and (b) could reasonably be expected to have been obtained and taken into account in the preparation and presentation of those financial statements. Such errors include the effects of mathematical mistakes, mistakes in applying accounting policies, oversights or misinterpretations of facts, and fraud.

private placement An issue of shares by private invitation.

proprietary company A company that has up to 50 shareholders and whose shares are not available for sale to the general public; also called a private company.

prospectus A document issued with an invitation to subscribe for shares, containing information about the offering company.

public company A company that may have thousands of shareholders and which may raise money from the public through debt or equity issues.

retained earnings The accumulated profit from the current and previous accounting periods that has not been distributed to owners.

return on ordinary shareholders' equity (ROE) A measure of the dollars of profit earned for each dollar invested by the owners, calculated as profit available to ordinary shareholders divided by average ordinary shareholders' equity.

revenue reserves A component of equity, other than retained earnings, that may be distributed as a dividend.

share dividend A pro rata distribution of the company's own shares to shareholders; also called a bonus issue.

share split The issue of additional shares to shareholders accompanied by a proportionate reduction in the stated value of the shares.

statement of profit or loss and other comprehensive income A statement that reports total comprehensive income during a period.

total comprehensive income The change in equity during a period resulting from transactions and other events, other than those changes resulting from transactions with owners/shareholders in their capacity as owners.

treasurer The person with custody of a company's funds and responsibility for maintaining the company's cash position.

DEMONSTRATION PROBLEM 1

Sydney Software Ltd successfully developed a new spreadsheet program. However, to produce and market the program, the company needed $1.5 million of additional financing. Sydney Software Ltd already had retained earnings of $100 000 and share capital of 100 000 $10 shares. The following transactions occurred:

1. Issued 150 000 ordinary shares for $10 each by private placement on 21 January 2019.
2. Dividends of $0.20 per share were declared on 8 September 2019 and paid on 30 September 2019. Sydney Software Ltd's reporting period ends on 31 December.

Required
(a) Journalise the issue of the shares on 21 January 2019.
(b) Prepare the entry for the declaration and payment of dividends.
(c) Prepare a statement of the movement in retained earnings for the year ended 31 December 2019. Profit was $60 000.

SOLUTION TO DEMONSTRATION PROBLEM 1

(a) Jan. 21	Cash	1 500 000	
	Share capital		1 500 000
	(To record issue of ordinary shares at $10 each)		

(b) Sept. 8	Cash dividend declared	50 000	
	Dividend payable		50 000
	(To record cash dividend declared)		

Sept. 30	Dividend payable	50 000	
	Cash		50 000
	(To record cash dividend paid)		

(c)	Retained earnings 1/1/19	$100 000
	Profit year ended 31/12/19	60 000
	Dividends declared and paid	(50 000)
	Retained earnings 31/12/19	**$110 000**

DEMONSTRATION PROBLEM 2

Hamilton Ltd prepared the following statement of profit or loss and movement in retained earnings for the year ended 31 December 2019:

HAMILTON LTD **Statement of profit or loss** for the year ended 31 December 2019	
	$'000
Net sales	4 400
Cost of sales	(2 600)
Finance costs	(300)
Other expenses (selling and administration expenses)	(1 000)
Additional depreciation expense resulting from change of estimated useful life	(100)
Tax expense	(150)
Profit for the period	**250**

HAMILTON LTD **Movement in retained earnings** for the year ended 31 December 2019	
	$'000
Balance at the start of the period	400
Profit for the period	250
Profit from plastics division and loss from restatement of the assets of that division, net of tax (discontinued operation)	(500)
Balance at the end of the period	**150**

Helpful hint: The movement in retained earnings is part of the statement of changes in equity.

Hamilton Ltd entered into negotiations with Townsville Trading for the sale of the plastics division assets. The sale is expected to be completed by April 2020. The plastics division formed part of the industrial products business segment, and generated revenue of $800 000, expenses of $600 000 and profit before tax of $200 000 for the year ended 31 December 2019. The profit after tax was $120 000. The loss resulting from the restatement of the assets of the plastics division was $1 000 000 before tax and $620 000 after tax.

Required

Prepare the statement of profit or loss, movement in retained earnings and any required disclosures in the notes to the financial statements.

SOLUTION TO DEMONSTRATION PROBLEM 2

HAMILTON LTD **Statement of profit or loss** for the year ended 31 December 2019	
	$'000
Revenue	4 400
Cost of sales	(2 600)
Gross profit	1 800
Expenses excluding finance costs	(1 100)
Finance costs	(300)
Profit before income tax expense	**400**
Income tax expense	(150)

	$'000
Profit from continuing operations for the period	250
Profit from plastics division and loss from restatement of the assets of that division, net of tax (discontinued operation)	(500)
Loss for the period	**(250)**

HAMILTON LTD
Movement in retained earnings
for the year ended 31 December 2019

	$'000
Balance at the start of the period	400
Loss for the period	(250)
Balance at the end of the period	**150**

HAMILTON LTD
Notes to the financial statements

Additional depreciation expense resulting from a change in estimated useful life has affected the line item 'Expenses excluding finance costs' by increasing depreciation expenses by $100 000. The carrying amount of property plant and equipment has decreased by $100 000 as a result of the change in estimated useful life.

The plastics division has been discontinued. It formed part of the industrial products business segment. Hamilton Ltd has commenced negotiations with Townsville Trading for the sale of the assets of the plastics division and it is anticipated that the sale will be completed in April 2020. The plastics division generated revenue of $800 000, expenses of $600 000 and profit before tax of $200 000 for the year ended 31 December 2019. The profit after tax was $120 000. The loss resulting from the restatement of the assets of the plastics division was $1 000 000 before tax and $620 000 after tax.

The notes to the financial statements should also identify the operating, financing and investing cash flows generated or used by the plastics division. These may be located with the other notes about the statement of cash flows.

SELF-STUDY QUESTIONS

10.1 Which of these is *not* a major advantage of the corporate form of business organisation?   **LO2**
(a) Separate legal existence.
(b) Continuous life.
(c) Separation of ownership and management.
(d) Limited liability of shareholders.

10.2 Which of these statements is *false*?   **LO2, 3**
(a) Ownership of ordinary shares gives the owner a voting right.
(b) The equity section begins with share capital (contributed equity).
(c) The transfer of shares between shareholders does not result in a formal accounting entry.
(d) Shares can be issued only for cash.

10.3 A share split has the effect of: **LO4**
(a) increasing the number of shares.
(b) increasing the amount of share capital.
(c) decreasing the amount of share capital.
(d) increasing equity.

10.4 Entries for cash dividends reduce equity on: **LO5**
    (a) both declaration date and payment date.
    (b) payment date only.
    (c) declaration date only.
    (d) neither declaration date nor payment date.

10.5 Which of these statements about share dividends is *true*? **LO5**
    (a) A credit entry should be made to retained earnings for the dollar amount of the shares issued.
    (b) A share dividend increases share capital.
    (c) A share dividend decreases total equity.
    (d) A share dividend ordinarily will increase total equity.

10.6 Which of the following conditions is necessary for a company to pay cash dividends? **LO5**
    (a) Dividends must be paid from retained earnings.
    (b) The company must pay the cash dividend at least once a year.
    (c) After paying the dividend, the company must be able to pay its other debts, i.e. the company must be solvent.
    (d) All of the above.

10.7 Which of the following is *not* true in relation to earning power? **LO6**
    (a) Earning power is the most likely level of profit to be obtained in the future.
    (b) Earning power is the extent to which this year's profit is a good predictor of future profits.
    (c) Profit adjusted for irregular items is referred to as earning power.
    (d) Profit including irregular items is referred to as earning power.

10.8 Which of the following is *not* classified as an irregular item? **LO6**
    (a) Change in accounting policy.
    (b) Bad debts expenses.
    (c) Changes in accounting estimates.
    (d) Prior period errors.

10.9 Which of the following is *not* part of comprehensive income? **LO7**
    (a) Prior period errors.
    (b) Discontinuing operations.
    (c) Changes in accounting estimates.
    (d) Dividends paid.

10.10 Retained earnings are: **LO8**
    (a) increased by cash dividends declared.
    (b) increased by all dividends declared.
    (c) decreased by transfers to reserves.
    (d) increased by losses after tax.

10.11 Which of the following is *not* an equity account? **LO3, 8**
    (a) Share capital.
    (b) Reserves.
    (c) Retained earnings.
    (d) Dividends payable.

10.12 Which of the following decreases retained earnings? **LO8**
    (a) Share dividends declared.
    (b) Payment of a cash dividend previously declared.
    (c) Transfer from reserves.
    (d) Profit after tax.

10.13 A low dividend payout may indicate that the company: **LO9**
    (a) generated low levels of profit.
    (b) paid high dividends.

(c) is retaining profit to pursue a growth strategy.

(d) has share capital surplus to needs.

10.14 A low return on ordinary shareholders' equity indicates: **LO9**

(a) shareholder confidence.

(b) low profitability on shareholders' funds.

(c) low return on assets.

(d) high leverage.

10.15 Duncan Ltd had the following account balances at 30 June 2018: Share capital $100 000, Retained earnings $30 000, General reserve $8000, Dividends payable $2000, and Cash $12 000. What is the total equity for Duncan Ltd at 30 June 2018? **LO9**

(a) $152 000.

(b) $140 000.

(c) $138 000.

(d) $136 000.

10.16 Which of the following increases the dividend payout? **LO9**

(a) An increase in average equity.

(b) An increase in profits, while the payout per share remains the same.

(c) A decrease in profits, while the payout per share remains the same.

(d) A decrease in average equity.

10.17 Which of the following directly increases return on ordinary shareholders' equity? **LO9**

(a) A decrease in average equity.

(b) A decrease in profit available to ordinary shareholders.

(c) A lower dividend payout.

(d) A share split.

10.18 Which of the decision-making tools would you recommend for a manager choosing between debt finance and issuing shares to raise funds for an investment project? **LO10**

(a) Compare profit before tax for each funding alternative.

(b) Choose debt finance because interest is tax deductible.

(c) Choose issuing shares to avoid paying interest.

(d) Compare return on ordinary shareholders' equity for each funding alternative.

QUESTIONS

10.1 Identify three groups that use equity information in decision making and distinguish between the nature and the sources of information each group requires.

10.2 Jie Li, a student, asks your help in understanding some characteristics of a company. Explain each of these to Jie:

(a) Separate legal existence.

(b) Limited liability of shareholders.

(c) Transferable ownership rights.

(d) Company management.

10.3 (a) Your friend Stuart cannot understand how the characteristic of company management is both an advantage and a disadvantage. Clarify this problem for Stuart.

(b) Identify and explain other disadvantages of a company.

10.4 What are the basic ownership rights of ordinary shareholders?

10.5 What conditions in Australia and in New Zealand must be met before a cash dividend is paid?

10.6 Contrast the effects of a cash dividend and a share dividend on a company's statement of financial position.

10.7 Explain the effect of a 2-for-1 share split on the following:
(a) the number of issued shares.
(b) the share capital account.
(c) equity.

10.8 During 2018, the accountant for Lu Ltd discovered an error in the 2017 statements. The effect of the error was to overstate an asset and understate expenses. How should the accountant correct the error in 2018?

10.9 Buck Ltd purchased a machine with an expected useful life of 4 years and nil residual value. After 2 years the estimated useful life was revised to 3 years. The manager of Buck Ltd suggested that the resulting additional depreciation should be charged against retained earnings. Is this correct? Give reasons for your answer.

10.10 Button Ltd has been in operation for 3 years. All of its manufacturing equipment, which has a useful life of 10 to 12 years, has been depreciated on a straight-line basis. During the fourth year, Button Ltd changes to an accelerated depreciation method for all of its equipment.
(a) Will Button Ltd report more profit as a result of this change?
(b) How will this change be reported?

10.11 Describe the interrelationship between the statement of profit or loss, the statement of profit or loss and other comprehensive income, and the statement of changes in equity.

10.12 List the three components of equity and give examples of transactions or events that can increase each component.

10.13 Specialist Brewers Ltd is considering buying more equipment but is concerned that the additional debt it needs to borrow will make its liquidity and solvency ratios look bad. What options does the company have other than borrowing to buy the equipment, and how will these options affect the financial statements?

10.14 Why do some companies have low dividend payout rates?

10.15 Amber is a shareholder of Southern Ferns Ltd. The company's return on ordinary shareholders' equity increased in 2019, but Amber received less dividends. Explain to Amber how this can occur.

BRIEF EXERCISES

BE10.1 Journalise private issue of ordinary shares.   **LO3**

On 1 June, Walrus Ltd issues 4800 shares by private invitation at a cash price of $2.50 per share. Journalise the issue of the shares.

BE10.2 Prepare entries for a share dividend.   **LO5**

Connor Ltd has 400 000 $3 shares issued. It declares a 10% share dividend on 1 December. The dividend shares are issued as $5 shares on 31 December. Prepare the entries for the declaration and payment of the share dividend.

BE10.3 Journalise the issue of shares.   **LO3**

On 2 March, Makayla Ltd invited the public to subscribe for 5000 shares at $1.50 each, $1.00 payable on application and $0.50 payable on allotment. By 31 March, applications were received for 5000 shares, and these were allotted on 1 April. All amounts owing on allotment were received by 30 April. Prepare the journal entries required to record the issue of the shares and proceeds of the share issue.

BE10.4 Journalise cash dividends.   **LO5**

Spinning Ltd had 15 000 shares issued. On 30 June 2019, a cash dividend of $0.15 per share was declared. The dividend was paid on 31 July 2019. Prepare journal entries to record the declaration and payment of the dividend.

BE10.5 Determine the effect of a share split and journalise cash dividends.   **LO4, 5**

At 1 July, TriTop Ltd had 1500 shares issued. An interim cash dividend of $0.25 per share was declared on 31 December and paid on 31 January. The shareholders agreed to a 3-for-1 share split, which occurred on 31 May. After the share split, a final cash dividend of $0.10 per share was declared on 30 June. Prepare journal entries to record the interim and final dividends declared and/or paid by TriTop Ltd.

BE10.6 Prepare a corrected statement of profit or loss.   **LO6**

An inexperienced accountant for Basil Ltd showed the following in Basil Ltd's statement of profit or loss: profit before income tax $600 000; income tax expense $180 000; correction of prior period error $90 000; and profit $330 000. The correction of the prior period error has no effect on tax expense. Prepare a corrected statement of profit or loss beginning with 'Profit before income tax'.

BE10.7 Evaluate a company's dividend and earnings performance from a shareholder's perspective.   **LO9**

The average shareholders' equity of Jonty James Ltd was $500 000 for the year ended 30 June 2019. During that year, Jonty James Ltd had a profit of $90 000 and declared cash dividends of $20 000. Calculate the dividend payout and the return on ordinary shareholders' equity.

BE10.8 Compare debt financing with equity financing.   **LO10**

Brianna Ltd is considering these two alternatives to finance its construction of a new $3 million factory:

(a) Issue 600 000 shares at the market price of $5 per share.

(b) Issue $3 million, 6% unsecured notes at face value.

Complete the table and indicate which alternative is preferable.

	Issue shares	Issue unsecured notes
Profit before interest and tax	$1 000 000	$1 000 000
Interest expense from unsecured notes		
Profit before income tax		
Income tax expense (30%)		
Profit	$	$
Equity	$	$ 800 000
Return on ordinary shareholders' equity	%	%

EXERCISES

E10.1 Journalise issue of ordinary shares.   **LO3**

During its first year of operations, SunLand Ltd had the following transactions pertaining to its capital.

Jan. 10	Issued 60 000 shares for cash at $5 per share.
July 1	Issued 20 000 shares for cash at $9 per share.

Required

(a) Journalise the transactions, assuming that the share issues were private placements.

(b) Journalise the 1 July and subsequent call issue assuming that it was a public offer, and that the public were invited to subscribe for 20 000 shares at $9 each, $4.50 payable on application and $3 on allotment. Applications closed and shares were allotted on 1 July. All allotment money was received by 31 July. The remaining capital of $1.50 per share is called on 1 December and all call money was received by 31 December.

E10.2 Journalise transactions and indicate statement presentation. LO3, 5

On 1 January 2019 Otter Ltd's share capital comprised 95 000 issued ordinary shares ($950 000) and retained earnings of $350 000. During the year, the following transactions occurred.

Apr.	1	Issued 3000 additional ordinary shares for $15 per share.
June	15	Declared a cash dividend of $2.50 per share to ordinary shareholders.
July	10	Paid the $2.50 cash dividend.
Dec.	1	Issued 4000 additional ordinary shares for $18 per share.
	15	Declared a cash dividend on issued ordinary shares of $2.80 per share to shareholders.
	31	Profit for the year was $925 000.

Required

(a) Prepare the journal entries to record the above transactions.
(b) Prepare the equity section of the statement of financial position as at 31 December 2019.
(c) What are the requirements for a company to pay a dividend?

E10.3 Compare effects of a share dividend and a cash dividend. LO5

On 31 October the equity section of Summer Ltd's statement of financial position consists of contributed equity $550 000 and retained earnings $240 000. Summer Ltd is considering the following two courses of action: (1) declaring a 6% share dividend on the 550 000 $1 issued ordinary shares or (2) paying a cash dividend of $0.06 per share. If the company issues shares as a dividend, the shares will have a nominal value of $1 each.

Required

Prepare a tabular summary of the effects of the alternative actions on the company's equity, the number of issued shares and share capital. Use these column headings: *Original balances*, *After share dividends* and *After cash dividends* (as illustrated in the section 10.5 'Learning reflection and consolidation' box), and comment on any assumption made and which course of action you would advise Summer Ltd to take.

E10.4 Prepare correcting entries for dividends. LO5, 8

Before preparing financial statements for the current year, the chief accountant for Jeckel Ltd discovered the following errors in the accounts:

1. The declaration and payment of a $15 000 cash dividend were recorded as a debit to interest expense $15 000 and a credit to cash $15 000.
2. A 10% share dividend (1500 shares) was declared on the $15 shares. The directors had determined that the share dividend should be at the market value of $18. The only entry made was: Retained earnings (Dr) $15 000 and Dividend payable (Cr) $15 000. The shares have not been issued.

Required

Prepare the correcting entries at 31 December.

E10.5 Calculate earning power. LO6

Bettie Ltd reported a current year's profit of $2 500 000.

Additional information:

- Prior period sales included in current sales revenues, $15 600.
- Gain on sale of a division of the entity, $45 200.
- New asset acquired — related depreciation expense for the period, $6000.
- Contingent liability of $32 000 reported in the notes to the financial statements.

Required

(a) Determine Bettie Ltd's earning power.
(b) Why is it important for potential investors to understand the concept of earning power when deciding whether to invest in an entity?

E10.6 Determine changes in retained earnings.

LO8

Gold Ltd had the following equity accounts at 1 July 2017:

Share capital (200 000 shares)	$400 000
General reserve	30 000
Retained earnings	20 000

During the year ended 30 June 2018, the following occurred:

1. A profit of $40 000 was generated.
2. $8000 was transferred to the general reserve.
3. An interim dividend of 4c per share was declared and paid.
4. A final dividend of 6c per share was declared.

Required

Prepare a statement of the changes in retained earnings.

E10.7 Determine changes in retained earnings.

LO8

Speedy Deliveries Ltd had the following equity accounts at 1 January 2018:

Share capital (30 000 shares)	$150 000
Dividend equalisation reserve	10 000
Retained earnings	34 000

During the year ended 31 December 2018, the following occurred:

1. A profit of $20 000 was generated.
2. $5000 was transferred to the dividend equalisation reserve.
3. An interim dividend of 15c per share was declared and paid.
4. A final dividend of 10c per share was declared.

Required

Prepare a statement of the changes in retained earnings.

E10.8 Journalise share transactions, post, and calculate share capital.

LO3

South Island Skiwear Ltd was registered on 5 January 2019. The following private share issues were completed during the first year:

Jan.	10	Issued 90 000 ordinary shares for cash at $1 per share.
Mar.	1	Issued 6000 ordinary shares for cash at $1.25 per share.
May	1	Issued 50 000 ordinary shares for cash at $2.50 per share.
Sept.	1	Issued 20 000 ordinary shares for cash at $3 per share.
Nov.	1	Issued 2000 10% preference shares for cash at $4 per share.

Required

(a) Journalise the transactions.
(b) Post to the share capital account. (Use T accounts.)
(c) Calculate the share capital at 31 December 2019.

E10.9 Journalise share transactions, post, and calculate share capital.

LO3

Young Ltd was registered on 3 January 2019. The following private share issues were completed during the first year:

Jan.	10	Issued 240 000 ordinary shares for cash at $2 per share.
Mar.	1	Issued 30 000 ordinary shares for cash at $3 per share.
May	1	Issued 90 000 ordinary shares for cash at $3.50 per share.
Sept.	1	Issued 20 000 ordinary shares for cash at $4 per share.
Nov.	1	Issued 21 000 ordinary shares for cash at $5 per share.

Required

(a) Journalise the transactions.

(b) Post to the share capital account. (Use T accounts.)

(c) Calculate the share capital at 31 December 2019.

E10.10 Calculate return on ordinary shareholders' equity and dividend payout.   **LO9**

The equity of Yang Pty Ltd was $210 000 at 30 June 2018. During the year ended 30 June 2019, Yang made a profit of $70 000 and declared dividends of $40 000.

Required

Calculate the dividend payout and the return on ordinary shareholders' equity for the year ended 30 June 2019.

E10.11 Compare equity financing with debt financing.   **LO10**

SpringTime Ltd is considering these two alternatives for financing extensions:

1. Issue 70 000 shares at $20 per share. (Cash dividends have not been paid; nor is the payment of any cash dividend contemplated.)

2. Issue 10%, 10-year debentures at face value for $1.4 million. (Assume that 10% is also the market rate for similar securities.)

It is estimated that the company will earn $500 000 before interest and taxes as a result of the extension. The company has an estimated tax rate of 30% and has equity of $2 million prior to the new financing.

Required

(a) Determine the effect on profit and return on ordinary shareholders' equity for (1) issuing shares and (2) issuing debentures.

(b) Discuss factors the company would need to consider in deciding the financing options.

PROBLEM SET A

PSA10.1 Journalise share transactions, post, and calculate share capital.   **LO3**

Sport's Field Ltd was registered on 31 January 2019. It invited the public to subscribe to the issue of 35 000 ordinary shares for $1 per share: $0.60 due on application, $0.30 due on allotment and the balance due on call.

Jan. 10	Prospectus issued.
Mar. 1	Received applications for 35 000 shares.
Mar. 2	Allotted 35 000 ordinary shares.
Mar. 31	All allotment money received.
Nov. 1	Remaining capital called.
Nov. 30	All money due on call is received.

Required

(a) Journalise the transactions.

(b) Post to the equity accounts (use T accounts).

(c) What is the share capital of Sport's Field Ltd at 1 December?

PSA10.2 Record share issues and dividends.   **LO3, 5**

On 31 December 2018, CoffeeForU Ltd had 2 000 000 shares. The equity accounts at 31 December 2018 had the balances listed as follows.

Share capital	$2 000 000
Revaluation surplus	400 000
Retained earnings	1 300 000

Transactions during 2019 and other information related to equity accounts were as follows.
1. On 9 January 2019, issued 200 000 shares for $4 cash.
2. On 10 June 2019, declared a cash dividend of 15% of share capital, payable on 10 July 2019 to shareholders.

Required

(a) Prepare journal entries to record the above transactions.

(b) Prepare the equity section of CoffeeForU Ltd's statement of financial position as at 30 June 2019.

PSA10.3 Journalise transactions with GST.   **LO3, 5**

Amber started her own consulting firm, Amber Consulting Pty Ltd, on 1 October 2020. Assume Amber Consulting and all suppliers are registered for GST. If GST applies to a transaction, it is included at a rate of 10%. (*Hint:* Share transactions, dividends, loans, and salaries and wages do not have GST.) The following transactions occurred during the month of October.

Oct.	1	Shareholders invested $12 000 cash in the business.
	2	Paid $990 for office rent for the month.
	3	Purchased $660 of supplies on account.
	5	Paid $110 to advertise in the *Daily News*.
	9	Received $4422 cash for services provided.
	12	Paid $500 cash dividend.
	15	Performed $6600 of services on account.
	17	Paid $3200 for employee salaries after PAYG withheld tax of $590.
	20	Paid for the supplies purchased on account on 3 October.
	23	Received a cash payment of $5600 for services provided on account on 15 October.
	26	Borrowed $10 000 from the bank.
	29	Purchased office equipment for $3520 on account.
	30	Paid $220 for electricity.

Required

Journalise the transactions for the month of October 2020. Include narrations.

PSA10.4 Prepare dividend entries and post to ledger accounts.   **LO5**

On 1 January 2019, Rake Ltd had equity accounts as follows.

Share capital (60 000 shares issued for $30 each)	$1 800 000
General reserve	250 000
Retained earnings	900 000

During the year, the following transactions occurred.

Feb.	1	Declared a $0.60 cash dividend per share to shareholders, payable on 1 March.
Mar.	1	Paid the dividend declared in February.
July	1	Declared a 10% share dividend to shareholders, distributable on 31 July. On 1 July the market price of the shares was $40 per share and this was determined to be the amount at which the dividend shares would be issued.
July	31	Issued the shares for the share dividend.
Dec.	1	Declared a cash dividend of $0.50 per share on 15 December, payable on 5 January 2020.

Required

(a) Journalise the transactions.

(b) Enter the beginning balances and post the entries to the equity T accounts.

(c) Prepare the equity section of Rake Ltd's statement of financial position as at 31 December.

PSA10.5 **Prepare journal entries, determine changes in retained earnings and calculate dividend payout.**   **LO4, 5, 7, 8, 9**

CanDo Ltd had the following equity accounts at 1 July 2018.

Share capital (20 000 shares)	$20 000
Retained earnings	18 000

The following transactions occurred during the year ended 30 June 2019.

2018	
Dec. 31	CanDo Ltd declared an interim dividend of $0.20 per share.
2019	
Jan. 15	The interim dividend was paid.
Feb. 10	CanDo Ltd effected a 3-for-1 share split.
June 30	A final dividend of $0.10 per share was declared.

Profit for the year was $12 000. There were no other transactions or events affecting equity accounts.

Required

(a) Prepare journal entries to record the dividends.
(b) Prepare a statement showing the change in retained earnings for the year.
(c) Calculate the dividend payout.
(d) By how much did equity change during the period?

PSA10.6 **Prepare journal entries, determine changes in retained earnings and calculate dividend payout.**   **LO5, 7, 8, 9**

Rocky Ltd had the following equity accounts at 1 April 2018.

Share capital (50 000 shares)	$100 000
Retained earnings	60 000

The following occurred during the year ended 31 March 2019.

2018	
Sept. 30	Rocky Ltd declared an interim share dividend of $0.30 per share. The assigned value of each share was $2.
Oct. 10	Shares were issued as dividends.
2019	
Mar. 31	A final cash dividend of $0.30 per share was declared.

Profit for the year was $30 000. There were no other transactions or events affecting equity accounts.

Required

(a) Prepare journal entries to record the dividends.
(b) Prepare a statement showing the change in retained earnings for the year.
(c) Calculate the dividend payout.
(d) By how much did equity change during the period?

PSA10.7 **Prepare journal entries, determine changes in retained earnings and calculate ratios.**
                                                                    LO5, 7, 8, 9

Harre Pty Ltd is a small proprietary company. Its owners invested $3 capital in the company and it has grown considerably since. The following section is taken from Harre Pty Ltd's statement of financial position as at 30 June 2019.

Share capital (20 shares)	$ 20
Reserves	18 000
Retained earnings	30 000

Additional information:
1. Harre Pty Ltd's profit for the year ended 30 June 2019 was $35 000.
2. Cash dividends declared for the year ended 30 June 2019 were $19 000.
3. The directors of the company approved a transfer of $8000 to reserves. This was recorded in the ledger and is the only item affecting reserves during the year.

Required
(a) Journalise the dividends declared.
(b) Calculate the dividend payout.
(c) Calculate the return on ordinary shareholders' equity.
(d) Prepare a statement of changes in equity for the year ended 30 June 2019.

PSA10.8 Record dividends, show changes in retained earnings and calculate ratios.   **LO5, 7, 8, 9**
The following section is taken from Silk Ltd's statement of financial position at 31 December 2019.

Share capital	$5 000 000
Reserves	212 000
Retained earnings	42 000

Additional information:
1. Equity was $5 225 000 at 31 December 2018.
2. Silk Ltd's profit for the year ended 31 December 2019 was $60 000.
3. Cash dividends declared for the year ended 31 December 2019 were $31 000.
4. The directors of the company approved a transfer of $20 000 to reserves. This was recorded in the ledger and is the only item affecting reserves during the year.

Required
(a) Journalise the dividends declared.
(b) Calculate the dividend payout.
(c) Calculate the return on ordinary shareholders' equity.
(d) Prepare a statement of changes in equity for the year ended 31 December 2019.

PSA10.9 Prepare journal entries, determine retained earnings and calculate ratios.   **LO3, 5, 7, 8, 9**
Wellington Ltd had the following equity accounts at 1 July 2019.

Share capital, 100 000 fully paid shares	$300 000
Revaluation surplus	60 000
Retained earnings	150 000

The following transactions occurred during the year ended 30 June 2020.

Aug. 15	Final dividend for the year ended 30 June 2019 of 15 cents a share was declared.
Oct. 1	Paid final cash dividend.
Jan. 6	Wellington Ltd declared an interim share dividend of 12%. The shares were to be issued at $3 per share.
Mar. 15	Shares were issued as dividends. The assigned value of each share was $3.
June 30	$12 000 was transferred to general reserve.

During the year, Wellington Ltd generated a profit of $180 000. After the end of the reporting period, the directors declared a final dividend of 15 cents per share. There were no other transactions or events affecting equity accounts.

Required

(a) Prepare journal entries to record the dividend transactions and the transfer to general reserve.

(b) Prepare a statement of changes in equity for the year ended 30 June 2020.

(c) By how much did equity change during the period?

(d) Calculate the dividend payout and the return on ordinary shareholders' equity for the year ended 30 June 2020.

PSA10.10 **Compare financing alternatives using return on ordinary shareholders' equity.**   **LO10**

Donkey Ltd's equity is as follows:

Share capital	$5 000 000
Retained earnings and reserves	2 000 000
Equity	$7 000 000

Donkey Ltd plans to expand its operations by establishing a branch in Thailand. The new branch will cost $3.5 million. Expected profit before tax and interest when the new branch is operational is $2.2 million. The tax rate is 30%. Donkey Ltd is considering two financing alternatives:

1. Borrow $3.5 million at 8% interest.
2. Issue 100 000 $35 shares.

Required

Which funding alternative yields the higher return on equity? What other factors should be considered?

PROBLEM SET B

PSB10.1 **Journalise share transactions, post, and calculate share capital.**   **LO3**

Jumping Jack Ltd was registered on 31 March 2019. It invited the public to subscribe to the issue of 200 000 ordinary shares for $6 per share: $3 due on application, $2 due on allotment and the balance due on call.

Mar.	31	Prospectus issued.
May	1	Received applications for 200 000 shares.
	2	Allotted 200 000 ordinary shares.
	31	All allotment money received.
Aug.	1	Remaining capital called.
	15	All money due on call received.

Required

(a) Journalise the transactions.

(b) Post to the equity accounts. (Use T accounts.)

(c) What is the share capital of Jumping Jack Ltd at 1 September?

PSB10.2 **Record share issues and dividends.**   **LO3, 5**

On 31 December 2018, Luke Ltd had 2 000 000 shares. The equity accounts at 31 December 2018 had the following balances.

Share capital	$6 000 000
Revaluation surplus	200 000
Retained earnings	2 100 000

Transactions during 2019 and other information related to equity accounts are as follows.
1. On 15 March 2019, issued 300 000 shares for $2.50 cash.
2. On 10 June 2019, declared a cash dividend of 10% of share capital, payable on 31 July 2019 to shareholders.

Required

(a) Prepare journal entries to record the above transactions.

(b) Prepare the equity section of Luke Ltd's statement of financial position as at 30 June 2019.

PSB10.3 Journalise transactions with GST. LO3, 5

On 1 April, Treetops Ltd was established. Treetops Ltd is registered for GST and if GST is applicable, it is included in the figures given. (*Hint:* Share transactions, dividends, loans, and salaries and wages do not have GST.) The GST rate is 10%. Assume all suppliers are registered for GST. The following transactions were completed during the month:
1. Shareholders invested $30 000 cash in the company in exchange for shares.
2. Paid $550 cash for April office rent.
3. Purchased office equipment for $2200 cash.
4. Incurred $2420 of advertising costs in *The Age* on account.
5. Paid $990 for office supplies.
6. Provided $25 520 of services. Received $5500 cash from customers. The balance was invoiced to customers on account.
7. Paid $500 cash dividends.
8. Paid *The Age* the amount due in transaction (4).
9. Paid employees' salaries $2200; PAYG withheld tax $600.
10. Received $12 500 in cash from customers who had previously been invoiced in transaction (6).

Required

Journalise the transactions for the month of April. Include narrations.

PSB10.4 Prepare dividend entries and post to ledger accounts. LO5

On 1 July 2019, Ellie Ltd had the following equity accounts:

Share capital (200 000 shares)	$2 000 000
General reserve	250 000
Retained earnings	900 000

During the year, the following transactions occurred:

Aug.	1	Declared a $0.45 cash dividend per share to shareholders, payable on 1 September.
Sept.	1	Paid the dividend declared in August.
Oct.	1	Declared a 5% share dividend to shareholders, distributable on 31 October. On 1 October the market price of the shares was $10 per share and this was determined to be the amount at which the dividend shares would be issued.
	31	Issued the shares for the share dividend.
Dec.	1	Declared a cash dividend of $0.40 per share, payable on 5 January 2020.

Required

Journalise the transactions.

Enter the beginning balances and post the entries to the equity T accounts.

PSB10.5 Record dividends, show changes in retained earnings and calculate ratios. LO4, 5, 7, 8, 9

Beta Ltd had the following equity balances at 1 July, the beginning of the year.

Share capital (15 000 shares)	$150 000
Reserves	90 000
Retained earnings	100 000

Beta Ltd's profit for the year ending 30 June 2019 was $100 000. During the year the following events and transactions occurred.

Dec. 30	Declared interim cash dividend of $1.5 per share.
Jan. 15	Paid interim cash dividend.
Mar. 31	4-for-1 share split.
June 30	Declared cash dividend of $1.25 per share.
30	Transferred $5000 to general reserve.

Required

(a) Prepare journal entries to record the transactions and events affecting equity during the year.

(b) Prepare a statement showing the changes in retained earnings during the year.

(c) Prepare the equity section of the statement of financial position.

(d) Calculate the dividend payout and the return on ordinary shareholders' equity.

(e) Explain why some companies engage in share splits.

PSB10.6 **Prepare journal entries, determine changes in retained earnings and calculate dividend payout.** **LO5, 7, 8, 9**

Brownstone Ltd had the following equity accounts at 1 July 2018.

Share capital (10 000 shares)	$50 000
Retained earnings	12 500

The following occurred during the year ended 30 June 2019.

2018	
Dec. 31	Brownstone Ltd declared an interim share dividend of $0.25 per share. The shares were to be issued at $5 per share.
2019	
Jan. 10	Shares were issued as dividends. The assigned value of each share was $5.
June 30	A final cash dividend of $0.15 per share was declared.

During the year Brownstone Ltd generated a loss of $5000. There were no other transactions or events affecting equity accounts.

Required

(a) Prepare journal entries to record the dividends.

(b) Prepare a statement showing the change in retained earnings for the year.

(c) By how much did equity change during the period?

(d) Why do you think Brownstone Ltd issued the share dividend?

PSB10.7 **Record dividends, show changes in retained earnings and calculate ratios.** **LO5, 7, 8, 9**

Pansies Pty Ltd is a small proprietary company. Its owners invested $3 capital in the company and it has grown considerably since. The following section is taken from Pansies Pty Ltd's statement of financial position at 30 June 2019.

Share capital (two shares)	$ 3
Reserves	5 000
Retained earnings	10 000

Additional information:

1. Pansies Pty Ltd's profit for the year ended 30 June 2019 was $8000.

2. Cash dividends declared for the year ended 30 June 2019 were $5000.

3. The directors of the company approved a transfer of $5000 to reserves. This was recorded in the ledger and is the only item affecting general reserves during the year.

Required

(a) Journalise the dividends declared.

(b) Calculate the dividend payout.

(c) Calculate the return on ordinary shareholders' equity.

(d) Prepare a statement of changes in equity for the year ended 30 June 2019.

PSB10.8 Record dividends, show changes in retained earnings and calculate ratios.   LO5, 7, 8, 9

The following section is taken from Swedish Ltd's statement of financial position at 30 June 2019.

Share capital	$5 000 000
Reserves	330 000
Retained earnings	92 000

Additional information:

1. Equity was $5 362 000 at 30 June 2018.

2. Swedish Ltd's profit for the year ended 30 June 2019 was $285 000.

3. Cash dividends declared for the year ended 30 June 2019 were $225 000.

4. The directors of the company approved a transfer of $45 000 to reserves. This was recorded in the ledger and is the only item affecting general reserves during the year.

Required

(a) Journalise the dividends declared.

(b) Calculate the dividend payout.

(c) Calculate the return on ordinary shareholders' equity.

(d) Prepare a statement of changes in equity for the year ended 30 June 2019.

PSB10.9 Prepare journal entries, show changes in equity and calculate ratios.   LO4, 5, 7, 8, 9

Gemini Ltd had the following equity accounts at 1 July 2019.

Share capital, 200 000 fully paid shares	$400 000
General reserve	50 000
Retained earnings	150 000

The following transactions occurred during the year ended 30 June 2020.

Aug. 15	Final dividend for the year ended 30 June 2019 of 10 cents a share was declared.
Oct. 1	Paid final cash dividend.
Jan. 6	Gemini Ltd declared an interim share dividend of 12%. The shares were to be issued at $2.50 per share.
Mar. 15	Shares were issued as dividends. The assigned value of each share was $2.50.
June 30	$15 000 was transferred to general reserve.

During the year, Gemini Ltd generated a profit of $100 000. After the end of the reporting period, the directors declared a final cash dividend of 9 cents per share. There were no other transactions or events affecting equity accounts.

Required

(a) Prepare journal entries to record the dividend transactions and the transfer to general reserve.

(b) Prepare a statement of changes in equity for the year ended 30 June 2020.

(c) By how much did equity change during the period?

(d) Calculate the dividend payout and the return on ordinary shareholders' equity for the year ended 30 June 2020.

PSB10.10 **Compare financing alternatives using return on ordinary shareholders' equity.** **LO10**

Donald Ltd's equity is as follows:

Share capital	$5 000 000
Retained earnings and reserves	600 000
Equity	$5 600 000

Donald Ltd plans to expand its operations by acquiring substantial landholdings in Scotland. The expansion will cost $4 million. Expected profit before tax and interest after the expansion is $$1 000 000. The tax rate is 30%. The managers of Donald Ltd are considering two financing alternatives:

1. Borrow $4 million at 10% interest.
2. Issue 1 million $4 shares.

Required

Which funding alternative yields the higher return on equity? What other factors should be considered?

BUILDING BUSINESS SKILLS

FINANCIAL REPORTING AND ANALYSIS

Financial reporting problem: Health Care Equipment and Services Industry

BBS10.1 Go to the ASX website (www.asx.com.au) and search for the latest annual report for a company in the Health Care Equipment & Services industry group. Select **Prices and research**, then **Company information**, then select **View all companies** under the Company directory. Using the chosen company's financial statements and notes determine the following.

Required

Answer these questions:

(a) How many shares had been issued by the end of the reporting period?
(b) How many shares were issued during the reporting period?
(c) How much capital (if any) was returned during the reporting period?
(d) What is the amount of issued capital at the beginning of the reporting period?
(e) Calculate the dividend payout for the current and previous reporting periods, and the return on ordinary shareholders' equity for the current reporting period.

Financial reporting problem: Energy Industry

BBS10.2 Go to the ASX website (www.asx.com.au) and search for the latest annual report for a company in the Energy industry group. Select **Prices and research**, then **Company information**, then select **View all companies** under the Company directory. Using the chosen company's financial statements and notes determine the following:

(a) What was the date that the company first listed on the ASX?
(b) Has the company had a recent change of name?
(c) Does the company have an Executive Share and Option Plan? If yes, how many shares were issued during the current reporting period under this plan and how was the issue price determined? Why would such a plan exist?
(d) During the current financial year were shares issued under a Dividend Reinvestment Plan? If yes, how many shares were issued and for what price? How was the issue price determined?

Comparative analysis problem: Blue Heeler Limited vs. Jack Russell Limited

BBS10.3 Information from the June 2019 financial statements of Blue Heeler Limited and Jack Russell Limited is presented below.

	Blue Heeler Limited		Jack Russell Limited	
	2019 $'000	2018 $'000	2019 $'000	2018 $'000
Share capital/Contributed equity	$216 290	$217 972	$72 668	$54 706
Reserves	—	—	1 370	22
Retained earnings	169 680	171 432	64 570	47 956
Profit	27 016	41 976	32 004	18 408
Cash dividends declared and paid	21 594	26 712	19 440	14 580

Required

(a) Calculate the dividend payout for each company for two years and the return on ordinary shareholders' equity for the 2019 year.

(b) What do the ratios indicate about the profitability and dividend record of the two companies?

A global focus

BBS10.4 Many multinational companies find it beneficial to have their shares listed on the securities exchanges in more than one country. This exercise introduces you to the global nature of capital markets.

Address: www.sgx.com

Steps:

1. Choose **Home**.
2. Click on **Listing** on the SGX and scroll down the page until the section headed **Learn the benefits of listing with Asia's financial gateway** to explore that section.
3. Answer question (a) below.
4. Return to **Home**.
5. Click on **Company Information**, then choose **Corporate information** from the drop-down menu. Click on **Select Country** and read the drop-down menu.
6. Answer question (b) below.
7. Choose **Australia** from the **Select Country** drop-down menu, then select a country by clicking on it.
8. Answer question (c) below.

Required

(a) Explain the benefits for a multinational company of listing on the Singapore Stock Exchange.

(b) Which countries have companies listed on the SGX (ignore 'other')?

(c) After selecting an Australian company, find out the following information about it (you will need to go to the company's website to answer some of these questions):
   1. Name
   2. Place of incorporation
   3. Address of registered office
   4. Web site
   5. When it was listed on the SGX
   6. What other exchanges, if any, it is listed on
   7. Name of auditor
   8. Nature of its operations (see web site)
   9. Largest shareholder (see annual report)

10. Contributed Equity and Total Equity in AUD (see annual report)
11. Countries in which the company — or its subsidiaries — operates (see annual report).

CRITICAL THINKING

Group decision-making case

BBS10.5 Dianaton Ltd is considering a risky investment in offshore drilling. To finance the ongoing working capital needs of the project over 15 years, $10 million will be needed if it continues to be successful. Several suggestions for finance have been put before the board of directors:
1. Issue more shares to the public or by private placement.
2. Borrow the required cash.
3. Establish another company (in which Dianaton Ltd will be the only shareholder) and use that company to borrow the money, relying on the limited liability principle if the project fails.

Assume that the expected returns on ordinary shareholders' equity are the same for all options.

Required

Divide the class into groups, and consider the following questions as Dianaton Ltd's board of directors:

(a) How should the board rank the first two options?

(b) What are the advantages and disadvantages of the third option? Should the board undertake the third option? Consider multiple stakeholders.

Communication activity

BBS10.6 Marama Fisher, chief executive officer of Purple Regs Ltd, is considering the issue of debt to finance an expansion of the business. She has asked you to (1) discuss the advantages of debt over equity financing, (2) indicate the type of debt that might be issued, and (3) explain the issuing procedures used in share transactions for both public issues and private placements.

Required

Write a memorandum to the chief executive officer, answering her request.

Communication activity

BBS10.7 Goodman Fielder is a leading food company in Australia, New Zealand and Asia Pacific. To answer the following questions, access Goodman Fielder's Sustainability & Environment section from its web site (http://goodmanfielder.com/).

Required

(a) What reporting guidelines does Goodman Fielder use to prepare the sustainability part of the review?

(b) Summarise Goodman Fielder's goal and how it measures achievements in three of the following areas:
- our people
- environment
- community
- products.

Ethics case

BBS10.8 Persuasive Ltd has paid 60 consecutive quarterly cash dividends (15 years). However, the last 6 months have been a real cash drain on the company because profit margins have been greatly narrowed by increasing competition. With a cash balance sufficient to meet only day-to-day operating needs, the chief executive officer, Valerie Flamingo, has decided that a share dividend instead of a cash dividend should be declared. She tells Persuasive Ltd's financial director, Jonty James, to issue a press release stating that the company is extending its consecutive dividend record with the issue of a 5% share dividend. 'Write the press release convincing the shareholders that the share dividend is just as good as a cash dividend,' she orders. 'Just watch our share price rise when we announce the share dividend; it must be a good thing if that happens.'

Required

(a) Who are the stakeholders in this situation?

(b) Is there anything unethical about Flamingo's intentions or actions?

(c) What is the effect of a share dividend on a company's equity accounts? Might it affect future dividends? Which would you rather receive as a shareholder — a cash dividend or a share dividend? Would it make a difference if you did not intend to invest in the long term in Persuasive Ltd?

ANSWERS

Answers to self-study questions

10.1 (c) 10.2 (d) 10.3 (a) 10.4 (c) 10.5 (b) 10.6 (c) 10.7 (c) 10.8 (b) 10.9 (d) 10.10 (c) 10.11 (d)
10.12 (a) 10.13 (c) 10.14 (b) 10.15 (c) 10.16 (c) 10.17 (a) 10.18 (d)

ACKNOWLEDGEMENTS

Photo: © Phongphan / Shutterstock.com
Photo: © racorn / Shutterstock.com
Photo: © LittlePigPower / Shutterstock.com

CHAPTER 11

Statement of cash flows

LEARNING OBJECTIVES

After studying this chapter, you should be able to:

11.1 indicate the main purpose of the statement of cash flows

11.2 distinguish among operating, investing and financing activities

11.3 prepare a statement of cash flows

11.4 explain the impact of the product life cycle on an entity's cash flows

11.5 use the statement of cash flows to evaluate an entity.

Chapter preview

The statement of profit or loss and statement of financial position do not always show the whole picture of the financial condition of an entity. In fact, looking at these two financial statements, a thoughtful investor might ask questions like 'How does a company finance its investments and day-to-day operations?' Answers to this and similar questions can be found in this chapter, which presents the statement of cash flows.

The content and organisation of this chapter are as follows.

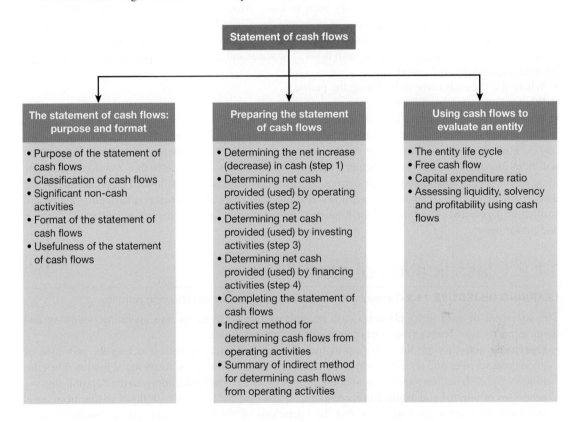

Statement of cash flows		
The statement of cash flows: purpose and format	**Preparing the statement of cash flows**	**Using cash flows to evaluate an entity**
• Purpose of the statement of cash flows • Classification of cash flows • Significant non-cash activities • Format of the statement of cash flows • Usefulness of the statement of cash flows	• Determining the net increase (decrease) in cash (step 1) • Determining net cash provided (used) by operating activities (step 2) • Determining net cash provided (used) by investing activities (step 3) • Determining net cash provided (used) by financing activities (step 4) • Completing the statement of cash flows • Indirect method for determining cash flows from operating activities • Summary of indirect method for determining cash flows from operating activities	• The entity life cycle • Free cash flow • Capital expenditure ratio • Assessing liquidity, solvency and profitability using cash flows

11.1 The statement of cash flows: purpose

LEARNING OBJECTIVE 11.1 Indicate the main purpose of the statement of cash flows.

The basic financial statements we have presented so far provide only limited information about an entity's cash flows (cash receipts and cash payments). For example, statements of financial position provide comparative figures that show the increase in property, plant and equipment during the year, but they do not show to what extent the change has involved the payment or receipt of cash. The statement of profit or loss shows profit, but it does not indicate the amount of cash generated by operating activities. Users of financial statements, namely equity investors, lenders and creditors, need information about the effects on cash of operating, investing and financing activities when deciding whether to provide resources to an entity.

Helpful hint: Recall we introduced the Conceptual Framework for Financial Reporting *in chapter 1. The* Conceptual Framework *outlines the objective of general purpose financial reporting and the primary users, namely the resource providers.*

Purpose of the statement of cash flows

The main purpose of the **statement of cash flows** is to provide information about cash receipts, cash payments and the net change in cash resulting from the operating, investing and financing activities of an entity during a period for external users of financial information. The operating, investing and financing activities involving cash are reported in a format that reconciles the beginning and ending cash balances.

Reporting the causes of changes in cash is useful because investors, creditors and other interested parties who provide resources to the entity want to know what is happening to an entity's most liquid resource, its cash, when making lending or investing decisions. Managers also find cash flow data an essential input in managing the day-to-day operations of the entity. To understand an entity's financial position it is essential to understand its cash flows. The statement of cash flows provides answers to these important questions about an entity.

- Where did the cash come from during the period?
- What was the cash used for during the period?
- What was the change in the cash balance during the period?

The answers to these questions provide important information for managers' decision-making processes. For example, for entities like Apple Inc. and Domino's Pizza Enterprises Ltd this information will help managers to determine whether the entity will be able to continue to thrive and invest in new ideas with the cash generated by their current operations, or whether they will need external funding for their investments. The statement of cash flows also provides clues about whether a struggling entity will survive or perish and where management needs to take action to improve the entity's financial position and performance.

11.2 Classification of cash flows

LEARNING OBJECTIVE 11.2 Distinguish among operating, investing and financing activities.

The statement of cash flows classifies cash receipts and cash payments into operating, investing and financing activities. Transactions within each activity are as follows.

- **Operating activities** are the entity's principal revenue-generating activities such as the provision of goods and services and activities which are not classified as investing or financing activities. The cash inflows and cash outflows arising from operating activities are a valuable input into the decision-making processes of internal and external users of financial information. Positive cash flows arising from operating activities are a good indicator that the operations of the business can generate sufficient cash flows to maintain or expand the current level of operations, repay debt and pay dividends.
- **Investing activities** are the acquisition and disposal of long-term assets, including activities such as purchasing and selling non-current assets, and lending money and collecting the loans. The cash inflows and cash outflows arising from investing activities also inform the decision-making processes of internal and external users of financial information. For example, cash outflows arising from investing activities are an indicator that the entity has invested in non-current assets that are intended to generate income and cash flows for future dividends to equity investors or expansion.
- **Financing activities** are those that affect the size and composition of contributed equity and borrowing, and include obtaining cash from issuing debt, repaying the amounts borrowed, obtaining cash from shareholders, and paying them dividends or buying back shares. The cash inflows and cash outflows arising from financing activities are another source of data for the decision-making processes of internal and external users of financial information. For example, cash inflows from financing activities are useful in predicting future cash outflows in the form of interest to lenders.

In IAS 7/AASB 107 *Statement of Cash Flows* the classification of certain items is debatable. For example, there are alternative treatments for interest and dividends. Interest received and dividends received may be classified as operating cash flows as they impact the calculation of profit or loss. Alternatively, interest and dividends received can be classified as investing cash flows because they are returns on investments. Most companies classify interest received and dividends received as operating activities, which is the method used in this chapter.

On the other hand, dividends paid may be classified as a financing cash flow because they relate to the cost of obtaining financial resources. An alternative classification for dividends paid is as a component of cash flows from operating as this can assist users to determine the ability of a business to pay dividends out of its operating cash flows.

Operating activities is the most important category because it shows the cash provided or used by operations. This source of cash is generally considered to be the best measure of whether an entity can generate sufficient cash to continue as a going concern by paying its debts as they fall due and whether there is additional cash for dividends or expansion. Monitoring operating cash inflows and outflows enables management of an entity to assess whether the entity will be able to finance its future expansion internally, or if additional funds are needed, to decide whether they will be obtained through borrowing and/or issuing shares.

Figure 11.1 lists typical cash receipts and cash payments within each of the three types of activities.

FIGURE 11.1 Typical cash receipts and payments classified by activity

Types of cash inflows and outflows

Operating activities
Cash inflows:
   From sale of goods or services
   From returns on loans (interest received) and on equity securities (dividends received)
Cash outflows:
   To suppliers for inventory
   To employees for services
   To governments for taxes
   To lenders for interest
   To others for expenses
Investing activities
Cash inflows:
   From sale of property, plant and equipment
   From sale of investments (debt or equity instruments of other entities)
   From collection of principal on loans to other entities
Cash outflows:
   To purchase property, plant and equipment
   To purchase investments (debt or equity instruments of other entities)
   To make loans to other entities
Financing activities
Cash inflows:
   From issue of the company's own shares
   From issue of debt (debentures and notes)
Cash outflows:
   To shareholders as dividends
   To redeem (repay) long-term debt
   To buy back the company's own shares
   To lessor as lease payments (finance lease)

Helpful hint 1: Operating activities generally relate to changes in current assets and current liabilities. Investing activities generally relate to changes in investments and non-current assets. Financing activities generally relate to changes in non-current liabilities and equity accounts.

Helpful hint 2: The lease payment to the lessor reduces the lease liability. The interest component is an operating cash outflow.

You may be wondering why interest paid to lenders is classified as an operating cash flow when it is a finance cost. Shouldn't it be classified as cash used by financing activities? This was one of the most controversial issues when accounting standards first required entities to prepare statements of cash flows. Some preparers argued that interest paid to lenders should be a financing cash flow, while others favoured operating cash flows because such interest was an expense. International accounting standard setters give preparers the choice of classification. Interest is classified as an operating cash flow in this text in accordance with the approach taken by most Australian and New Zealand entities.

Significant non-cash activities

Not all of an entity's significant activities involve cash. Here are four examples of significant non-cash activities:

- issue of shares to purchase assets
- conversion of debt, such as convertible notes, into ordinary shares
- issue of debt to purchase assets
- exchanges of property, plant and equipment.

Significant financing and investing activities that do not affect cash are not reported in the body of the statement of cash flows. However, these activities are reported in the notes to the financial statements. The reporting of significant non-cash investing and financing activities of the business (in the notes to the financial statements), together with the investing and financing cash flows (in the body of the statement of cash flows), provides users with a more comprehensive picture of the entity's investing activities and how it has financed them. For example, assume an entity reports inflows of cash from the sale of non-current assets, together with a significant non-cash investment in non-current assets. This could signal increased future cash flows from operations as the entity replaces old assets with new to increase production. Furthermore, if the non-current asset purchases were financed by debt, this indicates that there will be increased outflows of cash in the future to repay interest and loans. Reporting both the cash flows and significant non-cash flows for investing and financing activities together (along with other financial and non-financial information) is helpful when current and potential investors and lenders are deciding whether to provide resources in the form of investments or loans to the entity.

Format of the statement of cash flows

The three activities discussed previously — operating, investing and financing — make up the general format of the statement of cash flows. A widely used form of the statement of cash flows is shown in figure 11.2.

FIGURE 11.2 Format of the statement of cash flows

COMPANY NAME Statement of cash flows Period covered		
CASH FLOWS FROM OPERATING ACTIVITIES		
(List of individual items)	XX	
Net cash provided (used) by operating activities		XXX
CASH FLOWS FROM INVESTING ACTIVITIES		
(List of individual inflows and outflows)	XX	
Net cash provided (used) by investing activities		XXX
CASH FLOWS FROM FINANCING ACTIVITIES		
(List of individual inflows and outflows)	XX	
Net cash provided (used) by financing activities		XXX
Net increase (decrease) in cash		XXX
Cash at beginning of period		XXX
Cash at end of period		XXX

There are two methods of presenting cash provided (used) by operating activities: the direct method and the indirect method. The **direct method** presents cash payments as deductions from cash receipts to determine 'Net cash provided (used) by operating activities'. The cash receipts and payments may be determined by adjusting items in the statement of profit or loss from the accrual basis to the cash basis. The **indirect method** starts with profit and adjusts it for timing differences, non-cash items, and any investing or financing items included in profit, to determine 'Net cash provided (used) by operating activities'. The indirect method reconciles profit to net cash provided (used) by operating activities. Both methods arrive at the same result for 'Net cash provided (used) by operating activities', but differ in the disclosure of items on the face of the statement of cash flows. The direct method is more consistent with the objective of a statement of cash flows because it shows operating cash receipts and payments. Note that the two different methods affect only the operating activities section; the sections of the statement of cash flows pertaining to investing activities and financing activities are not affected by the choice of method for the operating activities section.

International accounting standard IAS 7/AASB 107 *Statement of Cash Flows* encourages entities to use the direct method for published financial statements. The direct method provides information that is helpful to users in their decision-making processes when estimating future cash flows. Both shareholders and lenders are interested in predicting future cash flows as this is an indicator of whether there will be sufficient cash to pay dividends and repay loans in the future. Furthermore, once you review both the direct and indirect methods illustrated below, you will see that the direct method contains information for users that is not available when an entity uses the indirect method.

If an entity uses the direct method, the standard requires a reconciliation of profit and net cash provided (used) by operating activities, i.e. the indirect method, to be disclosed in a note. Accordingly, in this chapter we will use the direct method for preparation of the statement of cash flows and the indirect method for the reconciliation, which is normally disclosed in a note to the statement. It is also important to note that a number of years ago, IAS 1/AASB 101 *Presentation of Financial Statements* was revised. Commencing 1 January 2009, among the changes was a change in terminology for the names of the financial statements. Prior to 1 January 2009 the statement of cash flows was called the cash flow statement. However, while it is mandatory for the new titles to be used in all accounting standards wherever the relevant statements are referred to, it is not mandatory for the financial reports produced in accordance with the standards to change their name. The new title, statement of cash flows, is used throughout this text.

Helpful hint: When an entity uses the direct method for the statement of cash flows, users benefit by having access to the unique information that arises from each method — the direct method reported in the body of the statement and the indirect method in a note to the statement of cash flows.

As illustrated, the section of cash flows from operating activities always appears first, followed by the investing activities and the financing activities sections. Also, the individual inflows and outflows from investing and financing activities are reported separately. Thus, the cash outflow for the purchase of property, plant and equipment is reported separately from the cash inflow from the sale of property, plant and equipment. Similarly, the cash inflow from the issue of debt is reported separately from the cash outflow for the repayment of debt (also referred to as the *redemption* or *retirement* of debt). If an entity does not report the inflows and outflows separately, it will obscure the investing and financing activities of the business and thus make it more difficult for the user to assess future cash flows.

The reported operating, investing and financing activities result in net cash either *provided* or *used* by each activity. The net cash provided or used by each activity is totalled to show the net increase (decrease) in cash for the period. The net increase (decrease) in cash for the period is then added to or subtracted from the beginning-of-period cash balance to obtain the end-of-period cash balance. Profit is not the same as net cash generated by operations. The differences are illustrated by the following results from recent annual reports for the 2019 financial year ($ in millions).

Entity	Profit/(Loss)	Net cash provided by operations
Original Furnishings Limited	$35 900	$79 425
Giorgina's Pizza Limited	21 400	24 885
Artistry Furniture Limited	16 600	18 800
Dovetail Limited	1 672	120

Note that Original Furnishings reported a profit of $35 900 million, but a net cash inflow from operations of $79 425 million. It is also interesting to observe the wide disparity between industries in term of the difference between profit/(loss) and net cash provided by operations.

Usefulness of the statement of cash flows

Many investors believe that 'Cash is cash and everything else is accounting'; that is, cash flow is less susceptible to creative accounting than traditional accounting measures such as profit. Although we suggest that reliance on cash flows to the exclusion of accrual accounting is inappropriate, when users of financial statements are making decisions about allocating their scarce resources, comparing cash from operations with profit can reveal important information that may help users decide whether to invest in, or lend funds to, an entity. The information in a statement of cash flows should help investors, creditors and others evaluate these aspects of the entity's financial position.

Helpful hint: Recall in chapter 1 that multiple sources of information — financial and non-financial — are needed to make sound decisions about resource allocations. These include: ratios, economic and industry data, as well as any other entity-specific information that could have a significant impact on the decision.

1. *The entity's ability to generate future cash flows.* By examining relationships between such items as sales and net cash provided by operating activities, investors, lenders and others can predict the amount, timing and uncertainty of future cash flows better than from accrual-based data.
2. *The entity's ability to pay dividends and meet obligations.* If an entity does not have adequate cash, it cannot pay employees, settle debts or pay dividends. Employees, creditors, shareholders and customers should be particularly interested in this statement because it alone shows the flows of cash in a business. Given an entity must generate sufficient cash flows for investors to receive future dividends as a return on their investment, and sufficient cash flows are needed to repay lenders interest and principal, being able to predict the amount, timing and uncertainty of future cash flows is an important input into the decision-making processes of these users. Recall that liquidity is a measure of the entity's ability to meet its short-term obligations and solvency is its ability to meet long-term obligations.
3. *The reasons for the difference between profit and net cash provided (used) by operating activities.* Profit is important because it provides information on the success or shortcomings of a business. However, some are critical of accrual-based profit because it requires many estimates such as bad debts expense. As a result, the reliability of the amount is often challenged. Such is not the case with cash because if cash is received by the entity in a period or is paid by the entity in that same period it is included in the statement of cash flows for that period. This is regardless of whether the payment is a prepayment rather than an expense or if the receipt of cash is a revenue received in advance rather than a revenue. Note that cash flows could, however, be manipulated by management's choice of timing of the cash payments. Management has less control over the receipts of cash by the entity. Many users of the financial statements want to know the reasons for the difference between profit and net cash provided by operating activities. The indirect method of calculating the cash flows from operating activities is helpful in this regard as you will see later in the chapter.

Helpful hint 1: Review the ratios explored in chapter 1 to refresh your memory and consolidate your understanding of how to measure liquidity and solvency of an entity using accrual-based numbers. Later in the chapter we will explore these same measures using information from the statement of cash flows.

Helpful hint 2: The term cash flow is sometimes used to refer to cash provided by operating activities. However, throughout this text we will use the term cash flow in the generic sense and identify when we are referring specifically to operating cash flows.

4. *The cash investing and financing transactions during the period.* By examining an entity's investing activities and financing activities, a financial statement user can better understand how assets and liabilities increased or decreased during the period.

In summary, the statement of cash flows can provide information that is helpful to shareholders, potential investors, lenders and other creditors when making decisions about the allocation of scare resources. It can provide insights into the following key questions.

- How did cash increase when there was a loss for the period?
- Why were dividends not increased?
- How was the retirement of debt accomplished?
- How much money was borrowed during the year?
- Is operating cash flow greater or less than profit?

LEARNING REFLECTION AND CONSOLIDATION

Review it

1. What is the main purpose of a statement of cash flows?
2. What are the major classifications on the statement of cash flows?
3. What are some examples of significant non-cash activities?
4. Why is the statement of cash flows useful? What key information does it convey?

Do it

During the first week of its existence, Fox Hauling Pty Ltd had these transactions:

1. Issued 100 000 shares for $800 000 cash.
2. Borrowed $200 000 from Castle Bank, signing a 5-year note bearing 8% interest.
3. Purchased two semi-trailers for $170 000 cash.
4. Paid employees $12 000 for salaries and wages.
5. Collected $20 000 cash for services rendered.
   Classify each of these transactions by type of cash flow activity.

Reasoning

All cash flows are classified into three activities for purposes of reporting cash inflows and outflows: operating activities, investing activities and financing activities. Operating activities include the principal revenue-producing activities and activities that are not classified as investing or financing activities. Investing activities include (a) purchasing and disposing of investments and long-term assets using cash and (b) lending money and collecting the loans. Financing activities include (a) obtaining cash from borrowing and repaying the amounts borrowed and (b) obtaining cash from shareholders.

Solution

1. Financing activity; 2. Financing activity; 3. Investing activity; 4. Operating activity; 5. Operating activity

---

11.3 Preparing the statement of cash flows

LEARNING OBJECTIVE 11.3 Prepare a statement of cash flows.

The statement of cash flows is prepared differently from the other basic financial statements. First, it is not prepared from an adjusted trial balance. Because the statement requires detailed information concerning the changes in account balances that occurred between two periods of time, an adjusted trial balance does not provide the data necessary for the statement. Second, the statement of cash flows deals with cash receipts and payments. As a result, the *accrual concept is not used* in the preparation of a statement of cash flows.

In computerised accounting systems, a statement of cash flows may be prepared automatically if cash receipts and payments are entered appropriately. An alternative approach, which is illustrated in this text, is to derive cash flows from information contained in other financial statements.

The information to prepare this statement usually comes from three sources.

1. *Statement of financial position.* Information in this statement indicates the amount of the changes in assets, liabilities and equity from the beginning to the end of the period.

    Helpful hint: A statement of financial position generally provides at least 2 years of data. Hence, the statement indicates changes in assets, liabilities and equity between periods.

2. *Current statement of profit or loss.* Information in this statement helps determine the amount of cash provided or used by operations during the period.

3. *Additional information.* Additional information includes transaction data that are needed to determine how cash was provided or used during the period.

Note that internal reports are used rather than their more aggregated external counterparts when preparing the statement of cash flows.

Recall from previous chapters, that income, expenses, assets and liabilities (except for accounts receivable and accounts payable) are shown net of the GST and the net amount payable to (recoverable from) the tax authority is classified also as a payable (receivable). Please also note that, while the implications of the goods and services tax (GST) have been excluded from this chapter, it is helpful to understand that cash flows are actually included in the statement of cash flows on a gross basis, i.e. cash flows include the GST received or paid. Further, the GST component of cash flows arising from investing and financing activities, which is either recoverable from or payable to the tax office, is classified as operating cash flows. This is reflected in the net payments to suppliers and employees.

Preparing the statement of cash flows from the data sources listed above involves the four steps explained in figure 11.3. First, to see where you are headed, start by identifying the change in cash during the period. Has cash increased or decreased during the year? Second, determine the net cash provided (used) by operating activities. Third, determine the net cash provided (used) by investing activities. Fourth, determine the net cash provided (used) by financing activities.

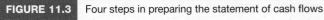

FIGURE 11.3	Four steps in preparing the statement of cash flows

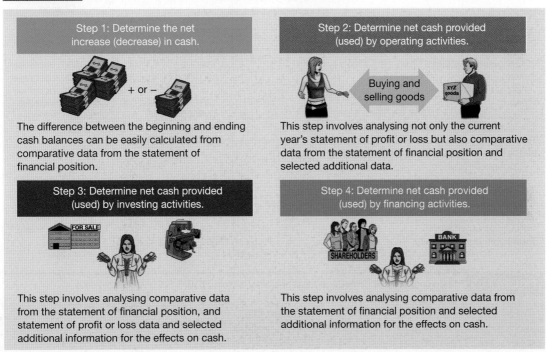

To explain the preparation of a statement of cash flows, we will use the transactions of Pacific Ltd for 2019. The statement of cash flows for 2019 is prepared using the detailed internal statement of profit or loss and statement of financial position and other information. The statement of financial position for 2018 is also used to determine the movement in accounts, such as accounts payable and accounts receivable.

The statement of financial position at the end of 2019 with 2018 comparatives is shown in figure 11.4. The net change in each account is also displayed. The statement of profit or loss for 2019 and additional information for Pacific Ltd are shown in figure 11.5.

Figure 11.6 provides an overview of the different ways to prepare a statement of cash flows. You can use the overview to gain the 'big picture' of the whole process. The details for calculating each amount are provided. Please note that some students may prefer to reconstruct accounts to calculate the cash amounts while others will prefer to use the formulas. Hence, both are provided in this chapter and both will yield the same solution.

Determining the net increase (decrease) in cash (step 1)

The statement of financial position for Pacific Ltd (figure 11.4) shows a cash balance of $159 000 at 30 June 2018, and a cash balance of $191 000 at 30 June 2019. Therefore, the change in cash for 2019 was a net increase of $32 000.

Statement of financial position, 2019, and calculation of the net change in each account

PACIFIC LTD
Statement of financial position
as at 30 June 2019

	2019	2018	Change Increase/decrease	
ASSETS				
Cash	$191 000	$159 000	$ 32 000	increase
Accounts receivable	12 000	15 000	3 000	decrease
Inventory	130 000	160 000	30 000	decrease
Prepaid expenses	6 000	8 000	2 000	decrease
Land	180 000	80 000	100 000	increase
Equipment	160 000	—	160 000	increase
Accumulated depreciation—equipment	(16 000)	—	16 000	increase
Total assets	**$663 000**	**$422 000**		
LIABILITIES AND EQUITY				
Accounts payable	$ 52 000	$ 60 000	$ 8 000	decrease
Accrued expenses payable	15 000	20 000	5 000	decrease
Income tax payable	12 000	—	12 000	increase
Notes payable (non-current)	90 000	—	90 000	increase
Share capital	400 000	300 000	100 000	increase
Retained earnings	94 000	42 000	52 000	increase
Total liabilities and equity	**$663 000**	**$422 000**		

FIGURE 11.5 Statement of profit or loss and additional information, 2019

PACIFIC LTD
Statement of profit or loss
for the year ended 30 June 2019

Revenue from sales		$975 000
Cost of sales	$ 660 000	
Operating expenses (excluding depreciation)	176 000	
Depreciation expense	18 000	
Loss on sale of store equipment	1 000	855 000
Profit before income tax		**120 000**
Income tax expense		36 000
Profit		**$ 84 000**

Additional information:
(a) In 2019 Pacific Ltd declared and paid a $32 000 cash dividend.
(b) Notes were issued at face value for $90 000 in cash. These are a long-term source of borrowing.
(c) Equipment items costing a total of $180 000 were purchased for cash.
(d) One item of equipment was sold for $17 000 cash. The equipment cost $20 000 and had a carrying amount of $18 000.
(e) Ordinary shares of $100 000 were issued to acquire land. The vendor (seller) of the land received the shares in payment for the land.

Determining net cash provided (used) by operating activities (step 2)

Under the direct method, net cash provided by operating activities is calculated by adjusting each item in the statement of profit or loss from the accrual basis to the cash basis. To simplify and condense the operating activities section, only major classes of operating cash receipts and cash payments are reported. The difference between these major classes of cash receipts and cash payments is the net cash provided by operating activities, as shown in figure 11.7.

FIGURE 11.6 Overview: Preparing a statement of cash flows

Information needed: statements of financial position (SOFP), current statement of profit or loss (P/L) and additional information (AI) on transactions that explain how cash was provided or used during the period. **Process**: first draft a template or blank statement of cash flows (SOCF), as in the example given below in the first column and then fill in the amounts as each of the following steps are completed. **Step 1:** Determine the net increase/decrease in cash. **Step 2:** Determine the net cash provided (used) by operating activities. **Step 3:** Determine the net cash provided (used) by investing activities. **Step 4:** Determine the net cash provided (used) by financing activities. Once the information has been used, place a tick (✓) beside each amount. Then review information for any amounts that remain unticked to ensure you have included all cash flows.

PACIFIC LTD **Statement of cash flows** for the year ended 30 June 2019*	**Information used**	**Accounts reconstructed** (*or use the formula illustrated* in the text)
CASH FLOWS FROM OPERATING ACTIVITIES		
Cash receipts from customers[1]	SOFP — Accounts receivable Allowance for doubtful debts P/L — Sales revenue Bad/doubtful debts expense	Accounts receivable Allowance for doubtful debts
Cash payments:		
To suppliers[2]	SOFP — Inventory and accounts payable P/L — Cost of sales	Inventory Accounts payable
For operating expenses[3]	SOFP — Prepaid expenses Accrued expenses payable P/L — Operating expenses (excluding depreciation)	Prepaid expenses and accrued Expenses payable (combined)
For income taxes	SOFP — Income tax payable P/L — Income tax expense	Income tax payable
Net cash provided (used) by operating activities		
CASH FLOWS FROM INVESTING ACTIVITIES		
Purchase of equipment[4]	SOFP — Equipment & accumulated depreciation—equipment	Equipment
Sale of equipment	P/L — Depreciation expense Loss on sale of equipment AI items (c) & (d) (figure 11.5)	Accumulated depreciation— equipment Disposal of equipment
[Land — this item is shown as a note to the statement of cash flows][5]	SOFP — Land and share capital AI item (e) (figure 11.5)	Land Share capital
Net cash provided (used) by investing activities		
CASH FLOWS FROM FINANCING ACTIVITIES		
Issue of notes payable[6]	SOFP and AI item (b) (figure 11.5)	Notes payable
Payment of cash dividends[7]	SOFP and AI item (a) (figure 11.5)	Retained earnings
Net cash provided (used) by financing activities		
Net increase in cash		
Cash at beginning of period[8]	SOFP (figure 11.4)	Cash
Cash at end of period	SOFP (figure 11.4)	Cash

*The title of the SOCF includes the name of the entity, the name of the financial statement and the period covered by the statement.

[1] See heading 'Cash receipts from customers' later in this section.

[2] See heading 'Cash payments to supplies' later in this section.

[3] See heading 'Cash payments for operating expenses' later in this section.

[4] See heading 'Increase in equipment' later in this section.

[5] See heading 'Significant non-cash activities' earlier in section 11.2.

[6] See heading 'Increase in notes payable' later in this section.

[7] See heading 'Increase in retained earnings' later in this section.

[8] See heading 'Determining the net increase (decrease) in cash (step 1)' earlier in this section.

FIGURE 11.7 Major classes of cash receipts and payments

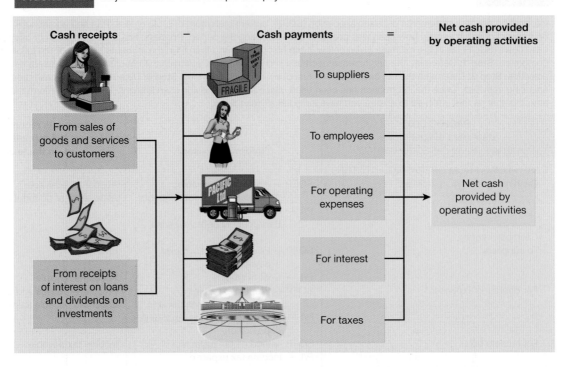

An efficient way to apply the direct method is to analyse the revenues and expenses reported in the statement of profit or loss in the order in which they are listed and then determine cash receipts and cash payments related to these revenues and expenses. The direct method adjustments for Pacific Ltd to determine net cash provided by operating activities in 2019 are presented in the following sections.

Cash receipts from customers

The statement of profit or loss for Pacific Ltd (figure 11.5) reported revenue from sales of $975 000. Revenue includes both cash sales and credit sales. To determine the *cash receipts* from customers, it is necessary to consider the change in accounts receivable during the year. When accounts receivable increase during the year, this means that revenues on an accrual basis are higher than cash receipts from customers. This is because a credit sale results in an increase in accounts receivable (debit) and a corresponding increase in revenue (credit). When accounts receivable increase you can see that revenue has increased but the cash *has not* been received.

In other words, operations led to increased revenues, but not all of these revenues resulted in cash receipts. To determine the amount of cash receipts, the increase in accounts receivable is deducted from sales revenues. This represents the amount of credit sales that have not been collected in cash. Conversely, a decrease in accounts receivable is added to sales revenues because cash receipts from customers then exceed sales revenues.

As a general rule, the effects of the timing differences between recording revenues and expenses under accrual accounting and the recording of cash receipts and payments are found in the current asset and current liability accounts in the statement of financial position.

Pacific Ltd's accounts receivable decreased by $3000. Thus, cash receipts from customers were $978 000, calculated as shown in figure 11.8.

FIGURE 11.8 Calculation of cash receipts from customers

Revenues from sales	$975 000
Add: Decrease in accounts receivable	3 000
Cash receipts from customers	**$978 000**

Cash receipts from customers may also be determined from an analysis of the accounts receivable control account, as shown in figure 11.9. For simplicity, the accounts receivable control account will be referred to as accounts receivable in this chapter.

FIGURE 11.9 Analysis of accounts receivable

Accounts receivable

2018					
July 1	Balance	15 000	**Receipts from customers**		978 000
	Revenue from sales	975 000	June 30 Closing balance		12 000
		990 000			990 000
2019					
July 1	Balance	12 000			

Helpful hint: The statement of financial position provides 2 years of data, indicating the changes in assets, liabilities and equity between periods. When reconstructing accounts, it is helpful to note that the balance reported at the end of one period is the opening balance in the following period. In this example, the closing balance of accounts receivable at 30 June 2018 becomes the opening balance for accounts receivable on 1 July 2018. Hence, the balance of accounts receivable at 30 June 2019 becomes the opening balance for accounts receivable on 1 July 2019. The closing balance goes on the opposite side to the opening balance as shown in figure 11.9, as it is merely a 'balancing' item to make the debit and credit sides of the account equal or 'balance' the account.

Review figure 2.33 in chapter 2 and the related text on how to balance accounts if you need help. This is a crucial skill in supporting your mastery of this topic.

Are all credit entries to accounts receivable for cash receipts? Unfortunately not. Recall from chapter 7 that bad debts are written off by crediting accounts receivable. If the direct write-off method is used, the amount will be easily identified from the statement of profit or loss. If the allowance method is used, the amount of bad debts written off can be determined by reconstructing the allowance for doubtful debts account. Recall that when the allowance method is used, bad debts are written off by debiting allowance for doubtful debts and crediting accounts receivable.

The relationships among cash receipts from customers, revenues from sales, and changes in accounts receivable are shown in figure 11.10.

FIGURE 11.10 Formula to calculate cash receipts from customers

Cash receipts from customers	=	Revenues from sales	{ + Decrease in accounts receivable – bad debts written off or – Increase in accounts receivable – bad debts written off

Helpful hint: The illustration and formula assume that there is no discount allowed for prompt payment of accounts receivable. If the entity allows discounts, they should be included in the reconstruction of accounts receivable to calculate cash receipts.

As illustrated in figure 11.11, the statement adds accounts receivable and sales. The amount owed by customers at the beginning of the year and the sales made during the year represent the amount that could be collected from customers. The amount of accounts receivable uncollected at the end of the year is deducted from the sum of the opening accounts receivable and sales balances, to calculate the amount of cash collected.

FIGURE 11.11 Statement presentation of calculation of cash received from customers

Opening accounts receivable	$ 15 000
+ Sales	975 000
	990 000
− Closing accounts receivable	12 000
= Cash received from customers	$ 978 000

For simplicity, bad debts have been omitted. However, the statement can be modified to incorporate bad debts, as illustrated in figure 11.12.

FIGURE 11.12 Statement presentation of calculation of cash received from customers with bad debts written off

Opening accounts receivable
+ Sales
  Subtotal
− Bad debts written off
− Closing accounts receivable
= Cash received from customers

Now we will look at a more complicated example in which the allowance for doubtful debts account is used. Assume that the following information is extracted from the financial statements of Chocolate Indulgence Ltd:

Accounts receivable at 30 June 2020	$120 debit
Allowance for doubtful debts at 30 June 2020	$15 credit
Sales revenue for the year ended 30 June 2020	$2400
Bad debts expense for the year ended 30 June 2020	$50

Account balances at the end of the previous year, 30 June 2019, were:

Accounts receivable	$100 debit
Allowance for doubtful debts	$10 credit

To calculate the amount of cash received we need to know how much of the accounts receivable has been written off as a bad debt. This is not necessarily the same amount as the bad debts expense when the allowance method is used to account for bad debts. We can reconstruct the allowance for doubtful debts to determine the amount of bad debts written off against it.

Allowance for doubtful debts				
		2019		
Accounts receivable (for bad		July 1	Balance	10
debt written off)	45		Bad debts expense	50
June 30 Closing balance	15			
	60			60
		2020		
		July 1	Balance	15

The amount of bad debts written off against accounts receivable is determined by adding the opening balance of the allowance for doubtful debts and the doubtful debts expense on the credit side of the account and then subtracting the closing balance shown on the debit side of the account, that is, $10 + $50 − $15 = $45.

Having identified the bad debts written off against accounts receivable, we can now calculate the cash collected from customers as follows:

Opening accounts receivable	$ 100
+ Sales	2 400
Sub-total	2 500
− Bad debts written off	(45)
− Closing accounts receivable	(120)
= Cash received from customers	$2 335

Cash payments to suppliers

Pacific Ltd reported cost of sales of $660 000 on its statement of profit or loss. Cash payments to suppliers is determined using a two-step process. First, it is necessary to find purchases for the year and only then can cash paid to suppliers be determined. To find purchases, cost of sales is adjusted for the change in inventory. When inventory increases during the year, it means that purchases this year exceed cost of sales. In other words, the company purchased more inventory than it sold, so the balance of inventory increases. As a result, the increase in inventory is added to cost of sales to arrive at purchases for the period. If the periodic inventory system is used, purchases are shown on the statement of profit or loss.

In 2019, Pacific Ltd's inventory decreased $30 000. This means that cost of sales exceeded purchases. In this case, the company sold all of the inventory purchased during the period *and* it also sold inventory that was available at the beginning of the period (opening inventory) and inventory decreased. Hence, the cost of sales figure includes both the inventory purchased during the current period as well as the sale of inventory that was not purchased during the period, but was available as opening inventory. As a result, to calculate purchases, the decrease in inventory must be subtracted from cost of sales, as shown in figure 11.13.

FIGURE 11.13   Calculation of purchases

Cost of sales	$660 000
Less: Decrease in inventory	30 000
Purchases	$630 000

Second, after purchases are calculated, cash payments to suppliers are determined by adjusting purchases for the change in accounts payable. Purchases can be made for cash or on credit (increase in accounts payable). When accounts payable increase during the year, purchases on an accrual basis are higher than they are on a cash basis; that is, some of the purchases have not been paid for in cash, but are instead still payable. As a result, an increase in accounts payable is deducted from purchases to arrive at cash payments for purchases that have been made to suppliers. Conversely, a decrease in accounts payable (which represents a payment to a supplier) is added to purchases because cash payments to suppliers exceed purchases. In other words, in addition to the cash purchases made during the period, cash outflows occurred to pay off amounts owing on previous purchases (accounts payable). Cash payments to suppliers were $638 000, calculated as in figure 11.14.

| **FIGURE 11.14** | Calculation of cash payments to suppliers |

Purchases	$630 000
Add: Decrease in accounts payable	8 000
Cash payments to suppliers	**$638 000**

Cash payments to suppliers may also be determined from an analysis of the accounts payable account, as shown in figure 11.15. Throughout this chapter we provide practical illustrations for determining cash flows in two ways. First, using a T-account reconstruction as shown in figure 11.15. Second, using a formula to calculate cash payments to suppliers as shown in figure 11.16. You can choose the method that gives you the greatest understanding of how to determine cash inflows and outflows.

| **FIGURE 11.15** | Analysis of accounts payable |

Accounts payable

			2018		
Payments to suppliers	638 000	July 1	Balance		60 000
June 30 Closing balance	52 000		Purchases		630 000
	690 000				690 000
		2019			
		July 1	Balance		52 000

The relationship between cash payments to suppliers, cost of sales, changes in inventory, and changes in accounts payable is shown in the formula in figure 11.16.

| **FIGURE 11.16** | Formula to calculate cash payments to suppliers |

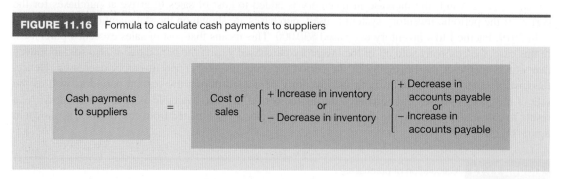

Helpful hint: The illustration and formula assume that the entity has received no discount for prompt payment. A discount, if received, should be included in the reconstruction of accounts payable to calculate cash payments to suppliers. A worked example is provided in demonstration problem 2 at the end of this chapter.

The equation in figure 11.16 can be rearranged and presented as a statement. This is illustrated in figure 11.17. The sum of the closing inventory and the cost of sales is the cost of goods available for sale. Subtracting the opening inventory from the cost of goods available for sale gives the cost of purchases. Purchases do not usually equal cash paid for inventory because purchases are typically made on credit. The purchases are added to the opening accounts payable to determine the total amount owed to suppliers of inventory throughout the year. The closing balance of accounts payable is subtracted from this subtotal to calculate the amount paid to suppliers. In figure 11.17, the total amount owed to suppliers throughout the year is $690 000. Of this amount, $52 000 had not been paid by the end of the year. Thus, the amount that had been paid during the year is $638 000 (i.e. $690 000 − $52 000). As you can see from the figures, the different methods of calculating cash flows produce the same result.

FIGURE 11.17   Statement presentation of calculating cash paid to supplier

Closing inventory	$ 130 000
+ Cost of sales	660 000
= Cost of goods available for sale	790 000
− Opening inventory	160 000
= Purchases	630 000
+ Opening accounts payable	60 000
	690 000
− Closing accounts payable	52 000
= Cash paid to suppliers	$ 638 000

Cash payments for operating expenses

Operating expenses of $176 000 excluding depreciation were reported in Pacific Ltd's statement of profit or loss. Recall that expenses can arise from cash payments or accrual accounting entries. Furthermore, some cash payments are not recorded as expenses, but prepayments. Hence, to determine the cash paid for operating expenses, the amount for operating expenses must be adjusted for any changes in prepaid expenses and accrued expenses payable. For example, when prepaid expenses decreased $2000 during the year, cash paid for operating expenses was $2000 lower than operating expenses reported in the statement of profit or loss. To convert operating expenses to cash payments for operating expenses, the decrease of $2000 must be subtracted from operating expenses as the decrease represents a debit to operating expenses and a credit to prepaid expenses and not a cash outflow. Conversely, if prepaid expenses increase during the year, the increase must be added to operating expenses to calculate cash payments as the increase in prepaid expenses represents a cash outflow.

Operating expenses must also be adjusted for changes in accrued expenses payable. The term accrued expenses payable is used to describe all liability accounts, such as accrued wages, warranty provisions and expenses payable, that arise from accrual accounting. Recall that an accrued expense is recorded as a debit to the expense account and a credit to the corresponding accrued expenses payable account. So, when accrued expenses payable increase during the year, operating expenses on an accrual basis are higher than they are on a cash basis. For example, if accrued wages were $1000 at the beginning of the year and $2000 at the end of the year, the cash payments for wages would include $1000 that was not a current-year expense and exclude $2000 that was a current-year expense. Thus, expenses on an accrual basis would be higher than on a cash basis. As a result, an increase in accrued expenses payable is deducted from operating expenses to arrive at cash payments for operating expenses. Conversely, in the case of Pacific Ltd the decrease in accrued expenses payable of $5000 in 2019 (refer to figure 11.4) is added to operating expenses because cash payments exceed operating expenses.

Pacific Ltd's cash payments for operating expenses were $179 000, calculated as shown in figure 11.18.

FIGURE 11.18   Calculation of cash payments for operating expenses

Operating expenses	$176 000
Deduct: Decrease in prepaid expenses	(2 000)
Add: Decrease in accrued expenses payable	5 000
Cash payments for operating expenses	$179 000

The relationships among cash payments for operating expenses, changes in prepaid expenses, and changes in accrued expenses payable are shown in the formula in figure 11.19.

FIGURE 11.19 Formula to calculate payments for operating expenses

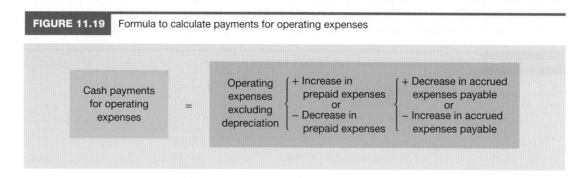

The formula in figure 11.19 can be rearranged and presented as a statement. This is illustrated in figure 11.20. The closing balance of the prepaid expenses account is added to the current period expenses because some cash payments become expenses in the current period and some are prepaid expenses classified as assets. The opening amount of the prepaid expenses account is deducted because it was paid in a previous period. The opening balance of the accrued expenses payable account is added because this is an amount that was paid in the current period but not included in expenses as it relates to the previous period's expenses. The closing balance of the accrued expenses payable account is deducted because it had not been paid by the end of the period.

FIGURE 11.20 Statement presentation of calculation of cash paid for expenses

Closing prepaid expenses	$ 6 000
+ Expenses	176 000
	182 000
− Opening prepaid expenses	8 000
	174 000
+ Opening accrued expenses payable	20 000
	194 000
− Closing accrued expenses payable	15 000
= Cash paid for operating expenses	$179 000

Depreciation expense and loss on sale of equipment

Operating expenses are shown exclusive of depreciation. Depreciation expense in 2019 was $18 000. Depreciation expense is not shown on a statement of cash flows under the direct method because it is a non-cash charge. If the amount for operating expenses includes depreciation expense, operating expenses must be reduced by the amount of depreciation expense to determine cash payments for operating expenses.

The loss on sale of store equipment of $1000 must also be excluded. The loss on the sale of equipment reduces profit, but it does not affect operating cash flows. A gain or loss on the sale of equipment comprises two items: proceeds from the sale, which are included in the investing cash flows; and the carrying amount of the asset sold, which is a non-cash item. Thus, a gain or loss on the sale of equipment is not reported on a statement of cash flows prepared using the direct method.

Other charges to expense that do not require the use of cash, such as the amortisation of intangible assets, leased assets and depletion expense, are treated in the same manner as depreciation.

Cash payments for income tax

Income tax expense reported on the statement of profit or loss was $36 000. Income tax payable, however, increased $12 000, which means that $12 000 of the income tax has not been paid. As a result, income tax paid was less than income tax reported on the statement of profit or loss. Cash payments for income tax were therefore $24 000, as shown in figure 11.21.

FIGURE 11.21	Calculation of cash payments for income tax

Income tax expense	$36 000
Deduct: Increase in income tax payable	12 000
Cash payments for income tax	$24 000

The relationship among cash payments for income tax, income tax expense, and changes in income tax payable are shown in the formula in figure 11.22.

FIGURE 11.22	Formula to calculate cash payments for income tax

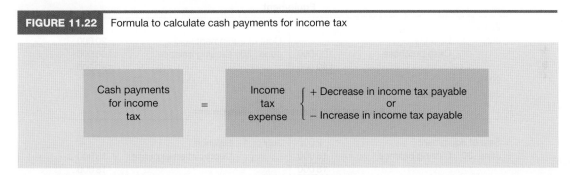

The formula in figure 11.22 can be rearranged and presented as a statement. This is illustrated in figure 11.23. The sum of the opening balance of the income tax payable and income tax expense accounts for the period is the amount of tax paid or payable. To calculate the tax paid during the year, deduct the closing balance of income tax payable because it has not been paid during the year.

FIGURE 11.23	Statement presentation of cash paid for income tax

Opening income tax payable	$ nil
+ Income tax expense	36 000
	36 000
− Closing income tax payable	12 000
= Cash paid for income tax	$24 000

Determining net cash provided (used) by investing activities (step 3)

Increase in land

Land increased $100 000. The additional information indicates that ordinary shares were issued to purchase the land. Although the issue of ordinary shares for land has no effect on cash, it is a significant non-cash investing and financing transaction. This transaction requires disclosure in a separate note to the statement of cash flows.

Increase in equipment

The statement of financial position shows that equipment increased $160 000 in 2019. The additional information in figure 11.5 indicates that the increase resulted from two investing transactions: (1) equipment items costing $180 000 were purchased for cash, and (2) an item of equipment costing $20 000 was sold for $17 000 cash when its carrying amount was $18 000. The relevant data for the statement of cash flows are the cash paid for the purchase and the cash proceeds from the sale. For Pacific Ltd the investing activities section will show purchase of equipment $180 000 as an outflow of cash, and sale of equipment $17 000 as an inflow of cash. The two amounts should *not* be netted; both flows should be shown separately.

While a lot of information was provided in this illustration, often you will need to reconstruct noncurrent asset accounts to determine amounts paid for acquisitions, or other key items needed to calculate cash flows. To assist in this task the equipment account is reconstructed and illustrated. The analysis of the changes in equipment should include the related accumulated depreciation account. These two accounts for Pacific Ltd are shown in figure 11.24.

FIGURE 11.24 | Analysis of equipment and related accumulated depreciation

Equipment

2018						
July	1	Balance	—	Cost of equipment sold		20 000
		Cash purchase	180 000	June 30 Closing balance		160 000
			180 000			180 000
2019						
July	1	Balance	160 000			

Accumulated depreciation—equipment

				2018			
Sale of equipment		2 000		July	1	Balance	—
June 30 Closing balance		16 000				Depreciation expense	18 000
		18 000					18 000
				2019			
				July	1	Balance	16 000

Note that if we didn't know the cost of the equipment purchased, we could have used the equipment account reconstruction to calculate it by adding the cost of equipment sold to the closing balance and then subtracting the opening balance, i.e. $160 000 + $20 000 − $nil = $180 000.

Determining net cash provided (used) by financing activities (step 4)

Increase in notes payable

Notes payable increased $90 000. The additional information in figure 11.5 indicates that notes with a face value of $90 000 were issued for $90 000 cash. The issue of notes is a financing activity. For Pacific Ltd, there is an inflow of cash of $90 000 from the issue of notes.

Increase in ordinary shares

The share capital account increased $100 000. As indicated in the additional information, land was acquired from the issue of ordinary shares. This transaction is a significant non-cash investing and financing transaction that should be reported in a note to the statement of cash flows.

Increase in retained earnings

The net increase in retained earnings of $52 000 resulted from profit of $84 000 and the declaration and payment of a cash dividend of $32 000. Profit is not reported in the statement of cash flows under the direct method. Cash dividends paid of $32 000 are reported in the financing activities section as an outflow of cash.

Completing the statement of cash flows

The statement of cash flows for Pacific Ltd is shown in figure 11.25.

FIGURE 11.25	Statement of cash flows — direct method

PACIFIC LTD Statement of cash flows for the year ended 30 June 2019		
CASH FLOWS FROM OPERATING ACTIVITIES		
Cash receipts from customers		$ 978 000
Cash payments:		
To suppliers	$ 638 000	
For operating expenses	179 000	
For income taxes	24 000	841 000
Net cash provided by operating activities		137 000
CASH FLOWS FROM INVESTING ACTIVITIES		
Purchase of equipment	(180 000)	
Sale of equipment	17 000	
Net cash used by investing activities		(163 000)
CASH FLOWS FROM FINANCING ACTIVITIES		
Issue of notes payable	90 000	
Payment of cash dividends	(32 000)	
Net cash provided by financing activities		58 000
Net increase in cash		32 000
Cash at beginning of period		159 000
Cash at end of period		**$ 191 000**
Note:		
Non-cash investing and financing activities		
Issue of ordinary shares to purchase land		$ 100 000

Helpful hint 1: Although cash payments to suppliers are shown separately from cash payments for operating expenses in figure 11.25, they may be reported as a single line item in a statement of cash flows.

Helpful hint 2: Notice the issue of shares to purchase land is not included in the body of the statement of cash flows but in the notes as it is a significant non-cash activity.

Indirect method for determining cash flows from operating activities

As noted in section 11.2, there are two methods to present the cash flows from the operating activities section in the main statement of cash flows. The presentation of the investing and financing activities sections are the same. Earlier in this chapter we demonstrated the direct method for calculating the operating cash flows. The alternative method is the indirect method, which starts with profit and converts/reconciles it to net cash provided (used) by operating activities. Profit is calculated as income (revenues and gains) less expenses (expenses and losses). Cash flows from operating activities is calculated by subtracting operating cash inflows from operating cash outflows. To reconcile these two figures we need to 'undo' the effects of accrual accounting from profit to arrive at the cash flows from operating activities as illustrated below.

If the direct method is used to calculate the operating cash flows, the reconciliation of profit to cash provided (used) by operations must be disclosed as a note to the statement of cash flows. There are three types of differences between profit and cash provided (used) by operations:
- items that affect reported profit but do not affect cash, such as depreciation

- timing differences arising from accrual accounting, such as changes in accounts receivable
- cash flow items that are included in profit but not classified as operating activities in the statement of cash flows, such as proceeds from the sale of land.

The reconciliation adjusts profit for non-cash items, timing differences and cash flow items that are not classified as operating cash flows. The relationship between profit and net cash provided (used) by operations is illustrated in figure 11.26. Examples of accrual accounting timing differences depicted as adjustments in figure 11.26 are for revenue received in advance and prepayments.

FIGURE 11.26 Profit versus net cash provided (used) by operating activities

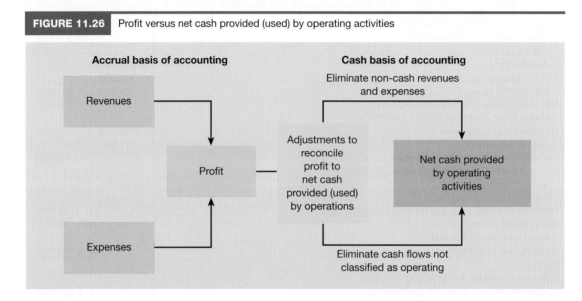

As a general rule, the effect of the timing differences between the recording of revenues and expenses under accrual accounting and the receipts and payments of cash are found in the current asset and current liability accounts in the statement of financial position. Hence, a useful starting place in identifying the adjustments to profit is the current asset and current liability accounts other than cash. Those accounts, such as receivables, payables and inventories, should be analysed for their effects on cash. Some of the adjustments are identical or similar to those made to individual revenue or expense items to determine cash flows displayed in the statement of cash flows using the direct method, illustrated earlier in the chapter.

Change in accounts receivable

Revenue includes both cash sales and credit sales. When accounts receivable increase during the year, this means that revenues on an accrual basis are higher than revenues on a cash basis. In other words, operations of the period led to revenues, but not all of these revenues resulted in an increase in cash; some of the revenues resulted in an increase in accounts receivable. Conversely, when cash collected from customers exceeds revenue during the year, accounts receivable decreases for the cash received.

To determine the amount of cash collected by Pacific Ltd, we need to start with the 2019 revenue for Pacific Ltd of $975 000 and then adjust this amount by the decrease in accounts receivable of $3000. That is, cash collected by Pacific Ltd includes the $975 000 in cash for revenue and a further $3000 for accounts receivable, totalling $978 000 in cash collected (refer also to the analysis of the accounts receivable ledger account in figure 11.9). To convert profit to net cash provided by operating activities, the decrease of $3000 in accounts receivable must be added to profit.

How do bad debt write-offs affect the reconciliation? If the direct write-off method is used, the bad debt expense does not appear in the reconciliation of profit after tax and cash provided (used) by operations. To illustrate, assume that an entity has an opening balance of $10 000 in accounts receivable, generates sales of $110 000, collects $100 000 from debtors, writes off a bad debt of $5000, and thus has a closing accounts receivable balance of $15 000. The effect on profit of those transactions is $105 000, being the sales revenue less the bad debt expense. The cash provided by these transactions is $100 000. The only reconciliation item between profit resulting from the sales and receivables transactions and cash provided by the sales and accounts receivable transactions is the increase in accounts receivable: $105 000 profit less the increase in accounts receivable, $5000 equals cash collected. What happened to the bad debts expense? It was charged against revenue in the calculation of profit, and it was an amount of sales that never resulted in a cash receipt. The bad debt write-off is already reflected in the lower accounts receivable balance at the end of the period; instead of increasing by $10 000, accounts receivable increased by only $5000.

If the allowance method is used, bad debts are written off against the allowance for doubtful debts account, thus reducing the contra accounts receivable account. If the allowance for doubtful debts account has absorbed bad debt write-offs during the period, a greater charge against bad debts expense will be needed to achieve the required credit balance in the allowance for doubtful debts account at the end of the period. The bad debts expense is a non-cash item included in profit. The amount of the bad debts expense reflects the change in the allowance for doubtful debts account plus any bad debts written off against accounts receivable. Thus, the bad debts expense is reflected in the changes in the allowance for doubtful debts and in accounts receivable. The changes in each of these accounts can be included separately in the reconciliation of profit and cash provided (used) by operations. However, as the allowance for doubtful debts account is a contra accounts receivable account, the change in net accounts receivable can be used in the reconciliation of profit and cash provided (used) by operations to reflect the bad debts expense.

Change in inventory

When inventory purchases during the period exceed cost of sales recognised in the statement of profit or loss, the amount of inventory increases. In other words, the entity purchased more inventory than it sold during the period, so the balance of inventory increases. Conversely, when cost of sales is greater than purchases, the amount of inventory decreases. That is, the entity sold more inventory than it purchased, so the balance of inventory decreases (some of the opening inventory is sold). The differences between purchases and cost of sales form part of the reconciliation between profit and net cash provided (used) by operating activities.

To convert profit to net cash provided (used) by operating activities, increases in inventory must be deducted from profit because purchases during the period exceed the expense (cost of sales) included in profit. That is, profit must be decreased to account for the purchase of inventory during the period that is not included in cost of sales. Some of the purchases were sold (cost of sales) and some of the purchases were included in ending inventory. In this way cost of sales does not include all of the purchases for the period and must therefore be deducted from profit in determining the net cash provided (used) by operating activities.

Conversely, decreases in inventory must be added to profit because the expense (cost of sales) included in the calculation of profit not only represents inventory that was purchased, it also includes inventory that was sold out of existing inventory (that is purchased in a previous period). In this case cost of sales is greater than purchases during the period and only payments for inventory in the current period are included as cash outflows. The total cash outflow will be picked up by the net change in inventory and accounts payable, similarly to the two-step process for the direct method explained above.

To illustrate, Pacific Ltd's cost of sales in 2019 were $660 000, and purchases were only $630 000, as illustrated in figure 11.13. The decrease in inventory of $30 000 is added to profit to convert it to net cash provided by operations. Note that in figure 11.13 the decrease in inventory is being subtracted from cost of sales to calculate the amount of purchases.

Differences between purchases during the period and payments for purchases are reflected in the change in accounts payable. Taken together, the adjustments to profit for the change in inventory and the change in accounts payable reflect the difference between the cost of sales expense included in profit and cash paid for purchases of inventory, assuming all accounts payable pertain to the purchase of inventory.

Change in accounts payable

Purchases are typically made on credit terms. Consequently, the amount of cash paid for purchases usually differs from purchases recorded during the period. For Pacific Ltd, purchases for 2019 were $630 000 and payments to suppliers for purchases were $638 000, as shown in figure 11.14. When payments for purchases exceed purchases made during the year, accounts payable decreases as shown in figure 11.15. Conversely, an increase in accounts payable results from purchases exceeding the amount of cash paid for purchases during the period.

To convert profit to net cash provided (used) by operating activities, a decrease in accounts payable should be deducted from profit because it is the amount by which cash payments exceed purchases. Conversely, an increase in accounts payable should be added to profit to convert it to net cash provided (used) by operating activities.

Change in accrued expenses payable

Recall that, under accrual accounting, expenses can be paid in cash or accrued. Accrued expenses payable are treated the same way as accounts payable in the reconciliation of profit to cash provided (used) by operations. Accrued expenses payable increase during a period as a result of expenses exceeding cash payments. That is, expenses are debited and accrued expenses payable credited. Expenses are subtracted from revenues in determining profit; however, when expenses payable increase, then not all expenses are paid in cash. Accordingly, an increase in accrued expenses payable should be added to profit to convert it to net cash provided (used) by operations.

Conversely, when cash payments exceed expenses included in the statement of profit or loss, accrued expenses payable decrease during the period; that is, accrued expenses payable is debited and cash credited. A decrease in accrued expenses payable should be deducted from profit to convert it to net cash provided (used) by operations to account for the cash payment of accrued expenses. For Pacific Ltd, accrued expenses payable decreased by $5000 during 2019. This amount should be deducted from profit to convert it to net cash provided by operations.

Change in prepaid expenses

Prepaid expenses increase during a period because cash paid for expenses is greater than expenses reported on an accrual basis. Conversely, prepaid expenses decrease when expenses exceed cash paid. Cash payments have been made in the current period, but expenses (as charges to the statement of profit or loss) include the decrease in prepaid expenses, as the amounts that were paid in the previous year become current period expenses. To convert profit to net cash provided by operating activities, the decrease of $2000 in prepaid expenses must be added to profit as the decrease in a prepaid expense is not a cash outflow (the entry is a debit to expense and a credit to prepaid expense). An increase in prepaid expenses, on the other hand, means that cash paid for expenses and cash payments that are prepayments exceed the amount recognised as an expense under accrual accounting. Accordingly, an increase in prepaid expenses is deducted from profit to convert it to net cash provided (used) by operating activities.

Change in income tax payable

During 2019 Pacific Ltd's reported income tax payable increased by $12 000. Income tax payable increases during a period as a result of the income tax expense exceeding income tax payments. Conversely, when income tax payments exceed income tax expense, income tax payable decreases. Accordingly, an increase in income tax payable should be added to profit to convert it to net cash provided (used) by operations; and a decrease in income tax payable should be subtracted from profit to convert it to net cash provided (used) by operations. In the Pacific Ltd illustration, the $12 000 increase in income tax payable should be added to profit to convert it to net cash provided by operations.

You may have noticed deferred tax liabilities and deferred tax assets in some of the statements of financial position illustrated in this text or examined in the course of your studies. Deferred tax assets and deferred tax liabilities are reported in the non-current assets section and the non-current liabilities section, respectively. They result from the application of tax-effect accounting, which is usually covered in intermediate and advanced accounting texts. The movements in the deferred tax asset and the deferred tax liability accounts form part of the reconciliation between profit and cash provided (used) by operations. However, in this text, deferred tax asset and deferred tax liability accounts are not used in the illustration of the preparation of the statement of cash flows.

Depreciation expense

During 2019 Pacific Ltd reported depreciation expense of $18 000. The depreciation expense can also be calculated by reconstructing the accumulated depreciation account, as illustrated in figure 11.24. Because depreciation expense is a non-cash charge, it is added back to profit in order to arrive at net cash provided by operating activities. Other charges to expense that do not require the use of cash, such as the amortisation of intangible assets, are treated in the same manner as depreciation.

Gain/loss on the sale of non-current assets

The gain or loss on the sale of a non-current asset has two components: (1) the sale proceeds and (2) the carrying amount of the asset sold. The carrying amount of the asset is a non-cash expense. Although the sale proceeds typically involve the receipt of cash, the sale is classified as an investing activity and not an operating activity. Thus, neither component of the gain or loss on the sale of a non-current asset is included in net cash provided (used) by operating activities.

Since a gain on the sale of a non-current asset increases profit, it should be deducted from profit to convert it to net cash provided (used) by operating activities. Conversely, a loss on the sale of a non-current asset, which reduces profit, should be added to profit to convert it to net cash provided (used) by operating activities.

As a result of the preceding adjustments, Pacific Ltd's net cash provided by operating activities is calculated as $137 000, as shown in figure 11.27. Note that this is the same as the amount of net cash provided by operating activities as calculated using the direct method in figure 11.25.

FIGURE 11.27 Operating activities section of statement of cash flows — indirect method

PACIFIC LTD Statement of cash flows (extract) for the year ended 30 June 2019		
CASH FLOWS FROM OPERATING ACTIVITIES		
Profit		$ 84 000
Adjustments to reconcile profit to net cash provided by operating activities:		
Depreciation expense	$18 000	
Loss on sale of equipment	1 000	
Decrease in accounts receivable	3 000	
Decrease in inventory	30 000	
Decrease in prepaid expenses	2 000	
Decrease in accounts payable	(8 000)	
Decrease in accrued expenses	(5 000)	
Increase in income taxes payable	12 000	53 000
Net cash provided by operating activities		**$137 000**

Summary of indirect method for determining cash flows from operating activities

As shown in the previous illustration, the indirect method starts with profit and adds or deducts items not affecting cash, timing differences and any investing cash flows included in profit to arrive at net cash provided by operating activities. The additions and deductions consist of (1) changes in specific current assets and current liabilities and (2) certain items reported in the statement of profit or loss. A summary of the adjustments for current assets and current liabilities is provided in table 11.1.

TABLE 11.1 Indirect method — adjustments for current assets and current liabilities

Current assets and current liabilities	Adjustments to convert profit to net cash provided by operating activities	
	Add to profit	**Deduct from profit**
Accounts receivable	Decrease	Increase
Inventory	Decrease	Increase
Prepaid expenses	Decrease	Increase
Accounts payable	Increase	Decrease
Accrued expenses payable	Increase	Decrease

Adjustments for items reported in the statement of profit or loss that are non-cash or not classified as operating activities are shown in table 11.2.

TABLE 11.2	Indirect method — adjustments for non-cash items and cash flow items not classified as operating activities	
Non-cash charges	**Adjustments to convert profit to net cash provided by operating activities**	
Depreciation expense	Add	
Patent amortisation expense	Add	
Loss on sale of non-current assets	Add	
Gain on sale of non-current assets	Deduct	

LEARNING REFLECTION AND CONSOLIDATION

Review it

1. What is the format of the operating activities section of the statement of cash flows using the direct method?
2. What is the format of the operating activities section of the statement of cash flows using the indirect method?
3. Why is depreciation expense added to profit in the reconciliation?

Do it

The information below relates to Reynolds Ltd. Use it to prepare a statement of cash flows using the direct method and a reconciliation of profit to cash provided by operating activities.

REYNOLDS LTD Statement of financial position as at 31 December 2019			
	2019	2018	Change Increase/decrease
ASSETS			
Cash	$ 54 000	$ 37 000	$ 17 000 increase
Accounts receivable	68 000	26 000	42 000 increase
Inventories	54 000	—	54 000 increase
Prepaid expenses	4 000	6 000	2 000 decrease
Land	45 000	70 000	25 000 decrease
Buildings	200 000	200 000	—
Accumulated depreciation—buildings	(21 000)	(11 000)	10 000 increase
Equipment	193 000	68 000	125 000 increase
Accumulated depreciation—equipment	(28 000)	(10 000)	18 000 increase
Total assets	**$ 569 000**	**$ 386 000**	
LIABILITIES AND EQUITY			
Accounts payable	$ 23 000	$ 40 000	$ 17 000 decrease
Accrued expenses payable	10 000	—	10 000 increase
Convertible notes payable	110 000	150 000	40 000 decrease
Share capital	220 000	60 000	160 000 increase
Retained earnings	206 000	136 000	70 000 increase
Total liabilities and equity	**$ 569 000**	**$ 386 000**	

Helpful hint: A convertible note is a note payable that may be converted into ordinary shares.

▶

<table>
<tr><td colspan="3">**REYNOLDS LTD**
Statement of profit or loss
for the year ended 31 December 2019</td></tr>
<tr><td>Revenues</td><td></td><td>$890 000</td></tr>
<tr><td>Cost of sales</td><td>$ 465 000</td><td></td></tr>
<tr><td>Operating expenses</td><td>221 000</td><td></td></tr>
<tr><td>Interest expense</td><td>12 000</td><td></td></tr>
<tr><td>Loss on sale of equipment</td><td>2 000</td><td>700 000</td></tr>
<tr><td>**Profit before tax**</td><td></td><td>190 000</td></tr>
<tr><td>Income tax expense</td><td></td><td>65 000</td></tr>
<tr><td>**Profit**</td><td></td><td>$125 000</td></tr>
</table>

Additional information:
(a) Operating expenses include depreciation expense of $33 000.
(b) Land was sold at its carrying amount for cash in 2019.
(c) Cash dividends of $55 000 were declared and paid in 2019.
(d) Interest expense of $12 000 was paid in cash.
(e) During 2019, equipment with a cost of $166 000 was purchased for cash. Equipment with a cost of $41 000 and a carrying amount of $36 000 was sold.
 (f) In 2019, convertible notes of $10 000 were redeemed at their carrying amount for cash; convertible notes of $30 000 were converted into ordinary shares issued at $30 000 in total.
(g) Ordinary shares were issued for $130 000 in cash during 2019.
(h) Accounts payable pertain to inventory suppliers.

Reasoning

The direct method reports cash receipts less cash payments to arrive at net cash provided by operating activities. For clarification, payments to suppliers are shown separately from payments for expenses in the solution. However, they are usually combined in external statements of cash flows. Similarly, the sale of land and the sale of equipment are shown separately in the solution but are usually combined and shown as proceeds from the sale of property, plant and equipment in external statements of cash flows.

Solution

Helpful hint: To prepare the statement of cash flows complete the following steps.
1. *Determine the net increase (decrease) in cash.*
2. *Determine net cash provided (used) by operating activities.*
3. *Determine net cash provided (used) by investing activities. Investing activities generally relate to changes in non-current assets.*
4. *Determine net cash provided (used) by financing activities. Financing activities generally relate to changes in non-current liabilities and equity accounts.*

<table>
<tr><td colspan="3">**REYNOLDS LTD**
Statement of cash flows
for the year ended 31 December 2019</td></tr>
<tr><td>CASH FLOWS FROM OPERATING ACTIVITIES</td><td></td><td></td></tr>
<tr><td>Cash receipts from customers</td><td></td><td>$848 000[a]</td></tr>
<tr><td>*Cash payments:*</td><td></td><td></td></tr>
<tr><td>To suppliers</td><td>$536 000[b]</td><td></td></tr>
<tr><td>For operating expenses</td><td>176 000[c]</td><td></td></tr>
<tr><td>For interest</td><td>12 000</td><td></td></tr>
<tr><td>For income taxes</td><td>65 000</td><td>789 000</td></tr>
<tr><td>Net cash provided by operating activities</td><td></td><td>59 000</td></tr>
</table>

CASH FLOWS FROM INVESTING ACTIVITIES		
Sale of land	25 000	
Sale of equipment	34 000[d]	
Purchase of equipment	(166 000)	
Net cash used by investing activities		(107 000)
CASH FLOWS FROM FINANCING ACTIVITIES		
Redemption of convertible notes	(10 000)	
Issue of ordinary shares	130 000	
Payment of dividends	(55 000)	
Net cash provided by financing activities		65 000
Net increase in cash		17 000
Cash at beginning of period		37 000
Cash at end of period		$ __54 000__

Calculations:

[a]$848 000 = $890 000 – $42 000 (Sales – increase in accounts receivable)

[b]$536 000 = $465 000 + $54 000 + $17 000 (Cost of sales + increase in inventories + decrease in accounts payable)

[c]$176 000 = $221 000 – $33 000 – $2000 – $10 000 (Operating expenses – depreciation expense – decrease in prepaid expenses – increase in accrued expenses payable)

[d]$34 000 = $36 000 – $2000. (The loss of $2000 arose because the carrying amount of the equipment sold exceeded the sale proceeds by $2000.)

Note 1: Non-cash investing and financing activities

Conversion of notes payable into ordinary shares		$ __30 000__

Note 2: Reconciliation of profit to net cash provided by operating activities

Profit		125 000
Adjustments to reconcile profit to net cash provided by operating activities:		
Depreciation expense	$ 33 000	
Increase in accounts receivable	(42 000)	
Increase in inventories	(54 000)	
Decrease in prepaid expenses	2 000	
Decrease in accounts payable	(17 000)	
Increase in accrued expenses payable	10 000	
Loss on sale of equipment	2 000	(66 000)
		$ __59 000__

11.4 Using cash flows to evaluate an entity

LEARNING OBJECTIVE 11.4 Explain the impact of the product life cycle on an entity's cash flows.

Before we can begin an evaluation of an entity we need to understand the impact of the product life cycle on an entity's cash flows.

The entity life cycle

All products go through a series of phases called the *product life cycle*. The phases (in order of their occurrence) are often referred to as the introductory phase, growth phase, maturity phase and decline phase. The introductory phase occurs when the entity is purchasing plant and equipment, and beginning to produce and sell. During the growth phase, the entity is striving to expand its production and sales. In the maturity phase, sales and production level off. And during the decline phase, sales of the product fall due to a weakening in consumer demand. Users of financial statements must consider the entity life cycle when interpreting financial information as it is a key input for their analysis and decision to invest in or lend funds to the entity. Depending on where an entity is in its life cycle will have a significant impact on the cash flow, as explained in detail shortly.

If an entity had only one product and that product was, for example, nearing the end of its saleable life, we would say that the entity was in the decline phase. Entities generally have more than one product, however, and not all of an entity's products are in the same phase of the product life cycle at the same time. We can still characterise an entity as being in one of the four phases if the majority of its products are in a particular phase.

Figure 11.28 shows how the phase an entity is in affects its cash flows. In the *introductory stage*, we expect that the entity will be spending considerable amounts to purchase productive assets, but it will not be generating much (if any) cash from operations. To support its product development and asset purchases, it may have to issue shares or debt. Thus, we expect cash from operations to be negative, cash from investing to be negative, and cash from financing to be positive.

FIGURE 11.28   Impact of product life cycle on cash flows

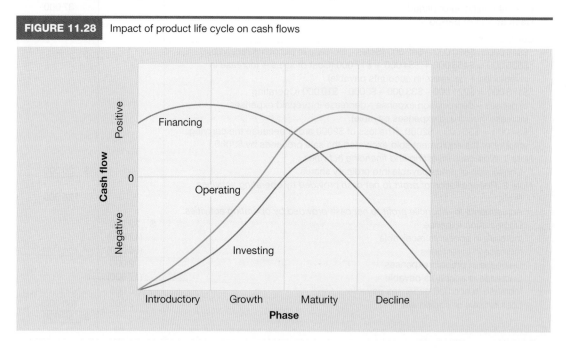

During the *growth phase*, we expect to see the entity start to generate small amounts of cash from operations. Cash from operations continues to be less than profit during this phase, to the extent that inventory must be purchased for future projected sales. Since those sales are projected to be increasing, the size of inventory purchases must usually increase. Thus, less inventory will be expensed on an accrual basis than purchased on a cash basis in the growth phase. Also, collections on accounts receivable will lag behind sales, and because sales are growing, accrual sales during a period will exceed cash collections during that period. Cash needed for asset acquisitions will continue to exceed cash provided by operations, requiring that the entity make up the deficiency by issuing new shares or debt. Thus, the entity continues to show negative cash from investing and positive cash from financing in the growth phase. During the growth phase, entities often do not pay dividends because they need to spend cash on investment in operations. Investors and shareholders need to consider the life cycle of an entity when making investment decisions. When potential investors are interested in short-term returns on their investment, then entities in the introductory or early growth stages are generally not an ideal investment given they are unlikely to pay dividends in the short term. However, entities in the introductory or early growth stages are generally more suitable for potential investors interested in long-term returns, providing these entities continue to grow and prosper in the future.

During the *maturity phase*, cash from operations and profit are approximately the same. Cash generated from operations exceeds investing needs. Thus, in the maturity phase the entity can actually start to retire debt or buy back shares, and pay dividends. A share buy-back is when a company pays an agreed amount to shareholders and cancels the shares. Lenders and creditors need to consider the life cycle of an entity when making lending decisions. Creditors are more likely to be repaid when entities are in the maturity phase and have positive cash flows. Lending to entities in the introductory or early stages of growth is generally more risky.

Finally, during the *decline phase*, cash from operations decreases. Cash from investing might actually become positive as the business sells off excess assets, and cash from financing may be negative as the company buys back shares and retires debt.

Managers need to consider the entity life cycle when planning for and managing cash inflows and outflows of the entity. Consider Microsoft. During its early years it had significant product development costs with little revenue. Microsoft was fortunate in that its agreement with IBM to provide the operating system for IBM PCs gave it an early steady source of cash to support growth. One way it conserved cash was to pay employees with stock options rather than cash. Today Microsoft could best be characterised as being between the growth and maturity phases. Managers of Microsoft need to make many decisions about the strategic direction and day-to-day operations of the business to maintain its success. In the Shareholder Letter in the 2016 annual report, Satya Nadella, Microsoft's CEO, reported that the company had advanced its mission to 'empower every person and every organisation on the planet to achieve more'. During 2016, new product innovations and increased customer usage of cloud platforms and Microsoft packages such as Office 365 and Windows 10 led to revenue of $85 billion, with operating income of $20.2 billion. The company also maintained their commitment to shareholders and returned $26.1 billion to its shareholders through dividends and stock repurchases. Microsoft continues to spend considerable amounts on research and development and investment in new assets. For example, during 2016 the research and development expense was almost $12 billion and the company revealed plans to continue to make significant investments in a broad range of research and development efforts. In the last few years, its cash from operations has exceeded its profit. For Microsoft, as for any large entity, the challenge is to maintain its growth. In the software industry, where products become obsolete very quickly and the competition from Apple is fierce, the challenge is particularly great.

Helpful hint: Remember that the term stock is used to refer to shares in the United States.

Traditionally, to evaluate an entity the ratios most commonly used by investors and creditors have been based on accrual accounting. In this section we introduce you to some cash-based ratios that are gaining increased acceptance among analysts.

11.5 Free cash flow

LEARNING OBJECTIVE 11.5 Use the statement of cash flows to evaluate an entity.

In the statement of cash flows, cash provided by operating activities is intended to indicate the cash-generating capability of the entity. Analysts have noted, however, that net cash provided by operating activities fails to take into account that an entity must invest in new property, plant and equipment just to maintain its current level of operations, and it may need to maintain dividends at current or minimum levels to satisfy investors. **Free cash flow** is the term used to describe the cash from operations available for expansion or the payment of dividends. It is the amount of cash flow from operating activities remaining after deducting investment in capital expenditure necessary to maintain the current level of operations. Alternative definitions are also used. Some analysts define free cash flow as discretionary cash flow and deduct a minimum level of dividends because they are non-discretionary.

According to Telstra's 2017 annual report, free cash flow 'represents the cash that a company is able to generate from its operations after spending money required to maintain or expand its asset base'. Free cash flow generated from operating and investing activities was $3496 million in the year, a significant decrease of 41%. As outlined in the Chairman and CEO's message to shareholders, Telstra's vision for the financial years 2017–19 is 'to be a world class technology company that empowers people to connect'.

It aims to do this by building better customer experiences and connectivity through new and improved products and services. In 2018, Telstra expects free cash flow of between $4.4 billion and $4.9 billion and capital expenditure of around 18% of sales.

Free cash flow is difficult to measure because financial statements do not distinguish between investment expenditure that maintains the current level of operations and investment expenditure incurred for expansion. Respondents to the exposure draft preceding the introduction of an accounting standard for the statement of cash flows argued that free cash flow should not be reported. Two common reasons were: (1) there is not a generally accepted definition of free cash flow, and (2) it is often not possible, due to the rapid developments in technology, to distinguish between capital expenditure incurred to maintain operations and that which expands capacity. Investment expenditure may often both maintain and expand operating capacity. For example, if you replaced your old computer, it would be difficult to do so without upgrading its capacity.

Throughout this text we will adopt the formula shown in figure 11.29 to estimate free cash flow.

FIGURE 11.29 Estimate of free cash flow

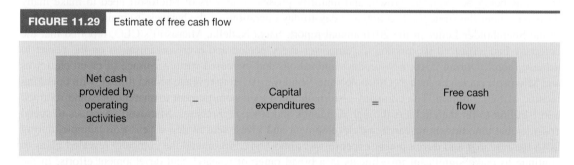

Figure 11.30 provides basic information extracted from the 2019 statement of cash flows of Artistry Furniture Limited.

FIGURE 11.30 Cash flow information

ARTISTRY FURNITURE LIMITED Statement of cash flows (partial) for the year ended 30 June 2019 $'000		
Net cash provided by operating activities		$18 800
CASH FLOWS FROM INVESTING ACTIVITIES		
Additions to property, plant and equipment	$(9 000)	
Net cash used by investing activities		(9 000)
Net cash used by financing activities		(5 600)

Artistry Furniture's free cash flow (again noting that we do not have details to differentiate between amounts spent to maintain the current level of operations and amounts spent to expand production) is calculated as shown in figure 11.31.

FIGURE 11.31 Calculation of free cash flow ($'000)

Net cash provided by operating activities	$18 800
Less: Expenditures on property, plant and equipment	(9 000)
Free cash flow	**$ 9 800**

Free cash flow of $9 800 000 is available for the acquisition of new assets, the retirement of debt, or the payment of dividends. Artistry Furniture chose to use some of its free cash flow to pay dividends.

Using the decision-making toolkit, managers and external users can evaluate the entity's ability to generate cash from its normal operating activities and determine whether this is at an adequate level to finance future expansion and pay dividends to its shareholders. The decision demonstrated looks at the relationship between net cash provided by operating activities and capital expenditure to determine the entity's free cash flow. This figure is of particular interest to managers and shareholders as it provides an indication of the entity's capacity to finance future growth in their business. Both parties would prefer a higher free cash flow as this indicates a greater potential to finance new investments and pay dividends, which, in turn, would have a direct impact on future profits and returns to shareholders.

DECISION-MAKING TOOLKIT

Decision/issue	Info needed for analysis	Tool or technique to use for decision		How to evaluate results to make decision
How much cash did the entity generate to either expand operations or pay dividends?	Net cash provided by operating activities and cash spent on property, plant and equipment (Ideally, the measure would use cash spent to maintain the current level of operations, but that is rarely available.)	$\dfrac{\text{Free}}{\text{cash}} = \dfrac{\text{Net cash provided by operating activities}}{}$	$- \dfrac{\text{Capital expenditures}}{}$	A higher free cash flow indicates a greater potential to finance new investment and pay dividends.

Capital expenditure ratio

Another indicator of an entity's ability to generate sufficient cash to finance the purchase of new property, plant and equipment is the **capital expenditure ratio** — net cash provided by operating activities divided by capital expenditures. This measure is similar to free cash flow, except that free cash flow reveals the amount of cash available for discretionary use by management, whereas the capital expenditure ratio provides a *relative measure* of cash provided by operations compared with cash used for the purchase of productive assets. Amounts spent on capital expenditures are listed in the investing activities section of the statement of cash flows. Using the information from Artistry Furniture's 2019 annual report, as presented in figure 11.30, we can calculate its capital expenditure ratio as shown in figure 11.32.

FIGURE 11.32   Capital expenditure ratio ($'000)

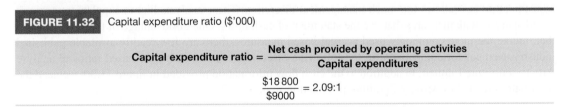

$$\text{Capital expenditure ratio} = \frac{\text{Net cash provided by operating activities}}{\text{Capital expenditures}}$$

$$\frac{\$18\,800}{\$9000} = 2.09{:}1$$

The ratio of 2.09:1 shows that there was $2.09 of net cash provided by operating activities to finance each $1 of capital expenditure. This figure suggests that Artistry Furniture could have purchased more than two times as much property, plant and equipment as it did *without requiring any additional outside financing*. This ratio will vary across industries depending on the capital intensity of the industry. That is, we would expect a manufacturing entity to have a lower ratio (because it has higher capital expenditures) than a software entity, which spends less of its money on non-current assets and more on intellectual capital. The phase of an entity's life cycle will also affect the expected capital expenditure ratio. It is likely to be lower in the introductory and growth phases and higher in the maturity and decline phases.

In deciding whether to invest, potential investors and existing shareholders would be interested in the entity's management and its ability to generate sufficient cash to finance the purchase of new property, plant and equipment. The capital expenditure ratio provides some insight as it compares the net cash provided by operating activities to the investment in capital expenditure. A ratio greater than or equal to one indicates that the entity is generating sufficient cash from its normal operations and there is no need for management to source external financing for capital expenditures. This would be preferable as an entity with a high capital expenditure ratio would be a more attractive investment option as it provides investors with greater confidence in the entity's ability to finance new investments which may lead to an increase in profit and share price in the future. The relevance of this ratio in management and investment decisions is summarised in the decision-making toolkit below.

DECISION-MAKING TOOLKIT

Decision/issue	Info needed for analysis	Tool or technique to use for decision	How to evaluate results to make decision
Can the entity finance its capital expenditures with cash provided by operating activities?	Net cash provided by operating activities and cash spent on property, plant and equipment (capital expenditures)	$\text{Capital expenditure ratio} = \dfrac{\text{Net cash provided by operating activities}}{\text{Capital expenditures}}$	A ratio greater than or equal to 1 indicates no need for outside financing for capital expenditures. It may indicate that the entity is in the mature or declining phase of its life cycle.

Assessing liquidity, solvency and profitability using cash flows

Previous chapters have presented ratios used to analyse an entity's liquidity, solvency and profitability. With the exception of chapter 1, the ratios were calculated using accrual-based numbers from the statement of profit or loss and statement of financial position. Now we explore, in more detail, ratios that are *cash-based* rather than accrual-based, i.e. instead of using numbers from the statement of profit or loss, these ratios use numbers from the statement of cash flows.

Many analysts do not confine their calculations to accrual-based numbers because they feel that the adjustment process allows too much management discretion. These analysts like to supplement accrual-based analysis with measures that use the statement of cash flows. One disadvantage of these measures is that, unlike the more commonly used accrual-based measures, there are few readily available published industry averages for comparison. In the following discussion we use cash flow-based ratios to analyse Artistry Furniture Limited. In addition to the cash flow information provided in figure 11.30, we need the information related to Artistry Furniture provided in figure 11.33.

FIGURE 11.33 Additional data

	2019 $'000	2018 $'000
Current liabilities	29 130	21 250
Total liabilities	39 140	29 080
Sales	135 000	112 000
Profit after tax	16 600	9 450

Liquidity

Liquidity is the ability of an entity to meet its immediate obligations. One measure of liquidity is the *current ratio*: current assets divided by current liabilities. A disadvantage of the current ratio is that it uses year-end balances of current asset and current liability accounts, and these year-end balances may not be representative of the entity's position during most of the year.

A measure that partially corrects this problem is the **current cash debt coverage**, which is the net cash provided by operating activities divided by average current liabilities. Because net cash provided by operating activities involves the entire year rather than a balance at one point in time, it is often considered a better representation of liquidity. The calculation is shown in figure 11.34, using the data for Artistry Furniture Limited for 2019.

Helpful hint: Liquidity is discussed in more detail in chapter 12.

FIGURE 11.34	Current cash debt coverage ($'000)

$$\text{Current cash debt coverage} = \frac{\text{Net cash provided by operating activities}}{\text{Average current liabilities}}$$

$$\frac{\$18\,800}{(\$29\,130 + \$21\,250)/2} = 0.75{:}1$$

Artistry Furniture's current cash debt coverage in 1 year is 0.75:1 or 75%. This ratio indicates that the entity has 75 cents of net cash provided by operating activities to cover each $1 of current liabilities. Artistry Furniture generates enough cash from its operating activities to meet 75% of the obligations that are due within 1 year.

Using the decision-making toolkit below, managers and creditors can use the current cash debt coverage to determine the entity's ability to generate sufficient cash from its operating activities to pay its current liabilities. A higher coverage ratio indicates a higher level of liquidity. This is preferable, as it would provide managers and creditors with greater confidence in the entity's capacity to pay its short-term obligations as they fall due.

DECISION-MAKING TOOLKIT

Decision/issue	Info needed for analysis	Tool or technique to use for decision	How to evaluate results to make decision
Is the entity generating sufficient cash provided by operating activities to meet its current obligations?	Net cash provided by operating activities and average current liabilities	$\text{Current cash debt coverage} = \dfrac{\text{Net cash provided by operating activities}}{\text{Average current liabilities}}$	The higher the current cash debt coverage, the better the liquidity. Since the numerator contains a cash flow measure, it provides a good supplement to the current ratio.

Solvency

Solvency is the ability of an entity to survive over the long term. A measure of solvency that uses cash figures is the **cash debt coverage** which is measured as the net cash provided by operating activities divided by total debt as represented by average total liabilities. This measure indicates an entity's ability to repay its liabilities from cash generated from operations, i.e. without having to liquidate productive assets such as property, plant and equipment. The cash debt coverage for Artistry Furniture for 2019 is given in figure 11.35.

FIGURE 11.35 Cash debt coverage ($'000)

$$\text{Cash debt coverage} = \frac{\text{Net cash provided by operating activities}}{\text{Average total liabilities}}$$

$$\frac{\$18\,800}{(\$39\,140 + \$29\,080)/2} = 0.55{:}1$$

Artistry Furniture's net cash provided by operating activities is 0.55:1 or 55%. This means that the entity has 55 cents net cash provided by operating activities to cover each $1 of average total liabilities. Another way to consider this measure is to look at the reciprocal $(1/0.55 = 1.82)$. It would take Artistry Furniture 1.82 years to repay all of its liabilities from cash provided by operating activities at the current level. Artistry Furniture's reliance on non-current assets has increased substantially in 2019. As the entity's total liabilities have increased at a higher rate than the increase in current liabilities, its cash debt coverage (55%) is significantly lower than its current debt coverage (75%).

Using the decision-making toolkit below, managers and creditors can use the cash debt coverage to determine the entity's ability to generate sufficient cash from its operating activities to pay its total liabilities. A higher coverage ratio indicates a higher level of solvency. This is preferable as it would provide managers and creditors with greater confidence in the entity's capacity to pay its short-term and long-term obligations as they fall due.

DECISION-MAKING TOOLKIT

Decision/issue	Info needed for analysis	Tool or technique to use for decision	How to evaluate results to make decision
Is the entity generating sufficient cash provided by operating activities to cover its total debt?	Net cash provided by operating activities and average total liabilities	$\text{Cash debt coverage} = \dfrac{\text{Net cash provided by operating activities}}{\text{Average total liabilities}}$	The higher the cash debt coverage, the higher the level of solvency, which is the capacity to pay short-term and long-term obligations. The cash debt coverage should be considered in conjunction with the maturity dates of liabilities.

Profitability

Profitability refers to an entity's ability to generate a reasonable return. In chapter 12, accrual-based ratios that measure profitability are discussed, such as gross profit rate, profit margin and return on assets. In measures of profitability the potential differences between cash accounting and accrual accounting are most pronounced. Although some differences are expected because of the difference in the timing of revenue and expense recognition under cash versus accrual accounting, significant differences should be investigated. A cash-based measure of performance is the cash return on sales ratio.

The **cash return on sales ratio** is calculated as net cash provided by operating activities divided by net sales. This ratio indicates the entity's ability to convert sales into cash. The cash return on sales ratio should be compared with the corresponding accrual-based ratio. A lower cash return on sales ratio should be investigated because it might indicate that the entity is recognising sales that will never be collected in cash, or incurring a high level of expenditure relative to revenue. Alternatively, it may reflect payments for increased inventory and other lags occurring in the growth phase. The cash return on sales ratio for Artistry Furniture Limited for 2019 is presented in figure 11.36.

FIGURE 11.36	Cash return on sales ratio ($'000)

$$\text{Cash return on sales ratio} = \frac{\text{Net cash provided by operating activities}}{\text{Net sales}}$$

$$\frac{\$18\,800}{\$135\,000} = 0.14{:}1$$

Artistry Furniture's cash return on sales ratio is 0.14:1 or 14%. This means the entity generates 14 cents in cash for each $1 of sales. This compares favourably with the ratio of its profit to sales ($16\,600\,000/\$135\,000\,000$), which represents a profit margin of 12% for 2019. The cash return on sales is expected to be greater than the profit margin in the long term, because profit includes a charge for depreciation, which is a non-cash expense.

Using the decision-making toolkit below, managers, existing shareholders and potential investors can use the cash return on sales ratio to determine the entity's ability to convert sales into cash. A higher ratio is preferable as it indicates a higher level of efficiency in the entity's management of accounts receivable and overall productivity.

DECISION-MAKING TOOLKIT

Decision/issue	Info needed for analysis	Tool or technique to use for decision	How to evaluate results to make decision
Is the entity efficient in converting sales into cash?	Net cash provided by operating activities and sales	$\text{Cash return on sales ratio} = \dfrac{\text{Net cash provided by operating activities}}{\text{Net sales}}$	Cash return on sales ratio should be compared with the profit margin. Lower cash return on sales ratios or differences over a series of years should be investigated further.

LEARNING REFLECTION AND CONSOLIDATION

Review it

1. What is the difference between cash from operating activities and free cash flow?
2. Why might an analyst want to supplement accrual-based ratios with cash-based ratios?
3. Identify four cash-based ratios that are relevant to the decision-making process.

Designer Decor Ltd (a hypothetical entity) undertook a major expansion in the year ended 30 June 2019. Financial statement data for Designer Decor Ltd are provided below.

Required

Calculate the following cash-based measures for Designer Decor Ltd for 2019 and compare them with those provided for Artistry Furniture.

(a) Capital expenditure ratio.
(b) Current cash debt coverage.
(c) Cash debt coverage.
(d) Cash return on sales ratio.

DESIGNER DECOR LTD
Statement of financial position (partial)
as at 30 June 2019

	2019 ('000)	2018 ('000)
ASSETS		
Current assets	$169 880	$ 80 838
Property, plant and equipment	85 659	40 229
Deferred tax assets	6 401	2 705
Intangible assets	95 586	44 030
Other assets	385	494
Total assets	**$357 911**	**$168 296**
LIABILITIES AND EQUITY		
Current liabilities	$209 144	$ 92 337
Non-current liabilities	69 020	37 660
Total liabilities	278 164	129 997
Equity	79 747	38 299
Total liabilities and equity	**$357 911**	**$168 296**

DESIGNER DECOR LTD
Statement of cash flows (partial)
for the year ended 30 June 2019

	2019 ('000)	2018 ('000)
Net cash provided by operating activities	$ 18 314	$ 19 724
Gross cash used for investing activities	(53 322)	(21 918)
Proceeds from the sale of property, plant and equipment	411	180
Net cash provided by financing activities	49 965	184
Net increase (decrease) in cash	**$ 15 368**	**$ (1 830)**

Designer Decor Ltd's sales revenue for 2019 was $646 734 000.

The comparative data for Artistry Furniture for the year ended 30 June 2019 is presented below.

1. Capital expenditure ratio   2.09:1
2. Current cash debt coverage   0.75:1
3. Cash debt coverage   0.55:1
4. Cash return on sales ratio   0.14:1

Solution

Ratio	Formula	Designer Decor $'000	Artistry Furniture $'000
1. Capital expenditure ratio	Net cash provided by operating activities / Capital expenditures	$\dfrac{\$18\,314}{\$53\,322} = 0.34{:}1$	$\dfrac{\$18\,800}{\$9\,000} = 2.09{:}1$
2. Current cash debt coverage	Net cash provided by operating activities / Average current liabilities	$\dfrac{\$18\,314}{(\$209\,144 + \$92\,337)/2} = 0.12{:}1$	$\dfrac{\$18\,800}{(\$29\,130 + \$21\,250)/2} = 0.75{:}1$
3. Cash debt coverage	Net cash provided by operating activities / Average total liabilities	$\dfrac{\$18\,314}{(\$278\,164 + \$129\,997)/2} = 0.09{:}1$	$\dfrac{\$18\,800}{(\$39\,140 + \$29\,080)/2} = 0.55{:}1$
4. Cash return on sales ratio	Net cash provided by operating activities / Net sales	$\dfrac{\$18\,314}{\$646\,734} = 0.03{:}1$	$\dfrac{\$18\,800}{\$135\,000} = 0.14{:}1$

(a) Designer Decor Ltd's capital expenditure ratio of 0.34 is very low compared to Artistry Furniture's ratio of 2.09. This figure shows that, even though Designer Decor Ltd was able to generate $18 314 000 net cash provided by operating activities, it was not sufficient to cover its significant capital expenditure of $53 322 000. The ratio of 0.34 shows that net cash provided by operating activities financed only 34 cents of each $1 of capital expenditure. Designer Decor Ltd's cash-generating ability relative to its expenditures is significantly lower than Artistry Furniture's. The low capital expenditure ratio for Designer Decor Ltd reflects the significant expansion undertaken in 2019. Note that Designer Decor Ltd's capital expenditure ratio for 2019 was substantially higher at 0.90 ($19 724 000/ $21 918 000).

(b) Designer Decor Ltd's current cash debt coverage of 0.12 indicates that it generates 12 cents of net cash provided by operating activities for each $1 of current liabilities. This coverage is significantly lower than Artistry Furniture's coverage of 0.75 which indicates that Designer Decor Ltd is less liquid than Artistry Furniture.

(c) Designer Decor Ltd's cash debt coverage of 0.09 indicates that it generates 9 cents of net cash provided by operating activities for each $1 of total liabilities. This coverage is significantly lower than Artistry Furniture's coverage of 0.55 which indicates that Designer Decor Ltd is considerably less solvent than Artistry Furniture.

(d) Designer Decor Ltd's cash return on sales ratio is 0.03 which means it converts 3 cents into cash from each $1 of sales. This is very low in comparison to Artistry Furniture's cash return on sales ratio of 0.14. These figures indicate that Artistry Furniture has the greater ability to convert its sales into cash.

SUMMARY

11.1 Indicate the main purpose of the statement of cash flows.

The statement of cash flows provides information about the cash receipts and cash payments of an entity during a period. A secondary objective is to provide information about the operating, investing and financing activities of the entity during the period.

11.2 Distinguish among operating, investing and financing activities.

Operating activities include the principal revenue-generating activities of the entity, and activities that are not classified as investing or financing. Investing activities include the acquisition and disposal of non-current assets. Financing activities are activities that affect the composition of borrowing and equity.

11.3 Prepare a statement of cash flows.

The preparation of the statement of cash flows involves four major steps: (a) determine the net increase or decrease in cash, (b) determine net cash provided (used) by operating activities, (c) determine net cash provided (used) by investing activities and (d) determine net cash provided (used) by financing activities. The direct method reports cash receipts less cash payments to arrive at net cash provided by operating activities. The indirect method reconciles profit to net cash provided (used) by operating activities.

11.4 Explain the impact of the product life cycle on an entity's cash flows.

During the introductory stage, cash provided by operating activities and cash from investing are usually negative, whereas cash from financing is positive. During the growth stage, cash provided by operating activities becomes positive. During the maturity stage, cash provided by operating activities typically exceeds investing needs, so the entity may begin to retire debt. During the decline stage, cash provided by operating activities is reduced, cash from investing may become positive, and more cash is used in financing activities such as retiring debt.

11.5 Use the statement of cash flows to evaluate an entity.

A number of measures can be derived by using information from the statement of cash flows as well as the other required financial statements. Free cash flow indicates the amount of cash an entity generated during the current year that is available for the payment of dividends or for expansion. The capital expenditure ratio (cash provided by operating activities divided by capital expenditures) complements free cash flow by giving a relative indicator of the sufficiency of cash from operations to fund capital expenditures. Liquidity can be measured with the current cash debt coverage (cash provided by operating activities divided by average current liabilities), solvency by the cash debt coverage (cash provided by operating activities divided by average total liabilities), and profitability by the cash return on sales ratio (cash provided by operating activities divided by sales).

The relevance of these four important cash-based ratios in the decision-making process is summarised in the decision-making toolkit below.

DECISION-MAKING TOOLKIT — A SUMMARY

DECISION-MAKING TOOLKIT

Decision/issue	Info needed for analysis	Tool or technique to use for decision	How to evaluate results to make decision
How much cash did the entity generate to either expand operations or pay dividends?	Net cash provided by operating activities and cash spent on property, plant and equipment (Ideally, the measure would use cash spent to maintain the current level of operations, but that is rarely available.)	$\text{Free cash flow} = \text{Net cash provided by operating activities} - \text{Capital expenditures}$	A higher free cash flow indicates a greater potential to finance new investment and pay dividends.

Decision/issue	Info needed for analysis	Tool or technique to use for decision	How to evaluate results to make decision
Can the entity finance its capital expenditures with cash provided by operating activities?	Net cash provided by operating activities and cash spent on property, plant and equipment (capital expenditures)	$$\text{Capital expenditure ratio} = \frac{\text{Net cash provided by operating activities}}{\text{Capital expenditures}}$$	A ratio greater than or equal to 1 indicates no need for outside financing for capital expenditures. It may indicate that the entity is in the mature or declining phase of its life cycle.
Is the entity generating sufficient cash provided by operating activities to meet its current obligations?	Net cash provided by operating activities and average current liabilities	$$\text{Current cash debt coverage} = \frac{\text{Net cash provided by operating activities}}{\text{Average current liabilities}}$$	The higher the current cash debt coverage, the better the liquidity. Since the numerator contains a cash flow measure, it provides a good supplement to the current ratio.
Is the entity generating sufficient cash provided by operating activities to cover its total debt?	Net cash provided by operating activities and average total liabilities	$$\text{Cash debt coverage} = \frac{\text{Net cash provided by operating activities}}{\text{Average total liabilities}}$$	The higher the cash debt coverage, the higher the level of solvency, which is the capacity to pay short-term and long-term obligations. The cash debt coverage should be considered in conjunction with the maturity dates of liabilities.
Is the entity efficient in converting sales into cash?	Net cash provided by operating activities and sales	$$\text{Cash return on sales ratio} = \frac{\text{Net cash provided by operating activities}}{\text{Net sales}}$$	Cash return on sales ratio should be compared with the profit margin. Lower cash return on sales ratios or differences over a series of years should be investigated further.

KEY TERMS

capital expenditure ratio A cash-basis ratio that indicates the extent to which cash provided by operating activities was sufficient to fund capital expenditure (non-current asset) purchases during the year.

cash debt coverage A cash-basis ratio used to evaluate solvency, calculated as net cash provided by operating activities divided by average total liabilities.

cash return on sales ratio A cash-basis ratio used to evaluate profitability, calculated as net cash provided by operating activities divided by net sales.

current cash debt coverage A cash-basis ratio used to evaluate liquidity, calculated as net cash provided by operating activities divided by average current liabilities.

direct method A method of presenting cash payments as deductions from cash receipts to determine net cash provided by operating activities.

financing activities Activities that affect the size and composition of contributed equity and borrowings.

free cash flow Cash provided by operating activities less investments made to maintain the current level of operations.

indirect method A method of preparing a statement of cash flows in which profit is adjusted for timing differences, non-cash items and cash flows classified as investing to determine net cash provided (used) by operating activities.

investing activities The acquisition and disposal of long-term assets.

operating activities The entity's principal revenue-generating activities and activities that are not classified as investing or financing activities.

statement of cash flows A basic financial statement that provides information about the cash receipts and cash payments of an entity during a period, classified as operating, investing and financing activities, in a format that reconciles the beginning and ending cash balances.

DEMONSTRATION PROBLEM 1

The statement of profit or loss for Kosinski Manufacturing Ltd contains the following condensed information:

KOSINSKI MANUFACTURING LTD Statement of profit or loss for the year ended 31 December 2019		
Revenues		$6 583 000
Cost of sales	$4 000 000	
Operating expenses, excluding depreciation	893 000	
Depreciation expense	880 000	
Loss on sale of machinery	27 000	5 800 000
Profit before income tax		**783 000**
Income tax expense		353 000
Profit		**$ 430 000**

Machinery was purchased at a cost of $750 000. The following balances are reported on Kosinski's 2019 statement of financial position at 31 December:

	2019	2018
Cash	$ 672 000	$ 130 000
Accounts receivable	775 000	610 000
Inventories	834 000	867 000
Accounts payable	521 000	501 000
Provision for warranty	103 000	106 000
Machinery	3 020 000	2 400 000
Accumulated depreciation	1 647 000	800 000
Loan payable	1 200 000	1 000 000
Share capital	1 500 000	1 500 000
Retained earnings	330 000	100 000

Required

(a) Prepare the statement of cash flows using the direct method.

(b) Prepare the reconciliation of profit and cash provided by operating activities.

SOLUTION TO DEMONSTRATION PROBLEM 1

(a)

KOSINSKI MANUFACTURING LTD
Statement of cash flows
for the year ended 31 December 2019

CASH FLOWS FROM OPERATING ACTIVITIES		
Cash collections from customers		$ 6 418 000[1]
Cash payments to suppliers and employees		(4 843 000)[2]
Cash payments for income tax		(353 000)[3]
Net cash provided by operating activities		1 222 000
CASH FLOWS FROM INVESTING ACTIVITIES		
Sale of machinery	$ 70 000[4]	
Purchase of machinery	(750 000)	
Net cash used by investing activities		(680 000)
CASH FLOWS FROM FINANCING ACTIVITIES		
Proceeds from borrowing	200 000[5]	
Payment of cash dividends	(200 000)[6]	
Net cash used by financing activities		—
Net increase in cash		542 000
Cash at beginning of period		130 000
Cash at end of period		**$ 672 000**

Direct method calculations

[1]Calculation of cash collections from customers:

Revenues per the statement of profit or loss	$ 6 583 000
Less increase in accounts receivable	(165 000)
Cash collections from customers	$ 6 418 000

[2]Calculation of cash payments to suppliers and employees:

Payments for the purchase of inventory:

Cost of sales	$ 4 000 000	
Less decrease in inventories	(33 000)	
Less increase in accounts payable	(20 000)	
Cash paid to suppliers of merchandise		$ 3 947 000

Payments for operating expenses:

Operating expenses per the statement of profit or loss	893 000	
Add decrease in provision for warranty	3 000	896 000
Cash paid to suppliers and employees		$ 4 843 000

[3]Tax expense equals tax paid because there is neither an opening nor closing income tax liability in 2019.

[4]The sale proceeds of $70 000 are derived by subtracting the loss ($27 000) on disposal from the carrying amount of the machine sold ($97 000). The carrying amount of the machine sold is $97 000 ($130 000 – $33 000). This is determined by reconstructing the accumulated depreciation account and the machinery account as follows:

Machinery

2019				
Jan. 1	Balance	2 400 000	Cost of machine sold	130 000
	Purchased machine	750 000	Closing balance	3 020 000
		3 150 000		3 150 000

Accumulated depreciation

			2019		
Machine sold	33 000		Jan. 1	Balance	800 000
Closing balance	1 647 000			Depreciation expense	880 000
	1 680 000				1 680 000

[5]Increase in loan payable ($1 200 000 – $1 000 000)
[6]Retained earnings 2018 + profit – retained earnings 2019 ($100 000 + $430 000 – $330 000)

(b) Reconciliation of profit to cash provided by operating activities

Profit		$ 430 000
Adjustments to reconcile profit to cash provided by operating activities:		
Depreciation expense	$ 880 000	
Loss on sale of machinery	27 000	
Increase in accounts receivable	(165 000)	
Decrease in inventories	33 000	
Increase in accounts payable	20 000	
Decrease in provision for warranty	(3 000)	792 000
Net cash provided by operating activities		$1 222 000

DEMONSTRATION PROBLEM 2 — COMPREHENSIVE

The following information relates to Kim Ltd.

KIM LTD			
Statement of financial position			
as at 30 June 2019			
	2019 ('000)	2018 ('000)	Change — Increase/(decrease) ('000)
---	---:	---:	---:
Current assets			
Cash	$ 773	$ 340	$433
Accounts receivable	585	625	(40)
Allowance for doubtful debts	(35)	(25)	10
Inventory	550	420	130
Prepaid insurance	35	30	5
	1 908	1 390	
Non-current assets			
Land	1 170	1 100	70
Buildings	1 225	955	270
Accumulated depreciation—buildings	(385)	(350)	(35)
Plant and equipment	942	723	219
Accumulated depreciation—plant and equipment	(430)	(400)	(30)
Patents	65	80	(15)
	2 587	2 108	
Total assets	**$4 495**	**$3 498**	
Current liabilities			
Accounts payable	$ 310	$ 390	(80)
Accrued expenses	130	140	(10)
Interest payable	35	30	5
Income tax payable	450	390	60
Final dividend payable	300	200	100
	1 225	1 150	
Non-current liabilities			
Borrowings	1 100	800	300
Total liabilities	2 325	1 950	
Equity			
Share capital	800	500	300
General reserve	180	250	(70)
Retained earnings	1 190	798	392
Total equity	2 170	1 548	
Total liabilities and equity	**$4 495**	**$3 498**	

KIM LTD		
Statement of profit or loss		
for the year ended 30 June 2019		
('000)		
Sales revenue		$5 040
Gain from sale of land		75
Gain on sale of equipment		30
Discount received		15
		5 160
Less: Expenses		
Cost of sales	$2 565	
Bad debts expense	22	
Depreciation—building	35	
Depreciation—plant and equipment	95	
Insurance expense	80	
Interest expense	110	
Amortisation—patents	15	
Other expenses	766	
Total expenses		3 688
Profit before income tax		**1 472**
Income tax expense		450
Profit for the period		**$1 022**

Additional information:

1. Land with a cost of $50 000 was sold during the year.
2. Land with a cost of $100 000 was acquired during the year in exchange for $100 000 of ordinary shares in Kim Ltd.
3. Equipment with an original cost of $100 000 and accumulated depreciation of $65 000 was sold during the year.
4. There were cash acquisitions of land, buildings, and plant and equipment during the year.
5. A share dividend of $100 000 was paid from retained earnings. An interim cash dividend of $300 000 was paid during the year.
6. During the year $70 000 was transferred from general reserve to Retained Earnings.
7. Accounts payable pertain to inventory suppliers, and during the year $15 000 of settlement discount was received from suppliers.

Required

(a) Prepare a statement of cash flows using the direct method.
(b) Prepare the reconciliation of profit and cash provided by operating activities.

SOLUTION TO DEMONSTRATION PROBLEM 2

Reasoning

The direct method reports cash receipts less cash payments to arrive at net cash provided by operating activities. The sale of land and the sale of equipment are shown separately in the solution but are usually combined and shown as proceeds from the sale of property, plant and equipment in external statements of cash flows.

Refer to figure 11.6 for an overview of how to prepare a statement of cash flows. (*Hint:* As you use each piece of information and figures in the statement of financial position and statement of profit or loss, tick the items off to ensure you do not omit any information.)

Workings (cash flows are in red bold)

1. Cash receipts from customers

Cash	=	Revenue from sales	+	Decrease in accounts receivable	+	Increase in allowance for doubtful debts	–	Bad debts expense
$5 068 000	=	$5 040 000	+	$40 000	+	$10 000	–	$22 000

Reconstruct using T accounts — the advantages of using the T-account reconstructions is that you do not need to memorise formulas. This can be shown by the reconstruction of the accounts below.

First reconstruct the allowance for doubtful debts account to determine the bad debt written off. Then reconstruct the accounts receivable account to determine the cash received from customers.

Helpful hint: The 'o/b' is the opening balance and the 'c/b' is the closing balance. Recall that when we balance accounts, the closing balance is always on the wrong side in order to balance the account. For example, the closing balance in the allowance for doubtful debts account is a debit to balance the account. However, the actual account balance, the one you would see in the trial balance, is a credit. This is reflected in the opening balance for the next period.

Allowance for doubtful debts

Accounts receivable (bad debt write-off)	12 000	Balance o/b	25 000
Balance c/b	35 000	Bad debts expense	22 000
	47 000		47 000
		Balance o/b	35 000

Accounts receivable

Balance o/b	625 000	**Cash**	**5 068 000**
Sales	5 040 000	Allowance for doubtful debts (bad debt write-off)	12 000
		Balance c/b	585 000
	5 665 000		5 665 000
Balance o/b	585 000		

2. Cash payments to suppliers and employees

Need to determine the expenses paid during the year:

Cash	=	Cost of sales	+	Increase in inventory	+	Decrease in accounts payable	–	Discount received
$2 760 000	=	$2 565 000	+	$130 000	+	$80 000	–	$15 000

This can be shown by the reconstruction of the accounts below.

First reconstruct the inventory account to determine purchases. Then reconstruct the accounts payable account to determine cash paid to suppliers.

Inventory

Balance o/b	420 000	Cost of sales	2 565 000
Purchases	2 695 000	Balance c/b	550 000
	3 115 000		3 115 000
Balance o/b	550 000		

Accounts payable

Discount received	15 000	Balance o/b	390 000
Cash	2 760 000	Purchases	2 695 000
Balance c/b	310 000		
	3 085 000		3 085 000
		Balance o/b	310 000

Other payments:

Cash payments for operating expenses	=	Operating expenses excluding depreciation	+	Increase in prepaid expenses	+	Decrease in accrued expenses
$861 000	=	$ 80 000	+	$5 000	+	$10 000
	+	766 000				

This can be shown by the reconstruction of the following accounts.

Prepaid insurance

Balance o/b	30 000	Insurance expense	80 000
Cash	85 000	Balance c/b	35 000
	115 000		115 000
Balance o/b	35 000		

Accrued expenses

Cash	776 000	Balance o/b	140 000
Balance c/b	130 000	Other expenses	766 000
	906 000		906 000
		Balance o/b	130 000

$85 000 + $776 000 = $861 000 total cash expenses other than inventory.
Total paid to suppliers and employees = $2 760 000 + $861 000 = $3 621 000.

3. Interest paid

Cash payments for interest	=	Interest expense	−	Increase in interest payable
$105 000	=	$110 000	−	$5 000

This can be shown by the reconstruction of the account below.

Interest payable

Cash	105 000	Balance o/b	30 000
Balance c/b	35 000	Interest expense	110 000
	140 000		140 000
		Balance o/b	35 000

4. Taxes paid

Cash payments for income tax	=	Income tax expense	−	Increase in income tax payable
$390 000	=	$450 000	−	$60 000

This can be shown by the reconstruction of the account below.

Income tax payable

Cash	390 000	Balance o/b	390 000
Balance c/b	450 000	Profit or loss	450 000
	840 000		840 000
		Balance o/b	450 000

5. After reviewing the additional information, determine the movement in retained earnings to determine the dividend declared and the transfers from retained earnings to other equity accounts.

The additional information indicates $70 000 was transferred to retained earnings from general reserve and that there was a share dividend of $100 000.

Cash dividend declared	=	Profit	−	Increase in retained earnings	+	Transfer from general reserve	−	Share dividend
$600 000	=	$1 022 000	−	$392 000	+	$70 000	−	$100 000

The cash dividend declared is used to determine the cash dividend paid (see item 6 below).

Cash flows from equity can be from the issue of share capital. During the year share capital increased by $300 000.

The additional information reveals that $100 000 in shares was issued to fund the purchases of land (item 7) and that there was a share dividend of $100 000 (out of retained earnings). Therefore, only $100 000 ($300 000 − $100 000 − $100 000) was a cash share issue.

This can be shown by the reconstruction of the accounts below.

Share capital

Balance c/b	800 000	Balance o/b	500 000
		Land	100 000
		Share dividend	100 000
		Cash	100 000
	800 000		800 000
		Balance o/b	800 000

Retained earnings

Share dividend	100 000	Balance o/b	798 000
Dividend declared	600 000	General reserve	70 000
Balance c/b	1 190 000	Profit	1 022 000
	1 890 000		1 890 000
		Balance o/b	1 190 000

6. Financing cash flows from liabilities

From the movement in retained earnings (item 5 above), dividends declared were $600 000.

Cash dividend paid	=	Dividend declared	−	Increase in dividend payable
$500 000	=	$600 000	−	$100 000

The increase in borrowings of **$300 000** is a cash inflow. The additional information does not indicate there were any other transactions involving borrowings.

This can be shown by the reconstruction of the accounts below.

Dividend payable

Cash	500 000	Balance o/b	200 000
Balance c/b	300 000	Dividends declared	600 000
	800 000		800 000
		Balance o/b	300 000

Borrowings

Balance c/b	1 100 000	Balance o/b	800 000
		Cash	300 000
	1 100 000		1 100 000
		Balance o/b	1 100 000

7. Cash flows from investing activities

Returning to the non-current assets section of the statement of financial position we can determine the cash flows from investing activities using the additional information and the information in the statement of profit or loss.

The additional information indicates that ordinary shares were issued to purchase the land (see item 5). Although the issue of ordinary shares for land has no effect on cash, it is a significant non-cash investing and financing transaction. This transaction requires disclosure in a separate note to the statement of cash flows.

The additional information also indicates that land was sold. The land had an original cost of $50 000 and the statement of profit or loss shows a gain of $75 000. This means that proceeds were **$125 000** (gain = proceeds − cost).

(a)

Cash purchases of land		Increase in land	−	Non-cash purchase (by share issue)	+	Disposal
$20 000	=	$70 000	−	$100 000	+	$50 000

The gain on sale of land was $75 000 and in the additional information the land sold cost $50 000, so the proceeds are $125 000 (gain = proceeds − cost).

(b) The movement in patents is the amortisation, which is not a cash outflow. This can be shown by the reconstruction of the asset accounts below.

Land

Balance o/b	1 100 000	Disposal	50 000
Shares	100 000	Balance c/b	1 170 000
Cash	20 000		
	1 220 000		1 220 000
Balance o/b	1 170 000		

Patents

Balance o/b	80 000	Amortisation expense	15 000
		Balance c/b	65 000
	80 000		80 000
Balance o/b	65 000		

(c) There is no additional information concerning the buildings. The statement of profit or loss reflects depreciation expense of $35 000.

The net increase in buildings of $270 000 is a cash outflow. The increase in the accumulated depreciation—building account is the depreciation charge in the statement of profit or loss.

This can be shown by the reconstruction of the accounts below.

Buildings

Balance o/b	955 000	Balance c/b	1 225 000
Cash	270 000		
	1 225 000		1 225 000
Balance o/b	1 225 000		

Accumulated depreciation—buildings

Balance c/b	385 000	Balance o/b	350 000
		Depreciation expense	35 000
	385 000		385 000
		Balance o/b	385 000

(d) The additional information reveals that equipment with a carrying value of $35 000 (cost of $100 000 and accumulated depreciation of $65 000) was sold during the year. The statement of profit or loss reveals a gain of $30 000, which means the proceeds were **$65 000** (gain = proceeds − carrying value).

Cash purchases	=	Increase in plant and equipment	+	Disposal
$319 000	=	$219 000	+	$100 000
Net increase in accumulated depreciation	=	Depreciation expense	−	Disposal
$30 000	=	$95 000	−	$65 000

This can be shown by the reconstruction of the accounts below.

Plant and equipment

Balance o/b	723 000	Disposal	100 000
Cash	319 000	Balance c/b	942 000
	1 042 000		1 042 000
Balance o/b	942 000		

Accumulated depreciation—plant and equipment

Disposal	65 000	Balance o/b	400 000
Balance c/b	430 000	Depreciation expense	95 000
	495 000		495 000
		Balance o/b	430 000

Now all the movements in the statement of financial position have been ticked off, all the bold figures can be listed in the following statement of cash flows.

<table>
<tr><td colspan="3" align="center">**KIM LTD**
Statement of cash flows
for the year ended 30 June 2019
('000)</td></tr>
<tr><td>CASH FLOWS FROM OPERATING ACTIVITIES</td><td></td><td></td></tr>
<tr><td>Receipts from customers</td><td>$ 5 068</td><td></td></tr>
<tr><td>Payments to suppliers and employees</td><td>(3 621)</td><td></td></tr>
<tr><td>Interest paid</td><td>(105)</td><td></td></tr>
<tr><td>Income tax paid</td><td>(390)</td><td></td></tr>
<tr><td>Net cash provided by operating activities</td><td></td><td>$ 952</td></tr>
<tr><td>CASH FLOWS FROM INVESTING ACTIVITIES</td><td></td><td></td></tr>
<tr><td>Purchase of land</td><td>(20)</td><td></td></tr>
<tr><td>Purchase of building</td><td>(270)</td><td></td></tr>
<tr><td>Purchase of plant and equipment</td><td>(319)</td><td></td></tr>
<tr><td>Proceeds from sale of equipment</td><td>65</td><td></td></tr>
<tr><td>Proceeds from sale of land</td><td>125</td><td></td></tr>
<tr><td>Net cash outflow from investing activities</td><td></td><td>(419)</td></tr>
<tr><td>CASH FLOWS FROM FINANCING ACTIVITIES</td><td></td><td></td></tr>
<tr><td>Proceeds from issue of shares</td><td>100</td><td></td></tr>
<tr><td>Cash from borrowings</td><td>300</td><td></td></tr>
<tr><td>Dividends paid</td><td>(500)</td><td></td></tr>
<tr><td>Net cash from financing activities</td><td></td><td>(100)</td></tr>
<tr><td>Net increase in cash held</td><td></td><td>433</td></tr>
<tr><td>Cash at the beginning of the financial year</td><td></td><td>340</td></tr>
<tr><td>**Cash at the end of the financial year**</td><td></td><td>$ 773</td></tr>
<tr><td>*Note 1: Non-cash investing and financing activities*</td><td></td><td></td></tr>
<tr><td>Purchase of land by the issue of ordinary shares</td><td></td><td>100 000</td></tr>
<tr><td colspan="3">*Note 2: Reconciliation of profit to net cash provided by operating activities*</td></tr>
<tr><td></td><td>$'000</td><td>$'000</td></tr>
<tr><td>Profit</td><td></td><td>1 022</td></tr>
<tr><td>Adjustments to reconcile profit to net cash provided by operating activities:</td><td></td><td></td></tr>
<tr><td>Gain from sale of land</td><td>(75)</td><td></td></tr>
<tr><td>Gain on sale of equipment</td><td>(30)</td><td></td></tr>
<tr><td>Depreciation expense—building</td><td>35</td><td></td></tr>
<tr><td>Depreciation expense—plant and equipment</td><td>95</td><td></td></tr>
<tr><td>Amortisation—patents</td><td>15</td><td></td></tr>
<tr><td>Decrease in accounts receivable (net)</td><td>50</td><td></td></tr>
<tr><td>Increase in inventory</td><td>(130)</td><td></td></tr>
<tr><td>Increase in prepaid insurance</td><td>(5)</td><td></td></tr>
<tr><td>Decrease in accounts payable</td><td>(80)</td><td></td></tr>
<tr><td>Decrease in accrued expenses</td><td>(10)</td><td></td></tr>
<tr><td>Increase in interest payable</td><td>5</td><td></td></tr>
<tr><td>Increase in income tax payable</td><td>60</td><td>(70)</td></tr>
<tr><td></td><td></td><td>952</td></tr>
</table>

SELF-STUDY QUESTIONS

11.1 Which of the following is *incorrect* about the statement of cash flows? **LO1**
  (a) It is the third basic financial statement.
  (b) It provides information about cash receipts and cash payments of an entity during a period.
  (c) It reconciles the ending cash account balance to the balance as per the bank statement.
  (d) It provides information about the operating, investing and financing activities of the business.
11.2 Which of the following is not a non-cash activity? **LO2**
  (a) Issue of shares to purchase assets.
  (b) Issue of debt to purchase assets.

(c) Payment of cash dividends.

(d) Exchange of property, plant and equipment.

11.3 Which is an example of a cash flow from an operating activity?   **LO2**

(a) Payment of wages.

(b) Receipt of cash from the issue of shares.

(c) Payment of cash dividends to the company's shareholders.

(d) None of the above.

11.4 Which is an example of a cash flow from an investing activity?   **LO2**

(a) Receipt of cash from the issue of debentures.

(b) Payment of dividends.

(c) Receipt of cash from the sale of equipment.

(d) Payment of cash to suppliers for inventory.

11.5 Cash dividends paid to shareholders are classified on the statement of cash flows as: **LO2**

(a) operating activities.

(b) investing activities.

(c) a combination of (a) and (b).

(d) financing activities.

11.6 Which is an example of a cash flow from a financing activity?   **LO2**

(a) Receipt of cash from sale of land.

(b) Issue of debt for cash.

(c) Purchase of equipment for cash.

(d) None of the above.

11.7 The beginning balance in accounts receivable is $44 000, the ending balance is $42 000, and sales during the period are $129 000. What are cash receipts from customers, assuming no bad debts or discounts allowed?   **LO3**

(a) $127 000.

(b) $129 000.

(c) $131 000.

(d) $141 000.

11.8 Which of the following items is reported on a statement of cash flows prepared using the direct method?   **LO3**

(a) Bad debts expense.

(b) Increase in accounts receivable.

(c) Depreciation expense.

(d) Cash payments to suppliers.

11.9 Profit is $132 000, accounts payable increased $10 000 during the year, inventory decreased $6000 during the year, and accounts receivable increased $12 000 during the year. Using the indirect method, what is net cash provided by operations?   **LO3**

(a) $104 000.

(b) $116 000.

(c) $124 000.

(d) $136 000.

11.10 Non-cash charges that are added back to profit in determining cash provided by operations under the indirect method do *not* include: **LO3**

(a) depreciation expense.

(b) an increase in inventory.

(c) amortisation expense.

(d) loss on sale of equipment.

11.11 During the introductory phase of an entity's life cycle, one would normally expect to see: **LO4**
    (a) negative cash from operations, negative cash from investing, and positive cash from financing.
    (b) negative cash from operations, positive cash from investing, and positive cash from financing.
    (c) positive cash from operations, negative cash from investing, and negative cash from financing.
    (d) positive cash from operations, negative cash from investing, and positive cash from financing.

11.12 During the growth phase of an entity's life cycle, you would normally expect to see: **LO4**
    (a) negative cash from operations, positive cash from investing, and positive cash from financing.
    (b) negative cash from operations, negative cash from investing, and positive cash from financing.
    (c) positive cash from operations, negative cash from investing, and negative cash from financing.
    (d) positive cash from operations, negative cash from investing, and positive cash from financing.

11.13 The statement of cash flows should *not* be used to evaluate an entity's ability to: **LO5**
    (a) earn profit.
    (b) generate future cash flows.
    (c) pay dividends.
    (d) meet obligations.

11.14 Free cash flow provides an indication of a company's ability to: **LO5**
    (a) generate profit.
    (b) generate cash to pay dividends.
    (c) generate cash to expand investment.
    (d) both (b) and (c).

11.15 Which of the following provides a useful comparison with the profit margin?   **LO5**
    (a) Capital expenditure ratio.
    (b) Cash return on sales ratio.
    (c) Cash debt coverage.
    (d) Current cash debt coverage.

QUESTIONS

11.1 What questions about cash are answered by the statement of cash flows?

11.2 Distinguish among the three activities reported in the statement of cash flows.

11.3 Why is it important to disclose certain non-cash transactions? How should they be disclosed?

11.4 (a) What are the phases of the life cycle of an entity?
    (b) What effect does each phase have on the amounts reported in a statement of cash flows?

11.5 Contrast the advantages and disadvantages of the direct and indirect methods of reporting on cash flows from operating activities.

11.6 Cameron's Cars reported sales of $2 million for 2018. Accounts receivable increased $200 000 and accounts payable increased $400 000. Calculate cash receipts from customers, assuming that the receivable and payable transactions related to operations.

11.7 The managing director of Fancy Fashion Pty Ltd is puzzled. During the last year, the entity experienced a loss for the period of $800 000, yet its cash increased $300 000 during the same period of time. Explain to the managing director how this could occur.

11.8 Identify five items that form part of the reconciliation of profit and net cash provided by operating activities.

11.9 During 2018, Pencils and More Ltd purchased equipment but paid for it with the issue of 2 million $1 ordinary shares. Indicate how the transaction would be reported in a statement of cash flows, if at all.

11.10 Give an example of a cash-based ratio to measure these characteristics of an entity:
    (a) liquidity
    (b) solvency
    (c) profitability.

BRIEF EXERCISES

BE11.1 Indicate statement presentation of selected transactions.   **LO2**

Each of these items must be considered in preparing a statement of cash flows for Vong's Thongs Ltd for the year ended 30 June 2018. For each item, state how it should be classified in the statement of cash flows for 2018.

(a) Issued unsecured notes for $100 000 cash.

(b) Purchased land for $75 000 cash.

(c) Sold land costing $10 000 for $10 000 cash.

(d) Declared and paid a $25 000 cash dividend.

BE11.2 Identify financing activity transactions.   **LO2**

The following T account is a summary of the cash account of King Fisheries Pty Ltd.

Cash (summary form)

2018			
Balance, 1 Jan.	8 000	Payments for goods	180 000
Receipts from customers	264 000	Payments for operating expenses	140 000
Dividends received	6 000	Interest paid	30 000
Proceeds from sale of equipment	36 000	Taxes paid	8 000
Proceeds from issue of debentures	200 000	Dividends paid	40 000
		Balance, 31 Dec.	116 000
	514 000		514 000
2019			
Balance, 1 Jan.	116 000		

What amount of net cash provided (used) by financing activities should be reported in the statement of cash flows?

BE11.3 Calculate receipts from customers.   **LO3**

Cheong's Chinese Herbs Ltd has accounts receivable of $14 000 at 1 July 2018, and $24 000 at 30 June 2019. Sales revenues were $600 000 for 2019. Bad debts written off directly against accounts receivable were $2000 in 2019. What is the amount of cash receipts from customers in 2019?

BE11.4 Calculate cash payments for operating expenses — direct method.   **LO3**

Pete's Pies Ltd reports operating expenses of $216 000 excluding depreciation expense of $18 000 for 2018. During the year prepaid expenses decreased $7920 and accrued expenses payable increased $5280. Calculate the cash payments for operating expenses in 2018.

BE11.5 Calculate net cash provided by operating activities — indirect method.   **LO3**

Rotorua Rides Ltd's profit for the year is $200 000. The comparative statement of financial position shows these changes in non-cash current asset accounts: Accounts receivable decrease $80 000, Prepaid expenses increase $12 000, and Inventories increase $30 000. Reconcile net cash provided by operating activities to profit.

BE11.6 Determine cash received from sale of equipment.   **LO3**

The T accounts for equipment and the related accumulated depreciation for Lau Pty Ltd at the end of 2018 are shown here.

Equipment				Accumulated depreciation			
2018						2018	
Op. bal.	225 000	Disposals	33 000	Disposals	9 000	Op. bal.	54 000
Acquisitions	62 400	Clos. bal.	254 400	Clos. bal.	63 000	Dep'n	18 000
	287 400		287 400		72 000		72 000
2019						2019	
Op. bal.	254 400					Op. bal.	63 000

In addition, Lau Pty Ltd's statement of profit or loss reported a gain on the sale of equipment of $4500. What amount was reported on the statement of cash flows as 'cash flow from sale of equipment'?

BE11.7 Answer questions related to the phases of product life cycle.   **LO4**

(a) Why is cash from operations likely to be lower than reported profit during the growth phase?

(b) Why is cash from investing often positive during the late maturity phase and during the decline phase?

(c) Why is cash from financing often positive during introductory and growth phases?

EXERCISES

E11.1 Classify transactions by type of activity.   **LO2**

Wilderness Equipment Ltd had these transactions during 2018:

(a) Purchased a machine for $37 500, giving a long-term note in exchange.

(b) Issued ordinary shares for $62 500 in cash.

(c) Collected $20 000 of accounts receivable.

(d) Declared and paid a cash dividend of $31 250.

(e) Sold a long-term investment with a cost of $18 750 for $18 750 cash.

(f) Convertible notes with a carrying amount of $250 000 were converted to ordinary shares at $250 000.

(g) Paid $22 500 on accounts payable.

Required

(a) Analyse the above transactions and indicate whether each transaction resulted in a cash flow from operating activities, investing activities or financing activities, or was a non-cash investing and financing activity.

(b) What are the differences between operating, investing and financing activities?

E11.2 Prepare the operating activities section — indirect method.   **LO3**

Madonna Ltd reported profit of $200 000 for 2018. Madonna Ltd also reported depreciation expense of $35 000 and a loss of $5000 on the sale of equipment. The statement of financial position shows an increase in accounts receivable of $15 000 for the year, an $8000 increase in accounts payable, and a $5000 increase in prepaid expenses.

Required

Prepare the operating activities section of the statement of cash flows using the indirect method.

E11.3 Identify phases of product life cycle.   **LO4**

The information in the following table is from the statement of cash flows for an entity at four different points in time (A, B, C and D). Negative values are presented in parentheses.

| | Point in time | | | |
	A	B	C	D
Cash provided by operations	$100 000	$ 30 000	$ 60 000	$ 10 000
Cash provided by investing	30 000	50 000	(100 000)	(40 000)
Cash provided by financing	(50 000)	(110 000)	70 000	120 000
Profit	100 000	40 000	(40 000)	(5 000)

Required

For each point in time, state whether the entity is most likely to be in the introductory phase, growth phase, maturity phase or decline phase. In each case explain your choice.

E11.4 Prepare a statement of cash flows (direct method), and calculate cash-based ratios.   **LO3, 5**

Here is a statement of financial position for Big Bang Balloons Pty Ltd:

BIG BANG BALLOONS PTY LTD Statement of financial position as at 30 June 2018		
	2018	2017
ASSETS		
Cash	$ 72 000	$ 26 400
Accounts receivable	102 000	91 200
Inventories	216 000	226 800
Land	90 000	120 000
Equipment	312 000	240 000
Accumulated depreciation	(79 200)	(50 400)
Total assets	**$712 800**	**$654 000**
LIABILITIES AND EQUITY		
Accounts payable	$ 40 800	$ 56 400
Notes payable (long term)	180 000	240 000
Share capital	256 800	196 800
Retained earnings	235 200	160 800
Total liabilities and equity	**$712 800**	**$654 000**

Additional information:
1. Profit for 2018 was $126 000. Total expenses were $1 047 600 and included cost of sales expense $633 600, interest paid $18 000, and tax expense $54 000.
2. Cash dividends of $51 600 were declared and paid.
3. Notes payable amounting to $60 000 were redeemed for cash $60 000.
4. Ordinary shares were issued for $60 000 cash.
5. Sales for 2018 were $1 173 600.
6. Land was sold at cost.

Required
(a) Prepare a statement of cash flows for 2018 using the direct method.
(b) Calculate these cash-basis ratios and comment on the cash adequacy indicated by the calculations:
    1. current cash debt coverage
    2. cash return on sales
    3. cash debt coverage.

E11.5 Classify transactions by type of activity.   **LO2**

An analysis of the statement of financial position, the current year's statement of profit or loss, and the general ledger accounts of Simpson Ltd uncovered the following items. Assume all items involve cash unless there is information to the contrary.
(a) Purchase of plant and equipment
(b) Payment of dividends
(c) Sale of building
(d) Exchange of land for patent
(e) Depreciation
(f) Redemption of debentures
(g) Receipt of interest on notes receivable
(h) Issue of ordinary shares
(i) Amortisation of patent
(j) Issue of unsecured notes
(k) Payment of interest on overdraft

(l) Conversion of notes into ordinary shares

(m) Sale of land

(n) Receipt of dividends on investment in Telstra shares

Required

Indicate how each item should be classified in the statement of cash flows using these four major classifications: operating activity, investing activity, financing activity, and non-cash investing and financing activity.

E11.6 Calculate cash provided by operating activities — direct method.   **LO3**

Christchurch Motors Pty Ltd completed its first year of operations on 30 June 2018. Its statement of profit or loss showed that the business had revenues of $170 000 and operating expenses of $80 000 including bad debts expense of $1000. Accounts receivable and accounts payable at year-end were $43 000 and $33 000, respectively. Assume that accounts payable related to operating expenses. Ignore income tax. The allowance for doubtful debts is $1000. There has been no direct write-off of accounts receivable.

Required

Calculate net cash provided by operating activities using the direct method.

E11.7 Calculate cash payments — direct method.   **LO3**

The statement of profit or loss for Colin Ltd shows cost of sales $355 000 and operating expenses (exclusive of depreciation) $230 000. The statement of financial position for the year shows that inventory increased $6000, prepaid expenses decreased $6000, accounts payable (inventory suppliers) decreased $8000, and accrued expenses payable decreased $12 000.

Required

Using the direct method, calculate (a) cash payments to suppliers and (b) cash payments for operating expenses.

E11.8 Calculate cash provided by operating activities — direct method.   **LO3**

The 2018 accounting records of Outdoor Adventures Ltd reveal the following transactions and events.

Payment of interest	$ 15 000	Collection of accounts receivable	$190 000
Cash sales	60 000	Payment of salaries and wages	68 000
Receipt of dividend revenue	14 000	Depreciation expense	16 000
Payment of income tax	16 000	Proceeds from sale of aircraft	812 000
Profit	38 000	Purchase of equipment for cash	22 000
Payment of accounts payable for		Loss on sale of aircraft	3 000
inventory	100 000	Payment of dividends	14 000
Payment for land	74 000	Payment of operating expenses	20 000

Required

Prepare the cash flows from operating activities section of the statement of cash flows using the direct method. (Not all of the items will be used.)

E11.9 Calculate cash flows — direct method.   **LO3**

The following information is taken from the general ledger of Chau Ltd.

Rent	Rent expense	$ 93 000
	Prepaid rent, 1 January	17 700
	Prepaid rent, 31 December	9 000
Salaries	Salaries expense	162 000
	Salaries payable, 1 January	15 000
	Salaries payable, 31 December	24 000
Sales	Revenue from sales	540 000
	Accounts receivable, 1 January	36 000
	Accounts receivable, 31 December	27 000

Required

In each case, calculate the amount that should be reported in the operating activities section of the statement of cash flows under the direct method.

E11.10 Compare two entities by using cash-based ratios. **LO5**

Presented here is information for two entities in the shipping industry: Kang Ltd and Jang Ltd:

	Kang Ltd	Jang Ltd
Cash provided by operations	$220 000	$240 000
Average current liabilities	50 000	100 000
Average total liabilities	200 000	250 000
Profit	200 000	200 000
Sales	400 000	800 000

Required

Using the cash-based ratios presented in this chapter, compare the (a) liquidity, (b) solvency and (c) profitability of the two entities, and discuss their meaning.

E11.11 Calculate cash provided by operating activities — direct method. **LO3**

The 2019 accounting records of Home and Away Travels Ltd reveal the following transactions and events.

Payment of interest	$ 21 000	Collection of accounts receivable	$ 266 000
Cash sales	84 000	Payment of salaries and wages	95 200
Receipt of dividend revenue	19 600	Depreciation expense	22 400
Payment of income tax	22 400	Proceeds from sale of aircraft	1 136 800
Profit	53 200	Purchase of equipment for cash	30 800
Payment of accounts payable for		Loss on sale of aircraft	4 200
inventory	140 000	Payment of dividends	19 600
Payment for land	103 600	Payment of operating expenses	28 000

Required

Prepare the cash flows from the operating activities section of the statement of cash flows using the direct method. (Not all of the items will be used.)

E11.12 Prepare the operating activities section of the statement of cash flows — indirect method. **LO3**

The current section of Opotiki Ltd statement of financial position at 30 June 2019 is presented below.

	2019	2018
Current assets		
Cash	$105 000	$ 99 000
Accounts receivable	120 000	89 000
Inventory	161 000	186 000
Prepaid expenses	27 000	22 000
Total current assets	$431 000	$396 000
Current liabilities		
Accounts payable	$ 85 000	$ 92 000
Accrued expenses payable	15 000	5 000
Total current liabilities	$100 000	$ 97 000

Other information:
1. Profit for the year ended 30 June 2019 was $153 000.
2. Depreciation expense was $19 000.

Required

Prepare the net cash provided by the operating activities section of Opotiki's statement of cash flows for the year ending 30 June 2019 using the indirect method.

E11.13 Prepare a partial statement of cash flows using the indirect method.   **LO3**

The following accounts appear in the ledger of Castle Ltd during 2019.

Equipment

Date	Description	Debit $	Credit $	Balance $
01/07/18	Balance			40 000
31/01/19	Purchase of equipment	17 500		57 500
02/03/19	Cost of equipment constructed	13 250		70 750
10/05/19	Cost of equipment sold		8 750	62 000

Accumulated depreciation—equipment

Date	Description	Debit $	Credit $	Balance $
01/07/18	Balance			17 750
10/05/19	Accumulated depreciation on equipment sold	7 500		10 250
30/06/19	Depreciation for the year		7 000	17 250

Retained earnings

Date	Description	Debit $	Credit $	Balance $
01/07/18	Balance			26 250
23/02/19	Dividends (cash)	3 500		22 750
30/06/19	Profit for the year		16 750	39 500

Required

From the postings in the accounts, indicate how the information is reported in the statement of cash flows using the indirect method. The loss on the sale of the equipment was $750. (*Hint:* The purchase of equipment is reported in the investing activities section as a decrease in cash of $17 500.)

PROBLEM SET A

PSA11.1 Prepare the investing activities section of the statement of cash flows.   **LO3**

The following selected account balances relate to the plant asset accounts of Waihi Beach Surfboards Pty Ltd at year-end.

	2018	2017
Accumulated depreciation—buildings	$125 000	$100 000
Accumulated depreciation—equipment	100 000	97 500
Buildings	500 000	500 000
Depreciation expense	47 750	40 000
Equipment	200 000	177 500
Land	485 000	425 000
Gain on sale of equipment	3 000	—

Additional information:
1. In 2018, Waihi Beach Surfboards Pty Ltd purchased $50 000 of equipment and $60 000 of land for cash.
2. Waihi Beach Surfboards Pty Ltd also sold equipment in 2018. (*Hint:* Reconstruct the accumulated depreciation account to determine carrying value and then determine the proceeds from sale of equipment.)

Required

Determine the amounts of any investing cash inflows or outflows in 2018.

PSA11.2 **Prepare the operating activities section — direct and indirect methods.**   LO2, 3

The statement of profit or loss of Phillips Screwdrivers Ltd is presented here.

PHILLIPS SCREWDRIVERS LTD Statement of profit or loss for the year ended 31 March 2020		
Sales		$6 900 000
Cost of sales		
Beginning inventory	$1 900 000	
Purchases	4 400 000	
Goods available for sale	6 300 000	
Ending inventory	1 600 000	
Total cost of sales		4 700 000
Gross profit		2 200 000
Operating expenses		
Selling expenses	450 000	
Administrative expenses	600 000	1 050 000
Profit before tax		**1 150 000**
Tax expense		100 000
Profit		**$1 050 000**

Additional information:

1. Accounts receivable decreased $300 000 during the year.
2. Prepaid expenses increased $150 000 during the year.
3. Accounts payable to suppliers of inventory decreased $300 000 during the year.
4. Accrued expenses payable decreased $100 000 during the year.
5. Administrative expenses include depreciation expense of $60 000.
6. All tax expense was paid in cash.

Required

(a) Prepare the operating activities section of the statement of cash flows for the year ended 31 March 2020 for Phillips Screwdrivers Ltd using the direct method.

(b) Reconcile profit to cash provided by operations for the year ended 31 March 2020.

(c) The statement of cash flows classifies cash receipts and cash payments into operating, investing and financing activities. Discuss why operating activities is the most important category of the three?

PSA11.3 **Prepare the operating activities section — direct and indirect methods.**   LO3

Peebody Enterprises Ltd's statement of profit or loss contained the condensed information below.

PEEBODY ENTERPRISES LTD Statement of profit or loss for the year ended 30 June 2018		
Revenues		$1 176 000
Operating expenses, excluding depreciation	$873 600	
Depreciation expense	84 000	
Loss on sale of equipment	36 400	994 000
Profit before income tax		**182 000**
Income tax expense		56 000
Profit		**$ 126 000**

Peebody Enterprises Ltd's statement of financial position contained the following comparative data.

	2018	2017
Accounts receivable	$65 800	$79 800
Accounts payable	57 400	46 200
Income tax payable	5 600	14 000
Accounts payable pertain to operating expenses.		

Required

(a) Prepare the operating activities section of the statement of cash flows using the direct method.

(b) Prepare the operating activities section of the statement of cash flows using the indirect method, i.e. prepare a reconciliation of profit to cash provided by operations.

PSA11.4 **Prepare a statement of cash flows — direct and indirect methods — and calculate cash-based ratios.** **LO3, 5**

These are the financial statements of Metro Meats Ltd.

METRO MEATS LTD
Statement of financial position
as at 31 December 2018

	2018	2017
ASSETS		
Cash	$ 29 000	$ 15 000
Accounts receivable	28 000	14 000
Inventory	25 000	35 000
Property, plant and equipment	60 000	78 000
Accumulated depreciation	(20 000)	(24 000)
Total assets	**$122 000**	**$118 000**
LIABILITIES AND EQUITY		
Accounts payable	$ 26 000	$ 25 000
Dividends payable	3 000	—
Income tax payable	5 000	8 000
Debentures payable	27 000	33 000
Share capital	18 000	14 000
Retained earnings	43 000	38 000
Total liabilities and equity	**$122 000**	**$118 000**

METRO MEATS LTD
Statement of profit or loss
for the year ended 31 December 2018

Sales	$250 000
Cost of sales	210 000
Gross profit	40 000
Selling expenses	18 000
Administrative expenses	6 000
Interest expense	2 000
Profit before income tax	**14 000**
Income tax expense	4 000
Profit	**$ 10 000**

The following additional data were provided:

1. The entity paid an interim dividend of $2000 and declared a final dividend.
2. During the year equipment was sold for $8500 cash. This equipment cost $18 000 originally and had a carrying amount of $8500 at the time of sale.
3. All depreciation expense is in the selling expense category.
4. All operating expenses except for depreciation were paid in cash.

Required

(a) Prepare a statement of cash flows using the direct method.
(b) Reconcile profit to cash provided by operating activities.
(c) Calculate these cash-basis measures:
  1. current cash debt coverage
  2. cash return on sales ratio
  3. cash debt coverage.
(d) Comment on the cash adequacy as indicated by the ratios calculated in part (c).

PSA11.5 Prepare a statement of cash flows — direct and indirect methods. LO3

The condensed financial data of Freshest Farmers Ltd follow.

FRESHEST FARMERS LTD
Statement of financial position
as at 31 March 2019

	2019	2018
ASSETS		
Cash	$147 000	$ 57 600
Accounts receivable	136 200	49 500
Inventories	168 750	154 275
Prepaid expenses	27 600	24 000
Investments	162 000	141 000
Plant and machinery	405 000	363 750
Accumulated depreciation	(75 000)	(78 000)
Total assets	**$971 550**	**$712 125**
LIABILITIES AND EQUITY		
Accounts payable	$138 000	$100 950
Accrued expenses payable	25 050	25 500
Debentures payable	127 500	150 000
Share capital	330 000	277 500
Retained earnings	351 000	158 175
Total liabilities and equity	**$971 550**	**$712 125**

FRESHEST FARMERS LTD
Statement of profit or loss
for the year ended 31 March 2019

Sales		$513 000
Less:		
Cost of sales	$173 190	
Operating expenses, excluding depreciation	18 615	
Depreciation expense	69 750	
Income tax	10 500	
Interest expense	3 345	
Loss on sale of machinery	11 250	286 650
Profit		**$226 350**

Additional information:

1. New machinery costing $127 500 was purchased for cash during the year.
2. Old machinery having an original cost of $86 250 was sold for $2250 cash.

3. Debentures matured and were paid off at face value for cash.
4. A cash dividend of $33 525 was declared and paid during the year.
5. Accounts payable pertain to inventory creditors.

Required

(a) Prepare a statement of cash flows for Freshest Farmers Ltd using the direct method for operating cash flows.
(b) Prepare a reconciliation of profit and cash from operations. (*Note:* This is also the indirect method of calculating the operating activities section of the statement of cash flows.)

PSA11.6 **Prepare the operating activities section — direct and indirect methods.**   **LO3**

The statement of profit or loss of Sticky Stationery Supplies Ltd is presented here.

STICKY STATIONERY SUPPLIES LTD Statement of profit or loss for the year ended 30 June 2018		
Sales		$7 100 000
Cost of sales		
Beginning inventory	$1 700 000	
Purchases	5 430 000	
Goods available for sale	7 130 000	
Ending inventory	1 920 000	
Total cost of sales		5 210 000
Gross profit		1 890 000
Operating expenses		
Selling expenses	400 000	
Administrative expense	525 000	
Depreciation expense	75 000	
Amortisation expense	30 000	1 030 000
Profit		$ 860 000

Additional information:

1. Accounts receivable increased $510 000 during the year.
2. Prepaid expenses increased $170 000 during the year.
3. Accounts payable to inventory suppliers increased $50 000 during the year.
4. Accrued expenses payable decreased $180 000 during the year.

Required

(a) Prepare the operating activities section of the statement of cash flows for the year ended 30 June 2018 for Sticky Stationery Supplies Ltd using the direct method.
(b) Prepare the operating activities section of the statement of cash flows for the year ended 30 June 2018 for Sticky Stationery Supplies Ltd using the indirect method.

PSA11.7 **Prepare the operating activities section — direct and indirect methods.**   **LO3**

The statement of profit or loss of Yu's Shoes Ltd reported the following condensed information.

YU'S SHOES LTD Statement of profit or loss for the year ended 31 March 2018	
Revenues	$1 160 000
Operating expenses	560 000
Profit from operations	600 000
Income tax expense	180 000
Profit	$ 420 000

Yu's Shoes statement of financial position contained the following comparative data at 31 March 2018.

	2018	2017
Accounts receivable	$100 000	$80 000
Accounts payable	60 000	82 000
Income tax payable	12 000	8 000

Yu's Shoes has no depreciable assets and no inventory. Accounts payable pertain to operating expenses.

Required

(a) Prepare the operating activities section of the statement of cash flows using the direct method.

(b) Prepare the operating activities section of the statement of cash flows using the indirect method.

PSA11.8 **Prepare a statement of cash flows — direct and indirect methods — and calculate cash-based ratios.** **LO3, 5**

Here are the financial statements of Mountain King Tours Ltd.

MOUNTAIN KING TOURS LTD Statement of financial position as at 31 December 2019				
	2019		2018	
ASSETS				
Cash		$ 30 000		$ 13 000
Accounts receivable		18 000		14 000
Inventory		34 000		35 000
Equipment	$ 70 000		$ 78 000	
Less: Accumulated depreciation	(30 000)	40 000	(24 000)	54 000
Total assets		**$122 000**		**$116 000**
LIABILITIES AND EQUITY				
Accounts payable		$ 29 000		$ 33 000
Income tax payable		15 000		20 000
Debentures payable		15 000		10 000
Share capital		30 000		25 000
Retained earnings		33 000		28 000
Total liabilities and equity		**$122 000**		**$116 000**

MOUNTAIN KING TOURS LTD Statement of profit or loss for the year ended 31 December 2019		
Sales		$250 000
Cost of sales		180 000
Gross profit		70 000
Selling expenses	$28 000	
Administrative expenses	16 000	44 000
Interest expense		2 000
Profit before income tax		24 000
Income tax expense		7 000
Profit		$ 17 000

The following additional data were provided:

1. Dividends of $12 000 were declared and paid.

2. During the year equipment was sold for $10 000 cash. This equipment cost $15 000 originally and had a carrying amount of $10 000 at the time of sale.

3. All depreciation expense, $11 000, is in the selling expense category.
4. All sales and purchases are on account.
5. Additional accessories for the climbing equipment were purchased for $7000 cash. The accessories are reported as part of the asset, climbing equipment.
6. Accounts payable pertains to inventory creditors. Inventory comprises food and liquor sold on tours.
7. All operating expenses except depreciation are paid in cash.

Required

(a) Prepare a statement of cash flows using the direct method for operating cash flows.
(b) Prepare a reconciliation of profit and cash provided by operations.
(c) Calculate these cash-based measures:
    1. current cash debt coverage
    2. cash return on sales ratio
    3. cash debt coverage
    4. free cash flow.
(d) Discuss the cash adequacy as indicated by the ratios.

PSA11.9 Prepare a statement of cash flows — direct and indirect methods.   **LO3**

Condensed financial data of Takahashi Electronics Pty Ltd follow.

TAKAHASHI ELECTRONICS PTY LTD Statement of financial position as at 30 June 2020		
	2020	2019
ASSETS		
Cash	$ 47 500	$ 23 625
Accounts receivable	43 400	28 500
Inventory	60 950	51 325
Investments (long term)	42 300	43 500
Plant and equipment	125 000	102 500
Accumulated depreciation	(24 750)	(20 000)
Total assets	**$294 400**	**$229 450**
LIABILITIES AND EQUITY		
Accounts payable	$ 26 350	$ 24 140
Accrued expenses payable	6 050	9 415
Debentures payable	50 000	35 000
Share capital	125 000	100 000
Retained earnings	87 000	60 895
Total liabilities and equity	**$294 400**	**$229 450**

TAKAHASHI ELECTRONICS PTY LTD Statement of profit or loss for the year ended 30 June 2020		
Sales		$150 000
Gain on sale of equipment		4 375
Less:		154 375
Cost of sales	$49 730	
Operating expenses, excluding depreciation expense	7 335	
Depreciation expense	24 850	
Income tax	3 635	
Interest expense	2 720	88 270
Profit		**$ 66 105**

Additional information:

1. New equipment and machinery were purchased for cash during the year.
2. Investments were sold at cost.
3. Equipment costing $23 500 was sold for $7775, resulting in a gain of $4375.
4. A cash dividend of $40 000 was declared and paid during the year.
5. Accounts payable pertain to inventory creditors.

Required

(a) Prepare a statement of cash flows using the direct method.

(b) Prepare a reconciliation of profit to cash provided by operations.

PSA11.10 Prepare a statement of cash flows, including asset revaluations, transfer to reserves, and purchase of assets by issuing debt, using the direct and indirect methods.   **LO3**

The statement of financial position and statement of profit or loss for DVDs and More Limited is presented as follows.

DVDS AND MORE LIMITED Statement of financial position as at 30 June 2019		
	2019 $'000	2018 $'000
ASSETS		
Current assets		
Cash	165	80
Accounts receivable	190	210
Allowance for doubtful debts	(20)	(12)
Inventory	200	170
Prepaid rent	20	60
Total current assets	555	508
Non-current assets		
Land	420	360
Buildings	510	470
Accumulated depreciation — buildings	(230)	(210)
Equipment	250	280
Accumulated depreciation — equipment	(110)	(90)
Patents	30	40
Total non-current assets	870	850
Total assets	**1 385**	**1 318**
LIABILITIES AND EQUITY		
Current liabilities		
Accounts payable	170	190
Accrued expenses	80	75
Income tax payable	92	45
Final dividend payable	50	40
Total current liabilities	392	350
Non-current liabilities		
Borrowings	310	410
Total liabilities	702	760
Equity		
Share capital	400	350
Revaluation surplus	108	48
General reserve	45	35
Retained earnings	130	125
Total equity	683	558
Total liabilities and equity	**1 385**	**1 318**

DVDS AND MORE LIMITED
Statement of profit or loss
for the year ended 30 June 2019

	$'000	$'000
Sales revenue		620
Profit on sale of land		20
		640
Less: Expenses		
Cost of sales	240	
Rent expense	40	
Bad debts expense	12	
Depreciation and amortisation	90	
Other expenses	28	
Loss on sale of office equipment	20	430
Profit before income tax		**210**
Income tax expense		
Current year	92	
Under-provision from previous year	18	110
Profit for the period		**100**

Additional information (dollar amounts expressed in full units):

1. Equipment with an original cost of $90 000 and accumulated depreciation of $40 000 was sold.
2. Land with a cost of $80 000 was sold for $100 000. The remaining land was revalued upwards by $60 000.
3. Equipment to the value of $20 000 and buildings to the value of $40 000 were acquired with the issue of a long-term note. The amount payable has been included in borrowings on the statement of financial position.

Required

(a) Prepare a statement of cash flows using the direct method.
(b) Reconcile profit to cash provided by operating activities.

> (*Hint:* This statement of cash flows is more complex, so you will need to reconstruct all the statement of financial position accounts to solve it.)

PROBLEM SET B

PSB11.1 Prepare the investing activities section of the statement of cash flows. **LO3**

The following selected account balances relate to the plant asset accounts of Wholesale Foods Ltd at year-end.

	2018	2017
Accumulated depreciation — buildings	$337 500	$300 000
Accumulated depreciation — equipment	144 000	96 000
Buildings	750 000	750 000
Depreciation expense	101 500	85 500
Equipment	300 000	240 000
Land	100 000	70 000
Loss on sale of equipment	1 000	0

Additional information:

1. Wholesale Foods Ltd purchased $80 000 of equipment and $30 000 of land for cash in 2018.
2. Wholesale Foods Ltd also sold equipment in 2018.

Required

Determine the amounts of any investing cash inflows or outflows in 2018.

PSB11.2 Prepare the operating activities section — direct and indirect method. LO3

The statement of profit or loss of Okamoto Motors Ltd is presented here.

OKAMOTO MOTORS LTD Statement of profit or loss for the year ended 31 December 2018		
Sales		$1 350 000
Cost of sales		
Beginning inventory	$ 445 000	
Purchases	857 500	
Goods available for sale	1 302 500	
Ending inventory	480 000	
Total cost of sales		822 500
Gross profit		527 500
Operating expenses		
Selling expenses	100 000	
Administrative expense	131 250	
Depreciation expense	31 250	
Amortisation expense	5 000	267 500
Profit		**$ 260 000**

Additional information:

1. Accounts receivable decreased $127 500 during the year.
2. Prepaid expenses increased $42 500 during the year.
3. Accounts payable to merchandise suppliers increased $12 500 during the year.
4. Accrued expenses payable increased $41 250 during the year.

Required

(a) Prepare the operating activities section of the statement of cash flows for the year ended 31 December 2018 using the direct method.

(b) Prepare the operating activities section of the statement of cash flows for the year ended 31 December 2018 using the indirect method.

PSB11.3 Prepare the operating activities section — direct and indirect method. LO3

The statement of profit or loss of Nguyen and Tran Ltd reported the following condensed information.

NGUYEN AND TRAN LTD Statement of profit or loss for the year ended 31 March 2020	
Revenues	$430 000
Operating expenses	280 000
Income from operations before income tax	150 000
Income tax expense	47 000
Profit	**$103 000**

Nguyen and Tran's statement of financial position contained the following comparative data at 31 March.

	2020	2019
Accounts receivable	$50 000	$40 000
Accounts payable	30 000	41 000
Income taxes payable	6 000	4 000

Nguyen and Tran Ltd has no depreciable assets and no inventory. Accounts payable pertain to operating expenses.

Required

(a) Prepare the operating activities section of the statement of cash flows using the direct method.

(b) Prepare the operating activities section of the statement of cash flows using the indirect method.

(c) There are two methods of presenting cash provided (used) by operating activities: the direct method and the indirect method. Discuss the differences between the two methods.

PSB11.4 **Prepare a statement of cash flows and calculate cash-based ratios.** **LO3, 5**

Here are the financial statements of Kiwi Ltd.

KIWI LTD
Statement of financial position
as at 31 December 2018

		2018		2017
ASSETS				
Cash		$ 33 800		$ 42 900
Accounts receivable		36 400		18 200
Inventory		49 400		32 500
Property, plant and equipment	$ 91 000		$101 400	
Less: Accumulated depreciation	(35 100)	55 900	(31 200)	70 200
Total assets		**$175 500**		**$163 800**
LIABILITIES AND EQUITY				
Accounts payable		$ 40 300		$ 55 900
Income tax payable		33 800		26 000
Bonds payable		26 000		13 000
Contributed equity		32 500		32 500
Retained earnings		42 900		36 400
Total liabilities and equity		**$175 500**		**$163 800**

KIWI LTD
Statement of profit or loss
for the year ended 31 December 2018

Sales		$371 800
Cost of sales		252 200
Gross profit		119 600
Selling expenses	$36 400	
Administrative expenses	11 700	
Interest expense	9 100	57 200
Profit before income taxes		**62 400**
Income tax expenses		9 100
Profit		**$ 53 300**

Additional information:

1. Dividends were declared and paid.
2. During the year equipment was sold for $13 000 cash. This equipment cost $19 500 originally and had a book value of $13 000 at the time of sale.
3. All depreciation expense, $10 400, is in the selling expense category.
4. All sales and purchases are on account.
5. Additional equipment was purchased for cash.

6. Accounts payable pertains to merchandise creditors.

7. All operating expenses except for depreciation are paid in cash.

Required

(a) Prepare a statement of cash flows using the direct method.

(b) Prepare a reconciliation between profit and cash provided by operating activities. (*Note:* This is also the indirect method of calculating operating activity cash flows.)

(c) Calculate these cash-based measures:
1. current cash debt coverage
2. cash debt coverage
3. free cash flow.

(d) Discuss the cash adequacy as indicated by the ratios.

PSB11.5 Prepare a statement of cash flows — direct and indirect. LO3

Condensed financial data of Aleksia Ltd follows.

ALEKSIA LTD Statement of financial position as at 31 December 2019		
	2019	2018
ASSETS		
Cash	$ 92 700	$ 33 400
Accounts receivable	80 800	37 000
Inventory	121 900	102 650
Investments (long term)	84 500	107 000
Plant and equipment	310 000	205 000
Accumulated depreciation	(49 500)	(40 000)
Total assets	**$640 400**	**$445 050**
LIABILITIES AND EQUITY		
Accounts payable	$ 62 700	$ 48 280
Accrued expenses payable	12 100	18 830
Bonds payable	140 000	70 000
Contributed equity	250 000	200 000
Retained earnings	175 600	107 940
Total liabilities and equity	**$640 400**	**$445 050**

ALEKSIA LTD Statement of profit or loss for the year ended 31 December 2019		
Sales		$297 500
Gain on sale of plant assets		5 000
Less:		302 500
Cost of sales	$99 460	
Operating expenses, excluding depreciation expense	14 670	
Depreciation expense	35 500	
Income taxes	7 270	
Interest expense	2 940	159 840
Profit		**$142 660**

Additional information:

1. Plant and equipment costing $141 000 were purchased for cash during the year.

2. Investments were sold at cost.

3. Plant and equipment costing $36 000 were sold for $15 000.

4. A cash dividend was declared and paid during the year.

Required

(a) Prepare a statement of cash flows using the direct method.

(b) Prepare a reconciliation of profit to cash provided by operations. (*Note:* This is also the indirect method of calculating operating activity cash flows.)

PSB11.6 Distinguish among operating, investing, and financing activities. **LO2**

You are provided with the following transactions that took place during a recent fiscal year.

Transaction	Where reported on statement	Cash inflow, outflow, or no effect?
(a) Recorded depreciation expense on the plant assets.		
(b) Recorded and paid interest expense.		
(c) Recorded cash proceeds from a sale of equipment.		
(d) Acquired land by issuing shares.		
(e) Paid a cash dividend to shareholders.		
(f) Distributed a share dividend to shareholders.		
(g) Recorded cash sales.		
(h) Recorded sales on account.		
(i) Purchased inventory for cash.		
(j) Purchased inventory on account.		

Required

Complete the table indicating whether each item (1) should be reported as an operating (O) activity, investing (I) activity, financing (F) activity, or as a non-cash (NC) transaction reported in a separate schedule; and (2) represents a cash inflow or cash outflow or has no cash flow effect. Assume use of the direct approach.

PSB11.7 Prepare the operating activities section — direct and indirect. **LO3**

The statement of profit or loss of Bear's Chairs Ltd is presented here.

BEAR'S CHAIRS LTD Statement of profit or loss for the year ended 30 November 2018		
Sales		$7 700 000
Cost of sales		
Beginning inventory	$1 900 000	
Purchases	4 400 000	
Goods available for sale	6 300 000	
Ending inventory	1 400 000	
Total cost of sales		4 900 000
Gross profit		2 800 000
Operating expenses		
Selling expenses	450 000	
Administrative expenses	700 000	1 150 000
Profit		**$1 650 000**

Additional information:

1. Accounts receivable increased $200 000 during the year.
2. Prepaid expenses increased $150 000 during the year.
3. Accounts payable to suppliers of inventory decreased $340 000 during the year.
4. Accrued expenses payable decreased $100 000 during the year.
5. Administrative expenses include depreciation expense of $110 000.

Required

(a) Prepare the operating activities section of the statement of cash flows for the year ended 30 November 2018 for Bear's Chairs Ltd using the direct method.

(b) Prepare the operating activities section of the statement of cash flows for the year ended 30 November 2018 for Bear's Chairs Ltd using the indirect method.

PSB11.8 **Prepare a statement of cash flows, using direct and indirect methods, and calculate cash-based ratios.** **LO3, 5**

Here are the financial statements of XYZ Children's Centre Ltd.

XYZ CHILDREN'S CENTRE LTD Statement of financial position as at 31 December 2019				
		2019		2018
ASSETS				
Cash		$ 72 000		$ 31 200
Accounts receivable		43 200		33 600
Inventory		81 600		84 000
Plant	$168 000		$187 200	
Less: Accumulated depreciation	(72 000)	96 000	(57 600)	129 600
Total assets		**$292 800**		**$278 400**
LIABILITIES AND EQUITY				
Accounts payable		$ 69 600		$ 79 200
Income tax payable		36 000		48 000
Debentures payable		36 000		24 000
Share capital		72 000		60 000
Retained earnings		79 200		67 200
Total liabilities and equity		**$292 800**		**$278 400**

XYZ CHILDREN'S CENTRE LTD Statement of profit or loss for the year ended 30 June 2019		
Sales		$600 000
Cost of sales		432 000
Gross profit		168 000
Selling expenses	$60 000	
Administrative expenses	45 600	
Interest expense	4 800	110 400
Profit before income tax		**57 600**
Income tax expense		16 800
Profit for the period		**$ 40 800**

The following additional data were provided:

1. Dividends of $28 800 were declared and paid.
2. During the year furniture was sold for $24 000 cash. This furniture originally cost $36 000 and had an accumulated depreciation of $12 000 at the time of sale.
3. All the depreciation expense, $26 400, is in the selling expense category.
4. All sales and purchases are on account.
5. Additional equipment was purchased for $16 800 cash.
6. Accounts payable pertains to inventory creditors. Inventory comprises food and drinks for staff and children.
7. All operating expenses except depreciation are paid in cash.

Required

(a) Prepare a statement of cash flows using the direct method for operating cash flows.

(b) Prepare a reconciliation of profit and cash provided by operations.

(c) Calculate these cash-based measures:

  1. current cash debt coverage.

  2. cash return on sales ratio.

  3. cash debt coverage.

  4. free cash flow.

(d) Discuss the cash adequacy of XYZ Children's Centre Ltd, as revealed by the ratios calculated in part (c).

PSB11.9 Prepare a statement of cash flows, using direct and indirect methods.　　　　**LO3**

Below is information relating to ABC Manufacturing Pty Ltd for the year ended 30 June 2018.

ABC MANUFACTURING PTY LTD Comparative statement of financial position as at 30 June 2018		
	2018	2017
ASSETS		
Cash	$ 96 700	$ 47 250
Accounts receivable	86 800	57 000
Inventory	121 900	102 650
Investments	84 500	87 000
Plant and equipment	250 000	205 000
Accumulated depreciation	(49 500)	(40 000)
Total assets	**$590 400**	**$458 900**
LIABILITIES AND EQUITY		
Accounts payable	$ 52 700	$ 48 280
Accrued expenses payable	12 100	18 830
Debentures payable	100 000	70 000
Share capital	250 000	200 000
Retained profits	175 600	121 790
Total liabilities and equity	**$590 400**	**$458 900**

ABC MANUFACTURING PTY LTD Statement of profit or loss for the year ended 30 June 2018		
Sales		$297 500
Gain on sale of equipment		8 750
Less:		$306 250
Cost of sales	$99 460	
Operating expenses, excluding depreciation expense	14 670	
Depreciation expense	49 700	
Interest expense	2 940	
Income tax	7 270	174 040
Profit		**$132 210**

Additional information:

1. New equipment and machinery costing $92 000 were purchased for cash during the year.

2. Investments were sold at cost.

3. Equipment costing $47 000 was sold for $15 550, resulting in a gain of $8750.

4. A cash dividend of $78 400 was declared and paid during the year.

5. Accounts payable pertain to inventory creditors.

Required

(a) Prepare a statement of cash flows using the direct method.

(b) Prepare a statement of cash flows using the indirect method.

PSB11.10 Prepare a statement of cash flows, including asset revaluations, bonus share issue and transfer to reserves, using direct and indirect methods. **LO3**

Below is the information relating to Simic and Nikolic Ltd for the year ended 30 June 2019.

SIMIC AND NIKOLIC LTD Statement of financial position as at 30 June 2019		
	2019 $'000	2018 $'000
ASSETS		
Current assets		
Cash	3 150	1 220
Accounts receivable	1 240	1 100
Allowance for doubtful debts	(60)	(50)
Inventory	1 520	1 300
Prepaid insurance	60	40
Total current assets	5 910	3 610
Non-current assets		
Land	1 630	1 900
Buildings	2 100	1 670
Accumulated depreciation—buildings	(540)	(500)
Plant and equipment	1 454	1 258
Accumulated depreciation—plant and equipment	(440)	(610)
Office equipment	430	380
Accumulated depreciation—office equipment	(270)	(190)
Patents	260	280
Total non-current assets	4 624	4 188
Total assets	**10 534**	**7 798**
LIABILITIES AND EQUITY		
Current liabilities		
Accounts payable	750	500
Accrued expenses	260	280
Interest payable	100	80
Income tax payable	1 100	1 120
Final dividend payable	600	500
Total current liabilities	2 810	2 480
Non-current liabilities		
Borrowings	3 000	2 200
Total liabilities	5 810	4 680
Equity		
Share capital	1 400	1 000
Revaluation surplus	260	300
General reserve	300	200
Retained earnings	2 764	1 618
Total equity	4 724	3 118
Total liabilities and equity	**10 534**	**7 798**

SIMIC AND NIKOLIC LTD		
Statement of profit or loss		
for the year ended 30 June 2019		
	$'000	$'000
Sales revenue		14 126
Gain from sale of land		210
Gain on sale of equipment		230
		14 566
Less: Expenses		
Cost of sales	8 876	
Bad debts expense	28	
Depreciation	250	
Insurance expense	140	
Interest expense	180	
Amortisation patents	20	
Other expenses	1 796	11 290
Profit before income tax		**3 276**
Income tax expense		
Current year	1 100	
Under-provision from previous year	80	1 180
Profit for the period		**2 096**

Additional information (dollar amounts expressed in full units):

1. Equipment with an original cost of $500 000 was sold during the year.
2. Land with an original value of $600 000 was revalued upwards by $160 000 during the year.
3. A bonus share dividend of $200 000 was paid from the revaluation surplus.
4. An interim dividend was paid during the year.

Required

(a) Prepare a statement of cash flows, using the direct method.
(b) Reconcile profit to cash provided by operating activities.

(*Hint:* This statement of cash flows is more complex, so you will need to reconstruct all the statement of financial position accounts to solve it.)

BUILDING BUSINESS SKILLS

FINANCIAL REPORTING AND ANALYSIS

Financial reporting problem: Giorgina's Pizza Limited

BBS11.1 Refer to the financial statements of Giorgina's presented in chapter 1, figures 1.13, 1.15 and 1.16.

Required

Answer these questions:

(a) What was the amount of net cash provided by operating activities for the year ended 30 June 2019? For the year ended 30 June 2018? Are Giorgina's cash flows consistent with the introductory growth, maturity or decline phase?
(b) What was the amount of increase or decrease in cash for the year ended 30 June 2018 and for the year ended 30 June 2019?
(c) From your analysis of the 2019 cash flow statement, what was the amount of the change in borrowings and was it a decrease or an increase?
(d) What was the total (net) cash used for investing activities for 2019?

(e) What was the amount of interest paid in 2019? What was the amount of income tax paid in 2019?

Comparative analysis problem: Company A vs. Company B

BBS11.2 The following data have been extracted from the financial statements of two competitors in the retail industry:

Company A

	2020 $'000	2019 $'000
Sales revenue	505 754	461 205
Net cash provided by operations	113 393	101 126
Current liabilities	112 907	130 769
Total liabilities	124 497	149 139

Company B

	2020 $'000	2019 $'000
Sales revenue	744 285	693 007
Net cash provided by operations	131 615	71 926
Current liabilities	188 896	162 582
Total liabilities	387 638	334 298

Required

(a) Based on the information in these financial statements, calculate the following ratios for each entity for 2020:
   1. current cash debt coverage
   2. cash return on sales ratio
   3. cash debt coverage.
(b) What conclusions concerning the management of cash can be drawn from these data?

Interpreting financial statements

BBS11.3 The following information was taken from the financial statements of Peter's of Buckingham Ltd (in millions), reported on its web site:

	2021	2020	2019	2018
Total liabilities	$19 632	$20 177	$24 113	$23 751
Current liabilities	7 576	5 834	8 230	9 279
Net cash provided (used) by operations	7 433	7 057	7 098	
Net cash provided (used) by investing	(3 270)	(2 492)	(3 258)	
Net cash provided (used) by financing	(4 776)	(4 317)	(3 817)	
Sales revenue	20 737	20 495	20 196	
Capital expenditure	(3 683)	(3 332)	(3 662)	

Required

Discuss the change in Peter's solvency, liquidity and ability to generate cash from operations to finance capital expenditure. Use the capital expenditure ratio, free cash flow, current cash debt coverage, cash debt coverage and the cash return on sales ratio to support your position.

Research case

BBS11.4 Obtain the latest annual report of a public company. Some companies provide them on their web sites. Refer to BBS11.5 if you have difficulty finding an annual report.

Required

Answer these questions:

(a) Explain the differences between profit after tax and net cash provided by operating activities.

(b) How has the company financed the acquisition of non-current assets, if applicable?

(c) Calculate the cash debt coverage for the current year.

(d) Calculate the cash return on sales for the current year and the previous year. Discuss the trend, stating whether it indicates improvement in cash generating ability. Explain the key factors driving any identified change in the cash return on sales.

Financial analysis on the web

BBS11.5 Purpose: Locating a statement of cash flows in an annual report.

Address: www.asx.com.au or https://m.nzx.com/#

Steps:

1. On the Australian Securities Exchange home page, you will notice a series of tabs on the menu bar of the screen. Place your cursor on the **Prices and research** tab, and you will get a drop-down menu. Then click on **Company information**, and then find the heading **Company directory** and select **View all companies**.

2. You are now at the index for listed companies. Choose a letter and select a particular company (don't just choose the first company, find one that interests you) by clicking on the ASX code.

3. From this page browse down to the internet address and click on the address which will take you to the company's web site.

4. From the web site, search around and find the latest annual report.

OR

For the New Zealand Stock Exchange:

1. Go to the home page and click on the top menu.

2. Click on **Markets**. This will take you to a drop down menu. Click on **NZSX Main Board**. You are now at the index for listed entities.

3. Scroll down the names and click the code for a company. This will take you to their page. Click on the link of the company's name (after issued by) and under contact info it will provide the company's web site address.

Required

Answer the following questions:

(a) What company did you select?

(b) Did it provide financial statements on its web site? If so, how easy or difficult was it to locate the latest annual report? If not, choose another company web site that does.

(c) Determine how much cash the company generated from/used in operating activities by referring to the statement of cash flows.

CRITICAL THINKING

Communication activity

BBS11.6 Peter Sole, the owner-manager of Cool Shooz Pty Ltd, is unfamiliar with the statement of cash flows that you, as his accountant, prepared. He asks for further explanation.

Required

Write a brief presentation explaining the form and content of the statement of cash flows as shown in figure 11.2.

BBS11.7 Have you heard of the 'The B Team'? The B team was initiated by Richard Branson to explore how people in business can develop a better version of capitalism that considers how people are treated and how businesses impact the cultures they are based in, economically, socially and environmentally.

Required

Go to http://bteam.org and find a B Team Project that interests you.

Answering the questions that follow, prepare summary notes that would allow you to give a five-minute in-class presentation on the project to your peers. You may like to prepare two to three PowerPoint slides to focus your talk.

1. What is the project about? Provide some background to *the problem* this project is aiming to address.
2. What are businesses being asked to *do differently* based on the objectives of this project?
3. What are social and environmental impacts — the intended benefits of this project? Have any been achieved?

Ethics case

BBS11.8 Big Rubber Ltd is a wholesaler of truck tyres. It has shareholders who have been paid a total of $1 million in cash dividends for 8 consecutive years. The board of directors' policy requires that in order for this dividend to be declared, net cash provided by operating activities as reported in Big Rubber Ltd's statement of cash flows must exceed $1 million. The managing director's job is secure so long as she produces annual operating cash flows to support the usual dividend.

At the end of the current year, the accountant reports some disappointing news. The net cash provided by operating activities is calculated as only $970 000. The managing director says, 'We must get that amount above $1 million. Isn't there some way to increase operating cash flow by another $30 000?' The accountant replies, 'I'll go back to my office and see what I can do.' The managing director replies, 'I know you won't let me down.'

On close scrutiny of the statement of cash flows, the accountant concludes that he can get the operating cash flows above $1 million by reclassifying a $60 000, 2-year note payable listed in the financing activities section as 'Proceeds from bank loan — $60 000'. He will add the 2-year note to accounts payable, thus reducing the net payment of accounts payable. He returns to the managing director, saying, 'You can tell the board to declare their usual dividend. Our net cash flow provided by operating activities is $1 030 000.' 'I knew I could count on you,' exults the managing director.

Required

(a) Is there anything unethical about the managing director's actions? Is there anything unethical about the accountant's actions?
(b) Are the board members or anyone else likely to discover the misclassification?
(c) Explain how the key stakeholders in this situation could be positively or negatively impacted by the note reclassification.
(d) What ethical actions could the accountant take? Explain the implications of these actions.

Sustainability

BBS11.9 Minimising the negative impact of business operations on the environment is a key concern of government. Environmental laws are put in place to achieve this aim. The Waste Electrical and Electronic Equipment (WEEE) Regulation is a directive of the European Union that requires safe and responsible collection, recycling and disposal procedures for all types of electronic waste, including phones, computers and kitchen appliances. Electronic waste can harm the environment and can pose health risks if it is disposed of incorrectly as electronic products often contain lead, mercury and other heavy metals. The WEEE Regulation aims to reduce the health and environmental risks by providing a safe way to dispose of these materials in the short term. In the long term, the aim is to phase out dangerous materials and use safer alternatives to reduce the impact on the environment and human wellbeing.*

---

*Rouse, M n.d., 'Waste Electrical and Electronic Equipment Regulation (WEEE)', retrieved from TechTarget, http://searchdatacenter.techtarget.com/definition/Waste-Electrical-and-Electronic-Equipment-Regulation-WEEE.

Required

(a) Phones R 4 U Pty Ltd is a manufacturer of phones in Australia and they sell their products all over the world. Prepare a report for the management of Phones R 4 U Pty Ltd explaining how compliance with the Waste Electrical and Electronic Equipment Regulation directive would impact the company. Discuss both the potential positive and negative impacts.

(b) Download the latest annual report for Telstra Corporation Ltd and discuss the measures they have taken to recycle e-waste. (*Hint:* See the environmental impact section under sustainability.)

ANSWERS

Answers to self-study questions

11.1 (c) 11.2 (c) 11.3 (a) 11.4 (c) 11.5 (d) 11.6 (b) 11.7 (c) 11.8 (d) 11.9 (d) 11.10 (b) 11.11 (a) 11.12 (b) 11.13 (a) 11.14 (d) 11.15 (b)

ACKNOWLEDGEMENTS

Photo: © Andrey_Popov / Shutterstock.com
Photo: © patpitchaya / Shutterstock.com
Photo: © Gordon Bell / Shutterstock.com

CHAPTER 12

Financial statement analysis and decision making

LEARNING OBJECTIVES

After studying this chapter, you should be able to:

12.1 discuss the need for comparative analysis and identify the tools of financial statement analysis

12.2 explain and apply horizontal analysis

12.3 explain and apply vertical analysis

12.4 identify and calculate ratios and describe their purpose and use in analysing the liquidity, solvency and profitability of a business

12.5 discuss the limitations of financial statement analysis.

Chapter preview

If you are thinking of granting a loan to a company or purchasing some of its shares, how can you assess that company's creditworthiness and profitability? How can you compare the financial position and profitability of different entities? To answer these types of questions, it is helpful to understand how to analyse financial statement information.

Financial statement analysis, the topic of this chapter, enhances the usefulness of published financial statements for making decisions about a company or another entity. The content and organisation of this chapter are as follows.

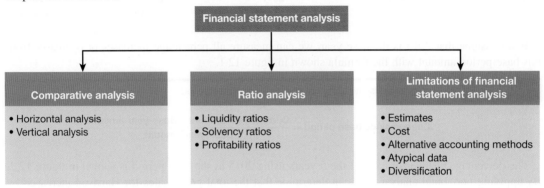

12.1 Comparative analysis

LEARNING OBJECTIVE 12.1 Discuss the need for comparative analysis and identify the tools of financial statement analysis.

The statement of profit or loss shows the dollar amounts for various types of income and expense to determine whether the entity made a profit or loss. Similarly, the statement of financial position reports aggregate dollar amounts for various categories of assets, liabilities and equity at a point in time. For example, in its annual report, a company reported a profit after tax of $120 million and total assets of $18 250 million. But whether that represents an increase over previous years, or whether it is adequate in relation to the entity's needs, cannot be determined from the amount alone. The amount must be compared with other financial data to provide more information.

Three types of comparisons increase the decision usefulness of financial information.

- *Intra-entity basis.* Comparisons within an entity are often useful to detect changes in financial relationships and significant trends. For example, a comparison of the current year's cash amount with the previous year's cash amount shows either an increase or a decrease. Likewise, a comparison of the year-end cash amount with the amount of the entity's total assets at year-end shows the proportion of total assets in the form of cash.
- *Industry averages.* Comparisons with industry averages provide information about an entity's relative position within the industry. For example, Woolworths' financial data can be compared with the averages for its industry compiled by financial ratings organisations such as Dun & Bradstreet and Moody's.
- *Inter-entity basis.* Comparisons with other entities provide insight into an entity's competitive position. For example, Woolworths' profit can be compared with the profit of its competitors in the retail industry, such as Wesfarmers or Aldi.

Three basic tools are used in financial statement analysis to highlight the significance of financial statement data:

- horizontal analysis
- vertical analysis
- ratio analysis.

12.2 Horizontal analysis

LEARNING OBJECTIVE 12.2 Explain and apply horizontal analysis.

Horizontal analysis is a technique for evaluating a series of financial statement data over a period of time. Its purpose is to determine the increase or decrease that has taken place, expressed as either an amount or a percentage. For example, here are 5 years of total group sales figures (in $ millions) of a fictitious company, Harrison Ltd, a retailer of fresh food.

2019	2018	2017	2016	2015
$87 774	$82 165	$81 217	$77 542	$74 390

If we assume that 2015 is the base year, we can measure all percentage increases or decreases from this base-period amount with the formula shown in figure 12.1.

FIGURE 12.1 Horizontal analysis calculation of changes since base period

$$\text{Change since base period} = \frac{\text{Current-year amount} - \text{Base-year amount}}{\text{Base-year amount}}$$

The percentage change for each of the 5 years using 2015 as the base period is shown in figure 12.2. By applying horizontal analysis, we can determine that the total group sales for Harrison increased by approximately 4% [($77 542 − $74 390)/$74 390] from 2015 to 2016. Similarly, we can also determine that the total group sales increased by around 18% [($87 774 − $74 390)/$74 390] from 2015 to 2019.

FIGURE 12.2 Horizontal analysis of total group sales

HARRISON LIMITED Total group sales (in $m) Base period 2015				
2019	**2018**	**2017**	**2016**	**2015**
$87 774	$82 165	$81 217	$77 542	$74 390
118%	110%	109%	104%	100%

Total group sales increased by $5609 million from 2018 to 2019, which represented an 8% improvement from the previous year. This significant growth in sales is mainly attributed to a combination of two key factors. In 2019, Harrison opened 23 supermarkets in Australia. Its food business continued to increase its market share and customer numbers. This additional information was provided in Harrison Ltd's 2019 annual report.

To further illustrate horizontal analysis, we use the 2019 comparative financial statements of Harrison Ltd. Extracts from the statement of financial position (also called the *balance sheet*) and the statement of profit or loss are illustrated in figures 12.3 and 12.4, respectively. Both the dollar change and percentage change in each line item from 2018 to 2019 are shown. For simplification, some line items have been combined.

The horizontal analysis of the statement of financial position shows that a number of changes occurred in Harrison' financial position from 2018 to 2019. As part of the analysis, we can examine individual items in each category of the statement of financial position as well as totals for each major category. For example, we can examine individual items such as receivables in the current assets section, where receivables increased by $147 000 000 or 11.3% ($147 000 000/$1 305 000 000). In the non-current assets section, we can examine property, plant and equipment which decreased by $514 000 000 or 3.6% ($514 000 000/$14 383 000 000). We can also examine totals for each major category. For example, in 2019 Harrison's total assets increased by $902 000 000 or 2.8% ($902 000 000/$32 369 000 000). There was an overall increase across both current and non-current assets with the exception of other assets, non-current receivables and deferred tax assets.

Helpful hint: It is difficult to comprehend the significance of a change when only the dollar amount of the change is examined. When the change is expressed in a percentage format, it is easier to understand the relative magnitude of the change.

Horizontal analysis can provide insights into underlying conditions for entities that may not be apparent from the individual components presented in financial statements. Horizontal analysis is even more meaningful if it is supplemented with further information such as inter-company comparisons with a competitor in the same industry, as well as other relevant information such as general economic conditions, industry trends or averages, information from directors' reports and media releases. For example, it was reported in the managing director's report in Harrison Ltd's 2019 annual report that, while the entity opened 23 new stores, there was a considerable decrease in the value of property, plant and equipment due to the sale of one of its subsidiaries.

FIGURE 12.3	Horizontal analysis of a statement of financial position

HARRISON LIMITED **Statement of financial position (and analysis)** as at 30 June 2019			Increase/(decrease) during 2019	
	2019 $m	2018 $m	Amount $m	%
Current assets				
Cash assets	1 273	1 250	23	1.8%
Receivables	1 452	1 305	147	11.3%
Inventories	6 307	5 547	760	13.7%
Other financial assets	81	35	46	131.4%
Other assets	223	565	(342)	(60.5)%
Total current assets	9 336	8 702	634	7.3%
Non-current assets				
Receivables	25	36	(11)	(30.6)%
Other financial assets	538	358	180	50.3%
Property, plant and equipment	13 869	14 383	(514)	(3.6)%
Intangible assets	8 676	7 923	753	9.5%
Deferred tax assets	827	967	(140)	(14.5)%
Total non-current assets	23 935	23 667	268	1.1%
Total assets	33 271	32 369	902	2.8%
Current liabilities				
Payables	8 085	7 863	222	2.8%
Borrowings	254	81	173	213.6%
Current tax liabilities	289	332	(43)	(13.0)%
Other financial liabilities	218	161	57	35.4%
Provisions	1 450	1 409	41	2.9%
Other	0	301	(301)	—
Total current liabilities	10 296	10 147	149	1.5%
Non-current liabilities				
Borrowings	6 423	7 042	(619)	(8.8)%
Other financial liabilities	1 488	1 330	158	11.9%
Provisions	823	791	32	4.0%
Other	389	388	1	0.3%
Total non-current liabilities	9 123	9 551	(428)	(4.5)%
Total liabilities	19 419	19 698	(279)	(1.4)%
Net assets	**13 852**	**12 671**	**1 181**	9.3%

▶

	2019 $m	2018 $m	Increase/(decrease) during 2019 Amount $m	%
Equity				
Issued capital	6 783	6 504	279	4.3%
Shares held in trust	(270)	(90)	(180)	200.0%
Reserves	37	(364)	401	—
Retained earnings	6 846	6 244	602	9.6%
Other	456	377	79	21.0%
Total equity	**13 852**	**12 671**	**1 181**	**9.3%**

Helpful hint: Some entities refer to retained earnings *as* retained profits.

We can continue our horizontal analysis by examining the liabilities and equity sections. Current liabilities increased by $149 000 000 or 1.5% whereas non-current liabilities decreased by $428 000 000 or 4.5%. Under the equity section, there were increases in each of the listed equity items which contributed to the overall increase of $1181 000 000 or 9.3%. The most substantial increase was in retained profits for $602 000 000 or 9.6% for the period.

FIGURE 12.4 Horizontal analysis of a statement of profit or loss

HARRISON LIMITED
Extract from statement of profit or loss (and analysis)
for the year ended 30 June 2019

	2019 $m	2018 $m	Increase/(decrease) during 2019 Amount $m	%
Revenue from sale of goods	87 774	82 165	5 609	6.8%
Other operating revenue	236	208	28	13.5%
Total revenue	88 010	82 373	5 637	6.8%
Cost of sales	(64 368)	(60 682)	3 686	6.1%
Gross profit	23 642	21 691	1 951	9.0%
Other revenue	371	335	36	10.7%
Branch expenses	(14 698)	(13 165)	1 533	11.6%
Administrative expenses	(3 921)	(3 840)	81	2.1%
EBIT	5 394	5 021	373	7.4%
Financial expenses	(615)	(474)	141	29.7%
Financial income	45	52	(7)	−13.5%
Profit before income tax	**4 824**	**4 599**	**225**	4.9%
Income tax expense	(1 438)	(1 327)	111	8.4%
Profit for the period*	**3 386**	**3 272**	**114**	3.5%
Basic earnings per share* (cents per share)	272.7	267.4	5.3	2.0%
Diluted earnings per share* (cents per share)	271.5	266.1	5.4	2.0%

*Figures are based on continuing operations.

Helpful hint 1: In a horizontal analysis, the amount column is additive *whereas the profit figure of $3 272 000 000 in the statement of profit or loss is the total figure after expense items have been deducted from revenue items. However, the % column is* not additive *as the 3.5% increase is not a total figure as it refers only to the change to the profit for the period. For more detailed analysis, both dollar amount changes and percentage changes need to be examined. For instance, percentage changes in line items may seem very large but the amount in the base year may be low and the impact on profit very small.*

Helpful hint 2: Some entities refer to cost of sales *as* cost of goods sold *and refer to* financial expenses *as* interest expense.

The horizontal analysis of Harrison Ltd's statement of profit or loss shows the following changes.

- Revenue from sale of goods increased by $5 609 000 000 or 6.8% ($5 609 000 000/$82 165 000 000).
- Other operating revenue increased by $28 000 000 or 13.5% ($28 000 000/$208 000 000).
- Cost of goods sold increased by $3 686 000 000 or 6.1% ($3 686 000 000/$60 682 000 000).

Overall, gross profit increased by $1 951 000 000 or 9%. Although all categories of expenses increased in 2019, Harrison's profit for the period increased by $114 000 000 or 3.5% as the revenue from sales of goods and other revenue increased at a greater rate than the overall increase in expenses. The entity's improved financial performance is also evident in both measures of earnings per share showing a 2% increase from 2018 to 2019.

The measurement of changes from period to period in percentages is relatively straightforward and quite useful. However, complications can result in making the calculations. If an item has no value in a base year or preceding year and a value in the next year, no percentage change can be calculated. An example of this appears in the current liabilities section, under the category of *other* where $301 000 000 appears in 2018 but there is no value in 2019.

Also, if a negative amount appears in the base or preceding period and a positive amount exists the following year, or vice versa, no meaningful percentage change can be calculated. An example of this appears in the equity section. Under the category of reserves, ($364 000 000) appears in 2018 and this increases to $37 000 000 in 2019.

Using the decision-making toolkit, management, along with other users such as potential investors, shareholders and lenders, can use horizontal analysis to determine whether the entity's operating results and financial position has improved from the previous year. Financial statements should be compared over at least 2 years, with the first year reported being the base year. Changes in each line item relative to the base year should be presented by both amount and percentage. An analysis of the statement of profit or loss will provide an indication of the changes in revenue, expenses and its effect on profit. An analysis of the statement of financial position will highlight changes in assets and financial structure. Any significant changes in these line items that have impacted on overall profitability and financial position should be investigated further.

DECISION-MAKING TOOLKIT

Decision/issue	Info needed for analysis	Tool or technique to use for decision	How to evaluate results to make decision
How do the entity's operating results and financial position compare with those of a previous period?	Statement of profit or loss and statement of financial position	Financial statements should be compared over at least 2 years, with the first year reported being the base year. Changes in each line item relative to the base year should be presented by both amount and percentage. This is called horizontal analysis.	Significant changes should be investigated to determine the reason for the change.

LEARNING REFLECTION AND CONSOLIDATION

Review it

1. What is the purpose of horizontal analysis?
2. Describe the limitations of horizontal analysis.

Do it

The following historical information is an extract from the 2019 annual report of Music and Games Ltd. All figures are in thousands of dollars. Use horizontal analysis to describe the trend in sales revenue and profit.

	2019	2018	2017	2016	2015
Sales revenue	3 308 396	3 127 792	2 959 253	2 731 320	2 327 266
Profit after tax	116 632	104 641	109 695	118 652	94 438

Reasoning

Using 2015 as a base year, the sales revenue and profit for each year can be compared relative to a common starting point so that any trends can be more readily observed and understood.

Solution

	2019	2018	2017	2016	2015
Sales revenue	3 308 396	3 127 792	2 959 253	2 731 320	2 327 266
	*142%	134%	127%	117%	100%
Profit after tax	116 632	104 641	109 695	118 652	94 438
	**124%	111%	116%	126%	100%

Calculations for each year are shown below.

	2019	2018	2017	2016	2015
Sales revenue*	3 308 396	3 127 792	2 959 253	2 731 320	2 327 266
	2 327 266	2 327 266	2 327 266	2 327 266	2 327 266
Profit after tax**	116 632	104 641	109 695	118 652	94 438
	94 438	94 438	94 438	94 438	94 438

Since the base year of 2015, Music and Games Ltd has reported a significant increase in sales revenues and profits. In 2019 it reported its highest sales revenue of $3 308 396 000 which is an increase of 42% from the base year. The entity's profit after tax has also increased since 2015, but the trend has been inconsistent over the five-year period. Music and Games Ltd's profit after tax peaked in 2016 with an increase of 26% from the base year. There was a substantial drop in 2017 and another decline in 2018 in which the entity reported its lowest level of growth of 11% since the base year. A considerable improvement can be seen in 2019 in which a profit after tax of $116 632 000 was reported — this is the largest increase in profit since 2016. The historical data provides a context for interpreting what is happening in the current context.

12.3 Vertical analysis

LEARNING OBJECTIVE 12.3 Explain and apply vertical analysis.

Vertical analysis is a technique for evaluating financial statement data that expresses each item in a financial statement as a percentage of a base amount. For example, on a statement of profit or loss, selling expenses are expressed as a percentage of total revenue. When analysing a statement of financial position, current assets are expressed as a percentage of total assets.

Figure 12.5 presents the vertical analysis of extracts from the statement of profit or loss for Harrison Ltd for the year ended 30 June 2019. Each line on the statement of profit or loss is presented as a percentage of total revenue.

Vertical analysis of Harrison's statement of profit or loss reveals that cost of goods sold as a percentage of total revenue has decreased from 73.7% in 2018 to 73.1% in 2019. This reduction in the cost of goods sold has increased the entity's gross profit from 26.3% to 26.9% over the same period; however, the profit for the period dropped slightly from 4% in 2018 to 3.8% in 2019. This was mainly attributed to the increase in branch expenses as there were minimal changes noted for all other line items.

| FIGURE 12.5 | Vertical analysis of a statement of profit or loss (percentages are rounded) |

HARRISON LIMITED
Extract from statement of profit or loss (and analysis)
for the year ended 30 June 2019

	2019		2018	
	Amount $m	%	Amount $m	%
Revenue from sale of goods	87 774	99.7%	82 165	99.7%
Other operating revenue	236	0.3%	208	0.3%
Total revenue	88 010	100.0%	82 373	100.0%
Cost of sales	(64 368)	(73.1)%	(60 682)	(73.7)%
Gross profit	23 642	26.9%	21 691	26.3%
Other revenue	371	0.4%	335	0.4%
Branch expenses	(14 698)	(16.7)%	(13 165)	(16.0)%
Administrative expenses	(3 921)	(4.5)%	(3 840)	(4.7)%
EBIT	5 394	6.1%	5 021	6.1%
Financial expenses	(615)	(0.7)%	(474)	(0.6)%
Financial income	45	0.1%	52	0.1%
Profit before income tax	**4 824**	5.5%	**4 599**	5.6%
Income tax expense	(1 438)	(1.6)%	(1 327)	(1.6)%
Profit for the period*	**3 386**	3.8%	**3 272**	4.0%

*Profit after tax from continuing operations

Like horizontal analysis, vertical analysis can provide insights into underlying conditions for entities that may not be apparent from the individual components presented in financial statements. However, vertical analysis is even more meaningful if it is supplemented with further information such as general economic conditions, industry trends or averages, information from web sites, directors' reports and media releases. For example, given the current economic uncertainty, many of us may be concerned about our current or future employment opportunities and therefore more conscious about how we spend our cash. In light of this, it is generally more difficult for entities to increase their prices without potentially losing sales to competitors. However, despite these challenging economic conditions, Harrison reported its highest group sales of $87 774 million in 2019 due to significant increases in sales in their supermarket and general merchandise operations. This is perhaps due to the nature of their core business which would be regarded as necessities despite the overall economic conditions. Harrison is very competitive with its major rival Forever Fresh, which aims to offer the lowest possible prices to its customers and provide the best value for money while maintaining profit margins.

Vertical analysis of the statement of financial position shows the relative size of each category. Each line item on the statement of financial position is presented as a percentage of total assets or total liabilities and equity. When applied to comparative financial statements, vertical analysis shows the relative change in the composition of assets from one year to the next, as well as changes in the extent of reliance on various forms of debt and equity financing.

Helpful hint: The statement of financial position can be presented in two main formats: $A = L + E$ or $A - L = E$. In Harrison's 2019 annual report, the statement of financial position is presented as $A - L = E$, as shown in figure 12.3. However, for the purposes of vertical analysis in figure 12.6, the statement of financial position has been presented in the $A = L + E$ format.

The vertical analysis of extracts from Harrison's statement of financial position for 30 June 2019 is shown in figure 12.6.

FIGURE 12.6 Vertical analysis of a statement of financial position

HARRISON LIMITED
Statement of financial position (and analysis)
as at 30 June 2019

	2019		2018	
	Amount $m	%	Amount $m	%
Current assets				
Cash assets	1 273	3.8%	1 250	3.9%
Receivables	1 452	4.4%	1 305	4.0%
Inventories	6 307	19.0%	5 547	17.1%
Other financial assets	81	0.2%	35	0.1%
Other assets	223	0.7%	565	1.7%
Total current assets	9 336	28.1%	8 702	26.9%
Non-current assets				
Receivables	25	0.1%	36	0.1%
Other financial assets	538	1.6%	358	1.1%
Property, plant and equipment	13 869	41.7%	14 383	44.4%
Intangible assets	8 676	26.1%	7 923	24.5%
Deferred tax assets	827	2.5%	967	3.0%
Total non-current assets	23 935	71.9%	23 667	73.1%
Total assets	**33 271**	100.0%	**32 369**	100.0%
Current liabilities				
Payables	8 085	24.3%	7 863	24.3%
Borrowings	254	0.8%	81	0.3%
Current tax liabilities	289	0.9%	332	1.0%
Other financial liabilities	218	0.7%	161	0.5%
Provisions	1 450	4.4%	1 409	4.4%
Other	0	0.0%	301	0.9%
Total current liabilities	10 296	30.9%	10 147	31.3%
Non-current liabilities				
Borrowings	6 423	19.3%	7 042	21.8%
Other financial liabilities	1 488	4.5%	1 330	4.1%
Provisions	823	2.5%	791	2.4%
Other	389	1.2%	388	1.2%
Total non-current liabilities	9 123	27.4%	9 551	29.5%
Total liabilities	**19 419**	58.4%	**19 698**	60.9%

The statement of financial position should be read in conjunction with the accompanying notes.

From the vertical analysis of Harrison's statement of financial position in figure 12.6, we can see that the proportion of current assets to total assets increased from 26.9% in 2018 to 28.1% in 2019. During the same period, the proportion of current liabilities to total liabilities and equity decreased slightly from 31.3% to 30.9%. The proportion of total equity to total liabilities and equity increased from 39.1% in 2018 to 41.6% in 2019. This was mainly attributed to increases in issued capital and retained earnings. Given all of the changes are relatively small, we can conclude that the underlying relationships between statement of financial position items have not changed significantly between 2018 and 2019. It seems that Harrison's operations are relatively stable despite the general economic uncertainty during this period.

An associated benefit of vertical analysis is that it enables you to compare entities in the same industry even if they are different in size. For example, one of Harrison Ltd's competitors is Williams Holdings Ltd. By expressing each line item in the statement of profit or loss as a percentage of revenue, we have a common basis of comparison for each entity's statement of profit or loss, as shown in figure 12.7.

The first part of the analysis is to use the statement of profit or loss data to match up the items that Harrison and Williams report in their respective statements of profit or loss. The format and figures presented in figure 12.7 have been modified and simplified to enable a comparative analysis between these two entities. These amendments were necessary as the presentations of the statements of profit or loss for each entity were considerably different in their classifications of revenue and expense items. For example, the majority of Harrison's operating expenses are categorised under branch or administration expenses, whereas Williams separates operating expenses into more specific categories such as employee benefits and occupancy-related expenses. Despite these limitations, we can still make a number of useful observations from the information available.

| FIGURE 12.7 | Inter-entity comparison by vertical analysis |

Statement of profit or loss (extracts and analysis) for the year ended 30 June 2019				
	Harrison Limited		Williams Holdings Limited	
	Amount $m	%	Amount $m	%
Revenue from sale of goods	87 774	99.7%	89 748	100.0%
Other operating revenue	236	0.3%	0	0%
Total revenue	88 010	100.0%	89 748	100.0%
Cost of sales	(64 368)	−73.1%	(59 425)	−66.2%
Gross profit	23 642	26.9%	30 323	33.8%
Other revenue	371	0.4%	423	0.5%
Financial income	45	0.1%	192	0.2%
Interest expense	(615)	−0.7%	(648)	−0.7%
Branch and general expenses	(12 384)	−14.1%	(8 221)	−9.2%
Depreciation and amortisation	(597)	−0.7%	(1 605)	−1.8%
Employee expenses	(4 438)	−5.0%	(11 868)	−13.2%
Occupancy expenses	(1 200)	−1.4%	(3 590)	−4.0%
Profit before income tax	4 824	5.5%	5 006	5.6%
Income tax expense	(1 438)	−1.6%	(1 327)	−1.5%
Profit after tax	3 386	3.8%	3 679	4.1%

(*Note:* The percentage column expresses each amount as a percentage of the total revenue, rounded to one decimal place. This column is additive and errors in additions can arise due to rounding.)

From the revenue figures we can see that in 2019 Williams generated $1974 million or 2% more than Harrison for the same period. Vertical analysis eliminates this difference by measuring each line item relative to revenue. This is sometimes referred to as a common-size format. Harrison's gross profit is 26.9% of revenue which is significantly lower than the gross profit of 33.8% for Williams.

The most significant difference between the two entities is the branch and general expenses as a percentage of revenue. This category of expenses accounts for 14.1% of revenue for Harrison in comparison to 9.2% for Williams. These substantially higher costs for Harrison are likely to be associated with the opening of 23 new stores in 2019. We can approximate each entity's operating expenses by combining the branch and general expenses, depreciation and amortisation along with the employee and occupancy expenses. Harrison's operating expenses account for 21.2% of revenue whereas Williams' operating expenses account for 28.2% of revenue. These figures suggest that Harrison has better control of its operating expenses.

Using the decision-making toolkit next, management along with other users such as potential investors, shareholders and lenders can use vertical analysis to determine the relationships between items in this year's financial statements and how they compare with those of last year, or those of competitors. A vertical analysis of the statement of profit or loss shows the relationship between revenue, expenses and profit. Each line item on the statement of profit or loss should be presented as a percentage of net sales revenue. A vertical analysis of the statement of financial position shows the relationship between assets, liabilities and equity. Each line item on the statement of financial position should be presented as a percentage of total assets or total liabilities and equity. These percentages should be investigated for any significant differences within the same entity over consecutive years or between different entities for the same year.

LEARNING REFLECTION AND CONSOLIDATION

Review it

1. What is vertical analysis?
2. What different bases can be used to compare financial information?

12.4 Ratio analysis

LEARNING OBJECTIVE 12.4 Identify and calculate ratios and describe their purpose and use in analysing the liquidity, solvency and profitability of a business.

In this section we provide a comprehensive coverage of financial ratios, discuss some important relationships among the ratios, and focus on their interpretation.

For analysing the main financial statements, ratios can be classified into three types:

- **liquidity ratios**: measures of the short-term ability of an entity to pay its maturing obligations and to meet unexpected needs for cash
- **solvency ratios**: measures of the ability of an entity to survive over a long period of time
- **profitability ratios**: measures of the profit or operating success of an entity for a given period of time.

As a tool of analysis, ratios can provide clues to underlying conditions that may not be apparent from an inspection of the individual components of a particular ratio. But a single ratio by itself is not very meaningful. Accordingly, in this discussion we use the following comparisons.

- *Intra-entity comparisons* covering two years for Harrison. Calculations are provided for some 2019 ratios which use data from the statement of profit or loss, statement of financial position and statement

of cash flows, so that you can trace the numbers back to the financial statements in figures 12.6, 12.7 and 12.10.
- *Inter-entity comparisons* using Williams as one of Harrison's main competitors.

Ratios can be expressed in several ways: as a percentage, such as 20%; as a decimal, such as 0.2; and in ratio form, such as 0.2:1.

Alternatively, liquidity can refer to how quickly liabilities need to be paid and how quickly assets can be converted to cash. For example, accounts receivable are more liquid than plant and machinery.

Liquidity ratios

Liquidity ratios measure the short-term ability of the entity to pay its maturing obligations and to meet unexpected needs for cash. Short-term creditors such as bankers and suppliers are particularly interested in assessing liquidity. The measures that can be used to determine the entity's short-term debt-paying ability are the current ratio, the quick ratio (or acid test), current cash debt coverage, receivables turnover, the average collection period, inventory turnover, and average days in inventory.

Helpful hint: The term liquidity *has two meanings. It can refer to the ability to pay obligations and meet unexpected cash needs in the short term. Alternatively, liquidity can refer to how quickly liabilities need to be paid and how quickly assets can be converted to cash. For example, accounts receivable are more liquid than plant and machinery.*

1. *Current ratio.* The **current ratio** expresses the relationship of current assets to current liabilities, calculated by dividing current assets by current liabilities. It is widely used for evaluating an entity's liquidity and short-term debt-paying ability. The 2019 and 2018 current ratios for Harrison and comparative data are shown in figure 12.8, together with the ratio for Williams for 2019. (Amounts have been rounded to $millions.)

FIGURE 12.8	Current ratio				
			Harrison		Williams
Ratio	Formula	Indicates	2019	2018	2019
Current ratio	$\dfrac{\text{Current assets}}{\text{Current liabilities}}$	Short-term debt-paying ability	$\dfrac{\$9\,336}{\$10\,296} = 0.91{:}1$	$\dfrac{\$8\,702}{\$10\,147} = 0.86{:}1$	$\dfrac{\$15\,879}{\$14\,358} = 1.11{:}1$

What do these measures actually mean? A higher current ratio is considered more favourable than a lower current ratio. The 2019 ratio for Harrison means that for every dollar of current liabilities Harrison has $0.91 of current assets. This suggests that Harrison has insufficient cash to meet liabilities as they fall due. Although there was a small increase from $0.86 in 2018 there was no significant change in liquidity. In both years Harrison's current ratio was significantly lower than Williams' current ratio of $1.11 in 2019. What is considered to be an acceptable ratio varies from industry to industry. However, around 1.5:1 is generally considered to be an acceptable current ratio for most industries. Based on this rule of thumb, it is clear that both companies are not in a strong position to repay short-term liabilities as they fall due.

The current ratio is only one measure of liquidity. It does not take into account the composition of the current assets. For example, an entity may have a high current ratio because it has a lot of slow-moving inventory. A dollar of cash is more readily available to pay the bills than is a dollar's worth of slow-moving inventory. This weakness is resolved to some extent by the quick ratio.

2. *Quick ratio.* The **quick ratio** (or acid test) is a measure of an entity's immediate short-term liquidity. It is calculated by dividing the sum of cash, marketable securities and net receivables by current liabilities. Therefore, it is an important complement to the current ratio. Note that it does not include inventory or prepaid expenses. Of the current assets, cash, marketable securities and net receivables

are considered highly liquid as they are more quickly converted to cash when compared with inventory and prepaid expenses. The inventory may not be readily saleable and the prepaid expenses are not generally convertible into cash. The quick ratios for Harrison and Williams are shown in figure 12.9.

FIGURE 12.9 Quick ratio

Ratio	Formula	Indicates	Harrison		Williams
			2019	2018	2019
Quick ratio or acid test	$Cash + \dfrac{Marketable\ securities + Net\ receivables}{Current\ liabilities}$	Immediate short-term liquidity	$\dfrac{\$1\,273 + \$81 + \$1\,452}{\$10\,296} = 0.27{:}1$	0.26:1	0.38:1

The difference between the quick ratios indicates marginal change in liquidity from 0.26 to 0.27 for Harrison in 2018 and 2019 respectively. Compared with Williams' quick ratio of 0.38, Harrison's ratio indicates considerably fewer quick assets for every dollar of current liabilities in both years. As a rule of thumb, some analysts suggest that a ratio of approximately 1:1 is adequate. However, this is arbitrary and subject to debate and exception. In any case, deviations from the general rule of thumb are worthy of further investigation. However, in the retail segment of the market, where sales are generally made in cash (this includes credit card sales), a lower ratio is acceptable. This would be applicable to entities such as Harrison and Williams as their core business is in supermarkets where sales are generally cash or credit sales. As this provides a continual inflow of cash, it can be used to meet debts as they fall due.

3. *Current cash debt coverage.* A disadvantage of the current and quick ratios is that they use year-end balances of current asset and current liability accounts. These year-end balances may not be representative of the entity's current position during most of the year. A ratio that partially corrects for this problem is the ratio of net cash provided by operating activities to average current liabilities, called the **current cash debt coverage**. Because the numerator consists of net cash provided by operating activities rather than a balance at one point in time, and the denominator consists of average current liabilities, the ratio may provide a better representation of liquidity. The simplified statement of cash flows for Harrison is provided in figure 12.10. The current cash debt coverage ratios for Harrison and Williams are shown in figure 12.11.

FIGURE 12.10 Statement of cash flows (simplified)

HARRISON LIMITED
Statement of cash flows (extract)
for the year ended 30 June 2019

	2019 $m	2018 $m
Net cash inflow from operating activities	4 080	4 310
Net cash (outflow) from investing activities	−1 804	−3 120
Net cash (outflow) from financing activities	−2 280	−2 204
Net (decrease)/increase in cash held	**−4**	**−1 014**

From this current cash debt coverage ratio based on cash flow information, Harrison's coverage of its current liabilities improved slightly in 2019 from 0.39 to 0.40. These figures have remained stable over the 2 years and are similar to Williams' current cash debt coverage at 0.39 in 2019. This ratio indicates the entity's ability to generate sufficient cash to meet its short-term needs. While the acceptable level for the current cash debt coverage ratio will vary between industries, in general a value below 0.40:1 times is considered cause for additional investigation of an entity's liquidity. Harrison's current cash debt coverage of 0.40 in 2019 is within the acceptable level. Williams' ratio of 0.39 in 2019 is marginally below the rule of thumb, which may warrant further investigation to ensure it does not have cash flow shortages in the future.

FIGURE 12.11 Current cash debt coverage

Ratio	Formula	Indicates	Harrison 2019	2018	Williams 2019
Current cash debt coverage	Net cash provided by operating activities / Average current liabilities	Short-term debt-paying ability (cash basis)	$\dfrac{\$4\,080}{(\$10\,296 + \$10\,147)/2} = 0.40{:}1$	0.39:1	0.39:1

4. *Receivables turnover.* Liquidity may be measured by how quickly certain assets can be converted to cash. Low values of the previous ratios can sometimes be compensated for if some of the entity's current assets are highly liquid. How liquid, for example, are the receivables? The ratio used to assess the liquidity of the receivables is the **receivables turnover**, which measures the number of times, on average, that receivables are collected during the period. The higher the receivables turnover, the shorter the period of time between an entity making a credit sale and collecting the cash for the receivable. The receivables turnover is calculated by dividing net credit sales (net sales less cash sales) by average net trade receivables during the year. Receivables reported on the statement of financial position may include amounts not related to sales. If this is the case, trade receivables are disclosed in the notes. The receivables turnover figures for Harrison and Williams are shown in figure 12.12. Users of external financial statements use total sales revenue because net credit sales are not separately identified in published financial statements.

FIGURE 12.12 Receivables turnover

Ratio	Formula	Indicates	Harrison 2019	2018	Williams 2019
Receivables turnover	Net credit sales / Average net trade receivables	Liquidity of receivables	$\dfrac{\$87\,774}{(\$1\,452 + \$1\,305)/2} = 63.7$ times	69.3 times	33.6 times

Helpful hint: Note that net sales is gross sales less sales returns and allowances.

Harrison's receivables turnover decreased from 69.3 times per year in 2018 to 63.7 times per year in 2019. However, these ratios are not a true reflection of the turnover. Retail entities typically make most of their sales as cash sales or credit card sales and this exaggerates turnover when the net sales figure is substituted for net credit sales.

5. *Average collection period.* This is a variation of the receivables turnover which converts the turnover into an **average collection period** in days. This is done by dividing the receivables turnover into 365 days. The ratio can be used to assess the effectiveness of an entity's credit and collection policies. A general rule is that the collection period should not greatly exceed the credit term period, which is the time allowed for payment. For example, if an entity offers 30-day credit terms and has an average collection period of 27 days, this provides an indication that the entity's credit policy is appropriate and the monitoring of receivables collection is effective. A company whose average collection period is significantly above its credit terms suggests that it may be granting credit to customers who are not creditworthy or needs to change its credit policies or collection procedures. The average collection periods for Harrison and Williams are shown in figure 12.13.

FIGURE 12.13 Average collection period

Ratio	Formula	Indicates	Harrison		Williams
			2019	2018	2019
Average collection period	$\dfrac{365 \text{ days}}{\text{Receivables turnover}}$	Liquidity of receivables and collection success	$\dfrac{365}{63.7} = 5.73$ days	$\dfrac{365}{69.3} = 5.27$ days	$\dfrac{365}{33.6} = 10.86$ days

Both Harrison and Williams have relatively low average collection periods; however, Harrison's collection period is faster with an average of around 5.5 days in 2018 and 2019 compared to Williams' collection period of approximately 11 days. It should be noted that customers making purchases on credit terms are unlikely to pay for them in 5 days. These very low numbers reflect the invalidity of assuming all sales are credit sales for a retailer. However, these ratios would be calculated internally using the actual credit sales figures providing more useful information for management.

6. *Inventory turnover.* The **inventory turnover** measures the number of times on average the inventory is sold during the period. Its purpose is to measure the liquidity of the inventory. Further, the higher the turnover, the less chance stock will be slow moving or become obsolete and unsaleable. It is important to monitor the amount of resources invested in inventory, as part of managing the business. Entities do not want to unnecessarily have too much cash tied up in inventories. At the same time, they do not want to be understocked and miss out on sales because of lack of stock. Inventory turnover is calculated by dividing the cost of sales by the average inventory during the period. Unless seasonal factors are significant, average inventory can be calculated from the beginning and ending inventory balances. Harrison's and Williams' inventory turnovers are shown in figure 12.14.

FIGURE 12.14 Inventory turnover ratio

Ratio	Formula	Indicates	Harrison		Williams
			2019	2018	2019
Inventory turnover	$\dfrac{\text{Cost of sales}}{\text{Average inventory}}$	Liquidity of inventory	$\dfrac{\$64\,368}{(\$6\,307 + \$5\,547)/2} = 10.86$ times	10.88 times	7.88 times

Harrison's inventory turnover has remained consistent over the 2 years, wherein inventory was sold and replaced 10.88 times in 2018 and 10.86 times in 2019. Harrison is more efficient in managing its inventory with a substantially faster turnover than Williams' turnover of 7.88 times in 2019. Generally, a high inventory turnover is preferable as this minimises the cost of obsolescence and less cash is tied up in inventory. The downside of a very high inventory turnover is that the entity can run out of inventory and this may result in lost sales. Inventory turnover ratios are much higher in industry sectors such as supermarkets that sell perishable items.

7. *Average days in inventory.* This is a variation of the inventory turnover that converts the turnover into days. This is done by dividing the inventory turnover by 365 days. The **average days in inventory** ratio measures the average number of days it takes to sell the inventory. The average number of days in inventory for Harrison and Williams are shown in figure 12.15.

Harrison's average days in inventory remained relatively unchanged from 33.5 days in 2018 to 33.6 days in 2019. This is considerably faster than Williams' average days in inventory of 46.3 days. An inventory turnover of 100 days may be acceptable for non-perishable items such as computers or furniture, but a much higher turnover would be necessary for perishables such as fresh food items. Both Williams and Harrison are retailers of perishables and general merchandise as well as consumer durables which have a longer shelf-life than many of their grocery and fast-food lines. This would contribute to the average number of days that inventory is held.

FIGURE 12.15 | Average days in inventory

Ratio	Formula	Indicates	Harrison 2019	Harrison 2018	Williams 2019
Average days in inventory	$\dfrac{365 \text{ days}}{\text{Inventory turnover}}$	Liquidity of inventory and inventory management	$\dfrac{365}{10.86} = 33.6$ days	33.5 days	46.3 days

Solvency ratios

Solvency ratios measure the ability of the entity to survive over a long period of time. Long-term creditors and shareholders are interested in a company's long-term solvency, particularly its ability to pay interest as it comes due and to repay the face value of the debt at maturity. The debt to total assets ratio, times interest earned, and cash debt coverage provide information about debt-paying ability. In addition, free cash flow provides information about the company's solvency and its ability to pay dividends or invest in new projects.

8. *Debt to total assets ratio.* The **debt to total assets ratio** measures the percentage of the total assets financed by creditors. It is calculated by dividing total liabilities by total assets. This ratio indicates the degree of leveraging; it provides some indication of the entity's ability to withstand losses without impairing the interests of its creditors. The higher the percentage of total liabilities to total assets, the greater the financial risk that the entity may be unable to meet its maturing obligations. The lower the debt to total assets ratio, the greater the equity available to creditors if the entity becomes insolvent. Therefore, from the creditors' point of view, a low ratio of debt to total assets is usually desirable. Harrison's and Williams' debt to total assets ratios are shown in figure 12.16.

Helpful hint: Leveraging is borrowing money at a lower rate of interest that can be earned by using the borrowed money; also referred to as trading on equity.

FIGURE 12.16 | Debt to total assets ratio

Ratio	Formula	Indicates	Harrison 2019	Harrison 2018	Williams 2019
Debt to total assets ratio	$\dfrac{\text{Total liabilities}}{\text{Total assets}}$	Percentage of total assets provided by creditors	$\dfrac{\$19\,419}{\$33\,271} = 0.58{:}1$	0.61:1	0.40:1

Harrison's debt to total assets ratio of 0.58 in 2019 indicates that creditors provided 58 cents for every dollar invested in assets compared to 61 cents in 2018. The adequacy of this ratio is often judged in the light of the entity's profits. Generally, entities with relatively stable profits have higher debt to total assets ratios than do cyclical entities with widely fluctuating profits, such as many high-tech companies. Stable profits reflect low operating risk, whereas fluctuating profits are interpreted as high operating risk. Leverage, measured by the debt to total assets ratio, is an indicator of financial risk. Creditors consider the total risk and are reluctant to lend to entities that combine high finance risk with high operating risk.

Another ratio with a similar meaning is the *debt to equity ratio*. It shows the relative use of borrowed funds (total liabilities) and resources invested by the owners. Because this ratio can be calculated in several ways, care should be taken when making comparisons. Debt may be defined to include only the non-current portion of liabilities, and intangible assets may be deducted from equity (which would equal tangible net worth). If debt and assets are defined as above (all liabilities and all assets), when the debt to total assets ratio equals 50% the debt to equity ratio is 1:1.

9. *Times interest earned.* **Times interest earned** (also called interest coverage) indicates the entity's ability to meet interest payments as they come due. It is calculated by dividing earnings before income tax plus interest expense (finance costs) by interest expense. Note that this ratio uses earnings before income tax and interest expense (EBIT) because this amount represents what is available to cover interest. A general rule of thumb is that earnings should be approximately 3–4 times the interest expense. Harrison's and Williams' times interest earned are shown in figure 12.17.

FIGURE 12.17 Times interest earned

Ratio	Formula	Indicates	Harrison 2019	Harrison 2018	Williams 2019
Times interest earned	Earnings before interest and tax / Interest expense	Ability to meet interest payments as they fall due	$\dfrac{\$5\,394}{\$615} = 8.77$ times	10.56 times	8.47 times

Harrison's interest coverage has decreased from 10.56 times in 2018 to 8.77 times in 2019. Although Harrison's EBIT had increased significantly in 2019, the interest expense increased at a higher rate. Williams' interest coverage of 8.47 times in 2019 is similar to that of Harrison. These figures indicate that both entities have very strong ability to cover interest expense, well above the rule of thumb of 3–4 times.

10. *Cash debt coverage.* Net cash provided by operating activities to average total liabilities, called the **cash debt coverage**, is a cash-basis measure of solvency. This ratio indicates an entity's ability to repay its liabilities from cash generated from operating activities, without having to liquidate the assets used in its operations. The cash debt coverage ratio is calculated as cash provided by operating activities divided by average total liabilities. While what is considered an acceptable ratio varies between industries, a general rule of thumb is that a ratio below 0.20 times is considered cause for additional investigation. Figure 12.18 shows Harrison's and Williams' cash debt coverage.

FIGURE 12.18 Cash debt coverage

Ratio	Formula	Indicates	Harrison 2019	Harrison 2018	Williams 2019
Cash debt coverage	Net cash provided by operating activities / Average total liabilities	Long-term debt-paying ability (cash basis)	$\dfrac{\$4\,080}{(\$19\,419 + \$19\,698)/2} = 0.21{:}1$	0.22:1	0.23:1

Harrison's cash debt coverage decreased slightly from 0.22:1 in 2018 to 0.21:1 in 2019. These figures are similar to that of Williams' cash debt coverage of 0.23:1 in 2019. The cash debt coverage for Harrison and Williams are within the recommended minimum level of 0.2:1, which suggests that both entities appear solvent.

An alternative way of interpreting this ratio is that, in 2019, net cash provided by operations is sufficient to pay 21% of Harrison's average liabilities and it could take approximately 4.76 years to pay existing liabilities from cash surpluses from operations at the 2019 level.

11. *Free cash flow.* One indication of an entity's solvency, as well as its ability to pay dividends, reduce long-term debt, or expand operations, is the amount of excess cash it generated after investing to maintain its current productive capacity. This measure is referred to as **free cash flow**. For example, if you generate $100 000 of net cash from operations but spend $40 000 to maintain and replace productive facilities at their current levels, you have a free cash flow of $60 000 to use to either expand operations or to pay dividends.

As a practical matter, entities do not disclose what percentage of their capital expenditure was made to maintain existing production and what percentage was made to expand operations. Therefore, external users normally calculate free cash flow by simply subtracting gross property, plant and equipment (non-current assets) expenditures from cash from operations. Harrison's and Williams' free cash flows are shown in figure 12.19. Harrison's capital expenditures were $3562 million in 2019 and $3550 million in 2018.

FIGURE 12.19 | Free cash flow

| Ratio | Formula | Indicates | Harrison | | Williams |
			2019	2018	2019
Free cash flow	Net cash provided by operating activities – Capital expenditures	Cash available for paying dividends or expanding operations	$4 080 – $3 562 = $518	$760	$2400

Using the formula above, Harrison's free cash flow is positive in both years. This means that capital expenditures are paid for using surpluses from operating activities. Sufficient cash is generated from operations net of capital expenditure to provide for dividends and liabilities. Harrison's free cash flow showed a significant decrease from $760 million in 2018 to $518 million in 2019. These figures are well below Williams' free cash flow of $2400 million in 2019.

Profitability ratios

Profitability ratios measure the profit or operating success of an entity for a given period of time. An entity's profit, or lack of it, affects its ability to obtain debt and equity financing, its liquidity position and its ability to grow. As a consequence, creditors and investors alike are interested in evaluating profitability. Profitability is frequently used as the ultimate test of management's operating effectiveness. Some commonly used measures of profitability are discussed in the following pages.

The relationships among these profitability measures are very important. Understanding them can help management determine where to focus its efforts to improve the entity's profitability. Figure 12.20 illustrates the interrelationships between these ratios. The following discussion of Harrison's profitability is structured around this diagram.

FIGURE 12.20 | Relationships among profitability measures

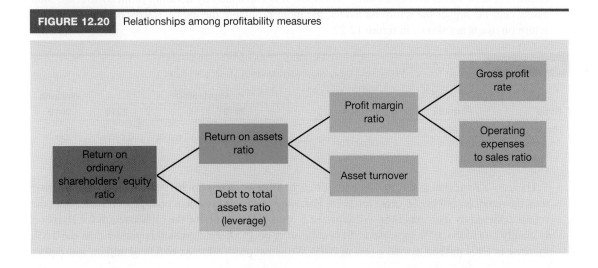

12. *Return on ordinary shareholders' equity.* A widely used measure of profitability from the perspective of the ordinary shareholder is the **return on ordinary shareholders' equity (ROE)**. This ratio shows the amount of profit carned for each dollar invested by the shareholders. The ROE is calculated by dividing the profit available to ordinary shareholders by average ordinary shareholders' equity. To determine the profit available to ordinary shareholders, we need to subtract any dividends for preference shareholders. The return on ordinary shareholders' equity for Harrison and Williams is shown in figure 12.21.

FIGURE 12.21 Return on ordinary shareholders' equity

Ratio	Formula	Indicates	Harrison 2019	2018	Williams 2019
Return on ordinary shareholders' equity	Profit available to ordinary shareholders / Average ordinary shareholders' equity	Profitability of ordinary shareholders' investment	$\dfrac{\$3\,386}{(\$13\,852 + \$12\,671)/2} = 25$ cents	22 cents	9 cents

Harrison's return on equity of 25 cents for each dollar of equity in 2019 was slightly higher than the return on equity of 22 cents for 2018. There was a 9.6% increase of $602 million in profit available to ordinary shareholders and a 9.3% increase of $1181 million in equity. The combination of these factors increased Harrison's return on equity in 2019. The return on equity for Harrison for both years was much higher than the 9 cent return on equity for Williams in 2019. Williams' profit available to ordinary shareholders of $3679 million in 2019 was actually higher than that of Harrison in both years. The reason for the low return on equity for Williams is mainly due to the fact that it had $39 033 million of equity in 2019 compared to $13 852 million of equity for Harrison. As a potential investor, based on these results for 2019, Harrison appears to be the more attractive investment as it provides the greater return on shareholder funds invested. Furthermore, given that Harrison's return on equity is much greater than the market interest rate, investing in the company provided each shareholder with a greater return than if they had kept the money and earned interest on it in a bank account or if the money had been used to finance debt.

13. *Return on assets.* The return on ordinary shareholders' equity is affected by two factors: the **return on assets (ROA)** and the degree of leverage. The return on assets measures the overall profitability of assets in terms of the profit earned on each dollar invested in assets. It is a measure of management's effectiveness based on normal business activities. It is calculated by dividing profit by average total assets, and the higher the return on assets, the more profitable the entity. Harrison's and Williams' return on assets are shown in figure 12.22.

FIGURE 12.22 Return on assets

Ratio	Formula	Indicates	Harrison 2019	2018	Williams 2019
Return on assets	Profit after tax / Average total assets	Overall profitability of assets	$\dfrac{\$3\,386}{(\$33\,271 + \$32\,369)/2} = 10$ cents	6 cents	5 cents

Harrison's return on assets of 10 cents for each dollar of assets in 2019 was considerably higher than the return on assets of 6 cents for 2018. Harrison's return on assets in both years is better than the return achieved by its competitor, Williams, of 5 cents. The reason for the higher return for Harrison is mainly due to the 3.5% increase of $114 million in profit after tax, which is greater than the 2.8% increase of $902 million in total assets in 2019. Williams' profit after tax of $3679 million was higher than Harrison's $3386 million in 2019. The reason for the low return on assets for Williams in 2019 is mainly attributed to its total assets of $64 732 million, which is almost twice the size of Harrison's total assets of $33 271 million. The return on assets indicates that Harrison has been more effective in generating relatively high profits from a much smaller asset base.

14. *Profit margin.* The return on assets is affected by two factors, the first of which is the profit margin. The **profit margin**, or rate of return on sales, is a measure of the amount of each dollar of sales that results in profit. It is calculated by dividing profit by net sales for the period. Harrison's and Williams' profit margins are shown in figure 12.23.

FIGURE 12.23	Profit margin				
			Harrison		**Williams**
Ratio	Formula	Indicates	2019	2018	2019
Profit margin	$\dfrac{\text{Profit after tax}}{\text{Net sales}}$	Profit generated by each dollar of sales	$\dfrac{\$3\,386}{\$87\,774} = 4$ cents	6 cents	4 cents

Harrison's profit margin indicates that 4 cents of profit was generated from each dollar of sales in 2019 compared to 6 cents of profit in 2018. These results are similar to the profit margin for Williams in 2019.

Profit margins vary from industry to industry, as can be seen in the following hypothetical business examples. High-volume businesses such as supermarkets generally experience low profit margins, which can be below 7 cents as shown in the results for Harrison and Williams. In contrast, Blue Water Resorts Ltd, which operates in the hotels, restaurants and leisure industry, had a higher profit margin of 14 cents and Giorgina's Pizza Limited, which operates in the food retail industry, had a profit margin of 15 cents.

15. *Asset turnover.* The other factor that affects the return on assets is the asset turnover. The **asset turnover** measures how efficiently an entity uses its assets to generate sales. It is determined by dividing net sales by average total assets for the period. The resulting number shows the dollar of sales produced by each dollar invested in assets. Figure 12.24 shows asset turnover for Harrison and Williams.

FIGURE 12.24	Asset turnover				
			Harrison		**Williams**
Ratio	Formula	Indicates	2019	2018	2019
Asset turnover	$\dfrac{\text{Net sales}}{\text{Average total assets}}$	How efficiently assets are used to generate sales	$\dfrac{\$87\,774}{(\$33\,271 + \$32\,369)/2} = \$2.67$	$2.58	$1.34

The asset turnover for 2019 shows that Harrison generated sales of $2.67 for each dollar it had invested in assets compared to $2.58 in 2018. This significant improvement was mainly attributed to the 6.8% increase of $5609 million in sales, which was greater than the 2.8% increase of $902 million in total assets. Williams had an asset turnover of $1.34 in 2019, which indicates a much lower level efficiency than Harrison in generating sales revenue from its assets.

Asset turnovers vary considerably across different industry sectors. For example, Blue Water Resorts Ltd, which operates in the hotels, restaurants and leisure industry, had a low turnover ratio of 50 cents. In contrast, Music and Games Ltd, which operates in the specialty retail industry, had a high asset turnover of $4.10.

16. *Gross profit margin.* Two factors strongly influence the profit margin. One is the gross profit margin. The **gross profit margin** is determined by dividing gross profit (net sales less cost of sales) by net sales. This rate indicates an entity's ability to maintain an adequate selling price above its costs. As an industry becomes more competitive, this ratio declines. For example, when smart phones and mobile technology were newly released into the retail sector, the gross profit margins for these products were quite high. However, due to the intense competition across a diversity of new and innovative products, the gross profit margins have become relatively lower. Gross profit margins should be closely monitored over time. Figure 12.25 shows Harrison's and Williams' gross profit margins.

FIGURE 12.25 Gross profit margin

| | | | Harrison | | Williams |
Ratio	Formula	Indicates	2019	2018	2019
Gross profit margin	$\dfrac{\text{Gross profit}}{\text{Net sales}}$	Margin between selling price and cost of sales	$\dfrac{\$23\,642}{\$87\,774} = 27\%$	26%	31%

Harrison's gross profit margin increased slightly from 26% in 2018 to 27% in 2019. As stated in its 2019 annual report, its gross profit margin continued to improve due to better buying, increased freight efficiencies and more effective promotions. Harrison's gross profit margins are slightly lower than that of its competitor, Williams, at 31%. This difference may be due to the nature of Williams' diverse business operations. In addition to supermarkets, department stores and home improvement, which are similar to Harrison, its operations also include coal production and export; insurance; chemicals, energy and fertilisers; and industrial and safety products.

17. *Operating expenses to sales ratio.* This is the other factor that directly affects the profit margin. Management can influence an entity's profitability by maintaining adequate prices, cutting expenses, or both. The **operating expenses to sales ratio** measures the costs incurred to support each dollar of sales. It is calculated by dividing operating expenses (selling and administrative expenses) by net sales. The operating expenses to sales ratios for Harrison and Williams are shown in figure 12.26.

FIGURE 12.26 Operating expenses to sales ratio

| | | | Harrison | | Williams |
Ratio	Formula	Indicates	2019	2018	2019
Operating expenses to sales ratio	$\dfrac{\text{Operating expenses}}{\text{Net sales}}$	The costs incurred to support each dollar of sales	$\dfrac{\$14\,698 + \$3\,921}{\$87\,774} = 0.21\!:\!1$	0.21:1	0.29:1

These figures relate back to Harrison's statement of profit or loss (refer to figure 12.5). Harrison's operating expenses are classified under branch expenses and administration expenses. From the operating expenses to sales ratio, we can see that Harrison has maintained a constant level of 21 cents of operating expenses for each sales dollar over the 2-year period. In comparison, Williams spends 29 cents of each sales dollar on operating expenses. These figures show that Harrison is able to manage its operating costs more effectively.

An alternative approach is to include finance costs as well as the expenses used in the formula provided above. However, when comparing the operating expenses to sales ratios of different entities, it is preferable to exclude finance costs so that the comparison is not distorted by differences in financial structure. Obviously, entities that rely more heavily on debt financing will have higher total expenses because interest is recognised as an expense. Entities that rely more heavily on equity may pay more dividends. It is important to note that dividends are a distribution of profit and therefore not an expense. This is particularly relevant in the case of comparisons between Harrison and Williams, given that Harrison has a greater reliance on debt finance. In 2019, the debt to assets ratio was 58% and 40% for Harrison and Williams respectively.

18. *Cash return on sales ratio.* The profit margin discussed earlier is an accrual-based ratio using profit as a numerator. The cash-basis counterpart to that ratio is the **cash return on sales ratio**, which uses net cash provided by operating activities as the numerator and net sales as the denominator. The difference between these two ratios should be explainable as differences between accrual accounting and cash-basis accounting, such as differences in the timing of revenue and expense recognition. The cash return on sales ratios for Harrison and Williams are shown in figure 12.27.

FIGURE 12.27	Cash return on sales ratio				

			Harrison		Williams
Ratio	Formula	Indicates	2019	2018	2019
Cash return on sales ratio	Net cash provided by operating activities / Net sales	Net cash flow generated by each dollar of sales	$\dfrac{\$2\,719.9}{\$58\,516.4} = 0.05{:}1$	0.05:1	0.07:1

Harrison' cash return on sales remained the same with a return of 5 cents from each sales dollar in 2018 and 2019. This ratio is similar to Williams' return of 7 cents from each sales dollar in 2019. Despite the diversity of each entity's business operations, the net cash provided by operating activities and sales generated were similar over the 2-year period.

19. *Earnings per share (EPS).* Shareholders usually think in terms of the number of shares they own or plan to buy or sell. Expressing profit earned on a per share basis provides a useful perspective for determining profitability. **Earnings per share** is a measure of the profit earned on each ordinary share. It is calculated by dividing profit available to ordinary shareholders by the weighted average number of ordinary shares issued. When we use 'profit per share' or 'earnings per share', it refers to the amount of profit applicable to each ordinary share. Therefore, when we calculate earnings per share, if there are preference dividends declared for the period, they must be deducted from profit to determine the profit available to the ordinary shareholders. The reporting of earnings per share is regulated by accounting standard IAS 33/AASB 133 *Earnings per Share*. Harrison's and Williams' earnings per share are shown in figure 12.28.

FIGURE 12.28	Earnings per share				

			Harrison		Williams
Ratio	Formula	Indicates	2019	2018	2019
Earnings per share (EPS)	Profit available to ordinary shareholders / Weighted average number of ordinary shares	Profit per ordinary share	$\dfrac{\$3\,386}{1\,854} = 182.6$ cents	148.7 cents	195.9 cents

Harrison's EPS has increased significantly from 148.7 cents in 2018 to 182.6 cents in 2019. This was due to an increase in profit available to ordinary shareholders of $114 million with a relatively small increase of 15 million to the number of issued shares in 2019. Williams' EPS is greater than Harrison's in 2019 at 195.9 cents per share. The EPS is a commonly quoted figure and can be found in many daily newspapers and securities exchange reports. Companies are also required to disclose it in their annual reports. Comparison of EPS between companies is not valid when companies vary in the number of issued shares without further information about the share price. To some extent, the price/earnings ratio overcomes this limitation.

20. *Price/earnings ratio*. Like EPS, the **price/earnings ratio (P/E ratio)** is another statistic that is often quoted as it measures the ratio of the market price of each ordinary share to the earnings per share. The price/earnings ratio is a reflection of investors' assessments of a company's future earnings and indicates how much an investor would have to pay in the market for each dollar of earnings expected. It is calculated by dividing the market price per share by earnings per share. Harrison's and Williams' price/earnings ratios are shown in figure 12.29.

FIGURE 12.29 Price/earnings ratio

Ratio	Formula	Indicates	Harrison 2019	Harrison 2018	Williams 2019
Price/ earnings ratio	$\dfrac{\text{Share price}}{\text{Earnings per share}}$	Relationship between market price per share and earnings per share	$\dfrac{\$32.80}{\$1.826} = 17.96$ times	17.82 times	20.22 times

At the end of the 2019 financial period, Harrison's share price of $32.80 was 17.96 times higher than the amount of earnings per share. This means that an investor who buys one share in Harrison at a market price of $32.80 can expect to earn an average return of 5.6% ($1.826/$32.80) at the current level of profit. In 2019, Williams' P/E ratio of 20.22 times is much higher than that of Harrison's P/E ratio which remained close to 18 times in 2018 and 2019. Both companies had strong P/E ratios. Investing in shares in either company would have provided a return greater than simply earning interest on the money invested in a fixed term deposit with a bank if the prevailing rate was about 3% to 4.5%.

Price/earnings ratios vary between industries. Generally, financially strong, or 'blue chip', companies, and companies experiencing growth have higher P/E ratios. Companies in the maturity and decline phase of the life cycle tend to have lower P/E ratios. Calculating the P/E ratios enables an investor to compare the market value of one ordinary share relative to profits with that of other companies. It also provides an indication of shareholder confidence in the company. A greater level of shareholder confidence would be reflected in a higher P/E ratio as shareholders would be prepared to pay a higher price for the share. For example, Harrison's share price rose from $26.50 in 2018 to $32.80 in 2019.

21. *Dividend payout rate*. The **dividend payout rate** measures the percentage of profit distributed in the form of dividends. It is calculated by dividing dividends paid on ordinary shares by profit. Companies that have high growth rates are characterised by low payout rates because often they reinvest most of their profit back into the business. The dividend payout rates for Harrison and Williams are shown in figure 12.30. Harrison paid dividends of $2396 million in 2019.

FIGURE 12.30 Dividend payout rate

Ratio	Formula	Indicates	Harrison 2019	Harrison 2018	Williams 2019
Dividend payout rate	$\dfrac{\text{Dividends}}{\text{Profit}}$	Percentages of profit distributed in the form of dividends	$\dfrac{\$2\,396}{\$3\,386} = 71\%$	83%	88%

Harrison's dividend payout rate decreased from 83% of profit paid as dividends in 2018 to 71% in 2019. This is mainly due to the decrease of $588 million in dividends paid in 2019. Management determines the amount of dividends paid each year and companies are generally reluctant to reduce a dividend below the amount paid in a previous year except in this case where it was unusually high and not sustainable. Therefore, sometimes the payout rate will actually increase if a company's profit declines but the company maintains its dividend payments. Of course, unless the company returns to its previous level of profitability, maintaining this higher dividend payout rate is probably not possible over the long term.

Harrison's dividend payout rate of 71% and 83% for 2019 and 2018 respectively was lower compared to Williams' dividend payout rate of 88% of profit in 2019. In the absence of low profits, a high dividend payout rate is indicative of a company in the maturity stage. The decline of Harrison's dividend payout rate in 2019 also may have been attributed to the reinvestment of profits in the business to finance new store openings in 2019. This can be seen in the substantial increase of $602 million in retained earnings in 2019. Before drawing any conclusions regarding the company's dividend payout rate, we should calculate this ratio over a longer period of time to evaluate any trends, and also try to find out whether management's philosophy regarding dividends has changed in recent times.

In terms of the types of financial information available and the ratios used by various industries, what can be practically covered in this text gives you only the 'Titanic approach' — you are seeing only the tip of the iceberg compared with the vast databases and types of ratio analysis that are available on computers. The availability of information is not a problem. The challenge is to be discriminating enough to perform relevant analyses and select pertinent comparative data. It also must be restated that ratios provide useful information about a company that may not be immediately evident from simply observing the data provided in financial reports, additional information about general economic conditions, industry trends or averages, and information from directors' reports and media releases.

Potential investors, shareholders, lenders and other users are interested in evaluating whether the entity is profitable and whether it can meet its short- and long-term obligations. These decision makers feel more confident investing in a company that is highly profitable and financially stable, with adequate funds to not only meet financial obligations but also to expand its future operations. Financial data can be found in the entity's statement of profit or loss and statement of financial position. To evaluate an entity's profitability, liquidity and solvency, key ratios specific to each of these categories can be calculated and used for analysis and interpretation, for example, profit margin for profitability, current ratio for liquidity and debt to assets ratio for solvency. For a more meaningful analysis, it is useful to use appropriate benchmarks for comparison such as intra-company comparisons and inter-company comparisons as well as industry trends and averages.

From this chapter it is evident that there is a lot of information that users can draw upon to analyse, evaluate and make decisions about an entity. The decision-making and analysis process using ratio analysis is summarised in the decision-making toolkit below.

DECISION-MAKING TOOLKIT

Decision/issue	Info needed for analysis	Tool or technique to use for decision	How to evaluate results to make decision
Is the entity profitable and can it meet its short- and long-term obligations?	Statement of profit or loss, statement of financial position and other relevant information such as general economic conditions, industry trends and/or averages, information from annual reports and media releases	Calculate a variety of ratios to indicate an entity's profitability, liquidity and solvency. This is called ratio analysis.	A single ratio on its own is not very meaningful, hence it is useful to interpret ratios using: (1) intra-company comparisons, (2) inter-company comparisons, (3) other relevant information such as general economic conditions and industry trends and averages.

Review it

1. What are liquidity ratios? Explain the current ratio, quick ratio, receivables turnover, inventory turnover, and current cash debt coverage.
2. What are solvency ratios? Explain the debt to total assets ratio, times interest earned, and cash debt coverage.
3. What are profitability ratios? Explain return on ordinary shareholders' equity, return on assets, asset turnover, cash return on sales ratio, earnings per share, price/earnings ratio and dividend payout rate.

12.5 Limitations of financial statement analysis

LEARNING OBJECTIVE 12.5 Discuss the limitations of financial statement analysis.

Significant business decisions are often made using one or more of the three analytical tools presented in this chapter — horizontal, vertical and ratio analysis. You should be aware of some of the limitations of these tools and of the financial statements on which they are based.

Estimates

Financial statements contain numerous estimates. Estimates are used, for example, in determining the allowance for uncollectable receivables, periodic depreciation and the costs of warranties. To the extent that these estimates are inaccurate, the financial ratios and percentages are also inaccurate.

Cost

Traditional financial statements are based on cost and are not adjusted for price-level changes. Comparisons of unadjusted financial data from different periods may be rendered invalid by significant inflation or deflation. For example, if a 5-year comparison of revenues shows a growth of 24% and the general price level also increased by 24%, the entity's real growth would be nil. Also, some assets such as property, plant and equipment might be many years old. The carrying amount (cost less accumulated depreciation) at which they are shown on the statement of financial position might be significantly lower than their current market value. Therefore, ratios such as return on investment would appear more favourable than if the entity had new assets.

Alternative accounting methods

Variations among entities in the application of generally accepted accounting principles may hamper comparability. For example, one entity may use the straight-line method of depreciation, whereas another entity in the same industry may use the diminishing-balance method. This would affect ratios that use profit and, to a lesser extent, ratios that use total assets. Although these differences in accounting methods might be detectable from reading the notes to the financial statements, adjusting the financial data to compensate for the different methods is difficult, if not impossible, in some cases. For example, many entities have changed accounting policies effective from the commencement of the first reporting period beginning on or after 1 January 2005. This is the result of the Financial Reporting Council's decision for Australia to converge with international financial reporting standards as discussed in chapter 1. While entities must in most cases restate comparative data, horizontal analysis over earlier periods would be distorted unless the entities also restated earlier figures.

Atypical data

Financial year-end data may not be typical of an entity's financial condition during the year. In such cases, certain account balances (cash, receivables, payables and inventories) may not be representative of the balances in the accounts during the year. Data may also be atypical across years if, for example, unusual events have occurred. If a gain or loss is not expected to recur, an analyst may exclude its effects from the analysis.

Diversification

Diversification within entities also limits the usefulness of financial statement analysis. Many entities today are so diversified that they cannot be classified by industry. Others appear to be comparable but are not. You might think that Seven Network Ltd and Ten Network Holdings Ltd would be comparable as commercial television network operators. But are they comparable when Seven Network, through Seven Media Group, lists activities including broadcast television and magazine publishing with online and expanding new communications platforms in a joint venture with Yahoo in Australia, while Ten Network Holdings' principal activities include out-of-home advertising, in particular large-format outdoor signage? Diversification hampers comparisons with competitors and industry statistics. This problem is somewhat mitigated by segmental reporting.

When entities have significant operations in different industries or groups of related products that have different risks and returns, they are required to report **segmental data**, i.e. information about the financial performance and position of each reportable segment. For example, Harrison Ltd provides information about its business segments: supermarkets (including retail liquor and petrol outlets), general merchandise, consumer electronics and hotels. The disclosures include sales revenue, other revenue, segment revenue, total revenue, capital expenditure, depreciation and amortisation, and other non-cash expenses for each segment as well as geographic information.

Many analysts and other users of financial statements consider the segment disclosures to be among the most important information in the financial statements. Without the segment disclosures, comparing diversified entities becomes very difficult.

Decision/issue	Info needed for analysis	Tool or technique to use for decision	How to evaluate results to make decision
Are efforts to evaluate the entity significantly hampered by any of the common limitations of financial statement analysis?	Financial statements as well as a general understanding of the entity and its business	The main limitations of financial statement analysis are estimates, cost, alternative accounting methods, atypical data and diversification.	If any of these factors is significant, the analysis should be relied upon with caution.

LEARNING REFLECTION AND CONSOLIDATION

Review it

What are some of the limitations of financial statement analysis?

USING THE DECISION-MAKING TOOLKIT

Extracts from the Taupiri Group annual report for 2019 are presented below.

TAUPIRI GROUP
Statement of comprehensive income (extract)
for the year ended 30 June 2019

	2019 NZ$'000	2018 NZ$'000
Sales	575 975	520 656
Cost of sales	(212 937)	(191 339)
Gross profit	363 038	329 317
Other income	1 296	72
Selling expenses	(182 700)	(170 661)
Administration and general expenses	(86 550)	(73 281)
Finance income	281	216
Finance expenses	(6 891)	(8 975)
Profit before income tax	**88 474**	**76 688**
Income tax	(22 212)	(24 411)
Profit after income tax	**66 262**	**52 277**

TAUPIRI GROUP
Statement of financial position (extract)
as at 30 June 2019

	2019 NZ$'000	2018 NZ$'000
Current assets		
Cash assets	3 518	2 717
Trade and other receivables	5 502	5 255
Financial assets	11 831	0
Inventories	120 047	109 943
Total current assets	140 898	117 915

	2019 NZ$'000	2018 NZ$'000
Non-current assets		
Property, plant and equipment	65 069	62 867
Intangibles	352 295	373 638
Derivative financial instruments	41	0
Deferred tax assets	6 026	4 827
Total non-current assets	423 431	441 332
Total assets	564 329	559 247
Current liabilities		
Trade and other payables	49 548	43 956
Derivative financial instruments	87	4 692
Interest bearing liabilities	335	0
Current tax liabilities	8 261	9 414
Total current liabilities	58 231	58 062
Non-current liabilities		
Derivative financial instruments	942	1 127
Interest bearing liabilities	63 870	80 606
Total non-current liabilities	64 812	81 733
Total liabilities	123 043	139 795
Net assets	**441 286**	**419 452**
Equity		
Share capital	296 055	295 947
Reserves	(7 002)	7 587
Retained earnings	152 233	115 918
Total equity	**441 286**	**419 452**

Required

Calculate the following ratios for Taupiri Group for 2019 and 2018 and comment on each ratio for 2019 relative to the corresponding ratio for 2018.

(a) Liquidity:
    1. Current ratio
    2. Inventory turnover (inventory as at the end of 30 June 2017 was $81 002)
    3. Days in inventory

(b) Solvency:
    1. Debt to total assets ratio
    2. Times interest earned

(c) Profitability:
    1. Return on ordinary shareholders' equity (equity as at 30 June 2017 was $382 389)
    2. Return on assets (assets on 30 June 2017 were $509 835)
    3. Profit margin

Solution

(a) Liquidity

Ratio	Formula	2019	2018
1. Current ratio	$\dfrac{\text{Current assets}}{\text{Current liabilities}}$	$\dfrac{\$140\,898}{\$58\,231} = 2.42{:}1$	$\dfrac{\$117\,915}{\$58\,062} = 2.03{:}1$
2. Inventory turnover	$\dfrac{\text{Cost of sales}}{\text{Average inventory}}$	$\dfrac{\$212\,937}{(\$120\,047 + \$109\,943)/2}$ $= 1.85$ times	$\dfrac{\$191\,339}{(\$109\,943 + \$81\,002)/2}$ $= 2$ times
3. Days in inventory	$\dfrac{365 \text{ days}}{\text{Inventory turnover}}$	$\dfrac{365}{1.85} = 197$ days	$\dfrac{365}{2} = 183$ days

Taupiri's current ratio increased from $2.03 to $2.42 of current assets to cover each $1.00 of current liabilities in 2019. This was due to a significant increase in current assets and a relatively small increase in current liabilities. Taupiri's inventory turnover slowed down slightly from 2 times to 1.85 times per year in 2019. The days in inventory ratio converts into 183 days in 2018 and 197 days in 2019. Although the cost of sales increased in 2019, there were greater levels of inventory held.

(b) Solvency

Ratio	Formula	2019	2018
1. Debt to total assets ratio	$\dfrac{\text{Total liabilities}}{\text{Total assets}}$	$\dfrac{\$123\,043}{\$564\,329} = 0.22{:}1$	$\dfrac{\$139\,795}{\$559\,247} = 0.25{:}1$
2. Times interest earned	$\dfrac{\text{Earnings before interest and tax}}{\text{Interest expense}}$	$\dfrac{\$95\,365}{\$6\,891} = 13.84 \text{ times}$	$\dfrac{\$85\,663}{\$8\,975} = 9.54 \text{ times}$

Taupiri's debt to total assets ratio indicates a slight improvement. The level of debt used to finance assets decreased from 25% to 22% in 2019. This is reflected in the decline in liabilities and increase in the asset base in 2019. Taupiri's lower use of debt has also had a positive impact on the times interest earned ratio which increased substantially from 9.54 times to 13.84 times in 2019. This increase is due to a higher EBIT along with a lower interest expense. Taupiri's interest cover is very strong and well exceeds the 'rule of thumb' of 3 to 4 times coverage.

(c) Profitability

Ratio	Formula	2019	2018
1. Return on ordinary shareholders' equity	$\dfrac{\text{Profit available to ordinary shareholders}}{\text{Average ordinary shareholders' equity}}$	$\dfrac{\$66\,262}{(\$441\,286 + \$419\,452)/2}$ $= 15.4 \text{ cents}$	$\dfrac{\$52\,277}{(\$419\,452 + \$382\,389)/2}$ $= 13 \text{ cents}$
2. Return on assets	$\dfrac{\text{Profit after tax}}{\text{Average total assets}}$	$\dfrac{\$66\,262}{(\$564\,329 + \$559\,247)/2}$ $= 11.8 \text{ cents}$	$\dfrac{\$52\,277}{(\$559\,247 + \$509\,835)/2}$ $= 9.8 \text{ cents}$
3. Profit margin	$\dfrac{\text{Profit after tax}}{\text{Net sales}}$	$\dfrac{\$66\,262}{\$575\,975} = 11.5 \text{ cents}$	$\dfrac{\$52\,277}{\$520\,656} = 10 \text{ cents}$

Taupiri's return on ordinary shareholders' equity profitability increased from 13% to 15.4% in 2019. This is attributed to an increase in profit available to ordinary shareholders and a concurrent increase in the average ordinary shareholders equity in 2019. Taupiri's return on assets increased from 9.8% to 11.8% in 2019. This is mainly due to the significant increase in profit after tax, which was greater than the increase in the average total assets. Taupiri's profit margin showed a slight increase from 10% to 11.5% in 2019. As the increase in profit after tax was substantially greater than the increase in sales, this suggests Taupiri had better control over its expenses in 2019.

SUMMARY

12.1 Discuss the need for comparative analysis and identify the tools of financial statement analysis.

Comparative analysis is performed to evaluate an entity's short-term liquidity, profitability and long-term solvency. Comparisons can detect changes in financial relationships and significant trends, and can provide insight into an entity's competitive position and relative position within its industry. Financial statements may be analysed horizontally, vertically, and with ratios.

12.2 Explain and apply horizontal analysis.

Horizontal analysis is a technique for evaluating a series of data over a period of time to determine the increase or decrease that has taken place, expressed as either an amount or a percentage.

12.3 Explain and apply vertical analysis.

Vertical analysis is a technique that expresses each item in a financial statement as a percentage of a relevant total or base amount.

12.4 Identify and calculate ratios and describe their purpose and use in analysing the liquidity, solvency and profitability of a business.

Ratios can be used to measure profitability, liquidity and solvency for purposes of comparison over time, between entities, and with industry statistics.

12.5 Discuss the limitations of financial statement analysis.

The usefulness of analytical tools is limited by the use of estimates, the cost basis, the application of alternative accounting methods, atypical data at year-end, and the diversification of entities.

DECISION-MAKING TOOLKIT — A SUMMARY

DECISION-MAKING TOOLKIT

Decision/issue	Info needed for analysis	Tool or technique to use for decision	How to evaluate results to make decision
How do the entity's operating results and financial position compare with those of a previous period?	Statement of profit or loss and statement of financial position	Financial statements should be compared over at least 2 years, with the first year reported being the base year. Changes in each line item relative to the base year should be presented both by amount and by percentage. This is called horizontal analysis.	Significant changes should be investigated to determine the reason for the change.
How do the relationships between items in this year's financial statements compare with those of last year or those of competitors?	Statement of profit or loss and statement of financial position	Each line item on the statement of profit or loss should be presented as a percentage of net sales revenue, and each line item on the statement of financial position should be presented as a percentage of total assets or total liabilities and equity. These percentages should be investigated for any significant differences within the same entity over consecutive years or between different entities for the same year. This is called vertical analysis.	Significant differences either across years or between entities should be investigated to determine the cause.

▶

Decision/issue	Info needed for analysis	Tool or technique to use for decision	How to evaluate results to make decision
Is the entity profitable and can it meet its short- and long-term obligations?	Statement of profit or loss, statement of financial position and other relevant information such as general economic conditions, industry trends and/or averages, information from annual reports and media releases	Calculate a variety of ratios to indicate an entity's profitability, liquidity and solvency. This is called ratio analysis.	A single ratio on its own is not very meaningful, hence it is useful to interpret ratios using: (1) intra-company comparisons, (2) intercompany comparisons, (3) other relevant information such as general economic conditions and industry trends and averages.
Are efforts to evaluate the entity significantly hampered by any of the common limitations of financial statement analysis?	Financial statements as well as a general understanding of the entity and its business	The main limitations of financial statement analysis are estimates, cost, alternative accounting methods, atypical data and diversification.	If any of these factors is significant, the analysis should be relied upon with caution.

KEY TERMS

asset turnover A measure of how efficiently an entity uses its assets to generate sales, calculated as net sales divided by average total assets.

average collection period The average number of days that receivables are outstanding, calculated as receivables turnover divided into 365 days.

average days in inventory A measure of the average number of days it takes to sell the inventory, calculated as inventory turnover divided into 365 days.

cash debt coverage A cash-basis ratio used to evaluate solvency, calculated as net cash provided by operating activities divided by average total liabilities.

cash return on sales ratio A cash-basis ratio used to evaluate profitability, calculated as net cash provided by operating activities divided by net sales.

current cash debt coverage A cash-basis ratio used to evaluate liquidity, calculated as net cash provided by operating activities divided by average current liabilities.

current ratio A measure used to evaluate an entity's liquidity and short-term debt-paying ability, calculated as current assets divided by current liabilities.

debt to total assets ratio A measure of the percentage of total financing provided by creditors, calculated as total liabilities divided by total assets.

dividend payout rate A measure of the percentage of profit distributed in the form of dividends, calculated as dividends divided by profit.

earnings per share (EPS) The profit earned per ordinary share, calculated as profit available to ordinary shareholders divided by the weighted average number of ordinary shares.

free cash flow Cash provided by operating activities less investments made to maintain the current level of operations.

gross profit margin An indicator of an entity's ability to maintain an adequate selling price of goods above their cost, calculated as gross profit divided by net sales.

horizontal analysis A technique for evaluating a series of financial statement data over a period of time to determine the increase (decrease) that has taken place, expressed as either an amount or a percentage.

inventory turnover A measure of the liquidity of inventory, calculated as cost of sales divided by average inventory.

liquidity ratios Measures of the short-term ability of an entity to pay its maturing obligations and to meet unexpected needs for cash.

operating expenses to sales ratio A measure of the costs incurred to support each dollar of sales, calculated as operating expenses divided by net sales.

price/earnings ratio (P/E ratio) A comparison of the market price of each ordinary share with the earnings per share, calculated as the market price of the share divided by earnings per share.

profit margin A measure of the profit generated by each dollar of sales, calculated as profit divided by net sales.

profitability ratios Measures of the profit or operating success of an entity for a given period of time.

quick ratio A measure of an entity's immediate short-term liquidity, calculated by dividing the sum of cash, marketable securities and net receivables by current liabilities; also called the acid test.

receivables turnover A measure of the liquidity of receivables, calculated as net credit sales divided by average net trade receivables.

return on assets (ROA) An overall measure of profitability, calculated as profit divided by average total assets.

return on ordinary shareholders' equity (ROE) A measure of the dollars of profit earned for each dollar invested by the owners, calculated as profit available to ordinary shareholders divided by average ordinary shareholders' equity.

segmental data A required note disclosure for diversified entities in which the entity reports financial information such as sales, profit and identifiable assets by geographic and/or industry segments.

solvency ratios Measures of the ability of the entity to survive over a long period of time.

times interest earned A measure of an entity's ability to meet interest payments as they come due, calculated as profit before income tax plus interest expense divided by interest expense.

vertical analysis A technique for evaluating financial statement data that expresses each item in a financial statement as a percentage of a base amount, such as total assets or sales revenue.

DEMONSTRATION PROBLEM

Selected Soda Pop Inc. 2019 and 2018 figures and 2018 ratios are provided below.

	Soda Pop 2019 US$m	Soda Pop 2018 US$m
Net credit sales	99 623	98 238
Profit after tax	10 181	9 321
Profit available to ordinary shareholders	10 110	9 417
Income tax	3 156	3 135
Interest expense	1 367	1 349
Earnings before income tax and interest expense	14 703	13 805
Cost of sales	46 865	46 937
Gross profit	52 758	51 302
Operating expenses	38 201	37 917
Current assets	33 305	28 080
Cash + Receivables + Marketable securities	34 948	20 490

▶

	Soda Pop 2019 US$m	Soda Pop 2018 US$m
Net receivables	10 431	10 562
Inventory	5 114	5 372
Total assets	116 217	111 957
Current liabilities	26 759	25 634
Total liabilities	79 634	78 359
Net cash flows from operating activities	14 532	12 719
Capital expenditures	4 193	4 071
Total equity	36 584	33 599
Weighted average no. of ordinary shares	2 312	2 336
Share price	$124.41	$103.00
Dividends	5 151	4 958
Earnings per share	$6.56	$6.00

Ratios	2018
Liquidity	
1. Current ratio	1.10:1
2. Quick ratio	0.80:1
3. Current cash debt coverage	0.32:1
4. Receivables turnover	9.39 times
5. Average collection period	38.88 days
6. Inventory turnover	8.45 times
7. Average days in inventory	43.21 days
Solvency	
8. Debt to total assets	0.70:1
9. Times interest earned	10.24 times
10. Cash debt coverage	0.16:1
11. Free cash flow	$8 648
Profitability	
12. Return on ordinary shareholders' equity	28.5%
13. Return on assets	8.4%
14. Profit margin	9%
15. Asset turnover	$1.34
16. Gross profit margin	53%
17. Operating expenses to sales	39%
18. Cash return on sales	0.13:1
19. Earnings per share	$5.95
20. Price/earnings ratio	17.25 times
21. Dividend payout rate	53%

Required

Calculate the liquidity, solvency and profitability ratios listed above for Soda Pop Inc. for 2019 and comment on the changes between 2018 and 2019.

SOLUTION TO DEMONSTRATION PROBLEM

Liquidity, solvency and profitability ratios for Soda Pop Inc. for 2019 are shown on the following pages. Also shown are the formulas for each ratio calculation.

Ratio analysis is more meaningful if it is supplemented with further information such as inter-company comparisons with a competitor in the same industry as well as other relevant information such as general economic conditions, industry trends or averages, company web sites, media releases, information from directors' reports and management's discussion and analysis in annual reports. This is illustrated in the analysis that follows the ratio calculations.

Liquidity

Liquidity ratios measure the short-term ability of the entity to pay its maturing obligations and to meet unexpected needs for cash.

Ratio	Formula	2019	2018
1. Current ratio	$\dfrac{\text{Current assets}}{\text{Current liabilities}}$	$\dfrac{\$33\,305}{\$26\,759} = 1.24{:}1$	1.10:1
2. Quick ratio	$\dfrac{\text{Cash + Marketable securities + Net receivables}}{\text{Current liabilities}}$	$\dfrac{\$24\,948}{\$26\,759} = 0.93{:}1$	0.80:1
3. Current cash debt coverage	$\dfrac{\text{Net cash provided by operating activities}}{\text{Average current liabilities}}$	$\dfrac{\$14\,532}{(\$26\,759 + \$25\,634)/2} = 0.55{:}1$	0.32:1
4. Receivables turnover (times)	$\dfrac{\text{Net credit sales}}{\text{Average net trade receivables}}$	$\dfrac{\$99\,623}{(\$10\,431 + \$10\,562)/2} = 9.49$ times	9.39 times
5. Average collection period (days)	$\dfrac{\text{365 days}}{\text{Receivables turnover}}$	$\dfrac{365}{9.49} = 38.5$ days	38.9 days
6. Inventory turnover (times per annum)	$\dfrac{\text{Cost of sales}}{\text{Average inventory}}$	$\dfrac{\$46\,865}{(\$5\,114 + \$5\,372)/2} = 8.94$ times	8.45 times
7. Average days in inventory	$\dfrac{\text{365 days}}{\text{Inventory turnover}}$	$\dfrac{365}{8.94} = 41$ days	43 days

Soda Pop's current ratio increased from 1.10:1 in 2018 to 1.24:1 in 2019 as the increase in current assets was greater than the increase in current liabilities. Soda Pop's competitor, Soft Drink Co., reported a current ratio of 1.13:1 in 2019, which is lower than Soda Pop's ratio of 1.24 in 2019 but similar to its ratio in 2018. What is considered to be an acceptable ratio may vary from industry to industry; however, around 1.5:1 is generally considered to be an acceptable current ratio for most industries. Although Soda Pop's ratio is below 1.5:1, it still has more current assets than current liabilities. This suggests that it can meet its current obligations when they fall due.

Soda Pop's quick ratio has improved from 0.80:1 in 2018 to 0.93:1 in 2019. As a rule of thumb, some analysts suggest that a quick ratio of approximately 1:1 is adequate; however, this is arbitrary and subject to debate and exception. Soda Pop's quick ratio for both years is below 1:1, which suggests that it may have difficulties in meeting its current obligations when they fall due.

Soda Pop's current cash debt coverage has increased from 0.32:1 in 2018 to 0.55:1 in 2019. The acceptable level for current cash debt coverage may vary between industries; however, a value below 0.40:1 is considered cause for additional investigation of an entity's liquidity. Soda Pop's current cash debt coverage in 2019 is above this benchmark, which indicates that it is in a strong position to meet its current liabilities.

Soda Pop's receivables turnover improved slightly from 9.39 in 2018 to 9.49 times per annum in 2019. To assess the effectiveness of an entity's credit and collection policies, the average collection period should be calculated. The general rule is that the collection period should not greatly exceed the credit term period; the time allowed for payment. Soda Pop's average collection period remained relatively unchanged from 38.9 days in 2018 to 38.5 days in 2019. To assess this ratio we need to know Soda Pop's credit policy, which is explained under the accounting policies section of Soda Pop's 2019 annual report and indicates that payment is required within 30 days of delivery in the United States and within 30 to 90 days internationally and discounts may be allowed for early payment. To evaluate Soda Pop's credit and collection policies more accurately we would need the break-up between international and local receivables. As this data is not available in the information provided, we need to evaluate the results with caution. However, Soda Pop's average collection period of 38.5 days in 2019 is close to the 30-day credit terms for its US customers, which indicates its credit policy is appropriate and its monitoring of receivables collection is effective.

The inventory turnover measures the number of times on average the inventory is sold during the period. Its purpose is to measure the liquidity of the inventory. The higher the turnover, the less chance stock will be slow moving or become obsolete or spoiled and unsaleable. It is important to monitor the amount of resources invested in inventory as part of managing the business. Entities do not want to unnecessarily have too much cash tied up in inventories. At the same time, they do not want to be understocked and miss out on sales because of a lack of stock. Soda Pop's inventory turnover improved slightly from 8.45 times to 8.94 times per annum in 2019.

The days in inventory ratio converts the inventory turnover into days. Soda Pop's days in inventory decreased slightly from 43 days in 2018 and 41 days in 2019. Although the cost of sales had decreased in 2019, there were significantly lower levels of inventory held. This suggests more efficient management of inventory during 2019. In order to analyse these results, we need to understand the nature of the inventory. An inventory turnover of 100 days is acceptable for non-perishable items such as furniture and machinery, but a much higher turnover would be necessary for perishables such as fresh food items. For example, Harrison reported an inventory turnover of 10.86 times per annum which is an average of 34 days in inventory in 2019. General merchandise and consumer durables have a longer shelf life than many grocery and fast food lines, contributing to the average number of days that inventory is held. Soda Pop sells a smaller variety of products than Harrison, including soft drinks and snack foods. Snack foods have a shorter shelf life than soft drinks; therefore, the 41 days in inventory reported in 2019 should be evaluated with caution. We would need more detailed data for each type of product to evaluate these figures with accuracy. However, 41 days in inventory does not seem excessive for soft drinks, which have expiry dates greater than one year. The figure is comparable to Harrison, which sells both soft drinks and snack foods.

Summary — liquidity

From the analysis of the liquidity ratios along with the other information, including comparisons with competitors and information from Soda Pop's annual report, it appears that Soda Pop is able to meet its short-term obligations as they fall due, has effective credit and collection policies for receivables and is adequately turning its inventory over to avoid stock spoilage and wasted resources invested in inventory but maintain adequate supplies to meet product demand. Although slight improvements have been noted in each of the liquidity ratios from 2018 to 2019, Soda Pop's current ratio and quick ratio are slightly below expected benchmarks. Although there is no cause for concern at this stage, this should be monitored and investigated further if the decline continues in future.

Solvency

Solvency ratios measure the financial stability of the entity and its ability to survive over a long period of time. Long-term creditors and shareholders are interested in a company's long-term solvency, particularly its ability to pay interest as it falls due and to repay the face value of debts at maturity. The debt to total assets, times interest earned and cash debt coverage provide information about debt-paying ability. The higher the percentage of total liabilities to total assets, the greater the financial risk that the entity may be unable to meet its maturing obligations. The lower the ratio, the more equity 'buffer' is available to creditors if the entity becomes insolvent. Therefore, from the creditors' point of view, a low ratio of debt to total assets is usually desirable.

Ratio	Formula	2019	2018
8. Debt to total assets ratio	$\dfrac{\text{Total liabilities}}{\text{Total assets}}$	$\dfrac{\$79\,634}{\$116\,217} = 0.69{:}1$	0.70
9. Times interest earned	$\dfrac{\text{Earnings before interest and tax}}{\text{Interest expense}}$	$\dfrac{\$14\,703}{\$1\,367} = 10.76 \text{ times}$	10.24 times
10. Cash debt coverage	$\dfrac{\text{Net cash provided by operating activities}}{\text{Average total liabilities}}$	$\dfrac{\$14\,532}{(\$79\,634 + \$78\,359)/2} =$ 0.18:1	0.16:1
11. Free cash flow ($ millions)	Net cash provided by operating activities – Capital expenditures	$\$14\,532 - \$4\,193 = \$10\,339$	$\$8\,648$

Soda Pop's debt to total assets ratio indicates a marginal improvement with the level of debt used to finance assets decreased slightly from 0.70:1 in 2018 to 0.69:1 in 2019 as the increase in liabilities was relatively smaller than the increase in the asset base in 2019. Generally, entities with relatively stable profits have a higher debt to total assets than cyclical entities with widely fluctuating profits, such as many high-tech companies. Stable profits reflect low operating risk, whereas fluctuating profits are interpreted as reflecting high operating risk. Soda Pop has relatively stable profits as evidenced in the profitability ratios shown in the final section of this analysis.

To assess whether the entity's profit is adequate to meet interest payments we can calculate the times interest earned. Soda Pop's slightly lower debt to total assets ratio has had a similar impact on the times interest earned ratio which increased from 10.24 times in 2018 to 10.76 times in 2019. This was attributed to an increase in Soda Pop's EBIT which offset a marginally higher interest expense. Soda Pop's interest coverage is very strong and well exceeds the rule of thumb of 3 to 4 times interest coverage.

The cash debt coverage ratio provides additional insight into an entity's ability to repay its liabilities from cash generated from operating activities without having to liquidate the assets used in its operations. Soda Pop's cash debt coverage increased slightly from 0.16:1 in 2018 to 0.18:1 in 2019. Both ratios are below the general rule of thumb of 0.20:1 which indicates additional investigation may be required; however, this may vary between industries. Soda Pop's ratio is considerably lower than its competitor, Soft Drink Co., which reported a ratio of 0.25:1 in 2019.

To complete our analysis of Soda Pop's solvency, free cash flow provides information about the company's solvency and its ability to pay dividends or invest in new projects. The free cash flow has increased substantially from $8 648 000 in 2018 to $10 339 000 in 2019. In 2019, Soda Pop spent $4 193 000 on capital expenditures. According to Soda Pop's management, capital spending is essential to maintaining product innovation initiatives and operational capabilities and is a necessary and ongoing use of cash.

Summary — solvency

Based on the solvency ratios calculated and other relevant information, it appears that Soda Pop is able to meet its long-term obligations as they fall due and can meet its planned capital expenditures to maintain innovation and efficiency. Financial ratings organisations can provide a comparison rating of Soda Pop's financial data to other companies. Moody's is one of the world's leading credit rating agencies. In June 2019, Moody's lowered the long-term ratings of Soda Pop from Aa3 (high quality and very low credit risk) down to A1 (upper-medium grade and low credit risk). Soda Pop's short-term rating was affirmed at P-1 Prime-1 (best ability to repay short-term debt) and the outlook for the company was evaluated as stable. The downgrade reflects Soda Pop's gradually increasing financial leverage as well as continued challenges in the North American beverage market. The significance of this downgrade by Moody's is significant for Soda Pop as it could increase its future borrowing costs.

Profitability

Profitability ratios measure the profit or operating success of an entity for a given period of time. An entity's profit affects its ability to obtain debt and equity financing, its liquidity position and its ability to grow. As a consequence, creditors and investors alike are interested in evaluating profitability. Profitability is frequently used as the ultimate test of management's operating effectiveness.

Ratio	Formula	2019	2018
12. Return on ordinary shareholders' equity	Profit available to ordinary shareholders / Average ordinary shareholder's equity	$\dfrac{\$10\,110}{(\$36\,584 + \$33\,599)/2} = 28.8$ cents or 28.8%	28.5 cents or 28.5%
13. Return on assets	Profit after tax / Average total assets	$\dfrac{\$10\,181}{(\$116\,217 + \$111\,957)/2} = 8.9$ cents or 8.9%	8.4 cents or 8.4%

▶

Ratio	Formula	2019	2018
14. Profit margin	$\dfrac{\text{Profit after tax}}{\text{Net sales}}$	$\dfrac{\$10\,181}{\$99\,623} = 10.2$ cents or 10.2%	9.5 cents or 9.5%
15. Asset turnover	$\dfrac{\text{Net sales}}{\text{Average total assets}}$	$\dfrac{\$99\,623}{(\$116\,217 + \$111\,957)/2} = \$0.87$	$0.89
16. Gross profit margin	$\dfrac{\text{Gross profit}}{\text{Net sales}}$	$\dfrac{\$52\,758}{\$99\,623} = 53\%$	53.0%
17. Operating expenses to sales	$\dfrac{\text{Operating expenses}}{\text{Net sales}}$	$\dfrac{\$38\,201}{\$99\,623} = 38.3\%$	38.6%
18. Cash return on sales	$\dfrac{\text{Net cash provided by operating activities}}{\text{Net sales}}$	$\dfrac{\$14\,532}{\$99\,623} = 0.15{:}1$	0.13:1
19. Earnings per share (EPS)	$\dfrac{\text{Profit available to ordinary shareholders}}{\text{Weighted average number ordinary shares}}$	$\dfrac{\$10\,110}{2\,312} = \$4.37$	$3.97
20. Price/earnings ratio (times)	$\dfrac{\text{Share price}}{\text{Earnings per share}}$	$\dfrac{\$124.41}{\$6.56} = 18.96$ times	17.25 times
21. Dividend payout	$\dfrac{\text{Dividends}}{\text{Profit}}$	$\dfrac{\$5\,151}{\$10\,181} = 51\%$	53%

The return on ordinary shareholders' equity (ROE) shows the amount of profit earned for each dollar invested by the shareholders. Soda Pop's return increased marginally from 28.5 cents in 2018 to 28.8 cents in 2019. These results are reflective of the minimal change in the profit available to ordinary shareholders and the average ordinary shareholders equity in 2019. The higher the ROE, the more attractive investment in the company is, as it indicates a greater return on shareholder funds invested.

The return on assets measures the overall profitability of assets in terms of the profit earned on each dollar invested in assets. It is a measure of management's effectiveness based on normal business activities. Soda Pop's return on assets increased slightly from 8.4 cents in 2018 to 8.9 cents in 2019. Although there was a marginal increase in Soda Pop's profit after tax in 2019, this was offset by a greater increase in the asset base. The combination of these two factors explains the modest increase. Soda Pop's return on assets over the 2 years is comparable to that of its competitor, Soft Drink Co., whose return on assets was 9.7 cents in 2019.

Soda Pop's profit margin showed a slight increase from 9.5% in 2018 to 10.2% in 2019. As the increase in profit after tax was greater than the increase in sales, this suggests that Soda Pop had better control over its expenses in 2019.

The asset turnover decreased slightly over the 2-year period. In 2019, Soda Pop generated 89 cents in sales for every dollar invested in assets compared to 87 cents in 2018. These figures are significantly higher than Soft Drink Co.'s asset turnover of 53 cents in 2019, which suggests that Soda Pop is using its assets more effectively in generating greater sales from its assets.

Soda Pop's gross profit margin remained unchanged between 2018 and 2019. This indicates that Soda Pop continued to have good control over its cost of sales in 2019. Its operating expenses to sales ratio has declined slightly from 38.6% to 38.3% in 2019, which contributed to the marginal increase in the profit margin in 2019.

The cash return on sales focuses on the cash generated from operating activities and therefore eliminates the impact of non-cash expenses such as depreciation, which are included in the calculation of profit-based ratios. Soda Pop's cash return on sales shows a slight increase from 13% to 15% in 2019. Soda Pop's principal source of liquidity is its operating cash flows, which is one of its fundamental strengths and offers the company financial flexibility in meeting its financing, investing and operating requirements.

Earnings per share (EPS) is a measure of the profit earned on each ordinary share. Soda Pop's EPS increased from $3.97 in 2018 to $4.37 in 2019. The EPS is a commonly quoted figure and can be found in many newspapers and on securities exchange web sites. Companies are also required to disclose this figure in their annual reports.

The price/earnings ratio (P/E ratio) is a reflection of shareholder confidence in a company's future earnings and indicates how much a shareholder would have to pay for the share compared to the earnings expected. The higher the P/E ratio, the more confident the shareholder is about the future earning capacity of the company. In the case of Soda Pop, the P/E ratio increased from 17.25 times in 2018 to 18.96 times in 2019. This is mainly due to the large increase in share price from $68.43 to $82.94 in 2019. At the end of the 2019 reporting period, Soda Pop's shares were selling for $82.94, and its EPS was $4.37, therefore the share price is approximately 19 times higher than the EPS of $4.37. Soda Pop's P/E ratio was slightly lower than Soft Drink Co.'s P/E ratio of approximately 21 times in 2019. Both companies would be considered profitable investments.

Soda Pop's dividend payout ratio decreased slightly from 53% in 2018 to 51% in 2019. Companies that have high growth rates are characterised by low payout rates because they often reinvest most of the profit back into the business. Soda Pop has a relatively high dividend payout ratio which is indicative of a company in maturity; however, it also recognises that to maintain innovation and effectiveness it needs to reinvest funds into the business. Soda Pop has a balanced approach to distributing funds to shareholders and reinvesting funds into the business.

Summary — profitability
Based on the ratios calculated and discussed in this section as well as the information gleaned from the annual report, Soda Pop is a profitable entity. Profitability is frequently used as the ultimate test of management's operating effectiveness. It appears that management is operating Soda Pop's assets efficiently and controlling prices and expenses adequately. This enables Soda Pop to generate sufficient cash to continue its investments in innovation as well as pay out generous dividends to shareholders.

SELF-STUDY QUESTIONS

12.1 Intra-entity analysis is useful to detect: LO1
  (a) changes in financial relationships and significant trends within the entity.
  (b) differences between entities within an industry.
  (c) differences between entities.
  (d) all of the above.

12.2 Industry average analysis is useful to detect: LO1
  (a) differences between entities within an industry.
  (b) changes in financial relationships and significant trends within the entity.
  (c) differences between entities.
  (d) all of the above.

12.3 Comparison of data with other entities is an example of the following comparative basis: LO1
  (a) Intra-entity.
  (b) Inter-entity.
  (c) Industry averages.
  (d) Both (a) and (b).

12.4 Which of the following are the basic tools used in financial statement analysis? LO1
  (a) Horizontal analysis.
  (b) Vertical analysis.
  (c) Ratio analysis.
  (d) All of the above.

12.5 In horizontal analysis, each item is expressed as a percentage of the: **LO2**
    (a) profit amount.
    (b) equity amount.
    (c) total assets amount.
    (d) base-year amount.

12.6 Canterbury Ltd reported net sales of $300 000, $330 000 and $360 000 in the years 2018, 2019 and 2020 respectively. If 2018 is the base year, what is the trend percentage for 2020?   **LO2**
    (a) 77%.
    (b) 108%.
    (c) 120%
    (d) 130%.

12.7 In vertical analysis, the base amount for depreciation expense is generally: **LO3**
    (a) net sales.
    (b) depreciation expense in a previous year.
    (c) gross profit.
    (d) non-current assets.

12.8 The following schedule is a display of what type of analysis?   **LO3**

	Amount	Percentage
Current assets	$200 000	25%
Property, plant and equipment	600 000	75%
Total assets	$800 000	

    (a) Horizontal analysis.
    (b) Differential analysis.
    (c) Vertical analysis.
    (d) Ratio analysis.

12.9 Which measure is an evaluation of an entity's ability to pay current liabilities?   **LO4**
    (a) Quick ratio.
    (b) Current ratio.
    (c) Both (a) and (b).
    (d) None of the above.

12.10 Which measure is useful in evaluating the efficiency in managing inventories?   **LO4**
    (a) Inventory turnover.
    (b) Average days in inventory.
    (c) Both (a) and (b).
    (d) None of the above.

12.11 Which of these is *not* a liquidity ratio?   **LO4**
    (a) Current ratio.
    (b) Asset turnover.
    (c) Inventory turnover.
    (d) Receivables turnover.

12.12 Silver Fern Limited reported profit $24 000; net sales $400 000; and average assets $600 000 for 2019. What is the 2019 profit margin?   **LO4**
    (a) 6%.
    (b) 12%.
    (c) 40%.
    (d) 200%.

12.13 Which of the following is generally not considered to be a limitation of financial statement analysis? **LO5**
- (a) Use of ratios.
- (b) Use of estimates.
- (c) Use of cost.
- (d) Use of alternative accounting methods.

12.14 Which of the following is *not* considered to be true in relation to segmental data? **LO5**
- (a) Entities which make significant sales in different industries are required to report segment data.
- (b) Entities which are highly diversified are required to report segment data.
- (c) Segment data includes information about each reportable segment.
- (d) Entities which have significant operations in different industries are required to report segment data.

12.15 Which of the following are generally considered to be limitations of financial statement analysis? **LO5**
- (a) Use of estimates, e.g. for depreciation.
- (b) Use of cost for asset purchases.
- (c) Use of alternative accounting methods, e.g. for inventory valuation.
- (d) All of the above.

QUESTIONS

12.1 (a) Distinguish among the following bases of comparison: intra-entity, industry averages and inter-entity.
(b) Give the principal purpose of using each of the three bases of comparison.

12.2 Two popular methods of financial statement analysis are horizontal analysis and vertical analysis. Explain the difference between these two methods.

12.3 The current ratio and the quick ratio are both measures of liquidity. Explain how the quick ratio overcomes some of the limitations of the current ratio.

12.4 Explain how calculating current cash debt coverage for an entity overcomes a disadvantage of the current and quick ratios.

12.5 Discuss the advantages of calculating the average collection period of receivables. How does an entity determine if there is an issue with receivables collection based on the average collection period calculation?

12.6 Megasonic Ltd, a retail store, has an inventory turnover of 8 times. The industry average is 14 times. Does Megasonic Ltd have a problem with its inventory?

12.7 Which ratios should be used to help answer each of these questions?
- (a) How efficient is an entity in using its assets to produce sales?
- (b) How long does it take for customers to pay their accounts?
- (c) How many dollars of profit were generated for each dollar of sales?
- (d) How liquid is this entity?

12.8 The price/earnings ratio of Domino's Pizza Enterprises Limited was 54.8 and the price/earnings ratio of Telstra Corporation Limited was 16.4. Which company did the securities market favour? Explain.

12.9 Indicate whether each of the following changes generally signals good or bad news about an entity:
- (a) Decrease in gross margin rate.
- (b) Decrease in inventory turnover.
- (c) Decrease in quick ratio.
- (d) Increase in return on assets.

(e) Increase in price/earnings ratio.

(f) Increase in debt to total assets ratio.

(g) Increase in current cash debt coverage.

12.10 Identify and briefly explain five limitations of financial analysis.

BRIEF EXERCISES

BE12.1 Identify inter-entity and intra-entity comparison data.   **LO2**

Identify the inter-entity and intra-entity comparisons from the following data:

(a) Madison Ltd's current ratio has increased from 1.78:1 in 2018 to 1.90:1 in 2019.

(b) Broadway Ltd's quick ratio has decreased from 0.71:1 in 2018 to 0.69:1 in 2019.

(c) Madison Ltd's quick ratio of 0.51:1 in 2019 is lower than Broadway Ltd's quick ratio of 0.69:1 in 2019.

(d) Madison Ltd's current debt coverage of 0.80:1 is greater than the industry average.

(e) Madison Ltd's receivables turnover of 1.23 times in 2019 is higher than the receivables turnover in 2018.

(f) Madison Ltd's average collection period of 34.5 days in 2019 is lower than Broadway Ltd's average collection period of 40.3 days in 2019.

BE12.2 Prepare horizontal analysis.   **LO2**

Using these data from the statement of financial position, prepare a horizontal analysis using 2018 as a base year.

	30 June 2020	30 June 2019	30 June 2018
Accounts receivable	$ 800 000	$ 600 000	$ 700 000
Inventory	950 000	420 000	530 000
Total assets	4 600 000	3 800 000	2 400 000

BE12.3 Prepare vertical analysis.   **LO3**

Using the data presented in BE12.2, prepare a vertical analysis.

BE12.4 Calculate change in profit.   **LO2**

Horizontal analysis percentages for Jayden Ltd's sales, cost of sales and expenses are presented below.

Horizontal analysis	2020	2019	2018
Sales	92%	105%	100%
Cost of sales	105%	93%	100%
Expenses	107%	96%	100%

Explain whether Jayden Ltd's profit increased, decreased or remained unchanged over the 3-year period.

BE12.5 Calculate liquidity ratios.   **LO4**

The following selected condensed data are taken from a recent statement of financial position of Sunnydale Ltd. What are the (a) current ratio and (b) quick ratio?

Cash	$ 640 000
Marketable securities	84 500
Accounts receivable	106 300
Inventories	924 000
Other current assets	375 000
Total current assets	2 129 800
Total current liabilities	1 810 000

BE12.6 Evaluate collection of accounts receivable.

LO4

The following data are taken from the financial statements of Bristol Ltd.

	2020	2019
Accounts receivable (net), end of year	$ 672 000	$ 564 000
Net sales on account	6 600 000	4 920 000
Terms for all sales are 1/10, n/45.		

Calculate for each year (a) the receivables turnover and (b) the average collection period. What conclusions about the management of accounts receivable can be drawn from these data? At the end of 2018 accounts receivable (net) was $588 000.

BE12.7 Calculate cash-basis liquidity, profitability and solvency ratios.

LO4

Selected data taken from the 2019 financial statements of Madison Ltd are as follows.

Net sales	$8 232 000
Current liabilities, 1 July 2018	216 000
Current liabilities, 30 June 2019	288 000
Net cash provided by operating activities	912 000
Total liabilities, 1 July 2018	1 800 000
Total liabilities, 30 June 2019	1 560 000

Calculate these ratios at 30 June 2019: (a) current cash debt coverage, (b) cash return on sales ratio, and (c) cash debt coverage.

EXERCISES

E12.1 Calculate intra-entity liquidity ratios and discuss comparative analysis.

LO1, 4

The following data is available for White Ltd and Wong Ltd.

	White 2019 $'000	White 2018 $'000	Wong 2019 $'000	Wong 2018 $'000
Cost of sales	17 988	18 038	15 762	16 002
Current assets	9 998	10 151	9 130	10 200
Cash + receivables + marketable securities	6 800	6 870	6 547	7 300
Net receivables	3 995	4 389	3 725	3 500
Inventory	3 100	2 290	1 926	2 001
Total assets	35 648	34 628	29 930	33 000
Current liabilities	7 770	7 753	6 860	7 200
Total liabilities	18 231	17 394	14 562	12 450

Required

(a) Calculate all the intra-entity comparisons in relation to liquidity that the data allows for White Ltd.

(b) Why is it helpful to prepare intra-entity, inter-entity and industry comparisons when evaluating an entity?

E12.2 Prepare a horizontal analysis.

LO2

The financial information for Spencer Ltd is provided below.

	30 June 2020	30 June 2019
Current assets	$150 000	$103 000
Property, plant and equipment (net)	380 000	315 000
Current liabilities	85 000	72 000
Non-current liabilities	140 000	104 000
Share capital, $1 each	175 000	100 000
Retained earnings	130 000	142 000

Required

Prepare a horizontal analysis for 2020 using 2019 as the base year.

E12.3 Prepare horizontal analysis. LO2

The financial information for Forrester Ltd is provided below.

	30 June 2020	30 June 2019
Current assets	$ 96 000	$ 88 000
Property, plant and equipment (net)	680 000	630 000
Current liabilities	45 000	50 000
Non-current liabilities	72 000	78 000
Share capital, $1 each	450 000	365 000
Retained earnings	209 000	225 000

Required

(a) Prepare a schedule showing a horizontal analysis for 2020 using 2019 as the base year.

(b) Explain the changes that have occurred for Forrester Ltd between 2019 and 2020.

E12.4 Prepare vertical analysis and discuss the usefulness of horizontal and vertical analysis. LO3

Operating data for Spectre Ltd are presented here.

	2020	2019
Sales	$900 000	$870 000
Cost of sales	520 000	460 000
Selling expenses	140 000	93 000
Administrative expenses	65 000	61 000
Income tax expense	52 500	76 800
Profit	122 500	179 200

Required

(a) Prepare a schedule showing a vertical analysis for 2020 and 2019.

(b) Why is it helpful to prepare horizontal and vertical analysis when evaluating an entity?

E12.5 Prepare a vertical analysis. LO3

Financial information for Ridge Ltd is as follows.

	2019	2018
Sales	$1 500 000	$1 350 000
Cost of sales	745 000	738 000
Selling expenses	123 000	105 000
Administrative expenses	92 000	81 000
Income tax expense	162 000	127 800
Profit	378 000	298 200

Required

(a) Prepare a schedule showing a vertical analysis for 2019 and 2018.

(b) Prepare a brief report outlining the results of your analysis for a potential investor.

E12.6 Prepare horizontal and vertical analyses. LO2, 3

The statement of financial position for Jai's Jeans Ltd is presented below.

JAI'S JEANS LTD Partial statement of financial position as at 30 June 2020		
	2020	2019
ASSETS		
Current assets	$ 27 000	$ 36 000
Property, plant and equipment (net)	951 000	862 000
Intangibles	56 000	52 000
Total assets	**$1 034 000**	**$950 000**

	2020	2019
LIABILITIES AND EQUITY		
Current liabilities	$ 45 000	$ 50 000
Non-current liabilities	320 000	311 000
Equity	669 000	589 000
Total liabilities and equity	**$1 034 000**	**$950 000**

Required

(a) Prepare a horizontal analysis of the statement of financial position data for Jai's Jeans Ltd using 2019 as a base.

(b) Prepare a vertical analysis for Jai's Jeans Ltd for 2020 and 2019.

(c) If you were deciding whether to invest in this business, which analysis would you find more useful? Provide reasons for your answer.

E12.7 **Prepare horizontal and vertical analyses.** LO2, 3

The statement of financial position for Bondi Ltd is presented below.

BONDI LTD Statement of financial position as at 30 June 2020		
	2020	2019
ASSETS		
Current assets	$ 88 000	$ 80 000
Property, plant and equipment (net)	81 000	90 000
Intangibles	31 000	40 000
Total assets	**$200 000**	**$210 000**
LIABILITIES AND EQUITY		
Current liabilities	$ 52 000	$ 48 000
Non-current liabilities	135 000	150 000
Equity	13 000	12 000
Total liabilities and equity	**$200 000**	**$210 000**

Required

(a) Prepare a horizontal analysis of the statement of financial position data for Bondi Ltd using 2019 as a base. Show the amount of increase or decrease as well.

(b) Prepare a vertical analysis for Bondi Ltd for 2019 and 2020.

E12.8 **Calculate liquidity ratios and compare results.** LO4

Selected financial statement data for Grayson Ltd are presented below.

	End of year $m	Beginning of year $m
Cash and cash equivalents	33	91
Receivables (net)	378	271
Inventory	628	586
Prepaid expenses	61	52
Total current assets	1 100	1 000
Total current liabilities	690	627

For the year, net sales were $3894 million, cost of sales was $2600 million, and cash from operations was $215 million.

Required

Calculate the current ratio, quick ratio, current cash debt coverage, receivables turnover, average collection period, inventory turnover, and average days in inventory.

E12.9 **Perform current and quick ratio analysis.**   **LO4**

Global Ltd had the following transactions involving current assets and current liabilities during February 2019.

Feb.	3	Collected accounts receivable of $15 000.
	7	Purchased equipment for $25 000 cash.
	11	Paid $3000 for a 1-year insurance policy.
	14	Paid accounts payable of $14 000.
	18	Declared cash dividends of $6000 to be paid in March.

Additional information:

1. As of 1 February 2019, current assets were $200 000 and current liabilities were $100 000.
2. As of 1 February 2019, current assets included $25 000 of inventory and $5000 of prepaid expenses.

Required

(a) Calculate the current ratio as of the beginning of the month and after each transaction.
(b) Calculate the quick ratio as of the beginning of the month and after each transaction.

E12.10 **Calculate selected ratios.**   **LO4**

Sonic Ltd has the following comparative data.

SONIC LTD Statement of financial position as at 30 June 2019		
	2019	2018
Cash	$ 20 000	$ 30 000
Receivables (net)	65 000	60 000
Inventories	60 000	50 000
Property, plant and equipment (net)	200 000	180 000
	$345 000	$320 000
Accounts payable	$ 50 000	$ 60 000
Loan payable (15%)	100 000	100 000
Share capital, $10 each	140 000	120 000
Retained earnings	55 000	40 000
	$345 000	$320 000

Additional information for 2019:

1. Profit was $20 000.
2. Sales on account were $380 000. Sales returns and allowances amounted to $30 000.
3. Cost of sales was $200 000.
4. Net cash provided by operating activities was $50 000.
5. The loan payable is a non-current liability in both years.

Required

Calculate the following at 30 June 2019:

(a) Current ratio.
(b) Quick ratio.
(c) Receivables turnover.
(d) Average collection period.
(e) Inventory turnover.
(f) Average days in inventory.
(g) Cash return on sales ratio.
(h) Cash debt coverage.
(i) Current cash debt coverage.

E12.11 Calculate selected ratios.   **LO4**

Selected comparative statement data for Cyber Ltd are presented here.

	2020	2019
Net sales	$950 000	$830 000
Cost of sales	534 000	390 000
Finance cost	8 700	6 300
Profit	164 000	142 000
Accounts receivable (30 June)	56 000	52 000
Inventory (30 June)	35 000	41 000
Total assets (30 June)	710 000	670 000
Ordinary shareholders' equity (30 June)	610 000	580 000
Cash provided by operating activities	95 000	78 000

Required

Calculate the following for 2020:

(a) Profit margin.

(b) Asset turnover.

(c) Return on assets.

(d) Return on ordinary shareholders' equity.

(e) Cash return on sales ratio.

(f) Gross profit margin.

E12.12 Calculate selected ratios.   **LO4**

Centro Ltd's statement of profit or loss follows.

CENTRO LTD Statement of profit or loss (extract) for the year ended 30 June 2019	
Sales	$ 580 000
Cost of sales	(210 000)
Gross profit	370 000
Expenses (excluding finance costs)	(160 000)
Finance costs	(36 000)
Profit before tax	**174 000**
Tax expense	(52 200)
Profit for the period	**$ 121 800**

Additional information:

1. The weighted average number of ordinary shares was 20 000.
2. The market price of Centro Ltd shares was $23 on 30 June 2019.
3. Cash dividends of $18 000 were paid, $3000 of which were to preference shareholders.
4. Net cash provided by operating activities was $95 000.

Required

Calculate the following measures for 2019:

(a) Earnings per share.

(b) Price/earnings ratio.

(c) Dividend payout rate.

(d) Times interest earned.

(e) Cash return on sales ratio.

E12.13 Calculate amounts from ratios.   **LO4**

Xander Ltd experienced a fire on 30 June 2019 in which its financial records were partially destroyed. It has been able to salvage some of the records and has ascertained the following balances.

	30 June 2019	1 July 2018
Cash	$ 30 000	$ 10 000
Receivables (net)	72 500	126 000
Inventory	200 000	180 000
Accounts payable	50 000	90 000
Notes payable (non-current)	30 000	60 000
Ordinary shares, $100 each	400 000	400 000
Retained earnings	113 500	101 000

Additional information:

1. The inventory turnover is 3.6 times.
2. The return on ordinary shareholders' equity is 22%. Xander Ltd had no additional paid-up capital or reserves.
3. The receivables turnover is 9.4 times. All sales are on credit.
4. The return on assets is 12.5% (12.5 cents).
5. Total assets at 30 June 2018 were $805 000.

Required

Calculate the following for Xander Ltd:

(a) Cost of sales for 2019.
(b) Net sales for 2019.
(c) Profit for 2019.
(d) Total assets at 30 June 2019.

PROBLEM SET A

PSA12.1 Prepare vertical analysis and comment on profitability.   **LO3, 4**

Here are comparative statement data for Spencer Ltd and Forrester Ltd, two competitors. All data relating to the statement of financial position are as at 30 June, the end of the reporting period for both entities.

	Spencer Ltd		Forrester Ltd	
	2019	2018	2019	2018
Net sales	$1 250 000		$410 000	
Cost of sales	690 000		257 000	
Operating expenses	321 000		62 000	
Finance costs	6 000		1 200	
Income tax expense	69 900		26 940	
Profit	163 100		62 860	
Current assets	325 975	$312 410	188 000	$180 000
Non-current assets	521 310	500 000	240 000	216 000
Current liabilities	79 595	75 815	36 000	32 000
Non-current liabilities	108 500	90 000	27 000	24 000
Share capital, $10 each	500 000	500 000	320 000	300 000
Retained earnings	159 190	146 595	45 000	40 000

Required

(a) Prepare a vertical analysis of the 2019 statement of profit or loss data for both entities.
(b) Comment on the relative profitability of the entities by calculating the return on assets and the return on ordinary shareholders' equity for both entities.

PSA12.2 Calculate ratios from financial statements.   **LO4**

The comparative statements of Bayview Ltd are presented below.

BAYVIEW LTD
Statement of profit or loss (extract)
for the years ended 30 June

	2019	2018
Net sales	$1 818 500	$1 750 500
Cost of sales	1 005 500	996 000
Gross profit	813 000	754 500
Selling and administrative expenses	506 000	479 000
Finance costs	18 000	19 000
Profit before income tax	**289 000**	**256 500**
Income tax expense	86 700	77 000
Profit for the period	**$ 202 300**	**$ 179 500**

BAYVIEW LTD
Statement of financial position
as at 30 June 2019

	2019	2018
ASSETS		
Current assets		
Cash	$ 64 900	$ 64 200
Marketable securities	100 000	50 000
Accounts receivable (net)	150 000	102 800
Inventory	200 000	115 500
Total current assets	514 900	332 500
Non-current assets		
Property, plant and equipment (net)	625 300	520 300
Total assets	**$1 140 200**	**$852 800**
LIABILITIES AND EQUITY		
Current liabilities		
Accounts payable	$ 150 000	$145 400
Income taxes payable	43 500	42 000
Total current liabilities	193 500	187 400
Non-current liabilities		
Notes payable	210 000	200 000
Total liabilities	403 500	387 400
Equity		
Share capital ($5 each)	450 000	300 000
Retained earnings	286 700	165 400
Total equity	736 700	465 400
Total liabilities and equity	**$1 140 200**	**$852 800**

All sales were on account. Net cash provided by operating activities for the year ended 30 June 2019 was $280 000. The weighted average number of shares is 80 137.

Required

Calculate the following for 2019:
(a) Earnings per share.
(b) Return on ordinary shareholders' equity.
(c) Return on assets.
(d) Current ratio.
(e) Quick ratio.
(f) Receivables turnover.

(g) Average collection period.

(h) Asset turnover.

(i) Debt to total assets ratio.

(j) Current cash debt coverage.

(k) Inventory turnover.

(l) Average days in inventory.

(m) Times interest earned.

(n) Cash return on sales ratio.

(o) Cash debt coverage.

PSA12.3 **Prepare ratio analysis and discuss change in financial position operating results.** **LO4**

Condensed financial statements for Metro Ltd are presented as follows.

METRO LTD Statement of financial position as at 30 June 2020			
	2020	2019	2018
Cash	$ 25 000	$ 20 000	$ 18 000
Receivables (net)	50 000	45 000	48 000
Other current assets	90 000	85 000	64 000
Investments	75 000	70 000	45 000
Plant and equipment (net)	400 000	370 000	358 000
	$640 000	$590 000	$533 000
Current liabilities	$ 75 000	$ 80 000	$ 70 000
Long-term debt	80 000	85 000	50 000
Share capital, $10 each	340 000	300 000	300 000
Retained earnings	145 000	125 000	113 000
	$640 000	$590 000	$533 000

METRO LTD Statement of profit or loss for the years ended 30 June		
	2020	2019
Sales	$740 000	$700 000
Less: Sales returns and allowances	40 000	50 000
Net sales	700 000	650 000
Cost of sales	420 000	400 000
Gross profit	280 000	250 000
Operating expenses (including income tax)	236 000	218 000
Profit	$ 44 000	$ 32 000

Additional information:

1. The market price of Metro Ltd's shares was $4.00 at 30 June 2018, $5.00 at 30 June 2019 and $7.95 at 30 June 2020.

2. All dividends were paid in cash.

3. On 1 January 2020, 4000 ordinary shares were issued.

Required

(a) Discuss the need for comparative analysis and identify the tools of financial statement analysis.

(b) Calculate the following for 2020 and 2019:

1. Profit margin ratio.

2. Gross profit margin.

3. Asset turnover.
4. Earnings per share.
5. Price/earnings ratio.
6. Cash dividend payout ratio.
7. Debt to total assets ratio.

(c) Based on the ratios calculated, provide an overview of the changes in the financial position and operating results from 2019 to 2020.

PSA12.4 **Calculate ratios; comment on overall liquidity and profitability.** **LO4**

The following financial information is for Digimax Ltd.

DIGIMAX LTD		
Statement of financial position		
as at 30 September 2019		
	2019	2018
ASSETS		
Cash	$ 70 000	$ 65 000
Short-term investments	45 000	40 000
Receivables (net)	94 000	90 000
Inventories	130 000	125 000
Prepaid expenses	25 000	23 000
Land	130 000	130 000
Building and equipment (net)	190 000	175 000
Total assets	**$684 000**	**$648 000**
LIABILITIES AND SHAREHOLDERS' EQUITY		
Notes payable (30 days)	$100 000	$100 000
Accounts payable	45 000	42 000
Accrued liabilities	40 000	40 000
Notes payable, due March 2020	150 000	150 000
Contributed equity, $10 per share	200 000	200 000
Retained earnings	149 000	116 000
Total liabilities and shareholders' equity	**$684 000**	**$648 000**

DIGIMAX LTD		
Statement of profit or loss		
for the years ended 30 September		
	2019	2018
Sales	$850 000	$790 000
Cost of sales	620 000	575 000
Gross profit	230 000	215 000
Operating expenses (including tax)	194 000	180 000
Profit	**$ 36 000**	**$ 35 000**

Additional information:
1. Inventory at 1 October 2017 was $115 000.
2. Receivables at 1 October 2017 were $88 000.
3. Total assets at 1 October 2017 were $630 000.
4. No transactions affected share capital during the years ended 30 September 2018 and 2019.

Required

By using ratios, explain the change in liquidity and profitability of Digimax Ltd from 2018 to 2019. (*Note:* Not all profitability ratios or cash-based ratios can be calculated.)

PSA12.5 **Calculate selected ratios, and compare liquidity, profitability and solvency for two entities.**

LO4

Selected financial data of two intense competitors in a recent year are presented here (in millions).

	Eastco Ltd	Westco Ltd
	Statement of profit or loss data	
Net sales	$ 40 000	$ 82 000
Cost of sales	(32 000)	(65 000)
Selling and administrative expenses	(7 200)	(13 000)
Finance expense	(600)	(1 000)
Gain on sale of equipment	800	200
Income tax expense	(300)	(1 200)
Profit	$ 700	$ 2 000
	Statement of financial position data (end-of-year)	
Current assets	$ 11 000	$ 11 000
Property, plant and equipment (net)	9 000	17 481
Total assets	$ 20 000	$ 28 481
Current liabilities	$ 5 500	$ 9 000
Non-current liabilities	8 200	11 000
Total equity	6 300	8 481
Total liabilities and equity	$ 20 000	$ 28 481
	Beginning-of-year balances	
Total assets	$ 17 504	$ 26 441
Current liabilities	5 698	9 981
Total equity	6 093	10 753
	Other data	
Average net receivables	$ 5 500	$ 2 200
Average inventory	5 000	8 000
Net cash provided by operating activities	1 000	2 500

Required

(a) For each entity, calculate the following:
1. Current ratio.
2. Receivables turnover.
3. Average collection period.
4. Inventory turnover.
5. Average days in inventory.
6. Profit margin.
7. Asset turnover.
8. Return on assets.
9. Return on ordinary shareholders' equity.
10. Debt to total assets ratio.
11. Times interest earned.
12. Current cash debt coverage.
13. Cash return on sales ratio.
14. Cash debt coverage.

(*Hint:* Use beginning of year information provided to calculate beginning of year balance for total liabilities.)

(b) Compare the liquidity, solvency and profitability of the two entities.

PSA12.6 Calculate numerous ratios.   **LO4**

The comparative statements of Diva Ltd are presented here.

DIVA LTD Statement of profit or loss for the year ended 31 December		
	2019	2018
Net sales (all on account)	$580 000	$520 000
EXPENSES		
Cost of sales	400 000	354 000
Selling and administrative	120 800	114 800
Interest expense	7 200	6 000
Income tax expense	18 000	14 000
Total expenses	546 000	488 800
Profit	**$ 34 000**	**$ 31 200**

DIVA LTD Statement of financial position as at 31 December		
	2019	2018
ASSETS		
Current assets		
Cash	$ 15 000	$ 18 000
Marketable securities	18 000	15 000
Accounts receivable (net)	92 000	74 000
Inventory	84 000	70 000
Total current assets	209 000	177 000
Non-current assets		
Property, plant and equipment (net)	423 000	383 000
Total assets	**$632 000**	**$560 000**
LIABILITIES AND EQUITY		
Current liabilities		
Accounts payable	$112 000	$110 000
Income taxes payable	23 000	20 000
Total current liabilities	135 000	130 000
Non-current liabilities		
Notes payable	130 000	80 000
Total liabilities	265 000	210 000
Equity		
Share capital ($5 each)	150 000	150 000
Retained earnings	217 000	200 000
Total equity	367 000	350 000
Total liabilities and equity	**$632 000**	**$560 000**

Additional information:
1. Diva Ltd's shares recently sold at $19.50 per share.
2. All dividends are cash dividends.
3. All sales are credit sales.

Required

Calculate the following ratios for 2019:
 (a) Current ratio.
 (b) Quick ratio.
 (c) Receivables turnover.
 (d) Average collection period.

(e) Inventory turnover.

(f) Average days in inventory.

(g) Profit margin.

(h) Asset turnover.

(i) Return on assets.

(j) Return on ordinary shareholders' equity.

(k) Earnings per share.

(l) Price/earnings ratio.

(m) Dividend payout rate.

(n) Debt to total assets ratio.

(o) Times interest earned.

PSA12.7 **Calculate missing information given a set of ratios.** LO4

Presented here are incomplete financial statements of Ascot Ltd.

ASCOT LTD Statement of profit or loss for the year ended 30 June 2019	
Sales	$11 000 000
Cost of sales	?
Gross profit	?
Operating expenses	1 665 000
Interest expense	?
Profit before income tax	?
Income tax expense	560 000
Profit	$?

ASCOT LTD Statement of financial position as at 30 June 2019		
	2019	2018
ASSETS		
Current assets		
Cash	$ 450 000	$ 375 000
Accounts receivable (net)	?	950 000
Inventory	?	1 720 000
Total current assets	?	3 045 000
Non-current assets	4 620 000	3 955 000
Total assets	$?	$7 000 000
LIABILITIES AND EQUITY		
Current liabilities	$?	$ 825 000
Non-current liabilities	?	2 800 000
Total liabilities	?	3 625 000
Equity		
Share capital ($1 each)	3 000 000	3 000 000
Retained earnings	400 000	375 000
Total equity	3 400 000	3 375 000
Total liabilities and equity	$?	$7 000 000

Additional information:

1. The receivables turnover for the year ended 30 June 2019 is 10 times.
2. All sales are on account.
3. The profit margin for the year ended 30 June 2019 is 14.5%.
4. Return on assets is 22% (22 cents) for the year ended 30 June 2019.

5. The current ratio on 30 June 2019 is 3:1.

6. The inventory turnover for the year ended 30 June 2019 is 4.8 times.

Required

Calculate the missing information given for the ratios. Show your calculations. (*Note:* Start with one ratio and derive as much information as possible from it before trying another ratio. List all missing amounts under the ratio used to find the information.)

PSA12.8 **Use the statement of cash flows to evaluate an entity.** **LO4**

Presented below is a simplified statement of cash flows for Calgary Ltd.

CALGARY LTD Statement of cash flows (simplified) for the year ended 31 December 2020 $'000		
Net cash provided by operating activities		$101 344
Cash flows from investing activities		
Additions to property, plant and equipment	$ (32 560)	
Proceeds from the sale of non-current assets	164	
Net cash used by investing activities		(32 396)
Net cash used by financing activities		(35 692)

Additional information:

1. Sales were $608 000.

2. Current liabilities were $202 800 in 2020 and $203 500 in 2019.

3. Total liabilities were $505 000 in 2020 and $306 500 in 2019.

Required

(a) Calculate:

    1. Free cash flow.

    2. Capital expenditure ratio.

    3. Current cash debt coverage.

    4. Cash debt coverage.

    5. Cash return on sales ratio.

(b) Based on your calculations, what is your evaluation of this entity? Explain your answer.

PSA12.9 **Identify and discuss the limitations of ratio analysis.** **LO5**

Presented below are extracts of financial information for two companies: Yin Ltd and Yan Ltd. Assume they both began operations at the beginning of 2019 with identical assets, liabilities and equity and that their revenues and expenses were identical except for their choice of accounting method for inventories and depreciation. Yin Ltd uses FIFO for inventories and straight line for depreciating property, plant and equipment. Yan Ltd uses the weighted average method for inventories and diminishing balance for depreciating property, plant and equipment. Ignore the effects of income tax for this question.

Statement of profit or loss (extracts) for the year ended 31 December 2019		
	Yin Ltd	Yan Ltd
Sales revenue	$1 000 000	$1 000 000
Less: Cost of sales	552 000	600 000
Gross profit	448 000	400 000
Less: Expenses		
Finance costs	32 000	32 000
Depreciation expense	40 000	80 000
Other expenses	100 000	100 000
Total expenses	172 000	212 000
Profit	$ **276 000**	$ **188 000**

Statement of financial position (extracts) for the year ended 31 December 2019		Yin Ltd	Yan Ltd
Cash		$ 80 000	$ 80 000
Accounts receivable		200 000	200 000
Inventories		208 000	160 000
Property, plant and equipment		260 000	260 000
Less: Accumulated depreciation		(40 000)	(80 000)
Total assets		**$708 000**	**$620 000**
Current liabilities		$120 000	$120 000
Non-current liabilities		180 000	180 000
Equity		408 000	320 000
Total liabilities and equity		**$708 000**	**$620 000**

Required

(a) Calculate the following ratios for each entity:
1. Return on assets.
2. Return on equity.
3. Profit margin.
4. Current ratio.
5. Receivables turnover.
6. Debt to equity ratio.

(b) Explain the effect that the use of different accounting methods can have on the calculations of ratios.

PROBLEM SET B

PSB12.1 Prepare vertical analysis and comment on profitability.   **LO3, 4**

Presented below is the statement of financial position data as at 31 December 2019 for two competitors, Black Ltd and White Ltd.

	Black Ltd		White Ltd	
	2019	**2018**	**2019**	**2018**
Net sales	$350 000		$1 400 000	
Cost of sales	180 000		720 000	
Operating expenses	51 000		278 000	
Finance expense	3 000		10 000	
Income tax expense	11 000		68 000	
Current assets	130 000	$100 000	700 000	$650 000
Non-current assets	405 000	270 000	1 000 000	750 000
Current liabilities	60 000	52 000	250 000	275 000
Non-current liabilities	50 000	68 000	200 000	150 000
Share capital	360 000	210 000	950 000	700 000
Retained earnings	65 000	40 000	300 000	275 000

Required

(a) Calculate profit and prepare the 2019 statement of profit or loss with vertical analysis for Black Ltd and White Ltd.

(b) Comment on the relative profitability of the entities by calculating the return on assets and return on ordinary shareholders' equity for both entities.

PSB12.2 Calculate ratios from statement of financial position and statement of profit or loss. **LO4**

The financial statements with comparative figures of Halifax Ltd are presented here.

HALIFAX LTD Statement of profit or loss for the year ended 30 June		
	2019	2018
Net sales	$ 780 000	$ 624 000
Cost of sales	(440 000)	(405 600)
Gross profit	340 000	218 400
Selling and administrative expense	(143 880)	(149 760)
Finance expense	(9 920)	(7 200)
Profit before income taxes	**186 200**	**61 440**
Income tax expense	(29 000)	(24 000)
Profit for the period	**$ 157 200**	**$ 37 440**

HALIFAX LTD Statement of financial position as at 30 June		
	2019	2018
ASSETS		
Current assets		
Cash	$ 23 100	$ 21 600
Short-term investments	34 800	33 000
Trade receivable (net allowance for doubtful accounts		
of $4800 for 2019 and $4200 for 2018)	106 200	93 800
Inventory	116 400	64 000
Total current assets	280 500	212 400
Property, plant and equipment (net)	455 300	459 600
Total assets	**$735 800**	**$672 000**
LIABILITIES AND EQUITY		
Current liabilities		
Accounts payable	$168 200	$132 000
Income taxes payable	25 300	24 000
Total current liabilities	193 500	156 000
Bonds payable	132 000	120 000
Total liabilities	325 500	276 000
Equity		
Share capital	140 000	150 000
Retained earnings	270 300	246 000
Total equity	410 300	396 000
Total liabilities and equity	**$735 800**	**$672 000**

All sales were on account. Net cash provided by operating activities was $41 000.

Required

Calculate the following ratios for 2019:

(a) Gross profit margin.
(b) Return on ordinary shareholders' equity.
(c) Return on assets.
(d) Current ratio.
(e) Receivables turnover.
(f) Average collection period.
(g) Inventory turnover.
(h) Days in inventory.

(i) Times interest earned.
(j) Asset turnover.
(k) Debt to total assets.
(l) Current cash debt coverage.
(m) Cash debt coverage.

PSB12.3 Perform ratio analysis, and discuss change in financial position, operating results and limitation of financial statement analysis. **LO4**

Condensed financial statements for Jasmine Ltd are presented below.

JASMINE LTD Statement of financial position as at 30 June			
	2019	2018	2017
Cash	$ 60 000	$ 40 000	$ 18 000
Receivables (net)	70 000	60 000	48 000
Inventory	90 000	85 000	64 000
Investments	75 000	70 000	45 000
Plant and equipment (net)	500 000	410 000	358 000
	$795 000	$665 000	$533 000
Current liabilities	$ 75 000	$ 80 000	$ 70 000
Long-term debt	80 000	85 000	50 000
Share capital, $10 each	340 000	300 000	300 000
Retained earnings	300 000	200 000	113 000
	$795 000	$665 000	$533 000

JASMINE LTD Statement of profit or loss for the year ended 30 June		
	2019	2018
Sales	$780 000	$710 000
Less: Sales returns and allowances	(40 000)	(50 000)
Net sales	740 000	660 000
Cost of sales	420 000	450 000
Gross profit	320 000	210 000
Operating expenses (including income tax)	200 000	110 000
Profit	**$120 000**	**$100 000**

Additional information:
1. The market price of Jasmine Ltd's shares was $4 at 30 June 2017, $10 at 30 June 2018 and $15 at 30 June 2019.
2. All dividends were paid in cash.
3. The weighted average number of shares was 30 000 in 2018 and 31 984 in 2019.

Required
(a) Calculate the following for 2019 and 2018.
    1. Profit margin
    2. Gross profit margin
    3. Asset turnover
    4. Earnings per share
    5. Price/earnings ratio
    6. Cash dividend payout ratio
    7. Debt to total assets ratio

(b) Based on the ratios calculated, discuss briefly the improvement or lack thereof in the financial position and operating results from 2018 to 2019 of Jasmine Ltd.

(c) Discuss the limitations of financial statement analysis.

PSB12.4 Calculate ratios; comment on overall liquidity and profitability.　　　　　　　　**LO4**

Financial information for Multimedia Ltd is presented here.

MULTIMEDIA LTD Statement of financial position as at 31 December		
	2019	2018
ASSETS		
Cash	$ 50 000	$ 42 000
Short-term investments	80 000	50 000
Receivables (net of allowance for doubtful accounts of $4000 for 2017 and $3000 for 2016)	100 000	87 000
Inventories	440 000	300 000
Prepaid expenses	25 000	31 000
Land	75 000	75 000
Building and equipment (net)	570 000	400 000
Total assets	**$1 340 000**	**$985 000**
LIABILITIES AND EQUITY		
Short-term provisions	$ 125 000	$ 25 000
Accounts payable	160 000	90 000
Accrued liabilities	50 000	50 000
Bonds payable, due 2019	200 000	100 000
Share capital (100 000 shares)	500 000	500 000
Retained earnings	305 000	220 000
Total liabilities and equity	**$1 340 000**	**$985 000**

MULTIMEDIA LTD Statement of profit or loss for the year ended 31 December		
	2019	2018
Sales	$1 000 000	$ 940 000
Cost of sales	(650 000)	(635 000)
Gross profit	350 000	305 000
Finance cost	(20 000)	(10 000)
Operating expenses	(115 000)	(145 000)
Profit before tax	**215 000**	**150 000**
Tax expense	(100 000)	(70 000)
Profit	**$ 115 000**	**$ 80 000**

Additional information:

1. Inventory at the beginning of 2018 was $350 000.
2. Receivables at the beginning of 2018 were $80 000, net of an allowance for doubtful accounts of $3000.
3. Total assets at the beginning of 2018 were $1 175 000.
4. No share capital transactions occurred during 2018 or 2019.
5. All sales were on account.

Required

(a) By using ratios, explain the change in liquidity and profitability of the entity from 2018 to 2019. (*Note:* Not all profitability ratios can be calculated, nor can cash-basis ratios be calculated.)

(b) Your friend is a first-year accounting student and has asked you to explain, in simple terms, what the ratios calculated in part (a) mean.

PSB12.5 Calculate selected ratios and compare liquidity, profitability and solvency for two entities.

LO4

Selected financial data of two intense competitors are presented below.

	Angel Ltd $m 2019	Buffy Ltd $m 2019
	Statement of profit or loss data	
Net sales	34 025	82 494
Cost of sales	25 992	65 586
Selling and administrative expenses	7 701	12 858
Interest expense	494	706
Gain on sale of equipment	572	918
Income tax expense	114	1 581
Profit	296	2 681
	Statement of financial position data (end-of-year)	
Current assets	9 187	15 338
Property, plant and equipment (net)	7 842	17 481
Total assets	17 029	32 819
Current liabilities	5 626	9 973
Non-current liabilities	5 371	10 120
Total shareholders' equity	6 032	12 726
Total liabilities and shareholders' equity	17 029	32 819
	Beginning-of-year balances	
Total assets	17 504	26 441
Total shareholders' equity	6 093	10 753
Current liabilities	5 698	9 981
	Other data	
Average net receivables	1 570	695
Average inventory	7 317	12 539
Net cash provided by operating activities	351	3 106

Required

(a) For each entity, calculate the following:
1. Current ratio.
2. Receivables turnover.
3. Average collection period.
4. Inventory turnover.
5. Average days in inventory.
6. Profit margin ratio.
7. Asset turnover.
8. Return on assets ratio.
9. Return on shareholders' equity ratio.
10. Debt to total assets ratio.
11. Times interest earned.
12. Current cash debt coverage.
13. Cash return on sales ratio.
14. Cash debt coverage.

(b) Compare the liquidity, solvency and profitability of the two companies.

PSB12.6 Calculate numerous ratios.   **LO4**

The comparative statements of Beachcombers Ltd are presented below.

BEACHCOMBERS LTD Statement of profit or loss for the year ended 31 December 2019		
	2019	2018
Net sales (all on account)	$704 000	$645 000
EXPENSES		
Cost of sales	376 000	360 000
Selling and administrative	145 000	138 000
Interest expense	9 500	7 500
Income tax expense	52 050	41 850
Total expenses	582 550	547 350
Profit	**$121 450**	**$ 97 650**

BEACHCOMBERS LTD Statement of financial position as at 31 December 2019		
	2019	2018
ASSETS		
Current assets		
Cash	$ 25 000	$ 22 500
Marketable securities	15 600	19 000
Accounts receivable (net)	110 000	95 000
Inventory	90 000	78 000
Total current assets	240 600	215 000
Non-current assets		
Property, plant and equipment (net)	520 000	465 000
Total assets	**$760 600**	**$680 000**
LIABILITIES AND EQUITY		
Current liabilities		
Accounts payable	$ 83 600	$ 80 700
Income taxes payable	28 000	24 300
Total current liabilities	111 600	105 000
Non-current liabilities		
Notes payable	184 000	150 000
Total liabilities	295 600	255 000
Equity		
Share capital ($5 each)	200 000	180 000
Retained earnings	265 000	245 000
Total equity	465 000	425 000
Total liabilities and equity	**$760 600**	**$680 000**

Additional information:
1. Beachcombers Ltd shares recently sold at $28.50 per share.
2. All dividends are cash dividends.
3. You are required to reconstruct the Retained Earnings account to calculate the dividend amount.
4. All sales are credit sales.

Required

Calculate the following ratios for 2019:

(a) Current ratio.

(b) Quick ratio.

(c) Receivables turnover.

(d) Average collection period.

(e) Inventory turnover.

(f) Average days in inventory.

(g) Profit margin.

(h) Asset turnover.

(i) Return on assets.

(j) Return on ordinary shareholders' equity.

(k) Earnings per share.

(l) Price/earnings ratio.

(m) Dividend payout.

(n) Debt to total assets ratio.

(o) Times interest earned.

PSB12.7 **Calculate missing information given a set of ratios.**   **LO4**

The incomplete financial statements of Jade Ltd are presented below.

JADE LTD
Statement of profit or loss
for the year ended 30 June 2019

Sales	$5 500 000
Cost of sales	?
Gross profit	?
Operating expenses	832 500
Interest expense	?
Profit before income tax	?
Income tax expense	280 000
Profit	$?

JADE LTD
Statement of financial position
as at 30 June 2019

	2019	2018
ASSETS		
Current assets		
Cash	$ 225 000	$ 187 500
Accounts receivable (net)	?	475 000
Inventory	?	860 000
Total current assets	?	1 522 500
Non-current assets	2 310 000	1 977 500
Total assets	$?	$3 500 000
LIABILITIES AND EQUITY		
Current liabilities	$?	$ 412 500
Non-current liabilities	?	1 400 000
Total liabilities	?	1 812 500
Equity		
Share capital ($1 each)	1 500 000	1 500 000
Retained earnings	200 000	187 500
Total equity	1 700 000	1 687 500
Total liabilities and equity	$?	$3 500 000

Additional information:

1. The receivables turnover for the year ended 30 June 2019 is 10 times.
2. All sales are on account.
3. The profit margin for the year ended 30 June 2019 is 14.5%.
4. Return on assets is 22% (22 cents) for the year ended 30 June 2019.
5. The current ratio on 30 June 2019 is 3:1.
6. The inventory turnover for the year ended 30 June 2019 is 4.8 times.

Required

Calculate the missing information, given the ratios. Show your calculations. (*Hint:* Start with one ratio and derive as much information as possible from it before trying another ratio. List all missing amounts under the ratio used to find the information.)

PSB12.8 Calculate missing information given a set of ratios.   **LO4**

The incomplete financial statements of Kalamata Ltd are presented below.

KALAMATA LTD Statement of profit or loss for the year ended 30 June 2019	
Sales	$2 750 000
Cost of sales	?
Gross profit	?
Operating expenses	416 250
Interest expense	?
Profit before income tax	?
Income tax expense	140 000
Profit	$?

KALAMATA LTD Statement of financial position as at 30 June 2019		
	2019	2018
ASSETS		
Current assets		
Cash	$ 112 500	$ 93 750
Accounts receivable (net)	?	237 500
Inventory	?	430 000
Total current assets	?	761 250
Non-current assets	1 155 000	988 750
Total assets	$?	$1 750 000
LIABILITIES AND EQUITY		
Current liabilities	$?	$ 206 250
Non-current liabilities	?	700 000
Total liabilities	?	906 250
Equity		
Share capital ($1 each)	750 000	750 000
Retained earnings	100 000	93 750
Total equity	850 000	843 750
Total liabilities and equity	$?	$1 750 000

Additional information:

1. The receivables turnover for the year ended 30 June 2019 is 10 times.
2. All sales are on account.
3. The profit margin for the year ended 30 June 2019 is 14.5%.
4. Return on assets is 22% (22 cents) for the year ended 30 June 2019.
5. The current ratio on 30 June 2019 is 3:1.
6. The inventory turnover for the year ended 30 June 2019 is 4.8 times.

Required

(a) Given the ratios, calculate the missing information. Show your calculations.

(*Note:* Start with one ratio and derive as much information as possible from it before trying another ratio. List all missing amounts under the ratio used to find the information.)

(b) Based on the ratios provided, would you invest in this business? Justify your answer.

PSB12.9 Use the statement of cash flows to evaluate an entity. **LO4**

Presented below is a simplified statement of cash flows for Spectre Ltd.

SPECTRE LTD Statement of cash flows (extract) for the year ended 31 December 2019 ('000)		
Net cash provided by operating activities		$202 688
Cash flows from investing activities		
Additions to property, plant and equipment	($65 120)	
Proceeds from the sale of non-current assets	328	
Net cash used by investing activities		(64 792)
Net cash used by financing activities		(71 384)

Additional information:

1. Sales were $1 216 000.
2. Current liabilities were $403 000 in 2019 and $406 500 in 2018.
3. Total liabilities were $990 800 in 2019 and $608 500 in 2018.

Required

(a) Calculate:
  1. Free cash flow.
  2. Capital expenditure ratio.
  3. Current cash debt coverage.
  4. Cash debt coverage.
  5. Cash return on sales ratio.

(b) Based on your calculations, what is your evaluation of this entity? Explain your answer.

PSB12.10 Identify and discuss the limitations of ratio analysis. **LO5**

Extracts of financial information for two companies, Victoria Ltd and Conrad Ltd, are presented below. Assume they both began operations at the beginning of 2019 with identical assets, liabilities and equity and that their revenues and expenses were identical except for their choice of accounting method for inventories and depreciation. Victoria Ltd uses FIFO for inventories and straight line for depreciating property, plant and equipment. Conrad Ltd uses the weighted average method for inventories and diminishing balance for depreciating property, plant and equipment. Assume no income tax for this question.

Statement of profit or loss (extracts) for the year ended 31 December 2019		
	Victoria Ltd	Conrad Ltd
Sales revenue	$500 000	$500 000
Less: Cost of sales	276 000	300 000
Gross profit	224 000	200 000
Less: Expenses		
Finance costs	16 000	16 000
Depreciation expense	20 000	40 000
Other expenses	50 000	50 000
Total expenses	86 000	106 000
Profit	$138 000	$ 94 000

Statement of financial position (extracts) as at 31 December 2019		
	Victoria Ltd	Conrad Ltd
Cash	$ 40 000	$ 40 000
Accounts receivable	100 000	100 000
Inventories	104 000	80 000
Property, plant and equipment	130 000	130 000
Less: Accumulated depreciation	(20 000)	(40 000)
Total assets	**$354 000**	**$310 000**
Current liabilities	60 000	60 000
Non-current liabilities	90 000	90 000
Equity	204 000	160 000
Total liabilities and equity	**$354 000**	**$310 000**

Required

(a) Calculate the following ratios for each entity:
1. Return on assets.
2. Return on equity.
3. Profit margin.
4. Current ratio.
5. Receivables turnover.
6. Inventory turnover.
7. Debt to equity ratio.

(b) Explain the effect that the use of different accounting methods can have on the calculations of ratios.

BUILDING BUSINESS SKILLS

FINANCIAL REPORTING AND ANALYSIS

Financial reporting problem

BBS12.1 Your parents are considering investing in Gayle Murray Ltd (GMY) shares. They ask you, an accounting expert, to make an analysis of the entity for them. An extract from the five-year summary included in Gayle Murray Ltd 2019 annual report is presented below. All figures are in thousands.

GAYLE MURRAY LTD Five-year summary 2015–2019 $'000					
	2019	2018	2017	2016	2015
Sales	2 767 518	2 801 726	2 942 616	3 079 631	2 978 235
Gross profit	1 059 216	1 049 745	1 150 904	1 223 594	1 179 219
Department store—EBIT	149 298	157 493	298 505	307 197	276 566
Financial services—EBIT	74 199	74 127	71 561	66 569	61 911
Total EBIT	223 497	231 620	370 065	373 766	338 477
Profit after tax	152 331	151 655	252 209	256 149	234 783
Total assets	1 856 678	1 861 346	1 821 825	1 792 382	1 687 011
Total liabilities	655 034	697 790	643 605	676 025	659 748
Total equity	1 201 644	1 163 556	1 178 220	1 116 357	1 027 263
Basic earnings per share (cents)	28.8	29.1	49.5	51.0	47.3
Dividends per share (cents)	25.5	26.3	42.0	45.0	42.0

Required

(a) Prepare a 5-year trend (horizontal) analysis of sales, gross profit, department store EBIT, financial services EBIT and profit after tax using 2015 as the base year. Comment on the significance of the trend results.

(b) Calculate the following for 2019 and 2018:
   1. Debt to total assets ratio.
   2. Profit margin.
   3. Asset turnover.
   4. Return on shareholders' equity.
   5. Dividend payout.

(c) How would you evaluate Gayle Murray Ltd's profitability, solvency and investment potential?

(d) What other information may be useful in making a decision about investing in Gayle Murray Ltd (GMY) shares?

Interpreting financial statements

BBS12.2 In 2019, Digitech Ltd decided to sell its low-performing e-business and concentrate efforts on showroom sales. The 2018 comparative figures were restated to reflect discontinued operations. The statement of profit or loss, statement of financial position and selected note disclosures from the annual report of Digitech Ltd for 2019 are presented below.

	Notes	Consolidated 2019 $'000	Consolidated 2018 $'000
DIGITECH LTD Statement of profit or loss for the year ended 30 June 2019			
Revenue	2	$ 627 708	$ 550 324
Changes in inventories of work in progress and finished goods		(2 961)	(11 448)
Raw materials and consumables used		(276 558)	(221 865)
Employee benefits expense		(149 173)	(137 848)
Depreciation and amortisation expenses		(18 764)	(17 166)
Finance costs		(8 529)	(6 440)
Other expenses from ordinary activities		(160 000)	(149 727)
Profit before income tax expense		11 723	5 830
Income tax expense	5	(5 000)	(2 711)
Profit for the period from continuing operations	3	6 723	3 119
Profit after tax from discontinued operations net of loss on restatement of assets	21	(5 223)	(500)
Profit for the period		$ **1 500**	$ **2 619**
NOTE 3: PROFIT Includes the following income and expense items:			
Loss on asset write-down on impairment		(766)	(760)
Research and development costs		(2 620)	(3 931)
Defined benefit superannuation expense		(164)	(502)
Long service leave		(993)	(952)
Annual leave		(1 168)	(1 151)
Doubtful debts—trade debtors		(306)	(310)
Rent expense relating to operating leases		(49 368)	(43 574)
Bad debts recovered—trade debtors		39	60
Dividends received		470	600
Interest received		823	300
Gain on sale of non-current assets		1 800	500

DIGITECH LTD Statement of financial position as at 30 June 2019	Consolidated	
	2019 $'000	2018 $'000
Current assets		
Cash assets	$ 31 691	$ 18 422
Receivables	47 583	63 908
Inventories	55 117	88 853
Other—prepayments	8 324	10 014
Total current assets	142 715	181 197
Non-current assets		
Investments	13 965	6 295
Property, plant and equipment	108 000	110 860
Intangibles	27 000	35 000
Total non-current assets	148 965	152 155
Total assets	291 680	333 352
Current liabilities		
Payables	37 915	57 882
Current portion of long-term borrowings	4 000	142
Current tax liabilities	3 000	2 000
Short-term provisions	31 704	26 818
Total current liabilities	76 619	86 842
Non-current liabilities		
Borrowings	87 453	118 154
Long-term provisions	3 734	2 733
Total non-current liabilities	91 187	120 887
Total liabilities	167 806	207 729
Net assets	**$123 874**	**$125 623**
Equity		
Parent entity interest		
Share capital	$ 61 390	$ 61 390
Reserves	8 000	11 249
Retained earnings	54 484	52 984
Total equity	**$123 874**	**$125 623**

Required

(a) Calculate the following ratios for 2018 and 2019 and then evaluate Digitech's profitability:
1. Profit margin based on profit for the period and on profit from continuing operations. Use data in note 3 to calculate sales revenue.
2. Return on ordinary shareholders' equity, using both profit for the period and profit from continuing operations.
3. Return on assets, using both profit for the period and profit from continuing operations.
4. Times interest earned, using profit from continuing operations before finance cost and tax expense.

Note that, at 30 June 2017, equity was $124 million and total assets were $330 million.

(b) All sales were on credit. Cost of sales were $279 519 000 in 2019 and $233 313 000 in 2018.
1. Calculate Digitech's inventory turnover for 2019.
2. Calculate Digitech's receivables turnover for 2019. Use sales revenue calculated in (a).
3. Calculate Digitech's gross profit margin for 2018 and 2019, using sales revenue calculated in (a).

(c) Discuss the change in profitability from 2018 to 2019 and prospects for 2020. Explain which profitability ratios are more useful as an indicator of future profitability.

Managerial analysis

BBS12.3 Grayson Global Ltd has excess cash that it wishes to invest in the ordinary shares of Nolan E-Corp Ltd. Daniel Grayson, finance director of Grayson Global Ltd, has a copy of Nolan E-Corp Ltd's most recent financial statements and a summary of key information is presented below.

	2020	2019	2018
Current ratio	2.5:1	2.0:1	1.3:1
Quick ratio	0.5:1	0.9:1	1.4:1
Accounts receivable turnover	7.2 times	8.4 times	6.8 times
Inventory turnover	6.1 times	7.3 times	7.6 times
Sales as a % of 2018 base year	142%	121%	100%
Dividends per share	$3.00	$3.00	$3.00
Dividend payout rate	50%	60%	70%
Return on total assets ratio using profit before tax	14 cents	12.4 cents	9.7 cents
Return on ordinary shareholders' equity	14.7 cents	13 cents	10.2 cents
(No additional shares issued from 2018 to 2020)			
Gross profit margin	40%	40%	40%

Required

To make this investment decision, Daniel would like to know about the financial trends of Nolan E-Corp Ltd over the past 3 years. As Daniel's assistant, you are required to answer each of the following questions using the data above and explain your reasoning for each answer.

(a) Are customers of Nolan E-Corp Ltd paying their invoices faster or slower now than they did in 2018?

(b) Is it becoming easier or harder for Nolan E-Corp Ltd to pay its invoices as they come due?

(c) Has the balance in Nolan E-Corp Ltd's accounts receivable been increasing, decreasing or staying constant?

(d) Has the amount carried in Nolan E-Corp Ltd's inventory increased, decreased or stayed constant since 2018?

(e) Is the amount of earnings per share increasing or decreasing?

(f) Is Nolan E-Corp Ltd financially leveraging to the advantage of its shareholders? Nolan E-Corp Ltd is charged 10% interest by the bank.

Financial analysis on the web

BBS12.4 Purpose: Financial statements communicate to investors, creditors and management the financial status of the organisation. Entities are aware that financial statements are read by individuals who have varying degrees of understanding of financial matters. IBM's 'Guide to Financials', which is located on its web site, provides online information for novice users. This guide takes an investor's approach to understanding the different financial statements.

Address: www.ibm.com/investor/help/

Steps: Go to the given address and select **How to Read Annual Reports**. You will then be able to answer questions (a)–(d).

Required

Answer the following questions:

(a) What is the purpose of an annual report? Who prepares the financial statements?

(b) What is the auditor's report?

(c) What are the three financial statements required in an annual report? What are key numbers in the statement of profit or loss and statement of financial performance?

(d) From an investor's perspective, list two general suggestions for an approach to analysing financial statements. (Refer to the **Guide to Financial Statements** on the above web address, then **Statement Basics: Analysing the Statements**.)

Comprehensive financial analysis exercise with web search

BBS12.5 Selected figures and ratio calculations for The Flash Company and selected ratio calculations for Green Arrow Inc. are provided below. All figures are presented in US$ millions, except the share data.

The Flash Company			
	2019	2018	2017
Net credit sales	$46 854	$48 017	$46 542
Profit after tax	8 626	9 086	8 646
Profit available to ordinary shareholders	8 584	9 019	8 584
Income tax	2 851	2 723	2 812
Interest expense	463	397	417
Earnings before income tax and interest expense	11 940	12 206	11 875
Cost of sales	18 421	19 053	18 215
Gross profit	28 433	28 964	28 327
Operating expenses	18 205	18 185	18 154
Current assets	31 304	30 328	25 497
Cash + Receivables + Market securities	25 141	21 310	18 955
Net receivables	4 873	4 759	4 920
Inventory	3 277	3 264	3 092
Total assets	90 055	86 174	79 974
Current liabilities	27 811	27 821	24 283
Total liabilities	56 615	53 006	48 053
Net cash flows from operating activities	10 542	10 645	9 474
Capital expenditures	2 550	2 780	2 920
Total equity	33 440	33 168	31 921
Weighted average no. of ordinary shares (in millions)	4 425	4 510	4 566
Share price	$ 41.31	$ 36.25	
Dividends	4 969	4 595	
Earnings per share	$ 1.94	$ 2.00	

Ratios	The Flash Company 2018	The Flash Company 2019	Green Arrow Inc. 2019
LIQUIDITY			
1. Current ratio	1.09:1		1.24:1
2. Quick ratio	0.77:1		0.93:1
3. Current cash debt coverage	0.27:1		0.37:1
4. Receivables turnover	9.92 times		9.49 times
5. Average collection period	36.79 days		38.46 days
6. Inventory turnover	6.00 times		8.94 times
7. Average days in inventory	60.88 days		40.83 days
SOLVENCY			
8. Debt to total assets	0.62:1		0.69:1
9. Times interest earned	30.75 times		10.76 times
10. Cash debt coverage	0.21:1		0.18:1
11. Free cash flow (in millions)	$7 865		$6 893

▶

Ratios	The Flash Company 2018	The Flash Company 2019	Green Arrow Inc. 2019
PROFITABILITY			
12. Return on ordinary shareholders' equity	28 cents		29 cents
13. Return on assets	11 cents		9 cents
14. Profit margin	19 cents		10 cents
15. Asset turnover	58 cents		87 cents
16. Gross profit margin	60%		61%
17. Operating expenses to sales	0.38:1		0.38:1
18. Cash return on sales	0.22:1		0.15:1
19. Earnings per share	$2.00		$4.37
20. Price/earnings ratio	18.13 times		18.96 times
21. Dividend payout rate	51%		51%

Required

(a) Calculate the liquidity, solvency and profitability ratios listed above for The Flash Company for 2019. Show all workings in the format provided in the demonstration problem in this chapter. Then enter the results in the table above. (*Hint:* If you are familiar with spreadsheets, you may like to enter all of the data provided on The Flash Company into a spreadsheet and enter each of the ratio formulas so that the spreadsheet calculates the amounts for you.)

(b) Compare The Flash Company's liquidity, solvency and profitability ratios for 2018 and 2019 and comment on any changes that have occurred between the years.

(c) Compare the 2019 liquidity, solvency and profitability ratios for Green Arrow Inc. and The Flash Company and comment on any differences between the entities. (*Hint:* For each of the ratios, go back to the relevant section in the chapter and the demonstration problem to help guide your analysis and discussion.)

CRITICAL THINKING

Group decision case

BBS12.6 You are a loan officer at Corporate Bank. Penny Wise, manager of Leverage Ltd, is interested in a 5-year loan to expand the entity's operations. The borrowed funds would be used to purchase new equipment. As evidence of Leverage Ltd's debt-worthiness, Penny provided you with the following facts.

	2019	2018
Current ratio	3.1	2.1
Quick ratio	0.8	1.4
Asset turnover	2.8	2.2
Cash debt coverage	0.1	0.2
Profit	Up 32%	Down 8%
Earnings per share	$3.30	$2.50

When you told Penny that you would need additional information before making your decision, she was offended, and said, 'What more could you possibly want to know?' You responded that, as a minimum, you would need complete audited financial statements.

Required

With the class divided into groups, answer the following:

(a) Explain why you would want the financial statements to be audited.

(b) Discuss the implications of the ratios provided for the lending decision you are to make. Does the information paint a favourable picture? Are these ratios relevant to the decision?

(c) List three other ratios that you would want to calculate for Leverage Ltd, and explain why you would use each.

(d) What are the limitations of ratio analysis for credit and investing decisions?

Communication activity

BBS12.7 Shannon Leahy is the chief executive officer of Digital Designs Ltd. Shannon is an expert in web site design and development but a novice in accounting. Shannon requires your assistance as an accounting student, to explain (a) the basis for comparison in analysing Digital Designs Ltd's financial statements and (b) the limitations of financial statement analysis.

Required

Write a memo to Shannon explaining the basis for comparison and the limitations of financial statement analysis.

Ethics case

BBS12.8 The management team of Positive Perception Ltd was faced with a financial crisis. The entity was in breach of a loan agreement and had to repay a major loan at short notice. To raise the necessary cash, one of Positive Perception Ltd's successful subsidiaries (a company owned by another company) was sold. While this solved the liquidity and solvency problems, it reduced future earning potential. As chief accountant, you have been asked to provide a list of 20 financial ratios along with some other operating statistics relative to Positive Perception Ltd's first-quarter financial data and operations.

Two days after you provide the ratios and data requested, you are asked by the public relations officer to prove the accuracy of the financial and operating data contained in the press release. In the press release, the managing director highlights the sales increase of 25% over last year's first quarter and the positive change in the current ratio from 1.5:1 last year to 3:1 this year. The managing director also emphasises that production was up 50% over the previous year's first quarter. You note that the release contains only positive or improved ratios and none of the negative or deteriorated ratios. For instance, the profit margin, which showed slight improvement from 6% to 7%, was reported, but the interest cover, which had declined, was excluded. None of the ratios used profit from continuing operations, which was considerably lower. For instance, the profit margin from continuing operations was only 3%. The public relations office emphasises: 'The managing director wants this release by early this afternoon'.

Required

(a) Who are the stakeholders in this situation?

(b) Is there anything unethical in the management team's actions?

(c) Should you as chief accountant remain silent? Does the accountant or public relations officer have any responsibility?

(d) If you do not want to remain silent, who should you speak or write to?

Sustainability

BBS12.9 Many companies today provide information on their objectives and strategies to ensure a sustainable future for the company and the planet.

Required

Download PepsiCo's 2016 annual report and summarise the key initiatives outlined for ensuring sustainable growth in relation to:

• its products
• the marketplace
• communities.

ANSWERS

Answers to self-study questions

12.1 (a) 12.2 (a) 12.3 (b) 12.4 (d) 12.5 (d) 12.6 (c) 12.7 (a) 12.8 (c) 12.9 (c) 12.10 (c) 12.11 (b)
12.12 (a) 12.13 (a) 12.14 (a) 12.15 (d)

ACKNOWLEDGEMENTS

Photo: © Zadorozhnyi Viktor / Shutterstock.com
Photo: © DragonImages / Getty Images

CHAPTER 13

Analysing and integrating GAAP

After studying this chapter, you should be able to:

13.1 explain and apply the concepts and principles underlying the recording of accounting information

13.2 describe the *Conceptual Framework for Financial Reporting* (the *Conceptual Framework*)

13.3 explain the objective of general purpose financial reporting

13.4 identify the primary and other users, and their uses of financial reports

13.5 explain the nature of a reporting entity

13.6 identify and apply the qualitative characteristics and constraint on financial reporting

13.7 define assets, liabilities, equity, income and expenses and apply recognition criteria

13.8 integrate principles, concepts, standards and the *Conceptual Framework*

13.9 appreciate, at an introductory level, various future developments in financial reporting.

Chapter preview

Well here we are at chapter 13 — let's begin with an analogy. Have you ever pieced together a jigsaw puzzle? You might have begun by putting all of the pieces that form the edge or outline of the puzzle together first. Then you might have grouped all of the pieces of a similar colour together, and then piece by piece with a lot of trial and error and a bit of luck and patience you eventually put it all together. Woo hoo! Yippee! Hooray! After all those hours of hard work, you probably stood back to admire your work, and saw the jigsaw puzzle as a whole and observed how everything fits together to make a complete picture.

The organisation and content of the chapter are as follows.

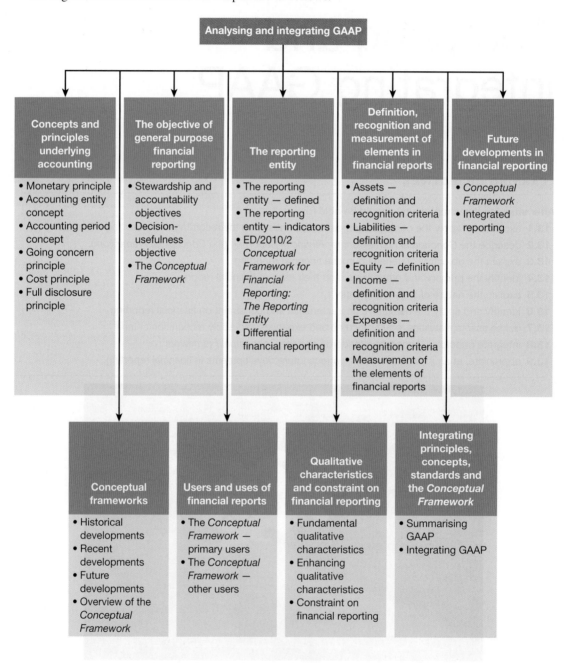

The *process* involves putting the jigsaw puzzle together piece by piece, but unless you stand back and look at the finished *product* you will never see it as an interrelated whole. We have used this analogy to explain the purpose of this chapter. Piece by piece, chapter by chapter, we have put together the various aspects of accounting theory and practice. The aim of this chapter is to help you stand back and review what you have learned so you can see it as an integrated whole — just like the finished picture of a jigsaw puzzle.

So, now that you know the objective of this chapter, let's review some of the concepts you have learned so far. Recall that in chapter 1 we explained that the objective of general purpose financial reporting is to provide financial information about the reporting entity that is useful to existing and potential investors, lenders and other creditors in making decisions about providing resources to the entity. Decisions for potential and existing shareholders include whether to buy, retain or sell shares in an entity; and for creditors decisions include whether to supply goods or services on credit or to lend funds to the entity. It is the accounting process that underlies the development of financial statements and accounting is defined as the process of identifying, measuring, recording and communicating the economic transactions and events of a business entity. Then, in the chapters that followed, we illustrated in detail each of these processes. By now you have had many opportunities to identify, measure and record transactions and prepare financial reports.

Take some time to reflect on your learning. How did you know which economic events were accounting transactions? How did you know how to record a purchase of equipment? How did you know what was to be recorded as an asset or a liability? How did you know when to recognise revenues and expenses? How did you know what to report and who you were reporting to? The answer to all of these questions is that you integrated and applied the rules, principles, theories and the *Conceptual Framework for Financial Reporting* (the *Conceptual Framework*) underlying accounting.

This chapter is entitled 'Analysing and integrating GAAP'. The accounting concepts, accounting principles and qualitative characteristics, together with the accounting standards, are collectively referred to as Australian **generally accepted accounting principles (GAAP)**. Australian GAAP is similar to New Zealand GAAP with the exception of differential reporting discussed later in the chapter.

Throughout the chapter we will explore the *Conceptual Framework* as well as some of the future developments in accounting.

13.1 Concepts and principles underlying accounting

LEARNING OBJECTIVE 13.1 Explain and apply the concepts and principles underlying the recording of accounting information.

In chapter 1, we introduced the concepts and principles that underlie the recording of accounting transactions. You have used those concepts and principles time and time again in recording the transactions in the numerous exercises and problems you have completed. Let's revisit them briefly to integrate your understanding of how to apply them and how important they are to preparing financial reports useful for decision making.

Monetary principle

The **monetary principle** requires that the items included in the accounting records must be able to be expressed in monetary terms. Given the many transactions you have recorded to date, this might seem so obvious that it doesn't bear revisiting; however, we need to do so, as the monetary principle has important implications for financial reporting. Recall that only economic events that can be quantified in dollar terms are recorded in the financial reports. This means that some information that may in fact be helpful to a variety of users in making decisions will not be found in the financial reports (e.g. land — size, location and zoning). It is easy to identify transactions that can be quantified in monetary terms. Just look at the items that are listed in the main financial reports, including sales, cost of sales, administrative expenses, interest expenses, cash, accounts receivable and payable, bank loans and issued share capital just to name a few.

We also need to consider *how* we measure these items. Measurement is discussed in various accounting standards and in the *Conceptual Framework*. This will be explored with examples in a later part of this chapter.

Accounting entity concept

The **accounting entity concept** states that every entity can be separately identified and accounted for. This is particularly important for sole proprietorships and partnerships as they are not separate legal entities. It is important that the owners do not confuse the entity's transactions with their personal transactions, or the transactions of any other entity. For example, if a sole trader purchased a car for personal use, obtaining the funds from their personal bank account, when applying the accounting entity concept, it would not be recorded in the accounts of the entity. However, if the owner purchased a car from their personal bank account for use within the business, then, based on the accounting entity concept, this transaction would be a capital contribution and would be recorded as a debit to an asset (motor vehicles), and a credit to equity (capital).

A related concept is the *reporting entity concept*. While the accounting entity concept applies to all accounting entities, not all entities are reporting entities. Currently the *Conceptual Framework* does not deal with this important concept. An exposure draft (ED/2010/2 *Conceptual Framework for Financial Reporting: The Reporting Entity*) which sets out the proposed views on the *reporting entity concept* has been released. The reporting entity is discussed in a later section.

Helpful hint: The reporting entity concept is discussed in the statement of accounting concepts 1. Australian business entities and standard setters will use this concept until the new concept is added to the Conceptual Framework.

Accounting period concept

The **accounting period concept** states that the life of a business entity can be divided into artificial periods and that useful reports covering those periods can be prepared for the entity. Most, if not all, entities report on cash flows and performance for periods of 1 year and on the financial position at the end of each period. However, listed companies (reporting entities) report at least every 6 months to shareholders, and many prepare monthly reports for internal purposes. Throughout the text we have provided financial reports for numerous fictitious companies. For example, in chapter 1 we provided the financial reports for Giorgina's Pizza Limited, and in chapter 12 we provided the financial reports for Harrison Limited and Williams Limited. These companies report their performance and cash flows for one financial period and prepare a statement of their financial position at the end of the period. It is important to note that this concept has implications for the recording of transactions that affect more than one period.

Recall that in chapter 3 we discussed that for revenues, expenses, assets and liabilities to be recorded in the correct accounting period we need to record adjusting entries for prepayments and accruals. In short, adjusting entries are needed to ensure that the recognition criteria are followed for assets, liabilities, revenues and expenses. For example, an insurance premium may cover more than one accounting period. It is important to recognise as an expense the portion of the insurance payment that relates to the current period, while the portion that relates to the next accounting period is recognised as an asset (prepaid insurance). Numerous examples of adjusting entries are provided in chapter 3. We suggest you review this chapter if you cannot recall all of the types of adjusting entries or how to prepare them.

Helpful hint: Recall that entities provide comparative figures for one or more previous years in addition to the current period figures in the financial statements.

At this point it is helpful to reflect on how accounting concepts and principles and recognition criteria are interrelated. In the insurance example provided above we can see that the accounting period concept and the expense recognition criteria are interrelated.

Going concern principle

The going concern principle is that the business will remain in operation for the foreseeable future. The **going concern principle** states that financial statements are prepared on a going concern basis unless management either intends to or must liquidate the business or cease trading (IAS 1/AASB 101, paragraph 25). Of course, many businesses do fail but, in general, it is reasonable to assume that the business will continue operating. Management must make an assessment of the validity of the going concern principle when preparing financial reports in accordance with accounting standards. The going concern principle underlies much of what we do in accounting. To give you just one example: if the going concern principle is not assumed, then plant and equipment should be stated at their liquidation value (selling price less cost of disposal), not at their cost. Liquidation values are the most indicative of an entity's current financial position if it will not be operating in the future, as it is likely that the assets will be sold, the creditors paid and any remaining funds distributed to owners. The going concern principle is inappropriate only when liquidation of the business appears likely.

Cost principle

The **cost principle** states that all assets are initially recorded in the accounts at their purchase price or cost. This is applied not only at the time the asset is purchased, but also over the time the asset is held. For example, if Woolworths Limited was to purchase land for $500 000, it would initially be recorded at $500 000. But what would the company do if, by the end of the next year, the land had increased in value to $600 000? The answer is that under the cost principle the land would continue to be reported at $500 000. However, we also know that the purpose of general purpose financial reports is to provide useful information for decision makers. Are outdated land values useful? Perhaps not; therefore, to provide useful information, sometimes entities need to deviate from the cost principle.

Helpful hint: Critics of the cost principle contend that fair value would be more useful to decision makers. Proponents of cost measurement say that cost is the best measure because it can be verified easily from transactions between two parties, whereas fair value is often subjective.

In chapter 8 we discussed the recording and reporting of non-current assets. In that chapter, examples of asset revaluations were provided. Recall that after the initial recognition of an asset at cost (which is its fair value at the time of acquisition), an entity may choose to revalue its non-current assets to fair value. A revaluation is a reassessment of the fair value of a non-current asset at a particular date. After the initial recognition of a property, plant and equipment (PPE) asset at cost, IAS 16/AASB 116 requires each class of PPE to be measured on either the cost basis or the revalued basis. Assets can be revalued upwards or downwards as relevant. When the PPE asset is measured using the revaluation basis, any impairment loss is treated as a revaluation decrease. As you can see, the principles and the standards need to be applied together when preparing financial statements. Please review chapter 8 if you cannot recall how to record non-current assets.

Helpful hint: General purpose financial reports are reports intended to meet the information needs of existing and potential investors, lenders and other creditors who cannot require reporting entities to provide information directly to them.

Full disclosure principle

The **full disclosure principle** requires that all circumstances and events that could make a difference to the decisions that users of general purpose financial reports might make should be disclosed in the financial reports. Some important financial information is not easily reported in the financial reports due to its uncertainty or difficulty in terms of its measurement. Recall that in chapter 9 we discussed the recording and reporting of liabilities. In that chapter we introduced contingent liabilities. Liabilities are classified as contingent when the amount of the future sacrifice is so uncertain that it cannot be measured reliably, or when they do not satisfy the probability criterion, or when they are dependent upon the occurrence of an uncertain future event outside the control of the entity. Examples include an unresolved lawsuit brought against the entity and the potential liability resulting from a tax audit in progress. Contingent liabilities are not recognised in the financial reports as they are either not probable or they are not able to be measured reliably, or both. This means they do not satisfy the probability criterion and the measurement criterion for the recognition of liabilities. So, once again we see how the principles must be applied in conjunction with accounting standards. Despite the entity not being able to measure contingent liabilities with accuracy, under the full disclosure principle, information about contingent liabilities must be disclosed in the notes to the financial reports if this information can have a material impact on the decisions made by users of financial reports.

To summarise, the accounting concepts and principles are shown graphically in figure 13.1.

FIGURE 13.1 Accounting concepts and principles

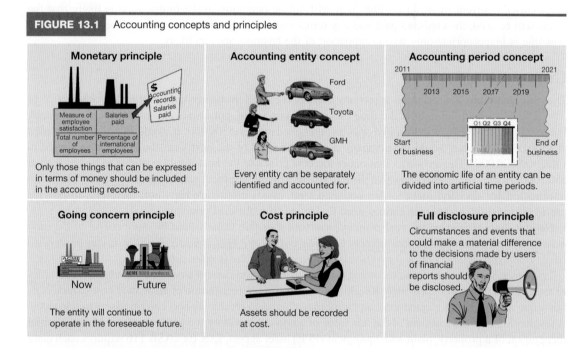

LEARNING REFLECTION AND CONSOLIDATION

Review it

1. Explain the two concepts and four principles underlying the recording of accounting information.
2. Describe any interrelationships between the concepts, principles, accounting standards and the *Conceptual Framework*.
3. Explain how both the cost principle and asset revaluations can coexist.

Do it

Peter Liu has recently begun his accounting studies and is very confused about the concepts and principles underlying the recording of accounting information. He has been asked prepare a class presentation on one of the homework questions on this topic. His tutorial is only 1 day away; he is very nervous

---

and needs help. Given you have nearly finished your introductory accounting unit he has asked you for assistance. The question Peter needs to present is: For each of the following transactions, explain the *main* concept or principle that underlies its recording:

1	Buildings	3 000 000	
	Mortgage liability		3 000 000
	(Purchased buildings using a mortgage loan for funding)		
2	Insurance expense	20 000	
	Prepaid insurance	20 000	
	Cash		40 000
	(Paid 2 years' insurance in cash)		

Include in your discussion any other relevant guidance that should be considered when recording these transactions.

Reasoning

To answer this question, you explain to Peter that he first needs to review each of the concepts and principles underlying the recording of accounting information. These include the monetary principle, accounting entity concept, accounting period concept, going concern principle, cost principle and full disclosure principle. Then, once he has a good understanding of the concepts and principles, he will be able see which of these apply to the cases in the homework problem. It is important to notice that the question asks for the *main* concept or principle. Sometimes more than one can apply, so the main one must be chosen. For example, the monetary principle may apply in both cases as the transactions are recorded in dollars; however, the monetary principle may not be the main one, as explained below. Finally, while the focus of the question is on concepts and principles, as requested, it is important to explain to Peter that in practice the principles and concepts aren't considered in isolation but work together with accounting standards and the *Conceptual Framework* which provide guidance for recording transactions, for example, the recognition criteria for assets, liabilities, revenues and expenses.

Solution

After some discussion with you, Peter was able to come up with the following solution for his class presentation.

The first transaction involved the purchase of buildings using a mortgage loan for funding. The main underlying principle is the *cost principle,* which states that all assets are initially recorded in the accounts at their purchase price or cost. After initial recognition of a non-current asset at cost, it is important to consider the standard on non-current assets, IAS 16/AASB 116, which requires each class of property, plant and equipment to be measured on either the cost basis or the revalued basis.

Helpful hint: Recall from chapter 8 that if an item of PPE is revalued, the entire class of PPE to which that asset belongs shall be revalued (IAS 16/AASB 116, paragraph 36).

The second transaction involved the payment of 2 years' insurance in cash. Half the payment was recorded as an expense and half as an asset. The main underlying concept is the *accounting period concept,* which states that the life of a business can be divided into artificial periods and that useful reports covering those periods can be prepared for the business. In this case, only half of the insurance payment belonged as an expense in the first reporting period. The other half would be an expense in the next reporting period, and so it was recorded as a prepayment (an asset) in the current period.

As noted in the reasoning section above, concepts and principles are not applied in isolation, and in this case expense and asset recognition criteria as outlined in the *Conceptual Framework* are also relevant. Recognition criteria are discussed in a later section.

13.2 Conceptual frameworks

LEARNING OBJECTIVE 13.2 Describe the *Conceptual Framework for Financial Reporting* (the *Conceptual Framework*).

In this section we explore some of the historical, recent and future developments in conceptual frameworks. We also overview the current version of the *Conceptual Framework for Financial Reporting* (the *Conceptual Framework* (2010)) issued by the International Accounting Standards Board (IASB) as well as various ongoing developments. The *Conceptual Framework* applies in Australia and New Zealand although they have a different standard-setting process (refer to chapter 1 for the differences). A **conceptual framework** consists of a set of concepts defining the nature, purpose and content of general purpose financial reporting to be followed by preparers of general purpose financial reports and standard setters. At the time of writing, the IASB was in the process of revising the *Conceptual Framework* (2010), with a new version expected to be released in mid-2018. Given the revised *Conceptual Framework* was not available at the time of writing this chapter, the *Conceptual Framework* content in this chapter is based on the 2010 version with insights into potential changes where relevant. For example, in 2015, the IASB issued the *Conceptual Framework for Financial Reporting Exposure Draft* (ED 2015/3). A summary of the 2015 ED and its potential effects on the financial statements of reporting entities is explored in the following section.

As will be abundantly evident, the development of the *Conceptual Framework* is a long-term project that has taken many, many years. Historians would argue that to understand where we are now and where we are headed in the future, we need to know where we've come from. So, let's begin with a brief history of the development of conceptual frameworks.

Historical developments

While many theories of accounting have developed over time, prior to the late 1970s there was no generally accepted theory of financial accounting. This meant that the development of accounting standards for financial accounting practice was piecemeal as the standards were not based on any particular theory. This resulted in some inconsistencies between standards and therefore inconsistencies in accounting practice. To improve the standard-setting process and consistency in accounting practice, the development of a generally accepted theory of financial reporting was necessary. The theory was needed to outline the objectives of financial reporting and the required qualitative characteristics for financial information, and to provide clear guidance on how to measure and account for economic events when recording transactions and preparing financial reports. The theory could be used to guide the standard-setting process and accounting practice.

Developing a generally accepted, normative theory of financial accounting and reporting has been attempted by several countries including the United States and the United Kingdom, as well as New Zealand and Australia. Historically, these countries have drawn upon one another's frameworks and exposure drafts in developing a conceptual framework that suited the particular country's economic and financial reporting environments. For example, in Australia, unlike the United States, the *Conceptual Framework* applies to both the private and public sectors. There are many similarities between conceptual frameworks from around the world; however, most conceptual frameworks are only partially complete and there has never been a conceptual framework completed in any country which is broadly applicable across countries.

The United States has been particularly active in developing a conceptual framework and its Financial Accounting Standards Board (FASB) was actually among the first to develop a framework. The FASB defined their conceptual framework as a 'coherent system of interrelated objectives and fundamentals that is expected to lead to consistent standards ... [prescribing] ... the nature, function and limits of financial accounting and reporting' (Statement of Accounting Concepts 1: 'Objectives of financial reporting by business enterprises', 1978). This was way back in 1978. In 1989, the International Accounting Standards Board (IASB) issued the *Framework for the Preparation and Presentation of Financial Statements* — referred to as the *Framework* (1989). Historically, Australia was also quite active in developing a conceptual framework.

Prior to 2005, a conceptual framework was jointly under development in Australia by the Australian Accounting Standards Board (AASB) and the Australian Accounting Research Foundation (AARF). Like the US *Framework*, the Australian conceptual framework consisted of a series of Statements of Accounting Concepts (SACs). These statements outlined the nature, purpose and content of general purpose financial reporting for both the private and the public sectors. SAC 1 was concerned with the reporting entity, SAC 2 with the objective of general purpose financial reporting, SAC 3 with the qualitative characteristics of financial information and SAC 4 with the elements of financial statements.

Helpful hint: These organisations are discussed in chapter 1. Please refer to chapter 1 if you would like further detail.

In 2002, it was decided that Australian standards would converge with international accounting standards from 1 January 2005. However, some of the content in the Australian conceptual framework differed from that in the International Accounting Standards Board's *Framework* (1989). As part of the international convergence program, the AASB issued a conceptual framework (the *Framework*) which was equivalent to the *Framework* (1989) issued by the IASB. This resulted in the four SACs issued by the AASB prior to the decision to converge either being subsumed or retained alongside the *Framework*.

The statements concerned with qualitative characteristics (SAC 3) and the elements of financial statements (SAC 4) were subsumed in the *Framework*. The statements that covered the scope (SAC 1) and the objectives (SAC 2) of general purpose financial reports were temporarily retained as they were not already encompassed in the *Framework* like SAC 3 and SAC 4 were.

Helpful hint: Note that the conceptual framework issued by the AASB was called the Framework; *the conceptual framework issued by the IASB in 1989 is referred to as the* Framework *(1989); and the conceptual framework released in 2010 is called the* Conceptual Framework.

In 2006, the International Accounting Standards Board (IASB) and the Financial Accounting Standards Board (FASB) issued the first of a series of publications arising from a joint project to develop an improved conceptual framework (the *Conceptual Framework*). The comprehensive project was initially divided into eight phases.

Phase A	Objectives and qualitative characteristics
Phase B	Definitions of elements, recognition and derecognition
Phase C	Measurement
Phase D	Reporting entity concept
Phase E	Boundaries of financial reporting, and presentation and disclosure
Phase F	Purpose and status of the framework
Phase G	Application for the framework to not-for-profit entities
Phase H	Remaining issues, if any

The project was designed to span a number of years and it is currently ongoing. The extended time period was considered necessary to enable extensive consultation with the many and varied stakeholders at all stages of the project.

The consultation process involves the boards inviting interested parties to comment on the various phases of the proposed improved framework (the *Conceptual Framework*) by providing publicly available exposure drafts, discussion papers and holding roundtable discussions.

The aim of the joint project was to develop an improved common conceptual framework which could provide a sound foundation for the development of future accounting standards. This, in turn would support the development of internally consistent, principle-based standards that result in financial reporting practices that provide users with the information they need to make decisions.

When complete, the *Conceptual Framework* will be one document with several chapters rather than a series of concept statements as was the case with the FASB conceptual framework and the former Australian conceptual framework. The proposed improved *Conceptual Framework* will be focused on the private sector. However, once the project is complete, the boards will consider the applicability of the concepts for the not-for-profit and government sectors.

The *Conceptual Framework* project progressed in 2008, when the IASB and FASB issued a number of consultative documents for public comment. The first document, issued May 2008, was an exposure draft (ED) of the first two chapters of the *Conceptual Framework*. Chapter 1 of the ED discussed the proposed changes surrounding the objective of financial reporting and chapter 2 of the ED re-examined the qualitative characteristics and constraints of decision-useful financial reporting information. Comments on these chapters were accepted until the closing date of 29 September 2008.

Helpful hint: The consultation process is part of the **due process***, where standard setters invite interested parties to contribute to the development of accounting standards.*

In 2010, an exposure draft was released exploring the changes to the definition of the reporting entity. The closing date for feedback on that exposure draft was 16 July 2010. Soon after, in September 2010, the IASB finally issued the *Conceptual Framework for Financial Reporting* (*Conceptual Framework*). It consists of an introduction, purpose and status, scope, three chapters (Chapter 2 'The reporting entity' is to be added when complete), as well as the board approval of the *Conceptual Framework*, the basis for conclusions and a table of concordance.

Given that Chapter 2 'The reporting entity' has yet to be added to the *Conceptual Framework*, Australia has retained SAC 1 on the reporting entity from the Australian conceptual framework developed many years ago.

Helpful hint: Recall that the current Conceptual Framework *for Australia and New Zealand is based on the IASB's 2010 version.*

In July 2013, a discussion paper entitled *A Review of the Conceptual Framework for Financial Reporting* (DP/2013/1) was released because the IASB identified a number of issues with the existing *Conceptual Framework*. Problems included little guidance on how to identify a reporting entity and little guidance on measurement, presentation and disclosure in financial reports. Furthermore, the current definitions of liabilities and assets required improvement and some aspects of the *Conceptual Framework* did not reflect the current views of the IASB and so were out of date. The discussion paper was the IASB's first step towards developing a revised *Conceptual Framework*. Responses to the discussion paper were received at the beginning of 2014.

In July 2014, the IASB issued a paper entitled *Effect of Board Redeliberations on DP: A Review of the Conceptual Framework for Financial Reporting*. This paper reflected the tentative decisions made by the IASB that were to be made available for public comment in an exposure draft of the revised *Conceptual Framework*.

At that time the *Conceptual Framework* was still incomplete and there were a number of future developments to come. DP/2013/1 (p. 15) outlined the key areas the IASB intended to focus on when developing the revised *Conceptual Framework*:

(a) elements of the financial statements (including the boundary between liabilities and equity)
(b) recognition and derecognition
(c) measurement
(d) presentation and disclosure (including the question of what should be presented in other comprehensive income (OCI))
(e) the reporting entity.

The IASB (www.ifrs.org) and FASB (www.fasb.org) web sites provide information on the progress of the project.

In May 2015, the IASB issued an Exposure Draft (ED 2015/3) *Conceptual Framework for Financial Reporting* for public comment to be received by October 2015. The ED was developed to overcome the limitations of the existing *Conceptual Framework*. The revised *Conceptual Framework* was more complete than the existing *Conceptual Framework* because it addressed the areas that were either not covered, or not covered in enough detail, in the existing *Conceptual Framework*.

Given we now have a number of documents on the *Conceptual Framework* including the *Conceptual Framework for Financial Reporting* (*Conceptual Framework*) issued in September 2010; the discussion paper entitled *A Review of the Conceptual Framework for Financial Reporting* (DP/2013/1), the paper entitled *Effect of Board Redeliberations on DP: A Review of the Conceptual Framework for Financial Reporting* issued in July 2014, and ED 2015/3 *Conceptual Framework for Financial Reporting*, it is challenging to write up the current status of the *Conceptual Framework*.

The current 2010 version of the *Conceptual Framework* is based on these three key documents and is discussed in some detail in the sections that follow. But, before we go into the detail, let's briefly recap where we are now and provide an overview of the *Conceptual Framework*.

Future developments

At the time of writing this chapter, the IASB was in the process of revising the 2010 version of the *Conceptual Framework*, with a new version expected to be released in mid-2018. Given the *Conceptual Framework* applies in both Australia and New Zealand, the amendments made to the *current Conceptual Framework* will eventually have a flow-on effect in Australia and New Zealand. However, Exposure Draft (ED 2015/3) *Conceptual Framework for Financial Reporting* explains that the proposed changes to the *Conceptual Framework* will not have an immediate impact on financial reporting as the changes will still need to be incorporated into the relevant accounting standards through the normal standard-setting processes in each country. To the extent that the existing accounting standards operate effectively in current practice, the IASB will not require an amendment to the standard if the revised *Conceptual Framework* results in an inconsistency with the existing accounting standard.

Given that this project is still unfinished and still evolving and the new version of the *Conceptual Framework* had not been released at the time of writing, up-to-date information and the latest version of the *Conceptual Framework* should be obtained from the IASB website www.ifrs.org.

Overview of the *Conceptual Framework*

We first introduced the *Conceptual Framework* in chapter 1. We used the image of a window to present the *Conceptual Framework*, because a window is a lens through which we can view the world, in the same way as preparing external financial statements using a conceptual framework allows users to view the economic world in a particular way. Put simplistically, the *Conceptual Framework* consists of a set of concepts defining the nature, purpose and content of general purpose financial reporting to be followed by preparers of general purpose financial reports and standard setters.

In this section we revisit the *Conceptual Framework* and discuss its content at the time of writing this chapter. We begin with a brief overview of the *Conceptual Framework* as set out in chapter 1; however, we have changed the order of quadrants 3 and 4 of the illustrative window to facilitate the flow of the discussion in this chapter. In the sections that follow we explore in more depth some of the aspects of the *Conceptual Framework*. Given the *Conceptual Framework* is currently under development, where available the proposed changes are also explained. For example, it is important to note that in ED 2015/3, issued by the IASB, the *Conceptual Framework* has a different structure to the four quadrants based on the 2010 version of the *Conceptual Framework* discussed in this chapter. The 2015 version is as follows:

- Chapter 1 — The objective of general purpose financial reporting
- Chapter 2 — Qualitative characteristics of useful financial information
- Chapter 3 — Financial statements and the reporting entity
- Chapter 4 — The elements of financial statements.

In chapter 1 it was explained that the *Conceptual Framework* consists of four sections: the objective of general purpose financial reports, the reporting entity (SAC 1), the qualitative characteristics, and the definition of elements in financial statements which contains the remaining text from the *Framework* (1989) issued by the IASB. The main components from the 2010 *Conceptual Framework* plus SAC 1 are depicted in figure 13.2.

FIGURE 13.2 The current *Conceptual Framework*

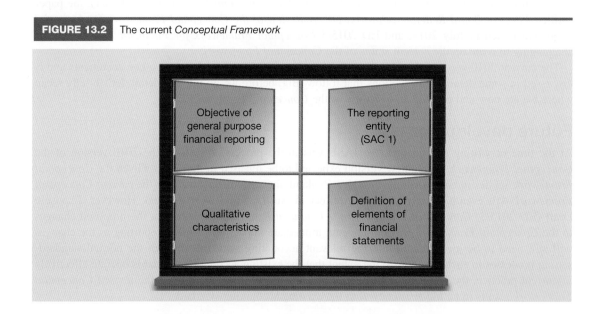

Review it

1. Many countries throughout the world have at various times worked on the development of a conceptual framework. Discuss the advantages of developing a generally accepted normative theory of financial accounting and reporting.
2. The AASB had issued four SACs prior to the decision to converge with international accounting standards. What were they?
3. Briefly describe the *Conceptual Framework*. (*Hint:* See figure 13.2 for an overview and refer back to chapter 1 for more detail.)

The *Conceptual Framework* provides guidance to preparers of financial information by defining the objective of general purpose financial reporting. Now let's look at this in greater detail.

13.3 The objective of general purpose financial reporting

LEARNING OBJECTIVE 13.3 Explain the objective of general purpose financial reporting.

Do you think it is important to have a clear common objective for financial reporting? Perhaps we can think about this question by using a simple analogy. If you were going to construct a building, how would you know what type of building to build unless you knew the purpose the building was intended to serve and who would be using the building? If you were told the building was to house people, it would be helpful to know more details such as whether those people would require single or family accommodation and whether they had a low or high income to cover the rent payments. A building constructed to house people would be quite different in structure to a building constructed to serve as a shopping centre. So, as you can see, if you know the intended purpose for the building and who will use the building, you have a clearer idea of what kind of building is required and you are more likely to satisfy the needs of the inhabitants of the building. The same goes for financial reporting.

Stewardship and accountability objectives

If we understand the objective of financial reporting, the users of the information and the decisions these users make, we are more likely to prepare financial reports that serve those users' needs. A number of different objectives or purposes of financial reporting have been suggested, for example the *stewardship* or *accountability* objectives (or perspectives) of financial reporting. These perspectives suggest that for entities where there is a separation of ownership from control (e.g. in a company where the shareholders do not manage the business), general purpose financial reports can support the stewardship or accountability function. Managers can use general purpose financial reports to show the owners they are fulfilling their stewardship function effectively and that the resources are being managed effectively and appropriately, and shareholders can use the reports to *check* on managers to make them accountable and make decisions about whether they are carrying out their stewardship duties effectively and efficiently to maximise shareholder value. In fact, in the July 2014 Board's redeliberations paper (p. 16), the IASB explained that it had decided tentatively to amend Chapter 1 of the *Conceptual Framework* to increase the prominence of stewardship as part of the objective of financial reporting by recognising that the information required to assess management's effectiveness as stewards does not fully overlap with the information required when users are assessing the future cash flows of the entity. The importance of providing information that can be used to help assess management's stewardship of the entity's resources to meet the objective of financial reporting is clarified in ED 2015/3.

Decision-usefulness objective

An alternative purpose or objective of financial reporting is the decision-usefulness perspective. This was the perspective adopted in the Australian conceptual framework Statement of Accounting Concepts 2 (SAC 2), which stated the objective of general purpose financial reports was to 'provide information to users that is useful for making and evaluating decisions about the allocation of scarce resources'. This is similar to the objective in the FASB's Concept Statement 1. However, Concept Statement 1 provides more specificity in that some of the users and some of their decisions are specifically mentioned. In particular, the statement specifies that a major objective of financial reporting is that it should provide information 'that is useful to present and potential investors and creditors and other users in making rational investment, credit and similar decisions'. In 2013, SAC 2 was withdrawn from the AASB CF 2013-1 *Amendments to the Australian conceptual framework* pronouncement. The objectives of general purpose financial reports in the *Conceptual Framework* now apply as outlined in the next section.

The dual purposes of decision making and stewardship are highlighted in the following section on how measurement contributes to the objective of general purpose financial reports. The board's redeliberations paper (2014) explains that measurement contributes to the overall objective of financial reporting in that 'measurement is the process of quantifying in monetary terms information about the resources of an entity, claims against the entity and changes in those resources and claims. Such information helps users to assess the entity's *prospects for future cash flows* and assess *management's stewardship* of the entity's resources' (p. 10, *emphasis added*).

The *Conceptual Framework* is also based on the decision-usefulness perspective.

The *Conceptual Framework*

Chapter 1, 'The objective of general purpose financial reporting', forms the foundation of the *Conceptual Framework*. All the other elements flow from the objective. If we know why we need to report, then it follows we can determine who needs to report, what information should be provided and how the information is to be reported. This section is primarily based on the *Conceptual Framework* published in 2010.

In the *Conceptual Framework* published in 2010, the **objective of general purpose financial reporting** is to provide information that will be useful for existing and potential users (investors, lenders and other creditors) to make decisions about the reporting entity. The types of decisions to be made by the users of the information will include buying, selling or holding their investments, and providing loans or other forms of credit to the reporting entity. Decisions include: buying, selling or retaining shares, and providing loans, goods or services on credit or settling amounts owed to the entity. To make those decisions, users need information to help them assess the prospects for future net cash inflows to an entity. This will allow them to estimate the return they can expect from the resources they provide to the entity.

This definition highlights that the primary users of general purpose financial reports are existing and potential investors, lenders and other creditors; however, these users cannot generally require a reporting entity to provide information directly to them so they rely on **general purpose financial reports**.

It is acknowledged that general purpose financial reports cannot provide all of the information that each of the primary users may need, neither do they provide a valuation of an entity. However, they seek to provide information that will meet the needs of the maximum number of primary users. Hence, financial reports, together with other sources of information such as general economic conditions, political climate and industry conditions, allow primary users to estimate the value of the reporting entity and assess the prospects for future net cash inflows to an entity when making resource allocation decisions like investing and lending.

It is, however, acknowledged that other groups may also be interested in the financial reports. For example, the management of the reporting entity is one such group, but it was decided that management does not need to rely on general purpose financial reports because managers can obtain the financial information they need internally. Other parties such as regulators and members of the public may also find general purpose financial reports useful.

In the building analogy introduced at the beginning of this section, we saw that understanding who the primary users of the building were to be, as well as details of their needs, would more likely result in a building that would satisfy their needs and achieve the purpose the building was to be constructed to fulfil. The same is true for financial reporting.

13.4 Users and uses of financial reports

LEARNING OBJECTIVE 13.4 Identify the primary and other users, and their uses of financial reports.

Now that we know the objective for financial reporting, let's take a closer look at the users of financial reports and their information needs. We begin with an exploration of the primary users and their information needs as outlined in the *Conceptual Framework* and then discuss other users of financial reporting.

The *Conceptual Framework* — primary users

Figure 13.3 sets out the primary users of general purpose financial reports as **resource providers**, i.e. those users who provide resources to the entity and therefore require information to make decisions concerning the provision of those resources. Equity investors provide resources to an entity usually by investing cash for the purpose of receiving a return, and include shareholders, holders of partnership interests and other equity owners. Lenders provide resources to an entity by lending cash for the purpose of receiving a return in the form of interest.

FIGURE 13.3 Categories of resource providers — *Conceptual Framework*

*Only in their capacity as resource providers, otherwise they are not considered primary users.

Some questions that may be asked by investors and lenders about a company include the following.
- Is the company earning satisfactory profit?
- How does the company compare in size and profitability to its competitors?
- Will the company be able to pay its debts as they fall due?
- Is the company paying regular dividends to its shareholders?
- What is the company's potential for generating future cash flows?

To assess future net cash inflows, users require information about the entity's resources, the claims against the entity and how efficiently the entity's management and governing board have discharged their responsibilities in relation to the use of the entity's resources. So it appears that while the objective of general purpose financial reporting is founded on a decision-usefulness perspective, it is acknowledged that a stewardship perspective is also relevant.

Has management put in place systems to protect the entity's resources against the unfavourable effects of economic factors such as price and technology change? Has management complied with applicable laws, regulations and contractual commitments? This information concerning management's responsibilities is partly provided in the corporate governance statement in an entity's financial report.

Helpful hint: Shareholders, who can vote on retaining or replacing directors and determining management's remuneration, need information on which to base their decisions. Hence, information about stewardship is also important to these resource providers.

Other creditors may also provide resources to an entity as a result of their relationship with the entity, even though they are not primarily resource providers. The exposure draft on the objectives of general purpose financial reporting provided more explanation on the other creditors category of primary users of financial reports when compared with Chapter 1 of the *Conceptual Framework*.

Suppliers are considered to be other creditors when they extend credit to facilitate a sale, employees are considered to be other creditors when they provide their services (human resources) in exchange for remuneration, and customers are considered to be other creditors when they prepay for goods or services which are to be provided in the future. These parties are only considered resource providers to the extent that they provide the entity with resources in the form of credit or services, and they make decisions based on providing such resources. When they are not in this capacity they are referred to as other users.

ED 2015/3 refers to the primary user categories as: existing and potential investors, lenders and other creditors.

The *Conceptual Framework* — other users

Other users include government agencies, members of the public as well as suppliers, customers and employees (when not resource providers, as explained above). The information needs and questions of other users vary considerably. For example, taxation authorities, such as the Australian Taxation Office (ATO), want to know whether the entity complies with taxation laws. Regulatory agencies, such as the Australian Securities and Investments Commission (ASIC) or the Australian Competition and Consumer Commission (ACCC), want to know whether the entity is operating within prescribed rules.

While these other users have specialised information needs, they may find the financial reporting that meets the needs of resource providers useful. As with the primary users, the common information needs of other users include an assessment of the entity's future cash flows (amount, timing and uncertainty) and evidence that management has discharged its responsibilities to use the entity's resources efficiently and effectively. However, it is made clear in the *Conceptual Framework* that financial reporting is not primarily directed to other users but rather to equity investors, lenders and other creditors. Figure 13.3 summarises the three main categories of users.

LEARNING REFLECTION AND CONSOLIDATION

Review it
1. Explain the objective of general purpose financial reporting as outlined in the *Conceptual Framework*.
2. Identify the primary users of financial reporting as outlined in the *Conceptual Framework*.
3. Under what circumstances are employees, suppliers and customers considered as primary users?
4. Identify the other users of financial reporting as outlined in the *Conceptual Framework*.

Now that the objective of general purpose financial reporting and the primary users of that information have been discussed, the next step is to decide who needs to prepare general purpose financial reports.

13.5 The reporting entity

LEARNING OBJECTIVE 13.5 Explain the nature of a reporting entity.

At the time of writing this chapter, the section on the reporting entity was not available in the *Conceptual Framework* (2010). In ED 2015/3, a reporting entity is described as: 'an entity that chooses, or is required, to prepare general purpose financial statements' (ED 2015/3, p. 10). Given the revised conceptual framework was not available at the time of writing, currently in Australia SAC 1 provides a definition of the reporting entity, as explained below.

The reporting entity — defined

In chapter 1 of this text we described a number of different forms of business organisation including sole trader, partnership and company. While each of these forms of business prepares some kind of information for a variety of users, not all businesses are classified as reporting entities. The Australian conceptual framework defines the **reporting entity** in Statement of Accounting Concepts 1 (SAC 1) as an entity in which it is reasonable to expect the existence of users who depend on general purpose financial reports for information to enable them to make economic decisions.

Recall that, based on the entity perspective, the reporting entity is viewed as separate from its owners, having substance of its own. The resources provided to the entity by the owners, creditors and other capital providers become the resources of the entity, and resource providers receive, in exchange, a claim on the resources of the entity. Hence, general purpose financial reports present the economic resources of the entity and the claims on those resources held by the resource providers.

Entity theory can be contrasted with proprietary theory, where the reporting entity doesn't have a substance of its own. Within this perspective, general purpose financial reports present the economic resources of the owners, the liabilities of the owners to various lenders and creditors, and the owners' residual equity in the reporting entity (i.e. assets minus liabilities).

The reporting entity — indicators

When deciding whether an entity is required to provide general purpose financial reports, we can use the decision-making toolkit provided below to guide the analysis. We need to begin by consulting SAC 1 to access the information needed for the decision. SAC 1 *Definition of the Reporting Entity* identifies three main indicators (decision-making tools) to determine which of the forms of business organisation discussed so far in this chapter fall into the category of a reporting entity. That is, an entity is more likely to be classified as a reporting entity if it is (1) managed by individuals who are not owners of the entity, (2) politically or economically important, and (3) sizable in any of the following ways — sales, assets, borrowings, customers or employees. It appears then, in applying the indicators, subjective judgements must be made. For example, what value of sales or how many employees are considered sizeable enough for the business to be a reporting entity? In the main, reporting entities include public companies, some large private companies and government authorities.

It is important to determine whether an organisation is a reporting entity as reporting entities must prepare *external* general purpose financial reports that comply with accounting standards. All other entities will prepare information for internal use.

Reporting entities tend to be larger organisations and the financial information provided in external general purpose financial reports tends to be quite condensed. Both reporting and non-reporting entities also prepare internal reports that contain more detailed information. Examples of both internal and external reports were provided in chapter 1.

Let's see how the definition and indicators of a reporting entity as described in the Australian conceptual framework compare with the definition and features of a reporting entity as outlined in the exposure draft issued by the IASB on the reporting entity.

DECISION-MAKING TOOLKIT

Decision/issue	Info needed for analysis	Tool or technique to use for decision	How to evaluate results to make decision
Is the entity required to provide general purpose financial reports?	Characteristics of the entity as outlined in SAC 1	Make a judgement about whether the entity is a reporting entity based on SAC 1 indicators. An organisation is more likely to be classified as a reporting entity if it has separation of ownership and management; is politically or economically important; and is sizeable in relation to sales, assets, borrowings, customers and employees.	If the entity is classified as a reporting entity, the entity is required to provide general purpose financial reports in accordance with GAAP.

ED/2010/2 *Conceptual Framework for Financial Reporting: The Reporting Entity*

As defined in paragraph 2 of ED/2010/2, 'a reporting entity is a circumscribed area of economic activities whose financial information has the potential to be useful to existing and potential equity investors, lenders and other creditors who cannot directly obtain the information they need in making decisions about providing resources to the entity in assessing whether management and the governing board of that entity have made efficient and effective use of the resources provided'. This definition is consistent with the definition in the Australian conceptual framework and is linked to the objective of general purpose financial reporting in the *Conceptual Framework*.

Rather than referring to indicators as in the Australian conceptual framework, the exposure draft identifies three features as necessary — but not always sufficient conditions — to identify a reporting entity. First, a reporting entity conducts, has conducted or will conduct economic activities. Second, the economic activities can be distinguished from those of other entities and the economic environment. Third, linking back to the objective of financial reporting, financial information about the economic entity will be useful in making decisions on providing resources to the entity and in assessing the efficiency and effectiveness of management and the governing board.

Helpful hint: In DP/2013/1 the IASB noted that important areas were not covered in the Conceptual Framework. *For example, the existing* Conceptual Framework *provides very little guidance on how to identify a reporting entity. SAC 1 offers guidance as provided in the decision-making toolkit. ED 2015/3 and the revised* Conceptual Framework *seek to remedy this gap in the 2010* Conceptual Framework.

Differential financial reporting

In chapter 1, we outlined the financial reporting requirements where reporting entities are required to prepare general purpose financial reports (GPFRs) in accordance with the accounting standards. **Differential reporting** means applying different sets of rules for different categories of entities preparing general purpose financial reports.

The standards issued by the IASB are intended for the preparation of general purpose financial reports of profit-seeking entities that meet the definition of a reporting entity as discussed above. The issue is: what GAAP rules to apply to *for-profit* entities that do not meet the reporting entity criteria? The IASB has developed an *International Financial Reporting Standard for Small and Medium-sized Entities* (IFRS for SMEs), a self-contained standard of 230 pages, designed to meet the needs and capabilities of small- and medium-sized entities (SMEs). The IASB estimated over 95% of all companies around the world are SMEs.

There is another set of accounting standards, International Public Sector Accounting Standards (IPSAS) issued by the International Public Sector Accounting Standards Board (IPSASB) for use by public sector entities around the world in the preparation of GPFRs. These standards are based on IFRSs issued by the IASB but are tailored to meet the needs of public sector bodies. Thus, there are three sets of rules for the preparation of GPFRs.

Until recently, Australia and New Zealand used *sector neutral* accounting standards; that is, the same standards were applied to for-profit companies and entities, public sector entities and not-for-profit entities that prepared external general purpose financial reports (GPFRs). Thus, a one-size-fits-all approach was in place. The reporting entity concept as discussed above is used to determine if an entity needs to prepare GPFRs. Non-reporting entities prepare special purpose financial reports (SPFRs).

However, with the revisions to the *Conceptual Framework* it would no longer be possible to issue GPFRs. The AASB response was to modify the reporting entity concept by allowing reporting entities that were not publicly accountable to apply a reduced disclosure version of the AASB standards and not to adopt the IASB's IFRS for small- and medium-sized entities (SMEs).

AASB 1053 *Application of Tiers of Australian Accounting Standards* establishes a differential financial reporting framework consisting of two tiers of reporting requirements for preparing general purpose financial reports. Tier 1 entities are required to apply the full AASB standards. Tier 1 entities are for-profit entities in the private sector that have public accountability, the Australian government, and State, Territory and Local governments entities.

Tier 2 entities are: for-profit private sector entities that do not have public accountability; all not-for-profit private sector entities; and public sector entities other than the Australian government and State, Territory and Local governments. Tier 2 entities are required to apply the full recognition, measurement and presentation requirements of IFRSs, but have substantially reduced disclosure requirements. The disclosures required by Tier 2 and the disclosures required by the IASB's IFRS for SMEs are similar. However, the IFRS for SMEs does not include all the recognition and measurement requirements corresponding to those in IFRSs.

In 2011, the New Zealand government announced changes to the financial reporting requirements for New Zealand entities. These changes are enacted in the Financial Reporting Act 2013. The main change is that many small- and medium-sized New Zealand companies no longer need to prepare accounting reports using New Zealand generally accepted accounting practice (GAAP). Complementary to this, the External Reporting Board (XRB) announced that, for financial reporting, New Zealand would change from a single set of sector-neutral accounting standards to a multi-sector and standards approach. This change took effect in 2016. Now, New Zealand's reporting standards are similar to the international standards where the for-profit publicly accountable entities use New Zealand equivalents of the International Financial Reporting Standards (NZ IFRS) and public benefit entities (PBE) (not-for-profit and government sector) report using PBE standards, which are based primarily on International Public Sector Accounting Standards (IPSAS), modified as necessary for the New Zealand environment by the XRB. Further, within the two-sector reporting regime there are four tiers. Tier 1 in both sectors will use the full standards with fewer requirements as the tiers go down.

For reporting entities, the usefulness of the information is dependent upon its qualitative characteristics, that is, the attributes that make information useful. The qualitative characteristics of information as outlined in the *Conceptual Framework* are discussed below. Once again, it is important to reflect on the interrelatedness of all aspects of the *Conceptual Framework*. Reporting entities are required to prepare general purpose financial reports. The objective of general purpose financial reports is to provide decision-useful information to resource providers. Usefulness is dependent upon its qualitative characteristics. Are you beginning to see the links? Are you beginning to see the *Conceptual Framework* coming together and how the parts are interrelated?

13.6 Qualitative characteristics and constraint on financial reporting

LEARNING OBJECTIVE 13.6 Identify and apply the qualitative characteristics and constraint on financial reporting.

In chapter 1 we discussed in detail the fundamental and enhancing qualitative characteristics of information contained in general purpose financial reports outlined in the *Conceptual Framework*. They include: relevance, faithful representation, comparability, verifiability, timeliness and understandability. These are reviewed in the following section with examples of their application as relevant. Please read chapter 1 again if you cannot recall the qualitative characteristics in sufficient detail.

Now let's turn our attention to the needs of the primary users of financial reports. The *Conceptual Framework* identifies the objective of general purpose financial reporting as the provision of financial information about the reporting entity that is useful to existing and potential equity investors, lenders and other creditors in making their decisions about providing resources to the entity. But how is that objective best served? In what format should financial information be presented? These questions are addressed by Chapter 3 of the *Conceptual Framework*. The *Conceptual Framework* provides guidance on the qualitative characteristics that information contained in general purpose financial reports should have to achieve the objective of providing useful information for decision making. That is, the qualitative characteristics are the attributes that make the information in financial reports useful.

According to the *Conceptual Framework*, the qualitative characteristics are classified as either fundamental or enhancing depending on how they affect the usefulness of financial information. Enhancing qualitative characteristics and fundamental qualitative characteristics are complementary.

Fundamental qualitative characteristics

For the information in general purpose financial reports to be useful, it must be relevant and provide a faithful representation of the economic phenomena it represents. Relevance and faithful representation are therefore classified as fundamental qualitative characteristics.

Relevance

Information is considered **relevant** if it is capable of making a difference to the decisions made by users. Information that has predictive value and/or confirmatory value is considered to be relevant. Information is considered to have predictive value if it can be used to develop expectations for the future. Information is considered to have confirmatory value if it confirms or contests users' past or present expectations. Information can often be both predictive and confirmatory.

Users of financial reports need to make many decisions based on the information contained in general purpose financial reports (which include a statement of profit or loss and other comprehensive income, a statement of financial position, a statement of cash flows, a statement of changes in equity and the relevant notes). Decisions such as 'shall I invest in this entity?' or 'should I lend money to this entity?' require information on the entity's future profitability and ability to pay its debts as they fall due. It seems then that for information to be relevant it must have predictive value, to help users make predictions about the future, or provide feedback, to help users assess the accuracy of their past predictions and decisions.

The *Conceptual Framework* suggests that information about past cash flows, financial performance and financial position can be used in predicting future cash flows, financial performance and financial position. Recall from chapter 11 that the cash inflows and cash outflows arising from operating activities are a valuable input into the decision-making processes of internal and external users of financial information. Positive cash flows arising from operating activities are a good indicator that the operations of the business can generate sufficient cash flows to maintain or expand the current level of operations, repay debt and pay dividends in the future. This text focuses on all aspects of financial accounting: recording, reporting and analysing, and decision making; that is why at the end of most chapters there is a section on analysing financial reports. The information provided in financial reports is relevant for use in ratio analysis, which can be used to assess an entity's profitability, liquidity and solvency. Based on these assessments, users of financial information can make decisions about resource allocations. Given an entity must generate sufficient cash flows for investors to receive future dividends as a return on their investment and sufficient cash flows are needed to repay lenders interest and principal, being able to predict the amount, timing and uncertainty of future cash flows is an important input into the decision-making processes of these users. Recall that liquidity is a measure of the entity's ability to meet its short-term obligations and solvency is its ability to meet long-term obligations.

Helpful hint: You can refer back to chapter 12 if you need to review ratio analysis and how measures of liquidity, solvency and profitability are valuable in making resource allocation decisions.

In concluding this section, it is helpful to note yet another example of the interrelationships and overlaps between the *Conceptual Framework* and the accounting concepts and principles described earlier in the chapter. For example, the purpose of the full disclosure principle is that all *relevant* information must be provided. The relevance of the information is also affected by its **materiality**. Information is material if its omission or misstatement could affect users' decisions. In relation to a specific reporting entity, a practical application of materiality is that small expenditures for non-current assets (e.g. tools) are often expensed immediately rather than depreciated over their useful lives to save the additional administrative costs of recording depreciation year after year for an insignificant amount. These are considered immaterial because the effects on general purpose financial reports over their useful lives are not large enough to affect users' decisions about resource allocations. Another example of the practical application of materiality is the common practice by large companies of rounding amounts in their financial statements to the nearest thousand dollars. Sometimes materiality has nothing to do with size. For example, financial fraud, no matter what amount, would be considered material. Deciding whether an item is material or not requires professional judgement and is not always straightforward. In making judgements about the materiality of an item, accountants need to consider the nature and size of the entity and the decisions that the primary users of financial statements make.

Helpful hint: Materiality is relative; that is, what is material for one entity may be immaterial for another. A $10 000 error may not be important in the financial statements of a multimillion-dollar company, but it may be critical to a small business.

Faithful representation

Information is a **faithful representation** of the economic phenomena it purports to represent if it is complete, neutral and free from material error. It is important that the information depicts the economic substance of the transactions, events or circumstances. At times, economic substance may not be the same as the legal form. To be complete, all of the information needed to represent the economic phenomena faithfully is included and there is no omission which could make the information misleading. Hence, like relevance, faithful representation is also linked to the full disclosure principle.

Information that is considered to be neutral is free from bias. Information is biased if it is intended to attain or induce a particular behaviour or result. Some of the information in general purpose financial reports is measured using estimates in conditions of uncertainty. Hence, it is not reasonable to expect that reports will be completely error free. However, despite this limitation, faithful representation is achieved when the inputs used to make the judgements and estimates reflect the best available information at the time.

As explained above, in the *Conceptual Framework* (2010) relevance and faithful representation work together in enhancing the decision usefulness of information. Relevance is applied to determine which economic phenomena to represent and then faithful representation is applied to determine which depictions best represent the underlying economic phenomena to assist users in making resource allocation decisions.

In a meeting on 21 September 2017 the IASB discussed the comments on the pre-ballot draft of the revised *Conceptual Framework for Financial Reporting* (*Conceptual Framework*) with regards to measurement uncertainty and the application of the fundamental qualitative characteristics of useful financial information. The Board tentatively decided that Chapter 2 *Qualitative characteristics of useful financial information* in the revised *Conceptual Framework* should:

(a) clarify that a trade-off may need to be made between relevance and faithful representation and specifically between relevance and measurement uncertainty; but

(b) not discuss how such a trade-off is made.

All 14 Board members agreed with that decision. Further information is available at www.ifrs.org/projects/work-plan/conceptual-framework/#.

Enhancing qualitative characteristics

Enhancing qualitative characteristics include comparability, verifiability, timeliness and understandability. These characteristics are called enhancing characteristics as they enhance the decision usefulness of relevant information faithfully represented in financial statements. The enhancing qualitative characteristics are summarised in figure 13.4.

FIGURE 13.4 Enhancing qualitative characteristics of financial information in general purpose financial reports

Which is better?

Comparability
1. Between different companies
2. Between different years of the same company

Verifiability
1. Faithful representation
2. Independent observer consensus

Timeliness
Capable of influencing decisions

Understandability
Able to be understood by proficient users

Comparability

Information that is comparable facilitates users identifying similarities and differences between different economic phenomena. Consistency refers to the use of the same accounting policies between entities, at the same point in time, or the same entity over time. Consistency supports the achievement of **comparability**.

In accounting, comparability is achieved when an entity uses the same or consistent accounting principles each year and different entities use the same accounting principles. At one level, we could argue that accounting information is comparable because it is based on certain qualitative characteristics, principles and concepts. However, standards still allow for some variation in methods of measurement and presentation. For example, recall from chapter 5 that there are different ways to measure inventory (e.g. specific identification; first in, first out; or average cost). Recall from chapter 8 that there are different ways to record depreciation (e.g. straight-line or diminishing balance). In the examples provided in chapters 5 and 8, it was clear that the different methods resulted in different amounts for profit and different amounts for assets, impacting comparability.

To make comparisons across entities easier, within the *Conceptual Framework* and IAS 8/AASB 108 'Accounting Policies, Changes in Accounting Estimates and Errors' each entity must disclose the accounting methods used. From these disclosures, the external user can determine whether the financial information is comparable and try to make adjustments. Unfortunately, converting the accounting numbers of entities that use different methods is not simple. To further complicate matters, accounting standards differ between countries, making the comparison of entities from different countries more difficult. Through the IASB, standard setters around the world have worked towards harmonising accounting standards based on IFRSs, thus increasing comparability.

Users of financial reports are not only interested in comparing different entities but also in comparing the same entity's financial results over time when making resource allocation decisions. Recall that in chapter 12 we looked at statement of financial position data for Harrison Limited and Williams Limited and explored a number of tools for comparative analysis, for example, horizontal analysis, which is a technique for evaluating a series of financial data to determine trends. However, for this analysis to be meaningful we needed to confirm that the same principles were used from year to year, otherwise we could be 'comparing apples with oranges', so to speak.

Verifiability

Information is verifiable if it faithfully represents the economic phenomena it is meant to represent. **Verifiability** means that independent observers can reach a consensus — but not necessarily 100% agreement — that a particular depiction is a faithful representation. Direct verification is through direct observation, like counting cash to verify cash balance reported on the statement of financial position or counting inventory to determine quantities in stock. Indirect verification is where techniques or calculations are used to check the representation. For example, verifying the ending inventory balance in the statement of financial position by checking quantities and costs using the same cost flow assumption. See chapter 5 for more information on calculating ending inventory using different cost flow assumptions.

Timeliness

Timeliness is measured by whether the information is available to users before it ceases to be relevant; that is, the information is received while it is still capable of influencing the decisions users make based on the information. Financial information may lose its relevance if it is not reported in a timely manner; however, some information may remain timely long after the reporting period as the information is used to determine trends.

Application of timeliness means that the preparer should not take so long to collect and prepare financial information that the reported information loses its relevance. Application of this principle may mean that some transactions and events are reported before all the facts are known. For example, recall in chapter 3 that accruals for electricity or telephone expenses are estimated when the invoice has not been received by year-end but the expense has been incurred. Recall also in chapter 7 that estimates for the allowance for doubtful debts are reported in the accounts rather than waiting for the debts to go bad. Hence, if preparers of financial reports waited until all the information was available, it could be too late for users who have to make decisions about investing in or lending to an organisation in the interim.

Understandability

Understandability is the last of the enhancing qualitative characteristics and relates to the quality of information that assists users to understand the meaning of the information provided when making resource allocation decisions. Let's face it, what would be the point of having information if it were incomprehensible. It makes sense, then, that the *Conceptual Framework* lists understandability as an enhancing qualitative characteristic of general purpose financial reports.

Understandability refers to the extent to which information can be understood by proficient users; that is, users who have reasonable knowledge of accounting and business activities. It is not practicable to require financial reports to be understandable to novices. That is why, ultimately, whether information is understandable depends on the capabilities of the individual user, and why novice users should seek professional advice if the information is too complex for their level of understanding.

When you first began your accounting studies and saw the Giorgina's Pizza Limited accounts in chapter 1, you may have found that you did not really understand the information contained in the financial reports. However, by chapter 12, as you worked through the analysis of financial reports in each chapter, perhaps you'd acquired sufficient knowledge about accounting and business to be able to understand the Harrison Limited and Williams Limited accounts and the resulting ratio analyses. So, understandability is not about simplifying the information provided; in fact, the *Conceptual Framework* requires that information about complex matters be included in reports if it is relevant to users in making their decisions.

Understandability depends on the capabilities of users; however, classifying, characterising and presenting information clearly and concisely will enhance understandability. While enhancing qualitative characteristics improve the usefulness of financial information and should be maximised where possible, it is important to note that they are only enhancing because they cannot make information decision-useful if the information is irrelevant or not faithfully represented. The decision-usefulness objective of general purpose financial reporting ensures that the information is helpful to shareholders, potential investors, lenders and other creditors when making decisions about the allocation of scare resources. It can provide insights into many key questions that form the basis for resource allocation decisions as follow.

- Is the company generating sufficient cash flows to repay debts and distribute dividends?
- Will the company generate sufficient funds to replace assets as needed?
- Can the organisation survive in the short and long term?
- Will I receive an adequate return on my investment?

The qualitative characteristics we have discussed are intended to provide users of financial reports with the most useful information for decision making. However, if taken to the extreme, the pursuit of useful financial information could be far too costly to an entity. Therefore, cost is a constraint on the information provided by financial reporting.

Constraint on financial reporting

Providing decision-useful information imposes costs, and the benefits of providing the information should outweigh the costs. Costs can include those associated with collecting, processing, verifying and disseminating information. Assessing whether benefits outweigh costs is usually more qualitative than quantitative and is often incomplete. In an attempt to ensure benefits outweigh costs, it is important to consider whether one or more enhancing qualitative characteristics may be sacrificed to reduce costs.

Table 13.1 summarises the fundamental and enhancing qualitative characteristics of financial information and the constraint of providing financial information as outlined in the *Conceptual Framework*.

TABLE 13.1	Fundamental and enhancing qualitative characteristics and constraint of financial information	
Fundamental qualitative characteristics	**Enhancing qualitative characteristics**	**Constraint of providing financial information**
Relevance	Comparability	Cost
Faithful representation[*]	Verifiability	
	Timeliness	
	Understandability	

[*]Complete, neutral, free from material error.

Review it

1. Define reporting entity as outlined in the Australian conceptual framework.
2. Explain the indicators of a reporting entity as outlined in the Australian conceptual framework.
3. Discuss the definition and features of a reporting entity as outlined in the exposure draft on the reporting entity.
4. Explain differential reporting.
5. Explain the fundamental qualitative characteristics of financial information.
6. Explain the enhancing qualitative characteristics of financial information.
7. Describe the constraint underlying financial statements in the *Conceptual Framework*.

To recap and summarise the discussion thus far, Chapter 1 of the *Conceptual Framework* discusses the objective of general purpose financial reporting. Chapter 2 on the reporting entity is yet to be added, hence in Australia SAC 1 (from the Australian conceptual framework) applies. The qualitative characteristics of useful information are outlined in Chapter 3. The final chapter has not been replaced and is in fact the text from the framework for the preparation of financial statements (*Framework* (1989)). Chapter 4 discusses the definition, recognition criteria and measurement of elements in financial statements.

13.7 Definition, recognition and measurement of elements in financial reports

LEARNING OBJECTIVE 13.7 Define assets, liabilities, equity, income and expenses and apply recognition criteria.

When you first began your studies, you needed to learn many new terms and concepts; that is, you needed to learn the language of accounting. These concepts were introduced in chapter 1. Then, in chapter 3, you learned about the accrual basis of recording transactions and events. You now know that reporting entities record accounting transactions and events using **accrual-based accounting** rather than cash-based accounting. For accrual-based accounting the transactions and events are recorded in the periods in which they meet the revenue, expense, asset and liability recognition criteria. This can occur before, as, or after cash has been received or paid. You also now understand what general purpose financial reports are and how they communicate information about an entity to users.

General purpose financial reports include a statement of profit or loss and other comprehensive income, a statement of financial position, a statement of cash flows, a statement of changes in equity and the notes to the financial statements. These statements portray the effects of transactions and events in relation to the entity, by grouping them into broad classes or elements. The *Conceptual Framework* defines assets, liabilities, equity, income and expenses, that is, each of the main **elements in financial statements**. It also sets out the criteria for their recognition. Definitions and recognition criteria are crucial in recording transactions. For example, if you don't define assets, how will you know what an asset is? How will you know when and how to record an asset if you don't have recognition criteria? The definitions and recognition criteria for the main elements of financial statements are discussed in the next section.

Assets — definition and recognition criteria

At the time of writing, the IASB noted in the board's redeliberations paper 2014 that the definitions of assets and liabilities as provided in the *Conceptual Framework* could be clarified. These were made available for public comment in ED 2015/3 and a revised conceptual framework is expected in mid-2018. For this reason, the definitions for assets and liabilities, as provided in the 2010 *Conceptual Framework*, are discussed as follows.

Definition

Assets are defined in the *Conceptual Framework* as 'a resource controlled by the entity as a result of past events and from which future economic benefits are expected to flow to the entity' (paragraph 4.4a). Let's look at the essential characteristics individually.

First, the entity must have control over the asset. In chapter 8 we illustrated the recording of a number of ways assets could be acquired, for example, by cash, as an exchange or on credit. While control often means ownership of the asset, ownership is not an essential characteristic. Take, for example, the case of a finance lease, where the legal ownership of the leased asset remains with the lessor; however, the substance and therefore the economic reality is that the lessee acquires the right to use the leased asset. The leased asset is a resource providing future economic benefits to the lessee. Hence, a finance lease satisfies the definition of an asset (and a liability) and is recognised as such in the lessee's statement of financial position, even though the legal title to the leased asset remains with the lessor.

Helpful hint: Finance leases are discussed in more detail in chapter 9.

A second essential characteristic is that the control of the future economic benefits must be as a result of a past transaction or event. Generally, this is after the purchase of the asset has taken place. We have recorded the purchase of many assets throughout the chapters. Recall that, based on the cost principle, assets are initially recorded at cost. It is important to note that resources to be purchased in the future are not considered an asset of the entity until the exchange takes place. For example, recall our discussion of consignment stock in our chapters on inventory. While the consignee might have possession of goods on consignment, the consignee does not have control. If the consignee does not sell the consigned goods within the agreed consignment period, the goods are returned to the consignor. However, to further complicate matters, payment is not an essential characteristic of an asset; a donated resource, once the entity has control of the future economic benefits, meets the definition of an asset as well.

Finally, the resource must be able to provide future economic benefits or service potential, such that it can contribute directly or indirectly to the future cash flows or cash equivalents of the entity. Of the numerous transactions involving assets that you have recorded, can you remember the many different ways assets can provide future economic benefits? For example, an asset can be sold for cash or exchanged for another asset; it can be used to settle a liability; or it can be used to produce goods or services that result in future cash flows from clients and customers. How many did you recall correctly?

The definition of an asset identifies its essential features but does not attempt to specify the criteria that need to be met before it can be recognised in the statement of financial position. Hence, it is not sufficient to record assets based only upon the definition of assets. We also need the recognition criteria, which are discussed next.

Recognition criteria

Recognition is the process of recording in the financial reports any item that meets the definition of an element and satisfies the criteria for recognition. If you look at a statement of profit or loss or statement of financial position you will see each item depicted both in words and with a monetary amount. When recording transactions, preparers need to make decisions about when to recognise assets in the accounting records and on the statement of financial position. The decision-making toolkit guides this analysis by identifying the relevant information as well as the tools for analysis — the asset recognition criteria. Assets that satisfy the recognition criteria should be incorporated in the statement of financial position when:

(a) it is probable that the future economic benefits will flow to the entity

(b) the asset has a cost or value that can be measured with reliability (paragraph 4.38).

Helpful hint: Reliability is not a qualitative characteristic in the Conceptual Framework*; however, it was in the* Framework *(1989). In that context information was considered reliable when it was complete, neutral and free from error.*

The first recognition criterion results from the fact that business entities operate in uncertain environments. We use the concept of probability to refer to the degree of uncertainty that surrounds whether the future economic benefits will flow to or from the entity in relation to a transaction or event. To assess the degree of probability of the future economic benefits, all of the evidence available when the financial reports are prepared is used. To illustrate, recall in chapter 7 where we needed to assess the likelihood of the flow of future economic benefits from receivables. When it was probable that a receivable would be collected, it was recognised as an asset. However, we also knew that some degree of non-payment was normally considered probable and, as such, a doubtful debts expense representing the expected reduction in economic benefits was also recognised, meeting the expense recognition criteria.

The second recognition criterion requires that each item possess a cost or value that can be measured with reliability. In most of the exercises and examples illustrated throughout this text, determining cost has been straightforward as the cost of the asset was provided. Based on the decision-making toolkit analysis, assets should be recognised when it is probable that the future economic benefits will flow to the entity and the asset has a cost or value that can be measured with reliability. General purpose financial reports are prepared to provide resource providers with information to make their resource allocation decisions such as lending or investing. Recognising assets too early overstates current period assets; recognising assets too late understates current period assets, which distorts the financial information available to users and can adversely affect their ability to make informed decisions.

However, for some items such as a provision for warranties, the cost or value is not straightforward and must be estimated. This is considered to be an essential part of the preparation of financial reports and does not undermine their reliability. However, for cases where a reasonable estimate cannot be made, the item is not recognised in the financial reports. For example, internally developed brand names are not recognised in the financial reports. However, when a brand name is purchased, the exchange provides a cost that can be measured with reliability.

There are a number of circumstances where an asset is not recorded in the statement of financial position. The first is when an item meets the definition of an asset but fails to meet the criteria for recognition. Under these circumstances, the item should be disclosed in the notes if it is considered to be relevant to users' evaluations of the financial position, financial performance and/or cash flows of the entity. Finally, an asset is not recognised in the statement of financial position if it is considered improbable that economic benefits will flow to the entity beyond the current accounting period. In this case, the expenditure is recorded as an expense in the statement of profit or loss. You have recorded numerous examples of this type of transaction, for example, payment of electricity, wages, fuel, stationery and advertising. You can refer to chapters 2, 3 and 4 for examples. The important thing to note for these transactions is that the economic benefits will not flow to the entity *beyond* the current accounting period. To the extent that they do, the cost is recorded as an asset. For example, when insurance is paid in advance for the following accounting period, a prepayment (an asset) is recorded.

DECISION-MAKING TOOLKIT

Decision/issue	Info needed for analysis	Tool or technique to use for decision	How to evaluate results to make decision
At what point should the entity recognise (record) assets?	Need to understand the nature of the entity's business and the definition and recognition criteria for assets.	Assets should be recognised when it is probable that the future economic benefits will flow to the entity and the asset has a cost or value that can be measured with reliability.	Recognising assets too early overstates current period assets; recognising them too late understates current period assets.

Liabilities — definition and recognition criteria

Definition

A **liability** is defined in the *Conceptual Framework* as an outflow of economic benefits that the entity is presently obliged to make as a result of past events. As mentioned earlier, this definition of liabilities is currently being reviewed and is expected to be updated in the new conceptual framework. A similarly worded definition is provided in IAS 37/AASB 137 *Provisions, Contingent Liabilities and Contingent Assets*. Let's look at the essential characteristics individually.

First, the entity must have a present obligation. This means the entity has a duty to act or perform in a certain way in the future. For example, in chapter 3 we illustrated transactions involving revenue received in advance (recorded as a liability). In this case, the entity had a present obligation to deliver goods or provide services at a future date. In chapter 9, we illustrated the recording of many other types of liabilities including mortgage and lease liabilities. In the case of a mortgage, the future obligation was a payment of cash to cover the principal and interest components for each repayment. In general, a legal debt constitutes a liability; however, liabilities do not have to be legal debts. For example, a warranty provision is not a legal liability; however, an entity will honour this liability when it arises if it is one of the entity's business practices for maintaining good customer relations.

A second essential characteristic is that the obligation must be as a result of a past transaction or event. To illustrate, an intention to buy an asset in the future does not give rise to a present obligation. Generally, the obligation arises after the purchase of the asset has taken place.

Finally, a liability must result in an outflow of resources or economic benefits such that it can reduce directly or indirectly the future cash flows or cash equivalents of the entity. Of the many transactions involving liabilities you have recorded, can you remember the many different ways liabilities can be settled or discharged? For example, a liability can be settled by paying cash; this is the most obvious. Can you remember other ways? As mentioned above, in the case of revenue received in advance, the liability can be discharged by providing goods or services. In the case of accounts payable, these can be discharged by issuing another liability such as notes payable. Liabilities can also be discharged by issuing shares instead of repaying the liability in cash. How many did you recall correctly?

It is not sufficient to record liabilities based only upon the definition of liabilities. We also need the recognition criteria, which are discussed below.

Recognition criteria

When recording transactions, preparers need to make decisions about when to recognise liabilities in the accounting records and on the statement of financial position. The decision-making toolkit guides this analysis by identifying the relevant information as well as the tools for analysis — the recognition criteria for liabilities. As outlined in the *Conceptual Framework*, a liability is recognised in the statement of financial position when:

(a) it is probable that an outflow of resources embodying economic benefits will result from the settlement of a present obligation

(b) the amount at which the settlement will take place can be measured reliably (paragraph 4.46).

Based on the decision-making toolkit analysis, liabilities (also called *debts*) should be recognised when it is probable that an outflow of resources embodying economic benefits will result from the settlement of a present obligation and the amount at which the settlement will take place can be measured reliably. General purpose financial reports are prepared to provide resource providers with information to make their resource allocation decisions such as lending or investing. Recognising liabilities too early overstates current period liabilities; recognising them too late understates current period liabilities, which distorts the financial information available to users, adversely affecting their ability to make informed decisions.

Simply put, a liability is reported when the future sacrifice of economic benefits is probable and can be reliably measured. Many liabilities are straightforward. To illustrate, accounts payable are recorded as liabilities once the goods are delivered or the service has been provided. A bank loan is recorded once the money is transferred from the bank to the entity's bank account.

Liabilities for which the amount of the future sacrifice is so uncertain that they cannot be measured reliably are classified as contingent liabilities. Liabilities are also classified as contingent if they do not satisfy the probability criterion, or if they are dependent upon the occurrence of an uncertain future event outside the control of the entity. Examples include an unresolved lawsuit brought against the entity and the potential liability resulting from a tax audit in progress. While contingent liabilities are not recognised because they are not probable and/or are unable to be measured reliably, the information about contingent liabilities must be disclosed in the notes to the financial statements if the liability is possible and considered to be material.

DECISION-MAKING TOOLKIT

Decision/issue	Info needed for analysis	Tool or technique to use for decision	How to evaluate results to make decision
At what point should the entity recognise (record) liabilities?	Need to understand the nature of the entity's business and the definition and recognition criteria for liabilities.	Liabilities should be recognised when it is probable that an outflow of resources embodying economic benefits will result from the settlement of a present obligation and the amount at which the settlement will take place can be measured reliably.	Recognising liabilities too early overstates current period liabilities; recognising them too late understates current period liabilities.

Proposed changes to the definitions and recognition criteria for assets and liabilities

Based on the feedback from DP/2013/1, the board believed that the definitions of assets and liabilities could be clarified. In ED 2015/3 (p. 11), the IASB proposes to define the elements of the financial statements as follows:

> An asset is a present economic resource controlled by the entity as a result of past events. An economic resource is a right that has the potential to produce economic benefits.

> A liability is a present obligation of the entity to transfer an economic resource as a result of past events.

Given the revised *Conceptual Framework* was not available at the time of writing this chapter, the definitions of assets and liabilities and recognition criteria as outlined in the *Conceptual Framework* (2010) apply.

Equity — definition

Equity is defined in the *Conceptual Framework* as 'the residual interest in the assets of the entity after deducting all its liabilities' (paragraph 4.4c). Put simply, equity is what remains when we subtract liabilities from assets. The accounting equation can be restated from Assets = Liabilities + Equity to Equity = Assets − Liabilities. This equation shows that equity cannot be defined independently of the other elements in the statement of financial position; that is, equity is the residual. In the board's redeliberations paper (2014), the IASB noted that the *Conceptual Framework* should retain the current definition of equity as the residual interest in the assets of the entity after deducting all its liabilities. This is consistent with ED 2015/3 'Equity is the residual interest in the assets of the entity after deducting all its liabilities' (p. 11).

Can you recall what transactions or events affect equity? The most obvious is that gains increase equity and losses decrease equity. Owners can also affect equity. For example, injections of capital into the business by owners, such as share purchases, increase equity, whereas drawings, dividends or share buybacks decrease equity.

Can you think of any other transactions or events that affect equity? Here's a hint, it has to do with asset valuations. Have you got it now? That's right, asset revaluations can affect equity. Recall that a revaluation upwards is recorded as a debit to the revalued asset and a credit to the revaluation surplus, which is an equity account. A reversal of a previous increase will decrease equity. If you can't remember how to record the journal entries, please review chapter 8.

Equity can be presented in subcategories. For example, in a corporate entity, equity can be classified into funds contributed by shareholders (share capital), retained earnings and reserves representing appropriations of retained earnings.

This completes the discussion of the elements found in the statement of financial position. We now turn to the elements in the statement of profit or loss.

Income — definition and recognition criteria

Profit is generally used as the main measure of performance. The elements directly related to the measurement of profit are income and expense. The statement of profit or loss reports on income less expenses, resulting in profit. However, you already knew that, right?

Definition

Income is defined in the *Conceptual Framework* as 'increases in economic benefits during the accounting period in the form of inflows or enhancements of assets or decreases of liabilities that result in increases in equity, other than those relating to contributions from equity participants' (paragraph 4.25a). In ED2015/3 'Income is increases in assets or decreases in liabilities that result in increases in equity, other than those relating to contributions from holders of equity claims' (p. 12). It is important to note that, like the definition of equity, the definition of income is linked to the definitions of assets and liabilities.

Can you recall the many types of income you have recorded over the period you have been studying accounting? If you are thinking about sales revenue, interest income, gains on the sale of non-current assets and discounts received, then you would be correct. Well done! As you can see, the definition of income is wide in its scope and includes any increases in equity except contributions of capital; that is, income includes revenue and gains.

Income is defined in the *Conceptual Framework* as encompassing both revenue and gains. The *Conceptual Framework* defines revenue as increases in economic benefits arising in the course of ordinary activities of an entity. It includes sales revenue, fees, interest, dividends, royalties and rent. Gains are other increases in economic benefits. They are no different in nature from revenue but are labelled as gains either because they do not arise in the ordinary course of business or because they are reported as a net amount, such as the gain on the sale of non-current assets.

How wide is the definition of income? Let's test the definition by looking at revenue received in advance. Would this be classified as income based on this definition? The answer is no, as the economic benefits that flow to the entity in the form of cash are matched with an increase in a liability. According to the definition, a decrease in liabilities is needed, not an increase, therefore revenue received in advance is initially classified as a liability, not income. Once the entity discharges its obligation the income can be recorded. Recall that the entry to record the income is a debit to revenue received in advance and a credit to sales revenue. The definition of income identifies the essential features of income but does not attempt to specify the criteria that would need to be met before it is recognised in the statement of profit or loss.

Recognition criteria

A definition of income is helpful in determining *what* is to be recorded as income but preparers also need guidelines on *when* to record or recognise income in preparing financial statements. For example, entities that sell goods (merchandising entities) need to first purchase goods, then sell them to customers and collect the cash. The operating cycle is the length of time it takes for a business to acquire goods, sell them to customers and collect the cash from the sale. The decision that arises is to determine at which point in the operating cycle sales revenue should be recognised.

Determining the amount of revenue to be reported in a given accounting period can be difficult. Generally, revenue should be recognised in the accounting period in which the service is performed or the goods are delivered. Proper reporting requires a thorough understanding of the nature of the entity's business and the appropriate application of the criteria for the recognition of revenues to facilitate the recording process. In short, adjusting entries are needed to ensure that the recognition criteria are followed for assets, liabilities, revenues and expenses. The *Conceptual Framework* (2010) outlines income recognition criteria.

As outlined in the *Conceptual Framework,* income (which includes revenues and gains) is recognised in the income statement 'when an increase in future economic benefits related to an increase in an asset or a decrease of a liability has arisen that can be measured reliably' (paragraph 4.47). The decision-making toolkit guides the analysis by identifying the relevant information as well as the tools for analysis, including the recognition criteria for income in determining when to recognise income in the financial statements; that is, the recognition of income occurs simultaneously with the recognition of increases in assets or decreases in liabilities. To illustrate, a sale of goods on credit results in an increase in accounts receivable (asset) and a corresponding increase in sales revenue (income). For revenue received in advance, once the service has been provided there is a decrease in revenue received in advance (liability) and an increase in sales revenue (income).

In the context of revenue recognition, the concept of probability refers to the degree of uncertainty that the future economic benefits will flow to the entity. The assessment of probability, or the degree of uncertainty, is made on the basis of evidence available when the financial statements are prepared. Ordinarily, this assessment is also made at the time the transaction that gives rise to the revenue occurs, thereby allowing the transaction to be recorded. However, when preparing the financial statements, the accountant must reconsider any information available at this time to assess whether the revenue should be reported as such in financial reports.

The requirement that revenue can be measured reliably does not mean it must be measured with absolute certainty. In some routine transactions, such as cash sales, measurement may be certain. However, in many instances, revenue must be estimated. In ED 2015/3 the criterion of 'reliable measurement' is no longer present in the recognition criteria for income or expenses.

In applying the recognition criteria, many businesses adopt procedures for recognising revenue when it is earned. For example, when a surgeon earns revenue by conducting surgery on a patient, a claim against the patient arises for the doctor's fee. At that time, the amount of the fee could be measured reliably because the doctor would know what surgery has been performed, and the flow of benefits would be probable because the doctor would have a valid claim against the patient for the fee. Based on the decision-making toolkit analysis, recognising income too early overstates current period income; recognising it too late understates current period income. Because general purpose financial reports are prepared to provide primary users with information to make their resource allocation decisions, such as lending or investing, the correct application of income recognition criteria is essential.

Standards for revenue recognition

As explained in chapter 3, a new standard for revenue recognition, IFRS 15/AASB 15 *Revenue from Contracts with Customers,* became mandatory for reporting periods from 1 January 2017. The new standard prescribes a five-step model for the recognition of revenue. Please refer to chapter 3 for an explanation of the five steps. Basically, revenue is recognised when the entity satisfies the performance obligation. The application of revenue recognition for a service business is described below.

In a service entity, revenue is recognised at the time the service is performed. For example, assume a dry-cleaning business cleans clothing on 30 June, but customers do not pick up and pay for their clothes until the first week of July. Using the revenue recognition criteria, revenue is recorded in June when the service is performed, not in July when the cash is received. At 30 June, the tests for the recognition of revenue are met.

DECISION-MAKING TOOLKIT

Decision/issue	Info needed for analysis	Tool or technique to use for decision	How to evaluate results to make decision
At what point should the entity recognise (record) income?	Need to understand the nature of the entity's business, the definition and the recognition criteria for income.	Income should be recognised when an increase in future economic benefits related to an increase in an asset or a decrease of a liability has arisen that can be measured reliably. Generally, for a service business, revenue is recognised when the service is performed. For a business that sells goods, revenue is recognised when the goods have been delivered.	Recognising income too early overstates current period income; recognising it too late understates current period income.

Expenses — definition and recognition criteria

Recall that profit is generally used as the main measure of performance. The elements directly related to the measurement of profit are income and expense.

Definition

As defined in the *Conceptual Framework,* **expenses** are 'decreases in economic benefits during the accounting period in the form of outflows or depletions of assets or incurrences of liabilities that result in decreases in equity, other than those relating to distributions to equity participants' (paragraph 4.25b). In ED 2015/5 expenses are defined as 'decreases in assets or increases in liabilities that result in decreases in equity, other than those relating to distributions to holders of equity claims' (p. 12).

It is important to note that, like the definitions of equity and income, the definition of expenses is linked to the definitions of assets and liabilities.

Can you recall the many types of expenses you have recorded during your accounting studies? If you recall electricity, insurance, wages and interest expenses, just to name a few, you would be correct! As you can see, the definition of expenses is wide in its scope and includes any decreases in equity except distributions of equity to equity participants (owners and shareholders).

The *Conceptual Framework* defines expenses as encompassing both losses and expenses. Expenses are decreases in economic benefits. They include expenses that arise in the ordinary activities of the entity such as cost of sales, wages and payments for rent. Losses refer to expenses that do not necessarily arise in the ordinary course of business such as the loss from a fire or flood, as well as reductions in economic benefits that are reported on a net basis (i.e. net of any associated revenue) such as a loss on the sale of non-current assets. Put simply, expenses are decreases in equity during an accounting period that are not distributions to the owner(s).

The consumption of economic benefits is easily determined for some transactions such as using cash to pay rent for the current period. However, some economic benefits such as buildings and equipment last for numerous accounting periods. Measuring the amount of economic benefits consumed in each accounting period can be difficult which, in turn, makes it difficult to determine how much of the cost of assets such as buildings and equipment should be allocated to expenses in each accounting period. The allocation of a cost of an asset to expense is called depreciation. If you need to review the different methods of depreciation, please refer to chapter 8.

Recognition criteria

The definition of expenses is helpful in determining what is to be recorded as an expense but, as for revenues, we need guidelines on when to record or recognise expenses. The *Conceptual Framework* provides expense recognition criteria. Expenses should be recognised when 'a decrease in future economic benefits related to a decrease in an asset or an increase of a liability has arisen that can be measured reliably' (paragraph 4.49). Many expenses for merchandising and service entities involve little uncertainty as they result from the production or delivery of goods or services during an accounting period. Examples include wages and salaries expense, supplies (e.g. stationery) and electricity or gas. It is important to note that an expense is recognised when the reduction in assets or the increase in liabilities is recognised, and that this may occur before, as or after cash is paid. Referring to the previous dry-cleaning business example, although wages may not be paid on 30 June for the hours worked by employees in providing dry-cleaning services, the expense is recognised as the increase in liabilities (wages payable) has occurred and the future outflow can be measured reliably.

Based on the decision-making toolkit analysis, expenses should be recognised when a decrease in future economic benefits related to a decrease in an asset or an increase of a liability has arisen that can be measured reliably. General purpose financial reports are prepared to provide resource providers with information to make their resource allocation decisions such as lending or investing. Recognising expenses too early overstates current period expenses; recognising them too late understates current period expenses, which distorts the financial information available to users, adversely affecting their ability to make informed decisions.

Decision/issue	Info needed for analysis	Tool or technique to use for decision	How to evaluate results to make decision
At what point should the entity recognise (record) expenses?	Need to understand the nature of the entity's business, and definition and recognition criteria for expenses.	Expenses should be recognised when a decrease in future economic benefits related to a decrease in an asset or an increase of a liability has arisen that can be measured reliably.	Recognising expenses too early overstates current period expenses; recognising them too late understates current period expenses.

Where the expenses result directly and jointly from the same transaction as the revenues, e.g. the cost of services provided or the cost of sales, expenses should be recognised on the basis of a direct association with revenues. This recognition technique is sometimes referred to as 'matching' of expenses with revenues — the simultaneous recognition of revenues and related expenses. The nature of, and methods for, recording cost of sales were explored in chapters 4 and 5.

Determining the amount of revenues and expenses to be reported in each accounting period is facilitated by revenue and expense recognition criteria. Relationships between revenue recognition, expense recognition and the accounting period concept which form part of GAAP are depicted in figure 13.5.

FIGURE 13.5 Relationships between revenue recognition, expense recognition and the accounting period concept

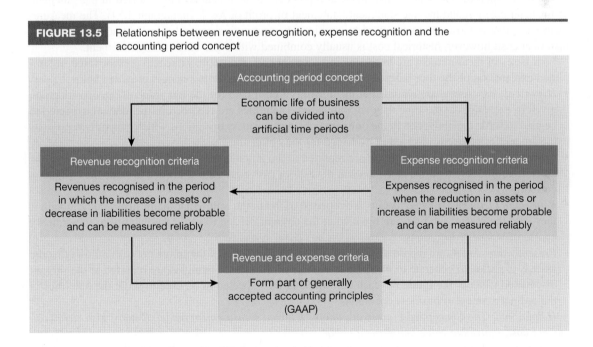

Note: The recognition criteria in figure 13.5 are the same as those in the *Conceptual Framework* which is currently under revision. The criteria in the decision-making toolkit are from the new accounting standard IFRS 15/AASB 15 *Revenue from Contracts with Customers*.

To sum up and conclude this section on the definition and recognition criteria of elements in financial statements, we'd like you to reflect on any similarities you may have noticed in the recognition criteria.

If you noticed that an item that meets the definition of an element should be recognised if *it is probable that any future economic benefit associated with the item will flow to or from the entity, and the item has a cost or value that can be measured with reliability,* you have correctly recognised the basic criteria that are applied to assets, liabilities, revenues and expenses.

You may have also noticed the interrelationships between the elements. That is, an item that meets the definition and recognition criteria for a particular element, for example, an asset, automatically requires the recognition of another element, for example, income or a liability. Further, if an item fails to meet the recognition criteria at a certain point in time, it may qualify for recognition at a later date as a result of a change in circumstances or events. If, on the other hand, an item possesses the essential characteristics of an element but fails to meet the recognition criteria, it may warrant disclosure in the notes if it is considered to be relevant to the users of the financial statements in making decisions.

Finally, you may have noticed that the definitions of equity, income and expenses are related to the definitions of assets and liabilities. For example, income is defined as 'increases in economic benefits during the accounting period in the form of inflows or enhancements of assets or decreases of liabilities that result in increases in equity, other than those relating to contributions from equity participants' (*Conceptual Framework*, paragraph 4.25(a)). Thus, the measurement of equity, income and expenses are dependent on the measurement of assets and liabilities. Measurement of the elements of financial reports is discussed below.

Measurement of the elements of financial reports

The *Conceptual Framework* states that **measurement** 'is the process of determining the monetary amounts at which the elements of the financial reports are to be recognised and carried in the statement of financial position and income statement [statement of profit or loss]' (paragraph 4.54). The measurement basis that is most commonly used by entities when preparing general purpose financial reports is historical cost; however, historical cost is usually combined with other bases of measurement.

Four bases of measurement are historical cost, current cost, realisable value and present value. A simplified explanation of the four bases as outlined in the *Conceptual Framework* is provided below.

- *Historical cost.* Assets are recorded at the amount of cash paid (or the fair value of the consideration given in exchange) at the time they are purchased. Liabilities are recorded in the amount expected to be paid to settle the obligation in the ordinary course of business operations which generally represents the amount of proceeds received in exchange for the obligation.
- *Current cost.* Under this base, assets are reported at the amount that would be required to replace the asset. Liabilities are reported at the amount of cash (or cash equivalents) needed to settle the obligation currently.
- *Realisable (settlement) value.* Assets are reported at the dollar value that the business could obtain if they sold the asset. Liabilities are reported at the amount needed to settle the liability in the ordinary course of business operations.
- *Present value.* Assets are reported at the present discounted value of the future net cash inflows that the asset is expected to generate in the ordinary course of business. Liabilities are reported at the present discounted value of the future net cash outflows that are expected to be used to settle the liabilities in the ordinary course of business operations.

Helpful hint: The Conceptual Framework *adopts a mixed measurement model, namely, historical cost, current cost, realisable value and present value.*

Can you recall the use of alternative measurement bases discussed in the preceding chapters? For example, in chapter 1 we explained that assets are initially recorded at their historical cost based on the cost principle. However, subsequently, in chapter 8 we illustrated that they may also be accounted for based on the revalued basis; hence, they may be revalued upwards or downwards to their fair value. Fair value is a subset of the realisable (settlement) value in the *Conceptual Framework*. Another example of a possible measure of realisable value is the fair value less any costs incurred in selling the asset. In chapter 5 we explored the reporting of inventories. Inventories are usually carried at the lower of cost and net realisable value. We can see from these examples that a number of different measurement bases can be used in the preparation of financial reports, and so measurement can have an impact on the decisions users of general purpose financial reports make based on the measurements reported.

In DP/2013/1 the board noted that the existing *Conceptual Framework* provides little guidance on measurement and when particular measurements should be used. Hence, the IASB intends to provide further guidance in the revised *Conceptual Framework*. ED 2015/3 notes that the revised *Conceptual Framework* will be more complete than the existing *Conceptual Framework* (2010) because it addresses measurement in more detail.

Furthermore, the number of different measurements used by an entity should be the smallest number needed to provide relevant information to users of general purpose financial reports. Unnecessary measurement changes should be avoided and the benefits of providing the information to users must outweigh the costs to the reporting entity.

Helpful hint: Note how measurement is linked to the purpose of financial reports — to provide information to the primary users for their resource allocation decisions as well as helping managers discharge their stewardship responsibilities.

LEARNING REFLECTION AND CONSOLIDATION

Review it
1. Define assets, liabilities, equity, income and expenses as defined in the *Conceptual Framework*.
2. Explain asset, liability, revenue and expense recognition criteria as outlined in the *Conceptual Framework*.

Do it
During year 1, Ray Ltd invoiced its customers $100 000 for services performed. It received $75 000 cash in year 1 and the balance in year 2. Expenses paid during year 1 amounted to $45 000 but another $13 000 of expenses were not paid until year 2. Calculate the profit for year 1 based on the income and expense recognition criteria.

Reasoning
Income is recognised when an increase in future economic benefits related to an increase in an asset or a decrease of a liability has arisen that can be measured reliably. Expenses are recognised when a decrease in future economic benefits related to a decrease in an asset or an increase of a liability has arisen that can be measured reliably.

Solution
Profit is $42 000, calculated as $100 000 (invoiced) less $45 000 (cash expenses paid) and $13 000 (incurred but still unpaid) or $100 000 − ($45 000 + $13 000) = $42 000.

13.8 Integrating principles, concepts, standards and the *Conceptual Framework*

LEARNING OBJECTIVE 13.8 Integrate principles, concepts, standards and the *Conceptual Framework*.

The aim of this section is to provide an overview of GAAP and summarise how the various aspects of GAAP are related. This section is necessarily brief to keep it simple, and the detail is provided in this and other chapters throughout the text.

Summarising GAAP

Recall that GAAP consists of accounting standards, underlying accounting concepts and principles and the *Conceptual Framework*. Table 13.2 summarises the various aspects of GAAP. The text that follows summarises how it all fits together.

TABLE 13.2   Summarising the various aspects of GAAP

Generally accepted accounting principles (GAAP)		
Reporting question	**Conceptual element of GAAP**	**Source authority**
Who is required to prepare general purpose financial reports (preparers)?	Reporting entity	Statement of Accounting Concepts 1 (the Australian conceptual framework)
What is the purpose of general purpose financial reporting?	Objective of financial reporting	*Conceptual Framework*
Who uses general purpose financial reports (recipients)?	Users of financial reports	*Conceptual Framework*
What is reported in general purpose financial reports?	Qualitative characteristics and constraints	*Conceptual Framework*
How are items reported in general purpose financial reports?	Definition of elements and recognition criteria	*Conceptual Framework*
	Concepts and principles	Evolved over time, *Conceptual Framework*, accounting standards
	Rules	Accounting standards, Corporations Act
	Measurement	*Conceptual Framework*, accounting standards

Helpful hint: Recall that Chapter 2 on the reporting entity is yet to be added to the Conceptual Framework, *hence SAC 1 from the Australian conceptual framework is still used.*

Helpful hint 2: Statement of Accounting Concepts is abbreviated to SAC.

The section on the reporting entity in the Australian conceptual framework (SAC 1) defines which entities are required to prepare general purpose financial reports. Recall that a reporting entity is defined as an entity in which it is reasonable to expect the existence of users who depend on general purpose financial reports for information to enable them to make economic decisions.

The *Conceptual Framework* not only identifies *who* is required to report, it also explains the *objective* of general purpose financial reports. The objective is 'to provide financial information about the reporting entity that is useful to existing and potential investors, lenders and other creditors in making decisions about providing resources to the entity' (paragraph OB2). Once we know who is required to report and why they report, it is important to understand who is being reported to, that is, the users of general purpose financial reports.

Three categories of primary users are identified: existing potential investors, lenders and other creditors. These are summarised in figure 13.3. The *Conceptual Framework* also outlines *what* is reported in general purpose financial reports in the sections outlining the qualitative characteristics and constraint on financial information, and provides guidance on *how* items are reported. The guidance is provided in the sections on the definition of elements and recognition criteria. Thus, the *Conceptual Framework* is an important part of GAAP.

In addition to the *Conceptual Framework*, other aspects of GAAP outline *what* is reported in general purpose financial reports as well as *how* those items are reported in general purpose financial reports. The various other aspects include the concepts and principles, the accounting standards backed by legislation, and the measurement rules as outlined in the standards and the *Conceptual Framework*. Recall from earlier in this chapter that the concepts and principles have evolved over time and include the monetary principle, the accounting entity concept, the accounting period concept, the going concern principle, the cost principle and the full disclosure principle.

Integrating GAAP

It is important to recognise that the various aspects of GAAP do not operate in isolation, but are inter-related. Examples of the interrelationships have been provided throughout this chapter. For example, recall that reporting entities are required to prepare general purpose financial reports; the objective of general purpose financial reporting is to provide decision-useful information to users, and usefulness is dependent upon the information's qualitative characteristics. Recall also that the accounting period concept and the revenue and expense recognition criteria are interrelated. Are you beginning to see some of the links?

Before we complete this section, it is important to identify the *order* in which the various aspects of GAAP must be applied. After the Corporations Act, accounting standards are the first point of guidance for preparers. Accounting standards and authoritative interpretations of accounting standards must be followed as they have legislative backing, which means they are required by law. If the standards are silent on an accounting issue, preparers can seek guidance from the *Conceptual Framework*. The concepts and principles that traditionally underlie accounting are applied where there is no guidance on an issue in the *Conceptual Framework*. Further, if any conflicts arise between standards, the *Conceptual Framework* and concepts and principles, the various aspects of GAAP are still applied in the order listed above. To summarise, GAAP is applied as follows: first the Corporations Act, then accounting standards and interpretations are consulted, then the *Conceptual Framework*, and finally the underlying concepts and principles.

Helpful hint: The IFRS Interpretations Committee issues authoritative interpretations clarifying how to apply accounting standards. Standard-setting boards like the AASB adopt them.

13.9 Future developments in financial reporting

LEARNING OBJECTIVE 13.9 Appreciate, at an introductory level, various future developments in financial reporting.

Earlier in this chapter in the section on conceptual frameworks we explained that the International Accounting Standards Board (IASB) and the US Financial Accounting Standards Board (FASB) are currently conducting a joint project to develop the *Conceptual Framework*. Throughout the chapter we have discussed its current status and the proposed changes that have been developed to date.

Other developments in financial reporting include integrated reporting.

Integrated reporting

You have probably heard the term 'sustainability' used many times and in many contexts. One aspect focuses on the environment and humanity's impact on it. While each of us makes an imprint on our environment with daily use of electricity, driving of cars and adding huge amounts of household waste to public waste facilities, businesses have the capacity to have an even larger effect on the environment.

Mining, deforestation, toxic wastes in rivers and oceans, and natural resource consumption are only some of the negative impacts that businesses all around the world have on our natural environment. It is not sufficient just to talk about it; it is more important to look at what we are doing to try to reduce the effects. Have you ever thought about your impact on the environment? Are you doing anything to reduce your environmental footprint?

There is no one definition of sustainability; however, there appears to be some agreement that it is concerned with three main areas: economic, environmental and social. In a business context, most major businesses now report on their performance in relation to their economic, social and environmental impacts.

The social dimension of sustainability focuses on the impact of business on individuals as well as communities; for example, the negative impact of timber and mining companies on local communities and the lack of rights for workers in international 'sweatshops' who work under appalling working conditions and receive low pay. It also includes the positive impacts, such as the development of infrastructure, that businesses can bring to a local community.

The environmental dimension is concerned with the impact of business on the environment; for example, negative impacts such as air, water and land pollution or positive impacts such as supporting and replenishing ecosystems.

Sustainability is about making sure the social, economic and environmental needs of our world are met and kept healthy for future generations.

As you can imagine, running a successful organisation becomes even more complex when the leadership team needs to take into account the financial, social, environmental and economic implications of the day-to-day operations of the organisation and when developing future strategic plans. In the same way that we are moving towards one *Conceptual Framework* and one set of international standards for financial reporting, we need a framework and set of standards for sustainability reporting. The International Integrated Reporting Framework, developed by the International Integrated Reporting Council (IIRC), provides a set of guidelines to support organisations to integrate sustainability into their objectives and to account more fully for the value organisations create in the short, medium and long term. Improving the quality of information available to financial capital providers enables a more efficient and productive allocation of capital. Capital is used by organisations to create value over time. A more efficient and productive allocation of capital ultimately supports a more financially stable global economy. Integrated reporting (IR) is becoming the new norm for corporate reporting. The guidelines have been primarily prepared for business organisations but can be adapted for government and not-for-profit entities.

Figure 13.6 lists the IR framework's guiding principles and content elements that underpin the preparation of an integrated report.

FIGURE 13.6 International Integrated Reporting Framework guiding principles and content elements

Guiding principles

The following Guiding Principles underpin the preparation of an integrated report, informing the content of the report and how information is presented.

- *Strategic focus and future orientation:* An integrated report should provide insight into the organization's strategy, and how it relates to the organization's ability to create value in the short, medium and long term, and to its use of and effects on the capitals
- *Connectivity of information:* An integrated report should show a holistic picture of the combination, interrelatedness and dependencies between the factors that affect the organization's ability to create value over time
- *Stakeholder relationships:* An integrated report should provide insight into the nature and quality of the organization's relationships with its key stakeholders, including how and to what extent the organization understands, takes into account and responds to their legitimate needs and interests
- *Materiality:* An integrated report should disclose information about matters that substantively affect the organization's ability to create value over the short, medium and long term
- *Conciseness:* An integrated report should be concise
- *Reliability and completeness:* An integrated report should include all material matters, both positive and negative, in a balanced way and without material error
- *Consistency and comparability:* The information in an integrated report should be presented: (a) on a basis that is consistent over time; and (b) in a way that enables comparison with other organizations to the extent it is material to the organization's own ability to create value over time.

Integrated reporting supports integrated thinking, which improves the way organisations strategise, manage and report on how they go about creating value and the ways they minimise negative impacts on society, the economy and the environment. Putting it more simply, integrated reporting helps businesses take an integrated approach to their business and sustainability goals, in order to develop truly sustainable business practices.

In late 2017, the IIRC published the International Framework Implementation Feedback Summary Report on the first worldwide consultation to determine how companies were adopting integrated reporting since the introduction of the framework in 2013. The report revealed that over 1500 businesses in 62 countries globally were integrating the goals of sustainable development and financial stability to support their reporting. The report also noted that more guidance, examples and other measures were needed to further support the adoption of integrated reporting worldwide.

Further information about the International Integrated Reporting Council (IIRC), integrated reporting and future developments can be found on the IIRC website, www.integratedreporting.org.

Measuring environmental impact is a difficult task. Accounting has traditionally measured business activities in dollar terms. How can accountants measure the impact that businesses have on the environment? How do we measure the impact of an open-cut mine on the landscape? How do we measure the effects of an oil spill that kills marine life? Is it possible to standardise our measurement of environmental impacts?

LEARNING REFLECTION AND CONSOLIDATION

Review it

Explain possible developments in financial reporting that may occur in the future.

USING THE DECISION-MAKING TOOLKIT

Forden Ltd is a sizeable Australian car manufacturer selling cars all over the world. It employs many thousands of Australians in its factories and showrooms. Many of the shareholders of Forden Ltd attend

▶

annual general meetings to ensure management has been operating the business as efficiently and effectively as possible. The company has spent a significant amount for property, plant and equipment financed largely through borrowings.

Provided below are several transactions and events in relation to Forden Ltd for the year ended 30 June 2019.

1. The company paid for a 1-year insurance policy from Insurance Brokers Ltd on 1 March 2019, costing $12 000, paid in advance.
2. The company sub-leased part of its premises to Sheet Metals R Us Ltd for a period of 3 years, beginning 1 January 2019. Sheet Metals R Us Ltd paid $50 000 on this date, and is required to pay further instalments of $50 000 in 2020 and 2021.
3. Currently there is a lawsuit against the company as a local environmental group found the company was polluting a local lake with toxic waste from its factory. The payout is estimated to be somewhere between $100 000 and $200 000 if the lawsuit is successful.
4. In the past, the company has donated $20 000 each year to a local charity. This has been the case for the last 10 years. At 30 June 2019, nothing has been recorded in the accounts.
5. On 31 December 2018, the company issued a further $90 000 share capital to raise funds for a possible expansion.

Required

(a) For each transaction or event, determine the appropriate amount of income, expenses, assets, liabilities and equity that should be recorded by the company and record the journal entry. Include in your answer your reasoning based on the recognition criteria for the elements in financial statements as outlined in the *Conceptual Framework*. Ignore the effects of GST.

(b) Explain how Forden Ltd can determine if it is a reporting entity.

Solution

1. The company paid for a 1-year insurance policy from Insurance Brokers Ltd on 1 March 2019, costing $12 000, paid in advance. The company should recognise $8000 as an asset and $4000 for insurance expense.

Prepaid insurance	8 000	
Insurance expense	4 000	
Cash		12 000
(To record 8 months prepaid insurance July 2019–February 2020 and 4 months insurance expense March–June 2019)		

Reasoning

As outlined in the *Conceptual Framework*, assets should be recognised when it is probable that the future economic benefits will flow to the entity and the asset has a cost or value that can be measured with reliability. In this case, it is probable that the firm will enjoy the economic benefits of being insured for 8 months of the following accounting period and the amount can be reliably measured. Both recognition criteria have been met for assets and so the prepaid insurance asset should be recognised.

Expenses should be recognised when decreases in assets or increases in liabilities that result in a decrease in equity are probable. In this case, there was a decrease in cash and a decrease in equity for the insurance expense that can be measured reliably. Recall that an asset is not recognised in the statement of financial position if it is considered improbable that economic benefits will flow to the entity beyond the current accounting period. In this case, $4000 of the expenditure is recorded as an expense in the statement of profit or loss as it will not provide economic benefits beyond the current accounting period.

2. The company sub-leased part of its premises to Sheet Metals R Us Ltd for a period of 3 years, beginning on 1 January 2019. Sheet Metals R Us Ltd paid $50 000 on this date, and is required to pay further instalments of $50 000 in 2020 and 2021.

Cash	50 000	
Rent revenue		25 000
Rent received in advance		25 000
(To record revenue and revenue received in advance)		

Forden Ltd should recognise $50 000 as an asset (cash), $25 000 as income and $25 000 as a liability (rent received in advance).

As outlined in the *Conceptual Framework*, assets should be recognised when it is probable that the future economic benefits will flow to the entity and the asset has a cost or value that can be measured with reliability. In this case, $50 000 cash has flowed into the organisation, meeting both recognition criteria. Income should be recognised when an inflow of future economic benefits is probable and can be measured reliably. Generally, for a service business, revenue is recognised when the service is performed. In this case, at 30 June, Forden Ltd has completed the service (providing the rental premises to Sheet Metals R Us for 6 months) and the economic benefits (cash) have been received by the company and can therefore be reliably measured. All income recognition criteria have been satisfied.

Liabilities should be measured when it is probable that an outflow of resources embodying economic benefits will result from the settlement of a present obligation and the amount at which the settlement will take place can be measured reliably. As at 30 June 2019, Sheet Metals R Us Ltd has paid 6 months' rental income in advance. Hence, the present obligation, the outflow of resources, is to either provide rental premises for a period of 6 months or repay the cash. The amount has already been received so it can be determined reliably. Both criteria for recognising liabilities have been met.

3. Currently there is a lawsuit against the company as a local environmental group found the company was polluting a local lake with toxic waste from its factory. The payout is estimated to be somewhere between $100 000 and $200 000 if the lawsuit is successful.

    In this case, no amount would be recognised in the financial statements but would be disclosed in the notes, as a lawsuit of this nature is classified as a contingent liability. Contingent liabilities are liabilities for which the amount of the future sacrifice is so uncertain that it cannot be measured reliably, that do not satisfy the probability criterion, or are dependent upon the occurrence of an uncertain future event outside the control of the entity. Contingent liabilities are not recognised in the financial statements. However, information about contingent liabilities must be disclosed in the notes to the financial statements if they are material.

4. In the past, the company has always donated $20 000 each year to a local charity. This has been the case for the last 10 years. At 30 June 2019, nothing has been recorded in the accounts. In this case, no liability is recorded as there is currently no present obligation for an outflow of resources. This case does not meet the liability recognition criteria.

5. On 31 December 2018, the company issued a further $90 000 share capital to raise funds for a possible expansion. In this case, $90 000 should be recognised as an asset (cash) and $90 000 as equity (share capital).

Cash	90 000	
Share capital		90 000
(To record an increase in paid up capital)		

The inflow of cash meets both of the recognition criteria for assets as outlined in part 2. There are no specific recognition criteria for equity; hence, we can turn to the definitions of income and equity for guidance. Income is defined in the *Conceptual Framework* as 'increases in economic benefits during the accounting period in the form of inflows or enhancements of assets or decreases of liabilities that result in increases in equity, other than those relating to contributions from equity participants' (paragraph 4.25(a)). As this inflow of cash is from equity participants, it is not income.

Equity is defined in the *Conceptual Framework* as 'the residual interest in the assets of the entity after deducting all its liabilities' (paragraph 4.4(c)). Put simply, equity is what remains when we subtract liabilities from assets; that is, Equity = Assets − Liabilities.

In this case, Equity = $90 000 − $0. This equation shows that equity cannot be defined independently of the other elements in the statement of financial position; that is, equity is the residual.

We also know that equity can be presented in subcategories. In a corporate entity, equity can be classified into funds contributed by shareholders (share capital), retained earnings, and reserves representing appropriations of retained earnings.

▶

The Australian conceptual framework defines the reporting entity as an entity in which it is reasonable to expect the existence of users who depend on general purpose financial reports for information to enable them to make economic decisions (Statement of Accounting Concepts 1). Three main indicators are used to decide whether a business organisation is a reporting entity. First, if the entity is managed by individuals who are not the owners of the entity. Second, if the entity is politically or economically important. Third, if the entity is sizeable measured in relation to sales, assets, borrowings, customers and employees. Based on the criteria, and the information about Forden Ltd provided in the question, we can make a judgement about whether Forden Ltd is a reporting entity:

1. Separation of ownership and management — many of the shareholders of Forden Ltd attend annual general meetings to ensure management has been operating the business as efficiently and effectively as possible.
2. Is economically important — Forden Ltd employs many thousands of Australians.
3. Sizeable — sales — Forden Ltd is a sizeable Australian car manufacturer selling cars all over the world.
4. Sizeable — assets/borrowings — the company has spent a significant amount for property, plant and equipment financed largely through borrowings.

Based on the above analysis, it appears that Forden Ltd satisfies many of the indicators of a reporting entity and is likely to be a reporting entity.

SUMMARY

13.1 Explain and apply the concepts and principles underlying the recording of accounting information.

There are two concepts and four principles that underlie the recording of accounting information. In many cases, more than one principle or concept can apply to each transaction. For example, the monetary principle requires that only those things that can be expressed in monetary terms be included in the accounting records. Hence, all accounting transactions will be based on the monetary principle, but may also be based on others. The accounting entity concept states that every entity can be separately identified and accounted for. The accounting period concept states that the life of a business can be divided into artificial periods and that useful reports covering those periods can be prepared for the business. The going concern principle states that the business will remain in operation for the foreseeable future. The full disclosure principle requires that all circumstances and events that could make a difference to the decisions financial statement users might make should be disclosed in the financial statements. The cost principle states that all assets are initially recorded in the accounts at their purchase price or cost. It is important to note that the concepts and principles are not applied in isolation but in conjunction with accounting standards and the *Conceptual Framework*.

13.2 Describe the *Conceptual Framework for Financial Reporting* (the *Conceptual Framework*).

The *Conceptual Framework* consists of a set of concepts defining the nature, purpose and content of general purpose financial reporting to be followed by preparers and standard setters. It has four main components: the objective of general purpose financial reporting, the reporting entity (SAC 1), the definition of elements in financial statements, and the qualitative characteristics. A definition of the reporting entity is missing from the *Conceptual Framework* issued by the IASB, hence Australia retains SAC 1 from the Australian conceptual framework. Currently the joint project being undertaken by the IASB and US FASB is yet to be completed.

13.3 Explain the objective of general purpose financial reporting.

The objective of general purpose financial reporting is to provide financial information about the reporting entity that is useful to present and potential equity investors, lenders and other creditors in making their decisions about providing resources to the entity.

13.4 Identify the primary and other users, and their uses of financial reports.

Two categories of users of financial information are identified. Primary users include: equity investors, lenders and other creditors. Other users include: government agencies and members of the public, as well as suppliers, customers and employees (when not resource providers and therefore other creditors).

13.5 Explain the nature of a reporting entity.

The Australian conceptual framework defines the reporting entity as an entity in which it is reasonable to expect the existence of users who depend on general purpose financial reports for information to enable them to make economic decisions (Statement of Accounting Concepts 1). Three main indicators are used to decide whether a business organisation is a reporting entity. First, if the entity is managed by individuals who are not the owners of the entity. Second, if the entity is politically or economically important. Third, if the entity is sizeable measured in relation to sales, assets, borrowings, customers and employees. Based on these criteria, reporting entities include public companies and some large private companies as well as government authorities.

At the time of writing, the section on the reporting entity was not available in the *Conceptual Framework*. However, an exposure draft (ED/2010/2 *Conceptual Framework for Financial Reporting: The Reporting Entity*) was released which set out the proposed views on the reporting entity concept, and ED 2015/3 explores The Reporting Entity in detail.

13.6 Identify and apply the qualitative characteristics and constraint on financial reporting.

The objective of general purpose financial reporting is to provide useful information for decision making. Qualitative characteristics are the attributes that make the information in financial reports useful. The qualitative characteristics are classified as either fundamental or enhancing depending on how they affect the usefulness of financial information. Fundamental qualitative characteristics include relevance and faithful representation. Enhancing qualitative characteristics include comparability, verifiability, timeliness and understandability. While the qualitative characteristics are intended to provide users of financial statements with the most useful information for decision making, if taken to the extreme, the pursuit of useful financial information may be far too costly to the entity. Therefore, cost is a constraint on financial reporting.

13.7 Define assets, liabilities, equity, income and expenses and apply recognition criteria.

The *Conceptual Framework* defines assets, liabilities, equity, income and expenses, that is, each of the main elements included in financial statements. It also sets out the criteria for their recognition. Definitions and recognition criteria are crucial in recording transactions. In the *Conceptual Framework*, assets are defined as a resource controlled by the entity as a result of past events and from which future economic benefits are expected to flow to the entity. Liabilities are present obligations of the entity arising from past events, the settlement of which is expected to result in an outflow from the entity of resources embodying economic benefits. Equity is the residual interest in the assets of the entity after deducting all its liabilities. Income is defined as increases in economic benefits during the accounting period in the form of inflows or enhancements of assets or decreases of liabilities that result in increases in equity, other than those relating to contributions from equity participants. Expenses are decreases in economic benefits during the accounting period in the form of outflows or depletions of assets or incurrences of liabilities that result in decreases in equity, other than those relating to distributions to equity participants.

An item that meets the definition of an element included in financial statements should be recognised if it is probable that any future economic benefit associated with the item will flow to or from the entity, and the item has a cost or value that can be measured with reliability. These are the basic criteria that are applied when recognising assets, liabilities, revenues and expenses.

13.8 Integrate principles, concepts, standards and the *Conceptual Framework*.

Generally accepted accounting principles (GAAP) consist of accounting standards, underlying accounting concepts and principles, and the *Conceptual Framework*. The various aspects of GAAP do not operate in isolation, but are interrelated. For example, the accounting period concept and the revenue and expense recognition criteria are interrelated. The *order* in which the various aspects of GAAP must be applied is as follows: accounting standards are the first point of guidance for preparers and must be followed as they have legislative backing. Where the standards are silent on an accounting issue, preparers can seek guidance from the *Conceptual Framework*. The concepts and principles that underlie accounting are applied where there is no guidance in the *Conceptual Framework*.

13.9 Appreciate, at an introductory level, various future developments in financial reporting.

There are a number of future developments in financial reporting, including the International Accounting Standards Board (IASB) and US Financial Accounting Standards Board (FASB) joint project to develop a *Conceptual Framework*. This comprehensive project is yet to be completed. Hence, there are future developments on the horizon. Other developments in financial reporting include sustainability reporting.

DECISION-MAKING TOOLKIT — A SUMMARY

Decision/issue	Info needed for analysis	Tool or technique to use for decision	How to evaluate results to make decision
Is the entity required to provide general purpose financial reports?	Characteristics of the entity as outlined in SAC 1	Make a judgement about whether the entity is a reporting entity based on SAC 1 indicators. An organisation is more likely to be classified as a reporting entity if it has separation of ownership and management; is politically or economically important; and is sizeable in relation to sales, assets, borrowings, customers and employees.	If the entity is classified as a reporting entity, the entity is required to provide general purpose financial reports in accordance with GAAP.
At what point should the entity recognise (record) assets?	Need to understand the nature of the entity's business and the definition and recognition criteria for assets.	Assets should be recognised when it is probable that the future economic benefits will flow to the entity and the asset has a cost or value that can be measured with reliability.	Recognising assets too early overstates current period assets; recognising them too late understates current period assets.
At what point should the entity recognise (record) liabilities?	Need to understand the nature of the entity's business and the definition and recognition criteria for liabilities.	Liabilities should be recognised when it is probable that an outflow of resources embodying economic benefits will result from the settlement of a present obligation and the amount at which the settlement will take place can be measured reliably.	Recognising liabilities too early overstates current period liabilities; recognising them too late understates current period liabilities.
At what point should the entity recognise (record) income?	Need to understand the nature of the entity's business and the definition and the recognition criteria for income.	Income should be recognised when an increase in future economic benefits related to an increase in an asset or a decrease of a liability has arisen that can be measured reliably. Generally, for a service business, revenue is recognised when the service is performed. For a business that sells goods, revenue is recognised when the goods have been delivered.	Recognising income too early overstates current period income; recognising it too late understates current period income.
At what point should the entity recognise (record) expenses?	Need to understand the nature of the entity's business, and definition and recognition criteria for expenses.	Expenses should be recognised when a decrease in future economic benefits related to a decrease in an asset or an increase of a liability has arisen that can be measured reliably.	Recognising expenses too early overstates current period expenses; recognising them too late understates current period expense.

KEY TERMS

accounting entity concept A concept that every entity can be separately identified and accounted for. Economic events can be identified with a particular unit of accountability, so that financial reports are prepared from the perspective of the entity, not its owners or other parties.

accounting period concept An accounting concept that the economic life of an entity can be divided into discrete periods of time and that useful reports covering these periods can be prepared by the entity.

accrual-based accounting The accounting basis in which transactions and events are recorded in the periods in which they meet the recognition criteria for assets, liabilities, revenues and expenses. Recognition can occur before, as or after cash is paid or received.

assets Resources controlled by an entity as a result of past events and from which future economic benefits are expected to flow to the entity.

comparability Ability to compare the accounting information of different entities or the same entity over time because the same accounting measurement and principles are used.

conceptual framework A conceptual framework consists of a set of concepts to be followed by the preparers of financial statements and standard setters.

cost principle All assets are initially recorded in the accounts at their purchase price or cost.

differential reporting The application of different sets of rules for different categories of entities when preparing general purpose financial reports.

due process A consultation process where standard setters invite interested parties to contribute to the development of accounting standards.

elements in financial statements As defined in the *Conceptual Framework* include assets, liabilities, equity, income and expenses.

equity The residual interest in the assets of the entity after deducting all its liabilities; also known as shareholders' or owners' equity.

expenses Decreases in economic benefits during the accounting period in the form of outflows or depletions of assets or incurrences of liabilities that result in decreases in equity, other than those relating to distributions to equity participants.

faithful representation Information is a faithful representation of the economic phenomena it purports to represent if it is complete, neutral and free from material error.

full disclosure principle Accounting principle dictating that circumstances and events that make a difference to financial statement users should be disclosed.

general purpose financial reports Financial reports intended to meet the information needs of users who are unable to command reports to suit their specific needs.

generally accepted accounting principles (GAAP) Accounting concepts, principles, qualitative characteristics and standards having substantial authoritative support, and are recognised as a general guide for financial reporting purposes.

going concern principle States that the financial statements are prepared on a going concern basis unless management either intends to or must liquidate the business or cease trading.

income Increases in economic benefits during the accounting period in the form of inflows or enhancements of assets or decreases of liabilities that result in increases in equity, other than those relating to contributions from equity participants.

liability A present obligation of the entity arising from past events, the settlement of which is expected to result in an outflow from the entity of resources embodying economic benefits.

materiality The condition on reporting information if its omission or misstatement could influence the decisions of users of financial reports.

measurement The process of determining the monetary amounts at which the elements of the financial reports are to be recognised and carried in the statement of financial position and the statement of profit or loss.

monetary principle A principle stating that the items included in an entity's accounting records must be able to be expressed in monetary terms.

objective of general purpose financial reporting Is to provide financial information about the reporting entity that is useful to existing and potential investors, lenders and other creditors in making decisions about providing reserves to the entity.

recognition Process of recording in the statement of profit or loss or statement of financial position any item that meets the definition of an element in financial statements and satisfies the recognition criteria.

relevant Accounting information is considered to be relevant if the information makes a difference to a decision.

reporting entity An entity in which it is reasonable to expect the existence of users who depend on general purpose financial reports for information to enable them to make economic decisions.

resource providers The primary users of financial reports — those with a claim on the entity's resources as expected in the *Conceptual Framework*.

timeliness Whether the communication of financial information is in the time frame within which decisions are made.

understandability The extent to which information can be understood by proficient users.

verifiability The extent to which independent observers could reach a consensus that a particular depiction is a faithful representation of the economic phenomena it is meant to represent.

DEMONSTRATION PROBLEM

A number of independent situations are provided below:

(a) The owner of a small hairdressing salon recorded the purchase of a Mercedes sports car using funds from the business as indicated below. The car was purchased for personal use.

Motor vehicles	60 000	
Cash		60 000

(b) The size of the entity's land was listed in the statement of financial position (see below). The entity did not want to disclose an outdated land value.

Non-current assets	
Land	100 000 acres

(c) A company is currently undergoing a tax audit. It is probable that the company will be required to pay a substantial amount in unpaid taxes, but the exact amount will not be determined until the audit is complete. The entity has not recorded any amount in the financial statements.

(d) The auditors for a large company made an incorrect assumption that the company was headed for bankruptcy.

(e) A magazine company recorded $9000 cash received for 1-year subscriptions as income even though half related to magazines to be delivered in the next accounting period.

Cash	9 000	
Subscription revenue		9 000

Required

For each of the situations presented, explain which accounting principles or concepts have been violated. Where possible, provide the correct journal entry to record the transaction or event (ignore GST). Where relevant, provide any other applicable generally accepted accounting principles to support your answer.

PROBLEM-SOLVING STRATEGIES

1. Review the accounting concepts and principles discussed in the chapter.
2. Recall that the concepts and principles are not applied in isolation but in conjunction with other generally accepted accounting principles (GAAP).
3. GAAP in Australia is a combination of statutory rules (accounting standards) and interpretations, the concepts and principles, as well as the *Conceptual Framework*.
4. Determine which accounting concepts and principles have been violated and determine if there are any other relevant GAAP that apply to the situation.
5. Explain the violation based on the concepts and principles and other relevant GAAP.
6. Finally, prepare the correct journal entry where relevant (ignore GST).

SOLUTION TO DEMONSTRATION PROBLEM

(a) The accounting entity concept states that every entity can be separately identified and accounted for. It is important that the owners do not confuse the entity's transactions with their personal transactions, or the transactions of any other entity. The correct journal entry would be:

Drawings	60 000	
Cash		60 000

(b) This situation violates two accounting principles: the cost principle and the monetary principle. The monetary principle requires that only those things that can be expressed in monetary terms be included in the accounting records. The cost principle states that all assets are initially recorded in the accounts at their purchase price or cost. The entity should record its assets either at cost or fair value. Recall that, after the initial recognition of an asset at cost, an entity may choose to revalue its non-current assets to fair value. IAS 16/AASB 116 requires each class of property, plant and equipment to be measured on either the cost basis or the revalued basis. The entity could therefore recognise the land at its cost or at its revalued amount in the statement of financial position.

(c) The full disclosure principle requires that all circumstances and events that could make a difference to the decisions financial statement users might make should be disclosed in the financial statements. The fact that it is likely that the company will need to pay a substantial amount in unpaid taxes should be disclosed. This situation represents a contingent liability, which is a liability for which the amount of the future sacrifice is so uncertain that it cannot be measured reliably. While contingent liabilities are not recognised in the financial statements, information about contingent liabilities must be disclosed in the notes to the financial statements.

(d) This situation is a violation of the going concern principle. The going concern principle states that the business will remain in operation for the foreseeable future.

(e) This situation is a violation of the accounting period concept, which states that the life of a business can be divided into artificial periods and that useful reports covering those periods can be prepared for the business.

In this case, income was overstated by $4500. Also relevant to this situation are the recognition tests for assets, income and liabilities. As outlined in the *Conceptual Framework*, assets should be recognised when it is probable that the future economic benefits will flow to the entity and the asset has a cost or value that can be measured with reliability. In this case, $9000 cash has flowed into the organisation, meeting both recognition criteria, and is correctly recorded. Income should be recognised when an inflow of future economic benefits is probable and can be measured reliably. For a business that sells goods, revenue is recognised when the goods have been delivered. In this case, the company has provided goods worth $4500 and the economic benefits (cash) have been received by the company and can therefore be reliably measured. For the $4500, the income recognition criteria have been satisfied.

Liabilities should be measured when it is probable that an outflow of resources embodying economic benefits will result from the settlement of a present obligation and the amount at which the settlement will take place can be measured reliably. At the end of the accounting period, the magazine company customers have paid 6 months' magazine subscriptions in advance. Hence, the present obligation, the outflow of resources, is to either provide the magazines for a period of 6 months or repay the cash. The amount has already been received so it can be determined reliably. Both criteria for recognising liabilities have been met and the $4500 should be recorded as a liability.

The correct journal entry would be as follows:

Cash	9 000	
Subscription revenue		4 500
Subscription revenue received in advance		4 500

SELF-STUDY QUESTIONS

13.1 The accounting entity concept states that: **LO1**
- (a) the life of an entity can be divided into artificial periods.
- (b) useful reports covering an accounting period can be prepared for the entity.
- (c) activities of an entity should be kept separate and distinct from the activities of its owner(s).
- (d) the entity's assets and the owner's assets are accounted for together.

13.2 The cost principle states that: **LO1**
- (a) assets should be recorded at cost and subsequently adjusted when the market value changes.
- (b) every entity can be separately identified and accounted for.
- (c) all assets should be initially recorded at their cost.
- (d) only transaction data capable of being expressed in monetary amounts should be included in the accounting records.

13.3 Valuing assets at their market value rather than at their cost is inconsistent with the: **LO1**
- (a) monetary concept.
- (b) accounting entity concept.
- (c) cost principle.
- (d) all of the above.

13.4 Which of the following is not a concept or a principle underlying the recording of accounting information? **LO1**
- (a) The monetary concept.
- (b) The accounting entity concept.
- (c) The going concern principle.
- (d) The reliability principle.

13.5 The *Conceptual Framework*: **LO2**
- (a) consists of 4 sections.
- (b) includes the objective of general purpose financial reporting.
- (c) defines the elements in financial reports and the qualitative characteristics.
- (d) all of the above.

13.6 The *Conceptual Framework*: **LO2**
- (a) has been completed and is awaiting approval by the International Accounting and Reporting Board (IARB).
- (b) is in the process of being prepared by the IARB.
- (c) is the result of a joint project between the International Accounting Standards Board (IASB) and Financial Accounting Standards Board (FASB).
- (d) none of the above.

13.7 Due process is: **LO2**
- (a) where governments from around the world work together to prepare unified accounting standards.

(b) the process where all interested parties are consulted and invited to provide feedback when standards are developed.

(c) the process entities go through to collect cash when payments are due.

(d) the process reporting entities go through to make sure that all users who are due the information receive the information as part of the due process.

13.8 The objective of general purpose financial reporting as defined in the *Conceptual Framework* is to provide: **LO3**

(a) information that is useful to present and potential investors in making rational investment, credit and similar decisions.

(b) information that is useful to creditors in making rational investment, credit and similar decisions.

(c) financial information about the reporting entity that is useful to primary users in making decisions about providing resources to the entity.

(d) information that is useful to present and potential investors for making and evaluating decisions about the allocation of scarce resources.

13.9 The primary users of financial information as outlined in the *Conceptual Framework* are: **LO4**

(a) resource providers, recipients of goods and services and parties performing a review or oversight function.

(b) existing and potential equity investors, lenders and other creditors.

(c) resource providers, existing equity investors and other creditors.

(d) potential equity investors, recipients of goods and services and other creditors.

13.10 The primary users of financial information in the category of other creditors as outlined in the *Conceptual Framework* include: **LO4**

(a) employees, suppliers and customers.

(b) employees, lenders and customers.

(c) lenders, suppliers and customers.

(d) employees, lenders, customers and suppliers.

13.11 Accounting entities are: **LO5**

(a) all reporting entities.

(b) never reporting entities.

(c) sometimes also reporting entities.

(d) both accounting entities and reporting entities.

13.12 The criteria used to determine if an entity is a reporting entity include: **LO5**

(a) separation of ownership from management.

(b) size measured in relation to sales, assets, borrowings, customers and employees.

(c) political and economic importance.

(d) all of the above.

13.13 Reporting entities generally don't include: **LO5**

(a) public companies.

(b) government authorities.

(c) some large private companies.

(d) sole traders.

13.14 The enhancing qualitative characteristics of financial information outlined in the *Conceptual Framework* include: **LO6**

(a) understandability, timeliness, verifiability and comparability.

(b) understandability, verifiability, reliability and comparability.

(c) understandability, relevance, faithful representation and timeliness.

(d) understandability, relevance, reliability and confidentiality.

13.15 Which of the following is a fundamental qualitative characteristic of information as outlined in the *Conceptual Framework*? **LO6**
   (a) Comparability.
   (b) Understandability.
   (c) Faithful representation.
   (d) Verifiability.

13.16 Which of the following is considered to be a constraint of providing financial information in the *Conceptual Framework*? **LO6**
   (a) Full disclosure.
   (b) Understandability.
   (c) Materiality.
   (d) Cost.

13.17 In the *Conceptual Framework*, an asset is defined as a resource: **LO7**
   (a) owned by the entity as a result of past events and from which future economic benefits are expected to flow to the entity.
   (b) controlled by the entity from which future economic benefits are expected to flow to the entity.
   (c) controlled by the entity as a result of past events and from which future economic benefits are expected to flow to the entity.
   (d) controlled by the entity as a result of past events and from which future economic benefits are expected to flow out of the entity.

13.18 In the *Conceptual Framework*, expenses are defined as: **LO7**
   (a) decreases in economic benefits during the accounting period in the form of outflows or depletions of assets or incurrences of liabilities that result in decreases in equity, other than those relating to distributions to equity participants.
   (b) increases in economic benefits during the accounting period in the form of outflows or depletions of assets or incurrences of liabilities that result in decreases in equity, other than those relating to distributions to equity participants.
   (c) decreases in economic benefits during the accounting period in the form of inflows of assets or incurrences of liabilities that result in decreases in equity, other than those relating to distributions to equity participants.
   (d) decreases in economic benefits during the accounting period in the form of outflows or depletions of assets or incurrences of liabilities that result in decreases in equity, including those relating to distributions to equity participants.

13.19 As outlined in the *Conceptual Framework*, income should be recognised when: **LO7**
   (a) an inflow of future economic benefits is certain and can be measured reliably.
   (b) the cash is received.
   (c) an inflow of future economic benefits is probable and can be measured reliably.
   (d) an outflow of future economic benefits is probable and can be measured reliably.

13.20 Which of the following statements is not true in relation to the definitions and/or recognition criteria for elements in financial reports as outlined in the *Conceptual Framework*? **LO7**
   (a) The definitions of equity, income and expenses are related to the definitions of assets and liabilities.
   (b) The measurement of equity, income and expenses is dependent on the measurement of assets and liabilities.
   (c) The measurement of income and expenses is dependent on the measurement of equity.
   (d) Income is defined as increases in economic benefits during the accounting period in the form of inflows or enhancements of assets or decreases of liabilities that result in increases in equity, other than those relating to contributions from equity participants.

13.21 When preparing general purpose financial reports, the elements of GAAP should be applied in the following order: **LO8**

(a) underlying concepts and principles, accounting standards, the *Conceptual Framework*.

(b) accounting standards, the *Conceptual Framework*, underlying concepts and principles.

(c) the *Conceptual Framework*, accounting standards, underlying concepts and principles.

(d) none of the above.

13.22 Which of the following has/have been identified as future developments for financial reporting? **LO8**

(a) A definition of the reporting entity as part of the *Conceptual Framework* for financial reporting.

(b) Integrated reporting.

(c) Emissions trading as part of sustainability reporting.

(d) All of the above.

QUESTIONS

13.1 Explain the concepts and principles that underlie accounting.

13.2 Explain how accounting concepts, principles and recognition criteria are interrelated and provide guidance when recording certain transactions. Provide at least one example to illustrate your answer.

13.3 What is the *Conceptual Framework*?

13.4 What are the advantages or benefits of the *Conceptual Framework* for financial reporting? Do you believe that these benefits can actually be achieved?

13.5 Explain what is meant by the reporting entity concept as proposed in the exposure draft ED/2010/2. In your answer, discuss the feature. Do you believe that the accounting entity concept is helpful?

13.6 Differential reporting means applying different sets of rules for different categories of entities preparing general purpose financial reports. Identify the different categories of entities and explain their reporting requirements.

13.7 Explain the objective of general purpose financial reporting as defined in the *Conceptual Framework*. Why is it necessary to have an objective?

13.8 Identify the primary users and their uses of financial information as outlined in the *Conceptual Framework*.

13.9 Compare and contrast the primary users of financial reports and their information needs as outlined in the *Conceptual Framework* with the other users of financial reports.

13.10 Provide a brief summary of each of the qualitative characteristics and the constraint on providing financial information as outlined in the *Conceptual Framework*.

13.11 Two qualitative characteristics that financial information should possess are relevance and faithful representation. Explain these concepts and discuss whether you believe one is more important than the other, or if they are equally important?

13.12 The *Conceptual Framework* identifies a number of qualitative characteristics that financial information should possess if it is to be useful for decision making. Faithful representation is one such characteristic. Do you believe that financial information can, in reality, be neutral and free from material error? Explain your answer.

13.13 The *Conceptual Framework* outlines a constraint on providing financial reports. Explain this constraint.

13.14 General purpose financial reports are only one source of information for users when making a variety of decisions. What other sources of information are available to users and why is it important that they obtain them? Support your discussion with examples.

13.15 Explain why general purpose financial reports should be seen more as models of transactions and events that have occurred in relation to an entity rather than as an exact depiction of transactions and events.

13.16 The *Conceptual Framework* identifies qualitative characteristics as fundamental or enhancing. Describe each of the qualitative characteristics. What makes a qualitative characteristic fundamental or enhancing? Do you believe this is an important distinction?

13.17 Cost is a constraint that limits the information provided by financial reporting. Explain whether fundamental or enhancing qualitative characteristics can be sacrificed to reduce costs. Justify the reasons for your answer.

13.18 Define liabilities and outline the recognition criteria for liabilities as outlined in the *Conceptual Framework*.

13.19 Define income and expenses as outlined in the *Conceptual Framework*.

13.20 Define assets and explain the recognition criteria for assets as outlined in the *Conceptual Framework*.

13.21 How is equity defined in the *Conceptual Framework*? Provide examples of transactions or events that affect equity. Provide examples of transactions and events that do not affect equity.

13.22 At what point should an entity recognise income? Provide examples to support your explanation.

13.23 What are the two basic common recognition criteria that are applied to assets, liabilities, revenues and expenses?

13.24 There are four bases of measurement outlined in the *Conceptual Framework*. Briefly describe each of these. Identify common alternative measurement bases that can be found in general purpose financial reports.

13.25 Briefly outline how the elements of GAAP are applied.

13.26 Outline two future developments in financial reporting.

BRIEF EXERCISES

BE13.1 Identify the concepts and principles underlying accounting.   **LO1**

The statements below refer to the concepts and principles underlying the recording of accounting information. Identify if they are true or false.

(a) The accounting period concept states that the life of a business can be divided into various periods to more accurately reflect the profit and smooth out seasonal fluctuations in profit between different periods.

(b) The cost principle states that all accounting transactions and events are recorded in the accounts at their cost.

(c) The going concern principle states that the business will remain in operation for the foreseeable future.

BE13.2 Apply the concepts and principles underlying accounting.   **LO1**

A number of independent economic events are presented below. Comment on each case. In your discussion, identify if any concepts and/or principles underlying the recording of accounting transactions have been incorrectly applied.

(a) The owner of the business included his personal vehicle expenses in the entity's statement of profit or loss.

(b) A major lawsuit has been filed against a children's toy manufacturer as a number of children were injured due to the manufacturer's products not complying with safety standards. The solicitors acting for the company believe there is a high probability of the company having to pay out a large amount in damages; however, nothing is reported in the financial statements as the amount is unknown.

(c) Land and buildings were reported in the statement of financial position at their estimated selling price. This amount was substantially higher than the outdated cost figures.

BE13.3 **Identify and explain the concepts and principles underlying accounting.** **LO1**

Each of the concepts and principles underlying the recording of accounting transactions is *incorrectly* stated below. Correct each of the statements.

(a) The going concern principle states that if the business will remain in operation for the foreseeable future, assets should not be recorded at cost but at the amount they can be sold for. This will provide current and future investors with more up-to-date information with which to assess future profitability.

(b) The full disclosure principle requires that any circumstances and events that might be of interest to financial statement users should be disclosed in the financial statements.

(c) The accounting entity concept states that the personal transactions of the owners should be accounted for separately from the entity's transactions, unless the entity is a sole trader or a partnership as they are not separate legal entities.

BE13.4 **Describe conceptual frameworks.** **LO2**

A number of statements in relation to conceptual frameworks are provided below. Identify if they are true or false.

(a) Prior to 1970 there was no generally accepted theory of financial reporting.

(b) One of the many theories of accounting is the capitalist theory of accounting.

(c) The development of a generally accepted theory of accounting is necessary to improve the standard-setting process and consistency in accounting practice.

(d) A conceptual framework for accounting consists of a set of concepts defining the nature, purpose and content of general purpose financial reporting.

(e) Preparers of general purpose financial reports are bound by law to follow the *Conceptual Framework*.

BE13.5 **Identify the primary and other users of financial reports.** **LO4**

In the table listing *categories of users* provided below, place a tick (✓) in the correct column to identify which user categories are primary users or other users as outlined in the *Conceptual Framework*.

User category	Primary users	Other users
Potential equity investors		
Regulators		
Existing equity investors		
Lenders		
Members of the public		
Other creditors		
Financial advisers		
Customers		

BE13.6 **Identify the primary and other users of financial reports.** **LO4**

A list of users and a list of financial information needs are provided. Identify the most likely information needs for each user by drawing a line between the columns to link each user with their information needs. One example is provided to illustrate the process.

Users	Information needs
Managers	Information to calculate the amount of tax owing and whether the entity complies with tax laws
Investors	Information on whether an entity will continue to honour product warranties and support its product lines
Creditors	Information to determine whether the entity is operating within prescribed rules
Customers	Information on whether the entity has the ability to pay increased wages and benefits, and offer job security
Employees and trade unions	Information to determine whether to grant credit based on risks and ability of the entity to repay debts
Government authorities	Information to determine whether to invest based on future profitability, return or capital growth
Regulatory agencies	Information to plan, organise and run a business

BE13.7 Identify and apply the indicators of a reporting entity. **LO5**

Identify which of the following indicators is more likely to result in an entity being classified as a reporting entity.

(a) The entity is owned and managed by the same individuals.
(b) The entity is politically or economically important.
(c) The entity is sizeable measured in relation to customer satisfaction.
(d) The entity is sizeable measured in relation to sales.
(e) The entity has a small number of assets.
(f) The entity has large borrowings.

BE13.8 Identify the qualitative characteristics and constraint on financial reports. **LO6**

From the list below, identify which of the items are considered to be qualitative characteristics or a constraint on financial information as outlined in the *Conceptual Framework*.

(a) Cost
(b) Reliability
(c) Comparability
(d) Understandability
(e) Affordability
(f) Transferability
(g) Timeliness
(h) Relevance

BE13.9 Identify the qualitative characteristics of financial information. **LO6**

In the *Conceptual Framework*, the qualitative characteristics underlying financial reporting are classified as fundamental and enhancing. From the list below, identify which are fundamental and which are enhancing.

(a) Relevance
(b) Materiality
(c) Timeliness
(d) Comparability
(e) Cost
(f) Verifiability
(g) Conservatism
(h) Faithful representation
(i) Understandability

BE13.10 Define the elements in financial statements as outlined in the *Conceptual Framework*. **LO7**

Each of the following definitions has one or more errors. Identify the error and correct it.

(a) **Assets** are defined in the *Conceptual Framework* as future economic benefits controlled by the entity as a result of past events and from which resources are expected to flow from the entity.

(b) **Expenses** are defined in the *Conceptual Framework* as increases in economic benefits during the accounting period in the form of outflows or depletions of assets or incurrences of liabilities that result in decreases in equity, other than those relating to distributions to equity participants.

(c) **Equity** is defined in the *Conceptual Framework* as the residual interest in the equity of the entity after deducting all of its liabilities.

(d) **Income** is defined in the *Conceptual Framework* as increases in economic benefits during the accounting period in the form of inflows or enhancements of assets or decreases of liabilities that result in increases in equity, as well as contributions from equity participants.

EXERCISES

E13.1 Apply the concepts and principles underlying accounting. **LO1**

Brief definitions of the concepts and principles that underlie the recording of accounting transactions are provided below.

- The **accounting entity concept** states that every entity can be separately identified and accounted for.
- The **accounting period concept** states that the life of a business can be divided into artificial periods and that useful reports covering those periods can be prepared for the business.
- The **going concern principle** states that the business will remain in operation for the foreseeable future.
- The **cost principle** states that all assets are initially recorded in the accounts at their purchase price or cost.
- The **full disclosure principle** requires that all circumstances and events that could make a difference to the decisions financial statement users might make should be disclosed in the financial statements.

Required

For each of the definitions listed above, provide one transaction that illustrates the application of that concept or principle.

E13.2 Apply the concepts and principles underlying accounting. **LO1**

Slavko Mitrovic is one of the owners of Salami 4 U, a small business that manufactures and sells organic salami and other smallgoods. Slavko also manages the business on a part-time basis, sharing responsibilities with the other partners. Using the business cheque book by accident, Slavko recently purchased a car for his beautiful wife Natasha Mitrovic as a birthday present. Natasha is a sales representative for a large computer company and will be using the car in her job. Based on the cheque butt, the accountant recorded the transaction in the accounts of Salami 4 U as follows.

Motor vehicles	20 000	
Cash		20 000
(Purchase of motor vehicle)		

One day later, Slavko realised his error and decided to purchase some salami-making equipment worth $20 000 out of his personal account to correct his error. Not realising the transactions were linked, the accountant recorded the transaction in the accounts as follows.

Plant and equipment	20 000	
Owner's capital—Slavko Mitrovic		20 000
(Capital contribution by owner—purchase of equipment for business by Slavko Mitrovic from personal funds)		

Required

(a) For each of the transactions recorded above:
  (i) Determine if they have been recorded correctly or incorrectly based on the concepts and principles that underlie the recording of accounting transactions.
  (ii) If any transactions have been recorded incorrectly, discuss how the accounting concept(s) or principle(s) have been breached.
  (iii) If any transactions have been recorded incorrectly, prepare BOTH the correcting entry to correct the recorded error as well as the correct journal entry that should have been recorded by the accountant in the first instance. Ignore GST.
(b) What if the car had been purchased for use by Slavko when he was working only in the business? Under these circumstances, explain whether the transactions have been recorded correctly or incorrectly based on the concepts and principles that underlie the recording of accounting transactions.

E13.3 Apply the concepts, principles, recognition criteria and constraint underlying accounting.

LO1, 6, 7

A list of concepts, principles and recognition criteria are provided below.

1	Accounting entity concept
2	Monetary principle
3	Accounting period concept
4	Cost principle
5	Materiality
6	Full disclosure principle
7	Going concern principle
8	Revenue recognition criteria
9	Expense recognition criteria

Required

For each of the situations provided below, identify, by number, the applicable accounting concept, principle, recognition criterion or constraint. Do not use each number more than once.
(a) Plant assets were not reported at liquidation value in the entity's accounts. (*Hint:* Do not use the cost principle.)
(b) Personal and business record keeping was kept separate for the entity.
(c) All relevant financial information was reported in the general purpose financial reports for the entity.
(d) The dollar was used as the 'measuring stick' to report financial performance and position.
(e) Accounting standards were followed for all items that were reasonably expected to affect decisions made by users of financial statements.
(f) Information on financial performance was provided for the year ending June 2020.
(g) Expenses were recorded when the flow of economic benefits from the entity was probable and could be reliably measured.
(h) Market value changes subsequent to purchase were not recorded in the financial statements.

E13.4 Apply the concepts, principles, recognition criteria and constraint underlying accounting.

LO1, 6, 7

A number of accounting reporting situations are provided below.
(a) Tick Tock Ltd recognises revenue at the end of the production cycle but before sale has been made. The selling price as well as the quantity that can be sold are not certain.

(b) Cap, Caps and Hats Ltd is a medium-sized firm listed on the Australian and New Zealand securities exchanges. It is currently in its third year of operations; however, it has not issued one set of financial statements. (*Hint:* Do not use the full disclosure principle.)

(c) Books and More Ltd is carrying inventory at its current net realisable value of $90 000. Inventory had an original cost of $110 000.

(d) Aunty Jane's Toy Emporium Ltd reports only current assets and current liabilities on its statement of financial position. Property, plant and equipment and bills payable are reported as current assets and current liabilities, respectively. Property, plant and equipment is reported at the amount for which it could be sold at short notice. Liquidation of the entity is unlikely.

(e) Surf's Up Ltd has inventory on hand that cost $400 000. The entity reports inventory on its statement of financial position at its current net realisable value of $425 000.

(f) Brad Spit, the manager of Top Time Movies Ltd, purchased a computer for his personal use. He paid for the computer with company funds and debited the Computers account.

Required

For each situation, explain whether a concept, principle, recognition criterion or constraint has been violated. Provide only one answer for each situation.

E13.5 **Apply the concepts, principles, recognition criteria and constraint underlying accounting.**

LO1, 6, 7

A list of concepts, principles and recognition criteria are provided below.

1	Accounting entity concept
2	Monetary principle
3	Accounting period concept
4	Cost principle
5	Full disclosure principle
6	Going concern principle
7	Revenue recognition criteria
8	Expense recognition criteria

Required

For each of the items in the list above, prepare a journal entry (ignore GST) and explain how the journal entry is guided by the accounting concept, principle, recognition criterion or constraint. For example, for the accounting entity concept:

Drawings	25 000	
Cash		25 000
(Purchase of motor vehicle from entity funds for personal use)		

In this case, the accounting entity concept guides the recording of the transaction. The accounting entity concept indicates that the personal transactions of the owner should be recorded separately from the transactions of the entity. Hence, the purchase of the vehicle for personal use out of company funds is recorded as a withdrawal of capital rather than an asset of the entity.

E13.6 **Apply recognition criteria as outlined in the *Conceptual Framework*.** **LO7**

Liabilities can be classified as provisions, contingent liabilities or other liabilities.

Required

Classify each of the following liabilities as (1) provisions, (2) contingent liabilities or (3) other liabilities.

(a) An unquantifiable liability for restoring a polluted river.

(b) Accounts payable.

(c) Wages payable.

(d) Obligation for unexpired warranty costs.

(e) Trade creditors.

(f) Obligations for employees' long service leave.

(g) Accrued interest liability.

(h) Mortgage loan.

(i) Guarantee for another's loan, which will be payable if the other party defaults.

E13.7 Apply recognition criteria underlying accounting. **LO7**

Computer Games Ltd reported a profit of $50 560 for the year ending 31 December 2019. However, upon closer examination of the accounting records, the chief financial officer noticed the following important information:

1. Service revenues included an advance of $20 000 for computer games to be delivered in March of the following year.

2. There was $2300 of advertising supplies on hand at 31 December that was recorded as supplies expense.

3. Prepaid insurance included an amount of $12 000, which is the whole amount paid on 1 October 2019 for a 1-year policy.

4. The following invoices had not been paid: advertising for week of 24 December, $2500; repairs made on 10 December, $2000; and electricity expense, $800.

5. At 31 December, 2 days' wages had not been accrued or paid, amounting to $400.

6. The business took out a loan of $240 000 on 1 January 2019 at an annual interest rate of 10%. The amount for interest expense for the month of December was not accrued.

Required

Explain the generally accepted accounting principles that were not followed in preparing the statement of profit or loss and their effect (under or overstatement) on the results.

E13.8 Apply recognition criteria as outlined in the *Conceptual Framework*. **LO7**

Using the information provided in E13.7 above:

(a) Prepare the journal entries to record the missing transactions or events. Ignore GST.

(b) What if the accountant had in fact recorded the missing transactions correctly? Calculate the correct income for the year ended 31 December 2019. Show all workings.

E13.9 Apply recognition criteria as outlined in the *Conceptual Framework*. **LO7**

A list of independent transactions is provided below.

(a) Steel Tubes Ltd received $200 000 cash from a customer in December 2019 in payment for special-purpose tubing that is to be manufactured and shipped to the customer in February 2020. Ignore GST.

(b) Tough Tyres Ltd received an item of equipment as settlement for goods sold on credit for $3000. Ignore GST.

(c) The court has ordered Mining Deep Ltd to repair the environmental damage the mining has caused. The company has not yet received a quote of the estimated costs from a specialist environmental repair landscaping company and, as such, does not know the cost of the repair.

Required

Identify if an asset, liability, revenue or expense should be recognised in the year ending December 2019 and prepare the journal entry to record each transaction. Ignore GST.

E13.10 Apply definition and recognition criteria for assets. **LO7**

The *Conceptual Framework* defines assets and outlines a number of criteria for their recognition. Shiny Shoes Ltd has the following items:

(a) Large inventory of shoes.

(b) One antique boot in a display cabinet donated by a customer. The boot looks nice in the store and is a talking point; however, it has no commercial value as the other boot is missing.

(c) Shoes held on consignment.

(d) Three staff members.

(e) Shelving to display shoes.

Required

For each of the items listed above, explain whether you would recognise it as an asset in the statement of financial position. Refer to the definition and recognition criteria outlined in the *Conceptual Framework* to support your answer.

E13.11 Apply definition and recognition criteria for liabilities.   **LO7**

The *Conceptual Framework* defines liabilities and outlines a number of criteria for their recognition. a-Forden and a-Holden Custom Cars Ltd identifies the following items:

(a) Purchased tyres, glass and steel on account.

(b) Received $100 000 in deposits for custom cars to be built in the next financial period.

(c) Employed two new staff members and agreed to pay them $75 000 per annum. They begin work next week.

(d) One of a-Forden and a-Holden Custom Cars Ltd's customers is sueing the company as he is not happy with the colour scheme the company used to paint the custom car. The customer chose the colour scheme at the time of signing the contract and has now changed his mind. The lawsuit is for $15 000. a-Forden and a-Holden Custom Cars believe they might lose the case.

(e) When constructing a car in the factory, one of a-Forden and a-Holden Custom Cars Ltd's employees dumped excess paint and other waste products into the local river running behind the factory. The company has been ordered by the court to pay damages; however, the exact amount is yet to be determined.

Required

For each of the items listed above, explain whether you would recognise it as a liability in the statement of financial position. Refer to the definition and recognition criteria outlined in the *Conceptual Framework* to support your answer.

E13.12 Apply definition and recognition criteria for revenues.   **LO7**

The *Conceptual Framework* defines revenues and outlines a number of criteria for their recognition. Surfin' Magazines Ltd identifies the following independent transactions and events:

(a) Received $24 000 in subscriptions for magazines to be delivered once per month for the next 12 months.

(b) Received dividends from IAG for shares owned by the business.

(c) Paid interest on a loan to purchase a delivery vehicle.

(d) Received a discount for early payment of a supplier's invoice.

(e) Delivered magazines for the month for customers who had paid in advance.

(f) Delivered magazines and invoices to customers who had not prepaid their subscriptions.

Required

For each of the items listed above, explain whether you would recognise it as revenue in the statement of profit or loss. Refer to the definition and recognition criteria outlined in the *Conceptual Framework* to support your answer.

E13.13 Apply definition and recognition criteria for expenses.   **LO7**

The *Conceptual Framework* defines expenses and outlines a number of criteria for their recognition. Night Golf Course Ltd identifies the following independent transactions and events:

(a) Paid $240 000 for public liability insurance for the next 12 months.

(b) Paid dividends to shareholders.

(c) Paid interest on the mortgage on the property.

(d) Allowed $2000 in discounts for early payment of accounts due from purchases made by customers at the pro shop.

(e) Received $3 million from members who paid their yearly fee in advance.

(f) Received the electricity bill which had not yet been paid.

Required

For each of the items listed above, explain whether you would recognise it as an expense in the statement of profit or loss. Refer to the definition and recognition criteria outlined in the *Conceptual Framework* to support your answer.

PROBLEM SET

PSA13.1 Identify the concepts or principles violated. **LO1**

Beautiful Wedding Memorabilia Pty Ltd had a number of major business transactions and events during 2020. An extract is provided below.

(a) Merchandise inventory with a cost of $68 000 is reported at its net realisable value of $100 000 in the statement of financial position.

(b) The owner of Beautiful Wedding Memorabilia Pty Ltd, Ima McBride, used company funds to purchase a computer for personal use for $2500. She recorded it as a decrease in Cash and an increase in Office Equipment.

(c) The manager of Beautiful Wedding Memorabilia Pty Ltd wanted to make its 2020 profit look better, so she added in memorabilia sales that occurred on the first two days of 2021.

(d) The manager of Beautiful Wedding Memorabilia Pty Ltd wanted to make its 2020 profit look even better, so she did not record an interest payment of $15 000 incurred but not due to be paid until 1 January 2021.

(e) Beautiful Wedding Memorabilia Pty Ltd is currently being sued by a bride as she was injured when one of the company's wedding snow globes shattered. It is expected that the company will have to pay damages; however, the amount is currently uncertain and so the accountant has decided not to include it anywhere in the financial statements.

Required

For each situation:

(a) Identify if any concept or principle has been violated.

(b) Discuss what should have been done and provide evidence for your answer.

(c) Record the correct journal entries and discuss the correct accounting treatment for each of the transactions or events as appropriate.

PSA13.2 Apply concepts, principles, constraint and recognition criteria. **LO1, 6, 7**

The accountant for Moo Cow Farm Ltd has identified the following independent situations.

(a) Fence repair tools are expensed when purchased.

(b) Unpaid farm hand salaries are recognised as an expense.

(c) The accountant assumes that the dollar is the measuring unit used to prepare general purpose financial reports.

(d) The accountant separates financial information into time periods for reporting purposes.

(e) The market value changes subsequent to purchase of farm land, and buildings are not recorded in the accounts. (*Hint:* Do not use the revenue recognition criteria.)

(f) The accountant ensures that personal and business record keeping are separately maintained.

(g) The auditor ensures that all relevant financial information is reported.

(h) The accountant ensures the recognition of revenues when increases in assets or decreases in liabilities result in a reliably measured increase in equity, other than capital contributions.

(i) The accountant would like to provide more detailed information to shareholders; however, it would be too costly to provide over and above what is currently required.

Required

Explain the accounting concept, principle constraint or recognition criterion that describes each of the situations listed above. Use the list of concepts, principles, constraint and recognition criteria provided below and do not use each one more than once. Refer to the relevant GAAP in your discussion to justify your answer.

(a) Accounting entity concept
(b) Going concern principle
(c) Monetary principle
(d) Accounting period concept
(e) Full disclosure principle
(f) Revenue recognition criteria
(g) Expense recognition criteria
(h) Cost principle
(i) Materiality

PSA13.3 Describe the *Conceptual Framework*. LO2

A first-year accounting student provided the following answer to an examination question on the *Conceptual Framework*:

What is the *Conceptual Framework*? (15 marks)

The *Conceptual Framework* looks like a window that you can see the world through and has four sections. It talks about accounting concepts. It talks about what accounting is about. It tells accountants how to prepare financial statements. It is helpful to standard setters.

The four parts are:

(a) the accounting entity, which states that the transactions of the owners should be separate from that of the business

(b) the objective of businesses, which states the objective of a business is to make profit to be able to pay dividends to the owners

(c) the qualitative characteristics, which include the monetary principle, the accounting period concept and the going concern and cost principles

(d) the definition of elements in the financial statements, which is the last window. For example, accounts receivable is defined as 'the right to receive cash upon the sale of goods or provision of services to a customer'.

Required

Assume you are the teacher marking this answer.

(a) For each of the points made by the student in their answer, identify which are correct and which are incorrect. Justify your assessment of their work by referring to the *Conceptual Framework* to support your discussion.

(b) Provide the student with a model or correct answer to the question to assist their learning.

PSA13.4 Explain the objective of general purpose financial reports. LO3

In a recent annual general meeting of Thrifty Tyres Ltd, one of the shareholders stated: 'the objective of general purpose financial reports is to make the directors and management accountable'. The other shareholders at the meeting cheered and agreed.

Required

As a director of Thrifty Tyres Ltd, you feel obligated to respond to the shareholders to ensure they understand the objective of general purpose financial reports as defined in the *Conceptual Framework*. Your response includes the following points:

(a) Explain two suggested alternative objectives for general purpose financial reporting.

(b) Identify the objective for general purpose financial reporting adopted in the *Conceptual Framework*.

(c) What information about management and the governing board would be useful to users as outlined in the *Conceptual Framework*?

PSA13.5 Identify the primary and other users of financial reports.   **LO4**

A group of first-year accounting students are in the library preparing their homework exercises for next week's class. A disagreement arises as one student claims that 'in the *Conceptual Framework* it suggests that the primary users of general purpose financial reports are the resource providers. That means the shareholders. I think this is unfair as in the *Conceptual Framework* creditors should be identified as the primary users as they have more to lose.' A second student steps in and says 'well you really don't have a clue. You have it all mixed up. I think you need to review the *Conceptual Framework* before you confuse everyone.'

Required

You have just reviewed the users of general purpose financial reports as outlined in the *Conceptual Framework* and the proposed improved conceptual framework and have been asked to explain your findings to the other students. In your answer, you include a discussion of:

(a) the primary categories of users as identified in the *Conceptual Framework*

(b) the other users as identified in the *Conceptual Framework*

(c) why the *Conceptual Framework* distinguishes between primary and other users.

PSA13.6 Explain the nature of a reporting entity.   **LO5**

The following statement was set as a class discussion question: 'All accounting entities are reporting entities'.

Required

(a) Explain the accounting entity concept.

(b) Define a reporting entity as outlined in the *Framework*.

(c) Do you agree with the statement above? Explain your answer.

(d) Outline the three main indicators used to decide whether a business organisation is a reporting entity.

(e) Based on the main indicators outlined in your answer to part (d), identify the main categories of organisation that are generally classified as reporting entities.

(f) Why is it important to link the definition of a reporting entity to the objective of financial reporting?

PSA13.7 Identify and apply the qualitative characteristics of financial information.   **LO6**

The financial controller and managing director of Busy B Cleaning Ltd were arguing over how to report the company's recent land acquisition. The land was purchased at 2 million and due to rezoning it now has a fair value of 5 million. The financial controller claims it should be presented at cost as this provides reliable information and that is what the shareholders want. The managing director claims that the cost is outdated information as it is no longer relevant to shareholders and the current fair value is more useful.

Required

You have been called in as an independent consultant to help resolve this issue. You are required to prepare a report for the company. The report should include discussion on the following points:

(a) Relevance and faithful representation as defined in the *Conceptual Framework*.

(b) Whether relevance is more or less important than reliability.

(c) The alternative ways land can be reported based on GAAP.

(d) Your recommendation as to how the land should be reported, including justification for your answer.

(e) Whether financial information can be neutral and free from material error.

PSA13.8 **Apply definition and recognition criteria as outlined in the *Conceptual Framework*.** **LO7**

You are the accountant for Braidwood Hair Ltd. The managing director of the company has asked you to stop purchasing assets for the company and to start leasing them using finance leases. He claims that, given the ownership of the leased asset remains with the lessor, Braidwood Hair Ltd will not have to report the asset nor the liability in the statement of financial position. You are not sure if this is true or not and have decided to research the topic and prepare a report for the managing director on your findings.

Required

Prepare a report which includes the following information:

(a) Define assets and liabilities as outlined in the *Conceptual Framework*.

(b) Outline the recognition criteria for assets and liabilities as explained in the *Conceptual Framework*.

(c) Explain the difference between a finance and an operating lease. (*Hint:* Also see the discussion on leases in chapter 9.)

(d) Identify whether finance leases meet the definition and recognition criteria for assets and liabilities as outlined in the *Conceptual Framework*.

PSA13.9 **Apply definition and recognition criteria as outlined in the *Conceptual Framework*.** **LO5, 7**

You are the assistant accountant for Travel the World Bags Ltd. The following transactions and events occurred during the year ending 31 December 2020.

(a) In December 2020, Travel the World Bags Ltd received a payment from a customer for $2500 for roller bags that were out of stock and would not be delivered until January 2021.

(b) Travel the World Bags Ltd made $400 000 net credit sales in 2020. As at the end of the year, $300 000 had been collected from customers. Based on the receivable collection history of the company, 96% of net credit sales are usually collected.

(c) During the stocktake, the accountant noticed that $3000 of inventory was no longer saleable as it had been damaged by water.

(d) Consignment stock totalling $15 000 was counted during the stocktake.

(e) Travel the World Bags Ltd paid $9900, which was the amount owing to a supplier less an early settlement discount of $100.

(f) One of Travel the World Bags Ltd's trucks overturned during a delivery and caused serious injury to two people involved in the accident. The driver was negligent and the company is being sued for damages. While the amount for the payout is yet to be determined, it is estimated that it could be in the vicinity of $500 000.

(g) Travel the World Bags Ltd paid a 1-year insurance policy for $12 000 on 1 November 2020.

(h) The electricity bill arrived on 31 December 2020 for $2500. The amount is due to be paid on 15 January 2021.

Required

For each of the items listed above:

(a) Discuss the appropriate way to account for each item. Include in your discussion references to the definitions and recognition criteria outlined in the *Conceptual Framework* to support your answer.

(b) Prepare the journal entries as required (ignore the effects of GST).

(c) Discuss how Travel the World Bags Ltd would determine if it was a reporting entity.

PSA13.10 **Summarise and integrate GAAP.** **LO8**

In the last week of semester, the accounting lecturer stated that there would definitely be a 20% essay question on GAAP in the final exam. Imagine you are preparing the summary notes to assist your revision for the final exam.

Required

Prepare notes for the final exam that:

(a) summarise and explain the main aspects of GAAP.

(b) identify and explain three of the many interrelationships between the elements of GAAP. Go to www.globalreporting.org/ and answer the following questions.

    (i) What is the GRI?

    (ii) What are the benefits of GRI Reporting?

    (iii) Explain the GRI Reporting Framework.

BUILDING BUSINESS SKILLS

FINANCIAL REPORTING AND ANALYSIS

Financial reporting problem: Domino's Pizza Enterprises Ltd

BBS13.1 Access the latest annual report for Domino's Pizza. In the notes to the financial statements, Domino's identify the various ways that revenues, expenses, assets and liabilities are recognised.

Required

(a) Review the section on 'Revenue recognition' in 'Note 3 Significant accounting policies'. Explain the different forms of revenue recorded by Domino's and, in particular, the different ways the company recognises each type of revenue.

(b) Are the methods Domino's uses for revenue recognition consistent with the revenue recognition criteria discussed in the chapter?

(c) Review the section on 'Goods and services tax' in 'Note 3 Significant accounting policies'. How are revenues, expenses and assets recognised?

(d) Review the section on inventories 'Note 3 Significant accounting policies'. How are inventories measured and reported?

Financial analysis on the web

BBS13.2 Purpose: This exercise explores information contained in notes to the financial statements for an Australian company.

Required

(a) Access Coca-Cola Amatil Ltd's annual report for the year ending 2016 from the company's web site www.ccamatil.com.

(b) Review section (a) on 'Revenue' in 'Note 1 Summary of significant accounting policies'. Explain the different forms of revenue recorded by Coca-Cola and, in particular, the different ways the company recognises each type of revenue.

(c) Are Coca-Cola's methods of revenue recognition consistent with the revenue recognition criteria discussed in the chapter?

(d) Compare Coca-Cola's types of revenue and methods of revenue recognition with those of Domino's Ltd.

A global focus

BBS13.3 Purpose: This exercise explores information contained in notes to the financial statements for a US-based company, The Coca-Cola Company.

Address: www.thecoca-colacompany.com

Steps:

1. Select **Investors, Financial Reports & Information, 2016 Annual Report on Form 10-K**.

2. Select the PDF file.

Required

(a) In the annual report, find the note on 'Critical accounting policies and estimates' and read the sections on revenue recognition. Explain Coca-Cola's policy for recognising revenue.

(b) Is the way that Coca-Cola recognises revenue consistent with the revenue recognition criteria discussed in the chapter?

CRITICAL THINKING

Group decision case

BBS13.4 Vital Health Ltd is a vitamin shop that commenced business on 1 April 2019. Wang Jiànkāng is a health fanatic and a good manager but a poor accountant. From the trial balance prepared by a part-time bookkeeper, Wang prepared a statement of profit or loss for the year ended 31 March 2020. Wang knew something was wrong with the statement because profit up to February had not exceeded $28 000. Knowing that you are an experienced accountant, he asks you to review the statement of profit or loss and other data. You first look at the trial balance. In addition to the account balances reported in the statement of profit or loss, the general ledger contains the following selected balances at 31 March 2020.

Advertising supplies on hand	$14 000
Prepaid insurance	22 400
Bank loan	28 000

VITAL HEALTH LTD **Statement of profit or loss** for the year ended 31 March 2020		
REVENUES		
Service revenue		$168 000
OPERATING EXPENSES		
Advertising	$ 8 540	
Wages	59 080	
Electricity	5 460	
Depreciation	1 680	
Repairs	5 600	
Total operating expenses		80 360
Profit		**$ 87 640**

You then make further enquiries and discover the following:

1. Service revenues include advanced money for vitamins to be delivered after March, $16 800.
2. There was $3220 of advertising supplies on hand at 31 March 2020.
3. Prepaid insurance resulted from the payment of a 1-year policy on 1 October 2019.
4. The following invoices have not been paid: advertising for week of 24 March 2020, $3500; repairs made on 10 March 2020, $2800; and electricity expense, $1120.
5. At 31 March 2020, two days' wages had not been paid, amounting to $560.
6. The business took out the loan on 1 January 2020 at an annual interest rate of 10%.

Required

With the class divided into groups, answer the following.

(a) Prepare a correct statement of profit or loss for the year ended 31 March 2020.

(b) Explain to Wang the generally accepted accounting principles that he did not follow in preparing the statement of profit or loss and the effect on the results.

Sustainability

BBS13.5 Coca-Cola Amatil Ltd (CCA): Corporate Social Responsibility reporting.

Required

(a) Access CCA's sustainability report on their latest annual report at www.ccamatil.com.

(b) Summarise CCA's achievements in the areas of environment and community.

Communication activity

BBS13.6 On 15 June 2018, Statistics R Us Pty Ltd signed a contract to provide market research services to a client for $1 million. The research would be undertaken during the years ended 30 June 2019 and 30 June 2020. Half of the research would be performed in the year ended 30 June 2019 and an amount of $600 000 would be received that year. The remaining half of the research would be performed in the year ended 30 June 2020 and $300 000 would be received. The remaining $100 000 would be received in August 2020. The managing director, Prime Numbers, believes that the $1 million should be recognised as revenue in June 2018 because the contract has been signed. The finance director, Square Root, argues that no amount should be recognised in 2018; that $600 000 should be recognised as revenue in the year ending 30 June 2019 and $300 000 in the year ended 30 June 2020; and that the remaining $100 000 should be recognised in August 2020.

Required

Prepare a report to the board of directors outlining the appropriate treatment for the revenue arising from the research contract. In your report, refer to the relevant definitions and recognition criteria as outlined in the *Conceptual Framework* to support your recommendations.

Ethics cases

BBS13.7 Toffee and More Ltd produces several varieties of candy. An action has been brought against the entity by a customer who broke a tooth while eating one of the entity's fudge bars. The managing director of Toffee and More Ltd, Sweet Tooth, has suggested that this should not be reported as a contingent liability because the entity might win the case, and any mention of this in the financial statements could encourage more lawsuits and increase the entity's liability.

Required

(a) Who are the stakeholders in this situation?

(b) Who would be potentially harmed or disadvantaged by non-disclosure of the contingent liability?

(c) Are the managing director's actions ethical?

BBS13.8 Healthy Living Ltd provides private healthcare cover for its customers. At the end of the reporting period, the business information system manager, Con Puter, found that the company's accounting system had been infected by a computer virus and any general ledger account balances could not be relied upon. Con advised the chief financial officer, Abit Crooked, and the chief executive officer, Alot Crooked, that the profit reports would be delayed extensively while the software was cleaned up and the virus removed. Alot Crooked said that he needed to issue a press release for the profit figures and didn't want this to be delayed because shareholders would think something was wrong with the company. He explained to his brother, Abit Crooked, it was not in the shareholders' best interest to delay profit figures and asked him to estimate them so that the press release would not be late. Abit Crooked argued that he did not have documentation or other sources of information on which to base the estimates because they depended on the computer to determine how many health cover insurance contracts had been sold. Alot Crooked suggested that this should not be a problem because accounting uses a lot of estimates and judgements. He added that this was what was meant by timeliness, which Alot Crooked recalled was mentioned in an accounting textbook he had read a long time ago.

Required

(a) Who are the stakeholders in this situation?

(b) Is Alot Crooked correct about the estimation of revenue, expenses and profit for the period being consistent with the timeliness constraint?

(c) Would the actions requested by Alot Crooked be consistent with generally accepted accounting principles?

(d) Would reporting estimated figures be ethical?

(e) What do you think would be the possible consequences of a significant error in the estimation that overestimated profit?

ANSWERS

Answers to self-study questions

13.1 (c) 13.2 (c) 13.3 (c) 13.4 (d) 13.5 (d) 13.6 (c) 13.7 (b) 13.8 (c) 13.9 (b) 13.10 (a)
13.11 (c) 13.12 (d) 13.13 (d) 13.14 (a) 13.15 (c) 13.16 (d) 13.17 (c) 13.18 (a) 13.19 (c)
13.20 (c) 13.21 (b) 13.22 (d)

ACKNOWLEDGEMENTS

Photo: © franckreporter / iStockphoto

Photo: © Klaus Vedfelt / Getty Images

Photo: © Steve Debenport / Getty Images

Photo: © Andrei Rahalski / Shutterstock.com

Photo: © tweetlebeetle / Shutterstock.com

Figure 13.6: Copyright © December 2013 by the International Integrated Reporting Council 'the IIRC'. All rights reserved. Used with permission of the IIRC. Contact the IIRC info@theiirc.org for permission to reproduce, store, transmit or make other uses of this document.

Text: © 2018 Australian Accounting Standards Board AASB. The text, graphics and layout of this publication are protected by Australian copyright law and the comparable law of other countries. No part of the publication may be reproduced, stored or transmitted in any form or by any means without the prior written permission of the AASB except as permitted by law. For reproduction or publication permission should be sought in writing from the Australian Accounting Standards Board. Requests in the first instance should be addressed to the National Director, Australian Accounting Standards Board, PO Box 204, Collins Street West, Melbourne, Victoria, 8007.

CHAPTER 14

Technology concepts

After studying this chapter, you should be able to:

14.1 appreciate the use of a computerised accounting information system such as Xero

14.2 understand why organisations are motivated to implement or upgrade to an enterprise resource planning (ERP) system

14.3 categorise the key business processes that ERP systems support

14.4 describe the main modules in an ERP system through using SAP as an example

14.5 explain how XBRL is used in reporting systems

14.6 compare and contrast the different ways XBRL can be used

14.7 justify the benefits of XBRL

14.8 understand the various concepts in using XBRL

14.9 categorise the different types of cloud-based computing including Software as a Service

14.10 appreciate new technologies and how they may impact the future of accounting.

Chapter preview

Different types of systems or technologies are used in organisations to capture transactions and produce reports that are used for planning, decision making and reporting. Several of those systems have been developed for different sized businesses, more or less complexity and different information needs. As discussed in chapter 6, many businesses in Australia use accounting software systems such as Xero to record and capture accounting information.

The chapter begins with a discussion of the computerised accounting information system, Xero. We then consider an enterprise resource planning system (ERP), using Systems Applications & Products (SAP) as an example. An ERP is used by larger, more complex organisations where information needs to be recorded, verified and communicated to various stakeholders. We next discuss **eXtensible Business Reporting Language (XBRL)**, which is standard for the electronic communication of business and financial data and is revolutionising business reporting around the world. Other advancements in technology including cloud computing, artificial intelligence, big data, blockchain and bitcoin are briefly described in the latter part of the chapter where we also consider the impact of these new technologies on accounting as we now know it.

The content and organisation of this chapter are as follows.

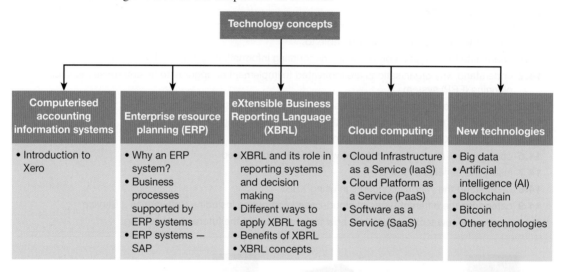

Technology concepts				
Computerised accounting information systems	**Enterprise resource planning (ERP)**	**eXtensible Business Reporting Language (XBRL)**	**Cloud computing**	**New technologies**
• Introduction to Xero	• Why an ERP system? • Business processes supported by ERP systems • ERP systems — SAP	• XBRL and its role in reporting systems and decision making • Different ways to apply XBRL tags • Benefits of XBRL • XBRL concepts	• Cloud Infrastructure as a Service (IaaS) • Cloud Platform as a Service (PaaS) • Software as a Service (SaaS)	• Big data • Artificial intelligence (AI) • Blockchain • Bitcoin • Other technologies

14.1 Computerised accounting information systems

LEARNING OBJECTIVE 14.1 Appreciate the use of a computerised accounting information system such as Xero.

In chapter 6, we looked at the basic concepts of accounting information systems. One of the main principles of these systems is that they provide an efficient and effective means of recording business transactions. An accounting system that is cost-effective, useful and flexible can contribute to an organisation's goals. As mentioned throughout this text, there are many computerised accounting software packages available on the market. Examples of the best known packages include Sage, ACCPAC, Attaché, MYOB, QuickBooks, Xero and Sybiz. In this chapter we have a brief look at the Xero accounting software package.

Xero accounting software

Xero is a well-known accounting software package that is popular with small businesses as it is simple and easy to use, allowing more time for business owners to improve and grow their business. The software can be accessed anywhere, anytime on a variety of electronic devices, making it easy to run the business while 'on the go'.

Before using the Xero software package the business needs to be set up and created. This is done via the Settings tab on the home page and involves entering the business name, address, Australian Business Number (ABN), and the type of business, e.g. whether it is a company, partnership, sole trader or not-for-profit. Once the business details are entered, the chart of accounts is created. Xero can provide a predetermined list of accounts or the business can use their existing chart of accounts if they are converting to Xero from another system. The choice of a predetermined list or use of specific accounts for your business is important. Having the correct chart of accounts for the type of business will ensure that useful accounting information that suits the decision-making needs of both external and internal users is provided from the computerised system. Access to the various accounting functions is gained via the home page. The Xero home page is also known as the dashboard and can be set up to show, at a glance, how the business is performing. Figure 14.1 shows a sample dashboard which includes a view of the current invoices owing from customers and bills due to be paid to suppliers.

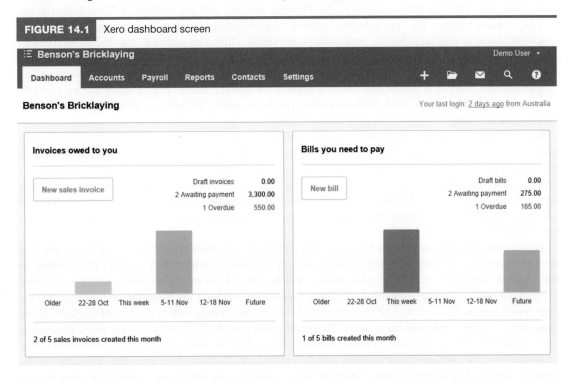

FIGURE 14.1 Xero dashboard screen

Clicking on the 'Awaiting payment' or 'Overdue' links will provide more details of those amounts such as the customer or supplier and the due dates. New sales invoices or new bills can quickly be added from the dashboard by clicking on the appropriate box. There are other features that can be added to the dashboard to allow monitoring of specific areas of a business. Some of these features include the following.

- *Business bank accounts.* Allows monitoring of any bank and/or credit card account in use by the business. The dashboard provides an up-to-date view of the current balances and reconciliations of the chosen accounts.
- *Account watch list.* You can choose specific general ledger accounts (e.g. sales, advertising, materials) to allow you to see the current status of the month's sales and monitor spending in particular areas, and compare the current amounts to the year-to-date totals.
- *Total cash in and out.* Provides simple charts and graphs to allow the business to monitor its cash flow.

All the business accounting functions can be accessed by clicking on the specific tab at the top of the dashboard and selecting the required function from the drop-down menu.

1. *Accounts tab.* This tab allows access to the main functions of a business: Bank Accounts, Sales, Purchases, Inventory, Expense Claims and Fixed Assets. A sample of the main page for the Sales function is shown in figure 14.2.

2. *Payroll tab.* This tab allows access to an Overview (where the payroll accounts and calendar can be set up), Employees, Pay Runs, Leave, Timesheets and Superannuation.

3. *Reports tab.* This is where all the business reports can be customised and accessed. The reports are categorised as Financial, Tax, Accounting, Fixed Assets, Sales, Purchases, Inventory and Payroll. The reports that are frequently used can be flagged and listed in the drop-down menu as 'favourites' to allow quick and easy access.

4. *Contacts tab.* All customers, suppliers and employees can be added and edited via this tab. They can be set up into various Groups, and Smart Lists can be used to look at an account history or to monitor the status of overdue accounts.

5. *Settings tab.* This tab allows access to the General Settings and the business's Xero Subscription. The General Settings are split into four groups: Organisation, Connect, Reports and Features. The Organisation setting includes the general business details, financial settings, conversion balances (if converting to Xero from another accounting software package), and tax rates. The Connect setting provides automatic linking to other Xero users, apps, and online payment services. The Reports setting includes the chart of accounts and tracking options for specific items. The Features setting provides templates for documents, such as invoices and purchase orders, so they can be customised with the business branding.

Entering new transactions into Xero is a quick and easy process. As mentioned, new sales invoices can be entered from the dashboard or alternatively they can be entered from the Sales page. Figure 14.2 shows the main page for the Sales function. This page provides an overview of the status of invoices and quotes and includes a list of customers, with those owing the most listed first, and indicating whether the amount owing is current or overdue. From this main page new invoices, quotes, credit notes and repeating invoices can be entered and sent directly to customers by email. Statements can also be emailed to customers automatically on a regular basis.

To illustrate how data is entered for a sale and receipt of cash from the customer, let us assume that we have a sale for Benson's Bricklaying of 4 bags of concrete, valued at $25 each, to Peter Smith. In this example we ignore GST. The sales invoice will be created via the Sales menu, which is accessed by clicking on the Accounts tab. From the main Sales page, click on the New box and a blank invoice screen will appear. This can then be completed with the relevant details such as the date of the transaction, description of goods sold and the quantity. Xero will allow you to add a new customer while processing the transaction, but the customer's contact details will need to be completed later via the Contacts tab. (Alternatively, the new customer's details can be entered via Contacts first, then the customer can be selected when filling in the invoice). Once the details for the sale have been entered, the sales invoice can be printed or emailed directly to the customer. Any supporting documentation can be uploaded to the sales invoice and kept on file. Clicking on the Approve button near the bottom right of the screen will post the invoice details to the ledger accounts. Therefore, the entries made in the general ledger will be to debit the accounts receivable control account for $100 and credit the sales account for $100. In the accounts receivable subsidiary ledger, the account of Peter Smith will be debited for $100. Figure 14.3 shows the completed invoice screen.

If the customer is paying at the time of sale, the payment details can be added at the bottom of the screen in the Receive a Payment section. If the customer is paying at a later date, the invoice can be reopened and the payment details completed in this section at that later date. There are other ways in which the customer's payment can be recorded but they are not covered in this text. Clicking on the Add Payment button will post the receipt of cash to the ledger accounts, resulting in a debit entry to the cash account and a credit entry to the accounts receivable control account in the general ledger. In the accounts receivable subsidiary ledger, the account of Peter Smith will be credited for $100.

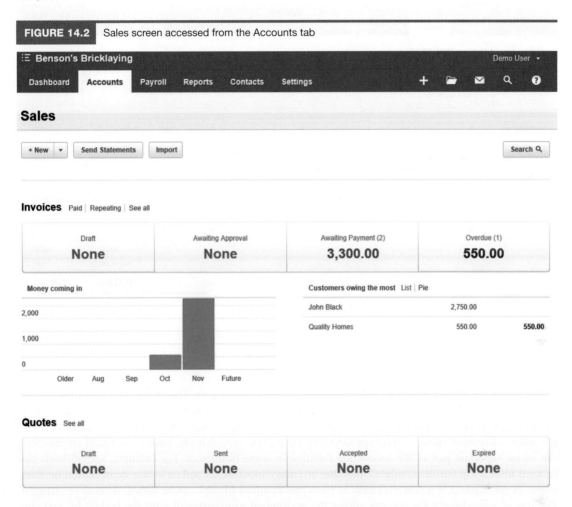

FIGURE 14.2 Sales screen accessed from the Accounts tab

The procedures for recording other types of accounting transactions (e.g. purchases of goods, cash payments and general journal entries) are similar to those illustrated.

There are many computerised accounting systems on the market. These accounting systems offer computer packages with various subsystems covering all the accounting functions. Most accounting software providers also sell a range of subpackages consisting of various modules that can be purchased separately to suit the needs of the particular business. For example, a business providing only services would not require an inventory subsystem, whereas a business selling goods would find an inventory module useful in recording and managing inventories. Thus, integrated accounting packages and various modules can be purchased based on the nature of the business (service, manufacturing or merchandising), its size (small, medium or large) and the number of employees.

Some computerised accounting systems are cloud-based systems which can be accessed anywhere, anytime, either on a PC, Mac, tablet or phone. Examples of these are the Xero accounting package and MYOB AccountRight Live. Where packages can be run on a desktop or as a cloud-based system, management need to decide which access they wish to have and would base their decision on considerations such as accessibility (anywhere, anytime would be available if it was a cloud-based solution as discussed later in this chapter) and risk.

FIGURE 14.3 | Xero completed invoice screen

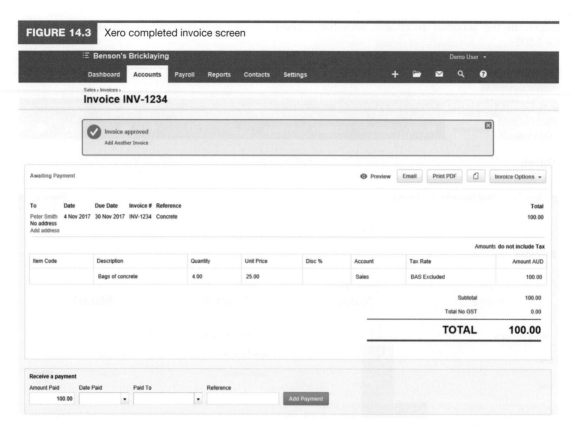

Recall that not all businesses run fully integrated accounting systems. This means that data from reports produced in one subsystem needs to be entered into other subsystems either manually or by using data export/import processes. In addition to computerised accounting packages like Xero, companies will also use other subsystems such as Excel spreadsheets. Electronic spreadsheets, such as an Excel spreadsheet, can be an important part of the accounting function in some businesses. For example, spreadsheets can be used to develop business budgets, monitor inventory movements and calculate depreciation on fixed assets. A spreadsheet is a powerful tool, as rows and columns of data can be added, deleted or changed. The use of spreadsheets for budgets allows the accountant to experiment with the budget by applying and testing 'what if?' questions simply by changing one number of one formula in the spreadsheet. This saves hours of manual calculations.

14.2 Enterprise resource planning (ERP)

LEARNING OBJECTIVE 14.2 Understand why organisations are motivated to implement or upgrade to an enterprise resource planning (ERP) system.

Why an ERP system?

As we know, an accounting information system is concerned with financial data and accounting transactions. For example, a sale will be captured by the accounting system through the accounting software package, resulting in a debit to accounts receivable and a credit to sales. However, other potentially useful non-financial information about the sale, e.g. the time of day the sale was made, can also be important. Such information can be gathered in an enterprise resource planning (ERP) system. An ERP system integrates all aspects of a company's operations with the accounting information system. It collects, processes and stores data in a centralised database and shares up-to-date information across business processes so that business activities can be coordinated. It is an effective means of capturing data and providing information to managers to facilitate communication and decision making among operational and financial departments within an organisation. SAP is an example of an ERP system, and is a leading provider of enterprise business applications which allow businesses to manage operations and customer relations. SAP products are available for small and large businesses and are discussed later in this chapter.

ERP systems are designed to capture a wide range of information about all business transactions and processes related to the typical four major areas in an organisation: sales and marketing, finance, manufacturing and human resources. These systems link the typical major functions of an organisation and the organisation's suppliers and customers in the value chain.

ERP systems link:

- sales and marketing: the division of the organisation that sells the products and services
- accounting and finance: the division of the organisation that manages the business's financial assets and maintains its financial records
- manufacturing: the division of the organisation that purchases raw materials to be converted into products and services that provide customer value
- human resources: the division of the organisation that attracts, develops and maintains the business's labour resources and employee records
- suppliers: the businesses that provide direct and indirect raw materials to the manufacturing division of the organisation
- customers: the people who purchase products and services from the organisation because they value those products and services.

Given these links in the system, this is the main reason why an ERP system is attractive to businesses. As ERP systems can capture a wide range of information about all key business processes within an organisation and share this information between its business departments and other organisations, this integration of all departments and functions in a business into one system means that redundant information is not held by each department. The information can easily be shared between the departments.

14.3 Business processes supported by ERP systems

LEARNING OBJECTIVE 14.3 Categorise the key business processes that ERP systems support.

ERP systems support key business processes that involve the major functions in an organisation. These processes include:

1. revenue, sales or order to cash
2. payments, purchases or purchase to pay
3. production, manufacturing or conversion
4. human resources and payroll
5. general ledger and financial reporting.

Each of these key business processes brings together different functions or divisions in the organisation. For example, the revenue process brings together the sales and marketing department and accounts receivable in the accounting department (which records the sales), while manufacturing (which produces the product or service to sell) brings together human resources (which provides the sales, finance and manufacturing staff for the revenue process to be executed).

14.4 ERP systems — SAP modules

LEARNING OBJECTIVE 14.4 Describe the main modules in an ERP system through using SAP as an example.

There are many commercial ERP vendors, of which SAP is one. It is a leading provider of enterprise business applications which allow businesses to manage operations and customer relations. SAP products are suitable for large businesses.

Core modules of the SAP Business Suite ERP system are as follows.

- *Financial accounting* (general ledger and financial reporting). This module is connected to all of the other ERP system modules and processes the monetary transactions in the ERP system. This module collects all the transactional data to enable it to prepare the balance sheet, income statement and statement of cash flows for statutory reporting. It also maintains customer and vendor balances through fully integrated accounts receivable and accounts payable sub-modules. Other sub-modules are included in this module, with fixed assets being the most utilised.

- *Controlling and profitability analysis* (management accounting and decision making). This is the management accounting module and is designed to collect the data for preparing internal reports that support decision making in the organisation relating to effective cost and revenue control through analysis of sales, costs and budgets. These are the areas about which managers most often ask questions in order to make decisions to improve the performance of the business.

- *Human resources* (human resources management and payroll process). This module contains functions that relate to the recruitment, management and administration of personnel; payroll processing; and personnel training and travel. It captures employee details, changes in those details and the distribution of pay to those employees. When employees undertake training or travel for work purposes, it also captures this information.

- *Sales and distribution* (revenue process). This module contains functions related to the revenue or sales order to cash process. It provides the ability to capture and record customer orders, check the customer's ability to pay, execute customer orders, ship products to customers and bill customers. It also contains a process that records each step during picking and packing so that the system can provide the latest status on a customer's order. The module is linked to the materials management module to facilitate checking of product availability, and the financial accounting module to post the sales transactions to the general ledger.

- *Materials management*. This module contains functions related to the payment or purchase to pay process, including the management of products while they are in stock. The module also contains the processes for purchase orders. It connects with the financial accounting module when purchases are made from suppliers, and with the sales and distribution module when customer orders are processed. When products arrive from suppliers, it compares what is received with what was ordered, then adjusts the records of stock on hand. The data for accounts payable and the cash payment are updated when all the source documents (purchase order, product receipt and invoice) are verified.

The modules provide the necessary support for the five key business processes and functions in any business. Most ERP systems contain similar modules and have similar functionality. The modules and functionality mimic the key business processes that occur in reality in organisations.

ERP systems support key internal business processes and financial transactions with suppliers and customers. These systems are also increasingly reaching out toward the non-financial activities associated with suppliers and customers. For example, while an ERP system can record a purchase of raw materials from suppliers, modules within SAP can also suggest ways of improving the sourcing of raw materials. While an ERP system can record the sale of a product to a customer, SAP modules can also suggest ways of improving the revenue process or the customer's buying experience. There are two modules that extend the internal capabilities of ERP systems to suppliers and customers by offering mechanisms to improve supply chain management and customer relationship management respectively. These are **supply chain management (SCM)** and **customer relationship management (CRM)** modules. We will not discuss them here, but they are examples of how the ERP system extends beyond the current organisation.

We have discussed how ERP systems combine all the processes for a business into one system. If an organisation wants to send data to another organisation that can be directly written into the other organisation's computerised accounting/ERP system, they can use **eXtensible Markup Language (XML)**. Having their ERP system coded with XBRL tags is one way to ensure that their data is easily extracted and sent to regulatory agencies. The next section discusses the technology that is capable of doing this: XBRL.

14.5 eXtensible Business Reporting Language (XBRL)

LEARNING OBJECTIVE 14.5 Explain how XBRL is used in reporting systems.

XBRL and its role in reporting systems and decision making

The idea behind XBRL is simple: instead of treating financial information as simply a block of text — as in a standard web page or a printed document — XBRL provides a computer-readable tag for each item of data. A tag can be thought of as being similar to a barcode. If we think of it this way, each piece of data in an accounting report has a barcode attached to it and the barcode explains what the piece of data is. By attaching meaning to strings of text, XBRL adopts a **semantic approach**. Companies can use XBRL to save costs and streamline their processes for collecting and reporting financial information. Consumers of financial data, including investors, analysts, financial institutions and regulators, can receive, find, compare and analyse data much more rapidly and efficiently if it is in XBRL format. XBRL is freely licensed and available to the public. It is based on XML, which is a hypertext language used to add syntax to strings of data by embedding meaningful tags, and therefore is widely available in software applications. The major benefit of XBRL is a result of introducing a set of industry-accepted standards that provide consistency and therefore comparability of financial information.

XBRL is a data standard used when generating financial reports. The importance of this standard is that it allows semantics, or meaning, to be embedded within strings of financial data, allowing more efficient and in-depth analysis to be conducted by users or recipients of the data. This meaning is conveyed by embedded tags that identify where individual pieces of data start and end within larger strings of data. XBRL makes financial reporting to various user groups much more efficient. It can be used for internal users and external financial reporting.

For internal users of business information, one of the prime motivations behind the development of XBRL was the number of times in traditional financial reporting circles that differing information needed to be supplied in paper documents, or electronic formats, when communicating financial results to investors, regulators, government agencies and other stakeholders.

For external users of business information, XBRL represents a significant step forward in their ability to analyse publicly available information. The vast majority of companies have websites, on which they typically publish information relating to employment opportunities, company history and financial information. Financial information is often presented on a web page, using **HTML (HyperText Markup Language)** standards, or the annual report is published as an Adobe PDF (portable document format) file, which can be downloaded and then viewed or printed. The problem with both of these approaches is that it is difficult for users, such as analysts, to manipulate the information with any degree of efficiency. The advantage of PDF files is that they can be securely locked so that figures cannot be changed — ensuring that financial reports can be printed but not changed ensures the integrity of the financial reports. This gives the company assurance that audited financial statements cannot be altered. For this reason, secure PDFs have become a standard way to publish financial reports. However, the advantage to companies in ensuring that their figures are correct on the website creates a disadvantage to those wishing to use the figures in financial statement analysis. For example, in order to conduct analysis, users need to view the PDF financial reports, identify data of interest and re-enter those data into other software, such as a Microsoft Excel spreadsheet. This extra data manipulation that the user must perform represents a time cost in the analysis of the information. It also introduces the risk of data errors when transferring the data from one source to another.

Corporate regulators worldwide are gradually moving towards mandating XBRL for corporate filings and reporting. The XBRL concept has strong international support, with many countries establishing local bodies to develop and implement XBRL. Detailed information about the use of XBRL is available at www.xbrl.org, the website of XBRL International, a consortium of companies and agencies. The Australian government's Standard Business Reporting website, www.sbr.gov.au, has additional information on Australian business reporting trends and standards.

In the United States, the Securities Exchange Commission (SEC) issued a rule 'Interactive Data to Improve Financial Reporting' in January 2009. The rule requires all public companies that prepare financial statements in accordance with at least US generally accepted accounting principles (GAAP) and all foreign private issuers that prepare their financial statements using International Financial Reporting Standards (IFRS), as issued by the International Accounting Standards Board (IASB), to provide their financial statements to the SEC and their corporate websites in XBRL format. In addition to all financial statement line items, companies must use XBRL to tag their footnotes in detail.

XBRL's use is reaching a tipping point for other countries. Regulatory authorities in Europe, Australia, Singapore, Japan, Korea and China have various XBRL financial requirements, and large banks around the world are beginning to require companies to use XBRL in their loan application and credit granting processes.

XBRL has become a standard for tagging data and transmitting it across networks and databases. Most current software is XML compliant and can import, export and process data in XML format. XML is an open standard for marking up data and adds meaning to individual pieces of data by surrounding it with tags. Since XBRL is an XML vocabulary, most current software is XBRL compliant.

As it becomes the standard for financial reporting, XBRL will deliver its promise of helping companies to automate required reporting processes and helping investors, analysts and users of all types to retrieve and use financial information for investment and other decision-making purposes.

XBRL can also be used for internal purposes, particularly management reporting that involves transferring information between different countries or branches within the same company. Regardless of the spoken or written language, the tag signifies what the item means. Using XBRL for internal purposes means that an organisation can set up the coding structure of the items they want to tag to match what is particularly suitable for that company.

We have reached a point where every accountant and financial professional should understand XBRL, how to navigate and use the XBRL taxonomies, and how to create XBRL instance documents. However, XBRL is not currently a standard for filing financial accounting reports with the stock exchanges in Australia and New Zealand. Australia's corporate regulator, the Australian Securities and Investments

Commission (ASIC) has been able to accept XBRL lodgements since July 2010, but as yet there is very little evidence that Australian companies are using this voluntary system to any great extent.

14.6 Different ways to apply XBRL tags

LEARNING OBJECTIVE 14.6 Compare and contrast the different ways XBRL can be used.

In this section we look at the different ways that XBRL tags may be applied to data. Tagging is the process of associating a dollar value in an account, such as debtors, to the XBRL element/item in an XBRL schema; for example, <debtors>10 000</debtors>. Along with the tagging of the items, the XBRL element contains content items such as date and currency type and whether the item is usually a debit or a credit. There are two main ways to code the financial accounts.
1. Attach XBRL to the accounting system.
2. Attach XBRL tags after the financial accounts have been produced.

There is debate in the accounting information systems community as to whether to tag data at the individual transaction level when capturing the original event data in the accounting system, or to tag the summarised outputs (i.e. at the general ledger account code level). The choice between the two options is very important. Coding accounts once they have been produced impacts on core processes and the data quality that will result, as mistakes are more likely using this method. However, while companies get to grips with XBRL, this will probably be the most common method. Over time, companies will work to incorporate the XBRL into their coding structures.

XBRL tags in the accounting system

XBRL tags are available in many ERP and accounting packages. The XBRL tags are attached to the chart of account codes. When the data in a particular code is transferred, the XBRL tags are attached to it. As a result, very little work needs to be done in external financial account presentation. Also, the data can be transferred internally and used internally using the XBRL tags. The main issue is to ensure the tags that are set up against the chart of account codes in the general ledger are correct and have been verified. Once that is done, it is easy to generate reports from the database.

Tagging accounts after reports have been produced

When tags are applied to the data after the reports have been created, internal control procedures are required to check the data before it is used or filed with regulatory agencies. Any XML-compliant software such as Microsoft Word or Excel can be used to add XBRL tags.

14.7 Benefits of XBRL

LEARNING OBJECTIVE 14.7 Justify the benefits of XBRL.

As mentioned earlier, Australia has had a voluntary system of lodging their corporate reports using XBRL since July 2010. It appears, though, that organisations in Australia have yet to be convinced that the benefits attributed to XBRL outweigh the costs. However, XBRL is a significant step forward for business reporting for several reasons. First, it represents the collaboration of some of the leading industrialised nations and some of the largest commercial firms. Together, they are developing standards for XBRL reporting that will apply internationally. XBRL is also significant for the impact that it will have on users of financial information. Financial statement analysis tasks, such as searching for particular items or information, will be made easier by the set of context-specific metadata tags that are developed through XBRL. This will yield benefits including reduced time for information searching, greater ease when comparing data across companies (since they will all be presenting information using XBRL conventions), easier interchanging of data and, potentially, paperless financial reporting. The advantages of XBRL are as follows.

Reduced data manipulation

Typically, companies report their financial information to shareholders in an annual report which is usually a glossy, magazine-like publication. The annual reports are also often available from the stock exchange and on the investor section of the company's website, usually as PDF files. It is not possible to analyse the data from these files until it is transcribed into a spreadsheet or word processing file. This requires the user to identify each item and enter it correctly into their software.

XBRL takes every item that appears in a set of financial statements, including the discussion and analysis, and applies a tag to it. This tag can then be used to search, sort and manipulate data. XBRL data prepared by an organisation can be loaded into users' software, and users thus will avoid the need to re-enter data (see figure 14.4). For example, if you want to search for data held by a stock exchange that uses XBRL, such as the Canadian Stock Exchange, you can select the stock exchange and download the XBRL reports directly into Microsoft Excel. The data tags can then be used as headings in the spreadsheet. Once you have downloaded the data, you can program formulae to perform financial statement analysis and compare the companies of interest. You can be assured that your headings for items in current assets or current liabilities are correct. Certainly, there will be no errors introduced by your trying to find items in a paper annual report and manually typing the figures into a spreadsheet. This is of course a significant step forward from what was previously possible in financial statement analysis.

| FIGURE 14.4 | After XBRL, data from financial statements can be put straight into other software for analysis |

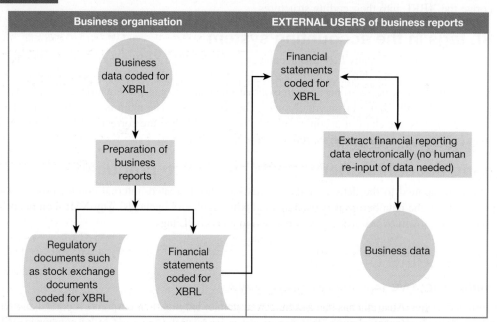

From the company's perspective, conventionally it has needed to reconfigure financial data, which typically originates from the accounting information system, into the different formats required by its external users, including shareholders, regulatory bodies such as stock exchanges and government agencies. This represents a significant preparation cost to the company. XBRL overcomes this problem. The underlying data are entered once, but tagged to capture the different ways in which the data will be presented. XBRL thus eliminates the need to manipulate the data to suit different users' requirements, and companies do not need to maintain separate documents for each reporting requirement they face.

Paperless reporting

XBRL is well suited to paperless reporting, as reports are able to be viewed online.

Industry-accepted standards

XBRL has been designed through the collaboration of software companies, governments and professional accounting communities. Therefore, there is only one version of XBRL. The XBRL standards have the support of the international and national accounting bodies and thus incorporate the international financial reporting standards that a company would use, or a country's generally accepted accounting practice if they do not use international financial reporting standards. This high degree of coordination has helped to develop industry-accepted standards and to avoid competition between different versions of XBRL. Once XBRL standards are defined, they can be taken and applied to different industries and environments through the creation of different taxonomies. For example, the Standards Based Reporting (SBR) initiative in Australia uses its own taxonomy for the reporting requirements of government agencies in Australia.

Reduced accounting time

Through the application of different taxonomies and standards, the time required to prepare accounting reports — whether for shareholders, regulators, creditors or auditors — is significantly reduced. The data tags that form XBRL enable accounting packages to interact with other organisational databases and prepare information to meet the requirements of different reporting formats in a quick and efficient way. Real-time reporting becomes a possibility.

Recognition by major accounting software vendors

XBRL has been incorporated into the vast majority of enterprise resource planning (ERP) systems, accounting packages and office software. As discussed earlier, ERP systems are used in larger, more complex organisations. The incorporation of XBRL into these systems means the data are relatively easily transferable between these packages.

Interchangeable data

The interchangeability of XBRL data between the major accounting software means that once the data is tagged it can be reused in many ways to meet differing financial reporting requirements. There is no need to re-enter the data just because a new reporting requirement arises.

Comparisons across companies

If stock exchanges have XBRL filing as part of their filing requirements, it will be easy to download and analyse the data of multiple companies. XBRL makes it feasible to analyse and compare huge numbers of companies and enables small investors to do their own efficient analyses using spreadsheet data. As mentioned previously, the data does not need to be identified, classified and re-entered, so it has an extra element of accuracy and integrity.

Improved audit quality

Improved audit quality can occur as long as the taxonomy has correctly classified items of data at its source. As part of this process, the coding or tagging of the items does itself need to be audited to ensure that the tagging is correct. Any changes made to the tags also need to be audited. In traditional audits, the output of the accounts is looked at; for example, the debtors' balances. Using XBRL, if the data is inputted correctly and the correct tag is applied, then the output produced from this *will* be correct. So the emphasis will be on tagging the data correctly in the input processes; if this is done correctly, the accounts will be correct.

Stakeholder benefits

XBRL can benefit both external and internal reporting. It is not just used for external stakeholders such as stock exchanges and regulatory authorities but for different purposes for different external stakeholders in different jurisdictions. XBRL can also be used by internal users. XBRL benefits the decision-making processes of external stakeholders by making it easier and faster to search, sort and compare financial information. From an internal user perspective, by using XBRL, companies and other producers of financial data and business reports can automate the processes of data collection. For example, data from different company divisions with different accounting systems can be assembled quickly, cheaply and efficiently if the sources of information have been upgraded to use XBRL. Once data is gathered in XBRL, different types of reports using varying subsets of the data can be produced with minimum effort. A company finance division, for example, could quickly and reliably generate internal management reports, financial statements for publication, tax and other regulatory filings, as well as credit reports for lenders.

Additionally, because XBRL is an external standard that supports financial reporting based on US GAAP and IFRS, companies will have the ability to respond to rapid changes in regulatory reporting requirements.

14.8 XBRL concepts

LEARNING OBJECTIVE 14.8 Understand the various concepts in using XBRL.

XBRL is a variant of XML for financial reporting. XML, or eXtensible Markup Language, is data about data, or **metadata**, specifying what different pieces of data are and how they may be used. XML enables us to tag items according to what content they contain. Therefore, XML tags enable us to code any data with a description of their content. Consider, for example, that our financial data includes a debtors' balance of $10 000. When the data for the debtors' balance is tagged, the XML code would read <debtors>$10 000</debtors>. In this way, regardless of how this figure is displayed or formatted, it is clear that the debtors' balance is $10 000 and, conversely, that this $10 000 is the debtors' balance. This example shows how the tags work as a semantic code to specify the meaning of the item. XBRL takes the concept of XML a step further by enabling the tags to contain more data than just its content; they also add additional metadata such as time period, currency and type of standard (e.g. IFRS). XBRL uses tags applied to data to specify what the piece of data is and how it is used, and also to make the data searchable.

The set of tags developed under XBRL represent a standard for the business environment, as the tags are obtained from taxonomies which are publicly available from the various taxonomies available on XBRL International's website, www.xbrl.org. There are internal and external taxonomies. For example, there are internal general ledger taxonomies which tag the chart of accounts. External taxonomies include those for IFRS (i.e. all the account names required to use all of the IFRS standards). **Taxonomies**, therefore, are the dictionaries that define each accounting item that can be tagged in XBRL. An Australian company, for example, would use the taxonomy for International Financial Reporting Standards (IFRS). The taxonomy contains one or more **schemas** which contain the individual **elements**, such as debtors or sales revenue, for tagging data. The set of tags developed under XBRL represents a standard for the business environment; thus the tag <SalesRevenue>, for example, has the same meaning — in terms of its calculation and what the value represents — for anyone using the XBRL standards. The schema contains additional information such as the time period and the currency used. When XBRL tagging is applied to a file containing data (e.g. an income statement), the XBRL-tagged document is called an **instance document**. The account figures, such as income, are coded for what they are — for income, the period to which that figure relates and the monetary value. The instance document contains information about the organisation's financial statements at one instant in time, along with other contextual information such as monetary items, debit or credit, and balance sheet or income statement items. The instance document can be used to store and transmit data between computers for various analyses, both internally and externally.

14.9 Cloud computing

LEARNING OBJECTIVE 14.9 Categorise the different types of cloud-based computing including Software as a Service.

Cloud computing is a model of computing that provides computer services through the internet to a pooled set of resources that provide these services. This pooled set of resources is usually infrastructure in data centres and software. There are various types of cloud computing, the most important to accountants probably being software services called Software as a Service (SaaS). Other services include Infrastructure as a Service (IaaS), **Hardware as a Service (HaaS)** and Platform as a Service (PaaS).

Each type of cloud service is discussed below; however, the cloud-computing model generally has some advantages. The main advantage is that these different services can be accessed on an as-needed basis. Therefore, as your business grows you can use more services or resources as you need them. The services are accessed through the internet on stand-alone computers on a 24/7 model, so no special set-up is needed to access them. The resources you wish to use are assigned to you on demand and you do not need to know where the computing resources are housed. Google has massive server farms in the USA. The number of resources you use can be increased or decreased to meet the changing user demand that you require. You are charged for what you actually use.

The computing services offered by each type of cloud computing is different.

Cloud Infrastructure as a Service (IaaS)

Cloud **Infrastructure as a Service (IaaS)** customers obtain the use of processing, storage, networking and other infrastructure resources from cloud service providers to run their information systems on, and pay for them on a usage basis rather than purchasing their own infrastructure. This can include storage services (HaaS).

Cloud Platform as a Service (PaaS)

With **Platform as a Service (PaaS)**, customers obtain the infrastructure services as discussed above in IaaS, as well as programming tools so that users can design their own applications, and pay for them on a usage basis.

Software as a Service (SaaS)

As part of the systems development effort, a common choice faced by organisations is whether they should buy the required software, develop it themselves or customise an existing package to suit their needs. In the modern environment of technology where the internet is omnipresent, a fourth option has emerged: the use of **Software as a Service (SaaS)** providers, previously known as *application service providers* (some vendors use the alternative term *on-demand computing*). SaaS providers are organisations that offer software applications that can be leased by a range of clients. The leased programs are typically made available to the customers through the use of internet and portal technology.[1] SaaS services are a derivative of the traditional outsourcing function, representing a way for small- and mid-sized organisations to gain access to the systems and technologies — such as ERP systems and CRM technology — that were traditionally only available to larger organisations. Motivations for using SaaS may include reducing the total cost of ownership, focusing on core competencies, arranging a more predictable expenditure pattern for IT, being more efficient and matching the technology used by competitors. Technological reasons for using SaaS may include a lack of adequate skills within the organisation, quicker implementation time, a shift of risk of ownership and the ability to have best technology in place.[2]

SaaS providers offer organisations several advantages that would not necessarily be available under conventional acquisition methods, including cost savings, lower initial investment, better performance and

---

[1] Smith, AD & Rupp, WT 2002, 'Application service providers (AS): Moving downstream to enhance competitive advantage', *Information Management and Computer Security*, vol. 10, no. 2/3, pp. 64–72; Smith David, J, McCarthy, WE & Sommer, BS 2001, 'Agility: The key to survival of the fittest in the software market', unpublished paper.

[2] Sofiane Tebboune 2001, 'Application service provision: Origins and development', *Business Process Management Journal*, vol. 9, no. 6, pp. 722–34.

---

the ability to focus on dealing with key strategy and competency issues rather than peripheral technology-based issues. Cost savings from the use of SaaS come from the economies of scale that SaaS providers enjoy in providing the required software. The SaaS provider can serve many users and is therefore able to develop and maintain the software at a cheaper cost per user than if firms were to develop the software themselves. Organisations using SaaS are potentially able to benefit from a lower total cost of ownership. Using the services of a SaaS provider can also present a way for the organisation to benefit from the use of applications without needing to make a large initial investment. This leads to the service being implemented within the organisation more quickly and also allows the organisation to place its emphasis on its competencies, rather than worrying about IT and peripheral issues associated with IT. SaaS thus allows an organisation to focus its attention on what it does best. The SaaS provider can also assist the subscribing organisation with its bank of support services and technical advice and training, thus ensuring qualified technical support, the cost of which is not the responsibility of the organisation but rather of the SaaS provider.

SaaS also presents some disadvantages that an organisation should take into consideration. These include the degree of customisation required, the reliability of the SaaS, security, speed and infrastructure. Speed, along with 24/7 access, can be addressed through the service agreement with the SaaS provider. Infrastructure, if it is needed, can be purchased from an IaaS provider, as discussed above. The degree of customisation of applications provided through a SaaS provider may not be as high as that for applications which have been developed in-house. This may mean that their applications may do all of the general tasks required by an organisation but not specific tasks unique to it.

A further issue for the potential customer to consider is the SaaS provider's reliability, which can be broken up into two main areas: quality of service and long-term stability. The issue of reliability of service is a fairly obvious consideration: is the SaaS provider able to offer the quality and level of support that is required? The level of service that is required from the SaaS provider will normally be specified in the **service level agreement**, a document specifying what responsibilities the SaaS provider has and how they are to be fulfilled. Typically, this document will specify responsibilities in periods of normal operation, as well as what is to happen in the event of maintenance, service and disaster.

The long-term stability aspect of reliability acknowledges that, for the subscribing organisation, a fair reliance is being placed on the SaaS provider to be able to provide the services in the mid to long term. This presupposes that the SaaS provider is able to keep operating in the mid to long term. As a result, organisations should consider factors such as the financial stability of the SaaS provider before committing to a particular one, because a SaaS provider that collapses can leave an organisation without valuable services, which can be disruptive, if not disastrous. One way of minimising this risk is for the client to require that the service level agreement provides for a copy of the software code to be deposited in *escrow* (i.e. in trust with a third party). If the SaaS provider fails for any reason, then the code is made available to the client to use on their own system. This requires, first, that the escrow copy is kept current and, second, that the code and associated documentation are sufficiently user-friendly for the code to be successfully installed by the client company. This may not be an option that the SaaS provider is open to.

A final issue for organisations to consider when evaluating a SaaS provider is the security of services offered. Security in this sense refers to how safe the data are that reside with the SaaS provider, especially if they are related to key strategic activities or areas of operation. Because the SaaS provider potentially can be providing the same set of services to many different organisations at once, concern about the security of proprietary data is a very real one.[3]

Software as a service is not a new concept. SaaS represents a different avenue for businesses to go down, allowing them to focus on their core competencies and strategically important activities. However, use of a SaaS provider is no different from any other systems project, requiring careful planning and investigation. At their best, SaaS providers 'offer the ability for a company to focus on its core competencies,

---

[3] Sofiane Tebboune 2001, p. 727.

reduce value chain activity costs and enhance overall competitive advantage'.[4] At their worst, however, they can cause disruption to an organisation's operations and result in significant down time and costs.

14.10 New technologies

LEARNING OBJECTIVE 14.10 Appreciate new technologies and how they may impact the future of accounting.

This section considers some technological enhancements which may have an impact on the future of accounting. This is by no means an exhaustive list, but the following are areas receiving quite a lot of media attention at the time of writing.

Big data

Over the past few years, we as users are creating more and more data that systems are recording. When we access Facebook or tweet or play YouTube clips, we are accessing social media, and information is now available on what tweets are being retweeted, what YouTube clips are going viral and what hash tags are trending. The quantity of social media transactions is enormous — and all this data is being recorded. Because it is being recorded, it can now be analysed. Previously this was not the case.

The data being generated by social media is semi-structured and comes from many sources: tweets, Facebook posts, blogs and browsing patterns of online shoppers. Other systems are also generating this sort of data: for example, traffic systems that monitor motorways in real time, environmental management systems that manage air-conditioning in buildings through the sensor data collected, and computerised monitoring of yacht races. All this data needs to be stored so that we can analyse it. However, this data does not fit with the traditional database models that have been developed for business, so a whole new area of database design has come about for recording this type of data. This data is called **big data** and databases have been designed to accommodate the huge amount of data from social media and real-time systems. Once data is stored in these databases, we can then interrogate it for information. These databases must have the capacity to store a lot of data and must be structured to store data that is incomplete. Think of how you would store browsing patterns of consumers on an online shopping site. Given the site has been operating for years, you would have a lot of information that a business could use, but not all of it would be useful.

The databases that have been created to contain this big data are not like traditional databases. They do not support relational database concepts and they do not support structured query language (SQL). They are called **noSQL databases** and the data they contain is known as **sparse data**. This is data generated from web services and sensor or environmental systems, for example, but not every option on a page is accessed and only data that is accessed is recorded. So, from the given options on a page, only a few may be accessed and recorded. Therefore, if you were looking at a normal database structure, you would have many empty attribute columns, and thus the data you have would be sparse. To illustrate what sparse data is, let's take another example. When an individual records data on their Facebook page, they do not record all their data. They may choose not to include a photo, or other information such as first name, last name, degree, employer, income, country of birth, favourite hobbies, friends, or relationship status. Some of the attributes may be applicable to them, but they may choose not to include them. This means the resulting data is sparse data.

Big data is currently being used to analyse sales and buyer behaviour by stores such as Walmart, Netflix and eBay to improve their operations, and it is likely that accountants will become involved in the world of big data as it involves data being searched on their websites. However, it is unlikely that social media data will form part of data analysis for marketing purposes in accounting firms. As an accountant, an organisation you may work for may be interested in big data because it contains patterns that are useful

---

[4] Smith & Rupp 2002, p. 67.

---

insights into customer behaviour or even financial markets behaviour. Capturing, storing and analysing big data can be expensive for a business and you would need to make sure that any investment in big data would be able to assist decision making or improve operations within the organisation.

Artificial intelligence

Artificial intelligence (AI) is a sub-area of computer science, and is devoted to creating software and hardware to get computers to do things that would be considered 'intelligent', as if people did them. In other words, it is where a machine imitates intelligent human behaviour through pattern recognition, algorithms and machine learning. Many associate artificial intelligence with human-like robots; however, many of us have encountered artificial intelligence in our daily lives. It assists us in finding similar products while shopping online, helps us search for websites and allows for advancements in machine technology, such as robotic vacuum cleaners and cars that park themselves. In addition, machine learning has enabled computerised grading of assignments and translation from one language to another via a product you may have used, Google Translate API.

AI has been implemented in many industries. In 2015 Amazon launched a cloud service that allows companies to build predictive models using their own data. This service works with spreadsheets or huge data sets to make predictions using statistical modelling. Stock traders and investors use AI to automatically analyse portfolio performance and predict market changes. This automation allows information to be analysed quickly, with little error, saving analysts large amounts of time and enabling them to work on more interesting areas, such as deciding on which stocks to invest in. This kind of innovation may eventually lead to investment advice being provided by a market-prediction system. A UK-based company, Arria, has developed a natural language generation software (NLG) which takes large quantities of data, identifies the key information contained in the data, and then delivers that information in natural language text or voice. The software imitates human behaviour and automatically recognises patterns in these large volumes of complex data, with the output being a narrative description of the most significant information, thus simplifying the analysis and communication of data-heavy reports.

In terms of the future of AI in accounting, AI offers many opportunities for accountants to improve their efficiency by allowing processing of large amounts of data, picking up weaker or more complex patterns from the data quickly, and providing more consistency in their decision making as AI does not suffer from human biases. This should enable accountants to provide added value to businesses in the long run. The future of AI in accounting could include the following: (1) improving fraud detection through training the computer on 'normal' activities and allowing for the prediction of fraudulent activities; (2) using machine learning based predictive models to forecast revenues; and (3) improving analysis of unstructured data such as contracts and emails. Indeed, audit firm KPMG has an alliance with IBM's cognitive computer, Watson, to do just that. Watson can read many thousands of pages of contracts or agreements and summarise the information very quickly based on a set of rules or criteria. However, it should be acknowledged that the outputs of machine learning models are predictions, or suggestions, based on mathematical calculations, which requires large training sets and a degree of repeatability in order for the machine learning to be effective and for the output to be meaningful.

The role of the accountant may also change over time as AI permeates the field of accounting. While accountants will still require technical accounting skills and expertise and the ability to apply human judgement, other roles may involve skills to help the organisation derive the right meaning from the data or models, being directly involved with the inputs or outputs of the data, being involved in training and testing the models, or auditing the mathematical calculations and algorithms.

Blockchain

As we have identified in earlier chapters, in a normal set of accounts accounting transactions are recorded in the one place, the general ledger, and each party to the transaction keeps separate records based on transaction source documents such as receipts. This general ledger, indeed the accounting system, can be housed in an accounting package such as Xero or by using cloud-based technology. A recent advancement, allowing digital currency transactions to be recorded, is blockchain technology. A **blockchain** is a distributed decentralised ledger which records digital currency transactions. A **distributed ledger** is a dynamic, independently maintained database that lives across a network of computers. The blockchain is a single ledger that records transactions between organisations, their suppliers and customers, and securely manages digital relationships.

Blockchain stores records in blocks. Each block is time stamped and linked to the previous block, forming a blockchain. Information contained in the blockchain is updated in real time, with the information being both permanent, that is, unable to be deleted, and publicly available to everyone involved in the network. Therefore, all parties to the transaction can see the information in real time. As the information is publicly viewable, it means the blockchain is completely transparent. Further, as entries recorded in the blockchain are cryptographically sealed, with participants to the transaction verifying the transaction in an electronic way, it makes it very difficult to falsify, conceal or destroy entries made. You cannot change a transaction without rewriting every single block in the chain, which means the blockchain is extremely secure.

You might be wondering how blockchain may impact accounting as we currently know it. First, as transactions in the blockchain are verified, it eliminates the need for both parties to enter the transactions in their own ledger. Second, in future it may allow for transactions to be entered into the blockchain and both parties' ledgers.

Once transactions are entered into the blockchain, they cannot be altered. While corrections can be made, and are able to be seen by all parties, it means the data cannot be falsified or manipulated. This adds to the trustworthiness of the data. This, in turn, should make the process of auditing, i.e. examining/checking an entity's accounting records, easier, more reliable and less prone to error. The important role of an auditor will still exist, but it may eliminate some of the more mundane tasks currently undertaken by an auditor. It may also allow auditors to verify automatically a large portion of the most important data behind the financials, freeing them up to spend time on areas where they can add value, for example, on internal control mechanisms.

While application of the blockchain technology in accounting is still in its infancy, there is growing interest in the technology. Australia's leading banks and the Australian Securities Exchange (ASX) are investing in blockchain experiments. For example, the Commonwealth Bank of Australia has tested the blockchain technology by making direct bank-to-bank international settlements. CBA, NAB and Westpac have joined a global consortium to develop standards for blockchain applications. Further, the ASX, working in collaboration with Digital Asset Holdings, a software company which develops and builds distributed ledger technology solutions for the financial services industry, is examining the use of blockchain technology in its clearing and settlement system for share trades in Australia.[5]

In summary, blockchain at its core is a database that is public, that is not owned by anyone; distributed, that is, not stored centrally on a computer but on many computers across the world; constantly synchronised to keep transactions up to date; and secured overall by the art of cryptography to make it hamper proof.

Bitcoin

Blockchain technology was originally developed for the cryptocurrency, **bitcoin**. Bitcoin is a digital currency created in 2009 by an unknown person using the alias Satoshi Nakamoto. Bitcoins are created and held electronically and are stored in a '**digital wallet**' which exists on a user's computer or in the cloud. The wallet is a virtual bank account that allows the user or investor to send or receive bitcoins, pay for goods where bitcoins are accepted or simply save their money. Bitcoins, therefore, buy things electronically; that is, people who own bitcoins can send them to each other using their computers or mobile applications. In this way, it is similar to sending cash digitally. Where sending cash digitally requires a bank to facilitate the transaction, bitcoin does not require the bank as the middle man.

Bitcoin is not physically printed; it is created digitally — that is, mined using computing power in a distributed network. The bitcoin protocol, that is, the rules that make bitcoin work, state that only 21 million bitcoins can ever be created by miners. However, these coins can be divided into smaller parts (one hundred millionth of a bitcoin), which is known as a 'Satoshi'.

Bitcoin is not controlled by one central authority — it is decentralised. Every machine that mines bitcoin and processes transactions makes up the network; that is, no single institution controls the bitcoin network. It is completely transparent as bitcoin stores details of every transaction that happens in the network in the digital general ledger, the blockchain.[6]

Currently, many use bitcoin as a form of investment. At the time of writing, the value of 1 bitcoin was A\$9000.[7] Bitcoin is traded, and given it is considered still to be in its infancy it has a lot of volatility with frequent daily price changes. Another reason for its high volatility is the increased media attention it is receiving, with any news about it ensuring changes in price.

---

[5] Meyer, D 2017, 'The Australian Securities Exchange just made blockchain history', *Fortune*, 7 December, retrieved from http://fortune.com/2017/12/07/blockchain-technology-australian-securities-exchange-asx/; Eyers, J 2016, 'CBA blockchain deal creates the future of trade finance', *Financial Review*, 24 October, retrieved from http://www.afr.com/technology/cba-blockchain-deal-creates-the-future-of-trade-finance-20161021-gs7w98; Eyers, J 2017, 'CBA, Westpac back R3 blockchain capital raising', *Financial Review*, 23 May, retrieved from http://www.afr.com/business/banking-and-finance/financial-services/cba-westpac-back-r3-blockchain-capital-raising-20170523-gwav5e; Eyers, J 2017, 'ASX to upgrade to Blythe Masters' blockchain Digital Asset Holdings technology', *Financial Review*, 7 December, retrieved from http://www.afr.com/business/banking-and-finance/asx%20to%20upgrade%20to%20blythe%20master's%20blockchain-inspired%20digital%20asset%20holdings%20technology-20171206-h00avz.

[6] Bitcoin.org 2018, 'Frequently asked questions', retrieved from https://bitcoin.org/en/faq.

[7] CoinSpot 2018, 'Bitcoin market', retrieved from https://www.coinspot.com.au/trade/btc.

Other technologies

Other technologies that may affect accounting information systems in the future are briefly discussed here. Wearable technology such as smart watches and cloth that are able to access your computer system already exists, although the use of this technology in accounting information systems isn't currently very high. However, with the release of the Apple Watch with apps, this may change over the next few years.

Then there is Google Glass — glasses that can record anything the wearer is looking at, access the internet and even post what they are seeing as a video — which may be an issue if employees wear them in an office that contains confidential information. This may also have an impact on privacy if the wearer's actions are being recorded without their knowledge. All of these issues seem to have transpired for the test group of Google Glass users, so the widespread use of this wearable technology does not seem likely at this stage.

Bring your own device (BYOD) has had a profound effect on businesses. Many individuals have phones, iPads and phablets. Phablets are phone/tablet devices that are bigger than a phone and smaller than a tablet and have increased functionality. Individuals who own these devices want to use them to access their work email systems, so organisations have had to prepare policies on the types of devices that are allowed to access their network and the type of security that has to be installed on an individually owned phone/phablet/iPad to enable it to access the organisation's information systems. In particular, these policies stipulate the type of access the user is permitted — email only or email and access to accounting systems. Given the devices are privately owned by individuals, any such data/access needs to be efficiently removed when the individual leaves the organisation and updates need to be made to the devices.

SUMMARY

14.1 Appreciate the use of a computerised accounting system such as Xero.

Xero accounting software is a well-known computerised accounting package available on the market. It is particularly popular with small businesses as it provides easy transaction processing, monitoring and reporting. It is also accessible anywhere, anytime from various mobile devices, allowing businesses to keep up to date while 'on the go', providing more time for growing their business.

14.2 Understand why organisations are motivated to implement or upgrade to an enterprise resource planning (ERP) system.

The motivation for implementing or upgrading to an ERP product lies in obtaining a product that contains accounts for all aspects of your business. For example, with production and accounting, the information that needs to flow between them such as the amount of product produced and the cost of production can flow between the modules without any need for re-keying data. The data from production is entered into the accounting module in the correct general ledger accounts under double-entry accounting. Stand-alone accounting systems that accommodate only the accounting function need to have another system for production and that data needs to be re-entered into the accounting module.

14.3 Categorise the key business processes that ERP systems support.

ERP systems support the five key business processes that involve the major functions in an organisation:
1. revenue, sales or order to cash
2. payment, purchases or purchase to pay
3. production, manufacturing or conversion
4. human resources and payroll
5. general ledger and financial reporting.

ERP supports these processes through allowing data capture, processing and report production for key decision making in these areas.

14.4 Describe the main modules in an ERP system through using SAP as an example.

The main modules in the SAP ERP system are financial accounting, controlling and profitability analysis, human resources, sales and distribution, and materials management. Most ERP systems have similar modules and similar functionality. These modules cover the five main business processes. The sales and distribution module enables the capture and processing of customer orders, checking of customers' ability to pay, shipping the products to customers and billing customers. The materials management module contains functions related to the payment process, including the management of products while they are in stock. The financial accounting module processes all the accounting transactions for the business, and the data from sales and distribution and materials management are integrated in its chart of accounts. The human resources module provides the functionality to recruit employees, manage employees and their remuneration, and enable payroll processing to occur, as well as additional functions such as employee training. The controlling and profitability module supports internal management accounting for the business, which includes budgets and variances to budgets, as well as analysis of sales and costs.

14.5 Explain how XBRL is used in reporting systems.

Different stakeholders such as company managers, employees, analysts and shareholders require information to make strategic and operational decisions. Information is only accurate, timely and relevant if data are captured, stored and managed efficiently and effectively. XBRL enables the data to be coded for its content. Data in an XBRL format can be easily managed and manipulated by common productivity packages.

14.6 Compare and contrast the different ways XBRL can be used.

XBRL can be attached to your ERP or accounting package if your accounting vendor provides this. Once XBRL is attached to the ERP or accounting package, accounts can be coded according to the taxonomy in use. Tags can be attached to the accounting system at the individual transaction level or to the summarised output, that is, once the reports are prepared.

14.7 Justify the benefits of XBRL.

XBRL provides efficiencies for internal and external users of financial data. Among the advantages are reduced data re-entry and manipulation, the ability for paperless reporting, widespread industry acceptance of data standards, reduced accounting time, recognition by major software vendors, interchangeability and comparability of data, and improved audit quality.

14.8 Understand the various concepts in using XBRL.

XML tags enable us to code any data with a description of its content. The tag travels with the data as it is transferred through multiple software packages. The coding system can be created internally as long as those who code the data have the coding system and those who receive the data also have the coding system to enable them to read the data. Alternatively, the tagging system can be an already created one. XBRL International's website, www.xbrl.org, contains the taxonomies for the financial reporting standards. This provides a consistent coding structure for companies that use International Financial Reporting Standards. These codes don't just code the data for its content; they also add additional metadata. The codes are contained in taxonomies that anyone can use. XBRL requires a taxonomy related to the applicable reporting rules; for example, the International Financial Reporting Standards. The taxonomy contains one or more schemas which contain the individual elements, such as debtors and creditors, for tagging data. The schema contains additional information such as the time period and the currency used.

14.9 Categorise the different types of cloud-based computing including Software as a Service.

The different types of cloud-based computing services include Software as a Service (SaaS), which allows various types of software to be leased and used. Examples of SaaS are Google Apps, Microsoft Office 365, ERPs such as SAP's Business byDesign and customer relationship management software such as e.Salesforce.com. There is also Infrastructure as a Service (IaaS), which provides cloud storage for data offline. With IaaS, customers buy from cloud service providers the use of processing, storage, networking and other infrastructure resources on which to run their information systems, rather than purchasing their own infrastructure. This can include the storage service, Hardware as a Service (HaaS). With HaaS, various components of hardware can be supplied over the internet. There is also Platform as a Service (PaaS), which consists of Infrastructure as a Service and programming tools that allow users to design their own applications.

14.10 Appreciate new technologies and how they may impact the future of accounting.

A number of technologies may affect the future of accounting and the role of the accountant including big data, artificial intelligence, the blockchain and bitcoin. Big data can be analysed for patterns so that a business can use the data to make operational decisions. Artificial intelligence (AI) is where a machine imitates intelligent human behaviour through pattern recognition, algorithms and machine learning. AI offers many opportunities for accountants to improve their efficiency through processing large amounts of data and picking up weaker or more complex patterns from the data quickly, and allows for more consistency in decision making as AI will not suffer from human biases. The role of the accountant may also change over time as AI permeates the field of accounting. While accountants will still require technical accounting skills and expertise and the ability to apply human judgement, other roles may involve skills to help the organisation derive the right meaning from the data or models, being involved in training and testing the models, or auditing the mathematical calculations and algorithms. Blockchain is a database that is public, distributed and constantly synchronised to keep transactions up to date, and secured overall by the art of cryptography. Blockchain has the potential to eliminate the need for both parties to the transaction to enter transactions in their own general ledger and has the potential to change auditor roles. The cryptocurrency bitcoin was also considered in this section.

KEY TERMS

artificial intelligence (AI) A sub-area of computer science that is devoted to creating software and hardware to get computers to do things that would be considered 'intelligent', as if people did them. In other words, it is where a machine imitates intelligent human behaviour.

big data The massive amount of web, system or sensor generated data that existing database management tools have difficulty capturing, storing and managing.

bitcoin A digital currency created in 2009. Bitcoins are created and held electronically and are stored in a 'digital wallet' which exists on a user's computer or in the cloud.

blockchain A database that is public, that is, not owned by anyone; distributed, that is, not stored centrally on a computer but on many computers across the world; constantly synchronised to keep transactions up to date; and secured overall by the art of cryptography to make it hamper proof.

cloud computing A model of computing whereby computing services are obtained from a cloud provider over the internet and paid for based on a usage model.

customer relationship management (CRM) Software designed with the specific purpose of viewing the organisation's data from a customer-centric perspective and that monitors and helps the management of customer interactions with the organisation. Examples include Siebel and SAP.

digital wallet A virtual bank account that allows the user or investor to send or receive bitcoins, pay for goods where bitcoins are accepted or simply save their money.

distributed ledger A dynamic, independently maintained database that lives across a network of computers.

elements Each specific item tagged in a financial statement is an element.

ERP systems Software designed to capture a wide range of information about all key business events including accounting and finance, human resources, sales and marketing, and manufacturing.

eXtensible Business Reporting Language (XBRL) A data standard used when generating financial reports.

eXtensible Markup Language (XML) A hypertext language which is used to add syntax to strings of data by embedding semantic tags. Useful for transaction processing where the data syntax is predictable and well defined.

Hardware as a Service (HaaS) A model of computing whereby hardware computing services are obtained from a cloud provider over the internet and paid for on a usage basis.

HTML (HyperText Markup Language) A language that a web browser uses to display a web page correctly, based on a set of standards.

Infrastructure as a Service (IaaS) A model of computing whereby computing infrastructure such as hardware, software, data, network and services are obtained from a cloud provider over the internet and paid for on a usage basis.

instance document An XBRL tagged document containing information about an organisation's financial statements at one instant in time.

metadata Data that describes other data.

noSQL databases Databases generally used for big data that do not follow relational database rules or have the ability to use SQL to interrogate the data for information.

Platform as a Service (PaaS) A model of computing whereby computing infrastructure as well as programming tools are obtained from a cloud provider over the internet and paid for on a usage basis.

schemas Formal descriptions of the structure and content of a database.

semantic approach An approach focused on meaning.

service level agreement A document specifying what responsibilities the Software as a Service provider has and how these are to be fulfilled.

Software as a Service (SaaS) Companies that provide software applications that can be leased by a range of clients.

sparse data Data from web services and sensor or environmental systems is considered to be sparse data in that it provides many attributes but the attributes instances recorded may be very small.

supply chain management (SCM) Systems that monitor and assist the management of supplier interactions with the organisation.

taxonomies The dictionaries that define each accounting item that can be tagged in XBRL.

SELF-STUDY QUESTIONS

14.1 The four major functions that are linked by an ERP system are: **LO2**
(a) sales/marking, manufacturing, accounting/finance, and human resources.
(b) sales/marketing, manufacturing, customer, and accounting/finance.
(c) customer, sales/marketing, production, accounting/finance and human resources.
(d) customer, sales/marketing, production, and accounting/finance.

14.2 Which of the following is not an advantage of XBRL? **LO7**
(a) Interchangeable data.
(b) Less accurate financial reporting.
(c) Recognition by major accounting package vendors.
(d) Paperless reporting.

14.3 Which of the following best describes the relationship between accounting information **LO5**
systems and accounting standards?
(a) Accounting information systems must comply with all accounting standards.
(b) Accounting standards dictate the way an accounting information system must store and handle financial data.
(c) Accounting information systems that recognise and comply with accounting standards are advantageous for tax purposes.
(d) There is no direct relationship between accounting standards and accounting information systems.

14.4 XBRL will potentially assist in strengthening information transparency because it: **LO7**
(a) offers greater search power and customised information for different stakeholders.
(b) is a typology based on specific business reporting requirements.
(c) is technically superior to HTML and reduces the reporting time by businesses.
(d) offers paperless reporting based on industry-specific standards.

14.5 Which of the following statements is not true about cloud computing? **LO9**
(a) It removes all concern about data and systems security for businesses.
(b) It relies on the internet as the platform for delivering services to users.
(c) It consists of three types of services: SaaS, IaaS (including HaaS) and PaaS.
(d) It allows smaller firms to use resources that may have been previously unaffordable.

14.6 What best describes the big data phenomenon? **LO10**
(a) Computing software that can heal itself.
(b) Green computing initiatives.
(c) Software services that can be leased.
(d) Data that has come from social media or environmental systems.

14.7 When using Xero, which accounting process is automatically performed when a sales
invoice is 'approved'? **LO1**
(a) Posting the transaction to the ledger accounts.
(b) Updating the bank reconciliation.

(c) Preparing the profit and loss statement.

(d) Recording the payment on the invoice.

14.8 Integrated accounting packages and various modules can be purchased based on the: **LO1**

(a) size of the business.

(b) nature of the business.

(c) number of employees.

(d) all of the above.

QUESTIONS

14.1	Describe each of the accounting functions that are available using Xero.	**LO1**
14.2	Explain how an ERP system integrates the activities within an organisation.	**LO2**
14.3	Explain the benefits of an ERP system.	**LO2**
14.4	What key business processes does an ERP system support?	**LO3**
14.5	Explain how an ERP system supports key business processes.	**LO2**
14.6	Describe the typical modules in the SAP ERP system.	**LO4**
14.7	Discuss how XBRL is used in reporting systems.	**LO5**
14.8	What are the benefits of XBRL for internal and external users of financial information?	**LO7**
14.9	Describe the current state of adoption of XBRL reporting.	**LO7**
14.10	Discuss what cloud computing is.	**LO10**
14.11	Explain the concept of big data.	**LO10**
14.12	Explain blockchain and bitcoin.	**LO10**
14.13	Define artificial intelligence.	**LO10**

EXERCISES

E14.1 Determine the use and usefulness of Xero for a small business. **LO1**

Mary White is the owner of a small florist shop. She currently records all her business transactions in an electronic spreadsheet at the end of the day after her shop has closed. She is looking to switch to a more efficient electronic accounting software package that will enable her to quickly and easily record her sales and purchases as they occur during the day. This will provide her with the ability to focus on expanding her business as well as having more time to spend with her family. As her accountant, Mary has approached you to ask if the Xero accounting software would be suitable for her business needs. Explain how using Xero will enable Mary to efficiently record her business transactions, assist her in monitoring the business's progress, and enable her to expand her business.

E14.2 Explain the benefits of using an ERP system. **LO2, 3**

Green Grocer is the name of a business that runs 8 bookstores around the country. It sells all types of books, from fiction, non-fiction and children's to technical and academic books. Green Grocer has decided to opt for an ERP system. Explain the importance of an ERP system for businesses and how it will benefit the Green Grocer book chain.

E14.3 Explain XBRL and the benefits of using XBRL. **LO6, 7**

Cafe Corner Ltd is a successful food company that has developed a large market presence in the meat pie industry. The company has several thousand shareholders, as well as many key suppliers of financial and production resources. In a heated discussion with one of its major lenders, Al's Bank, it was suggested to the CEO of Cafe Corner Ltd that, in order to acquire funding for further expansion plans to go ahead, the business would need to improve its reporting. Al's Bank wanted Cafe Corner Ltd to make its financial data more accessible and easier to analyse and compare, both across time and with that of other companies. Upon hearing this, the CEO of Cafe Corner Ltd, who did not have an information systems background, responded with 'We cannot do that without totally redesigning our system and totally altering our reporting system in order to give you direct access'. The bank manager responded, 'What about adopting XBRL? Some of our other clients have used it quite successfully.'

The CEO of Cafe Corner Ltd was dumbfounded — he thought XBRL was what controlled the display of web pages and could not see how it would answer the bank's problem. Thus he left the meeting confused, flustered and uncertain about where to head from here.

You have been asked by the CEO of Cafe Corner Ltd to clear up his confusion. He requests the following of you:

(a) Prepare an outline that describes the XBRL.

(b) Conduct a search and identify some of the organisations that are using XBRL. Briefly describe the benefits these organisations get from XBRL.

E14.4 Explain the benefits of using XBRL.   **LO7**

SBR was developed as a standard for governmental reporting in Australia. It is used to facilitate and cut compliance costs in reporting to the government. Rather than using XBRL, the Australian government came up with its own taxonomy for how items need to be classified for reporting. The accounting, financial and payroll software has the SBR codes applied for all government reporting. This means that, when a government organisation reports to government, they have exactly the same standards of reporting. SBR was designed in conjunction with the Australian, state and territory governments and their software professionals. The Australian government also consulted the Netherlands government who had used it on a smaller scale. They also ensured that the chief agency CEOs were supportive of SBR.

> The SBR model includes the adoption of a standards-based language to report to government, functionality in financial, accounting and payroll software to pre-fill and electronically lodge forms, a single authentication credential to report to many agencies, and a receipt in real time to confirm the report has been received. It sounds pretty simple as a business proposition and most leaders can understand this and learn to expect it.
>
> SBR requires 12 agencies to communicate their reporting needs and be able to receive reporting information in a single language. Rather than adopt one of the agency's reporting standards, **SBR adopted XBRL as a standard**, which was originally developed by the accounting community for financial reporting. A key task from the outset was to ensure the overall SBR design would reduce the reporting burden for business and generate the expected savings.[8]

The main issue faced with the adoption of the SBR standards by the Australian government was the need to find competent advisers with knowledge of its application. The other important issue was educating accounting staff on its adoption and use. It was a new technology but its adoption and use were reasonably straightforward. The use of internet software and XML meant that it did not require an investment in software. The development of SBR reporting has the potential to save the governmental reporting institutions significant time and money.

Given SBR adopted XBRL as the standard, discuss the advantages for preparers and users of adopting XBRL.

E14.5 Explain the different ways XBRL is used.   **LO6**

Prepare a report explaining the two approaches to XBRL tagging — tags at the end of the financial reporting process and during information processing.

E14.6 Explain the benefits of XBRL.   **LO7**

XBRL is ensuring the standardisation of financial reports. Why is this important in today's global environment?

---

[8] Madden, P 2010, 'Cut compliance costs', *CIO*, August, p. 19.

E14.7 Explain the benefits of XBRL. LO7

You have been asked to advise on a possible XBRL installation for Emporium. Emporium is a multistore retail business that sells products such as DVDs, CDs, mp3 players, game consoles and TVs. In addition to these retail sales, Emporium also sells music, games and DVDs via its website. The company is required to report to shareholders, regulatory bodies and the tax office/inland revenue department. Emporium currently has an ERP system with SAP installed on it. With reference to Emporium, discuss the benefits and costs of using XBRL in this organisation.

E14.8 Explain the relevance of XBRL to accountants. LO5, 6, 7

Why do accountants need an understanding of XBRL? Isn't this something we should leave up to the information technology people?

E14.9 Explain the importance of XBRL. LO5

Should XBRL be mandated in each reporting jurisdiction? Give arguments for and against.

E14.10 Determine the different types of cloud computing models applicable to accounting. LO9

As part of a team, individually search the Web for information on cloud computing models. Particularly look for accounting packages that use Software as a Service (SaaS) such as ERP SAP's Business byDesign. Discuss what is required to install this package.

E14.11 Determine the use of big data. LO10

Search for examples on the internet where big data has been used to generate new insights.

E14.12 Determine the current use of bitcoin. LO10

Search newspaper articles and the internet to identify the current price of bitcoin. Discuss whether bitcoin has become more widely accepted.

E14.13 Determine the use of the blockchain and its impact on accounting. LO10

Has blockchain disrupted or revolutionised the world of accounting as it was claimed to have the potential to do? Discuss.

E14.14 Explain the impact of artificial intelligence on accountants. LO10

'Artificial intelligence has the potential to change the role of the accountant.' Explain.

BUILDING BUSINESS SKILLS

COMPUTERISED ACCOUNTING PROGRAMS — AN INTRODUCTION

BBS14.1 There are many businesses that sell computerised accounting software packages such as Xero, MYOB and QuickBooks. Many businesses provide detailed product information on their web page and some will even allow potential customers to try the software before purchasing it. If you would like to try using a computerised accounting system, you can go to the Xero web page https://www.xero.com/au/, MYOB web page https://www.myob.com.au/products/accounting/ and the QuickBooks web page http://quickbooks.intuit.com/ to learn about and try the software.

COMMUNICATION ACTIVITY

BBS14.2 Quite a large amount of information is available regarding artificial intelligence. Update your knowledge on artificial intelligence by searching newspapers and the internet. Prepare a summary of the recent advancements in artificial intelligence and whether it has had an impact on accounting.

RESEARCH CASE

BBS14.3 There has been a shift in the trading opportunities for the amateur trader. In the 90s, the financial instruments people had access to were for use in the regular stock markets, whereas today, the opportunities are wider. The following is an excerpt from an article published in *Investment Insights* in October 2017.

All over the world we now have access to instruments that were previously only able to be touched by the financial elites. There are limitless amounts of things to access: futures, options, normal equity markets, CFDs (contracts for difference), forex and cryptocurrencies (Bitcoin).[9]

Compare and contrast forex and bitcoin. Have other cryptocurrencies joined bitcoin as an investment opportunity?

ANSWERS
Answers to self-study questions
14.1 (a) 14.2 (b) 14.3 (a) 14.4 (a) 14.5 (a) 14.6 (d) 14.7 (a) 14.8 (d)

ACKNOWLEDGEMENTS

Photo: © mapodile / Getty Images
Photo: © ipopba / Getty Images
Photo: © DragonImages / Getty Images
Photo: © fishbones / Getty Images
Photo: © Ociacia / Shutterstock.com
Figure 14.1: © Xero Limited
Figure 14.2: © Xero Limited
Figure 14.3: © Xero Limited
Text: © Australian Taxation Office for the Commonwealth of Australia

---

[9] Truelove, A 2017, 'Bitcoin v forex, which one is better for trading?', *Investment Insights*, 27 October, retrieved from https://www.nestegg.com.au/investment-insights/11102-bitcoin-vs-forex-which-one-is-better-for-trading.

MANAGERIAL ACCOUNTING SUPPLEMENT

CHAPTER 15

Introduction to management accounting

LEARNING OBJECTIVES

After studying this chapter, you should be able to:

15.1 explain the distinguishing features of management accounting

15.2 identify the three broad functions of management and discuss how management accounting tools assist these functions

15.3 define the three classes of manufacturing costs

15.4 distinguish between product and period costs

15.5 explain the difference between a merchandising and a manufacturing statement of profit or loss

15.6 explain the difference between a merchandising and a manufacturing statement of financial position

15.7 indicate how cost of goods manufactured and cost of sales are determined

15.8 describe contemporary developments in management accounting

15.9 prepare a worksheet and closing entries for a manufacturing entity.

Chapter preview

This and the next three chapters focus on issues associated with the strategic direction of a business. The accounting information system provides the necessary data for the management team. We examine the relationship between costs, volume and profit, and the function of budgets in managing a business.

In the previous financial accounting chapters, you studied the form and content of the financial statements for the external users of financial information such as shareholders and creditors. These financial statements represent the main product of financial accounting. The remaining chapters in this text concern management accounting, which focuses mainly on the preparation of reports for the internal users of financial information (i.e. managers at all levels of the entity). These reports are the main product of management accounting. The content and organisation of this chapter are as follows.

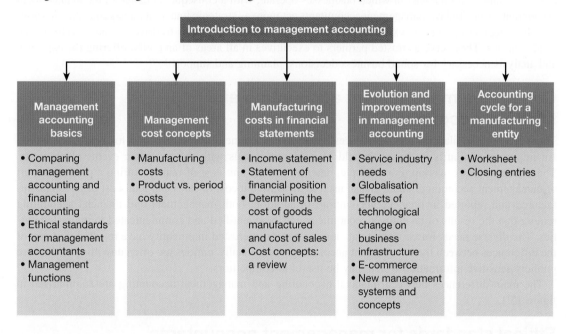

15.1 Management accounting basics

LEARNING OBJECTIVE 15.1 Explain the distinguishing features of management accounting.

Management accounting, also called *managerial accounting*, is the process of identifying, measuring, reporting and analysing information about economic events in an entity. In other words, it is a field of accounting that provides economic and financial information for managers and other internal users. The activities that are part of management accounting (and the chapters in which they are discussed) are as follows:

1. explaining manufacturing and non-manufacturing costs and how they are reported in the financial statements (this chapter)
2. calculating the cost of rendering a service or manufacturing a product (chapter 16)
3. determining the behaviour of costs and expenses as activity levels change and analysing cost–volume–profit relationships within an entity (chapter 17)
4. formalising budgets as a basis for controlling costs and expenses to assist management in profit planning and assigning responsibility for cost centres (chapter 18).

Management accounting applies to all types of businesses — service, merchandising and manufacturing — and to all forms of business entities — sole proprietorships, partnerships and companies. Although the information needs may be different, both a small corner store and a large service entity such as Air New Zealand require costing information to price their grocery items and airline services appropriately. Moreover, management accounting is needed in not-for-profit entities as well as in profit-oriented entities. For example, non-profit entities such as World Vision need to work out how much sponsorship income they require to provide assistance such as access to food, clean water and education to children in developing countries.

The traditional role of the management accountant was to provide information that enabled management to make decisions. Globalisation and changes in technology have led to many opportunities and risks associated with the way in which businesses operate, with a consequent change in the management accountant's role. Today, management accountants act more as strategic financial management professionals who integrate accounting expertise with advanced management skills to drive business performance inside entities. They serve as trusted partners to executives in all areas of an entity, offering the expertise and analysis necessary for sound business decisions, planning and support.[*]

Comparing management accounting and financial accounting

There are both similarities and differences between management accounting and financial accounting. An important similarity is that each field of accounting deals with the economic events of an entity. Thus, their interests overlap. For example, determining the unit cost of manufacturing a product is part of management accounting, and it is also used to measure the cost of sales and total cost of goods manufactured and reported in financial accounting. In addition, both management and financial accounting require that the results of an entity's economic events be quantified and communicated to interested parties. The diverse needs for economic data among parties interested in an entity have resulted in many of the differences between the two fields of accounting. Additionally, entities are often unwilling to disclose publicly sensitive information which may be useful to competitors.

The main differences between financial accounting and management accounting are summarised in figure 15.1.

Ethical standards for management accountants

Management accountants need to adhere to a high standard of ethical conduct. Australia does not have a professional body dealing specifically with management accountants, but many belong to the two main Australian professional accounting bodies (Chartered Accountants Australia & New Zealand (CA ANZ) and CPA Australia). The two accounting bodies established the Accounting Professional & Ethical Standards Board (APESB) to set the code of ethics and professional standards by which their members are required to abide. These ethical rules and standards promote the integrity of the accounting profession by setting out the principles of professional and ethical accounting practice.

Some Australian management accountants are members of overseas management accounting bodies, such as the Certified Institute of Management Accountants (CIMA) in the United Kingdom and the Institute of Management Accountants (IMA) in the United States. The US code, entitled *Statement of Ethical Professional Practice*, divides the management accountant's responsibility into four areas: (1) competence, (2) confidentiality, (3) integrity and (4) credibility. The code states that management accountants should not commit acts in violation of these standards, nor should they condone acts by others within their organisations.

---

[*]Institute of Management Accounting 1997–2018, 'About management accounting', www.imanet.org.

FIGURE 15.1 Differences between financial and management accounting

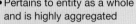

Financial accounting		Management accounting
• External users, who include shareholders, creditors and regulatory agencies.	**Main users of reports**	• Internal users, who are officers, department heads, managers and supervisors in the business.
• Classified financial statements. • Issued quarterly (for some entities), 6-monthly and annually.	**Types and frequency of reports**	• Internal reports. • Issued as frequently as the need arises.
• To provide general-purpose information for all users.	**Purpose of reports**	• To provide special-purpose information for a particular user for a specific reason.
• Pertains to entity as a whole and is highly aggregated (condensed). • Limited to double-entry accounting system and cost data. • Reporting standard is generally accepted accounting principles.	**Content of reports**	• Pertains to subunits of the entity and may be very detailed. • May extend beyond double-entry accounting system to any type of relevant data. • Reporting standard is relevance to the decision to be made.
• Annual independent audit by external auditor.	**Verification process**	• No independent audits.

15.2 Management functions

LEARNING OBJECTIVE 15.2 Identify the three broad functions of management and discuss how management accounting tools assist these functions.

The management of an entity performs three broad functions:
1. planning
2. directing and motivating
3. controlling.

   In performing these functions, management must make decisions that have a significant impact on the entity.

Planning requires management to look ahead and to establish objectives. These objectives are often as diverse as maximising short-term profits and market share, maintaining a commitment to environmental protection, and contributing to social programs. A key objective of management is to add value to the business under its control. Value for a company is usually measured by the trading price of the company's shares and by the potential selling price of the company. Planning also involves long-term strategic objectives which the entity strives towards.

Directing and motivating involve coordinating an entity's diverse activities and human resources to produce a smooth-running operation. This function relates to the implementation of planned objectives. For example, in entities such as Coca-Cola Amatil, Domino's Pizza Enterprises Ltd, JB Hi-Fi and BMW, purchasing, manufacturing, warehousing and selling must be coordinated. Similarly, it is necessary to select executives, appoint managers and supervisors, and hire and train employees. Most larger entities prepare organisation charts to show the interrelationship of activities and the delegation of authority and responsibility within the entity. Some entities may also use performance-linked bonus payments to reward and motivate employees to work towards achieving the organisation's goals.

The third management function, *controlling*, is the process of keeping the entity's activities on track. In controlling operations, management determines whether planned goals are being met and what changes are necessary when there are deviations from targeted objectives.

How do managers achieve control? In small entities, a manager might use personal observation. A smart manager in a small operation should know the right questions to ask and how to evaluate the answers. But such a system in a large entity would be chaotic. Imagine the CEO of Air New Zealand attempting to determine whether planned objectives are being met without some record of what has happened and what is expected to occur. Thus, a formal system of evaluation that includes such items as budgets, responsibility centres and performance evaluation reports is typically used in large entities.

As shown by the graphic, the three functions of management may be depicted as the spokes of a wheel that move around the axle or hub of decision making. Decision making is not a separate management function. Rather, it is the outcome of the exercise of judgement in planning, directing and motivating, and controlling.

You are now ready to study specific applications of management accounting. As you study these applications, you will encounter many new terms, concepts and reports. At the same time, you will find some new uses and interpretations of a number of familiar financial accounting terms.

LEARNING REFLECTION AND CONSOLIDATION

Review it

1. Compare and contrast financial accounting and management accounting, identifying the principal differences.
2. Identify and discuss the three broad functions of management.

Management cost concepts

To perform the three management functions effectively, management needs information. One very important type of information is related to costs. For example, questions such as the following need answering.

1. What costs are involved in making a product?
2. If production volume is decreased, how much will costs decrease?
3. What impact will automation have on total costs?
4. How can costs best be controlled in the entity?

To answer these questions, management needs reliable and relevant cost information. We now explain and illustrate the costs that management uses.

15.3 Manufacturing costs

LEARNING OBJECTIVE 15.3 Define the three classes of manufacturing costs.

Manufacturing consists of activities and processes that convert raw materials into finished goods. Contrast this type of operation with merchandising, which sells goods in the form in which they are purchased. Manufacturing costs are typically classified as shown in figure 15.2.

Direct materials

To obtain the materials that will be converted into the finished product, the manufacturer purchases raw materials. Raw materials represent the basic materials and parts that are to be used in the manufacturing process. For example, steel, plastics and tyres are raw materials used in making motor vehicles.

FIGURE 15.2 Classifications of manufacturing costs

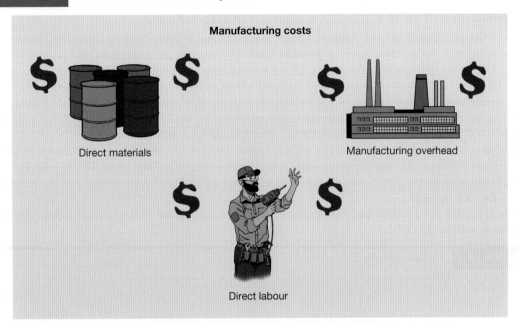

Raw materials that can be physically and economically traced to the finished product during the manufacturing process are called **direct materials**. Examples include flour in the baking of bread, syrup in the bottling of soft drinks, and steel in the making of motor vehicles.

Conversely, some raw materials cannot be easily associated with the finished product; these are considered indirect materials. **Indirect materials** (1) do not physically become part of the finished product, such as lubricants and polishing compounds used in the manufacturing process, or (2) cannot be traced in an economically feasible manner because their physical association with the finished product is too small in terms of cost, such as nails, washers and the like. Indirect materials are accounted for as part of *manufacturing overhead*.

Direct labour

The work of factory employees that can be physically and economically traced to converting raw materials into finished goods is considered **direct labour**. Bottlers in a soft-drink factory, bakers in a bakery, and print press operators in a printery are examples of employees whose activities are usually classified as direct labour. In contrast, the wages of maintenance people and supervisors are usually identified as **indirect labour** because their efforts have no physical association with the finished product, or it is not economically feasible to trace the costs to the goods produced. Like indirect materials, indirect labour is classified as manufacturing overhead.

Manufacturing overhead

Manufacturing overhead consists of costs that are indirectly associated with the manufacture of the finished product. Terms such as *factory overhead*, *indirect manufacturing costs* and *burden* are sometimes used instead of manufacturing overhead. These costs may also be defined as manufacturing costs that cannot be classified as either direct materials or direct labour. Manufacturing overhead includes indirect materials, indirect labour, depreciation on factory buildings and machinery, and insurance and maintenance on factory facilities.

The composition of overheads is further explored in the next chapter.

15.4 Product vs. period costs

LEARNING OBJECTIVE 15.4 Distinguish between product and period costs.

Each of the manufacturing cost elements (direct materials, direct labour and manufacturing overhead) are product costs. As the term suggests, **product costs** are costs that are a necessary and integral part of producing the finished product. These costs do not become expenses until the finished goods inventory is sold. The expense is cost of sales when sales occurred. Direct materials and direct labour are often referred to as **prime costs** because of their direct association with the manufacturing of the finished product. In addition, because direct labour and manufacturing overhead are incurred in converting direct materials into finished goods, these two cost elements are often referred to as **conversion costs**.

Period costs are costs that are identified with a specific time period rather than with a saleable product. These costs relate to non-manufacturing costs and therefore are not product costs. Period costs include selling, administrative expenses and financial expenses that are deducted from revenues in the period in which they are incurred.

The foregoing relationships and cost terms are summarised in figure 15.3. Our main concern in this chapter is with product costs.

FIGURE 15.3	Product versus period costs

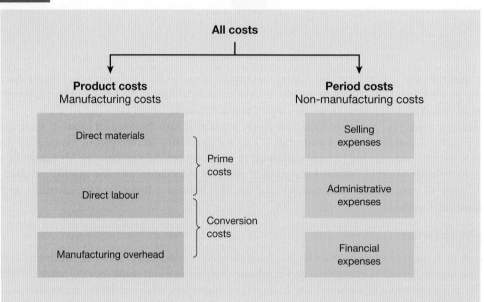

Helpful hint: What are the effects of absorbing office insurance expense in the ending inventory balances?

Answer: Office insurance expense is an administrative expense (period cost) not pertaining to production. Treating it as a product cost will overstate an asset (inventory), understate expenses and therefore overstate profit for the period.

LEARNING REFLECTION AND CONSOLIDATION

Review it

1. What are the major cost classifications involved in manufacturing a product?
2. What are product and period costs and their relationship to the manufacturing process?

15.5 Manufacturing costs in financial statements

LEARNING OBJECTIVE 15.5 Explain the difference between a merchandising and a manufacturing statement of profit or loss.

The financial statements of a manufacturing business are very similar to those of a merchandising entity. The main differences pertain to the cost of sales section of the statement of profit or loss and the current assets section of the statement of financial position.

Statement of profit or loss

Under a periodic inventory system, the statement of profit or loss of a merchandising entity and a manufacturing entity differ in the cost of sales section. For a merchandising entity, cost of sales is calculated by adding the beginning inventory and the cost of goods purchased and subtracting the ending inventory. For a manufacturing entity, cost of sales is calculated by adding the beginning finished goods inventory and cost of goods manufactured and subtracting the ending finished goods inventory. The different components are shown graphically in figure 15.4.

FIGURE 15.4	Cost of sales components

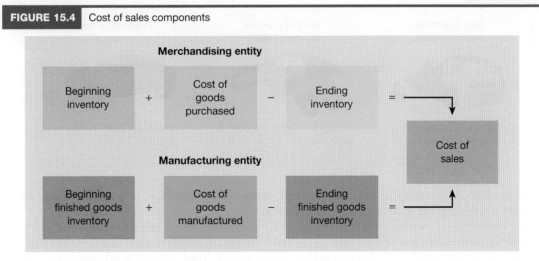

Helpful hint: Note that a periodic inventory system is used here.

The cost of sales sections for merchandising and manufacturing entities shown in figure 15.5 highlight the different presentations.

FIGURE 15.5 Cost of sales sections of merchandising and manufacturing statement of profit or loss

MERCHANDISING ENTITY Statement of profit or loss (partial) for the year ended 31 December		MANUFACTURING ENTITY Statement of profit or loss (partial) for the year ended 31 December	
COST OF SALES		COST OF SALES	
Inventory, 1 January	$ 70 000	Finished goods inventory, 1 January	$ 90 000
Cost of goods purchased	650 000	Cost of goods manufactured*	370 000
Cost of goods available for sale	720 000	Cost of goods available for sale	460 000
Inventory, 31 December	400 000	Finished goods inventory, 31 December	80 000
Cost of sales	**$320 000**	**Cost of sales**	**$380 000**

*See figure 15.9

The other sections of a statement of profit or loss are similar for both a merchandising and a manufacturing entity.

A number of accounts are involved in determining the cost of goods manufactured. To eliminate excessive detail in the statement of profit or loss, it is customary to show in the statement only the total cost of goods manufactured and to present the details in a cost of goods manufactured schedule. The form and content of this schedule are shown in figure 15.9.

15.6 Statement of financial position

LEARNING OBJECTIVE 15.6 Explain the difference between a merchandising and a manufacturing statement of financial position.

Unlike the statement of financial position for a merchandising entity, which shows just one category of inventory, the statement of financial position for a manufacturing entity may have three inventory accounts, as shown in figure 15.6.

FIGURE 15.6 Inventory accounts for a manufacturing entity

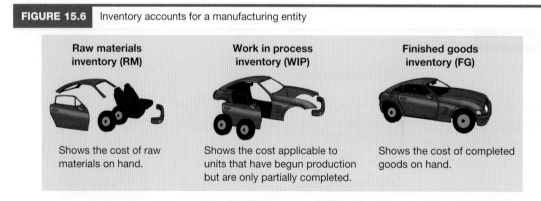

Raw materials inventory (RM)	Work in process inventory (WIP)	Finished goods inventory (FG)
Shows the cost of raw materials on hand.	Shows the cost applicable to units that have begun production but are only partially completed.	Shows the cost of completed goods on hand.

Finished goods inventory is to a manufacturing entity what inventory is to a merchandising entity because it represents the goods that are available for sale.

The current assets sections presented in figure 15.7 contrast the presentation of inventories of a merchandising entity with those of a manufacturing entity. Manufacturing inventories are generally listed in the order of their liquidity — their expected realisation in cash. Thus, finished goods inventory is listed first. The remainder of the statement of financial position is similar for the two types of entities.

MERCHANDISING ENTITY Statement of financial position (partial) as at 31 December		MANUFACTURING ENTITY Statement of financial position (partial) as at 31 December		
Current assets		Current assets		
Cash	$100 000	Cash		$180 000
Receivables (net)	210 000	Receivables (net)		210 000
Inventory	400 000	Inventories:		
Prepaid expenses	22 000	Finished goods	$80 000	
Total current assets	$732 000	Work in process	25 200	
		Raw materials	22 800	128 000
		Prepaid expenses		18 000
		Total current assets		$536 000

Each step in the accounting cycle for a merchandising entity is applicable to that of a manufacturing entity. For example, before financial statements are prepared, adjusting entries are required. The adjusting entries are essentially the same as those of a merchandising entity.

The closing entries for a manufacturing entity are also similar to those of a merchandising entity. The use of a worksheet in the accounting cycle and the journalising of closing entries for a manufacturing entity are illustrated in section 15.9.

DECISION-MAKING TOOLKIT

Decision/issue	Info needed for analysis	Tool or technique to use for decision	How to evaluate results to make decision
What is the composition of a manufacturing entity's inventory?	Amount of raw materials, work in process, and finished goods inventory	Statement of financial position	Determine whether there are sufficient finished goods inventory, raw materials and work in process to meet forecast demand.

15.7 Determining the cost of goods manufactured and cost of sales

LEARNING OBJECTIVE 15.7 Indicate how cost of goods manufactured and cost of sales are determined.

An example may be helpful in showing how the cost of goods manufactured for a period is determined. Assume that Ford has a number of motor vehicles in various stages of production on 1 January. In total, these partially completed units are recorded in the *work in process (WIP) inventory* as the beginning balance. The costs assigned to beginning WIP inventory are based on the manufacturing costs incurred in the previous period. In the current year, Ford continues the production of motor vehicles. The manufacturing costs incurred in the current year are used first to complete the work in process on 1 January and then to start the production of other vehicles. The sum of the direct materials costs, direct labour costs and manufacturing overhead incurred in the current year is the **total manufacturing costs**.

We now have two cost amounts: (1) the cost of the beginning WIP inventory and (2) the total manufacturing costs for the current period. The sum of these costs is the **total cost of work in process** for the year.

Helpful hint: Does the amount of 'total manufacturing costs for the current year' include the amount of 'beginning work in process inventory'?

Answer: No.

At the end of the year, some vehicles may be only partially completed. The costs of these units become the cost of the *ending WIP inventory*. To find the **cost of goods manufactured**, we subtract this cost from the total cost of work in process.

Assume that Ford also has a number of completed motor vehicles sitting in its warehouse, ready to be sold on 1 January. These completed units are recorded in the *finished goods (FG) inventory* as the beginning balance. These completed units, plus the units manufactured in the current period, make up the *total cost of goods available for sale*. Of course, Ford may not be able to sell all these completed vehicles at the end of the period. These unsold units become the cost of the *ending FG inventory*. To find the **cost of sales (COS)**, we subtract this cost from the total cost of goods available for sale.

The determination of the cost of goods manufactured and sales is shown graphically in figure 15.8.

FIGURE 15.8 Cost of goods manufactured and cost of sales formula

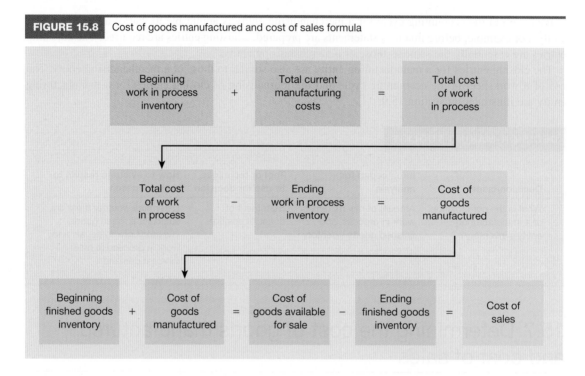

An internal financial schedule called the *cost of goods manufactured schedule* shows each of the cost elements explained in figure 15.8. The schedule for Olsen Manufacturing Ltd using assumed data is shown in figure 15.9. Note that detailed data are presented for direct materials and manufacturing overhead.

A review of figure 15.8 along with an examination of the cost of goods manufactured schedule, figure 15.9, should help you distinguish between 'total manufacturing costs' and 'cost of goods manufactured'. The difference is the effect of the change in work in process during the period. Once the cost of goods manufactured is calculated, we then consider the changes in beginning and ending FG inventory to work out the cost of sales. These relationships can be observed in figure 15.10.

OLSEN MANUFACTURING LTD
Costs of goods manufactured schedule
for the year ended 31 December 2019

Work in process, 1 January			$ 18 400
Direct materials			
Raw materials inventory, 1 January	$ 6 700		
Raw materials purchases	152 500		
Total raw materials available for use	169 200		
Less: Raw materials inventory, 31 December	(22 800)		
Direct materials used		$146 400	
Direct labour		175 600	
Manufacturing overhead			
Indirect labour	14 300		
Factory repairs	12 600		
Factory power	10 100		
Factory depreciation	9 440		
Factory insurance	8 360		
Total manufacturing overhead		54 800	
Total manufacturing costs for the year			376 800
Total cost of work in process			395 200
Less: **Work in process, 31 December**			(25 200)
Cost of goods manufactured			**$370 000**

FIGURE 15.10 Statement of profit or loss (partial)

OLSEN MANUFACTURING LTD
Statement of profit or loss (partial)
for the year ended 31 December 2019

Sales (net)		$660 000
COST OF SALES		
Finished goods inventory, 1 January	$ 90 000	
Cost of goods manufactured (from figure 15.9)	370 000	
Cost of goods available for sale	460 000	
Less: Finished goods inventory, 31 December	(80 000)	
Cost of sales		380 000
Gross profit		**$280 000**

DECISION-MAKING TOOLKIT

Decision/issue	Info needed for analysis	Tool or technique to use for decision	How to evaluate results to make decision
Is the entity maintaining control over the costs of production?	Cost of material, labour and overhead; expected revenue from product sales	Cost of goods manufactured schedule for current and previous periods	Compare the cost of goods manufactured with sales revenue; compare these figures with those of previous periods to analyse trends.

Cost concepts: a review

You have learned a number of cost concepts in this chapter. Because many of these concepts are new, we believe an extended example will be helpful in understanding how these various cost concepts are used. To illustrate, assume that Northridge Ltd manufactures and sells pre-hung metal doors. Recently, it decided to start selling pre-hung timber doors as well. An old warehouse that the business presently owns will be used to manufacture the new product. To manufacture and sell these pre-hung timber doors, Northridge identifies the following costs.

1. The material cost (timber) for each door is $10.
2. Labour costs involved in constructing a timber door are $8 per door.
3. Depreciation on the new equipment used to make the timber door using the straight-line method is $25 000 per year.
4. Rates and taxes on the old warehouse used to make the timber doors are $6000 per year.
5. Advertising costs for the pre-hung timber doors total $2500 per month or $30 000 per year.
6. Sales commissions related to pre-hung timber doors sold are $4 per door.
7. Maintenance salaries for the old warehouse are $28 000.
8. Salary of the factory manager in charge of pre-hung timber doors is $70 000.
9. Cost of shipping pre-hung timber doors is $12 per door sold.

These manufacturing and selling costs can be assigned to the various categories shown in figure 15.11.

FIGURE 15.11   Assignment of costs to cost categories

| | Product costs | | | | | |
Cost item	Direct materials	Direct labour	Manufacturing overhead	Period costs	Prime costs	Conversion costs
1. Material cost ($10) per door	X				X	
2. Labour costs ($8) per door		X			X	X
3. Depreciation on new equipment ($25 000 per year)			X			X
4. Rates and taxes ($6000 per year)			X			X
5. Advertising costs ($30 000 per year)				X		
6. Sales commission ($4 per door)				X		
7. Maintenance salaries ($28 000 per year)			X			X
8. Salary of factory manager ($70 000)			X			X
9. Cost of shipping pre-hung doors ($12 per door)				X		

Remember that total manufacturing costs are the sum of the product costs — direct materials, direct labour, and manufacturing overhead costs. Assume that Northridge Ltd produces 10 000 pre-hung timber doors in the first year. The total manufacturing costs are shown in figure 15.12.

FIGURE 15.12   Calculation of total manufacturing cost

Cost number and item	Manufacturing cost
1. Material cost ($10 × 10 000)	$100 000
2. Labour cost ($8 × 10 000)	80 000
3. Depreciation on new equipment	25 000
4. Rates and taxes	6 000
7. Maintenance salaries	28 000
8. Salary of factory manager	70 000
Total manufacturing costs	$309 000

If total manufacturing costs are $309 000, then the manufacturing cost per unit (cost to produce one pre-hung timber door) is $30.90 ($309 000 ÷ 10 000 units).

The cost concepts above will be used extensively in subsequent chapters. Study figure 15.11 carefully. If you do not understand any of these classifications, re-read the appropriate section in this chapter.

LEARNING REFLECTION AND CONSOLIDATION

Review it

1. How does the content of a statement of profit or loss differ between a merchandising entity and a manufacturing entity?
2. How are the work in process inventories reported in the cost of goods manufactured schedule?
3. How does the content of the statement of financial position differ between a merchandising entity and a manufacturing entity?

15.8 Evolution and improvements in management accounting

LEARNING OBJECTIVE 15.8 Describe contemporary developments in management accounting.

The business environment has changed rapidly in the past few decades. There have been shifts away from manufacturing into service industries, a globalisation of business activities, technology changes and new, progressive management approaches. These changes, together with increasing emphasis on corporate social responsibility, have been the catalysts for the expanding role of management accounting. This has forced many Australian and New Zealand businesses to find new strategies in order to be globally competitive, as well as to maintain sustainability. Such factors are discussed briefly next and in more detail in the following chapters.

Service industry needs

There is growing importance of the service sector at the expense of the manufacturing sector. A service industry produces services valuable to consumers as final products, such as the fitness program promoted by Fitness First or the academic degree provided by your university. A service industry also produces services valuable to other service and goods producers as intermediary inputs, such as wholesale trade or accounting services. According to the Australian Bureau of Statistics (ABS), service industries are the largest component of the Australian economy in terms of number of businesses, employment and gross value added (GVA).

According to the Australian and New Zealand Standard Industrial Classification (ANZSIC) used by ABS, service industries encompass the following activities: wholesale and retail trade; accommodation and food services; information, media and telecommunications; financial and insurance services; rental, hiring and real estate services; professional, scientific and technical services; administrative and support services; public administration and safety; education and training; health care and social assistance; and arts and recreation services. Figure 15.13 illustrates a variety of service industries and provides examples of businesses that fall into the various industry categories.

FIGURE 15.13 Service industries and entities, and the management accounting questions they face

	Industry/company	Questions faced by service-company managers
	Transportation (Qantas, Air New Zealand, Swiss Air)	Whether to buy new or used planes? Whether to service a new route?
	Package delivery services (DHL, Australia Post, TNT Express)	What fee structure to use? What mode of transportation to use? What technology to use to track deliveries?
	Telecommunications (Vodafone, Telstra, Optus, Telecom NZ)	What fee structure to use? Whether to service a new community? How many households will it take to break even? Whether to invest in a new satellite or lay new cable?
	Professional services (solicitors, public accountants, doctors, architects, engineers)	How much to charge for particular services? How much office overhead to allocate to particular jobs? How efficient and productive are individual staff members?
	Financial institutions (National Bank, Merrill Lynch, ANZ, HSBC, ING, AMP, insurance companies)	Which sevices to charge for, and which to provide for free? Whether to build a new branch or to install a new ATM? Should fees vary depending on the size of the customer's accounts?
	Health care (Affinity Health, Central Sydney Area Health, hospitals, nursing homes)	Whether to invest in new equipment? How much to charge for various services? How to measure the quality of services provided?

Some of the key differences between the service industry and the manufacturing industry are that normally in the service industry there is no inventory and services are consumed as they are produced. In some cases, however, there may be production (services) not yet invoiced. For example, when employees in an advertising agency have been working on a large advertising campaign or a public accountant has been working on the preparation of financial statements for a large client, the labour charge is often being accumulated as the basis of the amount that will eventually be charged to the client or customer.

How do Qantas or Telstra measure the efficiency and productivity of their call centre staff? How do KPMG or CommSec measure the cost of serving individual customers? What measures can be used to evaluate the quality of services provided by St George Hospital or Australia Post? Some new management accounting tools provide answers to these questions for managers of such service entities. For example, key performance indicators (KPIs) are management accounting tools designed to measure and control the cost of serving individual customers. KPIs are also used to track and measure business units' performances against set targets.

Helpful hint: Some common KPIs used by the banking industry include average interest earning assets, net interest margin, funds under administration and funds under management.

Many businesses are a mixture of service and retail. Vodafone, for example, provides mobile and internet services to 469.7 million customers around the globe. Additionally, it has more than 4500 exclusive branded stores including franchises and a broad network of distribution partners and third-party retailers that sell handsets and other communication devices to customers. Vodafone requires very detailed information and management systems to support management across different functions and areas in monitoring and improving business performance. Detailed cost information is needed in order to price the new services, so as to recover costs and meet profit targets.

Detailed cost information is required by all entities, regardless of whether they need information about manufacturing, retailing or services. The following chapters examine in more detail how to establish systems to control these costs.

Globalisation

Changes in world economic structure have increasingly moved us towards a 'borderless society' and, consequently, the Australian economy has undergone immense change in the past few decades. Globalisation presents both business opportunities and risks. Reduction in trade barriers is freeing up markets around the world. At the same time, businesses have to strive for excellence in providing products and services to customers while delivering shareholder value to investors. In response to intense international competition, businesses have to restructure their activities, improve their processes, reduce costs, differentiate their products or services and innovate in their application of technology.

Globalisation is a two-way street. Businesses have to become globally competitive to defend their domestic market share against foreign competitors, while at the same time entering overseas markets themselves. Australian businesses such as Brambles, CSR, Telstra and Qantas are expanding their markets overseas, and international entities are competing in the Australian market. For example, Vodafone is an international entity that directly competes with Telstra.

Effects of technological change on business infrastructure

Technological changes over the past few decades have had major impacts on both manufacturing and service businesses. Flexible manufacturing systems that combine robotics and *computer-integrated manufacturing (CIM)* are increasingly being used in production development, design and production. The resulting increase in flexibility, efficiency and productivity has enabled high-quality customised products to be supplied in shorter timeframes. An example is the use of robotic equipment in the steel and motor vehicle industries. Automation reduces the reliance on labour and enables numerous product variations on the production line.

Advancements in information technology have had an astronomical effect on service industries. Many businesses have taken advantage of electronic data management to completely revamp their workflows to reduce double-handling and improve their processes. For example, when you visit your GP, you might have noticed that the medical centre is now storing patients' files electronically instead of on paper files.

This eliminates the need for the receptionist to retrieve and handle your file and improves the accuracy of the recorded data.

Scientific discoveries and new technologies are opening up industries that were not even contemplated a few years ago (e.g. cochlear implants, genetic engineering, superconductivity, artificial hearts), and existing industries are changing and eliminating product lines. For example, Philips has announced that it will no longer manufacture the VCR recorder and instead will concentrate on the DVD and Blu-ray products and even they are under threat with online streaming of entertainment. Similarly, Kodak closed most of its camera film plants in favour of digital cameras and again this product is being challenged by the quality of the cameras integrated into mobile phones. Such changes present challenges to management accounting systems. Another effect of the new technologies and industries is the growing importance of intellectual capital and the overall concern with knowledge management. New techniques and methods have to be designed and implemented for measuring the value of intangible assets. One of these is the *intangible asset monitor*, which allows a number of indicators (e.g. growth/volume, renewal, efficiency, risk associated with the intangible) to be rated.

E-commerce

Another trend in business is the growth of e-commerce and internet sales. More people are embracing the online environment and digital media, spending more time and money online than ever before. This allows small businesses, as well as large businesses and multinationals, to provide goods and services via the internet. Many industries (for example, banking, real estate and retailing) have successfully combined e-commerce and traditional selling methods to reach a wider audience of customers. However, e-commerce presents additional challenges to businesses, including maintaining the integrity of electronic payment systems, addressing security issues such as business confidentiality, and ensuring the availability and authenticity of goods. It also has far-reaching implications for the taxation system.

New management systems and concepts

Fully automated systems have added reliability to the manufacturing process and freed resources. This has allowed manufacturers to place greater emphasis on product change and development, and to better respond to the increased competitive pressures caused by globalisation. Consequently, product life cycles have become shorter. For example, products in the computer industry are quickly outdated, so businesses must know the market and be familiar with the latest product developments in order to respond in a timely manner. New product development and marketing are essential if an entity is to remain competitive — this requires a good management information system.

Risk management

Accurately forecasting the future results of the business is one of management's roles. Doing so involves the measurement of traditional financial risk, as well as identifying and assessing the impact of the strategic, operational and other business risks.

Traditional financial risk is the risk that an investment will be unable to return a profit and hence the business loses the value in its assets. Strategic risk is broader than financial risk and is the potential loss that may prevent a business from achieving its goals and objectives. Operational risk is the risk of direct or indirect loss resulting from inadequate or failed internal processes, people and systems or from external events. Examples include employee fraud or incompetence, or a computer system failure. Other business risks include non-compliance with laws and regulations such as occupational health and safety or financial reporting regulations.

Enterprise performance management (EPM)

Some of the new performance management techniques used by businesses are the balance scorecard, values-based management, activity-based management, strategic cost management, customer relationship management and customer profitability analysis.

Balanced scorecard

The **balanced scorecard** is an approach to performance measurement that combines traditional financial measures with operating ones. It aims to provide a balanced presentation of financial performance, such as profit and turnover, with non-financial measures, such as customer and staff satisfaction. The balance scorecard highlights and communicates an entity's strategic goals into operable objectives and performance measures. This is achieved by measuring the entity's financial performance, internal business processes, business growth and customer satisfaction in order to plan its future strategic direction.

Values-based management

Values-based management acknowledges that there are difficulties associated with traditional accounting measures. It can focus on increasing the economic value (shareholder value) or it can be aimed at other constituents (e.g. stakeholder value). The stakeholder groups are shareholders, customers, suppliers and employees. Vodafone, for example, has adopted a values-based management system.

Activity-based management

Activity-based management (ABM) focuses on determining the entity's activities and associated costs, and assessing if the costs can be reduced or eliminated. Global competition and advances in information technology have permitted more detailed analysis to be made of the costs of carrying on a business. In order to obtain more accurate product costs, many businesses are accounting for overhead costs by the activities used in making the product. Activities include purchasing materials, handling raw materials, and production order scheduling. This costing technique, known as *activity-based costing (ABC)*, is further explained in chapter 16.

Additional activity-based techniques include: *strategic cost management*, which uses techniques such as target costing, competitive cost benchmarking, and value or supply chain management; *customer relationship management (CRM)*, where management learns about the customers' needs and the costs of meeting those needs; and *customer profitability analysis*, where the customer is seen as a cost/profit object and customer profitability is measured and managed. This involves expanding the traditional product and service costing to include tracing the selling, marketing and costs to individual customers to determine the most profitable customers. This then is used to change strategic direction of the business.

Data analytics

Data analytics uses past product or service costing and customer information to interpret patterns in the data and simulate scenarios about the future with the aid of computer programs.

In today's competitive environment where complexity and volatility are increasing, management is not concerned about past product costs but how to adapt to the current and future environments. Traditional strategies such as being the lowest cost supplier or using product differentiation are not sustainable as agile competitors can adapt very quickly by adjusting their prices, thereby reducing your market share. Data analytics embedded into the business management system, many believe, is the way to achieve sustainable long-term competitive advantage.

Quality

Quality is growing in importance in our increasingly competitive business environment. Many entities have recognised the need to pay close attention to quality in order to improve business performance. A number of quality management concepts have emerged over the past couple of decades. In particular, the approaches of total quality management and benchmarking have been widely adopted in the business community and are discussed here.

Total quality management (TQM) is a management philosophy emphasising quality, customer focus, total employee involvement, and continuous improvement. It attempts to eliminate all defects, waste and activities that do not add value to both internal and external customers. Because of its focus on customer satisfaction, the principles of TQM can be applied to any entity — large or small, not-for-profit or profit-oriented, in the public or private sector, or in service or manufacturing entities.

Benchmarking is a strategic management process of searching for and adopting best practice and innovative ideas to improve the performance of an organisation. In other words, it is a continuous process of measuring products, services or activities against the best levels of performance that may be found inside or outside the entity.

Economic sustainability

Increasing concerns about global warming and climate change have put pressure on entities to conduct business in a more sustainable fashion. Society today demands more information about the activities of businesses and their effects on the environment and the community in which the businesses operate. **Triple bottom line reporting** provides information about an entity's financial, social/ethical and environmental performance. As a result, accountants have had to develop narratives and qualitative performance measures for reporting on these issues. Many entities produce and include a corporate social responsibility report section in their annual reports.

Another growing trend of organisations responding to calls for action in combating global warming and climate change is the increasing disclosure of entities' carbon footprints. In Australia, the government established the National Carbon Accounting System (NCAS) to enable accounting for greenhouse gas emissions from corporate activities. **Greenhouse gas accounting** describes the way to inventory and audit greenhouse gas emissions. The management accountant, as a strategic partner in business activities, is well placed to incorporate carbon reporting in an entity's performance measurement framework. To meet this growing demand for specialist carbon reporting skills, some universities are offering courses in carbon accounting.

Final comment

The role of management accounting and the management accountant is constantly evolving as business meets the challenges of the twenty-first century. Many of the concepts discussed in this section are covered in greater detail in more advanced management accounting courses.

15.9 Accounting cycle for a manufacturing entity

LEARNING OBJECTIVE 15.9 Prepare a worksheet and closing entries for a manufacturing entity.

The accounting cycle for a manufacturing entity is the same as for a merchandising business when a periodic inventory system is used. Except for the additional manufacturing inventories and manufacturing cost accounts, the journalising and posting of transactions is the same. Similarly, the preparation of a trial balance and the journalising and posting of adjusting entries are the same. Some changes, however, occur in the use of a worksheet and in preparing closing entries.

To illustrate the changes in the worksheet, we will use the cost of goods manufactured schedule for Olsen Manufacturing Ltd presented in figure 15.9 of the chapter and other assumed data. For convenience, the cost of goods manufactured schedule is reproduced in figure 15.14.

FIGURE 15.14 Cost of goods manufactured schedule

OLSEN MANUFACTURING LTD
Cost of goods manufactured schedule
for the year ended 31 December 2019

Work in process, 1 January			$ 18 400
Direct materials			
Raw materials inventory, 1 January	$ 16 700		
Raw materials purchases	152 500		
Total raw materials available for use	169 200		
Less: Raw materials inventory, 31 December	(22 800)		
Direct materials used		$146 400	
Direct labour		175 600	
Manufacturing overhead			
Indirect labour	14 300		
Factory repairs	12 600		
Factory power	10 100		
Factory depreciation	9 440		
Factory insurance	8 360		
Total manufacturing overhead		54 800	
Total manufacturing costs for the year			376 800
Total cost of work in process			395 200
Less: Work in process, 31 December			(25 200)
Cost of goods manufactured			**$370 000**

Worksheet

When a worksheet is used in preparing financial statements, two additional columns are needed for the cost of goods manufactured schedule. As illustrated in the worksheet in figure 15.15, debit and credit columns for this schedule have been inserted before the statement of profit or loss columns.

In the cost of goods manufactured columns, the beginning inventories of raw materials and work in process are entered as debits. In addition, all the manufacturing costs are entered as debits. The reason is that each of these amounts increases cost of goods manufactured. Ending inventories for raw materials and work in process are entered as credits in the cost of goods manufactured columns because they have the opposite effect — they decrease cost of goods manufactured. The balancing amount for these columns is the cost of goods manufactured. Note that the amount, $370 000, agrees with the amount reported for cost of goods manufactured in figure 15.14. This amount is also entered in the statement of profit or loss debit column.

The statement of profit or loss and statement of financial position columns for a manufacturing entity are basically the same as for a merchandising entity. For example, the treatment of the finished goods inventories is identical to the treatment of inventory. That is, the beginning inventory is entered in the debit column, and the ending finished goods inventory is entered in the statement of profit or loss credit column and the statement of financial position debit column.

FIGURE 15.15 Partial worksheet

OLSEN MANUFACTURING LTD
Worksheet (partial)
for the year ended 31 December 2019

	Adjusted trial balance		Cost of goods manufactured		Statement of profit or loss		Statement of financial position	
	Dr $	Cr $	Dr $	Cr $	Dr $	Cr $	Dr $	Cr $
Cash	180 000						180 000	
Accounts receivable (net)	210 000						210 000	
Finished goods inventory	90 000				90 000	80 000	80 000	
Work in process inventory	18 400		18 400	25 200			25 200	
Raw materials inventory	16 700		16 700	22 800			22 800	
Prepaid expenses	18 000						18 000	
PPE assets	724 000						724 000	
Accumulated depreciation		278 400						278 400
Bills payable		264 000						264 000
Accounts payable		40 000						40 000
Income taxes payable		5 000						5 000
Share capital		400 000						400 000
Retained earnings		205 100						205 100
Sales		660 000				660 000		
Raw materials purchases	152 500		152 500					
Direct labour	175 600		175 600					
Indirect labour	14 300		14 300					
Factory repairs	12 600		12 600					
Factory power	10 100		10 100					
Factory depreciation	9 440		9 440					
Factory insurance	8 360		8 360					
Selling expenses	114 900				114 900			
Administrative expenses	75 000				75 000			
Financial expenses	2 600				2 600			
Income tax expense	20 000				20 000			
Totals	1 852 500	1 852 500	418 000	48 000				
Cost of goods manufactured				370 000	370 000			
Totals			418 000	418 000	672 500	740 000	1 260 000	1 192 500
Profit					67 500			67 500
Totals					**740 000**	**740 000**	**1 260 000**	**1 260 000**

As in the case of a merchandising entity, financial statements can be prepared from the statement columns of the worksheet. In addition, the cost of goods manufactured schedule can also be prepared directly from the worksheet.

Closing entries

The closing entries for a manufacturing entity are different from those for a merchandising entity. A **manufacturing summary account** is used to close all accounts that appear in the cost of goods manufactured schedule. The balance of the manufacturing summary account is the cost of goods manufactured for the period. Manufacturing summary is then closed to profit or loss summary. The closing entries can be prepared from the worksheet. As illustrated, the closing entries for the manufacturing accounts are prepared first. The closing entries for Olsen Manufacturing Ltd are as follows.

General journal		$	$
Dec. 31	Work in process inventory (31 Dec.)	25 200	
	Raw materials inventory (31 Dec.)	22 800	
	Manufacturing summary		48 000
	(To record ending raw materials and work in process inventories)		
31	Manufacturing summary	418 000	
	Work in process inventory (1 Jan.)		18 400
	Raw materials inventory (1 Jan.)		16 700
	Raw materials purchases		152 500
	Direct labour		175 600
	Indirect labour		14 300
	Factory repairs		12 600
	Factory power		10 100
	Factory depreciation		9 440
	Factory insurance		8 360
	(To close beginning raw materials and work in process inventories and manufacturing cost accounts)		
31	Finished goods inventory (31 Dec.)	80 000	
	Sales	660 000	
	Profit or loss summary		740 000
	(To record ending finished goods inventory and close sales account)		
31	Profit or loss summary	672 500	
	Finished goods inventory (1 Jan.)		75 000
	Manufacturing summary		370 000
	Selling expenses		114 900
	Administrative expenses		75 000
	Financial expenses		2 600
	Income tax expense		20 000
	(To close beginning finished goods inventory, manufacturing summary and expense accounts)		
31	Profit or loss summary	67 500	
	Retained earnings		67 500
	(To close profit or loss summary to retained earnings)		

After posting, the summary accounts will appear as shown in figure 15.16.

FIGURE 15.16   Summary accounts for a manufacturing entity, after posting

Manufacturing summary

Dec. 31	Closing entry	418 000	Dec. 31	Closing entry	48 000
			31	P or L summary	370 000
		418 000			418 000

Profit or loss summary

Dec. 31	Closing entry	672 500	Dec. 31	Closing entry	740 000
31	Retained earnings	67 500			
		740 000			740 000

These data precisely track the closing entries.

USING THE DECISION-MAKING TOOLKIT

Giant Ltd specialises in manufacturing different models of mountain bikes. Assume that a new model, the Jaguar, has been well accepted. As a result, the entity has established a separate manufacturing facility to produce these bicycles. Giant Ltd produces 1000 bicycles per month. Monthly manufacturing costs and other expenses related to these bicycles are as follows:

1. Rent on manufacturing equipment (lease cost) $2000/month
2. Insurance on manufacturing building $750/month
3. Raw materials (frames, tyres, etc.) $80/bicycle
4. Power costs for manufacturing facility $1000/month
5. Supplies for general office $800/month
6. Wages for assembly line workers in manufacturing facility $30/bicycle
7. Depreciation on office equipment $650/month
8. Miscellaneous materials (lubricants, solders, etc.) $1.20/bicycle
9. Rates and taxes on manufacturing building $2400/year
10. Manufacturing supervisor's salary $3000/month
11. Advertising for bicycles $30 000/year
12. Sales commissions $10/bicycle
13. Depreciation on manufacturing building $1500/month

Required

(a) Prepare an answer sheet with the following column headings. Enter each cost item on your answer sheet, placing an 'X' under the appropriate headings.

| | Product costs | | | | | |
Cost item	Direct materials	Direct labour	Manufacturing overhead	Period costs	Prime costs	Conversion costs

(b) Calculate total manufacturing costs for the month.

PROBLEM-SOLVING STRATEGIES

1. Remember the definitions of: Prime costs = Direct materials + Direct labour; Conversion costs = Direct labour + Manufacturing overhead costs incurred in converting direct materials into finished goods.
2. Make sure you are doing the calculations for the appropriate period — month, year, unit, etc.
3. Period costs are expenses, not manufacturing costs.
4. Product costs are manufacturing costs.

Solution

(a)

| | Product costs | | | | | |
Cost item	Direct materials	Direct labour	Manufacturing overhead	Period costs	Prime costs	Conversion costs
1. Rent on equipment ($2000/month)			X			X
2. Insurance on manufacturing building ($750/month)			X			X
3. Raw materials ($80/bicycle)	X				X	
4. Manufacturing power ($1000/month)			X			X
5. Office supplies ($800/month)				X		
6. Wages for workers ($30/bicycle)		X			X	X
7. Depreciation on office equipment ($650/month)				X		

Cost item	Direct materials	Direct labour	Manufacturing overhead	Period costs	Prime costs	Conversion costs
8. Miscellaneous materials ($1.20/bicycle)			X			X
9. Rates and taxes on building ($2400/year)			X			X
10. Manufacturing supervisor's salary ($3000/month)			X			X
11. Advertising cost ($30 000/year)				X		
12. Sales commissions ($10/bicycle)				X		
13. Depreciation on manufacturing building ($1500/month)			X			X

Helpful hint: Contrast item 13 with depreciation on office equipment (item 7). Although both items are depreciation, they are treated differently in terms of costing. Office equipment is non-manufacturing related, so its depreciation is classified as a period cost (an administrative expense). On the other hand, the manufacturing building is definitely relevant to manufacturing, so its depreciation is classified as a product cost (manufacturing overhead).

(b)

Cost item	Manufacturing cost (per month)
Rent on equipment	$ 2 000
Insurance	750
Raw materials ($80 × 1000)	80 000
Manufacturing power	1 000
Labour ($30 × 1000)	30 000
Miscellaneous materials ($1.20 × 1000)	1 200
Rates and taxes ($2400 ÷ 12)	200
Manufacturing supervisor's salary	3 000
Depreciation on manufacturing building	1 500
Total manufacturing costs	$119 650

SUMMARY

15.1 Explain the distinguishing features of management accounting.

The distinguishing features of management accounting are:

• Main users of reports — internal users, who are officers, department heads, managers and supervisors in the entity.
• Type and frequency of reports — internal reports that are issued as frequently as the need arises.
• Purpose of reports — to provide special-purpose information for a particular user for a specific decision.
• Content of reports — pertains to subunits of the entity and may be very detailed; may extend beyond double-entry accounting system; the reporting standard is relevant to the decision being made.
• Verification of reports — no independent audits.

15.2 Identify the three broad functions of management and discuss how management accounting tools assist these functions.

The three functions are planning, directing and motivating, and controlling. Planning requires management to look ahead and to establish objectives. Directing and motivating involves coordinating the diverse activities and human resources of an entity to produce a smooth-running operation. Controlling is the process of keeping the activities on track. Budgets, responsibility centres and performance evaluation reports are examples of management accounting tools which assist managers in managing a business.

15.3 Define the three classes of manufacturing costs.

Manufacturing costs are typically classified as either (1) direct materials, (2) direct labour or (3) manufacturing overhead. Raw materials that can be physically and economically traced to the finished product during the manufacturing process are called direct materials. The work of factory employees that can be physically and economically traced to converting raw materials into finished goods is considered direct labour. Manufacturing overhead consists of costs that are indirectly associated with the manufacture of the finished product.

15.4 Distinguish between product and period costs.

Product costs are costs that are a necessary and integral part of producing the finished product. These costs do not become expenses until the inventory to which they attach is sold. Period costs are costs that are identified with a specific time period rather than with a saleable product, and relate to non-manufacturing costs.

15.5 Explain the difference between a merchandising and a manufacturing statement of profit or loss.

The difference between a merchandising and a manufacturing statement of profit or loss is in the cost of sales section. A manufacturing cost of sales section shows beginning and ending finished goods inventories and the cost of goods manufactured.

15.6 Explain the difference between a merchandising and a manufacturing statement of financial position.

The difference between a merchandising and a manufacturing statement of financial position is in the current asset section. In the current asset section of a manufacturing entity's statement of financial position, three inventory accounts are presented: finished goods inventory, work in process inventory, and raw materials inventory. A merchandising statement of financial position has only finished goods inventory.

15.7 Indicate how cost of goods manufactured and cost of sales are determined.

The cost of the beginning work in process is added to the total manufacturing costs for the current year to arrive at the total cost of work in process for the year. The ending work in process is then subtracted from the total cost of work in process to arrive at the cost of goods manufactured. The cost of the beginning finished goods is added to the cost of goods manufactured to arrive at the total cost of goods available for sale. The ending finished goods is then subtracted from the total cost of goods available for sale to arrive at the cost of sales.

15.8 Describe contemporary developments in management accounting.

The business environment in the past few decades has changed rapidly. There has been a shift away from manufacturing into service industries, a globalisation of business activities, technology changes and new progressive management approaches taking advantage of new technologies.

15.9 Prepare a worksheet and closing entries for a manufacturing entity.

Two additional columns are needed in the worksheet for the cost of goods manufactured. In these columns, the beginning inventories of raw materials and work in process are entered as debits, and the ending inventories are entered as credits; all manufacturing costs are entered as debits. To close all the accounts that appear in the cost of goods manufactured schedule, a manufacturing summary account is used.

DECISION-MAKING TOOLKIT — A SUMMARY

DECISION-MAKING TOOLKIT

Decision/issue	Info needed for analysis	Tool or technique to use for decision	How to evaluate results to make decision
What is the composition of a manufacturing entity's inventory?	Amount of raw materials, work in process, and finished goods inventory	Statement of financial position	Determine whether there are sufficient finished goods inventory, raw materials and work in process to meet forecast demand.
Is the entity maintaining control over the costs of production?	Cost of material, labour and overhead; expected revenue from product sales	Cost of goods manufactured schedule for current and previous periods	Compare the cost of goods manufactured with sales revenue; compare these figures with those of previous periods to analyse trends.

KEY TERMS

activity-based management (ABM) A management tool that focuses on determining the entity's activities and associated costs, and assessing if the costs can be reduced or eliminated.

balanced scorecard An approach to performance measurement that combines traditional financial measures with operating ones.

benchmarking A strategic management process of searching for and adopting best practice to improve an entity's performance.

conversion costs Direct labour and manufacturing overhead costs incurred in converting raw materials into finished goods.

cost of goods manufactured Total cost of work in process less the cost of the ending work in process inventory.

cost of sales (COS) The total cost of inventories sold during the period.

direct labour The work of factory employees that can be physically and economically traced to converting raw materials into finished goods.

direct materials Raw materials that can be physically and economically traced to manufacturing the finished product.

greenhouse gas accounting A method of accounting that describes the way to inventory and audit greenhouse gas emissions.

indirect labour Work of factory employees that has no physical association with the finished product, or it is not economically feasible to trace the costs to the goods produced.

indirect materials Raw materials that do not physically become part of the finished product or cannot be traced because their physical association with the finished product is too small.

management accounting A field of accounting that provides economic and financial information for managers and other internal users.

manufacturing overhead Manufacturing costs that are indirectly associated with the manufacture of the finished product.

manufacturing summary account Used to close all accounts that appear in the cost of goods manufactured schedule. It is similar to the profit or loss summary account, in that they are both temporary accounts used to summarise certain closing entries.

period costs Costs that are identified with a specific time period and charged to expense as incurred.

prime costs Direct materials and direct labour.

product costs Costs that are a necessary and integral part of producing the finished product.

total cost of work in process Cost of the beginning work in process plus total manufacturing costs for the current period.

total manufacturing costs The sum of direct materials, direct labour and manufacturing overhead incurred in the current period.

total quality management (TQM) A management philosophy that emphasises quality, customer focus, employee involvement and continuous improvement.

triple bottom line reporting A measurement system that provides information about an entity's financial, social, ethical and environmental performance.

values-based management A management principle that focuses on increasing the economic value and interests of shareholders.

DEMONSTRATION PROBLEM

Superior Manufacturing Ltd has the following cost and expense data for the year ending 31 December 2019.

Raw materials, 1/1/19	$ 30 000	Insurance, factory	$ 14 000
Raw materials, 31/12/19	20 000	Rates and taxes, factory building	6 000
Raw materials purchased	205 000	Sales (net)	1 500 000
Indirect materials	15 000	Delivery expenses	100 000
Work in process, 1/1/19	80 000	Sales commissions	150 000
Work in process, 31/12/19	50 000	Indirect labour	90 000
Finished goods, 1/1/19	110 000	Factory machinery rent	40 000
Finished goods, 31/12/19	120 000	Factory power	65 000
Direct labour	350 000	Depreciation, factory building	24 000
Factory manager's salary	35 000	Administrative expenses	300 000

Required

(a) Prepare a cost of goods manufactured schedule for Superior Manufacturing Ltd for 2019.

(b) Prepare a statement of profit or loss for Superior for 2019.

(c) Assume that Superior's ledgers show the balances of the following current asset accounts: cash $17 000, accounts receivable (net) $120 000, prepaid expenses $13 000 and short-term investments $26 000. Prepare the current assets section of the statement of financial position for Superior Manufacturing Ltd as at 31 December 2019.

PROBLEM-SOLVING STRATEGIES

1. Beginning work in process is the first item in the cost of goods manufactured schedule.

2. Total manufacturing costs for the year are the sum of direct materials used, direct labour and total manufacturing overhead.

3. Total cost of work in process is the sum of beginning work in process and total manufacturing costs.
4. Cost of goods manufactured is the total cost of work in process less ending work in process.
5. The cost of sales section of the statement of profit or loss shows beginning and ending finished goods inventory and cost of goods manufactured.
6. In the statement of financial position, manufacturing inventories are listed in the order of their expected realisation in cash, with finished goods first.

SOLUTION TO DEMONSTRATION PROBLEM

(a)

SUPERIOR MANUFACTURING LTD
Cost of goods manufactured schedule
for the year ended 31 December 2019

Work in process, 1/1			$ 80 000
Direct materials			
Raw materials inventory, 1/1	$ 30 000		
Raw materials purchased	205 000		
Total raw materials available for use	235 000		
Less: Raw materials inventory, 31/12	(20 000)		
Direct materials used		$215 000	
Direct labour		350 000	
Manufacturing overhead			
Indirect labour	90 000		
Factory power	65 000		
Factory machinery rent	40 000		
Factory manager's salary	35 000		
Depreciation on building	24 000		
Indirect materials	15 000		
Factory insurance	14 000		
Rates and taxes	6 000		
Total manufacturing overhead		289 000	
Total manufacturing costs for the year			854 000
Total cost of work in process			934 000
Less: Work in process, 31/12			(50 000)
Cost of goods manufactured			**$884 000**

(b)

SUPERIOR MANUFACTURING LTD
Statement of profit or loss
for the year ended 31 December 2019

Sales (net)		$1 500 000
COST OF SALES		
Finished goods inventory, 1 January	$ 110 000	
Cost of goods manufactured	884 000	
Cost of goods available for sale	994 000	
Less: Finished goods inventory, 31 December	(120 000)	
Cost of sales		874 000
Gross profit		626 000
Operating expenses		
Administrative expenses	300 000	
Sales commissions	150 000	
Delivery expenses	100 000	
Total operating expenses		550 000
Profit		$ 76 000

(c)

SUPERIOR MANUFACTURING LTD		
Statement of financial position (partial)		
as at 31 December 2019		
Current assets		
Cash		$ 17 000
Short-term investments		26 000
Accounts receivable (net)		120 000
Inventories:		
Finished goods	$120 000	
Work in process	50 000	
Raw materials	20 000	190 000
Prepaid expenses		13 000
Total current assets		**$366 000**

SELF-STUDY QUESTIONS

15.1 Management accounting: **LO1**
(a) is governed by generally accepted accounting principles.
(b) places emphasis on special-purpose information.
(c) pertains to the entity as a whole and is highly aggregated.
(d) is limited to cost data.

15.2 The management of an organisation performs three broad functions. They are: **LO2**
(a) planning, directing and motivating, and selling.
(b) planning, directing and motivating, and controlling.
(c) planning, manufacturing and controlling.
(d) directing and motivating, manufacturing and controlling.

15.3 Which of the following is not an example of management accounting tools?   **LO2**
(a) Budgets.
(b) Sales forecast.
(c) Performance evaluation reports.
(d) Costing analysis reports.

15.4 Direct materials are a: **LO3**

	Conversion cost	Manufacturing cost	Prime cost
(a)	Yes	Yes	No
(b)	No	Yes	Yes
(c)	Yes	Yes	Yes
(d)	No	No	No

15.5 Which of the following costs would be included in manufacturing overhead of a computer manufacturer?   **LO3**
(a) The cost of the disk drives.
(b) The wages earned by computer assemblers.
(c) The cost of the memory chips.
(d) Depreciation on testing equipment.

15.6 Which of the following is *not* an element of manufacturing overhead?   **LO3**
(a) Sales manager's salary.
(b) Factory manager's salary.
(c) Factory repairman's wages.
(d) Product inspector's salary.

15.7 Indirect labour is a: **LO4**

(a) non-manufacturing cost.

(b) prime cost.

(c) product cost.

(d) period cost.

15.8 A cost of goods manufactured schedule shows beginning and ending inventories for: **LO5**

(a) raw materials and work in process only.

(b) work in process only.

(c) raw materials only.

(d) raw materials, work in process, and finished goods.

15.9 In a manufacturing entity statement of financial position, three inventories may be reported: (1) raw materials, (2) work in process, and (3) finished goods. Indicate in what sequence these inventories generally appear on a statement of financial position. **LO6**

(a) (1), (2), (3).

(b) (2), (3), (1).

(c) (3), (1), (2).

(d) (3), (2), (1).

15.10 James Surfboard Manufacturing Ltd has beginning and ending work in process inventory of $3500 and $7800 respectively for the year. Direct materials used amounts to $55 000, direct labour incurred is $80 000 and manufacturing overheads total $46 000. The cost of goods manufactured is: **LO7**

(a) $176 700.

(b) $181 000.

(c) $184 500.

(d) $162 800.

15.11 For the year, Redder Ltd has cost of goods manufactured of $600 000, beginning finished goods inventory of $200 000, and ending finished goods inventory of $250 000. The cost of sales is: **LO7**

(a) $450 000.

(b) $500 000.

(c) $550 000.

(d) $600 000.

QUESTIONS

15.1 (a) 'Management accounting is a field of accounting that provides economic information for all interested parties.' Do you agree? Explain.

(b) Pat Gonzalez believes that management accounting serves only manufacturing entities. Is Pat correct? Explain.

15.2 Distinguish between management and financial accounting as to (a) main users of reports, (b) types and frequency of reports, and (c) purpose of reports.

15.3 Karen Smith is studying for the next accounting examination. Summarise for Karen what she should know about management functions.

15.4 'Decision making is management's most important function.' Do you agree? Why or why not?

15.5 Carlos Mann is an interim management accountant in MFC Manufacturing Ltd. He is confused about whether depreciation on the office building should be a product cost or a period cost. Explain how Carlos should classify this depreciation.

15.6 In Fisher Ltd, direct materials are $12 000, direct labour $15 000 and manufacturing overhead is $9000. What is the amount of (a) prime costs and (b) conversion costs?

15.7 Harn Manufacturing has beginning raw materials inventory $32 000, ending raw materials inventory $29 000, and raw materials purchases $200 000. What is the cost of direct materials used?

15.8 Griggs Manufacturing Ltd has beginning work in process $27 200, direct materials used $280 000, direct labour $180 000, total manufacturing overhead $220 000, and ending work in process $36 400. What are (a) total manufacturing costs, (b) total cost of work in process and (c) cost of goods manufactured?

15.9 How, if at all, does the accounting cycle differ between a manufacturing entity and a merchandising entity?

15.10 What typical account balances are carried into the cost of goods manufactured columns of the manufacturing worksheet?

BRIEF EXERCISES

BE15.1 Distinguish between management and financial accounting. **LO1**

Complete the following comparison table between management accounting and financial accounting.

	Financial accounting	Management accounting
Main users		
Purpose of reports		
Frequency of reports		
Type of reports		
Content of reports		
Verification process		

BE15.2 Identify the three management functions. **LO2**

Below are three functions of the management of an entity:

(a) Planning

(b) Directing and motivating

(c) Controlling.

  Identify which of the following statements best describes each of the above functions.

1. _____ Require(s) management to look ahead and to establish objectives. A key objective of management appears to be to add value to the business.

2. _____ Involve(s) coordinating the diverse activities and human resources of an entity to produce a smooth-running operation. This function relates to the implementation of planned objectives.

3. _____ Is the process of keeping the activities on track. Management must determine whether goals are being met and what changes are necessary when there are deviations.

BE15.3 Classify manufacturing costs. **LO3**

Indicate whether each of the following costs of a motor vehicle manufacturer would be classified as direct materials, direct labour or manufacturing overhead:

(a) Windshield.

(b) Engine.

(c) Wages of assembly line worker.

(d) Depreciation of factory machinery.

(e) Factory machinery lubricants.

(f) Tyres.

(g) Steering wheel.

(h) Salary of painting supervisor.

BE15.4 Classify manufacturing costs. $\qquad$ **LO3, 4**

Presented below are Office Mate Pty Ltd's monthly manufacturing cost data relating to its stationery product:

(a)	Power for manufacturing equipment	$116 000
(b)	Raw material (plastic, ink etc.)	$ 85 000
(c)	Depreciation on manufacturing building	$880 000
(d)	Wages for production workers	$191 000

Enter each cost item on the following table, placing an 'X' under the appropriate headings.

	Product costs				
	Direct materials	Direct labour	Factory overhead	Prime costs	Conversion costs
(a)					
(b)					
(c)					
(d)					

BE15.5 Determine missing amounts in calculating total manufacturing costs. $\qquad$ **LO7**

Presented below are incomplete 2020 manufacturing cost data for Sunny Ltd. Determine the missing amounts.

	Direct materials used	Direct labour used	Factory overhead	Total manufacturing costs
(a)	$98 000	$122 000	$100 000	?
(b)	?	44 000	60 000	$148 000
(c)	11 000	?	19 000	60 000

BE15.6 Determine missing amounts in calculating cost of goods manufactured. $\qquad$ **LO7**

Use the same data from BE15.5. Calculate the cost of goods manufactured for Sunny Ltd in 2020.

	Total manufacturing costs	Work in process (1/1)	Work in process (31/12)	Cost of goods manufactured
(a)	?	$ 60 000	$43 000	?
(b)	$ 98 000	?	49 000	$159 000
(c)	150 000	235 000	?	358 000

BE15.7 Identify worksheet columns for selected accounts. $\qquad$ **LO9**

A worksheet is used in preparing financial statements for Lawney Manufacturing. The following accounts are included in the adjusted trial balance: Finished goods inventory $28 000, Work in process inventory $21 600, Raw materials purchases $175 000, and Direct labour $140 000. Indicate the worksheet column(s) to which each account should be extended.

EXERCISES

E15.1 Classify costs into three classes of manufacturing costs. $\qquad$ **LO3**

Below is a list of costs and expenses usually incurred by Mauer Ltd, a manufacturer of furniture, in its factory:

1. Salaries for assembly line inspectors.
2. Insurance on factory machines.

3. Rates and taxes on the factory building.
4. Factory repairs.
5. Upholstery used in manufacturing furniture.
6. Wages paid to assembly line workers.
7. Factory machinery depreciation.
8. Glue, nails, paint and other small parts used in production.
9. Factory supervisors' salaries.
10. Timber used in manufacturing furniture.

Required

Classify the above items into the following categories: (a) direct materials, (b) direct labour, and (c) manufacturing overhead.

E15.2 **Determine the total amount of various types of costs.** **LO3, 4**

Oscar Ltd reports the following costs and expenses in October:

Factory power	$ 10 200	Direct labour	$72 100
Depreciation on factory equipment	11 240	Sales salaries	51 700
Depreciation on delivery trucks	3 000	Rates and taxes on factory building	3 500
Indirect factory labour	52 600	Repairs to office equipment	1 500
Indirect materials	101 200	Factory repairs	2 100
Direct materials used	143 400	Advertising	16 000
Factory manager's salary	10 000	Office supplies used	4 000

Required

From the information, determine the total amount of:

(a) prime costs
(b) manufacturing overhead
(c) conversion costs
(d) product costs
(e) period costs.

E15.3 **Classify various costs into different cost categories.** **LO3, 4**

Tower Computers is a manufacturer of personal computers. Various costs and expenses associated with its operations are as follows:

1. Rates and taxes on the factory building.
2. Production supervisors' salaries.
3. Memory boards and chips used in assembling computers.
4. Depreciation on the factory equipment.
5. Salaries for assembly line quality-control inspectors.
6. Sales commissions paid to sell personal computers.
7. Electrical wiring in assembling computers.
8. Wages of workers assembling personal computers.
9. Soldering materials used on factory assembly lines.
10. Salaries for the night security guards for the factory building.

The entity intends to classify these costs and expenses into the following categories: (a) direct materials, (b) direct labour, (c) manufacturing overhead and (d) period costs.

Required

List the items 1 to 10. For each item, indicate the cost category to which it belongs.

E15.4 **Indicate in which schedule or financial statement(s) different cost items will appear.** **LO5, 6, 7**

Piazza Manufacturing Ltd produces blankets. From its accounting records it prepares the following schedule and financial statements on a yearly basis:

(a) cost of goods manufactured schedule
(b) statement of profit or loss
(c) statement of financial position.

The following items are found in its ledger and accompanying data:

1. Direct labour
2. Raw materials inventory, 1/1
3. Work in process inventory, 31/12
4. Finished goods inventory, 1/1
5. Indirect labour
6. Depreciation on factory machinery
7. Work in process, 1/1
8. Finished goods inventory, 31/12
9. Factory maintenance salaries
10. Cost of goods manufactured
11. Depreciation on delivery equipment
12. Cost of goods available for sale
13. Direct materials used
14. Gas and electricity for factory
15. Repairs to roof of factory building
16. Cost of raw materials purchases

Required

List the items 1 to 16. For each item, indicate by using the appropriate letter or letters the schedule and/or financial statement(s) in which it will appear.

E15.5 Determine the missing amount of different cost items.   **LO7**

Manufacturing cost data for Dalby Ltd are presented below:

	Case A	Case B	Case C
Direct materials used	(a)	$70 000	$130 000
Direct labour	$ 60 000	86 000	(g)
Manufacturing overhead	42 500	81 600	102 000
Total manufacturing costs	180 650	(d)	260 000
Work in process, 1/1/19	(b)	16 500	(h)
Total cost of work in process	221 500	(e)	327 000
Work in process, 31/12/19	(c)	9 000	70 000
Cost of goods manufactured	185 275	(f)	(i)

Required

Calculate the missing amount for each letter.

E15.6 Determine the missing amounts in cost of goods manufactured schedule.   **LO7**

The cost of goods manufactured schedule shows each of the cost elements.

SOLOMON MANUFACTURING COMPANY		
Cost of goods manufactured schedule		
for the year ended 31 December 2020		
Work in process (1/1)			$200 000
Direct materials		
Raw materials inventory (1/1)	$?	
Add: Raw material purchases	158 000	
Less: Raw material inventory (31/12)	(7 500)	
Direct materials used		$190 000
Direct labour		?
Manufacturing overhead		
Indirect labour	18 000	
Factory depreciation	36 000	
Factory utilities	68 000	

Total overhead		122 000
Total manufacturing costs		?
Total cost of work in process		?
Less: Work in process (31/12)		(81 000)
Cost of goods manufactured		**$560 000**

Required

Complete the schedule for Solomon Manufacturing.

E15.7 **Identify features of management accounting; identify functions of management and contemporary developments in management accounting.** **LO1, 2, 8**

Complete the following statements with one of the terms listed below:

Management accounting	Globalisation	Balanced scorecard
Creditors	Inventory	Shareholders
Budgets	External auditors	Total quality management

(a) Financial accounting reports are verified by _____.

(b) The key difference between a service and a manufacturing business is that the former does not have _____.

(c) Australian companies competing in overseas markets are made possible by _____.

(d) Businesses adopting _____ aim to eliminate all defects, waste and activities that do not add value to customers.

(e) Managers use _____ to formalise short-term and long-term plans.

(f) _____ combines financial and non-financial measures to evaluate an entity's performance.

(g) Financial accounting produces reports for external users such as _____ and _____.

(h) Departmental costing analysis is an example of _____ reports.

E15.8 **Explain the difference between a merchandising and a manufacturing statement of profit or loss; indicate how cost of goods manufactured is determined.** **LO5, 6**

Complete the following statements with one of the terms listed below:

Service company	Work in process inventory
Raw materials	Merchandising companies
Manufacturing companies	Finished goods inventory

(a) _____ resell products they purchased from suppliers.

(b) The cost applicable to units that have begun production but are not completed is recorded in _____.

(c) Accounting firm Ernst & Young is an example of a _____ which does not have tangible products intended for sale.

(d) _____ use labour and equipment to convert raw materials into new finished products.

(e) _____ consists of goods that have been fully completed, ready to be sold but not yet sold.

(f) For Domino's, flour, cheese and tomato are classified as _____.

E15.9 **Prepare a cost of goods manufactured schedule and a partial statement of profit or loss. LO5, 7**

Broadbeach Ltd has the following cost records for June 2020:

Indirect factory labour	$ 4 500	Factory electricity	$ 400
Direct materials used	20 000	Depreciation, factory equipment	1 700
Work in process, 1/6/20	3 000	Direct labour	25 000
Work in process, 30/6/20	3 500	Maintenance, factory equipment	1 300
Finished goods, 1/6/20	5 000	Indirect materials	2 200
Finished goods, 30/6/20	6 000	Factory manager's salary	3 000

Required

(a) Prepare a cost of goods manufactured schedule for June 2020.

(b) Prepare a statement of profit or loss to gross profit for June 2020 assuming net sales are $98 100.

E15.10 Prepare a cost of goods manufactured schedule and present the ending inventories of the statement of financial position. **LO6, 7**

An analysis of the accounts of Salazar Manufacturing reveals the following manufacturing cost data for the month ended 30 June 2019:

Inventories	Beginning	Ending
Raw materials	$8 800	$11 000
Work in process	5 000	7 000
Finished goods	8 000	6 000

Costs incurred: Raw material purchases $62 000, Direct labour $45 000, Manufacturing overhead $19 900.

The specific overhead costs were: Indirect labour $5500, Factory insurance $4000, Machinery depreciation $4800, Machinery repairs $1800, Factory power $2500, Miscellaneous factory costs $1300.

Required

(a) Prepare the cost of goods manufactured schedule for the month ended 30 June 2019.

(b) Show the presentation of the ending inventories on the 30 June 2019 statement of financial position.

E15.11 Prepare a partial worksheet for a manufacturing entity. **LO9**

The information for Salazar Manufacturing is presented in E15.10.

Required

Prepare a partial worksheet for Salazar Manufacturing.

E15.12 The cost of goods manufactured schedule shows each of the cost elements. Complete the following schedule for Lanier Manufacturing Ltd:

LANIER MANUFACTURING LTD Cost of goods manufactured schedule for the year ended 31 December 2019			
Work in process (1/1)			$200 000
Direct materials			
Raw materials inventory (1/1)	$?		
Add: Raw material purchases	132 000		
Less: Raw material inventory (31/12)	(6 500)		
Direct materials used		$135 500	
Direct labour		?	
Manufacturing overhead			
Indirect labour	21 000		
Factory depreciation	38 000		
Factory power	68 000		
Total overhead		127 000	
Total manufacturing costs			?
Total cost of work in process			?
Less: Work in process (31/12)			(87 000)
Cost of goods manufactured			**$560 000**

E15.13 **Determine the amount of cost to appear in various accounts and indicate in which financial statements these accounts would appear.** **LO5, 6, 7**

Fiero Motor Ltd manufactures motor vehicles. During September 2020 the entity purchased 5000 headlamps at a cost of $8 per lamp. Fiero withdraw 4650 lamps from the warehouse during the month. Fifty of these lamps were used to replace the headlamps in cars used by travelling sales staff. The remaining 4600 lamps were put in cars manufactured during the month.

Of the cars put into production during September 2020, 90% were completed and transferred to the entity's storage bay; 80% of the cars completed during the month were sold by 30 September.

Required

(a) Determine the cost of headlamps that would appear in each of the following accounts at 30 September 2020: Raw Materials, Work in Process, Finished Goods, Cost of Sales and Selling Expenses.

(b) Write a short memorandum to the chief accountant, indicating whether and where each of the accounts in (a) would appear on the statement of profit or loss or on the statement of financial position at 30 September 2020.

PROBLEM SET A

PSA15.1 **Classify manufacturing costs into different categories and calculate the unit cost.** **LO3, 4**

Galex Ltd, a manufacturer of stereo systems, started its production in October 2020. For the preceding 3 years Galex had been a retailer of stereo systems. After a thorough survey of stereo system markets, Galex decided to turn its retail store into a stereo equipment factory.

Raw materials cost for a stereo system will total $70 per unit. Workers on the production lines are on average paid $15 per hour. A stereo system usually takes 5 hours to complete. In addition, the rent on the equipment used to assemble stereo systems amounts to $4500 per month. Indirect materials cost $5 per system. A supervisor was hired to oversee production; her monthly salary will be $3500.

Cleaning costs were $1300 monthly. Advertising costs for the stereo system will be $8500 per month. The factory building depreciation expense is $7200 per year. Rates and taxes on the factory building will be $6000 per year.

Required

(a) Prepare an answer sheet with the following column headings.

Cost item	Product costs			Period costs
	Direct materials	Direct labour	Manufacturing overhead	

Assuming that Galex manufactures, on average, 1300 stereo systems per month, enter each cost item on your answer sheet, placing the dollar amount per month under the appropriate headings. Total the dollar amounts in each of the columns.

(b) Calculate the cost to produce one stereo system.

PSA15.2 **Classify manufacturing costs into different categories and calculate the unit cost.** **LO3, 4**

Glazier Ltd specialises in manufacturing motorcycles. The model is well accepted by consumers, and the entity has a large number of orders to keep the factory production at 100 motorcycles per month. Glazier's monthly manufacturing costs and other expense data are as follows.

Maintenance costs on factory building	$ 600
Factory manager's salary	5 000
Advertising for motorcycles	10 000
Sales commissions	5 000
Depreciation on factory building	800
Rent on factory equipment	6 200
Insurance on factory building	3 000
Raw materials (frames, tyres, etc.)	30 000
Power costs for factory	800
Supplies for general office	200
Wages for assembly line workers	45 000
Depreciation on office equipment	400
Miscellaneous materials (lubricants, solders, etc.)	600

Required

(a) Prepare an answer sheet with the following column headings. Enter each cost item on your answer sheet, placing the dollar amount under the appropriate headings. Total the dollar amounts in each of the columns.

	Product costs					
Cost item	Direct materials	Direct labour	Manufacturing overhead	Period costs	Prime costs	Conversion costs

(b) Calculate the cost to produce one motorcycle.

PSA15.3 Classify different cost items, and prepare a cost of goods manufactured schedule. LO3, 4, 7
Lucas Kids Town Ltd is a manufacturer of children's furniture. The following accounts and amounts are extracts from the records as at 30 June 2019.

Finished goods inventory, 30/6/19	$ 14 350
Depreciation—factory machinery	7 250
Depreciation—office equipment	3 800
Direct labour	41 000
Raw material inventory, 1/7/18	2 490
Administrative expense	7 800
Finished goods inventory, 1/7/18	8 000
Sales commissions	7 250
Factory supplies	2 800
Work in process, 1/7/18	3 825
Factory power	3 000
Raw material purchases	22 500
Sales revenue	132 000
Indirect labour	16 250
Work in process, 30/6/19	4 940
Insurance expense—factory	1 800
Rent—office building	24 000
Raw material inventory, 30/6/19	3 960

Required

(a) Use an Excel spreadsheet to prepare a cost of goods manufactured schedule for the year ended 30 June 2019.

(b) If Depreciation—office equipment was mistakenly included in manufacturing overhead, explain what effect this mistake would have on the cost of goods manufactured.

PSA15.4 Prepare a statement of profit or loss. **LO7**
Refer to the data for Lucas Kids Town Ltd in PSA15.3.

Required

(a) Indicate Lucas Kids Town's financial performance for the year ended 30 June 2019.

(b) What if Lucas Kids Town did not have any beginning finished goods. How would this affect the cost of sales and profit results?

PSA15.5 **Prepare a cost of goods manufactured schedule and a correct statement of profit or loss.**

LO7

Hawkinson Ltd is a manufacturer of garments. Its controller, Al Duryea, resigned in August 2019. An inexperienced assistant accountant has prepared the following statement of profit or loss for the month of August 2019.

HAWKINSON LTD Statement of profit or loss for the month ended 31 August 2019		
Sales (net)		$670 000
Less: Operating expenses		
Raw materials purchased	$200 000	
Direct labour cost	150 000	
Advertising expense	80 000	
Selling and administrative salaries	70 000	
Rent on factory	60 000	
Depreciation on sales equipment	55 000	
Depreciation on factory equipment	40 000	
Indirect labour cost	20 000	
Factory power	10 000	
Factory insurance	5 000	690 000
Net loss		**$ (20 000)**

Prior to August 2019 Hawkinson Ltd had been profitable every month. The entity's CEO is concerned about the accuracy of the statement of profit or loss above. As a friend of the CEO, you have been asked to review the statement of profit or loss and make necessary corrections. After examining other manufacturing cost data, you have acquired additional information as follows:

1. Inventory balances at the beginning and end of August were:

	1 August	31 August
Raw materials	$18 000	$33 000
Work in process	25 000	21 000
Finished goods	40 000	62 000

2. Only 70% of the power expense and 80% of the insurance expense apply to factory operations; the remaining amounts should be charged to selling and administrative activities.

Required

(a) Prepare a cost of goods manufactured schedule for August 2019.

(b) Prepare a correct statement of profit or loss for August 2019.

PSA15.6 **Indicate the missing amount of different cost items, and prepare a condensed cost of goods manufactured schedule, a statement of profit or loss and a partial statement of financial position.**

LO7

Incomplete manufacturing costs, expenses, and selling data for two different cases are as follows.

	Case	
	1	2
Direct materials used	$ 8 300	$ (g)
Direct labour	3 000	4 000
Manufacturing overhead	4 000	5 000
Total manufacturing costs	(a)	22 000
Beginning work in process inventory	1 000	(h)
Ending work in process inventory	(b)	2 000
Sales	21 500	(i)
Sales discounts	1 500	1 200
Cost of goods manufactured	12 800	21 000
Beginning finished goods inventory	(c)	4 000
Goods available for sale	17 300	(j)
Cost of sales	(d)	(k)
Ending finished goods inventory	1 200	2 500
Gross profit	(e)	6 000
Operating expenses	2 700	(l)
Profit	(f)	2 800

Required

(a) Indicate the missing amount for each letter.

(b) Prepare a condensed cost of goods manufactured schedule for Case 1.

(c) Prepare a statement of profit or loss and the current assets section of the statement of financial position for Case 1. Assume that in Case 1 the other items in the current assets section are as follows: Cash $4300, Receivables (net) $10 000, Raw materials $700, and Prepaid expenses $200.

PSA15.7 **Prepare a cost of goods manufactured schedule, a partial statement of profit or loss and a partial statement of financial position.** **LO5, 6, 7**

The following data were taken from the records of Mauro Manufacturing Ltd for the year ended 31 December 2020.

Raw materials inventory 1/1/20	$ 43 000	Accounts receivable	$ 45 000
Raw materials inventory 31/12/20	39 600	Factory insurance	5 400
Finished goods inventory 1/1/20	76 000	Factory machinery depreciation	18 090
Finished goods inventory 31/12/20	83 200	Freight-in on raw materials purchased	5 640
Work in process inventory 1/1/20	25 240	Factory power	36 000
Work in process inventory 31/12/20	23 600	Office power expense	8 600
Direct labour	250 600	Sales	890 900
Indirect labour	35 410	Sales discounts	10 120
		Factory manager's salary	60 000
		Factory rates and taxes	10 100
		Factory repairs	4 500
		Raw materials purchases	206 800
		Cash	15 000

Required

(a) Prepare a cost of goods manufactured schedule.

(b) Prepare a statement of profit or loss up to gross profit.

(c) Prepare the current assets section of the statement of financial position at 31 December.

PSA15.8 **Complete a worksheet; prepare a cost of goods manufactured schedule, a statement of profit or loss and a statement of financial position; journalise and post the closing entries.** **LO9**

Grayson Manufacturing Ltd uses a simple manufacturing accounting system. At the end of its year on 30 June 2020, the adjusted trial balance contains the following accounts.

Debits		Credits	
Cash	$ 30 500	Accumulated depreciation	$ 275 000
Accounts receivable (net)	72 100	Bills payable	42 000
Finished goods inventory	55 200	Accounts payable	31 000
Work in process inventory	17 400	Income tax payable	8 100
Raw materials inventory	23 400	Share capital	300 000
Plant assets	720 000	Retained earnings	190 400
Raw materials purchased	211 600	Sales	932 000
Direct labour	265 400		
Indirect labour	23 200		
Factory repairs	9 600		
Factory depreciation	18 000		
Factory manager's salary	40 000		
Factory insurance	4 700		
Factory rates and taxes	12 900		
Factory power	13 300		
Selling expenses	108 600		
Administrative expenses	120 800		
Income tax expense	31 800		
	$1 778 500		$1 778 500

Physical inventory accounts on 30 June 2020, show the following inventory amounts: Finished goods $51 400, Work in process $22 800, and Raw materials $21 700.

Required

(a) Enter the adjusted trial balance data on a worksheet in financial statement order and complete the worksheet.

(b) Prepare a cost of goods manufactured schedule for the year.

(c) Prepare a statement of profit or loss for the year and a statement of financial position at 30 June 2020.

(d) Journalise the closing entries.

(e) Post the closing entries to manufacturing summary and to profit or loss summary.

PROBLEM SET B

PSB15.1 **Classify manufacturing costs into different categories and calculate the unit cost.** **LO3, 4**

Molik Ltd, a manufacturer of tennis racquets, started production in November 2018. For the preceding 5 years Molik Ltd had been a retailer of sports equipment. After a thorough survey of tennis racquet markets, Molik Ltd decided to turn its retail store into a tennis racquet factory.

Raw materials cost for a tennis racquet total $28 per racquet. Workers on the production lines are on average paid $15 per hour. A racquet usually takes 2 hours to complete. In addition, the rent on the equipment used to produce racquets amounts to $4000 per month. Indirect materials cost is $3 per racquet. A supervisor was hired to oversee production; her monthly salary will be $2500.

Cleaning costs will be $2000 monthly. Advertising costs for the racquets will be $6000 per month. The factory building depreciation expense will be $19 200 per year. Rates and taxes on the factory building will be $4800 per year.

Required

(a) Prepare an answer sheet with the following column headings:

	Product costs					
Cost item	Direct materials	Direct labour	Manufacturing overhead	Period costs	Prime costs	Conversion costs

Assuming that Molik manufactures, on average, 3000 tennis racquets per month, enter each cost item on your answer sheet, placing the dollar amount per month under the appropriate headings. Total the dollar amounts in each of the columns.

(b) Calculate the cost of producing one racquet.

PSB15.2 Classify manufacturing costs into different categories and calculate the unit cost.   LO3, 4

Marek Accessories specialises in manufacturing a unique model of bicycle helmet. The model is well accepted by consumers, and the business has a large number of orders to keep the factory production at 10 000 helmets per month (80% of its full capacity). Marek Accessories' monthly manufacturing costs and other expense data are as follows.

Rent on factory equipment	$ 8 000
Insurance on factory building	1 500
Raw materials (plastics, polystyrene, etc.)	80 000
Power costs for factory	800
Supplies for general office	400
Wages for assembly line workers	106 000
Depreciation on office equipment	800
Miscellaneous materials (lubricants, solders, etc.)	1 500
Factory manager's salary	5 700
Rates and taxes on factory building	800
Advertising for helmets	11 000
Sales commissions	6 500
Depreciation on factory building	3 000

Required

(a) Prepare an answer sheet with the following column headings:

	Product costs					
Cost item	Direct materials	Direct labour	Manufacturing overhead	Period costs	Prime costs	Conversion costs

Enter each cost item on your answer sheet, placing the dollar amount under the appropriate headings. Total the dollar amounts in each of the columns.

(b) Calculate the cost of producing one helmet.

PSB15.3 Classify different cost items; prepare a cost of goods manufactured schedule.   LO3, 4

Greenspring Ltd is a manufacturer of organic skin care products. The following accounts and amounts are extracts from the records as at 30 June 2019.

Finished goods inventory, 30/6/19	$ 71 750
Depreciation—factory machinery	36 250
Depreciation—office equipment	19 000
Direct labour	205 000
Raw material inventory, 1/7/18	12 450
Administrative expense	39 000
Finished goods inventory, 1/7/18	40 000
Sales commissions	36 250
Factory supplies	14 000
Work in process, 1/7/18	19 125
Factory power	15 000
Raw material purchases	112 500
Sales revenue	660 000
Indirect labour	81 250
Work in process, 30/6/19	24 700
Insurance expense—factory	9 000
Rent—office building	120 000
Raw material inventory, 30/6/19	19 800

Required

(a) Use an Excel spreadsheet to prepare a cost of goods manufactured schedule for the year ended 30 June 2019.

(b) If Depreciation—office equipment was mistakenly included in manufacturing overhead, explain what effect this mistake would have on the cost of goods manufactured.

PSB15.4 **Prepare a statement of profit or loss.**　　　　　　　　　　　　　　　　**LO7**

Refer to the data for Greenspring Ltd in PSB15.3.

Required

(a) Indicate Greenspring Ltd's financial performance for the year ended 30 June 2019.

(b) What if Greenspring Ltd did not have any beginning finished goods. How would this affect the cost of sales and profit results?

PSB15.5 **Prepare a cost of goods manufactured schedule and a correct statement of profit or loss.**

LO7

Noonan Ltd is a manufacturer of computers. Its senior accountant resigned in October 2019. An inexperienced assistant accountant has prepared the following statement of profit or loss for the month of October 2019.

NOONAN LTD Statement of profit or loss for the month ended 31 October 2019		
Sales (net)		$840 000
Less: Operating expenses		
Raw materials purchased	$271 000	
Direct labour cost	210 000	
Advertising expense	85 000	
Selling and administrative salaries	81 000	
Rent on factory	72 000	
Depreciation on sales equipment	43 000	
Depreciation on factory equipment	30 000	
Indirect labour cost	32 000	
Factory power	12 000	
Factory insurance	8 625	844 625
Loss		$　(4 625)

Before October 2019 the entity had been profitable every month. The entity's CEO is concerned about the accuracy of the statement of profit or loss above. As a friend of the CEO, you have been asked to review the statement of profit or loss and make necessary corrections. After examining other manufacturing cost data, you have acquired additional information as follows:

1. Inventory balances at the beginning and end of October were:

	1 October	31 October
Raw materials	$20 000	$25 000
Work in process	13 000	16 000
Finished goods	30 000	48 000

2. Only 70% of the power expense and 80% of the insurance expense apply to factory operations; the remaining amounts should be charged to selling and administrative activities.

Required

(a) Prepare a cost of goods manufactured schedule for October 2019.

(b) Prepare a corrected statement of profit or loss for October 2019.

PSB15.6 Indicate the missing amount of different cost items; prepare a condensed cost of goods manufactured schedule, a statement of profit or loss, and a partial statement of financial position. **LO7**

Incomplete manufacturing costs, expenses and selling data for two different cases are as follows.

	Case	
	1	2
Direct materials used	$ 8 000	$ (g)
Direct labour	6 000	8 000
Manufacturing overhead	5 000	4 000
Total manufacturing costs	(a)	21 000
Beginning work in process inventory	1 000	(h)
Ending work in process inventory	(b)	3 000
Sales	24 500	(i)
Sales discounts	2 500	1 400
Cost of goods manufactured	16 500	22 000
Beginning finished goods inventory	(c)	3 500
Goods available for sale	18 000	(j)
Cost of sales	(d)	(k)
Ending finished goods inventory	3 000	2 500
Gross profit	(e)	7 000
Operating expenses	2 500	(l)
Profit	(f)	2 800

Required

(a) Indicate the missing amount for each letter.
(b) Prepare a condensed cost of goods manufactured schedule for Case 1.
(c) Prepare a statement of profit or loss and the current assets section of the statement of financial position for Case 1, assuming that in Case 1 the other items in the current assets section are as follows: Cash $4000, Receivables (net) $15 000, Raw materials $600, and Prepaid expenses $400.

PSB15.7 Prepare a cost of goods manufactured schedule, a partial statement of profit or loss, and a partial statement of financial position. **LO5, 6, 7**

The following data were taken from the records of Scheve Manufacturing Ltd for the financial year ended 30 June 2019.

Raw materials inventory, 1/7/18	$ 46 500	Accounts receivable	$ 27 000
Raw materials inventory, 30/6/19	39 600	Factory insurance	4 600
Finished goods inventory, 1/7/18	96 000	Factory machinery depreciation	15 000
Finished goods inventory, 30/6/19	95 900	Freight-in on raw materials purchased	8 600
Work in process inventory, 1/7/18	21 000	Factory electricity	24 600
Work in process inventory, 30/6/19	18 700	Office electricity expense	8 650
Direct labour	147 250	Sales	547 000
Indirect labour	24 460	Sales discounts	3 300
		Factory manager's salary	29 000
		Factory property rates	9 600
		Factory repairs	1 400
		Raw materials purchases	89 800
		Cash	32 000

Required

(a) Prepare a cost of goods manufactured schedule.
(b) Prepare a statement of profit or loss to gross profit.
(c) Prepare the current assets section of the statement of financial position as at 30 June 2019.

PSB15.8 Complete a worksheet; prepare a cost of goods manufactured schedule, a statement of profit or loss, and a statement of financial position; journalise and post the closing entries. LO9

Everheart Manufacturing Ltd uses a simple manufacturing accounting system. At the end of its financial year on 30 June 2020, the adjusted trial balance contains the following accounts.

Debits		Credits	
Cash	$ 16 700	Accumulated depreciation	$ 353 000
Accounts receivable (net)	62 900	Bills payable	45 000
Finished goods inventory	56 000	Accounts payable	38 200
Work in process inventory	27 800	Income tax payable	9 000
Raw materials inventory	37 200	Share capital	352 000
Plant assets	890 000	Retained earnings	205 300
Raw materials purchased	236 500	Sales	996 000
Direct labour	280 900		
Indirect labour	27 400		
Factory repairs	17 200		
Factory depreciation	19 000		
Factory manager's salary	40 000		
Factory insurance	11 000		
Factory rates and taxes	12 900		
Factory power	13 300		
Selling expenses	98 500		
Administrative expenses	115 200		
Income tax expense	36 000		
	$1 998 500		$1 998 500

Physical inventory accounts on 30 June 2020 show the following inventory amounts: Finished goods $54 600, Work in process $23 400, and Raw materials $46 500.

Required

(a) Enter the adjusted trial balance data on a worksheet in financial statement order and complete the worksheet.

(b) Prepare a cost of goods manufactured schedule for the year.

(c) Prepare a statement of profit or loss for the year and a statement of financial position as at 30 June 2020.

(d) Journalise the closing entries.

(e) Post the closing entries to manufacturing summary and to profit or loss summary.

BUILDING BUSINESS SKILLS

FINANCIAL REPORTING AND ANALYSIS

Managerial analysis

BBS15.1 Golf, Anyone? Ltd is a manufacturing entity located in Wellington. It manufactures golf clubs, golf balls, golf clothing and golf shoes, all bearing the entity's distinctive logo, a large green question mark on a white golf ball. The entity's sales have been increasing over the past 10 years. The golf club division has recently implemented several advanced manufacturing techniques. Robotic technology plus scanners test for defects, and the engineering and design team use computers to draft and test new products. The following managers work in the golf club division:

- Marshall Loadsman, sales manager (supervises all sales representatives)
- Anthony Chan, technical specialist (supervises computer programmers)
- Martine Clancy, management accounting manager (supervises management accountants)

- Jack Jones, production supervisor (supervises all manufacturing employees)
- Louise Parker, engineer (supervises all new product design teams).

Required

With the class divided into groups, answer the following questions:

(a) What are the main information needs of each manager?

(b) Which, if any, financial accounting report(s) is each likely to use?

(c) Name one special-purpose management accounting report that could be designed for each manager. Include the name of the report, the information it contains, and how frequently it should be issued.

Research case

BBS15.2 CSL Limited is Australia's leading biopharmaceutical company. Listed on the Australian Securities Exchange (ASX), the company specialises in pharmaceuticals, vaccines and plasma products. The web site of CSL Ltd has information about the company.

Address: www.csl.com.au

Required

(a) What are CSL Ltd's main activities?

(b) What is the sales revenue for the current year and cost of sales? Is this an improvement in sales revenue on the previous year? (*Hint:* Click on the latest annual financial report under the **Investors** heading on the home page.)

(c) What are the main industry segments? Calculate the percentage each segment contributes to total revenue for the entity. (*Hint:* Read through the relevant sections of the statement of profit or loss and Notes to the Financial Statements in the annual report.)

Research case

BBS15.3 Select from one of the following entities:

- Vodafone Group Plc (www.vodafone.com)
- Brisbane City Council (www.brisbane.qld.gov.au)
- Qantas Airways Ltd (www.qantas.com.au)
- Coca-Cola Amatil (www.ccamatil.com)

Required

Answer the questions below. (The information you will need may be contained within the entity's annual report or on its website. The annual reports are usually found under the investor relation sections of the website.)

(a) What is the main strategy for the entity in the current year?

(b) Outline the performance measures/indicators the entity uses to assess if the entity is meeting its stated objectives.

(c) Describe the entity's risk management policy (include an outline of monitoring mechanisms used by the entity).

(d) What performance measures are used to report on the social and environmental issues associated with the entity?

CRITICAL THINKING

Group decision case

BBS15.4 Deskins Manufacturing Ltd specialises in producing fashion outfits. On 31 January 2019, a cyclone tore through its factory and general office. The inventories in the warehouse and the factory were totally damaged due to heavy rain and moisture. The general office nearby was completely destroyed. Next morning, through a careful search of the disaster site, Ed Loder, the manager, and Susan Manning, the management accountant, were able to recover a small part of manufacturing cost data for the current month.

'What a horrible experience,' sighed Ed. 'And the worst part is that we may not have enough records to use in filing an insurance claim.'

'It was terrible,' replied Susan. 'However, I managed to recover some of the manufacturing cost data that I was working on yesterday afternoon. The data indicate that our direct labour cost in January totalled $280 000 and that we had purchased $360 000 of raw materials. In addition, I recall that the raw materials used for January was $362 000. But I'm not sure this information will help; the rest of our records are gone.'

'Well, not exactly,' said Ed. 'I was working on the year-to-date statement of profit or loss when the cyclone warning came. My recollection is that our sales in January were $1 300 000 and our gross profit ratio has been 40% of sales. Also, I can remember that our cost of goods available for sale was $850 000 for January.'

'Maybe we can work something out from this information,' said Susan. 'My experience tells me that our manufacturing overhead is usually 60% of direct labour. Also, someone found a copy of this January's statement of financial position, and it shows that our inventories as of 1 January are finished goods, $56 000, work in process, $22 000, and raw materials, $16 000.'

'Super,' yelled Ed. 'Let's work something out.'

In order to file an insurance claim, Deskins Manufacturing Ltd must determine the amount of its inventories as of 31 January 2019, the date of the cyclone.

Required

With the class divided into groups, answer the following questions:

(a) Determine the amount of cost in the raw materials, work in process and finished goods inventory accounts as of the date of the cyclone.

(b) Prepare a cost of goods manufactured schedule and a statement of profit or loss to gross profit line.

Communication activities

BBS15.5 Give examples of management accounting information that could help a manager decide in the following independent situations.

1. Billabong International is considering whether to open a new store in Canada.
2. Qantas management is deciding what routes are viable and whether to add/delete/alter routes.
3. Coca-Cola Amatil management is deciding whether to invest in a new flavour beverage.
4. The CSR Ltd divisional plant manager is planning production for the next 12 months.

BBS15.6 Steven Roger started a small business in the late 1970s which developed and grew over the years, expanding to 20 stores located throughout Australia and New Zealand. Although turnover seemed to be increasing, net profit was decreasing. Steven thinks some product lines must not be profitable. The reports prepared from the business's financial accounting system seemed to indicate that the declining 'bottom line' was from a blowout in costs. Steven is frustrated as the statement of profit or loss is not useful in assessing this and he also suspects that the quality, delivery and price of the goods from the suppliers could be improved.

Required

Write a memorandum to Steven explaining how management accounting could help him. Include in your discussion the role of management accounting techniques.

Ethics case

BBS15.7 John Shepherd, accountant for Casper Ltd, was reviewing production cost reports for the year. One amount in these reports continued to bother him: advertising. During the year, the company had instituted an expensive advertising campaign to sell some of its slower moving products. It was still too early to tell whether the advertising campaign was successful. There had been much internal debate regarding how to report advertising costs. The director of finance argued that advertising costs should be reported as a cost of production, just like direct materials and direct labour. He therefore recommended that this cost be identified as manufacturing overhead and reported as part of inventory costs until sold. Others disagreed. John believed that this cost should be reported as an expense of the current period based on the conservatism principle. Others argued that it should be reported as prepaid advertising and reported as a current asset.

The CEO finally had to decide the issue. He argued that these costs should be reported as inventory. His arguments were practical ones. He noted that the entity was experiencing financial difficulty and expensing this amount in the current period might jeopardise a planned debenture offering. Also, by reporting the advertising costs as inventory rather than as prepaid advertising, less attention would be directed to it by the financial community.

Required

(a) Who are the stakeholders in this situation?

(b) What are the ethical issues involved in this situation?

(c) What would you do if you were John Shepherd?

ANSWERS

Answers to self-study questions

15.1 (b) 15.2 (b) 15.3 (b) 15.4 (b) 15.5 (d) 15.6 (a) 15.7 (c) 15.8 (a) 15.9 (d) 15.10 (a) 15.11 (c)

ACKNOWLEDGEMENTS

Photo: © Abel Mitja Varela / iStockphoto
Photo: © Rawpixel.com / Shutterstock.com
Photo: © wavebreakmedia / Shutterstock.com

CHAPTER 16

Cost accounting systems

LEARNING OBJECTIVES

After studying this chapter, you should be able to:

16.1 explain the characteristics and purposes of cost accounting systems

16.2 describe the flow of costs in a job order cost system

16.3 explain a job cost sheet and the accounting entries for a job order cost system

16.4 describe the flow of costs in a process cost system

16.5 prepare the accounting entries for a process cost system

16.6 prepare a production cost report

16.7 recognise the difference between traditional costing and activity-based costing and identify the activity cost pools and activity drivers used in activity-based cost systems

16.8 understand the benefits and limitations of activity-based costing

16.9 differentiate between value-added and non-value-added activities

16.10 explain just-in-time (JIT) processing.

Chapter preview

Michael Hill International Limited, jewellery manufacturer and retailer, is an example of a company with a need for a costing system. Jewellery making is the manufacturing of mixed products: some unique special orders and other similar or homogeneous pieces. How does a business determine the cost of making its product and in turn ensure adequate pricing for a profitable business? This chapter discusses how costs are assigned to products and services. The content and organisation of this chapter are as follows.

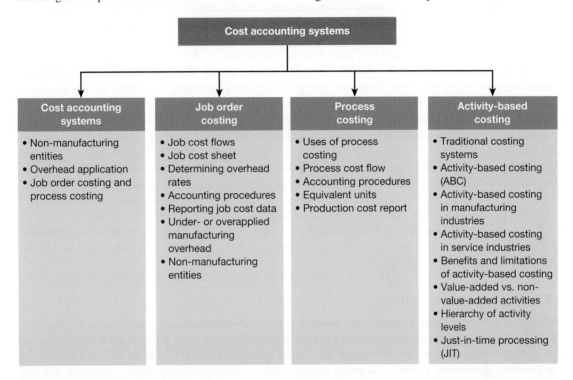

Cost accounting systems			
Cost accounting systems	**Job order costing**	**Process costing**	**Activity-based costing**
• Non-manufacturing entities • Overhead application • Job order costing and process costing	• Job cost flows • Job cost sheet • Determining overhead rates • Accounting procedures • Reporting job cost data • Under- or overapplied manufacturing overhead • Non-manufacturing entities	• Uses of process costing • Process cost flow • Accounting procedures • Equivalent units • Production cost report	• Traditional costing systems • Activity-based costing (ABC) • Activity-based costing in manufacturing industries • Activity-based costing in service industries • Benefits and limitations of activity-based costing • Value-added vs. non-value-added activities • Hierarchy of activity levels • Just-in-time processing (JIT)

16.1 Cost accounting systems

LEARNING OBJECTIVE 16.1 Explain the characteristics and purposes of cost accounting systems.

Cost accounting involves the measuring, recording and reporting of product or service costs. From the data accumulated, both the total cost and the unit cost of each product are determined.

A product **cost accounting system** consists of manufacturing cost accounts that are fully integrated into the general ledger of an entity. An important feature of a product cost accounting system is the use of a perpetual inventory system that provides information immediately on the cost of a product. For financial accounting, product costs are needed to value inventory in the statement of financial position and the cost of sales in the statement of profit or loss.

Recall from chapter 15 that management accounting is primarily concerned with providing economic and financial information to managers and other internal users for planning, directing and controlling business activities. As such, cost accounting is an integral part of the management accounting system. Accurate costing data provide any entity's management with high quality information for making better decisions. For example, having access to ingredient costing enables Domino's Pizza Enterprises Ltd to set competitive pricing for its fresh pizzas. Likewise, Coca-Cola Amatil needs accurate costing information about its diversified lines of products to compete with other food and beverage manufacturers in the markets.

Non-manufacturing entities

Cost accounting was designed mainly to determine product costs for manufacturing businesses. However, the need for product cost information is also important in other industries such as merchandising, mining, agricultural products and service industries. Service and non-profit entities do not have inventory but they still need to know the cost of their services for the purposes of pricing, planning, cost control and decision making. For example, Qantas management needs to know the cost of flying a proposed route, the Willoughby City Council can make a better decision about whether to provide library services in a new area if the cost of providing similar existing services is known, and Vodafone can decide when to launch new products in Australia if the costs of the new network are known.

In Australia, the service sector is a large and important part of the economy. Approximately 70% of gross domestic product (GDP) is derived from the service sector. The design of costing systems for service entities differs from manufacturers in that the service is normally consumed as it is produced and there is no inventory. However, for services that may take a longer time to complete, costs may be accumulated and charged at a later date (e.g. a solicitor involved in a complex legal case may accumulate unbilled labour and incidentals and invoice once a month). The service product is usually heterogeneous and tailored to meet the customer's (client's) needs. As outlined in the previous chapter, product costs are divided into direct materials, direct labour and manufacturing overhead, and the selling and administrative costs are period costs. In contrast, in service entities the main costs are direct labour; there are very little, if any, direct materials and it is often difficult to determine production overhead costs from other indirect costs. For financial accounting purposes, no special ledger accounts are required to accumulate the costs of the service provided as the costs are treated as period costs. The costs are recorded in individual expense accounts such as Salaries and Wages, Telephone and Depreciation. This is because the service is usually consumed as it is produced.

Overhead application

Whether a service is being provided or a product is being manufactured, establishing the costing systems for direct materials and direct labour presents a few difficulties. The difficult issue in establishing the costing systems is the classification of what constitutes overheads that can be assigned as costs to the products or services. For manufacturing entities, what constitutes manufacturing overheads that can be inventoried (product cost) is constrained by the requirements of IAS 2/AASB 102 *Inventories*. This will be discussed later in this chapter in the discussion of activity-based costing.

Theoretically, overhead costs are accumulated and then assigned to products and services in relation to the resources consumed, but many indirect costs have differing relationships to the products and services. Traditionally, many entities use a factory-wide rate such as direct labour hours or machine hours as the cost driver. A **cost driver** is any factor or activity that has a direct cause–effect relationship with the resources consumed. Thus, there should be some correlation between the incurrence of the overhead cost and the use of the cost driver. For example, the cost of machine maintenance may be driven by the number of hours each machine is used. The predetermined overhead rate can be applied to the whole factory where one rate is applied for all production. Some entities may use a two-stage cost allocation, where each production department is assigned the overhead costs that relate to that department and overheads are assigned only to products that use that department. A further refinement of the allocation process is the activity-based costing system. The processes of applying overheads are illustrated throughout this chapter.

Job order costing and process costing

All costing systems track the costs of providing a service or manufacturing a product. When deciding on a cost accounting system, the nature of the product or service must be considered. Where the product or service is unique (heterogeneous) with little standardisation (e.g. a tailor-made wedding gown or Flight Centre booking an itinerary for a customer), costs are assigned to each job. However, where there is a high volume, uniform, homogeneous products or services such as Mainland Cheese or bulk mail processing by Australia Post, then the costing is based on the volume of the standard product or service through each processing department. There are two basic types of accounting systems: (1) job order costing and (2) process costing. Although the costing systems differ widely from entity to entity, most are based on one of these two traditional costing systems. Figure 16.1 provides examples of businesses and the products or services suited to job order costing and process costing systems.

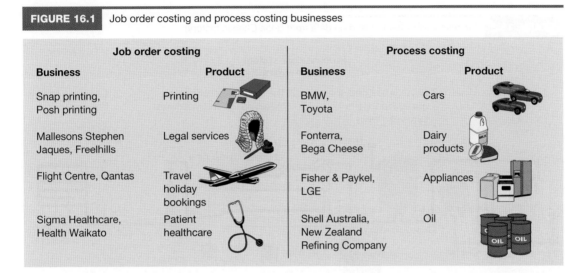

FIGURE 16.1 Job order costing and process costing businesses

Under a **job order cost system**, costs are assigned to each job, such as the manufacture of a high-speed drilling machine, or to each batch of goods, such as 500 wedding invitations. Jobs or batches may be completed to fill a specific customer order or to replenish inventory. An important feature of job order costing is that each job (or batch) has its own distinguishing characteristics. For example, each travel itinerary is developed to suit the traveller, each motion picture is unique, and each printing job is different. The objective is to calculate the cost per job. At each point in the manufacturing process, the job and its associated costs can be identified. A job order cost system measures costs for each completed job, rather than for set time periods. A job order cost system is illustrated in figure 16.2.

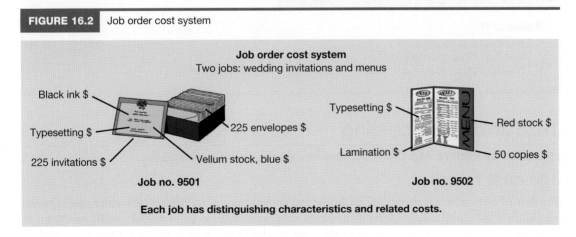

FIGURE 16.2 Job order cost system

A **process cost system** is used when a series of connected manufacturing processes or departments produce a large volume of uniform or relatively homogeneous products. Production is continuous to ensure that adequate inventories of the finished product(s) are on hand. A process cost system is used in the manufacture of whitegoods, the refining of petroleum, the manufacture of motor vehicles and the processing of cheese. Process costing accounts for and accumulates product-related costs for a period of time (such as a week or a month) as opposed to assigning costs to specific products or job orders. In process costing, the costs are assigned to or accumulated by departments or processes for a set period of time. A process cost system is illustrated in figure 16.3.

FIGURE 16.3 Process cost system (based on data from Bega Cheese factory)

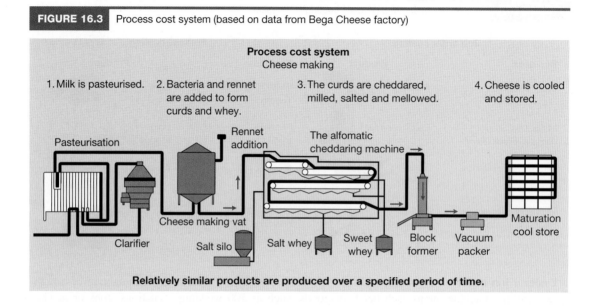

A business may use both types of cost systems. For example, BMW uses process cost accounting for its standard models and job order cost accounting for BMW individual models, which are custom-made orders with specific designs.

LEARNING REFLECTION AND CONSOLIDATION

Review it
1. What is cost accounting?
2. What is a cost accounting system?
3. How does a job order cost system differ from a process cost system?

16.2 Job order costing

LEARNING OBJECTIVE 16.2 Describe the flow of costs in a job order cost system.

Job cost flows

The flow of costs (direct materials, direct labour and manufacturing overhead) in job order cost accounting parallels the physical flow of the materials as they are converted into finished goods. As shown in figure 16.4, manufacturing costs are assigned to the work in process inventory account. When a job is completed, the cost of the job is transferred to finished goods inventory. Later when the goods are sold, their cost is transferred to cost of sales.

FIGURE 16.4 Flow of costs in job order cost accounting

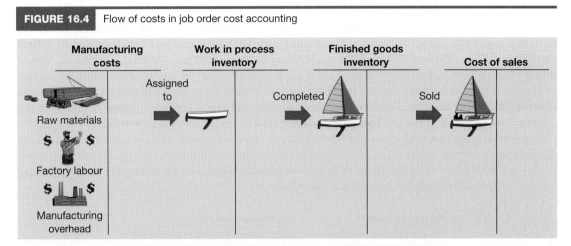

A job order cost system uses the perpetual inventory approach for accumulating costs. Details of costs are recorded on job cost sheets (subsidiary ledger) and summarised and recorded monthly in the general ledger.

A more detailed presentation of the flow of costs is shown in figure 16.5. This figure indicates that there are two major steps in the flow of costs: (1) *accumulating* the manufacturing costs incurred and (2) *assigning or allocating* the accumulated costs to the job done. In step one, manufacturing costs incurred are accumulated in entries 1–3 by debits to raw materials inventory, factory labour and manufacturing overhead. No attempt is made when costs are incurred to associate the costs with specific jobs at this stage.

FIGURE 16.5 Job order cost accounting system

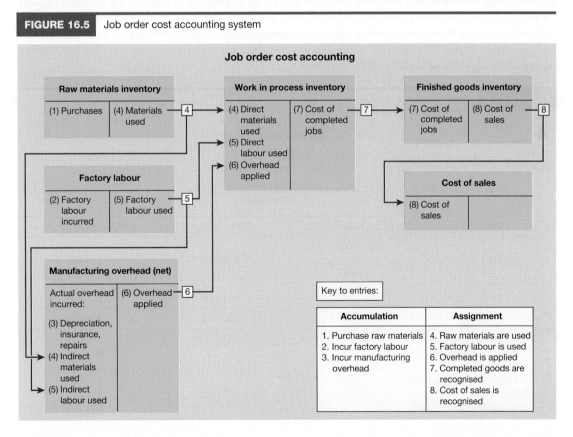

The second stage is assigning the accumulated costs to the work done. As raw materials are used, the costs are transferred to work in process (direct materials) and manufacturing overhead (indirect materials), as shown in entry 4. Labour is assigned in the same way. Direct labour hours are controlled by a **time sheet** that indicates the hours worked, the account/job to be charged and the total labour cost. This is shown as entry 5. Manufacturing overhead costs are assigned to work in process and to specific jobs on an estimated basis through the use of a predetermined overhead rate, as shown in entry 6. On completion of production, the accumulated costs are transferred to finished goods inventory (entry 7), and when the goods are sold the cost of the finished goods is transferred to cost of sales as shown in entry 8.

The general ledger accounts shown in figure 16.5 are control accounts with corresponding subsidiary accounts using job cost sheets. The control account and the link to the subsidiary ledger are shown below. Entries are made in the subsidiary ledgers daily as movement occurs and the entries are summarised and recorded in the general ledgers usually on a monthly basis.

Control account	Subsidiary ledger
Work in process inventory	Job cost sheets (incomplete jobs)
Finished goods inventory	Job cost sheets (completed jobs)
Cost of sales	Job cost sheets (for jobs sold)

16.3 Job cost sheet

LEARNING OBJECTIVE 16.3 Explain a job cost sheet and the accounting entries for a job order cost system.

A **job cost sheet** or job card is a form used to record the costs chargeable to a specific job and to determine the total and unit cost of the completed job. Postings to the job cost sheet are made daily directly from the supporting documentation that shows the cost and job to be charged. A separate job cost sheet is kept for each job. Job cost sheets constitute the subsidiary ledger for the work in process inventory account. Each entry to work in process inventory must be accompanied by a corresponding posting to one or more job cost sheets. Figure 16.6 shows a completed job cost sheet for customer Tanner Ltd. The information contained on the job cost sheet is explained below.

FIGURE 16.6	Completed job cost sheet

Job cost sheet

Job no.	101	Quantity	1000
Item	Magnetic sensors	Date ordered	5 March
For	Tanner Ltd	Date completed	31 March
		Date required	5 April

Date	Direct materials	Direct labour	Manufacturing overhead
6/3	$ 2 000		
10/3		$18 000	$14 400
12/3	14 000		
26/3	8 000		
31/3		12 000	9 600
	$24 000	$30 000	$24 000

Cost of completed job
    Direct materials $24 000
    Direct labour   30 000
    Manufacturing overhead   24 000
Total cost $78 000
Unit cost ($78 000 ÷ 1000) $ 78.00

Helpful hint: A job cost sheet is a source document detailing the costs associated with each job or order that a business is working on or has completed.

Each job requires a control number: Tanner's job is number 101 for 1000 magnetic sensors. It also shows that the job started on 6 March and was completed on 31 March, five days ahead of the scheduled required date and time. On 6, 12 and 26 March materials were requisitioned for the job and the direct labour of $30 000 was assigned from labour sheets. Overheads were allocated on the same date as the labour, which indicates that the overheads were allocated according to direct labour hours. The bottom half of the job sheet summarises the costs and calculates a per-unit cost for the job.

DECISION-MAKING TOOLKIT

Decision/issue	Info needed for analysis	Tool or technique to use for decision	How to evaluate results to make decision
What is the cost of a job?	Cost of material, labour and overhead assigned to a specific job	Job cost sheet	Compare costs with those of previous periods and with those of competitors to ensure that costs are in line. Compare costs with expected selling price to determine overall profitability.

Determining overhead rates

The **predetermined overhead application rate** (or **budgeted overhead rate**) is based on the relationship between estimated annual overhead costs and expected annual operating activity, expressed in terms of a common activity base. The common activity base may be stated in terms of direct labour costs, direct labour hours, machine hours or any other measure that will provide an equitable basis for applying overhead costs to jobs. The predetermined overhead application rate is established by the beginning of the year. The formula for a predetermined overhead application rate is shown in figure 16.7.

FIGURE 16.7 Formula for predetermined overhead application rate

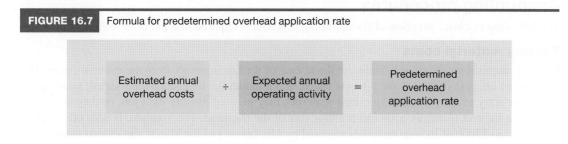

The reason for using a predetermined rate to assign overhead costs to jobs is that actual overheads are generally not known at the time when a job or order is being worked on. For example, the actual costs of factory overheads such as electricity and water rates are generally not available until the end of each month when the invoices are received. As jobs are being completed throughout the month, the time lag for the availability of actual overhead costs means that the information will be too late to be useful. As an alternative, management accountants estimate how much factory overheads will be and use a predetermined application rate to assign overhead costs so that the cost for a job can be determined immediately. Figure 16.8 indicates how manufacturing overhead is applied to work in process.

Helpful hint: In contrast to overhead, actual costs for direct materials and direct labour are used to assign costs to work in process because the time delay to get materials and labour cost information is short.

FIGURE 16.8 Using predetermined overhead application rates

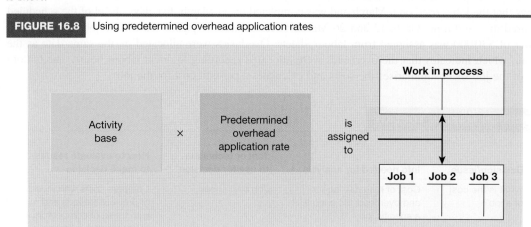

For example, if direct labour cost is the activity base, annual overhead costs are expected to be $280 000 and direct labour costs are anticipated to be $350 000, the overhead application rate is 80%, calculated as follows:

$$\$280\,000 \div \$350\,000 = 80\%$$

This means that for every dollar of direct labour, 80 cents of manufacturing overhead will be applied to a job. The use of a predetermined overhead application rate enables the business to determine the approximate total cost of each job when the job is completed.

Historically, direct labour costs or direct labour hours have often been used as the activity base because of the relatively high correlation between direct labour and manufacturing overhead. In recent years, however, there has been a significant trend towards using machine hours or a combination of other activity measures as the activity base because of increased reliance on automation in manufacturing operations. This is discussed in more detail later in the chapter.

Accounting procedures

The following is a brief overview of the recording procedures required in a job order cost system.

Factory material costs

Materials requisitions are made to authorise the release of the raw materials from the materials store. The requisitions are posted daily to the job cost sheets. Each month the requisitions are sorted, totalled and costed for entry to the general ledger. Raw materials may be used directly on a job, or they may form part of the indirect materials costs and are thus part of the overhead. For example, if $36 000 of direct materials and $3000 of indirect materials are used by Mackenzie Ltd for March, the journal entry is:

	(1)		
Mar. 31	Work in process inventory	36 000	
	Manufacturing overhead control	3 000	
	Raw materials inventory		
	(To assign materials to jobs and overhead)		39 000

A	=	L	+	E
+36 000				
+ 3 000				
−39 000				

Factory labour costs

Factory labour costs are assigned to jobs on the basis of time sheets prepared when the work is performed. The time sheet should indicate the employee's name, the hours worked, the account and the job to be charged, and the total labour cost. The time sheets are sent to the payroll department where the total time reported for an employee is reconciled for the pay period with the total hours worked. These time sheets are sorted and summarised for entry in the general ledger. For example, if in March the total factory labour cost incurred of $48 000 consists of $40 000 of direct labour and $8000 of indirect labour, the journal entry is:

	(2)		
Mar. 31	Work in process inventory	40 000	
	Manufacturing overhead control	8 000	
	Factory labour		48 000
	(To assign labour to jobs and overhead)		

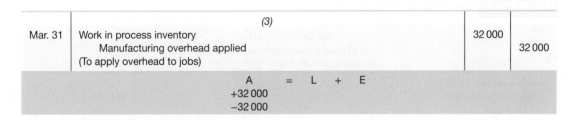

A = L + E
+40 000
+ 8 000
−48 000

Manufacturing overhead

The manufacturing overhead is applied using a predetermined overhead application rate. If the activity base is direct labour hours, then the entry is linked to the direct labour hours charged for the month. If the overhead rate is 80% of direct labour hours, then the entry for the month to apply overhead of $32 000 ($40 000 × 80%) is:

	(3)		
Mar. 31	Work in process inventory	32 000	
	Manufacturing overhead applied		32 000
	(To apply overhead to jobs)		

A = L + E
+32 000
−32 000

Helpful hint: The manufacturing overhead applied account accumulates the amount of factory overhead that has been assigned to work in process inventory.

Assigning costs to finished goods inventory

When a job is finished, an entry is made to transfer its total cost to finished goods inventory. Assuming the costing from the completed job cost sheets for the month totalled $98 000, the entry to record the finished goods is:

	(4)		
Mar. 31	Finished goods inventory	98 000	
	Work in process inventory		98 000
	(To record the completion of the jobs for the month)		

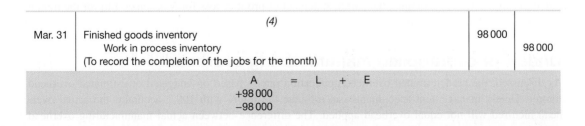

A = L + E
+98 000
−98 000

Assigning costs to cost of sales

The last entry is the recognition of the cost of goods when the sale is made. Assume Mackenzie Ltd sells, on account, a job costing $90 000 for $125 000. The entries are:

		(5)		
Mar. 31	Accounts receivable		125 000	
	Sales			125 000
	(To record the sale of job #842)			
	Cost of sales		90 000	
	Finished goods inventory			90 000
	(To record the cost of job #842)			

A	=	L	+	E	
+125 000				+125 000	

A	=	L	+	E	
−90 000				−90 000	

Reporting job cost data

At the end of a period, financial statements are prepared that present aggregate data on all jobs manufactured and sold. The cost of goods manufactured schedule in job order costing is the same as in chapter 15 with one exception — manufacturing overhead applied, rather than actual overhead costs, is added to direct materials and direct labour in determining total manufacturing costs. The schedule is prepared directly from the work in process inventory account. A condensed schedule for Mackenzie Ltd for March is shown in figure 16.9.

FIGURE 16.9 Cost of goods manufactured schedule

MACKENZIE LTD
Cost of goods manufactured schedule
for the month ended 31 March 2019

Work in process, 1 March		$ —
Direct materials used	$36 000	
Direct labour	40 000	
Manufacturing overhead applied	32 000	
Total manufacturing costs for the month		108 000
Total cost of work in process		108 000
Less: Work in process, 31 March		(10 000)
Cost of goods manufactured		**$ 98 000**

Helpful hint: Monthly financial statements are usually prepared for management use only.

Note that the cost of goods manufactured ($98 000) agrees with the amount transferred from work in process inventory to finished goods inventory in journal entry no. 4 above.

The statement of profit or loss and statement of financial position are the same as those that are illustrated in chapter 15. For example, the partial statement of profit or loss for Mackenzie Ltd for the month of March is shown in figure 16.10.

Under- or overapplied manufacturing overhead

As discussed, the predetermined overhead application rate is based on budgeted or estimated overhead figures. Unless management accountants can estimate the future with 100% accuracy, the actual overhead incurred will not equal overhead applied. The difference between actual manufacturing overhead and *applied* manufacturing overhead is called **underapplied manufacturing overhead** or **overapplied manufacturing overhead**.

FIGURE 16.10	Partial statement of profit or loss

MACKENZIE LTD
Statement of profit or loss (partial)
for the month ended 31 March 2019

Sales		$125 000
Cost of sales		
Finished goods inventory, 1 March	$ —	
Cost of goods manufactured (see figure 16.9)	98 000	
Cost of goods available for sale	98 000	
Finished goods inventory, 31 March	8 000	
Less: Total cost of sales		(90 000)
Gross profit		**$ 35 000**

When actual overheads exceed applied overheads (i.e. the entity spent more than it had budgeted for), overhead is said to be underapplied. Underapplied overhead means that the overhead assigned to work in process is less than the overhead incurred. This means that the cost of the job was underestimated and needs to be corrected by increasing the overhead application rate for future jobs. Conversely, when actual overheads are less than applied overheads (i.e. the entity spent less than it had planned for), overhead is overapplied. In other words, overapplied overhead means that the overhead assigned to work in process is greater than the overhead incurred. Thus, overapplied overhead overstated the cost of the job and needs to be adjusted by reducing the overhead application rate.

At the end of the year, any balances in the manufacturing overhead control and manufacturing overhead Applied accounts are eliminated by an adjusting entry. Usually, under- or overapplied overhead is considered to be an adjustment to cost of sales. Thus, underapplied overhead is debited to cost of sales (increasing the cost), and overapplied overhead is credited to cost of sales (reducing the cost). To illustrate, assume that Mackenzie Ltd has a $100 000 debit balance in manufacturing overhead control, representing actual overheads incurred; and a $102 500 credit balance in manufacturing overhead applied at 31 December.

This means that actual overheads were less than anticipated. The adjusting entry for the overapplied overhead is:

Dec. 31	Manufacturing overhead applied	102 500	
	Manufacturing overhead control		100 000
	Cost of sales		2 500
	(To transfer overapplied overhead to cost of goods sold)		

	A	=	L	+	E	
	+102 500				−2 500	
	−100 000					

After this entry is posted, manufacturing overhead and manufacturing overhead applied will have nil balances. In preparing a statement of profit or loss for the year, the amount reported for cost of sales will be the account balance after the adjustment for either under- or overapplied overhead.

Conceptually, it can be argued that under- or overapplied overhead at the end of the year should be allocated among ending work in process, finished goods and cost of sales. However, most management accountants do not believe allocation is worth the cost and effort. The bulk of the under- or overapplied amount will be allocated to cost of sales anyway, because most of the jobs will be sold during the year.

Non-manufacturing entities

Job order costing is also used in non-manufacturing entities. In these entities the terminology used to describe each 'job' reflects the service being provided. Advertising agencies and consulting firms have 'contracts'; hospitals, doctors and lawyers have 'cases'; building companies have 'projects'; and government agencies have 'programs'. No matter what the terminology, details of the costs associated with the output still need to be accumulated.

In service entities, fewer direct materials are used. Figure 16.11 illustrates the cost accumulation in a legal practice, Smithers Partners.

FIGURE 16.11 Overhead budget

SMITHERS PARTNERS Annual budgeted overhead	
Indirect labour (secretarial, clerical)	$140 000
Indirect materials	25 000
Rent, telephone, postage, photocopying	200 000
Electricity	5 000
Depreciation	30 000
Library services	40 000
Estimated annual overhead costs	$440 000
Budgeted direct professional labour (estimated annual operating activity)	$220 000
Overheads are assigned to cases based on professional labour as the activity base.	

The formula for a predetermined overhead application rate is applied to Smithers Partners in figure 16.12.

FIGURE 16.12 Using the predetermined overhead application rate for services

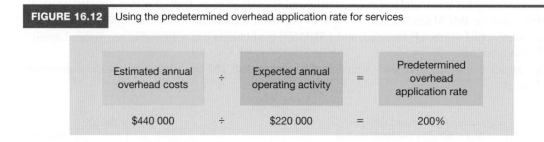

Estimated annual overhead costs	÷	Expected annual operating activity	=	Predetermined overhead application rate
$440 000	÷	$220 000	=	200%

If the job used no direct materials and $6000 of direct professional labour, then the cost for the case will be as shown below.

Direct materials	nil
Direct professional labour	$ 6 000
Overhead ($6000 × 200%)	12 000
Total cost	**$18 000**

Some entities (e.g. law firms) may keep separate records for secretarial and clerical labour, telephone and photocopying and charge them directly to the legal case.

Decision/issue	Info needed for analysis	Tool or technique to use for decision	How to evaluate results to make decision
Has the entity over- or underapplied overhead for the period?	Actual overhead costs and overhead applied	Manufacturing overhead control and manufacturing overhead applied accounts	Overapplied overhead occurs when the manufacturing overhead applied exceeds actual manufacturing overhead. Underapplied overhead occurs when actual manufacturing overhead exceeds manufacturing overhead applied.

LEARNING REFLECTION AND CONSOLIDATION

Review it

1. What source documents are used in assigning manufacturing costs to work in process inventory?
2. What is a job cost sheet, and what is its main purpose?
3. What is the formula for calculating a predetermined overhead application rate?
4. What is the difference between manufacturing and non-manufacturing entities?
5. When are entries made to record the completion of a job and the sale of a job?
6. What costs are included in total manufacturing costs in the cost of goods manufactured schedule?
7. How is under- or overapplied manufacturing overhead reported in monthly financial statements?

Do it

Danielle Ltd is working on two job orders. The job cost sheets show the following: direct materials — Job 120 $6000, Job 121 $3600; direct labour — Job 120 $4000, Job 121 $2000; and manufacturing overhead — Job 120 $5000, Job 121 $2500. Prepare the three summary entries to record the assignment of costs to work in process from the data on the job cost sheets.

Reasoning

Each cost charged to a job must be accompanied by a debit to the control account, work in process inventory. The credits in the summary entries are the accounts debited when the manufacturing costs were accumulated. The manufacturing overhead costs are accumulated in the manufacturing overhead account and, when applied/assigned to jobs, a contra account (manufacturing overhead applied) is credited. At the end of the period, these two accounts are offset and the balance is transferred to cost of sales.

Solution

The three summary entries are:

Work in process inventory ($6000 + $3600)	9 600	
Raw materials inventory		9 600
(To assign materials to jobs)		
Work in process inventory ($4000 + $2000)	6 000	
Factory labour		6 000
(To assign labour to jobs)		
Work in process inventory ($5000 + $2500)	7 500	
Manufacturing overhead applied		7 500
(To assign overhead to jobs)		

Process costing

Uses of process costing

Process cost systems are used to apply costs to similar products that are mass-produced in a continuous fashion.

BHP Billiton uses process costing in the manufacturing of steel, Fonterra uses process costing for processing milk products, Kellogg and Sanitarium use process costing for cereal production, and Dulux uses process costing for its paint products. At a bottling company like Coca-Cola Amatil, the manufacturing process begins with the blending of the beverages. Next the beverage is dispensed into bottles that are moved into position by automated machinery. The bottles are then capped, packaged and forwarded to the finished goods warehouse. This process is shown in figure 16.13.

FIGURE 16.13 Manufacturing processes

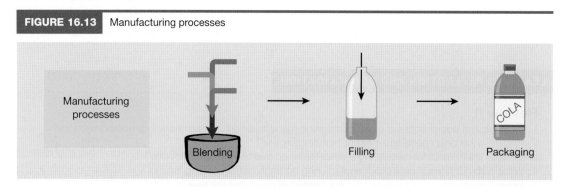

For Coca-Cola Amatil, as well as the other entities just mentioned, once the production begins, it continues until the finished product emerges. Process cost systems are used when a large volume of uniform or relatively homogeneous products are produced. The major differences between a job order and process cost system are summarised in figure 16.14.

FIGURE 16.14 Job order versus process cost systems

Features	Job order cost system	Process cost system
Work in process accounts	• One for multiple jobs	• One for each process
Documents used	• Job cost sheets	• Production cost reports
Determination of total manufacturing costs	• Each job	• Each period
Unit-cost calculations	• Cost of each job ÷ Units produced for the job	• Total manufacturing costs ÷ Units produced during the period

16.4 Process cost flow

LEARNING OBJECTIVE 16.4 Describe the flow of costs in a process cost system.

Figure 16.15 shows the flow of costs in the process cost system for Tyler Ltd, which manufactures automatic can openers that are sold to retail outlets. Manufacturing consists of two processes: machining and assembly which are performed in two departments. In the Machining Department (Department A), the raw materials are shaped, honed and drilled. In the Assembly Department (Department B), the parts are assembled and packaged.

FIGURE 16.15 Flow of costs in process cost system — Tyler Ltd

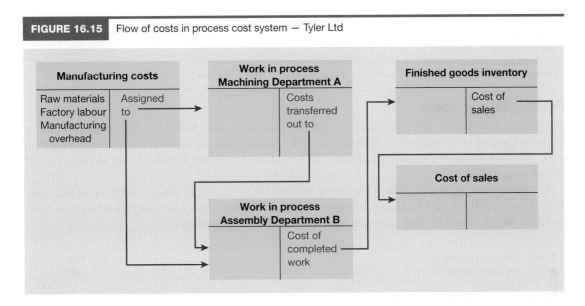

As the flow of costs indicates, materials, labour and manufacturing overhead can be added in both the Machining and Assembly departments. When the Machining Department finishes its work, the partially completed units are transferred to the Assembly Department. In the Assembly Department, with further processing, the goods are finished and are then transferred to the finished goods inventory. Upon sale, the goods are removed from the finished goods inventory. Within each department, a similar set of activities is performed on each unit processed.

16.5 Accounting procedures

LEARNING OBJECTIVE 16.5 Prepare the accounting entries for a process cost system.

Assignment of manufacturing costs — journal entries

As indicated earlier, the accumulation of the costs of materials, labour and manufacturing overhead is the same in a process cost system as in a job order cost system. All raw materials are debited to raw materials inventory when the materials are purchased. All factory labour is debited to factory labour when the labour costs are incurred. And overhead costs are debited to manufacturing overhead as they are incurred. However, the assignment of the three manufacturing cost elements to work in process in a process cost system is different from that for a job order cost system. Here we'll look at how these manufacturing cost elements are assigned in a process cost system.

Materials costs

All raw materials issued for production are a materials cost to the producing department. **Materials requisition slips** may be used in a process cost system, but fewer requisitions are generally required than in a job order cost system, because the materials are used for processes rather than for specific jobs. Requisitions are issued less frequently in a process cost system because the requisitions are for larger quantities.

Materials are usually added to production at the beginning of the first process. However, in subsequent processes, other materials may be added at various points. For example, in the manufacture of Mars Bars, the chocolate and other ingredients are added at the beginning of the first process, and the wrappers and cartons are added at the end of the packaging process. At Tyler Ltd, materials are added at the beginning of each process. The entry to record the materials used is:

Work in process—machining	XXX	
Work in process—assembly	XXX	
Raw materials inventory		XXX
(To record materials used)		

Factory labour costs

In a process cost system, as in a job order cost system, time tickets may be used in determining the cost of labour assignable to the production departments. Since labour costs are assigned to a process rather than a job, the labour cost chargeable to a process can be obtained from the payroll register or departmental payroll summaries.

All labour costs incurred within a producing department are a cost of processing the raw materials. Thus, labour costs for the Machining Department will include the wages of employees who shape, hone and drill the raw materials. The entry to assign these costs for Tyler Ltd is:

Work in process—machining	XXX	
Work in process—assembly	XXX	
Factory labour		XXX
(To assign factory labour to production)		

Manufacturing overhead costs

The objective in assigning overhead in a process cost system is to allocate the overhead costs to the production departments on an objective and equitable basis. That basis is the activity that 'drives' or causes the costs. A primary driver of overhead costs in continuous manufacturing operations is machine time used, not direct labour. Thus, machine hours are widely used in allocating manufacturing overhead costs. The entry to allocate overhead to the two processes is:

Work in process—machining	XXX	
Work in process—assembly	XXX	
Manufacturing overhead applied		XXX
(To apply overhead to production)		

Transfer to next department

At the end of the month, an entry is needed to record the cost of the goods transferred out of the department. In this case, the transfer is to the Assembly Department, and the following entry is made.

Work in process—assembly	XXX	
Work in process—machining		XXX
(To record transfer of units to the Assembly Department)		

Transfer to finished goods

The units completed in the Assembly Department are transferred to the finished goods warehouse. The entry for this transfer is as follows:

Finished goods inventory	XXX	
Work in process—assembly		XXX
(To record transfer of units to finished goods)		

Transfer to cost of sales

When finished goods are sold, the entry to record the cost of sales is as follows:

Cost of sales	XXX	
Finished goods inventory		XXX
(To record cost of units sold)		

LEARNING REFLECTION AND CONSOLIDATION

Review it

1. What type of manufacturing entities might use a process cost accounting system?
2. What are the main similarities and differences between a job order cost system and a process cost system?

Do it

Ruth Ltd manufactures ZEBO through two processes: blending and bottling. In June, raw materials used were blending $18 000 and bottling $4000; factory labour costs were blending $12 000 and bottling $5000; manufacturing overhead costs were blending $6000 and bottling $2500. Units completed at a cost of $19 000 in the Blending Department are transferred to the Bottling Department. Units completed at a cost of $11 000 in the Bottling Department are transferred to finished goods. Journalise the assignment of the blending and bottling costs to the two processes and the transfer of units as appropriate.

Reasoning

In process cost accounting, separate work in process accounts are kept for each process. Raw materials are accumulated in the account entitled Raw materials inventory. Factory labour is accumulated in the account entitled Factory labour. Overhead is accumulated in the account entitled Manufacturing overhead. These accounts are credited when the costs are assigned to production. When units are completed, they are transferred to the next process or to finished goods. To assign the costs to production, a contra account (manufacturing overhead applied) is used (see journal entry no. 3 in section 16.3).

Solution

The entries are:

Work in process—blending	18 000	
Work in process—bottling	4 000	
Raw materials inventory		22 000
(To record materials used)		
Work in process—blending	12 000	
Work in process—bottling	5 000	
Factory labour		17 000
(To assign factory labour to production)		
Work in process—blending	6 000	
Work in process—bottling	2 500	
Manufacturing overhead applied		8 500
(To assign overhead to production)		
Work in process—bottling	19 000	
Work in process—blending		19 000
(To record transfer of units to the Bottling Department)		
Finished goods inventory	11 000	
Work in process—bottling		11 000
(To record transfer of units to finished goods)		

Equivalent units

Suppose you were asked to calculate the cost of instruction at your university per full-time equivalent student. You are given the information in figure 16.16.

FIGURE 16.16 Information for full-time student example

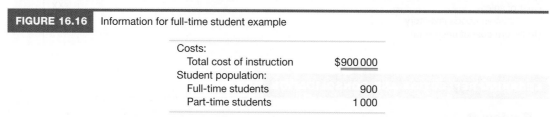

Costs:	
Total cost of instruction	$900 000
Student population:	
Full-time students	900
Part-time students	1 000

Part-time students take 60% of the classes of a full-time student during the year. You will need to calculate how many full-time students the 1000 part-time students are equivalent to. To work out the number of full-time equivalent students per year, you would make the calculation shown in figure 16.17.

FIGURE 16.17 Full-time equivalent unit calculation

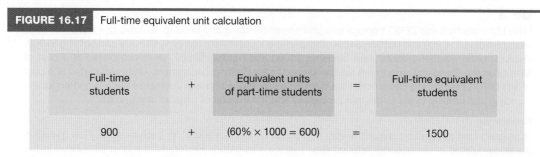

Full-time students	+	Equivalent units of part-time students	=	Full-time equivalent students
900	+	(60% × 1000 = 600)	=	1500

The cost of instruction per full-time equivalent student is therefore the total cost of instruction ($900 000) divided by the number of full-time equivalent students (1500), which is $600 ($900 000 ÷ 1500).

In a process cost system, the same idea, called equivalent units of production, is used. **Equivalent units of production** measure the work done during the period, expressed in fully completed units. This concept is used to determine the cost per unit of completed product, for internal and external reporting.

Weighted-average method

The formula to calculate equivalent units of production is shown in figure 16.18.

FIGURE 16.18 Formula for equivalent units of production

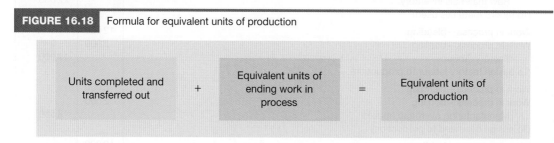

Units completed and transferred out	+	Equivalent units of ending work in process	=	Equivalent units of production

To better understand this concept of equivalent units, let's continue with the production processes at Tyler Ltd.

The Machining Department's entire output during the period consists of ending work in process of 4000 units which are 60% complete as to materials, labour and overhead. The equivalent units of production for the Machining Department are therefore 2400 units (4000 × 60%).

The Assembly Department's output during the period consists of 10 000 units completed and transferred out, and 5000 units in ending work in process which are 70% completed. The equivalent units of production are therefore 13 500 [10 000 + (5000 × 70%)].

This method of calculating equivalent units is referred to as the **weighted-average method**. It considers the degree of completion (weighting) of the units completed and transferred out and the ending work in process. It is the method most widely used in practice.

Refinements on the weighted-average method

Aunt Sally's Cereals makes muesli cakes. Three departments are used to produce the muesli cakes: Mixing, Baking and Packaging. In the Mixing Department dry ingredients, including flour, salt and baking powder, are mixed with liquid ingredients, including eggs and vegetable oil. Information related to the Mixing Department at the end of June is provided in figure 16.19.

FIGURE 16.19	Information for Mixing Department

Mixing Department

	Physical units	Percentage complete	
		Materials	**Conversion costs**
Work in process, 1 June	100 000	100%	70%
Started into production	800 000		
Total units	900 000		
Units transferred out	700 000		
Work in process, 30 June	200 000	100%	60%
Total units	900 000		

Figure 16.19 indicates that the beginning work in process is 100% complete as to materials cost and 70% complete as to conversion costs. In other words, both the dry and liquid ingredients (materials) are added at the beginning of the process to make the muesli cakes. The conversion costs (labour and overhead) related to the mixing of these ingredients were incurred uniformly and are 70% complete. The ending work in process is 100% complete as to materials cost and 60% complete as to conversion costs.

We then use the Mixing Department information to determine equivalent units. In calculating equivalent units, the beginning work in process is not part of the equivalent units of production formula. The units transferred out to the Baking Department are fully complete as to both materials and conversion costs. The ending work in process is fully complete as to materials, but only 60% complete as to conversion cost. Two equivalent unit calculations are therefore necessary: one for materials and the other for conversion costs. Figure 16.20 shows these calculations.

FIGURE 16.20	Calculation of equivalent units — Mixing Department

	Equivalent units	
	Materials	**Conversion costs**
Units transferred out	700 000	700 000
Work in process, 30 June		
200 000 × 100%	200 000	
200 000 × 60%		120 000
Total equivalent units	900 000	820 000

Helpful hint: Is it necessary to calculate equivalent units of production if the processing occurs quickly and is complete at the end of a day's operating activity?

Answer: No. If the production process does not extend beyond a day's operation, there is no work in process at the end of the day. A film processing business is an example; once the film or CD is loaded to the printing machine, photos are instantly printed and the process is complete — there is no 70% complete photograph at the end of the day.

The earlier formula in figure 16.18 used to calculate equivalent units of production can be refined to show the calculations for materials and for conversion costs (figure 16.21).

FIGURE 16.21 Refined equivalent units of production formula

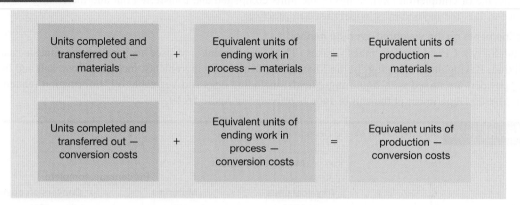

16.6 Production cost report

LEARNING OBJECTIVE 16.6 Prepare a production cost report.

As part of a performance evaluation procedure, a production cost report is prepared for each department in a process cost system. A **production cost report** is the key document used by management to understand the activities in a department because it shows the production quantity and cost data related to that department.

To complete a production cost report, the business must perform four steps.

1. Calculate the physical unit flow.
2. Calculate the equivalent units of production.
3. Calculate unit production costs.
4. Prepare a cost reconciliation schedule.

As a whole, these four steps make up the process cost system.

Production cost reports provide a basis for evaluating the productivity of a department. In addition, the cost data can be used to assess whether unit costs and total costs are reasonable. When the quantity and cost data are compared with predetermined goals, top management can also ascertain whether current performance is meeting planned objectives. By comparing actual results with budgeted cost data, management can highlight where variations exist and consider measures to address them.

The following is a brief example showing the calculation of a production cost report for Essence Ltd, which manufactures a high-quality after-shave lotion, Eternity, using three processes: mixing, filling and corking. Figure 16.22 provides unit and cost data for the Mixing Department.

FIGURE 16.22 Unit and cost data — Mixing Department

ESSENCE LTD Mixing Department	
UNITS	
Work in process, 1 May	1 000
Direct materials: 100% complete	
Conversion costs: 70% complete	
Units started into production during May	2 000
Units completed and transferred out to Filling Department	2 200
Work in process, 31 May	800
Direct materials: 100% complete	
Conversion costs: 50% complete	

COSTS	
Work in process, 1 May	
Direct materials: 100% complete	$ 49 100
Conversion costs: 70% complete	7 200
Cost of work in process, 1 May	**$ 56 300**
Costs incurred during production in May	
Direct materials	$100 000
Conversion costs	19 320
Costs incurred in May	**$119 320**

Figure 16.23 illustrates Essence Ltd's production cost report for the Mixing Department.

FIGURE 16.23 Production cost report

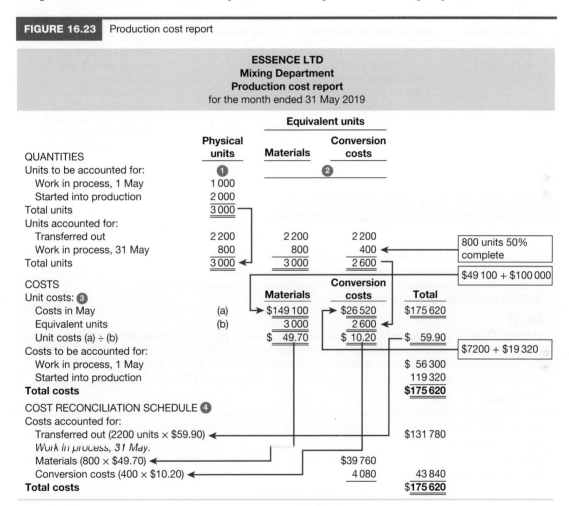

① *Calculate the physical unit flow.* On 1 May, 1000 units were in opening work in process. During May, 2000 more units entered into production, making a total of 3000 units. If 2200 units were transferred out, then 800 units must be in closing work in process on 31 May.

② *Calculate the equivalent units of production.* For materials, equivalent units are the same as the physical flow because materials are added at the beginning of the process (2200 + 800). Conversion costs are added as and when needed: 2200 units were completed, and 400 (800 × 50% complete) are in work in process. Accordingly, there are 2600 equivalent units (2200 + 400).

3 *Calculate unit production costs.*

(a) Materials are $49 100$ (opening) $+ \$100\,000$ incurred during May $= \$149\,100$. The equivalent units are 3000, so unit production is $\$149\,100 \div 3000 = \$49.70$.

(b) Conversion costs are $\$7200$ (opening) $+ \$19\,320$ incurred during May $= \$26\,520$. The equivalent units are 2600, so unit production is $\$26\,520 \div 2600 = \$10.20$.

4 *Prepare a cost reconciliation schedule.* Refer to figure 16.23.

DECISION-MAKING TOOLKIT

Decision/issue	Info needed for analysis	Tool or technique to use for decision	How to evaluate results to make decision
What is the cost of a product?	Costs of materials, labour and overhead assigned to processes used to make the product; selling price of the product	Production cost report	Compare costs with previous periods and with those of competitors to ensure that costs are in line. Compare with expected selling price to determine overall profitability.

LEARNING REFLECTION AND CONSOLIDATION

Review it

1. How do physical units differ from equivalent units of production?
2. What are the formulas for calculating unit costs of production?
3. How are costs assigned to units transferred out, and in ending work in process?
4. What are the four sections of a production cost report?

Do it

In March, Reece Manufacturing had the following unit production costs: materials $6 and conversion costs $9. On 1 March, it had zero work in process. During March, 12 000 units were transferred out, and 800 units that were 25% completed as to conversion costs and 100% complete as to materials were in ending work in process at 31 March. Assign the costs to the units transferred out and the units in process at 31 March.

Reasoning

The 12 000 units transferred should be assigned the total manufacturing cost of $16 per unit. The assignment of costs to units in process consists of the materials cost and conversion cost based on equivalent units of production.

Solution

The assignment of costs is as follows:

Costs accounted for:		
Transferred out (12 000 × $15)		$180 000
Work in process, 31 March		
Materials (800 × $6)	$4 800	
Conversion costs (200* × $9)	1 800	6 600
Total costs		**$186 600**

*800 × 25%

16.7 Activity-based costing (ABC)

LEARNING OBJECTIVE 16.7 Recognise the difference between traditional costing and activity-based costing and identify the activity cost pools and activity drivers used in activity-based cost systems.

Traditional costing systems

The primary aim of a costing system is to provide management with information about the exact cost of a product or service. Although, realistically, it may be impossible to ascertain the true cost, every effort to provide management with the best possible cost estimates must be made. The best estimate of costs occurs when the costs are traceable directly to the product produced or the service rendered. Direct material and direct labour costs are the easiest to trace directly to the product through the use of material requisition forms and payroll time sheets. Overhead, however, is an indirect or common cost that generally cannot be directly traced to individual products or services.

To illustrate, consider the cases of a furniture maker and a charter flight company. The cost of fabric (direct material) and carpenter time (direct labour) needed to make a desk is easy to calculate. But how much factory electricity a particular desk consumes is harder to determine. Likewise, gathering the cost of fuel (direct material) and pilot hour (direct labour) required to fly a chartered plane from the Gold Coast to Sydney is relatively straightforward. However, assessing how much aircraft maintenance is used up by a particular flight is more complicated.

As mentioned earlier, despite the difficulty in establishing a direct relationship between overhead and a product or service, a predetermined application rate is used to allocate overhead costs to each product or service. When overhead cost allocation systems were first developed, direct labour made up a large part of total manufacturing cost. It was widely accepted that there was a high correlation between direct labour and the incurrence of overhead cost. As a result, direct labour became the most popular basis for overhead allocation. Even in today's environment, direct labour is often the appropriate basis for assigning overhead cost to products. It is appropriate when (a) direct labour constitutes a significant part of total product cost, and (b) a high correlation exists between direct labour and changes in the amount of overhead costs.

The need for a new costing system

Advances in computerised systems, technological innovation, globalisation and automation have changed the manufacturing environment drastically. The amount of direct labour used in many industries is now greatly reduced, and total overhead costs (e.g. depreciation on expensive equipment and machinery, power, repairs and maintenance) have significantly increased. Entities that continue to use predetermined overhead rates based on direct labour, where the correlation between direct labour and overhead no longer exists, experience significant product cost distortions.

Recognising these distortions, many entities now use machine hours as the basis on which to allocate overhead in an automated manufacturing environment. But even machine hours may not suffice as the sole basis for allocating all overhead. If the manufacturing process is complex, then only multiple allocation bases can result in more accurate calculations. In such situations, managers need a new overhead cost allocation method — *activity-based costing*.

Activities and cost drivers

Activity-based costing (ABC) allocates overhead to multiple activity cost pools and assigns the activity cost pools to products by means of cost drivers. In activity-based costing, an **activity** is any event, action, transaction or work sequence that causes the incurrence of cost in the production of a product or the rendering of a service. A cost driver is any factor or activity that has a direct cause–effect relationship with the resources consumed.

ABC first allocates costs to activities, and then to the products based on each product's use of those activities. The reasoning behind ABC cost allocation is simple: products consume activities; activities consume resources; resources have a cost.

ABC allocates overhead in a two-stage process. In the first stage, overhead is allocated to **activity cost pools**, each of which is a distinct type of activity (e.g. ordering materials, setting up machines, assembling and inspecting), rather than to departments. In the second stage, the overhead allocated to the activity cost pools is assigned to products using cost drivers that represent and measure the number of individual activities undertaken or performed (e.g. number of purchase orders, number of set-ups, labour hours or number of inspections) to produce products or render services. Examples of activities and the possible cost drivers that measure them are shown in figure 16.24.

As you might imagine, not all products or services share equally in these activities. The more complex a product's manufacturing operation, the more activities and cost drivers it is likely to have. If there is little or no correlation between changes in the cost driver and consumption of the overhead cost, inaccurate product costs are inevitable. This can lead to incorrect product pricing and production decisions, which in today's competitive global environment may mean a loss of potential markets and hence profits.

Activity-based costing in manufacturing industries

The following is an example for Lift Jack Ltd. The design of an activity-based costing system with seven activity cost pools is graphically shown in figure 16.25 for Lift Jack Ltd. Lift Jack Ltd manufactures two automotive jacks — a car scissors jack and a truck hydraulic jack, with 200 000 units and 80 000 units respectively expected to be produced.

Helpful hint: Computers alleviate the problems of huge numbers of activities and promote the platform of ABC costing, enabling improved product costing.

In some entities the number of activities can be substantial. For example, in the United States, at Clark-Hurth (a division of Clark Equipment Company), a manufacturer of axles and transmissions, over 170 activities were identified; at the Compumotor Division of Parker Hannifin over 80 activities were identified in just the purchasing section of its Material Control Department.

Having identified its activity cost pools and the cost drivers for each cost pool, Lift Jack Ltd accumulated data relative to those activity cost pools and cost drivers shown in figure 16.26.

FIGURE 16.24 Activities and related cost drivers

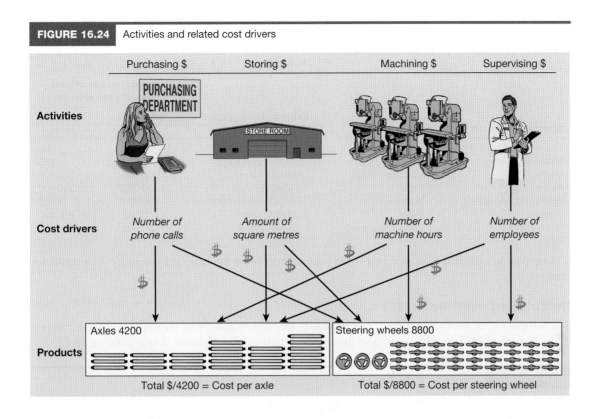

FIGURE 16.25 ABC system design — Lift Jack Ltd

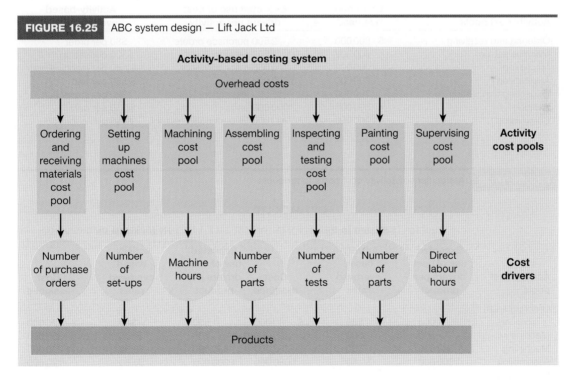

FIGURE 16.26 Cost drivers and expected use

LIFT JACK LTD

Activity cost pools	Cost drivers	Expected use of cost drivers per activity	Expected use of cost drivers per product	
			Scissors jacks	Hydraulic jacks
Ordering and receiving	Purchase orders	2 500 orders	1 000	1 500
Machine set-up	Set-ups	1 200 set-ups	500	700
Machining	Machine hours	800 000 hours	300 000	500 000
Assembling	Parts	3 000 000 parts	1 800 000	1 200 000
Inspecting and testing	Inspections	35 000 inspections	20 000	15 000
Painting	Parts	3 000 000 parts	1 800 000	1 200 000
Supervising	Labour hours	200 000 hours	130 000	70 000

Note that, in assigning overhead costs, it is necessary to know the expected use of the cost driver for each product.

Calculating overhead rates

The assignment of activity cost pools to products is then calculated using the expected use of the cost driver and the estimated overhead to give the activity-based overhead rate as shown in figure 16.27.

FIGURE 16.27 Calculation of activity-based overhead rates

LIFT JACK LTD

Activity cost pools	Estimated overhead	÷	Expected use of cost drivers per activity	=	Activity-based overhead rates
Ordering and receiving	$ 200 000		2 500 purchase orders		$80 per order
Machine set-up	600 000		1 200 set-ups		$500 per set-up
Machining	2 000 000		800 000 machine hours		$2.50 per machine hour
Assembling	1 800 000		3 000 000 parts		$0.60 per part
Inspecting and testing	700 000		35 000 inspections		$20 per inspection
Painting	300 000		3 000 000 parts		$0.10 per part
Supervising	1 200 000		200 000 labour hours		$6 per labour hour
	$6 800 000				

FIGURE 16.28 Assignment of activity cost pools to products

LIFT JACK LTD

Activity cost pools	Scissors jacks				Hydraulic jacks		
	Expected use of cost drivers per product ×	Activity-based overhead rates =	Cost assigned		Expected use of cost drivers per product ×	Activity-based overhead rates =	Cost assigned
Ordering and receiving	1 000	$80	$ 80 000		1 500	$80	$ 120 000
Machine set-up	500	$500	250 000		700	$500	350 000
Machining	300 000	$2.50	750 000		500 000	$2.50	1 250 000
Assembling	1 800 000	$0.60	1 080 000		1 200 000	$0.60	720 000
Inspecting and testing	20 000	$20	400 000		15 000	$20	300 000

	Scissors jacks				Hydraulic jacks			
Activity cost pools	Expected use of cost drivers per product	×	Activity-based overhead rates	= Cost assigned	Expected use of cost drivers per product	×	Activity-based overhead rates	= Cost assigned
Painting	1 800 000		$0.10	180 000	1 200 000		$0.10	120 000
Supervising	130 000		$6	780 000	70 000		$6	420 000
Total assigned costs				$3 520 000				$3 280 000

	Scissors jacks	Hydraulic jacks
Total costs assigned	$3 520 000	$3 280 000
Total units produced	200 000	80 000
Overhead cost per unit	$17.60	$41.00

Assigning overhead costs to products under ABC

Costs for each activity pool are then assigned to each product by multiplying the expected use of each cost driver by its activity-based overhead rate. The data shown in figure 16.28 show that the total overhead assigned to 80 000 hydraulic jacks is nearly as great as the overhead assigned to 200 000 scissors jacks. But the overhead cost per hydraulic jack is $41.00 and per scissors jack is only $17.60.

Comparing traditional and ABC overhead rates

If a traditional costing system based only on output volume is used to allocate overhead cost, what would be the overhead cost per unit for the two products? Since 200 000 units of scissors jacks and only 80 000 units of hydraulic jacks were produced, the total overhead of $6 800 000 would be spread over 280 000 units of jacks. Hence, the unit overhead cost would be $24.30. This is a significantly different allocation result compared with the unit overhead cost calculated under ABC, as summarised in the following table.

Overhead cost per unit based on:	Scissors jacks	Hydraulic jacks
Traditional costing	$24.30	$24.30
Activity-based costing	$17.60	$41.00
Effect on cost accuracy	Overcosted $6.70/unit (38%)	Undercosted $16.70/unit (40%)

If the management of Lift Jack Ltd relied solely on traditional costing data to set its product prices, scissors jacks would be overpriced and hydraulic jacks would be underpriced. The inaccuracy in costing would have a significant impact on the business's bottom line.

Activity-based costing in service industries

Although initially developed and implemented by manufacturing entities that produce products, activity-based costing has been widely adopted in service industries. ABC has been found to be a useful tool in such diverse industries as airlines, railroads, hotels, hospitals, banks, insurance companies, telephone companies and financial services entities. The overall objective of installing ABC in service entities is no different from that in a manufacturing entity: to identify the key activities that generate costs and to keep track of how many of those activities are performed for each service that is rendered (by job, service, contract or customer).

The general approach to identifying activities, activity cost pools and cost drivers is used by a service entity in the same manner as a manufacturing entity. Also, the labelling of activities as value-added and non-value-added and the attempt to reduce or eliminate non-value-added activities as much as possible is just as valid in service industries as in manufacturing operations. And the classification of activities into unit-level, batch-level, product-level, and facility-level activities also applies to service industries. What sometimes makes implementation of activity-based costing difficult in service industries is that a larger proportion of overhead costs are facility-level costs that cannot be directly traced to specific services rendered by the entity.

To illustrate the application of activity-based costing to a service entity, contrasted with traditional costing, we use a public accounting practice. This illustration is equally applicable to a law practice, consulting firm, architect, or any service entity that performs numerous services for a client as part of a job.

Traditional costing example

Assume that the public accounting practice of Check & Doublecheck prepares the following condensed annual budget (see figure 16.29).

FIGURE 16.29	Condensed annual budget of a service entity under traditional costing

CHECK & DOUBLECHECK Annual budget		
Revenue		$2 000 000
Direct labour	$ 600 000	
Overhead (expected)	1 200 000	
Total costs		1 800 000
Operating profit		**$ 200 000**

$$\frac{\text{Estimated overhead}}{\text{Direct labour cost}} = \text{Predetermined overhead rate}$$

$$\frac{\$1\,200\,000}{\$600\,000} = 200\%$$

Helpful hint: A budget is a quantified statement of planned or forecast activity.

Under traditional costing, the direct professional labour is the service performed and it forms the basis for overhead application to each audit job. To determine the operating profit earned on any job, overhead is applied at the rate of 200% of actual direct professional labour cost incurred. For example, assume that Check & Doublecheck records $70 000 of actual direct professional labour cost during its audit of Plano Moulding Ltd, which was invoiced an audit fee of $260 000. Under traditional costing, using 200% as the rate for applying overhead to the job, operating profit related to the Plano Moulding Ltd audit would be calculated as shown in figure 16.30.

FIGURE 16.30	Overhead applied under traditional costing system

CHECK & DOUBLECHECK Plano Moulding Ltd audit		
Revenue		$260 000
Less:		
Direct professional labour	$ 70 000	
Applied overhead (200% × $70 000)	140 000	210 000
Operating profit		**$ 50 000**

In this simple service industry example, under traditional costing only one direct cost item and only one overhead application rate is used.

Activity-based costing example

Under activity-based costing, Check & Doublecheck's estimated annual overhead costs of $1 200 000 are recast and related to several activity cost pools, and cost drivers are identified that relate those costs to the entity's audit activities. Figure 16.31 shows an annual overhead budget using an ABC system.

FIGURE 16.31 Condensed annual budget of a service entity under ABC

CHECK & DOUBLECHECK
Annual overhead budget

Activity cost pools	Cost drivers	Estimated overhead ÷	Expected use of cost drivers per activity =	Activity-based overhead rates
Secretarial support	Direct professional hours	$ 210 000	30 000	$7 per hour
Direct labour fringe benefits	Direct labour cost	240 000	$600 000	$0.40 per $1 labour cost
Printing and photocopying	Working paper pages	20 000	20 000	$1 per page
Computer support	CPU minutes	200 000	50 000	$4 per minute
Telephone and postage	None (traced directly)	71 000	$71 000	Based on usage
Legal support	Hours used	129 000	860	$150 per hour
Insurance (professional liability etc.)	Revenue invoiced	120 000	$2 000 000	$0.06 per $1 revenue
Recruiting and training	Direct professional hours	210 000	30 000	$7 per hour
		$1 200 000		

Note that some of the overhead can be directly assigned (see telephone and postage). The assignment of the individual overhead activity rates to the actual number of activities used in the performance of the Plano Moulding audit results in total overhead assigned of $165 100 as shown in figure 16.32.

FIGURE 16.32 Assignment of overhead in a service entity

CHECK & DOUBLECHECK
Assignment of overheads for Plano Moulding Ltd audit

Activity cost pools	Cost drivers	Actual use of drivers	Activity-based overhead rates	Costs assigned
Secretarial support	Direct professional hours	3 800	$7.00	$ 26 600
Direct labour fringe benefits	Direct labour cost	$70 000	$0.40	28 000
Printing and photocopying	Working paper pages	1 800	$1.00	1 800
Computer support	CPU minutes	8 600	$4.00	34 400
Telephone and postage	None (traced directly)			8 700
Legal support	Hours used	156	$150.00	23 400
Insurance (professional liability etc.)	Revenue invoiced	$260 000	$0.06	15 600
Recruiting and training	Direct professional hours	3 800	$7.00	26 600
				$165 100

Under activity-based costing, overhead of $165 100 is assigned to the Plano Moulding Ltd audit, compared with $140 000 under traditional costing. A comparison of total costs and operating margins is shown in figure 16.33.

The comparison shows that the assignment of overhead costs under traditional costing is distorted. The total cost assigned to performing the audit of Plano Moulding Ltd is greater under activity-based costing by $25 100, or 18% higher, and the profit margin is only half as great. Traditional costing gives the false impression of an operating profit of $50 000, more than double what it really is at $24 900.

	Traditional costing		ABC	
CHECK & DOUBLECHECK				
Plano Moulding Ltd audit				
Revenue		$260 000		$260 000
Expenses:				
Direct professional labour	$ 70 000		$ 70 000	
Applied overhead	140 000		165 100	
Total expenses		210 000		235 100
Operating profit		$ 50 000		$ 24 900
Profit margin		19.2%		9.6%

16.8 Benefits and limitations of activity-based costing

LEARNING OBJECTIVE 16.8 Understand the benefits and limitations of activity-based costing.

As the use of activity-based costing has grown, both its practical benefits and its limitations have now become apparent.

Benefits of ABC

The main benefit of ABC is *more accurate product costing* because of the following.

1. *ABC leads to more cost pools* used to assign overhead costs to products. Instead of one factory-wide pool (or even departmental pools) and a single cost driver, numerous activity cost pools with more relevant cost drivers are used. Costs are assigned more directly on a basis of the portion of multiple cost-driven activities that can be traced to each product.
2. *ABC leads to enhanced control of overhead costs.* Under ABC, many overhead costs can be traced directly to activities — some indirect costs become direct costs. Thus, managers become more aware of their responsibility to control the activities that generate those costs.
3. *ABC leads to better management decisions.* More accurate product costing should contribute to setting selling prices that will achieve desired product profitability levels. In addition, the more accurate cost data should be helpful in deciding whether to make or buy a product, part or component.

Activity-based costing does not, in itself, change the amount of overhead costs, but it does in certain circumstances allocate those costs in a more accurate manner. And if the score-keeping is more realistic, more accurate and better understood, managers should be able to better understand cost behaviour and overall profitability.

Limitations of ABC

Although ABC systems often provide better product cost data than traditional volume-based systems, there are limitations.

1. *ABC can be expensive to use.* Many entities are discouraged from using ABC by the higher cost of identifying multiple activities and applying numerous cost drivers. Activity-based costing systems are more complex than traditional costing systems — sometimes significantly more complex. Is the cost of implementation greater than the benefits of greater accuracy? For some entities there may be no need to consider ABC at all because their existing system is sufficient, or because the costs of ABC outweigh the benefits.
2. *Some arbitrary allocations continue.* Even though more overhead costs can be assigned directly to products through multiple activity cost pools, certain overhead costs remain to be allocated by means of some arbitrary volume-based cost driver such as labour or machine hours.

3. IAS 2/AASB 102 *Inventories* specifically prohibit administrative overheads unrelated to production, selling and distribution costs from being included in conversion costs. Thus the cost allocation achieved by ABC cannot be used for external reporting purposes.

When to switch to ABC

Activity-based costing is a useful tool and under certain conditions is the appropriate costing system to use. The presence of one or more of the following factors indicates that ABC would be the superior costing system.
1. Product lines differ greatly in volume and manufacturing complexity.
2. Product lines are numerous and diverse, and require differing degrees of support services.
3. Overhead costs constitute a significant portion of total costs.
4. The manufacturing process or the number of products has changed significantly — for example, from labour-intensive to automated.
5. Production or marketing managers are ignoring data provided by the existing system and are using other data when pricing or making other product decisions.

The redesign and installation of a new product costing system is a significant decision that requires considerable cost and a major effort to accomplish. Therefore, financial managers need to be very cautious and deliberative when initiating changes in costing systems.

DECISION-MAKING TOOLKIT

Decision/issue	Info needed for analysis	Tool or technique to use for decision	How to evaluate results to make decision
When should we switch to ABC?	Knowledge of the products or product lines, the manufacturing process, overhead costs and the needs of managers for accurate cost information	A detailed and accurate cost accounting system, cooperation between accountants and operating managers	Compare the results under both costing systems. If managers are better able to understand and control their operations using ABC, and the costs are not prohibitive, the switch would be beneficial.

LEARNING REFLECTION AND CONSOLIDATION

Review it
1. What are the benefits of activity-based costing (ABC)?
2. What are the limitations of ABC?
3. What factors indicate the applicability of ABC as the superior costing system?

16.9 Value-added vs. non-value-added activities

LEARNING OBJECTIVE 16.9 Differentiate between value-added and non-value-added activities.

Some entities that have experienced the benefits of activity-based costing have applied it to a broader range of management activities. **Activity-based management (ABM)** is an extension of ABC from a product costing system to a management function that focuses on reducing costs and improving processes and decision making. A refinement of activity-based costing used in ABM is the classification of activities as either value-added or non-value-added.

Value-added activities are the functions of actually manufacturing a product or performing a service. They increase the worth of a product or service to customers. Value-added activities involve resource usage and related costs that customers are willing to pay for. Examples of value-added activities in a manufacturing operation are engineering design, machining, assembly, painting and packaging.

Non-value-added activities are production- or service-related activities that simply add cost to, or increase the time spent on, a product or service without increasing its market value. Examples typical of a manufacturing operation include the repair of machines; the storage of inventory; the moving of raw materials, assemblies and finished product; building maintenance; inspections; and inventory control. Examples of non-value-added activities in service businesses might include taking appointments, reception, bookkeeping, invoicing, travelling, ordering supplies, advertising, cleaning and computer repair.

Identifying and labelling activities as value-added or non-value-added is part of the analysis of operations, the first step, in an ABC system. Figure 16.34 is an activity flowchart. Activity flowcharts are often used to help identify the activities that will be used in ABC costing. In the top part of this flowchart, activities are identified as value-added or non-value-added. The value-added activities are highlighted in red, and the non-value-added activities are highlighted in blue.

FIGURE 16.34 Flowchart showing value-added and non-value-added activities

HEARTLAND MANUFACTURING
Activity flowchart

Activities

NVA	NVA	NVA	NVA	VA		NVA	NVA	VA	NVA	NVA	NVA	VA
Receive and inspect materials	Move and store materials	Move materials to production and wait	Set up machines	Machining: Drill	Lathe	Inspect	Move and wait	Assembly	Inspect and test	Move to storage	Store finished goods	Package and ship
Current days 1	12	2.5	1.5	2	1	0.2	6	2	0.3	0.5	14	1

← ———————————— Total current average time = 44 days ———————————— →

| Proposed days 1 | 4 | 1.5 | 1.5 | 2 | 1 | 0.2 | 2 | 2 | 0.3 | 0.5 | 10 | 1 |

← ———————————— Total proposed average time = 27 days ———————————— →

Proposed reduction in non-value-added time = 17 days

VA = Value-added   **NVA** = Non-value-added

Note that in the lower part of the flowchart there are two rows showing the number of days spent on each activity. The first row shows the number of days spent on each activity under the current manufacturing process. The second row shows the number of days spent on each activity under management's proposed re-engineered manufacturing process. The proposed changes would reduce time spent on non-value-added activities by 17 days. This 17-day improvement is entirely due to moving inventory more quickly through the processes — that is, by reducing inventory time in moving, storage and waiting.

Not all activities labelled non-value-added are totally wasteful, nor can they be totally eliminated. For example, although inspection time is a non-value-added activity from a customer's perspective, few entities would eliminate their quality control functions. Similarly, moving and waiting time is non-value-added, but it would be impossible to completely eliminate. Nevertheless, because managers recognise the non-value-added characteristic of these activities, they are motivated to minimise them as much as possible. Attention to such matters is part of the growing practice of activity-based management which helps managers concentrate on continuous improvement of operations and activities.

DECISION-MAKING TOOLKIT

Decision/issue	Info needed for analysis	Tool or technique to use for decision	How to evaluate results to make decision
How can ABC help managers manage the business?	Activities classified as value-added and non-value-added; activities and costs classified by level of performance or incurrence	The activity analysis flowchart extended to identify each activity as value-added or non-value-added; activities and related costs classified as unit-level, batch-level, product-level or facility-level	The flowchart should motivate managers to minimise non-value-added activities. Managers should better understand the relationship between activities and the resources they consume.

Hierarchy of activity levels

Traditional costing systems are volume-driven — driven by units of output. Some activity costs are strictly variable and are caused by the production or acquisition of a single unit of product or the performance of a single unit of service. However, the recognition that other activity costs are not driven by output units has led to the development of a hierarchy of ABC activities, consisting of four levels. The four levels of activities are classified and defined as follows.

1. **Unit-level activities**. These are performed for each unit of production.
2. **Batch-level activities**. These are performed for each batch of products rather than each unit.
3. **Product-level activities**. These are performed in support of an entire product line, but are not always performed every time a new unit or batch of products is produced.
4. **Facility-level activities**. These are required to support or sustain an entire production process.

Greater accuracy in overhead cost allocation may be achieved by recognising these four different levels of activities and, from them, developing specific activity cost pools and their related cost drivers. Figure 16.35 graphically displays this four-level activity hierarchy, along with the types of activities and examples of costs traceable to those activities at each level.

This hierarchy provides managers and accountants with a structured way of thinking about the relationships between activities and the resources they consume. In contrast, traditional volume-based costing recognises only unit-level costs. Failure to recognise this hierarchy of activities is one of the reasons that volume-based cost allocation causes distortions in product costing.

As indicated earlier, allocating all overhead costs by bases that measure change in units produced can send false signals to managers — dividing batch-, product- or facility-level costs by the number of units produced gives the mistaken impression that these costs vary with the number of units. The resources consumed by batch-, product- and facility-level supporting activities do not vary at the unit level, nor can they be controlled at the unit level. The number of activities performed at the batch level goes up as the number of batches rises — not as the number of units within the batches changes. For example, machine set-up costs are incurred for each batch regardless of the number of units in the batch. Similarly, what product-level activities are performed depends on the number of different products — not on how many units or batches are produced. And facility-sustaining activity costs do not depend on the number of products, batches or units produced. Batch-, product- and facility-level costs can be controlled only by modifying batch-, product- and facility-level activities.

FIGURE 16.35 Hierarchy of activity levels

Four levels	Types of activities	Examples of costs
Unit-level activities		
	Machine-related: drilling, cutting, milling, trimming, pressing	Direct materials Depreciation of machine Power costs Machine maintenance
	Labour-related: assembling, painting sanding, sewing	Direct labour Employee entitlements Payroll tax
Batch-level activities		
	Equipment set-ups Purchase ordering Inspection Materials handling	Labour set-up costs Purchasing clerical costs Quality control costs Materials handling costs
Product-level activities		
	Product design Engineering changes Inventory management	Design costs Product engineering costs Inventory carrying costs
Facility-level activities		
	Factory management Personnel administration Training Security	Building depreciation Heating, airconditioning Rates and taxes Insurance

16.10 Just-in-time processing (JIT)

LEARNING OBJECTIVE 16.10 Explain just-in-time (JIT) processing.

The benefit of classifying activities as value-added and non-value-added is that managers know which activities to eliminate or minimise in order to reduce costs without affecting production efficiency or product quality. The activity analysis flowchart shown in figure 16.34 revealed lots of inventory storage and waiting time at several places in the operation. These are non-value-added activities. One way to minimise inventory storage and waiting time is to implement a **just-in-time (JIT) processing system**.

Traditionally, continuous process manufacturing has been based on a just-in-case philosophy: Inventories of raw materials are maintained just in case some items are of poor quality or a key supplier is shut down by a strike. Similarly, sub-assembly parts are manufactured and stored just in case they are needed later in the manufacturing process. Finished goods are completed and stored just in case unexpected and rush customer orders are received. This philosophy often results in a push approach in which raw materials and sub-assembly parts are pushed through each process. Traditional processing often results in the build-up of extensive manufacturing inventories.

Many entities have switched to just-in-time (JIT) processing primarily in response to cost reduction. JIT manufacturing is dedicated to having the right amount of materials, products, or parts at the time they are needed. Under JIT processing, raw materials are received just in time for use in production, sub-assembly parts are completed just in time for use in finished goods, and finished goods are completed just in time to be sold. Figure 16.36 shows the sequence of activities in just-in-time processing.

Helpful hint: Just-in-time processing is easier said than done. JIT requires a total commitment by management and employees, a complete change in philosophy and significant changes in the way production is organised. JIT takes time to implement.

Objective of JIT processing

A primary objective of JIT is to eliminate all manufacturing inventories. Inventories are considered to have an adverse effect on profit because they tie up funds and storage space that could be made available for more productive purposes. JIT strives to eliminate inventories by using a demand–pull approach in manufacturing. This approach begins with the customer placing an order with the entity. This order, which indicates product demand, starts the process of pulling the product through the manufacturing process. A signal is sent via a computer to the next preceding work station indicating the exact materials (parts and sub-assemblies) needed for a time period, such as an 8-hour shift, to complete the production of a specified product. The preceding process, in turn, sends its signal to other preceding processes. The goal is a smooth continuous flow in the manufacturing process, with no build-up of inventories at any point.

JIT processing has grown in importance in many supply chain management programs. For example, Fonterra has developed a 'do it once, do it right first time' structure and culture to eliminate unnecessary duplications in functions and costs.

FIGURE 16.36 Just-in-time processing

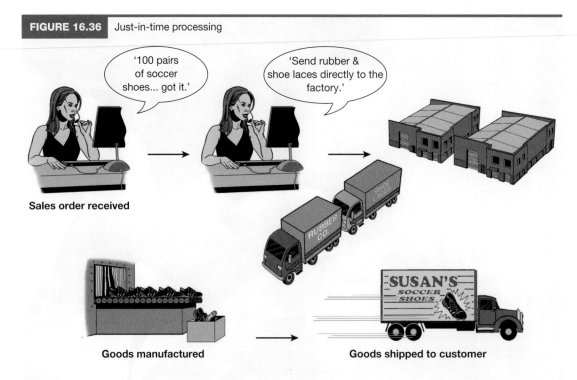

Sales order received

Goods manufactured

Goods shipped to customer

Elements of JIT processing

There are three important elements in JIT processing.

1. An entity must have dependable suppliers who are willing to deliver on short notice exact quantities of raw materials according to precise quality specifications. (This may even include multiple deliveries within the same day.) Suppliers must also be willing to deliver the raw materials at specified work stations rather than at a central receiving department. This type of purchasing requires constant and direct communication with suppliers, which is facilitated by an online computer linkage between the entity and its suppliers.
2. A multiskilled workforce must be developed. Under JIT, machines are often strategically grouped into work cells or centres and much of the work is automated. As a result, one worker may have the responsibility to operate and maintain several different types of machines.
3. A total quality control system must be established through the manufacturing operations. Total quality control means no defects. Since only required quantities are signalled by the demand–pull approach, any defects at a work station will shut down operations at subsequent work stations. Total quality control requires continuous monitoring by both employees and supervisors at each work station.

Benefits of JIT processing

The major benefits of implementing JIT processing are as follows.

1. Manufacturing inventories are significantly reduced or eliminated.
2. Product quality is enhanced.
3. Rework costs and inventory storage costs (i.e. rent and labour costs) are reduced or eliminated.
4. Production cost savings are realised from the improved flow of goods through the processes.

One of the major accounting benefits of JIT is the elimination of separate inventory accounts for raw materials and work in process. These accounts are replaced by one account called Raw and In-Process Inventory. All materials and conversion costs are charged to this account. Due to the reduction (or elimination) of in-process inventories, the calculation of equivalent units of production is simplified.

Helpful hint: Without its emphasis on quality control, JIT would be impractical or even impossible. In JIT, quality is engineered into the production process.

Decision/issue	Info needed for analysis	Tool or technique to use for decision	How to evaluate results to make decision
Can we benefit from installation and implementation of JIT processing?	Amounts of raw materials, work in process, and finished goods inventory; days that inventory is in storage or waiting to be processed or sold	Establish that we have dependable suppliers, a multiskilled workforce, and a total quality control system.	JIT should reduce or nearly eliminate inventories, storage and waiting time, and should minimise waste and defects. Inventory should be pulled rather than pushed through each production process.

LEARNING REFLECTION AND CONSOLIDATION

Review it

1. Of what benefit is classifying activities as value-added and non-value-added?
2. Of what importance to managers is the differentiation of activities into unit-level, batch-level, product-level and facility-level?
3. What are the major 'benefits' of implementing JIT?

Do it

Morgan Toy Ltd manufactures six main product lines in its factory. As a result of an activity analysis, the accounting department has identified eight activity cost pools. Each of the toy products is produced in large batches, with the whole factory devoted to one product at a time. Classify each of the following activities as either unit-level, batch-level, product-level or facility-level: (a) engineering design, (b) machine set-up, (c) inventory management, (d) cafeteria, (e) inspections after each set-up, (f) polishing parts, (g) assembling parts, (h) health and safety.

Reasoning

Unit-, batch-, product- and facility-level costs can be controlled only by modifying unit-, batch-, product- and facility-level activities. This hierarchy provides managers and accountants a structured way of thinking about the relationship between activities and the resources they consume.

Solution

(a) Product-level, (b) batch-level, (c) product-level, (d) facility-level, (e) batch-level, (f) unit-level, (g) unit-level, (h) facility-level.

USING THE DECISION-MAKING TOOLKIT

Speedy Ltd manufactures a line of up-market exercise equipment of commercial quality. The chief accountant has proposed changing from a traditional costing system to an activity-based costing system. The financial director is not convinced of making the changes, so she requests that the next large order for equipment be costed under both systems for purposes of comparison and analysis. An order from Slim-Way Salons for 150 low-impact treadmills is received and identified as the order to be subjected to dual costing. The following cost data relate to the Slim-Way order.

▶

Data relevant to both costing systems

Direct materials	$55 500
Direct labour hours	820
Direct labour rate per hour	$18

Data relevant to the traditional costing system

Predetermined overhead rate is 300% of direct labour cost.

Data relevant to the activity-based costing system

Activity cost pools	Cost drivers	Activity-based overhead rate	Expected use of cost drivers per treadmill
Engineering design	Engineering hours	$30 per hour	330 hours
Machine set-up	Set-ups	$200 per set-up	22 set-ups
Machining	Machine hours	$25 per hour	732 hours
Assembly	Number of subassemblies	$8 per subassembly	1450 subassemblies
Packaging and shipping	Packaging/shipping hours	$15 per hour	152 hours
Building occupancy	Machine hours	$6 per hour	732 hours

Required

Calculate the total cost of the Slim-Way Salons order under (a) the traditional costing system and (b) the activity-based costing system. (c) As a result of this comparison, which costing system is Speedy likely to adopt? Why?

Solution

(a) Traditional costing system:

Direct materials	$ 55 500
Direct labour (820 × $18)	14 760
Overhead assigned ($14 760 × 300%)	44 280
Total costs assigned to Slim-Way order	$114 540
Number of low-impact treadmills	150
Cost per unit	$ 763.60

(b) Activity-based costing system:

Direct materials		$ 55 500
Direct labour (820 × $18)		14 760
Overhead activities costs:		
Engineering design (330 hours @ $30)	9 900	
Machine set-up (22 set-ups @ $200)	4 400	
Machining (732 machine hours @ $25)	18 300	
Assembly (1450 subassemblies @ $8)	11 600	
Packaging and shipping (152 hours @ $15)	2 280	
Building occupancy (732 hours @ $6)	4 392	50 872
Total costs assigned to Slim-Way order		$121 132
Number of low-impact treadmills		150
Cost per unit		$ 807.55

(c) Speedy Ltd is likely to adopt ABC because of the differences in the cost per unit. More importantly, ABC provides greater insight into the sources and causes of the cost per unit. Managers are given greater insight into which activities to control in order to reduce costs.

SUMMARY

16.1 Explain the characteristics and purposes of cost accounting systems.
Cost accounting involves the procedures for measuring, recording and reporting product costs. From the data accumulated, the total cost and the unit cost of each product are determined.

16.2 Describe the flow of costs in a job order cost system.
In job order cost accounting, manufacturing costs are first accumulated in three accounts: Raw materials inventory, Factory labour, and Manufacturing overhead. The accumulated costs are then assigned to work in process inventory and eventually to finished goods inventory and cost of sales.

16.3 Explain a job cost sheet and the accounting entries for a job order cost system.
A job cost sheet is a form used to record the costs chargeable to a specific job and to determine the total and unit cost of the completed job. Job cost sheets constitute the subsidiary ledger for the work in process inventory control account. Costs are assigned to production and controlled via the job cost sheet. While jobs are in progress, the costs are accumulated in the work in process account. When jobs are completed, the cost is debited to finished goods inventory and credited to work in process inventory. When a job is sold, cost of sales is debited and finished goods inventory is credited for the cost of the goods.

16.4 Describe the flow of costs in a process cost system.
Manufacturing costs for raw materials, labour and overhead are assigned to work in process accounts for various departments or manufacturing processes, and the costs of units completed in a department are transferred from one department to another as those units move through the manufacturing process. The costs of completed work are transferred to finished goods inventory. When inventory is sold, costs are transferred to cost of sales.

16.5 Prepare the accounting entries for a process cost system.
The raw materials, labour and direct overhead are debited to the raw materials inventory, factory labour and manufacturing overhead accounts. Entries to assign the costs of raw materials, labour and overhead consist of a credit to raw materials inventory, factory labour and manufacturing overhead applied, and a debit to work in process for each of the departments doing the processing. Entries to record the cost of goods transferred to another department are a credit to work in process for the department whose work is finished and a debit to the department to which the goods are transferred. The entry to record units completed and transferred to the warehouse is a credit for the department whose work is finished and a debit to finished goods inventory. Finally, the entry to record the sale of goods is a credit to finished goods inventory and a debit to cost of sales.

16.6 Prepare a production cost report.
The production cost report contains both quantity and cost data for a production department. There are four sections in the report: (a) number of physical units, (b) equivalent units determination, (c) unit costs and (d) cost reconciliation schedule.

16.7 Recognise the difference between traditional costing and activity-based costing and identify the activity cost pools and activity drivers used in activity-based cost systems.
A traditional costing system allocates overhead to products on the basis of predetermined factory-wide or department-wide volume of output rates such as direct labour or machine hours. An ABC system allocates overhead to identified activity cost pools which are then assigned to products using related cost drivers that measure the activities (resources) consumed.

To identify activity cost pools, an entity must perform an analysis of each operation or process, documenting and timing every task, action or transaction. Cost drivers identified for assigning activity cost pools must reflect the actual consumption of the activity by the various products.

16.8 Understand the benefits and limitations of activity-based costing.

What makes ABC a more accurate product costing system is (1) the increased number of cost pools used to assign overhead, (2) the enhanced control over overhead costs and (3) the better management decisions. The limitations of ABC are (1) the higher analysis and measurement costs that accompany multiple activity centres and cost drivers, (2) the necessity still to allocate some costs arbitrarily, and (3) the preclusion of its use in external reports by IAS 2/AASB 102.

16.9 Differentiate between value-added and non-value-added activities.

Value-added activities increase the worth of a product or service, for which the customer is willing to pay. Non-value-added activities simply add cost to, or increase the time spent on, a product or service without increasing its market value. Awareness of these classifications encourages managers to reduce or eliminate the time spent on the non-value-added activities. Related to eliminating non-value-added activities is the implementation of just-in-time inventory management.

16.10 Explain just-in-time (JIT) processing.

JIT is a processing system that is dedicated to having on hand the right materials and products at the time they are needed, thereby reducing the amount of inventory and the time inventory is held. One of the principal accounting effects is that one account, Raw and In-Process Inventory, replaces both inventory accounts for raw materials and work in process.

DECISION-MAKING TOOLKIT — A SUMMARY

DECISION-MAKING TOOLKIT

Decision/issue	Info needed for analysis	Tool or technique to use for decision	How to evaluate results to make decision
What is the cost of a job?	Cost of material, labour and overhead assigned to a specific job	Job cost sheet	Compare costs with those of previous periods and with those of competitors to ensure that costs are in line. Compare costs with expected selling price to determine overall profitability.
Has the entity over- or underapplied overhead for the period?	Actual overhead costs and overhead applied	Manufacturing overhead and manufacturing overhead applied accounts	Overapplied overhead occurs when the manufacturing overhead applied exceeds actual manufacturing overhead. Underapplied overhead occurs when actual manufacturing overhead exceeds manufacturing overhead applied.
What is the cost of a product?	Costs of materials, labour and overhead assigned to processes used to make the product; selling price of the product	Production cost report	Compare costs with previous periods and with those of competitors to ensure that costs are in line. Compare with expected selling price to determine overall profitability.

Decision/issue	Info needed for analysis	Tool or technique to use for decision	How to evaluate results to make decision
When should we switch to ABC?	Knowledge of the products or product lines, the manufacturing process, overhead costs and the needs of managers for accurate cost information	A detailed and accurate cost accounting system, cooperation between accountants and operating managers	Compare the results under both costing systems. If managers are better able to understand and control their operations using ABC, and the costs are not prohibitive, the switch would be beneficial.
How can ABC help managers manage the business?	Activities classified as value-added and non-value-added; activities and costs classified by level of performance or incurrence	The activity analysis flowchart extended to identify each activity as value-added or non-value-added; activities and related costs classified as unit-level, batch-level, product-level or facility-level	The flowchart should motivate managers to minimise non-value-added activities. Managers should better understand the relationship between activities and the resources they consume.
Can we benefit from installation and implementation of JIT processing?	Amounts of raw materials, work in process, and finished goods inventory; days that inventory is in storage or waiting to be processed or sold	Establish that we have dependable suppliers, a multiskilled workforce, and a total quality control system	JIT should reduce or nearly eliminate inventories, storage and waiting time, and should minimise waste and defects. Inventory should be pulled rather than pushed through each production process.

KEY TERMS

activity Any event, action, transaction or work sequence that causes incurrence of cost in producing a product or rendering a service.

activity cost pool The overhead cost allocated to a distinct type of activity or related activities.

activity-based costing (ABC) An overhead cost allocation system that allocates overhead to multiple activity cost pools and assigns the activity cost pools to products or services by means of cost drivers.

activity-based management (ABM) A management tool that focuses on determining the entity's activities and associated costs, and assessing if the costs can be reduced or eliminated.

batch-level activities Activities performed for each batch of products.

cost accounting An area of accounting that involves the measuring, recording and reporting of product or service costs.

cost accounting system Manufacturing cost accounts that are fully integrated into the general ledger of an entity.

cost driver Any factor or activity that has a direct cause–effect relationship with the resources consumed. In ABC, cost drivers are used to assign activity cost pools to products or services.

equivalent units of production A measure of the work done during the period, expressed in fully completed units.

facility-level activities Activities required to support or sustain an entire production process and not dependent on number of products, batches or units produced.

job cost sheet A form used to record the costs chargeable to a job and to determine the total and unit cost of the completed job.

job order cost system A cost accounting system in which costs are assigned to each job or batch.

just-in-time (JIT) processing system A processing system dedicated to having the right amount of materials, products or parts arrive as they are needed, thereby reducing the amount of inventory.

materials requisition slip A document authorising the issue of raw materials from the storeroom to production.

non-value-added activity An activity that adds cost to, or increases the time spent on, a product or service without increasing its market value.

overapplied manufacturing overhead A situation in which overhead assigned to work in process is greater than the overhead incurred.

predetermined overhead application rate or budgeted overhead rate A rate based on the relationship between estimated annual overhead costs and expected annual operating activity, expressed in terms of a common activity base.

process cost system A system of accounting used by entities that manufacture a large volume of uniform or relatively homogeneous products through a series of continuous processes or operations.

product-level activities Activities performed for and identifiable with an entire product line.

production cost report An internal report for management that shows both production quantity and cost data for a production department.

time sheet A document that indicates the employee, the hours worked, the account and job to be charged, and the total labour cost.

underapplied manufacturing overhead A situation in which overhead assigned to work in process is less than the overhead incurred.

unit-level activities Activities performed for each unit of production.

value-added activity An activity that increases the worth of a product or service to customers.

weighted-average method Method used to calculate equivalent units of production which considers the degree of completion (weighting) of the units completed and transferred out and the ending work in process.

DEMONSTRATION PROBLEM

Spreadwell Paint manufactures two high-quality base paints — an oil-based paint and a latex paint. Both paints are manufactured in neutral white colour only. The white base paints are sold to franchised retail paint and decorating stores where pigments are added to tint (colour) the paint as desired by the customer. The oil-based paint is made from, thinned, and cleaned with organic solvents (petroleum products) such as mineral spirits or turpentine. The latex paint is made from, thinned, and cleaned with water; synthetic resin particles are suspended in the water and dry and harden when exposed to the air. Both paints are house paints. Spreadwell uses the same processing equipment to produce both paints in differing production runs. Between batches, the vats and other processing equipment must be washed and cleaned.

After analysing the entire operations, Spreadwell's accountants and production managers have identified activity cost pools and accumulated annual budgeted overhead costs by pool as follows:

Activity cost pools	Estimated overhead
Purchasing	$ 240 000
Processing (weighing and mixing, grinding, thinning and drying, straining)	1 400 000
Packaging ($\frac{1}{2}$ litre, 5 litres and 25 litres)	580 000
Testing	240 000
Storage and inventory control	180 000
Washing and cleaning equipment	560 000
Total annual budgeted overhead	**$3 200 000**

Following further analysis, activity cost drivers were identified and their expected use by product and activity were scheduled as follows:

Activity cost pool	Cost drivers	Expected cost drivers per activity	Expected use of drivers per product	
			Oil-based	Latex
Purchasing	Purchase orders	1 500 orders	800	700
Processing	Litres processed	1 000 000 litres	400 000	600 000
Packaging	Containers filled	400 000 containers	180 000	220 000
Testing	Number of tests	4 000 tests	2 100	1 900
Storing	Avg. litres on hand	18 000 litres	10 400	7 600
Washing	Number of batches	800 batches	350	450

Spreadwell has budgeted 400 000 litres of oil-based paint and 600 000 litres of latex paint for processing during the year.

Required

(a) Prepare a schedule showing the calculations of the activity-based overhead rates.
(b) Prepare a schedule assigning each activity's overhead cost pool to each product.
(c) Calculate the overhead cost per unit for each product.
(d) Classify each activity cost pool as value-added or non-value-added.

PROBLEM-SOLVING STRATEGIES

1. Identify the major activities that pertain to the manufacture of specific products and allocate manufacturing overhead costs to activity cost pools.
2. (a) Identify the cost drivers that accurately measure each activity's contribution to the finished product.
   (b) Calculate the activity-based overhead costs.
3. Assign manufacturing overhead costs for each activity cost pool to products, using the activity-based overhead rates.

SOLUTION TO DEMONSTRATION PROBLEM

(a) Calculations of activity-based overhead rates:

SPREADWELL PAINT

Activity cost pools	Estimated overhead	÷	Expected use of cost drivers	=	Activity-based overhead rates
Purchasing	$ 240 000		1 500 orders		$160 per order
Processing	1 400 000		1 000 000 litres		$1.40 per litre
Packaging	580 000		400 000 containers		$1.45 per container
Testing	240 000		4 000 tests		$60 per test
Storing	180 000		18 000 litres		$10 per litre
Washing	560 000		800 batches		$700 per batch
	$3 200 000				

(b) Assignment of activity cost pools to products:

SPREADWELL PAINT

Activity cost pools	Oil-based paint			Latex paint		
	Expected use of drivers	Overhead rates	Cost assigned	Expected use of drivers	Overhead rates	Cost assigned
Purchasing	800	$160	$ 128 000	700	$160	$ 112 000
Processing	400 000	$1.40	560 000	600 000	$1.40	840 000

Activity cost pools	Oil-based paint			Latex paint		
	Expected use of drivers	Overhead rates	Cost assigned	Expected use of drivers	Overhead rates	Cost assigned
Packaging	180 000	$1.45	261 000	220 000	$1.45	319 000
Testing	2 100	$60	126 000	1 900	$60	114 000
Storing	10 400	$10	104 000	7 600	$10	76 000
Washing	350	$700	245 000	450	$700	315 000
Total overhead assigned			$1 424 000			$1 776 000

(c) Calculation of overhead cost assigned per unit:

	Oil-based paint	Latex paint
Total overhead cost assigned	$1 424 000	$1 776 000
Total litres produced	400 000	600 000
Overhead cost per litre	$ 3.56	$ 2.96

(d) Value-added activities: processing and packaging.
Non-value-added activities: purchasing, testing, storing and washing.

SELF-STUDY QUESTIONS

16.1 Cost accounting involves the measuring, recording and reporting of: **LO1**
(a) product costs.
(b) future costs.
(c) manufacturing processes.
(d) managerial accounting decisions.

16.2 When incurred, factory labour costs are debited to: **LO2**
(a) work in process.
(b) factory wages expense.
(c) factory labour.
(d) factory wages payable.

16.3 A job cost sheet: **LO3**
(a) is used in process costing.
(b) is the subsidiary ledger record for work in process.
(c) records direct material requisitions only.
(d) is used to record a factory employee's total hours worked.

16.4 In Styler Manufacturing, the predetermined overhead rate is 80% of direct labour cost. During the month, $210 000 of factory labour costs are incurred, of which $180 000 is direct labour and $30 000 is indirect labour. Actual overheads incurred was $200 000. The amount of overhead debited to work in process inventory should be: **LO3**
(a) $120 000.
(b) $200 000.
(c) $144 000.
(d) $168 000.

16.5 In a process cost system, costs are assigned only to: **LO4**
(a) one work in process account.
(b) work in process and finished goods inventory.
(c) work in process, finished goods and cost of sales.
(d) work in process accounts.

16.6 In making the journal entry to assign raw materials costs in a process costing system the: **LO5**

(a) debit is to finished goods inventory.

(b) debit is often to two or more work in process accounts.

(c) credit is generally to two or more work in process accounts.

(d) credit is to finished goods inventory.

16.7 The Mixing Department's output during the period consists of 20 000 units completed and transferred out, and 5000 units in ending work in process 60% complete as to materials and conversion costs. Beginning work in process is 1000 units, 40% complete as to materials and conversion costs. The equivalent units of production are: **LO5**

(a) 25 000.

(b) 22 600.

(c) 24 000.

(d) 23 000.

16.8 Lister Ltd has a unit cost of $10 for materials and $30 for conversion costs. If there are 2500 units in ending work in process, 40% complete as to conversion, and fully complete as to materials cost, the total cost assignable to ending work in process inventory is: **LO6**

(a) $40 000.

(b) $55 000.

(c) $70 000.

(d) $10 000.

16.9 A production cost report: **LO6**

(a) is an external report.

(b) shows costs charged to department and costs accounted for.

(c) shows equivalent units of production but not physical units.

(d) contains six sections.

16.10 Activity-based costing: **LO7**

(a) is the initial phase of converting to a just-in-time operating environment.

(b) can be used only in a job order cost system.

(c) is a two-phase overhead cost allocation system that identifies activity cost pools and cost drivers.

(d) uses direct labour as its main cost driver.

16.11 Crawford Ltd has identified an activity cost pool to which it has allocated estimated overhead of $1 500 000 and determined the expected use of cost drivers per that activity to be 200 000 inspections. Widgets require 40 000 inspections, gadgets 60 000 inspections, and targets 100 000 inspections. The overhead assigned to each product is: **LO7**

(a) widgets $40 000, gadgets $60 000, targets $100 000.

(b) widgets $80 000, gadgets $80 000, targets $200 000.

(c) widgets $450 000, gadgets $300 000, targets $750 000.

(d) widgets $300 000, gadgets $450 000, targets $750 000.

16.12 Any activity that causes resources to be consumed is called a: **LO7**

(a) just-in-time activity.

(b) facility-level activity.

(c) cost driver.

(d) non-value-added activity.

16.13 Activity-based costing would be likely to be most beneficial to companies with: **LO8**

(a) a single product.

(b) few products, each of which consumes about the same amount of resources.

(c) many products, each of which consumes about the same amount of resources.

(d) many products, each of which consumes different amounts of resources.

16.14 Which activities are value-added?   **LO9**

    (a) Storage of raw materials.

    (b) Moving parts from machine to machine.

    (c) Turning a piece of metal on a lathe.

    (d) All of the above.

16.15 Just-in-time processing requires all of the following except: **LO10**

    (a) increasing operational efficiencies.

    (b) eliminating inventories.

    (c) basing production on future demand for the product.

    (d) controlling quality.

QUESTIONS

16.1 (a) Your friend is not sure about the differences between cost accounting and a cost accounting system. Explain the differences.

    (b) What is an important feature of a cost accounting system?

16.2 Your classmate asks for your help in understanding the major steps in the flow of costs in a job order cost system. Identify the steps.

16.3 What is the purpose of a job cost sheet?

16.4 Ron is confused about under- and overapplied manufacturing overhead. Define the terms for Ron and indicate the action that should be taken at the end of the year for under- or overapplied overhead.

16.5 A friend is confused about the features of process cost accounting. Identify and explain the distinctive features.

16.6 What steps are involved in developing an activity-based costing system?

16.7 (a) What are the main differences between activity-based costing (ABC) and traditional product costing?

    (b) What assumptions must be met for ABC costing to be useful?

16.8 Of what benefit is classifying activities as value-added and non-value-added?

16.9 (a) Describe the philosophy and approach of just-in-time processing.

    (b) Identify the major elements of JIT processing.

16.10 In what ways is the application of ABC to service entities the same as its application to manufacturing entities?

BRIEF EXERCISES

BE16.1 Distinguish between job and process costing.   **LO1**

Indicate whether job costing or process costing would be more appropriate for each of the following products:

    (a) Antique chairs.

    (b) Office chairs.

    (c) Mobile phones.

    (d) Aircraft.

    (e) Volleyballs.

BE16.2 Prepare a flowchart of a job order cost accounting system, and identify transactions.   **LO2**

Diamond Tool & Die Pty Ltd begins operations on 1 January. Because all work is done to customer specifications, the entity decides to use a job cost accounting system. Prepare a flowchart of a typical job order system with arrows showing the flow of costs. Identify the eight transactions.

BE16.3 Calculate equivalent units of production. **LO6**

Burrough Manufacturing has the following production data for selected months:

Month	Beginning work in process	Units transferred out	Ending work in process Units	Ending work in process % complete as to conversion cost
January	—	7 000	2 000	60
March	—	12 000	3 000	30
May	—	16 000	4 000	80
July	—	10 000	15 000	40

(a) Calculate the physical units for each month.
(b) Calculate equivalent units of production for materials and conversion costs for each month, assuming materials are entered at the beginning of the process.

BE16.4 Calculate equivalent units of production. **LO6**

The Smelting Department of Clark Manufacturing has the following production and cost data for March. Beginning work in process 3000 units that are 100% complete as to materials and 20% complete as to conversion costs; units transferred out 11 000 units; and ending work in process 2000 units that are 100% complete as to materials and 60% complete as to conversion costs. Calculate the equivalent units of production for (a) materials and (b) conversion costs for the month of March.

BE16.5 Calculate activity-based overhead rates. **LO7**

Smyth Ltd identifies three activities in its manufacturing process: machine set-ups, machining, and inspections. Estimated annual overhead cost for each activity is $180 000, $325 000 and $70 000, respectively. The cost driver for each activity and the expected annual usage are: number of set-ups 2000, machine hours 25 000 and number of inspections 1750. Calculate the overhead rate for each activity.

BE16.6 Classify activities as value-added or non-value-added. **LO9**

Dewey Novelty Pty Ltd identified the following activities in its production and support operations. Classify each of these activities as either value-added or non-value-added.
1. Purchasing.
2. Receiving.
3. Design engineering.
4. Storing inventory.
5. Cost accounting.
6. Moving work-in-process.
7. Inspecting and testing.
8. Painting and packing.

BE16.7 Classify activities according to level. **LO9**

Elburn Plastics Ltd operates 20 injection moulding machines in the production of fishing tackle boxes of four different sizes: the minnow, the bass, the mackerel, and the shark. Classify each of the following costs as unit-level, batch-level, product-level or facility-level.
(a) First shift supervisor's salary.
(b) Powdered raw plastic.
(c) Dies for casting plastic components.
(d) Depreciation on injection moulding machines.
(e) Changing dies on machines.
(f) Moving components to assembly department.
(g) Engineering design.
(h) Workers compensation insurance.

EXERCISES

E16.1 Analyse a job cost sheet and prepare entries for manufacturing costs.   **LO2, 3**

A job order cost sheet for Standish Ltd is shown below.

Job no. 92		Direct materials	Direct labour	Manufacturing overhead
Date				For 2000 units
Beg. bal. Jan.	1	7 000	8 000	5 200
	8	5 000		
	12		7 000	4 900
	25	4 000		
	27		5 000	3 500
		16 000	20 000	13 600

Cost of completed job:
Direct materials	$16 000
Direct labour	20 000
Manufacturing overhead	13 600
Total cost	$49 600
Unit cost ($49 600 ÷ 2000)	$ 24.80

Required

(a) Answer the following questions using the job order cost sheet above:
1. What are the source documents for direct materials, direct labour and manufacturing overhead costs assigned to this job?
2. What was the balance in work in process inventory on 1 January if this was the only unfinished job?
3. If manufacturing overhead is applied on the basis of direct labour cost, what overhead rate was used in each year?

(b) Prepare summary entries at 31 January to record the current year's transactions pertaining to job no. 92.

E16.2 Analyse costs of manufacturing and determine missing amounts.   **LO2, 3**

Manufacturing cost data for Kang Pty Ltd, which uses a job order cost system, are presented below:

	Case A	Case B	Case C
Direct materials	(a)	$83 000	$63 150
Direct labour used	$50 000	90 000	(h)
Manufacturing overhead applied	42 500	(d)	(i)
Total manufacturing costs	185 650	(e)	287 000
Work in process, 1/1/19	(b)	15 500	18 000
Total cost of work in process	203 100	(f)	(j)
Work in process, 31/12/19	(c)	11 800	(k)
Cost of goods manufactured	193 700	(g)	262 000

Required

Indicate the missing amount for each letter. Assume that in all cases manufacturing overhead is applied on the basis of direct labour cost and the rate is the same.

E16.3 Recognise a variety of cost accounting systems.   **LO2, 3, 7, 9, 10**

Complete the following statements with one of the terms listed below:

Job costing	Non-valued-added
Just-in-time processing	Underapplied
Overhead	Activity-based costing

(a) _____ is an approach to manufacturing which results in reduced inventory, stream-lined production processes and quality control.

(b) A design firm creates custom-made interior design plans for clients. The company would use a _____ system.

(c) _____ is a strategy for allocating factory overhead costs to activity cost pools based on appropriate cost drivers.

(d) Reworking and fixing defective parts is an example of _____ activity.

(e) The key difference between activity-based costing and traditional costing systems is the allocation of _____ costs.

(f) Overhead is considered _____ if overhead incurred exceeds applied overhead.

E16.4 Prepare entries for manufacturing costs.   **LO3**

Berg Printing Ltd uses a job order cost system. The following data summarise the operations related to the first quarter's production.

1. Materials purchased on account $172 000, and factory wages incurred $87 300.
2. Materials requisitioned and factory labour used by job:

Job number	Materials	Factory labour
A20	$ 32 240	$18 000
A21	42 920	26 000
A22	36 100	15 000
A23	39 270	25 000
General factory use	4 470	3 300
	$155 000	$87 300

3. Manufacturing overhead costs incurred on account $39 500.
4. Depreciation on machinery and equipment $14 550.
5. Manufacturing overhead rate is 75% of direct labour cost.
6. Jobs completed during the quarter: A20, A21, and A23.

Required

Prepare entries to record the operations summarised above. (Prepare a schedule showing the individual cost elements and total cost for each job in item 6.)

E16.5 Determine equivalent units, unit costs and assignment of costs.   **LO5, 6**

The Blending Department of Kohler Ltd has the following cost and production data for the month of July:

COSTS	
Work in process, 1 July	
Direct materials: 100% complete	$ 100 000
Conversion costs: 20% complete	70 000
Cost of work in process, 1 July	$ 170 000
Costs incurred during production in July	
Direct materials	$ 800 000
Conversion costs	350 000
Costs incurred in July	$1 150 000

Units transferred out 8000; ending work in process 1000 units that are 100% complete as to materials and 40% complete as to conversion costs.

Required

(a) Calculate the equivalent units of production for (1) materials and (2) conversion costs for the month of July.

(b) Calculate the unit costs for the month.

(c) Determine the costs to be assigned to the units transferred out and in ending work in process.

E16.6 Prepare a production cost report. **LO6**

The Welding Department of Nagano Manufacturing has the following production and manufacturing cost data for February 2019. All materials are added at the beginning of the process.

Manufacturing costs			Production data	
Beginning work in process			Beginning work in process	15 000 units
Materials	$18 000			1/10 complete
Conversion costs	14 175	32 175	Units transferred out	49 000
Materials		180 000	Units started	60 000
Labour		35 100	Ending work in process	26 000
Overhead		64 545		1/5 complete

Required

Prepare a production cost report for the Welding Department for the month of February.

E16.7 Journalise transactions for two processes. **LO5**

Henderson Manufacturing has two production departments: Cutting and Assembly. 1 July inventories are Raw materials $4200, Work in process—Cutting $2900, Work in process—Assembly $10 600; and Finished goods $31 000. During July, the following transactions occurred:

1. Purchased $35 600 of raw materials on account.
2. Incurred $56 000 of factory labour (credit wages payable).
3. Incurred $70 000 of manufacturing overhead; $42 000 was paid and the remainder is unpaid.
4. Requisitioned materials for Cutting $15 700 and Assembly $8900.
5. Used factory labour for Cutting $29 000 and Assembly $27 000.
6. Applied overhead at the rate of $20 per machine hour. Machine hours were Cutting 1740 and Assembly 1620.
7. Transferred goods costing $67 700 from the Cutting Department to the Assembly Department.
8. Transferred goods costing $134 900 from Assembly to finished goods.
9. Sold goods costing $130 000 for $200 000 on account.

Required

Journalise the transactions (narrations are not required).

E16.8 Explain the production cost report. **LO6**

Larry Lair has recently been promoted to production manager, and so he has just started to receive various management reports. One of the reports he has received is the production cost report that you prepared. It showed that his department had 1000 equivalent units in ending inventory. His department has had a history of not keeping enough inventory on hand to meet demand. He has come to you, very angry, and wants to know why you credited him with only 1000 units when he knows he had at least twice that many on hand.

Required

Explain to him why his production cost report showed only 1000 equivalent units in ending inventory. Write an informal memo. Be kind and explain very clearly why he is mistaken.

E16.9 Calculate activity-based overhead rates. **LO7**

Robina Jam Factory produces two types of jam: blueberry and raspberry. Planned production for August is 4500 bottles of blueberry jam and 13 500 bottles of raspberry jam. Estimated overhead for August is \$53 750. The following data summarises activities, overhead cost pools and cost drivers for August:

Activity cost pools	Cost driver	Estimated overhead	Expected use of cost drivers	Expected use of cost driver by blueberry	Expected use of cost driver by raspberry
Purchasing	Orders	\$12 000	500	200	300
Blending	Litres	35 000	9 800	2 400	7 400
Packaging	Cartons	6 750	540	180	360

Required

(a) Calculate the overhead allocation rate for each overhead cost pool.

(b) Calculate the total overhead costs allocated to each product.

E16.10 Identify activity cost drivers and classify activities as value-added or non-value-added.   LO7, 9

Valliance Vineyards produces three varieties of wine: Merlot, Shiraz and Pinot Noir. The wine master, Sue, has identified the following activities as cost pools for accumulating overhead and assigning it to products:

1. Culling and replanting — dead or overcrowded vines are culled and new vines are planted or relocated. (Separate vineyards by variety.)
2. Trimming — at the end of the harvest the vines are cut and trimmed back in preparation for the next season.
3. Tying — the posts and wires are reset and vines are tied to the wires for the dormant season.
4. Spraying — the vines are sprayed with chemicals for protection against insects and fungi.
5. Harvesting — the grapes are hand-picked, placed in carts and transported to the crushers.
6. Stemming and crushing — cartfuls of bunches of grapes of each variety are separately loaded into machines that remove stems and gently crush the grapes.
7. Pressing and filtering — the crushed grapes are transferred to presses that mechanically remove the juices and filter out bulk and impurities.
8. Fermentation — the grape juice, by variety, is fermented in either stainless-steel tanks or oak barrels.
9. Ageing — the wines are aged in either stainless-steel tanks or oak barrels for 1 to 3 years depending on variety.
10. Bottling and corking — bottles are machine-filled and corked.
11. Labelling and boxing — each bottle and each 9-bottle case is labelled with the name of the vintner, vintage and variety.
12. Storing — packaged and boxed bottles are stored awaiting shipment.
13. Shipping — the wine is shipped to distributors and private retailers.
14. Maintenance of buildings and equipment — printing, repairs, replacements and general maintenance are performed in the off-season.
15. Heating and air conditioning of plant and offices.

Required

(a) For each of Valliance's 15 activity cost pools, identify a probable cost driver that might be used to assign overhead costs to its three wine varieties.

(b) In an effort to expand the usefulness of its activity-based costing system, the vineyard uses activity-based management techniques. One of these ABM techniques is qualifying its activities as either value-added or non-value-added. Using the list of 15 activity cost pools, classify each of the activities as either value-added or non-value-added.

E16.11 Calculate overhead rates and assign overhead using ABC. **LO7, 8**

Amend Instrument Ltd manufactures two products: missile range instruments and space pressure gauges. During January, 50 range instruments and 300 pressure gauges were produced, and overhead costs of $89 000 were incurred. An analysis of overhead costs reveals the following activities:

Activity	Cost driver	Total cost
1. Materials handling	Number of requisitions	$35 000
2. Machine set-ups	Number of set-ups	27 000
3. Quality inspections	Number of inspections	27 000

The cost driver volume for each product was as follows:

Cost driver	Instruments	Gauges	Total
Number of requisitions	400	600	1 000
Number of set-ups	200	300	500
Number of inspections	200	400	600

Required

(a) Determine the overhead rate for each activity.

(b) Assign the manufacturing overhead costs for January to the two products using activity-based costing.

(c) Write a memorandum to the CEO of Amend Instrument Ltd explaining the benefits of activity-based costing.

E16.12 Assign overhead using traditional costing and ABC; classify activities as value- or non-value-added and by level. **LO7, 9**

Stylish Clothing Ltd manufactures its own designed and labelled sports attire and sells its products through catalogue sales and retail outlets. While Stylish has for years used activity-based costing in its manufacturing activities, it has always used traditional costing in assigning its selling costs to its product lines. Selling costs have traditionally been assigned to Stylish's product lines at a rate of 60% of direct material costs. Stylish's direct material costs for the month of March for its 'high intensity' line of attire are $400 000. The entity has decided to extend activity-based costing to its selling costs. Data relating to the 'high intensity' line of products for the month of March are as follows:

Activity cost pool	Cost driver	Overhead rates	Number of cost drivers used per activity
Sales commissions	Dollar sales	$0.05 per dollar sales	$930 000
Advertising (TV/radio)	Minutes	$300 per minute	250
Advertising (newspaper)	Column cm	$10 per column cm	3 000
Catalogues	Catalogues mailed	$2.50 per catalogue	60 000
Cost of catalogue sales	Catalogue orders	$1 per catalogue order	8 500
Credit and collection	Dollar sales	$0.03 per dollar sales	$930 000

Required

(a) Calculate the selling costs to be assigned to the 'high-intensity' line of attire for the month of March: (1) using the traditional product costing system (direct material cost is the cost driver), and (2) using activity-based costing.

(b) By what amount does the traditional product costing system undercost or overcost the 'high-intensity' product line?

(c) Classify each of the activities as value-added or non-value-added.

E16.13 Classify activities as value-added or non-value-added. **LO9**

Groat and Groat is a law firm that is initiating an activity-based costing system. Jim Groat, the senior partner and a strong supporter of ABC, has prepared the following list of activities performed by a typical solicitor in a day at the firm.

Activity	Hours
Writing contracts and letters	1.0
Attending staff meetings	0.5
Taking depositions	1.5
Doing research	1.0
Travelling to/from court	1.0
Contemplating legal strategy	1.5
Eating lunch	1.0
Instructing barristers	2.5
Entertaining a prospective client	1.5

Required

Classify each of the activities listed by Jim Groat as value-added or non-value-added; be able to defend your classification. How much was value-added time and how much was non-value-added?

PROBLEM SET A

PSA16.1 Prepare entries in a job cost system and cost of goods manufactured schedule. LO2, 3

Mercury Ltd is a construction company specialising in custom patios. The patios are constructed of concrete, brick, fibreglass and timber, depending upon customer preference. On 1 June 2019, the general ledger for Mercury Ltd contains the following data:

Raw materials inventory	$4 200	Manufacturing overhead applied	$32 640
Work in process inventory	$5 900	Manufacturing overhead incurred	$31 650

Subsidiary data for work in process inventory on 1 June are as follows:

	Job cost sheets		
	Customer job		
Cost element	Rockford	Aurora	Moline
Direct materials	$ 600	$ 800	$ 900
Direct labour	320	540	580
Manufacturing overhead	480	810	870
	$1 400	$2 150	$2 350

A summary of materials requisition slips and time sheets for June shows the following.

Customer job	Materials requisition slips	Time sheets
Rockford	$ 800	$ 450
Elgin	2 000	800
Aurora	500	360
Moline	1 300	800
Rockford	300	250
	4 900	2 660
General use	1 500	1 200
	$6 400	$3 860

During June, raw materials purchased on account were $3900, and all wages were paid. Additional overhead costs consisted of depreciation on equipment $700 and miscellaneous costs of $400 incurred on account. Overhead was charged to jobs at the same rate that was used in May. The patios for customers Rockford, Aurora and Moline were completed during June and sold for a total of $18 900. Each customer paid in full.

Required

(a) Journalise the June transactions.

(b) Post the entries to work in process inventory.

(c) Reconcile the balance in work in process inventory with the costs of unfinished jobs.

(d) Prepare a cost of goods manufactured schedule for June.

PSA16.2 Calculate predetermined overhead rate, apply overhead, and indicate statement presentation of under- or overapplied overhead. **LO3**

Urbana Manufacturing Ltd uses a job order cost system in each of its three manufacturing departments. Manufacturing overhead is applied to jobs on the basis of direct labour cost in Department D, direct labour hours in Department E, and machine hours in Department K.

In establishing the predetermined overhead rates for 2018 the following estimates were made for the year:

	Department		
	D	**E**	**K**
Manufacturing overhead	$1 170 000	$1 500 000	$1 248 000
Direct labour costs	$1 500 000	$1 250 000	$ 585 000
Direct labour hours	100 000	120 000	52 000
Machine hours	400 000	500 000	156 000

During January, the job cost sheets showed the following costs and production data:

	Department		
	D	**E**	**K**
Direct materials used	$140 000	$126 000	$93 600
Direct labour costs	$120 000	$110 000	$45 000
Manufacturing overhead incurred	$ 98 000	$129 000	$96 000
Direct labour hours	8 000	11 000	4 200
Machinery hours	34 000	45 000	12 480

Required

(a) Calculate the predetermined overhead rate for each department.

(b) Calculate the total manufacturing costs assigned to jobs in January in each department.

(c) Calculate the under- or overapplied overhead for each department at 31 January.

(d) Indicate the statement presentation of the under- or overapplied overhead in the financial statements.

PSA16.3 Journalise transactions. **LO5**

Vargas Ltd manufactures its product, Vitadrink, through two manufacturing processes: Mixing and Packaging. All materials are entered at the beginning of each process. On 1 October 2018, inventories consisted of Raw materials $26 000, Work in process—Mixing $0, Work in process—Packaging $250 000, and Finished goods $89 000. The beginning inventory for Packaging consisted of 10 000 units that were 50% complete as to conversion costs and fully complete as to materials. During October, 50 000 units were started into production in the Mixing Department and the following transactions were completed.

1. Purchased $400 000 of raw materials on account.

2. Issued raw materials for production: Mixing $210 000 and Packaging $45 000.

3. Incurred labour costs of $238 900.

4. Used factory labour: Mixing $182 500 and Packaging $56 400.

5. Incurred $790 000 of manufacturing overhead on account.

6. Applied manufacturing overhead on the basis of $25 per machine hour. Machine hours were 28 000 in Mixing and 7000 in Packaging.

7. Transferred 45 000 units from Mixing to Packaging at a cost of $999 000.

8. Transferred 53 000 units from Packaging to finished goods at a cost of $1 455 000.

9. Sold goods costing $1 540 000 for $2 500 000 on account.

Required

Journalise the October transactions.

PSA16.4 **Complete four steps necessary to prepare a production cost report.** **LO6**

Freedo Ltd manufactures in separate processes refrigerators and freezers for homes. In each process, materials are entered at the beginning and conversion costs are incurred uniformly. Production and cost data for the first process in making two products in two different manufacturing plants are as follows:

	Stamping department	
	Plant A	**Plant B**
Production data — June	**R12 refrigerators**	**F24 freezers**
Work in process units, 1 June	0	0
Units started into production	20 000	20 000
Work in process units, 30 June	2 000	2 500
Work in process percent complete	75%	60%
Cost data — June		
Work in process, 1 June	$ 0	$ 0
Materials	840 000	700 000
Labour	223 500	251 000
Overhead	420 000	319 000
Total	$1 483 500	$1 270 000

Required

(a) For each plant:

　1. Calculate the physical units of production.

　2. Calculate equivalent units of production for materials and for conversion costs.

　3. Determine the unit costs of production.

　4. Show the assignment of costs to units transferred out and in process.

(b) Prepare the production cost report for Plant A for June 2019.

PSA16.5 **Calculate equivalent units and complete production cost report.** **LO6**

Taylor Processing Ltd uses a weighted-average process costing system and manufactures a single product — a premium rug shampoo and cleaner. The manufacturing activity for the month of October has just been completed. A partially completed production cost report for the month of October for the Mixing and Blending Department is shown below.

TAYLOR PROCESSING LTD
Mixing and Blending Department
Production cost report
for the month ended 31 October

		Equivalent units	
	Physical units	**Materials**	**Conversion costs**
QUANTITIES			
Units to be accounted for:			
Work in process, 1 October (all materials, 70% conversion costs)	20 000		
Started into production	160 000		
Total units	180 000		

	Physical units	Equivalent units	
		Materials	Conversion costs
Units accounted for:			
Transferred out	140 000	?	?
Work in process, 31 October (50% materials, 25% conversion costs)	40 000	?	?
Total units accounted for	180 000	?	?

	Materials	Conversion costs	Total
COSTS			
Unit costs			
Costs in October	$240 000	$90 000	$330 000
Equivalent units	?	?	
Unit costs	$?	?	$?
Costs to be accounted for:			
Work in process, 1 October			$ 30 000
Started into production			300 000
Total costs			$330 000
COST RECONCILIATION SCHEDULE			
Costs accounted for:			
Transferred out			$?
Work in process, 31 October:			
Materials		$?	
Conversion costs		?	?
Total costs			$?

Required

Complete the production cost report for Taylor Processing Ltd.

PSA16.6 Assign overhead using traditional costing and ABC. **LO7**

Chris at Burleigh Ltd specialises in making two types of surfboards: short boards and long boards. The profitability in the last two years has deteriorated. Chris consulted Luke, who is a CPA, to help improve his business's bottom line. Luke analysed the profitability of the two products, firstly by investigating how overheads were allocated to each product line. The following information relates to overhead:

		Short boards	Long boards
Production units		200	150
Material moves per product line		300	200
Purchase orders per product line		450	350
Direct labour hours per product line		700	1 300
Annual material-handling costs	$120 000		
Annual purchasing activity costs	45 600		

Required

(a) Currently, a traditional costing system is in place. It assigns overhead on the basis of direct labour hours. Under this system:

1. What material handling costs are assigned to each unit of short board and long board?
2. What purchasing activity costs are assigned to each unit of short board and long board?

(b) Luke suggested adopting an activity-based costing (ABC) to allocate overheads. Under ABC:

1. What material handling costs are assigned to each unit of short board and long board?
2. What purchasing activity costs are assigned to each unit of short board and long board?

(c) After reviewing the costing from parts (a) and (b), what advice can Luke offer to Chris about improving the profitability of the two product lines?

PSA16.7 Assign overhead using traditional costing and ABC; compute unit costs; classify activities as value- or non-value-added. **LO7, 9**

Curly-Soo Ltd manufactures hair curlers and hair-dryers. The handheld hair curler is Curly-Soo's high-volume product (80 000 units annually). It is a 'large barrel', triple-heat appliance designed to appeal to the teenage market segment with its glow-in-the-dark handle. The handheld hair-dryer is Curly-Soo's lower-volume product (40 000 units annually). It is a three-speed appliance with a 'cool setting' and a removable filter. It also is designed for the teen market.

Both products require one hour of direct labour for completion. Therefore, total annual direct labour hours are 120 000 (80 000 + 40 000). Expected annual manufacturing overhead is $441 600. Thus, the predetermined overhead rate is $3.68 per direct labour hour. The direct materials cost per unit is $5.25 for the hair curler and $9.75 for the hair-dryer. The direct labour cost is $8.00 per unit for the hair curler and the hair-dryer.

Curly-Soo purchases most of the parts from suppliers and assembles the finished product at its Brisbane factory. It recently adopted activity-based costing, which after this year-end will totally replace its traditional direct labour-based cost accounting system. Curly-Soo has identified the following six activity cost pools and related cost drivers and has assembled the following information:

Activity cost pool	Cost driver	Estimated overhead	Expected use of cost drivers	Expected use of cost drivers per product Curlers	Dryers
Purchasing	Orders	$ 57 500	500	170	330
Receiving	Kilograms	42 000	168 000	70 000	98 000
Assembling	Parts	169 600	848 000	424 000	424 000
Testing	Tests	52 000	130 000	82 000	48 000
Finishing	Units	60 000	120 000	80 000	40 000
Packing and shipping	Cartons	60 500	12 100	8 040	4 060
		$441 600			

Required

(a) Under traditional product costing, calculate the total unit cost of both products. Prepare a simple comparative schedule of the individual costs by product.

(b) Under ABC, prepare a schedule showing the calculations of the activity-based overhead rates (per cost driver), using the information above.

(c) Prepare a schedule assigning each activity's overhead cost pool to each product based on the use of cost drivers. (Include a calculation of overhead cost per unit, rounding to the nearest cent.)

(d) Calculate total cost per unit for each product under ABC.

(e) Classify each of the activities as a value-added activity or a non-value-added activity.

(f) Comment on (1) the comparative overhead cost per unit for the two products under ABC, and (2) the comparative total costs per unit under traditional costing and ABC.

PSA16.8 Assign overhead costs using traditional costing and ABC; compare results; identify benefits and limitations of ABC. **LO7, 8**

Castro Cabinets Company Ltd designs and builds upscale kitchen cabinets for luxury homes. Many of the kitchen cabinet and counter arrangements are customer made, but occasionally the entity does mass production on order. Its budgeted manufacturing overhead costs for the year 2018 are as follows:

Overhead cost pools	Estimated overhead
Purchasing	$ 114 400
Handling materials	164 320
Production (cutting, milling, finishing)	400 000
Setting up machines	174 480
Inspecting	184 800
Inventory control (raw materials and finished goods)	252 000
Power	360 000
Total budget overhead costs	$1 650 000

For the last 3 years, Castro Cabinets has been charging overhead to products on the basis of machine hours. For the year 2018, 100 000 machine hours are budgeted.

Michael Castro, owner-manager of Castro, recently directed his accountant, John Kandy, to implement the activity-based costing system he has repeatedly proposed. At Michael's request, John and the production foreman identify the following cost drivers and their usage for the previously budgeted overhead cost pools:

Overhead cost pools	Activity cost drivers	Total drivers
Purchasing	Number of orders	650
Handling materials	Number of moves	8 000
Production (cutting, milling, finishing)	Direct labour hours	100 000
Setting up machines	Number of set-ups	1 200
Inspecting	Number of inspections	6 000
Inventory control (raw materials and finished goods)	Number of components	36 000
Power	Square metres occupied	90 000

Kathy Lawson, sales manager, has received an order for 50 kitchen cabinet arrangements from Bob the Builder. At Kathy's request, John prepares cost estimates for producing components for 50 cabinet arrangements so Kathy can submit a contract price per kitchen arrangement to Bob the Builder. He accumulates the following data for the production of 50 kitchen cabinet arrangements.

Direct materials	$180 000
Direct labour	$200 000
Machine hours	15 000
Direct labour hours	12 000
Number of purchase orders	50
Number of material moves	800
Number of machine set-ups	100
Number of inspections	450
Number of components (cabinets and accessories)	3 000
Number of square metres occupied	8 000

Required

(a) Calculate the predetermined overhead rate using traditional costing with machine hours as the basis. (Round to the nearest cent.)

(b) What is the manufacturing cost per complete kitchen arrangement under traditional costing?

(c) What is the manufacturing cost per kitchen arrangement under the proposed activity-based costing? (Prepare all of the necessary schedules.)

(d) Which of the two costing systems is preferable in pricing decisions and why?

PSA16.9 Assign overhead to products using ABC and evaluate decision. **LO7**

Jackson Electronics manufactures two large-screen television models: the Royale which sells for $1600, and a new model, the Majestic, which sells for $1300. The production cost calculated per unit under traditional costing for each model in 2019 was as follows:

Traditional costing	Royale	Majestic
Direct materials	$ 700	$420
Direct labour ($20 per hour)	120	100
Manufacturing overhead ($38 per DLH)	228	190
Total per unit cost	$1 048	$710

In 2019, Jackson manufactured 25 000 units of the Royale and 10 000 units of the Majestic. The overhead rate of $38 per direct labour hour was determined by dividing total expected manufacturing overhead of $7 600 000 by the total direct labour hours (200 000) for the two models.

Under traditional costing, the gross profit on the models was: Royale $552 or ($1600 − $1048), and Majestic $590 or ($1300 − $710). Because of this difference, management is considering phasing out the Royale model and increasing the production of the Majestic model.

Before finalising its decision, management asks Jackson's accountant to prepare an analysis using activity-based costing (ABC). The accountant accumulates the following information about overhead for the year ended 31 December 2019:

Activity	Cost driver	Estimated overhead	Expected use of cost drivers	Activity-based overhead rate
Purchasing	Number of orders	$1 200 000	40 000	$30
Machine set-ups	Number of set-ups	900 000	18 000	50
Machining	Machine hours	4 800 000	120 000	40
Quality control	Number of inspections	700 000	28 000	25

The cost drivers used for each product were:

Cost driver	Royale	Majestic	Total
Purchase orders	15 000	25 000	40 000
Machine set-ups	6 000	12 000	18 000
Machine hours	75 000	45 000	120 000
Inspections	8 000	20 000	28 000

Required

(a) Assign the total 2019 manufacturing overhead costs to the two products using activity-based costing (ABC).

(b) What was the cost per unit and gross profit of each model using ABC costing?

(c) Are management's future plans for the two models sound? Explain.

PSA16.10 Assign overhead costs to services using traditional costing and ABC; calculate overhead rates and unit costs; compare results. **LO7**

Horses and Dogs Veterinary Clinic is a small-town partnership that offers two primary services, farm animal services and pet care services. Providing veterinary care to farm animals requires travel to the farm animal (house calls), while veterinary care to pets generally requires that the pet be brought into the clinic. As part of an investigation to determine the contribution that each of these two types of services makes to overall profit, one partner argues for allocating overhead using activity-based costing while the other partner argues for a more simple overhead cost allocation on the basis of direct labour hours. The partners agree to use next year's budgeted data, as prepared by their public accountant, for analysis and comparison purposes. The following overhead data are collected to develop the comparison:

Activity cost pool	Cost driver	Estimated overhead	Total expected cost drivers	Expected use of drivers by service	
				Farm animals	Pets
Drug treatment	Treatments	$ 64 000	4 000	1 800	2 200
Surgery	Operations	65 000	800	200	600
Travel	Mileage	28 000	28 000	26 000	2 000
Consultation	Appointment/calls	33 000	3 000	600	2 400
Accounting/office	Direct labour hours	30 000	5 000	2 000	3 000
Boarding and grooming	100% pets	40 000			
		$260 000			

Required

(a) Using traditional product costing as proposed by the one partner, calculate the total overhead cost assigned to both services of Horses and Dogs Veterinary Clinic.

(b) 1. Using activity-based costing, prepare a schedule showing the calculations of the activity-based overhead rates (per cost driver).

   2. Prepare a schedule assigning each activity's overhead cost pool to each service based on the use of the cost drivers.

(c) Classify each of the activities as a value-added activity or a non-value-added activity.

(d) Comment on the comparative overhead cost assigned to the two services under both traditional costing and ABC.

PROBLEM SET B

PSB16.1 Prepare entries in a job cost system and partial statement of profit or loss.   **LO2, 3**

For the year ended 31 December 2019, the job cost sheets of Asticio Manufacturing contained the following data.

Job number	Explanation	Direct materials	Direct labour	Manufacturing overhead	Total costs
7650	Balance 1/1	$18 000	$20 000	$25 000	$ 63 000
	Current year's costs	22 000	30 000	37 500	89 500
7651	Balance 1/1	12 000	18 000	22 500	52 500
	Current year's costs	28 000	40 000	50 000	118 000
7652	Current year's costs	40 000	60 000	75 000	175 000

Additional information:

1. Raw materials inventory totalled $20 000 on 1 January. During the year, $100 000 of raw materials were purchased on account.

2. Finished goods on 1 January consisted of job no. 7648 for $98 000 and job no. 7649 for $62 000.

3. Job no. 7650 and job no. 7651 were completed during the year.

4. Job nos. 7648, 7649 and 7650 were sold on account for $390 000.

5. Manufacturing overhead incurred on account totalled $120 000.
6. Other manufacturing overhead consisted of indirect materials $12 000, indirect labour $18 000, and depreciation on factory machinery $6000.

Required

(a) Prove the agreement of work in process inventory with job cost sheets pertaining to unfinished work.

(b) Prepare the adjusting entry for manufacturing overhead, assuming the balance is allocated entirely to cost of sales.

(c) Determine the gross profit to be reported for 2019.

PSB16.2 Prepare entries in a job cost system and job cost sheets.   **LO3**

Han Wu Manufacturing uses a job order cost system and applies overhead to production on the basis of direct labour hours. On 1 January 2019, job no. 50 was the only job in process. The costs incurred prior to 1 January on this job were as follows: direct materials $10 000, direct labour $6000, and manufacturing overhead $10 500. As of 1 January, job no. 49 had been completed at a cost of $45 000 and was part of finished goods inventory. There was a $5000 balance in the raw materials inventory account.

During the month of January, Han Wu Manufacturing began production on jobs 51 and 52, and completed jobs 50 and 51. Jobs 49 and 50 were sold on account during the month for $67 000 and $74 000, respectively. The following additional events occurred during the month.
1. Purchased additional raw materials of $45 000 on account.
2. Incurred factory labour costs of $31 500. Of this amount $6500 related to employer payroll taxes.
3. Incurred manufacturing overhead costs as follows: indirect materials $10 000; indirect labour $7500; depreciation expense $1250; and various other manufacturing overhead costs on account $15 000.
4. Assigned direct materials and direct labour to jobs as follows:

Job no.	Direct materials	Direct labour
50	$ 5 000	$ 3 000
51	20 000	12 000
52	15 000	9 000

5. The company uses direct labour hours as the activity base to assign overhead. Direct labour hours incurred on each job were as follows: Job no. 50, 200; Job no. 51, 800; and Job no. 52, 600.

Required

(a) Calculate the predetermined overhead rate for 2019, assuming Han Wu Manufacturing estimates total manufacturing overhead costs of $500 000, direct labour costs of $300 000 and direct labour hours of 20 000 for the year.

(b) Open job cost sheets for jobs 50, 51 and 52. Enter the 1 January balances on the job cost sheet for job no. 50.

(c) Prepare the journal entries to record the purchase of raw materials, the factory labour costs incurred, and the manufacturing overhead costs incurred during the month of January.

(d) Prepare the journal entries to record the assignment of direct materials, direct labour, and manufacturing overhead costs to production. In assigning manufacturing overhead costs, use the overhead rate calculated in (a). Post all costs to the job cost sheets as necessary.

(e) Total the job cost sheets for any job(s) completed during the month. Prepare the journal entry (or entries) to record the completion of any job(s) during the month.

(f) Prepare the journal entry (or entries) to record the sale of any job(s) during the month.

(g) What is the balance in the finished goods inventory account at the end of the month? What does this balance consist of?

(h) What is the amount of over- or underapplied overhead for the month? How would this be reported in the financial statements for the month of January?

PSB16.3 Complete four steps necessary to prepare a production cost report.   **LO6**

Buehler Skis manufactures water-skis through two processes: moulding and packaging. In the Moulding Department, fibreglass is heated and shaped into the form of a ski. In the Packaging Department, the skis are placed in cartons and sent to the finished goods warehouse. Materials are entered at the beginning of both processes. Labour and manufacturing overhead are incurred uniformly throughout each process. Production and cost data for the Moulding Department for June 2019 are presented below.

Production data	June
Beginning work in process units	—
Units commenced	35 200
Ending work in process units	4 000
Per cent complete — ending inventory	65%
Cost data	
Materials	$400 400
Labour	159 600
Overhead	191 520
Total	$751 520

Required

(a) Calculate the physical units of production.

(b) Determine the equivalent units of production for materials and conversion costs.

(c) Calculate the unit costs of production.

(d) Determine the costs to be assigned to the units transferred out and in process.

(e) Prepare a production cost report for the Moulding Department for the month of June.

PSB16.4 Journalise transactions.   **LO5**

Pickard Pty Ltd manufactures a nutrient, Everlife, through two manufacturing processes: blending and packaging. All materials are entered at the beginning of each process. On 1 August 2019 inventories consisted of Raw materials $5000, Work in process—Blending $0, Work in process—Packaging $3945 and Finished goods $7500. The beginning inventory for Packaging consisted of 500 units, two-fifths complete as to conversion costs and fully complete as to materials. During August, 9000 units were started into production in Blending and the following transactions were completed:

1. Purchased $25 000 of raw materials on account.
2. Issued raw materials for production: Blending $16 930 and Packaging $7140.
3. Incurred labour costs of $18 770.
4. Used factory labour: Blending $13 320 and Packaging $5450.
5. Incurred $41 500 of manufacturing overhead on account.
6. Applied manufacturing overhead at the rate of $35 per machine hour. Machine hours were Blending 900 and Packaging 300.
7. Transferred 8200 units from Blending to Packaging at a cost of $54 940.
8. Transferred 8600 units from Packaging to finished goods at a cost of $74 490.
9. Sold goods costing $62 000 for $90 000 on account.

Required

Journalise the August transactions.

PSB16.5 Calculate equivalent units and complete production cost report. **LO5, 6**

Fluid Cleaners uses a weighted-average process cost system and manufactures a single product — an all-purpose liquid cleaner. The manufacturing activity for the month of March has just been completed. A partially completed production cost report for the month of March for the mixing and blending department is shown below.

FLUID CLEANERS
Mixing and blending department
Production cost report
for the month ended 31 March

		Equivalent units	
	Physical units	Materials	Conversion costs
QUANTITIES			
Units to be accounted for:			
Work in process, 1 March (40% materials, 20% conversion costs)	10 000		
Started into production	100 000		
Total units	110 000		
Units accounted for:			
Transferred out	95 000	?	?
Work in process, 31 March (60% materials, 20% conversion costs)	15 000	?	?
Total units	110 000	?	?

	Materials	Conversion costs	Total
COSTS			
Unit costs			
Costs in March	$156 000	$98 000	$254 000
Equivalent units	?	?	
Unit costs	$?	?	$?
Costs to be accounted for:			
Work in process, 1 March			$ 8 700
Started into production			245 300
Total costs			$254 000
COST RECONCILIATION SCHEDULE			
Costs accounted for:			
Transferred out			$?
Work in process, 31 March:			
Materials		?	
Conversion costs		?	?
Total costs			$?

Required

Complete the production cost report for Fluid Cleaners.

PSB16.6 Assign overhead using traditional costing and ABC. **LO7**

Prince Boat Ltd specialises in making two types of boat: sail boats and power boats. Profitability has deteriorated in the last few years. Owner, Scott, consulted his accountant, Jeff, who is a CPA to help improve his business's bottom line. Jeff analysed the profitability of the two products, firstly by investigating how overheads were allocated to each product line. The following information relates to overhead.

	Sail boats	Power boats
Production units	50	30
Material moves per product line	20	80
Purchase orders per product line	80	120
Direct labour hours per product line	175	285
Annual material-handling costs	$245 000	
Annual purchasing activity costs	69 800	

Required

(a) Currently a traditional costing system is in place. It assigns overhead on the basis of direct-labour hours. Under this system:
   1. What material handling costs are assigned to each unit of sail boat and power boat?
   2. What purchasing activity costs are assigned to each unit of sail boat and power boat?
(b) Jeff suggested adopting activity-based costing (ABC) to allocate overheads. Under ABC:
   1. What material handling costs are assigned to each unit of sail boat and power boat?
   2. What purchasing activity costs are assigned to each unit of sail boat and power boat?
(c) After reviewing the costing from parts (a) and (b), what advice can Jeff offer to Scott about improving the profitability of the two product lines?

PSB16.7 Assign overhead using traditional costing and ABC; calculate unit costs; classify activities as value-added or non-value-added. **LO7, 9**

Spartan Safety manufactures steel cylinders and nozzles for two models of fire extinguishers: (1) a home fire extinguisher and (2) a commercial fire extinguisher. The home model is a high-volume (54 000 units) 2-litre cylinder that holds 1 kilogram of multipurpose dry chemical at 480 PSI. The commercial model is a low-volume (10 200 units) 8-litre cylinder that holds 4 kilograms of multipurpose dry chemical at 390 PSI. Both products require 1.5 hours of direct labour for completion. Therefore, total annual direct labour hours are 96 300 [1.5 h × (54 000 + 10 200)]. Expected annual manufacturing overhead is $1 492 780. Thus, the predetermined overhead rate is $15.50 ($1 492 780 ÷ 96 300) per direct labour hour. The direct materials cost per unit is $18.50 for the home model and $26.50 for the commercial model. The direct labour cost is $19 per unit for both the home and the commercial models.

Spartan Safety's managers identified six activity cost pools and related cost drivers and accumulated overhead by cost pool as follows:

Activity cost pool	Cost driver	Estimated overhead	Expected use of cost drivers	Expected use of drivers by product	
				Home	Commercial
Receiving	Kilograms	$ 70 350	335 000	215 000	120 000
Forming	Machine hours	150 500	35 000	27 000	8 000
Assembling	Number of parts	381 600	212 000	162 000	50 000
Testing	Number of tests	51 000	25 500	15 500	10 000
Painting	Litres	52 080	6 510	4 510	2 000
Packing and shipping	Kilograms	787 250	335 000	215 000	120 000
		$1 492 780			

Required

(a) Under traditional product costing, calculate the total unit cost of both products using the information above. Prepare a simple comparative schedule of the individual costs by product.
(b) Under ABC, prepare a schedule showing the calculations of the activity-based overhead rates (per cost driver), using the information above.

(c) Prepare a schedule assigning each activity's overhead cost pool to each product based on the use of cost drivers (include a calculation of overhead cost per unit, rounding to the nearest cent).

(d) Calculate the total cost per unit for each product under ABC.

(e) Classify each of the activities as a value-added activity or a non-value-added activity.

(f) Comment on (1) the comparative overhead cost per unit for the two products under ABC and (2) the comparative total costs per unit under traditional costing and ABC.

PSB16.8 Assign overhead costs using traditional costing and ABC; compare results.   **LO7**

Designed Stairs designs and builds factory-made premium timber stairs for homes. The manufactured stair components (spindles, risers, hangers, hand rails) permit installation of stairs of varying lengths and widths, but all are of cedar timber. Its budgeted manufacturing overhead costs for the year 2018 are as follows:

Overhead cost pools	Amount
Purchasing	$ 57 000
Handling materials	82 000
Production (cutting, milling, finishing)	200 000
Setting up machines	84 840
Inspecting	90 000
Inventory control (raw materials and finished goods)	126 000
Power	180 000
Total budget overhead costs	**$819 840**

For the last four years, Designed Stairs has been charging overhead to products on the basis of machine hours. For the year 2018, 100 000 machine hours are budgeted.

Larry Morris, owner-manager of Designed Stairs, recently directed his accountant, Denise Cheung, to implement the activity-based costing system that she has repeatedly proposed. At Larry's request, Denise and the production foreman identify the following cost drivers and their usage for the previously budgeted overhead cost pools:

Overhead cost pools	Activity cost drivers	Expected use of cost drivers
Purchasing	Number of orders	600
Handling materials	Number of moves	8 000
Production (cutting, milling, finishing)	Direct labour hours	100 000
Setting up machines	Number of set-ups	1 200
Inspecting	Number of inspections	6 000
Inventory control (raw materials and finished goods)	Number of components	168 000
Power	Square metres occupied	90 000

Richard Way, sales manager, has received an order for 280 stairs from Acme Builders, a large housing development contractor. At Richard's request, Denise prepares cost estimates for producing components for 280 stairs so Richard can submit a contract price per stair to Acme Builders. She accumulates the following data for the production of 280 stairways.

Direct materials	$103 600
Direct labour	$112 000
Machine hours	14 500
Direct labour hours	5 000
Number of purchase orders	60
Number of material moves	800
Number of machine set-ups	100
Number of inspections	450
Number of components	16 000
Number of square metres occupied	8 000

Required

(a) Calculate the predetermined overhead rate using traditional costing with machine hours as the basis.

(b) What is the manufacturing cost per stairway under traditional costing?

(c) What is the manufacturing cost per stairway under the proposed activity-based costing? (Prepare all of the necessary schedules.)

(d) Which of the two costing systems is preferable in pricing decisions and why?

PSB16.9 **Assign overhead to products using ABC and evaluate decision.** **LO7**

Leto Plastics manufactures two plastic icebox containers at its plastics moulding facility. Its large container, called the Ice House, has a volume of 25 litres, side carrying handles, a snap-down lid, and a side drain and plug. Its smaller container, called the Cool Chest, has a volume of 10 litres and a carrying handle which is part of a tilting lid. Both containers and their parts are made entirely of hard-moulded plastic. The Ice House sells for $35.00 and the Cool Chest sells for $24.00. The production costs calculated per unit under traditional costing for each model in 2018 were as follows:

Traditional costing	Ice House	Cool Chest
Direct materials	$ 9.50	$ 6.00
Direct labour ($10 per hour)	8.00	5.00
Manufacturing overhead ($17.20 per direct labour hour)	13.76	8.60
Total per unit cost	$31.26	$19.60

In 2018, Leto Plastics manufactured 50 000 units of the Ice House and 20 000 units of the Cool Chest. The overhead rate of $17.20 per direct labour hour was determined by dividing total expected manufacturing overhead of $860 000 by the total direct labour hours (50 000) for the 2 models.

Under traditional costing, the gross profit on the two containers was Ice House $3.74 ($35 − $31.26) and Cool Chest $4.40 ($24 − $19.60). The gross margins on cost are Ice House 12% ($3.74 ÷ $31.26) and Cool Chest 22% ($4.40 ÷ $19.60). Because Leto can earn a gross margin nearly twice as great with less investment in inventory and labour costs, management is urging the sales staff to put its efforts into selling the Cool Chest over the Ice House.

Before finalising its decision, management asks the controller, Janet Plote, to prepare a product costing analysis using activity-based costing (ABC). Plote accumulates the following information about overhead for the year ended 31 December 2018:

Activity	Cost driver	Estimated overhead	Total expected cost drivers	Activity-based overhead rate
Purchasing	Number of orders	$180 000	4 500	$40 per order
Machine set-ups	Number of set-ups	200 000	800	$250 per set-up
Extruding	Machine hours	320 000	80 000	$4 per machine hour
Quality control	Tests and inspections	160 000	8 000	$20 per test

The cost drivers used for each product were:

Cost driver	Ice House	Cool Chest	Total
Purchase orders	2 500	2 000	4 500
Machine set-ups	500	300	800
Machine hours	60 000	20 000	80 000
Tests and inspections	5 000	3 000	8 000

Required

(a) Assign the total 2018 manufacturing overhead costs to the two products using activity-based costing (ABC).

(b) What was the cost per unit and gross profit of each model using ABC costing?

(c) Are management's future plans for the two models sound?

PSB16.10 Assign overhead costs to services using traditional costing and ABC; calculate overhead rates and unit costs; compare results. **LO7**

Wise and Otherwise is a public accounting firm that offers two main services, auditing and tax return preparation. A controversy has developed between the partners of the two service lines as to who is contributing the greater amount to the bottom line. The contentious area is the assignment of overhead. The tax partners argue for assigning overhead on the basis of 40% of direct labour dollars and the audit partners argue for implementing activity-based costing. The partners agree to use next year's budgeted data for purposes of analysis and comparison. The following overhead data are collected to develop the comparison:

Activity cost pool	Cost driver	Estimated overhead	Expected use of cost drivers	Expected use of cost drivers per service	
				Audit	Tax
Employee training	Direct labour dollars	$209 000	$1 900 000	$1 000 000	$900 000
Typing and secretarial	Number of reports/forms	76 200	2 500	600	1 900
Computing	Number of minutes	204 000	60 000	25 000	35 000
Facility rental	Number of employees	142 500	38	20	18
Travel	Per expense reports	128 300	Direct	86 800	41 500
		$760 000			

Required

(a) Using traditional product costing as proposed by the tax partners, calculate the total cost of both services (audit and tax) of Wise and Otherwise.

(b) 1. Using activity-based costing, prepare a schedule showing the calculations of the activity-based overhead rates (per cost driver).

  2. Prepare a schedule assigning each activity's overhead cost pool to each service based on the use of the cost drivers.

  3. Calculate the overhead cost per unit for each product under ABC.

(c) Classify each of the activities as a value-added activity or a non-value-added activity.

(d) Comment on the comparative overhead cost per unit for the two products under both traditional costing and ABC.

BUILDING BUSINESS SKILLS

FINANCIAL REPORTING AND ANALYSIS

Managerial analysis

BBS16.1 Davidson Furniture manufactures living-room furniture through two departments: Framing and Upholstering. Materials are entered at the beginning of each process. For May, the following cost data are obtained from the two work-in-process accounts:

	Framing	Upholstering
Work in process, 1 May	$ —	$?
Materials	420 000	?
Conversion costs	210 000	330 000
Costs transferred in	—	550 000
Costs transferred out	550 000	?
Work in process, 31 May	80 000	?

Required

Answer the following questions:

(a) If 3000 sofas were started into production on 1 May and 2500 sofas were transferred to Upholstering, what was the unit cost of materials for May in the Framing department?

(b) Using the data in (a) above, what was the per-unit conversion cost of the sofas transferred to Upholstering?

(c) Continuing the assumptions in (a) above, what is the percentage of completion of the units in process at 31 May in the Framing department?

BBS16.2 New Tech Pharmaceuticals, Brisbane, has supported a Research and Development (R&D) department that has for many years been the sole contributor to New Tech's new cancer drug. The R&D activity is an overhead cost centre that provides services only to in-house manufacturing departments (four different product lines), all of which produce pharmaceutical products. The department has never sold its services outside, but because of its long history of success, larger manufacturers of pharmaceutical products have approached New Tech to hire its R&D department for special projects. Because the costs of operating the R&D department have been spiralling uncontrollably, New Tech's management is considering entertaining these outside approaches to absorb the increasing costs. But (1) management doesn't have any cost basis for charging R&D services to outsiders and (2) it needs to gain control of its R&D costs. Management decides to implement an activity-based costing system in order to determine the charges for both outsiders and the in-house users of the department's services.

R&D activities fall into four pools with the following annual costs:

Market analysis	$1 050 000
Product design	2 280 000
Product development	3 600 000
Prototype testing	1 400 000

Activity analysis determines that the appropriate cost drivers and their usage for the four activities are:

Activity	Cost drivers	Total estimated drivers
Market analysis	Hours of analysis	15 000 hours
Product design	Number of designs	2 500 designs
Product development	Number of products	90 products
Prototype testing	Number of redesigns	700 redesigns

Required

(a) Calculate the activity-based overhead rate for each activity cost pool.

(b) How much cost would be charged to an in-house manufacturing department that consumed 1800 hours of market analysis time, was provided with 280 designs relating to 10 products, and requested 92 engineering redesigns?

(c) How much cost would serve as the basis for pricing an R&D bid with an outside entity on a contract that would consume 800 hours of analysis time, require 178 designs relating to 3 products, and result in 70 engineering redesigns?

(d) What is the benefit to New Tech of applying activity-based costing to its R&D activity for both in-house and outside charging purposes?

Surfing the net

BBS16.3 Search the internet and find the web sites of two manufacturers that you think are likely to use process costing. Are there any specifics included in their web sites that confirm the use of process costing for each of these entities? (*Hint:* Go to the ASX web site, www.asx.com.au, and search by company name.)

CRITICAL THINKING

Group decision cases

BBS16.4 Costello Products uses a job order cost system. For a number of months there has been an ongoing rift between the sales department and the production department concerning a special-order product, TC-1. TC-1 is a seasonal product that is manufactured in batches of 1000 units. TC-1 is sold at cost plus a mark-up of 40% of cost.

The sales department is unhappy because fluctuating unit production costs significantly affect selling prices. Sales personnel complain that this has caused excessive customer complaints and the loss of considerable orders for TC-1.

The production department maintains that each job order must be fully costed on the basis of the costs incurred during the period in which the goods are produced. Production personnel maintain that the only real solution to the problem is for the sales department to increase sales in the slack periods.

Linda Smart, the manager, asks you as the accountant to collect quarterly data for the past year on TC-1. From the cost accounting system, you accumulate the following production quantity and cost data:

	Quarter			
Costs	**1**	**2**	**3**	**4**
Direct materials	$150 000	$330 000	$120 000	$300 000
Direct labour	90 000	198 000	72 000	180 000
Manufacturing overhead	157 500	184 000	146 000	187 500
Total	$397 500	$712 000	$338 000	$667 500
Production in batches	5	11	4	10
Unit cost (per batch)	$ 79 500	$ 64 727	$ 84 500	$ 66 750

Required

With the class divided into groups, answer the following questions:
(a) What manufacturing cost element is responsible for the fluctuating unit costs? Why?
(b) What is your recommended solution to the problem of fluctuating unit cost?
(c) Restate the quarterly data on the basis of your recommended solution.

BBS16.5 Mendoza Ltd manufactures suntan lotion, called Surtan, in 50 mL plastic bottles. Surtan is sold in a competitive market. As a result, management is very cost-conscious. Surtan is manufactured through two processes: mixing and filling. Materials are entered at the beginning of each process, and labour and manufacturing overhead occur uniformly throughout each process. Unit costs are based on the cost per litre of Surtan using the weighted-average costing approach.

On 30 June 2019, Sue Noller, the chief accountant for the past 20 years, opted to take early retirement. Her replacement, Jeff Mura, had extensive accounting experience with motels in the area but only limited contact with manufacturing accounting.

During July, Jeff correctly accumulated the following production quantity and cost data for the Mixing Department:

Production quantities: Work in process, 1 July, 8000 litres 75% complete; started into production 100 000 litres; work in process, 31 July, 5000 litres 20% complete. Materials are added at the beginning of the process.

Production costs: Beginning work in process $88 000, comprising $21 000 of materials costs and $67 000 of conversion costs; incurred in July: materials $600 000, conversion costs $785 800.

Jeff then prepared a production cost report on the basis of physical units started into production. His report showed a production cost of $14.738 per litre of Surtan. Management was surprised at the high unit cost. The CEO comes to you, as Sue's top assistant, to review Jeff's report and prepare a correct report if necessary.

Required

With the class divided into groups, answer the following questions:

(a) Show how Jeff arrived at the unit cost of $14.738 per litre of Surtan.

(b) What error(s) did Jeff make in preparing his production cost report?

(c) Prepare a correct production cost report for July.

Communication activity

BBS16.6 Sue Smithers was a good friend of yours in high school. While you chose to major in accounting when you both went to university, she majored in marketing and management. You have recently been promoted to accounting manager for the Furniture Division of Easy Relax, and your friend was promoted to regional sales manager for the same division. Sue recently telephoned you. She explained that she was familiar with job cost sheets, which had been used by the Special Projects division where she had formerly worked. She was, however, very uncomfortable with the production cost reports prepared by your division. She emailed you a list of her particular questions. These included the following:

1. Since Easy Relax occasionally prepares furniture for special orders in the Furniture Division, why don't we track costs of the orders separately?

2. What is an equivalent unit?

3. Why am I getting four production cost reports? Isn't there only one work in process account?

Required

Prepare a memorandum to Sue. Answer her questions and include any additional information you think would be helpful. You may write informally, but be careful to use proper grammar and punctuation.

BBS16.7 The following is an extract from Bega Cheese Limited's web site, www.begacheese.com.au:

> Bega Cheese is committed to improving its sustainability and reducing the environmental impact of the business. Bega Cheese focuses on two core areas; Farm Sustainability and Factory Sustainability.

Required

1. What is meant by the term 'sustainability'?

2. Access Bega Cheese's latest sustainability information and complete the following.

   (a) Outline Bega Cheese's approach to sustainability and why it is important for the business.

   (b) Summarise Bega Cheese's achievements, and include a discussion of goals and how these achievements are measured in farming and factory sustainability.

ANSWERS

Answers to self-study questions

16.1 (a) 16.2 (c) 16.3 (b) 16.4 (c) 16.5 (c) 16.6 (b) 16.7 (d) 16.8 (b) 16.9 (b) 16.10 (c) 16.11 (d) 16.12 (c) 16.13 (d) 16.14 (c) 16.15 (c)

ACKNOWLEDGEMENTS

Photo: © Zadorozhnyi Viktor / Shutterstock.com

Photo: © Hero Images / Getty Images

Photo: © Monkey Business Images / Shutterstock.com

CHAPTER 17

Cost–volume–profit relationships

LEARNING OBJECTIVES

After studying this chapter, you should be able to:

17.1 distinguish between variable, fixed and mixed cost behaviour

17.2 explain the difference between absorption costing and variable costing

17.3 explain the five basic assumptions of cost–volume–profit (CVP) analysis

17.4 indicate the meaning of contribution margin and identify break-even point and the use of break-even analysis

17.5 determine target profit by applying formulas

17.6 explain how CVP analysis is used with multiple products

17.7 describe the essential features of a CVP statement of profit or loss.

Chapter preview

To manage any entity you must understand how costs respond to changes in sales volume and the effect of the interaction of costs and revenues on profits. A prerequisite to understanding cost–volume–profit (CVP) relationships is knowledge of the behaviour of costs. In this chapter, we first explain the considerations involved in cost behaviour analysis. Then we discuss and illustrate CVP analysis and variable costing. The content and organisation of the chapter are as follows.

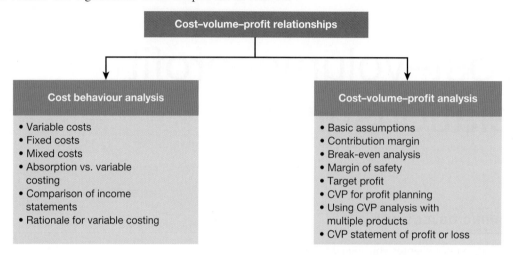

17.1 Cost behaviour analysis

LEARNING OBJECTIVE 17.1 Distinguish between variable, fixed and mixed cost behaviour.

Cost behaviour analysis is the study of how specific costs respond to changes in the level of business activity. When a business gets busier, some costs change and others remain the same. For example, many retailers employ extra staff to cater for the peak shopping period leading up to Christmas. As a result, you might expect an increase in labour costs, but the rent for the retail shop stays the same for that period. A sound knowledge of cost behaviour therefore helps management plan business operations and choose between alternative courses of action. Since cost is one of the key factors in any pricing or funding decision, cost behaviour analysis applies to all types of entities and businesses.

The starting point in cost behaviour analysis is measuring the key activities in the entity's business. Activity levels may be expressed in terms of sales dollars (in a retail business), kilometres driven (in a transport business), room occupancy (in a hotel) or number of courses offered (by a university). Many entities use more than one measurement base. A manufacturing entity, for example, may use direct labour hours or units of output for manufacturing costs and sales revenue or units sold for selling expenses.

For an activity level to be useful in cost behaviour analysis, there should be a correlation between changes in the level or volume of activity and changes in costs. The activity level selected is referred to as the activity (or volume) index. The **activity index** identifies the activity that causes changes in the behaviour of costs. Once an appropriate activity index is selected, it is possible to classify the behaviour of costs in response to changes in activity levels into three categories: variable, fixed or mixed.

Variable costs

Variable costs are costs that vary *in total* directly and proportionately with changes in the activity level. If the level increases by 10%, total variable costs will increase by 10%. If the level of activity decreases by 25%, variable costs will be reduced by 25%. Examples of variable costs include direct materials and direct labour in a manufacturing entity; cost of sales, sales commissions and freight-out in a retail entity;

and fuel in airline and transport entities. A common feature of all of these examples is that the higher the activity level, the higher the total variable costs. As you might expect, for instance, a Virgin Pacific flight from Sydney to Auckland will use more fuel in total than, say, a Virgin Blue flight between Sydney and Melbourne because of the difference in mileage.

Although total variable costs vary with activity levels, the *variable cost per unit* remains the same at every level of activity. Continuing with our Virgin flights example, although more fuel will be used for the Sydney to Auckland flight than for the Sydney to Melbourne flight, the fuel usage per kilometre remains the same for these two flights.

To further demonstrate the behaviour of a variable cost, assume that Damon Ltd manufactures radios that contain a $10 digital clock. The activity index is the number of radios produced. As each radio is manufactured, the total cost of the clocks increases by $10. As shown in part (a) of figure 17.1, total cost of the clocks will be $20 000 if 2000 radios are produced, and $100 000 when 10 000 radios are produced. The digital clocks example can also be used to show that a variable cost remains the same per unit as the level of activity changes. As shown in part (b) of figure 17.1, the unit cost of $10 for the clocks is the same whether 2000 or 10 000 radios are produced.

Entities that rely heavily on labour to manufacture a product or to render a service are likely to have many variable costs. In contrast, those that use a high proportion of machinery and equipment in producing revenue, such as automated factories, may have few variable costs other than materials.

Fixed costs

Fixed costs are costs that remain the same in total regardless of changes in the activity level. Examples include rates and taxes, insurance, rent, supervisory salaries, and depreciation on buildings. Because fixed costs remain constant in total as activity changes, it follows that fixed costs per unit vary inversely with activity. In other words, as activity level increases, the total fixed costs are shared by a bigger pool of outputs. Hence, each unit of output will share fewer of the fixed costs.

FIGURE 17.1   Behaviour of total and unit variable costs

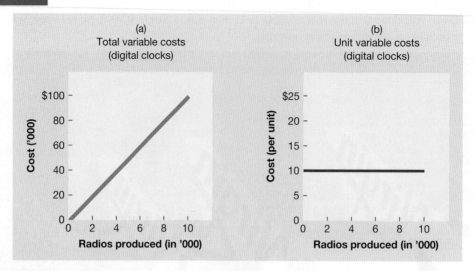

To demonstrate the behaviour of fixed costs, assume that Damon Ltd leases all of its productive facilities at a cost of $10 000 per month. Total rental of the facilities will remain constant at every level of activity, as shown in part (a) of figure 17.2. However, on a per-unit basis, the cost of rent will decline as activity increases, as shown in part (b) of figure 17.2. At 2000 units, the unit cost is $5 ($10 000 ÷ 2000); when 10 000 radios are produced, the unit cost is only $1 ($10 000 ÷ 10 000).

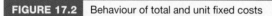

FIGURE 17.2   Behaviour of total and unit fixed costs

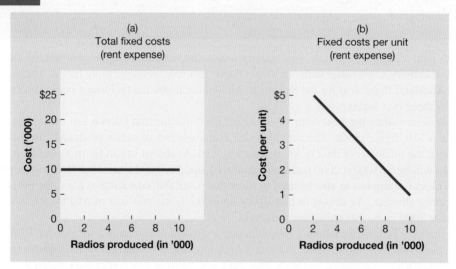

The trend in many manufacturing entities is to have more fixed costs and fewer variable costs. This development results from increased use of automation and less use of employees. As a result, depreciation and lease charges (fixed costs) increase, whereas direct labour costs (variable costs) decrease.

Relevant range

In figures 17.1 and 17.2, straight lines were drawn throughout the entire activity index for total variable costs and total fixed costs. In essence, the assumption was made that the costs were linear. It is now necessary to ask: Is the straight-line relationship realistic? Can the linear assumption produce useful data for CVP analysis?

In most business situations, a straight-line/linear relationship does not exist for variable costs throughout the entire range of activity. At abnormally low levels of activity, it may be impossible to be cost efficient, since the scale of operations may not allow the business to obtain quantity discounts in the purchase of raw materials or use specialisation of labour. In contrast, at abnormally high levels of activity, labour costs may increase sharply because of overtime pay, and materials costs may jump significantly because of excess spoilage caused by worker fatigue. Consequently, in the real world, the relationship between the behaviour of a variable cost and changes in the activity level is often curvilinear, as shown in part (a) of figure 17.3.

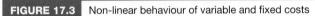

FIGURE 17.3 Non-linear behaviour of variable and fixed costs

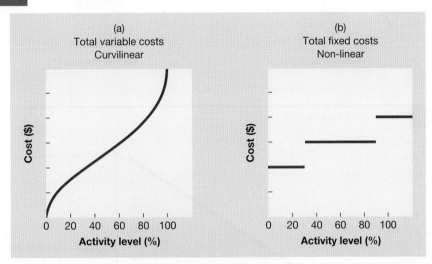

Helpful hint: Fixed costs that may be changeable include research, such as new product development, and management training programs.

Total fixed costs also do not have a linear relationship over the entire range of activity. Although some fixed costs will not change, it is sometimes necessary for management to add or change other fixed costs. For example, additional supervisors may be required to cover extra factory activity. The behaviour of total fixed costs through all levels of activity is shown in part (b) of figure 17.3.

For most entities, operating at almost nil activity or at 100% capacity are exceptions rather than the rule. Instead, they often operate over a somewhat narrower range, such as 40–80% of capacity. The range over which an entity expects to operate during a year is called the **relevant range** of the activity index. (The relevant range is also called the *normal* or *practical range*.) Within this range, as shown in both diagrams in figure 17.4, a linear relationship generally exists for both variable and fixed costs.

As you can see, although the linear relationship may not be completely realistic, the linear assumption produces useful data for CVP analysis as long as the level of activity remains within the relevant range.

Mixed costs

Mixed costs contain both a variable cost element and a fixed cost element. Sometimes called *semi-variable costs*, mixed costs change in total but not proportionately with changes in the activity level. The rental of a truck is a good example of a mixed cost. To demonstrate, assume that local rental terms for a truck, including insurance, are $50 per day plus 50 cents per kilometre. The daily charge is a fixed cost with respect to truck hire, whereas the kilometre charge is a variable cost. The graphic presentation of the rental cost for a one-day rental is shown in figure 17.5.

FIGURE 17.4 Linear behaviour within relevant range

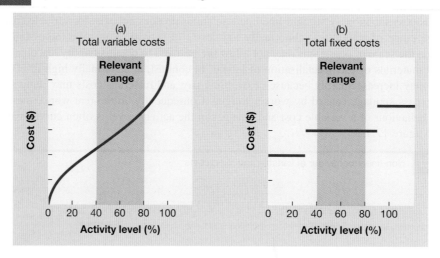

(a)
Total variable costs

(b)
Total fixed costs

FIGURE 17.5 Behaviour of a mixed cost

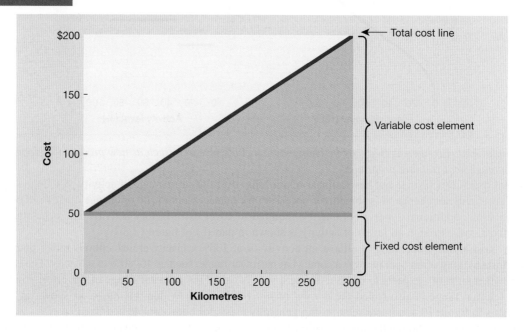

In this case, as in others, the fixed cost element is the cost of having the service available, whereas the variable cost element is the cost of actually using the service. Another example of a mixed cost is the cost of utilities (electricity, telephone and so on), where there is a flat service fee plus a usage charge.

For purposes of CVP analysis, an underlying assumption is that mixed costs must be classified into their fixed and variable elements. Accordingly, we must ask: How does management make the classification? One possibility is to determine the variable and fixed components each time a mixed cost is incurred. However, because of time and cost constraints, this approach is rarely followed. Instead, the customary approach is to determine variable and fixed costs on an aggregate basis at the end of a period of time, using the entity's past experience with the behaviour of the mixed cost at various levels of activity. Management may use several complex methods in making the determination, such as the high–low method, scatter diagrams and least-squares regression. These methods are covered in more advanced management accounting courses.

Importance of identifying variable and fixed costs

Why is it important to separate costs into variable and fixed elements? The answer may become apparent if we look at the following five business decisions.

1. If Harvey Norman wants to make a profit when it reduces the price of all printers by 20%, what reduction in costs or increases in volume would be required? *Answer:* To make a profit if it cuts the price of printers by 20%, Harvey Norman will need to increase its turnover (i.e. number of products sold) or cut its variable costs for that department. Its fixed costs will not change.
2. What increase in sales revenue will be needed to maintain current profit levels if Qantas meets the Transport Workers Union (TWU) demands for higher wages? *Answer:* Higher wages to TWU members at Qantas will increase the variable costs of maintaining aircraft. To maintain present profit levels, Qantas will have to cut other variable costs or increase the price of its airfares. The level of cuts in other variable costs will determine the level of increase in sales revenue.
3. If Fonterra was to modernise plant facilities and reduce the workforce by 20%, what would be the effect on the cost of producing its Mainland cheese? *Answer:* Modernising the plant facilities at Fonterra changes the proportion of fixed and variable costs. Fixed costs increase because of the higher depreciation charge, and variable costs decrease because of the reduction in the number of employees.
4. What level of sales will BMW need to cover its costs exactly for the X5 in the next model year? *Answer:* To cover its costs exactly on the X5 car for the next model year, BMW must determine the sales volume at which sales revenue will equal total costs, both fixed and variable.
5. What happens if Domino's Pizza Enterprises Ltd increases its advertising expenses? *Answer:* Sales volume must be increased to cover three items: (1) the increase in advertising, (2) the variable cost of the increased sales volume, and (3) the desired additional profit.

LEARNING REFLECTION AND CONSOLIDATION

Review it

1. What are the effects of a change in activity on (a) a variable cost and (b) a fixed cost?
2. What does the term relevant range mean? Describe the behaviour of costs within this range.

Do it

Helena Ltd reports the following total costs at two levels of production:

	10 000 units	20 000 units
Direct materials	$20 000	$40 000
Maintenance	8 000	10 000
Depreciation	4 000	4 000

Classify each cost as variable, fixed or mixed.

Reasoning

A variable cost varies in total directly and proportionately with each change. A fixed cost remains the same in total with each change. A mixed cost changes in total but not proportionately with each change.

Solution

Direct materials is a variable cost. Maintenance is a mixed cost. Depreciation is a fixed cost.

17.2 Absorption vs. variable costing

LEARNING OBJECTIVE 17.2 Explain the difference between absorption costing and variable costing.

In the previous chapter, both variable and fixed manufacturing costs were classified as product costs. In job order costing, for example, a job is assigned the costs of direct materials, direct labour, and both variable and fixed manufacturing overhead. This costing approach is referred to as full or **absorption costing**, because all manufacturing costs are charged to, or absorbed by, the product. An alternative approach is to use variable costing. Under **variable costing** (also called *direct costing*) only direct materials, direct labour and variable manufacturing overhead costs are considered product costs; fixed manufacturing overhead costs are recognised as period costs (expenses) when incurred. The difference between absorption costing and variable costing is shown graphically in figure 17.6.

FIGURE 17.6 | Difference between absorption costing and variable costing

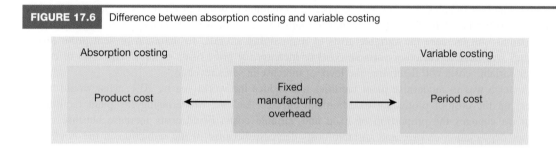

Selling, administrative and financial expenses are period costs under both absorption and variable costing.

To demonstrate the calculation of unit production cost under absorption and variable costing, assume that Premium Products Ltd manufactures a polyurethane sealant, called Fix-it, for car windshields. Relevant data for Fix-it in January 2018, the first month of production, are:

- *selling price:* $20 per unit
- *units:* Beginning inventory nil; produced 30 000; sold 20 000
- *variable unit costs:* Manufacturing $9 (direct materials $5, direct labour $3 and variable overhead $1), and selling and administrative expenses $2
- *fixed costs:* Manufacturing overhead $120 000 and selling and administrative expenses $15 000.

The per-unit production cost under each costing approach is as shown in figure 17.7.

FIGURE 17.7 | Calculation of per-unit production cost

Type of cost	Absorption costing	Variable costing
Direct materials	$ 5	$ 5
Direct labour	3	3
Variable manufacturing overhead	1	1
Fixed manufacturing overhead ($120 000 ÷ 30 000 units produced)	4	—
Total unit cost	$13	$ 9

The difference in total unit cost of $4 ($13 − $9) occurs because fixed manufacturing costs are a product cost under absorption costing and a period cost under variable costing. Based on these data, each unit sold and each unit remaining in inventory is costed at $13 under absorption costing and at $9 under variable costing.

Comparison of statements of profit or loss

The statements of profit or loss under the two costing approaches are shown in figures 17.8 and 17.9. Calculations are inserted parenthetically in the statements to help your understanding of the amounts.

FIGURE 17.8	Absorption costing statement of profit or loss

PREMIUM PRODUCTS LTD
Statement of profit or loss
for the month ended 31 January 2019
(absorption costing)

Sales (20 000 units × $20)		$ 400 000
Cost of sales		
Inventory, 1 January	$ —	
Cost of goods manufactured (30 000 units × $13)	390 000	
Cost of goods available for sale	390 000	
Less: **Inventory, 31 January (10 000 units × $13)**	(130 000)	
Cost of sales (20 000 units × $13)		(260 000)
Gross profit		140 000
Less: Selling and administrative expenses		
[(variable 20 000 units × $2) + (fixed $15 000)]		(55 000)
Profit from operations		$ 85 000

Helpful hint: This is the conventional statement that would result from job order and processing costing explained in chapter 16.

FIGURE 17.9	Variable costing statement of profit or loss

PREMIUM PRODUCTS LTD
Statement of profit or loss
for the month ended 31 January 2019
(variable costing)

Sales (20 000 units × $20)		$ 400 000
Cost of sales		
Inventory, 1 January	$ —	
Cost of goods manufactured (30 000 units × $9)	270 000	
Cost of goods available for sale	270 000	
Less: **Inventory, 31 January (10 000 units × $9)**	(90 000)	
Less: Cost of sales (20 000 units × $9)		(180 000)
Gross profit		220 000
Manufacturing overhead (fixed expenses)	120 000	
Selling and administrative expenses		
(variable 20 000 units × $2) + (fixed $15 000)]	55 000	
Less: Total expenses		(175 000)
Profit from operations		$ 45 000

Helpful hint: Note the difference in the calculation of the ending inventory: $9 per unit in figure 17.9, $13 per unit in figure 17.8.

Profit from operations under absorption costing, shown in figure 17.8, is $40 000 higher than under variable costing ($85 000 − $45 000), shown in figure 17.9.

As highlighted in the two statements of profit or loss, there is a $40 000 difference in the ending inventories ($130 000 under absorption costing and $90 000 under variable costing). Under absorption costing, $40 000 of the fixed overhead costs (10 000 units × $4) have been deferred to a future period as a product cost. In contrast, under variable costing the entire fixed manufacturing costs are expensed when incurred.

As shown, when units produced exceed units sold, profit under absorption costing is higher than under variable costing. Conversely, when units produced are less than units sold, profit under absorption costing is lower than under variable costing. The reason is that the cost of the beginning inventory will be higher under absorption costing than under variable costing. For example, if 30 000 units of Fix-it are sold in February and only 20 000 units are produced, profit from operations will be $40 000 less under absorption costing than under variable costing because of the $40 000 difference ($130 000 vs. $90 000) in the beginning inventories.

When units produced and sold are the same, profit from operations will be equal under the two costing approaches. Since there is no increase in ending inventory, fixed overhead costs of the current period deferred to future periods through the ending inventory are equal to the amount deferred from the previous period in beginning inventory. The foregoing effects of the two costing approaches on profit from operations may be summarised as shown in figure 17.10.

FIGURE 17.10 Summary of profit effects

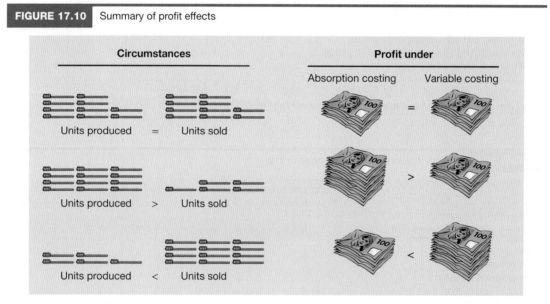

Rationale for variable costing

The rationale for variable costing centres on the purpose of fixed manufacturing costs, which is to have productive facilities available for use. Conceptually, these costs are incurred whether an entity operates at zero or at 100% of capacity. Thus, proponents of variable costing argue that these costs should be expensed in the period in which they are incurred.

Supporters of absorption costing defend the assignment of fixed manufacturing overhead costs to inventory on the basis that these costs are as much a cost of getting a product (such as Fix-it) ready for sale as direct materials or direct labour. Accordingly, these costs should not be recognised until the product is sold. Accounting standards IAS 2/AASB 102 *Inventories* do not permit the use of variable costing for external reporting. The use of variable costing in product costing is acceptable for internal reporting. The benefits of variable costing are that it forces management to evaluate the cost behaviour pattern of each cost item and it is presented in the profit or loss format, and so provides the basis for CVP analysis, flexible budgeting, cost control and resource allocation.

17.3 Cost–volume–profit analysis

LEARNING OBJECTIVE 17.3 Explain the five basic assumptions of cost–volume–profit (CVP) analysis.

Cost–volume–profit (CVP) analysis is the study of the effects of changes in costs and volume on an entity's profits. In other words, CVP analysis shows how profit is affected by changes in sales volume, selling prices of products and various costs. Therefore, CVP analysis is important in profit planning. It also is a critical factor in such management decisions as setting selling prices, determining the best product mix and making maximum use of production facilities.

Basic assumptions

CVP analysis involves a consideration of the interrelationships among the components shown in figure 17.11.

FIGURE 17.11 Components of CVP analysis

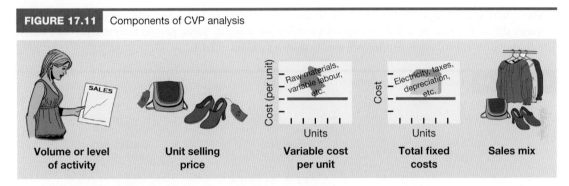

| Volume or level of activity | Unit selling price | Variable cost per unit | Total fixed costs | Sales mix |

The following assumptions underlie each CVP application.
1. The behaviour of both costs and revenues is linear throughout the relevant range of the activity index.
2. All costs can be classified as either variable or fixed with reasonable accuracy.
3. Changes in activity are the only factors that affect costs.
4. All units produced are sold.
5. When more than one type of product is sold, total sales will be in a constant sales mix. Sales mix complicates CVP analysis because different products will have different cost relationships.
   When these five assumptions are not valid, the results of CVP analysis may be inaccurate.

In the applications of CVP analysis that follow, we will assume that the term 'cost' includes *all* costs and expenses pertaining to production and sale of the product. That is, cost includes manufacturing costs plus selling and administrative expenses. To illustrate how CVP analysis can help management in making decisions, we will use Mike's Bikes Ltd as an example. Mike's Bikes specialises in producing and exporting mountain bicycles. Figure 17.12 shows the relevant data for the bikes produced by this business.

FIGURE 17.12 Assumed selling price and cost data for Mike's Bikes

Unit selling price	$800
Unit variable costs	$640
Total monthly fixed costs	$160 000

17.4 Contribution margin

LEARNING OBJECTIVE 17.4 Indicate the meaning of contribution margin and identify break-even point and the use of break-even analysis.

One of the key relationships in CVP analysis is contribution margin. **Contribution margin (CM)** is the amount of revenue remaining after deducting variable costs. For example, if we assume that Mike's Bikes sells 1500 mountain bikes in one month, sales are $1 200 000 (1500 × $800) and variable costs are $960 000 (1500 × $640). Thus, contribution margin is $240 000 calculated as shown in figure 17.13.

FIGURE 17.13 Formula for and calculation of contribution margin

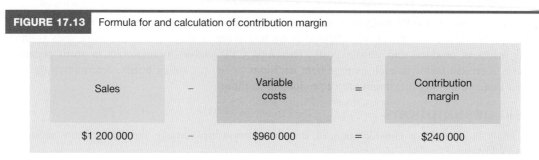

This contribution margin is then available to cover fixed costs and to contribute profit to the business. Views differ as to the best way to express contribution margin. Some people favour a per-unit basis. The formula for *contribution margin per unit* is shown in figure 17.14.

FIGURE 17.14 Formula for and contribution margin per unit

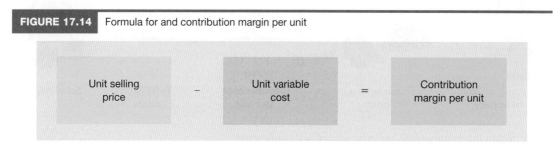

At Mike's Bikes, the contribution margin per unit is $160, calculated as follows:

$$\$800 - \$640 = \$160$$

Contribution margin per unit indicates that for every bike sold, Mike's Bikes will have $160 to cover fixed costs and contribute to profit. Since fixed costs are $160 000, Mike's Bikes must sell 1000 bikes ($160 000 ÷ $160) in a month before there is any profit. Above that sales volume, every sale will contribute $160 to profit. Thus, if 1500 units are sold, profit will be $80 000 (500 × $160).

Others prefer to use a *contribution margin ratio*. The formula for this ratio is shown in figure 17.15.

FIGURE 17.15 Formula for contribution margin ratio

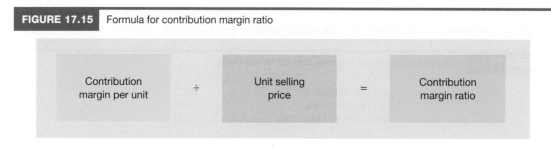

At Mike's Bikes, the ratio is 20%, as shown below:

$$\$160 \div \$800 = 20\%$$

Helpful hint: The same ratio results from dividing total CM by total sales: @ $1000 units: $160 000 ÷ $800 000 = 20%.

The CM ratio of 20% means that 20 cents of each sales dollar ($1 × 20%) is available to apply to fixed costs and to contribute to profit. This expression of contribution margin is very helpful in determining the effect of changes in sales on profit. To illustrate, if the management of Mike's Bikes wants to know the effect of a $50 000 increase in sales, they simply multiply $50 000 by the CM ratio (20%) to determine that profit will increase $10 000.

DECISION-MAKING TOOLKIT

Decision/issue	Info needed for analysis	Tool or technique to use for decision			How to evaluate results to make decision
What was the contribution towards fixed costs and profit from each unit sold?	Selling price per unit and variable cost per unit	Contribution margin per unit	= Unit selling price	= Unit variable cost	Every unit sold will increase profit by the contribution margin.

Break-even analysis

A second key relationship in CVP analysis is the level of activity at which total revenues equal total costs, both fixed and variable. This level of activity is called the **break-even point**. At this volume of sales, the entity will realise no profit and suffer no loss. Since no profit is involved when finding the break-even point is the objective, the analysis is often referred to simply as *break-even analysis*. Knowledge of the break-even point is useful to management in deciding whether to introduce new product lines, change sales prices on established products, or enter new market areas.

The break-even point can be:
- calculated from a mathematical equation
- calculated by using contribution margin
- derived from a cost–volume–profit (CVP) graph.

The break-even point can be expressed either in sales dollars or sales units.

Mathematical equation

In its simplest form, the equation for break-even sales is as shown in figure 17.16.

FIGURE 17.16   Break-even equation

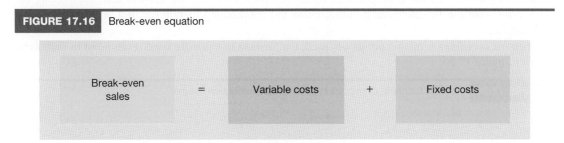

The break-even point in dollars is found by expressing variable costs as a percentage of unit selling price. For Mike's Bikes, the percentage is 80% ($640 ÷ $800). The calculation to determine sales dollars at the break-even point is shown in figure 17.17.

Sales, therefore, must be $800 000 for Mike's Bikes to break even.

The break-even point in units can be calculated directly from the mathematical equation by using unit selling prices and unit variable costs. The calculation is as shown in figure 17.18.

FIGURE 17.17 | Calculation of break-even point in dollars

$$X = 0.8X + \$160\,000$$
$$0.2X = \$160\,000$$
$$X = \$800\,000$$

where:

X = sales dollars at the break-even point

0.8 = variable costs as a percentage of unit selling price

$160 000 = total fixed costs per month

FIGURE 17.18 | Calculation of break-even point in units

$$\$800X = \$640X + \$160\,000$$
$$\$160X = \$160\,000$$
$$X = \mathbf{1000\ units}$$

where:

X = sales volume

$800 = unit selling price

$640 = variable cost per unit

$160 000 = total fixed costs per month

Thus, Mike's Bikes must sell 1000 units to break even. The accuracy of the calculations can be proved as shown in figure 17.19.

FIGURE 17.19 | Break-even proof

Sales (1000 × $800)		$800 000
Total costs:		
Variable (1000 × $640)	$640 000	
Fixed	160 000	800 000
Profit		$ —

Contribution margin technique

Because we know that contribution margin equals total revenues less variable costs, it follows that, at the break-even point, contribution margin must equal total fixed costs. On the basis of this relationship, the break-even point can be calculated by using either the contribution margin per unit or the contribution margin ratio.

When the contribution margin per unit is used, the formula to calculate break-even point in units is as shown in figure 17.20.

FIGURE 17.20 | Formula for break-even point in units using contribution margin

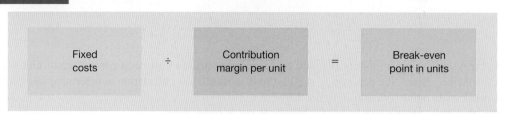

For Mike's Bikes, the contribution margin per unit is $160, as explained previously. Thus, the calculation is:

$$\$160\,000 \div \$160 = 1000\ \text{units}$$

When the contribution margin ratio is used, the formula to calculate break-even point in dollars is as shown in figure 17.21.

FIGURE 17.21 Formula for break-even point in dollars using contribution margin ratio

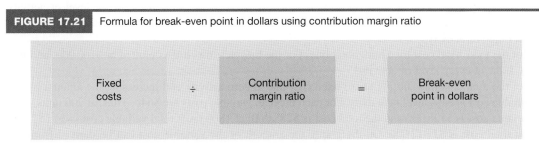

| Fixed costs | ÷ | Contribution margin ratio | = | Break-even point in dollars |

We know that the contribution margin ratio for Mike's Bikes is 20%. Thus, the calculation is:

$$\$160\,000 \div 20\% = \$800\,000$$

Graphic presentation

An effective way to derive the break-even point is to prepare a break-even graph. Because this graph also shows costs, volume and profits, it is referred to as the **cost–volume–profit (CVP) graph**.

In the graph in figure 17.22, sales volume is recorded along the horizontal axis. This axis should extend to the maximum level of expected sales. Both total revenues (sales) and total costs (fixed plus variable) are recorded on the vertical axis.

FIGURE 17.22 CVP graph, Mike's Bikes

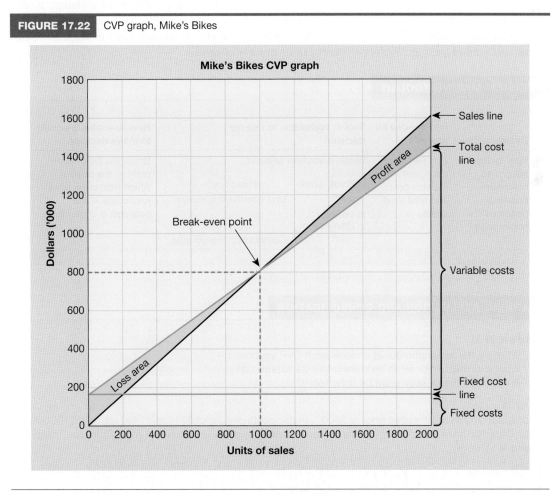

The construction of the graph, using the data for Mike's Bikes, is as follows.

1. Plot the total revenue line starting at the zero activity level. For every bicycle sold, total revenue increases by $800. For example, at 200 units, sales are $160 000, and at the upper level of activity (2000 units), sales are $1 600 000. Note that the revenue line is assumed to be linear throughout the full range of activity.

2. Plot the total fixed cost by a horizontal line. For the bicycles, this line is plotted at $160 000, and it is the same at every level of activity.

3. Plot the total cost line starting at the fixed cost line at zero activity and increasing the amount by the variable cost at each level of activity. For each bicycle, variable costs are $640. Thus, at 200 units, total variable cost is $128 000 and the total cost is $288 000; at 1800 units total variable cost is $1 152 000, and total cost is $1 312 000. On the graph, the amount of the variable cost can be derived from the difference between the total cost and fixed cost lines at each level of activity.

4. Determine the break-even point from the intersection of the total cost line and the sales line. The break-even point in dollars is found by drawing a horizontal line from the break-even point to the vertical axis. The break-even point in units is obtained by drawing a vertical line from the break-even point to the horizontal axis. For the bicycles, the break-even point is $800 000 of sales, or 1000 units. At this sales level, Mike's Bikes will cover costs but make no profit.

In addition to identifying the break-even point, the CVP graph shows both the profit and loss areas. Thus, the amount of profit or loss at each level of sales can be derived from the total sales and total cost lines.

A CVP graph is especially useful in management meetings because the effects of a change in any element in the CVP analysis can be promptly portrayed. For example, a 10% increase in selling price will change the location of the total revenue line. Similarly, the effects on total costs of wage increases to both office employees and factory workers can be quickly observed.

DECISION-MAKING TOOLKIT

Decision/issue	Info needed for analysis	Tool or technique to use for decision	How to evaluate results to make decision
How far can sales drop before the business becomes unprofitable?	Unit selling price, unit variable cost and total fixed costs	Break-even point analysis *In units:* $\text{Break-even point} = \dfrac{\text{Fixed costs}}{\text{Unit contribution margin}}$ *In dollars:* $\text{Break-even point} = \dfrac{\text{Fixed costs}}{\text{Contribution margin ratio}}$	Below the break-even point — the point at which total sales equal total costs — the business is unprofitable.

LEARNING REFLECTION AND CONSOLIDATION

Review it

1. What are the assumptions that underlie each CVP application?
2. What is contribution margin and how may it be expressed?
3. How can the break-even point be determined?

Do it

Lombardi Ltd has a unit selling price of $400, variable costs per unit of $240 and fixed costs of $160 000. Calculate the break-even point in units using (a) a mathematical equation and (b) contribution margin per unit.

Margin of safety

The margin of safety is another relationship that may be calculated in CVP analysis. **Margin of safety** is the excess of actual or expected sales above the break-even point. This relationship indicates the amount by which sales can drop before a loss is incurred. In other words, margin of safety measures the 'breathing space' or 'cushion' that a business has if expected sales fail to materialise. The margin of safety may be expressed in units or dollars or as a ratio.

The formula for stating the margin of safety in dollars is as shown in figure 17.23.

FIGURE 17.23 Formula for margin of safety in dollars

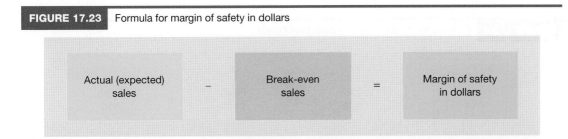

Let's continue our analysis for Mike's Bikes. Assume that the manager estimated that sales in the following month will be 1500 units or $1\,200\,000. As break-even point is 1000 units of bicycles or $800\,000, the margin of safety is:

$$\$1\,200\,000 - \$800\,000 = \$400\,000 \text{ (or 500 units @ \$800)}$$

We can also express the margin of safety as a ratio, as shown in figure 17.24.

FIGURE 17.24 Formula for margin of safety ratio

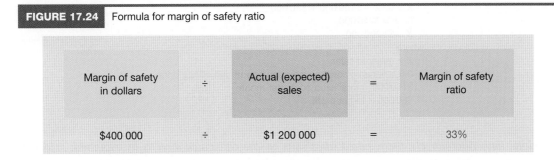

What are the implications of the margin of safety for the manager of Mike's Bikes? At an expected sales level of 1500 units, Mike's Bikes will still be profitable as long as sales do not drop by more than 500 units or 33% next month.

The higher the dollars or the percentage, the greater the margin of safety. The adequacy of the margin of safety should be evaluated by management in terms of such factors as the vulnerability of the product to competitive pressures and to downturns in the economy.

17.5 Target profit

LEARNING OBJECTIVE 17.5 Determine target profit by applying formulas.

Management usually sets a profit objective for individual product lines. This objective, called **target profit**, is extremely useful to management because it indicates the sales necessary to achieve a specified level of profit. The amount of sales necessary to achieve target profit can be determined from each of the approaches used in determining break-even sales.

Mathematical equation

We know that at the break-even point no profit or loss results for the entity. By adding a factor for target profit to the break-even equation, we obtain the formula shown in figure 17.25 for determining required sales.

FIGURE 17.25 Formula for required sales to meet target profit

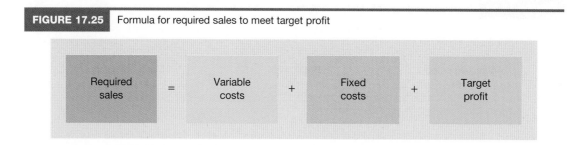

Required sales may be expressed in either sales dollars or sales units. Assuming that target profit is $80 000 for Mike's Bikes, the calculation of required sales in dollars is as shown in figure 17.26.

FIGURE 17.26 Calculation of required sales

$X = 0.8X + \$160\,000 + \$80\,000$
$0.2X = \$240\,000$
$X = \$1\,200\,000$
where:
X = required sales
0.8 = variable costs as a percentage of unit selling price
$\$160\,000$ = total fixed costs per month
$\$80\,000$ = target profit

Helpful hint: Alternatively, the required sales units can be calculated directly by using unit prices in the equation: $\$800X = \$640X + \$160\,000 + \$80\,000$; $\$160X = \$240\,000$; $X = 1500$ units.

The sales volume in units at the targeted profit level is found by dividing the sales dollars by the unit selling price ($\$1\,200\,000 \div \$800$) = 1500 units.

Contribution margin technique

As in the case of break-even sales, the sales required to meet a target profit can be calculated in either dollars or units. The formula using the contribution margin ratio is as shown in figure 17.27.

FIGURE 17.27 Formula for required sales in dollars using contribution margin ratio

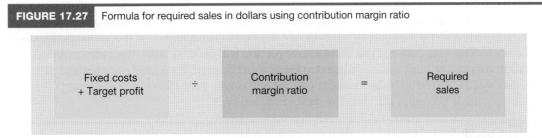

The calculation for Mike's Bikes is as follows:

$$\$240\,000 \div 20\% = \$1\,200\,000$$

Graphic presentation

The CVP graph presented in figure 17.22 can also be used to derive the sales required to meet target profit. In the profit area of the graph, the distance between the sales line and the total cost line at any point equals profit. Required sales are found by analysing the differences between the two lines until the desired profit is found.

CVP for profit planning

When the IBM personal computer (PC) was introduced, it sold for about $5000; today the same type of computer sells for much less. When oil prices rose, the break-even point for airline and transport entities increased dramatically. The point should be clear — business conditions change rapidly, and management must respond intelligently to these changes. CVP analysis can help.

To illustrate how CVP analysis can be used in responding to change, we will use the following independent situations that might occur at Mike's Bikes. Each case is based on the original bicycle monthly sales and cost data, as shown in figure 17.28.

FIGURE 17.28 Original bicycle sales and cost data

Unit selling price	$800
Unit variable cost	$640
Total fixed costs	$160 000
Break-even sales	$800 000 or 1000 units

Case I

A competitor is offering a 10% discount on the selling price of its mountain bikes. Management must decide whether to offer a similar discount. What effect will a 10% discount on selling price have on the break-even point for mountain bikes? *Answer:* A 10% discount on selling price reduces the selling price per unit to $720 [$800 − ($800 × 10%)]. Variable costs per unit remain unchanged at $640. Thus, the contribution margin per unit is $80. Assuming no change in fixed costs, break-even sales are 2000 units, calculated as shown in figure 17.29.

FIGURE 17.29 Calculation of break-even sales in units

Fixed costs	÷	Contribution margin per unit	=	Break-even sales
$160 000	÷	$80	=	2000 units

For Mike's Bikes, this change would require monthly sales to increase by 1000 units in order to break even. Mike's Bikes will need to look at how to increase the bike's contribution margin by reducing the variable costs.

Case II

To meet the continuing threat of foreign competition, management invests in new robotic equipment that will significantly lower the amount of direct labour required to make the bikes. It is estimated that total fixed costs will increase 20% and that variable cost per unit will decrease 25%. What effect will the new equipment have on the sales volume required to break even? *Answer:* Total fixed costs become $192 000 [$160 000 + (20% × $160 000)], and variable cost per unit is now $480 [$640 − (25% × $640)]. The new break-even point is 600 units, calculated as shown in figure 17.30.

FIGURE 17.30 | Revised calculation of break-even sales in units

Fixed costs	÷	Contribution margin per unit	=	Break-even sales
$192 000	÷	($800 − $480)	=	600 units

These changes appear to be advantageous for Mike's Bikes because the break-even point is reduced by 40%, or 400 units.

Case III

The main supplier of raw materials has just announced a price increase. It is estimated that the higher cost will increase the variable cost of mountain bikes by $60 per unit. Management is considering increasing the selling price to $1000. It also plans a cost-cutting program that will save $30 000 in fixed costs per month. Mike's Bikes is currently realising monthly profit of $32 000 on sales of 1200 bikes. What increase in sales will be needed to maintain the same level of profit? *Answer:* The variable cost per unit increases to $700 ($640 + $60), and fixed costs are reduced to $130 000 ($160 000 − $30 000). Because of the change in variable cost, the variable cost becomes 70% of sales ($700 ÷ $1000). Using the equation for target profit we find that required sales are $540 000, calculated as shown in figure 17.31.

FIGURE 17.31 | Calculation of required sales

Required sales = Variable costs + Fixed costs + Target profit
$X = 0.7X + \$130\,000 + \$32\,000$
$0.3X = \$162\,000$
$X = \$540\,000$

To achieve the required sales, 540 bicycles will have to be sold ($540 000 ÷ $1000). Because of the improvement in contribution margin, Mike's Bikes will need to sell only 540 bikes to earn the same level of profit. However, management will need to carefully assess the impact on sales volume of the 25% increase in selling price.

DECISION-MAKING TOOLKIT

Decision/issue	Info needed for analysis	Tool or technique to use for decision	How to evaluate results to make decision
How can a business increase its total contribution margin to improve profitability?	Data on what effect a price decrease, a fixed-cost increase, or a trade-off between fixed and variable costs would have on volume	Measurement of contribution margin at new volume levels	If contribution margin increases under proposed change, adopt change.

17.6 Using CVP analysis with multiple products

LEARNING OBJECTIVE 17.6 Explain how CVP analysis is used with multiple products.

One of the assumptions of CVP analysis is that, if more than one product is involved, the sales mix of the products remains constant. **Sales mix** is the relative combination in which an entity's products are sold. For example, if two units of Product A are sold for every one unit of Product B, the sales mix of the two products is 2:1.

Break-even sales

Break-even sales can be calculated for a mix of two or more products by determining the weighted average unit contribution margin of all the products. To demonstrate, we will assume that Mike's Bikes sells both mountain bikes and BMXs at the per-unit data shown in figure 17.32.

FIGURE 17.32 Per-unit data — sales mix

Unit data	Mountain bikes	BMXs
Unit selling price	$800	$1 150
Unit variable cost	640	830
Contribution margin	$160	$ 320
Sales mix	3	1

The total contribution margin for the sales mix of three mountain bikes to one BMX is $800, which is calculated as follows:

$$[(\$160 \times 3) + (\$320 \times 1)] = \$800$$

The weighted average unit contribution margin, which is total contribution margin divided by the number of units in the sales mix is $200, calculated as follows:

$$\$800 \div 4 \, \text{units} = \$200$$

We then use the weighted average unit contribution margin to calculate break-even sales, as shown in figure 17.33.

FIGURE 17.33 Break-even formula — sales mix

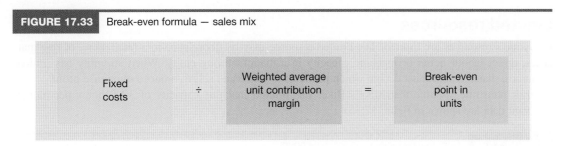

The calculation of break-even sales in units for Mike's Bikes, assuming $160 000 fixed monthly costs, is as follows:

$$\$160\,000 \div \$200 = 800 \, \text{units}$$

Note that a sales mix of 3 mountain bikes to 1 BMX means three-quarters of the units sold will be mountain bikes and one-quarter will be BMXs. Therefore, in order to break even, Mike's Bikes must sell 600 mountain bikes ($\frac{3}{4} \times 800$) and 200 BMXs ($\frac{1}{4} \times 800$). This can be verified as shown in figure 17.34.

FIGURE 17.34 | Break-even proof — sales mix

Product	Unit sales	×	Unit CM	=	Total CM
Mountain bikes	600	×	$160	=	$ 96 000
BMXs	200	×	320	=	64 000
	800				$160 000

Helpful hint: What are break-even sales in units if the sale mix is reversed?

Answer: Total contribution margin = $1120 ($160 + $960). Weighted average unit contribution margin = $280 ($1120 ÷ 4). Break-even units = 572 ($160 000 ÷ $280)

Management should continually review the entity's sales mix. At any level of units sold, profit will be greater if more high-contribution-margin units are sold than low-contribution-margin units. For Mike's Bikes, the BMXs produce the higher contribution margin. Consequently, if 500 BMXs and 300 mountain bikes are sold, profit would be higher than in the current sales mix even though total units sold has not changed. An analysis of these relationships shows that a shift from low-margin sales to high-margin sales may increase profit, even though there is a decline in total units sold. Likewise, a shift from high- to low-margin sales may result in a decrease in profit, even though there is an increase in total units sold.

Helpful hint: Continuing the preceding helpful hint: How many mountain bikes and BMXs must be sold?

Answer: Mountain bikes 143 ($572 \times \frac{1}{4}$); BMXs 429 ($572 \times \frac{3}{4}$)

DECISION-MAKING TOOLKIT

Decision/issue	Info needed for analysis	Tool or technique to use for decision	How to evaluate results to make decision
How many units of product A and product B do we need to sell to break even?	Fixed costs, weighted average contribution margin, sales mix	Break-even point in units $= \dfrac{\text{Fixed costs}}{\text{Weighted average contribution margin}}$	To determine number of units of Product A and B, allocate total units based on sales mix.

Limited resources

Everyone's resources are limited. The limited resource may be floor space in a retail store, or raw materials, direct labour hours or machine capacity in a manufacturing entity. When an entity has limited resources, management must decide which products to make and sell in order to maximise profit.

To demonstrate, assume that Mike's Bikes has limited machine capacity of 3000 hours per month. Relevant data are shown in figure 17.35.

FIGURE 17.35 | Contribution margin and machine hours

	Mountain bikes	BMXs
Contribution margin per unit	$160	$320
Machine hours required per unit	2	5

Helpful hint: CM alone is not enough to make this decision. The key factor is CM per unit of limited resource.

The BMXs may appear to be more profitable because they have a higher contribution margin ($320) than the mountain bikes ($160). However, note that the mountain bikes take fewer machine hours to produce than do the BMXs. Therefore, it is necessary to find the contribution margin per unit of limited resource; in this case, contribution margin per machine hour. This is obtained by dividing the contribution margin per unit of each product by the number of units of the limited resource required for each product, as shown in figure 17.36.

Contribution margin per unit of limited resource

	Mountain bikes	BMXs
Contribution margin per unit (a)	$160	$320
Machine hours required per unit (b)	2	5
Contribution margin per machine hour (a) ÷ (b)	$ 80	$ 64

The calculation shows that the mountain bikes have a higher contribution margin per unit of limited resource. This would suggest that, given sufficient demand for mountain bikes, the company should shift the sales mix to mountain bikes or increase machine capacity. If Mike's Bikes is able to increase machine capacity from 3000 hours to 4000 hours, the additional 1000 hours could be used to produce either the mountain bikes or BMXs. The total contribution margin under each alternative is found by multiplying the machine hours by the contribution margin per unit of limited resource, as shown in figure 17.37.

Incremental analysis — calculation of total contribution margin

	Produce mountain bikes	Produce BMXs
Machine hours (a)	1 000	1 000
Contribution margin per machine hour (b)	$ 80	$ 64
Contribution margin (a) × (b)	$80 000	$64 000

From this analysis, we can see that to maximise profit, all of the increased capacity should be used to make and sell the mountain bikes.

DECISION-MAKING TOOLKIT

Decision/issue	Info needed for analysis	Tool or technique to use for decision	How to evaluate results to make decision
How many units of products A and B should we produce in light of a limited resource?	Contribution margin per unit, limited resource required per unit	Contribution margin per unit of limited resource = $\dfrac{\text{Contribution margin per unit}}{\text{Limited resource per unit}}$	Any additional capacity of limited resource should be applied towards the product with higher contribution margin per unit of limited resource.

17.7 CVP statement of profit or loss

LEARNING OBJECTIVE 17.7 Describe the essential features of a CVP statement of profit or loss.

As you have learned, cost behaviour and contribution margin are key factors in CVP analysis. Because management makes its decisions on these factors, it often wants the results of these decisions reported in a similar format. This has led to the development *for internal use only* of a CVP or contribution margin format for the statement of profit or loss. The **CVP statement of profit or loss** classifies costs and expenses as variable or fixed and specifically reports contribution margin in the body of the statement. This is in contrast to the statement of profit or loss traditionally prepared for external use, in which no disclosure is made of the behaviour of costs and expenses. In the traditional statement, costs and expenses are classified usually by function, such as cost of sales, selling expenses, administrative expenses and financial expenses, or by nature, such as employee expenses, depreciation expense and changes in inventory.

To illustrate the CVP statement of profit or loss, assume that Mike's Bikes reaches its target profit of $80 000 (see figure 17.26 and surrounding text). From an analysis of the transactions, figure 17.38 shows the information obtained about the $1 120 000 of costs that were incurred in June.

FIGURE 17.38 Assumed cost and expense data

	Variable	Fixed	Total
Cost of sales	$585 000	$100 000	$ 685 000
Selling expenses	292 500	30 000	322 500
Administrative expenses	82 500	30 000	112 500
	$960 000	$160 000	$1 120 000

The CVP statement of profit or loss and the conventional statement based on these data are shown side by side for comparative purposes in figure 17.39.

Note that profit is the same ($80 000) in both of the statements. The major difference is the format for the expenses. As illustrated, the CVP statement classifies costs and expenses as either variable or fixed. Another difference is that the traditional statement shows gross profit, whereas the CVP statement shows contribution margin. Study the CVP format carefully. It will be used in the remaining chapters, and is often used by entities in internal reporting to management.

FIGURE 17.39	Traditional versus CVP statement of profit or loss

MIKE'S BIKES
Statement of profit or loss
for the month ended 30 June 2019

Traditional format			CVP format		
Sales		$1 200 000	Sales		$1 200 000
Less: Cost of sales		(685 000)	Variable expenses		
Gross profit		515 000	Cost of sales	$585 000	
Operating expenses			Selling expenses	292 500	
Selling expenses	$322 500		Administrative expenses	82 500	
Administrative expenses	112 500		*Less:* Total variable expenses		(960 000)
Less: Total operating expenses		(435 000)	**Contribution margin**		240 000
Profit		$ 80 000	Fixed expenses		
			Cost of sales	100 000	
			Selling expenses	30 000	
			Administrative expenses	30 000	
			Less: Total fixed expenses		(160 000)
			Profit		$ 80 000

Helpful hint: Why are statements of profit or loss in CVP format produced for internal use only?

Answer: CVP statements of profit or loss present highly sensitive information such as the breakdown of costs and expenses. No business would want external parties, particularly competitors, to obtain this information.

LEARNING REFLECTION AND CONSOLIDATION

Review it

1. What is the formula for calculating the margin of safety (a) in dollars and (b) as a ratio?
2. Explain how an entity that shifts its sales mix might actually increase its profit even though the total number of units it sells declines.
3. How does a CVP statement of profit or loss differ from a traditional statement of profit or loss?

USING THE DECISION-MAKING TOOLKIT

B.T. Hogan Ltd, maker of high-quality pipes, has experienced steady growth over the last 6 years. However, increased competition has led Ian Lee, the CEO, to believe that an aggressive campaign is needed next year to maintain the entity's present growth. The accountant has presented Ian with the following data for the current year, 2019, for use in preparing next year's advertising campaign:

Cost schedules	
Variable costs	
Direct labour per pipe	$ 8.00
Direct materials	4.00
Variable overhead	3.00
Variable cost per pipe	$15.00

▶

Fixed costs	
Manufacturing	$ 25 000
Selling	40 000
Administrative	70 000
Total fixed costs	$135 000
Selling price per pipe	$ 25.00
Expected sales, 2019 (20 000 pipes)	$500 000

Ian has set the sales target for the year 2020 at a level of $550 000 (22 000 pipes).

Required

(Ignore any income tax considerations.)

(a) What is the projected operating profit for 2019?

(b) What is the contribution margin per unit and ratio for 2019?

(c) What is the break-even point in units for 2019?

(d) Ian believes that to attain the sales target in the year 2020 requires an additional selling expense of $10 000 for advertising in 2020, with all other costs remaining constant. What will be the break-even point in dollar sales for 2020 if the entity spends the additional $10 000?

(e) If the entity spends the additional $10 000 for advertising in 2020, what is the sales level in dollars required to equal the 2019 operating profit?

Solution

(a)

Expected sales	$500 000
Less:	
Variable cost (20 000 pipes × $15)	300 000
Fixed costs	135 000
Projected operating profit	$ 65 000

(b)

Selling price per pipe	$25
Variable cost per pipe	15
Contribution margin per unit	$10
CM ratio ($10 ÷ $25)	40%

(c) Fixed costs ÷ Contribution margin per unit = Break-even point in units

$$\$135\,000 \div \$10 = 13\,500 \text{ units}$$

(d) Fixed costs ÷ Contribution margin ratio = Break-even point in dollars

$$\$145\,000 \div 40\% \text{ from (b)} = \$362\,500.$$

Calculated as follows:

Fixed costs (from 2019)	$135 000
Additional advertising expense	10 000
Fixed costs (2020)	$145 000

(e) Required sales = Variable costs + Fixed costs + Target profit

$$X = 0.6X + \$145\,000 + \$65\,000 \text{ (from (a))}$$
$$0.40X = \$210\,000$$
$$X = \$525\,000$$

SUMMARY

17.1 Distinguish between variable, fixed and mixed cost behaviour.
Variable costs are costs that vary in total directly and proportionately with changes in the activity level. Fixed costs are costs that remain the same in total regardless of changes in the activity level. Mixed costs contain both a variable cost element and a fixed cost element. Mixed costs change in total but not proportionately with changes in the activity level.

17.2 Explain the difference between absorption costing and variable costing.
Under absorption costing, fixed manufacturing costs are product costs; under variable costing, fixed manufacturing costs are period costs.

17.3 Explain the five basic assumptions of cost–volume–profit (CVP) analysis.
The five assumptions of CVP analysis are: (a) linearity of costs and revenues, (b) costs must be classified as either variable or fixed, (c) changes in activity are the only factors that affect costs, (d) all units produced are sold, and (e) when more than one type of product is sold, total sales will be in a constant sales mix.

17.4 Indicate the meaning of contribution margin and identify break-even point and the use of break-even analysis.
Contribution margin is the amount of revenue remaining after deducting variable costs. It can be expressed as a per-unit amount or as a ratio. The break-even point can be (a) calculated from a mathematical equation, (b) calculated by using a contribution margin technique, and (c) derived from a CVP graph. Break-even analysis is useful in deciding whether to introduce new product lines, change sales prices on established products, or enter new market areas.

17.5 Determine target profit by applying formulas.
One formula is: Required sales = Variable costs + Fixed costs + Target profit. Another formula is: Fixed costs + Target profit ÷ Contribution margin ratio = Required sales.

17.6 Explain how CVP analysis is used with multiple products.
Break-even sales are determined using the weighted average unit contribution margin of all products. When an entity has limited resources, it is necessary to find the contribution margin per unit of limited resource.

17.7 Describe the essential features of a CVP statement of profit or loss.
The CVP statement of profit or loss classifies costs and expenses as variable or fixed and reports contribution margin in the body of the statement.

DECISION-MAKING TOOLKIT — A SUMMARY

DECISION-MAKING TOOLKIT

Decision/issue	Info needed for analysis	Tool or technique to use for decision	How to evaluate results to make decision
What was the contribution towards fixed costs and profit from each unit sold?	Selling price per unit and variable cost per unit	Contribution margin per unit = Unit selling price − Unit variable cost	Every unit sold will increase profit by the contribution margin.

Decision/issue	Info needed for analysis	Tool or technique to use for decision	How to evaluate results to make decision
How far can sales drop before the business becomes unprofitable?	Unit selling price, unit variable cost and total fixed costs	Break-even point analysis *In units:* $$\text{Break-even point} = \frac{\text{Fixed costs}}{\text{Unit contribution margin}}$$ *In dollars:* $$\text{Break-even point} = \frac{\text{Fixed costs}}{\text{Contribution margin ratio}}$$	Below the break-even point — the point at which total sales equal total costs — the business is unprofitable.
How can a business increase its total contribution margin to improve profitability?	Data on what effect a price decrease, a fixed-cost increase, or a trade-off between fixed and variable costs would have on volume	Measurement of contribution margin at new volume levels	If contribution margin increases under proposed change, adopt change.
How many units of product A and product B do we need to sell to break even?	Fixed costs, weighted average contribution margin, sales mix	$$\text{Break-even point in units} = \frac{\text{Fixed costs}}{\text{Weighted average contribution margin}}$$	To determine number of units of Product A and B, allocate total units based on sales mix.
How many units of products A and B should we produce in light of a limited resource?	Contribution margin per unit, limited resource required per unit	$$\frac{\text{Contribution margin per unit of limited resource}}{} = \frac{\text{Contribution margin per unit}}{\text{Limited resource per unit}}$$	Any additional capacity of limited resource should be applied towards the product with higher contribution margin per unit of limited resource.

KEY TERMS

absorption costing A costing approach in which all manufacturing costs are charged to the product — direct materials, direct labour, and both variable and fixed manufacturing overhead.

activity index The activity that causes changes in the behaviour of costs.

break-even point The level of activity at which total revenues equal total costs.

contribution margin (CM) The amount of revenue remaining after deducting variable costs.

cost behaviour analysis The study of how specific costs respond to changes in the level of activity within an entity.

cost–volume–profit (CVP) analysis The study of the effects of changes in costs and volume on an entity's profits.

cost–volume–profit (CVP) graph A graph showing the relationship between costs, volume and profits.

cost–volume–profit (CVP) statement of profit or loss A statement for internal use that classifies costs and expenses as fixed or variable and reports contribution margin in the body of the statement.

fixed costs Costs that remain the same in total regardless of changes in the activity level within the relevant range.

margin of safety The difference between actual or expected sales and sales at the break-even point.

mixed costs Costs that contain both a variable and a fixed cost element and change in total, but not proportionately, with changes in the activity level.

relevant range The range of the activity index over which the entity expects to operate during the year.

sales mix The relative combination in which an entity's products are sold.

target profit The profit objective for individual product lines; it indicates the sales necessary to achieve a specified level of profit.

variable costing A costing approach in which only direct materials, direct labour and variable manufacturing overhead costs are product costs and fixed manufacturing overhead costs are period costs (expenses).

variable costs Costs that vary in total directly and proportionately with changes in the activity level within the relevant range.

DEMONSTRATION PROBLEM

Morris Ltd makes calculators that sell for $20 each. For the coming year, management expects fixed costs to total $220 000 and variable costs to be $9.00 per unit.

Required
(a) Calculate break-even sales in dollars using the mathematical equation.
(b) Calculate break-even sales using the contribution margin (CM) ratio.
(c) Calculate the margin of safety percentage assuming actual sales are $500 000.
(d) Calculate the sales required to earn profit of $165 000.

PROBLEM-SOLVING STRATEGIES
1. Know the formulas.
2. Recognise that variable costs change with sales volume; fixed costs do not.
3. Avoid calculation errors.
4. Prove your answers.

SOLUTION TO DEMONSTRATION PROBLEM
(a) Break-even sales = Variable costs + Fixed costs

$$X = 0.45X + \$220\,000$$
$$0.55X = \$220\,000$$
$$X = \$400\,000$$

(b) Contribution margin per unit = Unit selling price − Unit variable costs

$$\$11 = \$20 - \$9$$

Contribution margin ratio = Contribution margin per unit ÷ Unit selling price

$$55\% = \$11 \div \$20$$

Break-even sales = Fixed cost ÷ Contribution margin ratio

$$X = \$220\,000 \div 55\%$$
$$X = \$400\,000$$

(c) Margin of safety = (Actual sales − Break-even sales) ÷ Actual sales

$$= (\$500\,000 - \$400\,000) \div \$500\,000$$
$$= 20\%$$

(d) Required sales = Variable costs + Fixed costs + Profit

$$X = 0.45X + \$220\,000 + \$165\,000$$
$$0.55X = \$385\,000$$
$$X = \$700\,000$$

SELF-STUDY QUESTIONS

17.1 Variable costs are costs that: **LO1**
(a) vary in total directly and proportionately with changes in the activity level.
(b) remain the same per unit at every activity level.
(c) none of the above.
(d) both (a) and (b) above.

17.2 The relevant range is: **LO1**
(a) the range of activity in which variable costs will be curvilinear.
(b) the range of activity in which fixed costs will be curvilinear.
(c) the range over which the entity expects to operate during a year.
(d) usually from zero to 100% of operating capacity.

17.3 Mixed costs consist of a: **LO1**
(a) variable cost element and a fixed cost element.
(b) fixed cost element and a controllable cost element.
(c) relevant cost element and a controllable cost element.
(d) variable cost element and a relevant cost element.

17.4 Under variable costing, fixed manufacturing costs are classified as: **LO2**
(a) period costs.
(b) product costs.
(c) both (a) and (b).
(d) neither (a) nor (b).

17.5 Profit would be higher under absorption costing than under variable costing when: **LO2**
(a) units produced are less than units sold.
(b) units produced are more than units sold.
(c) units produced are the same as units sold.
(d) both (a) and (b).

17.6 One of the following is *not* involved in CVP analysis. That factor is: **LO3**
(a) sales mix.
(b) unit selling prices.
(c) fixed costs per unit.
(d) volume or level of activity.

17.7 Contribution margin: **LO4**
(a) is revenue remaining after deducting variable costs.
(b) may be expressed as contribution margin per unit.
(c) is selling price less cost of sales.
(d) both (a) and (b) above.

17.8 Gossen Pty Ltd is planning to sell 200 000 pliers for $4.00 per unit. The contribution margin ratio is 25%. If Gossen will break even at this level of sales, what are the fixed costs?   **LO4**
(a) $100 000.
(b) $160 000.
(c) $200 000.
(d) $300 000.

17.9 Marshall & Co. had actual sales of $1 000 000 when break-even sales were $400 000. What is the margin of safety ratio? **LO4**
   (a) 25%.
   (b) 30%.
   (c) 60%.
   (d) 40%.

17.10 The mathematical equation for calculating required sales to obtain target profit is: Required sales = **LO5**
   (a) Variable costs + Target profit.
   (b) Variable costs + Fixed costs + Target profit.
   (c) Fixed costs + Target profit.
   (d) No correct answer is given.

17.11 Assume Domino's sells 5 Supremes for every 3 Hawaiian and 2 Meatosaurus pizzas. What is the percentage of Supreme pizzas in the sales mix? **LO6**
   (a) 5%.
   (b) 30%.
   (c) 20%.
   (d) 50%.

17.12 Cournot Ltd sells 100 000 wrenches for $10.00 a unit. Fixed costs are $300 000 and profit is $200 000. What should be reported as variable expenses in the CVP statement of profit or loss? **LO7**
   (a) $700 000.
   (b) $900 000.
   (c) $500 000.
   (d) $1 000 000.

QUESTIONS

17.1 (a) What is cost behaviour analysis?
   (b) Why is cost behaviour analysis important to management?

17.2 (a) Jenny Beason asks your help in understanding the term 'activity index'. Explain the meaning and importance of this term for Jenny.
   (b) State the two ways that variable costs may be defined.

17.3 Distinguish between absorption costing and variable costing.

17.4 Ray Chang claims that the relevant range concept is important only for variable costs.
   (a) Explain the relevant range concept.
   (b) Do you agree with Ray's claim? Explain.

17.5 Explain the five basic assumptions of CVP analysis.

17.6 In Eusey Ltd, the Speedo pocket calculator sells for $40, and variable costs per unit are estimated to be $22. What is the contribution margin per unit and the contribution margin ratio?

17.7 Inwood Pty Ltd's break-even sales are $600 000. Assuming fixed costs are $210 000, what sales dollars are needed to achieve a target profit of $56 000?

17.8 Calculate the weighted average contribution margin for the following sales mix:

	Product A	Product B
Selling price	$20	$30
Unit variable cost	$12	$18
Sales mix	3	4

17.9 How is the contribution margin per unit of limited resources calculated?

17.10 The traditional statement of profit or loss for Reeves Ltd shows sales $900 000, cost of sales $500 000 and operating expenses $200 000. Assuming all costs and expenses are 70% variable and 30% fixed, prepare a CVP statement of profit or loss including contribution margin.

BRIEF EXERCISES

BE17.1 Classify costs as variable, fixed or mixed. **LO1**

Monthly production costs in Kiwi & Co. for two levels of production are as follows:

Cost	2000 units	4000 units
Indirect labour	$10 000	$20 000
Supervisors' salaries	5 000	5 000
Maintenance	3 000	3 600

Indicate which costs are variable, fixed and mixed, and give the reason for each answer.

BE17.2 Explain the difference in profit calculation between absorption costing and variable costing. **LO2**

Your friend Kate, who has recently completed a massage therapy course, is considering starting a mobile massage therapy business. Explain to Kate whether absorption and variable costing will give different profit figures for her business.

BE17.3 Determine missing amounts for contribution margin. **LO4**

Determine the missing amounts.

	Unit selling price	Unit variable costs	Contribution margin per unit	Contribution margin ratio
1.	$400	$240	(a)	(b)
2.	$700	(c)	$140	(d)
3.	(e)	(f)	$480	40%

BE17.4 Calculate the break-even point. **LO4**

Smart Ltd has a unit selling price of $500, variable costs per unit of $325 and fixed costs of $140 000. Calculate the break-even point in units using (a) a mathematical equation and (b) contribution margin per unit.

BE17.5 Calculate sales for target profit. **LO5**

In Ranch Ltd variable costs are 75% of sales, fixed costs are $180 000 and management's profit goal is $60 000. Calculate the required sales needed to achieve management's target profit of $60 000. (Use the mathematical equation approach.)

BE17.6 Prepare CVP statement of profit or loss. **LO7**

Whitehead Manufacturing Ltd has sales of $2 300 000 for the first quarter of 2019. In making the sales, the entity incurred the following costs and expenses:

	Variable	Fixed
Cost of sales	$785 000	$600 000
Selling expenses	195 000	80 000
Administrative expenses	78 000	112 000

Prepare a CVP statement of profit or loss for the quarter ended 31 March 2019.

BE17.7 Calculate break-even sales units for two products. **LO6**

Loos Pty Ltd sells three units of AA to one unit of BB; the two products have contribution margins of $100 and $200, respectively. Fixed costs are $300 000. Calculate the unit sales at the break-even point. How many units of each product must be sold?

BE17.8 Show allocation of limited resources. **LO6**

In Cruz Ltd, data concerning two products are: contribution margin per unit — Product A $10, Product B $12; machine hours required for one unit — Product A 2, Product B 3. Calculate the contribution margin per unit of limited resource for each product.

EXERCISES

E17.1 Define terms used in CVP analysis. **LO1, 2, 4**

Complete the following statements with one of the terms listed below (some terms may not be used):

Margin of safety	Total fixed costs	Mixed cost
Unit variable cost	Contribution margin	Total variable cost
Absorption costing	Variable cost	Break-even point

(a) _____ remain unchanged when activity level changes within the relevant range.
(b) The excess of selling price over variable costs is called the _____.
(c) Fixed manufacturing overhead is included in product costs under _____.
(d) An activity level where total revenues equal total costs is termed _____.
(e) Direct labour is an example of a _____.
(f) _____ measures the excess of sales over break-even sales volume.

E17.2 Define and classify variable, fixed, and mixed costs. **LO1**

Massey & Co. manufactures a single product. Annual production costs incurred in the manufacturing process are shown below for two levels of production:

	Costs incurred			
Production in units	**5000**		**10 000**	
Production costs	**Total cost**	**Cost/unit**	**Total cost**	**Cost/unit**
Direct materials	$8 250	$1.65	$16 500	$1.65
Direct labour	9 500	1.90	19 000	1.90
Electricity	1 400	0.28	2 300	0.23
Rent	4 000	0.80	4 000	0.40
Maintenance	800	0.16	1 100	0.11
Supervisors' salaries	1 000	0.20	1 000	0.10

Required

(a) Define the terms variable costs, fixed costs and mixed costs.
(b) Classify each cost above as either variable, fixed or mixed.

E17.3 Calculate cost and prepare a statement of profit or loss under variable costing. **LO2**

Deskmate Ltd manufactures and distributes printers. The following costs are available for the year ended 30 June 2019:

Variable costs per unit	
Direct materials	$60
Direct labour	45
Variable manufacturing overhead	30
Variable selling and administrative expenses	15
Annual fixed costs and expenses	
Manufacturing overhead	$150 000
Selling and administrative expenses	50 000
Selling price	$300
Number of units produced	2 500
Number of units sold	1 500
Finished goods inventory, 1 July 2018	0

Required

(a) Calculate the manufacturing cost per unit of printer, using variable costing.

(b) Prepare a 2019 statement of profit or loss for Deskmate Ltd, using variable costing.

E17.4 **Calculate contribution margin, break-even point and margin of safety.** **LO4**

In the month of March, Maria's Beauty Salon gave 2800 haircuts, shampoos and colour treatments at an average price of $40. During the month, fixed costs were $21 000 and variable costs were 70% of sales.

Required

(a) Determine the contribution margin in dollars, per unit and as a ratio.

(b) Using the contribution margin technique, calculate the break-even point in dollars and in units.

(c) Calculate the margin of safety in dollars and as a ratio.

E17.5 **Prepare a CVP graph and calculate break-even point and margin of safety.** **LO4**

True & Co. estimates that variable costs will be 50% of sales and fixed costs will total $700 000. The selling price of the product is $4.

Required

(a) Use an Excel spreadsheet to prepare a CVP graph, assuming maximum sales of $3 200 000. (*Note:* Use $400 000 increments for sales and costs and 100 000 increments for units.)

(b) Calculate the break-even point in (1) units and (2) dollars.

(c) Calculate the margin of safety in (1) dollars and (2) as a ratio, assuming actual sales are $2 million.

E17.6 **Calculate variable cost per unit, contribution margin ratio, and increase in fixed costs.** **LO4**

In 2019, Wiggins Ltd had a break-even point of $350 000 based on a selling price of $7 per unit and fixed costs of $105 000. In 2020, the selling price and the variable cost per unit did not change, but the break-even point increased to $455 000.

Required

(a) Calculate the variable cost per unit and the contribution margin ratio for 2019.

(b) Calculate the increase in fixed costs for 2020.

E17.7 **Calculate various components to derive target profit under different assumptions.** **LO5**

Vowell Ltd had $90 000 profit in 2018 when the selling price per unit was $150, the variable costs per unit were $90 and the fixed costs were $630 000. Management expects per-unit data and total fixed costs to remain the same in 2019. The CEO of Vowell Ltd is under pressure from shareholders to increase profit by $60 000 in 2019.

Required

(a) Calculate the number of units sold in 2018.

(b) Calculate the number of units that would have to be sold in 2019 to reach the shareholders' desired profit level.

(c) Assume that Vowell Ltd sells the same number of units in 2019 as it did in 2018. What would the selling price have to be to reach the shareholders' desired profit level?

E17.8 **Calculate profits under different alternatives.** **LO4**

Angel Ltd reports the following operating results for the month of August: Sales $400 000 (units 5000), variable costs $290 000 and fixed costs $90 000. Management is considering the independent courses of action shown below to increase profit.

1. Increase selling price by 10% with no change in total variable costs.

2. Reduce variable costs to 62% of sales.

3. Reduce fixed costs by $10 000.

Required

Calculate the profit to be earned under each alternative. Which course of action will produce the highest profit?

E17.9 Calculate profits under different alternatives. LO4

Pepper Ltd reports the following operating results for the month of April 2018: Sales $900 000 (units 10 000), variable costs $630 000 and fixed costs $230 000. Management is considering the following independent courses of action to increase profit.

1. Increase selling price by 5% with no change in total variable costs.
2. Reduce variable costs to 65% of sales.
3. Reduce fixed costs by $30 000.

Required

Calculate the profit to be earned under each alternative. Write a short memo to the CEO of Pepper Ltd to suggest which of the above options you would recommend.

E17.10 Calculate sales mix, weighted average unit contribution margin, and break-even point. LO6

The following information is selected from the records of Burnie Ltd, which produces and sells two products:

	Product X	Product Y
Selling price per unit	$11.00	$18.00
Units sold	80 000	40 000
Variable manufacturing cost per units	$4.00	$8.00

Fixed manufacturing overhead costs are $256 000 and fixed selling and administrative expenses are $80 000.

Required

(a) Calculate the sales mix for Burnie Ltd.
(b) Calculate the weighted average unit contribution margin.
(c) Calculate the break-even point in units, assuming the sales mix calculated in part (a).

E17.11 Calculate and prove the break-even point in units with sales mix. LO6

The Home Appliance Centre sells three models of Super Clean dishwashers. Selling price and variable cost data for the models are as follows:

	Economy	Standard	Deluxe
Unit selling price	$500	$650	$800
Unit variable costs	$400	$500	$600
Expected sales volume (units)	500	300	200

Required

(a) Calculate the break-even point in units, assuming total fixed costs are $297 000.
(b) Prove the correctness of your answer.

E17.12 Calculate contribution margin and determine the product to be manufactured. LO6

Sensor Pty Ltd manufactures and sells three products. Relevant per unit data concerning each product are given below:

	Product		
	A	B	C
Selling price	$8	$12	$14
Variable costs and expenses	$3	$ 8.50	$12
Machine hours to produce	2	1	2

Required

(a) Calculate the contribution margin per unit of the limited resource (machine hour) for each product.
(b) Assuming 1500 additional machine hours are available, which product should be manufactured?

(c) Prepare an analysis showing the total contribution margin if the additional hours are (1) divided equally among the products, and (2) allocated entirely to the product identified in (b) above.

E17.13 Prepare a CVP statement of profit or loss before and after changes in business environment. **LO6**

Chalet Ltd had sales in 2019 of $1 500 000 on 60 000 units. Variable costs totalled $720 000, and fixed costs totalled $500 000.

A new raw material is available that will decrease the variable costs per unit by 20% (or $2.40). However, to process the new raw material, fixed operating costs will increase by $50 000. Management feels that one-half of the decline in the variable costs per unit should be passed on to customers in the form of a sales price reduction. The marketing department expects that this sales price reduction will result in a 5% increase in the number of units sold.

Required

Prepare a CVP statement of profit or loss for 2019, assuming the changes are made as described.

PROBLEM SET A

PSA17.1 Determine variable and fixed costs, calculate break-even point, prepare a CVP graph, and determine profit. **LO1, 4**

May Wong owns the Cute Nails Salon. She employs seven manicurists and pays each a base rate of $1350 per month. One of the manicurists serves as the manager and receives an extra $600 per month. In addition to the base rate, each manicurist also receives a commission of $7.00 per client.

Other costs are as follows:

Advertising	$300 per month
Rent	$800 per month + 0.50 per manicure
Nail supplies	$0.50 per nail ($5.00 per manicure)
Power	$280 per month
Magazines	$45 per month
Depreciation	$400 per month

May currently charges $25 per manicure.

Required

(a) Determine the variable cost per manicure and the total monthly fixed costs.

(b) Calculate the break-even point in units and dollars.

(c) Use an Excel spreadsheet to prepare a CVP graph, assuming a maximum of 1800 manicures in a month. Use increments of 300 manicures on the horizontal axis and $7500 on the vertical axis.

(d) Determine profit, assuming 1500 manicures are given in a month.

PSA17.2 Prepare statements of profit or loss under absorption and variable costing. **LO2**

The following information relates to Poullas Ltd for the year ended 30 June 2019, the entity's first year of operation. During the year Poullas produced 200 000 units and sold 170 000 units. In 2020 the production and sales levels were reversed. In each year, selling price was $120, variable manufacturing costs were 70% of the sales price of units produced, variable selling expenses were 10% of the selling price of units sold, fixed manufacturing costs were $2 000 000 and fixed administrative expenses were $1 800 000.

Required

(a) Prepare comparative statements of profit or loss for each year using variable costing.

(b) Prepare comparative statements of profit or loss for each year using absorption costing.

(c) Reconcile the differences each year in profit from operations under the two costing approaches.

PSA17.3 Prepare statement of profit or loss under absorption and variable costing.   **LO2**

Karming Metal Ltd produces the steel wire that goes into the production of paperclips. In 2019, the first year of operations, Karming produced 40 000 kilometres of wire and sold 30 000 kilometres. In 2020, the production and sales results were exactly reversed. In each year, the selling price per kilometre was $80, variable manufacturing costs were 20% of the sales price, variable selling expenses were $8.00 per kilometre sold, fixed manufacturing costs were $1 200 000, and fixed administrative expenses were $200 000.

Required

(a) Prepare comparative statements of profit or loss for each year using variable costing.

(b) Prepare comparative statements of profit or loss for each year using absorption costing.

(c) Reconcile the differences each year in profit from operations under the two costing approaches.

PSA17.4 Calculate product cost and prepare statements of profit or loss, using absorption costing and variable costing.   **LO2**

Rain Heaven Ltd is a start-up company manufacturing umbrellas. The following data is an extract from the first month's operation:

Unit selling price	$40
Unit variable manufacturing costs	15
Unit variable selling and administrative expense	4
Fixed manufacturing overhead	10 000
Fixed selling and administrative expenses	8 000
Number of umbrellas produced	2 000
Number of umbrellas sold	1 000

Required

(a) Calculate the manufacturing cost of one unit of umbrella using:

1. absorption costing.
2. variable costing.

(b) Prepare a statement of profit or loss for Rain Heaven Ltd for the month ended 31 January 2018 using:

1. absorption costing.
2. variable costing.

(c) Explain why profits are different under the two costing methods.

PSA17.5 Prepare a CVP statement of profit or loss, calculate break-even point, contribution margin ratio, margin of safety ratio and sales for target profit.   **LO4, 5, 7**

Tyson Ltd bottles and distributes NO-KAL, a diet soft drink. The beverage is sold for 40 cents per 600 mL bottle to retailers, who charge customers 60 cents per bottle. At full (100%) plant capacity, management estimates the following revenues and costs:

Net sales	$1 800 000	Selling expenses—variable	$80 000
Direct materials	400 000	Selling expenses—fixed	65 000
Direct labour	280 000	Administrative expenses—variable	20 000
Manufacturing overhead—variable	300 000	Administrative expenses—fixed	52 000
Manufacturing overhead—fixed	283 000		

Required

(a) Prepare a CVP statement of profit or loss for 2019 based on management's estimates.

(b) Calculate the break-even point in (1) units and (2) dollars.

(c) Calculate the contribution margin ratio and the margin of safety ratio (round to nearest percentages).

(d) Determine the sales required to earn profit of $150 000.

PSA17.6 Calculate break-even point under alternative courses of action.   **LO5**

Cruz Manufacturing Ltd's sales slumped badly in 2019. For the first time in its history, it operated at a loss. The entity's statement of profit or loss showed the following results from selling 600 000 units of product: net sales $2 400 000; total costs and expenses $2 610 000; and net loss $210 000. Costs and expenses consisted of the following:

	Total	Variable	Fixed
Cost of sales	$2 100 000	$1 440 000	$ 660 000
Selling expenses	300 000	72 000	228 000
Administrative expenses	210 000	48 000	162 000
	$2 610 000	$1 560 000	$1 050 000

Management is considering the following independent alternatives for 2020.

1. Increase unit selling price 25% with no change in costs, expenses and sales volume.
2. Change the compensation of salespersons from fixed annual salaries totalling $210 000 to total salaries of $70 000 plus a 3% commission on net sales.
3. Purchase new high-tech machinery that will change the proportion between variable and fixed costs of sales to 60% variable and 40% fixed.

Required

(a) Calculate the break-even point in dollars for 2019.

(b) Calculate the break-even point in dollars under each of the alternative courses of action (round to nearest percentage). Which course of action do you recommend?

PSA17.7 Calculate fixed costs, contribution margin and break-even point.   **LO4**

You are interested in setting up a coffee kiosk called Mix n Match on the university's campus. After consulting with your parents who own a café in the city, you have gathered the following information:

Initial investments required:	
Coffee stand	$ 8 000
Coffee machine	4 000
	$12 000

Your parents have suggested that the coffee stand and coffee machine can last for 4 years or a total of 30 000 cups of coffee, after which they will need to be replaced. The space outside the library is available for lease from the university. Because of the prime location, you will have to pay a premium for the rent at $800 per month. You plan to charge $3.50 for each cup of coffee and the estimated variable cost per cup of coffee is $1.50.

Required

(a) Calculate the total monthly fixed costs for Mix n Match. (*Hint:* You will need to calculate the depreciation of your initial investments based on straight-line depreciation.)

(b) What is the unit contribution margin and contribution margin ratio? How do you interpret this ratio?

(c) How many cups of coffee do you have to sell in a month to break even?

PSA17.8 Calculate fixed costs, contribution margin and break-even point in sales mix.   **LO4, 6**

Continue with the data from PSA17.7. After 6 months of operation, coffee sales for Mix n Match reached 1000 cups last month. You have observed that the line of customers queuing up to place and pick up drink orders is getting longer and longer. And you are worried that the long line may turn some customers away. You are also planning to add fresh juice to the kiosk. Your new expansion plan will require an additional investment of $12 000 (depreciated over 4 years, with no residual value). The extension will incur a higher rent expense from the university of another $1100 per month.

Estimated sales and costs for coffee and juice are:

	Coffee	Juice
Selling price	3.5	4.5
Unit variable costs	1.5	1.5
Sales mix	3	2

Required

(a) Calculate the new total monthly fixed costs for Mix n Match.

(b) What is the contribution margin for the sales mix? How do you interpret this figure?

(c) What is the break-even point for the sales mix? Show the profit at the break-even point to confirm the accuracy of your break-even point calculation.

PSA17.9 **Calculate break-even point and margin of safety ratio and prepare a CVP statement of profit or loss before and after changes in business environment.** **LO4, 7**

Kathy Short is the advertising manager for Value Shoe Store. She is currently working on a major promotional campaign. Her ideas include the installation of a new lighting system and increased display space that will add $48 000 in fixed costs to the $240 000 currently spent. In addition, Kathy is proposing that a 5% price decrease ($40.00 to $38.00) will produce a 20% increase in sales volume (20 000 to 24 000). Variable costs will remain at $20.00 per pair of shoes. Management is impressed with Kathy's ideas but concerned about the effects that these changes will have on the break-even point and the margin of safety.

Required

(a) Calculate the current break-even point in units, and compare it with the break-even point in units if Kathy's ideas are used.

(b) Calculate the margin of safety ratio for current operations and after Kathy's changes are introduced (round to nearest full percentage).

(c) Prepare a CVP statement of profit or loss for current operations and after Kathy's changes are introduced. Would you make the changes suggested?

PSA17.10 **Calculate contribution margin, break-even point, and sales to meet target income.** **LO5, 6**

Vista Ltd manufactures two models of refrigerators, Clearfrost and Superfreeze. Unit data for each model are as follows:

	Clearfrost	Superfreeze
Selling price	$420	$630
Variable costs and expenses:		
Direct materials	90	125
Direct labour	50	90
Manufacturing overhead	60	100
Selling	32	70
Administrative	20	56
Total variable	$252	$441

Monthly fixed costs are: manufacturing overhead $80 000; selling expenses $54 000; and administrative expenses $34 000.

Required

(a) Calculate the contribution margin for each model.

(b) Calculate the break-even point in dollars for each model using the contribution margin, assuming fixed costs are divided equally between the products.

(c) Calculate the sales necessary to make a profit of $36 000 on Clearfrost and $48 000 on Superfreeze. Each model incurs 50% of all fixed costs.

PROBLEM SET B

PSB17.1 **Determine variable and fixed costs, calculate break-even point, prepare a CVP graph, and determine profit.** **LO1, 4**

The University Barber Shop employs four barbers. One barber, who also serves as the manager, is paid a salary of $1600 per month. The other barbers are paid $1200 per month. In addition, each barber is paid a commission of $4 per haircut. Other monthly costs are: shop rent $800 plus 60 cents per haircut, depreciation on equipment $500, barber supplies 40 cents per haircut, electricity $300 and advertising $200. The price of a haircut is $10.

Required

(a) Determine the variable cost per haircut and the total monthly fixed costs.
(b) Calculate the break-even point in units and dollars.
(c) Prepare a CVP graph, assuming a maximum of 1800 haircuts in a month. Use increments of 300 haircuts on the horizontal axis and $3000 increments on the vertical axis.
(d) Determine profit, assuming 1600 haircuts are given in a month.

PSB17.2 **Prepare a statement of profit or loss under absorption and variable costing.** **LO2**

Tinga Ltd produces the sheet metal that goes into the production of filing cabinets. In 2019, the first year of operations, Tinga produced 50 000 tonnes and sold 40 000 tonnes. In 2020, the production and sales results were exactly reversed. In each year, selling price per tonne was $100, variable manufacturing costs were 25% of the sales price, variable selling expenses were $6.00 per tonne sold, fixed manufacturing costs were $1 400 000, and fixed administrative expenses were $250 000.

Required

(a) Prepare comparative statements of profit or loss for each year using variable costing.
(b) Prepare comparative statements of profit or loss for each year using absorption costing.
(c) Reconcile the differences each year in profit from operations under the two costing approaches.

PSB17.3 **Prepare statements of profit or loss under absorption and variable costing.** **LO2**

Glowbus produces plastic that is used for injection moulding applications such as gears for small motors. In 2018, the first year of operations, Glowbus produced 4000 tonnes of plastic and sold 3000 tonnes. In 2019, the production and sales results were exactly reversed. In each year, selling price per tonne was $2000, variable manufacturing costs were 15% of the sales price of units produced, variable selling expenses were 10% of the selling price of units sold, fixed manufacturing costs were 2 400 000, and fixed administrative expenses were $600 000.

Required

(a) Prepare comparative statements of profit or loss for each year using variable costing.
(b) Prepare comparative statements of profit or loss for each year using absorption costing.
(c) Reconcile the differences each year in profit from operations under the two costing approaches.

PSB17.4 **Calculate product cost and prepare statements of profit or loss, using absorption costing and variable costing.** **LO2**

Ella Lang is a new designer specialising in making leather jackets. The following data were extracted from the designer's first year of operation:

Unit selling price	$400
Unit variable manufacturing costs	150
Unit variable selling and administrative expense	40
Fixed manufacturing overhead	100 000
Fixed selling and administrative expenses	80 000
Number of jackets produced	2 000
Number of jackets sold	1 000

Required

(a) Calculate the manufacturing cost of one unit of leather jacket using:
   1. absorption costing.
   2. variable costing.
(b) Prepare a statement of profit or loss for Ella Lang Design for the year ended 31 December 2018 using:
   1. absorption costing
   2. variable costing.
(c) Explain why profits are different under the two costing methods.

PSB17.5 Prepare a CVP statement of profit or loss, calculate break-even point, contribution margin ratio, margin of safety ratio, and sales for target profit.   **LO4, 7**

Corbin Ltd bottles and distributes LOKAL, a fruit drink. The drink is sold for 50 cents per 600 mL bottle to retailers, who charge customers 70 cents per bottle. At full (100%) factory capacity, management estimates the following revenues and costs:

Net sales	$2 000 000	Selling expenses—variable	$ 90 000
Direct materials	360 000	Selling expenses—fixed	150 000
Direct labour	450 000	Administrative expenses—variable	30 000
Manufacturing overhead—variable	270 000	Administrative expenses—fixed	60 000
Manufacturing overhead—fixed	380 000	Financial expenses—variable	4 000
		Financial expenses—fixed	6 000

Required

(a) Prepare a CVP statement of profit or loss for 2019 based on management's estimates.
(b) Calculate the break-even point in (1) units and (2) dollars.
(c) Calculate the contribution margin ratio and the margin of safety ratio.
(d) Determine the sales required to earn profit of $220 000.

PSB17.6 Calculate break-even point under alternative courses of action.   **LO4**

Unique Manufacturing had a bad year in 2018. For the first time in its history it operated at a loss. The statement of profit or loss showed the following results from selling 60 000 units of product: net sales $2 250 000; total costs and expenses $2 835 000; and loss $585 000. Costs and expenses consisted of the following:

	Total	Variable	Fixed
Cost of sales	$2 025 000	$1 395 000	$ 630 000
Selling expenses	630 000	110 000	520 000
Administrative expenses	180 000	70 000	110 000
	$2 835 000	$1 575 000	$1 260 000

Management is considering the following independent alternatives for 2019:
1. Increase unit selling price to $52.50 with no change in costs, expenses and sales volume.
2. Change the compensation of salespersons from fixed annual salaries totalling $300 000 to total salaries of $75 000 plus a 5% commission on net sales.
3. Purchase new high-tech factory machinery that will change the proportion between variable and fixed cost of sales to 50:50.

Required

(a) Calculate the break-even point in dollars for the year 2018.
(b) Calculate the break-even point in dollars under each of the alternative courses of action. Which course of action do you recommend?

PSB17.7 Calculate fixed costs, contribution margin and break-even point. **LO4**

You are interested in setting up a juice bar, called Super Charge, on the university campus. After consulting with your friend who owns a café in the city, you have gathered the following information:

Initial investments required:	
Juice bar setting	$20 000
Blending machines	4 000
	$24 000

Your friend suggested that the juice bar setting and blending machines can last for 4 years or a total of 30 000 glasses of juice, after which they will need to be replaced. The space outside the sport centre is available for lease from the university. Because of the good location, you will have to pay a premium for the rent at $1000 per month. You plan to charge $4.50 for each glass of juice and the estimated variable cost per glass is $1.50.

Required

(a) Calculate the total monthly fixed costs for Super Charge. (*Hint:* You will need to calculate the depreciation of your initial investments based on straight-line depreciation.)

(b) What is the unit contribution margin and contribution margin ratio? How do you interpret this ratio?

(c) How many glasses of juice do you have to sell in a month to break even?

PSB17.8 Calculate fixed costs, contribution margin and break-even point in sales mix. **LO4, 6**

Continue with the data from PSB17.7. After 6 months' operation, Super Charge's sales level reached 1000 glasses of juice last month. You have observed that the line of customers queuing up to place and pick up drink orders is getting longer and longer. And you are worried that the long line may turn some customers away. You are also planning to add yoghurt to the kiosk. Your new expansion plan will require an additional investment of $28 800 (depreciated over 4 years, with no residual value). The extension will incur a higher rent expense from the university of another $1200 per month.

Estimated sales and costs for coffee and juice are:

	Juice	Yogurt
Selling price	$4.5	$4.5
Unit variable costs	$1.5	$1.5
Sales mix	3	2

Required

(a) Calculate the new total monthly fixed costs for Super Charge.

(b) What is the contribution margin for the sales mix? How do you interpret this figure?

(c) What is the break-even point for the sales mix? Show the profit at the break-even point to confirm the accuracy of your break-even point calculation.

PSB17.9 Calculate break-even point and margin of safety ratio and prepare a CVP statement of profit or loss before and after changes in business environment. **LO4, 7**

Cheryl Henning is the advertising manager for Thrifty Shoe Store. She is currently working on a major promotional campaign. Her ideas include the installation of a new lighting system and increased display space that will add $37 000 in fixed costs to the $210 000 currently spent. In addition, Cheryl is proposing that a $6\frac{2}{3}\%$ price decrease (from $30.00 to $28.00) will produce an increase in sales volume from 16 000 to 21 000 units. Variable costs will remain at $15.00 per pair of shoes. Management is impressed with Cheryl's ideas but concerned about the effects that these changes will have on the break-even point and the margin of safety.

Required

(a) Calculate the current break-even point in units, and compare it with the break-even point in units if Cheryl's ideas are used.

(b) Calculate the margin of safety ratio for current operations and after Cheryl's changes are introduced (round to nearest full percentage).

(c) Prepare a CVP statement of profit or loss for current operations and after Cheryl's changes are introduced. Would you make the changes suggested?

PSB17.10 Calculate contribution margin ratio, break-even point, and sales to meet target profit. **LO4, 5**

Cashmere Ltd manufactures two models of washing machines, Turbotub and Ultraclean. Unit data for each model are as follows:

	Turbotub	Ultraclean
Selling price	$400	$500
Variable costs and expenses:		
Direct materials	80	91
Direct labour	60	101
Manufacturing overhead	54	67
Selling	40	56
Administrative	46	60
Total variable	$280	$375

Monthly fixed costs are: manufacturing overhead $90 000, selling expenses $56 000 and administrative expenses $34 000.

Required

(a) Calculate the contribution margin ratio for each model.

(b) Calculate the break-even point in dollars for each model using the contribution margin ratio, assuming fixed costs are divided equally between the products.

(c) Calculate the sales necessary to make profit of $36 000 on Turbotub and $30 000 on Ultraclean. Each model incurs 50% of all fixed costs.

BUILDING BUSINESS SKILLS

FINANCIAL REPORTING AND ANALYSIS

Managerial analysis

BBS17.1 The condensed statement of profit or loss for the Riverina and Murray partnership for 2018 is as follows:

RIVERINA AND MURRAY Statement of profit or loss for the year ended 30 June 2018		
Sales (300 000 units)		$1 500 000
Cost of sales		1 200 000
Gross profit		300 000
Operating expenses		
Selling	$275 000	
Administrative	180 000	
Financial	15 000	470 000
Loss		$ (170 000)

A cost behaviour analysis indicates that 70% of the cost of sales are variable, 60% of the selling expenses are variable, and 25% of the administrative expenses are variable.

Required

(Round to nearest unit, dollar and percentage, where necessary. Use the CVP statement of profit or loss format in calculating profits.)

(a) Calculate the break-even point in total sales dollars and in units for 2018.

(b) Riverina has proposed a plan to get the partnership 'out of the red' and improve its profitability. She feels that the quality of the product could be substantially improved by spending $0.55 more per unit on better raw materials. The selling price per unit could be increased to only $6.00 because of competitive pressures. Riverina estimates that sales volume will increase by 30%. What effect will Riverina's plan have on the profits and the break-even point in dollars of the partnership?

(c) Murray majored in marketing at university. He believes that sales volume can be increased only by intensive advertising and promotional campaigns. He therefore proposed the following plan as an alternative to Riverina's: (1) increase variable selling expenses to $0.65 per unit, (2) lower the selling price per unit by $0.20, and (3) increase fixed selling expenses by $20 000. Murray quoted an old marketing research report that said that sales volume would increase by 50% if these changes were made. What effect will Murray's plan have on the profits and the break-even point in dollars of the partnership?

(d) Which plan should be accepted? Explain your answer.

Surfing the net

BBS17.2 Select one of the following entities and go to their web site:

Address: CSR Ltd	www.csr.com.au
Nestlé	www.nestle.com
The Coca-Cola Company	www.coca-colacompany.com
Harvey Norman	www.harveynormanholdings.com.au

Required

Answer the following questions:

(a) Describe what the entity does.

(b) What are the major industry or geographical segments of the entity selected?

(c) Describe at least two fixed costs and two variable costs that are likely to affect the production of one of the entity's products.

Real-world focus

BBS17.3 BMW is a world-class car maker, producing many models of motor vehicles and motor cycles. The company's web site contains many interesting facts about its history and production process.

Address: www.bmwgroup.com

Steps:

1. On the company tab, Click on **Production**.

2. Click on **BMW video link**.

Required

Read the description of how motor cars are made and answer the following questions:

(a) Describe the main steps in making motor vehicles.

(b) Identify at least two variable and two fixed costs that are likely to affect the production of cars.

CRITICAL THINKING

Group decision cases

BBS17.4 Consider your personal financial situation. In groups, discuss your daily expenses during a semester while attending university. Summarise your key spending items and then identify whether they are fixed, variable or mixed expenses. Can you identify any expenses that are avoidable and where savings can be made?

BBS17.5 In CVP analysis there are many formulas. Your classmate asks your help on the following questions:

    (a) How can the mathematical equation for break-even sales show both sales dollars and sales units?

    (b) How do the formulas differ, if at all, for contribution margin per unit and contribution margin ratio?

    (c) How can contribution margin be used to determine break-even sales in dollars and in units?

Required

Write a report to your classmate stating the relevant formulas and the answers to each of the above questions.

Communication activity

BBS17.6 If variable costing is suitable only for internal use by management, then why prepare two sets of information? Why not just use the costing prepared for external financial reporting?

Required

Write a report to the CEO of the entity you work for explaining the benefits of variable costing.

Communication activity

BBS17.7 Access the BMW Group's web site (www.bmwgroup.com), select the **Responsibility** tab and answer the following.

Required

    (a) Outline BMW Group's approach to sustainability.

    (b) Download the latest Sustainable Value Report and discuss BMW Group's objectives, challenges and achievements in economics, product responsibility and one of the three following areas: product and services, employees and society, or production and value creation.

Ethics case

BBS17.8 Richard Blake is an accountant for Swan Ltd. Early this year Richard made a highly favourable projection of sales and profits over the next 3 years for its hot-selling computer PLEX. As a result of the projections Richard presented to senior management, they decided to expand production in this area. This decision led to relocation of some factory personnel who were reassigned to one of the entity's newer factories in another state. However, no-one was fired, and in fact the entity expanded its workforce slightly.

Unfortunately, Richard rechecked his calculations on the projections a few months later and found that he had made an error that, if corrected, would have reduced his projections substantially. Luckily, sales of PLEX have exceeded projections so far, and management is satisfied with its decision. Richard, however, is not sure what to do. Should he confess his honest mistake and jeopardise his possible promotion? He suspects that no-one will catch the error because sales of PLEX have exceeded his projections, and it appears that profits will materialise close to his projections.

Required

    (a) Who are the stakeholders in this situation?

    (b) Identify the ethical issues involved in this situation.

    (c) What are the possible alternative actions for Richard? What would you do in Richard's position?

ANSWERS

Answers to self-study questions

17.1 (d) 17.2 (c) 17.3 (a) 17.4 (a) 17.5 (b) 17.6 (c) 17.7 (d) 17.8 (c) 17.9 (d) 17.10 (b) 17.11 (d) 17.12 (c)

ACKNOWLEDGEMENTS

Photo: © Rido / Shutterstock.com
Photo: © Peter Gudella / Shutterstock.com
Photo: © Nonwarit / Shutterstock.com

CHAPTER 18

Budgeting

LEARNING OBJECTIVES

After studying this chapter, you should be able to:

18.1 outline the benefits and essential elements of effective budgeting

18.2 identify and describe the components of the master budget

18.3 explain and prepare the main sections of a cash budget

18.4 describe the sources of information for preparing the budgeted statement of profit or loss and statement of financial position

18.5 indicate the applicability of budgeting in non-manufacturing entities

18.6 explain the concept of budgetary control

18.7 compare and contrast the use of static and flexible budgets

18.8 describe the concept of responsibility accounting

18.9 identify the content of responsibility reports and their use in performance evaluation.

Chapter preview

Budgeting is an integral part of our society. As students, you budget your study time and your money. Families budget income and expenses, and government agencies budget revenues and expenditures. Business entities use budgets in planning and controlling their operations.

The main focus of this chapter is budgeting — specifically, how budgeting is used as a *planning tool* and to *control* operations. Through budgeting, management plans how the entity will maintain enough cash to pay creditors, to have sufficient raw materials to meet production requirements and to have adequate finished goods to meet expected sales. Budgets provide management with a tool for controlling operations to ensure that the planned objectives are met. Budgeting also permits performance evaluation and accountability of managers for the day-to-day decisions of matters directly under their control. The organisation and content of this chapter are as follows.

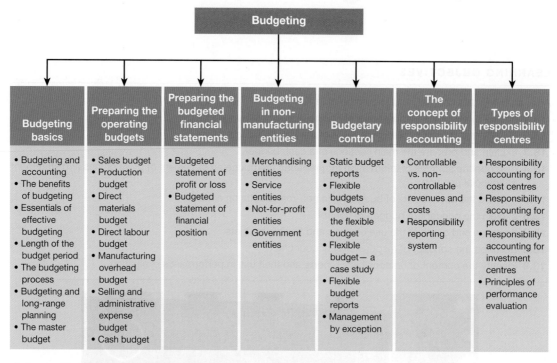

18.1 Budgeting basics

LEARNING OBJECTIVE 18.1 Outline the benefits and essential elements of effective budgeting.

One of management's major responsibilities is planning. As explained in chapter 15, *planning* is the process of establishing enterprise objectives. A successful entity establishes both long-term and short-term plans that set forth its objectives and the proposed means of accomplishing them.

A **budget** is a formal written summary (or statement) of management's plans for a specified future time period, expressed in financial terms. It normally represents the main way of communicating agreed-upon objectives throughout the entity. Once adopted, a budget becomes an important basis for controlling operations and evaluating performance. Thus, it promotes efficiency and serves as a deterrent to waste and inefficiency.

Budgeting and accounting

Budgets express management's goals and objectives in financial terms. In other words, budgets translate management's plans into monetary terms and provide the means of communicating plans to all areas of responsibility. Accountants play a key role in the budgeting process by preparing periodic budget reports. These budget reports form the basis for measuring performance and comparing actual results with planned financial objectives. However, the budget itself and the administration of the budget are entirely management responsibilities. These points are expanded on later in this chapter.

The benefits of budgeting

The main benefits of budgeting are as follows.
1. It requires all levels of management to *plan ahead* and to formalise their future goals on a recurring basis.
2. It provides *definite financial objectives* for evaluating performance at each level of responsibility.
3. It creates an *early warning system* for potential problems. With early warning, management has time to solve the problem before things get out of hand. For example, the cash budget may reveal the need for outside financing several months before an actual cash shortage occurs.
4. It facilitates the *coordination of activities* within the entity by aligning the goals of each segment with the entity's overall objectives. Thus, production and sales promotion can be integrated with expected sales.
5. It results in greater *management awareness* of the entity's overall operations and the impact of external factors, such as economic trends, on those operations.
6. It contributes to *positive behaviour patterns* throughout the entity by motivating personnel to meet planned financial objectives.

A budget is an aid to management; it is not a substitute for management. A budget cannot operate or enforce itself. The benefits of budgeting will be realised only when budgets are prepared carefully and administered properly by management.

Essentials of effective budgeting

Effective budgeting depends on a sound organisational structure in which authority and responsibility over all phases of operations are clearly defined. Budgets based on research of market and economic analysis and an understanding of factors of production should result in realistic goals that will contribute to the growth and profitability of an entity. The effectiveness of a budget program is directly related to its acceptance by all levels of management. In developing the budget, each level of management should be invited and encouraged to participate. When all levels participate, the budget has a greater chance of acceptance. The overall objective is to reach an agreement that all managers consider to be fair and achievable.

Once the budget has been adopted, it should be an important basis for evaluating performance. Variations between actual and expected results should be systematically and periodically reviewed to determine their cause(s). However, care should be exercised to see that individuals are not held responsible for variations that are beyond their control.

Length of the budget period

A budget may be prepared for any period of time. Such factors as the type of budget, the nature of the entity, the need for periodic appraisal and prevailing business conditions will influence the length of the budget period. For example, cash may be budgeted monthly, whereas a factory expansion program budget may cover a 10-year period.

The budget period should be long enough to provide an attainable goal under normal business conditions. Ideally, the time period should minimise the impact of seasonal and cyclical business fluctuations. On the other hand, the budget period should not be so long that reliable estimates are impossible.

The most common budget period is 1 year. The annual budget, in turn, is often supplemented by monthly and quarterly budgets. Many entities today use continuous 12-month budgets by dropping the month just ended and adding a future month. One advantage of continuous budgeting is that it keeps management planning a full year ahead. (*Continuous budgets* are also referred to as *rolling budgets*.)

The budgeting process

The development of the budget for the coming year generally starts several months before the end of the current year. The budgeting process usually begins with the collection of data from each of the organisational units of the entity. Past performance is often the starting point in budgeting, from which future budget goals are formulated.

The budget is developed within the framework of a **sales forecast** that shows potential sales for the industry and the entity's expected share of such sales. Sales forecasting involves a consideration of such factors as (1) general economic conditions, (2) industry trends, (3) market research studies, (4) anticipated advertising and promotion, (5) previous market share, (6) changes in prices, (7) new products and (8) technological developments. The input of sales and other marketing personnel and top management is essential in preparing the sales forecast.

Budgeting vs. long-range planning

In business, you may hear management talk about the need for long-range planning. Budgeting and long-range planning are not the same. One important difference is the time period involved. The maximum length of a budget is usually 1 year, and budgets are often prepared for shorter periods of time, such as a month or a quarter. In contrast, long-range planning usually encompasses a period of 3–5 years.

A second significant difference is in emphasis. Budgeting is concerned with the achievement of specific short-term goals, such as meeting annual profit objectives. **Long-range planning**, on the other hand, is a formalised process of selecting strategies to achieve long-term goals and developing policies and plans to implement the strategies. In long-range planning, management also considers its strategic response to the opportunities and challenges that arise from anticipated trends in the economic and political environment.

The final difference between budgeting and long-range planning pertains to the amount of detail presented. Budgets, as you will see later in this chapter, can be very detailed. The detail is needed to provide a basis for control. Long-range plans contain considerably less detail, because the data are intended for a review of progress towards long-term goals rather than for an evaluation of specific results to be achieved.

The main objective of long-range planning is to develop the best strategy to maximise the entity's performance over an extended future period.

18.2 The master budget

LEARNING OBJECTIVE 18.2 Identify and describe the components of the master budget.

When we discuss a 'budget', we actually are using a shorthand term to describe a variety of budget documents, all of which are combined into a master budget. The **master budget** (also known as *the plan*) is a set of interrelated budgets that constitutes a plan of action for a specified period of time. The individual budgets included in a master budget for Hayes Ltd are shown in figure 18.1.

FIGURE 18.1 Components of the master budget

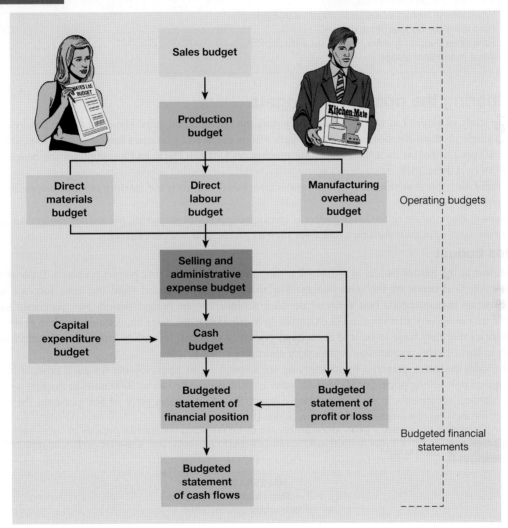

As shown in the figure, there are two classes of budgets in the master budget. **Operating budgets** are prepared within the framework of the sales forecast and culminate in the preparation of the cash budget and a budgeted statement of profit or loss. The main objective of these budgets is to establish goals for the sales and production personnel. The **budgeted financial statements** include a budgeted statement of profit or loss, budgeted statement of financial position and a budgeted statement of cash flows. These budgets focus mainly on the cash resources needed to fund expected operations and planned capital expenditures.

The master budget is prepared in the sequence shown in figure 18.1, although some parts of the master budget are often prepared simultaneously. The operating budgets are developed first, beginning with the sales budget. After these budgets have been determined, the financial statement budgets are prepared. We will explain and illustrate each budget shown in fgure 18.1 except the budgeted statement of cash flows (discussed in chapter 11) and the capital expenditure budget.

LEARNING REFLECTION AND CONSOLIDATION

Review it

1. What are the benefits of budgeting?
2. What are the factors essential to effective budgeting?
3. How does the budget process work?
4. How does budgeting differ from long-range planning?
5. What is a master budget?

Preparing the operating budgets

A case study of Hayes Ltd will be used in preparing the operating budgets. Hayes Ltd manufactures and sells a single product, Kitchen-mate. The budgets will be prepared by quarters for the year ending 30 June 2019. Hayes Ltd begins its annual budgeting process on 1 March 2018, and it completes the budget for 2018–19 by 1 June 2018.

Helpful hint: For a merchandising or manufacturing entity, what is the starting point in preparing the master budget, and why?

Answer: Preparation of the sales budget is the starting point in preparing the master budget because it sets the level of activity for other functions such as production and purchasing.

Sales budget

As shown in the master budget in figure 18.1, the sales budget is the first budget prepared. Each of the other budgets depends on the sales budget. The **sales budget** is derived from the sales forecast, and it represents management's best estimate of sales revenue for the budget period. An inaccurate sales budget may adversely affect profit. For example, an overly optimistic sales budget may result in excessive inventories that may have to be sold at reduced prices. In contrast, an unduly conservative budget may result in loss of sales revenue due to inventory shortages.

The sales budget is prepared by multiplying the expected unit sales volume for each product by its anticipated unit selling price. For Hayes Ltd, sales volume is expected to be 3000 units in the first quarter with 500-unit increments in each succeeding quarter. Based on a sales price of $60 per unit, the sales budget for the year, by quarters, is shown in figure 18.2.

FIGURE 18.2 Sales budget

HAYES LTD
Sales budget
for the year ended 30 June 2019

	Quarter 1	Quarter 2	Quarter 3	Quarter 4	Year
Expected unit sales	3 000	3 500	4 000	4 500	15 000
Unit selling price	× $60	× $60	× $60	× $60	× $60
Total sales	**$180 000**	**$210 000**	**$240 000**	**$270 000**	**$900 000**

The anticipated sales revenue may be classified as cash or credit sales and by geographical areas, territories and/or salespeople.

Production budget

The **production budget** shows the units that must be produced to meet anticipated sales. Production requirements are determined from the formula shown in figure 18.3. (This formula ignores any work in process inventories, which are assumed to be non-existent in Hayes Ltd.)

FIGURE 18.3 Production requirements formula

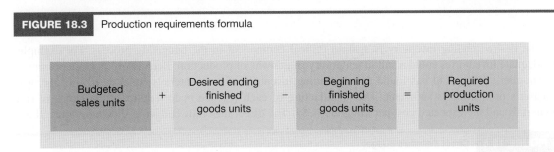

A realistic estimate of ending inventory is essential in scheduling production requirements. Excessive inventories in one quarter may lead to cutbacks in production and lay-offs of employees in a subsequent quarter. Conversely, inadequate inventories may result either in added costs for overtime work or in lost sales in a later period. On the basis of past experience, Hayes Ltd believes it can meet future sales requirements by maintaining an ending inventory equal to 20% of the next quarter's budgeted sales volume. For example, the ending finished goods inventory for the first quarter is 700 units (20% × anticipated second-quarter sales of 3500 units). The production budget is shown in figure 18.4.

FIGURE 18.4 Production budget

	Quarter					Quarter 1, 2020
HAYES LTD **Production budget** for the year ended 30 June 2019						
	1	**2**	**3**	**4**	**Year**	2020
Expected unit sales (figure 18.2)	3 000	3 500	4 000	4 500		5 000
Add: Desired ending finished goods units*	700	800	900	1 000**		1 100****
Total required units	3 700	4 300	4 900	5 500		6 100
Less: Beginning finished goods units	600***	700	800	900		1 000
Required production units	3 100	3 600	4 100	4 600	15 400	5 100

*20% of next quarter's sales
**Expected 2019–20 first-quarter sales, 5000 units × 20%
***20% of estimated first-quarter 2018–19 sales units, 3000 units × 20%
****20% of expected 2019–20 second-quarter sales, 5500 units × 20%

The production budget, in turn, provides the basis for determining the budgeted costs for each manufacturing cost element, as explained in the following sections.

Direct materials budget

The **direct materials budget** contains an estimate of both the quantity and cost of direct materials to be purchased. The quantities of direct materials are derived from the formula in figure 18.5.

The budgeted cost of direct materials to be purchased is then calculated by multiplying the required units of direct materials by the anticipated cost per unit.

FIGURE 18.5 Formula for direct materials quantities

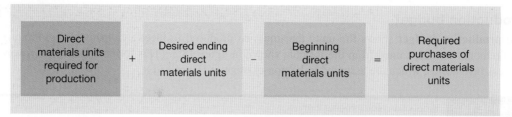

The desired ending inventory is again a critical component in the budgeting process. For example, inadequate inventories could result in temporary shutdowns of production. Because of its close proximity to suppliers, Hayes Ltd has found that an ending inventory of raw materials equal to 10% of the next quarter's production is sufficient. The manufacture of each Kitchen-mate requires 2 kilograms of raw materials and the expected cost per kilogram is $4. The direct materials budget is shown in figure 18.6.

FIGURE 18.6 Direct materials budget

HAYES LTD
Direct materials budget
for the year ended 30 June 2019

	Quarter				
	1	2	3	4	Year
Units to be produced (figure 18.4)	3 100	3 600	4 100	4 600	
Direct materials (kg) per unit	× 2	× 2	× 2	× 2	
Total kilograms needed for production	6 200	7 200	8 200	9 200	
Add: Desired ending direct materials (kg)*	720	820	920	1 020**	
Total materials required	6 920	8 020	9 120	10 220	
Less: Beginning direct materials (kg)	620***	720	820	920	
Direct materials purchases (kg)	6 300	7 300	8 300	9 300	
Cost per kilogram	× $4	× $4	× $4	× $4	
Total cost of direct materials purchases	$25 200	$29 200	$33 200	$37 200	$124 800

*10% of next quarter's production
**Estimated 2019–20 first-quarter kilograms needed for production, 5000 units × 2 × 10%
***10% of estimated first-quarter kilograms needed for production, 6200 × 10%

Direct labour budget

Like the direct materials budget, the **direct labour budget** contains the quantity (hours) and cost of direct labour necessary to meet production requirements. Direct labour hours are determined from the production budget. At Hayes Ltd, 2 hours of direct labour are required to produce each unit of finished goods, and the anticipated hourly wage rate is $10. These data are shown in figure 18.7. The direct labour budget is critical in maintaining a labour force that can meet the expected levels of production.

Manufacturing overhead budget

The **manufacturing overhead budget** shows the expected manufacturing overhead costs for the budget period. As shown in figure 18.8, this budget distinguishes between variable and fixed overhead costs. From previous experience, Hayes Ltd expects variable costs to fluctuate with production volume on the basis of the following rates per direct labour hour (DLH):
- indirect materials $1.00
- indirect labour $1.40
- electricity $0.40
- maintenance $0.20.

FIGURE 18.7 Direct labour budget

	Quarter				
HAYES LTD **Direct labour budget** for the year ended 30 June 2019					
	1	2	3	4	Year
Units to be produced (figure 18.4)	3 100	3 600	4 100	4 600	
Direct labour time (hours) per unit	× 2	× 2	× 2	× 2	
Total required direct labour hours	6 200	7 200	8 200	9 200	
Direct labour cost per hour	× $10	× $10	× $10	× $10	
Total direct labour cost	$62 000	$72 000	$82 000	$92 000	$308 000

Thus, for 6200 direct labour hours in the first quarter, budgeted indirect materials are $6200 (6200 × $1) and budgeted indirect labour is $8680 (6200 × $1.40).

Helpful hint: An important assumption here is that the entity can add and subtract from its workforce as needed so that the $10 per hour labour cost applies to a wide range of possible production activity.

Hayes Ltd also recognises that some maintenance is fixed. The amounts reported for fixed costs are assumed. At Hayes Ltd, overhead is applied to production on the basis of direct labour hours. Thus, as shown in figure 18.8, the annual rate is $8 per hour ($246 400 ÷ 30 800 DLH).

FIGURE 18.8 Manufacturing overhead budget

	Quarter				
HAYES LTD **Manufacturing overhead budget** for the year ended 30 June 2019					
	1	2	3	4	Year
Variable costs					
Indirect materials ($1/DLH)	$ 6 200	$ 7 200	$ 8 200	$ 9 200	$ 30 800
Indirect labour ($1.4/DLH)	8 680	10 080	11 480	12 880	43 120
Electricity ($0.4/DLH)	2 480	2 880	3 280	3 680	12 320
Maintenance ($0.2/DLH)	1 240	1 440	1 640	1 840	6 160
Total variable	18 600	21 600	24 600	27 600	92 400
Fixed costs					
Supervisors' salaries	20 000	20 000	20 000	20 000	80 000
Depreciation	3 800	3 800	3 800	3 800	15 200
Rates and taxes, and insurance	9 000	9 000	9 000	9 000	36 000
Maintenance	5 700	5 700	5 700	5 700	22 800
Total fixed	38 500	38 500	38 500	38 500	154 000
Total manufacturing overhead	$57 100	$60 100	$63 100	$66 100	$246 400
Direct labour hours (figure 18.7)	6 200	7 200	8 200	9 200	30 800
Manufacturing overhead rate per direct labour hour ($246 400 ÷ 30 800)					$ 8.00

Selling and administrative expense budget

Hayes Ltd combines its operating expenses into one budget, the **selling and administrative expense budget**. This budget is a projection of anticipated selling and administrative expenses for the budget period. In this budget, as in the preceding manufacturing overhead budget, expenses are classified as either variable or fixed. In this case, the variable expense rates per unit of sales are sales commissions

$3.00 and freight-out $1.00. Variable expenses per quarter are based on the unit sales projected in the sales budget (figure 18.2). For example, sales in the first quarter are expected to be 3000 units. Thus, Sales Commissions Expense is $9000 (3000 × $3), and Freight-out is $3000 (3000 × $1). Fixed expenses are based on assumed data. The selling and administrative expense budget is shown in figure 18.9.

FIGURE 18.9 Selling and administrative expense budget

HAYES LTD
Selling and administrative expense budget
for the year ended 30 June 2019

| | Quarter | | | | |
	1	2	3	4	Year
Expected unit sales (figure 18.2)	$ 3 000	$ 3 500	$ 4 000	$ 4 500	$ 15 000
Variable expenses					
Sales commissions ($3/unit)	9 000	10 500	12 000	13 500	45 000
Freight-out ($1/unit)	3 000	3 500	4 000	4 500	15 000
Total variable	12 000	14 000	16 000	18 000	60 000
Fixed expenses					
Advertising	5 000	5 000	5 000	5 000	20 000
Sales salaries	15 000	15 000	15 000	15 000	60 000
Office salaries	7 500	7 500	7 500	7 500	30 000
Depreciation	1 000	1 000	1 000	1 000	4 000
Rates and taxes, and insurance	1 500	1 500	1 500	1 500	6 000
Total fixed	30 000	30 000	30 000	30 000	120 000
Total selling and administrative expenses	$42 000	$44 000	$46 000	$48 000	$180 000

DECISION-MAKING TOOLKIT

Decision/issue	Info needed for analysis	Tool or technique to use for decision	How to evaluate results to make decision
Has the entity met its targets for sales, production expenses, selling and administrative expenses, and profit?	Sales forecasts, inventory levels, projected materials, labour, overhead, and selling and administrative requirements	Master budget — a set of interrelated budgets including sales, production, materials, labour, overhead, and selling and administrative budgets. Compare actual results to budget.	Results are favourable if revenues are equal to or exceed budgeted amounts, or if expenses are equal to or less than budgeted amounts.

18.3 Cash budget

LEARNING OBJECTIVE 18.3 Explain and prepare the main sections of a cash budget.

The **cash budget** shows anticipated cash flows. Because cash is so vital, this budget is considered to be the most important consideration in preparing financial budgets. The cash budget contains three sections (cash receipts, cash payments, and financing), and the beginning and ending cash balances as shown in figure 18.10.

ANY ENTITY Cash budget	
Beginning cash balance	$XXX
Add: Cash receipts (itemised)	XXX
Total available cash	XXX
Less: Cash payments (itemised)	XXX
Excess (deficiency) of available cash over cash payments	XXX
Financing	XXX
Ending cash balance	**$XXX**

The *cash receipts section* includes expected receipts from the entity's main source(s) of revenue such as cash sales and collections from customers on credit sales. This section also shows anticipated receipts of interest and dividends, and proceeds from planned sales of investments, plant and equipment, and the issue of shares.

The *cash payments section* shows expected payments for direct materials, direct labour, manufacturing overhead, and selling and administrative expenses. This section also includes projected payments for income tax, dividends, investments, and plant and equipment.

The *financing section* shows expected borrowings and the repayment of the borrowed funds plus interest. This section is needed when there is a cash deficiency or when the cash balance is below management's minimum required balance.

Data in the cash budget must be prepared in sequence because the ending cash balance of one period becomes the beginning cash balance for the next period. Data for preparing the cash budget are obtained from other budgets and from information provided by management. In practice, cash budgets are often prepared for the year on a monthly basis.

To minimise detail, we will assume that Hayes Ltd prepares an annual cash budget by quarters. The cash budget for Hayes Ltd is based on the following assumptions.

1. The 1 July 2018 cash balance is expected to be $38 000.
2. Sales (figure 18.2) — 60% are collected in the quarter sold and 40% are collected in the following quarter. Accounts receivable of $60 000 at 30 June 2018 are expected to be collected in full in the first quarter of 2018–19.
3. Marketable investments are expected to be sold for $2000 cash in the first quarter.
4. Direct materials (figure 18.6) — 50% is paid in the quarter purchased and 50% is paid in the following quarter. Accounts payable of $10 600 at 30 June 2018 are expected to be paid in full in the first quarter.
5. Direct labour (figure 18.7) — 100% is paid in the quarter incurred.
6. Manufacturing overhead (figure 18.8) and selling and administrative expenses (figure 18.9) — all items except depreciation are paid in the quarter incurred.
7. Management plans to purchase a truck in the second quarter for $10 000 cash.
8. The entity makes equal quarterly payments of its estimated annual income tax.
9. Loans are repaid in the first subsequent quarter in which there is sufficient cash; interest of $100 is payable with repayments.
10. It is Hayes Ltd's policy to maintain a minimum cash level of $15 000.

Schedules for collections from customers (assumption no. 2 above) and cash payments for direct materials (assumption no. 4 above) are useful in preparing the cash budget. The schedules are shown in figures 18.11 and 18.12.

FIGURE 18.11 Collections from customers

Schedule of expected collections from customers

	Quarter			
	1	2	3	4
Accounts receivable, 30/6/18	$ 60 000			
Sales, First quarter ($180 000)*	108 000*	$ 72 000**		
Sales, Second quarter ($210 000)		126 000*	$ 84 000**	
Sales, Third quarter ($240 000)			144 000*	$ 96 000**
Sales, Fourth quarter ($270 000)				162 000*
Total collections	$168 000	$198 000	$228 000	$258 000

*See item 2 above, $180 000 × 60% = $108 000 or 60% of current quarter's sales
**40% of previous quarter's sales

FIGURE 18.12 Payments for direct materials

Schedule of expected payments for direct materials

	Quarter			
	1	2	3	4
Accounts payable, 30/6/18	$10 600			
Purchases, First quarter ($25 200)	12 600*	$12 600		
Purchases, Second quarter ($29 200)		14 600	$14 600	
Purchases, Third quarter ($33 200)			16 600	$16 600
Purchases, Fourth quarter ($37 200)				18 600
Total payments	$23 200	$27 200	$31 200	$35 200

*See item 2 above, $25 200 × 50% = $12 600

The cash budget for Hayes Ltd is shown in figure 18.13. The budget indicates that $3000 of financing will be needed in the second quarter to maintain a minimum cash balance of $15 000. Since there is an excess of available cash over payments of $22 500 at the end of the third quarter, the borrowing is repaid in this quarter plus $100 interest (assume the interest is for 4 months at 10%).

FIGURE 18.13 Cash budget

HAYES LTD
Cash budget
for the year ended 30 June 2019

		Quarter			
	Assumption	1	2	3	4
Beginning cash balance	1	$ 38 000	$ 25 500	$ 15 000	$ 19 400
Add: Receipts					
Collections from customers	2	168 000	198 000	228 000	258 000
Sale of investments	3	2 000	–	–	–
Total receipts		170 000	198 000	228 000	258 000
Total available cash		208 000	223 500	243 000	277 400
Less: Payments					
Direct materials	4	23 200	27 200	31 200	35 200
Direct labour	5	62 000	72 000	82 000	92 000
Manufacturing overhead	6	53 300*	56 300	59 300	62 300
Selling and administrative expenses	6	41 000**	43 000	45 000	47 000
Purchase of truck	7	–	10 000	–	–
Income tax expense	8	3 000***	3 000	3 000	3 000
Total payments		182 500	211 500	220 500	239 500
Excess (deficiency) of available cash over payments		25 500	12 000	22 500	37 900
Financing					
Borrowings		–	3 000	–	–
Repayments — plus $100 interest	9	–	–	3 100	–
Ending cash balance		$ 25 500	$ 15 000	$ 19 400	$ 37 900

*$57 100 – $3800 depreciation
**$42 000 – $1000 depreciation
***See figure 18.15, budgeted statement of profit or loss, annual income tax $12 000 ÷ 4 quarters.

A cash budget contributes to more effective cash management. For example, it can show when additional financing will be necessary well before the actual need arises, and arrangements can be made with the bank ahead of time or you may be able to delay the payment of your suppliers in the short term. Conversely, it can indicate when excess cash will be available for investments or other purposes.

DECISION-MAKING TOOLKIT

Decision/issue	Info needed for analysis	Tool or technique to use for decision	How to evaluate results to make decision
Will the entity need to borrow funds in the coming quarter?	Beginning cash balance, cash receipts, cash payments, and desired cash balance	Examine the cash budget	The entity will need to borrow money if the cash budget indicates a projected cash deficiency of available cash over cash payments for the quarter.

18.4 Preparing the budgeted financial statements

LEARNING OBJECTIVE 18.4 Describe the sources of information for preparing the budgeted statement of profit or loss and statement of financial position.

Budgeted statement of profit or loss

The **budgeted statement of profit or loss** is the end product of the cash and operating budgets. This budget indicates the expected profitability of operations for the budget period. Once established, the budgeted statement of profit or loss provides the basis for evaluating performance. The budgeted statement of profit or loss is derived by drawing data from other components of the master budget, namely the operating budgets. For example, to find the cost of sales, it is first necessary to determine the unit product cost of producing one Kitchen-mate as shown in figure 18.14.

FIGURE 18.14 Calculation of unit product cost

Cost element	Cost of one Kitchen-mate			
	Figure	Quantity	Unit cost	Total
Direct materials	16.6	2 kilograms	$ 4.00	$ 8.00
Direct labour	16.7	2 hours	$10.00	20.00
Manufacturing overhead	16.8	2 hours	$ 8.00	16.00
Unit product cost				$44.00

Cost of sales can then be determined by multiplying units sold by unit product cost. For Hayes Ltd, budgeted cost of sales is $660 000 (15 000 × $44). All data for the statement are obtained from the individual operating budgets and the cash budget except income tax, estimated to be $12 000. The budgeted statement of profit or loss is shown in figure 18.15.

FIGURE 18.15 Budgeted statement of profit or loss

HAYES LTD Budgeted statement of profit or loss for the year ended 30 June 2019	
Sales (figure 18.2)	$ 900 000
Cost of sales (15 000 × $44)	(660 000)
Gross profit	240 000
Selling and administrative expenses (figure 18.9)	(180 000)
Profit from operations	60 000
Interest expense	(100)*
Profit before income tax	59 900
Income tax expense	(12 000)
Profit	$ 47 900

*See assumption 9 in figure 18.13.

Budgeted statement of financial position

The **budgeted statement of financial position** is a projection of the financial position at the end of the budget period. This budget is developed from the budgeted statement of financial position for the preceding year and the budgets for the current year. Pertinent data from the budgeted statement of financial position as at 30 June 2018 are shown below.

Property, plant and equipment	$182 000	Share capital	$225 000
Accumulated depreciation	$ 28 800	Retained earnings	$ 46 480

The budgeted statement of financial position as at 30 June 2019 is shown in figure 18.16.

FIGURE 18.16 Budgeted statement of financial position

HAYES LTD Budgeted statement of financial position as at 30 June 2019		
ASSETS		
Cash		$ 37 900
Accounts receivable		108 000
Finished goods inventory		44 000
Raw materials inventory		4 080
Property, plant and equipment	$192 000	
Less: Accumulated depreciation	(48 000)	144 000
Total assets		**$337 980**
LIABILITIES AND SHAREHOLDERS' EQUITY		
Accounts payable		$ 18 600
Share capital		225 000
Retained earnings		94 380
Total liabilities and shareholders' equity		**$337 980**

The calculations and sources of the amounts are explained below.
- *Cash* — ending cash balance $37 900, shown in the cash budget (figure 18.13).
- *Accounts receivable* — 40% of fourth-quarter sales $270 000, shown in the schedule of expected collections from customers (figure 18.11).
- *Finished goods inventory* — desired ending inventory 1000 units, shown in production budget (figure 18.4), times the total unit cost $44 (shown in figure 18.14).
- *Raw materials inventory* — desired ending inventory 1020 kilograms times the cost per kilogram $4, shown in the direct materials budget (figure 18.6).
- *Property, plant and equipment* — 30 June 2018 balance $182 000 plus purchase of truck for $10 000.
- *Accumulated depreciation* — 30 June 2018 balance $28 800 plus $15 200 depreciation shown in manufacturing overhead budget (figure 18.8) and $4000 depreciation shown in selling and administrative expense budget (figure 18.9).
- *Accounts payable* — 50% of fourth-quarter purchases $37 200, shown in schedule of expected payments for direct materials (figure 18.12).
- *Share capital* — unchanged from the beginning of the year.
- *Retained earnings* — 30 June 2018 balance $46 480 plus profit $47 900, shown in budgeted statement of profit or loss (figure 18.15).

LEARNING REFLECTION AND CONSOLIDATION

Review it
1. How may the individual budgets in the master budget be classified?
2. What is the sequence for preparing the operating budgets?
3. What are the three principal sections of the cash budget?

Do it
In Martian Pty Ltd, management wants to maintain a minimum monthly cash balance of $15 000. At the beginning of March, the cash balance is $16 500, expected cash receipts for March are $210 000, and

▶

cash payments are expected to be $220 000. How much cash, if any, must be borrowed to maintain the desired minimum monthly balance?

Reasoning

The best way to answer this question is to insert the dollar data into the basic form of the cash budget.

Solution

MARTIAN PTY LTD	
Cash budget	
for the month ended 31 March 2019	
Beginning cash balance	$ 16 500
Add: Cash receipts for March	210 000
Total available cash	226 500
Less: Cash payments for March	220 000
Excess of available cash over cash payments	6 500
Financing required	8 500
Ending cash balance	$ 15 000

To maintain the desired minimum cash balance of $15 000, $8500 of cash must be borrowed.

18.5 Budgeting in non-manufacturing entities

LEARNING OBJECTIVE 18.5 Indicate the applicability of budgeting in non-manufacturing entities.

Budgeting is not limited to manufacturing entities. Budgets may also be used in profit planning by merchandising entities, service entities, not-for-profit entities and government entities.

Merchandising entities

As in manufacturing operations, the sales budget is both the starting point and the key factor in the development of the master budget for a merchandising entity. The major differences between the master budgets of a merchandising entity and a manufacturing entity are that a merchandiser (1) uses a purchases budget instead of a production budget and (2) does not use the manufacturing budgets (direct materials, direct labour and manufacturing overhead). The **purchases budget** shows the estimated cost of goods to be purchased to meet expected sales. The formula for determining budgeted purchases is shown in figure 18.17.

FIGURE 18.17	Purchases formula

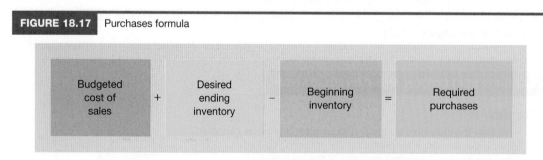

To demonstrate, assume that the budget committee of Lima Ltd is preparing the purchases budget for July. It estimates that budgeted sales will be $300 000 in July and $320 000 in August. Cost of sales is expected to be 70% of sales, and the entity's desired ending inventory is 30% of the following month's cost of sales. Required purchases for July are $214 200, calculated as shown in figure 18.18.

FIGURE 18.18 | Calculation of required purchases of inventory

Budgeted cost of sales (budgeted sales for July, $300 000 × 70%)	$210 000
Desired ending inventory (budgeted cost of sales for August, $320 000 × 70% × 30%)	67 200
Total	277 200
Less: Beginning inventory (budgeted sales for July, $300 000 × 70% × 30%)	(63 000)
Required purchases for July	**$214 200**

When the merchandising entity is departmentalised, separate budgets are prepared for each department. For example, a supermarket may start by preparing sales budgets and purchases budgets for each of its major departments, such as meat, dairy and produce. These budgets are then combined into a master budget for the store. When a retailer has branch stores, separate master budgets are prepared for each store. Then these budgets are incorporated into master budgets for the entity as a whole.

Service entities

In service entities, such as accounting practices, financial institutions, legal practices, public relations businesses or businesses engaged in hospitality and tourism, the critical factor in budgeting is coordinating professional staff needs with anticipated services. If an entity is overstaffed (1) labour costs will be disproportionately high, (2) profits will be lower because of the additional salaries, and (3) staff turnover may increase because of lack of challenging work. In contrast, if an entity is understaffed, revenue may be lost because existing and prospective client needs for service cannot be met, and professional staff may seek other positions because of excessive workloads.

Budget data for service revenue may be obtained from expected output or expected input. When output is used, it is necessary to determine the expected billings of clients for services rendered. In an accounting practice, for example, output would be the sum of its billings in auditing, tax and consulting services. When service revenue is derived from input data, each professional staff member is required to project his or her chargeable time. Billing rates are then applied to chargeable time to produce expected service revenue.

Not-for-profit entities

Budgeting is just as important for not-for-profit entities as for profit-oriented entities. The budget process, however, is significantly different. In some cases, not-for-profit entities budget on the basis of cash flows (expenditures and receipts), and in other cases on an accrual basis. If the not-for-profit entity is a reporting entity, then it must use accrual accounting and apply international accounting standards, but it may still use cash accounting for budgeting purposes. Often, the starting point in the process is expenditures, not receipts. For the not-for-profit entity, management's task generally is to find the receipts needed to support the planned expenditures. The activity index is also likely to be significantly different from that of a profit-oriented entity. For example, in a not-for-profit entity such as a university, budgeted faculty positions may be based on full-time equivalent students or credit hours expected to be taught in a department.

Government entities

Budgets are also an essential element for all government entities and all levels of government.

Such budgets must be approved by the relevant federal, state or local government bodies. The emphasis in preparing the budget is on expenditure. Once the programs have been costed, the focus changes to obtaining enough revenue from taxation, rates or service charges to fund the programs. For some councils, such as the Gold Coast City Council (GCCC), operations are conducted as commercial entities and fees are charged on a user-pays basis. The council can also obtain assets (such as roads, footpaths, water supply and sewerage mains) as a condition of building approval from major developments.

After the budget has been adopted it must be strictly followed. Part of the GCCC budget is a formal resolution that sets out the various rates levied by the council and associated charges, which determines the rates and charges the council may levy on users.* In government entities, authorisations tend to be on a line-by-line basis. The amount approved for expenditure in various programs must be followed, thereby limiting the discretion management can exercise. For example, the mayor cannot save on one line item, such as footpaths, and then cover extra garbage collections.

18.6 Budgetary control

LEARNING OBJECTIVE 18.6 Explain the concept of budgetary control.

How do budgets assist management in controlling operations? The use of budgets in controlling operations is known as **budgetary control**. The centrepiece of budgetary control is the use of budget reports that compare actual results with planned objectives. The preparation and use of budget reports is based on the belief that planned objectives lose much of their potential value without some monitoring of progress along the way. Just as your lecturers give mid-semester examinations to evaluate your progress, so top management requires periodic reports on the progress department or division managers are making towards planned annual financial objectives.

Budget reports provide the feedback needed by management to ascertain if actual operations are on course. The feedback for a crucial objective, such as having enough cash on hand to pay bills, may be made daily. For other objectives, such as meeting budgeted annual sales and operating expenses, monthly budget reports may suffice. Because of the flexibility of management accounting, budget reports can be prepared as often as needed. Budgetary differences occur when actual results differ from planned objectives. The differences can be favourable or unfavourable. For example, if actual sales exceed budgeted sales, the difference is considered favourable. On the other hand, actual operating expenses exceeding budgeted expenses is an unfavourable variance. By analysing the causes of unfavourable differences, management may take corrective action or decide to modify future plans.

Budgetary control involves the components shown in figure 18.19.

| **FIGURE 18.19** | Budgetary control |

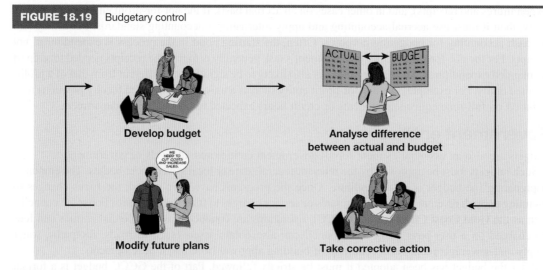

*Council of the City of Gold Coast n.d., 'Budget, plans and reports', retrieved from www.goldcoast.qld.gov.au.

Budgetary control works best when an entity has a formalised reporting system. The system should (1) identify the name of the budget report, such as the sales budget report or the manufacturing overhead budget report; (2) state the frequency of the report, such as weekly or monthly; (3) specify the purpose of the report; and (4) indicate the main recipient(s) of the report. The schedule in table 18.1 illustrates a partial budgetary control system for a manufacturing entity. Note the emphasis on control in the reports and the frequency of the reports. For example, there is a daily report on waste and a weekly report on labour.

TABLE 18.1 Budgetary control reporting system

Name of report	Frequency	Purpose	Main recipient(s)
Sales	Weekly	Determine whether sales goals are being met	Top management and sales manager
Labour	Weekly	Control direct and indirect labour costs	Director of production and production department managers
Waste	Daily	Determine efficient use of materials	Production manager
Departmental overhead costs	Monthly	Control overhead costs	Department manager
Selling expenses	Monthly	Control selling expenses	Sales manager
Statement of profit or loss	Monthly and quarterly	Determine whether profit objectives are being met	Top management

Static budget reports

The master budget formalises management's planned objectives for the coming year. When used in budgetary control, each budget included in the master budget is considered to be a static budget. A **static budget** is a projection of budget data at one level of activity. In such a budget, data for different levels of activity are ignored. As a result, actual results are always compared with budget data at the activity level used in developing the master budget.

Illustrations

To illustrate the role of a static budget in budgetary control, we will use selected budget data prepared for Hayes Ltd earlier in this chapter. Budget and actual sales data for the Kitchen-mate product in the first and second quarters of 2019–20 are shown in figure 18.20.

FIGURE 18.20 Budget and actual sales data

Sales	First quarter	Second quarter	Total
Budgeted	$180 000	$210 000	$390 000
Actual	179 000	199 500	378 500
Difference	$ 1 000	$ 10 500	$ 11 500

The sales budget report for Hayes Ltd's first quarter is shown in figure 18.21.

The report shows that sales are $1000 under budget — an unfavourable result. This difference is less than 1% of budgeted sales ($1000 ÷ $180 000 = 0.0056). Top management's analysis of unfavourable differences is often influenced by the materiality (significance) of the difference. Since the difference of $1000 is immaterial in this case, we will assume that the management of Hayes Ltd does not investigate the difference and takes no specific action. (Budget differences are also referred to as *budget variances*.)

FIGURE 18.21 Sales budget report — first quarter

HAYES LTD
Sales budget report
for the quarter ended 30 September 2019

Product line	Budget	Actual	Difference Favourable F Unfavourable U
Kitchen-mate*	$180 000	$179 000	$1 000 U

*In practice, each product line would be included in the report.

The budget report for the second quarter presented in figure 18.22 contains one new feature: cumulative year-to-date information. This report indicates that sales for the second quarter were $10 500 below budget, which is 5% of budgeted sales ($10 500 ÷ $210 000). Top management may conclude that the difference between budgeted and actual sales in the second quarter merits investigation.

FIGURE 18.22 Sales budget report — second quarter

HAYES LTD
Sales budget report
for the quarter ended 31 December 2019

Product line	Second quarter			Year-to-date		
	Budget	Actual	Difference Favourable F Unfavourable U	Budget	Actual	Difference Favourable F Unfavourable U
Kitchen-mate	$210 000	$199 500	$10 500 U	$390 000	$378 500	$11 500 U

Management's analysis should start by asking the sales manager the cause(s) of the shortfall. The need for corrective action should be considered. For example, management may decide to stimulate sales by offering sales incentives to customers or by increasing the advertising of Kitchen-mates. On the other hand, if management concludes that a downturn in the economy is responsible for the lower sales, it may decide to modify planned sales and profit goals for the remainder of the year.

Uses and limitations

From the examples just discussed, you can see that a master sales budget is useful in evaluating the performance of a sales manager. It is now necessary to ask: How appropriate is the master budget for evaluating a manager's performance in controlling costs? Recall that in a static budget, budget data are not modified or adjusted, regardless of changes in activity during the year. It follows, then, that a static budget is appropriate in evaluating a manager's effectiveness in controlling costs when:
1. the actual level of activity closely approximates the master budget activity level, and/or
2. the behaviour of the costs in response to changes in activity is fixed.

A static budget report is, therefore, appropriate for fixed manufacturing costs and fixed selling and administrative expenses. However, static budget reports may not be a proper basis for evaluating a manager's performance in controlling variable costs.

18.7 Flexible budgets

LEARNING OBJECTIVE 18.7 Compare and contrast the use of static and flexible budgets.

In contrast to a static budget — which is based on one level of activity — a **flexible budget** projects budget data for various levels of activity. In essence, the flexible budget is a series of static budgets at different levels of activity. The flexible budget is more useful to budgetary control because it is adaptable to changed operating conditions.

Flexible budgets can be prepared for each type of budget included in the master budget. For example, Hilton Hotels can budget revenues and profit on the basis of 60%, 80% and 100% of room occupancy. Similarly, Hertz car rentals can budget its operating expenses on the basis of various levels of kilometres driven. Likewise, the bottling department of Coca-Cola Amatil can budget manufacturing costs on the basis of 70%, 80% and 100% of machine hours. In the following, we will illustrate a flexible budget for manufacturing overhead.

Assume that you are the manager in charge of manufacturing overhead in the Forging Department of Smith Steel. In preparing the manufacturing overhead budget for 2019, you prepare the static budget shown in figure 18.23 based on a production volume of 10 000 units of steel ingots.

FIGURE 18.23 Static manufacturing overhead budget

SMITH STEEL
Forging Department
Manufacturing overhead budget (static)
for the year ended 31 December 2019

Budgeted production in units (steel ingots)	10 000
Budgeted costs	
Indirect materials	$ 250 000
Indirect labour	260 000
Electricity	190 000
Depreciation*	280 000
Rates and taxes*	70 000
Supervision*	50 000
	$1 100 000

---

*Fixed costs.

Fortunately for Smith Steel, the demand for steel ingots has increased, and 12 000 units are produced during the year, rather than 10 000. You are elated because increased sales means increased profitability, which should mean a large bonus for you and the employees in your department. Unfortunately, a comparison of the actual costs incurred with the budgeted costs for the year in the Forging Department has put you on the spot. The manufacturing overhead budget report is shown in figure 18.24.

FIGURE 18.24 Static manufacturing overhead budget report

SMITH STEEL
Forging Department
Manufacturing overhead budget report (static)
for the year ended 31 December 2019

	Budget	Actual	Difference Favourable F Unfavourable U
Production in units	10 000	12 000	
Costs			
Indirect materials	$ 250 000	$ 295 000	$ 45 000 U
Indirect labour	260 000	312 000	52 000 U
Electricity	190 000	225 000	35 000 U
Depreciation	280 000	280 000	—
Rates and taxes	70 000	70 000	—
Supervision	50 000	50 000	—
	$1 100 000	$1 232 000	$132 000 U

Note that this comparison is based on budget data based on the original activity level (10 000 steel ingots). The comparison indicates that the Forging Department is significantly over budget for three of the six overhead costs. Moreover, there is a total unfavourable difference of $132 000, which is 12% over budget ($132 000 ÷ $1 100 000). Your supervisor is very unhappy! Instead of sharing in the entity's success, you may find yourself looking for another job. What would you do in this situation?

When you calm down and carefully examine the manufacturing overhead budget report, you identify the problem — the budget data are not relevant! At the time the budget was developed, Smith Steel anticipated that only 10 000 units of steel ingots would be produced, *not* 12 000 ingots. As a result, the comparison of actual variable costs with budgeted costs is meaningless. The reason is that, as production increases, the budget allowances for variable costs should increase both directly and proportionately. The variable costs in this example are indirect materials, indirect labour and electricity.

Helpful hint: If an entity has substantial variable costs, a static budget will not provide useful information.

An analysis of the budget data for these costs at 10 000 units produces the per-unit results in figure 18.25.

FIGURE 18.25 Variable costs per unit

Item	Total cost	Per unit
Indirect materials	$250 000	$25
Indirect labour	260 000	26
Electricity	190 000	19
	$700 000	$70

The budgeted variable costs at 12 000 units, therefore, are as shown in figure 18.26.

FIGURE 18.26 Budgeted variable costs (12 000 units)

Item	Calculation	Total
Indirect materials	$25 × 12 000	$300 000
Indirect labour	26 × 12 000	312 000
Electricity	19 × 12 000	228 000
		$840 000

Because fixed costs do not change in total as activity changes, the budgeted amounts for these costs remain the same. The budget report based on the flexible budget for 12 000 units of production is shown in figure 18.27. (Compare this with figure 18.24.)

This report indicates that the Forging Department is below budget — a favourable difference. Instead of worrying about being fired, you may be in line for a pay rise or a promotion after all! As indicated from the foregoing analysis, the only appropriate comparison is between actual costs at 12 000 units of production and budgeted costs at 12 000 units of production. Flexible budget reports provide this comparison.

Developing the flexible budget

Comparing actual with budgeted figures from different activity levels does not yield meaningful comparison, as it is like comparing apples with pears. Hence, there is a need to develop a flexible budget, where data from a range of activity levels is formulated. The flexible budget is based on the master budget and is prepared by management, using the following steps.

1. Identify the activity index and the relevant range of activity.
2. Identify the variable costs and determine the budgeted variable cost per unit of activity for each cost.

3. Identify the fixed costs and determine the budgeted amount for each cost.
4. Prepare the budget for selected increments of activity within the relevant range.

| FIGURE 18.27 | Flexible manufacturing overhead budget report |

SMITH STEEL
Forging Department
Manufacturing overhead budget report (flexible)
for the year ended 31 December 2019

	Budget	Actual	Difference Favourable F Unfavourable U
Production in units	12 000	12 000	
Variable costs			
Indirect materials	$ 300 000	$ 295 000	$5 000 F
Indirect labour	312 000	312 000	—
Electricity	228 000	225 000	3 000 F
Total variable	840 000	832 000	8 000 F
Fixed costs			
Depreciation	280 000	280 000	—
Rates and taxes	70 000	70 000	—
Supervision	50 000	50 000	—
Total fixed	400 000	400 000	—
Total costs	**$1 240 000**	**$1 232 000**	**$8 000 F**

The activity index chosen should be one that significantly influences the costs that are being budgeted. For example, for manufacturing overhead costs, the activity index is usually the same as the index used in developing the predetermined overhead rate — that is, direct labour hours or machine hours. For selling and administrative expenses, the activity index usually is sales or net sales.

The choice of selected increments of activity is largely a matter of judgement. For example, if the relevant range is 8000 to 12 000 direct labour hours, increments of 1000 hours may be selected. The flexible budget is then prepared in columnar form for each increment within the relevant range.

DECISION-MAKING TOOLKIT

Decision/issue	Info needed for analysis	Tool or technique to use for decision	How to evaluate results to make decision
Are the increased costs resulting from increased production reasonable?	Variable costs projected at different levels of production	Compare actual costs to the flexible budget	After taking into account different production levels, results are favourable if expenses are less than budgeted amounts.

Flexible budget — a case study

To illustrate the preparation of the flexible budget, we will use Fox Manufacturing. The management of Fox Manufacturing wants to use the flexible budget for monthly comparisons of actual and budgeted manufacturing overhead costs of the Finishing Department. The master budget for the year ending 31 December 2019 shows expected annual operating capacity of 120 000 direct labour hours and overhead costs as shown in figure 18.28.

FIGURE 18.28 | Master budget data

Variable costs		Fixed costs	
Indirect materials	$180 000	Depreciation	$180 000
Indirect labour	240 000	Supervision	120 000
Power	60 000	Rates and taxes	60 000
Total	$480 000	Total	$360 000

The application of the four steps is as follows:

Step 1. Identify the activity index and the relevant range of activity. The activity index is direct labour hours. Management concludes that the relevant range is 8000–12 000 direct labour hours per month.

Step 2. Identify the variable costs and determine the budgeted variable cost per unit of activity for each cost. There are three variable costs. The variable cost per unit is found by dividing each total budgeted cost by the direct labour hours used in preparing the master budget (120 000 hours). For Fox Manufacturing, the calculations are shown in figure 18.29.

Step 3. Identify the fixed costs and determine the budgeted amount for each cost. There are three fixed costs. Since Fox Manufacturing desires monthly budget data, the budgeted amount is found by dividing each annual budgeted cost by 12. For Fox Manufacturing, the monthly budgeted fixed costs are: depreciation $15 000, supervision $10 000, and rates and taxes $5000.

Step 4. Prepare the budget for selected increments of activity within the relevant range. Management decides that the budget should be prepared in increments of 1000 direct labour hours.

FIGURE 18.29
Calculation of variable costs per direct labour hour

Variable cost	Calculation	Variable cost per direct labour hour
Indirect materials	$180 000 ÷ 120 000	$1.50
Indirect labour	240 000 ÷ 120 000	2.00
Electricity	60 000 ÷ 120 000	0.50
Total		$4.00

The flexible budget for the month of January 2019 is shown in figure 18.30.

FIGURE 18.30 Flexible monthly manufacturing overhead budget

FOX MANUFACTURING
Finishing Department
Flexible monthly manufacturing overhead budget
for the month ended 31 January 2019

Activity level					
Direct labour hours	8 000	9 000	10 000	11 000	12 000
Variable costs					
Indirect materials ($1.5/DLH)	$12 000	$13 500	$15 000	$16 500	$18 000
Indirect labour ($2/DLH)	16 000	18 000	20 000	22 000	24 000
Electricity ($0.5/DLH)	4 000	4 500	5 000	5 500	6 000
Total variable	32 000	36 000	40 000	44 000	48 000
Fixed costs					
Depreciation	15 000	15 000	15 000	15 000	15 000
Supervision	10 000	10 000	10 000	10 000	10 000
Rates and taxes	5 000	5 000	5 000	5 000	5 000
Total fixed	30 000	30 000	30 000	30 000	30 000
Total costs	$62 000	$66 000	$70 000	$74 000	$78 000

Alternatively, the formula in figure 18.31 may be used to determine total budgeted costs at any level of activity.

FIGURE 18.31 Formula for total budgeted costs

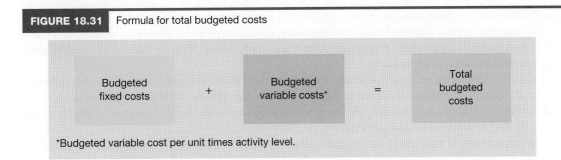

Budgeted fixed costs + Budgeted variable costs* = Total budgeted costs

*Budgeted variable cost per unit times activity level.

For Fox Manufacturing, fixed costs are $30 000, and total variable cost per unit is $4.00. Thus, at 9000 direct labour hours, total budgeted costs are $66 000 [$30 000 + ($4.00 × 9000)]. Similarly, at 8622 direct labour hours, total budgeted costs are $64 488 [$30 000 + ($4.00 × 8622)].

Helpful hint: Using the data given for Fox Manufacturing, what amount of total costs would be budgeted for 10 600 direct labour hours?

Answer:

Fixed	$30 000
Variable (10 600 × $4)	42 400
Total	$72 400

Total budgeted costs can also be shown graphically, as in figure 18.32. In the graph, the activity index is shown on the horizontal axis and costs are indicated on the vertical axis. The graph highlights two of the 1000 increments (10 000 and 12 000).

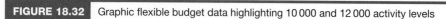

FIGURE 18.32 Graphic flexible budget data highlighting 10 000 and 12 000 activity levels

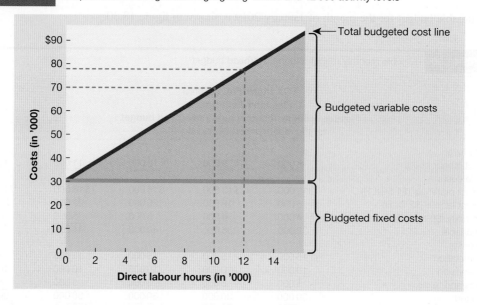

As shown in figure 18.32, total budgeted costs are $70 000 [$30 000 + ($4.00 × 10 000)] and $78 000 [$30 000 + ($4.00 × 12 000)], respectively.

Flexible budget reports

Flexible budget reports represent another type of internal report produced by management accountants. The flexible budget report consists of two sections: (1) production data such as direct labour hours and (2) cost data for variable and fixed costs. Consequently, the report provides a basis for evaluating a manager's performance in two areas: production control and cost control. Flexible budgets are widely used in production and service departments.

A flexible manufacturing overhead budget report for the Finishing Department of Fox Manufacturing for the month of January is shown in figure 18.33. In this month, 8800 direct labour hours were expected but 9000 hours were worked. The budget data are based on the flexible budget for 9000 hours in figure 18.30. The actual cost data are assumed.

How appropriate is this report in evaluating the Finishing Department manager's performance in controlling costs? The report provides a reliable basis for this. Both actual and budget costs are based on the activity level worked during January. Since variable costs generally are incurred directly by the department, the difference between the budget allowance for those hours and the actual costs are the responsibility of the department manager.

From the standpoint of production control, the report shows a 200-hour difference between actual direct labour hours and expected hours. This difference is not an issue if actual production orders required 9000 direct labour hours. The difference is unfavourable if actual production orders required only

8800 direct labour hours. In either case, the budget for purposes of cost control is based on 9000 direct labour hours.

FIGURE 18.33	Flexible manufacturing overhead budget report

FOX MANUFACTURING
Finishing Department
Flexible manufacturing overhead budget report
for the month ended 31 January 2019

				Difference
Direct labour hours (DLH)				
Expected	8800	**Budget at**	**Actual costs**	**Favourable F**
Actual	9000	**9000 DLH**	**9000 DLH**	**Unfavourable U**
Variable costs				
Indirect materials		$13 500	$14 000	$ 500 U
Indirect labour		18 000	17 000	1 000 F
Electricity		4 500	4 600	100 U
Total variable		36 000	35 600	400 F
Fixed costs				
Depreciation		15 000	15 000	—
Supervision		10 000	10 000	—
Rates and taxes		5 000	5 000	—
Total fixed		30 000	30 000	—
Total costs		**$66 000**	**$65 600**	**$ 400 F**

In subsequent months, other flexible budget reports will be prepared. For each month, the budget data are based on the actual activity level attained. In February that level may be 11 000 direct labour hours; in July, 10 000 and so on.

Management by exception

Management by exception means that top management's review of a budget report is directed either entirely or mainly to differences between actual results and budgeted objectives. This approach enables top management to focus on problem areas or opportunities that need attention. Management by exception does not mean that top management will investigate every difference. For this approach to be effective, there must be some guidelines for identifying an exception. The usual criteria are materiality and controllability of the item.

Materiality

Without quantitative guidelines, management would have to investigate every budget difference regardless of the amount. Materiality is usually expressed as a percentage difference from budget. For example, management may set the percentage difference at 5% for important items and 10% for other items. This means that all differences either over or under budget by the specified percentage will be investigated. Costs over budget warrant investigation to determine why they were not controlled. In contrast, costs under budget merit investigation to determine whether costs critical to the profitability of the division are being curtailed. For example, if maintenance costs are budgeted at $80 000 and only $40 000 is spent, major unexpected breakdowns in productive facilities may occur in the future.

Alternatively, an entity may specify a single percentage difference from budget for all items and supplement this guideline with a minimum dollar limit. For example, the exception criteria may be stated at 5% of budget or more than $10 000.

Controllability of the item

Exception guidelines are more restrictive for controllable items than for items that are not controllable by the manager being evaluated. In fact, there may be no guidelines for non-controllable items. For example, a large unfavourable difference between actual and budgeted rates and taxes expense may not be flagged by management for investigation because the only possible causes are an unexpected increase in the tax rate or in the revaluation of a property. An investigation into the difference will be useless because the manager cannot control either cause. It would still be investigated by top management.

LEARNING REFLECTION AND CONSOLIDATION

Review it

1. What is the meaning of budgetary control?
2. When is a static budget appropriate for evaluating a manager's effectiveness in controlling costs?
3. What is a flexible budget?
4. How is a flexible budget developed?
5. What are the criteria used in management by exception?

Do it

Your classmate asks your help in understanding how total budgeted costs are calculated at any level of activity. Calculate total budgeted costs at 30 000 direct labour hours, assuming that in the flexible budget graph, the fixed cost line and the total budgeted cost line intersect the vertical axis at $36 000 and that the total budget cost line is $186 000 at an activity level of 50 000 direct labour hours.

Reasoning

The formula for the calculation is: Fixed costs + Variable costs (Variable costs per unit × Activity level) = Total budgeted costs.

Solution

Using the graph, fixed costs are $36 000 and variable costs are $3 per direct labour hour [($186 000 − $36 000) ÷ 50 000]. Thus, at 30 000 direct labour hours, total budgeted costs are $126 000 [$36 000 + ($3 × 30 000)].

18.8 The concept of responsibility accounting

LEARNING OBJECTIVE 18.8 Describe the concept of responsibility accounting.

Like budgeting, responsibility accounting is an important part of management accounting. **Responsibility accounting** involves accumulating and reporting costs (and revenues, where relevant) on the basis of the individual manager who has the authority to make the day-to-day decisions about the items. Under responsibility accounting, the evaluation of a manager's performance is based on matters directly under that manager's control. Responsibility accounting can be used at every level of management in which the following conditions exist.

1. Costs and revenues can be directly associated with the specific level of management responsibility.
2. The costs and revenues are controllable at the level of responsibility with which they are associated.
3. Budget data can be developed for evaluating the manager's effectiveness in controlling the costs and revenues.

The levels of responsibility for controlling costs are depicted in figure 18.34.

Responsibility accounting personalises the management accounting system. Under responsibility accounting, any individual who has control and is accountable for a specified set of activities can be recognised as a responsibility centre. Thus, responsibility accounting may extend from the lowest level of control to the top strata of management. Once responsibility has been established, the effectiveness of the individual's performance is first measured and reported for the specified activity, and it is then reported upwards throughout the organisation.

Helpful hint: Virtually all entities use responsibility accounting. Without some form of responsibility accounting, there would be chaos in discharging management's control function.

Responsibility accounting is especially valuable in a decentralised entity. **Decentralisation** means that the control of operations is delegated by top management to many individuals (managers) throughout the organisation. Under responsibility accounting, reports are prepared periodically such as monthly, quarterly and annually, to provide a basis for evaluating the performance of each manager.

Responsibility accounting is an essential part of any effective system of budgetary control. The reporting of costs and revenues under responsibility accounting differs from budgeting in two respects.
1. A distinction is made between controllable and non-controllable items.
2. Performance reports either emphasise or include only items controllable by the individual manager.

Responsibility accounting applies to both profit and not-for-profit entities. The former seek to maximise profit, whereas the latter wish to minimise the cost of providing the service.

Controllable vs. non-controllable revenues and costs

All costs and revenues are controllable at some level of responsibility within an entity. This truth underscores the adage by the chief executive officer of any entity that 'the buck stops here'. Under responsibility accounting, the critical issue is whether the cost or revenue is controllable at the level of responsibility with which it is associated.

Helpful hint: Are there more or fewer controllable costs as you move to higher levels of management? Answer: More.

A cost is considered to be a **controllable cost** at a given level of managerial responsibility if that manager has the power to incur it within a given period of time. From this criterion, it follows that:
- all costs are controllable by top management because of the broad range of its authority
- fewer costs are controllable as one moves down to each lower level of managerial responsibility because of the manager's decreasing authority.

In general, costs incurred directly by a level of responsibility are controllable at that level. In contrast, costs incurred indirectly and allocated to a responsibility level are considered to be **non-controllable costs** at that level.

Helpful hint: The longer the time span, the more likely that the cost becomes controllable.

Responsibility reporting system

A **responsibility reporting system** involves the preparation of a report for each level of responsibility shown in the entity's organisation chart. To illustrate a responsibility reporting system, we will use the partial organisation chart and production departments of Francis Chairs Pty Ltd in figure 18.35.

The responsibility reporting system begins with the lowest level of responsibility for controlling costs and moves upwards to each higher level, as detailed in figure 18.36. A brief description of the four reports follows.

1. *Report D* is typical of reports that go to managers at the lowest level of responsibility shown in the organisation chart — department managers. In this report, additional detail may be presented for manufacturing overhead. Similar reports are prepared for the managers of the Enamelling and Assembly departments.
2. *Report C* is an example of reports that are sent to factory managers. This report shows the costs of the Wellington factory that are controllable at the second level of responsibility. In addition, report C shows summary data for each department that is controlled by the factory manager. Similar reports are prepared for the Adelaide and Perth factory managers.
3. *Report B* illustrates the reports at the third level of responsibility. It shows the controllable costs of the general manager of production and summary data on the three assembly factories for which this officer is responsible.
4. *Report A* is typical of the reports that go to the top level of responsibility — the managing director. This report shows the controllable costs and expenses of this office and summary data on the general managers who are accountable to the managing director.

FIGURE 18.35 | Partial organisation chart

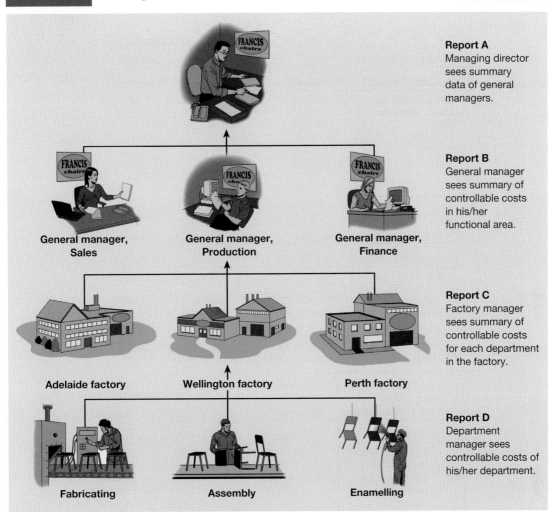

Report A
Managing director sees summary data of general managers.

General manager, Sales

General manager, Production

General manager, Finance

Report B
General manager sees summary of controllable costs in his/her functional area.

Adelaide factory

Wellington factory

Perth factory

Report C
Factory manager sees summary of controllable costs for each department in the factory.

Fabricating

Assembly

Enamelling

Report D
Department manager sees controllable costs of his/her department.

A responsibility reporting system permits management by exception at each level of responsibility within the entity. In addition to the information shown in figure 18.36, each higher level of responsibility can obtain the detailed report for each lower level of responsibility, e.g. the general manager of production may request the Wellington factory manager's report because this factory is $5300 over budget.

This type of reporting system also permits comparative evaluations. In figure 18.36, the Wellington factory manager can easily rank the department manager's effectiveness in controlling manufacturing costs. Comparative rankings provide further incentive for a manager to control costs. For example, the Adelaide factory manager will want to continue to be first in the report to the general manager of production, and the Perth factory manager will not want to remain third in future reporting periods.

Types of responsibility centres

There are three basic types of responsibility centres: cost centres, profit centres and investment centres. These centres indicate the degree of responsibility the manager has for the performance of the centre.

FIGURE 18.36 Responsibility reporting system

REPORT A

To Managing director   Month: January

Controllable costs:	Budget	Actual	Fav/unfav
Managing director	$ 150 000	$ 151 500	$ 1 500 U
General managers:			
Sales	185 000	187 000	2 000 U
Production	1 179 000	1 186 300	7 300 U
Finance	100 000	101 000	1 000 U
Total	$1 614 000	$1 625 800	$11 800 U

REPORT B

To General manager, Production   Month: January

Controllable costs:	Budget	Actual	Fav/unfav
G M Production	$ 125 000	$ 126 000	$1 000 U
Assembly factories:			
Adelaide	420 000	418 000	2 000 F
Wellington	304 000	309 300	5 300 U
Perth	330 000	333 000	3 000 U
Total	$1 179 000	$1 186 300	$7 300 U

REPORT C

To Factory manager — Wellington   Month: January

Controllable costs:	Budget	Actual	Fav/unfav
Wellington factory	$110 000	$113 000	$3 000 U
Departments:			
Fabricating	84 000	85 300	1 300 U
Enamelling	62 000	64 000	2 000 U
Assembly	48 000	47 000	1 000 F
Total	$304 000	$309 300	$5 300 U

REPORT D

To Fabricating department manager   Month: January

Controllable costs:	Budget	Actual	Fav/unfav
Direct materials	$20 000	$20 500	$ 500 U
Direct labour	40 000	41 000	1 000 U
Overhead	24 000	23 800	200 F
Total	$84 000	$85 300	$1 300 U

A **cost centre** incurs costs (and expenses) but does not directly generate revenues. Managers of cost centres have the authority to incur costs. They are evaluated on their ability to control costs. Cost centres are usually either production departments or service departments. The former participate directly in making the product and the latter provide support services. In a BMW factory, the welding, painting and assembling departments are production departments, and the maintenance, information technology, cafeteria and personnel departments are service departments. All of these departments are cost centres.

A **profit centre** incurs costs (and expenses) but also generates revenues. Managers of profit centres are judged on the profitability of their centres. Examples of profit centres include the individual departments of a retail store, such as clothing, furniture and automotive products, and branch offices of banks.

Like a profit centre, an **investment centre** incurs costs (and expenses) and generates revenues. In addition, an investment centre has control over the investment funds available for use. Managers of investment centres are evaluated on the profitability of the centre and on the rate of return earned on the funds invested. Investment centres are often associated with subsidiary companies. These three types of responsibility centres are depicted in figure 18.37.

FIGURE 18.37 Types of responsibility centres

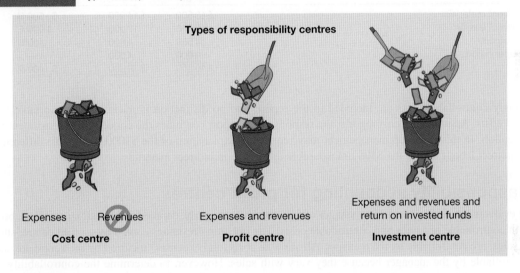

Types of responsibility centres

| Expenses | Revenues | Expenses and revenues | Expenses and revenues and return on invested funds |
| **Cost centre** | | **Profit centre** | **Investment centre** |

Helpful hint:
1. *Is the furniture department of a Harvey Norman store a profit centre or a cost centre?*
2. *Is Telecom New Zealand's payment processing department a profit centre or a cost centre?*
3. *Is AMP Financial Services' fund management division a profit centre or an investment centre?*
   Answers: 1. Profit centre; 2. Cost centre; 3. Investment centre.

The evaluation of a manager's performance in each type of responsibility centre is explained in the remainder of this chapter.

18.9 Responsibility accounting for cost centres

LEARNING OBJECTIVE 18.9 Identify the content of responsibility reports and their use in performance evaluation.

The evaluation of a manager's performance for cost centres is based on the manager's ability to meet budgeted goals for controllable costs. Responsibility reports for cost centres compare actual controllable costs with flexible budget data.

A manufacturing overhead responsibility report is illustrated in figure 18.38. The report is adapted from the budget report for Fox Manufacturing in figure 18.33. It assumes that the Finishing Department manager is able to control all manufacturing overhead costs except depreciation, rates and taxes, and the manager's own monthly supervisory salary of $6000. The remaining $4000 of supervision costs are assumed to apply to other supervisory personnel within the Finishing Department, whose salaries are controllable by the manager.

FIGURE 18.38	Responsibility report for a cost centre

FOX MANUFACTURING
Finishing Department
Manufacturing overhead responsibility report
for the month ended 31 January 2019

Controllable cost	Budget	Actual	Difference Favourable F Unfavourable U
Indirect materials	$13 500	$14 000	$ 500 U
Indirect labour	18 000	17 000	1 000 F
Electricity	4 500	4 600	100 U
Supervision	4 000	4 000	–
	$40 000	$39 600	$ 400 F

Only controllable costs are included in the report, and no distinction is made between variable and fixed costs. As in budget cost reports, the responsibility report continues the concept of management by exception. In this case, top management may request an explanation of the $1000 favourable difference in indirect labour and/or the $500 unfavourable difference in indirect materials.

Responsibility accounting for profit centres

To evaluate the performance of a manager of a profit centre properly, detailed information is needed about both controllable revenues and controllable costs. The operating revenues earned by a profit centre, such as sales, are controllable by the manager. All variable costs (and expenses) incurred by the centre are also controllable by the manager because they vary with sales. However, to determine the controllability of fixed costs, it is necessary to distinguish between direct and indirect fixed costs.

Helpful hint: For a production department manager, how should the expense of the staff canteen be classified?

Answer: Because the staff canteen is used by not just the production department, the costs are common costs and should be classified as indirect fixed costs.

Direct and indirect fixed costs

A profit centre may have both direct and indirect fixed costs. **Direct fixed costs** are costs that relate specifically to one centre and are incurred for the sole benefit of that centre. Examples of such costs include the salaries established by the profit centre manager for supervisory personnel and the cost of maintaining a time-keeping department for the centre's employees. Since these fixed costs can be traced directly to a centre, they are also called *traceable costs*. Most direct fixed costs are controllable by the profit centre manager.

In contrast, **indirect fixed costs** pertain to an entity's overall operating activities and they are incurred for the benefit of more than one profit centre. Indirect fixed costs are allocated to profit centres on some type of equitable basis. For example, rates and taxes on a building occupied by more than one centre may be allocated on the basis of square metres of floor space used by each centre. Alternatively, the cost of a personnel department may be allocated to profit centres on the basis of the number of employees in each centre. Because these fixed costs apply to more than one centre, they are also called *common costs*. Most indirect fixed costs are not controllable by the profit centre manager.

Responsibility report

The responsibility report for a profit centre shows budgeted and actual controllable revenues and costs. The report is prepared using the cost–volume–profit statement of profit or loss explained in chapter 16. In the report:

- controllable fixed costs are deducted from contribution margin
- the excess of contribution margin over controllable fixed costs is identified as **controllable margin**
- non-controllable fixed costs are not reported.

The responsibility report for the manager of the Marine Division, a profit centre of Mantle Manufacturing, is shown in figure 18.39. For the year, the Marine Division also had $60 000 of indirect fixed costs that were not controllable by the profit centre manager.

FIGURE 18.39	Responsibility report for a profit centre

MANTLE MANUFACTURING
Marine Division
Responsibility report
for the year ended 31 December 2019

	Budget	Actual	Difference Favourable F Unfavourable U
Sales	$1 200 000	$1 150 000	$50 000 U
Variable costs			
Cost of sales	500 000	490 000	10 000 F
Selling and administrative	160 000	156 000	4 000 F
Total	660 000	646 000	14 000 F
Contribution margin	540 000	504 000	36 000 U
Controllable fixed costs			
Cost of sales	100 000	100 000	—
Selling and administrative	80 000	80 000	—
Total	180 000	180 000	—
Controllable margin	$ 360 000	$ 324 000	$36 000 U

Helpful hint: Recognise that we are emphasising financial measures of performance. More effort is now being made to stress non-financial performance measures such as product quality, labour productivity, market growth, materials yield, manufacturing flexibility and technological capability.

Controllable margin is considered to be the best measure of the manager's performance in controlling revenues and costs. This report shows that the manager's performance was below budgeted expectations by approximately 10% ($36 000 ÷ $360 000). Top management would be likely to investigate the causes of this unfavourable result. Note that the report does not show the Marine Division's non-controllable fixed costs of $60 000. These costs would be included in a report on the profitability of the profit centre.

Responsibility reports for profit centres may also be prepared monthly. In addition, they may include cumulative year-to-date results.

Helpful hint: Responsibility reports are helpful tools for evaluating the performance of management. Too much emphasis on profits or investments, however, can be harmful if it ignores other important performance issues such as quality and social responsibility.

Decision/issue	Info needed for analysis	Tool or technique to use for decision	How to evaluate results to make decision
Have the individual managers been held accountable for the costs and revenues under their control?	Relevant costs and revenues, where the individual manager has authority to make day-to-day decisions about the items	Responsibility reports focused on cost centres, profit centres and investment centres as appropriate	Compare budget with actual costs for controllable items.

LEARNING REFLECTION AND CONSOLIDATION

Review it

1. What conditions are essential for responsibility accounting?
2. What is involved in a responsibility reporting system?
3. What is the main objective of a responsibility report for a cost centre?
4. What is the difference between direct fixed costs and indirect fixed costs relative to a responsibility report for a profit centre? Which of these costs are called traceable costs and which are called common costs?
5. How does contribution margin differ from controllable margin in a responsibility report for a profit centre?

Do it

New Zealand Division, which operates as a profit centre, reports the following actual results for the year: sales $1 700 000, variable costs $800 000, controllable fixed costs $400 000, non-controllable fixed costs $200 000. Annual budgeted amounts were $1 500 000, $700 000, $400 000 and $200 000, respectively. Prepare a responsibility report for the New Zealand Division for 31 December 2019.

Reasoning

In the responsibility report, variable costs are deducted from sales to show contribution margin. Controllable fixed costs are then deducted to show controllable margin. Non-controllable fixed costs are not reported; they would, however, be included in a report on the profitability of the profit centre.

Solution

NEW ZEALAND DIVISION
Responsibility report
for the year ended 31 December 2019

	Budget	Actual	Difference Favourable F Unfavourable U
Sales	$1 500 000	$1 700 000	$200 000 F
Variable costs	700 000	800 000	100 000 U
Contribution margin	800 000	900 000	100 000 F
Controllable fixed costs	400 000	400 000	—
Controllable margin	$ 400 000	$ 500 000	$100 000 F

Responsibility accounting for investment centres

As explained earlier, an important characteristic of an investment centre is that the manager can control or significantly influence the investment funds available for use. Thus, the main basis for evaluating the performance of a manager of an investment centre is **return on investment (ROI)**. The return on investment is considered to be superior to any other performance measurement because it shows the effectiveness of the manager in using the assets at the manager's disposal.

Return on investment (ROI)

The formula for calculating ROI for an investment centre, together with assumed illustrative data, is shown in figure 18.40. Both factors in the formula are controllable by the investment centre manager. Operating assets consist of current assets and property, plant and equipment used in operations by the centre and controlled by the manager. Non-operating assets such as idle property, plant and equipment assets and land held for future use are excluded. Average operating assets are usually based on the cost or carrying amount of the assets at the beginning and end of the year.

FIGURE 18.40 ROI formula

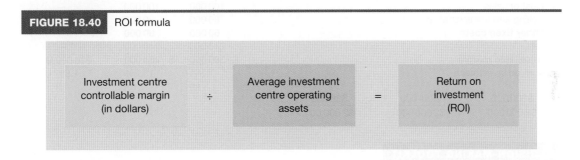

Responsibility report

The scope of the investment centre manager's responsibility significantly affects the content of the performance report. Since an investment centre is an independent entity for operating purposes, all fixed costs are controllable by the investment centre manager. For example, the manager is responsible for depreciation on investment centre assets. Accordingly, more fixed costs are identified as controllable in the performance report for an investment centre manager than in a performance report for a profit centre manager. In addition, the report shows budgeted and actual ROI below controllable margin.

To illustrate the responsibility report, we will now assume that the Marine Division of Mantle Manufacturing is an investment centre with budgeted and actual average operating assets of $2 000 000. In addition, we will assume that the manager can control the $60 000 of fixed costs that were not controllable when the division was a profit centre. The responsibility report is shown in figure 18.41.

The report shows that the manager's performance based on ROI was 12% below budget expectations (1.8% ÷ 15%). Top management would probably want an explanation of the reasons for this unfavourable result.

Judgemental factors in ROI

The return on investment approach includes two judgemental factors.
1. *Valuation of operating assets.* Assets may be valued at depreciated historical cost, fair value or an appraised value. The different measures will result in different ROI figures.
2. *Margin (profit) measure.* This measure may be controllable margin or profit.

However, the use of profit measures other than controllable margin will not result in a valid basis for evaluating the performance of an investment centre manager because they will include some non-controllable revenues and costs.

FIGURE 18.41 Responsibility report for an investment centre

MANTLE MANUFACTURING
Marine Division
Responsibility report
for the year ended 31 December 2019

	Budget	Actual	Difference Favourable F Unfavourable U
Sales	$1 200 000	$1 150 000	$50 000 U
Variable costs			
Cost of sales	500 000	490 000	10 000 F
Selling and administrative	160 000	156 000	4 000 F
Total	660 000	646 000	14 000 F
Contribution margin	540 000	504 000	36 000 U
Controllable fixed costs			
Cost of sales	100 000	100 000	—
Selling and administrative	80 000	80 000	—
Other fixed costs	60 000	60 000	—
Total	240 000	240 000	—
Controllable margin	$ 300 000	$ 264 000	$36 000 U
Return on investment	15%	13.2%	1.8% U
	(a)	(b)	(c)

(a) $\dfrac{\$300\,000}{\$2\,000\,000}$ (b) $\dfrac{\$264\,000}{\$2\,000\,000}$ (c) $\dfrac{\$36\,000}{\$2\,000\,000}$

DECISION-MAKING TOOLKIT

Decision/issue	Info needed for analysis	Tool or technique to use for decision	How to evaluate results to make decision
Has the investment centre performed to expectations?	Controllable margin (contribution margin minus controllable fixed costs), and average investment centre operating assets	Return on investment calculation	Compare actual ROI with expected ROI.

Principles of performance evaluation

Performance evaluation is at the centre of responsibility accounting. Performance evaluation is a management function that compares actual results with budget goals. It is based on internal reports prepared by the management accountant. Performance evaluation involves both behavioural and reporting principles.

Behavioural principles

The human factor is critical in evaluating performance. Behavioural principles include the following.

1. *Managers of responsibility centres should have direct input into the process of establishing budget goals of their area of responsibility.* Without such input, managers may view the goals as unrealistic or arbitrarily set by top management. Such views adversely affect managers' motivation to meet the targeted objectives.
2. *The evaluation of performance should be based entirely on matters that are controllable by the manager being evaluated.* Criticism of a manager on matters outside his or her control reduces the effectiveness of the evaluation process. Moreover, it leads to negative reactions by a manager and to doubts about the fairness of the evaluation policies.

3. *Top management should support the evaluation process.* As explained earlier, the evaluation process begins at the lowest level of responsibility and extends upwards to the highest level of management. Managers quickly lose faith in the process when top management ignores, overrules or bypasses established procedures for evaluating a manager's performance.
4. *The evaluation process must allow managers to respond to their evaluations.* Evaluation is not a one-way street. Managers should have the opportunity to explain their performance. Feedback from the manager concerned may provide useful insights into how targets may be better achieved. Evaluation without feedback is both impersonal and ineffective.
5. *The evaluation should identify both good and poor performance.* Praise for good performance is a powerful motivating factor. This is especially true when a manager's compensation includes rewards for meeting budget goals.

Reporting principles

Performance evaluation under responsibility accounting also involves reporting principles. These principles pertain mainly to the internal reports that provide the basis for evaluating performance. Performance reports should:

- contain only data that are controllable by the manager of the responsibility centre
- provide accurate and reliable budget data to measure performance
- highlight significant differences between actual results and budget goals
- be tailor-made for the intended evaluation
- be prepared at reasonable intervals.

In practice it may be difficult to differentiate between costs that can be controlled by a manager and those that cannot. For instance, labour costs are affected both by rates of pay and by hours worked. The supervisor may be able to control the hours worked by encouraging efficiency but may have no control over the amount paid per hour. For reporting purposes, it is necessary to classify costs as controllable or non-controllable.

LEARNING REFLECTION AND CONSOLIDATION

Review it
What is the formula for calculating return on investment (ROI)?

USING THE DECISION-MAKING TOOLKIT

The manufacturing overhead budget for Reebles Ltd contains the following items for the month of May 2019.

Variable expenses	
Indirect materials	$25 000
Indirect labour	12 000
Maintenance expenses	10 000
Manufacturing supplies	6 000
Total variable	53 000
Fixed expenses	
Supervision	17 000
Inspection costs	1 000
Insurance expenses	2 000
Depreciation	15 000
Total fixed	$35 000

▶

The budget was based on an estimated 2000 units being produced. During the past month, 1500 units were produced, and the following costs incurred:

Variable expenses	
Indirect materials	$25 200
Indirect labour	13 500
Maintenance expenses	8 200
Manufacturing supplies	5 100
Total variable	52 000
Fixed expenses	
Supervision	19 300
Inspection costs	1 200
Insurance expenses	2 200
Depreciation	14 700
Total fixed	$37 400

Required

(a) Determine which items would be predominantly controllable by Paul Webster, the production manager (assume 'supervision' excludes Webster's own salary).

(b) How much should have been spent during the month for the manufacture of the 1500 units?

(c) Prepare a flexible manufacturing overhead budget report for Webster.

(d) Prepare a responsibility report. Include only the costs that would have been controllable by Webster. In an attached memo, describe clearly for Webster the areas in which his performance needs to be improved.

Solution

(a) Paul Webster should be able to control all the variable expenses and the fixed expenses of supervision and inspection. Insurance and depreciation ordinarily are not the responsibility of the department manager.

(b) The total variable cost per unit is $26.50 ($53 000 ÷ 2000). The total budgeted cost during the month to manufacture 1500 units is variable costs $39 750 (1500 × $26.50) plus fixed costs, $35 000, for a total of $74 750 ($39 750 + $35 000).

(c)

REEBLES LTD
Production Department
Manufacturing overhead budget report (flexible)
for the month ended May 2019

Units		Budget at	Actual at	Difference
Expected	2000	**Budget at**	**Actual at**	**Favourable F**
Actual	1500	**1500 units**	**1500 units**	**Unfavourable U**
Variable costs				
Indirect materials		$18 750	$25 200	$ 6 450 U
Indirect labour		9 000	13 500	4 500 U
Maintenance expenses		7 500	8 200	700 U
Manufacturing supplies		4 500	5 100	600 U
Total variable		39 750	52 000	12 250 U
Fixed costs				
Supervision		17 000	19 300	2 300 U
Inspection costs		1 000	1 200	200 U
Insurance expenses		2 000	2 200	200 U
Depreciation		15 000	14 700	300 F
Total fixed		35 000	37 400	2 400 U
Total costs		**$74 750**	**$89 400**	**$14 650 U**

(d) Because a production department is a cost centre, the responsibility report should include only the costs that are controllable by the production manager. In this type of report, no distinction is made between variable and fixed costs. Budget data in the report should be based on the units actually produced.

REEBLES LTD
Production Department
Manufacturing overhead responsibility report
for the month ended May 2019

Controllable costs	Budget	Actual	Difference Favourable F Unfavourable U
Indirect materials	$18 750	$25 200	$ 6 450 U
Indirect labour	9 000	13 500	4 500 U
Maintenance expenses	7 500	8 200	700 U
Manufacturing supplies	4 500	5 100	600 U
Supervision	17 000	19 300	2 300 U
Inspection costs	1 000	1 200	200 U
Total	**$57 750**	**$72 500**	**$14 750 U**

To: Paul Webster, Production Manager
From: General Manager of Production
Subject: Performance Evaluation for the Month of May 2019

Your performance in controlling costs that are your responsibility was very disappointing in the month of May 2019. As indicated in the accompanying responsibility report, total costs were $14 750 over budget. On a percentage basis, costs were 26% over budget. As you can see, actual costs were over budget for every cost item. In three instances, costs were significantly over budget (indirect materials 34%, indirect labour 50%, and supervision 14%).

It is imperative that you get costs under control in your department as soon as possible.

We need to talk about ways to implement more effective cost control measures. Please meet in my office at 9 am on Wednesday to discuss possible alternatives.

SUMMARY

18.1 Outline the benefits and essential elements of effective budgeting.

The main advantages of budgeting are that it (a) requires management to plan ahead, (b) provides definite financial objectives for evaluating performance, (c) creates an early warning system for potential problems, (d) facilitates coordination of activities, (e) results in greater management awareness, and (f) contributes to positive behaviour patterns. The essentials of effective budgeting are (a) sound organisational structure, (b) research and analysis, and (c) acceptance by all levels of management.

18.2 Identify and describe the components of the master budget.

The master budget consists of the following budgets: (a) sales, (b) production, (c) direct materials, (d) direct labour, (e) manufacturing overhead, (f) selling and administrative expense, (g) cash budget, (h) capital expenditure budget, (i) budgeted statement of profit or loss, (j) budgeted statement of financial position and (k) budgeted statement of cash flows.

18.3 Explain and prepare the main sections of a cash budget.

The cash budget has three sections (receipts, payments, and financing) and the beginning and ending cash balances.

18.4 Describe the sources of information for preparing the budgeted statement of profit or loss and statement of financial position.

The budgeted statement of profit or loss and statement of financial position are prepared from (a) the sales budget, (b) the budgets for direct materials, direct labour and manufacturing overhead, and (c) the selling and administrative expense budget and the cash budget.

18.5 Indicate the applicability of budgeting in non-manufacturing entities.

Budgeting may be used in merchandising entities for development of a master budget. In service entities, budgeting is a critical factor in coordinating staff needs with anticipated services. In not-for-profit and government entities, the starting point in budgeting is usually expenditures, not receipts.

18.6 Explain the concept of budgetary control.

Budgetary control consists of (a) preparing periodic budget reports that compare actual results with planned objectives, (b) analysing the differences to determine their causes, (c) taking appropriate corrective action, and (d) modifying future plans, if necessary.

18.7 Compare and contrast the use of static and flexible budgets.

Static budget reports are useful in evaluating the progress towards meeting planned sales and profit goals. They are also appropriate in assessing a manager's effectiveness in controlling fixed costs and expenses when (a) actual activity closely approximates the master budget activity level and/or (b) the behaviour of the costs in response to changes in activity is fixed.

Flexible budget reports permit an evaluation of a manager's performance in controlling production and costs. To develop the flexible budget it is necessary to:
(a) identify the activity index and the relevant range of activity
(b) identify the variable costs and determine the budgeted variable cost per unit of activity for each cost
(c) identify the fixed costs and determine the budgeted amount for each cost
(d) prepare the budget for selected increments of activity within the relevant range.

18.8 Describe the concept of responsibility accounting.

Responsibility accounting involves the accumulation and reporting of revenues and costs on the basis of the individual manager who has the authority to make the day-to-day decisions about the items. Under responsibility accounting, the evaluation of a manager's performance is based on the matters directly under the manager's control. In responsibility accounting, it is necessary to distinguish between controllable and non-controllable fixed costs and to identify three types of responsibility centre — cost, profit and investment.

18.9 Identify the content of responsibility reports and their use in performance evaluation.
Responsibility reports for cost centres compare actual costs with flexible budget data. The reports show only controllable costs and no distinction is made between variable and fixed costs. Responsibility reports for profit centres show contribution margin, controllable fixed costs, and controllable margin for each profit centre. The main basis for evaluating performance in investment centres is return on investment (ROI). The formula for calculating ROI for investment centres is: Controllable margin (in dollars) ÷ Average operating assets.

DECISION-MAKING TOOLKIT — A SUMMARY

DECISION-MAKING TOOLKIT

Decision/issue	Info needed for analysis	Tool or technique to use for decision	How to evaluate results to make decision
Has the entity met its targets for sales, production expenses, selling and administrative expenses, and profit?	Sales forecasts, inventory levels, projected materials, labour, overhead, and selling and administrative requirements	Master budget — a set of interrelated budgets including sales, production, materials, labour, overhead, and selling and administrative budgets. Compare actual results to budget.	Results are favourable if revenues are equal to or exceed budgeted amounts, or if expenses are equal to or less than budgeted amounts.
Will the entity need to borrow funds in the coming quarter?	Beginning cash balance, cash receipts, cash payments, and desired cash balance	Examine the cash budget.	The entity will need to borrow money if the cash budget indicates a projected cash deficiency of available cash over cash payments for the quarter.
Are the increased costs resulting from increased production reasonable?	Variable costs projected at different levels of production	Compare the actual costs to the flexible budget.	After taking into account different production levels, results are favourable if expenses are less than budgeted amounts.
Have the individual managers been held accountable for the costs and revenues under their control?	Relevant costs and revenues, where the individual manager has authority to make day-to-day decisions about the items	Responsibility reports focused on cost centres, profit centres and investment centres as appropriate	Compare budget with actual costs for controllable items.
Has the investment centre performed to expectations?	Controllable margin (contribution margin minus controllable fixed costs), and average investment centre operating assets	Return on investment calculation	Compare actual ROI with expected ROI.

KEY TERMS

budget A formal written summary of management's plans for a specified future time period, expressed in financial terms.

budgetary control The use of budgets to control operations.

budgeted financial statements Individual budgets that indicate the cash resources needed for expected operations and planned capital expenditures.

budgeted statement of financial position A projection of financial position at the end of the budget period.

budgeted statement of profit or loss An estimate of the expected profitability of operations for the budget period.

cash budget A projection of anticipated cash flows.

controllable costs Costs that a manager has the authority to incur within a given period of time.

controllable margin Contribution margin less controllable fixed costs.

cost centre A responsibility centre that incurs costs but does not directly generate revenues.

decentralisation Control of operations is delegated by top management to many managers throughout the entity.

direct fixed costs Costs that relate specifically to a responsibility centre and are incurred for the sole benefit of the centre; also called traceable costs.

direct labour budget A projection of the quantity and cost of direct labour to be incurred to meet production requirements.

direct materials budget An estimate of the quantity and cost of direct materials to be purchased.

flexible budget A projection of budget data for various levels of activity.

indirect fixed costs Costs that are incurred for the benefit of more than one profit centre; also called common costs.

investment centre A responsibility centre that incurs costs, generates revenues, and has control over the investment funds available for use.

long-range planning A formalised process of selecting strategies to achieve long-term goals and developing policies and plans to implement the strategies.

management by exception The review of budget reports by top management directed entirely or mainly to differences between actual results and planned objectives.

manufacturing overhead budget An estimate of expected manufacturing overhead costs for the budget period.

master budget A set of interrelated budgets that constitutes a plan of action for a specific period of time.

non-controllable costs Costs incurred indirectly and allocated to a responsibility centre that are not controllable at that level.

operating budgets Individual budgets that culminate in the preparation of the cash budget and the budgeted statement of profit or loss.

production budget A projection of the units that must be produced to meet anticipated sales.

profit centre A responsibility centre that incurs costs and also generates revenues.

purchases budget The estimated cost of goods to be purchased in a retail entity to meet expected sales.

responsibility accounting A part of management accounting that involves accumulating and reporting revenues and costs on the basis of the individual manager who has the authority to make the day-to-day decisions about the items.

responsibility reporting system The preparation of reports for each level of responsibility shown in the entity's organisation chart.

return on investment (ROI) A measure of management's effectiveness in using assets at its disposal in an investment centre.

sales budget An estimate of expected sales for the budget period.

sales forecast The projection of potential sales for the industry and the entity's expected share of such sales.

selling and administrative expense budget A projection of anticipated selling and administrative expenses for the budget period.

static budget A projection of budget data at one level of activity.

DEMONSTRATION PROBLEM

Glenda Ltd uses a flexible budget for manufacturing overhead based on direct labour hours. For 2020 the master overhead budget for the Packaging Department at normal capacity of 300 000 direct labour hours was as follows:

Variable costs		Fixed costs	
Indirect labour	$360 000	Supervision	$ 60 000
Supplies and lubricants	150 000	Depreciation	24 000
Maintenance	210 000	Rates and taxes	18 000
Electricity	120 000	Insurance	12 000
Total	**$840 000**	**Total**	**$114 000**

During July, 24 000 direct labour hours were worked when 25 000 hours were expected to be worked. The business incurred the following variable costs in July: indirect labour $30 200, supplies and lubricants $11 600, maintenance $17 500, and electricity $9200. Actual fixed overhead costs were the same as monthly budgeted fixed costs.

Required

Prepare a flexible budget report for the Packaging Department for July.

PROBLEM-SOLVING STRATEGIES

1. Use budget data for actual direct labour hours worked.
2. Classify each cost as variable or fixed.
3. Determine the difference between budgeted and actual costs.
4. Identify the difference as favourable or unfavourable.
5. Determine the difference in total variable costs, total fixed costs and total costs.

SOLUTION TO DEMONSTRATION PROBLEM

GLENDA LTD
Packaging Department
Manufacturing overhead budget report (flexible)
for the month ended 31 July 2020

Direct labour hours (DLH)				Difference
Expected	25 000	**Budget**	**Actual costs**	**Favourable F**
Actual	24 000	**25 000 DLH**	**24 000 DLH**	**Unfavourable U**
Variable costs				
Indirect labour ($1.20)		$28 800	$30 200	$1 400 U
Supplies and lubricants ($0.50)		12 000	11 600	400 F
Maintenance ($0.70)		16 800	17 500	700 U
Electricity ($0.40)		9 600	9 200	400 F
Total variable ($2.80)		67 200	68 500	1 300 U
Fixed costs				
Supervision		5 000	5 000	—
Depreciation		2 000	2 000	—
Rates and taxes		1 500	1 500	—
Insurance		1 000	1 000	—
Total fixed		9 500	9 500	—
Total costs		**$76 700**	**$78 000**	**$1 300 U**

SELF-STUDY QUESTIONS

18.1 The benefits of budgeting include *all but one* of the following: **LO1**
   (a) Management can plan ahead.
   (b) An early warning system is provided for potential problems.
   (c) It enables disciplinary action to be taken at every level of responsibility.
   (d) The coordination of activities is facilitated.

18.2 The production budget shows: **LO2**
   (a) management's best estimate of sales revenue for the budget period.
   (b) the units that must be produced to meet anticipated sales.
   (c) an estimate of both the quantity and cost of direct materials to be purchased.
   (d) the expected manufacturing overhead costs for the budget period.

18.3 The formula for the production budget is budgeted sales in units plus: **LO2**
   (a) desired ending inventory less beginning inventory.
   (b) beginning finished goods units less desired ending finished goods units.
   (c) desired ending direct materials units less beginning direct materials units.
   (d) desired ending finished goods units less beginning finished goods units.

18.4 Each of the following budgets is used in preparing the budgeted statement of profit or loss *except* the: **LO3**
   (a) sales budget.
   (b) selling and administrative budget.
   (c) capital expenditure budget.
   (d) direct labour budget.

18.5 Expected direct materials purchases in Read Ltd are $70 000 in the first quarter and $90 000 in the second quarter; 40% of the purchases are paid in cash as incurred and the balance is paid in the following quarter. The budgeted cash payments for purchases in the second quarter are: **LO4**
   (a) $96 000.
   (b) $90 000.
   (c) $78 000.
   (d) $72 000.

18.6 The budget for a merchandising entity differs from a budget for a manufacturing entity because: **LO5**
   (a) a merchandise purchases budget replaces the production budget.
   (b) the manufacturing budgets are not applicable.
   (c) None of the above.
   (d) Both (a) and (b) above.

18.7 Which of the following is an example of a favourable budget difference? **LO6**
   (a) Actual sales are below budgeted sales.
   (b) Budgeted direct materials costs exceed actual direct material costs.
   (c) Actual operating expense is less than budgeted operating expense.
   (d) Both (b) and (c).

18.8 A static budget is useful in controlling costs when cost behaviour is: **LO7**
   (a) non-linear.
   (b) linear.
   (c) variable.
   (d) fixed.

18.9 The key difference between static and flexible budgets lies in: **LO7**
   (a) the source of information.
   (b) the number of activity levels displayed.

(c) the breakdown of variable and fixed costs.

(d) None of the above.

18.10 Under responsibility accounting, the evaluation of a manager's performance is based on matters that the manager: **LO8**

(a) directly controls.

(b) directly and indirectly controls.

(c) indirectly controls.

(d) has shared responsibility with another manager.

18.11 Responsibility reports for cost centres: **LO9**

(a) distinguish between fixed and variable costs.

(b) use static budget data.

(c) include both controllable and non-controllable costs.

(d) include only controllable costs.

18.12 In a responsibility report for a profit centre, controllable fixed costs are deducted from contribution margin to show: **LO9**

(a) profit centre margin.

(b) controllable margin.

(c) profit.

(d) profit from operations.

QUESTIONS

18.1 Matthew and Jacqui are discussing the benefits of budgeting. They ask you to identify the main advantages of budgeting. Comply with their request.

18.2 Christine Nguyen asks your help in understanding the essentials of effective budgeting. Identify the essentials for Christine.

18.3 Chen Ltd has 6000 beginning finished goods units. Budgeted sales units are 150 000. If management desires 10 000 ending finished goods units, what are the required units of production?

18.4 In preparing the direct materials budget for Parker Ltd, management concludes that required purchases are 54 000 units. If 50 000 direct materials units are required in production and there are 7000 units of beginning direct materials, what is the desired units of ending direct materials?

18.5 How may expected revenues in a service entity be calculated?

18.6 The following purposes are part of a budgetary reporting system: (a) determine efficient use of materials, (b) control overhead costs, and (c) determine whether profit objectives are being met. For each purpose, indicate the name of the report, the frequency of the report, and the main recipient(s) of the report.

18.7 'A flexible budget is really a series of static budgets.' Is this true? Why?

18.8 Kate Coulter is confused about how a flexible budget is prepared. Identify the steps for Kate.

18.9 Ann Wilkins is studying for an accounting exam. Describe for Ann what conditions are necessary for responsibility accounting to be used effectively.

18.10 What does return on investment (ROI) measure? What factors affect the ROI?

BRIEF EXERCISES

BE18.1 **Prepare a diagram of a master budget.** **LO2**

O'Connor Manufacturing uses the following budgets: statement of financial position, capital expenditure, cash, direct labour, direct materials, statement of profit or loss, manufacturing overhead, production, sales, and selling and administrative expense. Prepare a diagram of the interrelationships of the budgets in the master budget. Indicate whether each budget is an operating or a financial statement budget.

BE18.2 **Prepare a direct labour budget for two quarters.** **LO2**

For Haught & Son, units to be produced are 5000 in quarter 1 and 6000 in quarter 2. It takes 1.5 hours to make a finished unit, and the expected hourly wage rate is $12 per hour. Prepare a direct labour budget, by quarters, for the 6 months ending 30 June 2018.

BE18.3 **Prepare data for a cash budget.** **LO3**

Liang Industries expects credit sales for January, February and March to be $300 000, $275 000 and $450 000, respectively. It is expected that 60% of the sales will be collected in the month of sale, and 40% will be collected in the following month. Calculate cash collections from customers for each month.

BE18.4 **Prepare a budgeted statement of profit or loss for the year.** **LO4**

Birtles Pty Ltd has completed all of its operating budgets. The sales budget for the year shows 60 000 units and total sales of $3 000 000. The total unit cost of making one unit of sales is $35. Selling and administrative expenses are expected to be $600 000, and income tax is estimated to be $90 000. Prepare a budgeted statement of profit or loss for the year ending 31 December.

BE18.5 **Review business performance by preparing a budget report.** **LO6**

Marco Hass started his Marco Consulting business in 2019. The following is Marco's projection for the year:

Service revenue	$85 000
Salary expense	55 000
Rent expense	12 000
Other operating expenses	10 000

The actual results for 2019 are as follows:

Service revenue	$95 000
Salary expense	62 000
Rent expense	12 000
Other operating expenses	14 000

Assist Marco to review his business's first year of operation by preparing a budget report that highlights the various budget differences. Comment on whether the business had a successful first year.

BE18.6 **Show usefulness of flexible budgets in evaluating performance.** **LO7**

In Birch Ltd, direct labour is $20 per hour, and the business expects to operate at 10 000 direct labour hours each month. In January, direct labour totalling $207 000 is incurred in working 10 800 hours. Prepare a static budget report and a flexible budget report. Evaluate the usefulness of each report.

BE18.7 **Prepare a responsibility report for a profit centre.** **LO9**

Lehman Manufacturing accumulates the following summary data for the year ending 31 December 2019 for its Aqua Division, which it operates as a profit centre: sales — $2 500 000 budget, $2 600 000 actual; variable costs — $1 500 000 budget, $1 550 000 actual; and controllable fixed costs — $400 000 budget, $410 000 actual. Prepare a responsibility report for the Aqua Division.

BE18.8 Calculate return on investment using the ROI formula and under changed conditions. **LO9**

For its three investment centres, Dingo Ltd accumulates the following data:

	A	B	C
Sales	$2 400 000	$3 600 000	$4 800 000
Controllable margin	1 800 000	2 880 000	3 840 000
Average operating assets	7 200 000	9 600 000	12 000 000

(a) Calculate the return on investment (ROI) for each centre.

(b) The centres expect the following changes in the next year: (A) increase sales 10%; (B) decrease costs $240 000; (C) decrease average operating assets $480 000. Calculate the expected return on investment (ROI) for each centre. Assume centre A has a contribution margin percentage of 80%.

EXERCISES

E18.1 Prepare a sales budget for 2 quarters. **LO2**

L. Quick Electronics Ltd produces and sells two models of pocket calculators, XQ-103 and XQ-104. The calculators sell for $12 and $20, respectively. Because of the intense competition Quick faces, management budgets sales semi-annually. Its projections for the first 2 quarters of 2018 are as follows:

	Unit sales	
Product	Quarter 1	Quarter 2
XQ-103	45 000	40 000
XQ-104	18 000	20 000

No changes in selling prices are anticipated.

Required

Prepare a sales budget for the 2 quarters ending 30 June 2018. List the products and show for each quarter and for the 6 months, units, selling price, and total sales by product and in total.

E18.2 Prepare quarterly production budgets. **LO2**

S. Stahl Pty Ltd produces and sells two types of car batteries, the heavy-duty HD-240 and the long-life LL-250. The 2019 sales budget for the two products is as follows:

Quarter	HD-240	LL-250
1	7 000	12 000
2	9 000	20 000
3	10 000	22 000
4	12 000	40 000

The 1 January 2019 inventory of HD-240 and LL-250 units is 4200 and 7200 respectively. Management desires an ending inventory each quarter equal to 60% of the next quarter's sales. Sales in the first quarter of 2020 are expected to be 30% higher than sales in the same quarter in 2019.

Required

Prepare separate quarterly production budgets for each product by quarters for 2019.

E18.3 Define terms in budgeting and responsibility accounting.   **LO2, 7, 8, 9**

Complete the following statements with one of the terms listed below (some terms may not be used):

Sales budget	Return on investment	Cost centres
Master budget	Investment centres	Flexible budget
Profit centres	Static budget	Operating budgets

(a) Managers of _____ are responsible for revenues and costs of the business units.

(b) A set of interrelated budgets make up the _____.

(c) The _____ is often the starting point of budget preparation.

(d) A measure of the effectiveness of investment funds' use to generate profit is called _____.

(e) A _____ projects budget data for a number of activity levels.

(f) A responsibility centre that generates revenues, incurs costs and has control over investment funds is called a(n) _____.

E18.4 Prepare production and direct materials budgets by quarters for 6 months.   **LO2**

Kasper Ltd's budget committee has reached agreement on the following data for the 6 months ending 30 June 2019:

Sales units (by quarters)	(1) 6000, (2) 9000
Ending raw materials inventory	50% of the next quarter's production requirements
Ending finished goods inventory	25% of the next quarter's expected sales units

The ending raw materials and finished goods inventories at 31 December 2018 follow the same percentage relationships to production and sales that occur in 2019. Three kilograms of raw materials are required to make each unit of finished goods. Raw materials purchased are expected to cost $5 per kilogram. Sales of 8000 units and required production of 8500 units are expected in the third quarter of 2019.

Required

(a) Prepare a production budget by quarters for the 6 months.

(b) Prepare a direct materials budget by quarters for the 6 months.

E18.5 Prepare a direct labour budget.   **LO2**

Manies Pty Ltd is preparing its direct labour budget for 2018 from the following production budget based on a calendar year:

Quarter	Units	Quarter	Units
1	20 000	3	35 000
2	25 000	4	30 000

Each unit requires 1.6 hours of direct labour.

Required

Prepare a direct labour cost budget for 2018. Wage rates per hour are expected to be $14 for the first 2 quarters and $15 for quarters 3 and 4.

E18.6 Prepare a budgeted statement of profit or loss for the year.   **LO2, 4**

Sally Ltd has accumulated the following budget data for the year 2019:

1. Sales: 25 000 units; unit selling price $80.
2. Cost of one unit of finished goods: direct materials 2 kilograms at $5 per kilogram; direct labour 3 hours at $12 per hour; and manufacturing overhead $6 per direct labour hour.
3. Inventories (raw materials only): Beginning, 10 000 kilograms; ending 15 000 kilograms.
4. Raw materials cost: $5 per kilogram.

5. Selling and administrative expenses: $150 000.

6. Income tax: 30% of profit before income tax.

Required

(a) Prepare a budgeted statement of profit or loss for 2019. Show the calculation of cost of sales.

(b) Describe the sources of information for preparing the budgeted statement of profit or loss and budgeted statement of financial position.

E18.7 Prepare a cash budget for 2 months. **LO3**

Sala Pty Ltd expects to have a cash balance of $32 000 on 1 January 2019. Relevant monthly budget data for the first 2 months of 2019 are as follows:

1. Collections from customers: January $87 000; February $169 000.

2. Payments to suppliers: January $50 000; February $88 000.

3. Direct labour: January $40 000; February $45 000. Wages are paid in the month they are incurred.

4. Manufacturing overhead: January $21 000; February $30 000. These costs include depreciation of $1000 per month. All other overhead costs are paid as incurred.

5. Selling and administrative expenses: January $15 000; February $20 000. These costs are exclusive of depreciation. They are paid as incurred.

Sales of investments in January are expected to realise $15 000 in cash. Sala Pty Ltd has a line of credit at a local bank that enables it to borrow up to $25 000. The entity wants to maintain a minimum monthly cash balance of $20 000.

Required

Prepare a cash budget for January and February.

E18.8 Prepare a purchases budget and budgeted statement of profit or loss for a retail entity. **LO5**

In May 2018, the budget committee of Railway Street Stores assembles the following data in the preparation of budgeted inventory purchases for the month of June:

1. Expected sales: June $800 000, July $900 000.

2. Cost of sales is expected to be 60% of sales.

3. Desired ending inventory is 30% of the following (next) month's cost of sales.

4. The beginning inventory at 1 June will be the desired amount.

Required

(a) Calculate the budgeted inventory purchases for June.

(b) Prepare a partial budgeted statement of profit or loss for June to gross profit.

E18.9 Prepare a flexible manufacturing overhead budget and report and comment on findings. **LO7**

Deeva Ltd uses a flexible budget for manufacturing overhead based on direct labour hours. Variable manufacturing overhead costs per direct labour hour are as follows:

Indirect labour	$1.50
Indirect materials	0.75
Electricity	0.45

Fixed overhead costs per month are: supervision $4500, depreciation $2250, and rates and taxes $1200. The business believes it will normally operate in a range of 7000–10 000 direct labour hours per month.

Assume that in July 2018, Deeva Ltd incurs the following manufacturing overhead costs:

Variable costs		Fixed costs	
Indirect labour	$13 050	Supervision	$4 500
Indirect materials	6 450	Depreciation	2 250
Electricity	3 750	Rates and taxes	1 200

Required

(a) Prepare a monthly flexible manufacturing overhead budget for 2018 for the expected range of activity, using increments of 1000 direct labour hours.

(b) Prepare a flexible budget performance report, assuming 9000 direct labour hours were worked during the month. Deeva expected 9000 direct labour hours to be worked.

(c) Prepare a flexible budget performance report, assuming 8500 direct labour hours were worked during the month. Deeva expected 8500 direct labour hours to be worked.

(d) Comment on your findings.

E18.10 Prepare a flexible budget report and answer the question.   **LO7**

As sales manager, Todd Keyser was given the following static budget report for selling expenses in the Clothing Department of O'Keefe Pty Ltd for the month of October.

O'KEEFE PTY LTD Clothing Department Budget report for the month ended 31 October 2018			
	Budget	**Actual**	**Difference** **Favourable F** **Unfavourable U**
Sales in units	12 000	15 000	3 000 F
Variable costs			
Sales commissions	$ 3 600	$ 4 200	$ 600 U
Advertising expense	1 800	2 100	300 U
Travel expense	7 800	9 150	1 350 U
Free samples given out	1 200	1 550	350 U
Total variable	14 400	17 000	2 600 U
Fixed costs			
Rent	1 500	1 500	—
Sales salaries	1 200	1 200	—
Office salaries	800	800	—
Depreciation—motor vehicles (sales staff)	500	500	—
Total fixed	4 000	4 000	—
Total costs	**$18 400**	**$21 000**	**$2 600 U**

As a result of this budget report, Todd was called into the CEO's office and congratulated on his fine sales performance. He was reprimanded, however, for allowing his costs to get out of control. Todd knew something was wrong with the performance report that he had been given. However, he was not sure what to do, and has come to you for advice.

Required

(a) Prepare a budget report based on flexible budget data to help Todd.

(b) Should Todd have been reprimanded? Explain.

E18.11 Prepare reports in a responsibility reporting system.   **LO8**

Aza Steel's organisation chart includes the managing director; the production manager; three assembly factories — Brisbane, Adelaide and Perth; and two departments within each factory — Machining and Finishing. Budget and actual manufacturing cost data for July 2018 are as follows:

1. Finishing Department — Brisbane: direct materials $42 000 actual, $46 000 budget; direct labour $83 000 actual, $82 000 budget; manufacturing overhead $51 000 actual, $49 200 budget.

2. Machining Department — Brisbane: total manufacturing costs $218 000 actual, $214 000 budget.

3. Adelaide factory: Total manufacturing costs $426 000 actual, $421 000 budget.
4. Perth factory: Total manufacturing costs $494 000 actual, $499 000 budget.

The Brisbane factory production manager's office costs were $95 000 actual and $92 000 budget. The production manager's office costs were $132 000 actual and $130 000 budget. Office costs are not allocated to departments and factories.

Required

Prepare the reports in a responsibility system for (a) the Finishing Department — Brisbane, (b) the factory manager — Brisbane, and (c) the production manager. Use the format in figure 18.36.

E18.12 **Calculate missing amounts in responsibility reports for two profit centres and prepare a report.**
LO9

Amanda Media Ltd has two divisions that are operated as profit centres. Budgeted operating data for the divisions for 2019 are as follows:

Operating data	Print Media Division	Online Media Division
Contribution margin	$320 000	$450 000
Controllable fixed costs	180 000	(3)
Controllable margin	(1)	185 000
Service revenue	450 000	(4)
Variable expenses	(2)	230 000

Actual results for the year ended 30 June 2019 for the Online Media Division are as follows:

Sales	$600 000
Variable expenses	220 000
Contribution margin	380 000
Controllable fixed costs	265 000
Controllable margin	$115 000

Required

(a) Calculate the missing amounts. Show your calculations.
(b) Prepare a responsibility report for the Online Media Division for the year ended 30 June 2019.

E18.13 **Calculate ROI for current year and for possible future changes.**
LO9

The Mastercraft Division of Sands Ltd reported the following data for the current year:

Sales	$3 600 000
Variable costs	2 160 000
Controllable fixed costs	720 000
Average operating assets	6 000 000

Top management is unhappy with the investment centre's return on investment (ROI). It asks the manager of the Mastercraft Division to submit plans to improve ROI in the next year. The manager believes it is feasible to consider the following independent courses of action:

1. Increase sales by $384 000 with no change in the contribution margin percentage.
2. Reduce variable costs by $120 000.
3. Reduce average operating assets by 5%.

Required

(a) Calculate the return on investment (ROI) for the current year.
(b) Using the ROI formula, calculate the ROI under each of the proposed courses of action. (Round to one decimal.)

PROBLEM SET A

PSA18.1 Prepare budgeted statement of profit or loss and supporting budgets.   **LO2, 4**

Oakbrook Farm Supply Ltd manufactures and sells a pesticide called Snare. The following data are available for preparing budgets for Snare for the first 2 quarters of 2018:

1. Sales: Quarter 1, 35 000 bags; quarter 2, 50 000 bags. Selling price is $60 per bag.
2. Direct materials: Each bag of Snare requires 5 kilograms of Gumm at a cost of $3 per kilogram and 8 kilograms of Tarr at $1.50 per kilogram.
3. Desired inventory levels:

Type of inventory	1 January	1 April	1 July
Snare (bags)	8 000	12 000	18 000
Gumm (kilograms)	9 000	10 000	13 000
Tarr (kilograms)	14 000	20 000	25 000

4. Direct labour: Direct labour time is 15 minutes per bag at an hourly rate of $12 per hour.
5. Selling and administrative expenses are expected to be 8% of sales plus $175 000 per quarter.
6. Income taxes are expected to be 30% of profit from operations.

Your assistant has prepared two budgets: (1) The manufacturing overhead budget shows expected costs to be 150% of direct labour cost. (2) The direct materials budget for Tarr shows the cost of Tarr to be $477 000 in quarter 1 and $679 500 in quarter 2.

Required

Prepare the budgeted statement of profit or loss for the first 6 months and all required supporting budgets by quarters and in total. (*Note:* Use variable and fixed costs in the selling and administrative expense budget.)

PSA18.2 Prepare sales, production, direct materials, direct labour, and statement of profit or loss budgets.   **LO2, 4**

Joe Dunham Ltd is preparing its annual budgets for the year ending 30 June 2018. Accounting assistants furnish the following data for the company's two products — JB 50 and JB 60.

	Product JB 50	Product JB 60
Sales budget:		
Anticipated volume in units	480 000	180 000
Unit selling price	$20.00	$25.00
Production budget:		
Desired ending finished goods units	25 000	15 000
Beginning finished goods units	30 000	10 000
Direct materials budget:		
Direct materials per unit (kilograms)	2	3
Desired ending direct materials kilograms	30 000	15 000
Beginning direct materials kilograms	40 000	10 000
Cost per kilogram	$3.00	$4.00
Direct labour:		
Direct labour hours per unit	0.4	0.6
Direct labour rate per hour	$11.00	$11.00
Budgeted statement of profit or loss:		
Total unit cost	$12.00	$20.00

An accounting assistant has prepared the detailed manufacturing overhead budget and the selling and administrative expense budget. The latter shows selling expenses of $660 000 for product JB 50 and $360 000 for product JB 60, and administrative expenses of $420 000 for product JB 50 and $340 000 for product JB 60. Income taxes are expected to be 30%.

Required

Prepare the following budgets for the year. Show data for each product.

(a) Sales.

(b) Production.

(c) Direct materials.

(d) Direct labour.

(e) Statement of profit or loss. (*Note:* Income taxes are not allocated to the products.)

PSA18.3 **Prepare sales and production budgets and calculate cost per unit under two plans.** **LO2**

Hindu Industries had sales in 2019 of $6 300 000 and gross profit of $1 500 000. Management is considering two alternative budget plans to increase its gross profit in 2020.

Plan A would increase the selling price per unit from $9.00 to $9.40. Sales volume would decrease by 5% from its 2019 level. Plan B would decrease the selling price per unit by $0.50. The marketing department expects that the sales volume would increase by 150 000 units.

At the end of 2019, Hindu has 30 000 units of inventory on hand. If Plan A is accepted, the 2020 ending inventory should be equal to 4% of the 2020 sales. If Plan B is accepted, the ending inventory should be equal to 40 000 units. Each unit produced will cost $1.60 in direct labour, $2.00 in direct materials, and $0.90 in variable overhead. The fixed overhead for 2020 should be $1 800 000.

Required

(a) Prepare a sales budget for 2020 under each plan.

(b) Prepare a production budget for 2020 under each plan.

(c) Calculate the production cost per unit under each plan. Why is the cost per unit different for each of the two plans? (Round to 2 decimals.)

(d) Which plan should be accepted? (*Hint:* Calculate the gross profit under each plan.)

PSA18.4 **Prepare cash budget for 2 months.** **LO3**

Sierra Star prepares monthly cash budgets. Relevant data from operating budgets for 2020 are:

	January	February
Sales	$350 000	$400 000
Direct materials purchases	95 000	110 000
Direct labour	80 000	95 000
Manufacturing overhead	60 000	75 000
Selling and administrative expenses	75 000	85 000

All sales are on account. Collections are expected to be 50% in the month of sale, 30% in the first month following the sale, and 20% in the second month following the sale. Of direct material purchases, 40% are paid in cash in the month of purchase, and the balance due is paid in the month following the purchase. All other items above are paid in the month incurred. Depreciation has been excluded from manufacturing overhead and selling and administrative expenses.

Other data:

1. Credit sales: November 2019, $200 000; December 2019, $280 000.

2. Purchases of direct materials: December 2019, $90 000.

3. Other receipts: January — collection of 31 December 2019, interest receivable $3000; February — proceeds from sale of investments $5000.

4. Other disbursements: February — payment of $20 000 for land.

The cash balance on 1 January 2020 is expected to be $60 000. Sierra Star wants to maintain a minimum cash balance of $50 000.

Required

(a) Prepare schedules for (1) expected collections from customers and (2) expected payments for direct materials purchases.

(b) Using a spreadsheet program, prepare a cash budget for January and February.

PSA18.5 Prepare purchases and statement of profit or loss budgets for a retail entity.   **LO2, 4, 5**

The budget committee of Rex Ltd collects the following data for its Auckland Store to prepare the budgeted statements of profit or loss for July and August 2020.

1. Expected sales: July, $400 000; August, $450 000; September, $500 000.
2. Cost of sales is expected to be 70% of sales.
3. Company policy is to maintain ending inventory at 25% of the following month's cost of sales.
4. Operating expenses are estimated to be:

Sales salaries	$20 000 per month
Advertising	4% of monthly sales
Delivery expense	2% of monthly sales
Sales commissions	3% of monthly sales
Rent expense	$3000 per month
Depreciation	$700 per month
Electricity	$500 per month
Insurance	$300 per month

5. Income tax is estimated to be 30% of profit from operations.

Required

(a) Prepare the purchases budget for each month.

(b) Prepare budgeted statements of profit or loss for each month. Show the details of cost of sales in the statements.

PSA18.6 Prepare a budgeted statement of profit or loss and statement of financial position.   **LO4**

Sage Industries' statement of financial position as at 31 December 2018 is presented below.

SAGE INDUSTRIES Statement of financial position as at 31 December 2018		
ASSETS		
Current assets		
Cash		$ 9 000
Accounts receivable		87 500
Finished goods inventory (2500 units × $23)		57 500
Total current assets		$154 000
Property, plant and equipment		
Equipment	$40 000	
Less: Accumulated depreciation	10 000	30 000
Total assets		**$184 000**
LIABILITIES AND SHAREHOLDERS' EQUITY		
Liabilities		
Bank loan		$ 40 000
Accounts payable		64 000
Total liabilities		104 000
Shareholders' equity		
Share capital	$50 000	
Retained earnings	30 000	
Total shareholders' equity		80 000
Total liabilities and shareholders' equity		**$184 000**

Budgeted data for the year 2019 include the following:

	4th quarter of 2019	Year 2019 total
Sales budget (10 000 units at $40)	$100 000	$400 000
Direct material used	30 000	120 000
Direct labour	20 000	80 000
Manufacturing overhead applied	7 500	30 000
Selling and administrative expenses	12 500	50 000

Additional information:
1. Desired ending inventory of 4500 units is required to meet sales requirements for 2020.
2. The production budget shows 1200 required units of output in 2019 with a production unit cost of $23.
3. Selling and administrative expenses include $5000 for depreciation on equipment.
4. Interest expense is expected to be $5000 for the year.
5. Income tax is expected to be 30% of profit before income tax.
6. All sales and purchases are on account. It is expected that 60% of quarterly sales is collected in cash within the quarter and the remainder is collected in the following quarter.
7. Direct materials purchased from suppliers are paid 50% in the quarter incurred and the remainder in the following quarter. Purchases in the fourth quarter were the same as the materials used.
8. Accounts payable at 31 December 2019 include amounts due to suppliers plus other accounts payable of $8000.
9. In 2019, the business expects to purchase additional equipment costing $30 000.
10. Sage Industries expects to pay $10 000 on the bank loan plus all interest due and payable to 31 December (included in interest expense $5000).
11. In 2020, the business expects to declare and pay a $20 000 cash dividend.
12. Unpaid income tax at 31 December will be $15 000.
13. The cash budget shows an expected cash balance of $42 200 at 31 December 2019.

Required
Prepare a budgeted statement of profit or loss for 2019 and a budgeted statement of financial position at 31 December 2019. In preparing the statement of profit or loss, you will need to calculate cost of goods manufactured (materials + labour + overhead) and finished goods inventory (31 December 2019).

PSA18.7 Prepare flexible budget and budget report for manufacturing overhead.　　　　**LO6, 7**
Greish Ltd estimates that 240 000 direct labour hours will be worked during 2019 in the Assembly Department. On this basis, the following budgeted manufacturing overhead data are calculated.

Variable overhead costs		Fixed overhead costs	
Indirect labour	$ 72 000	Supervision	$ 72 000
Indirect materials	48 000	Depreciation	36 000
Repairs	24 000	Insurance	9 600
Power	19 200	Rent	7 200
Lubricants	9 600	Rates and taxes	6 000
	$172 800		$130 800

It is estimated that direct labour hours worked each month will range from 18 000 to 24 000 hours.

During January, 20 000 direct labour hours were worked and the following overhead costs were incurred.

Variable overhead costs		Fixed overhead costs	
Indirect labour	$ 6 200	Supervision	$ 6 000
Indirect materials	3 600	Depreciation	3 000
Repairs	1 600	Insurance	800
Power	1 250	Rent	700
Lubricants	830	Rates and taxes	500
	$13 480		$11 000

Required

(a) Prepare a monthly flexible manufacturing overhead budget for each increment of 2000 direct labour hours over the relevant range for the year ending 31 December 2019.

(b) Prepare a manufacturing overhead budget report for January, assuming 20 500 direct labour hours were expected.

(c) Explain the concept of budgetary control.

(d) Comment on management's efficiency in controlling manufacturing overhead costs in January.

PSA18.8 State total budgeted cost formula, and prepare flexible budget reports for 2 time periods.

LO6, 7

Nigh Ltd uses budgets in controlling costs. The August 2020 budget report for the entity's Assembling Department is as follows.

NIGH LTD
Budget report
Assembling Department
for the month ended 31 August 2020

Manufacturing costs	Budget	Actual	Difference Favourable F Unfavourable U
Variable costs			
Direct materials	$ 48 000	$ 47 000	$1 000 F
Direct labour	78 000	74 100	3 900 F
Indirect materials	24 000	24 200	200 U
Indirect labour	18 000	17 500	500 F
Power	15 000	14 900	100 F
Maintenance	9 000	9 200	200 U
Total variable	192 000	186 900	5 100 F
Fixed costs			
Rent	10 000	10 000	—
Supervision	17 000	17 000	—
Depreciation	7 000	7 000	—
Total fixed	34 000	34 000	—
Total costs	$226 000	$220 900	$5 100 F

The budget data in the report are based on the master budget for the year, which assumed that 720 000 units would be produced. The Assembling Department manager is pleased with the report and expects a raise, or at least praise for a job well done. The chief financial officer (CFO), however, is unhappy with the results for August, because only 58 000 units were produced. (*Hint:* The budget amounts above are one-twelfth of the master budget.)

Required

(a) State the total monthly budgeted cost formula.

(b) Prepare a budget report for August using flexible budget data. Why does this report provide a better basis for evaluating performance than the report based on static budget data? Assume 62 000 units were expected to be produced.

(c) In September, 64 000 units were produced when 65 000 were expected. Prepare the budget report using flexible budget data, assuming (1) each variable cost was 10% higher than its actual cost in August, and (2) fixed costs were the same in September as in August.

PSA18.9 Prepare a flexible budget, budget report and graph for manufacturing overhead. **LO7**

Tiger Manufacturing Pty Ltd produces one product: mingen. Because of wide fluctuations in demand for mingen, the Assembly Department experiences significant variations in monthly production levels. The master manufacturing overhead budget for the year, and actual costs incurred in July, are shown below. The master budget is based on 240 000 direct labour hours. In July, 22 000 labour hours were actually worked, whereas 22 500 hours were expected to be worked.

Overhead costs	Master budget (annual)	Actual in July
Variable		
Indirect labour	$240 000	$21 000
Indirect materials	180 000	15 000
Electricity	72 000	5 800
Maintenance	48 000	4 200
Fixed		
Supervision	150 000	12 500
Depreciation	90 000	7 500
Insurance and tax	60 000	5 000
Total	$840 000	$71 000

Required

(a) Prepare a monthly flexible overhead budget for the year ending 31 December 2019, assuming monthly production levels range from 18 000 to 24 000 direct labour hours. Use increments of 2000 direct labour hours.

(b) Prepare a budget performance report for July 2019, comparing actual results with budget data based on the flexible budget.

(c) Were costs effectively controlled? Explain your answer.

(d) State the formula for calculating the total monthly budgeted costs for Tiger Manufacturing Pty Ltd.

(e) Prepare a flexible budget graph showing total budgeted costs of 18 000 and 22 000 direct labour hours. Use increments of 2000 on the horizontal axis and increments of $10 000 on the vertical axis.

PSA18.10 Prepare reports for cost centres under responsibility accounting and comment on the performance of managers. **LO8, 9**

Ever Green Ltd is a fruit juice company that uses a responsibility reporting system. It has divisions in Brisbane, Sydney and Melbourne. Each division has three production departments: Squeezing, Bottling and Packaging. The responsibility for each department rests with a manager who reports to the division production manager. Each division manager reports to the general manager of production. There are also general managers for finance and sales. All general managers report to the managing director. In December 2018, controllable actual and budget manufacturing overhead cost data for the departments and divisions were as follows.

Manufacturing overhead	Budget	Actual
Individual costs — Bottling Department, Brisbane		
Indirect labour	$ 109 500	$ 136 000
Indirect materials	70 000	55 200
Maintenance	30 750	30 600
Electricity	30 150	28 900
Supervision	30 000	30 000
Total	$ 270 400	$ 280 700
Total costs		
Squeezing Department, Brisbane	$ 240 000	$ 228 000
Packaging Department, Brisbane	175 300	184 000
Sydney division	620 000	654 000
Melbourne division	548 000	553 000
	$ 1 583 300	$ 1 619 000
Additional overhead costs incurred		
Brisbane division — Production Manager	$ 38 000	$ 37 000
General Manager — Production	68 000	65 800
Managing Director	76 000	74 800

The general managers who report to the managing director, other than the general manager of production, had the following expenses:

Manufacturing overhead	Budget	Actual
General Manager — Finance	$115 000	$108 000
General Manager — Sales	167 000	172 000

Required

(a) Prepare the following responsibility reports:
1. Manufacturing overhead — Bottling Department manager, Brisbane division.
2. Manufacturing overhead — Brisbane division manager.
3. Manufacturing overhead — General manager of production.
4. Manufacturing overhead and expenses — Managing Director. Use the format in figure 18.36.

(b) Comment on the comparative performances of:
1. department managers in the Brisbane division.
2. division managers.
3. general managers.

PSA18.11 Prepare responsibility report for a profit centre. **LO8, 9**

Loco Manufacturing operates the Furniture Division as a profit centre. Operating data for this division for the year ended 31 December 2019 are as follows.

	Budget	Difference from budget
Sales	$2 500 000	$50 000 F
Cost of sales		
Variable	1 300 000	43 000 F
Controllable fixed	200 000	5 000 U
Selling and administrative		
Variable	220 000	7 000 U
Controllable fixed	50 000	2 000 U
Non-controllable fixed costs	70 000	4 000 U

In addition, Loco Manufacturing incurs $180 000 of indirect fixed costs that were budgeted at $175 000. Twenty per cent of these costs are allocated to the Furniture Division.

Required

(a) Prepare a responsibility report for the Furniture Division for the year.

(b) Comment on the manager's performance in controlling revenues and costs.

(c) Identify any costs excluded from the responsibility report and explain why they were excluded.

PSA18.12 Prepare responsibility report for an investment centre and calculate ROI.   **LO9**

Ridder Manufacturing Ltd manufactures a variety of garden and lawn equipment. The entity operates through three divisions. Each division is an investment centre. Operating data for the Lawnmower Division for the year ended 31 December 2020 and relevant budget data are as follows:

	Actual	Comparison with budget
Sales	$2 800 000	$200 000 unfavourable
Variable cost of sales	1 400 000	$150 000 unfavourable
Variable selling and administrative expenses	300 000	$50 000 favourable
Controllable fixed cost of sales	270 000	On target
Controllable fixed selling and administrative expenses	130 000	On target

Average operating assets for the year for the Lawnmower Division were $4 000 000, which was also the budgeted amount.

Required

(a) Prepare a responsibility report (in thousands of dollars) for the Lawnmower Division.

(b) Evaluate the manager's performance. Which items will likely be investigated by top management?

(c) Calculate the expected ROI in 2021 for the Lawnmower Division, assuming the following changes:

1. Variable cost of sales is decreased by 15%.

2. Average operating assets are decreased by 20%.

3. Sales are increased by $500 000 and this increase is expected to increase contribution margin by $200 000.

PROBLEM SET B

PSB18.1 Prepare a budgeted statement of profit or loss and supporting budgets.   **LO2, 4**

Blue Mountain Farm Supply manufactures and sells a fertiliser called Basic II. The following data are developed for preparing budgets for Basic II for the first two quarters of 2018:

1. Sales: quarter 1, 40 000 bags; quarter 2, 60 000 bags. Selling price is $60 per bag.

2. Direct materials: each bag of Basic II requires 6 kilograms of Trup at a cost of $3 per kilogram and 10 kilograms of Dert at $1.50 per kilogram.

3. Desired inventory levels:

Type of inventory	1 January	1 April	1 July
Basic II (bags)	10 000	15 000	20 000
Trup (kilograms)	9 000	12 000	15 000
Dert (kilograms)	15 000	20 000	25 000

4. Direct labour: direct labour time is 15 minutes per bag at an hourly rate of $10 per hour.

5. Selling and administrative expenses are expected to be 10% of sales plus $150 000 per quarter.
6. Income tax is expected to be 30% of profit from operations.

Your assistant has prepared two budgets: the manufacturing overhead budget, which shows expected costs to be 100% of direct labour cost, and the direct materials budget for Dert, which shows the cost of Dert to be $682 500 in quarter 1 and $982 500 in quarter 2.

Required

Prepare the budgeted statement of profit or loss for the first 6 months of 2018 and all required supporting budgets by quarters. (*Note:* Use variable and fixed costs in the selling and administrative expense budget.)

PSB18.2 Prepare sales, production, direct materials, direct labour and statement of profit or loss budgets.   **LO2, 4**

Royal Palm Ltd is preparing its annual budgets for the year ending 30 June 2018. Accounting assistants furnish the following data for the company's two products — RP 188 and RP 268.

	Product RP 188	Product RP 268
Sales budget:		
Expected sales in units	22 000	14 000
Unit selling price	$30	$40
Production budget:		
Desired ending finished goods units	4 840	3 080
Beginning finished goods units	4 400	2 800
Direct material budget:		
Direct material per unit (kg)	2	3
Desired ending direct materials (kg)	8 000	5 000
Beginning direct materials (kg)	10 000	7 000
Cost per kilogram	$4	$5
Direct labour:		
Direct labour hours per unit	0.4	0.6
Direct labour rate per hour	$15	$15
Budgeted statement of profit or loss:		
Total unit cost	$14	$24

An accounting assistant has prepared the detailed manufacturing overhead budget and the selling and administrative expense budget. The latter shows selling expenses of $110 000 for product RP 188 and $84 000 for product RP 268; and administrative expenses of $44 000 for product RP 188 and $28 000 for product RP 268. Income taxes are expected to be 30%.

Required

Prepare the following budgets for the year. Show data for each product.
(a) Sales.
(b) Production.
(c) Direct materials.
(d) Direct labour.
(e) Statement of profit or loss. (*Note:* Income taxes are not allocated to the products.)

PSB18.3 Prepare sales and production budgets and calculate cost per unit under two plans.   **LO2**

David Chambers Ltd has sales in 2019 of $5 250 000 (656 250 units) and gross profit of $1 587 500. Management is considering two alternative budget plans to increase its gross profit in 2020.

Plan A would increase the selling price per unit from $8.00 to $8.60. Sales volume would decrease by 10% from its 2019 level. Plan B would decrease the selling price per unit by 5%. The marketing department expects that the sales volume would increase by 100 000 units.

At the end of 2019, Chambers has 75 000 units on hand. If Plan A is accepted, the 2020 ending inventory should be equal to 87 500 units. If Plan B is accepted, the ending inventory should be equal to 100 000 units. Each unit produced will cost $2.00 in direct materials, $1.50 in direct labour and $0.50 in variable overhead. The fixed overhead for 2020 should be $965 000.

Required

(a) Prepare a sales budget for 2020 under each plan.

(b) Prepare a production budget for 2020 under each plan.

(c) Calculate the cost per unit under each plan. Explain why the cost per unit is different for each of the two plans. (Round to 2 decimals.)

(d) Which plan should be accepted? (*Hint:* Calculate the gross profit under each plan.)

PSB18.4 Prepare cash budget for 2 months. **LO3**

Zhang Ltd prepares cash budgets on a monthly basis. Relevant data from operating budgets for 2020 are:

	January	February
Sales	$ 360 000	$ 400 000
Direct materials purchases	125 000	130 000
Direct labour	90 000	100 000
Manufacturing overhead	70 000	75 000
Selling and administrative expenses	79 000	86 000

All sales are on account. Collections are expected to be 50% in the month of sale, 30% in the first month following the sale, and 20% in the second month following the sale. 60% of direct materials purchases are paid in cash in the month of purchase, and the balance due is paid in the month following the purchase. All other items above are paid in the month incurred. The selling and administrative expenses include $1000 of depreciation per month.

Other data:

1. Credit sales: November 2019, $260 000; December 2019, $300 000.
2. Purchases of direct materials: December 2019, $100 000.
3. Other receipts: January — collection of 31 December 2019, notes receivable $15 000; February — proceeds from sale of securities $6000.
4. Other disbursements: February — withdrawal of $5000 cash for personal use of owner, Joy Zhang.

The cash balance on 1 January 2020 is expected to be $70 000. The entity wants to maintain a minimum cash balance of $50 000.

Required

(a) Prepare schedules for (1) expected collections from customers and (2) expected payments for direct materials purchases.

(b) Using a spreadsheet program, prepare a cash budget for January and February.

PSB18.5 Prepare purchases and statement of profit or loss budgets for a retail entity. **LO2, 4, 5**

The budget committee of Morris Ltd collects the following data for its Darwin store when preparing the budgeted statement of profit or loss for January and February 2020:

1. Sales for January are expected to be $100 000. Sales in February and March are expected to be 10% higher than in the preceding month.
2. Cost of sales is expected to be 60% of sales.
3. Morris Ltd's policy is to maintain ending merchandise inventory at 30% of the following month's cost of sales.

4. Operating expenses are estimated to be:

Sales salaries	$8000 per month
Advertising	5% of monthly sales
Delivery	3% of monthly sales
Sales commissions	5% of monthly sales
Rent	$3000 per month
Depreciation	$800 per month
Electricity	$1000 per month
Insurance	$500 per month

5. Income taxes are estimated to be 30% of profit from operations.

Required

(a) Prepare the purchases budget for the months of January and February.

(b) Prepare a budgeted statement of profit or loss for January and February. Show in the statement the details of cost of sales.

PSB18.6 **Prepare budgeted statement of profit or loss and statement of financial position.** **LO4**

Viola Industries' statement of financial position at 31 December 2018 is presented below.

VIOLA INDUSTRIES Statement of financial position as at 31 December 2018		
ASSETS		
Current assets		
Cash		$ 7 500
Accounts receivable		82 500
Finished goods inventory (2000 units)		30 000
Total current assets		120 000
Property, plant and equipment		
Equipment	$40 000	
Less: Accumulated depreciation	10 000	30 000
Total assets		**$150 000**
LIABILITIES AND SHAREHOLDERS' EQUITY		
Liabilities		
Bank loan		$ 25 000
Accounts payable		45 000
Total liabilities		70 000
Shareholders' equity		
Share capital	$50 000	
Retained earnings	30 000	
Total shareholders' equity		80 000
Total liabilities and shareholders' equity		**$150 000**

Budgeted data for the year 2019 include the following:

	4th quarter of 2019	Year 2019 total
Sales budget (8000 units at $35)	$80 000	$280 000
Direct materials used	17 000	72 400
Direct labour	8 500	38 600
Manufacturing overhead applied	10 000	42 000
Selling and administrative expenses	18 000	76 000

To meet sales requirements and to have 2500 units of finished goods on hand at 31 December 2019, the production budget shows 8500 required units of output. The total unit cost of production is expected to be $18. Viola Industries uses the first-in, first-out (FIFO) inventory costing method. Selling and administrative expenses include $4000 for depreciation on equipment. Interest expense is expected to be $3500 for the year. Income tax is expected to be 30% of profit before income tax.

All sales and purchases are on account. It is expected that 60% of quarterly sales are collected in cash within the quarter and the remainder is collected in the following quarter. Direct materials purchased from suppliers are paid 50% in the quarter incurred and the remainder in the following quarter. Purchases in the fourth quarter were the same as the materials used. In 2019, the business expects to purchase additional equipment costing $24 000. It expects to pay $8000 on the bank loan plus all interest due and payable to 31 December (included in interest expense $3500 above). Accounts payable at 31 December 2019 includes amounts due to suppliers (see above) plus other accounts payable of $7500. In 2019, the business expects to declare and pay a $5000 cash dividend. Unpaid income tax at 31 December will be $5000. The cash budget shows an expected cash balance of $29 750 at 31 December 2019.

Required

Prepare a budgeted statement of profit or loss for 2019 and a budgeted statement of financial position at 31 December 2019. In preparing the statement of profit or loss, you will need to calculate cost of goods manufactured (materials + labour + overhead) and finished goods inventory (31 December 2019).

PSB18.7 **Prepare flexible budget and budget report for manufacturing overhead.** **LO6, 7**

Czernkowski & Co. estimates that 360 000 direct labour hours will be worked during the coming year, 2020, in the Packaging Department. On this basis, the following budgeted manufacturing overhead cost data are calculated for the year.

Fixed overhead costs		Variable overhead costs	
Supervision	$ 90 000	Indirect labour	$144 000
Depreciation	54 000	Indirect materials	90 000
Insurance	27 000	Repairs	54 000
Rent	36 000	Electricity	72 000
Rates and taxes	18 000	Lubricants	18 000
	$225 000		$378 000

It is estimated that direct labour hours worked each month will range from 27 000 to 36 000 hours.

During October, 27 000 direct labour hours were worked and the following overhead costs were incurred:

- Fixed overhead costs: supervision $7500, depreciation $4500, insurance $2225, rent $3000, and rates and taxes $1500.
- Variable overhead costs: indirect labour $11 760, indirect materials, $6400, repairs $4000, electricity $5900, and lubricants $1640.

Required

(a) Prepare a monthly flexible manufacturing overhead budget for each increment of 3000 direct labour hours over the relevant range for the year ending 31 December 2020.

(b) Prepare a flexible budget report for October, when 27 500 direct labour hours were worked.

(c) Comment on management's efficiency in controlling manufacturing overhead costs in October.

PSB18.8 **State total budgeted cost formula, and prepare flexible budget reports for 2 time periods.**

LO6, 7

Lorch Ltd uses budgets in controlling costs. The May 2019 budget report for the entity's Packaging Department is as follows.

			Difference
			Favourable F
Manufacturing costs	Budget	Actual	Unfavourable U

LORCH LTD
Budget report
Packaging Department
for the month ended 31 May 2019

Manufacturing costs	Budget	Actual	Difference Favourable F Unfavourable U
Variable costs			
Direct materials	$ 30 000	$ 32 000	$2 000 U
Direct labour	50 000	53 000	3 000 U
Indirect materials	15 000	15 200	200 U
Indirect labour	12 500	13 000	500 U
Power	7 500	7 100	400 F
Maintenance	5 000	5 200	200 U
Total variable	120 000	125 500	5 500 U
Fixed costs			
Rent	9 000	9 000	—
Supervision	9 000	9 000	—
Depreciation	5 000	5 000	—
Total fixed	23 000	23 000	—
Total costs	**$143 000**	**$148 500**	**$5 500 U**

The budget amounts in the report were on the master budget for the year, which assumed that 600 000 units would be produced. (*Hint:* The budget amounts above are one-twelfth of the master budget for the year.)

Lorch Ltd's chief financial officer (CFO) was displeased with the department manager's performance. The department manager, who thought she had done a good job, could not understand the unfavourable results. In May, 55 000 units were produced.

Required

(a) State the total budgeted cost formula.

(b) Prepare a budget report for May using flexible budget data. Why does this report provide a better basis for evaluating performance than the report based on static budget data? Assume 57 000 units were expected to be produced in the Packaging Department.

(c) In June, 40 000 units were produced when 39 000 were expected. Prepare the budget report using flexible budget data, assuming (1) each variable cost was 20% less in June than its actual cost in May, and (2) fixed costs were the same in the month of June as in May.

PSB18.9 **Prepare flexible budget, budget report, and graph for manufacturing overhead.**   **LO7**

Tariq Manufacturing Pty Ltd produces one product, Kebo. Because of wide fluctuations in demand for Kebo, the Assembly Department experiences significant variations in monthly production levels.

The master manufacturing overhead budget *for the year*, based on 300 000 direct labour hours, and the actual overhead costs incurred in July in which 27 500 labour hours were worked, and 27 500 hours were expected to be worked, are as follows:

Overhead costs	Master budget (annual)	Actual in July
Variable		
Indirect labour	$ 360 000	$32 000
Indirect materials	210 000	17 000
Electricity	90 000	8 100
Maintenance	60 000	5 400

Overhead costs	Master budget (annual)	Actual in July
Fixed		
Supervision	180 000	15 000
Depreciation	120 000	10 000
Insurance and tax	60 000	5 000
Total	**$1 080 000**	**$92 500**

Required

(a) Prepare a monthly flexible overhead budget for the year ending 31 December 2018, assuming monthly production levels range from 22 500 to 30 000 direct labour hours. Use increments of 2500 direct labour hours.

(b) Prepare a budget performance report for the month of July 2018 comparing actual results with budget data based on the flexible budget.

(c) Were costs effectively controlled? Explain.

(d) State the formula for calculating the total monthly budgeted costs of Tariq Manufacturing Pty Ltd.

(e) Prepare the flexible budget graph showing total budgeted costs at 25 000 and 27 500 direct labour hours. Use increments of 5000 on the horizontal axis and increments of $10 000 on the vertical axis.

PSB18.10 Prepare reports for cost centres under responsibility accounting and comment on performance of managers. **LO8, 9**

Otto Products uses a responsibility reporting system. It has divisions in Christchurch, Melbourne and Adelaide. Each division has three production departments: Cutting, Shaping, and Finishing. The responsibility for each department rests with a manager who reports to the division production manager. Each division manager reports to the general manager of production. There are also general managers for marketing and finance. All general managers report to the managing director.

In January 2018, controllable actual and budget manufacturing overhead cost data for the departments and divisions were as follows.

Manufacturing overhead	Actual	Budget
Individual costs—Cutting Department—Melbourne		
Indirect labour	$ 73 000	$ 70 000
Indirect materials	46 700	46 000
Maintenance	20 500	18 000
Electricity	20 100	17 000
Supervision	20 000	20 000
	$ 180 300	$ 171 000
Total costs		
Shaping Department—Melbourne	$ 158 000	$ 148 000
Finishing Department—Melbourne	210 000	208 000
Christchurch division	676 000	673 000
Adelaide division	722 000	715 000
	$1 766 000	$1 744 000

Additional overhead costs were incurred as follows: Melbourne division production manager — actual costs $52 500, budget $51 000; general manager of production — actual costs $65 000, budget $64 000; managing director — actual costs $76 400, budget $74 200. These expenses are not allocated.

The general managers who report to the managing director, other than the general manager of production, had the following expenses:

General manager	Actual	Budget
Marketing	$133 600	$130 000
Finance	107 000	105 000

Required

(a) Identify the content of responsibility reports and their use in performance evaluation.

(b) Prepare the following responsibility reports:

    1. Manufacturing overhead — Cutting Department manager — Melbourne division.

    2. Manufacturing overhead — Melbourne division manager.

    3. Manufacturing overhead — General manager of production.

    4. Manufacturing overhead and expenses — Managing Director.

    Use the format in figure 18.36.

(c) Comment on the comparative performances of:

    1. department managers in the Melbourne division.

    2. division managers.

    3. general managers.

PSB18.11 Prepare responsibility report for a profit centre.   **LO8, 9**

McCluskey Manufacturing operates the Home Appliance Division as a profit centre. Operating data for this division for the year ended 31 December 2020 are as follows:

	Budget	Difference from budget
Sales	$2 400 000	$100 000 U
Cost of sales		
Variable	1 200 000	60 000 U
Controllable fixed	200 000	10 000 F
Selling and administrative		
Variable	240 000	10 000 F
Controllable fixed	60 000	6 000 U
Non-controllable fixed costs	50 000	2 000 U

In addition, McCluskey Manufacturing incurs $150 000 of indirect fixed costs that were budgeted at $155 000. Twenty per cent of these costs are allocated to the Home Appliance Division. None of these costs is controllable by the division manager.

Required

(a) Prepare a responsibility report for the Home Appliance Division (a profit centre) for the year.

(b) Comment on the manager's performance in controlling revenues and costs.

(c) Identify any costs excluded from the responsibility report and explain why they were excluded.

PSB18.12 Prepare responsibility report for an investment centre and calculate ROI.   **LO9**

Kurian Manufacturing Ltd manufactures a variety of tools and industrial equipment. The entity operates through three divisions. Each division is an investment centre. Operating data for the Home Division for the year ended 31 December 2019 and relevant budget data are as follows:

	Actual	Comparison with budget
Sales	$1 500 000	$100 000 favourable
Variable cost of sales	700 000	$100 000 unfavourable
Variable selling and administrative expenses	125 000	$25 000 unfavourable
Controllable fixed cost of sales	170 000	On target
Controllable fixed selling and administrative expenses	100 000	On target

Average operating assets for the year for the Home Division were $2 000 000, which was also the budgeted amount.

Required

(a) Prepare a responsibility report (in thousands of dollars) for the Home Division.

(b) Evaluate the manager's performance. Which items will likely be investigated by top management?

(c) Calculate the expected ROI in 2020 for the Home Division, assuming the following changes:

1. Variable cost of sales is decreased by 6%.
2. Average operating assets are decreased by 10%.
3. Sales are increased by $200 000, and this increase is expected to increase contribution margin by $90 000.

BUILDING BUSINESS SKILLS

FINANCIAL REPORTING AND ANALYSIS

Managerial analysis

BBS18.1 Ergo Ltd manufactures ergonomic devices for computer users. Some of its more popular products include glare screens (for computer monitors), keyboard stands with wrist rests, and carousels that allow easy access to floppy disks. Over the past 5 years, the entity experienced rapid growth, with sales of all products increasing 20% to 50% each year.

Last year, some of the main manufacturers of computers began introducing new products with some of the ergonomic designs, such as glare screens and wrist rests, already built in. As a result, sales of Ergo Ltd's accessory devices have declined somewhat. The entity believes that the disk carousels will probably continue to show growth, but that the other products will probably continue to decline. When the next year's budget was prepared, increases were built in to research and development so that replacement products could be developed or the entity could expand into some other product line. Some product lines being considered are general-purpose ergonomic devices including back supports, foot rests, and sloped writing pads.

The most recent results have shown that sales of the glare screens decreased more than was expected. As a result, the entity may have a shortage of funds. Top management has therefore asked that all expenses be reduced 10% to compensate for these reduced sales. Summary budget information is as follows:

Raw materials	$336 000
Direct labour	154 000
Insurance	70 000
Depreciation	126 000
Machine repairs	42 000
Sales salaries	70 000
Office salaries	112 000
Factory salaries (indirect labour)	70 000
Total	$980 000

Required

Using the preceding information, answer the following questions:

(a) What are the implications of reducing each of the costs? For example, if the entity reduces raw materials costs, it may have to do so by purchasing lower quality materials. This may affect sales in the long term.

(b) Based on your analysis in (a), what do you think is the best way to obtain the $98 000 in cost savings requested? Be specific. Are there any costs that cannot or should not be reduced? Why?

BBS18.2 Outback manufactures expensive jewellery sold as souvenirs. Three of its sales departments are: Retail Sales, Wholesale Sales and Outlet Sales. The Retail Sales Department is a profit centre. The Wholesale Sales Department, however, is a cost centre, because its managers merely take orders from customers who purchase through the business's wholesale catalogue. The Outlet Sales Department is an investment centre, because each manager is given full responsibility for an outlet store location. The manager can hire and discharge employees, purchase, maintain and sell equipment, and in general is fairly independent.

Sally Worthington is manager in the Retail Sales Department; Guan Wei manages the Wholesale Sales Department; Owen Hadley manages the Harbourside outlet store in Sydney. Below are the budget responsibility reports for each of the three departments.

	Budget		
	Retail sales	Wholesale sales	Outlet sales
Sales	$1 500 000	$ 800 000	$ 400 000
Variable costs			
Cost of sales	300 000	200 000	50 000
Advertising	200 000	60 000	10 000
Sales salaries	150 000	30 000	6 000
Printing	20 000	40 000	10 000
Travel	40 000	60 000	4 000
Fixed costs			
Rent	100 000	60 000	20 000
Insurance	10 000	4 000	2 000
Depreciation	150 000	200 000	80 000
Investment in assets	2 000 000	2 400 000	1 600 000

	Actual results		
	Retail sale	Wholesale sales	Outlet sales
Sales	$1 500 000	$ 800 000	$ 400 000
Variable costs			
Cost of sales	390 000	240 000	52 500
Advertising	200 000	60 000	10 000
Sales salaries	150 000	30 000	6 000
Printing	20 000	40 000	10 000
Travel	30 000	40 000	3 000
Fixed costs			
Rent	80 000	100 000	24 000
Insurance	10 000	4 000	2 000
Depreciation	160 000	180 000	120 000
Investment in assets	2 000 000	2 400 000	1 600 000

Required
(a) Determine which of the items should be included in the responsibility report for each of the three managers.
(b) Compare the budgeted measures with the actual results. Decide which results should be called to the attention of each manager.

Real-world focus

BBS18.3 Earlier in this chapter, government budgets were discussed and the timing of the Australian and New Zealand governments' budget announcements was highlighted.

Addresses: New Zealand Treasury, www.treasury.govt.nz

Australian Government Budget, www.budget.gov.au

Required

Visit either government's web site and read the latest budget release, then answer the following questions.

(a) Describe the government's main sources of revenue.

(b) Identify the government's main types of expense.

(c) Does the government forecast a surplus or a deficit budget?

Financial analysis on the web

BBS18.4 Explore some aspects of the Gold Coast City Council budgeting process.

Address: www.goldcoast.qld.gov.au

Steps:

1. Go to the GCCC web site and explore the site.

2. Locate the budget documents.

Required

(a) Find the page where the rates are discussed, and answer the following.

    1. What are the components of the rates?

    2. How are the general rates calculated?

    3. How are the water charges calculated?

(b) Describe the major business activities of the council and how these services are priced. How does this affect the budget preparation for the council?

(c) Select one of the business groups and outline its activities. What are the sources of revenues for that particular business unit? How are funds generated for capital expenditure?

CRITICAL THINKING

Group decision case

BBS18.5 Green Pastures is a 200-hectare property on the outskirts of Campbelltown, specialising in the agistment of brood mares and their foals. A recent economic downturn in the thoroughbred industry has led to a decline in breeding activities, and it has made the agistment business extremely competitive. To meet the competition, Green Pastures planned in 2019 to entertain clients, advertise more extensively, and absorb expenses formerly paid by clients such as veterinary and blacksmith fees.

The budget report for 2019 is presented below. As shown, the static statement of profit or loss budget for the year is based on an expected 21 900 boarding days at $25 per mare. The variable expenses per mare per day were budgeted: feed $5, veterinary fees $3, blacksmith fees $0.30, and supplies $0.40. All other budgeted expenses were either partly or wholly fixed.

During the year, management decided not to replace a worker who quit in April, but it did issue a new advertising brochure and did more entertaining of clients.

GREEN PASTURES Static statement of profit or loss budget for the year ended 31 December 2019			
	Actual	Master budget	Difference
Number of mares	52	60	8*
Number of agistment days	18 980	21 900	2 920*
Sales	$379 600	$547 500	$167 900*
Less: Variable expenses			
Feed	104 390	109 500	5 110
Veterinary fees	58 838	65 700	6 862
Blacksmith fees	6 074	6 570	496
Supplies	7 402	8 760	1 358
Total variable expenses	176 704	190 530	13 826

▶

	Actual	Master budget	Difference
Contribution margin	202 896	356 970	154 074*
Less: Fixed expenses			
Depreciation	40 000	40 000	—
Insurance	11 000	11 000	—
Electricity	12 000	14 000	2 000
Repairs and maintenance	10 000	11 000	1 000
Labour	88 000	96 000	8 000
Advertisement	12 000	8 000	4 000*
Entertainment	7 000	5 000	2 000*
Total fixed expense	180 000	185 000	5 000
Profit	**$ 22 896**	**$171 970**	**$149 074***

*Unfavourable

Required

With the class divided into groups, answer the following.
(a) Based on the static budget report:
   1. what was the main cause(s) of the decline in profit?
   2. did management do a good, average, or poor job of controlling expenses?
   3. were management's decisions to stay competitive sound?
(b) Prepare a flexible budget report for the year.
(c) Based on the flexible budget report, answer the three questions in part (a) above.
(d) What course of action do you recommend for the management of Green Pastures?

Group decision case

BBS18.6 Fisher Ltd operates on a calendar-year basis. It begins the annual budgeting process in late August when the CEO establishes targets for the total dollar sales and profit before taxes for the next year.

The sales target is given first to the marketing department. The marketing manager formulates a sales budget by product line in both units and dollars. From this budget, sales quotas by product line in units and dollars are established for each of the entity's sales areas. The marketing manager also estimates the cost of the marketing activities required to support the target sales volume and prepares a tentative marketing expense budget.

The chief financial officer (CFO) uses the sales and profit targets, the sales budget by product line, and the tentative marketing expense budget to determine the dollar amounts that can be devoted to manufacturing and corporate office expense. The CFO prepares the budget for corporate expenses. She then forwards to the production department the product-line sales budget in units and the total dollar amount that can be devoted to manufacturing.

The production manager meets with the factory managers to develop a manufacturing plan that will produce the required units when needed within the cost constraints set by the CFO. The budgeting process usually comes to a halt at this point because the production department does not consider the financial resources allocated to be adequate.

When this standstill occurs, the CFO, the finance director, the marketing manager and the production manager meet together to determine the final budgets for each of the areas. This normally results in a modest increase in the total amount available for manufacturing costs and cuts in the marketing expense and corporate office expense budgets. The total sales and profit figures proposed by the CEO are seldom changed. Although the participants are seldom pleased with the compromise, these budgets are final. Each executive then develops a new detailed budget for the operations in his or her area.

None of the areas has achieved its budget in recent years. Sales often run below the target. When budgeted sales are not achieved, each area is expected to cut costs so that the CEO's profit target can be met. However, the profit target is seldom met because costs are not cut enough. In fact, costs often run above the original budget in all functional areas (marketing, production and corporate office).

The CEO is disturbed that Fisher Ltd has not been able to meet the sales and profit targets. He hires a consultant with considerable experience with entities in Fisher's industry, and the consultant reviews the budgets for the past 4 years. She concludes that the product-line sales budgets were reasonable and that the cost and expense budgets were adequate for the budgeted sales and production levels.

Required

With the class divided into groups, answer the following:

(a) Discuss how the budgeting process employed by Fisher Ltd contributed to the failure to achieve the CEO's sales and profit targets.

(b) Suggest how Fisher Ltd's budgeting process could be revised to correct the problems.

(c) Should the functional areas be expected to cut their costs when sales volume falls below budget? Explain your answer.

Ethics case

BBS18.7 You are an accountant in the budgetary, projections and special projects department of Vek-Tek Ltd, a large manufacturing entity. The managing director, Sue Lin, asks you on very short notice to prepare some sales and profit projections covering the next 2 years of the entity's much heralded new product lines. She wants these projections for a series of speeches she is making while on a 2-week trip to eight interstate brokerage firms. The managing director hopes to bolster Vek-Tek's share sales and price.

You work 23 hours in 2 days to compile the projections and hand deliver them to the managing director. A week later you find time to go over some of your calculations and discover a miscalculation that makes the projections grossly overstated. You quickly inquire about the managing director's itinerary and learn that she has made half of her speeches and has half yet to make. You are in a quandary as to what to do.

Required

(a) What are the consequences of telling the managing director of your gross miscalculations?

(b) What are the consequences of *not* telling the managing director of your gross miscalculations?

(c) What are the ethical considerations for you and the managing director in this situation?

Communication activities

BBS18.8 The monthly manufacturing overhead budget for Cathedral Ltd for 2018 contains the following items.

Variable factory expenses		Fixed factory expenses	
Indirect materials	$ 75 000	Supervision	$ 51 000
Indirect labour	36 000	Inspection costs	3 000
Maintenance expenses	30 000	Insurance expenses	6 000
Manufacturing supplies	18 000	Depreciation	45 000
Total variable	**$159 000**	**Total fixed**	**$105 000**

The budget was based on an estimated 6000 units being produced. During April 2018, 4500 units were produced, and the following costs incurred:

Variable factory expenses		Fixed factory expenses	
Indirect materials	$ 75 600	Supervision	$ 57 900
Indirect labour	40 500	Inspection costs	3 600
Maintenance expenses	24 600	Insurance expenses	6 600
Manufacturing supplies	15 300	Depreciation	44 100
Total variable	**$156 000**	**Total fixed**	**$112 200**

Required

(a) Determine which items would be controllable by B. Sherrick, the production manager.

(b) How much should have been spent to manufacture 4500 units?

(c) Prepare a flexible manufacturing overhead budget report for Ms Sherrick for the month of April 2018.

(d) Prepare a responsibility report for April 2018. Include only the costs that would have been controllable by Ms Sherrick. In an attached memo, describe clearly for Ms Sherrick the areas in which her performance needs to be improved.

BBS18.9 Budgeting is an important money management tool that can be used in our everyday life. In groups, discuss your sources of income and types of expense during a semester while attending university. Construct your cash budget for the semester to identify whether your budget will be in surplus or in deficit. Discuss how you will go about using the surplus or funding the deficit.

Sustainability

BBS18.10 The Gold Coast City Council's (GCCC) strategic vision is to work together with business and the community to make the Gold Coast the best place to live and visit. One of the key areas is the environment.

Address: www.goldcoast.qld.gov.au

Steps:

1. Go to the GCCC web site and explore the site.

2. Locate the 'Environment' Tab.

Required

(a) Identify the main environmental areas on which the council provides data.

(b) Explore in more depth by determining the key social issues under 'Sustainable living'.

(c) Summarise the council's information on the *state* of biodiversity and the *pressures* of biodiversity at http://www.goldcoastflorafauna.com.au/.

ANSWERS

Answers to self-study questions

18.1 (c) 18.2 (b) 18.3 (d) 18.4 (c) 18.5 (c) 18.6 (d) 18.7 (d) 18.8 (d) 18.9 (b) 18.10 (a) 18.11 (d) 18.12 (b)

ACKNOWLEDGEMENTS

Photo: © Tashatuvango / Shutterstock.com

Photo: © Christine Langer-Pueschel / Shutterstock.com

Photo: © hidesy / Shutterstock.com

Photo: © Diego Cervo / Shutterstock.com

Photo: © Goodluz / Shutterstock.com

Time value of money

LEARNING OBJECTIVES

After studying this appendix, you should be able to:

1 distinguish between simple and compound interest
2 solve for future value of a single amount
3 solve for future value of an annuity
4 identify the variables fundamental to solving present value problems and solve for present value of a single amount
5 solve for present value of an annuity
6 calculate the present values in capital budgeting situations.

Would you rather receive $1000 today or a year from now? You should prefer to receive the $1000 today because you can invest the $1000 and earn interest on it. As a result, you will have more than $1000 a year from now. What this example illustrates is the concept of the *time value of money*. Everyone prefers to receive money today rather than in the future because of the interest factor.

Nature of interest

LEARNING OBJECTIVE 1 Distinguish between simple and compound interest.

Interest is payment for the use of another person's money. It is the difference between the amount borrowed or invested (called the **principal**) and the amount repaid or collected. The amount of interest to be paid or collected is usually stated as a rate over a specific period of time. The rate of interest is generally stated as an annual rate.

The amount of interest involved in any financing transaction is based on three elements:
1. *principal (p)*: the original amount borrowed or invested
2. *interest rate (i)*: an annual percentage of the principal
3. *time (n)*: the number of years that the principal is borrowed or invested.

Simple interest

Simple interest is calculated on the principal amount only. It is the return on the principal for one period. Simple interest is usually expressed as shown in figure 1.

FIGURE 1 Interest calculation

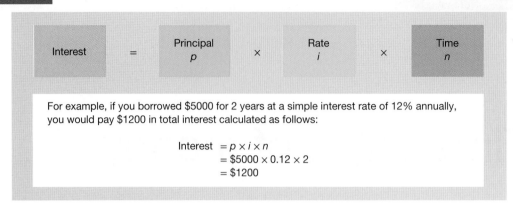

For example, if you borrowed $5000 for 2 years at a simple interest rate of 12% annually, you would pay $1200 in total interest calculated as follows:

$$\begin{aligned} \text{Interest} &= p \times i \times n \\ &= \$5000 \times 0.12 \times 2 \\ &= \$1200 \end{aligned}$$

Compound interest

Compound interest is calculated on principal *and* on any interest earned that has not been paid or withdrawn. It is the return on (or growth of) the principal for two or more time periods. Compounding calculates interest not only on the principal but also on the interest earned to date on that principal, assuming the interest is left on deposit.

To illustrate the difference between simple and compound interest, assume that you deposit $1000 in Bank One, where it will earn simple interest of 9% per year, and you deposit another $1000 in CityCorp, where it will earn compound interest of 9% per year compounded annually. Also assume that in both cases you will not withdraw any interest until 3 years from the date of deposit. The calculation of interest to be received and the accumulated year-end balances are indicated in figure 2.

FIGURE 2 Simple vs. compound interest

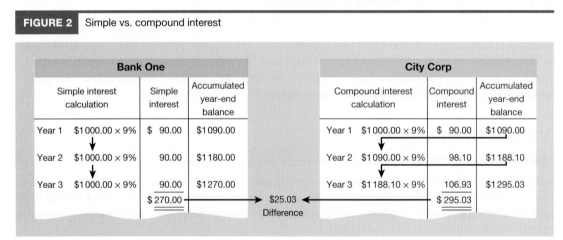

Bank One				City Corp		
Simple interest calculation	Simple interest	Accumulated year-end balance		Compound interest calculation	Compound interest	Accumulated year-end balance
Year 1 $1 000.00 × 9%	$ 90.00	$1 090.00		Year 1 $1 000.00 × 9%	$ 90.00	$1 090.00
Year 2 $1 000.00 × 9%	90.00	$1 180.00		Year 2 $1 090.00 × 9%	98.10	$1 188.10
Year 3 $1 000.00 × 9%	90.00	$1 270.00		Year 3 $1 188.10 × 9%	106.93	$1 295.03
	$ 270.00		$25.03 Difference		$ 295.03	

Note in figure 2 that simple interest uses the initial principal of $1000 to calculate the interest in all 3 years. Compound interest uses the accumulated balance (principal plus interest to date) at each year-end to calculate interest in the succeeding year — which explains why your compound interest account is larger.

Obviously, if you had a choice between investing your money at simple interest or at compound interest, you would choose compound interest, all other things — especially risk — being equal. In the example, compounding provides $25.03 of additional interest revenue. For practical purposes, compounding assumes that unpaid interest earned becomes a part of the principal, and the accumulated balance at the end of each year becomes the new principal on which interest is earned during the next year.

As can be seen in figure 2, you should invest your money at City Corp, which compounds interest annually. Compound interest is used in most business situations. Simple interest is generally applicable only to short-term situations of 1 year or less.

Future value concepts

LEARNING OBJECTIVE 2 Solve for future value of a single amount.

Future value of a single amount

The **future value of a single amount** is the value at a future date of a given amount invested assuming compound interest. For example, in figure 2, $1295.03 is the future value of the $1000 at the end of 3 years. The $1295.03 could be determined more easily by using the following formula:

$$FV = p \times (1 + i)^n$$

where:

FV = future value of a single amount
p = principal (or present value)
i = interest rate for one period
n = number of periods

Helpful hint: You can use this formula and a financial calculator as an alternative to the tables presented in this appendix.

The $1295.03 is calculated as follows:

$$
\begin{aligned}
FV &= p \times (1 + i)^n \\
&= \$1000 \times (1 + i)^3 \\
&= \$1000 \times 1.29503 \\
&= \$1295.03
\end{aligned}
$$

The 1.29503 is calculated by multiplying $(1.09 \times 1.09 \times 1.09)$. The amounts in this example can be depicted in the time diagram in figure 3.

FIGURE 3 | Time diagram

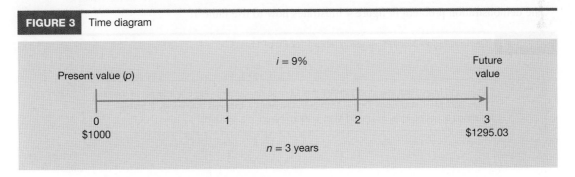

Another method that may be used to calculate the future value of a single amount involves the use of a compound interest table, which shows the future value of 1 for n periods. Table 1 is such a table.

In table 1, n is the number of compounding periods, the percentages are the periodic interest rates, and the 6-digit decimal numbers in the respective columns are the future value of 1 factors. In using table 1, the principal amount is multiplied by the future value factor for the specified number of periods and interest rate. For example, the future value factor for 2 periods at 9% is 1.18810. Multiplying this factor by $1000 equals $1188.10, which is the accumulated balance at the end of year 2 in the City Corp example in figure 2. The $1295.03 accumulated balance at the end of the third year can be calculated from table 1 by multiplying the future value factor for 3 periods (1.29503) by the $1000.

TABLE 1 Future value of 1

(n) Periods	4%	5%	6%	8%	9%	10%	11%	12%	15%
1	1.04000	1.05000	1.06000	1.08000	1.09000	1.10000	1.11000	1.12000	1.15000
2	1.08160	1.10250	1.12360	1.16640	1.18810	1.21000	1.23210	1.25440	1.32250
3	1.12486	1.15763	1.19102	1.25971	1.29503	1.33100	1.36763	1.40493	1.52088
4	1.16986	1.21551	1.26248	1.36049	1.41158	1.46410	1.51807	1.57352	1.74901
5	1.21665	1.27628	1.33823	1.46933	1.53862	1.61051	1.68506	1.76234	2.01136
6	1.26532	1.34010	1.41852	1.58687	1.67710	1.77156	1.87041	1.97382	2.31306
7	1.31593	1.40710	1.50363	1.71382	1.82804	1.94872	2.07616	2.21068	2.66002
8	1.36857	1.47746	1.59385	1.85093	1.99256	2.14359	2.30454	2.47596	3.05902
9	1.42331	1.55133	1.68948	1.99900	2.17189	2.35795	2.55803	2.77308	3.51788
10	1.48024	1.62889	1.79085	2.15892	2.36736	2.59374	2.83942	3.10585	4.04556
11	1.53945	1.71034	1.89830	2.33164	2.58043	2.85312	3.15176	3.47855	4.65239
12	1.60103	1.79586	2.01220	2.51817	2.81267	3.13843	3.49845	3.89598	5.35025
13	1.66507	1.88565	2.13293	2.71962	3.06581	3.45227	3.88328	4.36349	6.15279
14	1.73168	1.97993	2.26090	2.93719	3.34173	3.79750	4.31044	4.88711	7.07571
15	1.80094	2.07893	2.39656	3.17217	3.64248	4.17725	4.78459	5.47357	8.13706
16	1.87298	2.18287	2.54035	3.42594	3.97031	4.59497	5.31089	6.13039	9.35762
17	1.94790	2.29202	2.69277	3.70002	4.32763	5.05447	5.89509	6.86604	10.76126
18	2.02582	2.40662	2.85434	3.99602	4.71712	5.55992	6.54355	7.68997	12.37545
19	2.10685	2.52695	3.02560	4.31570	5.14166	6.11591	7.26334	8.61276	14.23177
20	2.19112	2.65330	3.20714	4.66096	5.60441	6.72750	8.06231	9.64629	16.36654

The demonstration problem in figure 4 illustrates how to use table 1.

FIGURE 4 Demonstration problem — using table 1 for FV of 1

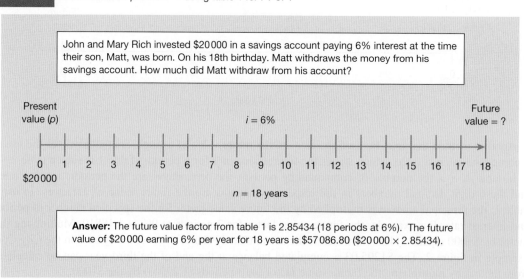

John and Mary Rich invested $20000 in a savings account paying 6% interest at the time their son, Matt, was born. On his 18th birthday. Matt withdraws the money from his savings account. How much did Matt withdraw from his account?

Present value (p)   i = 6%   Future value = ?

0 1 2 3 4 5 6 7 8 9 10 11 12 13 14 15 16 17 18
$20000

n = 18 years

Answer: The future value factor from table 1 is 2.85434 (18 periods at 6%). The future value of $20000 earning 6% per year for 18 years is $57086.80 ($20000 × 2.85434).

Future value of an annuity

LEARNING OBJECTIVE 3 Solve for future value of an annuity.

The preceding discussion involved the accumulation of only a single principal sum. Individuals and entities often encounter situations in which a series of equal dollar amounts are to be paid or received periodically, such as loans or lease (rental) contracts. Such payments or receipts of equal dollar amounts are referred to as **annuities**. The **future value of an annuity** is the sum of all the payments (receipts) plus the accumulated compound interest on them. In calculating the future value of an annuity, it is necessary to know (1) the interest rate, (2) the number of compounding periods, and (3) the amount of the periodic payments or receipts.

To illustrate the calculation of the future value of an annuity, assume that you invest $2000 at the end of each year for 3 years at 5% interest compounded annually. This situation is depicted in the time diagram in figure 5.

FIGURE 5 Time diagram for a 3-year annuity

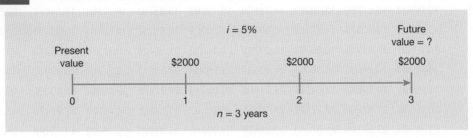

As can be seen in figure 5, the $2000 invested at the end of year 1 will earn interest for 2 years (years 2 and 3) and the $2000 invested at the end of year 2 will earn interest for 1 year (year 3). However, the last $2000 investment (made at the end of year 3) will not earn any interest. The future value of these periodic payments could be calculated using the future value factors from table 1 as shown in figure 6.

FIGURE 6 Future value of periodic payments

Year invested	Amount invested	×	Future value of 1 factor at 5%	=	Future value
1	$2 000	×	1.10250		$2 205
2	$2 000	×	1.05000		2 100
3	$2 000	×	1.00000		2 000
			3.15250		$6 305

The first $2000 investment is multiplied by the future value factor for 2 periods (1.1025) because 2 years' interest will accumulate on it (in years 2 and 3). The second $2000 investment will earn only 1 year's interest (in year 3) and therefore is multiplied by the future value factor for 1 year (1.0500). The final $2000 investment is made at the end of the third year and will not earn any interest. Consequently, the future value of the last $2000 invested is only $2000 since it does not accumulate any interest.

This method of calculation is required when the periodic payments or receipts are not equal in each period. However, when the periodic payments (receipts) are the same in each period, the future value can be calculated by using a future value of an annuity of 1 table. Table 2 is such a table.

Table 2 shows the future value of 1 to be received periodically for a given number of periods. From table 2 it can be seen that the future value of an annuity of 1 factor for 3 periods at 5% is 3.15250. The future value factor is the total of the three individual future value factors as shown in figure 6. Multiplying this amount by the annual investment of $2000 produces a future value of $6305.

The demonstration problem in figure 7 illustrates how to use table 2.

TABLE 2   **Future value of an annuity of 1**

(n) Periods	4%	5%	6%	8%	9%	10%	11%	12%	15%
1	1.00000	1.00000	1.00000	1.00000	1.00000	1.00000	1.00000	1.00000	1.00000
2	2.04000	2.05000	2.06000	2.08000	2.09000	2.10000	2.11000	2.12000	2.15000
3	3.12160	3.15250	3.18360	3.24640	3.27810	3.31000	3.34210	3.37440	3.47250
4	4.24646	4.31013	4.37462	4.50611	4.57313	4.64100	4.70973	4.77933	4.99338
5	5.41632	5.52563	5.63709	5.86660	5.98471	6.10510	6.22780	6.35285	6.74238
6	6.63298	6.80191	6.97532	7.33592	7.52334	7.71561	7.91286	8.11519	8.75374
7	7.89829	8.14201	8.39384	8.92280	9.20044	9.48717	9.78327	10.08901	11.06680
8	9.21423	9.54911	9.89747	10.63663	11.02847	11.43589	11.85943	12.29969	13.72682
9	10.58280	11.02656	11.49132	12.48756	13.02104	13.57984	14.16397	14.77566	16.78584
10	12.00611	12.57789	13.18079	14.48656	15.19293	15.93743	16.72201	17.54874	20.30372
11	13.48635	14.20679	14.97164	16.64549	17.56029	18.53117	19.56143	20.65458	24.34928
12	15.02581	15.91713	16.86994	18.97713	20.14072	21.38428	22.71319	24.13313	29.00167
13	16.62684	17.71298	18.88214	21.49530	22.95339	24.52271	26.21164	28.02911	34.35192
14	18.29191	19.59863	21.01507	24.21492	26.01919	27.97498	30.09492	32.39260	40.50471
15	20.02359	21.57856	23.27597	27.15211	29.36092	31.77248	34.40536	37.27972	47.58041
16	21.82453	23.65749	25.67253	30.32428	33.00340	35.94973	39.18995	42.75328	55.71747
17	23.69751	25.84037	28.21288	33.75023	36.97351	40.54470	44.50084	48.88367	65.07509
18	25.64541	28.13238	30.90565	37.45024	41.30134	45.59917	50.39593	55.74972	75.83636
19	27.67123	30.53900	33.75999	41.44626	46.01846	51.15909	56.93949	63.43968	88.21181
20	29.77808	33.06595	36.78559	45.76196	51.16012	57.27500	64.20283	72.05244	102.44358

FIGURE 7   *Demonstration problem — using table 2 for FV of an annuity of 1*

Henning Printing knows that in 4 years it must replace one of its existing printing presses with a new one. To ensure that some funds are available to replace the machine in 4 years, the business is depositing $25 000 in a savings account at the end of each of the next 4 years (four deposits in total). The savings account will earn 6% interest compounded annually. How much will be in the savings account at the end of 4 years when the new printing press is to be purchased?

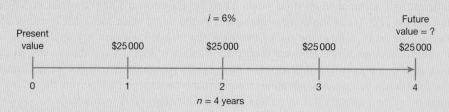

Answer: The future value factor from table 2 is 4.37462 (four periods at 6%). The future value of $25 000 invested at the end of each year for 4 years at 6% interest is $109 365.50 ($25 000 × 4.37462).

Present value concepts

LEARNING OBJECTIVE 4 Identify the variables fundamental to solving present value problems and solve for present value of a single amount.

Present value variables

The **present value**, like the future value, is based on three variables: (1) the dollar amount to be received (future amount), (2) the length of time until the amount is received (number of periods), and (3) the interest rate (the discount rate). The process of determining the present value is referred to as **discounting the future amount**.

In this text, present value calculations are used in measuring several items. For example, capital budgeting and other investment proposals are evaluated using present value calculations. All rate of return and internal rate of return calculations involve present value techniques.

Present value of a single amount

To illustrate present value concepts, assume that you are willing to invest a sum of money that will yield $1000 at the end of 1 year. In other words, what amount would you need to invest today to have $1000 in a year from now? If you want a 10% rate of return, the investment or present value is $909.09 ($1000 ÷ 1.10). The calculation of this amount is shown in figure 8.

| **FIGURE 8** | Present value calculation — $1000 discounted at 10% for 1 year |

$$
\begin{aligned}
\text{Present value} &= \text{Future value} \div (1 + i)^n \\
\text{PV} &= \text{FV} \div (1 + 10\%)^1 \\
\text{PV} &= \$1000 \div 1.10 \\
\mathbf{PV} &= \mathbf{\$909.09}
\end{aligned}
$$

The future amount ($1000), the discount rate (10%), and the number of periods (1) are known. The variables in this situation can be depicted in the time diagram in figure 9.

| **FIGURE 9** | Finding present value if discounted for one period |

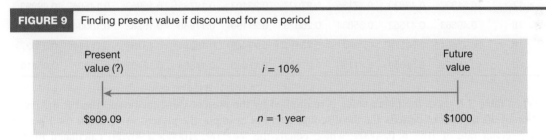

If the single amount of $1000 is to be received *in 2 years* and discounted at 10% [PV = $1000 ÷ $(1 + 10\%)^2$], its present value is $826.45 [$1000 ÷ (1.10 × 1.10)], as depicted in figure 10.

| **FIGURE 10** | Finding present value if discounted for two periods |

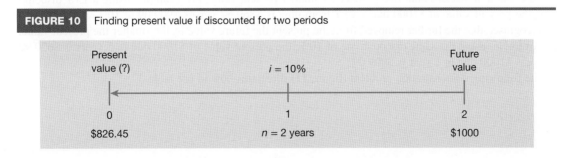

The present value of 1 may also be determined through tables that show the present value of 1 for n periods. In table 3, n is the number of discounting periods involved. The percentages are the periodic interest rates or discount rates, and the 6-digit decimal numbers in the respective columns are the present value of 1 factors.

TABLE 3   **Present value of 1 PV of $1 in n periods $= 1/(1 + i)^n$**

(n) Periods	4%	5%	6%	8%	9%	10%	11%	12%	15%
1	0.96154	0.95238	0.94340	0.92593	0.91743	0.90909	0.90090	0.89286	0.86957
2	0.92456	0.90703	0.89000	0.85734	0.84168	0.82645	0.81162	0.79719	0.75614
3	0.88900	0.86384	0.83962	0.79383	0.77218	0.75132	0.73119	0.71178	0.65752
4	0.85480	0.82270	0.79209	0.73503	0.70843	0.68301	0.65873	0.63552	0.57175
5	0.82193	0.78353	0.74726	0.68058	0.64993	0.62092	0.59345	0.56743	0.49718
6	0.79031	0.74622	0.70496	0.63017	0.59627	0.56447	0.53464	0.50663	0.43233
7	0.75992	0.71068	0.66506	0.58349	0.54703	0.51316	0.48166	0.45235	0.37594
8	0.73069	0.67684	0.62741	0.54027	0.50187	0.46651	0.43393	0.40388	0.32690
9	0.70259	0.64461	0.59190	0.50025	0.46043	0.42410	0.39092	0.36061	0.28426
10	0.67556	0.61391	0.55839	0.46319	0.42241	0.38554	0.35218	0.32197	0.24719
11	0.64958	0.58468	0.52679	0.42888	0.38753	0.35049	0.31728	0.28748	0.21494
12	0.62460	0.55684	0.49697	0.39711	0.35554	0.31863	0.28584	0.25668	0.18691
13	0.60057	0.53032	0.46884	0.36770	0.32618	0.28966	0.25751	0.22917	0.16253
14	0.57748	0.50507	0.44230	0.34046	0.29925	0.26333	0.23199	0.20462	0.14133
15	0.55526	0.48102	0.41727	0.31524	0.27454	0.23939	0.20900	0.18270	0.12289
16	0.53391	0.45811	0.39365	0.29189	0.25187	0.21763	0.18829	0.16312	0.10687
17	0.51337	0.43630	0.37136	0.27027	0.23107	0.19785	0.16963	0.14564	0.09293
18	0.49363	0.41552	0.35034	0.25025	0.21199	0.17986	0.15282	0.13004	0.08081
19	0.47464	0.39573	0.33051	0.23171	0.19449	0.16351	0.13768	0.11611	0.07027
20	0.45639	0.37689	0.31180	0.21455	0.17843	0.14864	0.12403	0.10367	0.06110

When table 3 is used, the future value is multiplied by the present value factor specified at the intersection of the number of periods and the discount rate. For example, the present value factor for 1 period at a discount rate of 10% is 0.90909, which equals the $909.09 ($1000 × 0.90909) calculated in figure 8. For 2 periods at a discount rate of 10%, the present value factor is 0.82645, which equals the $826.45 ($1000 × 0.82645) calculated previously.

Note that a higher discount rate produces a smaller present value. For example, using a 15% discount rate, the present value of $1000 due 1 year from now is $869.57 versus $909.09 at 10%. It should also be recognised that the further removed from the present the future value is, the smaller the present value. For example, using the same discount rate of 10%, the present value of $1000 due in 5 years is $620.92 whereas $1000 due in 1 year is $909.09.

The following demonstration problem (figure 11) illustrates how to use table 3.

FIGURE 11 *Demonstration problem — using table 3 for PV of 1*

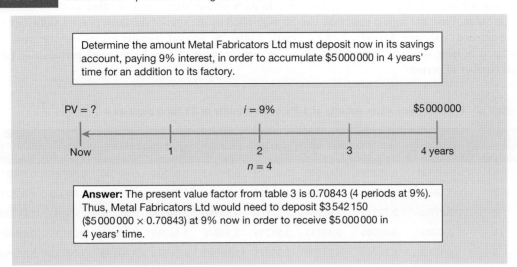

Determine the amount Metal Fabricators Ltd must deposit now in its savings account, paying 9% interest, in order to accumulate $5 000 000 in 4 years' time for an addition to its factory.

PV = ? $i = 9\%$ $5 000 000

Now   1   2   3   4 years

$n = 4$

Answer: The present value factor from table 3 is 0.70843 (4 periods at 9%). Thus, Metal Fabricators Ltd would need to deposit $3 542 150 ($5 000 000 × 0.70843) at 9% now in order to receive $5 000 000 in 4 years' time.

Present value of an annuity

LEARNING OBJECTIVE 5 Solve for present value of an annuity.

The preceding discussion involved the discounting of only a single future amount. Entities and individuals often engage in transactions in which a series of equal dollar amounts are to be received or paid periodically. Examples of a series of periodic receipts or payments are loan agreements, instalment sales, notes, lease (rental) contracts, and pension obligations. These series of periodic receipts or payments are called *annuities*. In calculating the **present value of an annuity**, it is necessary to know (1) the discount rate, (2) the number of discount periods, and (3) the amount of the periodic receipts or payments. To illustrate the calculation of the present value of an annuity, assume that you will receive $1000 cash annually for 3 years at a time when the discount rate is 10%. This situation is depicted in the time diagram in figure 12.

FIGURE 12 Time diagram for a 3-year annuity

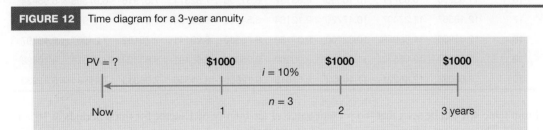

PV = ? $1000 $1000 $1000

          $i = 10\%$

Now   1   2   3 years

          $n = 3$

The present value in this situation may be calculated as shown in figure 13:

FIGURE 13 Present value of a series of future amounts calculation

Future amount	×	Present value of 1 factor at 10%	=	Present value
$1 000 (one year away)		0.90909		$ 909.09
1 000 (two years away)		0.82645		826.45
1 000 (three years away)		0.75132		751.32
		2.48686		**$2 486.86**

This method of calculation is required when the periodic cash flows are not uniform in each period. However, when the future receipts are the same in each period, there are two other ways to calculate present value. First, the annual cash flow can be multiplied by the sum of the three present value factors. In the previous example, $1000 × 2.48686 equals $2486.86. Second, annuity tables may be used. As illustrated in table 4 below, these tables show the present value of 1 to be received periodically for a given number of periods.

TABLE 4	Present value of an annuity of 1 PV of an annuity of $1 for n periods $= \dfrac{1 - 1/(1 + i)^n}{i}$								
(n) Periods	4%	5%	6%	8%	9%	10%	11%	12%	15%
1	0.96154	0.95238	0.94340	0.92593	0.91743	0.90909	0.90090	0.89286	0.86957
2	1.88609	1.85941	1.83339	1.78326	1.75911	1.73554	1.71252	1.69005	1.62571
3	2.77509	2.72325	2.67301	2.57710	2.53130	2.48685	2.44371	2.40183	2.28323
4	3.62990	3.54595	3.46511	3.31213	3.23972	3.16986	3.10245	3.03735	2.85498
5	4.45182	4.32948	4.21236	3.99271	3.88965	3.79079	3.69590	3.60478	3.35216
6	5.24214	5.07569	4.91732	4.62288	4.48592	4.35526	4.23054	4.11141	3.78448
7	6.00205	5.78637	5.58238	5.20637	5.03295	4.86842	4.71220	4.56376	4.16042
8	6.73274	6.46321	6.20979	5.74664	5.53482	5.33493	5.14612	4.96764	4.48732
9	7.43533	7.10782	6.80169	6.24689	5.99525	5.75902	5.53705	5.32825	4.77158
10	8.11090	7.72173	7.36009	6.71008	6.41766	6.14457	5.88923	5.65022	5.01877
11	8.76048	8.30641	7.88687	7.13896	6.80519	6.49506	6.20652	5.93770	5.23371
12	9.38507	8.86325	8.38384	7.53608	7.16073	6.81369	6.49236	6.19437	5.42062
13	9.98565	9.39357	8.85268	7.90378	7.48690	7.10336	6.74987	6.42355	5.58315
14	10.56312	9.89864	9.29498	8.24424	7.78615	7.36669	6.98187	6.62817	5.72448
15	11.11839	10.37966	9.71225	8.55948	8.06069	7.60608	7.19087	6.81086	5.84737
16	11.65230	10.83777	10.10590	8.85137	8.31256	7.82371	7.37916	6.97399	5.95424
17	12.16567	11.27407	10.47726	9.12164	8.54363	8.02155	7.54879	7.11963	6.04716
18	12.65930	11.68959	10.82760	9.37189	8.75563	8.20141	7.70162	7.24967	6.12797
19	13.13394	12.08532	11.15812	9.60360	8.95012	8.36492	7.83929	7.36578	6.19823
20	13.59033	12.46221	11.46992	9.81815	9.12855	8.51356	7.96333	7.46944	6.25933

From table 4 it can be seen that the present value of an annuity of 1 factor for three periods at 10% is 2.48685.* This present value factor is the total of the three individual present value factors as shown in figure 13. Applying this amount to the annual cash flow of $1000 produces a present value of $2486.85.

The demonstration problem in figure 14 illustrates how to use table 4.

Time periods and discounting

In the preceding calculations, the discounting has been done on an annual basis using an annual interest rate. Discounting may also be done over shorter periods of time such as monthly, quarterly or half-yearly. When the time frame is less than 1 year, it is necessary to convert the annual interest rate to the

---

*The difference of 0.00001 between 2.48686 and 2.48685 is due to rounding.

---

applicable time frame. Assume, for example, that the investor in figure 13 received $500 every 6 months for 3 years instead of $1000 annually. In this case, the number of periods becomes 6 (3 × 2), the discount rate is 5% (10% ÷ 2), the present value factor from table 4 is 5.07569, and the present value of the future cash flows is $2537.85 (5.07569 × $500). This amount is slightly higher than the $2486.86 calculated in figure 13 because interest is calculated twice during the same year; therefore interest is earned on the first 6 months' interest.

 FIGURE 14   *Demonstration problem — using table 4 for PV of an annuity of 1*

Steel Products Ltd has just signed an agreement to purchase equipment for instalment payments of $6000 each, to be paid at the end of each of the next 5 years. In setting the amount of the payments, the seller used a discount rate of 12%. What is the present value of the instalment payments — i.e. how much is Steel Products Ltd paying for the equipment and how much is it paying in total interest over the term of the instalment contract?

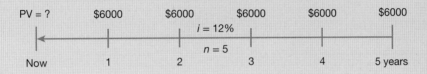

Answer: The present value factor from table 4 is 3.60478 (5 periods at 12%). The present value of 5 payments of $6000 each discounted at 12% is **$21 628.68** ($6000 × 3.60478). Therefore, the cost of the equipment to Steel Products Ltd is $21 628.68 and the interest is $8371.32 [($6000 × 5) − $21 628.68].

Calculating the present values in a capital budgeting decision

LEARNING OBJECTIVE 6 Calculate the present values in capital budgeting situations.

The decision to make long-term capital investments is best evaluated using discounting techniques that recognise the time value of money, i.e. the present value of the cash flows involved in a capital investment. The evaluation must reduce all cash inflows and outflows to a common comparable amount. That can be accomplished by either future valuing to some future date all the cash flows, or present valuing (discounting) to the present date all cash flows. Although both are useful for evaluating the investment, the present value (discounting) technique is more appealing and universally used.

Nagel Ltd is considering adding another truck to its fleet because of a purchasing opportunity. Navistar Ltd, Nagel Ltd's main supplier of trucks, is overstocked and offers to sell its biggest truck for $154 000 cash payable on delivery. Nagel Ltd knows that the truck will produce a net cash flow per year of $40 000 for 5 years (received at the end of each year), at which time it will be sold for an estimated residual value of $35 000. Nagel Ltd's discount rate in evaluating capital expenditures is 10%. Should Nagel Ltd commit to the purchase of this truck?

The cash flows that must be discounted to present value by Nagel Ltd are as follows:

Cash payable on delivery (now): $154 000.
Net cash flow from operating the rig: $40 000 for 5 years (at the end of each year).
Cash received from sale of truck at the end of 5 years: $35 000.

The time diagrams for the latter two cash flows are shown in figure 15.

FIGURE 15 Time diagrams for Nagel Ltd

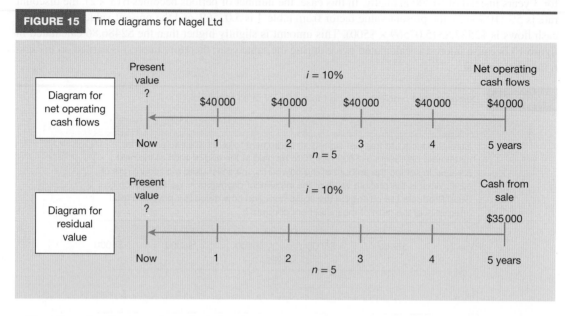

Note from the diagrams that calculating the present value of the net operating cash flows ($40 000 at the end of each year) is *discounting an annuity* (table 4) whereas calculating the present value of the $35 000 residual value is *discounting a single sum* (table 3).

The calculation of these present values is shown in figure 16.

FIGURE 16 Present value calculations at 10%

Present values using a 10% discount rate

Present value of net operating cash flows received annually over 5 years:	
$40 000 × PV of 1 received annually for 5 years at 10%	
$40 000 × 3.79079	$151 631.60
Present value of residual value (cash) to be received in 5 years:	
$35 000 × PV of 1 received in 5 years at 10%	
$35 000 × 0.62092	21 732.20
Present value of cash *inflows*	173 363.80
Present value of cash *outflows* (purchase price due now at 10%):	
$154 000 × PV of 1 due now	
$154 000 × 1.00000	154 000.00
Net present value	$ 19 363.80

Because the present value of the cash receipts (inflows) of $173 363.80 ($151 631.60 + $21 732.20) exceeds the present value of the cash payments (outflows) of $154 000.00, the net present value of $19 363.80 is positive and the decision to invest should be accepted.

Now assume that Nagel Ltd uses a discount rate of 15% not 10% because it wants a greater return on its investments in capital assets. The cash receipts and cash payments by Nagel Ltd are the same. The present values of these receipts and cash payments discounted at 15% are shown in figure 17.

Because the present value of the cash payments (outflows) of $154 000 exceeds the present value of the cash receipts (inflows) of $151 487.70 ($134 086.40 + $17 401.30), the net present value of $2512.30 is negative and the investment should be rejected.

FIGURE 17 Present value calculations at 15%

Present values using a 15% discount rate

Present value of net operating cash flows received annually over 5 years at 15%:	
$40 000 × 3.35216	$134 086.40
Present value of residual value (cash) to be received in 5 years at 15%:	
$35 000 × 0.49718	17 401.30
Present value of cash *inflows*	151 487.70
Present value of cash *outflows* (purchase price due now at 15%):	
$154 000 × 1.00000	154 000.00
Net present value	$ (2 512.30)

The above discussion relied on present value tables in solving present value problems. Electronic hand-held calculators may also be used to calculate present values without the use of these tables. Some calculators have present value (PV) functions that allow you to calculate present values by merely identifying the proper amount, discount rate and periods, then pressing the PV key.

SUMMARY

1 Distinguish between simple and compound interest.

Simple interest is calculated on the principal only whereas compound interest is calculated on the principal and any interest earned that has not been withdrawn.

2 Solve for future value of a single amount.

Prepare a time diagram of the problem. Identify the principal amount, the number of compounding periods, and the interest rate. Using the future value of 1 table, multiply the principal amount by the future value factor specified at the intersection of the number of periods and the interest rate.

3 Solve for future value of an annuity.

Prepare a time diagram of the problem. Identify the amount of the periodic payments, the number of compounding periods, and the interest rate. Using the future value of an annuity of 1 table, multiply the amount of the payments by the future value factor specified at the intersection of the number of periods and the interest rate.

4 Identify the variables fundamental to solving present value problems and solve for present value of a single amount.

The following three variables are fundamental to solving present value problems: (1) the future amount, (2) the number of periods, and (3) the interest rate (the discount rate).

To solve for present value of a single amount, prepare a time diagram of the problem. Identify the future amount, the number of discounting periods, and the discount (interest) rate. Using the present value of 1 table, multiply the future amount by the present value factor specified at the intersection of the number of periods and the discount rate.

5 Solve for present value of an annuity.

Prepare a time diagram of the problem. Identify the future amounts (annuities), the number of discounting periods, and the discount (interest) rate. Using the present value of an annuity of 1 table, multiply the amount of the annuity by the present value factor specified at the intersection of the number of periods and the interest rate.

6 Calculate the present values in capital budgeting situations.

Calculate the present values of all cash inflows and all cash outflows related to the capital budgeting proposal (an investment-type decision). If the *net* present value is positive, accept the proposal (make the investment). If the *net* present value is negative, reject the proposal (do not make the investment).

KEY TERMS

annuity A series of equal dollar amounts to be paid or received periodically.

compound interest The interest calculated on the principal and any interest earned that has not been paid or received.

discounting the future amount The process of determining present value.

future value of a single amount The value at a future date of a given amount invested assuming compound interest.

future value of an annuity The sum of all the payments or receipts plus the accumulated compound interest on them.

interest Cost of borrowing money.

present value The value today of an amount to be paid or received at some date in the future after taking into account current interest rates.

present value of an annuity A series of future receipts or payments discounted to their value now assuming compound interest.

principal The amount borrowed or invested.

simple interest The interest calculated on the principal only.

BRIEF EXERCISES (USE TABLES TO SOLVE EXERCISES)

BE1 **Calculate the future value of a single amount.** **LO2**

Don Smith invested $5000 at 6% annual interest, and left the money invested without withdrawing any of the interest for 10 years. At the end of the 10 years, Don withdrew the accumulated amount of money. (a) What amount did Don withdraw assuming the investment earns simple interest? (b) What amount did Don withdraw assuming the investment earns interest compounded annually?

BE2 **Using future value tables.** **LO2, 3**

For each of the following cases, indicate (a) to what interest rate columns and (b) to what number of periods you would refer in looking up the future value factor.

1. In table 1 (future value of 1):

	Annual rate	Number of years invested	Compounded
(a)	6%	5	Annually
(b)	5%	3	Half-yearly

2. In table 2 (future value of an annuity of 1):

	Annual rate	Number of years invested	Compounded
(a)	5%	10	Annually
(b)	4%	6	Half-yearly

BE3 **Calculate the future value of a single amount.** **LO2**

Porter Ltd signed a lease for an office building for a period of 10 years. Under the lease agreement, a security deposit of $10 000 is made. The deposit will be returned at the expiration of the lease with interest compounded at 5% per year. What amount will Porter receive at the time the lease expires?

BE4 **Calculate the future value of a single amount and of an annuity.** **LO2, 3**

David and Kathy Hatcher invested $5000 in a savings account paying 6% annual interest when their daughter, Sue, was born. They also deposited $1000 on each of her birthdays until she was 18 (including her 18th birthday). How much will be in the savings account on her 18th birthday (after the last deposit)?

BE5 **Calculate the future value of a single amount.** **LO2**

Ron Watson borrowed $20 000 on 1 July 2014. This amount plus accrued interest at 6% compounded annually is to be repaid on 1 July 2019. How much will Ron have to repay on 1 July 2019?

BE6 **Using present value tables.** **LO4, 5**

For each of the following cases, indicate (a) to what interest rate columns and (b) to what number of periods you would refer in looking up the discount rate.

1. In table 3 (present value of 1):

	Annual rate	Number of years involved	Discounts per year
(a)	12%	6	Annually
(b)	10%	15	Annually
(c)	8%	8	Half-yearly

2. In table 4 (present value of an annuity of 1):

	Annual rate	Number of years involved	Number of payments involved	Frequency of payments
(a)	12%	20	20	Annually
(b)	10%	5	5	Annually
(c)	8%	4	8	Half-yearly

BE7 Determining present values. **LO4, 5**
(a) What is the present value of $10 000 due 8 periods from now, discounted at 8%? (b) What is the present value of $10 000 to be received at the end of each of 6 periods, discounted at 9%?

BE8 Calculate the present value of a single amount investment. **LO4**
Smolinski Ltd is considering an investment which will return a lump sum of $500 000 in 5 years from now. What amount should Smolinski Ltd pay for this investment to earn a 15% return?

BE9 Calculate the present value of a single amount investment. **LO4**
Pizzeria Ltd earns 11% on an investment that will return $875 000 in 8 years from now. What is the amount Pizzeria should invest now to earn this rate of return?

BE10 Calculate the present value of an annuity investment. **LO5**
Kilarny Bros is considering investing in an annuity contract that will return $20 000 annually at the end of each year for 15 years. What amount should Kilarny Bros pay for this investment if it earns a 6% return?

BE11 Calculate the present value of an annuity investment. **LO5**
Jenna & Co. earns 11% on an investment that pays back $110 000 at the end of each of the next 4 years. What is the amount Jenna & Co. invested to earn the 11% rate of return?

BE12 Calculate the present value of a note. **LO4, 5**
Caledonia Pty Ltd receives a $50 000, 6-year note bearing interest of 11% (paid annually) from a customer at a time when the discount rate is 12%. What is the present value of the note received by Caledonia?

BE13 Calculate the present value of a machine for purposes of making a purchase decision. **LO6**
Brian Sands owns a garage and is contemplating purchasing a tyre-retreading machine for $16 280. After estimating costs and revenues, Brian projects a net cash flow from the retreading machine of $2790 annually for 8 years. He hopes to earn a return of 11% on such investments. What is the present value of the retreading operation? Should Brian purchase the retreading machine?

BE14 Calculate the present value of a note. **LO4, 5**
Hung-Chao Yu Ltd issues a 10%, 6-year mortgage note on 1 January 2019 to obtain financing for new equipment. The terms provide for half-yearly instalment payments of $112 825. What were the cash proceeds received from the issue of the note?

BE15 Calculate the maximum price to pay for a machine. **LO6**
Ramy Pty Ltd is considering purchasing equipment. The equipment will produce the following cash flows: Year 1, $30 000; Year 2, $40 000; Year 3, $50 000. Ramy Pty Ltd requires a minimum rate of return of 15%. What is the maximum price Ramy should pay for this equipment?

BE16 Calculate the interest rate on a single amount. **LO4**
Kerry Rogers invests $1827 now and will receive $10 000 at the end of 15 years. What annual rate of interest will Kerry earn on her investment? (*Hint*: Use table 3.)

BE17 Calculate the number of periods of a single amount. **LO4**
Michael Cork has been offered the opportunity of investing $24 719 now. The investment will earn 15% per year and at the end of that time will return Michael $100 000. How many years must Michael wait to receive $100 000? (*Hint*: Use table 3.)

BE18 **Calculate the interest rate on an annuity.**   **LO5**

Annie Dublin purchased an investment for $11 469.92. From this investment, she will receive $1000 annually for the next 20 years starting 1 year from now. What rate of interest will Annie's investment be earning for her? (*Hint*: Use table 4.)

BE19 **Calculate the number of periods of an annuity.**   **LO5**

Dylan Grey invests $8851.37 now for a series of $1000 annual returns beginning one year from now. Dylan will earn a return of 8% on the initial investment. How many annual payments of $1000 will Dylan receive? (*Hint*: Use table 4.)

INDEX

AASB 15 *Revenue from Contracts with Customers* 164, 240, 859, 861
AASB 16 *Leases* 507, 581
AASB 101 *Presentation of Financial Statements* 23, 533, 634, 640
AASB 102 *Inventories* 531
AASB 108 *Accounting Policies* 634
AASB 116 *Property, Plant and Equipment* 502, 509
AASB 123 *Borrowing Costs* 505
AASB 136 *Impairment of Assets* 518
AASB 137 *Provisions, Contingent Liabilities and Contingent Assets* 452, 565
AASB 138 *Intangible Assets* 525, 638
AASB 1053 *Application of Tiers of Australian Accounting Standards* 36, 845
absorption costing 1054
accelerated method 512
account 101
accountability objectives 839
accounting
  accrual *versus* cash basis 161–3
  business world 2–4
  concepts and principles 40
  cost principle 39, 831
  cycle 189–90
  entity concept 39, 830
  full disclosure principle 40, 831–2
  going concern principle 39, 831
  monetary principle 829–30
  period concept 39, 160, 830
  process 4–5
accounting equation 106
accounting information system 2, 14, 94, 346–8
accounting methods 781
accounting procedures 984–5
Accounting Professional & Ethical Standards Board (APESB) 930
accounting standard setting, structure of 36
accounting transactions
  analysing 95
  summary 100
accounting transactions and events 95
accounts payable 99, 365, 692, 698
accounts receivable 15, 98, 365, 449
accrual-based accounting 161, 852
accrued expenses 177
accrued interest 177–8
accrued revenues 176
accrued salaries 178–9
acid test 767

activity-based costing (ABC) 999–1000
  benefits 1006–7
  limitations 1006–7
  overhead rates 1003
  traditional costing systems 999–1000
activity-based management (ABM) 1007
activity cost pools 1000
activity index 1048
activity levels
  defined 1009
  hierarchy 1009–10
additions and improvements 518
adjusted trial balance 184
adjusting entries 167, 181
  types of 167–8
administrative expense budget 1101
administrative expenses 246
Adobe PDF 906
ageing the accounts receivable 452
agricultural activity 530
allowance method 452
amortisation 526
amortised cost method using the effective interest rate 576
annuities 1171
Apple 2, 235
application service providers 912
artificial intelligence (AI) 915–16
Artistry Furniture Limited 43–4, 46, 248, 448, 534–6, 710–1, 713
  statement of cash flows 51, 708
  statement of financial position 49
  statement of profit or loss 45
assets 17
  defined 853
  recognition criteria 853
assets and equity 310–11
assets and liabilities, Dr/Cr procedures for 103
asset turnover 536, 775
associations 10
ASX Corporate Governance Council 32
audit 5
Auditing and Assurance Standards Board (AUASB) 35
auditor 32–3
Australian Accounting Standards Board (AASB) 35, 36
Australian and New Zealand Standard Industrial Classification (ANZSIC) 942

Australian Bureau of Statistics (ABS) 942
Australian Business Number (ABN) 625, 899
Australian company number (ACN) 625
Australian Competition and Consumer Commission (ACCC) 14
Australian Forest Growers 9
Australian Securities and Investments Commission (ASIC) 13, 35, 624, 843, 906–7
  surveillance program 35
Australian Securities Exchange (ASX) 9, 32, 37, 350, 622
average age of PPE assets 535
average collection period 464, 769
average cost 306
average cost method 298
average days in inventory 770
average useful life 534

bad debts expense 450
bad debt write-off 457
balance sheet 758
Ballina Fishermen's Co-operative Ltd 9
Bankcard 466
bank loan 115
bank reconciliation 433–4, 436
bank statement 434, 437
basic accounting equation 21
batch-level activities 1009
benchmarking 946
Bermagui Pre School Co-operative Society Limited 9
BHP Billiton 990
big data 914–15
Big Mac 528
biological assets 530
bitcoin 917–18
Blue Chip Painting Company 161
Blue Water Resorts Ltd 775
BMW 1053
bonds 572
bonus share issue 631
bookkeeping 5
book value 172, 508
borrowing costs 566, 575
BPAY 429
brand name 528
break-even analysis
  contribution margin technique 1060–1
  mathematical equation 1059–60

break-even point 1059
break-even sales 1067
bring your own device (BYOD) 918
budget 1094
budgetary control 1110–11
budgeted financial statements 1097
budgeted overhead rate 983
budgeted statement of financial
    position 1106
budgeted statement of profit or
    loss 1106
budgeting
    benefits 1095
    essentials 1095–6
    period 1096
    process 1096
    vs. long-range planning 1096–7
business activity statement (BAS) 251
business bank accounts 899
business context 621–2
business organisation
    company 8–9
    cooperative 9–10
    partnership 8
    sole proprietorship 7–8
    trust 9
business transactions 427–9
business world 2

call on capital 627
Canadian Stock Exchange 908
capital expenditure 503
capital expenditure ratio 709–10
carrying amount 172, 508
cash 427
    managing and monitoring 441
    payment of insurance 120
    payment of rent 119
    services rendered for 118
cash account 439
cash adequacy 447
cash based accounting 161
cash budget 443, 1102
cash debt coverage 54, 711, 772
cash dividend, declared 630, 631
cash flows, statement 697
cash-generating unit 518
cash management, principles 442,
    443
cash payments 695
cash payments journal 384, 385
cash payments section 1103
cash payments to suppliers 691
cash payments transactions 384
cash receipts 465, 688
cash receipts journal 377, 380–1
cash receipts section 1103
cash receipts transactions 378
cash return on sales ratio 713, 777

Certified Institute of Management
    Accountants (CIMA) 930
Certified Practising Accountant
    (CPA) 38
change in accounting estimates 636
changes in accounting policies 637–8
chart of accounts 111
chief financial officer (CFO) 5
classified statement of financial
    position 23
class of non-current assets 520
closing entries 186
cloud computing 911–12
Coca-Cola Amatil 295, 299, 512, 528,
    990
commercial accountants 5
comparability 849–50
compound interest 1168
computer-integrated manufacturing
    (CIM) 943
computerised accounting information
    system 371
    Xero accounting software 898–9
computerised inventory systems 235
computerised systems
    advantages 373
    disadvantages 373–4
    features of 372
Conceptual Framework 10, 834, 840
    future developments 837–8
    historical development 10
    historical developments 835–7
    objective 11
    other users 842–3
    overview 838–9
    primary users 841–2
    qualitative characteristics 847–51
    reporting entity 11–12
*Conceptual Framework for Financial
    Reporting* 834, 849
*Conceptual Framework for Financial
    Reporting Exposure Draft* 10, 834
consigned goods 291
contingent liabilities 586
    classification of 585
    warranty 585, 587
    warranty provision 589
contra account 508
contra asset account 172
contra revenue account 243
contract interest rates 572, 573
contributed equity 627
contribution margin (CM) 1057
contribution margin per unit 1058
contribution margin ratio, formula
    1058
contribution margin technique 1065

control account 365
controllable cost 1121
controllable margin 1127
conversion costs 934
convertible notes 571
cooperative 9–10
copyright 528
corporate governance 350
*Corporate Governance Principles and
    Recommendations* 350
corporate governance statement 32
corporation
    advantages 624
    characteristics 622
    classification 622
    defined 622
    disadvantages 624
    organisation chart 624
    proprietary company 622
    public company 622
    types 622
corporation characteristics
    acquire capital 623
    company management 623
    continuous life 623
    government and other regulations
        624
    ownership rights 623
Corporations Act 2001 8, 625
cost 503, 509
cost accounting system 977–80
cost behaviour analysis 1048
cost centre 1125
cost concepts 940
cost constraints 42
cost flow assumptions
    average cost 294
    first-in, first-out (FIFO) 294
    last-in, first-out (LIFO) 294
cost flow methods 300
cost of goods available for sale 291
cost of goods manufactured 938
cost of goods purchased 289
cost of sales (COS) 232, 289
cost principle 39, 831
cost–volume–profit (CVP) analysis
    1057
    components of 1057
    statement of profit or loss 1069–70
cost–volume–profit (CVP) graph 1061
credit 102
credit cards to the retailer, advantages
    of 466
credit columns 380
credit risk 462
credit risk ratio 462
credit sales
    checking 377
    journalising 374–5

credit transactions 427
Crown Entities Act 2004 37
current assets 24
current cash debt coverage 52, 711, 768
current liabilities 26, 565
current ratio 50, 767
customer relationship management (CRM) 905
CVP analysis 1052

data analytics 946
days in inventory 303
debentures
  accounting issues 573–4
  determining market value of 572–3
  disadvantages 571
  redeeming at maturity 574
  redeeming before maturity 574–5
debit 102
debit columns 378
debt financing
  advantages over ordinary shares 571
  versus equity financing 648–51
debt to equity ratio 771
debt to total assets ratio 53, 771
decentralisation 1121
decision 3
decision-usefulness objective 840
declaration date 630
decline phase 707
Deloitte 5
depletion 532
depreciable amount 511
depreciation 26
depreciation disclosure 516
depreciation expense 694, 701
depreciation methods 510
  calculation 510
  comparison 515
  diminishing-balance method 512–14
  patterns of 515
  straight-line depreciation 511–12
depreciation process 171–3, 508
  factors calculation 509–10
DEXUS Property Group 9
differential financial reporting 845
diminishing-balance method 512
  formula 513
direct fixed costs 1126
direct labour 933
direct labour budget 1100
direct materials 933, 1103
direct materials budget 1099–100
direct write-off method 450, 451
  effects 451
discontinued operation 638–9
discount allowed 244
discounting processes 572

discounting future amount 1173
discount received 238
dishonoured cheque (RET) 434, 438
disposing of assets 522–4
  sale 522–3
  scrapping 524
distributed ledger 916
diverse roles of accountants
  commercial accounting 5
  government accounting 6
  not-for-profit accounting 6
  public accounting 5–6
diversification 781
dividend payout rate 778
dividend record 647
dividends 15
  cash 630
  payment 122
  payout 647
  share 631
documentation procedures 352–3
Domino's Pizza Enterprises Ltd 2, 299, 371, 512, 528, 621
double-entry system 103
Dun & Bradstreet 462, 757

earning power 633
earnings before income tax and interest expense (EBIT) 772
earnings per share 777
e-banking 429
e-commerce 944
economic phenomena 42
ED/2010/2 *Conceptual Framework for Financial Reporting: The Reporting Entity* 844–5
electronic banking processes 429
electronic funds transfer (EFT) 430
electronic funds transfer at point of sale (EFTPOS) 429
electronic spreadsheets, mortgage schedules 577
elements 911
employee salaries 123
end of the reporting period 39
enterprise performance management (EPM)
  activity-based management 945
  balanced scorecard 945
  data analytics 946
  quality 946
  values-based management 945
enterprise resource planning system (ERP) 372, 898, 902, 909
entries, perpetual *vs.* periodic 288–9
equity 21
  defined 856–7
  Dr/Cr procedures for 104

reserves 644
share capital 643
statement of changes in 20, 642
statement of financial position 642
equity financing, versus debt financing 648–51
equity investors 13
equity relationships 105–6
equivalent units 994
equivalent units of production 994
ERP systems 903–4, 904–5
errors 634
  rounding 578
Excel spreadsheets, mortgage schedules 577
expense claims and fixed assets 900
expense recognition criteria 165–6
expenses 15
  defined 860
  recognition criteria 860
eXtensible Business Reporting Language (XBRL) 898, 905–6
  benefits 907–8
  concepts 910–11
  tags 907
eXtensible Markup Language (XML) 905
External Reporting Board (XRB) 37, 846
external users 14

face value
  notes payable 566
  unsecured notes 572–3
facility-level activities 1009
factory labour costs 985, 992
fair value 503
finance leases 507, 582–4
financial accounting 3
Financial Accounting Standards Board (FASB) 295
financial and management accounting 931
financial data transformation 357
financial expenses 246
financial reporting 846, 851–2
  conceptual framework 840
  constraint 851
  decision-usefulness objective 840
  stewardship and accountability objectives 839
Financial Reporting Act 2013 37
Financial Reporting Council (FRC) 35, 781
financial reports, measurements 862
  current cost 862
  historical cost 862
  realisable (settlement) value 862

financial statement analysis
  cost 780
  estimates 780
  limitations of 780–4
  liquidity ratios 589
financial statements 17–34, 43, 185–6, 527
  accounting processes for generating 357–8
  analysis and decision making 43–4
  effect of cost flow methods 299–300
  elements in 852
  external users 354
  horizontal analysis 758–62
  liquidity ratios analysis 589–91
  non-current assets reporting 533
  prepared from adjusted trial balance 185–6
  presenting receivables in 461–7
financial year 160
financing activities
  ordinary shares 15
  share capital 15
financing section 1103
finished goods inventory 285
first-in, first-out (FIFO) method 295–6
fixed assets 26
fixed costs 1049
flexible budget 1112–14
  case study 1116–18
  development 1114–16
  reports 1118–19
FOB destination 291
Fonterra Co-operative Group Limited 621
forensic accounting 356
free cash flow 707–9, 773
freight costs 237–8, 287
full disclosure principle 40, 831–2
future value of an annuity 1171
future value of a single amount 1169–70

general journals 109, 124–5
  adjusting entries 181–2
  effect of special journals on 386–7
  journalising and posting 387
  using 368–70
general ledger 100, 112
  after write-offs 453–4
  cross-references 113
  recording adjustments 182–3
  relationship with subsidiary ledgers 365
generally accepted accounting principles (GAAP) 35, 37, 43, 781, 864, 906
  integrating 865
  summarising 864–5

general purpose financial reports (GPFRs) 845
Giorgina's financial reports
  director's report 32–3
  notes to financial statements 29, 32, 452, 461, 463, 516, 645
  statement of cash flows 30–1
  statement of changes in equity 28–9
  statement of financial position 25–7, 29–30
  statement of profit or loss 28
Giorgina's Pizza Limited 20, 24–33, 39, 40–1, 449, 452, 461–3, 516, 645, 682, 775, 830, 851
going concern principle 831
goods and services tax (GST) 94, 250, 457, 506, 684
  accounting for 252–3
  free supplies 251
  process 250
goods in transit 290
goodwill 530
Google 2, 918
government entities 1109–10
greenhouse gas accounting 946
gross domestic product (GDP) 978
gross profit 245
gross profit margin 776
gross profit ratio 247
gross value added (GVA) 942
growth phase 706

Hardware as a Service (HaaS) 912
horizontal analysis 757–62
HyperText Markup Language (HTML) 906

IAS 1 *Presentation of Financial Statements* 23–4
IAS 2 *Inventories* 294, 299, 301, 531, 1056
IAS 7 *Statement of Cash Flows* 678–9, 681
IAS 8 *Accounting Policies, Changes in Accounting Estimates and Errors* 634, 636
IAS 15 *Information Reflecting the Effects of Changing Prices* 164
IAS 16 *Property, Plant and Equipment* 509, 519
IAS 23 *Borrowing Costs* 505
IAS 33 *Earnings per Share* 777
IAS 36 *Impairments of Assets* 518–19
IAS 37 *Provisions, Contingent Liabilities and Contingent Assets* 452, 565
IAS 38 *Intangible Assets* 525, 638
IAS 41 *Agriculture* 530

IASB *See* International Accounting Standards Board (IASB)
IFRS 3 *Business Combinations* 526
IFRS 5 *Non-current Assets Held for Sale and Discounted Operations* 634, 639
IFRS 6 *Exploration for and Evaluation of Mineral Resources* 532
IKEA 528
impairments 518–20
  accounting 518–19
  loss 518
  revaluation 520
  reversal 519–20
implicit interest rate 582
income
  defined 857–8
  recognition criteria 858–9
  standards for revenue recognition 859
income tax payable 701
incremental borrowing rate 582
independent internal verification 354–5
indirect fixed costs 1126
indirect labour 933
indirect materials 933
industry-accepted standards 909
industry averages 757
Infrastructure as a Service (IaaS) 912
instance document 911
Institute of Management Accountants (IMA) 930
Institute of Public Accountants (IPA) 38
insurance 170–1
intangible assets 26, 528
  accounting for 525–6
  amortisation 526
  brand name 528
  copyright 528
  defined 525
  research and development costs 528
  trademark 528
  unidentifiable 525
integrated accounting systems 372
integrated reporting 865–7
inter-entity basis 757
interest
  calculation 1168
  compound 1168
  simple 1167–8
  simple *vs.* compound 1168
interest coverage 592
interest expenses 575
internal auditors 350
internal control 349
  establishment of responsibility 351
  forensic accounting 356
  limitations of 355

internal control *(continued)*
   principles of   351
      segregation of duties   352
internal control over cash payments
   431
internal control systems   348
   management's responsibility for
      349–50
internal users   14
International Accounting Standards
   Board (IASB)   10, 36, 834, 865,
   906
International Financial Reporting
   Standard for Small and
   Medium-sized Entities (IFRS for
   SMEs)   845
International Financial Reporting
   Standards (IFRS)   37, 846,
   906
International Public Sector Accounting
   Standards (IPSAS)   37, 845
International Public Sector Accounting
   Standards Board (IPSASB)
   845
internet banking   429
intra-entity basis   757
inventory   232
   analysis   302
   turnover   303
inventory cost flow methods   291
   first-in, first-out (FIFO)   305
   last-in, first-out (LIFO)   306
   specific identification   294
inventory errors   309
   effects on profit   309–10
inventory quantities   290
inventory systems
   computerised   235
   periodic   234
   perpetual   234
inventory turnover   303, 770
inventory write-down   243
investing activities   15
investment centre   1125, 1129
iPod   528
IPONZ   528
issue price   542, 626

JB Hi-Fi Ltd   364, 368, 371
   asset turnovers   775
job cost data   986
job cost flows   980–2
job cost sheet   982–3
job order costing   978–9, 988
job order cost system   979
job order *versus* process cost
   systems   990
journal   109
   recording transactions   110

journalising   109, 124–7
   cash payments journals   384–5
   cash receipts transactions   377–9
   purchases journals   381–4
   revaluations   520–1
just-in-time (JIT) processing
   system   1010–13
   benefits   1012
   elements   1012
   objective   1011

Kleenex   528
KPMG   5

last-in, first-out (LIFO)   297–8
leases
   advantages   581
   defined   581
   finance   582–4, 582–4
   operating   581
   reporting   584
lenders   13
lessee   506, 581
lessor   581
LG Electronics   235, 528, 621
liabilities
   definition   855
   recognition criteria   855–6
   recording payroll and deductions
      payable   567–9
licences   529
LIFO inventory method   295
limited liability   8
limited liability of shareholders
   622
limited resource   1068
liquidity   49, 711
liquidity measurement   591
liquidity ratios   48–9, 766, 767
loans payable by instalment   575–9
long-range planning   1096
long service leave   569
lower of cost and net realisable value
   (LCNRV)   302

management accountants   930
management accounting   3, 929
management accounting, evolution and
   improvements   941–6
   e-commerce   944
   globalisation   943
   service industry needs   942
   technological change on business
      infrastructure   943–4
management accounting *vs.* financial
   accounting   929
management by exception   1119
management functions
   controlling   932

   directing and motivating   931–2
   planning   931
management systems
   risk management   945
managerial accounting process   929
manual accounting system   372
manufacturing costs
   classifications   933
   direct labour   933
   direct materials   932
   manufacturing overhead   933
   statement of profit or loss   935–6
manufacturing entity
   closing entries   948–50
   partial worksheet   948
   worksheet   947
manufacturing overhead   933, 985
   budget   1100
   costs   992
manufacturing processes   990
manufacturing summary account   948
margin of safety   1063–4
market interest rates   572, 573
market value   572
master budget   1097
   components   1097
MasterCard   466
materiality   42
materials requisition slips   991
mathematical equation   1064
maturity phase   706
measurement process   4
merchandising entities   1108–9
   periodic inventory method   312
   perpetual inventory method   311–12
merchandising operations   232
   inventory systems   232–3
   operating cycles   232
metadata   910
Michael Hill International Limited
   626, 629
mixed costs   1051
modules   372
monetary principle   39, 829
mortgages   575–9
   rounding errors   578
   schedule   577
moving weighted average method
   306
MYOB   372
MYOB accounting package   353

narration   109
National Carbon Accounting System
   (NCAS)   946
natural resources   532
net purchases   289
net realisable value (NRV)   302
net sales   245

New Zealand Stock Exchange (NZX) 37, 622, 626
Nike 2
non-controllable costs 1121
non-current assets 25, 530, 701–2
  decision making regarding 501–2
  examples 531
non-current liabilities 26, 570–1
  calculating mortgage liabilities 579–80
  determining market value of unsecured notes 572–3
  issuing unsecured notes 573–4
  redeeming unsecured notes at maturity 574
  redeeming unsecured notes before maturity 574–5
  unsecured notes 571–2
non-manufacturing entities 978, 988
non-value-added activities 1008
notes 572
notes payable 566–7
notes receivable 450
notes to the financial statements 31
not-for-profit accountants 6
not-for-profit entities 6, 1109
not-for-profit organisations
  associations 10
  government 10

online banking 429
operating budgets 1097
operating cycle 24, 163
operating expenses 246
operating expenses to sales ratio 776
operating leases 507, 581, 582
ordinary repairs 517
ordinary shares, compared with debt financing 571
outstanding cheque 434
overapplied manufacturing overhead 986–7
overhead application 978
overhead budget 988
ownership rights of shareholders 626

paid-up capital 627
paperless reporting 908–9
partnership 8
Partnership Act 8
Partnership Act 1908 (NZ) 8
patent 528
pay-as-you-go (PAYG) withheld tax payable 567
payment date 631
payment of dividend 122
payments cycle 363
payroll and payroll deductions payable 567–9

performance evaluation 1130
period costs 934
periodic depreciation revision 516
periodic inventory system 234, 286–93
  closing entries (merchandising business) 311–12
  compared with perpetual 235, 287–8
  cost of goods purchased 289–90
  determining cost of sales 289–91
  determining inventory quantities 290–1
  inventory cost flow methods 293–9
  presentation of statement of profit or loss 292–3
  recording purchases 286–7
  recording sales 287–8
  recording transactions 286
permanent accounts 186
perpetual inventory system 232–4, 375
  average cost method 306–7
  closing entries (merchandising business) 311–12
  compared with periodic 235, 287–8
  FIFO method 305
  LIFO method 306
  recording purchases 237
  recording sales 240
  sales journals 374
petty cash fund 432
  fund establishment 468–9
  making payments from petty cash 469
  replenishing the fund 469
physical inventory 290
Platform as a Service (PaaS) 912
post-closing trial balance 189
posting errors 128
posting procedures 113–15, 124–6
  cash payments journals 384–5
  cash receipts journals 377–80
  purchases journals 381
  sales journals 375–6
  special journals 369–70
predetermined overhead application rate 983
prepaid expenses 169
prepayments 169
present value 1173
present value of an annuity 1175–6
present value of payments 572, 573
price/earnings ratio (P/E ratio) 778
Principles of Good Corporate Governance and Best Practice Recommendations 350
prior period errors 634
private placement 626
process costing 978–9, 990

process cost system 979
product costs 934
production budget 1099
production cost report 996, 997
product-level activities 1009
product versus period costs 934
profit 16
  compared with net cash 681, 698
  effect of inventory errors on 309–10
profitability 712
profitability ratios 45–6, 766, 773
profit centres 1125, 1126
profit effects 1056
profit margin 47, 775
profit measurement process 233
promissory note 458
property, plant and equipment (PPE) 26, 502–3, 524
  assets 533
proprietary company 622
prospectus 626
provisions, defined 585
public accountants 5
public benefit entities (PBE) standards 846
public companies, debt financing 571
public sector 10
purchase allowances 237
purchase discounts 238
purchase returns 253
purchase returns and allowances 237
  account 287
purchases account 286
purchases and payments cycle 362
purchases budget 1108
purchases cycle 363
purchases journal 381, 383
purchasing inventory 253

Qantas Airways Limited 512, 569
qualitative characteristics 40–1, 42, 874–51
QuickBooks 372
quick ratio 589, 767

ratio analysis 44
ratio of cash to daily cash expenses 447
raw materials 286
receivables 449
  accounting for 450
  extending credit 461
  financial statement presentation of 461
  monitoring collections 462
  payment period 462
receivables cycles 359, 360, 363
receivables turnover 464, 769
recognition process 853–4

recording inventory transactions 286
recording procedures for revaluation
    520
recording process 113–14
    sales invoice 108
    steps 107–8
recording purchases of inventory 286
recoverable amount 518
regulatory agencies 13
related purchasing activities 352
relevant range 1051
reporting and analysing issues,
    non-current assets 533
reporting entity 11–12
    defined 843
    indicators 844
reporting leases 584
reporting principles 1131
research and development costs 528
residual value 509
resource providers 841
responsibility accounting 1120
responsibility centres 1123
    types 1125
responsibility report 1129
responsibility reporting system 1122
retail business 441
retail inventory method 301
retained earnings 20, 104–5, 642
retained profits 634
return on assets (ROA) 46, 774
return on investment (ROI) 1129
return on ordinary shareholders' equity
    (ROE) 622, 648, 774
revenue cycle 359
revenue expenditure 503
revenue recognition criteria 163–5
revenue reserves 644
revenues and expenses 105
revenues received in advance 173–4,
    569–70
reversing entry 180

sales budget 1098
sales cycle 359, 363
sales discounts 243–4, 288
sales forecast 1096
sales invoice 240
sales journal 374, 375–6
    advantages of 377
sales mix 1067
sales of inventory 287–8
sales returns and allowances 242–3,
    254, 288
sales revenue 232, 245
salvage value 509
schedule of accounts payable 367
schedule of accounts receivable 366
schemas 911

Securities Exchange Commission
    (SEC) 906
segmental data 781
selling expense budget 1101
selling expenses 246
selling inventory 253–4
selling price 374
semantic approach 905
semivariable costs 1051
service entities 1109
service level agreement 913
service life 509
services rendered for cash 118
settlement discounts 238–40, 254–55
share capital 15, 96 See also
    contributed equity; stock
    debit and credit procedures 104–5
    reporting 682–84
share dividend 631
    effects 632
    entries 632
share issues 626
    private 627
    public 627
share split 628
shareholder rights 625
shareholders 8
simple interest 1167
small and medium-sized entities
    (SMEs) 845
Software as a Service (SaaS) 912,
    916
sole proprietorship 7
solvency 53, 711
solvency ratios 53, 592, 766, 771
source document 107
South Gippsland Herd Improvement
    Association Inc. 9
special journal 368–9
special purpose financial reports
    (SPFRs) 845
stakeholder benefits 909
Statement of Accounting Concept 1
    (SAC 1) 37, 835, 838, 840,
    843–4
Statement of Accounting Concept 2
    (SAC 2) 37, 835, 840
Statement of Accounting Concept 3
    (SAC 3) 37, 835
Statement of Accounting Concept 4
    (SAC 4) 37, 835
Statements of Accounting Concepts
    (SACs) 835–6
statement of cash flows 18, 22–3, 51
    assessing liquidity, solvency and
        profitability 710–16
    classification of 678–83
    purpose 677–8
    statement preparation 683–5

statement of ethical professional
    practice 930
statement of financial position 17,
    21–2
    after write-offs 453–4
    artistry furniture limited 49
    disclosures 24
    effect of 300–1
    equity 642–6
    formats of 763
    prepared from adjusted trial
        balance 186
    reporting leases 584
statement of profit or loss 19–20,
    357–8, 640
    effect of cost flow methods on
        299–300
    fully classified 246
    prepared from adjusted trial
        balance 185
    presentation in periodic system
        245–6
    presenting gross profit 245–6
    presenting operating expenses 246
    presenting other revenue 246–7
    presenting sales revenue 245–6
statements, interrelationships 23
static budget reports 1111–12
stewardship objectives 839
stock 96
straight-line depreciation method 511
straight-line method 512
subsidiary ledgers 364–5
    advantages of 367
supplier's invoice 236
supplies 169–70
supply chain management (SCM) 905
sustainability reporting 16
Sybiz 372
Systems Applications & Products
    (SAP) 898

T account 101
Tanner Ltd 982
target profit
    graphic presentation 1065
    mathematical equation 1063–4
    profit planning 1065
taxable supplies 250
taxation authority 251, 255–6
taxation effects 301
taxonomies 911
technologies
    artificial intelligence (AI) 915–16
    big data 914–15
    bitcoin 917–18
    block chain 916–17
    digital wallet 917
temporary accounts 186

timeliness 850
time periods and discounting 1176–7
time sheet 982
times interest earned 591, 772
time value of money 572
timing issues 160–1
Titanic approach 779
total comprehensive income 640
total cost of work in process 937
total manufacturing costs 937
total quality management (TQM) 946
trade discounts 240
trade-in value 509
trademark 528
transaction analysis 96
transactions 4
trial balance 127
    limitations of 128
triple bottom line reporting 946
trust 9

uncollectable accounts
    direct write-off method 451

understandability 850–1
unearned revenue 569
unit-level activities 1009
units-of-production method 514
unpresented cheque 434
unsecured notes 570
    accounting issues 573–4
    determining market value of 572–3
    disadvantages 571
    redeeming at maturity 574
    redeeming before maturity 574–5
US Financial Accounting Standards Board (FASB) 865

value-added activities 1008
value-added tax 250
variable costing 1053
variable cost per unit 1049
variable costs 1048–9, 1052
verifiability 850
vertical analysis 762
virtual banking 429
VISA 466
Vodafone 978

warranty 585–6
weighted-average method 995
weighted average unit cost 298
Wong Pty Ltd 18, 20, 22–3, 28, 67, 96–100, 102, 105, 109, 111–12, 122–5, 128, 133, 168–70
workers compensation 569
working capital 49
work in process (WIP) inventory 285, 937
worksheet 190, 313–15, 947–8
    form and procedure 191

XBRL 16, 898, 905–7
Xero 372, 898
    accounts tab 900
    contacts tab 900
    payroll tab 900
    reports tab 900
    settings tab 900
Xero accounting package 372, 901
Xero completed invoice screen 902
Xero dashboard screen 899
Xero software package 899